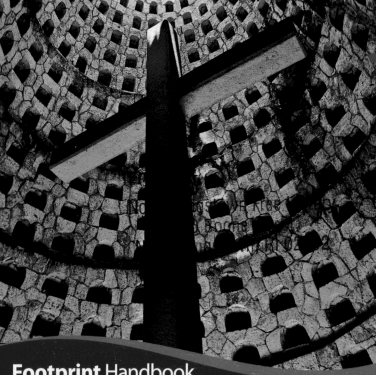

**Footprint** Handbook

# Central America

RICHARD ARGHIRIS

# This is
## Central America

The tapering isthmus of Central America is fast emerging from its tempestuous past as a place of breezy self-confidence. Throughout the 20th century, the often-squabbling family of nations running from Southern Mexico to Panama was plagued by civil strife, Cold War intrigue and a succession of dictatorial generals. Today, these former 'banana republics' enjoy lasting democracy and robust economic growth, encouraging foreign investors and foreign visitors alike. From mushrooming city skylines to burgeoning new mega-projects, the isthmus is changing – and fast.

Fortunately, the nations of Central America are far too self-assured to lose themselves any time soon. Spanish-speaking Latino culture – with its devout Catholic festivals, its love of a raucous fiesta and its eternally gregarious disposition – permeates the isthmus in a multitude of forms. Head to the Caribbean coast, however, and you'll find the lilting roots and thumping reggaeton of a people descended from Africa and the West Indies. Central America's famous indigenous peoples occupy the region's most remote and stunning locales. Hidden in vast jungles and mountain ranges, they practice ways of life that have changed little since their ancestors, the ancient Maya foremost among them.

Central America is, if anything, culturally diverse. But as a natural land bridge between the North and South American continents, it is one of the world's most biologically diverse places too. Exuberant swathes of rainforest host a staggering array of flora and fauna, protected by one of the finest national park systems on the planet. Hiking, diving, climbing, birding, caving, kayaking, surfing, snorkelling and whitewater rafting are all popular options. No wonder Central America is looking so bright.

*Richard Arghiris*

# Best of
## Central America

top things to do and see

### ❶ San Cristóbal de las Casas

The twin themes of indigenous mysticism and revolutionary struggle rarely fail to inspire. A favourite with anthropologists, activists and bohemian travellers, the colonial stronghold of San Cristóbal de las Casas is an administrative hub for Mexico's Chiapas highlands, fabled homeland of the Tzotzil Maya and the Zapatista Liberation Army. Page 54.

### ❷ Blue Hole

Recommended by Jacques Cousteau as one of the world's top 10 dive sites, Belize's Blue Hole is a giant, cavernous, perfectly circular underwater sinkhole, 1000 ft across and 400 ft deep; a true abyss habouring everything from delicate reef species to giant pelagics. Page 211.

### ❸ Lake Atitlán

Described by Alexander Von Humboldt as "the most beautiful lake in the world" and by Aldous Huxley as "too much of a good thing", Guatemala's Lake Atitlán is an entrancingly serene body of water fringed by Mayan villages and hazy blue volcanoes. Laze in a hammock or explore the local communities; it's up to you. Page 293.

## ❹ Tikal

The ruined city of Tikal earned its place in sci-fi history as the location for a rebel moon in George Lucas's *Star Wars*. Once one of the most powerful polities in the Mayan world, its astoundingly tall pyramids reach high above the rainforest canopy: the "New York of Mesoamerica". Page 394.

## ❺ Ruta de las Flores

Soak up the warmth, colour and disarming rural charm of El Salvador's beautiful Route of Flowers, dotted with handsome highland towns. There's a thriving arts and crafts scene, colonial architecture, great festivals and it's a foodie's heaven. Page 430.

## ❻ Gracias

Mighty Celaque, the highest peak in Honduras, beckons intrepid hikers from the refreshing mountain town of Gracias. Once you've climbed its slopes and explored its cloudforests, you can descend to nearby hot springs and soak your weary limbs. Page 503.

## ❼ La Mosquitia

The Río Coco on the Honduran/
Nicaraguan border marks the spiritual
heart of the Mosquitia, one of the most
remote indigenous regions in Central
America. Travel in this part of the country
is as rewarding as it is challenging – a
natural and cultural odyssey strictly for
experienced adventurers. Page 588.

## ❽ Isla de Ometepe

Sling a hammock on the magical island of
Ometepe, a bastion of peace, tranquility
and numinous volcanic beauty. Set on
the largest lake in Central America, Lago
Nicaragua, it's also home to twin volcanoes
and mysterious pre-Columbian idols.
Page 649.

## ❾ León

Propose a toast to revolution in Nicaragua's
hip and buzzing party town, home to
handsome plazas and a wealth of regal
colonial houses. León is surrounded by
active volcanoes, good for climbing,
hiking and sandboarding. Page 670.

## ⑩ Monteverde

Travel by boat and jeep up to the ethereal cloudforests of Monteverde in Costa Rica, which is in a magnificent setting that is seemingly straight out of a fantasy novel, and where it's easy to spot birds and other wildlife. Page 770.

## ⑪ Panama Canal

Marvel at one of the world's greatest engineering feats, as impressive today as it ever was. Whilst the Panama Canal may not be natural, it is spectacular, and pure Panamanian since the country took control of it in 1999. Page 884.

## ⑫ Guna Yala

Go native in Panama's indigenous Comarca Guna Yala (San Blas archipelago), a string of some 400 islets and a precious haven of calm and tranquility. Many of islands are entirely uninhabited, home only to verdant palm trees, resplendent coral reefs, gorgeous white-sand beaches and warm, gentle waters. Page 902.

CUBA

Caribbean Sea

Guna Yala
(San Blas
Islands)
PANAMA
CITY
Lago
Bayano
Panama
Canal
Campana
PANAMA
Yaviza
Pearl
Islands
Península
Azuero

# Route
## planner

One rewarding aspect of travel in Central America is the compact size of its countries. Three weeks is just enough time to sample a few countries, but a month or longer is recommended. Southern Mexico offers solid infrastructure and fascinating cultural heritage. Belize is the big Caribbean destination, increasingly geared to moneyed travellers rather than backpackers. Guatemala is a fascinating patchwork of Mayan cultures and sites, colonial towns, lakes and mountains. A vibrant nation, El Salvador's appeal lies in its ultra-compact size. Honduras' Bay Islands are a fabled dive mecca, but its mountainous mainland will appeal to slow travellers. Nicaragua is suited to thrifty adventurers. For beach-goers and nature-lovers, Costa Rica has reliable infrastructure, while Panama is an emerging eco-destination.

## Three to four weeks

Ruta Maya, Costa Rica or an overland trip

Three to four weeks is not long enough to cover the region, but you could explore a chunk of the Ruta Maya. In Guatemala, take a week or 10 days to take Antigua, Tikal and Lake Atitlán then head for Belize's Cayo district, and Caye Caulker for a bit of diving, for another week, before travelling north to Mexico's Yucatán and west to indigenous Chiapas, completing the loop in the remaining time. Any version of the Ruta Maya, taking in just the main Maya sites of Guatemala, Belize and southern Mexico, is possible in four weeks.

Another three- to four-week trip could focus on Costa Rica, with its great national parks. The most popular include Manuel Antonio National Park with rich flora and fauna, Monteverde Cloud Forest Reserve for world-class birdwatching, Tortuguero National Park

Right: Tortuguero National Park, Costa Rica
Opposite page: All Saints' Day, Santiago
Sacatepéquez, Guatemala

• 11

Above left: Chicken buses, Guatemala
Above: Ambergris Caye, Belize
Left: Sumidero Canyon, Chiapas, Mexico
Opposite page: El Zonte beach, El Salvador

for its coastal canals and turtle beaches, and Corcovado National Park with some of the country's best rainforest trails. The explosive Volcán Arenal never disappoints (unless it's shrouded in cloud). There's also whitewater rafting, surfing, horse riding and trekking. You could also easily pop in to Nicaragua or Panama too.

You could just about manage an overland trip from Guatemala through to Costa Rica in three to four weeks. If you're feeling particularly manic, you could even manage a mad dash down the Pan-American Highway from Mexico City all the way to Panama City.

## Six to eight weeks

Maya ruins, Spanish school and diving

Six to eight weeks is long enough to travel across a few countries without feeling you've rushed too much. Start in Chiapas and the Maya ruins of Palenque. From here, continue south to Guatemala or west out to the Yucatán Peninsula for beautiful beaches and more Maya ruins. Dropping south, Belize is worth some time. Diving, though pricier than Honduras, is some of the best in the world and includes the famed Blue Hole. Head west for Guatemala and the eerie cave and river trips of the Cayo District or, to the south, the serenity around Placencia, the jaguar sanctuary at Cockscomb Basin and Maya villages near Punta Gorda.

With six weeks you could squeeze in a Spanish course in Antigua, Quetzaltenango or Todos Santos, famous for its festival in November. Honduras offers affordable diving of the Bay Islands, which need at least a week. Other attractions include whitewater rafting on the Río Cangrejo. Inland, treks and hikes in the quiet hills around Gracias go through the very heart of Honduras.

An alternative six-week trip might arrive in Guatemala City and head south overland, flying out of San José, Costa Rica. As well as experiencing Guatemala and Costa Rica, you can travel through Honduras, dip into lakes and volcanic beauty in El Salvador and visit Nicaragua where revolutionary history merges with colonial legacy to create one of Central America's most endearing nations. Honduras and Nicaragua are, for many, the most challenging destinations, but also the most memorable.

## Three months

*remote adventures along the Pan-American Highway*

Three months allows for a thorough exploration of Central America. Use the Pan-American Highway as your guide and travel from southern Mexico to the Darién Gap. A month exploring the Ruta Maya is time well spent (see above), but a memorable trip through Honduras, El Salvador and Nicaragua could involve more daring expeditions to remote locales like the Mosquitia or the jungle-shrouded Río San Juan.

In Costa Rica, it's relatively easy to switch between Pacific and Caribbean shores before finally crossing the border into Panama, where, from the city of David, you can blend adventure and beauty with a visit to the Chiriquí Highlands, hiking Volcán Barú and sampling coffee at a local finca.

Alternatively, cross over the mountains and head for the dive sites of Bocas del Toro, sample the local nightlife and enjoy the easy-going Caribbean pace, then head back inland towards the capital. A voyage through the massive engineering feat of the Panama Canal and the protected rainforests around it would be the ideal way to end a trip of trans-continental travel, but don't miss island-hopping in the spectacular Guna Yala archipelago.

# Best
## Maya sites

### Palenque, Mexico

Built at the height of the Classic period on a series of artificial terraces, Palenque is one of the most beautiful of all the Maya ruins in Mexico, with a hillside setting backing onto the rainforest with wisps of cloud drifting across the site after rainfall. From about the fourth century AD, Palenque grew from a small agricultural village to one of the most important cities in the prehispanic world, although it really achieved greatness between AD 600 and 800. The pyramids once held ornate tombs of Maya rulers deep within. Page 83.

### Tulum, Mexico

The Maya-Toltec ruins of Tulum are perched on coastal cliffs in a beautiful setting above the azure Caribbean waters. The ruins are 12th century, with city walls of white stone. The temples were dedicated to the worship of the Falling God, or the Setting Sun, represented as a falling character over nearly all the

west-facing doors (Cozumel was the home of the Rising Sun). The same idea is reflected in the buildings, which are wider at the top than at the bottom. The main structure is the Castillo, which commands a view of both the sea and the forested Quintana Roo lowlands stretching westwards. Page 128.

### Chichén Itzá, Mexico

Voted one of the Seven New Wonders of the World, Chichén Itzá is one of the most spectacular of Maya sites. The Castillo, a giant stepped pyramid, dominates the site, watched over by Chacmool, a Maya fertility god who reclines on a nearby structure. The city was built by the Maya in late Classic times (AD 600-900). By the end of the 10th century, the city was more or less abandoned. It was re-established in the 11th-12th centuries, though much debate surrounds by whom. Page 161.

Left: Palenque
Above: Chichén Itzá

## Caracol, Belize

Caracol is a rediscovered Maya city and now part of a National Monument Reservation. The site was established about 300 BC and continued well into the Late Classic period (glyphs record a victorious war against Tikal). Why Caracol was built in such a poorly watered region is not known, but Maya engineers showed great ingenuity in constructing reservoirs and terracing the fields. The Sky Palace (Caana) pyramid, climbing 42 m above the site, is being excavated and satellite mapped by members of the University of Central Florida. Excavations take place February-May but there are year-round caretakers who will show you around. Page 225.

## Tikal, Guatemala

With its Maya skyscrapers pushing up through the jungle canopy, the massive site of Tikal will have you transfixed. Steep-sided temples for the mighty dead, stelae commemorating the powerful rulers, inscriptions recording the noble deeds and passing of time, and burials that were stuffed with jade and bone funerary offerings, make up the greatest Maya city in this pocket of Guatemala. And when you need a break from the expansive site, the area is packed with bird and other wildlife. Overall, it's a must-see of Guatemala, and a must-see for this part of the world. Page 394.

## Copán, Honduras

The magnificent ruins of Copán are one of Central America's major Maya sites, certainly the most significant in Honduras, and they mark the southeastern limit of Maya dominance. When John Lloyd Stephens and Frederick Catherwood examined the ruins in 1839, they were engulfed in jungle. In the 1930s, the Carnegie Institute cleared the ground and rebuilt the Hieroglyphic Stairway, and since then the ruins have been maintained by the government with a museum exhibit in Tegucigalpa. Some of the most complex carvings are found on the 21 stelae, or 3-m columns of stones on which the passage of time was originally believed to have been recorded. The stelae are deeply incised and carved with faces, figures and animals. There are royal portraits with inscriptions recording deeds and the lineage of those portrayed as well as dates of birth, marriage and death. Ball courts were revealed during excavation, and one of them has been fully restored. Page 513.

Above left: Tulum
Above right: Caracol
Right: Copán

15

# When to go

...and when not to

## Climate

If your trip is about clear skies, with a bit of beach life, then the best time to go is between November and April, when there is virtually no rain, although there are slight regional variations and a handful of microclimates that do not obey the rule. November is the best month to visit with the rains dropping off, or stopping, before large numbers of tourists arrive. The scenery also remains lush and green into November but by April many regions are arid and dusty.

From May to October, the rainy season works its way up from southern Central America. At the start of the season, rain falls for a just couple of hours a day, usually in the afternoon, but towards the end, it is more torrential and disruptive. However, don't be put off by the term 'rainy season'; most years, the rains only affect travellers for an hour or two a day.

Temperatures vary across the region, mostly due to altitude, but generally it's around 30-32°C in the day dropping to 21-22°C at night. Temperatures fall by a few degrees every 500 m from sea level, and by the time you've climbed up into the peaks of the highlands, daytime temperatures can dip under 20°C and be even cooler at night, so you'll need warm clothes.

### Southern Mexico

Due to its varied topography, there is a wide variety of climates in southern Mexico. The highlands tend to be warm during the day, and cool or chilly after dark. The lowlands tend to be blazing hot and, depending on the season, humid. During the dry season it becomes bone dry in parts of the Yucatán, but less so in the evergreen rainforests of lowland Chiapas.

### Belize

There are sharp annual variations in rainfall, with much higher rainfall in the south compared to the north. Around August the *mauger* occurs in some

> **Tip...**
> Some activities are better in the rainy season – such as birdwatching, whitewater rafting and some surf breaks – but others will be impossible with cloud cover, so plan carefully.

## ON THE ROAD

## Hurricane season

Note the rainy season corresponds to hurricane season in the Caribbean. Despite high-profile storms such as Hurricane Wilma, landfall is relatively rare. In Belize, an efficient warning system was put in place after Hurricane Mitch and most towns and large villages have hurricane shelters. You are strongly advised to heed local advice regarding incoming tropical storms. To track the position and trajectory of a hurricane, visit www.nhc.noaa.gov.

areas, a mini dry season of about six weeks. September to November tend to be overcast. Inland, in the west, day temperatures can be hot, but the nights are cooler and usually pleasant.

### Guatemala
Most of the population lives at between 900 m and 2500 m, with warm days and cool nights. The central region around Cobán has an occasional drizzle-like rain called *chipi chipi* in February and March. Some places enjoy a respite from the rains (the *canícula*) in July and August. On the Pacific and Caribbean coasts you can expect rain all year round, heaviest on the Pacific in June and September with a dry spell in between, but with no dry season on the Caribbean.

### El Salvador
El Salvador is fortunate in that temperatures are rarely excessively high. The average for San Salvador is 28°C with little variation. March to May are the hottest months; December to February the coolest.

### Honduras
Climate depends largely on altitude. In Tegucigalpa, at 1000 m, temperatures can be cold January to March but pleasantly hot April to May. On the Caribbean the dry season is from February to June, while the heaviest rains fall between August and December. Some of the central highland areas have a delightful climate, with a freshness that makes a pleasant contrast to the humidity and heat of the lowland zones.

### Nicaragua
December is an extraordinarily beautiful time to visit the Nicaraguan Pacific with all the landscape in bloom, the air still fresh and visibility excellent across the volcanic ranges. Later in the dry season, the Pacific Basin receives practically no rain at all. The dry season becomes shorter the further east you travel and on the Caribbean it can rain at any time of year.

## Costa Rica

In northwestern Costa Rica, temperatures can be unbearable in late April/May, before the cool rains arrive. The tourist-savvy Costa Ricans have rebranded the wet season the 'Green Season', and why not? Visiting the rainforest, there's a huge benefit in seeing the full force of nature.

## Panama

The southernmost country in Central America is also the wettest. Starting in November, the dry season technically lasts five to six months, but Panama City and the Darién often experience short thunderstorms from January. The seasons are more reliable in the western province of Chiriquí but the region is prone to floods during the rains. The Azuero peninsula is covered by the so-called *arco seco* (dry arch) and is typically hot and arid in the dry months. The Caribbean side tends to be wetter and less predictable than elsewhere. Bocas del Toro has its own microclimate and can be a good place to escape the rains on the Pacific side.

## Festivals

If the time and mood is right, there is little to beat a Latin American festival. Fine costumes, loud music, the sounds of firecrackers tipped off with the gentle wafting of specially prepared foods all (normally) with a drink or two. Whether you're seeking the carnival or happen to stumble across a celebration, the events – big or small – are memorable. If you want to hit the carnivals there are a few broad dates generally significant throughout the region. Carnival is normally the week before the start of Lent. It's more important in Mexico but you'll probably find regional celebrations in most places. Semana Santa (Easter Week) is an understandably more spiritual affair. On 2 November is Día de los Muertos (Day of the Dead), again most popular in Mexico but significant throughout the region when families visit cemeteries to honour the dead. Christmas and New Year result in celebrations of some kind, but not always public.

Beyond that each country celebrates wildly on Independence Day. Other important local fiestas are also busy times; book ahead. Keep an eye out for patron saints of villages and towns. August is holiday time for Mexicans and Central Americans so accommodation can be scarce, especially in the smaller resorts.

Public holidays throughout the region lead to a complete shut-down in services. There are no banks, government offices and usually no shops open, and often far fewer restaurants and bars. It is worth keeping an eye on the calendar to avoid changing money or trying to make travel arrangements on public holidays.

## Mexico

**Feb/Mar  Carnival/Mardi Gras.**
Traditionally throughout Latin America, this week is a time for celebration before the hardships of Lent; in Mexico it is particularly popular in Mérida.

**15 Sep  Cry for Independence.**
Celebrations which are held in the Zócalo of cities throughout Mexico.

**16 Sep  Independence Day.**
Regional festivities and parades.

**2 Nov  Día de los Muertos (Day of the Dead).** The souls of the deceased return to earth and family and friends turn out to meet them.

**12 Dec  Guadalupe Day.** Pilgrimage of thousands to the Basílica de Guadalupe, in northeast Mexico City, the most venerated shrine in Mexico. Well worth a visit. Also celebrated in places in southern Mexico, such as San Cristóbal de las Casas.

## Belize

**Feb  Weekend before or after Valentine's Day, Annual Sidewalk Arts Festival,** Placencia.

**Early Mar  San José Succotz Fiesta.**

**9 Mar  Baron Bliss Day;** see also Paddling the great Macal River box in Belize chapter.

**May (variable)  Cashew Festival** (Crooked Tree), **Cayo Expo** (San Ignacio), **Coconut Festival** (Caye Caulker).

**24 May  Commonwealth Day.**

**23-25 Jun  Lobster Fest,** Placencia.

**Early to mid-Jul  Benque Viejo Fiesta.**

**Aug  International Costa Maya Festival** (San Pedro, Ambergris Caye).

**10 Sep  St George's Caye Day.** With celebrations in Belize City that start with river races in San Ignacio.

**21 Sep  Independence Day.**

**19 Nov  Settlement Day.** Celebrating the liberation (or arrival) of the Garífuna from distant shores. Also celebrated in Guatemala.

## Guatemala

**Mar/Apr  Semana Santa.** Particularly colourful in Antigua with floats carrying Christ over wonderfully coloured and carefully placed carpets of flowers (see box in Antigua section of Guatemala chapter); also spectacular in Santiago Atitlán.

**15 Sep  Independence Day** and a public holiday in Guatemala City only.

**Nov  Día de los Muertos (All Saints' Day).** In the small town of Todos Santos there is a colourful and drunken horse race with lots of dancing and antics. See Todos Santos festival box in Guatemala chapter. In Santiago Sacatepéquez, it's characterized by colourful kite-flying (barriletes).

## El Salvador

**29 Nov  Nuestra Señora de la Paz.** Big celebrations in San Miguel.

## Honduras

**1-4 Feb  Supaya,** southeast of Tegucigalpa, the most important shrine in Honduras with a tiny wooden image of the Virgen de Supaya.

**15 May  San Isidro,** La Ceiba's patron saint, followed by a fortnight of celebrations. The highlight is a huge carnival on the 3rd Sat in May.

**3 Oct  Francisco Morazán.**

## Nicaragua

**19 Jul** Revolution of 1979.

**14 Sep** Battle of San Jacinto.

**Dec** La Purísima in honour of the patron saint of the Immaculate Virgin, celebrated with fireworks with 7 Dec being the high point.

## Costa Rica

**Late Jan/early Feb** Fiesta de los Diablos, in the small towns of Boruca and Rey Curre, southern Costa Rica, symbolic of the fight between cultures, religion and colonization.

**19 Mar** St Joseph.

**11 Apr** Battle of Rivas.

**25 Jul** Guanacaste Day.

**2 Aug** Virgin of Los Angeles, celebrated with pilgrimages to the basilica in Cártago.

**15 Sep** Independence Day, with celebrations and parades in the capital San José and throughout the country.

**12 Oct** Día de la Raza (Columbus Day) celebrated with particular gusto in the Caribbean city of Puerto Limón, the week before and after Columbus Day. There's music, dance, street processions and general festivities. Hotels book up, but it's definitely worth making the effort to go.

**28-31 Dec** San José only.

## Panama

**9 Jan** Martyrs' Day.

**Feb/Mar** Shrove Tuesday Carnival. Panama City carnival, held on the 4 days before Shrove Tuesday, is the best. During carnival, women who can afford it wear the voluminous *pollera* dress, while the men wear a *montuno* outfit: round straw hats, embroidered blouses and trousers, and carry the *chácara*, or small purse.

**12 Feb** The indigenous Ngöbe-Bugle (Guaymí) of Chiriquí province meet to transact tribal business, hold feasts and compete for brides by tossing balsa logs at one another; those unhurt in this contest, known as Las Balserías, are viewed as heroes.

**Mar/Apr** Easter ceremonies at Villa de Los Santos: the farces and acrobatics of the big devils – with their debates and trials in which the main devil accuses and an angel defends the soul – the dance of the 'dirty little devils' and the dancing drama of the Montezumas are all notable. The ceremonies at Pesé (near Chitré) are famous all over Panama.

**15 Aug** Founding of Panama. Panama City only.

**1 Nov** National Anthem Day.

**3 Nov** Independence Day.

**4 Nov** Flag Day.

**5 Nov** Independence Day in Colón.

**10 Nov** First Call of Independence.

**28 Nov** Independence from Spain.

# What to do

from caving to diving to whitewater rafting

## Archaeology

Archaeological sites run the gamut from a handful of unexcavated mounds to heavily restored citadels with vast pyramids and palatial complexes. The sheer scale of metropolises such as **Mexico's** Chichén Itzá is mind-boggling, but it is often the smaller, quieter, less popular sites, such as Yaxchilán and Toniná, which leave the deepest impressions.

Along with a quiet, contemplative attitude, solitude is key to experiencing the ruins and their subtle atmosphere. Set out as early as possible in the day, especially if the site lies within striking distance of Cancún and its hordes of package tourists; opening time is best. If the site is shrouded in forests, you have a better chance of seeing wildlife in the early morning too, and there may be photogenic mists. To comprehend the richness and complexity of Mayan civilization, it is worth reading in-depth before setting out. We recommend anything and everything by Linda Schele.

In **Guatemala**, archaeology is a big attraction and there are numerous organizations offering tours. Some companies operate out of Flores and Santa Elena in the Petén using local villagers to help with expeditions. **Maya Expeditions**, www.mayaexpeditions.com, offers archaeologist-led trips.

## Ballooning and bungee jumping

If you're looking for a last big-spending celebration, hot-air balloon rides in **Costa Rica** take you over the trees near Arenal Volcano and also the Turrialba region. Contact **Serendipity Adventures** (T2556-2222, www.serendipityadventures.com). Another suggestion is to jump off a bridge. Bungee jumping, that is, off the Colorado bridge, close to Grecia in the Meseta Central. In **Guatemala Maya Expeditions** (T2366-9950, www.mayaexpeditions. com), also arrange bungee jumping in Guatemala City and the Río Dulce.

## Canopy tours

The rainforest canopy is where most of Costa Rica's wildlife action takes place and there are now a multitude of ways of getting you up there. The calmest is probably exploring on a suspension bridge, strung out along the trees where you are free to walk at leisure, or on an aerial tram – essentially an adapted ski lift. The best high-adrenalin option is the zip-wire, which lets you whizz down high-tension steel cables strung between forest giants. You won't see much as you soar through the air, but it is good fun and you do get close to the forest canopy. Most of the country's canopy tour companies are concentrated in Santa Elena and Fortuna. Across the border in **Nicaragua**, there are some comparatively modest (but no less fun) ziplines around the city of Granada. Canopy tours have yet to take off in **Panama**, but the **Rainforest Discovery Centre** in Soberanía National Park has a 32-m-high tower with a viewing platform.

## Canyoning, caving and cenotes

Options for caving and canyoning are developing in **Mexico** and **Guatemala** but the best caving in the region and the western hemisphere is found in **Belize**, with some of the longest cave systems in the world. From San Ignacio, tours go to Chechem Ha, Barton Creek and Actun Tunichil Muknal Cave, known for their Maya artefacts.

Caving, or speleology, in Mexico is more than just going down into deep dark holes. Sometimes it is a sport more closely related to canyoning as there are some excellent underground river scrambles. The biggest cave systems in the country are in Chiapas, especially around Tuxtla Gutiérrez, with trips best organized from San Cristóbal de las Casas. You also have the option of diving in water-filled caves known as *cenotes*, a common and popular sport in the Yucatán, particularly around Tulum. Note some underground cavern diving is quite technical and requires special training beyond PADI certification.

## Diving

Opportunities for diving and snorkelling can be found throughout the region. As elsewhere in the world, the reefs in this region are under threat from mass tourism, climate change and hurricanes. Overall the best diving for safety and opportunity is probably in **Belize**, especially in the offshore cayes, but prices tend to be higher than elsewhere. 2 diving hotspots in the region are the Blue Hole in Belize and the Isla de Coco off **Costa Rica**.

In **Mexico**, the Yucatán is a world-class diving destination and learning to dive in the Cancún area is surprisingly affordable. The astonishing Mesoamerican Barrier Reef, the 2nd-largest reef system in the world, lies off the coast of Quintana Roo. Most serious divers head to Isla Cozumel, but there are dive centres at all the major resorts on the Riviera Maya. Near Cancún and Isla Mujeres, don't miss the superb Museo Subacuático de Arte, an underwater sculpture park.

The cheapest place to learn to dive in the region is off the Bay Island of Utila, **Honduras**. The Corn Islands off **Nicaragua** are another bastion of cheap diving instruction.

Good diving in **Costa Rica** is limited to the area around Puerto Viejo and Manzanillo on the Caribbean south coast. Generally, on the Caribbean side, you can see wrecks and coral reefs, particularly in the southeast towards the Panamanian border, while on the Pacific side you see large pelagics and sportfish. Liveaboard dive boats head for the islands of Caño and Isla del Coco. Divers are not permitted in national parks or reserves, nor within 500 m of the protected sea turtle zone north of Parque Nacional Tortuguero.

Good diving conditions continue south from Costa Rica to Bocas del Toro in **Panama**. The Caribbean coral reefs are similar to those of Belize and Honduras, extending southeast for 100 km along from the Costa Rica border and then from Colón 300 km to the border with Colombia. For information on these areas, see under Bocas del Toro, Portobelo and the San Blas islands. Places to go on Panama's Pacific coast include Taboga, the Pearl Islands, Iguana Island and Parque Nacional Coiba. A third, and perhaps unique experience, is diving in the lakes of the Panama Canal, mainly to visit wrecks, submerged villages and the odd train left behind by the filling of the canal.

## Fishing

Sea and freshwater fishing are world class, with marlin and sailfish in the deep waters off **Costa Rica**, **Panama** and **Mexico**, and bonefish a little closer to shore on the flats in **Belize**. There are freshwater dreams of snook and tarpon lurking in tropical streams along the Caribbean, with the largest snook being found in Sep and Oct, mostly north of Limón in Costa Rica (where there are fishing lodges), but also towards Panama. Costs, however, are generally prohibitive, running to several hundred dollars for the day. Anglers can save money in groups, since it is usually the same cost to rent a boat for 1 or 4 people.

**Note** In addition to the restrictions in Belize on turtle and coral extraction, the following regulations apply: no person may take, buy or sell crawfish (lobster) between 15 Feb and 14 Jun, shrimp between 15 Mar and 14 Jul, or conch between 1 Jul and 30 Sep.

## Hiking

A network of paths and tracks covers much of Central America. In Guatemala you can walk just about anywhere, but in other countries, particularly Costa Rica, you can be limited to the many excellent national parks with hiking trails.

In Chiapas, southern **Mexico**, there are good opportunities for hiking in the hills, as well as in the lowland Lacandón jungle, but seek current advice regarding Zapatista activity and narco-trafficking. The Yucatán is almost entirely flat and the hiking is monotonous. It is possible to trek between ruins and *cenotes*, but many of the forests shed their leaves in the dry season and thus offer little respite from the heat.

In **Guatemala**, the Petén is the most popular trekking destination with a variety of routes connecting jungle-shrouded ruins, some of them very remote. Flores is the usual jumping-off point. In the west of the country, the Cuchumatanes mountains, which claims the highest non-volcanic peak in the country at 3837 m, are a very mysterious and beautiful locale with a network of highland villages. The Sierra de las Minas in eastern Guatemala is relatively unexplored while the countryside around Quetzaltenango, Antigua and Lake Atitlán offers many opportunities for casual walking and volcano climbing, with more than 30 volcanoes on offer. Always check on the security situation before setting out.

In **El Salvador**, national parks provide opportunities for trekking and nature walks; in particular, at Parque Nacional Cerro Verde close to San Salvador and in the more remote parks of Montecristo and Parque Nacional El Imposible. In Nicaragua, the northern highlands and the Maribios volcanoes of León and Chinandega are popular destinations for trekking.

Volcán Barú, **Panama's** highest peak at 3475 m, and nearby Cerro Punta are the 2 best climbs in the country but there are several excellent long walks. The hike from Cañita on the Darién road over the continental divide to Cartí is an alternative to flying to San Blas. The Camino de Cruces and Camino Real are jungle walks that follow in the steps of the conquistadors crossing the continental divide and, if combined into an ocean-to-ocean hike, take 8 days. A good range for hiking is the Serranía de Majé east of Panama City, visiting Embera villages and its howler monkey population. Closer is the Parque Nacional Chagres and a 3-day walk from Cerro Azul to the coast.

**Equipment** Trekking should not be approached casually. Even if you only plan to be out a couple of hours you should have comfortable, safe waterproof footwear and a daypack to carry your sweater and waterproof. At high altitudes the difference in temperature between sun and shade is remarkable. The longer trips mentioned in this book require basic backpacking equipment. Essential items are: a good backpack, sleeping bag, foam mat, stove, tent or tarpaulin, dried food (not tins), water bottle, compass and trowel for burying human waste.

**Safety** Hikers have little to fear from the animal kingdom apart from insects; robbery and assault are rare. You are much more of a threat to the environment than vice versa.

**Responsible travel** Leave no evidence of your passing; don't litter and don't give gratuitous presents of sweets or money to rural villagers. Respect their system of reciprocity; if they give you hospitality or food, then is the time to reciprocate with presents.

**Maps** Most Central American countries have an Instituto Geográfico, which sells topographical maps of a scale 1:100,000 or 1:50,000. The physical features shown on these are usually accurate; the trails and place names less so. National parks offices also sell maps.

## Kayaking

The coasts of the Yucatán are filled with mangroves and wetlands rich in wildlife where you might spot crocodiles, manatees and scores of elegant waterbirds. One of the most popular areas to kayak is the Sian Ka'an Biosphere Reserve, where tours can be easily extended to include a visit to *cenotes* and ruins. Inland, the Laguna de Bacalar is another fun place for paddling about.

Casual sea kayaking is possible at numerous beach destinations throughout the region with many hotels renting equipment to their guests.

## Mountain biking

This is an increasingly popular activity in **Guatemala**. There are numerous tracks and paths weaving their way across the country. **Old Town Outfitters** (5 Av Sur 12"C", Antigua, T7832-4171, www.adventureguatemala.com) is a recommended operator, offering mountain-bike tours starting at US$25 for a half day. In **Nicaragua**, Granada is experiencing a steady rise in mountain-biking activities; one recommended tour operator is **Detour** (C Corales, Alcaldía, 150 vrs al lago, T2552-0155, www.detour-nicaragua.com). The rugged hills around Matagalpa have lots of potential too; for more information, contact **Matagalpa Tours** (BANRPRO, ½ c al este, T2772-0108, www.matagalpatours.com).

## Surfing

It's an endless summer of surfing all the way down the Pacific coast. If you're looking to learn, your best chance is probably in Mexico or Costa Rica.

**Mexico's** Soconusco coast in Chiapas is pleasant. In **Guatemala**, the beaches of the Costa Sur are black sand and sweltering, but also buffeted by refreshing sea breezes and waves, some of them fit for surfing. In **El Salvador** there are good breaks close to La Libertad, with several all down the Pacific coast of **Nicaragua**, particularly in the south.

Surfing is popular on the Pacific and southern Caribbean beaches in **Costa Rica**, attracting professionals who follow storm surges along the coast. The country has well-documented breaks with the main centres at Tamarindo, Malpaís, Jaco and Dominical, which also have classes for beginners. Particular breaks are mentioned in the text.

In **Panama**, surfing is best at Isla Grande, Playa Venado on the Azuero Peninsula, Santa Catalina on the Pacific coast of Veraguas and Bocas del Toro. In the capital, **Kenny Myers** (T6671-7777, www.panamasurftours.com), offers tours to the more out-of-the-way beaches. Also check out Playa Río Mar near San Carlos, just 1.5 km from Panama City, and **Río Mar Surf Camp** (T6516-5031, www.riomarsurf.com). Options range from turn-up-and-surf to rooms, boards, classes and transport.

## Textiles and weaving

It is possible to get weaving lessons in many places across the highlands in **Guatemala**. Weaving lessons can also be organized through the country's Spanish schools.

## Whitewater rafting

Being a potentially dangerous sport, whitewater rafting is not as widespread as it could be, but there are many world-class opportunities in the region. The variety of **Mexico's** rivers opens the activity up to all levels of experience. Rafting in Chiapas covers the spectrum from sedate floats on rivers such as the Lacan-Há through the Lacandón jungle to Grade IV/V rapids on the Río Jataté, which gathers force where the Lacan Tum enters it and gradually diminishes in strength as it nears the Río Usumacinta. Jan-Feb are the preferred months because the climate is cooler.

In **Guatemala** there are operators using the Cahabón, Motagua and Esclavos. **Maya Expeditions** (www.mayaexpeditions.com), is the country's best outfitter. It rafts the Río Cahabón in Alta Verapaz (Grade III-V), the Río Naranjo close to Coatepeque (Grade III), the Río Motagua close to Guatemala City (Grade III-IV), the Río Esclavos, near Barbarena (Grade III-IV), the Río Coyolate close to Santa Lucía Cotzumalguapa (Grade II-III) and the Río Chiquibul in the Petén (Grade II-III).

Rafting is growing steadily in **Honduras** with the hotspot being the River Cangrejal, near La Ceiba, where Grade II, III and IV rapids test both the novice and experienced paddler. The sport is relatively new to **Honduras** and more sites are sure to be found in the coming years.

In **Costa Rica** most trips start from San José. The Reventazón, Pacuare and Sarapiquí rivers on the Caribbean slope, and the General and Corobicí on the Pacific, offer a fantastic array of aquadventure. The Savegre, close to Quepos, is also a popular river.

Some of Central America's best rafting is in the Chiriquí highlands of **Panama**. Boquete is the centre of operations for most specialized rafting companies, which lead regular expeditions on the Río Chiriquí and the Chiriquí Viejo. There is also rafting in the Parque Nacional Chagres area, north of Panama City, with Grades II and III, which some consider better for tubing (generally best Aug-Dec).

## Wildlife and birdwatching

Central America offers spectacular wildlife-watching opportunities. In typical tropical exuberance, southern Mexico and Central America are brimming with wildlife and you won't have to venture far out of urban settings to encounter it. Casual strolling at any of the larger archaeological sites is often rewarded with the sight of iguanas sunning themselves on rocks, scampering agoutis, coatis and other rodents, mot-mots, hawks and occasional monkeys in the trees. The majority of tour operators listed in this guide will offer nature-oriented tours.

You have the chance to dive with whale sharks between Mar and May in southern **Belize** and the Bay Islands, whilst another popular animal to see is the manatee, often found in the coastal lagoons of Central America's rambling Caribbean coastline. Crocodiles are relatively common in the mangroves; a few have even begun lurking on golf courses in Cancún (with unpleasant consequences for one or two golfers). On land it is other mammals, particularly monkeys and the elusive wild cats, which quicken the heartbeat. The region's lowland rainforests conceal the most impressive wildlife of all, including jaguars and tapirs, but these are extremely difficult to spot. **Mexico's** Palenque is the best place to organize forays into the jungle.

In the air, or at least close to the ground, the sheer number of bird species – over 900 in **Panama** alone – mean ornithologists get positively overexcited by the prospect of Central America. The resplendent quetzal, with its beautifully flamboyant tail feather, is an essential sighting to start any twitcher's career. Although very rare, they populate the cloudforests around Cerro Punta, Panama, in great numbers. They can be spotted there without too much trouble.

In southern **Mexico**, the best places for birdwatching are the Río Largartos Biosphere Reserve and the Celestún Biosphere Reserve, both home to spectacular colonies of flamingos. Also good for aquatic birds is the Sian Ka'an Biosphere Reserve.

In **Nicaragua**, some 700 avian species are resident. The national bird is the beautiful turquoise-browed mot mot, fairly common in the highlands of Managua. Beyond the capital, the Reserva Biológica Indio-Maíz has primary rainforest that's home to green and scarlet macaws, whilst the Refugio de Vida Silvestre Los Guatuzos has gallery forest and wetlands teeming with aquatic birds. The northern mountains of Jinotega and Matagalpa are home to many prize bird species too, but for those with time, patience and rugged constitutions, the hard-to-reach Bosawás Biosphere Reserve promises some of the best birding in Central America.

Birdwatchers and butterfly lovers have long flocked to Costa Rica to see some of the 875 species of bird and untold varieties of butterfly. Birding is good year round in most national parks. See also Nature tourism box in **Costa Rica** chapter, for more on nature tourism.

**Panama** is home to 976 species of avifauna including 12 endemic and 20 endangered species. The lowland forests around the Panama Canal are a particularly fruitful and easy-to-access region; the Parque Nacional Soberanía is recommended for the world-class Pipeline Trail. The forests of Darién, eastern Panama, have particularly high rates of endemism and are home to some amazing species, but due to safety concerns are best visited as part of an organized tour. See also Nature tourism box in Panama chapter, for more on nature tourism.

For an introduction to the region's wildlife, see Background chapter.

# Where to stay

from homestays to hammocks

## Hotels and guesthouses

Hotels are widespread in all major towns and cities, but less prevalent in villages and small communities. Most rooms come with their own bathroom, running hot and/or cold water, cable TV, a fan, writing desk and Wi-Fi. Air conditioning will ratchet up the price, sometimes by an extra US$10-20. The very cheapest rooms have a shared bathroom (note that in the text the term 'with bath' usually means 'with shower and toilet', not 'with bathtub'). Couples should ask for a room with a *cama matrimonial* (double bed), which is cheaper than a room with two beds.

Rates vary seasonally, especially on the coast. You may also be charged 'gringo rates' based on your appearance and command of Spanish (in Spanish-speaking countries). Many hotels have a few cheap and very basic rooms set aside from their standards; politely ask if they have something *más económico*. Accommodation costs are highest in the tourist towns of southern Mexico, Belize, Costa Rica and Panama, where a 'cheap' and functional room with hot water and fan might cost US$20-35 (more on the beach during high season). You might pay US$15-20 for the same room in Guatemala, El Salvador, Nicaragua or Honduras, but these countries are no longer the great bargain they once were. In many popular destinations there is often an established preferred choice budget option.

## Price codes

**Where to stay**

$$$$ over US$150
$$$ US$66-150
$$ US$30-65
$ under US$30

Price of a double room in high season, including taxes.

**Restaurants**

$$$ over US$12
$$ US$7-12
$ US$6 and under

Prices for a two-course meal for one person, excluding drinks or service charge.

Making reservations is a good idea, particularly at times you know are going to be busy or if you are travelling a long distance and won't have the energy to look around for a room. At the lower end of the market, having reservations honoured can be difficult.

**Tip…**
Used toilet paper should be placed in the receptacle provided and not flushed down the pan, even in quite expensive hotels. Failing to do this blocks the pan or drain.

Ask the hotel if there is anything you can do to secure the room. If arriving late, make sure the hotel knows what time you plan to arrive. Beware 'helpers' who try to find you a hotel, as rates increase to pay their commission. Try www.airbnb.co.uk for stays with local hosts in apartments or houses. Although owners are not always necessarily present in the property while you're there, they will answer any questions before you get there and welcome you on arrival.

All-inclusive resorts tend to be concentrated on the Pacific and Caribbean coasts of southern Mexico, Belize, Costa Rica and Panama, and on the islands, especially in the Yucatán and Belize. Most resorts have beach access, pools, restaurants and a small army of staff to cater to your needs.

For those on a really tight budget, look for a boarding house, called a *casa de huéspedes, hospedaje, pensión, casa familial* or *residencial*; they are normally found in abundance near bus stations and markets and tend to be 20-50% cheaper than a hotel. They are usually quite basic and family-run and may or may not have television, running hot water, windows or sunlight. 'Love motels' can be found on highways, designed with discretion in mind. Although comfortable if occasionally seedy, their rates tend to be hourly.

## Youth hostels

Hostels have sprung up in all the big destinations across the region. They remain a cheap and sociable option for international backpackers, and useful for those who want to get together groups for tours. No two hostels are the same, as the cleanliness, quality and clientele vary greatly, but most offer a reliable range of amenities including free coffee, lockers, shared kitchen, Wi-Fi, tourist information and tours. Although you can save money by cooking your own meals, private rooms in hostels are not usually a good deal compared to hotels. Dorm accommodation, around US$7-15 per night, is the best bet for solo travellers on a budget. The **International Youth Hostel Association** ① *www.hihostels.com*, has a growing presence in the region, especially in Mexico and to a lesser extent, Panama and Costa Rica. With other affiliated hostels joining it is worth considering getting membership if you are staying in the country for a while.

## B&Bs

Throughout the region, the extent and popularity of B&Bs has taken off in recent years and most of them imply a level of quality, comfort and personal service above and beyond your bog-standard hotel. Some of the converted townhouses in the big colonial cities are especially beautiful. On the beach, luxury 'rustic chic' *cabañas* have become de rigueur. Most B&Bs cost upwards of US$50 per night and it's worth shopping around as style, comfort, intimacy and overall value vary greatly between establishments. Also check what kind of breakfast is included, as some do not extend to a full cooked spread. It's also worth checking out www.airbnb.co.uk too, see opposite page.

The web has spawned some great communities and independent travellers should take a look at www.couchsurfing.com. It's a way of making friends by kipping on their sofa. It's grown rapidly in the last few years and appears to be a great concept that works.

## Nature lodges

Nature lodges are famed for their romantic settings and access to areas of outstanding natural beauty, including rainforests, cloudforests, mountains and beaches. They are among the world's best places for wildlife observation, especially for birds. Although nature lodges are comparatively expensive – most fall in our $$$ and $$$$ range – they promise a unique and intimate experience of the wilderness that is sure to leave lasting impressions. Everyone should consider splashing out at least once.

## Homestays

Homestays are a great way to learn about local culture and are best arranged through Spanish schools or community tourism projects. Reasonably comfortable options are available in big towns and cities, but in more remote places, expect rustic conditions, including an outdoor toilet, little or no electricity, and cold running water (or just a bucket and wash bowl). Simple meals are usually included in rates. For homestays in Belize, see Guesthouse programme box in that chapter. See also **Experiment in International Living**, in Volunteering section of Practicalities chapter, which organizes homestays in Mexico and Central America.

## Camping

There are few official campsites in the region but camping is generally tolerated. Obey the following rules for wild camping: arrive in daylight and pitch your tent as it gets dark; ask permission to camp from a person in authority; never ask a group of people – especially young people; avoid camping on a beach (because of sandflies and thieves). If you can't get information, camp in a spot where you can't be seen from the nearest inhabited place and make sure no one saw you go there. Camping supplies are usually only available in the larger cities, so stock up on them when possible. In some national parks, simple rangers' station offer rustic lodging in cots. Bring your own food and water and some warm bedding; the rainforest can get quite chilly in the early hours.

## Hammocks

A hammock can be an invaluable piece of equipment, especially if travelling on the cheap. It will be of more use than a tent because many places have hammock hooks, or you can sling a hammock between trees or posts. A good tip is to carry a length of rope and some plastic sheeting. The rope gives a good choice of tree distances and the excess provides a hanging frame for the plastic sheeting to keep the rain off. Metal S-hooks or a couple of climbing karabiners can also be very useful, as can strong cord for tying out the sheeting. Don't forget a mosquito net if travelling in insect-infected areas.

# Food
# & drink

from poc chuc and pupusas to pulque and chicha

An excellent general rule when looking for somewhere to eat is to ask locally. Most restaurants serve a daily special meal, usually at lunchtime called a *comida corrida* or *comida corriente*, which works out much cheaper and is usually filling and nutritious. Vegetarians should list all the foods they cannot eat; saying '*Soy vegetariano/a*' (I'm a vegetarian) or '*No como carne*' (I don't eat meat) is often not enough. Street stalls are by far the cheapest – although not always the safest – option; another inexpensive place to eat is the local market. The best value is undoubtedly in small, family-run places. If self-catering, markets are cheaper than supermarkets.

**Safety** The golden rule is boil it, cook it, peel it or forget it, but if you did that every day, every meal, you'd never eat anywhere. A more practicable rule is that if large numbers of people are eating in a regularly popular place, it's more than likely going to be OK.

There are always plenty of non-alcoholic *refrescos* (soft drinks) and mineral water. *Agua fresca* – fresh fruit juices mixed with water or mineral water – and *licuados* (milk shakes) are good and usually safe, although hygiene varies in some countries such as Guatemala. Milk should be pasteurized. Water should be filtered or bottled. Herbal teas – for example chamomile (*manzanilla*) and mint (*hierba buena*) – are readily available. All imported food and drink is expensive.

## Mexico

Food for most Mexicans represents an integral part of their national identity and much has been written since the 1960s about the evolution of Mexican cooking. Experts suggest that there have been three important developmental stages: first, the combination of the indigenous and the Spanish traditions; later, the influence of other European cuisines, notably the French in the 19th century; and finally the adoption of exotic oriental dishes and fast food from the USA in the 20th century. In 2010, the importance of Mexican food was recognized by its inclusion on the UNESCO Intangible Cultural Heritage List.

Mexican cooking is usually perceived as spicy or hot due to the prolific use of chilli peppers, but equally, maize is a very typical ingredient and has been a staple crop since ancient times. It is mainly consumed in *antojitos* (snacks), including tacos, *quesadillas*, *flautas*, *sopes*, *tostadas*, *tlacoyos* and *gorditas*, which consist of various shapes and sizes of *tortillas*, with a variety of fillings and usually garnished with a hot sauce. Historically influenced by trade contact with the Caribbean, Europe and the southern US, Yucatec cuisine is distinctive. *Poc chuc* is grilled pork in a sour orange marinade. *Pollo pibil* is chicken marinated in sour orange and *achiote*, wrapped in banana leaves and baked; the same dish made with pork is called *cochinita pibil*. A *panucho* is a cooked tortilla with shredded chicken and a salad garnish; *salbutes* are *panuchos* with refried beans inside. *Huevos motuleños* is a breakfast dish consisting of fried eggs on a bed of tortilla and refried beans, all doused in tomato sauce, chopped ham, peas and cheese.

The native alcoholic drinks are *pulque*, made from the fermented juice of the agave plant, tequila and mescal, both made from distilled agave. *Mezcal* usually has a *gusano de maguey* (worm) in the bottle, considered to be a particular delicacy but, contrary to popular myth, is not hallucinogenic.

## Belize

Dishes suffer a wonderful preponderance of rice'n'beans – a cheap staple to which you add chicken, fish, beef and so on. For the cheapest meals, order rice which will come with beans and (as often as not) banana or plantain, or chicken, vegetables or even a blending of beef with coconut milk. Belize has some of the best burritos in Central America but you have to seek them out, normally in hidden-away stalls in the markets.

Along the coastal region and on the cayes seafood is abundant, fresh and reasonably cheap, but avoid buying lobster between 15 February and 14 June (when it's out of season) as stocks are worryingly low. (Conch is out of season between 1 July and 30 September; Nassau grouper, between 1 December and 31 March.)

Belikin beer is the local brew, costing US$3 a bottle. Many brands of local rum are available too. Several local wines and liqueurs are made from available fruit. One favourite, called *nanche*, is made from *crabou* fruit and is very sweet, as is the cashew wine, made from the cashew fruit rather than the nut.

## Guatemala

Traditional Central American/Mexican food such as tortillas, *tamales*, *tostadas*, etc, are found everywhere. Tacos are less spicy than in Mexico. *Chiles rellenos* (chillies stuffed with meat and vegetables) are a speciality in Guatemala and may be *picante* (spicy) or *no picante*. *Churrasco*, charcoal-grilled steak, is often accompanied by *chirmol*, a sauce of tomato, onion and mint. Guacamole is also excellent. Local dishes include *pepián* (thick meat stew with vegetables) in Antigua, *patín* (small lake fish wrapped in leaves and served in a tomato-based sauce) from Lake Atitlán and *cecina* (beef marinated in lemon and bitter orange) from the same region. *Fiambre* is widely prepared for families and friends who gather on All Souls' Day (1 November). It consists of all kinds of meat, fish, chicken, vegetables, eggs or cheese served as a salad with rice, beans and other side dishes. Desserts include *mole* (plantain and chocolate), *torrejas* (sweet bread soaked in egg and *panela* or honey) and *buñuelos* (similar to profiteroles) served with hot cinnamon syrup. For breakfast try *mosh* (oats cooked with milk and cinnamon), fried plantain with cream and black beans in various forms. *Pan dulce* (sweet bread), in fact bread in general, and local cheese are recommended. Try *borracho* (cake soaked in rum).

Local beers are good (Monte Carlo, Cabra, Gallo and Moza, a dark beer). By law alcohol cannot be consumed after 2000 on Sundays.

## El Salvador

*Pupusas*, stuffed tortillas made of corn or rice meal, are the quintessential Salvadorean dish. They come in several varieties including *chicharrón* (pork crackling), *queso* (cheese) and *revueltas* (mixed), and are typical, tasty and cheap. The ones sold at street stalls are better there than at restaurants, but beware stomach infection from the accompanying *curtido* (pickled cabbage). On Saturday and Sunday nights people congregate in *pupuserías*. *Pavo* (turkey) is common and good, as are *frijoles* (red beans). A *boca* is an appetizer, a small dish of yucca, avocado or chorizo, served with a drink before a meal. Apart from in San Salvador, restaurants tend to close early, around 2000.

*Chicha* is a traditional alcoholic drink made from corn, sometimes with a trace of pineapple; El Salvador also has a stronger, distilled version called *chaparro*. Although illegal to sell, everyone has their source. When made well *chicha* can taste similar to white wine. It is a trademark of the Maya and is particularly good in the western village of Izalco. Ask at the tourist office there for a *chicha* contact to purchase a sample. *Chaparro curado* contains fruit or honey. It is a favourite at election times when alcohol sales are banned. Water bottles are emptied and filled with the clear *chaparro* for illegal swigging on the streets.

## Honduras

*Carne asada* is charcoal-roasted meat and served with grated cabbage between tortillas; it is good, although rarely prepared hygienically. Make sure that pork is properly cooked. *Tajadas* are crisp, fried *plátano* chips topped with grated cabbage and sometimes meat; *nacatamales* are ground, dry maize mixed with meat and seasoning, boiled in banana leaves. *Baleadas* are soft flour tortillas filled with beans and various combinations of butter, egg, cheese and cabbage. *Pupusas* are also served; see El Salvador above. *Tapado* is a stew with meat or fish, plantain, yucca and coconut milk. *Pinchos* are meat, poultry, or shrimp kebabs. *Sopa de mondongo* (tripe soup) is very common.

Fish is sold on the beaches at Trujillo and Cedeño; also freshly fried at the roadside by the shore of Lago Yojoa. While on the north coast, look out for *pan de coco* (coconut bread) made by Garífuna (Black Carib) women, and *sopa de camarones* (prawn soup) prepared with coconut milk and lemon juice. Honduras is now a major producer of tilapia with exports to the US and fresh tilapia available in many restaurants.

*Horchata* is morro seeds, rice water and cinnamon. The main brands of **beer** are Port Royal Export, Imperial, Nacional, Barena and Salva Vida (more malty than the others). Local **rum** is cheap; try Flor de Caña white, or seven-year-old amber. Twelve-year-old Flor de Caña Centenario is regarded as the best.

## Nicaragua

A typical Nicaraguan breakfast is coffee with *gallo pinto* or *nacatamales*. *Gallo pinto*, the dish that keeps most of Nicaragua alive, is a mixture of fried white rice and kidney beans, which are boiled apart and then fried together with onions and sweet pepper, served with handmade corn tortillas. This can be breakfast, lunch and dinner for much of the population at home and for this reason is not found in most restaurants. *Nacatamales* are available; see under Honduras. A normal lunch includes a cabbage and tomato salad, white rice, beans, tortilla, onions, fried or boiled plantain and a meat or fish serving. *Asado* or *a la plancha* are key words for most foreigners. *Asado* is grilled meat or fish, which often comes with a chilli sauce. In the countryside *cuajada* is a must. It is a soft feta-style cheese made daily in people's homes, lightly salted and excellent in a hot tortilla. There are three traditional desserts that are worth trying: *tres leches*, a very sweet cake made with milk; *Pío V*, named after Pope Pius (though no one seems to know why), a corn cake topped with light cream and bathed in rum sauce; and if these are too heavy, there is the ubiquitous *cajeta*, milk mixed with cane sugar or endless varieties of blended or candied fruit. Look out, too, for *piñonate*, thinly sliced strips of candied green papaya.

Since Nicaragua is the land of a thousand fruits, the best drink is the *refresco* or *fresco*, fruit juices or grains and spices mixed with water and sugar. Two favourites are *cacao* and *pithaya*. *Cacao*, the raw cocoa bean, is ground and mixed with milk, rice, cinnamon, vanilla, ice and sugar and is refreshingly cold and filling. *Pithaya* is a cactus fruit, which is blended with lime and sugar and has a lovely, sensual deep purple colour and seedy pulp.

## Costa Rica

The food is simple, relying heavily on the staples of rice and beans. Mixed with shredded beef, chicken or sometimes fish, served with a couple of warmed tortillas and you have the dish of *casado* that fuels the majority of the country's workers. One way of spicing up the food is with liberal helpings of *Salsa Lizano* which is always somewhere near the dinner table.

*Sodas* (small restaurants) serve local food, which is worth trying. *Olla de carne* is a soup of beef, plantain, corn, yucca, *ñampi* and *chayote* (local vegetables). *Sopa negra* is made with black beans, and comes with a poached egg in it; *picadillo* is another meat and vegetable stew. Snacks are popular: *gallos* (filled tortillas), *tortas* (containing meat and vegetables), *arreglados* (bread filled with the same) and *empanadas*. *Pan de yuca* is a speciality, available from stalls in San José centre. For breakfast, try *gallo pinto* (rice and beans) with *natilla* (a slightly sour cream). The best ice cream can be found in Pops shops.

There are many types of cold drink made either from fresh fruit or milk drinks with fruit (*batidos*) or cereal flour whisked with ice cubes. The fruits range from the familiar to the exotic; other drinks include *cebada* (made with barley), *pinolillo* (made from roasted corn), *horchata* (rice-based with cinnamon) and *chan*, which, according to Michael Brisco, is "perhaps the most unusual, looking like mouldy frogspawn and tasting of penicillin". The coffee is excellent.

## Panama

In Panama City the range of food available is very broad with a profusion of restaurants and well-stocked supermarkets. In the interior tastes are simpler and available ingredients less varied. The staple of Panamanian food is white rice, grown not in paddies but on dry land, and usually served at every meal. Most food is boiled or fried in vegetable oil (usually soybean oil). A bowl of *sopa de carne* (beef broth with vegetables) or *de pescado* (fish chowder) is usually available as a first course for US$0.50. Breakfast normally consists of eggs, a small beefsteak or a slice of liver fried with onions and tomatoes, bread and butter and some combination of *frituras*.

The national dish is *sancocho de gallina*, a stew of chicken, yuca, *ñame* (dasheen), plantain, cut-up pieces of corn on the cob, potatoes and onions and strongly flavoured with *culantro*, an aromatic leaf similar in flavour to coriander (*cilantro*). *Ropa vieja* ('old clothes') is beef boiled or steamed until it can be shredded, then sautéed with onions, garlic, tomatoes and green or red peppers, often served with yellow rice (coloured with *achiote*). Piquant *ceviche*, eaten as a first course or a snack with cold beer, is usually raw *corvine* (sea bass) or shellfish seasoned with tiny red and yellow peppers, thin slices of onion and marinated in lime juice; it is served very cold with crackers (beware of the bite). A speciality of the Caribbean coast is *sao*, pig's trotters pickled with lime and hot peppers. Also try *arroz con coco*, coconut rice, or the same with *tití*, tiny shrimp; also *fufú*, a fish chowder with coconut milk. *Mondongo* is the stewed tripe dish.

Among the items sold at the roadside you may see bottles stopped with a corn cob, filled with *nance*, a strong-flavoured, yellow-green fruit packed with water and allowed to ripen and ferment slightly; *pifá/pixbae*, a bright orange fruit which, when boiled, tastes much like sweet potato; *níspero*, the tasty, acidic yellow fruit of the chicle tree.

There are dozens of sweetened fruit drinks: *naranja* (orange), *maracuyá* (passion fruit), *guayaba*, *zarzamora* (blackberry), *guanábana*, etc. The generic term is *chicha dulce* which also includes drinks made with rice or corn. Panamanian beer tends to be low in alcohol. *Chicha fuerte* is the alcoholic form of corn or rice drink fermented with sugar, brewed mostly in the countryside. The local rum is not bad. *Seco*, a harsh brand of 'white lightning' made from the juice of sugar cane, brand name *Herrerano*, deserves considerable respect.

# This is
## Southern
## Mexico

Forged in the flames of conquest, the deeply indigenous southern states of Mexico embody a vivid synthesis of European and Mesoamerican traditions: the merging of disparate worlds has spawned unique forms of art, cooking, song, dance, religion and philosophy.

A procession of vibrant colonial towns and cities echo the faded glory of imperial Spain, but beneath and behind them, at the foundations of lavish government palaces and grandiloquent baroque cathedrals, lie the hidden remnants of a much older and stranger reality. Millennia before Cortés and his conquistadors clambered ashore, southern Mexico was a crucible for competing civilizations: the Olmec, Zapotec, Mixtec and Maya chief among them. Today, their descendants breathe life into ancient traditions, for as much as the old gods are clothed in the respectable robes of Catholic saints, shamanism continues to thrive.

Perhaps no single indigenous symbol has become more firmly embedded in Mexican national identity than that of Lord Death. Encapsulating the ancient Mesoamerican concept of duality, death in Mexico is not a place of gloom or rest, but the source of spirited, irrepressible activity. Charged with colour, music, spectacle and celebration, Lord Death is an honoured guest at the feast, a garish skeleton festooned with flowers, drunk on mescal, delightfully raucous and dancing in the village square as church bells ring and fireworks explode. Death is a provocation to seize the moment for all it's worth. Death is Life, and by extension, so is Mexico.

# Chiapas & Tabasco

Encompassing jungles and mangrove swamps, the hot, humid, infrequently visited Gulf coast state of Tabasco holds special status as the forebear of all Mesoamerican societies. Out of this region came the Olmec with their shape-shifting jaguar shamans and their massive stone heads.

This was Mexico's first great culture, the mother culture. In the neighbouring state of Chiapas, lowland rainforests were home to the dazzling royal metropolises of Palenque, Bonampak, Yaxchilán, and Toniná. Today, many of their indigenous descendants still speak their native tongue, follow ancestral rites and observe the arcane procession of the Tzolk'in, an ancient Mayan calendar.

Isolated by convoluted highlands, western Chiapas is a remote landscape framed by desolate peaks, patchwork fields, wild flowers and clear clean mountain light. Daily life revolves around the cultivation of maize. So attuned to the symbols and lifestyles of its ancestors, it is no wonder that Chiapas has become a bastion for political movements focused on land rights, indigenous resistance, cultural preservation and food sovereignty.

**Best** for
Highland scenery ▪ Indigenous culture ▪ Mayan ruins ▪ Olmec heads

# Footprint picks

★ **Sumidero Canyon**, page 53

Take a boat trip on the reservoir that fills this stunning steep-sided chasm, with sheer walls up to 1 km high.

★ **San Cristóbal de las Casas**, page 54

Stay in the capital of Mexico's Mayan highlands, a fascinating stronghold of indigenous culture.

★ **San Juan Chamula**, page 69

Visit the atmospheric village church in this highland Mayan village where shamanism is practised.

★ **Lagunas de Montebello**, page 72

Swim in the crystal-clear magically multicoloured lakes set in pine forest.

★ **Palenque, Bonampak and Yaxchilán**, pages 83, 87 and 89

Explore these eerily atmospheric Mayan ruins buried deep in the rainforest.

★ **Parque Nacional La Venta**, page 92

Marvel at the huge Olmec stone heads that dominate this interesting outdoor museum.

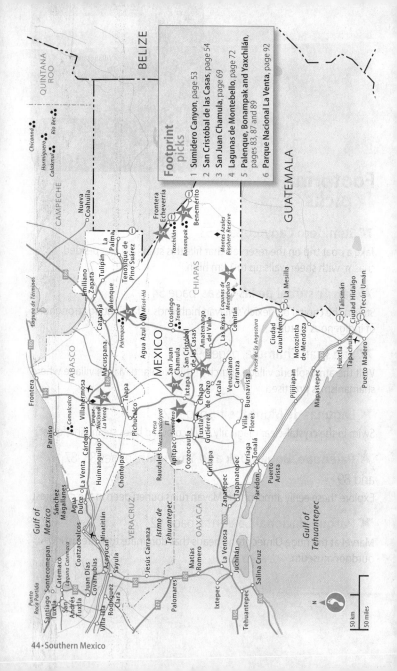

## Footprint picks

1 Sumidero Canyon, page 53
2 San Cristóbal de las Casas, page 54
3 San Juan Chamula, page 69
4 Lagunas de Montebello, page 72
5 Palenque, Bonampak and Yaxchilán, pages 83, 87 and 89
6 Parque Nacional La Venta, page 92

# Chiapas State

In Chiapas, the land of the Classic Maya (whose descendants still inhabit the highland villages today), the attractions are well known; San Cristóbal de las Casas is the end of the line for many travellers who base themselves in this delightful colonial and indigenous town while they soak up the atmosphere and explore the surrounding area. Around San Cristóbal are jungle waterfalls, the dramatic Sumidero Canyon; the multicoloured lakes, and – the highlight of any trip to Mexico – the ruins at Palenque, with a jungle setting that is arguably the most atmospheric and beautiful of all the Maya sites.

Chiapas is also a good entry point for Guatemala. You can head straight for northern Guatemala and the ruins of Tikal or take a more genteel entry through the western highlands and idyllic Lake Atitlán.

Chiapas seems largely impervious to the intrusion of outsiders. The Lost World feeling is created by indigenous inhabitants and their villages which make everything seem timeless. The appalling treatment the inhabitants have suffered over centuries was the fundamental cause of the rebellion on 1 January 1994, which led to the occupation of San Cristóbal by the revolutionaries of the EZLN (Zapatista Army of National Liberation) and their continuing struggle in and beyond the boundaries of Chiapas.

**humid and hectic, the largest and most developed city in Chiapas**

The state capital since 1892, Tuxtla Gutiérrez is an expanding business and transport hub. It is relatively modern and lacking in personality, but generally safe, clean and on the up. First settled by the Zoque and later incorporated into the Aztec empire, the city's name is derived from the Nahautl 'Tuchtlan', or Land of Rabbits ('Gutiérrez' refers to Joaquín Gutiérrez, a 19th-century politician). Today, you won't find many rabbits in Tuxtla, but like any capital, it has its share of decent museums, restaurants, shops and nightclubs. The downtown area can be walked but you may need a taxi to reach some outlying attractions. Streets follow a grid system with *avenidas* running east–west and *calles* running north–south around a central axis.

### Sights

At the intersection of Avenida and Calle Central, the **Plaza Cívica** is surrounded by government offices and historical buildings, including the **Catedral de San Marcos**, founded in the 16th century and renovated in modernist style. Its tower contains 48 bells and features an hourly parade of clockwork Apostles. One block east of the plaza, you'll find the **Museo del Café** ⓘ *2a Oriente Norte 236, T961-611 1478, www.museodelcafe.chiapas. gob.mx, Mon-Sat 0900-1700, US$0.75*, with exhibitions on the economy, history and culture of coffee production in Chiapas.

Marimba music is an integral part of Chiapaneco identity and its history, traditions and heroes are explored at the **Museo de la Marimba** ⓘ *9a Poniente Norte and Av Central, T961-616 0012, Tue-Sun 1000-2200, US$2.30*. Opposite the museum, the **Jardín de la Marimba** is the place to hear rousing live performances in the evening.

Approximately 1.2 km northeast of the Plaza Cívica (15 minutes' walk), **Parque Madero** is a parched park space with several museums strung along the **Calzada de los Hombres Ilustres**. The best and most important is the **Museo Regional de Antropología e Historia** ⓘ *T961-613 4375, Tue-Sun 0900-1800, US$3.50*, which charts the cultural and historical evolution of Chiapas with important exhibits of local archaeology and colonial antiques. Next door, you can observe a collection of 200 prehistoric fossils, including a reconstructed skeleton of a fearsome *megatherium* (giant sloth) inside the **Museo de Paleontología** ⓘ *Mon-Fri 1000-1700, Sat-Sun 1100-1700, US$1.25*. The **Jardín Botánico Faustino Miranda** ⓘ *Mon-Fri*

**Tuxtla Gutiérrez**

Ticketbus Office

Plaza Cívica

Palacio de Gobierno del Estado

Cathedral

Buses to Chiapa de Corzo

Bus to Zoo

**N**

200 metres
200 yards

**Where to stay** 🛏
Hilton Garden Inn **1**

Hostal San Miguel **2**
Hostel Tres Central **3**

**Restaurants** 🍴
Bonampak **1**
Las Pichanchas **2**
Los Molcajetes **3**

*0900-1500, Sat 0900-1300, free*, covers 4.4 ha with hundreds of botanical specimens but the space is now neglected.

### Zoológico Miguel Alvarez del Toro (Zoomat)

*Calzada Cerro Hueco s/n, T961-639 2856, www.zoomat.chiapas.gob.mx, Tue-Sun 0830-1630, US$4. Colectivos to 'Zoológico' and 'Cerro Hueco' depart every 20 mins from Mercado, Calle 1a Oriente Sur y 7 Sur Oriente; taxis charge around US$3 from centre or town buses charge US$0.20.*

Animal enclosures don't appeal to everyone, but Zoomat, Tuxtla's premier attraction, is a decent facility and internationally renowned for its efforts in conservation, outreach, environmental education and research. From highlands to lowlands, the zoo exclusively features fauna from Chiapas, Mexico's most biodiverse state. Here, you can observe a staggering cornucopia of magnificent neotropical beasts: tapirs, jaguars, ocelots, monkeys, coyotes, deer, snakes, lizards, insects, as well as scores of dazzling avian species, including raptors, macaws and quetzals. Originally founded in 1942, the zoo has changed locations twice and now enjoys verdant landscaped grounds inside the El Zapotal nature reserve. The enclosures are generally spacious.

## Listings Tuxtla Gutiérrez *map p46*

### Tourist information

There are municipal tourist information kiosks on the Plaza Cívica and inside the Museo de Marimba, 9a Calle Poniente Norte, www.turismo.tuxtla.gob.mx.

**SECTUR office**
*Blv Andrés Serra Rojas 1090, Edif Torre Chiapas, 5th floor, T961-617 0550, www.turismochiapas.gob.mx. Daily 0800-1900.*
Inconveniently located, has information on Chiapas state.

### Where to stay

**$$$ Hilton Garden Inn**
*Blv Belisario Domínguez 1641, T961-617 1800, www.hiltongardeninn3.hilton.com.*
Although not central, this is probably the best business-class hotel in the city, and there are many to choose from. The building is fairly new and it offers high quality, well-equipped standards and suites. A pool, gym, business centre, bar and restaurant are among the amenities. A good deal for the price.

**$$-$ Hostal San Miguel**
*3ra Sur Pte 510, T961-611 4459, www.hostalsanmiguel.com.mx.*
Hostal San Miguel offers 2 classes of lodging. The 'gold' rooms ($$) consist of smart, modern, above average mid-range quarters fully kitted with desk, cable TV and Wi-Fi. The 'hostal' rooms ($) are economical 6-bed dorms with lockers, a cooking area, shared bathroom, and a TV room.

**$ Hostal Tres Central**
*Calle Central Norte 393, T961-611 3674, hostaltrescentral@gmail.com.*
This socially and ecologically aware outfit has an excellent sustainable ethos, good value lodgings, great contemporary design and lots of attention to detail. Both private rooms and dorms are available: all crisp, clean, comfortable and well maintained. Upstairs there's a great rooftop terrace where you can sip mojitos or swing in a hammock. Relaxed and intimate. Highly recommended.

## Restaurants

### $$$-$$ Bonampak
*Blv Belisario Domínguez 180, T961-602 5916.*
Formerly an upmarket hotel, now only the restaurant remains. Decent Mexican and North American dishes, but quite pricey.

### $$-$ Las Pichanchas
*Av Central Ote 857, T961-612 5351, www. laspichanchas.com.mx. Daily 1200-2400.*
Pretty courtyard, typical food, live marimba music 1430-1730 and 2030-2330 and folkloric ballet 2100-2200 daily. Its sister restaurant **Mirador Copoya** overlooks Sumidero Canyon.

### $ Los Molcajetes
*In the arches behind the cathedral.*
Cheap all-day meal deals including tacos, *enchiladas suizas, chilaquiles* and other staples. Several other restaurants lining the arches offer similar good value.

## Transport

### Air
Tuxtla's international airport, **Aeropuerto Angel Albino Corzo (TGZ)**, is located 27 km south of the city. Fixed prices taxis into town cost US$16; to **San Cristóbal**, US$46. **OCC** minibuses also run from the airport to **San Cristóbal**, 4 daily, US$12.50.

Flights to **Mexcio City** with Interjet, Aeroméxico (Connect), TAR Aerolineas, and Volaris; **Oaxaca** with Aerotucán; **Cancún** with VivaAerobus; **Guadalajara** with Volaris and VivaAerobus; **Monterrey** with **Volaris** and **VivaAerobus**; **Tijuana** with **Volaris**; and **Houston** with **United**.

### Bus
The 1st class **ADO** bus station is on 5a Norte Poniente at the corner of Angel Albino Corzo, next to the large Plaza del Sol mall on the northwestern outskirts of the city; buses to the centre pass outside, US$0.50.

Departures to **Cancún**, 7 daily, 18-20 hrs, US$85-139; **Comitán**, every 45 mins, 3 hrs, US$7.50; **Mérida**, 8 daily, 13-15 hrs, US$66-92; **Mexico City**, hourly, 12-13 hrs, US$89-112; **Oaxaca City**, 5 daily, 10-11 hrs, US$41-62; **Palenque**, 6 daily, 6-7 hrs, US$20-25; **Puerto Escondido**, 3 daily, 2030, 2200, 2315, 11-12 hrs, US$45; **San Cristóbal de las Casas**, hourly, 1½ hrs, US$4-5; **Tapachula**, hourly, 4-6 hrs, US$30-51; **Tonalá**, hourly, 2 hrs, US$14-16; **Villahermosa**, 11 daily, 4-5 hrs, US$26-38. There's a 2nd-class terminal at 9a Av Sur Ote and 13a Calle Oriente Sur, about 1 km southeast of the centre, serving destinations in Chiapas.

### Colectivos
Shuttles to **Chiapa de Corzo** depart frequently from 1 Av Sur Ote and Calle 5a Ote Sur; and from the **Transportes Chiapa–Tuxtla** station, 2a Ote Sur and 1a Av Sur Ote, 20 mins, US$0.85. To **San Cristóbal de las Casas** (recommended, faster and more frequent than **ADO**), from 15a Calle Ote Sur and 4a Av Sur Ote; and from 13a Calle Ote Sur near Av Central Ote, 1 hr, US$3.50.

Backed by the peaks of the Sierra Madre de Chiapas, El Soconusco is a 200-km-long strip of fertile coastal lowlands fringed by brackish mangrove swamps, teeming estuarine outlets, rustic fishing villages, verdant fruit plantations, and miles of desolate, wave-swept beaches.

Settled in 2000 BC by the Mokaya, one of the oldest of Mesoamerican cultures, the region has always enjoyed a distinctive identity rooted in agriculture and trade, serving as a tribute province for various powers including the Aztecs. Its name is derived from the Nahuatl 'Xoconochco' (land of sour cactus fruit) and modern crops of bananas, coffee, cacao, mangos, maize, papaya, African palm and sesame seeds thrive in its rich volcano soil, staples of the local economy which are now complimented by tourism.

The beaches of the Soconusco are popular with weekenders from Tuxtla, but deserted during the week. The sands are grey and the currents can be strong (watch out for riptides, a definite danger), but the water is clear, clean and inviting, and the sunsets immense. If your final destination is Quetzaltenango or the Pacific coast of Guatemala, the crossing at Tapachula is the most convenient point of entry. **Note** The region is subject to high humidity, bloodthirsty bugs and torrential downpours during the wet season, May to October.

### Tonalá and around *Colour map 2, B1.*
Around 20 km east of the Oaxaca state border, the town of **Arriaga** marks an intersection of highways connecting Tehuantepec and Tuxtla Gutiérrez to the Soconusco. From here, Route 200 winds 24 km east to Tonalá, a small, sweltering agricultural city steeped in cattle pastures and farmlands. This is the gateway to more alluring destinations on the coast and you should stock up on supplies of cash as ATMs are non-existent beyond here. Around 14 km west of Tonalá, perched on Laguna del Mar Muerto, the village of **Paredón** is good for fresh seafood, but there is no beach.

The region's main tourist hub is the sleepy village of **Puerto Arista**, 19 km south of Tonalá, home to a 30-km-long grey-sand beach partly fronted by *palapas*, bars, restaurants, simple hotels and guesthouses. Turtles nest here from July to October and you'll find a sanctuary, the **Santuario Tortuguero Puerto Arista**, roughly 3 km northwest of town, which releases hatchlings and offers night tours. Around 14 km east of Puerto Arista, there are tranquil, low-key lodgings at the rustic fishing village of **Boca del Cielo**. A few kilometres further, **El Madresal** ① *T966-666 6147, www.elmadresal.com*, is a conservation and ecotourism operator with *cabañas*, restaurant, and knowledgeable guides for wildlife and birding excursions. From Tonolá, the best way to get to the beaches is by colectivo; they run from dawn till dusk from Matamoros, between 20 de Marzo and Belisario Domínguez, 20-45 minutes, US$1.50-3. Private taxis cost US$10-15.

### Reserva de la Biósfera La Encrucijada *Colour map 2, B2.*
A federally protected biosphere reserve since 1995, La Encrucijada encompasses 144,868 ha of mangroves and semi-deciduous forest, permanently flooded wetlands and seasonal canals. It is home to caiman, monkeys, raccoons, boa constrictors, abundant amphibians and at least 90 species of bird, including waders, waterfowl and seabirds, and the only bird species endemic to Chiapas, the giant wren. Tours of the park are offered by the **La Red de Ecoturismo la Encrucijada** ① *www.ecoturismolaencrucijada.com*, who can guide you

through the mangroves by *lancha* or kayak, connect you with local communities, or set you up with rustic accommodation on the beach; they offer various all-inclusive packages starting at around US$190 per person, contact in advance of travel. To get to the reserve, first travel to **Escuintla**, 150 km east of Tonalá on Route 200. From there, colectivos go to **Acapetahua**, 6 km south, US$0.50. Combis ply the last 18 km to the **Embarcadero Las Garzas**, US$1.50, where you can hire onward *lanchas*. Take plenty of cash and plan carefully to avoid getting stranded.

## Tapachula and around *Colour map 2, C3.*

Optimistically dubbed 'Pearl of the Soconusco', Tapachula is a busy border town and flood-prone regional capital. In pre-Columbian times, it belonged to a rural province controlled by the Mam Maya, until it was assimilated and urbanized by the Aztecs in the 13th century. Its Nahautl name is Tapachollan (appropriately 'Between the Waters' of 'Place of Floods'). Today, it is a small city built on coffee exports and cross-border trade. Its economy is heavily supplemented by its cargo port, **Puerto Chiapas** (Puerto Madero), which was upgraded in 2005 to accommodate cruise ships. Downtown, the action is focused on **Parque Miguel Hidalgo**, a large plaza flanked by historical buildings, including the **Casa de Cultura**, an art deco edifice constructed in 1929 and embellished with Mexican motifs. The plaza is home to the city's only recommended attraction, the **Museo Arqueológico del Soconusco** ⓘ *8a Av Norte, T962-626 4173, Tue-Sun 0900-1800, US$2.70 (plus US$3.50 to take photos)*, which houses a collection of artefacts from the site of Izapa (see below), including numerous stelae and a dazzling jade-encrusted human skull.

**Around Tapachula** If you have the time or inclination, there are several interesting diversions around Tapachula; for more details, including recommend guides, talk to the Sectur tourist office ⓘ *6a Av Sur s/n, entre 2a y Central Poniente, T962-625 5409*. Options include **La Ruta Café**, an agro-tourism development that includes more than a dozen coffee fincas, many of German origin. Some of them are stunningly located with luxury mountain-top accommodation and spas; others have facilities for adventure sports like biking and zip-lining. Hardcore adventurists should consider a guided hike up **Volcán Tacaná** (4150 m), Mexico's fourth largest mountain, which takes two to three days from the town of Unión Juárez. There are waterfalls on the lower slopes and some *cabañas* at the top; a sleeping bag is essential.

## Izapa *Colour map 2, B3.*
*Tapachula–Talismán highway Km10-12, 0900-1700, pay a donation to the caretaker. To get there, take any bus or a combi towards Talismán, US$0.80.*

Founded in 1500 BC, the ceremonial centre of Izapa is one of the oldest urban sites in Mesoamerica. Probably of Mixe-Zoque origin, it reached its zenith 600 BC-AD 100 and remained inhabited until AD 1200. Its main axis is aligned with Volcán Tacaná and its urban core of 161 buildings includes pyramids, platforms, and ball courts. Izapa is most notable for its 283 monuments, including 89 stelae and 61 altars depicting mythological entities such as frogs symbolizing rain gods.

Pointing to the site's distinctive artwork, the archaeologist Michael Coe argued that Izapa acted as a 'bridge culture' between the pre-Classic Olmec and Maya. Olmec motifs like downturned human mouths and scrolling skies are evident at Izapa, whilst distinctive Izapa motifs have also been discerned at Mayan sites in Guatemala. It has also been argued that Izapa is the birthplace of the 260-day Mesoamerican calendar. Although the site is historically important, it is visually underwhelming with around 100 mounds and restored platforms divided between three sections: F in the north, A and B in the south. A good guide will bring it to life; contact the archaeological museum in Tapachula for recommendations.

## Mexico to Guatemala: Tapachula–El Carmen/Ciudad Tecún *Colour map 2, C3.*

The Talismán bridge lies 20 km from Tapachula and connects the towns of **Talismán** in Mexico and **El Carmen** in Guatemala. It provides good onward connections to the Pacific coast and the western highlands, but it's also a fairly grubby crossing with sneaky and aggressive moneychangers who you should avoid doing business with.

Further south, 37 km from Tapachula, **Ciudad Hidalgo** connects with **Ciudad Tecún Umán** in Guatemala. Perched on the Pan-American Highway, this is a much busier border town and the preferred route of international buses. Start as early as possible to avoid travelling in Guatemala during the hours of darkness. See also Border crossings box in Practicalities chapter.

## Listings El Soconusco

### Where to stay

#### Tonalá and around

##### $$$-$$ Awa Hotel
*Blv Mariano Matamoros, Puerto Arista, T994-600 9187, awahotelboutiquespa@gmail.com.*
Situated on the coast road next to the beach, this small boutique hotel is one of the more upscale options in Puerto Arista. It is a modern, Mediterranean-style building with contemporary furnishings and clean comfortable rooms overlooking a pool and sunbeds. Spa facilities are available.

##### $$-$ Hotel Galilea
*Hidalgo 138, Tonalá, T966-663 0239.*
If you get stuck in Tonalá, or just need to make an early start, there are a few budget hotels and *posadas*. Hotel Galilea is one of the better ones, complete with adequate a/c and balconies overlooking the main plaza.

##### $$-$ José's Cabañas
*Niño Perdido 100, 1 block north of the beach, Puerto Arista, T994-600 9048, www.josescampingcabanas.com.*
This Canadian-owned camping park offers basic brick-built bungalows with own bath, rustic *cabañas* with shared bath, dorm accommodation, RV hook-up and campground. No frills, but quiet and restful.

##### $$-$ La Luna
*Boca del Cielo, T966-106 4893, www.lunachiapas.com.mx.*
This tranquil and remote place has rustic, wood-built *cabañas* on the sand, solar powered and complete with hammocks and mosquito nets. There's a restaurant serving good seafood and a fun evening bar called the 'Loco Mosquito'. To get there take a taxi to the dock at Rancho Don Lupe, then call the hotel for boat transit.

#### Tapachula

##### $$$$-$$$ Argovia Finca Resort
*Carretera Nueva Alemania Km 39+2, T962-692 3051, www.argovia.com.mx.*
Founded by a Swiss family in 1880, this handsome highland coffee finca holds numerous awards and certificates for its quality organic produce, sustainable practices and high standard of hospitality. They offer coffee tours, gourmet cuisine, nature walks, adventure sports and spa facilities. Lodging is in cosy rooms, wood cabins, houses and bungalows. Secluded and restful. Recommended.

##### $$$$-$$$ Finca Hamburgo
*Carretera Nueva Alemania Km 54, T962-626 7578, www.fincahamburgo.com.*
Established in 1888 by Arthur Edelmann from Germany, Finca Hamburgo has

also been recognized for its quality and distinction and has fabulous views of the countryside. Lodging includes tastefully decorated wood-panelled double rooms ($$$) and suites ($$$$). Restaurant, spa, coffee tours, nature tours, rappelling and zip-lining are among the services and amenities on offer.

### $$$ Hotel Boutique Casa Mexicana
*8a Av Sur 19, T962-626 6605,*
*www.casamexicanachiapas.com.*
There are scores of business hotels in Tapachula offering generic comfort for your pesos, but for something with style and personality head to this fabulous historic townhouse. It's strikingly adorned with folk art, antiques, paintings and statues. The superb atmosphere, quality rooms, intriguing decor, lush garden, pool, bar and restaurant combine to make this one of the best in town.

### $ Hotel Cervantino
*1a Calle Ote 6, T962-620 0008,*
*www.hotelcervantino.com.mx.*
Most of Tapachula's budget hotels are a bit insalubrious, but this place is a definite exception. They offer clean, simple rooms with Wi-Fi, parking, common areas and complimentary coffee. Friendly, helpful, good value and a good central location.

## Restaurants

### Tapachula

### $$ La Jefa
*1 Av Nte 16 esq, 1 Calle Ote.*
This friendly little joint serves up hearty tacos and other Mexican fare, best washed down with a cold beer. Wi-Fi is available and there are free snacks when you order booze.

## Transport

### Tapachula
### Air
**Tapachula airport (TAP)** is 25 mins from town centre, at Km 18.5 Carretera a Puerto

Madero. Flights to **Mexico City** with **Aeroméxico** and Volaris; **Tuxtla Gutiérrez** with **Ka'an Air**. Colectivos to downtown, US$6.50; US$13 for the whole vehicle.

### Bus
The 1st class **ADO** terminal is 1 km northeast of the Parque Central, Calle 17a Ote, between Av 3a and 5a Nte. There is a 2nd-class terminal at Calle 9a Pte 62; colectivos depart from Calle 5a Pte. From the **ADO** terminal, departures to **Comitán**, 11 daily, 4-5 hrs, US$26-38; **Escuintla**, 7 daily, 1½ hrs, US$7.70; **Mexico City**, 5 daily, 17-19 hrs, US$104; **Oaxaca City**, 2 daily, 1915, 2000, 12-13 hrs, US$41-54; **San Cristóbal de las Casas**, 8 daily, 8 hrs, US$26-33; **Tonalá**, hourly, 3½ hrs, US$18; **Tuxtla Gutiérrez**, hourly, 5-6 hrs, US$30-34.

**International buses** Several bus lines offer services from Tapachula's 1st-class bus station to **Guatemala City**, including **Ticabus**, www.ticabus.com, 0700, US$22, 6 hrs; **Línea Dorada**, www.lineadorada. com.gt, 0600, US$17; and **Trans Galgos Inter**, www.transgalgosinter.com.gt, 0600, 1215, 2345, US$22-32. For more information on crossing the border see page 51 and Border crossings box in Practicalities chapter.

### Colectivos
From Tapachula to **Ciudad Hidalgo** with onward connections to **Ciudad Tecún Umán**, combis depart from Calle 7a Pte, between Av 2 Norte and Av Central Norte, every 15 mins, US$1.90. Stamp out in Ciudad Hidalgo and cross the bridge into Guatemala to submit to formalities there. It is another 20-min walk from the border to Tecún Umán, or take a bici-taxi, US$1.50, where you can catch numerous onward connections.

From Tapachula to **Talismán** with onward connections to **El Carmen** in Guatemala, combis leave from near the Unión y Progreso bus station and from the colectivo terminal, Calle 5 Pte between Av 12 y Av 14 Norte, every 15 mins, 30 mins, US$1.15. Taxi

**Tapachula–Talismán**, negotiate fare to about US$4. You may have to walk 5 mins to the border. A taxi between Guatemalan and Mexican Immigration offices will cost US$2, but it may be worth it if you are in a hurry to catch an onward bus. If travelling to Quetzaltenango, you will need to change in Coatepeque or Retalhuleu, or take a colectivo taxi to Malacatán. Hitchhikers should note that there is little through international traffic at the Talismán bridge. As a rule, hitchhiking is not advisable in Chiapas.

## Chiapa de Corzo  Colour map 2, B2.

a thriving colonial town best known for its vertiginous canyon

Situated on a bluff overlooking the Grijalva River, Chiapa de Corzo, 15 km east of Tuxtla, is famous for its Parachico dancers, who descend on the streets in great numbers during the Great Feast, January 4-22 (see Festivals, below). Their striking attire includes colourful *sarapes* (blanket-type shawls), massive blond wigs, and lacquered wooden masks reminiscent of pale-faced Europeans.

Originally settled around 1400 BC by Mixe-Zoque speakers with close ties to the Olmec, the site evolved into an important city until its decline around 400 AD. By the time of the Spanish conquest, the war-like Chiapa tribe had established their capital less than 2 km away, which was subjugated by Diego de Mazariegos in 1528 only after fierce resistance. The administrative centre of Chiapa de los Indios was founded in the shade of La Pochota, an ancient and venerated ceiba tree, but soon abandoned for the cooler and more hospitable climes of San Cristóbal de las Casas. In the 19th century, the suffix of 'de Los Indios' was replaced to honour Liberal politician, Angel Albino Corzo.

### Sights

The town is laid out in a classic colonial grid with a plaza at the centre, municipal buildings, commercial *portales*, and a particularly handsome 16th-century Moorish fountain, **La Pila**, boasting numerous arches and a brick-built watchtower in the shape of a crown. By the river, the **Iglesia de Santo Domingo** is perched on a small hill. Built in Moorish style by Pedro de Barrientos and Juan Alonso, it boasts one of the largest bells in the country, said to weigh more than four tonnes. The adjoining *ex-convento* houses a cultural centre and the **Museo de la Laca** ① *Tue-Sun 1000-1700, free*, with fine examples of local lacquer work dating back to the 17th century. Remnants of the region's distant Zoque heritage can be encountered at the town's small but important **archaeological site** ① *Av Hidalgo, 0800-1630, free, 1.5 km from the plaza behind the Nestlé plant*. It includes some restored temple complexes, many unexcavated mounds, and the oldest known pyramid tomb in Mesoamerica. Around 10 km beyond Chiapa de Corzo is the **Cueva del Chorreadero**, with refreshing waterfalls and swimming pools. The underground cave system here should not be explored without a professional guide and safety equipment; there are several adventure and ecotourism operators in San Cristóbal de las Casas (see What to do, page 66).

### ★Sumidero Canyon

Engulfing the Río Grijalva with its vast and precipitous walls, the Sumidero Canyon, as deep as 1 km in some sections, is a truly sheer natural spectacle that rarely fails to impress. According to local legend, Chiapaneco warriors hurled themselves into this hungry chasm rather than submit to the Spanish conquistadors. In recent times, the construction of the Chicoasén Dam created a 25 km-long reservoir, allowing visitors to experience the canyon by motorboat. The journey takes around two hours. You'll see intriguing rock formations and prolific wildlife, such as crocodiles, monkeys, pelicans and vultures, but remember to pack a sweater, as it gets chilly when you're speeding along.

Boats depart from the riverside in **Chiapa de Corzo** when full, but you shouldn't have to wait long for other passengers. Tickets are available at the **Turística de Grijalva office** ① *west side of the plaza, 0800-1700, US$12.50*. If you have your own vehicle, you may wish to forgo Chiapa de Corzo (parking can be tricky) and use the *embarcadero* beneath Cahuaré bridge, 5 km north of town. It is also possible to view the canyon from on high at a sublime series of miradors. **Transporte Panorámico Cañón del Sumidero** ① *T961-166 3740*, visits the main ones, departing from Jardín de la Marimba in Tuxtla at 0930 and 1300, US$11.50, if there is sufficient demand (five people); call ahead to confirm.

## Listings Chiapa de Corzo

### Where to stay

**$$ Hotel La Ceiba**
*Av Domingo Ruíz 300, T961-616 0389,*
*www.laceibahotel.com.*
You'll find a handful of adequate *posadas* in Chiapa de Corzo, but La Ceiba is the only lodging of any decent standard. This handsome 3-storey colonial house boasts a rambling, leafy garden, pool, restaurant and spa facilities. Rooms are reasonable, but sometimes noisy due to tour groups.

### Festivals

The fiestas here are outstanding. Jan Daylight fiestas, **Los Parachicos**, on 15, 17 and 20 Jan to commemorate the miraculous healing of a young boy some 300 years ago, and the **Chunta Fiestas**, at night, 8-23 Jan. There are parades with men dressed up as women in the evenings of the 8, 12, 17 and 19 Jan. All lead to the climax, 20-23 Jan, in honour of **San Sebastián**, with a pageant on the river.
**25 Feb El Santo Niño de Atocha**.
**25 Apr Festival de San Marcos**, with various *espectáculos*.

### Transport

**Colectivos**
Frequent colectivos to **Tuxtla** depart from Av 21 de Octubre on the plaza. Buses to **San Cristóbal** now bypass Chiapa de Corzo, meaning you'll have to pick one up on the highway or go via Tuxtla.

## San Cristóbal de las Casas  Colour map 2, B2.

**a rambling colonial city with cobblestone streets and adobe houses**

★Nestled on the floor of a high green valley is the cool, bright, mysterious mountain enclave of San Cristóbal de las Casas, sometimes known by its Tzotzil name, 'Jovel'. It is the largest urban settlement in the Chiapas highlands and a vital hub of trade for Mayan communities dispersed in the surrounding hills and pine forests. Despite serving as the capital of Chiapas until its relocation to Tuxtla in 1892, it has always been an insular place, characterized by its many poor indigenous barrios, and during the colonial era, its devout monastic institutions and its somewhat over-privileged Spanish elite.

# Essential San Cristóbal de las Casas

## Getting around

Most places are within walking distance of each other although taxis are available in town and to the nearby villages; the cheaper colectivos run on fixed routes only.

### Best places to stay
Don Quijote, page 61
Na Bolom, page 61
Sol y Luna, page 61
Posada del Abuelito, page 62

## When to go

Daytime temperatures in the highlands are consistently warm throughout the year at around 20°C. However, evening temperatures can drop to 5°C or less from December to February, requiring a light jacket or sweater. December to February are the driest months; August to October can be extremely wet and buggy.

### Best restaurants
Tierra y Cielo, page 62
Cocoliche, page 63
El Punto Pizzería, page 63
Te Quiero Verde, page 63
Oh La La, page 64

In recent years, for better or worse, the outside world has intruded in the form of tourism: scores of international restaurants, youth hostels, boutique hotels, rowdy bars, art house cinemas, yoga schools and meditation centres give the city a vibrant, bohemian, New Age feel that may ultimately dissipate as gentrification intensifies. During the busiest tourist months, the atmosphere can verge on carnivalesque, sadly masking the city's essential character: beyond its fetching exterior and sociable vibe, a deeply political current here has long accented social divisions, inequalities and inequities.

## Sights
**Plaza 31 de Marzo**, named after the date of San Cristóbal's foundation in 1528, is the social heart of the city, informally known as the Zócalo or the Parque Central. Pleasantly landscaped with evergreens, tallipot palm trees, ornamentals, pathways, and benches, it is a hub for wandering pedestrians, shoe-shiners, and vendors, including traditionally attired Tzotzil and Tzeltal women who sell everything from hand-woven textiles to lovable Zapatista dolls, sweet organic strawberries and corn on the cob. At the centre of the plaza stands a Porfirato kiosk where jaunty marimba performances are staged on Sundays – there are terraced cafes on the south and east sides where you can enjoy hot Chiapaneco coffee, relax to the melodies and watch the world go by.

## Weather San Cristóbal de las Casas

| January | February | March | April | May | June |
|---------|----------|-------|-------|-----|------|
| 4°C | 4°C | 6°C | 8°C | 9°C | 11°C |
| 21°C | 22°C | 24°C | 24°C | 24°C | 23°C |
| 9mm | 8mm | 12mm | 45mm | 94mm | 229mm |

| July | August | September | October | November | December |
|------|--------|----------|---------|----------|----------|
| 10°C | 10°C | 11°C | 9°C | 7°C | 4°C |
| 23°C | 23°C | 22°C | 22°C | 21°C | 21°C |
| 174mm | 191mm | 226mm | 116mm | 35mm | 11mm |

The **Casa de la Sirena**, a late 16th-century mansion commissioned by the conquistador Diego de Mazariegos, stands on the southeast corner of the plaza. It is a rare but crude example of colonial residential architecture in the plateresque style (an ornate decorative style suggestive of silverware; literally 'in the manner of a silversmith'); the portals on

## San Cristóbal de las Casas

**Where to stay**
Axkan Arte **1** *D2*
Balam **2** *B3*
Bela's **3** *B2*
B˘o **4** *B1*
Don Quijote **5** *B3*
Guayaba Inn **6** *A4*
Iguana Hostel **7** *A2*
La Joya **8** *C3*
Los Camellos **9** *C4*
Na Bolom **10** *A4*

Posada del Abuelito **11** *A4*
Posada San Cristóbal **12** *C2*
Puerta Vieja **13** *C1*
Santo Tomás **14** *A4*
Sol y Luna **15** *A3*

**Restaurants**
Belil **1** *B3*
Cocoliche **2** *C3*
El Caldero **3** *D2*
El Cau **4** *C3*

El Mercadito **5** *B4*
El Punto Pizzeria **6** *C3*
Juguería Ana Banana **14** *D2*
La Casa del
  Pan Paplotl **33** *C3*
La Tertulia **7** *C2*
Madre Tierra **18** *D2*
Miura **9** *C2*
Oh La La **10** *C2*
Te Quiero Verde **11** *D2*
TierrAdentro **12** *C2*

Tierra y Cielo **23** *C2*

**Bars & clubs**
Dada Club **13** *B2*
El Cocodrilo **8** *C2*
Entropia **15** *B3*
Revolución **30** *B2*

## BACKGROUND
### San Cristóbal de las Casas

Throughout much of its colonial life, San Cristóbal was known as Ciudad Real, in reference to the birthplace of the Spanish conquistador, Diego de Mazariegos, who violently subjugated the region. It was later renamed in honour of the patron Saint Christopher, but the suffix referencing the 16th-century Dominican friar, Bartolomé de las Casas, the first Bishop of Chiapas, 'Protector of the Indians', who famously preached in the city and petitioned King Ferdinand over abuses committed against the indigenous peoples, was only added in the 19th century.

As a focal point for human rights activism, San Cristóbal hit global headlines on 1 January 1994 when the Zapatista Liberation Army (EZLN), driven by centuries of abuse and feudal injustice, came down from the hills and seized the city by force.

Avenida Insurgentes feature stucco coats of arms and the wide-eyed mermaids of its namesake. Built in 1885, the relatively modern **Palacio Municipal** (City Hall) stands on the west side of the plaza with rows of arches on Tuscan columns. It is the focal point of regular protests by students, *campesinos*, Zapatistas and other local activists.

San Cristóbal's mustard-coloured **cathedral** stands on the north side of the Zócalo. Construction of it probably began in the late 17th century to replace the modest brick and adobe structure that served as the principle house of worship from its foundation in 1528, the first public building in the city. The main façade was completed in the 18th century and numerous changes to the overall structure were made after the 1901 earthquake, including a complete remodeling of the cavernous interior. Today, it features rows of neoclassical Corinthian columns, three altars, and a gilded 16th-century wood pulpit. The cathedral's main west-facing façade overlooks a large open square, the **Plaza Catedral**, also known as the Plaza de la Paz, where concerts and other events are sometimes staged. Mayan women often gather on the steps here. The large cross in front of the church is not a Catholic crucifix, but a Mayan cross symbolizing the World Tree. Behind the cathedral, the much smaller, simpler **Templo San Nicolás** was built for the indigenous population by the Augustinian order in 1621.

Half a block north of Plaza Catedral you'll find the **Museo Mesoamericano de Jade** ① *Av 16 de Septiembre 16, T967-678 1121, www.eljade.com, Mon-Sat 1200-2000, Sun 1200-1800, US$2.30*, home to an extensive private collection of reproduction jade artefacts. This is more of a commercial jewellery shop than a true museum, but their exhibition does include a faithful recreation of the death mask of Lord Pakal of Palenque. Three blocks west of Plaza 31 de Marzo you'll find the modest **Museo de Cultura Popular** ① *Diego de Mazariegos 34 esq. 12 de Octubre*, which hosts small temporary exhibitions with ethnic or folkloric themes. On the opposite side of the street, the Iglesia Merced houses the **Museo de Ambar** ① *Diego de Mazariegos, T967-678 9716, www.museo delambar.com.mx, Tue-Sun 1000-2000, US$1.50*, not to be confused with jewellery shops bearing the same name. This one-room museum has a display of raw and cut amber, including some beautiful sculptures, and videos in Spanish explaining how jade is crafted. One block north of the Merced, it is well worth checking out the **Museo de Trajes Regionales** ① *Guadalupe Victoria 38, T967-678 4289, www.yokchij.org, guided visits by appointment only, various languages, at 1930, 1½ hrs, US$2.70*. This small but fascinating museum houses an array of traditional Mayan costumes, masks, musical

## ON THE ROAD
## Subcomandante Marcos and the Zapatistas

On New Year's Day 1994, at the moment when NAFTA came into force, the Ejército Zapatista de Liberación Nacional (EZLN) briefly took control of several towns in the southern state of Chiapas. Demanding social justice, indigenous people's rights, democracy at all levels of Mexican politics, an end to government corruption and land reform for the peasantry, the EZLN attracted international attention, helped by their use of modern communications technology. The government was forced to open peace talks.

President Zedillo later suspended the controversial PRI governor of Chiapas, but then allowed the army to launch a brief, but unsuccessful, campaign to capture the EZLN's leader, Subcomandante Marcos. Resumed talks between the government and the EZLN led to the first peace accord being signed in February 1996. The pace of change was slow, however, and in 1997 the EZLN renewed its protests, accusing the government of trying to change the terms of the agreed legal framework for indigenous rights. Physical conflict continued with 60,000 troops heavily outnumbering the Zapatista guerrillas.

In December 1997 45 civilians, mainly women and children, were massacred in Acteal near San Cristóbal de las Casas by paramilitaries linked to the PRI. Although the local mayor was implicated in the atrocity and arrested along with 39 others, there were calls for more senior government officials to be removed and in 1998 the Minister of the Interior and State Governor were forced to resign.

Tensions remained after Vicente Fox was elected in 2000 when the constitutional reforms long promised to the EZLN once again failed to materialize. Talks broke down and in 2003 the Zapatistas turned their attention inwards, consolidating support and developing self-governing committees – Juntas de Buen Gobierno (Committees of Good Government) – in those villages where approval was strongest. These, however, were criticized as unaccountable and bureaucratic.

In 2005, Subcomandante Marcos restyled himself Subdelegado Cero and attempted to broaden the Zapatista agenda by appealing to the whole country, not just the indigenous peasantry. He toured Mexico drumming up support for his broad leftist movement, although did not gain the same momentum as the mainstream parties, who were running their 2006 presidential election campaigns at the same time. In 2014, Marcos stepped down as an EZLN spokesman to make way for entirely indigenous leadership although he still writes for them from time to time. Today, the situation in Chiapas remains relatively stable, if tense.

instruments, textiles and more, comprising the personal collection of humanitarian Sergio Castro (who also offers interesting tours of the region).

Three important pedestrian streets lead off the two central plazas, all with an array of touristy restaurants, terraced cafés, bars, craft stores, and jade and amber workshops. Heading south off the southwest corner of Plaza 31 de Marzo, Manuel Hidalgo leads to the L-shaped **Templo El Carmen**, the only surviving part of the La Encarnación convent, founded in 1597. At its east side stands a superb Mudejár-style tower, squat, square and striking red. This unique architectural contribution was added to the convent in the 17th century to replace a belfry destroyed in a tornado. In the surrounding buildings, you'll find **El Carmen Cultural Centre** ⓘ *Tue-Sun, 0900-1700, free,* with chess tournaments and other events. Just north of the tower, a road, Hermanos Domínguez, heads west to Cerrito San Cristóbal – a small, isolated, tree-covered hill with a church and views over the city. Heading east off the northeast corner of Plaza 31 de Marzo, the pedestrianized street of **Real de Guadalupe** concludes at the **Templo de Guadalupe**, another small church perched on a hill. The surrounding indigenous barrio of Guadalupe was historically populated by candle-makers, saddle-makers and wooden toy makers. The third pedestrian street is Avenida 20 de Noviembre, which leads north off the northeast corner of Plaza Catedral past the **Teatro Daniel Zebadúa** (1931) and on to the sumptuous **Iglesia and ex-Convento de Santo Domingo**, arguably the finest building in the city (see below).

Running along the east side of Santo Domingo church, Avenida General Utrilla becomes Salomón González Blanco, home to the **Centro de Desarollo de la Medicina Maya** ⓘ *Salomón González Blanco 10, T967-678 5438, Mon-Fri 0900-1800, Sat-Sun 1000-1600, US$2.* This humble community museum maintains a working prayer room where healings are performed, a small garden filled with medicinal herbs, a *temazcal* (indigenous sauna) and several exhibitions relating to traditional Mayan medicine and bio-piracy (ask for the information cards). It is a very modest place that makes the best of its scant resources, but an excellent primer if you plan on visiting Tzotzil communities. Continuing north on Salomón González Blanco for 400 m, you'll meet the Periférico Norte. Turn right (east) and head straight for another 600 m and you'll arrive at the **Orquideas Moxviquil Botanical Garden** ⓘ *Periférico Norte 4, T967-678 5727, www.orchidsmexico.com, Mon-Sat 0900-1700, Sun 1000-1600, US$1.50.* Their gardens and greenhouses are home to a stunning collection of 3000 rescued and endangered plants, including specimens of roughly half the orchid species in Chiapas state.

## Iglesia and Ex-Convento de Santo Domingo

The west-facing Churriguersque façade of the church of Santo Domingo boasts the finest stonework in San Cristóbal: an incredibly extravagant tableau reminiscent of Oaxaca City's high-blown Dominican structures. Its sculpted surface features numerous Solomonic columns, niched saints and florid decorative details, best observed in the warm textured hues of the afternoon sun. Both the church and its adjoining monastery were originally constructed in the mid-16th century to house the first Dominican order in Chiapas, but little remains of those early adobe buildings. The current structures, which have been in constant use for four centuries, date to the late 17th century at the earliest.

Inside the ex-convent complex, on the ground floor, is the **Museo de los Altos de Chiapas** ⓘ *Calzada Lázaro Cárdenas, T967-678 1609, Tue-Sun 0900-1800, US$3.70.* This small regional museum charts the history of the Chiapas highlands from pre-Columbian times through the conquest to the colonial era. Its exhibitions comprise colonial antiques, religious art and archaeological finds: arrow heads, ceramics, stelae, implements, and ancient textiles. The ex-convent is also home to the highly recommended **Centro del Textiles Mundo Maya** ⓘ *upstairs on the first floor, T967-631 3094, www.fomentoculturalbanamex.org/ctmm, entrance included with the Museo de los Altos.* Opened in 2012, it documents the vast and extremely ancient heritage of Mayan textiles with examples of brilliantly woven pieces from Chiapas to El Salvador; hundreds of samples are exhibited in pull-out drawers. There are also interesting several videos that demonstrate the traditional methods of dyeing and weaving. Locally produced textiles can be purchased in the cooperatively managed store downstairs, or in the markets sprawled outside the church.

## Na Bolom Museum and Cultural Center

*Vicente Guerrero 33, T967-678 1418, www.nabolom.org. Guided tours daily, 1130 in Spanish, 1630 in English, US$4.50, US$3.50 without tour; library Mon-Fri 0930-1330 and 1630-1900.*

Founded in 1951 by the Danish archaeologist Frans Blom and his wife, the Swiss photographer Gertrudis Duby, both of them ardent Mayanists, Na Bolom ('Jaguar House' in Tzotzil) began life as a study centre for the universities of Harvard and Stanford. After the death of Frans Blom in 1963, Gertrudis Duby continued campaigning for the conservation of the Lacandón area. She died in 1993, aged 92, after which the centre continued to function as a non-profit-making organization dedicated to conserving the Chiapan environment and helping the Lacandón people.

Situated in a 19th-century neoclassical mansion, the museum and its photographic archives are fascinating and contain a detailed visual history of 50 years of daily life of the Maya people with beautifully displayed artefacts, pictures of Lacandones, and information about their present way of life. There are five galleries with collections of pre-Columbian Maya art and colonial religious paintings. There is also a great anthropological library. A shop sells products made by the indigenous people helped by the centre.

Na Bolom runs various projects, staffed by volunteers. Prospective volunteers spend a minimum of three months, maximum six, at the centre. They must have skills that can be useful to the projects, such as anthropology, organic gardening, or be multi-linguists. Volunteers are given help with accommodation and a daily food allowance. Na Bolom also has 12 rooms to rent (see Where to stay, below).

## Listings San Cristóbal de las Casas *map p56*

### Tourist information

**Municipal Office**
*Palacio Municipal on the main plaza, T967-678 0665.*
Has a good free map of the area. There is also a kiosk on the plaza with irregular opening hours.

### Where to stay

**$$$$ Guayaba Inn**
*Calle Comitan 55, T967-674 7699, www.guayabainn.com.*
This tranquil, beautiful and tasteful boutique B&B is the creation of Kiki and Gabriel Suárez, who have 40 years' experience in the hospitality industry. Set in a traditional converted home with koi ponds and orchid gardens, the inn has tranquil suites with fine wooden floors, original artwork, 4-poster beds and cosy fire places. Romantic and sublime.

**$$$$ Hotel B¨o**
*5 de Mayo 38, Barrio de Mexicanos, T967-678 1515, www.hotelbo.mx.*
The word 'B¨o' means 'water' and this luxury boutique hotel embodies a highly evolved contemporary design that will delight trendy young things and those with a discerning sense of aesthetics. Rooms and suites are the epitome of good taste.

**$$$$ La Joya**
*Francisco Madero 43A, T967-631 4832, www.lajoyahotelsancristobal.com.*
An impeccable upscale option built and managed by former Peace Corp volunteers, Ann and John. Secluded behind heavy wooden doors, there are 5 stylish boutique suites with names like 'The White Duchess' and 'The Black Orchid', all very unique, chic, extravagant and smart.

### $$$ Axkan Arte Hotel
*Álvaro Obregón 2, T967-116 0293,*
*www.axkanhotel.com.*
This modern new downtown hotel
has its own art gallery with works by
Chiapaneco artists. Set on 3 floors around
a central courtyard, it has 18 functional,
well-equipped, impeccably clean rooms.
Services include parking, travel agency,
and restaurant serving traditional food.
Breakfast included. Safe and reliable.

### $$$ Bela's
*Calle Dr Navarro 2, T967-678 9292, www.*
*belasbandb.com. 3-night minimum stay.*
Managed by the hospitable Bela, this
perfectly tranquil B&B features a verdant,
flowery and impeccably well-kept garden
complete with hummingbirds. Lodging is
in cosy rooms, with or without private bath,
including a suite and a top-floor quarter with
views. There are 4 friendly resident dogs too.

### $$$ Na Bolom
*Vicente Guerrero 33, T967-678 1418,*
*www.nabolom.org.*
Set in a 19th-century mansion that now
functions as the Na Bolom cultural centre
and museum (see above), this beautiful
17-room guesthouse was the former home
of Mayanists Franz Blom and Gertrude Duby.
Rooms are very cosy and feature popular art
and interesting photography. A traditional
Mexican meal is served every night at 1900
in the courtyard restaurant. A special place,
lots of atmosphere. Recommended.

### $$$ Sol y Luna
*Tonalá 27, T967-678 5727,*
*www.solylunainn.com.*
Centred around a patio with cacti, potted
plants, and orchids, this lovely little
family-run B&B has just 2 rooms, 'Sol' and
'Luna', both wonderfully decorated with
popular art, rustic furnishings, fine antiques
and books. There's a shared kitchen and
communal area with a chimney. Hospitable,
intimate, and bohemian. Book in advance.
Recommended.

### $$ Don Quijote
*Av Cristóbal Colón 7, T967-678 0346,*
*www.hoteldonquijote.com.mx.*
Popular with tour groups, this reliable option
has an ultra-convenient downtown location
just off Real de Guadalupe. Rooms are
simple, comfortable, affordable and down-
to-earth, and come complete with the usual
amenities like cable TV and Wi-Fi. The same
owners manage a much larger and more
upscale property, **Rincón del Arco ($$$)**,
www.rincondelarco.com, recommended
for its fine lawns and gardens.

### $$ Hotel Balam
*Calle Ejército Nacional 34, between Cristóbal*
*Colón and Diego Dugelay, T967-674 7771,*
*www.hotelbalam.mx.*
A small, friendly hotel with 16 impeccably clean
and comfortable quarters. Some rooms are on
the small side, but all are well-appointed with
modern facilities and solid wood furniture.
The hotel has been maintained with care
since its opening a few years ago and it
remains a good deal for your pesos. Reliable.

### $$ Hotel Posada San Cristóbal
*Insurgentes 3, T967-678 6881.*
Complete with a leafy patio and creaky
floorboards, this *posada* is housed in one of
the city's most historic buildings, the Casa de
la Sirena (see Sights, above) in an unbeatable
central location. It is an atmospheric place,
although the service is more functional than
fabulously hospitable. Unfussy travellers
who can tolerate flaws like musty aromas
and chipped paintwork will find good value
here; most rooms are massive for the price.

### $$ Hotel Santo Tomás
*Calle Franz Blom 1, T967-674 5227,*
*hotel_santothomas@hotmail.com.*
Off-the-beaten track around 15 mins
from the centre, this large colonial-
style hotel encloses a massive lawn
and courtyard like a rambling monastic
complex. Rooms are large, cosy and kitted
with chimneys, perfect for those chilly
winter nights. Secluded and good value.

### $ Iguana Hostel
*Chiapa de Corzo 16, T967-631 7731,*
*www.iguanahostel.com.*

A good, clean, well-managed hostel overlooking a pleasant neighbourhood plaza near the Santo Domingo church. The hosts and staff are exceptionally friendly and helpful with lots of good reports from former guests. Lodging is in dorms and rooms. There's a garden, hammocks, table tennis and travel agency. Sociable, relaxed and fun.

### $ Los Camellos
*Real de Guadalupe 110, T967-116 0097,*
*www.loscamellos.over-blog.com.*

This highly likeable French/Mexican-owned hostel is one of the oldest backpacker places in town. It's a quiet and chilled out place, very friendly, colourful, down-to-earth and bohemian. They have dorms and private rooms, free coffee and drinking water, book exchange, communal areas, a well-equipped kitchen and hammocks.

### $ Posada del Abuelito
*Tapachula 18, T967-678 1741,*
*www.posadadelabuelito.com.*

A homely little *posada* and one the city's best budget options. It has a handful of snug private rooms and dorm beds in a low-key colonial setting, with or without private bath. Facilities include chill-out patios and a common room with a toasty chimney. Laid-back, friendly and sociable, but not a party place. Recommended.

### $ Puerta Vieja
*Diego de Mazariegos 23, T967-631 4335,*
*www.puertaviejahostel.com.*

Set in a handsome colonial townhouse, Puerta Vieja is a very popular and sociable backpackers' hostel with an emphasis on shared activities like cinema and pizza, yoga, live music, parties and evening cocktails. Accommodation is in private rooms and dorms (mixed and female-only). Facilities include a garden, hammocks, lounge, kitchen and *temazcal* steam bath.

## Restaurants

As one of Mexico's busiest tourist hubs, there is an extensive and competitive restaurant scene in San Cristóbal, including lots of vegetarian places. Note many businesses close at 1700 on Sun.

### $$$ Miura
*Real de Guadalupe 26.*

Vegetarians are certainly at home in San Cristóbal, but carnivores need not despair. For mouth-watering cuts of certified Angus beef, including delectable fillet and rib-eye hand-picked from a selection and grilled to taste, head to Miura. Their burgers aren't bad either and there's a buffet option too. Good service.

### $$$ Tierra y Cielo
*Juárez 1, T967-678 1053,*
*www.tierraycielo.com.mx.*

With an award-winning chef, Tierra y Cielo is celebrated for its traditional Chiapaneco cuisine with an intriguing contemporary twist. Well-presented recipes use good, fresh, local ingredients and wholesome produce to creative effect. One of the best dining experiences in the city, the place for a special evening out. Recommended.

### $$$-$$ El Cau
*Real de Guadalupe 57A.*

Almost as if you've stepped into Barcelona, this cheery tapas joint serves authentic dishes from the motherland, including cod croquettes, Spanish tortilla and *escalivada* (grilled eggplant and red peppers). They have a fine stock of Spanish wine too and regular live jazz or acoustic guitar in the evenings. Trendy, friendly, warm and cosy, with a great atmosphere.

### $$ Belil
*María Adelina Flores 20B.*

'Belil' is a Tzotzil word that broadly translates as 'sustenance'. In that spirit, Belil is much more than a restaurant serving good coffee and tasty, organic Chiapaneco specialities, but a place of cultural nourishment. The manager, Ricardo, has spent years working in Chiapas in the field of human rights and can connect you with interesting guides and organizations for exploring the surrounding countryside.

## $$ Cocoliche
*Cristóbal Colón 3.*
Authentically bohemian with kitsch art house decor, this charismatic bar-restaurant has a fantastic international menu that includes flavourful curries from Thailand, Indonesia and Cambodia, enormous heart-warming bowls of pasta, generous salads, sandwiches and wraps. Evenings are an occasion for cabaret and live music. Great atmosphere, good food, lovely hosts, friendly service. Highly recommended.

## $$ El Punto Pizzería
*Real de Guadalupe 47.*
El Punto cooks up the best pizzas in town, no question. Authentically Italian and stone-baked in a wood-fired oven, they're close to perfect and large enough to satisfy 2 people. Seating is indoors or out and they have another branch on Calle Comitán, Barrio El Cerillo. Highly recommended.

## $$ La Casa del Pan Papalotl
*Inside the Centro Cultural El Puente, Real de Guadalupe 55, www.casadelpan.com.*
Using organic ingredients in many recipes, this is one of the city's first and oldest vegetarian restaurants with ties to many local farming cooperatives. They serve excellent bread, soups, salads, sandwiches, quesadillas, cooked breakfasts, juices and coffee. It's in a pleasant setting.

## $$ La Tertulia
*Cuauhtémoc 2. Closed Mon.*
This friendly, low-key little café is a great breakfast spot. They serve delicious *huevos rancheritos* with nopal cactus, spicy *chilaquiles*, sweet and savoury crêpes, pastas, thick fruity smoothies and a range of good, strong locally sourced coffee. There's

Wi-Fi too. If you were wondering about the name, a *tertulia* is a type of Spanish literary salon, or an informal meeting to discuss art, politics, or culture.

## $$ Te Quiero Verde
*Niños Héroes 5. Wed-Mon 0900-1100 and 1330-2100.*
This cosy, casual, chilled-out café with just a handful of tables serves excellent healthy fare such as veggie burgers made with love, including Moroccan and Indian options. They come complete with hand-cut fries and a side of hummus and nachos. Good fruit smoothies and *licuados* too. Friendly management. Recommended.

## $$-$ El Caldero
*Insurgentes 5A, www.elcaldero.com.mx.*
The perfect antidote to those chilly winter evenings: a bowl of piping hot stew. As the name might suggest, the popular locals' haunt of El Caldero (the Cauldron) serves nothing else. A range of flavourful meat-based and vegetarian broths are on offer, with or without an addition of local white cheese. Massive portions.

## $$-$ Madre Tierra
*Insurgentes 19, opposite Franciscan church, T967-678 4297.*
This long-established Anglo-Mexican café-bakery is recommended for its breakfasts, wholemeal breads, pies, brownies, cakes, and other sweet treats. There's cosy seating indoors or outdoors in an enclosed courtyard. Popular with travellers, Wi-Fi available.

## $$-$ TierrAdentro
*Real de Guadalupe 24.*
This cavernous cultural centre with Zapatista affiliation has an extensive menu of economical Mexican staples and international snacks, coffee, juices, breakfasts and lunches. Items can be a bit a hit and miss, but servings are reasonably generous and most people come for the EZLN connection and to meet other travellers.

## $ El Mercadito
*Diego Dugelay 11.*

Short on charm but rich in flavor, El Mercadito is a very low-key and unassuming locals' joint, and it serves great home-cooked grub at economical prices. They cook up a fresh buffet every day with an array of Mexican staples and regional specialities. A good casual lunch place.

## Coffee shops and bakeries

### Oh La La
*Miguel Hidalgo esq Cuauhtémoc.*

This exquisite French patisserie bakes an array of delicious treats every day: croissants, *pain au chocolate*, and a sumptuous variety of desserts. Friendly service and great coffee too. There's a smaller branch on Real de Guadalupe, just off Parque 31 de Marzo. Recommended.

## Bars and clubs

### Dada Club
*1 de Marzo 6, www.dadajazzclub.net. Thu-Sun, performances commence at 2200; hours vary with the seasons, see their website or Facebook page for more details.*

This intimate little club is the place to enjoy local jazz music performed live before Twin Peaks-style red curtains. In addition to beer, mescal and cocktails, they serve international cuisine.

### El Cocodrilo
*Insurgentes 1, opposite Parque 31 de Marzo.*

Adjoining **Hotel Santa Clara** in the historic premises of the Casa de la Sirena, **El Cocodrilo** is a popular and well-to-do lounge bar that's usually busy with tourists most evenings in high season. They host an eclectic range of talented local musicians for live performances.

### Entropia
*Maria Adelina flores 22, esq Cristóbal Colón.*

The preferred bohemian option, set inside a colonial townhouse with kitsch-style details, toasty fireplace and a handsome inner courtyard. They serve good grub and host live music most nights. One of the town's best watering holes. Good crowd, with a fun vibe. Highly recommended.

### Revolución
*20 de Noviembre and 1 de Marzo, www.elrevo.com. Open 1300-0200, live music daily 2000 and 2230.*

A San Cristóbal institution, lots of fun, but definitely touristy, with a grungy, alternative and bohemian vibe. They host good local bands and DJs with a buzzing crowd and a raucous atmosphere most nights. Skip the cocktails and food, stick to bottled beer.

## Entertainment

### Cinema and theatre
**Cinema El Puente,** *Real de Guadalupe 55, www.elpuenteweb.com.* Part of **El Puente** language school, this small cinema screens documentaries, art house films and classics at 1800, with later showings Fri-Sat at 2000. **Foro Cultural Kinoki,** *Belisario Domínguez 5A esq Real de Guadalupe, www.forokinoki. blogspot.com.* This excellent cultural centre shows thought-provoking documentaries and alternative, Latin American and art house films. They have 3 screening rooms, a bar, restaurant and a tea room with an upstairs terrace where you can sip herbal infusions and watch the bustle below. Recommended.

## Festivals

**Jan/Feb Carnival** is held during the 4 days before Lent, dates vary.
**Mar/Apr** There is a popular **spring festival** on **Easter Sun** and the week after.
**Early Nov Festival Maya-Zoque,** which lasts 4 days, promoting the 12 different Maya and Zoque cultures in the Chiapas region, with dancing and celebrations in the main plaza.
**12 Dec La Fiesta de Guadalupe.**

## Artesanías and produce

Colourful textiles, clay sculptures and other *artesanías* are sold on the streets by Mayan women at very low prices, mostly in the tourist hubs and plazas. Additionally, there are craft markets and cooperatives (see below). The following retail outlets are recommended:

**Casa Chiapas**, *Niños Héroes and Hidalgo, www.casachiapas.gob.mx*. This state-run shop sells high quality crafts from across Chiapas, including large furniture items you won't find at the market. Other offerings include textiles, lacquer boxes, baskets, costumed figurines.

**Poshería**, *Real de Guadalupe 46A, www. poxceremonial.com*. Consumed widely in Chiapas, for religious reasons as much as for pleasure, pox (pronounced 'posh') is a distilled alcoholic drink made from maize. This colourful little store sells artisanal varieties, some of them are not quite as strong as the crazy firewater the locals guzzle, but much more palatable.

## Bookshops

**La Abuelita**, *Cristóbal Colón 2, www.abuelita books.com*. A good stock of classics, non-fiction, guidebooks, Spanish-language, politics, history and spirituality titles. As well as hosting regular events, including movie screenings, they serve good local coffee and supply complimentary Wi-Fi. A good place to hang out.

**La Pared**, *Av Miguel Hidalgo 13B, near the Arco del Carmen, T967-678 6367, www.lapared bookstore.com*. A very good selection of Mexico books in English and a few in other European languages, and many travel books including **Footprint** guides. American owner Dana Burton is very helpful.

## Cooperatives

**El Camino de los Altos**, *Insurgentes 19, www.el-camino.fr*. A very successful association of 9 French designers and 130 Mayan weavers, **El Camino de los Altos** produces some lovely textiles that feature in many of Chiapas's upmarket hotels. Designs are contemporary, bold and beautiful.

**Sna Jolobil**, *Av 20 de Noviembre, next to the Museo de Textiles*. Meaning 'House of Weavers' in Tzotzil, this is the best cooperative and is comprised of 800 highland artisans producing some stunning traditional and contemporary textiles. Their very finest work can fetch thousands of dollars on international markets. Recommended.

**Taller Leñateros**, *Flavio A Paniagua 54, www.tallerlenateros.com*. Founded in 1975 by Mexican poet Ambar Past, this Mayan-operated paper-making workshop produces attractive paper and prints from natural materials. Their profits help support around 30 Maya families.

## Jewellery

Handmade jade and amber jewellery is widely available in San Cristóbal de las Casas. The quality of workmanship varies greatly. The finest pieces can be found in luxury boutiques and stores attached to the jade and amber museums (see above). More affordable productions – including some fine original work and a few hidden bargains – can be found in a multitude of small stores and workshops clustered in the streets around Parque 31 de Marzo, and on Real de Guadalupe. The very cheapest jewellery is available from market vendors (beware fakes, including glass that's peddled as amber). If you've never bought jade or amber before, it's best to shop around and ask lots of questions. Both stones come in a variety of hues (red amber is especially beautiful) and are often set in Taxco silver (look for the hallmark '.925').

## Markets

**Mercado de Artesanías**, *Av General Utrilla, outside the Iglesia y Convento de Santo Domingo*. This sprawling open-air market outside the church sells an array of textiles, woodwork, ceramics, basketry, and FZLN mementos. Lots of colour and bargains. Recommended.

**Mercado de Dulces y Artesanías**, *Av Insurgentes, next to the Templo de San Francisco.* A large indoor market purveying all the usual crafts as well as an assortment of local sweets, such as *cocada* (caramelized shredded coconut).

**Mercado Municipal**, *Av General Utrilla, a few blocks north of the Iglesia y Convento de Santo Domingo.* The bustling and pungent main city market where you can chow on street food or pick up some fruit and veg. Get some fresh organic strawberries if they're in season; you won't find any sweeter.

## What to do

### Adventure tourism
**Petra Vertical**, *Isabel La Católica 9b, T967-631 5173, www.petravertical.com.* The operator of choice for the hardcore adventurists. Their intensive packages include canyoning, abseiling, caving and hiking trips. Professional and knowledgeable. Recommended.
**Xaman Expediciones**, *1 de Marzo 45, T967-631 5376, www.xaman.com.mx.* **Xaman** offers a range of adrenalin-charged activities including explorations of the subterranean Río El Chorreadero (1 May-15 Nov), rappelling, whitewater kayaking on the Río Tzaconeja, zip-lining, and personalized expeditions. Rafting, birdwatching and trekking packages are planned for the near future.

### Body and soul
San Cristóbal is an alternative lifestyle hub and home to numerous New Age practitioners, yoga schools and Buddhist meditation centres.
**Ananda Healing Centre**, *Real de Guadalupe 55, T967-672 7477.* This healing centre offers a range of classes and private therapies including yoga, meditation, acupuncture, herbalism and reiki.

**Casa Plena**, *Diego Dugelay 22A, T967-678 7072, www.casaplena.org.* **Casa Plena** offers workshops and diplomas in dance, meditation, Tai Chi, Bach flower remedies and more. Healing therapies include a range of massage techniques, such as Mayan and Ayurvedic.
**Shaktipat Yoga**, *Niños Héroes 2, inside Casa Luz, 3rd floor, T967-130 3366, www.shaktipat yoga.com.mx.* Daily yoga and body work classes, including Kundalini, Vinyasa, Hatha and Shanti styles, as well as pilates. Cost per class is US$3.85 with reductions for 5- or 10-class packages.

### Community tourism
**Na Bolom**, *Vicente Guerrero 33, T967-678 1418, www.nabolom.org.* Any tour operator can take you for a spin around the Mayan villages, but as a trusted organization with well-established links to local communities, **Na Bolom** is uniquely placed to provide one of the most intimate, authentic and interesting community tours possible; their trips to Chamula and Zinacantán depart daily at 1000, US$23 per person. Na Bolom is also renowned for its tailor-made expeditions to the Selva Lacandona, where you can visit any or all of the 3 Lacandón communities, stay overnight in a jungle camp (or in more solid lodgings if you desire), costs are approximately US$250 per person per day, 4 person minimum. Highly recommended.

### Cultural centres
See also Na Bolom and Kinoki above and El Puente Spanish school in the Language schools box, opposite.
**Centro Cultural El Carmen**, *Hidalgo and Hermanos Domínguez.* Part of the colonial complex adjoining the Iglesia el Carmen, this cultural centre has a range of activities on offer: concerts, films, lectures, art exhibitions, chess games and conferences.
**El Paliacate**, *5 de Mayo 20, T967-125 3739, www.elpaliakate.blogspot.com.* A socially and ecologically aware cultural centre that

promotes artistic and cultural events such as theatre, live music and independent film screenings.

**Wapaní**, *Flavio Paniagua 10*. This low-key cultural centre hosts live music events, theatre, art exhibitions and film screenings. They also organize workshops in yoga, dance, and lay on a gastronomic market on Sun.

## Cycling tours

**Marcospata O En Bici**, *General Utrilla 18, T967-141 7216, www.marcosapata1.wordpress. com*. Guided cycling tours in the countryside around San Cristóbal, including trips to Chamula and Zinacantán. The length of trips varies, from 15 km to 80 km, or 3 hrs to a day.

## Language schools

**El Puente**, *Real de Guadalupe 55*, T967-678 3723. This long-established Spanish school offers 1-to-1 lessons at hourly or weekly rates, and homestays with local families. It also maintains a cultural centre with a small cinema; see their noticeboard for upcoming events. A good place to meet other travellers.
**Instituto Jovel**, *Madero 45, T967-678 4069, www.institutojovel.com*. Group or 1-to-1 classes, homestays arranged, said to be the best school in San Cristóbal as their teachers undergo an obligatory 6-week training course. Very good reports from students; all teachers are bilingual to some extent.
**La Casa en El Arbol**, *Madero 29, T967-674 5272, www.lacasaenelarbol.org*. This culturally aware school offers individual or group classes, medical Spanish, CME credits, DIE Exam and University credits. They also arrange homestays and apartments, and stage adventure activities and workshops in Tzotzil, weaving and cooking.

## Horse riding

Horse-riding tours are popular and widely available in San Cristóbal. Most go to Chamula and cost US$15 for 4-5 hrs. Hotels, tourist offices and travel agencies can easily organize them, or look for advertising flyers in tourist cafés and restaurants. Also, Señor Ismael rents out horses and organizes treks, T961-678 1511.

## Kayaking and rafting

**Explora**, *1 de Marzo 30, T967-631 7498, www.ecochiapas.com*. This eco-sensitive company with a sustainable ethos offers whitewater rafting, sea kayaking, river trips and multi-day camping expeditions on a variety of rivers, in addition to caving in El Chorreadero and conventional nature tours. Recommended.

## Tour operators

The lion's share of San Cristóbal's tour operators are clustered on Real de Guadalupe. There are many to choose from and their prices and services are broadly similar.
**Nichim Tours**, *Hermanos Domínguez 15, T678-3520, www.nichimtours.com.mx*. Daily tours of the city and surrounding villages, including Chamula and Zinacantán, 1-day tours to Palenque and Agua Azul, Sumidero, Montebello, rafting and kayaking, and multi-day packages to attractions across the state.
**Otisa Travel**, *Real de Guadalupe 3, T967-678 1933, otisatravel.com*. This smart, professional company runs daily tours to Sumidero Canyon, San Juan Chamula and Zinacantán, Lagunas de Montebello, Yaxchilán, Bonampak and the Yucatán, among other places.

### Transport

## Air

San Cristóbal has a small airport about 15 km from town, but at present does not serve passenger planes. Tuxtla Gutiérrez is now the principal airport.

## Bus

The 1st-class **ADO** bus terminal is at the junction of Insurgentes and Blv Sabines Gutiérrez, several blocks south of the Zócalo. 2nd-class lines, including **AEXA** and **Rodolfo Figueroa**, also have nearby terminals on Gutiérrez, which soon becomes the Pan-American Highway. Colectivo shuttles (combis) are more efficient for many regional destinations (see below). If you want to book tickets in advance without venturing to the terminal, there is a **Boletotal office**, Guadalupe 16, www.boletotal.mx, 0730-2030.

From the ADO terminal to **Campeche**, 1820, 10 hrs, US$42; **Cancún**, 1215, 1545, 1630, 17 hrs, US$91-95; **Chetumal**, 1215, 1545, 1630, 12 hrs, US$56-65; **Ciudad Cuauhtémoc**, 1140, 1530, 1730, 3 hrs, US$10; **Comitán**, frequent services, 1½ hrs, US$5; **Mérida**, 1820, 13 hrs, US$60; **Mexico City**, 12 daily most after 1550, 14 hrs, US$96-101; **Oaxaca City**, 1805, 2000, 2245, 10 hrs, US$46-55; **Palenque**, 7 daily, 5 hrs, US$16; **Pochutla**, 1915, 2200, 12 hrs, US$45; **Puerto Escondido**, 1915, 2200, 13 hrs, US$51; **Tapachula**, 7 daily, 8 hrs, US$27-33; **Tuxtla Gutiérrez**, many daily, 1 hr, US$4; **Tulum**, 1215, 1545, 1630, 14½ hrs, US$74-85; **Villahermosa**, 1000, 7 hrs, US$31.

## Colectivos

Colectivo shuttles (combis) are recommended for journeys of less than 4 hrs, including trips to the border. The terminals are clustered on Gutiérrez near the ADO terminal. To **Comitán**, with onward connections to **Ciudad Cuauhtémoc** and the **Guatemala border** (1½ hrs), every 20 mins, 1½ hrs, US$4-5; **Ocosingo**, with onward connections to **Palenque** and **Agua Azul**, every 20 mins, 2-3 hrs, US$4-5; **Tuxtla Gutiérrez**, every 15 mins, 1 hr, around

US$3.50. For those heading into Guatemala, numerous tour operators run direct shuttles to the border and beyond, including **Travesía Maya**. Destinations include **La Mesilla**, **Quetzaltenango**, **Antigua**, **Flores** and **Panajachel**, US$30-60. It's a convenient and comfortable option if you can afford it. There are also regular departures to **Guatemala** from the **ADO** terminal itself, all departing at 0745 daily.

For reasons of cultural sensitivity, it is recommended that you visit Mayan villages as part of a tour. If you go independently, be prepared for culture shock and possibly some suspicious treatment. Crowded microbuses to **Chamula**, **Zinacantán**, **San Andrés Larráinzar**, **Tenejapa** and other villages from around the market, north of the centre on Utrilla. Don't get stranded, as there isn't any tourist infrastructure.

## Car

Those travelling to Palenque by car will have fine views but should avoid travelling at night because of armed robberies.

**Car hire**  **Optima**, Diego de Mazariegos 39, T967-674 5409; and **Hertz**, Villas Mercedes, Panagua 32, T967-678 1886. Rental is for within Chiapas only; do not attempt to go beyond.

## Scooters

**Croozy Scooters**, Belisario Domínguez 7. Tue-Sun 0900, closing times vary. Swiss/British-run, rents out bikes and small scooters. Minimum payment US$20, 3 hrs, US$31 per day. They provide maps and suggested routes. Deposit and ID required. Friendly. Recommended.

## Taxi

US$1.75 anywhere in town, colectivo US$0.70.

The communities of San Juan Chamula and Zinacantán (see below) are near to the city, but several visitors have felt ashamed at going to look at the villagers as if they were in a zoo; there were many children begging, especially at Chamula. You are recommended to call at Na Bolom (see page 60) before setting out, to get cultural information and to seek advice on the reception you are likely to get. Good guides will introduce you to close contacts in the communities, personalizing the experience.

Travellers are strongly advised not to wander around in the hills surrounding San Cristóbal, as they could risk assault. Warnings can be seen in some places frequented by tourists. Remember that locals are particularly sensitive to proper dress (that is neither men nor women should wear shorts or revealing clothes) and manners; persistent begging should be countered with courteous, firm replies.

   **Note** Photography is strictly resisted by some of the indigenous people because they believe the camera steals their souls. Either leave your camera behind or ask your guide to let you know when you can and cannot take pictures. Cameras may be confiscated by villagers (and not returned) when photography is deemed inappropriate.

### ★San Juan Chamula

*For reasons of cultural understanding and safety, it is strongly recommended that you visit Chamula on a tour (see What to do, below). If you wish to go independently, you can catch a VW bus from the market in San Cristóbal every 20 mins, last at 1700, last one back at 1900, US$1 per person (or taxi, US$4). It is an interesting walk from San Cristóbal to Chamula, and onwards from Chamula to Zinacantán (see below), but these journeys may be currently unsafe, especially for solo travellers. Consult the tourist office for up-to-date information and for detailed instruction on the routes.*

In the Tzotzil village of San Juan Chamula, 10 km northwest of San Cristóbal, the men wear grey, black or light pink tunics, while the women wear black wool skirts, bright blouses with colourful braid and navy or bright blue shawls. It is a very conservative community and its religious leaders have expressed hostility to the missionary work of intrusive Protestant churches. Many of the street vendors in San Cristóbal, who live in shanty towns on the outskirts of the city, are religious exiles from Chamula.

   The community's main house of worship, the Catholic **Templo de San Juan**, is a fascinating esoteric experience. To enter, a permit (US$1.50) is needed from the village tourist office. **Note** Photography is absolutely forbidden. There are no pews but family groups sit or kneel on the floor, chanting in clouds of incense smoke, rows of candles lit in front of them, each representing a member of the family, a certain significance attached to their colours. The religion is centred on the 'talking stones' and three idols, as well as certain Christian saints. If you're lucky, you may witness shamans participating in the ritual consumption of *pox*, curing patients with eggs or even sacrificing chickens.

   At the end of August, Pagan rituals are held in small huts. The pre-Lent festival ends with celebrants running through blazing harvest chaff. This happens just after Easter prayers are held, before the sowing season starts. Festivals in Chamula should not be photographed; if you wish to take other shots ask permission, people are not unpleasant, even if they refuse (although children may pester you to take their picture for a small fee).

There are many handicraft stalls on the way up the small hill southwest of the village. This has a good viewpoint of the village and valley. Take the road from the southwest corner of the square, turn left towards the ruined church then up a flight of steps on the left.

## Zinacantán

*It is best to visit on a tour. To go independently, VW buses leave from San Cristóbal's market when full, 30 mins, US$0.75, sometimes with frequent stops while the conductor lights rockets at roadside shrines; taxi US$4.*

The community of Zinacantán is roughly 12 km northwest of San Cristóbal. The men of the village typically wear pink/red jackets with embroidery and tassels, the women vivid blue-purple shawls and navy skirts. Annual festival days here are 6 January, 19-22 January, 8-10 August; visitors are welcome. At midday every day the women prepare a communal meal, which they eat in shifts. The main gathering place is around the roofless fire-damaged church, US$1.50 for entering, official ticket from tourist office next door. Photography inside is strictly prohibited. There were two museums, but both appear to have closed; check on their status before planning a visit.

Above the municipal building on the right, the creative, resourceful Antonia has opened **Antonia's House** ① *Isabel la Católica 7*. There is a small crafts shop and she and her family will demonstrate back-strap weaving, the making of tortillas and many other aspects of life in the village. She usually has some *pox* (pronounced 'posh', a liquor made of sugar cane and corn) on the go; it's strong stuff, and the red variant will set your throat on fire – be ready with a couple of litres of water! Antonia is very easy going and she may not charge for a sample of *pox*; however, bear in mind that she makes her living from the shop, so buy something or leave a contribution.

## Tenejapa

Few tourists visit Tenejapa, 30 km northeast of San Cristóbal. The village is very friendly and many men wear local costume. Ask permission to take pictures and expect to pay. The Thursday market is traditionally for fruit and vegetables, but there are a growing number of other stalls. The market thins out by noon. Excellent woven items can be purchased from the weavers' cooperative near the church. They also have a fine collection of old textiles in their regional ethnographic museum adjoining the handicraft shop. The cooperative can also arrange weaving classes.

## Other Mayan villages

Two other excursions can be made, by car or local bus, from San Cristóbal. The first goes south on the Pan-American Highway (30 minutes by car) to Amatenango del Valle, a Tzeltal village where the women make and fire pottery in their yards – their creations include fearsome and beautiful jaguar sculptures – and then southeast (15 minutes by car) to **Aguacatenango**, a picturesque village at the foot of a mountain. Continue one hour along this road past Villa Las Rosas (which has a hotel) to **Venustiano Carranza**, where the women wear fine costumes, and there is an extremely good view of the entire valley. There is a good road from Las Rosas to Comitán as an alternative to the Pan-American Highway and there are frequent buses.

## Las Grutas de San Cristóbal

*Daily 0900-1700, US$1.50. To get there, take a combi towards Teopisca from the Pan-American highway and ask the driver to drop you at Km 94 for the 'grutas'. The caves are a 5-min walk south from the highway.*

Las Grutas (caves), 10 km southeast of the city, contain huge stalagmites and reach a depth of 2445 m. Only the first 350 m are lit, however, and there is a concrete walkway for admiring the carbonate sculptures. Snacks and refreshments are available. Horse can be hired for US$15-20 for a five-hour ride (guide extra) on lovely trails in the surrounding forest. Some of these are best followed on foot. Yellow diamonds on trees and stones mark the way to beautiful meadows. Stay on the trail to minimize erosion. The land next to the caves is taken up by an army football pitch, but once past this, it is possible to walk most of the way back to San Cristóbal through woods and fields.

## Comitán and around  *Colour map 2, B3.*

**friendly, tranquil highland city near the Guatemalan border**

Popular with Mexican tourists but largely overlooked by foreign visitors, Comitán de Domínguez is a small colonial city located south of San Cristóbal and close to the Guatemala border. It is an easy-going and elevated place, offering cool respite from the stifling lowlands, and a welcome pause before or after the frenetic environs of Guatemala. Flanked by handsome traditional edifices with overhanging eaves and clay-tile roofs, a large shady Zócalo marks the heart of the Centro Histórico with a host of modern art sculptures. Modest diversions lie within the city limits, but the best attractions are further afield in the surrounding countryside.

### Sights

Far from the madding crowd, Comitán is a pleasant place to simply hang out and unwind, but if you do need cultural stimulation, there are a few small museums worth checking out. **The Museo de Arte Hermila Domínguez de Castellanos** ① *Av Central Sur and 3a Sur Pte, Tue-Sat, 1000-1730, Sun 1000-1400, US$0.50,* maintains a collection of modern art and sculptures, including work by Rufino Tamayo, José Luis Cuevas, José Guadalupe Posadas and Francisco Toledo. The **Casa Museo Dr Belisario Domínguez** ① *Av Dr Belisario Domínguez Sur 35, Mon-Sat 1000-1845, Sun 0900-1245, US$0.40,* is the former home and birthplace of the good doctor Belisario, who was assassinated after speaking out against President Huerta. The museum includes memorabilia and historical exhibits dedicated to his professional and political life. For a dose of Mayan relics, head to the **Museo Arqueológico de Comitán** ① *1 Calle Sur Ote, Tue-Sun 0900-1800, free.*

### Around Comitán

The waterfalls of **El Chiflón** lie 41 km southwest of Comitán off Highway 226. Amenities and activities include wildlife tours (specialized in iguana observation), a zipline, swimming areas and *cabañas,* all managed by the **Centro Ecoturístico de Cascadas El Chiflón** ① *T963-596 9709, www.chiflon.com.mx.* Hourly vans run to the turn-off (where taxis continue to the site) with **Autotransportes Cuxtepeques** ① *Blv Belisario Domínguez, between 1a and 2a Calles Nte Pte, from 0400 to 2000, 45 mins, US$2.*

South of Comitán, you'll find the archaeological site of **Tenam Puente** ① *5 km off Highway 190, 0900-1600, US$2.50, the turn-off for the ruins is 10 km south of Comitán* on Highway 190; vans to the ruins depart from 3a Av Pte Sur 8, every 40 mins, 0800-1800 (last return at 1600), US$1.10, situated in a forest. Thought to have been a minor Mayan commercial centre, its construction dates back to the Classic era (AD 300-600) and includes three ball courts, a pyramid and some temple complexes. South of the turn-off, the tiny settlement of **La Trinitaria** marks the turn-off for Highway 307 and the Lagunas de Montebello (see below), frequently plied by colectivo vans. At Km 22, you'll pass the **Parador-Museo Santa María** ① *T963-632 5116, www.paradorsantamaria.com.mx*, a handsome 19th-century hacienda with a decent restaurant, eight fine guest rooms ($$$$), and a religious museum in its chapel. At Km 30, you'll pass the turn-off for the aesthetically situated ruins of **Chinkultic** ① *0900-1700, US$3*, with temples, ball court, and carved stone stelae; from the signpost the ruins are about 3 km along a dirt road. The structures are divided into two groups with striking views from the Acrópolis, a temple overlooking a massive *cenote* (deep round lake).

### ★Parque Nacional Lagunas de Montebello *Colour map 2, B3.*
*Highway 307, entrance to the park is around Km 37, US$2. From Comitán, combi vans or buses marked 'Tziscao' or 'Lagos' go to the lakes, every 20-40 mins, 1 hr, US$1.50, via the Lagunas de Siete Colores, departing from Av 2 Pte Sur y Calle 3 Sur Pte, four blocks from the plaza. The last bus and colectivo back from the lakes connecting with the 1900 bus to San Cristóbal is at 1600. For those with their own transport there are several dirt roads from Comitán to the Lagunas; a recommended route is the one via La Independencia, Buena Vista, La Patria and El Triunfo (beautiful views), eventually joining the road west of the Chinkultic ruins.*

The state's first national park and a designated UNESCO Biosphere Reserve since 2009, the Parque Nacional Lagunas de Montebello encompasses 6400 ha of rambling pine forests and no less than 59 multicoloured highland lakes, which due to their rich and varied mineral content, span multiple shades of blue and green from bright sapphire to turquoise. A trip to the lakes from Comitán can be easily done in a day and is also possible from San Cristóbal, but it's a bit tiring; bring your passport and tourist card for immigration checks.

From the ticket booth on Highway 307, the road forks north to the **Lagunas de Siete Colores**, a cluster of five tranquil lakes, including **Bosque Azul**, 3 km away. The area is noted for its orchids and birdlife, including the famous *quetzal*, but it gets very busy at weekends and holidays. There is a group of caves nearby called Grutas San Rafael del Arco, and several *cenotes*. Guides can be hired in the Bosque Azul cark park at the end of the road for horse tours, US$12 per person, two to three hours. East of the ticket booth, Highway 307 passes turn-offs for **Laguna de Montebello**, the **Cinco Lagunas**, and **Laguna Pojoj**, before arriving at the large **Laguna Tziscao** near the Guatemala border, and its village of the same name, 9 km from the entrance.

### Mexico to Guatemala: Ciudad Cuauhtémoc–La Mesilla *Colour map 2, B3.*
From Comitán the road winds down to the Guatemalan border at Ciudad Cuauhtémoc via La Trinitaria; see Transport, below. Despite its name, Ciudad Cuauhtémoc is not a city, but a very small hamlet. Before proceeding to the border, surrender your tourist card and get your exit stamp. Opposite the immigration office is the **Cristóbal Colón** bus station, with an overpriced restaurant and a hotel. Colectivo taxis run from here to Guatemalan immigration at La Mesilla a few kilometres away; they charge around US$0.60 per person, or US$2.50 for the whole vehicle. At La Mesilla, once you've stamped in, grab a mototaxi to the second-class bus station, where services depart for Huehuetenango,

two hours, and onwards to Quetzaltenango (Xela), four hours. The journey into the Guatemalan western highlands winds through remote villages and stunning canyons and is far more interesting than the crossing at Tapachula. See also Border crossings box in Practicalities chapter.

## Listings Comitán and around

### Tourist information

**Municipal tourist office**, in the green building on the north side of the Parque Central. Mon-Fri 0800-1800, Sat 0800-1600.

### Where to stay

**$$$ Hotel Casa Delina**
*1a Calle Sur Pte 6, T963-101 4793, www.hotelcasadelina.com.*
Set in a traditional 19th-century mansion, this stylish and aesthetic 'art hotel' show-cases work from emerging contemporary artists in its 8 boutique rooms. There's parking, a courtyard garden, café and a screening room where movies are shown in the evenings. Hip, interesting, and creative. Recommended.

**$$$-$$ Los Lagos de Montello**
*Belisario Domínguez 144, corner of 3 Av, T963-632 0657, www.hotelloslagosde montebello.com.*
Often overlooked by foreign tourists but popular with Mexicans, this excellent business hotel has 56 well-appointed rooms, restaurant, garden and a large indoor pool. Located 10 mins' walk from the Centro Histórico. A good deal, recommended for families.

**$$ Hotel Real Junchavin**
*2a Calle Norte, Oriente 8, T963-101 4337, www.realjunchavin.com.*
Located on a quiet street, this good, clean, budget option, recently renovated with crisp, simple rooms, modern decor, comfortable mattresses, cable TV and Wi-Fi. Good value.

### Around Comitán

**$$ Centro Ecoturístico El Chiflón**
*Tzimol, T963-596 9709, www.chiflon.com.mx.*
Cooperatively managed by the population of the San Cristobalito *ejido*, this place maintains 12 single and duplex *cabañas* complete with private bath, double beds, hot water, and lots of nice touches like attractive stone-work and clay sculptures from Amatenango. For more information on the park's attractions, including how to get there, see above.

**$$ Villas Tziscao**
*Carretera Fronteriza del Sur Km 61, T502-5780-2775, www.centro ecoturisticotziscao.com.mx.*
Overlooking the largest of Montebello's lakes, these wood-built cabins with high slanted roofs (ask to see a few before accepting) belong to the **Centro Ecoturistico Tziscao**, which is operated as part of a communally owned 300-ha *ejido*. Lots of activities are available from kayaking to hiking, and there's Wi-Fi in the common area. Conventional rooms inside the main building. It's a good place for families who like the outdoors.

### Restaurants

There are lots of terraced cafés and restaurants on the Zócalo.

**$$$-$$ Pasta di Roma**
*1 Av Pte Sur 1, www.pastadiroma.com.*
As the name might suggest, wholesome Italian fare including lasagna and spaghetti is served here. Simple and authentic, good reports.

## Transport

### Bus

The **ADO** terminal is at Blv Belisario Domínguez Sur 43. Daily departures to **Cancún**, 1420, 21 hrs, US$88; **Mexico City**, 8 daily, all after 1400, 15½ hrs, US$107-124; **Palenque**, 1420, 6½ hrs, US$25; **San Cristóbal de las Casas**, frequent services, 1½ hrs, US$5; **Tapachula**, 5 daily, 5½ hrs, US$14; **Tuxtla Gutiérrez**, many daily, 3 hrs, US$7.50.

### Colectivos

Shuttle terminals are clustered on Belisario Domínguez, a few blocks north from the **ADO** terminal and a 10- to 15-min walk to the Zócalo. To **Ciudad Cuauhtémoc** (Guatemala border), every 15 mins, 1½ hrs, US$4. To **San Cristóbal de las Casas**, 1½ hrs, US$4-5. To **Ocosingo** via an interesting back route, go to Altamirano and change, terminal on east side of town, take a taxi.

## Mexico to Guatemala: Ciudad Cuauhtémoc–La Mesilla

### Bus

The **ADO** terminal is inside the hotel opposite the Mexican Migración with infrequent services to **Palenque**, **San Cristóbal de las Casas**, **Tuxtla** and **Tapachula**. More national connections are available in Comitán, including services to **San Cristóbal** and **Tuxtla** (see colectivos, below).

### Colectivos

Colectivo taxis to **La Mesilla** and **Guatemala immigration**, around 6 km away, depart from opposite the **Mexican Migración**, US$0.75. Colectivo shuttles to **Comitán** depart from a small terminal around the corner from the Migración, 1½ hrs, US$4.

## Ocosingo  *Colour map 2, B3.*

**unpretentious town off the tourist track with an authentic market**

The friendly, if roughly hewn, provincial city of Ocosingo lies half way between San Cristóbal de las Casas and Palenque on Highway 199. The ride each way is astounding with wending mountain vistas and a patchwork of rolling maize fields and wood-built villages, many of them belonging to the Ejército Zapatista de Liberación Nacional (EZLN). If driving, you may be stopped occasionally to pay unofficial tolls of a few dollars, but it is worth it for this intriguing backdoor glimpse of highland Mayan communities. Ocosingo itself saw some of the fiercest fighting of all during the 1994 Zapatista uprising: pitched gun battles in the market and main plaza left dozens dead on both sides. There's a frenetic market but the big attraction is the Mayan ruin of Toniná, 12 km away (see below).

### Toniná  *Colour map 2, B3.*

*Daily 0800-1700, US$3.50, drinks are available at the site; also toilets and parking. The museum is closed Mon. Colectivos to the site depart from behind the market, every 30 mins, US$1.*

Toniná was one of the last Classic Maya sites and a powerful militaristic stronghold which terrorized and dominated lowland Chiapas before its final collapse. The site's history, only recently and partially deciphered, includes numerous bloodthirsty conflicts with surrounding regional powers, especially Palenque, that lasted several generations until its ultimate ascent. Much of the city's art and sculptures depict prisoners of war bound and poised for ritual decapitation, such as the ball court, which features torsos of captured Palenque vassals as markers.

The site's buildings – which include palaces and ritual labyrinths – are in the Palenque-style with internal sanctuaries in the back room. Architectural influences from many other different Maya styles have also been identified, suggesting that captured artists were incorporated into Toniná society, or else forced to work. The most important structure is the south-facing Acropolis, which fills seven terraces with temple-pyramids and climbs to 71 m over the plaza.

The fifth terrace contains an outstanding example of stucco work, for which Toniná is uniquely renowned, along with its famous sculptures in the round. Uncovered in 1992, the 'Frieze of the Four Suns' (sometimes called the Frieze of the Dream Lords) is a complex mystical representation featuring a sacrificial scaffold covered with feathers, four decapitated human heads – symbolic of four suns, four ages, and four races of man – and prominent Lords of the Underworld.

## Listings Ocosingo

### Where to stay

**$$-$ Hotel Central**
*Av Central 5, opposite the Parque Central, T919-673 0024.*
Conveniently located on the main square, reasonably priced and with friendly staff, this is the best place in town. Beyond the shabby lobby, it has several clean, comfortable, modest and perfectly adequate rooms with hot water, Wi-Fi and cable TV. There's a so-so restaurant downstairs and a communal balcony upstairs, ideal for watching life on the plaza.

### Transport

**Bus and colectivo**
Many buses and colectivos to **Palenque**, 2½ hrs, US$4-5, **Agua Azul** and **San Cristóbal de Las Casas**, terminals clustered outside the centre. For **Comitán**, go to Altamirano and change, colectivos leave from the market.

## Agua Azul and Misol-Há   *Colour map 2, A3.*
#### an entrancingly beautiful series of jungle waterfalls and rapids

### Agua Azul
*Entry US$2.90, US$4 for cars. Entry price is not always included in day trips from Palenque, which typically allow up to 3 hrs at the site. Due to the risk of theft, do not bring valuables. For information on getting there, see Transport, below.*

The main swimming area has many restaurants and indigenous children selling fruit. In good weather, the water is clear and blue; after the rains, it is muddy brown (but still very refreshing).

Swimmers should strictly stick to the roped areas where they can be seen by others; the various graves on the steep path up the hill alongside the rapids are testament to the risks of drowning. One of the falls is called 'The Liquidizer', an extremely dangerous area of white water which you must not enter. Even in the designated areas, the currents can be ferocious. Beware of hidden tree trunks and other obstacles if the water is murky.

The path on the left of the rapids can be followed for 7 km with superb views and secluded areas for picnics. There are also several *palapas* for hammocks, plenty of space for free camping and some rooms to rent (see Where to stay, below).

**Misol-Há** *Colour map 2, A3.*
*Entry US$2.*

At Misol-Há there is a stunning waterfall usually visited for 20 minutes or so before Agua Azul on day trips from Palenque. A narrow path winds around behind the falls, allowing you to stand behind the immense curtain of water. Swimming is possible in the large pool at the bottom of the tumbling cascade of water, but it is usually better to wait until you get to Agua Azul for a good swim. That said, during the rainy season, swimming is reported to be better at Misol-Há. Organized tours usually include only a brief stop at Misol-Há, so confirm with your operator or go by bus if you would like to spend longer there.

## Listings Agua Azul and Misol-Há

### Where to stay

#### Misol-Ha

**$$ Cabañas Misol-Ha**
*T55-5151 3377, www.misol-ha.com.*
Part of the tourist complex at Misol-Ha waterfall, these *cabañas* include 8 rustic units with hot and cold water, fan, mosquito net and simple furniture, and 4 bungalow-style units complete with kitchen appliances. All are nestled in lovely landscaped grounds on the edge of the jungle.

### Transport

Public buses travelling between Palenque and Ocosingo can drop you at the Agua Azul turn-off, US$1. There are some 2nd-class buses between San Cristóbal de las Casas and Palenque which will stop at the turn-off, but check before purchasing tickets. A tour or colectivo shuttle from Palenque is definitely the best option, as this includes a trip to Misol-Ha, see Palenque Transport, below.

From the Agua Azul turn-off, walk the 4 km downhill to the falls on a beautiful jungle-lined road (or hitch a ride in a taxi or minibus for US$1). If, after a long day at the falls, you have no desire to walk the steep 4 km back to the main road you may be able to catch a ride back to Palenque on tour buses that have extra space. They leave from the Agua Azul car park between 1500 and 1800. Tour companies can also arrange bus tickets with **AEXA** from the turn-off to San Cristóbal and other places if you don't wish to return all the way to Palenque to catch an onward bus.

**a hot, humdrum town and gateway to the famous ruins**

Palenque's inhabitants are very friendly and helpful, but the streets can be stifling and airless, especially in the months of June, July and August. The Fiesta de Santo Domingo is held on the first week of August.

Many travellers avoid downtown altogether, preferring to stay in the cool, quiet and leafy tourist barrio of **La Cañada**, a 10-minute walk northwest of the Parque Central. Flanked by alternating patches of rainforest and cattle pasture, the most appealing and isolated lodgings of all are strung along the **road to the ruins**. It is about 10°C cooler here than Palenque town thanks to the dense foliage cover (although it is also wetter, buggier, and much more humid). The highway begins near the western entrance to town, just south of the Mayan head near the **ADO** terminal. For details of travel along the highway to the ruins, see Transport, below. If walking on the highway during the rainy months, you may be approached by shifty-looking local entrepreneurs peddling bags of interesting Mayan *hongos* (mushrooms), which flourish in the fields thanks to the prodigious quantity of cow dung. These are hallucinogenic and their psilocybin content is astronomically high: consume at your own risk.

### Mexico to Guatemala: Tenosique–El Ceibo *Colour map 2, A3/A4.*

Approximately 80 km east of Palenque on Highway 203, Tenosique is a small, friendly town, and the starting point for a classic cross-border adventure that takes you by road to La Palma, by boat to El Naranjo in Guatemala, and finally, by road to Flores. However, since the completion of a new paved highway, this slow if somewhat scenic route is no longer used by the locals and thus impractical (for a price, a tourist operator in Palenque can probably arrange it for you).

The new road from Tenosique to Flores can be crossed in six to eight hours, but it is best to start at dawn and travel in daylight only. Colectivos to Tenosique with 'Transportes Palenque' leave from Allende Sur and 20 de Noviembre in Palenque, hourly, two hours,

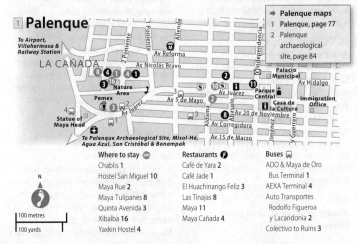

**Palenque maps**
1 Palenque, page 77
2 Palenque archaeological site, page 84

| Where to stay | Restaurants | Buses |
|---|---|---|
| Chablis **1** | Café de Yara **2** | ADO & Maya de Oro |
| Hostel San Miguel **10** | Café Jade **1** | Bus Terminal **1** |
| Maya Rue **2** | El Huachinango Feliz **3** | AEXA Terminal **4** |
| Maya Tulipanes **8** | Las Tinajas **8** | Auto Transportes |
| Quinta Avenida **3** | Maya **11** | Rodolfo Figueroa |
| Xibalba **16** | Maya Cañada **4** | y Lacandonia **2** |
| Yaxkin Hostel **4** | | Colectivo to Ruins **3** |

US$4. You may be dropped on the outskirts of Tenosique, in which case take a tuk-tuk to the market. From here, colectivo taxis travel to El Ceibo and the Guatemala border, one hour, US$3. After completing border formalities, you can catch onward connections to Flores, US$6, a straightforward four- to five-hour trip, but you may have to wait up to two hours for the bus to leave. See also Border crossings box in Practicalities chapter.

## Listings Palenque town *map p77*

### Tourist information

**Tourist office**
*Juárez, a block west of the plaza.*
*Daily 0900-2100.*
They are fairly useless but provide a good free map of the town and the ruins.

### Where to stay

There is a plethora of cheap lodgings here, but the town is generally a hot, dirty and unappealing place to stay.

**$$ Maya Rue**
*2a Av Pte, between Av Central and 1a Av Sur, T916-345 0743.*
**Maya Rue** wins the downtown style prize for its contemporary interior design that outshines the dated decor you'll find most other places. Rooms are spotlessly clean and have large, comfortable beds, Wi-Fi, hot water and cable TV. Good central location with a café downstairs. Recommended.

**$$-$ Quinta Avenida**
*Av Juárez 173, T916-345 0098.*
**Quinta Avenida** is chiefly recommended for its tranquil garden decking fringed by tropical foliage, and for its pool. The rooms are economical, modest and functional, but ask for one in the garden out back (the main building suffers street noise). It's not amazing, but for the money it's one of the best budget options in town. On the west side, within easy walking distance of the **ADO** terminal.

**$ Hostel San Miguel**
*Hidalgo and Aldama, above Unión Pharmacy, T916-345 0152.*

More of a budget hotel than a hostel, although they do have dorm space. The no-frills private rooms are spacious; some have balconies, TV and a/c. Good value for groups.

### La Cañada

**$$$ Chablis**
*Merle Green 7, T916-345 0870, www.hotelchablis.com.mx.*
Painted sunny yellow, this small resort-style hotel has 51 tidy if unadventurous rooms with king-size beds, a/c, 32-inch TVs, Wi-Fi and solar-heated hot water. The real draw is the leafy patio with a pool and jacuzzi, perfect for chilling out after a day at the ruins. Popular, helpful and well-maintained. Recommended for families.

**$$$ Maya Tulipanes**
*Cañada 6, T916-345 0201, www.mayatulipanes.com.mx.*
Another resort-style lodging with the same owners as Chablis down the road. The 78 slightly generic rooms vary in price, size and quality, but all are spotless and most have a/c, large TVs and Wi-Fi. Amenities include a garage, pool, karaoke bar, garden and restaurant. Check out the colourful murals inside the entrance.

**$$ Xibalba**
*Merle Green 9, T916-345 0411, www.hotelxibalba.com.*
A decent, popular, hospitable hotel with 2 wings (1 older, 1 newer). They offer clean, comfortable, simple, bug-free rooms with a/c. Fun archaeological decor, including an impressive and authentically proportioned Mayan arch and a reproduction lid of Pacal's

tomb, somewhat larger than the original. The owner is friendly and knowledgeable.

### $ Yaxkin Hostel
*Av Hidalgo corner with 5a Pte, T916-345 0102, www.hostalyaxkin.com.*
Popular with backpackers, this is La Cañada's best economical alternative, and reasonably smart for a hostel. It has tidy if small private rooms, which are simple, clean and comfortable, and cheap mixed and women-only dorms. Facilities include a *temazcal* and massage, Wi-Fi, movie lounge, free use of bikes, kitchen, lovely garden and a good bar and restaurant.

## Road to the ruins
The most alluring and atmospheric place to stay is along the road to the ruins. Lodgings are nestled inside the exuberant rainforest, but be aware that humidity is high and there are abundant creepy-crawlies, so bring repellent, especially in the wet season. Tropical decay is rampant too, meaning poorly maintained lodgings go downhill fast. Before accepting your room or *cabaña*, thoroughly check its security (thefts have been reported), screens and netting. Shop around and don't be pressured by touts. Note the highway to the ruins has opened up significantly in recent years and there is now plenty of robust competition to the long-established El Panchán.

### $$$$ Quinta Cha Nab Nal
*Carretera a las Ruinas Km 2.2, T916-345 5320, www.quintachanabnal.com.*
The owner of Quinta Cha Nab Nal is an enthusiastic Mayanist who set out to carefully create a hotel in the architectural style of a Classic-era Mayan palace complex. Surprisingly, it worked out quite tastefully, even if some of us prefer the aesthetic of ruin to reconstruction. Most guests leave this place enchanted and you won't find a higher standard of accommodation in Palenque. Recommended.

### $$$ La Aldea del Halach Huinic
*Carretera a las Ruinas Km 2.8, T916-345 1693, www.hotellaaldea.net.*
Rooms at the Aldea have been designed according to principles of classic Mayan architecture with curved edges, numerological proportions, solar and astronomical alignments. In effect, they're very tranquil and well-presented. The grounds are lush and include a good restaurant, *temazcal*, and a fabulous pool with wavy sides. Recommended.

### $$$ Piedra de Agua
*Carretera a las Ruinas Km 2.5, T999-924 2300, www.palenque.piedradeagua.com.*
A new boutique option with an aesthetic minimalist design and an emphasis on immersion in the environment. Thatched *cabañas* are crisp and simple and feature private terraces fully equipped with hot tub and hammocks where breakfast is served in the morning (at an extra cost). General services include spa, pool, tours and a welcome cocktail. There's no dinner, so it helps to have your own transport. Rustic chic, secluded and romantic.

### $$-$ Margarita and Ed's
*Carretera a las Ruinas Km 4.5, El Panchán, margaritaandedcabanas.blogspot.com.*
Margarita and Ed are very gracious and hospitable hosts and they offer a range of decent accommodation in simple, spacious rooms or economical *cabañas*, some with a/c and views of the forest. All of them all kept rigorously clean and fresh with floors scrubbed daily and mattresses regularly aired. An oasis of cleanliness in the jungle and easily the best lodgings in El Panchán. Recommended.

### $ El Panchán
*Carretera a las Ruinas Km 4.5, www.elpanchan.com.*
The classic travellers' haunt, a sprawling jungle resort that has long drawn backpackers, adventurers and hippies to its fabled enclaves. Its founder, Don Moisés,

first came to Palenque as an archaeologist and was one of the first guides to the ruins.

## Restaurants

The options below are adequate, but don't expect fine dining.

### $$$-$$ Restaurante Maya
*Hidalgo and Independencia.*
Overlooking the main square, this popular and reliable downtown option was established in 1958. It offers set menu lunches and à la carte breakfasts and dinners. Fare includes regional dishes, typical Mexican and international. Efficient service and free Wi-Fi.

### $$-$ Café de Yara
*Hidalgo 66.*
This sunny café on the corner serves good strong Chiapaneco coffee (recommended, try an Americano) and fair light meals including breakfasts, a *menú del día* and international and Mexican fare. Whole beans are sold in the shop next door if you want to take some of their coffee home. There's occasional live music in the evenings.

### $$-$ Las Tinajas
*20 de Noviembre 41 and Abasolo.*
This long-established family-run restaurant has seating indoors and out. They serve the usual Mexican fare and reasonable home-cooked grub in massive portions; the *pollo frito* is half a chicken on a bed of chunky chips. Good value, one of the better places to eat.

### La Cañada

### $$ El Huachinango Feliz
*Av Merle Green.*
A decent seafood joint and one of the better places for an evening meal in La Cañada. They serve ample plates of shrimp, grilled octopus, whole fish and more. Popular with locals and tourists and occasionally host to lively crowds. Slow service, but good value.

### $$ Maya Cañada
*Av Merle Green.*
Catering to a moneyed tourist crowd, the Maya Cañada has pleasant evening atmosphere and an appealing open-air setting. Offerings on the menu include Chiapaneco specialities and *comida típica*. Many rate the food highly, but we found the chicken in *mole* quite average. Hit and miss perhaps.

### $$-$ Café Jade
*Prolongación Av Hidalgo 1.*
Attached to Hostel Yaxchin, the best coffee shop in La Cañada. They serve decent light meals, including fruit breakfasts, soups, pastas, salads, stuffed peppers, tasty tacos, nachos and more. Also an array of indulgent desserts and refreshing fruit juices. Very mellow and popular with travellers. Recommended.

## Road to the ruins

### $$ Don Mucho
*El Panchán.*
This long-running outdoor restaurant is hugely popular in the high season and usually thronging with travellers and backpackers. It serves average international and Mexican fare and a good breakfast. Beyond the food, it's a place to sip beer and enjoy the spectacle of evening entertainment which may include travelling musicians, jugglers or fire-dancers. Quite exotic and a great atmosphere.

### $$ Monteverde Pizzeria
*Turn-off on the Carretera a las Ruinas, 1.5 km.*
Authentic Italian cuisine in a secluded jungle setting, including pastas and thin-crust pizzas. Occasional live music adds to the great atmosphere. One of the best in Palenque, but inconveniently located at the end of a dirt road; take a taxi, especially at night.

## What to do

### Tour operators

Palenque is the best place to arrange guided tours of Bonampak and Yaxchilán. To see both sites, it is recommended you take at least 2 days and stay overnight in Lacanjá or Frontera Corozal, otherwise expect a very long, tough day of at least 14 hrs. Note that some tours to Agua Azul include onward connections to San Cristóbal. This should be clarified before agreement as some travellers have reported being bundled onto a public bus after the waterfalls. There are many reasonable tour operators around town offering broadly similar services, we particularly recommend the following:

**Alonso Méndez**, *ask at Don Mucho's in El Panchán*. Available in high season only. Alonso is a well-versed guide with extensive knowledge of flora and fauna, medicinal uses of plants, and an intimate knowledge of Palenque ruins. A respected authority on ethnobotany in Chiapas, Alonso has the gift of academic and spiritual understanding of the rainforest. He speaks English, Spanish and Tzeltzal fluently.

**Center of Mayan Exploration**, *www.maya exploration.org*. Continuing the good work of Linda Schele and other key Mayanists, this excellent NGO has made significant research contributions to Mayan archaeology by mapping Palenque and uncovering hidden aspects of its astronomical alignments. They offer superb custom-made tours of the entire Mayan world, as far afield as Honduras and Guatemala. Contact well in advance of your trip.

**Transportadora Turística Scheerrer and Barb**, *Av Juárez 1, opposite the Burger King, T916-103 3649*. Managed by Fernando Mérida, a Lacandón guide with some interesting views on Mayan prophecy, this long-running tour operator offers solid excursions to Bonampak and Yaxchilán, as well as some more off-beat tours not offered by anyone else. Options include

multi-day trips to Metzabok and Na-Ha ecological reserves, Mitziha jungle treks, including options for zip-lining and kayaking, trips to Chinikiha Archaeological zone and Xibalba caves, kayaking on Sun Lagoon, and many others. Custom-made tours are also an option.

## Transport

### Air

**Palenque Airport (PQM)** recently opened to commercial flights with **ADO** minibuses shuttling arrivals into town. Flights to **Mexico City** with **Interjet** and **Tuxtla Gutiérrez** with **Ka'an Air**. Speak to a tour agent if you would like to organize chartered flights within Chiapas (including **Yaxchilán** and **Bonampak**), **Yucatán** or **Guatemala**.

### Bus

The new 1st-class **ADO** terminal is at the western end of Juárez near the Mayan head. The Rodolfo Figueroa y Lacandonia terminal is further east on Juárez with a few 2nd-class departures to San Cristóbal. An **AEXA** terminal is also on Juárez, serving a handful of destinations in Chiapas, as is **Autotransportes Tuxtla**, with 2nd-class departures to **Quintana Roo**.

From the **ADO** terminal to **Cancún**, 1740, 2230, 2300, 13 hrs, US$67-80; **Campeche**, 4 daily, 5 hrs, US$29; **Mérida**, 4 daily, 8 hrs, US$44; **Mexico City**, 1830, 14 hrs, US$91; **Oaxaca City**, 1730, 15 hrs, US$66; **San Cristóbal de las Casas**, 5 daily, mostly 5 hrs (some are 9 hrs), US$16; **Tulum**, 1740, 2230, 2300, 10-11 hrs, US$58-68; **Tuxtla Gutiérrez**, 6 daily, 6 hrs, US$20; **Villahermosa**, many daily, 2-3 hrs, US$11.50.

### Colectivos

For **Palenque ruins**, microbuses run back and forth along Av Juárez, turning onto the highway at the Mayan head, every 10 mins, US$1.50 (taxi US$8). Catch one of these for **El Panchán** and other nearby accommodation. For destinations in

Chiapas state, there are numerous colectivo shuttles leaving from many terminals. To **Agua Azul** and **Misol-ha**, Transportes Chambalú, Allende and Juárez, 0900, 1200, US$11.50 excluding entrance fees. They stop for 30 mins at Misol-Há and 3 hrs at Agua Azul. To **Frontera Corozal** (for **San Javier**, **Bonampak**, **Lacanjá** and **Yaxchilán**), **Transportes Chamoan**, Hidalgo 141, roughly hourly from 0500-1700, 2-3 hrs, US$9.20. To **Tenosique**, Transportes Palenque, Allende and 20 de Noviembre, hourly, 2 hrs, US$4. To **Playas de Catazajá** (for Escárcega and Campeche) **Transportes Pakal**, Allende between 20 de Noviembre and Corregidora, every 15 mins, US$3.

## Taxi

Taxis charge a flat rate of US$1.50 within the town, US$5 to **El Panchán**.

## Mexico to Guatemala: Tenosique–El Ceibo

### Bus

ADO services to **Emiliano Zapata**, hourly, 1 hr, US$5.50; **Mexico City**, 1700, 15 hrs, US$94; **Villahermosa**, 5 daily, 3½ hrs, US$16.

## Colectivos

Shuttles to **Palenque**, hourly with **Transportes Palenque**, US$4. Or catch a Villahermosa bus to **El Crucero de la Playa** and pick up a frequent colectivo from there. Colectivo taxis to El Ceibo and the border depart from the market in Tenosique, 1 hr, US$3; see also page 77.

★Enveloped in thick canopies of foliage, the ruined metropolis of Palenque is one of Mexico's most striking and enigmatic archaeological sites. It's this lush rainforest setting as much as its cultural and artistic achievements that conspire to make it one of Mexico's most vivid destinations.

Built at the height of the Classic period on a series of artificial terraces surrounded by jungle, Palenque was constructed for strategic purposes, with evidence of defensive apertures in some of the retaining walls. In the centre of the site is the Palace, a massive warren of buildings with an asymmetrical tower rising above them, and fine views to the north. The tower was probably used as an astronomical observatory and a watchtower. The outer buildings of the palace have an unusual series of galleries, offering shade from the jungle heat of the site.

From about the fourth century AD, Palenque grew from a small agricultural village to one of the most important cities in the prehispanic world, although it really achieved greatness between AD 600 and 800. During the long and illustrious reign of Lord Pacal, the city rapidly rose to the first rank of Maya states. The duration of Pacal's reign is still a bone of contention among Mayanists because the remains found in his sarcophagus do not appear to be those of an 81-year-old man, the age implied by the texts in the Temple of the Inscriptions.

## Essential Palenque ruins

### Site information

Daily 0800-1700, US$4.50; entrance to national park US$2.15, payable at the toll by El Panchán. Water at the site is expensive, so bring your own. The cheapest food is the tacos from the stalls. Colectivos back to the town leave from outside the main entrance, US$1.50, every 6-18 minutes. Guides of varying quality can be hired for around US$70 per group, two hours.

### Warning

The ruins are surrounded by thick, mosquito-infested jungle so wear insect repellent and make sure you're up to date with your tablets (May to November is the worst time for mosquitoes). It is extremely hot and humid at the ruins, especially in the afternoon, so it is best to visit early. Unfortunately, as well as mosquitoes, there have also been reports of criminals hiding in the jungle. Try and leave valuables at your hotel to minimize any loss.

Since its discovery, choked by the encroaching jungle that pushed against its walls and scaled the stairs of its temples once climbed by rulers, priests and acolytes, the architecture of Palenque has elicited praise and admiration and begged to be reconstructed. The corbelled vaults, the arrangement of its groupings of buildings, the impression of lightness created by walls broken by pillars and open spaces make Palenque-style architecture unique. It was only later that archaeologists and art historians realized that the architecture of Palenque was created mainly to accommodate the extraordinary sculptures and texts that referred not only to historical individuals and the important events in their lives, but also to mythological beings who endorsed the claims of dynastic continuity or 'divine right' of the rulers of this great city. The structures most illustrative of this function are the Palace, a group of buildings arranged around four patios to which a tower was later added, the Temple of the Inscriptions that rises above the tomb of Lord Pacal, and the temples of the Group of the Cross, used by Chan Bahlum, Pacal's successor, who made claims in the inscriptions carved on the tablets, pillars and balustrades of these exceptional buildings, claims which, in their audacity, are awe inspiring.

## The Palace

The Palace and Temple XI are located in the centre of the site. The Palace stands on an artificial platform over 100 m long and 9 m high. Chan Bahlum's younger brother, Kan Xul, was 57 when he became king. He devoted himself to enlarging the palace, and apparently built the four-storey tower in honour of his dead father. The top of the tower is almost at

➡ **Palenque maps**
1 Palenque, page 77
2 Palenque archaeological site, page 84

## ② **Palenque archaeological site**

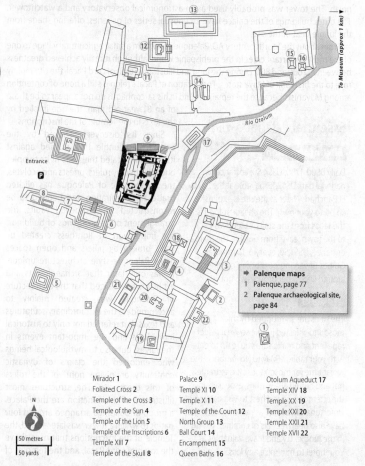

To Museum (approx 1 km) ▶

Río Otolum

Entrance

P

| | | |
|---|---|---|
| Mirador **1** | Palace **9** | Otolum Aqueduct **17** |
| Foliated Cross **2** | Temple XI **10** | Temple XIV **18** |
| Temple of the Cross **3** | Temple X **11** | Temple XX **19** |
| Temple of the Sun **4** | Temple of the Count **12** | Temple XXI **20** |
| Temple of the Lion **5** | North Group **13** | Temple XXII **21** |
| Temple of the Inscriptions **6** | Ball Court **14** | Temple XVII **22** |
| Temple XIII **7** | Encampment **15** | |
| Temple of the Skull **8** | Queen Baths **16** | |

N

50 metres
50 yards

## BACKGROUND

### Sarcophogus

Pacal's sarcophagus, or coffin, is carved out of a solid piece of rock, with a carved slab covering it. Every element in the imagery of the sarcophagus lid is consistent with Maya iconography. It is exquisitely beautiful. The central image is that of Lord Pacal falling back into the fleshless jaws of the earth monster who will transport him to Xibalba, the realm of the dead. A cruciform world-tree rises above the underworld maw. The same world-tree appears on the tablets in the sanctuaries at the backs of the buildings known as the Group of the Cross. A long inscription runs around the edge of the lid, which includes a number of dates and personal names that records a dynastic sequence covering almost the whole of the seventh and eight centuries.

Four plugs in the corners of the lid filled the holes used with ropes to lower the lid into place; the plug in the southeast corner had a notch cut in it so that the channel, built into the stairway leading to the upper world, would allow spiritual communion between the dead king and his descendants above. Although the imagery of the sarcophagus lid refers to Pacal's fall into Xibalba, the location of the tower of the palace ensures that he will not remain there. The sun, setting over the crypt on the winter solstice, will have to do battle with the Nine Lords of the Night before re-emerging triumphantly in the east; the nine tiers of the pyramid represent the nine battles to be fought during his downward journey. Pacal, who awaits the sun at the point where the final battle had been fought, will accompany the sun as he re-emerges from Xibalba in the east. Palenque, the westernmost city of the Classic Maya, was in the 'dead zone', which placed it in the perfect position to accommodate the descent of the sun and Lord Pacal into the underworld.

the level of Pacal's mortuary temple, and on the winter solstice the sun, viewed from here, sets directly above his crypt. Large windows where Maya astronomers could observe and chart the movement of the planets, ancestors of the royal lineage of Palenque, pierce the walls of the tower. Kan-Xul reigned for 18 years before being captured and probably sacrificed by the rulers of Toniná. During his reign Palenque reached its greatest degree of expansion, although recent excavations at the site may prove differently.

### Temple of the Inscriptions

The Temple of the Inscriptions, along with Temple XII and Temple XIII, lies to the south of the Palace group of buildings and is one of the rare Maya pyramids to have a burial chamber incorporated at the time of its construction. This building was erected to cover the crypt in which Lord Pacal, the founder of the first ruling dynasty of Palenque, was buried. Discovered in 1952 by Alberto Ruz-Lhuillier, the burial chamber measured 7 m long, 7 m high and 3.75 m across, an incredible achievement considering the weight of the huge pyramid pressing down upon it. According to the inscriptions, Lord Pacal was born in AD 603 and died in AD 684. Inside, Ruz-Lhuillier discovered his bones adorned with jade jewellery. Around the burial chamber were various figures carved in stucco, depicting the Bolontikú, the Nine Lords of the Night of Maya mythology. There was a narrow tube alongside the stairs, presumably to give Pacal spiritual access to the outside world. Pacal also left a record of his forebears in the inscriptions. These three great tablets contain one of the longest texts of any Maya monument. There are 620 glyph blocks; they tell of Pacal's ancestors, astronomical events and an astonishing projection into the distant future (AD 4772). One of the last inscriptions reveals that, 132 days after Pacal's death, his son, Chan Bahlum, ascended to power as the new ruler of Palenque.

While finishing his father's funerary monument, Chan Bahlum had himself depicted as a child being presented as heir by his father. The portraits of Chan Bahlum, on the outer pillars of the Temple of the Inscriptions, display features that are both human and divine. He took and assumed attributes that rightly belong to the gods, thus ensuring that the heir to the throne was perceived as a divine human.

## Group of the Cross

To the extreme southeast of the centre of the site lie Temple XIV and the buildings known as the *Grupo de la Cruz*. These include the Temple of the Sun, with beautiful relief carvings, which would probably have been painted in their day. The three temples in this group all have dramatic roof-combs, originally believed to have a religious significance, although traces of roof-combs have been found on buildings now known to have been purely residential. In all of the temples there was discovered a huge stone tablet with bas-relief, now removed to the museum, from whose images the name of each temple was taken.

Human and mythological time come together in the inscriptions of these temples. In each tableau carved on the tablets at the back of the temples, Chan Bahlum, the new ruler, receives the regalia of office from his father, Pacal, now in the underworld and shown much smaller than his living son. The shrines in the three temples are dedicated to the Palenque Triad, a sacred trinity linked to the ruling dynasty of the city, whose genealogy is explained in the inscriptions. They were certainly long lived: the parents of the triad were born in 3122 or 3121 BC and the children arrived on 19 October, 23 October and 6 November, 2360 BC. It has been shown that these were dates of extraordinary astronomical phenomena: the gods were intimately related to heavenly bodies and events. They also provided a mythological origin for the dynasty which is detailed on the three main tablets from the Group of the Cross. Rulers died and gods were born in an impressive merging of historical and mythological events. At their completion, the three temples of the Group of the Cross housed the divine sanction for the dynasty as a whole and gave the rationale for its descent through females and males.

On each set of balustrades, Chan Bahlum began his text with the birth of the patron god of each temple. On the left side of the stairs, he recorded the time elapsed between the birth of the god and the dedication of the temple. Thus, mythological time and contemporary time were fused. Each temple was named for the central image on its inner tablet. When Chan Bahlum died in 702 after ruling for 18 years, his younger brother and heir erected a fourth shrine to record the apotheosis of the departed king (Temple XIV). On these reliefs, Chan Bahlum emerges triumphantly from the underworld and dances towards his mother, Lady Ahpo-Hel.

The lengths to which the rulers of Palenque went to establish legitimacy for their claims of divine right could not guarantee the survival of Palenque after the collapse felt throughout the Classic Maya region, when the building of elite religious structures stopped and stelae were no longer engraved with the details of dynastic events. Toniná, the city that captured and probably sacrificed the Palenque ruler Kan-Xul, outlived the great centre made glorious by Pacal and Chan Bahlum. The last-known dated monument from the Maya region registers AD 909 at the lesser site; it is to be supposed that soon afterwards, Toniná went the way of the other centres of the Classic Maya world.

The **museum** ⓘ *Tue-Sun 0900-1630, free with ruins ticket,* is on the way back to the town, with an expensive restaurant and gift shop. Many of the stucco carvings retrieved from the site are here, as well as jade pieces of jewellery, funerary urns and ceramics. If you want to learn more about the iconography and writing system of the Classic Maya see *A Forest of Kings,* by L Schele and D Freidel (William Morrow and Company, NY 1992).

## East of Palenque: the Carretera Fronteriza
### jungle-clad remote border region with Mayan villages and archaeological sites

From Palenque, Highway 307, also known as the Carretera Fronteriza, follows the eastern outskirts of Chiapas state where it meets the frontier with Guatemala, eventually joining the Pan-American Highway at La Trinitaria, south of Comitán. This area encompasses tracts of pristine rainforests, isolated Lacandón Maya communities, endless enchanting waterfalls, lakes, and the lesser visited archaeological sites of Bonampak and Yaxchilán. The region is heavily militarized due to cross-border narco-trafficking and you may be stopped at a number of checkpoints during your journey. For safety, you should not travel on the highway after dark. The international crossings in this part of Chiapas provide an adventurous backdoor route into Guatemala's Petén.

### Lacanjá Chansayab

Lacanjá Chansayab, 6 km from the tiny hamlet of San Javier on the Carretera, is one of only three permanent Lacandón communities in Mexico. Forest-dwelling nomads until the late 20th century, the Lacandón settlers in this little village continue to speak their native language, but have otherwise abandoned their traditions and converted to Protestant Christianity. The experience of staying in the community is nonetheless fascinating, and the setting, on the edge of the rainforest, is certainly magical with its vast starry skies and swarms of twinkling fireflies. Accommodation consists of 'campamentos' with simple wood-built *cabañas* ($$-$) and shared dorms. Please contribute to the community by buying some artesanías from your hosts and/or by hiring the services of a guide: there are several jungle hikes, waterfalls and hidden ruins to check out, and it is also possible to hike to Bonampak, 12 km away (see below); expect to pay US$30-40 per group for a three- to four-hour tour. For more information on the community and Lacandón culture, drop into the **Na-Bolom** cultural centre in San Cristóbal de las Casas. In Lacanjá, Lucas Chambor at the **Casa de Cultura** is a good source of advice.

### ★Bonampak *Colour map 2, B4.*
*Open 0800-1645, US$3.50. To get there on public transport, ask the driver to drop you at 'Crucero Bonampak', 4 km from the site. If the bus only stops at San Javier, taxis can shuttle you 12 km to the entrance.*

Bonampak, originally under the political domination of Yaxchilán, was built in the late-Classic period on the Río Lacanjá, a tributary of the Usumacinta. It is famous for its murals, dated at AD 800. Painted on the walls, vault rises and benches of three adjoining but not interconnecting rooms, they depict the rituals surrounding the presentation at court of the future ruler. Some of the rituals were separated by considerable intervals which added to the solemnity of the ceremony. It is very likely that the rituals illustrated were only a small selection of a far greater series of events. The people participating were mainly elite, including the royal family, and a strict hierarchy was observed in which eminent lords were attended by minor nobility.

**Structure 1** The rituals portrayed on the walls of Structure 1 at Bonampak are thought to have been performed between 790 and 792, a time when the collapse of the Classic Maya was beginning to be felt. The extravagant use of enormous amounts of fine cloth, expensive jaguar pelts, jade beads and pectorals, elegant costumes, headdresses made from rare feathers, and spondylus shells was not enough to reverse the decadence of the civilization that had produced magnificent works in art, architecture, jewellery, mathematics, astronomy and glyphic writing: within a hundred years, the jungle was to claim it for its own.

**Room 1** In the first room of Structure 1, the celebration opens with the presentation of the young prince, in which a porter introduces the child to an assembly of lords, dressed for the occasion in white robes. The king watches from his throne. Also present are two representatives from Yaxchilán, one male and one female. It is probable that the female is the wife or consort of Chaan-Muan, the ruler of Bonampak. After this simple opening, the spectacle begins. Lords are represented dressed in sumptuous clothing and jewellery, musicians appear playing drums, turtle carapaces, rattles and trumpets and they all line up for a procession, which will bemuse the peasantry, labourers and artisans waiting outside. We never see the lower orders but, open-mouthed, we can stand with them to observe the spectacle. The headdresses alone are enough to bedazzle us and the great diversity in the attire of the participants illustrates the wide spectrum of social functions fulfilled by those attending the ceremony.

**Room 2** The imagery and text of the sculptured lintels and stelae at nearby Yaxchilán proclaim the right of the heir to accede to the throne while emphasizing the need to take captives to be sacrificed in honour of the king-to-be. This need is echoed in the paintings of Room 2, Structure 1, at Bonampak. A ferocious battle is in progress in which the ruler, Chaan-Muan, proves his right to the throne. In the midst of battle, he shines out heroically. The local warriors pull the hair of those of the opposite side, whose identity is not known. Many captives were taken. In the ensuing scene, the full horror of the fate of those captured by the Maya is illustrated.

On a stepped structure, the ruler Chaan-Muan oversees the torture and mutilation of the captives taken in the recent battle. This event is clearly in the open air and surely witnessed by the inhabitants of Bonampak, whose loyalty is rewarded by admission to the bloody circus. The torture of the captives consisted of mutilation of the hands; some disconsolate individuals hold up their hands dripping blood, while one has clearly been decapitated, his head resting on a bed of leaves. It is to be supposed that the torture of the captives would be followed by death, probably by decapitation. The gods demanded sacrifice, which was provided by the rulers in an extravaganza of bloodletting. It must be understood that what appears to be outright bloodthirstiness was a necessary part of Maya ritual and probably accepted by all the polities throughout the Classic Maya region. It is very probable that the heir would not have been acceptable without this gory ritual.

**Room 3** The murals of the third room at Bonampak express the events that were meant to close the series of rituals designed to consolidate the claim to the throne by the son of the ruler. At first sight, the paintings that cover the walls of room three of Structure 1 appear to celebrate the sacrifices of the previous depictions in an exuberant public display of music, dance and perhaps song. The background is a pyramid, and 10 elegantly dressed lords dance on different levels, colourful 'dance-wings' sprouting from their hips. The dominant dancer on the uppermost level is believed to be the ruler, Chaan-Muan. However, it has been noted that a very strong element of sacrifice accompanies the extrovert display. In a more private corner, the royal family is portrayed preparing to engage in blood sacrifice; a servant proffers them a container that the sacred bloodletting instruments. There are also indications that the male dancers had already drawn blood by means of penis perforation. As at Yaxchilán, blood endorsed the dynastic claims of the royal family.

## ★ Yaxchilán *Colour map 2, B4.*

*Yaxchilán 0800-1600, US$4.50. Lanchas to the site depart from Frontera Corozal on demand, 40-60 mins each way, costing from US$60 for 1-3 people up to US$120 for 8-10, with a 2- to 3-hr wait at the site. Prices are hard to negotiate so it's best to join a group to keep down costs.*

Yaxchilán was a powerful Maya city-state built on terraces and hills above a bend in the Río Usumacinta. Founded in the Pre-Classic era, it reached its apogee in the late Classic, dominating Bonampak and other regional population centres to become the most important city on the river. Now ruined and rather remote, the site is very haunting and tranquil, except for the troupes of occasionally vociferous howler monkeys who live in the surrounding forests.

Entering Yaxchilán on the west side, the Labyrinth is a three-level structure with numerous rooms and stairways, and a population of squeaking bats, which leads onto the Gran Plaza. Structures flank the plaza on all sides and climb the hills to the south. The finest building in Yaxchilán is Structure 33, dedicated in the 8th century and boasting an impressive roof-comb. A staircase leads to it from Stela 1 and the final step is engraved with hieroglyphs and a pictorial representation of the sacred ball game.

The site is generally renowned for its stelae and stone inscriptions, which include two hieroglyphic stairways, visual depictions of ceremonies and descriptions of the city's dynastic history. Sadly, some lintels have been removed from the site and taken out of Mexico, such as the famous Lintel 24, now on display in the British Museum in London. It depicts a blood-letting ritual performed by King Balam II and his wife Lady Kabal Xook. Lintel 15, also in the British Museum, depicts a similar scene Lady Wak Tuun, a wife of King Bird Jaguar IV, conjuring Vision Serpents from a bowl of blood-stained scrolls.

### Frontera Corozal *Colour map 2, B4.*

Formerly known as Frontera Echeverria, the town of Frontera Corozal is perched on the banks of the Río Usumacinta, the cradle of Classic Mayan civilization, and today the physical border between Mexico and Guatemala. The town serves as a small but important river port with connections by *lancha* downstream to the ruins of Yaxchilán, or across the frontier to Guatemala. There is an immigration office, a few adequate hotels, restaurants, a regional museum and a military presence. Colectivos travel directly from Palenque to Corozal, otherwise you can get a taxi from the highway turn-off (Crucero Corozal), US$1.50; or from San Javier, 16 km away, US$2 per person, plus a toll US$1 (retain your ticket until exiting). See also Mexico to Guatemala: Frontera Corozal–Bethel/La Técnica, below, and Border crossings box in Practicalities chapter.

**Mexico to Guatemala: Frontera Corozal–Bethel/La Técnica** *Colour map 2, B4.*
Adventurers will enjoy the remote Frontera Corozal crossing. The first leg includes a 40-minute *lancha* ride upstream to Bethel in Guatemala (see Transport, below). You must stamp out in Corozal and surrender your tourist card before proceeding. Once in Bethel, there is an immigration office for stamping into the country and buses run to Flores at least four times daily, four to five hours, US$3. A slightly cheaper alternative is to cross the river to La Técnica on the opposite bank (see Transport, below). From there, infrequent buses run to Bethel 12 km away (where you must submit to formalities) and onwards to Flores. The first hour or two of the trip to Flores is on a bumpy unpaved dirt road. Due to the unreliability of onward connections, some travellers like to have the whole journey booked on private transport. Tour operators in Palenque can organize this. See also Border crossings box in Practicalities chapter.

## Listings East of Palenque: the Carretera Fronteriza

### Transport

#### Frontera Corozal
#### Boat
From Frontera Corozal to **Yaxchilán** it costs from US$60 for 1-3 passengers; prices rise with additional people. You can try to bargain the boatmen down (be warned, they're stubborn), or hitch a ride with a tour group. If you are travelling from Frontera Corozal to **Guatemala**, ensure your papers are in order before crossing the border. Visit immigration offices on both sides for exit and entry stamps, and keep a photocopy of your passport handy for possible military inspection.

River crossings to La Técnica US$3.50, 5 mins, To Bethel in **Guatemala**, US$30 for 1-3 passengers, up to US$60 for 8-10.

#### Bus
A few different companies run hourly colectivo services to **Palenque**, including **Transportes Chamoan**, 0400-1600, 2-3 hrs, US$9.20 (see Palenque Colectivos, page 81). For Lacanjá or Bonampak, catch one of these and exit at the junction and military checkpoint at San Javier. From there, you will need to hike or take a taxi, if you can find one. Bear in mind this is a remote destination, so pack water, travel light and plan your time accordingly.

# Tabasco State

Until recently, low-lying, hot, steamy, swampy Tabasco was considered an oil state with little appeal for tourists. But oil wealth has brought Villahermosa, the state capital, a certain self-assurance and vibrancy, and the parks, nature reserves and huge meandering rivers in the eastern and southern regions of the state are beginning to attract visitors. Be sure to pack insect repellent, especially in the wet season.

## Villahermosa *Colour map 2, A1.*

*a busy, prosperous city, attracting mainly business travellers*

Capital of Tabasco state, Villahermosa is on the Río Grijalva, which is navigable to the sea. The cathedral, ruined in 1973, has been rebuilt, its twin steeples beautifully lit at night; it is not in the centre. There is a warren of modern colonial-style pedestrian malls throughout the central area.

The **Centro de Investigaciones de las Culturas Olmecas** (CICOM) is set in a modern complex with a large public library, expensive restaurant, airline offices and souvenir shops, a few minutes' walk south, out of town along the river bank. The **Museo Regional de Antropología Carlos Pellicer** ① *Pereférico Carlos Pellicer, www.iec.tabasco.gob.mx, Tue-Sun 0900-1700, US$3.80*, on three floors, has well laid-out displays of Maya and Olmec artefacts. Two other museums worth visiting are the **Museo de Cultura Popular** ① *Zaragoza 810, Tue-Sun 0900-2000, free*, and the **Museo de Historia de Tabasco** ① *Av 27 de Febrero corner of Juárez, Tue-Sun 0900-1900, US$1.50*. The **Mercado Pino Suárez** at Pino Suárez and Bastar Zozaya offers a sensory overload as every nook and cranny is taken up with a variety of goods; everything from barbecued *pejelagarto* (gar, a type of fish) to cowboy hats, colourful handmade fabrics, spices and dangling naked chickens en route to the kettle. The local drink, *pozol*, is believed to cure a hangover. You can watch it being made here as the *pozoleros* grind the hominy into a thick dough to then mix it with cacao and water; its grainy starchiness is somewhat of an acquired taste. Nonetheless it is popular, and the *pozoleros* will serve you the drink *al gusto*, that is, with as much or as little sugar as you want.

# ★Parque Nacional La Venta

*Adolfo Ruiz Cortines, T993-314 1652, Tue-Sun 0800-1600, US$4; it takes up to 2 hrs to do the park justice; excellent guides speak Spanish and English, recommended. Taxis charge US$2 to the Parque. Bus Circuito No 1 from outside 2nd-class bus terminal goes past Parque La Venta. From Parque Juárez in the city, take a 'Fraccionamiento Carrizal' bus and ask to be let off at Parque Tomás Garrido, of which La Venta is a part.*

In 1925, an expedition of archaeologists discovered huge sculptured human and animal figures, urns and altars at La Venta, the centre of the ancient Olmec culture, buried in near imprenetrable forest, 120 km west of Villahermosa. In the 1950s, the monuments were threatened with destruction by the discovery of oil nearby. The poet Carlos Pellicer got them hauled all the way to a woodland area near Villahermosa, now the Parque Nacional de La Venta, also called the Museo Nacional de la Venta. There is nothing to see now at the original site of La Venta.

The park, with scattered lakes, next to a children's playground, is almost opposite the old airport entrance (west of downtown). There, the 33 exhibits are dispersed in various small clearings. The huge heads, one of them weighing 20 tonnes, are Olmec, a culture that flourished about 1150-150 BC. The figures have suffered a certain amount of damage through being exposed to the elements (those in the Xalapa Anthropological Museum are in far better condition) but to see them here, in natural surroundings, is an experience not to be missed.

There is also a zoo with creatures from the Tabasco jungle, including monkeys, alligators, deer, wild pigs and birds. Outside the park, on the lakeside, is an observation tower, **Mirador de las Aguilas** ⓘ *free*, with excellent views, but only for the fit as there are lots of stairs.

## Listings Villahermosa

### Tourist information

**Institute of Tourism**
*Av Paseo Tabasco 1504, T993-316 8271, www.vistetabasco.com. Daily 0800-1800.*
English spoken, good for maps and advice on Tabasco state. There is also a tourist information kiosk at the ADO terminal.

### Where to stay

**$$$-$$ One Villahermosa Centro**
*Carranza 101 esq Zaragoza, T993-131 7100, www.onehotels.com.*
Unlike many other chain hotels, this reliable business class lodging is conveniently located downtown. Its rooms are crisp, minimalist and somewhat generic, but

they are all well equipped with the usual comforts and amenities.

**$$ Hotel Santo Domingo Express**
*Madero 802, T993-131 2674, www.santodomingohotel.com.mx.*
Immaculately clean, modern and stylish, this small business hotel has 27 well-attired rooms with Wi-Fi and plasma TVs. Good comfort to value ratio. Recommended.

**$$-$ Hotel Oriente**
*Madero 425, T993-312 0121, hotel-oriente@hotmail.com.*
A reliable budget option; nothing special, charming or fancy, but fair and adequate. Rooms are clean and modest, and those with fan and no a/c are slightly cheaper.

## Restaurants

In the high season a number of eateries, bars and discos open up along the riverfront. Good for sunset drinks and dining, but take mosquito repellent. For good tacos head to Calle Aldama, Nos 611, 613 and 615, where there are 3 decent places. These are cheap and cheerful, but excellent value, with great selections.

**$$$-$$ Los Manglares**
*Madero 418, inside Hotel Olmeca Plaza.*
Attractive restaurant serving seafood, meat, chicken and breakfast. Excellent 4-course lunch buffet.

**$$$-$$ Rodizio do Brasil**
*Parque la Choca, Stand Grandero, T993-316 2895, informacion@ restauranterodizio.com.*
Speciality *espadas*, good Brazilian food.

**$$ El Matador**
*Av César Sandino No 101a, www.elmatador. com.mx. Daily 24 hrs.*
Local meat dishes, *tacos al pastor*, good value.

### Cafés

**Café La Cabaña**
*Juárez 303-A, across the way from the Museo de Historia de Tabasco.*
Has outdoor tables where town elders congregate to debate the day's issues over cappuccinos. Very entertaining to watch. No meals.

## Festivals

**Feb Ash Wednesday** is celebrated from 1500 to dusk by the throwing of water bombs and buckets of water at anyone who happens to be on the street!

## Transport

### Air
**Airport Carlos R Pérez (VSA)**, 18 km from town, has international flights to **Havana** and **Houston**, and has good national connections. VW bus to town US$5 each, taxi US$11.

### Bus
Reserve your seat as soon as you can; buses to Mexico City can sometimes be booked up well in advance. 1st-class **ADO** bus terminal is on Javier Mina and Lino Merino, 12 blocks north of centre, computerized booking system. The **Central Camionera** 2nd-class bus station is on Av Ruiz Cortines, near the roundabout with the fisherman statue, 1 block east of Javier Mina, opposite Castillo, 4 blocks north of **ADO**.

    1st-class **ADO** services to **Cancún**, many daily, 13-14 hrs, US$61-113; **Chetumal**, 6 daily, 8½ hrs, US$44; **Campeche**, many daily, 6 hrs, US$36; **Emiliano Zapata**, many daily, 2½ hrs, US$12; **Mérida**, many daily, 8 hrs, US$49-86; **Mexico City**, many daily, 10-12 hrs, US$77-97; **Palenque**, many daily, 2½ hrs, US$11.50; **San Cristóbal de las Casas**, 2340, 7 hrs, US$31; **Tenosique**, many daily 3½ hrs, US$16.

### Taxi
City taxis charge US$1 for journeys in the centre.

# Yucatán Peninsula

Once a vast coral reef in a prehistoric ocean, the Yucatán Peninsula now divides the Gulf of Mexico from the Caribbean. Relentlessly flat, its inhospitable interior is consumed by arid scrubland, swamps lagoons and impenetrable jungle.

Yet the Yucatán thrived as a hub of civilization long before the Spanish arrived. Its horizon is broken by the ruins of skyward-reaching pyramids, overgrown temples, fallen palaces and astronomical observatories: sprawling Mayan metropolises where great dynasties once reigned.

None of it would have been possible without the peninsula's network of *cenotes* (sink holes), a subterranean labyrinth of submerged caverns and canyons. The ancient Maya venerated their sacred wells as sources of life and as portals to another dimension.

The Yucatán is a fiercely independent place and can often seem more like an island. It took three brutal campaigns by Francisco de Montejo to 'pacify' the region, and today, scores of rambling old haciendas, sumptuous mansions and religious buildings are testament to the grandeur of the colonial era. But beyond them, in remote rural enclaves, determined Mayan communities stage rituals to honour the ancestral gods of thunder and rain.

**Best** for
Beaches ▪ Caves & cenotes ▪ Diving ▪ Mayan ruins

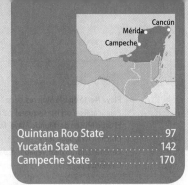

# Footprint
## picks

★ **Playa Norte on Isla Mujeres**, page 108

A white-sand beach on the Campeche Gulf Coast.

★ **Palancar Reef off Isla Cozumel**, page 125

This section of the Mesoamerican Barrier Reef has some spectacular coral and great diving opportunities.

★ **El Gran Museo del Mundo Maya**, Mérida, page 145

An impressive contemporary museum with lots of interactive exhibits on the Maya.

★ **Chichén Itzá**, page 161

The Toltec-influenced El Castillo pyramid looms over these Mayan ruins, the peninsula's most visited archaeological site.

★ **Cenote Dzitnup near Valladolid**, page 166

A beautiful underground lake with limestone features and tunnels leading off it.

★ **Calakmul**, page 181

The highlight of this archaeological site, one of the ancient Maya's most important capitals, is the huge pyramid of Structure II.

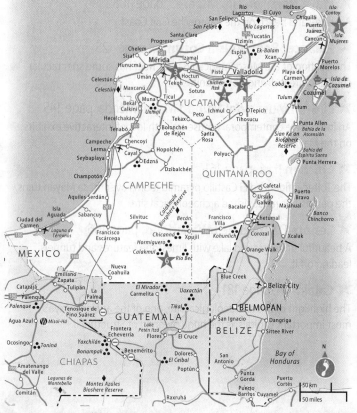

# Quintana Roo
## State

With its Caribbean shoreline and coral reefs, Quintana Roo is marketed to tourists as the exotic land of the Maya. Amply serviced by the international resorts of Cancún and Playa del Carmen, it is the most visited place in Mexico and, given its natural assets, it's easy to see why: soft white-sand beaches, sapphire blue waters and reclining palms… images of paradise so heavily traded they have become an oversold travel brochure cliché.

Is Quintana Roo a paradise? As a traveller, that depends on you. Some will delight in the region's well-oiled tourist infrastructure; others will want to run away. If so, forgo the resorts and head out to the islands, bastions of low-key tranquility where you can swim, dive, snorkel or eat delicious fresh seafood right on the beach. Or instead, explore the region's intriguing Mayan heritage: the many remnants of ancient Mayan ports and city states, including Tulum.

For some, paradise means getting as far from the crowds as possible, and fortunately Quintana Roo still has many unspoiled pockets: remote wetlands where you might glimpse grazing manatees, tropical rainforests with birds and vociferous howler monkeys, and forgotten Mayan villages where Yucatec is still spoken. If you look beneath the surface, Quintana Roo is far from a travel brochure cliché.

# Essential Yucatán Peninsula

## Getting around

Most destinations on the peninsula are well connected and easy to reach. The exceptions are Calakmul and some other ruins in the south, which require extra time and planning. Zipping up and down the coast of Quintana Roo on ADO buses is very easy. Ferries and high-speed *pangas* travel between the mainland and the islands of Holbox, Mujeres and Cozumel, as well as south from Chetumal to the Cayes of Belize.

## When to go

The Caribbean coast is inundated with tourists during the summer and winter holiday period. Spring break is notorious for its unfettered hedonism, especially in Cancún. The region is very hot year round and positively sweltering April to September. Hurricane season corresponds to the wet season, May to October, with a mini-dry season July and August.

## Time required

Seven to 10 days is enough for some chill-out time on one of the islands, a trip to Tulúm, a few days in Mérida, and day trips to a ruin or two. Two to three weeks is necessary to see Campeche, rural Yucatán and the lesser visited ruins.

## Cancún  Colour map 1, A3.
### a bold, brassy pleasure resort

Love or hate Cancún, its presence on the world tourism market is indisputable. From spring breakers to honeymooners to conference goers to cruise ship passengers, more than three million visitors flock to the city annually. When the Mexican tourist board 'discovered' the place in 1967, it was little more than a tiny fishing village, barren and inaccessible, but blessed with miles of white-sand beaches.

Two decades later, meticulous planning and massive international investment saw Cancún transformed into a city of more than 600,000 inhabitants. Clambering skyward from a sinuous spit of land that flanks the Caribbean Sea on one side, mangrove-fringed lagoons on the other, its high-density Zona Hotelera has become a potent symbol of mass tourism – and all the convenience, sterility and cynicism it brings. For those seeking cloistered protection and 24-hour creature comforts, the amenities are many: high-class shopping malls, international restaurants, gaudy theme parks, rambling golf courses, hedonistic night clubs and a procession of grandiose resort complexes that recall everything from Disney's Cinderella Castle to Nicolae Ceausescu's Palace of the People. By contrast, the city outside is a gritty urban sprawl, down-to-earth and unapologetically real.

## Weather Cancún

| January | February | March | April | May | June |
|---|---|---|---|---|---|
| 20°C 27°C 105mm | 20°C 27°C 50mm | 21°C 28°C 46mm | 23°C 29°C 29mm | 24°C 31°C 89mm | 25°C 31°C 141mm |

| July | August | September | October | November | December |
|---|---|---|---|---|---|
| 25°C 32°C 70mm | 25°C 32°C 88mm | 24°C 31°C 184mm | 23°C 30°C 282mm | 22°C 28°C 128mm | 20°C 29°C 70mm |

The city centre is laid out in street blocks called *manzanas* (M), grouped between major avenues as *supermanzanas* (SM). The precise building is a *lote* (L). Thus a typical address might read, for example, SM24, M6, L3. Streets also have names, often not mentioned in addresses, which can lead to confusion. If lost, look closely at the street signs for the SM/M number. Taxi drivers generally respond better to addresses based on the *manzana* system.

## Sights

**Cancún Centro**, or downtown Cancún, is a world apart from the Zona Hotelera. It evolved from a collection of temporary workers' shacks and is today a massive city with very little character. The main avenue is Tulum, formerly the highway running through the settlement when it was first conceived.

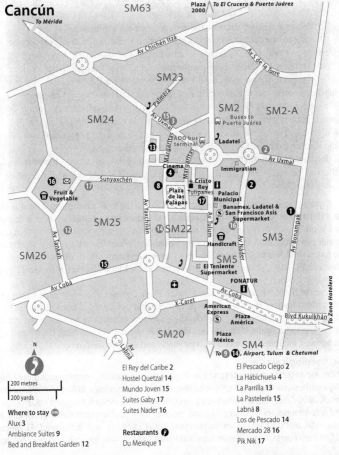

**Cancún**

**Where to stay**
Alux 3
Ambiance Suites 9
Bed and Breakfast Garden 12
El Rey del Caribe 2
Hostel Quetzal 14
Mundo Joven 15
Suites Gaby 17
Suites Nader 16

**Restaurants**
Du Mexique 1
El Pescado Ciego 2
La Habichuela 4
La Parrilla 13
La Pastelería 15
Labná 8
Los de Pescado 14
Mercado 28 16
Pik Nik 17

## BACKGROUND

### A brief history of the Caste War

Throughout the colonial era, the Yucatán enjoyed considerable independence from Mexico City, thanks to its geographic distance and its international trade. In the 19th century, as the capital relented to instability, the Yucatán enjoyed a prodigious economic boom fuelled by its expanding sugar and henequen (sisal) plantations.

But beyond the façade of urban gentrification, ethnic tensions festered in the countryside, especially when the sprawl of Yucatec haciendas began encroaching on communal Mayan lands. Against a backdrop of high taxes and shifting political transformations – independence from Spain, the emergence of a short-lived independent Yucatán, and its eventual incorporation into a federal Mexico – the Caste War broke out in 1847. Marred by atrocities on both sides, the conflict claimed 200,000 lives and very nearly resulted in an autonomous Mayan state.

The roots of the conflict lay far back in the Spanish conquest. In 1526, Francisco de Montejo and Alonso de Dávila were sent to conquer the Yucatán, but it was not until 1560 that the region fell decisively under the jurisdiction of the *audencia* of Mexico. Like other parts of New Spain, a strict racial hierarchy pervaded the colonial way of life: government was made up of Spanish-born upper classes only and based on the subordination of the *indígenas* and *mestizos*. In the same spirit, the prevailing *encomienda* system was tantamount to slavery, but it was soon replaced by the hacienda system with its feudal airs and absolute title to land. Christianization of the Yucatán intensified in 1571, the year of the Inquisition.

But despite the best efforts of the church to suppress Mayan culture – including those of Bishop Diego de Landa, who destroyed scores of Mayan idols and ancient

A good place for people-watching and soaking up the local atmosphere is **Parque de las Palapas**, a large plaza with cheap restaurants and wandering street vendors. It comes to life on Sunday evenings, an occasion for live music and dancing, ambling couples, families and children. Nearby, a mildly enthralling 'Zona Rosa' (entertainment district) can be found on **Avenida Yaxchilán**. The city's largest and most visited *artesanía* market is **Mercado 28** ① *0900-1800*, but many prefer the laid-back locals' market, **Mercado 23** (see Shopping, below).

If you're based in Cancún Centro, a trip to **Playa Delfines**, the white-sand beach on the eastern flank of the Zona Hotelera, is somewhat obligatory, if not to bathe in the calm Caribbean waters then to behold the panorama of high-rise hotels. On the other side of the spit, **Laguna Nichupté** separates the Zona from the mainland; it is fringed by mangroves, inhabited by crocodiles, a bit smelly and unfit for swimming.

### Archaeological sites

There are several very modest archaeological sites in Cancún, recommended only for Maya enthusiasts and those unable to visit any of the larger sites. **El Rey** ① *Blv Kukulcán Km 18, 0800-1700, US$3.25*, inhabited from 1200 AD, was a minor fishing and trade centre and a contemporary of Tulum. The site includes the foundations of two palaces and a pyramidal platform where an extravagant burial chamber was discovered. **El Meco** ① *Carretera Puerto Juárez–Punta Sam, 0800-1700, US$3.25*, was formerly occupied by the manuscripts in a single day of religious zeal – the *indígenas* managed to preserve their customs and spiritual beliefs. Rebellions and armed uprisings against the Spanish Yucatecos were frequent, but none were as bloody and protracted as the Caste War.

During the conflict, the Maya received considerable military support from the British, who smuggled weapons into the region from their own colony in British Honduras. By 1848, having taken the entire peninsula except the cities of Campeche and Mérida, the Maya seemed poised for victory. What happened next is a matter of academic debate. Some historians claim that the Maya ran out of supplies and were forced to retreat. Another more poetic version recounts how the annual emergence of swarms of flying ants, a phenomenon traditionally signaling the onset of planting season, prompted the Maya to return to their beloved crops of maize.

Seizing the moment, the Yucatecos mounted a formidable counter-offensive with the help of the Mexican government and US mercenaries, driving the rebels into the southeastern corner of the peninsula. But the Maya, undaunted by their defeats and unfettered from Spanish oppression, soon declared their own independent state at the newly forged settlement of Noh Cah Santa Cruz Xbalam Nah, better known as Chan Santa Cruz (today, Felipe Carrillo Puerto), where a fervent religious revival had culminated in the 'cult of the talking cross' (the cross predated Christianity as a symbol of the Mayan World Tree).

Their military theocracy enjoyed some years of stability and autonomy, but sporadic skirmishes with the Yucatecos continued. The war officially ended when President Porfirio Díaz negotiated the border of British Honduras and the British agreed to stop supplying arms to the Maya. Soon after, General Ignacio Bravo was sent to stamp out any remaining dissent in the region. In 1901, he occupied Chan Santa Cruz, ending the experiment in Mayan autonomy.

Itzas of Chichén Itzá. It features a palace with structural columns and a pyramidal temple with vestiges of serpent iconography; to get there, take a Punta Sam bus from Avenida Tulum (US$0.90) or a taxi (US$3-4).

## Museo Maya de Cancún
*Blv Kukulcán Km 16.5, T998-885 3842, www.inah.gob.mx, Tue-Sun 0900-1800, US$4.50, expository text in Spanish and English, labels mostly Spanish.*

Opened in 2012, the Museo Maya showcases a small but compelling collection of archaeological pieces from across southern Mexico. Ceramic gourds, incense burners, carved stelae and statuary depicting feathered serpents and shamans are on display, fine examples of Mayan art and its other-worldly motifs. The first exhibition room is dedicated to the state of Quintana Roo and its historical development from early settlement to the Spanish conquest. The second room explores Mayan civilization by theme: culture, agriculture, commerce, science and religious ritual. The third room features temporary exhibits. Outside, the excavated site of San Miguelito is underwhelming, but offers a shady stroll through mangrove forest where you might see an iguana or two.

## Museo Subacuático de Arte (MUSA)

*www.musacancun.org; costs vary, consult a local tour operator. A typical 2-tank dive from Cancún (4 hrs), US$70-80; snorkel tour (2 hrs), US$50.*

One of the world's largest and most thought-provoking underwater art attractions, the MUSA contains more than 500 life-size sculptures, all fixed to the seabed and crafted from material that promotes rapid coral growth. Installations include crowds of people modelled on real persons, a sleeping dog, a piano and a Volkswagen beetle. Inaugurated in 2010, the sculptures are now 'in bloom' and the overall effect is stunning. There are two galleries: **Salón Manchones**, 8 m deep, lies just off the southern tip of Isla Mujeres and should be dived. Off the southern edge of the Zona Hotelera, **Salón Nizuc**, 4 m deep, is suitable only for snorkelling. The stated aim of MUSA is to promote recovery of local reefs and offset the damages caused by climate change, hurricanes and 800,000 tourists to the region annually.

## Listings Cancún *map p99*

### Tourist information

See also the official Cancún tourism portal, www.cancun.travel, which is a good source of information.

**FONATUR tourist office**
*Av Nader and Cobá, SM5, T998-884 1426, www.fonatur.gob.mx. Mon-Fri 0800-1500.*
Flyers, maps, brochures and general information about Cancún and the surrounding attractions.

**SEDETUR office**
*Av Yaxchilán, SM17, T998-881 9000, www.caribemexicano.gob.mx.*
Not well located and deals with tourism in the state of Quintana Roo.

### Where to stay

By law, beaches in Mexico are public, so you don't have to stay in a pricey seafront resort to enjoy them. Nonetheless, meandering along the strand is not encouraged by some of the larger hotels. Cancún Centro or downtown area has many economical no-frills options, but prices are still higher than other parts of the Yucatán Peninsula. Rates everywhere in Cancún can fall by 25-50% in low season (and double or triple during Christmas and New Year).

**Zona Hotelera**
Almost all accommodation in the Zona Hotelera – decent or otherwise – starts at around US$100, rises quickly and is best arranged as part of a package holiday. The increased costs, already the highest in Mexico, are partly the result of a government-mandated rebuilding drive after 2 devastating hurricanes, which required all existing hotels to upgrade structures for safety. Just 2 reputable options are:

**$$$$ Le Blanc Spa Resort**
*Blv Kukulcán Km 10, T1800-712-4236, www.leblancsparesort.com.*
Sublime, all-inclusive luxury accommodation, complete with first-rate service and spa treatments that promise to take pampering, just like their nightly rates, to a 'transcendent level'.

**$$$$ Sun Palace**
*Blv Kukulcán Km 20, T1-888-414-5538, www.cancunpalaceresorts.com.*
A romantic and highly luxurious couples-only resort that's sure to ignite passions. From the same chain as **Le Blanc**.

**Cancún Centro**
Many downtown hotels, especially the budget ones, tend to be full during Semana

Santa, in Jul and over the Dec-Jan holidays. It is best to get a room as early as possible in the morning, or make a reservation if you are returning to Cancún after an overnight trip. Outside the ADO bus terminal, beware 'friendly' and persistent touts looking to make a commission.

### $$$ Ambiance Suites
*Av Tulum 227, SM20, T998-892 0392, www.ambiancecancun.com.*
Immaculately clean, professionally managed business hotel with helpful English-speaking staff, located close to Plaza de las Américas. Rooms and suites are crisply attired with modern furnishings, all in great condition. Amenities include small pool and business centre. Toast and coffee in the morning, welcome cocktail on arrival.

### $$$ El Rey del Caribe
*Av Uxmal 24 and Nader, SM2, T998-884 2028, www.reycaribe.com.*
El Rey del Caribe is an ecologically aware B&B with solar hot water and other green technologies. Its leafy courtyard, complete with small pool and jacuzzi, is tranquil and shady, a quiet place to unwind. Rooms are clean, comfortable and include kitchenettes. Spa treatments are available, including massage. Good for couples and families. An oasis of the calm in the chaos of downtown Cancún.

### $$$-$$ Suites Gaby
*Av Sunyaxche 46-47, SM25, T998-887 8037, www.suitesgaby.com.*
The exterior of **Suites Gaby** is utilitarian and uninspired, but inside you'll find simple, comfortable, recently remodelled rooms with a modern touch. Hot-water showers are strong and the rooms are generally quiet, although the walls are thin. Convenient for Mercado 28 and the restaurants on Yaxchilán.

### $$$ Suites Nader
*Av Nader 5, SM5, T998-884 1584, www.suitesnadercancun.com.*
The rooms at this downtown lodging are just adequate, but the suites are definitely

worth a look – all are very comfortable, clean, spacious and quite good value. Each has a fully equipped kitchen and living area, and 2 beds, good for small families with young children. The adjoining restaurant is an excellent breakfast spot and always buzzing with customers.

### $$ Alux
*Av Uxmal 21, T998-884 0556, www.hotelalux.com.*
Conveniently located a block from the ADO bus terminal and a stone's throw from the action on Yaxchilán, Hotel Alux has clean, safe, simple, comfortable rooms with a/c, TV, Wi-Fi and hot-water showers; rates include coffee and toast in the morning. Recommended for budget travellers, good rates off season ($). An *alux*, if you were wondering, is a kind of mythical Mayan elf.

### $$-$ Bed and Breakfast Garden
*Jícama 7, SM25, T998-267 7777, www.bedand breakfastcancun.com.mx.*
A cross between a hostel and B&B, this homely, cosy lodging has small dorms ($) and simple rooms ($$), shared kitchen and a comfortable living room with TV and reading material. Located in a quiet, residential part of town, 5 mins from Mercado 28. Surf and yoga lessons available. Breakfast included.

### $$-$ Hostel Quetzal
*Orquídeas 10, SM22, T998-883 9821, www.quetzal-hostel.com.*
Lots of good reports about Hostel Quetzal, a fun, sociable place that will suit outgoing backpackers and whippersnappers. Amenities include single- and mixed-sex dorms ($), private rooms ($$), rooftop terrace, bar and garden. Daytime excursions to the local sights are available, as well as legendary nights out to the clubs in the Zona.

### $$-$ Mundo Joven
*Av Uxmal 25, SM23, T998-271 4740, www.mundojoven.com.*
Conveniently located 1 block from the ADO bus terminal, this clean and professionally

managed hostel is part of an international franchise. This one has functional dorms ($) and rooms ($$), and a great rooftop terrace complete with bar, barbecue and hedonistic hot tub. Rock on.

## Restaurants

The Hotel Zone is lined with expensive restaurants, with every type of international cuisine imaginable, but with a predominance of Tex-Mex and Italian. Restaurants are cheaper in the centre, where the emphasis is on local food.

### Cancún Centro

#### $$$ Du Mexique
*Bonampak 109, SM3, T998-884-5919.*
Intimate and extravagant fine dining with superb French/Mexican fusion cuisine by Chef Alain Grimond; try the delicious rack of lamb. Courses are served in 3 different areas: sala, dining room and garden. Smart-casual attire and just 7 tables; advance reservations a must.

#### $$$ La Habichuela
*Margaritas 25, SM22, www.lahabichuela. com; a new branch is now open in the Zona Hotelera, Blv Kukulcán Km 12.6 Hotel Zone.*
Award-winning restaurant serving delicious Caribbean seafood in a tropical garden setting. Good ambience, attentive service, Mayan-themed decor and jazz music. Recommended.

#### $$$ Labná
*Margaritas 29, SM22, www.labnaonline.com.*
The best in Yucatecan cooking, serving dishes like *poc chuc* and *pollo pibil*. Try the platter and sample a wide range of this fascinating regional cuisine. Good lunchtime buffet ($$). Highly recommended.

#### $$$ La Parrilla
*Yaxchilán 51, SM22, www.laparrilla.com.mx.*
A buzzing, lively joint, always busy and popular, especially with Mexican families.

They serve mouth-watering grill platters, ribs, steaks and other carnivorous fare. Try the enormous margaritas in exotic flavours – hibiscus flower and tamarind.

#### $$$-$$ El Pescado Ciego
*Av Nader esquina Rubia, SM3. Closed Thu and Sun.*
Low-key and relaxed, a good place for friends and lovers, El Pescado Ciego serves flavourful contemporary seafood dishes with a Mexican twist. Offerings include tasty shrimp tacos, lobster quesadillas, tuna steaks and filleted catch of the day.

#### $$ Pik Nik
*Calle Tulipanes, SM22.*
A fun, local, friendly place to kick back and gorge on hearty Mexican food and drink. Expect the usual staples, including tacos, burritos and quesadillas, as well as Mexican beers and cocktails. Good service, a great place for groups, with terraced seating on a pedestrian street near Plaza del las Palapas.

#### $ Los de Pescado
*Av Tulum 32, SM20, www.losdepescado.com. Lunch and early supper only.*
Excellent Baja California-style fish burritos and tacos, prawn ceviche, beer, soda and absolutely nothing else. Charmless setting and service, but great fast food. Recommended.

#### $ Mercado 28
*SM28. Open for lunch and early supper.*
The half dozen or so kitchens nestled inside in the *artesanía* market serve the best budget meals in the city; **Mi Rancho** is one of the better ones. Set meals include generous Mexican staples and specialities, such as *pollo con mole poblano* (chicken in chocolate and chilli sauce). Most come with a soup starter, tortillas, nachos, salsa and a drink, all for US$5. If the waiter hands you the more expensive à la carte menu, insist on *comida del día*. Wandering mariachis may serenade you. Recommended.

## ON THE ROAD

## Know your hammock

Different materials are available for hammocks. Some you might find include sisal, which is very strong, light, hard-wearing but rather scratchy and uncomfortable, and is identified by its distinctive smell; cotton, which is soft, flexible, comfortable, not as hard-wearing but, with care, is good for four or five years of everyday use. It is not possible to weave cotton and sisal together, although you may be told otherwise, so mixtures are unavailable. Cotton/silk mixtures are offered, but will probably be an artificial silk. Nylon is very strong and light but it's hot in hot weather and cold in cold weather.

Never buy your first hammock from a street vendor and never accept a packaged hammock without checking the size and quality. The surest way to judge a good hammock is by weight: 1.5 kg (3.3 lb) is a fine item, under 1 kg (2.2 lb) is junk (advises Alan Handleman, a US expert). Also, the finer and thinner the strands of material, the more strands there will be, and the more comfortable the hammock. The best hammocks are the so-called 3-ply, but they are difficult to find. There are three sizes: single (sometimes called *doble*), *matrimonial* and family (buy a *matrimonial* at least for comfort). If judging by end-strings, 50 would be sufficient for a child, 150 would suit a medium-sized adult, 250 a couple. Prices vary considerably so shop around and bargain hard.

### Cafés

#### La Pastelería
*Av Cobá and Guanábana, SM25.*
La Pastelería, formerly known as **La Crepería**, is a European-style café-patisserie serving aromatic coffee and a host of elegant desserts, including sumptuous cakes and pastries adorned with lashings of rich, dark Mexican chocolate.

### Bars and clubs

Cancún is famous for its debauched nightlife. Clubs are mostly concentrated at Blv Kukulcán Km 9 in the Zona Hotelera. All tastes are catered to, but most of the action gravitates to chic lounge bars and enormous discos, invariably packed to the rafters with revellers during spring break.

Establishments come and go with the seasons, but one that has withstood the test of time is **Coco Bongo** (www.cocobongo. com.mx), famous for its vivid dance and acrobatic displays. Some tour agencies offer 'club crawl' excursions, allowing you to sample a few different places in one evening, a good option for groups; try **Party Rockers Cancún** (T998-883-0981, www.partyrockerscancun.com). Downtown, you'll find comparatively low-key bars and pubs in the Zona Rosa on Av Yaxchilán.

### Shopping

There are several shopping malls in the Zona Hotelera. The main one is **Kukulcán Plaza** (Blv Kukulcán Km 13, www.kukulcanplaza. com), with more than 170 retail outlets. There are others, including **La Isla** (Blv Kukulcán Km 12.5), mostly catering to the luxury shopper. Downtown, the big *artesanía* market is **Mercado 28**, where you'll find a plethora of handmade items including silver jewellery from Taxco, hammocks from Mérida, ceramic Mayan figurines, cowboy boots, sombreros, masks, sarapes, T-shirts and more; the quality of production varies. Note prices are hiked to the limit and

## ON THE ROAD
### Cenote diving

There are more than 50 *cenotes* in this area – accessible from Ruta 307 and often well signposted – and cave diving has become very popular. However, it is a specialized sport and, unless you have a cave diving qualification, you must be accompanied by a qualified Dive Master.

A cave diving course involves over 12 hours of lectures and a minimum of 14 cave dives using double tanks, costing around US$600. Accompanied dives start at around US$60. Specialist dive centres offering courses are: **Aquatech**, Villas de Rosa, PO Box 25, T984-875 9020, www.cenotes.com. **Aventuras Akumal** No 35, Tulum, T984-875 9030; **Aktun Dive Centre**, PO Box 119, Tulum, T984-871 2311, and **Cenote Dive Center**, Tulum, T984-876 3285, www.cenotedive.com, Norwegian owned.

Two of the best *cenotes* are 'Carwash', on the Cobá road, good even for beginners, with excellent visibility; and 'Dos Ojos', just off Ruta 307 south of Aventuras, the second largest underground cave system in the world. It has a possible link to the Nohoch Nah Chich, the most famous *cenote* and part of a subterranean system recorded as the world's largest, with over 50 km of surveyed passageways connected to the sea.

A word of warning: *cenote* diving has a higher level of risk than open-water diving – do not take risks and only dive with recognized operators.

---

the salesmen are mean and aggressive. Whatever happens, smile politely and bargain hard; most vendors expect to get at least half what they originally asked. Due to credit card rip-offs, it is safer to pay cash only. You could also try the locals' market, **Mercado 23**, at the end of Calle Cedro, off Av Tulum. It's a bit tatty and tacky, but has cheaper souvenirs and friendlier salesmen. For an American-style mall experience in Cancún Centro, your best option is **Plaza de las Américas** on Av Tulum.

### What to do

From booze cruises to canopy tours, parasailing to paintballing, the array of activities on offer in Cancún is vast. The listings below highlight some of the more interesting options, but are in no way exhaustive. Consult your hotel or the tourist information office for more possibilities.

### Cooking

**Can Cook in Cancún**, *T998-147 4827, www.cancookincancun.com.* A master of Mexican cuisine, chef Claudia has been in kitchens all her life. Classes are fun and intimate, take place in Claudia's home and include an overview of traditions and regional specialities, as well as practical instruction in ingredients and flavours.

### Diving and snorkelling

See box, above, for information on cave diving.
**Scuba Cancun**, *Kukulcán Km 5, T998-849 7508, www.scubacancun.com.mx.* A medium-sized dive centre run by Captain Luis Hurtado who has more than 3 decades' diving experience. He offers a range of sea, cavern and *cenote* dives, including trips to the MUSA, snorkelling tours and accelerated PADI courses.

## Sports cars

**Exotic rides**, *Carretera Cancún Airport Km 7.5, T998-882 0558, www.exoticridescancun.com.* Experience the speed, power and performance of Ferrari, Lamborghini and other 'exotic' sports cars. Training and test driving takes place at a private race track.

## Surfing

**360 Surf school**, *Blv Kukulcán Km 9.5, opposite Señor Frog, T998-241 6443, www.360surfschoolcancun.com.* The waves in Cancún are relatively gentle, making it a great place to learn how to surf. Managed by David '360Dave' Wanamaker, **360 Surf School** has been getting beginners up onto boards for more than 14 years. You'll surf, or your money back.

## Tour operators

**Ecocolors**, *Calle Camarón 32, SM27, T998-884 3667, www.ecotravelmexico.com.* Socially responsible and environmentally aware tours of the Yucatán Peninsula and beyond. Specialities include biking, birdwatching, hiking and wildlife photography.

### Transport

### Air

The airport is 16 km south of the city. Shared fixed-price shuttles to the **Zona Hotelera** or the centre depart hourly Mon-Fri 0800-2000, US$12; pay at the kiosk outside airport. Private taxis are US$45 one way, US$70 round trip. Be sure to know the name and address of your hotel, or the driver may offer to take you to a lodging of their own choice.

Cancún airport (CUN), *Carretera Cancún–Chetumal Km 22, T998-848 7200, www.cancun-airport.com,* has expensive shops, restaurants, currency exchange, car rental, hotel reservation agencies and ATMs. Terminal 1 serves domestic airlines; Terminal 2 and Terminal 3 serve international airlines. ADO buses go from the airport to **Cancún Centro**, every 30 mins, ½ hr, US$4; **Puerto Morelos**, every 30-40 mins, ½ hr, US$6,

and **Playa del Carmen**, every 30-40 mins, 1½ hrs, US$10.

### Bus

**Local**  Ruta 1 and Ruta 2 buses travel between Cancún Centro (downtown) and the Zona Hotelera, US$0.70. Ruta 1 runs 24 hrs and follows Av Tulum, the city's principal thoroughfare. Ruta 2 runs 0500-0330 and goes via Av Cobá. Shuttle buses to **Puerto Juárez** for the ferry to Isla Mujeres follow Av Tulum, US$0.65, opposite side to the bus station.

**Long distance**  Cancún's ADO bus terminal, C Pino, SM23, at the junction of Av Tulum and Uxmal, is a hub for routes west to Mérida and south to Tulum and beyond to Chetumal, open 24 hrs, left luggage, rates vary depending on size, open 0600-2200. Rapid ticket booths for the airport and Playa del Carmen.

To **Cancún Airport**, every 30 mins, ½ hr, US$4. To **Chetumal**, frequent departures, 6 hrs, US$27. To **Chichén Itzá**; all 2nd-class buses to Mérida stop here, fewer 1st-class buses, 4 hrs, US$14. To **Mérida**, frequent departures, 4½ hrs, US$25. To **Palenque**, 1st class, 1545, 2030, 12½ hrs, US$62; and an ADO GL, 1745, 13 hrs, US$68. To **Playa del Carmen**, every 10 mins, 1½ hrs, US$4. To **Puerto Morelos**, frequent departures, 30 mins, US$2.30. To **San Cristóbal**, OCC, 1545, 2030 18 hrs, US$69, ADO GL, 1745, US$83. To **Tulum**, ADO, frequent departures, 2½ hrs, US$9, and many cheaper 2nd-class buses. To **Valladolid**, frequent departures, 2½ hrs, US$12.50. To **Villahermosa**, 1st class, many departures, 13 hrs, US$62. **Expreso de Oriente** also has services to the more obscure destinations of **Tizimín** (3 hrs, US$10), **Izamal**, **Cenotillo** and **Chiquilá**.

### Car

**Car hire**  There are many car hire agencies, including **Dollar**, **Hertz**, **Thrifty**, **Budget** and others, with offices on Av Tulum, in the Hotel Zone and at the airport; look out for special deals, but check vehicles carefully.

**Car parking** Do not leave cars parked in side streets; there is a high risk of theft. Use the car park on Av Uxmal.

### Ferry

For ferries to **Isla Mujeres**, regular *combis* and buses travel along Av Tulum en route to **Puerto Juárez** (marked Pto Juárez or Punta Sam), US$0.80, where services to the island depart from the **Ultra Mar** terminal, T998-843 2011, www.granpuerto.com.mx, at Gran Puerto (recommended), every 30 mins, 0500-2330, US$5.50, children US$3.50; and from the **Magaña Express** terminal, T998 877 0618, 2 blocks north of Ultra Mar, hourly,

0800-2000. **Ultra Mar** services also depart from the Zona Hotelera (Playa Caracol, Playa Tortugas and El Embarcadero), every 1-2 hrs, US$11. Car ferries depart 4-5 times daily from **Punta Sam**, north of Puerto Juárez on the coast, US$20 for a car and driver, US$1.50 for each additional passenger.

### Taxi

Taxis are abundant in Cancún. Fares are based on a zone system and most short journeys downtown cost US$2. Overcharging is common; avoid taxis waiting outside hotels or restaurants.

## Isla Mujeres   *Colour map 1, A3.*

**a refreshing antidote to the urban sprawl of Cancún**

Blending Caribbean and Mexican styles, and more than faintly recalling the Mediterranean too, Isla Mujeres (Women Island) is a place to unwind, unravel and forget about the hurly burly of package tourism. In prehispanic times, the island served as a shrine to Ixchel, the Mayan goddess of childbirth, traditionally associated with midwifery, fertility, femininity and the moon. It received its current name after Spanish conquistadors came ashore in the 16th century and discovered scores of clay idols depicting the goddess and her daughters: Ixchebeliax, Ixhunie and Ixhunieta.

Blessed with one of the finest beaches in Mexico, kaleidoscopic coral reefs and, of course, an appropriately alluring name, Isla Mujeres has been a popular tourist destination since the 1960s. Unlike its younger sibling on the mainland, Cancún, it has endured remarkably well; even with the pressure of big dollars on its doorstep, it remains defiantly low-key, a sanctuary for travellers everywhere. The magic begins after dusk, once the day-trippers have gone.

### Sights

An unkempt seasonal refuge for pirates and fishermen, Isla Mujeres was largely uninhabited in the colonial era. It saw significant settlement only in 19th century when the violence and persecution of the Caste War drove scores of refugees to its shores. Today, tourism has all but replaced fishing as the mainstay of the local economy. Fortunately, **Isla Mujeres Town** remains strictly low-rise and unobtrusive, its colourful grid of streets boasting scores of intimate little restaurants, bars, cafés and *artesanía* shops. The island is 7 km long and 650 m wide. The town, at the northern end, can be easily covered on foot. For explorations further afield, hire a golf cart, moped or bicycle, or take the bus. The best beach on the island, ★ **Playa Norte**, is conveniently located on the fringe of the action.

Heading south from the town, the main seafront artery, **Avenida Rueda Medina**, becomes the **Carretera Garrafón** and skirts the airport, marinas and a series brackish lagoons which the ancient Maya harvested for their salt. Inland, near the southern tip of Laguna Makax, the ruined **Hacienda Mundaca** ① *0900-1700, US$2.50*, was constructed in 1860 on the site of a Mayan temple. Originally called 'Vista Alegre', its owner, a notorious Spanish slave trader,

Fermín Antonio Mundaca, fell madly in love with a local girl, Martiniana (Prisca) Pantoja, but she rejected him for a younger lover. Mundaca eventually went insane, dying alone in the city of Mérida on the mainland. His tomb on Isla Mujeres remains empty, but its bitter epitaph was carved by his own hand: "As you were, so was I. As I am, so you will be."

For something a bit lighter, the **Capitán Dulché Beach Club** ① *Cra Garrafon Km 4, T998-849 7594, www.capitandulche.com, daily 1030-1930*, is a new addition to the island, complete with sun loungers, bar, restaurant and a small museum of maritime artefacts, historic photos and handsome model ships. To the northwest, the **Carretera Sac Bajo** doubles back on a narrow spit, passing between the Caribbean sea and the shores of Laguna Makax. The government-sponsored **Tortugranja** ① *Cra Sac Bajo Km 5, daily 0900-1700, US$2.50*, is a small turtle hatchery with fish-filled aquariums and young turtles at different stages of development; knowledgeable staff explain their life cycles and migratory habits.

At the southern end of the island, the **Garrafón Natural Reef Park** ① *Cra Garrafón, Km 6, T01-866-393 5158, www.garrafon.com*, is a luxury adventure resort offering snorkelling, kayaking, zip-lining and bike tours; packages from US$59. Nearby, the **Santuario a la Diosa Ixchel** ① *daily 0900-1700, US$2.50*, is a crumbling ruin of a temple dedicated to Ixchel. The structure has been sadly damaged by hurricanes, but nonetheless commands a potent position on cliffs above the crashing ocean (take care on the slippery paths). If you can get there, it is a magical place to experience the sunrise.

# Isla Mujeres town

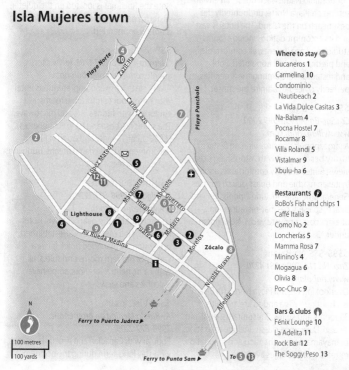

**Where to stay** 🛏
Bucaneros **1**
Carmelina **10**
Condominio
Nautibeach **2**
La Vida Dulce Casitas **3**
Na-Balam **4**
Pocna Hostel **7**
Rocamar **8**
Villa Rolandi **5**
Vistalmar **9**
Xbulu-ha **6**

**Restaurants** 🍴
BoBo's Fish and chips **1**
Caffé Italia **3**
Como No **2**
Loncherías **5**
Mamma Rosa **7**
Minino's **4**
Mogagua **6**
Olivia **8**
Poc-Chuc **9**

**Bars & clubs** 🍸
Fénix Lounge **10**
La Adelita **11**
Rock Bar **12**
The Soggy Peso **13**

## Tourist information

The official online information portal is www.isla-mujeres.com.mx.

### Tourist office
*Av Rueda Medina 130, T998-877 0767.*
Located on the seafront opposite the ferry terminals, the tourist office has maps, flyers and helpful staff, some of whom speak English.

## Where to stay

### $$$$ Condominio Nautibeach
*Playa Los Cocos, T998-877 0606, www.nautibeach.com.*
Condominio Nautibeach boasts an enviable setting on Playa Norte, undoubtedly the best beach on the island. The hotel is vast and its accommodations include rooms, studios and apartments, all comfortable and predictably well appointed. Pool and restaurant are among the amenities, perfectly placed to admire the sunset.

### $$$$ Hotel Villa Rolandi
*Cra Sac-Bajo, T998-999 2000, www.villarolandi.com.*
A large, popular, award-winning 5-star luxury beach resort with astonishing ocean views. Suites are very comfortable, adorned in Italian marble and boast jacuzzi terraces. General amenities include 2 pools, 'private' beach, spa services, bar-restaurant and, at extra cost, a private yacht. No children under 13.

### $$$$-$$$ Na Balam
*Zazil Ha 118, T998-881 4770, www.nabalam.com.*
Overlooking blissful Playa Norte, Na Balam is a boutique yoga and spa resort with 35 rooms and suites, 2 restaurants, pool and jacuzzi. Daily yoga classes include relaxation, pranayama, asana, chanting and meditation; retreats and packages available.

### $$$ La Vida Dulce Casitas
*Juárez 13, T515-974 6777, www.islatrip.com.*
A lot of love has gone into this *hotelito*, a very popular lodging that will suit couples or small families. Managed by attentive and hospitable hosts, Steve and Jerri, they offer 3 comfortable, cosy apartments that sleep 3-4. Book in advance.

### $$$ Rocamar
*Nicolás Bravo and Zona Marítima, T998-877 0101, www.rocamar-hotel.com.*
Crisp and minimalist, the Rocamar is an island favourite, now more than 30 years old. Its rooms and suites are clean and unfussy; the best of them enjoy expansive views of the Caribbean sea and sunrise. Note the Rocamar is located on the quieter, eastern side of the island, where swimming is not recommended.

### $$$-$$ Xbulu-ha
*Guerrero 4, T998-877 1783, www.sites. google.com/site/hotelxbuluha.*
A very clean, cosy and unpretentious hotel with simple but comfortable rooms, all equipped with fridges, a/c and microwave. The suites are best and have kitchenettes ($$$). Quiet, friendly and good value. Recommended. The name means 'bubbling water' in Yucatec Maya.

### $$ Hotel Bucaneros
*Hidalgo 11, T998-877 1228, www.bucaneros.com.*
Located right in the heart of town, Hotel Bucaneros is a pleasant, well-established, professionally managed hotel. It has a variety of modern rooms and suites, all with calm, neutral interiors; some have balconies and views.

### $$-$ Vistalmar
*Av Rueda Medina on promenade, T998-877 0209.*
Popular with Canadian and American retirees, who stay long-term during the northern

winter. The friendly Vistalmar has a range of reasonable rooms, some better equipped than others. Ask for one on the top floor, where you will enjoy sea breezes. Better to reserve in advance Jan-May. $ for longer stays.

### $ Hotel Carmelina
*Guerrero 4, T998-877 0006, hotel_carmelina@hotmail.com.*
Locally owned motel-style place with parking. The rooms are simple, sparse and clean, all with a/c, Wi-Fi and hot water, some with fridge. Good value, recommended for budget travellers.

### $ pp Pocna Hostel
*Top end of Matamoros on the northeast coast, T998-877 0090, www.pocna.com.*
An island institution, popular with backpackers, but not beloved by all. Grounds are large and warren-like with scores of scruffy dorms and rooms, as well as a campground. There's internet access, lounge and beach bar, dive shop, bike rental, spa services, free activities like yoga and drumming, and DJs and live music in the evenings, often continuing until 0300. Book in advance in high season.

## Restaurants

### $$$ Olivia
*Av Matamoros between Juárez and Medina, www.olivia-isla-mujeres.com. Dinner only, closed Mon except Jan-Mar.*
Founded by an Israeli couple, Lior and Yaron, Olivia serves fabulous Mediterranean home cooking, including old family recipes, and Greek, Moroccan and Middle Eastern specialities, such as kebabs, home-baked breads and sweet baklava. A great spot for a romantic meal. Recommended.

### $$$-$$ Como No
*Hidalgo 7, www.isla mujeresdining.com.*
A popular rooftop restaurant-bar that serves tasty Mediterranean food alongside eclectic international dishes including schnitzel, tapas and Thai curry. The

mojitos are particularly delicious and highly recommended. A joint venture with **The Patio**, downstairs, also good.

### $$$-$$ Mamma Rosa
*Hidalgo and Matamoros.*
A well-attired and authentic Italian restaurant with a relaxed, romantic ambiance. They serve good pasta, pizzas and seafood, with a fine selection of Italian wines. Personable service with dining inside or al fresco.

### $$ BoBo's Fish and Chips
*Av Matamoros 14A.*
A casual little joint with a few seats on the street outside. They serve wholesome beer-battered fish, burgers, chicken wings, chips and cheap beer; comfort food for weary travellers. Owner Brian is friendly and talkative, tending bar as he serves.

### $$ Minino's
*Av Rueda Medina.*
One of the best seafood restaurants in town, unpretentious, scruffy and often recommended by the locals. They offer delicious fresh fish fillets, squid, octopus, ceviche and lobster. Dining is on the sand at plastic tables. Good place, good food.

### $$ Mogagua
*Av Juárez and Madero.*
Closely resembling a North American coffeeshop, Mogagua has a laid-back, arty vibe. They serve good coffee from Chiapas (try the iced frappés), Spanish tapas and other international fare, and in the evening, sangria. A sociable place for breakfast before hitting the beach. Good, friendly service. Recommended.

### $$-$ Caffé Italia
*Av Hidalgo between Morelos and Madero.*
A cute little eatery serving breakfast, lunch and light snacks. Offerings include sweet and sour crêpes ($), fresh fruit juices, excellent strong coffee and authentic Italian home-cooking, including pizzas and pasta. Friendly, hospitable owner.

### $ Loncherías
*Northwest end of Guerrero, around the municipal market. Open till 1800.*
Busy and bustling, good for breakfast, snacks and lunch. All serve the same local fare at similar prices.

### $ Poc-Chuc
*Juárez and Abasolo.*
A simple little locals' joint on the corner serving good-value Mexican staples in large portions. Good, cheap and tasty.

## Bars and clubs

### Fénix Lounge
*Playa Norte, next to Na Balam, www.fenixisla.com.*
Low-lit and laid-back, Playa Norte's premier beach club and bar often features live music in the day time, there's shaded futon beds for chilling out. A fun, casual place and a superb location.

### La Adelita
*Hidalgo 12.*
Adelita stocks over 200 types of tequila, the bar staff really know their stuff and are happy to make recommendations. Pull up a stool, roll up your sleeves – it's going to be a long night.

### Rock Bar
*Av Hidalgo 8.*
As the name suggests, the haunt of spirited rock 'n rollers and other wild things. Great crowd and music at this intimate little downtown bar, not to mention killer cocktails. Cool place, recommended.

### The Soggy Peso
*Av Rueda Medina, www.soggypeso.com, south out of town, halfway down the airstrip. No under 21s.*
This quirky little tiki bar attracts its share of castaways and raconteurs. It's a friendly place, scruffy, unpretentious and laid back. They serve good margaritas and Tex-Mex on the side.

## What to do

### Diving and snorkelling
There are numerous good dive shops on Isla Mujeres, more than can be mentioned here. 2 established options are:
**Carey Dive Center**, *Matamoros 13 and Av Rueda Medina, T877-0763, www.carey divecenter.com.* Reef, drift, deep, night and cenote dives, PADI certification up to Dive Master, snorkelling and fishing. 2-tank dives cost US$65-140, dependent on destination.
**Sea Hawk**, offers PADI certification up to Dive Master, deep-sea fishing, snorkelling, and a range of Adventure Dives (2 tanks, US$75-85) including wreck sites, night dives, sleeping shark caves and the MUSA subaquatic museum. They have simple lodging in the attached guesthouse.

### Tour operators
**Co-operativa Isla Mujeres**, *Muelle 7, Av Rueda Medina.* The oldest tourism co-operative on the island, established 1977 and committed to sustainable practice. All their guides are qualified to take tourists to Isla Contoy (US$60 per person). Additionally, they offer sports fishing (US$200, 4 hrs) and snorkelling (US$25).
**Co-operativa Isla Bonita**, *Av Rueda Medina, T998-897 1095 (Adolfo), find them outside Restaurant Macambo.* This local co-operative specializes in half-day snorkel tours, including dolphin watching, shark handling, and a traditional Yucatec meal (US$25). They also offer trips to Isla Contoy (U$60), fishing (US$200, 4 hrs) and sell *artesanías*.

## Transport

### Air
The small airstrip in the middle of the island is mainly used for private planes, best arranged with a tourist office in Cancún.

### Bicycle, golf cart and moped
Lots of people like to zip around the island in their own transport. You'll find rental places concentrated on the seafront, Av Rueda

Medina and the surrounding streets. Rates vary with age and quality of vehicle: bicycles, US$15 per day; mopeds/motorbikes, US$8-11 per hr or US$25-35 per day; golf carts, US$40-50 per day; a credit card is often required as a deposit.

### Bus
A public bus runs from the ferry dock to Playa Paraíso every 30 mins, US$0.80. Timings can be erratic, especially on Sun.

### Ferry
**Ultramar** operate ferries to Isla Mujeres every 30 mins from Puerto Juárez, to the north of Cancún (and at slightly higher cost, from the Zona Hotelera); **Magaña Express** ferries depart from their own terminal 2 blocks north of Ultramar.

### Taxi
Fixed-rate taxis depart from a rank on Av Rueda Medina, opposite the **HSBC**. A taxi from town to **El Garrafón** and vice versa is US$6. For the return journey, sharing a taxi will work out marginally more expensive than the bus for 4 people. Taxis charge an additional US$1 at night.

## Isla Contoy   Colour map 1, A3.
### an uninhabited and strictly protected wildlife refuge

Encompassing 317 ha, Isla Contoy (www.islacontoy.org), 30 km north of Isla Mujeres, is covered in mangroves, tropical forests and white-sand beaches. It is one of the most important seabird nesting sites in the Mexican Caribbean, closely studied by biologists, and home to some 150 migratory and resident avian species, including vociferous colonies of frigates, pelicans and cormorants. Additionally, four species of sea turtle (loggerhead, green, hawksbill and leatherback) nest on the island.

Visitor numbers are limited to 200 per day and only licensed guides may conduct tours (see Isla Mujeres Tour operators, above). Facilities include a visitor centre, museum, souvenir store, observation tower, interpretive trails, resting area with benches and *palapas*. You can snorkel at the Ixlachxé Reef en route to the island.

## Isla Holbox   Colour map 1, A3.
### an indolent island with a white-sand beach and colourful village

As yet unspoiled by mass tourism, Isla Holbox, whose name means 'Black Hole' in Yucatec Maya, is a remote and sparsely populated island off the northern coast of Quintana Roo. It has a tiny wood-built village, home to robust fishing people and a small but thriving band of expats. Enclosed by the 154,000-ha Yum Balam Ecological Reserve, Isla Holbox has opportunities for swimming, diving, snorkelling, fishing, kitesurfing and wildlife observation, along with the timeless and strongly recommended pursuit of simply lolling in a hammock.

### Sights
Many visitors and locals enjoy a dip in the **Yalahau swimming hole** ⓘ *US$0.80*, a refreshing cold-water spring that has long been an important source of fresh water for islanders; keep an eye out for crocodiles and bring bug repellent.

# BACKGROUND

## First contact: the ill-fated journey of the Santa Lucía

Lost in a small boat in the Caribbean sea, the sight of land must have seemed like divine providence. After 13 days at the mercy of prevailing winds, the band of shipwrecked Spanish travellers were wretched, starved, thirsty and sick. They clambered ashore at Cabo Catoche in Quintana Roo, the first Europeans to set foot in Mexico. But as hordes of hungry Mayan warriors surrounded them, it became clear that their ordeal was only beginning…

The Spaniards had come from the tenuous colony of Santa María la Antigua del Darién, a tempestuous Spanish settlement forged in the wilderness of eastern Panama. In 1511, Captain Enciso y Valdivia had felt compelled to sail to the island of Santo Domingo to report on the colony's troubles – a matter of intrigue had culminated in the exile in a leaky boat of a Spanish nobleman, Diego de Nicuesa, never to be seen again. En route, Valdivia's caravel, the *Santa Lucía*, struck a sandbar and sunk. The 18 survivors were captured by a Mayan chief at Cabo Catoche and, one by one, sacrificed to the gods.

Just two survived. Gerónimo de Aguilar was a devout Franciscan friar from Ecija; Gonzalo Guerrero a sailor from Palos de la Frontera. They escaped but were soon captured and forced into slavery by the Mayan chief Xamanzana.

Months turned to years and Aguilar, who maintained his Catholic vows of celibacy, became a domestic servant for Xamanzana, watching over his wives and daughters. Guerrero ended up in the city of Chaacte'mal (Chetumal), under the dominion of Ah Nachan Kan Xiu, where he impressed the population with his skills in sailing, fishing and carpentry, eventually embraced Mayan customs, and in a historic union of indigenous and Spanish bloodlines, married the chief's daughter, the haughty Zazil Há.

In 1519, Hernán Cortés sailed from Cuba with 500 men, horses and goods for barter and, whilst exploring the island of Cozumel, heard stories about bearded men on the mainland. Following correspondence with messengers, Aguilar soon joined his campaign, becoming a vital informant and translator. But Guerrero remained in the Yucatán, writing to Aguilar: "I am married and have three children, and they look on me as a cacique here… My face is tattooed and my ears are pierced. What would the Spaniards say about me if they saw me like this?"

As the Aztec empire fell, Guerrero organized the Maya of the south, teaching them Spanish war craft and strategy. His efforts were not in vain: under the relentless onslaughts of Francisco de Montejo, it took 30 years to subjugate the Yucatán, a bastion of fierce resistance during the conquest of the New World. Guerrero himself died in battle in 1532, having brought 50 war canoes from Chetumal to aid a Honduran cacique in his fight against Pedro de Alvarado. Reviled by his 16th-century Spanish compatriots as a traitor, Guerrero is today lauded as a Mexican cultural icon. Misfortune or divine providence, the landing at Cabo Catoche was fateful in so many ways.

Offshore, there are several interesting islands and islets, many of them rich in wildlife. **Isla Pájaros** is home to some 140 avian species, mostly waterfowl and seabirds, including pelicans, flamingos, ducks and cormorants. It has two observation towers connected by a walkway designed to minimize human impact. **Isla Pasión**, 15 minutes away by boat, has a white-sand beach with facilities for day trippers. **Cabo Catoche** lies on the mainland 53 km north of Cancún, the point where European explorers are purported to have infamously first set foot on Mexican soil in 1517 (see box, opposite). The area is good for snorkelling and with some planning you can visit the ruins of the ancient church at **Boca Iglesia**, some say the oldest Catholic structure in the country.

From June to September the waters east of Holbox are visited by hundreds of gentle whale sharks, the world's largest fish, who come to feast on plankton blooms and tuna eggs. In the past, the island had a monopoly on tours, but now Cancún is in on the act, partly because the sharks have begun aggregating closer to Isla Mujeres than Isla Holbox. Despite the good intentions of many ecotourism operators, there are some concerns about lax environmental regulation and unchecked negative impacts. For the moment, whale shark tours cannot be recommended.

## Listings Isla Holbox

### Tourist information

Most hotels will be able to help with tourist information. Online, consult www.holbox.gob.mx.

### Where to stay

**$$$ La Palapa**
*Av Morelos 231, T984-875 2121, www.hotellapalapa.com.*
La Palapa is a very comfortable and relaxing boutique lodge on the beach, good for couples and families. They have 19 rooms, studios and bungalows, most with sea view, balconies or wooden verandas. Attentive service, spa therapies available.

**$$$ Mawimbi**
*T984-875 2003, www.mawimbi.com.mx.*
An intimate and well-kept boutique hotel with attractive decor and a good reputation. Rooms and bungalows are arty, chic and rustic; very romantic and relaxing. The grounds are private and secluded, yet close to town. Recommended.

**$$$-$ Hostel y Cabañas Ida y Vuelta**
*Av Paseo Kuka, between Robalo y Chacchi, www.holboxhostel.com.*

Popular with backpackers and budget travelers, Ida y Vuelta offers accommodation in a private house ($$$), simple *cabañas* with sand floors ($$), or *cabañas* with a/c and concrete floor ($$$). For the ultra-thrifty there are dorm beds, tents or hammocks ($).

**$$-$ Hostel Tribu**
*Av Pedro Joaquín Coldwell 19, T984-875 2507, www.tribu hostel.com.*
A new hostel, brightly painted, cheerful and brilliantly done. The crowd at Tribu is young, fun and sociable. Lots of activities on offer from Spanish lessons to kite surfing to jam sessions in the bar. Clean, comfortable, simple rooms ($$) and dorms ($) available. Recommended.

### Restaurants

**$$$ La Guaya**
*Calle Palomino s/n, on the plaza. Closed Mon, dinner only.*
Creative and authentic Italian cuisine professionally prepared with fresh, organic ingredients. Dishes include seafood, steak cuts and handmade pastas; try the lobster ravioli. Good desserts, cocktails and wine are also available. Gracious service. Recommended.

### $$$ Zarabanda
*Palomino 249, a block from the plaza.*
Long-established Holbox favourite serving typical island cuisine with a Cuban twist. There is an emphasis on fresh seafood and locally sourced ingredients. Zarabanda also has a bar and features occasional live music.

### $$$-$$ Los Peleones
*On the plaza.*
An international menu with an emphasis on seafood and Italian. Los Peleones offers a laid-back, friendly ambience, quirky *lucha libre* decor, great mojitos and excellent hospitable service. A good spot for watching the coming and going of the town in the plaza below. Recommended.

### $$$-$$ Pizzeria Edelyn
*On the plaza.*
There are certainly better Italian restaurants in town, but Edelyn is casual, reliable and local, and open late. Most people rate their famous thin-crust lobster pizza quite highly, but don't expect gourmet. A good place to see local life.

### $$-$ La Tortillería
*Tiburón Ballena. Open breakfast and lunch only.*

A modest and friendly little eatery run by a young Spanish couple. They serve great Spanish tortillas, good salads, smoothies, coffee, pies and vegetarian dishes. Recommended.

### Cafés and bakeries

Le Jardin
*Calle Lisa.*
An authentic French bakery and café serving croissants, baguettes, sandwiches, fruit and omelettes. Good coffee and muffins too.

## Transport

### Isla Holbox
**Bicycle and golf cart hire**
There are no cars on the island, but golf carts and bicycle rentals are available.

**Ferry**
Ferries to Isla Holbox depart from the town of **Chiquilá**, hourly, 0600-2130, US$6.25. Public transport to Chiquilá is infrequent, 4 buses daily from **Cancún**, 3½ hrs, US$8. If driving, there are car parks in Chiquilá, US$2-3 daily.

## South on the Riviera Maya *Colour map 1, A3.*
**sandy beach resorts strung along the Caribbean coast**

Formerly known as the 'Cancún–Tulum Corridor', the Mayan Riviera unfolds along the Caribbean shore with a procession of luminous white-sand bays, fishing villages, lively beach towns, gated resort complexes, palatial health spas and immaculately manicured lawns, where the only sounds to disturb your meditations are the occasional thwack of a club and the persistent hiss of water sprinklers. There isn't much authentically Mayan about it, but a lot of businesses trade shamelessly on the beauty and exoticism of Mayan culture.

### Adventure parks
The exact boundaries of the Riviera, a marketing concept introduced in 1999, appear to be expanding too. Once limited to a stretch of the Federal Highway, some maps now show it engulfing half the state of Quintana Roo from Isla Holbox to Felipe Carrillo Puerto. Whatever its limits, the service and convenience of the Riviera between Cancún and

Tulum will appeal to families, especially its ecologically themed adventure parks, which make fun use of caves, *cenotes*, lagoons and beaches.

Near Playa del Carmen, perhaps the oldest and most famous is **Xcaret** ① *www.xcaret.com.mx, US$89*, built on the ruins of a Mayan port. Its theatrical displays are iffy, but many visitors enjoy the outdoor element. **Xplor** ① *www.xplor.travel, US$109 adults, children US$55*, is a new one, offering zip-lining, amphibious vehicles and other adrenalin-charged thrills. Further south, 13 km from Tulum, **Xel-Ha** ① *www.xelha.com, US$79 adults, US40 children*, is an aquatic park with snorkelling, tubing through mangroves and other water-based activities. You can get a package for all three parks: US$197 adults, US$149 children; note certain experiences may cost extra. And there are more: **Labna Ha Ecopark Adventures** ① *Cancún–Tulum Km 240, T984-100 1362, www.labnaha.com*; and near the resort of Akumal, **Parque Natural Aktun Chen** ① *T984-806 4962, www.aktunchen.com*; both these offer a cave, *cenote* and zipline combo.

## Puerto Morelos

Despite the advent of tourism and a more than tenfold population increase in the last 10 years, Puerto Morelos, 34 km south of Cancún, has managed to retain the intimacy of its former existence as a fishing village, for now. Look out for the tilted lighthouse, an emblem of the port that has survived some of the region's worst hurricanes since 1967.

Many travellers find relief in Puerto's lazy ambience: the dusty main plaza overlooks the beach, a handful of roads skirt the mangroves. For divers and snorkellers, the **Mesoamerican Barrier Reef**, the second largest reef system in the world, lies just 500 m offshore. To get to Puerto Morelos, public transport from Cancún drops passengers on the **Carretera Cancún–Chetumal**, every 15 minutes; it's 2 km to the beach on an access road; bus US$0.70, taxi US$3; you can walk but cover up and bring insect repellent. Back on the highway, there's an interesting botanical garden by Dr Alfredo Barrera Marín, **Yaax Che** ① *Carretera Cancún–Chetmual Km 320, T998-206 9233, www.ecosur.mx/jb/YaaxChe, Mon-Sat 0900-1700*, and a zoo.

## Playa del Carmen *See map, page 119.*

Unlike Cancún, the entertainment hub of Playa del Carmen has not evolved into a gritty metropolitan sprawl, but it doesn't glisten either; few of its buildings exceed four storeys and most of the action is concentrated into a relatively small downtown area. And yet 'Playa', as it is affectionately known, is to the European tourist what Cancún is to the North American: a well-oiled resort where you are invited to gorge your appetites, flop about on the sand and forget about the world of toil you left behind. Fun, perhaps, but something got lost in the throng of gaudy souvenir stores, fast-food joints, jewellers, boutiques and department stores and, just like Cancún, you'll either love it or hate it.

Many travellers use Playa as a base for exploring ruins and *cenotes* in the region, otherwise there isn't much to do besides the obvious: eat, shop and drink. The town is laid out on a grid with most establishments within walking distance. Day and night, the herds ramble up and down the main commercial drag, **Quinta Avenida** (Fifth Avenue), a pedestrianized thoroughfare running from Calle 1 Norte to Calle 40. During high season, the swell of crowds and persistent attention of touts can be tiresome (just keep smiling). The **beach**, two blocks east of Quinta Avenida, is lovely and somewhat redeeming. The main plaza, next to the ADO bus terminal, has an intimate, modern church. In the afternoon, you'll see Totonac dancers – *voladores* – from Veracruz State, who spiral down a 30-m-high pole with rope around their ankles; please tip kindly if you watch the show.

## Where to stay

### Puerto Morelos

**$$$ Rancho Sak-Ol Libertad**
*Next door to Caribbean Reef Club,
T998-871 0181, www.ranchosakol.com.*
Pleasant B&B accommodation in 2-storey
thatched bungalows; each unit has a
wooden terrace and hammock for chilling
out. A very tranquil, restful spot, right next to
the beach. Spa therapies, shared kitchen and
snorkelling gear available. Recommended.

**$$ Posada Amor**
*Av Javier Rojo Gómez, opposite the beach,
T998-871 0033, www.posada-amor.wix.com/
puertom.*
A small, charming *posada*, well established
and affordable, but also quite simple with no
frills. A good central location, fine restaurant-
bar and friendly Mexican owners.

### Playa del Carmen
Accommodation in Playa del Carmen
is generally expensive and poor value
compared to other parts of Mexico,
particularly around the beach and Av 5.
The prices given below are for the high
season and can drop by as much as
50% at other times of the year.

**$$$$ Viceroy Riviera Maya**
*Playa Xcalacoco, Fracc 7, 10 km north
of Playa del Carmen, T984-877 3000,
www.viceroyhotelsandresorts.com.*
Secluded, exclusive, chic and tasteful, this
impeccable spa resort on the beach has
41 luxurious villas in a verdant jungle setting,
and excellent, attentive service. A host of
facilities include pool, sun deck and gym.

**$$$$-$$$ Alhambra**
*Calle 8 Norte con playa, T984-873 0735,
www.alhambra-hotel.net.*
The interior of the family-run Alhambra has a
light, clean, airy, palatial feel. All rooms have

balcony or sea view and general amenities
include yoga instruction, jacuzzi, massage,
spa and excellent restaurant. Quiet and
peaceful, despite its setting near beach bars.
French and English spoken. Recommended.

**$$$ Casa de Gopala**
*Calle 2 Norte s/n, entre Av 10 y 15 Centro,
T984-873 0054, www.casadegopala.com.*
The interior of Casa de Gopala is handsomely
attired in traditional Mexican style. The
rooms are spacious, airy and comfortable,
but the suite has more character. There's a
dive shop, rooftop pool, relaxing garden and
jacuzzi. Helpful staff.

**$$$ Hotel Cielo**
*Calle 4, between 5 and 10, T984-873 1227,
www.hotelcielo.com.*
Appropriately named Hotel Cielo
boasts commanding views from its
rooftop terrace. Located just off Av 5,
accommodation includes standard rooms,
*cabañas* and studios, all tastefully attired
in traditional Mexican style. Rates include
a 50% breakfast discount in **Carboncitos**
restaurant, 10% off other meals. Good
service, cheaper if paying cash.

**$$$-$$ Casa Tucán**
*Calle 4 Norte, between Av 10 and 15,
T984-873 0283, www.casatucan.de.*
German-owned hotel with simple, rustic
*cabañas*, studios and no-frills rooms. The
grounds are rambling and labyrinthine
with a lovely lush garden, painted murals
and a deep pool where diving instruction
takes place.

**$$$-$$ Mom's Hotel**
*Calle 4 and Av 30, about 5 blocks from
bus station or beach, T984-873 0315,
www.momshotel.com.*
Excellent value, friendly, family-run hotel
with pleasant, colourful rooms and a small
pool. There are also studios and apartments
and good rates for long-term stays. The

attached restaurant serves international food in the evening. Recommended.

### $$-$ Hostel Playa
*Av 25 with Calle 8, T984-803 3277, www.hostelplaya.com.*
There's a comfortable, friendly atmosphere at this well-maintained and professionally run hostel. Amenities include a single- and mixed-sex dorms ($), private rooms ($$), a superb, well-equipped shared kitchen,

lounge space, paddling pool and rooftop *palapa*. Shared bathrooms are clean. Recommended for backpackers and solo budget travellers.

### $$-$ The Yak
*Calle 10 Norte, between Av 10 and 15, T984-148 0925, www.yakhostel.com.*
A bohemian new hostel, very intimate and friendly, and home to a sociable backpacker scene. They offer clean, homely rooms ($$),

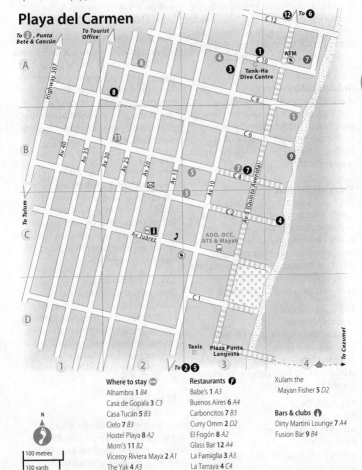

## Playa del Carmen

To **2**, Punta Bete & Cancún
To Tourist Office
Tank-Ha Dive Centre
To **6**
ATM
To Cozumel
To Tulum
Av Juárez
ADO, OCC, ATS & Mayab
Taxis
Plaza Punta Langosta
To **2 5**
100 metres
100 yards

**Where to stay**
Alhambra **1** B4
Casa de Gopala **3** C3
Casa Tucán **5** B3
Cielo **7** B3
Hostel Playa **8** A2
Mom's **11** B2
Viceroy Riviera Maya **2** A1
The Yak **4** A3

**Restaurants**
Babe's **1** A3
Buenos Aires **6** A4
Carboncitos **7** B3
Curry Omm **2** D2
El Fogón **8** A2
Glass Bar **12** A4
La Famiglia **3** A3
La Tarraya **4** C4

Xulam the Mayan Fisher **5** D2

**Bars & clubs**
Dirty Martini Lounge **7** A4
Fusion Bar **9** B4

dorm beds ($), shared kitchen, popular bar and garden, and activities such as movie night. Good hosts, good reports.

## Restaurants

### Puerto Morelos

#### $$$ El Merkadito
*Rafael Melgar lote 8-B, www.elmerkadito.mx.*
Perched on the edge of the beach, El Merkadito is a popular seafood restaurant that serves hearty plates of octopus *tostadas*, shrimp ceviche, tuna steak, marlin tacos and more. A casual option with open-air seating under a terraced palm-thatched *palapa*.

#### $$-$ El Nicho
*Av Tulum and Rojo Gómez, www.elnicho.com.mx. Closes 1400.*
Laid-back, pleasant, low-key eatery serving great brunch and breakfasts, including most excellent eggs benedict. Good juices, waffles, coffee and iced tea. Mexican staples served at lunchtime.

### Playa del Carmen

The majority of the town's restaurants line Quinta Avenida, where most tourists limit themselves and a meal costs no less (and usually a bit more) than US$10. Popular, big-name restaurants dominate the southern end of the street. Quieter, subtler settings lie north, beyond Calle 20. For budget eating, head west, away from the main drag.

#### $$$ Buenos Aires
*5a Av and Calle 34.*
Probably the best meat dishes in town, professionally prepared and authentically Argentine. Offerings include succulent cuts of fillet and mixed grill platters. Occasional displays of tango dancing.

#### $$$ Curry Omm
*10a Av and Calle 3 Sur, www.letseat.at/Curryomm.*
Great, authentic Indian cuisine, good and spicy. Offerings include old favourites like samosas, papadums and naan, a range of

hearty curries, including masala, madras and vindaloo, along with tasty traditional drinks such as mango lassi and chai. Great friendly service. Recommended.

#### $$$ The Glass Bar
*5a Av and Calle 12, www.theglassbar.com.mx.*
The place for an intimate, romantic dinner, The Glass Bar is a sophisticated Italian restaurant serving Mediterranean cuisine and seafood. It is recommended chiefly for its stock of fine wine, however, a rarity in Playa.

#### $$$ Xulam the Mayan Fisher
*10a Av and Calle 3 Sur, www.xulam.com.mx.*
Good seafood and traditional Mayan dishes, creatively prepared and presented. The themed decor is reminiscent of a ruined Mayan temple, complete with archaeological relics, colourful chattering parrots and creeping vegetation. Touristy, but lots of fun.

#### $$$-$$ Babe's
*Calle 10, between 5a and 10a Av, www.babesnoodlesandbar.com.*
Casual Thai noodle bar with kitsch decor and a superb menu of red, yellow and green curries, spring rolls, samosas, soups and more. Belting flavours, decent service and a fine stock of liquor at the bar. Highly recommended.

#### $$$-$$ Carboncitos
*Calle 4, between 5a and 10a Av.*
Seafood and steaks with a Mexican twist. Popular offerings include grilled jumbo shrimps, the salsa sampler and the frozen mojitos. Breakfast is very good too, try the *huevos rancheros*. Good service and al fresco dining on the pedestrian street. Recommended.

#### $$ La Famiglia
*10a Av and Calle 10.*
In a town with no shortage of Italian restaurants, La Famiglia is one of the better and more affordable ones. They serve wholesome traditional fare from

the motherland, including handmade pastas, lasagne and stone-baked pizzas. Casual dining.

### $$-$ El Fogón
*Av 30 and Calle 6.*
A buzzing locals' joint, hugely popular and economical. They serve grilled meat, wholesome *tortas*, tacos, quesadillas and other Mexican staples. Highly recommended.

### $$-$ La Tarraya
*Calle 2 and the beach.*
Economical seafood on the shore, including shrimp tacos and fried whole fish. Very simple and no frills, sometimes hit and miss, but a nice place to soak up ocean views and knock back a beer or two. Check your bill.

## Bars and clubs

### Playa del Carmen
Playa competes with Cancún as a major entertainment hub. Overall, the scene is a little quieter and more nuanced, offering many down-to-earth alternatives alongside the usual big-name clubs like **Coco Bongo** and **Señor Frog**.

### Dirty Martini Lounge
*1a Av, between Calle 10 and 12.*
There's a good boozy atmosphere at the Dirty Martini Lounge, the place to settle in for a long, hard drink. Fun crowd, seasoned bartenders and no shortage of Martini, naturally.

### Fusion Bar
*Calle 6 and the beach,*
*www.fusionhotelmexico.com.*
One of the better beach lounges, Fusion Bar has a romantic ambience with low-lighting rustic oil lanterns, tables and *palapas* on the sand. They often feature live music in the evenings and the kitchen serves good food.

## What to do

### Playa del Carmen
### Diving and snorkelling
**The Abyss**, *T984-876 3285, www.abyssdive center.com.* The Abyss is a professional, first-rate operation with more than 14 years' experience of local waters. Owned and managed by Canadian Dave Tomlinson, who offers ocean and *cenote* dives, certification, and a host of specialized and technical training. No physical premises, contact in advance by email.

**Tank-Ha**, *T984-873 0302, tankha.com.* The only dive shop in town with a licence to go to Cozumel, cutting out the ferry trip. They offer certification up to Dive Master, speciality courses, ocean and *cenote* dives, as well as the interesting option to hunt lion fish, an invasive species that apparently makes good ceviche.

### Language schools
**Playalingua**, *Calle 20 between Av 5 and 10, T984-873 3876, www.playalingua.com.* Weekend excursions, a/c, library, family stays, from US$225 per week (20 hrs).
**Solexico Language and Cultural Center**, *Av 35 between 6 and 6 bis, T984-873 0755, www.solexico.com.* Variable programme with workshops, also have schools in Oaxaca and Puerto Vallarta.

### Tour operators
**Alltournative**, *Carretera Chetumal–Puerto Juárez Km 287, T984-803 9999, www.alltournative.com.* A well-established ecotourism 'pioneer' with a proven commitment to sustainability. They offer adventure tours to the Yucatán's *cenotes* and national parks, as well as cultural visits to archaeological sites and Mayan communities.

## Transport

### Puerto Morelos
#### Bus
ADO buses (and others) travelling between Cancún and Playa del Carmen stop on the Carretera Cancún–Chetumal outside Puerto Morelos every 15 mins. Taxi to/from the beach, US$3.

### Playa del Carmen
#### Bus
The ADO bus terminal is on the corner of Av Juárez and Quinta Avenida (5a Av).

To **Cancún**, frequent departures, 1½ hrs, US$4; 2nd-class services with **Mayab**, less frequent, US$3. To **Cancún airport**, frequent between 0700 and 1915, 1 hr, US$10. To **Chetumal**, ADO, frequent departures, 4½ hrs, US$21; and many 2nd-class buses. To **Chichén Itzá**, ADO, 0800, 4 hrs, US$22; also with 2nd-class buses bound for Mérida. To **Cobá**, ADO, 0800, 0900, 1000, 2 hrs, US$7. To **Mérida**, frequent departures, 5 hrs, US$28. To **San Cristóbal de las Casas**, OCC, 1715, 2155, 16 hrs, US$66; an ADO GL, 1900, US$78. To **Tulum**, frequent departures, 1 hr, US$6; many 2nd class. To **Valladolid**, frequent, 3 hrs, US$12.50 (most buses going to Mérida stop at Valladolid. 2nd-class buses to Valladolid go via Tulum). To **Xcaret**, frequent departures, 15 mins, US$4. To **Xel Há**, frequent departures, 1 hr, US$5.

### Car
#### Car hire
**Alamo**, 5a Av and Calle 6 Norte, T984-826 6893, www.alamo.com; **Fiesta**, Av 144 No 35, T984-803 3345, www.fiesta carrental.com; **Hertz**, 5a Av between Calles 10 and 12, T984-873 0703, www.hertz.com; and many others.

### Ferry
Ferries to **Cozumel** depart from the main dock, just off the plaza. There are 2 competing companies, **Ultramar**, T998 843-2011, www.granpuerto.com.mx, and right next door, **Mexico Water Jets**, T987-879 3112, www.mexicowaterjets.com.mx, departures every 2-4 hrs each from 0500 until 2200, US$11.50 one way. Buy ticket 1 hr before journey. Car ferries to Cozumel, 4 daily (2 on Sun) with **Transcaribe**, www.transcaribe.net, family-sized car US$60, departing from Calica (Punta Venado) south of Playa del Carmen, but they will not transport rental vehicles.

### Taxi
**Cancún airport** US$40 for 4 persons. Tours to **Tulum** and **Xel-Há** from kiosk by boat dock US$35-40; tours to Tulum, Xel-Há and **Xcaret**, 5-6 hrs, US$60-70; taxi to Xcaret US$10. Taxis congregate on the Av Juárez side of the square (**Sindicato Lázaro Cárdenas del Río**, T998-873 0032).

## Cozumel   *Colour map 1, A3.*

a mecca for divers

The 'discovery' and popularization of Isla Cozumel and its dazzling coral reefs is often incorrectly attributed to the French oceanographer and documentary filmmaker, Jacques Cousteau. In fact, it was a Mexican director, René Cardona, who first documented Cozumel's vivid underwater world with his 1957 film *Un Mundo Nuevo* (he was, to an extent, inspired by Cousteau's 1956 explorations of the Mediterranean and Red Sea in *Un Monde du Silence*). Cousteau himself did visit the island in 1960 and famously declared, "Cozumel is one of the best places around the world for diving, thanks to its fantastic visibility and its wonderful marine life..." but by then, the word was already out.

Today, despite more than 50 years of touristic development, the controversial intrusion of cruise ships and the devastating impact of hurricanes, many of Cozumel's reefs remain healthy and vibrant, if endangered. Isla Cozumel, the largest of Mexico's Caribbean islands, continues to serve as a world-class scuba destination.

## Sights

The town, **San Miguel de Cozumel**, is touristic and commercial, increasingly marketed to cruise ship passengers arriving from Miami and Cancún, and lacking much nightlife or a discernible personality, a rather uninspired and overpriced destination. There isn't much to detain you apart from the **Museo de la Isla** ⓘ *Calle 4 and 6, Mon-Sat 0900-1600, US$2.50*, which charts the historical development of Cozumel.

### 1 Cozumel

➡ **Cozumel maps**
1  Cozumel, page 123
2  San Miguel de Cozumel, page 124

Similarly, the island's beaches are pleasant enough, but not worth a special trip from the mainland. The northern and western shores are generally sandy and good for swimming (poor for snorkelling), if a bit narrow; popular stretches include **Playa San Francisco** ① US$8, with a beach club that caters to cruisers and, 14 km south of town, **Playa Paradise**, also resort-style. Swimming on the rugged, exposed east coast is very dangerous due to ocean underflows; the exception is the sheltered bay at **Chen Río**. Surfers could try **Punta Morena**.

Like the Mayan Riviera, Cozumel now boasts adventure parks for day-trippers. Perched between a lagoon and a sandy beach, **Parque Chankanaab** ① *Carretera Costera Sur Km 9.5, www.cozumelparks.com, Mon-Sat 0800-1600, US$21, children US$14, some activities cost extra*, offers a world of fun including botanical garden, crocodile sanctuary, spa facilities, dolphinarium, snorkelling, restaurants, hammocks and *palapas*. **Punta Sur Park** ① *Carretera Costera Sur Km 30, T987-872 0914, www.cozumelparks.com, Mon-Sat 0900-1600, US$12, children US$8, some activities cost extra*, is a much wilder 1 sq km ecological park encompassing reefs, beaches and lagoons. Sights include the **Celarain lighthouse**, now converted to a nautical museum, Mayan ruins (see below) and wildlife observation towers.

## ② San Miguel de Cozumel

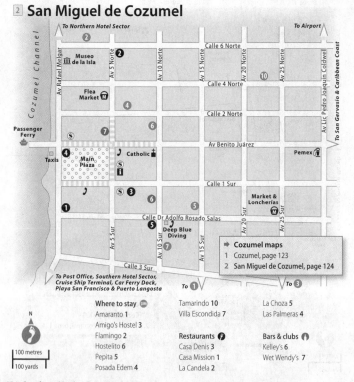

➡ Cozumel maps
1  Cozumel, page 123
2  San Miguel de Cozumel, page 124

| Where to stay | Tamarindo **10** | La Choza **5** |
| --- | --- | --- |
| Amaranto **1** | Villa Escondida **7** | Las Palmeras **4** |
| Amigo's Hostel **3** | | |
| Flamingo **2** | **Restaurants** 🍴 | **Bars & clubs** 🍸 |
| Hostelito **6** | Casa Denis **3** | Kelley's **6** |
| Pepita **5** | Casa Mission **1** | Wet Wendy's **7** |
| Posada Edem **4** | La Candela **2** | |

100 metres
100 yards

## ★Dive sites

Cozumel's reef system is part of the **Mesoamerican Barrier Reef** with sections on the southern side of the island protected by the 120 sq km **Parque Nacional Arrecifes de Cozumel**. There are dozens of sites to suit beginners and advanced divers. Favourites include **Palancar Reef**, which has deep and shallow sections, impressive coral outcrops, troughs and canyons. **Santa Rosa Wall** is a steep vertical shelf with very impressive blooms. **Colombia Reef** has shallow sections with a pretty coral garden and gentle currents; the deep section has massive corals and swim-throughs where you are likely to glimpse pelagic species. For more experienced divers, the reefs at **Punta Sur**, **Maracaibo** and **Baracuda** should not to be missed. Almost all Cozumel diving is drift diving, so if you are not used to a current, choose an operator you feel comfortable with. Snorkelling on Isla Cozumel is possible, but many sites were badly damaged by Hurricane Wilma in 2005 and have not yet recovered.

## Archaeological sites

Inhabited from 300 AD, Cozumel, whose name means 'Island of Swallows' in Yucatec Maya, was an ancient centre of worship for Ixchel. The journey to her temples involved a perilous passage by sea canoe and her pilgrims, according to the Bishop of Yucatán in the 16th century, Diego de Landa, "held Cozumel in the same veneration as we have for pilgrimages to Jerusalem and Rome". Sadly, the mysteries of Cozumel were lost forever after the Spaniards brought a devastating plague of small pox.

Today, all that remains are some 32 very modest archaeological sites, mostly single buildings thought to have been lookouts and navigational aids. The most interesting and easy to reach (and therefore often overrun with tour groups) is the post-Classic site of **San Gervasio** ⓘ *Carretera Transversal Km 7, 0800-1545, US$8, Spanish-speaking guides are on hand, US$18*. There are *sacbés* (sacred roads) between the groups of buildings, no large or monumental structures, but an interesting plaza and an arch, and surviving pigment in places. The site is located in the north of the island, 7 km from San Miguel, then 6 km to the left up a paved road, toll US$1; taxis are expensive, US$45 with two-hour wait; consider cycling. **Castillo Real** is one of many sites on the northeastern coast, but the road to this part of the island is in bad condition and the ruins themselves are very small. **El Cedral** in the southwest (3 km from the main island road) is a two-room temple, overgrown with trees, in the centre of the village of the same name. **El Caracol**, where the sun in the form of a shell was worshipped, is 1 km from the southernmost Punta Celarain.

## Listings Cozumel *maps p123 and p124*

## Tourist information

### Tourist office

*Plaza del Sol, Av 5 Sur, between Av Juárez and Calle 1 Sur, upstairs above the bank, T987-869 0211, www.cozumel.travel. Mon-Fri 0800-1500.*
Maps, flyers and general information.

## Where to stay

### $$$ Flamingo

*Calle 6 Norte 81, T987-872 1264, www.hotelflamingo.com.*
An intimate boutique lodging with a range of rooms and a penthouse suite, all spacious, tastefully attired and equipped with modern conveniences. Spa, diving and sports fishing

packages available, see website for more. Friendly and helpful staff.

### $$$ Tamarindo
*Calle 4 Norte 421, between Av 20 and 25, T987-872 6190, www.tamarindobedand breakfast.com.*
This tranquil B&B accommodation is located in a residential street and offers restful rooms and a leafy garden complete with plunge pool. A second property near the seafront has apartments and bungalows.

### $$$ Villa Escondida
*Av 10 Sur 299, T987-120 1225, www.villaescondidacozumel.com.*
Villa Escondida is a cosy B&B with 4 very clean, comfortable rooms and a well-tended garden with hammocks and plunge pool. Breakfasts are excellent and the Canadian/Mexican owners, David and Magda, are great hosts. Adults only. Recommended.

### $$ Amaranto
*Calle 5 Sur, between Av 15 and 20, T987-872-3219, www.amarantobedandbreakfast.com.*
Attractive thatched-roof Mayan-style bungalows and suites, complete with hammocks and kitchenettes. Spanish, English and French are spoken by the owners, Elaine and Jorge. There's a pool, and childcare is available on request. Rustic, tasteful and good value. Recommended.

### $$ Pepita
*Av 15 Sur 120 y Calle 1 Sur, T987-872 0098, www.hotelpepitacozumel.com.*
A well-established and family-run budget hotel with simple rooms set around a plant-filled courtyard, each with fridge and a/c. Clean, quiet and inexpensive for the island. Free coffee in the morning.

### $$-$ Amigos Hostel
*Calle 7 Sur 571, between Av 30 and 25, T987-872 3868, www.cozumelhostel.com.*
Formerly a B&B, Amigos Hostels features a large leafy garden with pool, various communal areas, a shady *palapa*, pool table, hammocks, simple shared kitchen,

mixed dorms ($) and clean rooms ($$). The owner, Kathy, has lots of information about the island.

### $$-$ Hostelito
*Av 10 No 42, between Juárez and 2 Nte, T987-869 8157, www.hostelito.com.mx.*
This downtown backpackers' hostel has large dorms ($) and simple whitewashed rooms ($$), suites, sun-decks and a shared kitchen. Clean and hip.

### $ Posada Edém
*Calle 2 Norte 124, T987-872 1166, gustarimo@hotmail.com.*
Very basic, economical rooms with Wi-Fi and the usual bare necessities, including fan or a/c. A little run-down these days, but friendly.

## Restaurants

There are few eating options for budget travellers. The cheapest places for breakfast, lunch or an early dinner are the *loncherías* next to the market on A R Salas, between Av 20 and 25. They serve fairly good local *comida corrida*, 0800-1930.

### $$$ Casa Mission
*Av 55, between Juárez and Calle 1 Sur, www.missioncoz.com. Daily 1700-2300.*
Established in 1973, this restaurant survived hurricanes Wilma and Gilbert and is now a Cozumel institution. Fine Mexican, international and seafood in an elegant hacienda setting. Recommended.

### $$$ La Choza
*Salas 198 and Av 10, www.lachoza restaurant.com.*
A large, airy restaurant serving classic Mexican dishes, seafood and regional cuisine. Good service and atmosphere, colourful decor. Popular with both tourists and nationals.

### $$ La Candela
*Calle 5 Norte 298. Closed Sun.*
Modest and affordable little restaurant serving good breakfasts and set lunches, Cuban and Mexican staples, including

fish tacos. A Cozumel favourite with pleasant service.

## $$ Las Palmeras
*At the pier, Av Melgar, www.restaurante palmeras.com. Open 0700-1400.*
Las Palmeras serves reliable and wholesome grub, a popular spot for breakfast. The restaurant overlooks the pier and is a great place for people-watching.

## $$-$ Casa Denis
*Calle 1 Sur 164, close to plaza, www.casadenis.com.*
An charming, intimate little eatery, one of the oldest on the island, owned by Denis and Juanita Angulo. They serve excellent and affordable tacos, tortas and other Mexican fare. Former diners include Jackie Onassis. Recommended.

## Bars and clubs

The big-name clubs like Señor Frog's and Carlos 'n' Charlie are clustered around the pier. They tend to draw tourists and very few locals. For something casual, try:

### Kelley's
*Av 10, www.kelleyscozumel.com.*
A grungy Irish sports bar, recommended chiefly because it serves beer on tap, including Guinness. Bring pesos, poor exchange rate.

### Wet Wendy's
*Av 5, between Calle 2 and Juárez, www.wetwendys.com.*
A popular place serving the most insane margaritas anywhere. Wet Wendy, the bar's namesake, is a legendary local mermaid, not an adult entertainer.

## What to do

### Diving
There are 2 different types of dive centre: the larger ones, where the divers are taken out to sea in big boats with many passengers; the smaller, more personalized dive shops,

with a maximum of 8 people per small boat, some of which are recommended below:
**Deep Blue**, *A R Salas 200, corner of Av 10 Sur, T987-872 5653, www.deepbluecozumel.com.*
A PADI facility since 1995, Deep Blue specializes in deep dives, including trips to Punta Sur, Maracaibo and Barracuda reefs. They also offer PADI, NAUI and SSI certification up to Dive Master. All dives are computerized for maximum bottom time and increased safety. Helpful and knowledgeable.
**Scuba Tony**, *Av Xel Ha 151, T987-869 8268, www.scubatony.com.* Tony loves diving so much he quit an 11-year career with the Los Angeles Sheriff's department to establish a dive shop on Cozumel. He offers reef, twilight and night dives, certification up to Advanced Open water, private charters and accommodation. No physical premises, contact through the website.

## Transport

### Air
The airport is just north of the town with a minibus shuttle service to the hotels.
There are 10-min flights to and from the airstrip near Playa del Carmen, as well as flights linking to Mexico City, Cancún and some international destinations.

### Bicycle and moped
The best way to get around the island is by hired moped or bicycle. Mopeds cost US$25-35 per day, credit card needed as deposit; bicycles are around US$15-20 per day, US$20 cash or TC deposit. Rental stalls at the ferry terminal, or try **El Aguila**, Av Melgar, between 3 and 5 Sur, T987-872 0729; and **El Dorado**, Av Juárez, between 5 and 10, T987-872 2383.

### Bus
There are no buses, but Cozumel town is small enough to visit on foot, or you can hire a moped or bicycle (see above) or take a taxi (see below).

## Car

**Car rental** There are many agencies, including **Avis**, airport, T987-872 0219; **Budget**, Av 5 between 2 and 4 Norte, T987-872 0219; **Hertz**, Av Melgar, T987-872 3955.

## Ferry

The passenger ferry to and from Playa del Carmen runs every 2 hrs and the car ferry leaves 4 times daily from Calica (see page 122).

## Taxi

Taxis are plentiful. Beware taxis looking for kick-backs.

## Tulum and around   *Colour map 1, A3.*

**compact clifftop Mayan site overlooking the turquoise Caribbean**

★Perched high on a sea cliff overlooking the eastern horizon, Tulum was originally named Zama, meaning 'City of the Dawn' in Yucatec Maya. Rising to prominence during the late post-Classic era (1200-1450 AD), it was an important trade hub where itinerant merchants exchanged precious commodities such as obsidian, jade and copper. Home to approximately 1500 inhabitants, the settlement was accessed by sea canoe through a gap in the offshore reef. The word 'Tulum' means wall or fence in Maya and the entire city was surrounded by walls, partially standing today.

Compared with the jungle-shrouded metropolises further inland, Tulum is a very small site, easily explored in an hour or two. Its buildings are small, squat versions of the architecture at Chichén Itzá, very typical of the east coast style. The **Temple of the Descending God** contains a well-preserved stucco sculpture of a downward diving deity, a recurring motif and the personification of the setting sun, to whom all west-facing buildings were consecrated. Nearby, the **Temple of Frescoes** was an observatory for tracking the sun. The façades of its inner temple have murals depicting deities and serpents, sadly no longer open to the public; its outer temple has stucco figures in bas-relief, including masks on the corners. The grandest building in Tulum is **El Castillo**, a fortress-like structure built in several phases on the edge of the cliff. It contains shrines and vaulted rooms, but you are not permitted to climb its steps. Bring a swimsuit if you want to scramble down from the ruins to one of the beaches for a swim. Do not attempt to swim out to the reef, 600 m to 1 km away.

## Essential Tulum

### Site information

www.inah.gob.mx, 0800-1700, US$4.50, parking, US$2.50, guides US$20. Buses drop passengers 1 km from the ruins at an access road on the Carretera Cancún–Chetumal. Taxis from Tulum village, US$5.50. The site is very popular and swamped with tour groups after 0900 or 1000.

### Tulum town

Approximately 3 km from the ruins, Tulum town, until recently, was nothing more than a dusty strip of houses on the edge of the highway. Today it is blossoming into a minor tourist town complete with international restaurants, coffee houses, dive shops and lodgings to suit all budgets. You'll find the ADO bus terminal and taxi ranks on the Carretera Cancún–Chetumal, which changes its name to Avenida Tulum as it enters the town. A small tourist information kiosk, irregularly staffed, is on the plaza. Just outside town, on the highway to Cobá, you'll find the **Tulum Monkey Sanctuary** ⓘ *T984-115 4296, www. tulummonkeysanctuary.com*, a private reserve with many spider monkeys and two refreshing *cenotes*; reservations essential.

## Tulum beach

Fronted by a procession of luxury hotels, upscale boutiques, B&Bs and *cabañas*, the sublime white-sand beach running south of the ruins was 'discovered' by property speculators some years ago. The treatment has been relatively rustic and low-rise (many establishments lack electricity during daylight hours), but there are now limited economical lodging options on this fabled stretch. If determined, you may find a

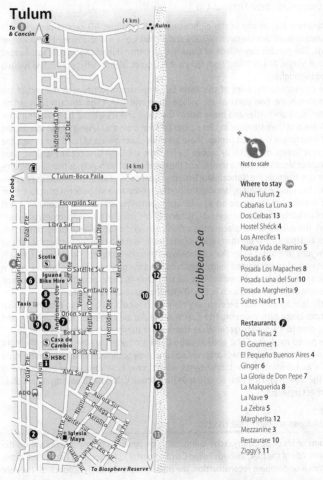

**Tulum**

To ⑧ & Cancún

Ruins (4 km)

Av Tulum
Andrómeda Ote
Sol Ote

③

To Cobá

(4 km)

C Tulum-Boca Paila

Escorpión Sur

Libra Sur
Polar Pte

Géminis Sur
Gamma Ote

Scotia Ⓢ ⑥
Sagitario Pte
Iguana
Bike Hire ⑥
Satélite Sur
Sol Ote
Venus Ote
Centauro Sur
Mercurio Ote
Asteroides Ote

Caribbean Sea

⑨
⑫

⑩

Taxis
⑧
Andrómeda Ote
①
Orión Sur
Neptuno Ote
③
①
⑪ ⑦
⑨ ④
Beta Sur
⑪
②
Casa de
Cambio Ⓢ
Osiris Sur

Ⓢ HSBC
ⓘ
Alfa Sur
Polar Pte
Av Tulum

⑤
⑤

ADO 🚌

Aurora Sur
Neptuno Pte
Omega Sur
Aerolito
Sol Pte

②
Júpiter Sur
Iglesia
Maya
Sol Pte
Luna Sur
Leo Sur
Saturno Pte
Acuario Sur

⑩
⑬

To Biosphere Reserve

Not to scale

### Where to stay 🛏
Ahau Tulum **2**
Cabañas La Luna **3**
Dos Ceibas **13**
Hostel Shéck **4**
Los Arrecifes **1**
Nueva Vida de Ramiro **5**
Posada 6 **6**
Posada Los Mapaches **8**
Posada Luna del Sur **10**
Posada Margherita **9**
Suites Nadet **11**

### Restaurants 🍴
Doña Tinas **2**
El Gourmet **1**
El Pequeño Buenos Aires **4**
Ginger **6**
La Gloria de Don Pepe **7**
La Malquerida **8**
La Nave **9**
La Zebra **5**
Margherita **12**
Mezzanine **3**
Restaurare **10**
Ziggy's **11**

scruffy cabin with a sand floor and shared bathroom for around US$30, but you should bring padlocks, carefully check the security situation and consider stashing valuables elsewhere. Access to the beach is via the Carretera Tulum–Boca Paila, which branches south from a crossroad on the Carretera Cancún–Chetumal and skirts the shore as far as Punta Allen. Taxis from the town to the beach US$5.50 minimum; cycling is an option.

## Around Tulum

ruined Mayan city, jungle-fringed lake and vast biosphere

### Cobá *Colour map 1, A3.*
*www.inah.gob.mx, 0800-1700, US$4.50.*

An important Mayan city in the eighth and ninth centuries AD, whose population is estimated to have been between 40,000 and 50,000, Cobá was abandoned for unknown reasons. The present-day village of Cobá lies on either side of Lago Cobá, surrounded by dense jungle, 47 km inland from Tulum. It is a quiet, friendly village, with few tourists staying overnight.

The entrance to the ruins of this large but little-excavated city is at the end of the lake between the two parts of the village. A second lake, **Lago Macanxoc**, is within the site. There are turtles and many fish in the lakes, and it's a good birdwatching area. Both lakes and their surrounding forest can be seen from the summit of the **Iglesia**, the tallest structure in the **Cobá Group**. There are three other groups of buildings to visit: the **Macanxoc Group**, mainly stelae, about 1.5 km from the Cobá Group; **Las Pinturas**, 1 km northeast of Macanxoc, with a temple and the remains of other buildings that had columns in their construction; the **Nohoch Mul Group**, at least another kilometre from Las Pinturas. Nohoch Mul has the tallest pyramid in the northern Yucatán, a magnificent structure, from which the views of the jungle on all sides are superb. You will not find at Cobá the great array of buildings that can be seen at Chichén Itzá or Uxmal, or the compactness of Tulum. Instead, the delight of the place is the architecture in the jungle, with birds, butterflies, spiders and lizards, and the many uncovered structures that hint at the vastness of the city in its heyday (the urban extension of Cobá is put at some 70 sq km). An unusual feature is the network of *sacbés* (sacred roads), which connect the groups in the site and are known to have extended across the entire Maya Yucatán. Over 40 *sacbés* pass through Cobá, some local, some of great length, such as the 100-km road to Yaxuná in Yucatán State.

At the lake, toucans may be seen very early; also look out for greenish-blue and brown mot-mots in the early morning. The guards at the site are very strict about opening and closing time so it is hard to get in to see the dawn or sunset from a temple.

The paved road into Cobá ends at **Lago Cobá**; to the left are the ruins, to the right **Villas Arqueológicas**. The roads around Cobá are badly potholed. Cobá is becoming more popular as a destination for tourist buses, which come in at 1030; arrive before that to avoid the crowds and the heat (ie on the 0430 bus from Valladolid, if not staying in Cobá). Take insect repellent.

### Muyil *Colour map 1, A3.*
*www.inah.gob.mx, 0800-1700, US$2.70.*

The ruins of Muyil at **Chunyaxché** comprise three pyramids (partly overgrown) on the left-hand side of the road towards Felipe Carrillo Puerto, 18 km south of Tulum. One of the pyramids is undergoing reconstruction; the other two are relatively untouched. They are very quiet, with interesting birdlife, but also mosquito infested. Beyond the last pyramid is Laguna Azul, which is good for swimming and snorkelling in blue, clean water (you do not have to pay to visit the pool if you do not visit the pyramids).

## Sian Ka'an Biosphere Reserve *Colour map 1, B3.*
*Daily 0900-1500, 1800-2000, US$2. For information, visit Los Amigos de Sian Ka'an in Cancún, T998-892 2958, www.amigosdesiankaan.org; they are very helpful.*

Meaning 'where the sky is born', the enormous reserve of Sian Ka'an, the third largest and one of the most diverse in all Mexico, was declared a UNESCO World Heritage Site in 1987 and now covers 652,000 ha (4500 sq km) of the Quintana Roo coast. About one-third is covered in tropical forest, one-third is savannah and mangrove, and one-third coastal and marine habitats, including 110 km of barrier reef. Mammals include jaguar, puma, ocelot and other cats, monkeys, tapir, peccaries, manatee and deer; turtles nest on the beaches; there are crocodiles and a wide variety of land and aquatic birds. If you want to see wildlife, it is best to use a qualified guide or tour operator (see Tour operators, below). You can drive into the reserve from Tulum village as far as Punta Allen (58 km; the road is opposite the turning to Cobá; it is not clearly marked and the final section is badly potholed), but beyond that you need a boat. Do not try to get there independently without a car.

## Listings Tulum and around *map p129*

### Where to stay

#### Tulum town
Scores of new budget hotels and restaurants are opening apace, making it a good base for backpackers and cost-conscious travellers. However, expect to offset those lower hotel rates with additional transport costs. There are no buses to the beach, only taxis and infrequent colectivos. For places to stay in Sian Ka'an Biosphere Reserve, see below.

#### $$$ Posada 6
*Andrómeda Ote, between Gemini Sur and Satélite Sur, T984-116 6757, www.posada06tulum.com.*
A stylish Italian-owned hotel with an interesting interior design that employs curves and enclaves to aesthetic effect. Rooms and suites are clean and comfortable, and amenities include garden, terraces, pool and jacuzzi.

#### $$$ Posada Luna del Sur
*Luna Sur 5, T984-871 2984, www.posadalunadelsur.com.*
An intimate downtown lodging with light, airy, elegantly attired rooms, all with

crisp white linen. The owner, Tom, is very hospitable and attentive, with lots of useful knowledge on the area. Immaculately clean and comfortable, and breakfast is included in the price. Recommended.

#### $$ Suites Nadet
*Orion Norte by Polar Ote and Av Tulum.*
The recently remodelled rooms at Suites Nadet are clean, simple and comfortable, all with smart new furnishings, a/c, hot water and cable TV. The suites ( $$$ ) are much better and have kitchen and dining room. A good overall deal for the quality, cleanliness and location.

#### $ Hostel Shéck
*Av Satelite Norte and Sagitario, T984-133 3992, www.hostelsheck.com.*
A clean, laid-back hostel with a sociable vibe and accommodation in mixed dorms only. The garden is lush and tranquil with inviting hammocks and seating areas, and amenities include a full-service bar and well-equipped industrial kitchen. Good cooked breakfast is included. Recommended for thrifty backpackers.

### $ Posada Los Mapaches
*Carretera Cancún–Chetumal, T984-871 2700,*
*www.posadalosmapaches.com. 1.5 km*
*north of the village, near the entrance to*
*the ruins.*
A very sweet and basic lodging bursting
with colourful flowers. The rooms are clean
and simple, with shared bath. Mother and
son hosts, Chela and Joaquín, are helpful
and hospitable. Complimentary bikes and
breakfast included. Highly recommended.

## Tulum beach
A plethora of lodgings run the length of
the coast from Tulum ruins to the Sian
Ka'an Biosphere reserve. There is little
infrastructure beyond these hotels and it's
best to reach them by taxi; official rates are
posted on a sign at the rank in the village.

### $$$$ Cabañas La Luna
*Carretera Tulum–Boca Paila Km 6.5,*
*T1-818-631 9824 (US reservations),*
*www.cabanaslaluna.com.*
Lots of love and care has gone into La Luna,
a very popular and reputable boutique
hotel with interesting and creative lodgings,
including 9 themed *cabañas*, an ocean-view
room, a garden suite and 2 villas. Stunning
setting, great service and attention to detail.

### $$$$-$$$ Nueva Vida de Ramiro
*Carretera Tulum–Boca Paila Km 8.5, No 17,*
*T984-877 8512, www.tulumnv.com.*
Nueva Vida de Ramiro prides itself
on attentive service and sustainable,
ecologically aware practices. They offer
luxury lodging in 30 wooden bungalows
situated on a 7.5-ha beachfront property.
Each unit boasts comfortable and tasteful
furnishings, the height of rustic chic.

### $$$$-$$$ Posada Margherita
*T984-801 8493, www.posadamargherita.com.*
There's a shabby-chic aesthetic at the
Posada Margherita, with some furnishings
made from reclaimed driftwood. The vibe is
relaxed, the crowd trendy. A generally
decent and hospitable lodging with 24-hr

electricity and wheelchair access. Many
people come for the excellent Italian food,
but be warned, it's not cheap (**$$$**).

### $$$ Dos Ceibas
*9 km from the ruins, T984-877 6024,*
*www.dosceibas.com.*
This verdant ecolodge on the edge of the
Sian Ka'an Biosphere Reserve has a range of
comfortable and cheerful *cabañas*. Massage,
cleansing rituals, New Age therapies and
yoga instruction available. Friendly and
tranquil ambience.

### $$$-$$ Los Arrecifes
*7 km from ruins, T984-155 2957,*
*www.losarrecifestulum.com.*
Clean, simple and affordable rooms and
*cabañas*, a little tired, but with an excellent
location on the beach and superb views
of the ocean. The ambience is quiet and
peaceful, the service adequate.

### $$ Ahau Tulum
*Carretera Tulum–Boca Paila Km 7.5,*
*T984-167 1154, www.ahau tulum.com.*
Named after the Mayan sun god, Ahau
Tulum is a community-oriented resort with
a New Age philosophy. They offer yoga,
retreats and spa treatments. Recommended
as one of the few reasonable budget beach
options; rustic lodging is in the guesthouse.
Asian-style *cabañas* are more expensive
(**$$$-$$**), as are the luxurious suites (**$$$$**).
Book in advance.

## Cobá

### $$ Hotelito Sac-Be
*Calle Principal, 150 m from Town Hall.*
Simple, clean, adequate rooms below a
restaurant. Nothing outstanding, not great
value, but the best available. Amenities
include hot water and a/c. Friendly owner.

## Sian Ka'an Biosphere Reserve

### $$$$ Rancho Sol Caribe
*Punta Allen, T984-139 3839,*
*www.solcaribe-mexico.com.*

Luxurious, extravagant and exclusive, Rancho Sol Caribe boasts a handful of handsome suites and *cabañas*, and an enviable location on the beach. Very hospitable and deeply relaxing, but not cheap. All-inclusive packages available. Recommended.

### $$$ Centro Ecológico Sian Ka'an
*T984-871 2499, www.cesiak.org.*
Environmentally considerate and sensitive accommodation in the heart of the Reserve, profits contribute to conservation and education programmes in the region. Tours, kayaking and fly fishing arranged.

## Restaurants

### Tulum Town

### $$$ El Pequeño Buenos Aires
*Av Tulum, www.pequenobuenosaires.com.*
High-quality cuts of beef, including rib eye, tenderloin, sirloin and more, all prepared and cooked to perfection the Argentine way, as the name suggests. Cosy setting with open-air seating on the main drag. One great meat feast, the servings are large.

### $$$ Ginger
*Calle Polar between Av Satélite and Centauro, www.gingertulum.com.*
A very decent, creative restaurant, if not the best in town. Starters include ceviche with mango and green apple and balsamic-glazed strawberry salad with goat cheese. For the main course, try the pan-seared fish fillet in passion fruit salsa or the grilled chicken in Yucatán spices. Recommended.

### $$$ La Gloria de Don Pepe
*Orion Sur 57.*
An intimate little Spanish restaurant with just a few tables and a welcoming host. They serve authentic tapas, including *albóndigas* (meatballs) and *chistorra* (cured sausages), Catalan salads, tasty seafood paella, sangria and crisp white wine.

### $$$-$$ La Malquerida
*Calle Centauro Sur and Av Tulum.*
A cheery Mexican restaurant serving tacos, fajitas, nachos, quesadillas and the usual local fare, with a smattering of Caribbean and seafood. Large portions, friendly service and a laid-back, sociable ambience. A good stock of tequila.

### $$ La Nave
*Av Tulum.*
A very popular Italian restaurant and pizzeria. Good, authentically Italian stone-baked pizzas and a lively atmosphere most evenings.

### $$-$ El Gourmet
*Av Tulum corner of Centauro Sur.*
An Italian deli stocking good cheeses and cured hams, salami, olives and other treats. They do delicious panini and ciabatta sandwiches for picnics or food on the go.

### $ Doña Tinas
Good basic and cheap, in a grass hut at southern end of town. **El Mariachito** next door also does good, cheap and cheerful grub.

### Ice cream parlours

### La Flor de Michoacán
*Av Tulum.*
This ice cream parlour on the main drag offers a wide variety of flavoured cones (try the coconut), a refreshing antidote to the searing Caribbean heat.

### Tulum beach
Restaurants on the beach tend to be owned by hotels. For dinner, book in advance where possible. Strolling between establishments after dark isn't advisable.

### $$$ Mezzanine
*Carretera Tulum–Boca Paila Km 1.5.*
Excellent authentic Thai cuisine conceived by TV personality Chef Dim Geefay, who has successfully infused old family recipes with local, Mexican flavours. Specialities include Pad Thai and a host of flavourful curries. Highly recommended.

### $$$ Restaurant Margherita
*Carretera Tulum–Boca Paila Km 4.5,
in Posada Margherita, www.posada
margherita.com. Closed Sun.*
Excellent, freshly prepared Italian food in
an intimate setting. Hospitable, attentive
service. Book in advance. Recommended.

### $$$ La Zebra
*Carretera Tulum–Boca Paila Km 7.5,
www.lazebratulum.com.*
Fresh, tasty barbequed fish, shrimps, ceviche
and Mexican fare. Lashings of Margarita at
the **Tequila Bar**.

### $$$-$$ Restaurare
*Carretera Tulum–Boca Paila Km 6.*
Excellent vegan cuisine, healthy and
flavourful, all served under the trees in a
verdant jungle garden (bring repellent).
Offerings include avocado soup, coconut
curry and delicious fresh fruit juices. No
alcohol served, bring your own if desired.

### $$$-$$ Ziggy's
*Carretera Tulum–Boca Paila Km 7,
www.ziggybeachtulum.com.*
Ziggy's serves seafood and vegetarian
dishes, all creatively prepared with local
ingredients. Offerings include mushroom
ceviche, coconut shrimp and smoked pork
chop and pineapple wrap. The sun loungers
and *palapas* are part of the beach club.

## What to do

### Cenote diving
**Koox Diving**, *Av Tulum, between Osiris and
Beta Norte, T984-131 6543, www.kooxdiving.
com.* Koox is a friendly, personable and
professional company with a solid team
headed by Jesús 'Chucho' Guzmán. They
offer reef and *cenote* dives, snorkel tours
and certification up to Dive Master.
**Xibalba Dive Center**, *Andrómeda,
between Libra and Gemini, T529-848 7129,
www.xibalbahotel.com/diving.asp.* Headed
by Robert Schmittner, Xibalba has been
diving *cenotes* in the Yucatán for more
than a decade. They visit around a dozen

sites and offer PADI certification up to
Dive Master, as well as NACD technical
cave and cavern certification.

### Kitesurfing
**Extreme control**, *El Paraíso Beach Club, T984-
745 4555, www.extremecontrol.net.* Managed
by Marco and Heather, Extreme Control is a
very successful kite-boarding operation with
branches across Mexico and Brazil. Basic
lessons for groups start at US$60 per person.
They also offer paddle-boarding and diving.

### Tour operators
**Community Tours Si'an Kaan**, *Osiris Sur,
between Sol Ote and Andrómeda Ote,
T984-871 2202, www.siankaantours.org.*
A socially responsible and environmentally
aware tour operator entirely operated by
Maya from local communities. They offer
a range of professional cultural and
adventure excursions, including wetland
kayaking, birding and visits to *chicle*
(chewing gum) farms.
**Yucatán Outdoors**, *T984-133 2334, www.
yucatanoutdoors.com.* Yucatán Outdoors
offers ecotourism for adventurous souls,
including personalized kayaking, hiking,
birding and biking tours. Committed to
sustainability and passionate about the
local culture and environment.

## Transport

### Bicycle
Bikes can be hired in the village from **Iguana
Bike Shop**, *Calle Satélite Sur and **Andrómeda
Ote**, T984-119 0836 (mob) or T984-871 2357.*

### Bus
Regular buses go up and down the coastal
road travelling from Cancún to Tulum
en route to Chetumal, stopping at most
places in between. Some buses may be
full when they reach Tulum; very few buses
begin their journeys here.

To **Chetumal**, frequent departures, 4 hrs,
2nd class, US$14, 1st class US$17. To **Cobá**,

mostly 2nd class, 1 hr, US$4. To **Escárcega**, ADO, 1825, 2300, 7 hrs, US$35. To **Felipe Carrillo Puerto**, frequent departures, 1½ hrs, US$6; also colectivos from the highway. To **Mérida**, ADO, 10 daily, 4 hrs, US$20; and numerous 2nd-class departures. To **Mexico City**, ADO, 1340, 23½ hrs, US$130. To **Palenque**, OCC, 1825, 2300, 10-11 hrs, US$52; and **ADO GL**, 2015, US$58. To **San Cristóbal**, OCC, 1825, 15 hrs, US$61; and an **ADO GL**, 2015, US$74. To **Villahermosa**, ADO, 4 daily, 11 hrs, US$54.

## Taxi
Tulum town to Tulum **ruins** US$5.50. To the **beach** US$5.50 minimum, check the board by the taxi stand on Av Tulum for a full list of fixed rates. **Tucan Kin** run shuttles to Cancún airport, T01-800-702-4111 for reservations, www.tucankin.com, from US$29, 1½ hrs.

## Cobá
### Bus
Buses into the village turn round at the road end. To **Playa del Carmen**, ADO, 1510, 1530, 2 hrs, US$9. To **Tulum**, ADO, 1510, 1530, 1 hr, US$5.

---

## Felipe Carrillo Puerto and around *Colour map 1, B3.*
### obscure Mayan administrative centre and Caste War rebel stronghold

The cult of the 'talking cross' started in Felipe Carrillo Puerto, a small town founded Chan Santa Cruz by Mayan rebels in 1850. The Santuario de la Cruz Parlante is five blocks west of the Pemex station on Highway 307. The beautiful main square is dominated by the Balam Nah Catholic church. Legend has it that the unfinished bell tower will only be completed when the descendants of those who heard the talking cross reassert control of the region.

### Mahahual *Colour map 1, B3.*
Further south on Route 307, at Cafetal, a good road heads east to Mahahual (Majahual) on the coast (56 km from Cafetal), a peaceful place with clear water and beautiful beaches. Unfortunately, the Costa Maya cruise ship dock, 3 km from the village, means occasional interruptions to the peace and calm. From Mahahual, an offshore excursion is possible to **Banco Chinchorro**, where there is a coral bank and a white-sand beach. There is an ADO bus stop in Mahahual, but services from Cancún and Chetumal are quite infrequent (see Transport, page 136).

## Listings Felipe Carrillo Puerto and around

### Where to stay

#### Felipe Carrillo Puerto

**$$ Hotel Esquivel**
*Calle 65 No746, between 66 y 68, T983-834 0344, www.hotelesquivel.blogspot.mx.*
The best in town, but simple. Rooms are clean and spacious, and include good hot water,

a/c and Wi-Fi. Helpful service, close to the bus station, but perhaps not the best value.

**$$-$ Chan Santa Cruz**
*Calle 68, 782, just off the plaza, T983-834 0021.*
The 2nd best option, generally good, clean and friendly. Rooms have a/c, cable TV, fridge and disabled access.

## Mahahual and around

### $$$ El Hotelito
*Av Mahahual, T983-834 5702,*
*www.elhotelitomahahual.com.*
A new, comfortable, tastefully decorated boutique hotel located at the southern end of the *malecón*, just across the street from the beach. Rooms on the top floor enjoy unobstructed ocean views and refreshing breezes. Good hosts and friendly, attentive service. Recommended.

### $$$ Posada Pachamama
*Huachinango s/n, T983-834 5762.*
A homely little *posada* with clean, cosy, smallish rooms, modern conveniences and attractive decor. Italian owners Max and Michela are helpful and hospitable. Not quite on the beach, 1 min away, but most guests don't seem to mind. Recommended.

### $$ Kabah-na
*Camino Costero Mahahual–Xcalak Km 8.6, T983-838 8861, www.kabah na.com.*
Simple, comfortable, relaxing beach *cabañas*, located several kilometres out of town, far from the hurly burly of the cruise-ship crowds. Neither chic nor rustic, but somewhere in between. Best accessed with own vehicle.

## Restaurants

### Mahahual

### $$$-$$ Tropicante
*Av Mahahual, on the Malecón, www. sandalsandskis.com/Tropicante.html.*
Mexican and American food served on the beach. They have sun loungers too, if you prefer to simply rest up with a beer or cocktail. Note Tropicante often caters to the cruise-ship crowd, so time your visit accordingly. Steve, the owner, is a good host.

### $$ Pizza Papi
*Av Paseo del Puerto.*
Casual little Italian eatery serving very good, authentic, stone-baked pizzas. Good service. Recommended.

## Transport

### Felipe Carrillo Puerto
### Bus
Bus station opposite Pemex. To **Cancun**, frequent 1st- and 2nd-class departures, 4 hrs, US$16. To **Chetumal**, frequent departures, 2½ hrs, US$10. To **Playa del Carmen**, frequent departures, 2½ hrs, US$11.50. To **Tulum**, frequent departures, 1½ hrs, US$7.50; also frequent colectivo minibuses.

## Chetumal and around  Colour map 1, B3.

*a small, non-touristy Mexican city with an authentic feel*

The state capital of Quintana Roo, Chetumal, 240 km south of Tulum, is a necessary stopover for travellers en route to Mayan sites in the south of the peninsula and across the frontier to Belize and Guatemala; see Border crossings box in Practicalities chapter. Although attractions are thin on the ground, Chetumal does have the advantage of being not devoted to tourism unlike other towns on the Riviera Maya. The Chetumal bay has been designated a natural protected area for manatees and includes a manatee sanctuary.

### Sights
The avenues are broad, busy and in the centre lined with huge shops selling cheap imported goods. The main local activity is window-shopping and the atmosphere is more like a North American city, with an impression of affluence that can be a culture shock to the visitor arriving from the much poorer country of Guatemala. The

downtown area is compact and can be navigated on foot; Avenida Héroes is the main commercial thoroughfare.

The *paseo* near the waterfront on Sunday night is worth seeing. The State Congress building has a mural showing the history of Quintana Roo. The **Museo de la Cultura Maya** ① *Av Héroes de Chapultepec by the market, Tue-Sun 0900-1900, US$5*, is highly recommended. It has good models of sites and touch-screen computers explaining the Mayan calendar and glyphs. Although there are few original Mayan pieces, it gives an excellent overview; some explanations are in English, guided tours are available.

## Chetumal

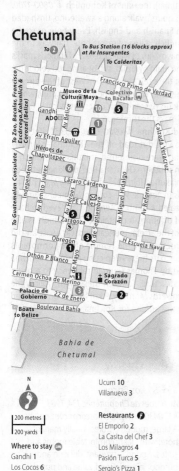

N

200 metres
200 yards

**Where to stay** 🛏
Gandhi **1**
Los Cocos **6**
Paakal's Hostel **2**

Ucum **10**
Villanueva **3**

**Restaurants** 🍴
El Emporio **2**
La Casita del Chef **3**
Los Milagros **4**
Pasión Turca **5**
Sergio's Pizza **1**

## Around Chetumal

Some 6 km north of Chetumal are the stony beaches of **Calderitas**, bus every 30 minutes from Colón, between Belice and Héroes, US$1.80, or taxi US$5, which has many fish restaurants. Beyond are the unexcavated archaeological sites of **Ichpaatun** (13 km), **Oxtancah** (14 km) and **Nohochmul** (20 km). Sixteen kilometres north on Route 307 to Tulum is the **Laguna de los Milagros**, a beautiful lagoon for swimming. Further on, 34 km north of Chetumal, is **Cenote Azul**, over 70 m deep, with a waterside restaurant serving inexpensive and good seafood and regional food (but awful coffee) until 1800. Both the *laguna* and the *cenote* are deserted in the week.

## Bacalar

About 3 km north of Cenote Azul is the village of Bacalar on the **Laguna de Siete Colores**, good for swimming and skin-diving; colectivos from terminal (Suchaa) in Chetumal, corner of Miguel Hidalgo and Primo de Verdad, 0700-1900 every 30 minutes, US$3, return from the plaza when full; also buses from Chetumal bus station every two hours or so, US$3. Built 1725-1733, the Spanish fort of **San Felipe** overlooks the shallow, clear, freshwater lagoon. It is a structure designed to withstand attacks by English pirates and smugglers who regularly looted Spanish galleons laden with Peruvian gold. Today, there are many old shipwrecks on the reef and around the Banco Chinchorro, 50 km out in the Caribbean. At the fort, there is a plaque praying for protection from the British and a small **museum** ① *Tue-Sun*

*0900-1700, US$4*. There is a dock for swimming north of the plaza, with a restaurant and disco next to it.

## Towards Campeche State *Colour map 1, B2.*

From Chetumal you can visit the fascinating Mayan ruins that lie west on the way (Route 186) to Francisco Villa and Escárcega, if you have a car. There are few tourists in this area and few facilities. Take plenty of drinking water. About 25 km from Chetumal at **Ucum** (where fuel is available), you can turn off 5 km south to visit **Palmara**, located along the Río Hondo, which borders Belize; there are swimming holes and restaurant.

Just before Francisco Villa (61 km from Chetumal), the ruins of **Kohunlich** ① *0800-1700, US$4.25*, lie 8.5 km south of the main road, 1½ hours' walk along a sweltering, unshaded road; take plenty of water. Descriptions are in Spanish and English. Every hour or so the van passes for staff working at **Explorer Kohunlich**, a luxury resort halfway to the ruins, which may give you a lift, but you'll still have 4 km to walk. There are fabulous masks (early Classic, AD 250-500) set on the side of the main pyramid, still bearing red colouring; they are unique of their kind (allow an hour for the site). About 200 m west of the turning for Kohunlich is an immigration office; wait here for buses to Chetumal or Xpujil, which have to stop, but first-class buses will not pick up passengers. Colectivos 'Nicolás Bravo' from Chetumal, or buses marked 'Zoh Laguna' pass the turning.

Other ruins in this area are **Dzibanché** and **Knichná** ① *0900-1700, US$3.50*. Both are recent excavations and both are accessible down a dirt road off the Chetumal–Morocoy road. In the 1990s the remains of a Mayan king were disinterred at Dzibanché, which is thought to have been the largest Mayan city in southern Quintana Roo, peaking between AD 300 and 1200. Its discoverer, Thomas Gann, named it in 1927 after the Maya glyphs he found engraved on the sapodilla wood lintels in Temple VI – *Dzibanché* means 'writing on the wood' in Maya. Later excavations revealed a tomb in Temple I, believed to have belonged to a king because of the number of offerings it contained. This temple is also known as the **Temple of the Owl** because one of the artefacts unearthed was a vase and lid carved with an owl figure. Other important structures are the **Temple of the Cormorants** and **Structure XIII**, known as 'The Captives', due to its friezes depicting prisoners. Knichná means 'House of the Sun' in Maya, christened by Thomas Gann in reference to a glyph he found there. The **Acropolis** is the largest structure. To reach these sights follow the Chetumal–Escárcega road, turn off at Km 58 towards Morocoy, 9 km further on. The road to Dzibanché is 2 km down this road, crossing the turning for Knichná.

## Listings Chetumal *map p137*

### Tourist information

**Municipal tourist office**
*Corner of 5 de Mayo and Carmen Ochoa de Merino, T983-833 2465.*
Stocks of maps and flyers, and enthusiastic staff.

### Where to stay

**$$$-$$ Los Cocos**
*Av Héroes de Chapultepec 134, T983-835 0430, www.hotelloscocos.com.mx.*
A large, modern, professionally managed hotel with clean, comfortable rooms and suites, a good restaurant, decking and outdoor jacuzzi. Good value and popular, if a bit generic.

### $$$-$$ Villanueva
*Carmen Ochoa de Merino 166, T983-267 3370, www.hotel-villanueva.com.*
A swish new business hotel with sparse contemporary furnishings and a wealth of facilities including pool, gym, business centre, restaurant and room service. Good value when promotions are available ($$).

### $$ Hotel Gandhi
*Av Gandhi 166, T983-285 3269, www.hotelgandhichetumal.com.*
A step up from the bare-bones Ucum across the street, Hotel Gandhi is a reliable business hotel with clean, comfortable a/c rooms, complete with Wi-Fi, a/c and cable TV. Convenient for a night, but ultimately unremarkable.

### $$-$ Paakal's Hostel
*Av Juárez 364A, T983-833 3715.*
Paakal's is a good, clean, friendly hostel with both private rooms ($$) and dorms ($), a well-equipped shared kitchen, lounge space, table tennis, plunge pool and relaxing garden. A newish property in excellent condition, very quiet and chilled out. Recommended for budget travellers.

### $$-$ Ucum
*Av Gandhi 167, corner of 16 de Septiembre, T983-832 6186.*
Motel-style lodging with parking, centrally located and no frills. Rooms are ultra-basic, with a bed, a/c, hot water, Wi-Fi and cable TV. Charmless, but a good deal for thrifty wanderers.

---

## Bacalar

### $$$$ Akal Ki
*Carretera Federal 307, Km 12.5, Bacalar Lagoon, T983-106 1751, www.akalki.com.*
A marvellously peaceful retreat with romantic thatched bungalows built right over the water. Though surrounded by jungle, this strip of the lagoon has few rocks and little vegetation, making it crystal clear and ideal for swimming.

### $$$ Rancho Encantado
*3 km north of Bacalar, Carretera Federal 307, Km 24, on the west shore of the lagoon, T983-839 7900, www.encantado.com.*
Comfortable, clean, spacious *cabañas*, suites and rooms, all in verdant surroundings by the lagoon. Services include private dock, tour boat, paddle boat, kayaks, restaurant and spa treatments.

### $$ Casita Carolina
*T983-834 2334, Costera 15, between Calle 16 and 18, www.casitacarolina.com.*
Colourful, comfortable, good-value rooms at this friendly guesthouse, the best budget option in the village. The garden backs directly onto the lagoon and the plaza is just 2 blocks away. There are kayaks for rent, a shared kitchen and hammocks. Recommended.

## Restaurants

### $$$-$$ El Emporio
*Merino 106.*
Delicious Uruguayan steaks served in a historic old house near the bay. Popular with businessmen at lunchtime.

### $$$-$$ Sergio's Pizza
*Av Obregón 182.*
A convenient downtown location for a popular family restaurant serving pizzas, fish and steaks. Good drinks and service, and a refreshing a/c interior. Very reasonable, but not amazing.

### $$ La Casita del Chef
*Obregón 163.*
Featuring 100-year-old photos of Chetumal, La Casita del Chef is a pleasant little eatery serving traditional Mexican dishes with contemporary flair. Convenient downtown location and a traditional wooden building.

### $$-$ Pasión Turca
*Av Héroes and Ignacio Zaragoza, www.pasionturca.com.mx.*
Chetumal is home to a large Turkish community and the Pasión Turca is one of

the best places to sample Turkish cuisine, with a Mexican twist, naturally. A simple place with slightly tired decor, but the food makes up for it.

### $ Los Milagros
*Zaragoza and 5 de Mayo.*
This locals' café serves economical Mexican fare, *comida corrida* and breakfasts. Busy with patrons in the morning, worth a look.

### $ Mercado.
Cheap meals in the market at the top of Av Héroes, but the service is not too good and tourists are likely to be stared at. Lots of cheap *taquerías* on the streets nearby.

## Bacalar

### Los Hechizos
*Hotel Rancho Encantado, Carretera Federal 307, www.encantado.com/restaurante.htm.*
A rustic *palapa* with great views of the lagoon and refreshing breezes. Good food, the best in town, including a range of well-presented Mexican, seafood and meat dishes. Recommended.

## Cafés

### In Chiich
*Calle 22, on the plaza.*
Cute little café serving crêpes, smoothies, ice cream, snacks and good coffee.

## Transport

For more information on crossing the border to Belize, see box in Practicalities chapter.

### Air
The airport (CTM), T983-834-5013, is 2.5 km from town. There are no local buses so take a taxi into town.

Flights to **Cancún**, **Mérida**, **Belize City**, **Mexico City**, **Monterrey** and **Tijuana**.

### Boat
Boats from Belize dock at the pier on the waterfront on the south side of the city.

**To Belize** You can avoid a lot of the hassle of travelling overland to Belize, skipping Belize City altogether, by taking a boat from the Muelle Fiscal on the south side of the city, journey time 2 hrs (excluding immigration formalities). There are 2 companies, both with departures at 1500 to San Pedro, US$40, and on to Caye Caulker, US$45; fares rise by US$10 at weekends and holidays. Try **Water Jets International**, www.sanpedrowatertaxi. com, or **Belize Express Water Taxi**, T983-832 1648, www.belizewatertaxi.com. Buy tickets at least 24 hrs in advance.

### Bus
The **ADO** bus terminal is 3 km out of town at the intersection of Insurgentes y Belice. Taxi into town US$2. There is a bus into the centre from Av Belice. 2nd-class buses from Belize arrive at the **Nuevo Mercado Lázaro Cárdenas**, on Calle Antonio Coria s/n, near the concrete tower in the market. Shuttles from Santa Elena and the border arrive at their own terminal, **Primo de Verdad**, between 16 de Septiembre and Hidalgo.

Bus information, T983-832 5110. At the ADO bus terminal left-luggage lockers cost US$0.30 per hr. If buying tickets in advance, go to the ADO office on Av Belice esq Gandhi, 0800-1600. There are often more buses than those marked on the display in the bus station, always ask at the information desk. Long-distance buses are often all booked a day ahead, so avoid unbooked connections. For local destinations in southern Quintana Roo, speedy minibuses depart from the terminal at Av Hidalgo and Primo de Verdad.

To **Bacalar**, very frequent 1st- and 2nd-class departures, 1 hr, US$3.50. To **Campeche**, ADO, 1200, 6 hrs, US$29. To **Cancún**, many 1st-class departures, 6 hrs, US$25. To **Escárcega**, ADO, 11 daily, 4 hrs, US$19. To **Felipe Carrillo Puerto**, many 1st- and 2nd-class departures, 2½ hrs, US$11. To **Mérida**, ADO, 5 daily, 5½ hrs, US$30. To **Palenque**, OCC, 0220, 2150, 7 hrs, US$32; and ADO GL, 2350, US$39. To **Playa del Carmen**, frequent 1st- and 2nd-class departures, 5 hrs, US$21. To **San Cristóbal**, OCC, 0220, 2150, 12 hrs, US$47; and **ADO GL** 0005, US$56. To **Tulum**, frequent 1st- and 2nd-class departures, 4 hrs, US$17. To **Villahermosa**, ADO, 6 daily, 8½ hrs, US$38. To **Xpujil**, ADO, Sur and OCC, 2 hrs, US$9.

**To Belize** Battered 2nd-class buses to Belize depart from a parking area in the Nuevo Mercado Lázaro Cárdenas, Calle Antonio Coria s/n, every 30-60 mins. To **Corozal**, 30-60 mins, US$1.50; to **Orange Walk**, 2 hrs, US$3.50; to **Belize City**, 3-4 hrs, US$5. Alternatively, if light on luggage, take a local bus to Santa Elena from the terminal on Primo de Verdad, between 16 de Septiembre and Hidalgo, 15 mins, US$0.80, cross the border on foot and pick up Belizean transport on the other side. Taxi from downtown Chetumal to the border, US$6. Money-changers in the bus terminal offer marginally poorer rates than those at the border. If intending to stay in Belize City, do not take a bus that arrives at night as you are advised not to look for a hotel in the dark.

**To Guatemala** San Juan Travel Services provide 1 daily service between Chetumal, Belize City and Flores in Guatemala, departs from **ADO** bus terminal 0700, US$31. Schedules are subject to change so always check times in advance, and be prepared to spend a night in Chetumal if necessary.

**Taxi**
There are no city buses; taxis run on fixed-price routes, US$1.50 on average. Cars with light-green licence plates are a form of taxi.

# Yucatán State

Yucatán State is a vivid celebration of Yucatecan history and traditions: its wealth of cathedrals, convents and rambling haciendas, frequently set against a backdrop of crumbling Mayan pyramids, recall the passion and drama of another age.

The state capital of Mérida was the seat of power for the colonial administration. Today, it is a deeply cultural place filled with museums, theatres and art galleries, teeming markets and plazas, historic mansions, churches and bright townhouses. The city of Valladolid, although much smaller, is no less romantic.

Beyond its urban centres, the state is peppered with bucolic towns and villages, many rich in Mayan heritage and specializing in *artesanía*, while communities on the Convent Route are so called for their ancient religious architecture.

As the once-thriving heart of the Mayan world, Yucatán State is also home to the vast city of Chichén Itzá, laden with sculpted feathered serpents and pyramids, ball courts and sacrificial slabs, a tremendous monument to an ancient culture. It is also worth exploring Uxmal, a stunning example of sumptuous Puuc-style architecture. Yucatán State has natural attractions too, including mysterious limestone cave systems and refreshing cenotes. On the coast, the wetlands Río Lagartos and Celestún are places to observe pelicans, egrets and flamingos.

**bold colonial buildings in varying states of repair and a state-of-the-art museum**

Mérida, the cultural and intellectual capital of the Yucatán Peninsula, is a bustling, tightly packed city. There is continual activity in the centre, with a huge influx of tourists during the high season mingling with busy *Meridanos* going about their daily business. Although the city has been developed over many years for tourism, there is plenty of local flavour, including the pungent and warren-like city market, a throng of commotion, noise and colour. Whether sipping coffee in a leafy colonial courtyard or admiring the mansions on the regal Paseo de Montejo, much of the pleasure in Mérida comes from exploring its architecture, a rich blend of European styles that spans the centuries. In the evenings, there is usually open-air dancing, music or singing. It is perhaps no surprise that many inhabitants of Mexico City are now relocating to the infinitely more civilized and urbane destination of Mérida.

You can see most of Mérida on foot. Although the city is big, there is not much to see outside the blocks radiating from the Plaza Grande; it is bound by Calles 60, 61, 62 and 63. The city centre is laid out in a classic colonial grid with even-numbered streets running north–south, odd-numbered east–west.

### Plaza Grande and around

The city revolves around the large, shady Plaza Grande, site of the **cathedral**, completed in 1559, the oldest cathedral in Latin America, which has an impressive baroque façade. It contains the Cristo de las Ampollas (Christ of the Blisters), a statue carved from a tree that burned for a whole night after being hit by lightning, without showing any damage at all. Placed in the church at Ichmul, it suffered only a slight charring (hence the name) when the church was burned to the ground. To the left of the cathedral on the adjacent side of the plaza is the **Palacio de Gobierno**, built 1892. It houses a collection of 27 enormous murals by Fernando Castro Pacheco, depicting the bloody struggle of the Maya to integrate with the Spanish. The murals can be viewed until 2100 every day. The **Casa de Montejo** ⓘ *www.casasdeculturabanamex.com, Tue-Sun 1000-1900, Sun 1000-1400, free*, is on the south side of the plaza, a 16th-century palace built by the city's founder, today a branch of Banamex and a minor art museum. It features elaborate stonework above the doorway flanked by statues of conquistadors standing victorious on the necks of their (presumably Maya) enemies.

Away from the main plaza along Calle 60 is **Parque Hidalgo**, a charming tree-filled square, which borders the 17th-century **Iglesia de Jesús.** A little further along Calle 60 is the **Teatro Peón Contreras**, built at the beginning of the 20th century by an Italian architect, with a neoclassical façade, marble staircase and Italian frescoes.

There are several 16th- and 17th-century churches dotted about the city: **La Mejorada**, behind the Museum of Peninsular Culture (Calle 59 between 48 and 50), **Tercera Orden**, **San Francisco** and **San Cristóbal** (beautiful, in the centre). The **Ermita**, an 18th-century chapel with beautiful grounds, is a lonely, deserted place, 10 to 15 minutes from the centre.

Mérida's wealth of museums is enough to keep most visitors busy for a few days. The **Museo de la Ciudad** ⓘ *Calle 56 between Calles 65 and 65-A, Tue-Fri 0900-2000, Sat 0900-1400, free*, has modest visual exhibits outlining the history of the city. The **Museo Macay** ⓘ *Calle 60, on the main plaza, www.macay.org, daily 1000-1800, free*, has a permanent exhibition of Yucatec artists, with temporary exhibits by contemporary local artists.

# Mérida

Museo de Antropología e Historia

Parque Santa Ana

Plaza Santa Lucía

Felipe Carrillo Puerta Monument

To El Gran Museo del Mundo Maya & Progreso

Paseo de Montejo

Teatro Peón Contreras

Jesús

Museo de Arte Popular

Museo de la Canción Yucateca

La Mejorada

Museum of Peninsular Culture

Mercado Municipal 2

Casa Catherwood

Parque Hidalgo

Palacio de Gobierno

Palacio Municipal

Zócalo

Cathedral

Museo Macay

Las Monjas

Casa de Montejo

Museo de la Ciudad

Combis to Izamal

Noreste

Municipal

San Cristóbal

Colectivos to Plaza de Los Americas

Autoprogreso

Colectivos to Ticul

Parque San Juan

CAME

Terminal de Autobuses

To Campeche & Mexico City

To Chichen-Itzá & Cancún

Parque San Sebastián

La Ermita

N

300 metres
300 yards

**Where to stay**

Aventura Hotel **1** *C1*
Casa Alvarez **2** *B2*
Casa Ana **3** *B4*
Casa Lecanda **4** *A3*
Hacienda Mérida VIP **5** *B2*
Hacienda Xcanatún **8** *A3*
Hostal Zócalo **17** *C2*
Hotel del Pelegrino **6** *B3*
Julamis **7** *B3*
Los Arcos **9** *B2*
Luz en Yucatán **10** *B3*

Medio Mundo **19** *B2*
Nómadas Youth
  Hostal **13** *B2*
Rosas and Xocolate
  Boutique **11** *A3*
Santa María **12** *B3*
Trinidad **22** *B2*

**Restaurants**

Amaro **1** *B2*
Bistro Rescoldos **13** *A2*
Café Chocolate **23** *B3*

Café El Hoyo **7** *B2*
Cafetería Pop **2** *B2*
Casa de Piedra **24** *A3*
Chile Habanero **6** *B3*
El Colón Sorbetes y
  Dulces Finos **10** *C3*
El Nuevo Tucho **4** *B3*
El Trapiche **3** *C2*
La Chaya **8** *B2*
La Recova **9** *A3*
Manjar Blanco **11** *A3*
Marlín Azul **18** *B2*

Mérida **20** *C2*
Pizzeria Raffaello **12** *A3*
Rosas and Xocolate **14** *A3*
Trotter's **16** *A3*

**Bars & clubs**

Cantina La Negrita **21** *A2*
Hennessy's Irish Pub **17** *A3*
Mayan Pub **22** *B2*

The **Museo de Arte Popular** ① *Calle 50-A No 487 and Calle 57, Tue-Sat 0900-1700, Sun 1000-1500, free,* has a permanent exhibition of Mayan art, handicrafts and clothing, with a good souvenir shop attached. In the Casa de Cultura, the **Museo de la Canción Yucateca** ① *Calles 57 and 48, Tue-Fri 0900-1700, Sat-Sun 0900-1500, US$1.50,* has an exhibition of objects and instruments relating to the history of music in the region. For contemporary painting and sculpture, head to the **Pinacoteca Juan Gamboa Guzmán** ① *Calle 59, between Calles 58 and 60, Tue-Sat 0900-1700, Sun 1000-1700, US$2.40.*

Established in 2007, the **Galería de Arte Municipal** ① *Calle 56, between Calles 65 and 65-A, Tue-Fri 1000-1900, Sun 1000-1400,* exhibits and promotes work by local Meridano artists. **Galería Tataya** ① *Calle 60 No 409, between Calles 45 and 47, www.tataya.com.mx, Mon-Fri 1000-1400 and 1600-2000, Sat 1000-1400,* is a private gallery specializing in Mexican and Cuban contemporary art and high quality *artesanías*. Dedicated exclusively to local artists, **Galería Mérida** ① *Calle 59 No 452, between Calles 52 and 54, Tue-Fri 1000-1230 and 1430-1700, www.galeriamerida.com,* is a small gallery featuring a range of fine and contemporary art; exhibits change monthly.

Railway fanatics might get some joy in the **Museo de los Ferrocarriles** ① *Calle 43 between Calles 46 and 58, Col. Industrial, Wed-Sun 0900-1400, US$1.50,* but there's little for the casual visitor. Fans of John Lloyd Steven's seminal travelogue *Incidents of Travel in Central America, Chiapas and Yucatán* should check out **Casa Catherwood** ① *Calle 59 between 72 and 74, www.casa-catherwood.com, Mon-Sat 0900-1400 and 1700-2100, US$5.* Dedicated to Steven's companion and illustrator, Mr Catherwood, this museum contains stunning colour lithographs of Mayan ruins, as they were found in the 19th century.

## Paseo de Montejo

Attempts to create a sophisticated Champs Elysées-style boulevard in the north of the city at Paseo Montejo have not been quite successful; the plan almost seems to go against the grain of Mérida's status as an ancient city, which has gradually evolved into a place with its own distinct identity. Nonetheless, the Paseo, which is the principal parade route during the city's fantastic carnival celebrations, features numerous impressive mansions dating to the late 19th century. You can take a casual stroll or hire a horse-drawn carriage and do it in style. For a glimpse of the *paseo* at its heyday, the **Casa Museo Montes Molina** ① *Paseo de Montejo No 469 between Calles 33 and 35, www.laquintamm.com, English tours Mon-Fri 0900, 1100, 1500, Sat 0900, 1100; Spanish tours Mon-Fri 1000, 1200, 1400, 1600, Sat 1000, 1200, US$4,* is a finely attired mansion with sumptuous antiques and art deco pieces.

The **Museo Regional de Antropología** ① *Paseo de Montejo 485, Tue-Sun 0800-1700, US$3.70,* housed in the beautiful neoclassical Palacio Cantón, has a collection of Mayan crafts and changing anthropological exhibits. However, most of its archaeological pieces have now been relocated to the Gran Museo del Mundo Maya (see below).

## ★El Gran Museo del Mundo Maya

*Paseo Montejo and Calle 60, on the outskirts of the city, www.granmuseodelmundo maya.com, Wed-Mon 0800-1700, closed Tue, US$11.50; buses to the museum depart from the corner of Plaza Grande, Calle 62 and 61, check with the driver first, US$0.70, or take a taxi, US$5.50. To return to the city centre, take a bus directly outside the museum.*

Mérida's Gran Museo Mundo Maya is a state-of-the-art interactive museum dedicated to Mayan history and identity. Opened in 2012, its collection of 1160 cultural and archaeological pieces is supplemented by scores of touch screens, computers, projection rooms and a full-sized cinema. The museum has one temporary exhibition wing and a

# BACKGROUND

## Mérida

Mérida was originally a large Mayan city called Tihoo. It was conquered on 6 January 1542, by Francisco de Montejo. He dismantled the pyramids of the Maya and used the stone as the foundations for the cathedral of San Ildefonso, built 1556-1559. For the next 300 years, Mérida remained under Spanish control, unlike the rest of Mexico, which was governed from the capital. During the Caste Wars of 1847-1855, Mérida held out against the marauding forces of indigenous armies, who had defeated the Mexican army in every other city in the Yucatán Peninsula except Campeche. Reinforcements from the centre allowed the Mexicans to regain control of their city, but the price was to relinquish control of the region to Mexico City.

permanent collection wing with four main sections. The first section deals with the geographic and social landscape of the Yucatán, its ethnic and ecological diversity, its various territories, forms of social organization and languages. The second section is a detailed exploration of the Yucatán's present-day economy and culture, including exhibitions on education, health, tradition and work. The colonial era is the theme of the third section with an array of antiques and old machines relating to the colonial industries, the conquest, the church and Mayan rebellions. The fourth and final section hosts an impressive array of archaeological pieces from statues depicting Mayan deities to examples of Mayan hieroglyphs. It explores the ancient Mayan world through the diverse themes of cosmovision, art, architecture, astronomy, time and more.

## Around Mérida

birdwatching, beaches and Mayan ruins

**Celestún** Colour map 1, A1.
A small, dusty fishing resort west of Mérida much frequented in summer by Mexicans, Celestún stands on the spit of land separating the Río Esperanza estuary from the ocean. The long beach is relatively clean except near the town proper, with clear water ideal for swimming, although rising afternoon winds usually churn up silt and there is little shade; along the beach are many fishing boats bristling with *jimbas* (cane poles), used for catching local octopus. There are beach restaurants with showers.

The immediate region is a biosphere reserve, created to protect the thousands of migratory waterfowl who inhabit the lagoons; fish, crabs and shrimp also spawn here, and kingfishers, black hawks, wood storks and crocodiles may sometimes be glimpsed in the quieter waterways. In the winter months Celestún plays host to the largest flamingo colony in North America, perhaps more than 20,000 birds – in the summer most of the flamingos leave Celestún for their nesting grounds in the Río Lagartos area. Boat trips to view the wildlife can be arranged at the beach or the **visitor centre** ① *below the river bridge 1 km back along the Mérida road, US$100 for 1-6 people, plus US$4 per person for the reserve entrance fees, 1½ hrs.* Make sure your boatman takes you through the mangrove channel and to the Baldiosera freshwater spring in addition to visiting the flamingos. It is often possible to see flamingos from the bridge early in the morning and the road to it may be alive with egrets, herons and pelicans. January to March is the best time to see them. It's important to wear a hat and use sunscreen. There are hourly buses to Mérida's terminal at Calle 50 and 67, 0530-2000, two to three hours, US$5.

## Progreso and around *Colour map 1, A1.*

Some 36 km north of Mérida, Progreso has the nearest beach to the city. It is a port and slow-growing resort town, with the facilities improving to service the increasing number of US cruise ships that arrive every Wednesday. Progreso is famous for its industrial pier, which at 6 km is the longest in the world. It has been closed to the public since someone fell off the end on a moped. The beach is long and clean and the water is shallow and good for swimming.

A short bus journey (4 km) west from Progreso are **Puerto Yucalpetén** and **Chelem**. Balneario Yucalpetén has a beach with lovely shells, but also a large naval base with further construction in progress.

Some 5 km east of Progreso is another resort, **Chicxulub**; it has a narrow beach, quiet and peaceful, on which are many boats and much seaweed. Small restaurants sell fried fish by the *ración*, or kilogram, served with tortillas, mild chilli and *cebolla curtida* (pickled onion). Chicxulub is reputed to be the site of the crater made by a meteorite crash 65 million years ago, which caused the extinction of the dinosaurs. (The site is actually offshore on the ocean floor.) The beaches on this coast are often deserted and, between December and February, 'El Norte' wind blows in every 10 days or so, making the water turbid and bringing in cold, rainy weather.

## Dzibilchaltún *Colour map 1, A1.*
*0800-1700, US$9. Combis to the ruins depart from Calle 58 between Calles 59 and 57.*

Halfway between Mérida and Progreso turn right for the Mayan ruins of Dzibilchaltún. This unique city, according to carbon dating, was founded as early as 1000 BC. The site is in two halves, connected by a *sacbé* (sacred road). The most important building is the **Templo de Las Siete Muñecas** (Temple of the Seven Dolls), at the east end, which is partly restored. At the west end is the ceremonial centre with temples, houses and a large plaza in which the open chapel, simple and austere, sticks out like a sore thumb. The evangelizing friars had clearly hijacked a pre-Conquest sacred area in which to erect a symbol of the invading religion. At its edge is the **Cenote Xlaca** containing very clear water that is 44 m deep (you can swim in it, take mask and snorkel as it is full of fascinating fish); there's a very interesting nature trail starting halfway between the temple and the *cenote*; the trail rejoins the *sacbé* halfway along. The **museum** is at the entrance by the ticket office (site map available). *Combis* stop here en route to **Chablekal**, a village along the same road.

## South to Campeche State *Colour map 1, A1.*

South of the city, 18 km away, the first place of any size is **Umán**, a henequen- (sisal-) processing town with a large 17th-century church and convent dedicated to St Francis of Assisi; there are many *cenotes* in the flat surrounding limestone plain. Further south, a turn-off leads to the turn-of-the-20th-century Moorish-style henequen hacienda at **San Bernardo**, one of a number in the state that can be visited; an interesting museum chronicling the old Yucatán Peninsula tramway system is located in its spacious grounds. At **Maxcanú**, the road to Muná and Ticul branches east; a short way down it is the recently restored Mayan site of **Oxkintoc** ① *US$3*. The Pyramid of the Labyrinth can be entered (take a torch) and there are other ruins, some with figures. Ask for a guide at the village of Calcehtoc, which is 4 km from the ruins and from the Grutas de Oxkintoc (no bus service). These, however, cannot compare with the caves at Loltún or Balankanché (see pages 157 and 164).

## Tourist information

It's worth getting hold of a copy of the excellent free tourist magazine, *Yucatan Today*, www.yucatantoday.com, published monthly and packed with useful information about the state and its attractions. Online, *Yucatán Living*, www.yucatanliving.com, is an informative expat site with news, reviews and current events.

### Municipal tourist office
*Calle 62, between Calles 61 and 63, T999-942 0000, www.yucatan.travel.*
In the Palacio Municipal on the Plaza Grande, this main municipal tourist office is helpful and well stocked with maps and flyers; additional modules are in the Museo de Ciudad, TAME Terminal and the Paseo Montejo.

### State tourist office
*Calles 60 and 62, T999-930 3101, www.yucatan.travel.*
In the Palacio de Gobierno, also on the Plaza Grande, with additional branches in the Teatro José Peón Contreras and the airport.

## Where to stay

### Mérida
If booking into a central hotel, always try to get a room away from the street side, as noise on the narrow streets begins as early as 0500.

### $$$$ Casa Lecanda
*Calle 47 No 471, between Calle 54 and 56, T999-928 0112, www.casalecanda.com.*
Recalls the beauty and elegance of a traditional Meridano home with handsome interior patios and gardens. It has 7 rooms, all impeccably attired and luxurious.

### $$$$ Hacienda Mérida VIP
*Calle 62 No 441A, between Calle 51 and 53, T999-924 4363, www.hotel haciendamerida.com.*

An elegant art deco townhouse in the Centro Histórico, complete with pool, spa and parking. Boutique rooms have all modern amenities, artistic and tasteful furnishings, and luxurious touches such as Egyptian cotton sheets.

### $$$$ Hacienda Xcanatún
*Carretera Mérida–Progreso Km 12, 10 mins out of town, T999-930 2140, www.xcanatun.com.*
A very elegant and carefully restored former henequen hacienda. They boast 18 sumptuous suites, spa facilities and one of the best restaurants in Mérida. Luxurious and romantic.

### $$$$ Rosas & Xocolate Boutique Hotel & Spa
*Paseo de Montejo No 480 and Calle 41, T999-924 2992, www.rosasandxocolate.com.*
A stylish and romantic lodging with smart rooms in shades of pink, superb contemporary decor that echoes the traditional Yucatec style, excellent restaurant, and spa facilities. This boutique hotel would suit couples and hip young things.

### $$$ Los Arcos
*Calle 66 No 448-B, between Calle 53 and 49, T999-926 0145, www.losarcosmerida.com.*
Classically elegant, Los Arcos is a 19th-century colonial house converted to an intimate B&B. It has rooms with high ceilings, fantastic displays of folk art and antiques, swimming pool and verdant garden. Friendly, personable service.

### $$$ Medio Mundo
*Calle 55 No 533 between Calle 64 and 66, T999-924 5472, www.hotelmediomundo.com.*
Renovated old home now a charming classically Yucatec hotel with 12 tasteful, high-ceiling rooms, lush garden patio and pool. Friendly, pleasant and quaint. Nice handicraft shop forms part of the hotel.

### $$$-$$ Julamis
*Calle 53 No 475B and Calle 54, T999-924 1818, www.hoteljulamis.com.*

An award-winning B&B with stylish high-ceilinged rooms and a superb rooftop terrace, great for sipping tequila after dusk. Owner, Alex, is Swiss and a good host. A generous breakfast is included in the rates.

### $$$-$$ Luz en Yucatán
*Calle 55 No 499, between Calle 60 and 58, T999-924 0035, www.luzenyucatan.com.*
A very welcoming, relaxed and slightly quirky 'urban retreat' with a range of comfortable rooms, studios and apartments. All have a contemporary look and good furnishings, including fridge. Outside, there's a pool and chilled-out garden. Interestingly, nightly rates vary according to your ability to pay, so those of modest means can stay too.

### $$ Casa Alvarez
*Calle 62 No 448 and Calle 53, T999-924 3060, www.casaalvarez guesthouse.com.*
A pleasant, homely little guesthouse with a small pool and comfortable rooms, all well equipped with TV, a/c and other modern amenities. Family-run and friendly.

### $$ Casa Ana
*Calle 52 No 469, T999-924 0005, www.casaana.com.*
A sweet little B&B with 5 rooms (a/c costs extra) and a family atmosphere, tropical garden and a small pool. Homely and quaint.

### $$ Hotel del Pelegrino
*Calle 51 No 488, between Calle 54 and 56, T999 924-3007 www.hoteldelperegrino.com.*
This remodelled colonial house with its original tile work has 14 rooms, all different and very clean, and an outdoor terrace with a jacuzzi that's accessible at all hours. A small, friendly, family-run place, helpful and good value.

### $$ Hotel Santa María
*Calle 55 No 493, between Calle 58 and 56, T923-6512, www.hotelsantamariamerida.com.*
A bit generic and uninspiring, but rooms are spacious, comfortable and fully equipped with cable TV, a/c and hot water. Pleasant lobby and a small pool. Modern and good value.

### $$-$ Trinidad
*Calle 62 No 464 esq 55, T999-923 2033, www.hotelestrinidad.com.*
A bit dishevelled, but irresistibly bohemian. The lightly crumbling courtyard features trees, art work and signs reading "don't feed the possum". Friendly owners, a range of rooms, some much better (and more pricey) than others, the cheapest have shared bathroom. There's a 2nd **Hotel Trinidad** with a pool. Bring mosquito repellent.

### $ Aventura Hotel
*Calle 61 No 580, between Calle 74 and 76, T999-923 4801, www.aventurahotel merida.com.*
Small, simple, basic rooms along a leafy outside corridor, peaceful, 5-min walk from the centre, well-kept and clean, excellent value with a/c, hot water, cable TV and Wi-Fi.

### $ Hostal Zócalo
*On the south of the plaza, T999-930 9562, www.hostalzocalo.com.*
Popular hostel with economical rooms and clean dormitories. There's TV, DVD, kitchen, laundry, chilled-out balconies and sunny terraces, tours and Wi-Fi. Full breakfast buffet included with the private rooms. Friendly management and good location.

### $ Nómadas Youth Hostal
*Calle 62 No 433, end of Calle 51, 5 blocks north of the plaza, T999-924 5223, www.nomadas travel.com.*
A sociable hostel with private rooms and dorms. General services include hot water, full kitchen, drinking water, hammocks, swimming pool and internet. Owner Raúl speaks English and is very helpful. Good value and a great place to meet other travellers. Lots of activities, including salsa, trova music, yoga and cooking classes. Bring mosquito repellent.

---

## Celestún
Most lodgings are along Calle 12.

### $$$$ Hotel Xixim
*Km 10 off the old Sisal Hwy, T988-916 2100, www.hotelxixim.com.*

Tranquil luxury bungalows and suites in a coconut grove on the edge of the beach and the reserve. They offer spa facilities, yoga, bicycles, kayaks, pool, and ecotours to surrounding area including flamingos, turtle nesting, etc.

### $$ Gutiérrez
*Calle 13 s/n, between Calles 12 and 14, T988-916 2609.*

Modest and functional hotel on the beach. Rooms on top floor get ocean views and breezes. Amenities include Wi-Fi, patio and restaurant. Check the room and bed before accepting.

## Progreso and around

### $$ Hotel Quinta Progreso
*Calle 23 No 64-C, between Calles 48 and 50, 600 m from the malecón, T969-934 4414, www.hotelquinta progreso.com.*

A handsome colonial building with beautiful tile work and large, clean, tastefully decorated rooms. Amenities include swimming pool and tea bar. Prices include breakfast. Recommended.

### $ Hostel Progreso
*Calle 21 and 54, T969-103 0294, www.hostelprogreso.com.*

This budget hostel is housed by an impressive 2-storey restored mansion 2 blocks from the *malecón*. It has dorm beds and simple private rooms, shared kitchen, ocean-facing decks, hammocks, and breakfast included.

## Restaurants

There are a number of taco stands, pizzerias and sandwich places in Pasaje Picheta, a small plaza off the Palacio de Gobierno.

### $$$ Casa de Piedra
*Hacienda Xcanatún, Calle 20 s/n, Carretera Mérida–Progreso Km12.*

Live music Fri-Sat. Inside an old machine room with high ceiling, this award-winning restaurant serves French-Yucatec fusion, creative appetizers and mains, local seafood

and meat. The place for a very romantic dinner or special occasion.

### $$$ La Recova
*Paseo de Montejo No 382, T999-944 0215, www.larecovamerida.com.*

A popular Argentine steakhouse serving all certified 'Aberdeen Angus' and Kobe beef, huge cuts of meat, burgers and seafood. Modern and elegant interior, smart-casual and often busy. A good stock of wine.

### $$$ Rosas and Xcolate
*Paseo de Montejo No 480 and Calle 41, T999-924 2992, www.rosasandxocolate.com.*

The place for a romantic candlelit dinner. They serve fusion cuisine by chef David Segovia, including courgette salad, catch of the day and chocolate tart, among other treats. Try the 6-course taster menu. Elegant, creative and interesting.

### $$$ Trotter's
*Circuito Colonias, between Paseo Montejo and Calle 60 Norte, www.trottersmerida.com.*

Stylish steakhouse with a good wine list and a mouth-watering array of Angus steaks, fresh fish and tapas. Includes a smart wine bar and great ambience in the romantic garden. Classy place, sophisticated. Take a taxi.

### $$$-$$ Bistro Rescoldos
*Calle 62 No 366, between Calles 41 and 43, T999-286 1028, www.rescoldosbistro.com.*

Bistro Rescoldos, meaning 'burning embers', serves flavourful Italian and Greek cuisine with love, including falafels, hummus, tzatziki, calzones and wood-fired pizzas. Lovely outdoor patio, wonderful atmosphere. Recommended.

### $$$-$$ Chile Habanero
*Calle 60 No 483B, www.elchilehabanero restaurante.com.*

Good clean place with attentive staff, pleasant evening atmosphere and art work on the walls. Recommended for its Yucatec specialities, including *pollo pibil* and a good sample platter *delicias de Yucatán*. Pizzas look good; they also do hamburgers.

### $$$-$$ La Chaya
*Calle 62 and 57, www.lachayamaya.com.*
A famous and massively popular restaurant
specializing in Yucatec dishes such as *poc
chuc* and *pollo pibil*. Tortillas are prepared
in front of diners and waitresses wear
traditional clothes. Often busy and buzzing
with locals and fun. Another branch on
Calle 55, between Calles 60 and 62, is a larger
and more atmospheric building with antique
carriage, often serving big tour groups.

### $$ Amaro
*Calle 59 No 507 between Calle 60 and 62,
near the plaza. Open late daily.*
Good vegetarian food served in an open
courtyard and covered patio. Try *chaya* drink
from the leaf of the *chaya* tree; their curry,
avocado pizza and home-made bread are
also very good.

### $$ El Nuevo Tucho
*Calle 60 near University.*
Local dishes, mostly meat and fish, and an
extensive drinks menu. A rousing locals'
joint, good fun place in the evenings, often
with live music. Give it a go.

### $$ Manjar Blanco
*Calle 47 between Calles 58 and 60.*
A very pleasant family-run restaurant with
a smart, clean interior. Friendly service,
Yucatec specialities and 'grandmother's
authentic recipes'.

### $$ Pizzeria Raffaello
*Calle 60 440A.*
Italian-style thin-crust pizzas, many to
choose from, stone-baked in an oven
outside. There's seating in the garden
or casual dining indoors. Relaxed place,
friendly owner, good service and pizzas.

### $ Cafetería Pop
*Calle 57, between 60 and 62.*
Low-key café attached to a hotel, they serve
Mexican staples and international fare,
breakfast, lunch and dinner. The *pollo con
mole poblano* (chicken in chocolate and chilli
sauce) is good. Clean and casual.

### $ El Trapiche
*Calle 62 half a block north of the plaza.*
Sizzling spit of meat outside, hearty specials
at lunchtime and economical grub à la
carte. Staff are very friendly. Reasonable and
cheap food, usually good. Sometimes a fun
atmosphere in the evenings. Unpretentious.

### $ Marlín Azul
*Calle 62, between Calle 57 and 59.*
Looks like a grotty hole in the wall, but
there's an a/c section next door. Amazing
fresh seafood, including fileted catch of the
day and ceviche, very simple and delicious,
completely local. Recommended for a quick,
casual lunch.

### $ Mérida
*Calle 62 between Calle 59 and 61.*
This economical restaurant has been in
Mérida for at least 10 years, always cheap
and reliable, and now with an attractive
remodelled interior and smartly attired
waiters. Breakfast and lunch specials are
popular with local office workers. They serve
simple Yucatec and Mexican food, not bad.

## Cafés and ice cream parlours

### Café Chocolate
*Calle 60 No 442 y Calle 49, T999-928 5113,
www.cafe-chocolate.com.mx.*
In addition to coffee, this café and art space
does good *mole*, an economical breakfast
buffet, a lunchtime menu and evening
meals. Cosy and bohemian, free Wi-Fi, sofas
indoors or outdoor courtyard seating.

### Café El Hoyo
*Calle 62, between Calle 57 and 59.*
Chilled-out tea house serving refreshing
fruit and herbal infusions, coffee too, good
sandwiches. Literature, board games.

### El Colón Sorbetes y Dulces Finos
*Calle 61 and 60, on the plaza.*
Serving ice cream since 1907, great sorbets,
*meringue*, good menu with explanation of
fruits in English. About 30 different flavours
of delicious ice cream.

### Celestún

Many beachside restaurants along Calle 12, but be careful of food in the cheaper ones; recommended is **La Playita**, for simple fried fish, seafood cocktails. Food stalls along Calle 11 beside the bus station should be approached with caution.

**$ Chivirico**
*Across the road from La Playita.*
Offers descent fish, shrimp and other seafood.

**$$ El Lobo**
*Calle 10 and 13, on the corner of the main square.*
Best spot for breakfast, with fruit salads, yoghurt, pancakes, etc. Celestún's best pizza in the evenings.

### Progreso and around

The Malecón at Progreso is lined with seafood restaurants, some with tables on the beach. For cheaper restaurants, head for the centre of town, near the bus terminal.

**$$ Flamingo's**
*Calle 69 No 144-D and Calle 72.*
Overlooking the ocean, Flamingo's serves wholesome fresh seafood, including fillets and coconut shrimp, standard Yucatec fare and good hot sauce. Strolling musicians may serenade you.

**$$-$ Las Palmas and El Cocalito**
2 of several reasonable fish restaurants in Chelem.

## Bars and clubs

See also the free listings magazine *Yucatán Today*.

### Cantina La Negrita
*Calle 62 and 49 No 415.*
Neighbourhood bohemian bar with lots of history, founded 1918. Buzzing, good crowd, fun vibe. Drinking up front, hearty food available out back. Modern and young, not a *cantina* in the traditional sense. Recommended.

### Hennessy's Irish Pub
*Paseo Montejo No 486-A, between 41 and 43.*
Remarkably authentic Irish pub in a fantastic building on the Paseo Montejo, a social hub for the city's expatriates. Good cold beer, expensive food.

### Mayan Pub
*Calle 62, between Calles 55 and 57, www. mayanpub.com. Wed-Sun 0700-0300.*
Superb outdoor colonial patio with ambient lighting, live music, jam sessions, Banksy wall art, beer, tequila, happy hours, snacks.

## Entertainment

See the free listings magazine *Yucatán Today*.

### Cinema
There is a cinema showing subtitled films in English on Parque Hidalgo.

**Teatro Mérida** (Calle 62 between 59 and 61), shows European, Mexican and independent movies as well as live theatre productions. The 14-screen multiplex **Cinépolis** is in the huge Plaza de las Américas, north of the city; colectivo and buses take 20 mins and leave from Calle 65 between 58 and 60. For art house films, head to the intimate **Cairo Cinema Café** (Calle 20 No. 98A between Calles 15 and 17, Col Itzimná (take a taxi), www.cairocinemacafe.com).

### Theatre
There are many fine playhouses in Mérida, including:
**Teatro Peón Contreras**, *Calle 60 with 57.* One of the most beautiful theatres in Mexico, showing plays, ballet and orchestral performances. Shows start at 2100. For the latest programme, see www.merida.gob.mx/cultura.

## Festivals

The city lays on a weekly programme of free cultural events. On Mon at 2100, there is a *vaquería*, with traditional Yucatec dancing, outside the Palacio Municipal; Tue at 2030, big band music in Parque de Santiago; Wed at 2100, a concert in the Centro Cultural Olimpio; Thu at 2100, Yucatec music, dance and song in the Parque Santa Lucía; Fri, usually an event in the University building, but not always; Sat at 2100, the 'Heart of Mérida' festival on the plaza and Calle 60; Sun, the central streets are closed to traffic, the plaza comes alive with music, performances and stalls.

**6 Jan** Mérida celebrates its birthday.
**Feb/Mar** **Carnival** takes place the week before Ash Wed (best on Sat). Floats, dancers in regional costume, music and dancing around the plaza and children dressed in animal suits.

Shopping

### Crafts and souvenirs

You'll find an abundance of craft shops in the streets around the plaza. They sell hammocks (see box, page 105), silver jewellery, Panama hats, *guayabera* shirts, *huaraches*, baskets and Mayan figurines. The salesmen are ruthless, but they expect to receive about half their original asking price. Bargain hard, but maintain good humour, patience and face. And watch out for the many touts around the plaza, using all sorts of ingenious ploys to get you to their shops (and away from their competitors).

There are 2 main craft markets in the city: the **Mercado Municipal** (Calle 56a and 67) and the **García Rejón Bazaar** (Calle 65 and 60). The former sprawls, smells and takes over several blocks, but it's undeniably alive and undeniably Mexican. It sells everything under the sun and is also good for a cheap, tasty meal, but check the stalls for cleanliness. The latter is excellent for handicrafts and renowned for clothing, particularly leather *huaraches* and good-value cowboy boots – good, cheap Yucatecan fare. The state-sponsored **Casa de las Artesanías** (www.artesanias. yucatan.gob.mx), has several branches around the Yucatán, including **Tienda**

**Matriz** (Calle 63 between Calle 64 and 66), and **Tienda Montejo** (Av Paseo de Montejo, opposite the Palacio Cantón); they sell everything from hammocks to *huipiles*, all made in the Yucatán, and provide social and economic programmes to support local artistic talent. For something special, **Artesanaria** (Calle 60 No 480 and Calle 55), deals in high-quality work.

If you're looking for a hammock, several places are recommended, but shop around for the best deal (also see box, page 105). **El Mayab** (Calle 58 No 553 and 71), are friendly, have a limited choice but good deals available; **La Poblana** (Calle 65 between Calle 58 and 60), will bargain, especially for sales of more than 1 – they have a huge stock. **El Aguacate** (Calle 58 No 604, corner of Calle 73), good hammocks and no hard sell. Recommended. **Casa de Artesanías Ki-Huic** (Calle 63, between Calle 62 and 64), is a friendly store with all sorts of handicrafts from silver and wooden masks, to hammocks and batik. Shop owner Julio Chay is very knowledgeable and friendly, sometimes organizes trips for visitors to his village, **Tixkokob** (daily, 0900-2100), which specializes in hammocks. Julio can also organize trips to other nearby villages and the shop has tequilas for sampling.

For silver, there are a handful of stores on Calle 60, just north of the plaza.

Mexican folk art, including *calaveras* (Day of the Dead skeletons), is available from **Minaturas** (Calle 59 No 507A); and **Yalat** (Calle 39 and 40).

If you're in the market for a *guayabera* shirt, you'll find stores all over the city, particularly on Calle 62, between 57 and 61.

What to do

### Language schools
**Centro de Idiomas del Sureste**, *Calle 52 No 455, between 49 and 51, T999-923 0954, www.cisyucatan.com.mx*. A well-established Spanish school offering tried and tested language and cultural programmes.

**Modern Spanish Institute**, *Calle 15, No 500B, between 16A and 18, T999-911 0790, www. modernspanish.com*. Courses in Spanish, Mayan culture, homestays.

## Tour operators

Most tour operators can arrange trips to popular local destinations including Chichén Itzá, Uxmal, Celestún and nearby *cenotes*. **Carmen Travel Services**, *Calle 27 No 151, between 32 and 34, T999-927 2027, www. carmentravel.com*. 3 other branches. This well-established agency can organize flights, hotels and all the usual trips to the sights. Recommended.

**Ecoturismo Yucatán**, *Calle 3 No 235, between Calle 32A and 34, T999-920 2772, www.ecoyuc.com.mx*. Specializes in educational and ecotourism tours including jungle trips, birding expeditions and turtle-hatching tours. Also offers adventure and archaeological packages.

**Mayan Ecotours**, *Calle 51 No 488 between Calles 54 and 56, T999-987 3710, www.mayan ecotours.com*. An adventure and ecotourism operator offering high-quality tailor-made tours focussed on a variety of adrenalin-charged activities including rappelling, kayaking and mountain biking. They also offer trips to haciendas, archaeological sites and little-known *cenotes*.

## Transport

### Air

The airport is 8 km from the city. Bus 79 takes you to the centre; taxis to the centre charge US$12.

From Calle 67, 69 and 60, bus 79 goes to the airport, **Aeropuerto Rejón (MID)**, T999-946 1530, marked 'Aviación', US$0.50, roughly every 20 mins. Taxi set price voucher system US$8; colectivo US$2.50. Good domestic flight connections. International flight connections with **Belize City**, **Houston**, **Miami**, San José (Costa Rica), Orlando and **Havana**. Package tours Mérida–Havana–Mérida available (be sure

to have a confirmed return flight). For return to Mexico ask for details at Secretaría de Migración Av Colón and Calle 8.

### Bus

All buses from outside Yucatán State arrive at the CAME terminal on Calle 70 between Calle 69 and 71, several blocks south of the centre. There is a 2nd-class bus terminal, **TAME**, around the corner on Calle 69, where buses from local destinations such as Uxmal arrive.

There are several bus terminals in Mérida, as well as various *combis* for some local destinations (often more rapid).

The 1st-class bus station, **Terminal CAME**, Calle 70, between Calles 69 and 71, serves major destinations in Mexico and Yucatán State. Bus companies include **ADO**, **ADO GL**, **UNO**, **Platino** and **OCC**. The station has lockers and is open 24 hrs; left luggage charges from around US$0.50 per bag, depending on size. The walk to the centre is about 20 mins, taxi US$2.50. Schedules change frequently.

To **Cancún**, hourly, 4 hrs, US$24. To **Campeche**, hourly, 2 hrs, US$14. To **Chichén Itzá** (ruins and Pisté), 0630, 0915, 1240, 2 hrs, US$9; more frequent services from the 2nd-class Terminal TAME. To **Palenque**, 0830, 1915, 2200, 2300, 8 hrs, US$37. To **Tulum**, 1040, 1240, 1740, 2340, 4-5 hrs, US$20. To **Valladolid**, every 1-2 hrs, 1½ hrs, US$13. To **Villahermosa**, every 1-2 hrs, 9 hrs, US$43; and several ADO GL services, US$52. To **Tuxtla Guitérrez**, 5 daily with OCC and ADO GL, US$57-79. To **San Cristóbal de las Casas**, 1 daily with OCC, 1915, 15-16 hrs, US$52.

There are also 1st-class departures from the Hotel Fiesta Americana, Calle 60 and Colón, which are mostly 'luxury' services to **Cancún**.

Around the corner from CAME, the main 2nd-class bus station, **TAME Terminal**, Calle 69 between Calles 68 and 70, mostly serves destinations in the Yucatán Peninsula, including Uxmal, Chichén Itzá and the Ruta

Puuc. Bus companies include **OCC**, **Mayab**, **Sur**, **FTS**, **Oriente** and **TRT**.

To **Cancún**, frequent departures, 5 hrs, US$15. To **Chichén Itzá**, hourly, 2-3 hrs, US$5.50. To **Ruta Puuc**, 2nd-class **ATS** service, Sun 0800, US$14. To **Uxmal**, 2nd-class **SUR** services at 0600, 0905, 1040, 1205, 1705, 1½ hrs, US$3.50. To **Valladolid**, hourly, 2 hrs, US$7.50

There is another 2nd-class terminal, **Terminal del Noreste**, near the market at Calle 50 and 65. It deals with obscure local destinations, including villages on the convent route, 11 departures daily, including **Acanceh**, **Tekit**, **Tecoh**, **Mamá**, **Chumayel**, **Teabo**, **Tipikal**, **Mani** and **Oxckutzcab**, US$1.25-3.60. To **Celestún**, frequent 2nd-class **Oriente** services, 2 hrs, US$3.50.

Buses to **Progreso** depart every 15 mins, US$1.25, from their own Autoprogreso terminal at Calle 62 No 524, between 65 and 67. For **Izamal**, it is fastest to use the *combis* that depart from Calles 65 and 54, 1 hr, US$3.50.

**To Guatemala** Take a bus from Mérida to San Cristóbal and change there for Comitán, or to Tenosique for the route to Flores. Another alternative would be to take the bus from Mérida direct to Tuxtla Gutiérrez (times given above), then connect to Ciudad Cuauhtémoc or to Tapachula.

**To Belize** Take a bus to **Chetumal**, **ADO** services at 0730 (except Wed and Sat), 1300, 1800, 2300, 6 hrs, US$30.50 and cross the border.

### Car
**Car hire** Car reservations should be booked well in advance if possible. Hire firms charge around US$45-50 a day although bargains can be found in low season. All agencies allow vehicles to be returned to Cancún for an extra charge, and most have an office at the airport where they share the same counter and negotiating usually takes place. Agencies include: **Budget**, at the airport, T999-946 0762; **Easy Way Car Rental**, Calle 60, between 55 and 57, T999-930 9021, www.easywayrentacar-yucatan.

com; **Mexico Rent a Car**, Calle 57A Depto 12, between 58 and 60, T999-923 3637, mexicorentacar@hotmail.com.

### Taxi
Both fixed-priced and metered taxis are available. Metered taxis are identified by a 'Taximetro' sign on the roof; if using an unmetered taxi, always arrange the price beforehand. Most fares start at US$3.

There are various *sitio* stands, including **Sitio Santa Ana**, Calle 47 between Calle 58 and 60, T999-928 5000, www.taxiyturismo. com. Sample fares from downtown to Terminal CAME, US$4; to Gran Museo del Mundo Maya, US$5.50; to airport, US$11.50, to Hacienda Xcanatún, US$11.50; to Dzibilchaltún, US$15.

## Celestún
### Bus
Buses leave every 1-2 hrs from the local bus station on Calle 65 between 50 and 52, in **Mérida**, 2-hr journey, 2nd class US$3.50.

## Progreso and around
### Boat
Boats can be hired to visit the reef of **Los Alacranes** where many ancient wrecks are visible in clear water.

### Bus
Buses from **Mérida** leave from the terminal on Calle 62 between 67 and 65, next to Hotel La Paz, every 10 mins. US$1.25. Returns every 10 mins until 2200.

## Dzibilchaltún
### Bus
5 direct buses a day on weekdays, from Parque San Juan, marked 'Tour/Ruta Polígono'; returns from the site entrance on the hour, passing the junction 15 mins later, taking 45 mins from the junction to **Mérida** (US$1).

**Shuttles** Leave from Parque San Juan in Mérida, corner of Calle 62 y 67A, every 1 or 2 hrs between 0500 and 1900.

For this route it's best to be on the road by 0800 with a full fuel tank. It's possible to explore the route using public transport (departures from the Noreste terminal on Calle 50), but keep an eye on the clock (few or no buses after dark) and consider overnighting in Ticul or Oxkutzcab. If driving, get on the Periférico to Ruta 18 (signs say Kanasín, not Ruta 18).

At **Kanasín**, La Susana is known especially for local delicacies like *sopa de lima*, *salbutes* and *panuchos*; it's clean, and there is excellent service and abundant helpings at reasonable prices. Follow the signs to **Acanceh**. Here you will see the unusual combination of the Grand Pyramid, a colonial church and a modern church, all on the same small plaza (similar to the Plaza de las Tres Culturas in Tlatelolco, Mexico City). About four blocks away is the Temple of the Stuccoes, with hieroglyphs. Eight kilometres further south is **Tecoh**, with an ornate church and convent dedicated to the Virgin of the Assumption. There are some impressive carved stones around the altar. The church and convent both stand at the base of a large Mayan pyramid. Nearby are the caverns of **Dzab-Náh**; you must take a guide as there are treacherous drops into *cenotes*. Next on the route is **Telchaquillo**, a small village with an austere chapel and a beautiful *cenote* in the plaza, with carved steps for easy access.

### Mayapán and around
*US$2.70.*

A few kilometres off the main road to the right (west) you will find the Mayan ruins of Mayapán, a walled city with 4000 mounds, six of which are in varying stages of restoration. Mayapán, along with Uxmal and Chichén Itzá, once formed a triple alliance, and the site is as big as Chichén Itzá, with some buildings being replicas of those at the latter site. The restoration process is ongoing; the archaeologists can be watched as they unearth more and more buildings of this large, peaceful, late-Maya site. Mayapán is easily visited by bus from Mérida (every 30 minutes from terminal at Calle 50 y 67 behind the municipal market, one hour, US$1 to Telchaquillo). It can also be reached from Oxcutzcab.

Some 30 km along the main road is **Tekit**, a large village containing the church of San Antonio de Padua, with many ornate statues of saints. The next village, 7 km further on, is called **Mama**, with the oldest church on the route, famous for its ornate altar and bell-domed roof. Another 9 km is **Chumayel**, where the legendary Mayan document *Chilam Balam* was found. Four kilometres ahead is **Teabo**, with an impressive 17th-century church. Next comes **Tipikal**, a small village with an austere church.

### Maní

Twelve kilometres further on is Maní, the most important stop on this route. Here you will find a large church, convent and museum with explanations in English, Spanish and one of the Mayan languages. It was here that Fray Diego de Landa ordered important Mayan documents and artefacts to be burned, during an intense period of Franciscan conversion of the Maya people to Christianity. When Diego realized his great error, he set about trying to write down all he could remember of the 27 scrolls and hieroglyphs he had destroyed, along with 5000 idols, 13 altars and 127 vases. The text, entitled *Relation of Things in Yucatán*, is still available today, unlike the artefacts. To return to Mérida, head for Ticul, to the west, then follow the main road via Muná.

## Ticul and Oxkutzcab

Eighty kilometres south of Mérida, Ticul is a small, pleasant little village known for its *huipiles*, the embroidered white dresses worn by the older Maya women. You can buy them in the tourist shops in Mérida, but the prices and quality of the ones in Ticul will be much better. It is also a good base for visiting smaller sites in the south of Yucatán State, such as Sayil, Kabah, Xlapak and Labná (see page 158).

Sixteen kilometres southeast of Ticul is **Oxkutzcab**, a good centre for catching buses to Chetumal, Muná, Mayapán and Mérida. It's a friendly place with a market by the plaza and a church with a 'two-dimensional' façade on the other side of the square.

## Grutas de Loltún and around

*Tue-Sun 0930, 1100, 1230 and 1400. US$8 Guided tours are at 0930, 1100, 1230, 1400, 1500, 1600; please tip generously.*

Nearby, to the south, are the caverns and pre-Columbian vestiges at Loltún (supposedly extending for 8 km). Take a pickup (US$0.30) or truck from the market going to Cooperativa (an agricultural town). For return, flag down a passing truck. Alternatively, take a taxi, US$10 (can be visited from Labná on a tour from Mérida). The area around Ticul and Oxkutzcab is intensively farmed with citrus fruits, papayas and mangoes. After Oxkutzcab on Route 184 is **Tekax** with restaurant **La Ermita** serving excellent Yucatecan dishes at reasonable prices. From Tekax a paved road leads to the ruins of **Chacmultún**. From the top you have a beautiful view. There is a caretaker. All the towns between Muná and Peto, 14 km northeast of Oxkutzcab off Route 184, have large old churches. Beyond the Peto turn-off the scenery is scrub and swamp as far as the Belizean border.

## Listings The Convent Route

### Where to stay

#### Ticul

**$$-$ Posada El Jardín**
*Calle 27 No 216c, between Calles 28 and 30, T997-972 0401, www.posadajardin.com.*
Sweet little guesthouse with a handful of simple, economical, brightly painted rooms, a verdant garden, relaxing patios and a pool. Charming hosts.

#### Oxkutzcab

**$$-$ Hotel Puuc**
*Calle 55 No 80 and Calle 40, 997-975 0103 www.hotelpuuc.com.mx.*
Convenient, functional and modest motel-style lodgings, but very clean and comfortable. There's a splendid pool, a restaurant and parking. Rooms are cheaper without a/c.

### Restaurants

#### Ticul

**$$$-$$ Tutul-Xiu**
*Calle 29 No 191, between Calles 20 and 22.*
Good-quality Yucatec and Mexican cuisine, including *poc chuc*, *queso relleno* and a host of turkey dishes, served by waitresses in traditional Yucatec dress. Also branches in Oxkutzcab, Maní and Mérida.

**$$ Pizzería La Góndola**
*Calle 23, Ticul.*
Good, moderately priced pizzas.

### Transport

#### Ticul and Oxkutzcab
**Colectivo**
There are frequent VW colectivos to Ticul from Parque San Juan, **Mérida**, US$3.

Taking in the four sites of Kabah, Sayil, Xlapak and Labná, as well as Uxmal, this journey explores the hilly (or *puuc* in Maya) region to the south of Mérida. All five sites can be visited in a day on the 'Ruta Puuc' bus, which departs from the first-class bus station in Mérida on Sunday at 0800, US$14, entry to sites not included, returns from Uxmal to Mérida at 1500. This is a good whistle-stop tour, but does not give you much time at each of the ruins, although five sites in one day is normally enough for most enthusiasts; if you want to spend longer seeing these sites, stay overnight in Ticul.

### Kabah
*0800-1700, US$3.25.*

On either side of the main road, 37 km south of Uxmal and often included in tours of the latter, are the ruins of Kabah. On one side there is a fascinating **Palace of Masks** (*Codz-Poop*), whose façade bears the image of Chac, mesmerically repeated 260 times, the number of days in the Almanac Year. Each mask is made up of 30 units of mosaic stone. Even the central chamber is entered via a huge Chac mask whose curling snout forms the doorstep. On the other side of this wall, beneath the figure of the ruler, Kabal, are impressive carvings on the door arches, which depict a man about to be killed, pleading for mercy, and two men duelling. This side of the road is mostly reconstructed; across the road the outstanding feature is a reconstructed arch marking the start of the *sacbé* (sacred road), which leads all the way to Uxmal, and several stabilized but impossible to climb mounds of collapsed buildings being renovated. The style is Classic Puuc.

### Sayil, Xlapak and Labná
*Entrance US$3.25 at each site.*

**Sayil** means 'The Place of the Ants'. Dating from AD 800-1000, this site has an interesting palace, which in its day included 90 bathrooms for some 350 people. The simple, elegant colonnade is reminiscent of the architecture of ancient Greece. The central motif on the upper part of the façade is a broad mask with huge fangs, flanked by two serpents surrounding the grotesque figure of a descending deity. From the upper level of the palace you can see a tiny ruin on the side of a mountain called the Nine Masks.

Some 13 km from Sayil, the ruins of **Xlapak** have not been as extensively restored as the others in this region. There are 14 mounds and three partially restored pyramids.

**Labná** has a feature that ranks it among the most outstanding sites of the Puuc region: a monumental arch connecting two groups of buildings (now in ruins), which displays an architectural concept unique to this region. Most Mayan arches are purely structural, but the one at Labná has been constructed for aesthetic purposes, running right through the façade and clearly meant to be seen from afar. The two façades on either side of the arch differ greatly; the one at the entrance is beautifully decorated with delicate latticework and stone carving imitating the wood or palm-frond roofs of Mayan huts.

### Uxmal
*Daily 0800-1700, US$14 including light and sound show; rental of translation equipment US$3. Shows are at 2000 in summer and 1900 in winter. Mixed reports. Guides available with 1½-hr*

*tours. Tours in Spanish US$40, in English, French, German and Italian US$45. For transport to Uxmal, see Transport, below.*

Built during the Classic period, Uxmal is the most famous of the ruins in the Puuc region. The characteristic features of Mayan cities in this region are the quadrangular layout of the buildings, set on raised platforms, and an artificially created underground water-storage system. The **Pyramid of the Sorcerer** is an unusual oval-shaped pyramid set on a large rectangular base; there is evidence that five stages of building were used in its construction. The pyramid is 30 m tall, with two temples at the top. The **Nunnery** is set around a large courtyard, with some fine masks of Chac, the rain god, on the corners of the buildings. The east building of the Nunnery is decorated with double-headed serpents on its cornices. There are some plumed serpents in relief, in excellent condition, on the façade of the west building.

The **House of the Governor** is 100 m long, and is considered one of the most outstanding buildings in all of Mesoamerica. Two arched passages divide the building into three distinct sections that would probably have been covered over. Above the central entrance is an elaborate trapezoidal motif, with a string of Chaac masks interwoven into a flowing, undulating serpent-like shape extending to the façade's two corners. The stately two-headed jaguar throne in front of the structure suggests a royal or administrative function.

The **House of the Turtles** is sober by comparison, its simple walls adorned with carved turtles on the upper cornice, above a short row of tightly packed columns, which resemble the Mayan *palapas*, made of sticks with a thatched roof, still used today. The **House of the Doves** is the oldest and most damaged of the buildings at Uxmal. It is still impressive: a long, low platform of wide columns topped by clusters of roof combs, whose similarity to dovecotes gave the building its name.

## Listings The Puuc Route

### Where to stay

#### Uxmal
There is no village at Uxmal, just some high end hotels. For cheap accommodation, go to Ticul, 28 km away (see above) or to Santa Elena, 10 mins from the ruins by car.

**$$$$ The Lodge at Uxmal**
*30 m from the entrance to ruins, T997-976 2102, www.mayaland.com/lodgeuxmal.*
Luxurious Mayan-style *casitas* with tasteful wood furniture. Facilities include pool, restaurants, and spa. The same owners operate the comfortable **Hacienda Uxmal** ($$$), 400 m from the ruins (see website for more).

**$$$-$$ The Fly-catcher Inn**
*Near the corner of Highway 261 and Calle 20, Santa Elena, T997-978 5350, www.flycatcherinn.com.*

Pleasant B&B with verdant grounds and clean, comfortable rooms and *casitas* with a/c and screened windows. Prices include full breakfast.

**$$ The Pickled Onion B&B**
*Highway 261 Uxmal–Kabah, Santa Elena, T997-111 7922, www.thepickledonion yucatan.com.*
Friendly and helpful B&B with quaint Mayan-style accommodation, leafy garden and a pool. Rooms are simple, clean, comfortable and pleasant. Reiki and massage are available, there's Wi-Fi in public areas and a continental breakfast is included.

**$$-$ Sacbé Bungalows**
*Highway 261 Km 159, Santa Elena, T997-978 5158, www.sacbebungalows.com.mx.*
Set in 3 ha of verdant grounds, Sacbé Bungalows offers 8 simple, comfortable,

clean, quiet and shaded bungalows. There's Wi-Fi and a pool.

## Transport

### Uxmal
**Bus**

5 buses a day from **Mérida**, from the terminal on Calle 69 between Calle 68 and 70, US$4. Return buses run every 2 hrs, or go to the entrance to the site on the main road and wait for a colectivo, which will take you to Muná for US$0.50. From there, many buses (US$1.70) and colectivos (US$1.40) go to Mérida.

**Car**

Parking at the site costs US$1 for the whole day. Uxmal is 74 km from **Mérida**, 177 km from **Campeche**, by a good paved road. If going by car from Mérida, there is a circular road round the city: follow the signs to Campeche, then 'Campeche via ruinas', then to 'Muná via Yaxcopoil' (long stretch of road with no signposting). Muná–Yaxcopoil is about 34 km. Parking US$1.

## Izamal and around   *Colour map 1, A2.*

**a friendly little town with a vast convent and important Mayan ruins**

Some 68 km east of Mérida is Izamal. Once a major Classic Maya religious site founded by the priest Itzamná, Izamal became one of the centres of the Spanish attempt to convert the Maya to Christianity.

Fray Diego de Landa, the historian of the Spanish conquest of Mérida (of whom there is a statue in the town), founded the huge **convent** and **church**, which now face the main **Plaza de la Constitución**. This building, constructed on top of a Mayan pyramid, was begun in 1549 and has the second largest atrium in the world. If you carefully examine the walls that surround the magnificent atrium, you will notice that some of the faced stones are embellished with carvings of Mayan origin, confirming that, when they had toppled the pre-Columbian structures, the Spaniards re-used the material to create the imported architecture. There is also a throne built for the Pope's visit in 1993. The image of the Inmaculada Virgen de la Concepción in the magnificent church was made the Reina de Yucatán in 1949, and the patron saint of the state in 1970.

Just 2½ blocks away, visible from the convent across a second square and signposted, are the ruins of a great mausoleum known as the **Kinich-Kakmo pyramid** ① *0800-1700, free, entrance next to the tortilla factory*. You climb the first set of stairs to a broad, tree-covered platform, at the end of which is a further pyramid (still under reconstruction). From the top there is an excellent view of the town and surrounding henequen and citrus plantations. Kinich-Kakmo is 195 m long, 173 m wide and 36 m high, the fifth highest in Mexico.

In all, 20 Mayan structures have been identified in Izamal, several on Calle 27. Another startling feature about the town is that the entire colonial centre, including the convent, the arcaded government offices on Plaza de la Constitución and the arcaded second square, is painted a rich yellow ochre, giving it the nickname of the 'golden city'.

From Izamal you can go by bus to **Cenotillo**, where there are several fine *cenotes* within easy walking distance from the town (avoid the one in town), especially **Ucil**, excellent for swimming, and **La Unión**. Take the same bus as for Izamal from Mérida. Past Cenotillo is Espita and then a road forks left to Tizimín (see page 167).

The cemetery of **Hoctún**, on the Mérida–Chichén road, is also worth visiting; indeed it is impossible to miss, there is an 'Empire State Building' on the site. Take a bus from Mérida (last bus back 1700) to see extensive ruins at **Aké**, an unusual structure. Public transport in Mérida is difficult: from an unsigned stop on the corner of Calle 53 y 50, some buses to Tixkokob and Ekmul continue to Aké; ask the driver.

## Listings Izamal

### Where to stay

**$$ Macan Ché**
*Calle 22 No 305 between Calle 33 and 35,*
*T988-954 0287, www.macanche.com.*
Intimate and friendly B&B with a lush tropical garden setting, pool, restaurant and hammocks. They offer comfortable rooms and *casitas*, all uniquely decorated. Recommended.

### Restaurants

There are several restaurants on Plaza de la Constitución.

**$$$-$$ Kinich**
*Calle 27 No 299 between Calle 28 and 30,*
*www.kinichizamal.com.*
Kinich serves very good Mexican and Yucatec cuisine in an open-air colonial courtyard. Rustic ambience and good service. It's located near the ruins of the same name.

**$$-$ Los Arcos**
*Calle 28, between Calles 31 and 34,*
*opposite Parque Zamná.*
Simple and reasonably priced little eatery on the plaza serving wholesome tacos, quesadillas and other Mexican fare. Wi-Fi, breakfast and coffee too.

### Shopping

**Hecho a mano**, *Calle 31A No 308 between 36 and 38*. A fine collection of Mexican folk art, postcards, textiles, jewellery, papier-mâché masks.
**Market**, *Calle 31, on Plaza de la Constitución, opposite convent*. Closes soon after lunch.

### Transport

**Bus**
Bus station is on Calle 32 behind government offices, can leave bags, but better to take the *combi*, every 30 mins, US$4. 2nd class to **Mérida**, every 45 mins, 1½ hrs, US$1.50, lovely countryside. 6 a day to/from **Valladolid** (96 km), about 2 hrs, US$2.30-3.

## Chichén Itzá  *Colour map 1, A2.*

**one of the most spectacular Mayan sites**

★Chichén Itzá means 'mouth of the well of the water-sorcerer'. The Castillo, a giant-stepped pyramid, overlooks the site, watched over by Chacmool, a Maya fertility god who reclines on a nearby structure. The city was built by the Maya in late Classic times (AD 600-900). By the end of the 10th century, the city was more or less abandoned. It was re-established in the 11th to 12th centuries, but much debate surrounds by whom. Whoever the people were, a comparison of some of the architecture with that of Tula, north of Mexico City, indicates they were heavily influenced by the Toltecs of Central Mexico.

The major buildings in the north half display a Toltec influence. Dominating them is **El Castillo** ① *1100-1500, 1600-1700, closed if raining*, its top decorated by the symbol of Quetzalcoatl/Kukulcán, the plumed serpent god. The balustrade of the 91 stairs up each of the four sides is also decorated at its base by the head of a plumed, open-mouthed serpent. The interior ascent of 61 steep and narrow steps leading to a chamber is currently closed; the red-painted jaguar that probably served as the throne of the high priest once burned bright, its eyes of jade, its fangs of flint.

There is a **ball court** with grandstand and towering walls, each set with a projecting ring of stone high up; at eye-level is a relief showing the decapitation of the winning captain (sacrifice was an honour; some theories, however, maintain that it was the losing captain who was killed). El Castillo stands at the centre of the northern half of the site, and almost at a right angle to its northern face runs the *sacbé* (sacred road), to the **Cenote Sagrado** (Well of Sacrifice). Into the Cenote Sagrado were thrown valuable propitiatory objects of all kinds, animals and human sacrifices. The well was first dredged by Edward H Thompson, the US Consul in Mérida, between 1904 and 1907; he accumulated a vast quantity of objects in pottery, jade, copper and gold. In 1962 the well was explored again by an expedition sponsored by the National Geographic Society and some 4000 further artefacts were recovered, including beads, polished jade, lumps of *copal* resin, small bells, a statuette of rubber latex, another of wood, and a quantity of animal and human bones. Another *cenote*, the Cenote Xtoloc, was probably used as a water supply. To the east of El Castillo is the **Templo de los Guerreros** (Temple of the Warriors) with its famous reclining **Chacmool** statue. This pyramidal platform is closed off to avoid erosion.

**Chichén Viejo** (Old Chichén), where the Mayan buildings of the earlier city are found, lies about 500 m by path from the main clearing. The famous **El Caracol**, or Observatory, is included in this group, as is the **Casa de las Monjas** (Nunnery). A footpath to the right of the Casa de las Monjas leads to the **Templo de los Tres Dinteles** (Temple of the Three Lintels) after 30 minutes' walking. It requires at least one day to see the many pyramids, temples, ball courts and palaces, all of them adorned with astonishing sculptures. Excavation and renovation is still going on. Interesting birdlife and iguanas can also be seen around the ruins.

## Essential Chichén Itzá

### Entry fees

US$14 including light and sound show, free bag storage, free for Mexicans on Sun and holidays, when it is incredibly crowded; you may leave and re-enter as often as you like on day of issue.

### Tours

Guided tours US$40 per group of any size; it is best to try and join one, many languages available.

### Opening hours

Daily 0800-1730. It's best to arrive before 1030 to beat the crowds.

### Facilities

The tourist centre at the entrance to the ruins has a restaurant and small museum, bookshop and souvenir shop with exchange facilities. Drinks, snacks and toilets are available at the entrance and at the *cenote*.

### What to take

Take a hat, suncream, sunglasses, shoes with good grip and drinking water.

### Tip...

On the morning and afternoon of the spring and autumn equinoxes, the alignment of the sun's shadow casts a serpentine image on the side of the steps of El Castillo.

# Chichén Itzá

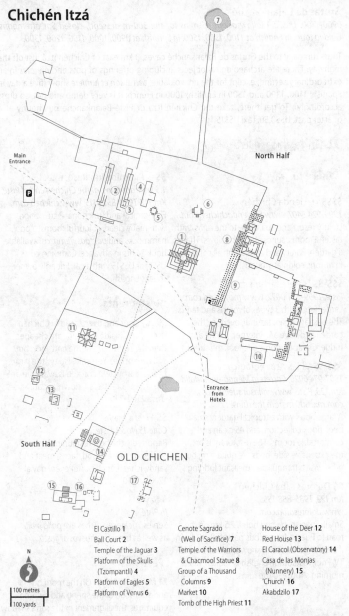

Main Entrance

North Half

Entrance from Hotels

South Half

OLD CHICHEN

N

| 100 metres |
| 100 yards |

El Castillo **1**
Ball Court **2**
Temple of the Jaguar **3**
Platform of the Skulls
  (Tzompantli) **4**
Platform of Eagles **5**
Platform of Venus **6**

Cenote Sagrado
  (Well of Sacrifice) **7**
Temple of the Warriors
  & Chacmool Statue **8**
Group of a Thousand
  Columns **9**
Market **10**
Tomb of the High Priest **11**

House of the Deer **12**
Red House **13**
El Caracol (Observatory) **14**
Casa de las Monjas
  (Nunnery) **15**
'Church' **16**
Akabdzilo **17**

### Grutas de Balankanché

*0900-1700, US$7.50 (allow about 45 mins for the 300-m descent), closed Sat afternoons. Guided tours in English at 1100, 1300, 1500; in Spanish at 0900, 1000, 1100, 1200, 1300.*

Tours run daily to the Grutas de Balankanché caves, 3 km east of Chichén Itzá just off the highway. There are archaeological objects, including offerings of pots and *metates* in an extraordinary setting, except for the unavoidable, awful *son et lumière* show (five a day in Spanish; 1100, 1300 and 1500 in English; 1000 in French; it is very damp and hot, so dress accordingly). To get there, take the Chichén Itzá or Pisté-Balankanché bus hourly at a quarter past, US$0.50, taxi US$15.

## Listings Chichén Itzá *map p.163*

### Where to stay

**$$$$ Hacienda Chichén**
*T999-924 8407, www.haciendachichen.com.*
Luxury resort and spa, close to the ruins, with tasteful rooms, suites and bungalows. There's a garden, library and restaurant, all contained in historic colonial grounds.

**$$$-$$ Hotel Chichén Itzá**
*Pisté, T999-851 0022, www.mayaland.com.*
Large hotel with 3 types of rooms and tariffs. The best are clean, tasteful, overlook the garden and have a/c, internet, phone and fridge. Cheaper rooms overlook the street.

**$$$-$$ Villas Arqueológicas**
*T997-974 6020, Carretera Mérida–Valladolid Km 120, Piste, www.villasarqueologicas. com.mx, 800 m from the ruins.*
A large hotel with a tropical garden, small pool, book collection, and 45 clean and comfortable rooms. The restaurant is on the expensive side, beds are quite firm, but otherwise a tranquil and pleasant lodging.

**$$ Dolores Alba Chichén**
*Km 122, T985-858 1555, www.doloresalba.com.*
Small, Spanish-owned hotel, 2.5 km on the road to Puerto Juárez (bus passes it), 40 clean if old bungalows with shower, a/c and cable TV. Pool, restaurant, English is spoken, free morning shuttle to the ruins.

**$$-$ Pirámide Inn Resort**
*1.5 km from ruins, at the Chichén end of Pisté, Km 117, T999-851 0115, www.chichen.com.*
Economical and functional Pisté option with many clean, colourful rooms, a pool, hammocks and *palapas*. *Temazcal* available, book 24 hrs in advance. Camping costs US$5, or US$15 with a car. Friendly owner, speaks English.

### Restaurants

Mostly poor and overpriced in Chichén itself (cafés inside the ruins are cheaper than the restaurant at the entrance, but still expensive). You can also try the larger hotels. Barbecued chicken is available on the streets of Pisté, sit-down restaurants close 2100-2200.

**$$ Fiesta Maya**
*Calle 15 No 59, Pisté.*
Reportedly the best restaurant in town. Serves Yucatecan food, tacos, meat and sandwiches. Lunch buffet every day at 1200, US$10.

**$ Sayil**
*In Pisté.*
Serves Yucatecan dishes like *pollo pibil*, as well as breakfast *huevos al gusto*.

### Festivals

**21 Mar and 21 Sep** On the morning and afternoon of the spring and autumn equinoxes, the alignment of the sun's shadow casts a serpentine image on the side of the steps of El Castillo. This occasion is popular and you'll be lucky to get close enough to see the action. Note that this phenomenon can also be seen on the days before and after the equinox, 19th-23rd of the month.

## Transport

ADO bus office in Pisté is between Stardust and Pirámide Inn. Budget travellers going on from Mérida to Isla Mujeres or Cozumel should visit Chichén from Valladolid (see below), although if you plan to go through in a day you can store luggage at the visitor centre.

### Bus

Frequent 2nd-class buses depart from Mérida to Cancún, passing Chichén Itzá and Pisté. Likewise, there are frequent departures to/from Valladolid. To **Mérida**, 2nd class, hourly, US$5.50; and 1st class, 1420 and 1700, US$9. To **Cancún**, 2nd class, hourly, US$9. To **Valladolid**, 2nd class, hourly, US$2.50. To **Tulum**, 2nd class, 0810, 1420, 1615, US$11. The ruins are a 5-min ride from Pisté – the buses drop off and pick up passengers until 1700 at the top of the coach station opposite the entrance.

## Valladolid and around   Colour map 1, A2.

**a handsome colonial city unspoilt by tourism**

Situated roughly halfway between Mérida and Cancún, Valladolid is filled with colourful houses, cobblestone streets, historic churches and plazas. There is a slightly medieval feel to the place, some of the streets tapering off into mud tracks. The *Vallisoletanos*, as they are known, are friendlier than their *Meridano* neighbours, and Valladolid's location makes it an ideal place to settle for a few days while exploring the ruins of Chichén Itzá, the fishing village of Río Lagartos, and the three beautiful *cenotes* in the area, one of which is right in the town itself. Valladolid is still relatively untouched by tourism (aside from the cavalcade of monstrous tour buses on the plaza every afternoon), but it is now showing signs of gentrification. The town is small and easily explored on foot.

### Sights

Valladolid is set around a large plaza flanked by the imposing Franciscan **cathedral** (which is more impressive outside than in) and the **Palacio de Gobierno**, which has striking murals inside. Most of the hotels are clustered around the centre, as well as numerous restaurants catering for all budgets. Just off the plaza, **Casa de los Venados** ⓘ *Calle 40 No 204, T985-856-2289, www.casadelosvenados.com, guided tours Mon-Fri 1000, suggested donation US$3*, is a private home with a stunning collection of Mexican folk art, painstakingly acquired over a decade by enthusiasts John and Dorianne Venator.

The **Calzada de los Frailes** is a historic lane running diagonally southwest from the corner of Calles 46 and 41. Near its entrance, there is a tequila tour, **Los Tres Toños** ⓘ *Calle 41 No 222, 1000-2000*, where you can learn about production techniques and sample some local liquor; the tour is free, essentially a sales pitch for the distillery. Further down the Calzada is a little chocolate factory also offering 'free' tours with samples at the end. At the conclusion of the calzada, the 16th-century **Ex-Convento de San Bernardino** ⓘ *Mon-Sat, 0900-1800, US$2*, is one of Mexico's most important Franciscan structures, more of a fortress than a convent. It contains interesting frescoes and sacred art, as well as gardens pleasant for strolling.

**Cenote Zací** ⓘ *Calle 36 between Calle 37 and 39, daily 0800-1800, US$3, half price for children*, right in town, is an artificially lit *cenote* where you can swim, except when it is occasionally prohibited due to algae in the water. There is a thatched restaurant and lighted promenades. A small town **museum** ⓘ *Calle 41, free*, housed in Santa Ana church, shows the history of rural Yucatán and has some exhibits from recent excavations at the ruins of Ek-Balam.

## ★Cenote Dzitnup
*Daily 0800-1800, US$2.50. Colectivos leave when full from in front of Hotel María Guadalupe, US$1, returning until 1800, after which you'll have to get a taxi back to Valladolid, US$6.*

Seven kilometres from Valladolid is the beautiful **Cenote X-Kekén**, at **Dzitnup**, the name by which it is more commonly known. It is stunningly lit with electric lights, the only natural light source being a tiny hole in the cavernous ceiling dripping with stalactites. Swimming is excellent, the water is cool and refreshing, although reported to be a little dirty, and harmless bats zip around overhead. Exploratory walks can also be made through the many tunnels leading off the *cenote*, for which you will need a torch. There is also the easily reached *cenote* close by, called **Samulá** ⓘ *US$3*, only recently opened to the public.

**Valladolid**

N
100 metres
100 yards

**Where to stay** 🛏
Antonio 'Negro' Aguilar **2**
Casa Tía Micha **1**
Hostel Candelaria **3**
Las Hamacas **4**
Mesón del Marqués **5**
San Clemente **6**
Zaci **8**

**Restaurants** 🍴
Bazar **1**
Conato **3**
La Casona de Valladolid **4**
Las Campanas **2**
Squimz **5**
Taberna de los Frailes **6**
Yerbabuena del Sisal **7**

### Ek-Balam
*Daily 0800-1700, US$7.50. To get there by car, take Route 295 north out of Valladolid. Just after the village of Temozón, turn right for Santa Rita. The ruins are 5 km further on. Colectivos to Ek Balam depart from Calle 44 between Calle 37 and 35, 4-person minimum, US$3. A round-trip taxi with a wait is around US$20.*

Some 25 km north of Valladolid are the Mayan ruins of Ek-Balam, meaning 'Black Jaguar'. The ruins contain an impressive series of temples, sacrificial altars and residential buildings grouped around a large central plaza. The main temple, known as 'The Tower', is an immaculate seven-tiered staircase leading up to a flattened area with the remains of a temple. The views are stunning and, because they are not on the tourist trail, these ruins can be viewed at leisure, without the presence of hordes of tour groups from Cancún.

### Río Lagartos and around *Colour map 1, A2.*
**Tizimín** is a dirty, scruffy little town en route to Río Lagartos, where you will have to change buses. If stuck, there are several cheap *posadas* and restaurants, but with frequent buses to Río Lagartos, there should be no need to stay the night here.

Río Lagartos is an attractive little fishing village on the north coast of Yucatán State, whose main attraction is the massive biosphere reserve containing thousands of pink flamingos, as well as 250 other species of bird. The people of Río Lagartos are extremely friendly and very welcoming to tourists. The only route is on the paved road from Valladolid; access from Cancún is by boat only, a journey mainly made by tradesmen ferrying fish to the resort. Development in Río Lagartos, however, is on the horizon.

Boat trips to see the flamingo reserve can be easily arranged by walking down to the harbour and taking your pick from the many offers you'll receive from boatmen. You will get a longer trip with fewer people, due to the decreased weight in the boat. As well as flamingos, there are 250 other species of bird, some very rare, in the 47-sq-km reserve. Make sure your boatman takes you to the larger colony of flamingos near **Las Coloradas** (15 km), recognizable by a large salt mound on the horizon, rather than the smaller groups of birds along the river. Early morning boat trips can be arranged in Río Lagartos to see the flamingos (US$40-55, in eight to nine seater, 2½ to four hours, cheaper in a five-seater, fix the price before embarking; in midweek few people go so there is no chance of negotiating, but boat owners are more flexible on where they go; at weekends it is very busy, so it may be easier to get a party together and reduce costs). Check before going whether the flamingos are there; they usually nest here during May and June and stay through July and August (although salt mining is disturbing their habitat).

## Listings Valladolid and around *map p166*

## Tourist information

**Tourist office**
*Southeast corner of the plaza.*
Maps, general information and flyers.

## Where to stay

**$$$ Casa Tía Micha**
*Calle 39 No 197, T985-856 0499, www. casatiamicha.wix.com/casatiamicha.*
Boutique colonial-style hotel with 1 room and 2 suites, very intimate and romantic; 1 'luxury suite' with jacuzzi and wine, 1 'honeymoon suite' with 4-poster bed.

Very helpful staff and hospitable hosts. Recommended.

### $$$ Hotel Las Hamacas
*Calle 49 No 202-A, T985-100 4270, www.casahamaca.com.*
Denis Larsen has done an extraordinary and commendable job with his friendly and hospitable B&B, which is set in verdant grounds, with a pool, 8 comfortable suites and an English-language library. It's adorned with indigenous art and artefacts; shamanic therapies are available. A storehouse of information on the area.

### $$$ Mesón del Marqués
*Calle 39 with Calle 40 and 42, north side of Plaza Principal, T985-856 2073, www.mesondelmarques.com.*
Housed in a handsome colonial edifice, this hotel has 90 tasteful rooms, all with a/c and cable TV. There's a pool, Wi-Fi, garden and laundry service. Check the room before accepting. Recommended.

### $$ Hotel Zaci
*Calle 44 No 191, between Calles 37 and 39, T985-856 2167, www.hotelzaci.com.mx.*
Large hotel with good-value rooms overlooking a narrow central courtyard, with a small pool, 48 standards, 12 premier, solid wood furniture, simple, comfortable.

### $$ San Clemente
*Calle 42 No 206, T985-856 2208, www.hotelsanclemente.com.mx.*
Located right on the plaza, rooms are large, comfortable and overlook a central courtyard. They are cleaned daily, although some are a bit musty. It's good value and a great price for the location. There's also a pool and a café.

### $ Antonio 'Negro' Aguilar
Rents rooms for 2, 3 or 4 people. The best budget deal in the town for 2 or more, clean, spacious rooms on a quiet street, garden, volleyball/ basketball court. The rooms are on Calle 41 No 225, but you need to book them at Aguilar's shop (Calle 44 No 195, T985-856

2125). If the shop's closed, knock on the door of the house on the right of the shop.

### $ Hostel Candelaria
*Calle 35 No 201F, between Calles 42 and 44, Parque de Candelaria, T985-856 2267, www.hostelvalladolidyucatan.com.*
Fantastic location on the lovely Plaza Candelaria, townhouse with a great garden, benches, tree growing through the centre. Best hostel in town.

## Río Lagartos and around

### $$ Villa de Pescadores
*Calle 14 No 93, on the Malecón T986-862 0020, www.hotelriolagartos.com.mx.*
The best option in town, functional, simple and clean. They have 11 rooms, some with balconies, breezes and expansive views over the harbour, worth the extra pesos.

## Restaurants

### $$$ Conato
*Calle 40 No 226, between Calles 45 y 47.*
Atmospheric bohemian bar-restaurant with Frida Kahlo artwork, antiques and vibrant Mexican folk art. They serve Mexican staples, hearty and reasonable international fare too. Kitsch place, mellow vibe.

### $$$ La Casona de Valladolid
*Calle 41 and 44, T985-100 7040.*
People come for the lunch buffet ($$$), which includes Yucatec specialities. Good setting and atmosphere with a splendid colonial building and lots of folk art. Seating is on a large outdoor patio, many tables, frequent tour groups.

### $$$ Taberna de los Frailes
*Calle 49 No 235, www.tabernadelos frailes.com.*
Romantic setting near the Convent of San Bernardino, lots of character, fabulous building and garden. They serve Yucatec and Mayan specialities, a bit pricey for the town, but very beautiful.

## $$ Las Campanas
*Calle 42, Parque Central.*
Reasonable Mexican fare, some of it good. An atmospheric building and lots of diners in the evenings.

## $$-$ Squimz
*Calle 39 No 219, between Calles 44 and 46, www.squimz.com.mx.*
Modern, airy café with casual booth seating up front and a relaxing patio out back. They serve good breakfasts, coffee, smoothies, sandwiches and some international fare. Wi-Fi and attentive service.

## $$-$ Yerbabuena del Sisal
*Calle 54A No 217.*
Lovely lunch café serving Yucatec treats and staple snacks made with healthy fresh ingredients, including revitalizing fruit and juices, spicy salsas, hot tortillas and salads prepared with love.

## $ Bazar
*Northeast corner of Plaza Principal, next to Mesón del Marqués.*
Wholesome grub, a bit hit and miss, it's best to choose a popular kitchen and ignore the excitable waiters trying to lure you in.

### Río Lagartos and around
For a fishing village, the seafood is not spectacular, as most of the good fish is sold to restaurants in Mérida and Cancún.

## $$ Isla Contoy
*Calle 19 No 134.*
Average seafood, not cheap for the quality.

## $$ Los Negritos
*Off the plaza.*
Moderately priced seafood.

Festivals

### Río Lagartos and around
**17 Jul** A big local **fiesta**, with music, food and dancing in the plaza.
**12 Dec** **Virgen de Guadalupe**. The whole village converges on the chapel built in 1976 on the site of a vision of the Virgin Mary by a local non-believer, who suddenly died, along with his dog, shortly after receiving the vision.

## Transport

### Bus
The **ADO** bus terminal is on Calle 39 and 46, 2 blocks from the main plaza. To **Cancún**, **ADO**, frequent, 2½ hrs, US$12.50; and many 2nd class, 3-4 hrs, US$6. To **Chichén Itzá**, **ADO**, 4 daily, 30 mins; US$5.25; and many 2nd class, US$2.50. To **Mérida**, **ADO**, 16 daily, 2½ hrs, US$13. To **Playa del Carmen**, 6 daily, 3 hrs, US$12.50. To **Tizimín** (for Río Lagartos), frequent 1 hr, US$2. To **Tulum**, 4 daily, US$7.50.

### Río Lagartos and around
### Bus
There are 2 terminals side by side in Tizimín. If coming from Valladolid en route to Río Lagartos, you will need to walk to the other terminal. Tizimín–Río Lagartos, 7 per day, 1½ hrs, US$2. To **Valladolid**, frequent, 1 hr, US$2. To **Mérida**, several daily, 4 hrs, US$4. There are also buses to **Cancún**, **Felipe Carrillo Puerto** and **Chetumal**.

It is possible to get to Río Lagartos and back in a day from **Valladolid**, if you leave on the 0630 or 0730 bus (taxi Tizimín–Río Lagartos US$25, driver may negotiate). Last bus back from Río Lagartos at 1730.

# Campeche State

The state of Campeche embraces the torpid Gulf coast of the Yucatán Peninsula. It enjoys a special prosperity thanks to its offshore oil reserves, exploited by Pemex since the 1970s. Despite its huge potential as a destination, next to the big tourist hubs of Quintana Roo and Yucatán states, relatively few travellers take the time to explore Campeche. But those who do invariably discover a land steeped in history and legends, as vivid and compelling as any of the Yucatán's hot spots.

The state capital, Campeche City, recalls the age of seafarers and pirates with its crumbling city walls and defensive forts, a bastion of colonial grandeur standing sentinel on the coast. Inland, the landscape alternates between savannah and rainforest, the setting for scores of distinctive Mayan ruins. The Chenes, Puuc and Río Bec architectural styles are all represented, triumphs of extraordinary aesthetic form, but nothing beats the mighty Calakmul for sheer size, its behemoth pyramids and temples testament to the vast power of the early Mayan city states. South of the capital, the sweltering Gulf coast is a lesser visited stretch of windswept beaches, sluggish mangroves, yawning estuaries and wildlife-rich lagoons, including Laguna de Términos.

For those willing to get off the beaten track, Campeche promises adventure and intrigue, blissfully free from crowds.

Oil profits have gone a long way to revitalizing the economy of the ancient fortified city of Campeche: neatly hidden behind traffic-choked streets, its Centro Histórico has enjoyed an extensive programme of restoration since the 1980s. It is now rapidly becoming gentrified and has been a UNESCO World Heritage Site since 1999. Replete with cafés and art galleries, the area also has pretty pastel-shaded town houses and cobblestone streets. Beyond the city walls, the seafront *malecón* is an extensive promenade where people stroll, cycle, walk and relax in the evening in the light of the setting sun.

Like many Yucatán towns, Campeche's streets in the Old Town are numbered rather than named. Even numbers run north–south beginning at Calle 8 (no one knows why) near the

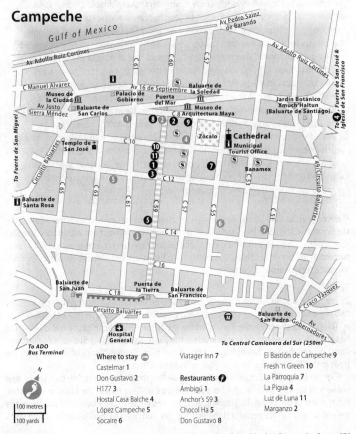

**Campeche**

| Where to stay | | Restaurants | |
|---|---|---|---|
| Castelmar 1 | Viatager Inn 7 | Ambigú 1 | El Bastión de Campeche 9 |
| Don Gustavo 2 | | Anchor's 59 3 | Fresh 'n Green 10 |
| H177 3 | | Chocol Ha 5 | La Parroquia 7 |
| Hostal Casa Balche 4 | | Don Gustavo 8 | La Pigua 4 |
| López Campeche 5 | | | Luz de Luna 11 |
| Socaire 6 | | | Marganzo 2 |

## BACKGROUND
## Campeche

Highway 180 enters the city as the Avenida Resurgimiento, passing either side of the huge **Monumento al Resurgimiento**, a stone torso holding aloft the Torch of Democracy. Originally the trading village of Ah Kim Pech, it was here that the Spaniards, under Francisco Hernández de Córdoba, first disembarked on Mexican soil (22 March 1517) to replenish their water supply. For fear of being attacked by the native population, they quickly left, only to be attacked later by the locals further south in Champotón, where they were forced to land by appalling weather conditions at sea. It was not until 1540 that Francisco de Montejo managed to conquer Ah Kim Pech, founding the city of Campeche on 4 October 1541, after failed attempts in 1527 and again in 1537.

The export of local dyewoods, *chicle*, timber and other valuable cargoes soon attracted the attention of most of the famous buccaneers, who constantly raided the port from their bases on Isla del Carmen, then known as the Isla de Tris. Combining their fleets for one momentous swoop, they fell upon Campeche on 9 February 1663, wiped out the city and slaughtered its inhabitants. Five years later the Crown began fortifying the site, the first Spanish colonial settlement to be completely walled. Formidable bulwarks, 3 m thick and 'a ship's height', and eight bastions (*baluartes*) were built in the next 36 years. All these fortifications soon put a stop to pirate attacks and Campeche prospered as one of only two Mexican ports (the other was Veracruz) to have had the privilege of conducting international trade.

After Mexican Independence from Spain, the city declined into an obscure fishing and logging town. Only with the arrival of a road from the 'mainland' in the 1950s and the oil boom of the 1970s has Campeche begun to see visitors in any numbers, attracted by its historical monuments and relaxed atmosphere (*campechano* has come to mean an easy-going, pleasant person).

Malecón, east to Calle 18 inside the walls; odd numbers run east (inland) from Calle 51 in the north to Calle 65 in the south. Most of the points of interest are within this compact area. Connecting sea and land gates, Calle 59 has now been pedestrianized with great success. A full circuit of the walls is a long walk; buses marked 'Circuito Baluartes' provide a regular service around the perimeter.

### Sights

Of the original walls, seven of the *baluartes* and an ancient fort (now rather dwarfed by two big white hotels on the seafront) remain; some house museums (see below).

The heart of the city is the Zócalo, where the austere Franciscan **cathedral** (1540-1705) has an elaborately carved façade; inside is the Santo Entierro (Holy Burial), a sculpture of Christ on a mahogany sarcophagus with a silver trim. There is plenty of shade under the trees in the Zócalo and a small pagoda with a snack bar.

Right in front of the Zócalo is the **Baluarte de Nuestra Señora de la Soledad**, the central bulwark of the city walls, from where you can do a walking tour of the **Circuito Baluartes**, the remains of the city walls. Heading east, you will come to the **Puerta del Mar**, formerly the entrance for those permitted to enter the city from the sea, which used to come up to this point. Next along the *circuito* is a pair of modern buildings, the **Palacio de Gobierno** and the **Congreso**. The latter looks like a flying saucer and makes for a bizarre sight when viewed with the 17th-century **Baluarte de San Carlos** in the background. Baluarte de San Carlos now houses the **Museo de la Ciudad**. Heading west on the continuation of the *circuito*, you will come to **Templo de San José**, on Calle 10, an impressive baroque church with a beautifully tiled façade. It has been de-consecrated and is now an educational centre. Back on to the *circuito*, you will next reach the **Baluarte de Santa Rosa**, now the home of the tourist information office. Next is **Baluarte de San Juan**, from which a large chunk of the old city wall still extends, protecting you from the noisy traffic on the busy road beyond. The wall connects with **Puerta de la Tierra** ① *Tue, Fri and Sat 2000 (for information, contact the tourist office), US$4*, where a *Luz y Sonido* (Light and Sound) show takes place. The continuation of the *circuito* will take you past the **Baluarte de San Francisco** and then past the market, just outside the line of the city walls. **Baluarte de San Pedro** flanks the northeast corner of the city centre and now houses a museum. The *circuito* runs down to the northwest tip of the old city, where the **Baluarte de Santiago** houses the Botanical Gardens.

There are a few cultural centres in Campeche. The **Casa del Teniente de Rey** ① *Calle 59 No 38 between 14 and 16, T981-811 1314, www.inah.gob.mx*, houses the Instituto Nacional de Antropología e Historia (INAH), dedicated to the restoration of Mayan ruins in the state of Campeche, as well as supporting local museums. INAH can be visited for information regarding any of the sites in the state. The **Centro Cultural Casa 6** ① *Calle 57, between Calle 8 and 10, daily 0900-2100, US$0.35*, is housed in a handsome building on the main plaza. It conjures the opulence and splendour of Campeche's golden days.

Further from the city walls is the **Batería de San Luis**, 4 km south from the centre along the coast road. This was once a lookout post to catch pirates as they approached the city from a distance. The **Fuerte de San Miguel**, 600 m inland, is now a museum. A 20-minute walk along Avenida Miguel Alemán from Baluarte de Santiago is the 16th-century **San Francisco** church, with wooden altars painted in vermilion and white. Nearby is the **Portales de San Francisco**, a beautifully restored old entrance to the city, with several good restaurants in its shadow.

The **Museo de Arquitectura Maya** ① *Baluarte de Nuestra Señora de la Soledad, Tue-Sun, 0800-1930, US$2.70*, has three well-laid-out rooms of Mayan stelae and sculpture. **Jardín Botánico Xmuch'Haltun** ① *Baluarte de Santiago, Mon-Sat 0900-2100, Sun 0900-1600, US$0.80*, is a small but perfectly formed collection of tropical plants and flowers in a peaceful setting. The **Fuerte de San Miguel** ① *Tue-Sun 0900-1930, US$2.50*, on the Malecón 4 km southwest, is the most atmospheric of the forts (complete with drawbridge and a moat said to have once contained either crocodiles or skin-burning lime, take your pick!); it houses the **Museo de Cultura Maya** ① *Tue-Sun 0900-1730*, with a well-documented display of pre-Columbian exhibits including jade masks and black funeral pottery from Calakmul and recent finds from Jaina.

## Around Campeche

**Lerma** is virtually a small industrial suburb of Campeche, with large shipyards and fish-processing plants; the afternoon return of the shrimping fleet is a colourful sight. The **Fiesta de Polk Kekén** is held on 6 January, with traditional dances. The nearest decent beaches are at Seybaplaya (see page 179), 20 km south of Campeche. There, the beaches are clean and deserted; take your own food and drink as there are no facilities. Crowded, rickety buses marked 'Lerma' or 'Playa Bonita' run from Campeche, US$1.50, 8 km.

## Tourist information

For a good orientation take the Centro Histórico tour, a regular tourist tram running daily from the main plaza on the hour 0900-1200 and 1700-2000, 45 mins, US$7.50, English and Spanish spoken.

### Municipal tourist office
*Calle 55 No 3, T019 816 3989, www.campeche.travel.*
Located next to the cathedral and supplemented by an information booth on the plaza.

### State tourist office
*Av Ruiz Cortines s/n, T981-127 3300, www.campeche.travel. On the malecón.*

## Where to stay

### $$$$ Don Gustavo
*Calle 59 No 4, T01800-839 0959, www.casadongustavo.com.*
Classic colonial beauty at this upmarket boutique hotel, a converted townhouse. Suites are simple and elegant, crisply attired and adorned with delicate antiques. Pleasant patios, spa facilities and a superb restaurant. The best in town.

### $$$$ Hacienda Uayamon
*Carretera Uayamon–China–Edzná Km 20, T981-813 0530, www.hacienda uayamon.com.*
This beautiful old hacienda has been tastefully restored to its former elegance and now serves as a luxury hotel. Rooms are handsome, combining traditional and contemporary flourishes. The grounds, setting and architecture are superb.

### $$$ Castelmar
*Calle 61, between Calle 8 and 10, T981-811 1204, www.castelmar hotel.com.*
Fantastic early 19th-century building, a former military barracks, now one of the oldest hotels in town and decorated in grand

colonial style. Its 26 rooms are smart, clean, spacious and decorated with solid wooden furniture and fine tiled floors.

### $$$ Hotel Socaire
*Calle 55 No 22, between Calles 12 and 14, T981-811 2130, www.hotelsocaire.com.mx.*
A youthful new hotel with 8 good, clean, well-equipped rooms, simple, stylish and modern. There's also a decent restaurant attached, friendly staff and a small pool. Calm and welcoming colours. Recommended.

### $$$-$$ Hotel H177
*Calle 14 No 177, between Calles 59 and 61, T981-816 4463, www.h177hotel.com.mx.*
A modern lodging with a trendy look. Brand new rooms include comfortable singles, doubles and suites, all crisply attired with white linen and red curtains. Facilities include spa and jacuzzi.

### $$ Hotel López Campeche
*Calle 12 No 189 between Calles 61 and 63, T981-816 3344, www.hotellopezcampeche. com.mx.*
An interesting art deco building with 50 clean, simple, comfortable rooms overlooking an inner courtyard. Facilities include a small pool, café and all modern conveniences. Central and good value.

### $$-$ Hostal Casa Balche
*Calle 57 No 6, T981-811 0087, www.casabalche.com.*
A bit more expensive than your usual hostel, but very new, comfortable, stylish and unique, and a superb location overlooking the plaza. There's just 1 private room ($$) and a few small clean dorms with bunks. Services include free Wi-Fi, breakfast and laundry. Attractive, hospitable and recommended.

### $ Viatger Inn
*Calle 51 No 28, between Calles 12 and 14, T981-811 4500, www.viatgerinn.com.*

A small, crisp, clean and stylish youth hostel with mixed and single-sex dorms. Coffee and Wi-Fi included. Brand new and in great shape.

## Restaurants

Campeche is known for its seafood, especially *camarones* (large shrimps), *esmedregal* (black snapper) and *pan de cazón* (baby hammerhead shark sandwiched between corn tortillas with black beans). Food stands in the market serve *tortas*, tortillas, *panuchos* and *tamales* but hygiene standards vary widely; barbecued venison is also a marketplace speciality.

### $$$ Anchor's 59
*Calle 59 between Calles 10 and 12.*
A plush new seafood restaurant, recommended chiefly for its stock of wine. Smart, pleasant interior and a tempting menu of grilled coconut prawns, seafood tostadas, snapper, pasta and more.

### $$$ Don Gustavo
*Calle 59 No 4, T01800-839 0959, www.casadongustavo.com.*
Don Gustavo's is the place for a romantic evening meal. They serve creatively prepared local specialities, steaks, pasta and fusion cuisine. The setting, inside the hotel, is a handsome colonial house with an elegant dining room and intimate patio seating. Attentive service.

### $$$ La Pigua
*Av Miguel Alemán 179A, www.lapigua.com.mx.*
La Pigua is well established, modern and clean. It has a traditional kitchen specializing in fresh fish, prawn cocktails, calamari, Campeche caviar and other seafood. Pleasant dining, open for lunch and dinner.

### $$$-$$ Ambigú
*Calle 59 between Calles 10 and 12.*
A cool place with a friendly atmosphere and a simple but elegant interior and additional al fresco seating on the pedestrian street.

They serve home-cooked regional cuisine and great cocktails made with traditional plants, fruits and *nance* liquor.

### $$$-$$ El Bastión de Campeche
*Calle 57 No 2a, www.elbastion.mx.*
A good spot on the plaza, clean and pleasant. They serve Mexican, Yucatec and international cuisine, specialities include chicken stuffed with cream cheese and chaya, filet mignon and shrimp in mango sauce. Breakfast, lunch and dinner.

### $$$-$$ Luz de Luna
*Calle 59 No 6, between Calles 10 and 12.*
A good Mexican restaurant serving national and local classics, including flavourful burritos, tacos, enchiladas and fish fillet with lemon and pepper. Friendly, attentive service and al fresco seating.

### $$$-$$ Marganzo
*Calle 8, www.marganzo.com.*
Highly regarded by the locals, Marganzo is a colonial-style restaurant serving good seafood and Mexican fare, including Yucatec specialities. They regularly lay on music with a trio of musicians and regional dancing. Good evening atmosphere. Recommended.

### $$-$ La Parroquia
*Calle 55 No 8, part of the hotel with the same name.*
This busy locals' joint – staffed by smartly attired and friendly waiters – is open 24 hrs and packed at breakfast time. They serve reliable grub, reasonable and casual, but not gourmet. Free Wi-Fi.

### $ Fresh 'n Green
*Calle 59 No 5.*
A simple sandwich and salad bar, very casual and cheap, fast food, and popular with students.

## Cafés

### Chocol Ha
*Calle 59 No 30.*
A chilled-out little patio, great for after-dinner crêpes, frappés and hot chocolate.

They have some tasty local produce on sale too, including honey and chocolate.

## Festivals

Feb/Mar Good **Carnival.**
7 Aug Campeche State holiday.
Sep **Feria de San Román**, 2nd fortnight.
4-13 Oct **Fiesta de San Francisco.**

## Shopping

### Handicrafts

Excellent cheap Panama hats (*jipis*), finely and tightly woven so hat they retain their shape even when crushed into your luggage (within reason); cheaper at the source in Becal. Handicrafts are generally cheaper than in Mérida. There are souvenir shops along Calle 8, such as **Artesanía Típica Naval** (Calle 8 No 259), with exotic bottled fruit like *nance* and *marañón*. Many high-quality craft items are available from the **Exposición** in the Baluarte San Pedro and **Casa de Artesanías Tukulná** (Calle 10 No 333, between C59 and C31, www.tukulna.com.mx, open daily 0900-2000).

The market, from which most local buses depart, is beside Alameda Park at the south end of Calle 57. There are plenty of bargains here. Try the ice cream, although preferably from a shop rather than a barrow.

## What to do

### Tour operators

**Kankabi'Ok**, *Calle 59 No 3, between Calles 8 and 10, T981-811 2792, www.kankabiok.com.* Eco and adventure tours, including kayaking, camping and ruins. A tour to Edzná is around US$25 per person (2-person minimum), including transport and guide. Other popular excursions include the 'Camino Real', a half-day tour of rural villages and workshops, including a traditional meal.
**Viajes Xtampak Tours**, *Calle 57 No 14, T981-816 6473, www.xtampak.com.* Daily transport

to ruins including Edzná, Calakmul, Uxmal and Palenque – they'll collect you from your hotel with 24 hrs' notice. There's a discount for groups and guide services at an extra cost. Recommended.

## Transport

### Air

The modern, efficient airport (**CPE**) on Porfirio is 10 km northeast of town. If on a budget, walk 100 m down service road (Av Aviación) to Av Nacozari, turn right (west) and wait for 'China–Campeche' bus to the Zócalo.
**Aeroméxico** direct daily to **Mexico City**, T981-816 3109.

### Bus

Long-distance buses arrive at the **ADO** bus terminal on Av Casa de Justicia 237, 3 km from downtown; buses to the centre pass outside, US$0.70, taxis cost US$3.
Buses to **Seybaplaya** leave from the tiny Cristo Rey terminal opposite the market, 9 a day from 0615, 45 mins, US$1.50.

**Long distance** See above for the location of the 1st-class **ADO** terminal. The 2nd-class bus terminal is about 1 km east of the centre along Av Gobernadores, but services are steadily moving to the main terminal. To **Cancún**, 8 daily with **ADO** and **ADO GL**, 7 hrs, US$38-45. To **Chetumal**, 1400, 6 hrs, US$38. To **Ciudad del Carmen**, frequent **ADO** services, 3 hrs, US$16. To **Escárcega**, 6 daily, 2 hrs, US$11. To **Mérida**, frequent **ADO** services, 2½ hrs, US$14. To **San Cristóbal de las Casas**, **OCC** at 2145, 11 hrs, US$36. To **Veracruz**, luxury only, **ADO GL** at 2010, 11½ hrs, US$62. To **Villahermosa**, frequent **ADO** services, 6-7 hrs, US$31.

### Car

**Car hire** Maya Nature, Av Ruiz Cortines 51, inside Hotel del Mar, T981-811 9191. **Hertz** and **Autorent** car rentals at airport.

A number of city remains (mostly in the Chenes architectural style) are scattered throughout the rainforest and scrub to the east of Campeche; little excavation work has been done and most receive few visitors. Getting to them by the occasional bus service is possible in some cases, but return trips can be tricky. The alternatives are one of the tours run by travel agencies in Campeche (see Tour operators, above) or renting a vehicle (preferably with high clearance) in Campeche or Mérida. Whichever way you travel, you are strongly advised to carry plenty of drinking water.

### Edzná

*Tue-Sun 0800-1700, US$3.50; local guides available. The easiest way to reach Edzná is on a tourist minibus. They depart hourly and operators include Xtampak, Calle 57 No 14, between Calle 10 and 12, T981-812 8655, xtampac_7@ hotmail.com, US$21.50 (prices drop depending on number of passengers); and Transportadora Turística Jade, Av Díaz Ordaz No 67, T981-827 4885, Jade_tour@hotmail.com, US$14. To get there on public transport, catch a morning bus to Pich and ask to be let out at Edzná – it's a 15-min walk from the highway. Ask the driver about return schedules, as services are quite infrequent and subject to change. There's no accommodation at Edzná and hitchhiking isn't recommended.*

The closest site to the state capital is Edzná ('House of Grimaces'), reached by the highway east to Cayal, then a right turn onto Highway 261, a distance of 61 km. A paved shortcut southeast through China and Poxyaxum (good road) cuts off 11 km; follow Avenida Nacozari out along the railway track.

Gracefully situated in a lovely, tranquil valley with thick vegetation on either side, Edzná was a huge ceremonial centre, occupied from about 600 BC to AD 200, built in the simple Chenes style mixed with Puuc, Classic and other influences. The centrepiece is the magnificent, 30-m-tall, 60-sq-m **Temple of the Five Storeys**, a stepped pyramid with four levels of living quarters for the priests and a shrine and altar at the top; 65 steep steps lead up from the Central Plaza. Opposite is the **Paal U'na**, Temple of the Moon. Excavations are being carried out on the scores of lesser temples by Guatemalan refugees under the direction of Mexican archaeologists, but most of Edzná's original sprawl remains hidden away under thick vegetation. Imagination is still needed to picture the network of irrigation canals and holding basins built by the Maya along the valley below sea level. Some of the stelae remain in position (two large stone faces with grotesquely squinting eyes are covered by a thatched shelter); others can be seen in various Campeche museums. There is also a good example of a *sacbé* (sacred road).

Edzná is well worth a visit especially in July, when a Mayan ceremony to honour Chac is held, to encourage or to celebrate the arrival of the rains (exact date varies). There is a small *comedor* at the entrance.

### Hochob

*Daily 0800-1700, US$2.70.*

Of the more remote and less-visited sites beyond Edzná, Hochob and Dzibilnocac are the best choices for the non-specialist. Hochob is reached by turning right at Hopelchén on Highway 261, 85 km east of Campeche. This quiet town has an impressive fortified 16th-century church but only one hotel. From here a narrow paved road leads 41 km south to the village of **Dzibalchén**.

Don Willem Chan will guide tourists to Hochob (he also rents bikes), is helpful and speaks English. Directions can be obtained from the church here (run by Americans); you need to travel 18 km southwest on a good dirt road (no public transport, hopeless quagmire in the rainy season) to the village of **Chenko**, where locals will show the way (4 km through the jungle). Bear left when the road forks; it ends at a small *palapa* and, from here, the ruins are 1 km uphill with a magnificent view over the surrounding forest.

Hochob once covered a large area but, as at Edzná, only the hilltop ceremonial centre (the usual plaza surrounded by elaborately decorated temple buildings) has been properly excavated; although many of these are mounds of rubble, the site is perfect for contemplating deserted, yet accessible Mayan ruins in solitude and silence. The one-room temple to the right (north) of the plaza is the most famous structure: deep-relief patterns of stylized snakes moulded in stucco across its façade were designed to resemble a mask of the ferocious rain god Chac. A door serves as the mouth. A fine reconstruction of the building is on display at the Museo de Antropología in Mexico City. Early morning second-class buses serve Dzibalchén, but returning to Campeche later in the day is often a matter of luck.

### Dzibilnocac
*Daily 0800-1700, free.*

Some 20 km northeast of Dzibalchén at Iturbide, this site is one of the largest in Chenes territory. Only three temples have been excavated here (many pyramidal mounds in the forest and roadside *milpas*); the first two are in a bad state of preservation, but the third is worth the visit: a unique narrow edifice with rounded corners and remains of a stucco façade, primitive reliefs and another grim mask of Chac on the top level. Much of the stonework from the extensive site is used by local farmers for huts and fences.

Several buses daily travel to Iturbide, three hours, US$6.70, and there is no accommodation. If driving your own vehicle, well-marked 'km' signs parallel the rocky road to Iturbide (no accommodation); bear right around the tiny Zócalo and its attendant yellow church and continue (better to walk in the wet season) for 50 m, where the right branch of a fork leads to the ruins. Other sites in the region require 4WD transport and appeal mostly to archaeologists.

### Becal
Becal is the centre for weaving Panama hats, here called *jipis* (pronounced 'hippies') and ubiquitous throughout the Yucatán. Many of the town's families have workshops in cool, moist backyard underground caves, which are necessary for keeping moist and pliable the shredded leaves of the *jipijapa* palm from which the hats are made. Most vendors give the visitor a tour of their workshop, but are quite zealous in their sales pitches. Prices are better for *jipis* and other locally woven items (cigarette cases, shoes, belts, etc) in the **Centro Artesanal**, **Artesanías de Becaleña** ① *Calle 30 No 210*, than in the shops near the plaza, where the hat is honoured by a hefty sculpture of three concrete *sombreros*! More celebrations take place on 20 May during the **Feria del Jipi**.

## Listings Mayan sites east of Campeche

### Festivals

**13-17 Apr** A traditional **Honey and Corn Festival** is held in Holpechén.

**3 May** **Día de la Santa Cruz**.

Opening to expansive views of the ocean, Campeche's Gulf coast sweeps south from Campeche City. The Highway 180 clings to the narrow shore, crumbling into the sea in places and usually ignored by tourists, but scenic. Running parallel, the toll road connecting Campeche City to Champotón is rapid, but bypasses Seybaplaya and Sihoplaya.

## Seybaplaya and Sihoplaya

The low-key Mexican resort of **Seybaplaya**, 32 km south of Campeche City, is a dusty, mellow place where fishermen mend nets and pelicans dry their wings along the beach. On the highway there are open-air restaurants serving red snapper, but in general there's little to explore. Only the **Balneario Payucán** at the north end of the bay makes a special trip worthwhile; it is the closest decent beach to Campeche, but quite isolated. A short distance further south of Seybaplaya is the smaller resort of **Sihoplaya** (regular buses from Campeche US$1).

## Champotón

Run-down but relaxed, Champotón, 66 km south of Campeche City, is a fishing and shrimping port sprawled at the mouth of the Río Champotón. In prehispanic times, it was an important trade link between Guatemala and Central Mexico. Toltec and Maya mingled here, followed by the Spaniards, including ill-fated Francisco Hernández de Córdoba, fatally wounded in a skirmish with the inhabitants in 1517. The remnants of the 1719 San Antonio fort, built as a defence against the pirates, can be seen the south side of town. The **Feast of the Immaculate Conception** (8 December) is celebrated with a joyous festival lasting several days. At Champotón, Highway 261 runs 86 km due south to Escárcega, joining Highway 186, giving access to southern Campeche State and Chetumal in Quintana Roo.

## Ciudad del Carmen  *Colour map 2, A3.*

Perched between the Gulf of Mexico and Laguna de Términos (named during the first Spanish expedition when it thought it had reached the end of the 'island' of Yucatán), Ciudad del Carmen is the hot, bursting-at-the-seams principal oil port of the region.

The site was established in 1588 by a pirate named McGregor, as a lair from which to raid Spanish shipping; it was infamous until the pirates were wiped out in 1717 by Alfonso Felipe de Andrade, who named the town after its patroness, the Virgen del Carmen. The patroness is honoured with a cheerful fiesta each year between 15 and 30 June.

The attractive, cream-coloured **cathedral** (Parroquia de la Virgen del Carmen), begun 1856, is notable for its stained glass. **La Iglesia de Jesús** (1820) opposite Parque Juárez is surrounded by elegant older houses. Nearby is the Barrio del Guanal, the oldest residential quarter, with the church of the **Virgen de la Asunción** (1815) and houses with spacious balconies and tiles brought from Marseille. There are several good beaches with restaurants and water sports, the most scenic being **Playa Caracol** (southeast of the centre) and **Playa Norte**, which has extensive white sand and is safe for bathing. The lagoon is rich in tarpon (*sábalo*) and bonefish.

## West of Ciudad del Carmen

A few kilometres west of Ciudad del Carmen, the **Zacatal** bridge crosses the lagoon to connect with the mainland; at 3.2 km it is the longest bridge in Latin America (celebrated with a light and sound show every evening). Near the exit, the lighthouse of **Xicalango** stands at the site of an important pre-Columbian trading centre. Cortés landed near here in 1519 on his way to Veracruz and was given 20 female slaves, including 'La Malinche', the indigenous princess baptized as Doña Marina who, as the Spaniards' interpreter, played an important role in the Conquest. A series of lagoons lie further west on Highway 180, good for birdwatching. Thereafter, the highway crosses the state border into Tabasco, skirting the Gulf up to the US border.

## Listings Ciudad del Carmen

### Where to stay

Hotel accommodation is generally poor value and can be difficult to come by Mon-Thu; book in advance and arrive early. You'll find a handful of 'economical' hotels opposite the ADO bus station.

**$$$ EuroHotel**
*Calle 22 No 208, T938-382 3044,*
*reganem@prodigy.net.mx.*
Large and modern, 2 restaurants, pool, a/c, disco, built to accommodate the flow of Pemex traffic.

**$ Lino's**
*Calle 31 No 132, T938-382 0788.*
A/c, pool, restaurant, also has 10 RV spaces with electricity hook-ups.

### Restaurants

**$$ El Kiosco Calle 33 s/n**
*Between Calle 20 and 22, in Hotel del Parque with view of the Zócalo.*
Modest prices, eggs, chicken, seafood and Mexican dishes.

**$$-$ El Pavo**
*Tucked away down Calle 36A, in Col Guadalupe.*
This superb, family-run restaurant serves excellent seafood dishes at cheap prices. Very popular with the locals.

**$$-$ La Fuente**
*Calle 20.*
24-hr snack bar with view of the Laguna.

**$ La Mesita**
*Outdoor stand across from the old ferry landing.*
Well-prepared shrimp, seafood cocktails, extremely popular all day.

### Transport

#### Air
**Carmen's airport** (**CME**, 5 km east of the plaza) currently only has direct flights to **Mexico City**, from where there are connections to the rest of the country.

#### Bus
The **ADO** bus terminal is some distance from the centre. Take bus or colectivo marked 'Renovación' or 'ADO'; they leave from around the Zócalo. There are frequent **ADO** and **ATS** services to **Campeche**, 2½-3 hrs, US$16. To **Mérida**, frequent, 6 hrs, US$29. To **Villahermosa** via the coast, 3 hrs, US$14, where connections can be made to **Palenque**. Buses also travel via **Escárcega**, where you can connect to **Chetumal** and **Belize**.

#### Car
**Car hire** **Budget**, Calle 31 No 117, T938-382 0908. **Auto-Rentas del Carmen**, Calle 33 No 121, T938-382 2376.

This region encompasses part of the vast lowland forest that reaches into northern Guatemala's Petén, much of it inaccessible without a guide and a good machete. For vehicles, the Escárcega–Chetumal highway bisects the region and eventually connects with Chetumal in Quintana Roo. From the hamlet of Xpujil, 150 km east of Escárcega, you can access the sites of Xpujil, Becán and Chicanná, all intriguing examples of the Río Bec architectural style, which is characterized by heavy masonry towers simulating pyramids and temples, usually found rising in pairs at the ends of elongated buildings. Encompassing a densely forested wilderness, the Calakmul Biosphere Reserve is an exceptional destination, home to one of the most powerful capitals in Mayan history, a site of monumental proportions.

## Francisco Escárcega Colour map 1, B1.

The town of Francisco Escárcega grew up on the Coatzacoalcos–Mérida railway line, which once transported the state's bounty of precious wood, rubber and gum. Today, at the junction of Highways 261 and 186, it is a major hub for travellers on their way to and from Mayan sites in southern Campeche, as well as south to Tabasco and Chiapas and north to Campeche City. The town itself is not particularly enticing, set on a busy highway with a dusty Wild West atmosphere. If stuck here overnight, there are a few hotels, a bank and several cheap restaurants (see Listings, below).

## ★Calakmul Colour map 1, B1.

*Daily 0800-1700, US$3.70, cars US$4, entrance to biosphere reserve US$4. Calakmul is only accessible by car; take Route 186 until Km 95, then turn off at Conhuás, where a paved road leads to the site, 60 km.*

Some 300 km southeast from Campeche town and a further 60 km off the main Escárcega–Chetumal road are the ruins of Calakmul. The site has been the subject of much attention in recent years, due to the previously concealed scale of the place. It is now believed to be one of the largest archaeological sites in Mesoamerica, and certainly the biggest of all the Mayan cities, with somewhere in the region of 10,000 buildings in total, many of them as yet unexcavated. The scale of the site is vast and many buildings are still under excavation, which means that information on Calakmul's history is continually being updated. There is evidence that Calakmul was begun in 300 BC, and continually added to until AD 800.

At the centre of the site is the **Gran Plaza**, overlooked by Structure II, a massive 45-m-high pyramid built in several phases; its core dates to the middle pre-Classic era (200-400 BC) with numerous reconstructions and layers added over the centuries until the end of the Classic era (AD 900). One of the buildings grouped around the Gran Plaza is believed, due to its curious shape and location, to have been designed for astronomical observation. The **Gran Acrópolis**, the largest of all the structures, is divided into two sections: **Plaza Norte**, with the ball court, was used for ceremonies; **Plaza Sur** was used for public activities.

### Chicanná *Colour map 1, B1.*
*Daily 0800-1700. US$3.40.*

. . . . . . . . . . . . . . . . . . . . . . . . . . . . . . . . . . . . . . .

Located 12 km from Xpujil, Chicanná was named upon its discovery in 1966 in reference to Structure II: *chi* (mouth), *can* (serpent) and *ná* (house), 'House of the Serpent's Mouth'. Due to its dimensions and location, Chicanná is considered to have been a small residential centre for the rulers of the ancient regional capital of Becán. It was occupied during the late pre-Classic period (300 BC-AD 250); the final stages of activity at the site have been dated to the post-Classic era (AD 1100). Typical of the Río Bec style are numerous representations of the Maya god Itzamná, or Earth Mother. One of the temples has a dramatic entrance in the shape of a monster's mouth, with fangs jutting out over the lintel and more fangs lining the access stairway. A taxi will take you from Xpujil bus stop to Becán and Chicanná for US$10, including waiting time.

### Becán *Colour map 1, B2.*
*Daily 0800-1700, US$3.70.*

. . . . . . . . . . . . . . . . . . . . . . . . . . . . . . . . . . . . . . .

Seven kilometres west of Xpujil, Becán is another important site in the Río Bec style. Its most outstanding feature is a moat, now dry, which surrounds the entire city and is believed to be one of the oldest defence systems in Mesoamerica. Seven entrance gates cross the moat to the city. The large variety of buildings on the site are a strange combination of decorative towers and fake temples, as well as structures used as shrines and palaces. The twin towers, typical of the Río Bec style, feature on the main structure, set on a pyramid-shaped base supporting a cluster of buildings that seem to have been used for many different functions.

### Xpujil *Colour map 1, B2.*
*Tue-Sun 0800-1700, US$3.40, US$3 to use a camcorder. To get there, see Transport, below.*

. . . . . . . . . . . . . . . . . . . . . . . . . . . . . . . . . . . . . . .

The name means a type of plant similar to a cattail. The main building at Xpujil features an unusual set of three towers, with rounded corners and steps that are so steep they are unscalable, suggesting they may have been purely decorative. The façade features the open jaws of an enormous reptile in profile on either side of the main entrance, possibly representing Itzamná, the Maya god of creation. Xpujil's main period of activity was AD 500-750; it began to go into decline around 1100. Major excavation on the third structure was done as recently as 1993, and there are still many unexcavated buildings dotted about the site. It can be very peaceful and quiet in the early mornings, compared with the throng of tourist activity at the more accessible sites such as Chichén Itzá and Uxmal.

### Hormiguero *Colour map 1, B1/B2.*
*Daily 0800-1700, free.*

. . . . . . . . . . . . . . . . . . . . . . . . . . . . . . . . . . . . . . .

Some 20 km southwest of Xpujil, Hormiguero is the site of one of the most important buildings in the Río Bec region, whose elaborate carvings on the façade show a fine example of the serpent's-mouth entrance, with huge fangs and a gigantic eye.

### Río Bec *Colour map 1, B2.*

Río Bec is south off the main highway, some 10 km further along the road to Chetumal. Although the site gave its name to the architectural style seen in this area, there are better examples of the style at the ruins listed above. Río Bec is a cluster of numerous small sites, all of which are difficult to reach without a guide.

## Where to stay

### Francisco Escárcega

**$$ Escárcega**
*Justo Sierra 86, T982-824 0187, around the corner from the bus terminal (turn left twice).*
Clean, bath, parking, hot water, good restaurant, small garden.

**$$ María Isabel**
*Justo Sierra 127, T982-824 0045.*
A/c, restaurant, comfortable, back rooms noisy from highway.

## Restaurants

### Francisco Escárcega
There are few places used to serving tourists, but there is a good and cheap *lonchería* opposite the bus terminal.

**$$ Titanic**
*Corner of the main highway and the road to the train station (1st turning on the right after turning right out of the bus terminal).*
For a more expensive meal with a/c.

## Transport

### Francisco Escárcega
**Bus**
Most buses from Chetumal or Campeche drop you off at the 2nd-class terminal on the main highway. To buy tickets, you have to wait until the outgoing bus has arrived; sit near the ticket office and wait for them to call out your destination, then join the scrum at the ticket office. There is an **ADO** terminal west of the 2nd-class terminal, a 20-min walk. From there, 1st-class buses go to **Palenque**, 5 daily, 3-4 hrs, US$15. To **Chetumal**, 7 daily, 4 hrs, US$18. To **Campeche**, 9 daily, 2 hrs, US$11. To **Mérida**, frequent, 4½ hrs, US$24.

From the 2nd-class terminal, there are buses to **Campeche**, 16 a day, 2½ hrs, US$8. To **Chetumal**, 7 daily, 4 hrs, US$15. To **Playas de Catazajá**, connecting with colectivos to **Palenque**, frequent, US$7. To **Villahermosa**, 12 a day, 4 hrs, US$16. Colectivos to **Palenque** leave from outside the 2nd-class terminal, US$11.

### Xpujil
You are strongly advised to use your own transport when exploring southern Campeche as passing buses on Highway 186 (Escárcega–Chetumal) are infrequent (every 3-4 hrs). From Xpujil, you'll need to hire a taxi to visit the ruins.

**Bus**
2nd-class buses from **Chetumal** and **Escárcega** stop on the highway in the centre of Xpujil, some 800 m east of the 2 hotels. There are 4 buses a day to **Escárcega**, between 1030 and 1500, 3 hrs, US$8. 8 buses a day to **Chetumal**, 2 hrs, US$7. Change at Escárcega for buses to **Palenque** or **Campeche**. 1st-class buses will not stop at Xpujil.

# This is
## Belize

Belize is a smorgasbord of landscapes, from mountainous jungle with abundant wildlife to fertile subtropical foothills where cattle are reared, and sugar, rice and fruit trees are cultivated, or coastal wetlands filled with birds and small islands – known as cayes – with beautiful beaches.

Measuring 174 miles north to south and just 80 miles across, the country nestles on the coast between Mexico and Guatemala, with a land area of about 8860 sq miles, including hundreds of cayes. The reefs and cayes form a 184-mile barrier reef with crystal-clear water and are a major attraction for world-class diving, snorkelling and sport fishing. And hidden beneath the depths is the magnificent Blue Hole, one of the world's best dives.

Inland, rivers and rainforest invite you to head out, trekking, paddling and biking, to visit the ancient ruins of the Maya, or to cave in their spiritual underworld. For the beginner and the specialist birdwatching is an endless pleasure.

With a Caribbean history and a Central American geography, Belize is a subtle blend of cultures that encourages the laid-back attitude of the small (just 311,000) but ethnically diverse population, who paint an intriguing picture in this culturally different, English-speaking Central American nation.

**N**

20 km
20 miles

MEXICO

Chetumal
Consejo
Corozal
Cerros
Sarteneja
Libertad
Chunox
Buena Vista
Progresso
San Pablo
Shipstern
Reserve
San Estevan
Orange Walk
Cuello
Ambergris
Caye
Tres Leguas
San Felipe
Maskall
San Pedro
Hol Chan
Marine Reserve
La Milpa
Blue Creek
Crooked Tree
Wildlife
Sanctuary
Caye Caulker
Lamanai
Altún Ha
Rio Bravo
Conservation Area
Indian Church
Burrell Boom
Sand Hill
GUATEMALA
Chan Chich
Community Baboon Sanctuary
Bermudian Landing
Ladyville
Gallon Jug
Hattieville
Belize City
Turneffe Islands
Guanacaste Park
Belize Zoo
Northern Lagoon
BELMOPAN
La Democracia
Blue Hole
Roaring Creek
Southern Lagoon
Gales Point
San Ignacio
Georgeville
Xunantunich
Actun Tunichil Muknal Cave
Blue Hole National Park
Melinda Forest Reserve
Benque Viejo
San Antonio
Augustine
Caribbean Sea
Dangriga
Caracol
Mayflower
Maya Mountains
Cockscomb Basin Wildlife Sanctuary
Hopkins
Sittee River
Sittee Point
Savannah Forest Reserve
Placencia Lagoon
Maya Beach
Mango Creek
Placencia
Barrier Reef
Big Creek
Nim Li Punit
San Antonio
Lubaantun
Pueblo Viejo
Blue Creek
Punta Gorda
Bay of Honduras
Rio Sarstoon
Livingston
Puerto Barrios

## Footprint picks

1 **Northern cayes**, page 198
2 **Blue Hole**, page 211
3 **Actun Tunichil Muknal Cave**, page 219
4 **Caracol**, page 225
5 **Crooked Tree Wildlife Sanctuary**, page 228
6 **Cockscomb Basin Wildlife Sanctuary**, page 248

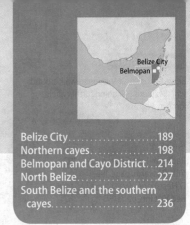

# Footprint picks

★ **Northern cayes**, page 198

Sling a hammock, pour yourself a glass of rum and soak up the easy-going Caribbean vibe on these palm-fringed paradise islands.

★ **Blue Hole**, page 211

Marvel at the incredible underwater wonders of this subterranean sinkhole, one of the world's most famous dive sites.

★ **Actun Tunichil Muknal Cave**, page 219

Descend into the shimmering Mayan underworld, filled with haunting rock formations, ancient ritual artefacts and crystallized sacrificial remains.

★ **Caracol**, page 225

Scramble over the ruins of Caracol, a major power centre during the Classic era of Mayan civilization.

★ **Crooked Tree Wildlife Sanctuary**, page 228

Admire the jabiru stork – the largest flying bird in the western hemisphere – and many other avian species in this sanctuary managed by the Belize Audubon Society.

★ **Cockscomb Basin Wildlife Sanctuary**, page 248

Promising an unforgettable encounter with neotropical fauna, this superb reserve is the world's premier destination for jaguar observation.

# Essential Belize City

## Getting around

Belize City is small enough to walk around when exploring. If going further afield, jump in a cab.

## Best places to stay

**Radisson Fort George**, page 192
**Villa Boscardi**, page 192
**D'Nest**, page 192
**Red Hut Inn**, page 193

## Safety

Tourist police wearing dark green uniforms patrol the city centre in an attempt to control crime and give advice; their introduction has been encouraging and crime in the city is greatly reduced.

## Tip...

Try the local drink, anise and peppermint, known as 'A and P'; also the powerful Old Belizeno rum. The local beer, Belikin, is good, as is the stout, strong and free of gas.

## Best restaurants

**De Barcelona**, page 193
**Sumathi Indian**, page 193
**Bird's Isle**, page 193

A common-sense approach is needed and a careful eye on your possessions recommended. Watch out for conmen. Guides have to be licensed and should carry a photo ID. Street money changers are not to be trusted. It is wise to avoid small, narrow sidestreets and stick to major thoroughfares, although even on main streets you can be the victim of unprovoked threats and racial abuse. Travel by taxi is advisable, particularly at night and in the rain.

Cars should only be left in guarded car parks. For a tip, the security officer at hotels with secure parking will look after cars for a few days while you go to the cayes.

## When to go

Humidity is high, but the summer heat is offset by the northeast trades.

## Weather Belize City

| January | February | March | April | May | June |
|---------|----------|-------|-------|-----|------|
| 21°C | 21°C | 23°C | 24°C | 26°C | 26°C |
| 26°C | 26°C | 28°C | 29°C | 30°C | 30°C |
| 110mm | 60mm | 40mm | 40mm | 100mm | 210mm |

| July | August | September | October | November | December |
|------|--------|-----------|---------|----------|----------|
| 26°C | 25°C | 25°C | 23°C | 22°C | 21°C |
| 30°C | 30°C | 30°C | 28°C | 27°C | 26°C |
| 200mm | 170mm | 240mm | 250mm | 170mm | 170mm |

# Belize City

Clapboard houses line dusty streets while people huddle in groups as the world drifts idly by. Hardly large enough to warrant the title 'city', in any other country Belize City would be a dusty backwater, but here, it is the country's largest settlement, home to a quarter of Belize's population, and an enticing blend of Latin American and Caribbean influences. It is the main centre for maritime communications with boat services to the northern cayes and it is also a flight hub, home to the country's only international airport. For many years, Belize City functioned as the capital of British Honduras, as the country was then known. After it was levelled by Hurricane Hattie in 1961, the government was transferred to the planned city of Belmopan, now the official capital, 80 km west in Cayo District.

Many of the houses are wooden, with galvanized-iron roofs. Most stand on 2-m-high piles – signs of when the city was regularly flooded. The city has improved greatly in recent years. Reclaimed land and building around the Eyre Street area, the Museum of Belize, renovation of the Bliss Institute and the House of Culture show plans to improve the city are well underway.

Hurricane Iris hit in 2002 and Hurricane Richard in 2010, acting as reminders of the inherent risks of Belize City's lowland location.

**Best** for
Finding your feet ▪ Colonial history

## Sights *Colour map 2, A6.*

**Haulover Creek** divides the city and is crossed by the antiquated **swing-bridge**, which opens to let large vessels pass, if required, usually between 1730 and 1800. Three narrow canals further divide the city. The main commercial area is either side of the swing-bridge, with most shops on the south side, many being located on Regent and Albert streets and with offices and embassies generally on the northern side.

The area around **Battlefield Park** (formerly Central Park) is always busy, with the former colonial administration and court buildings bordering the overgrown park adding to the sense of mischief in the area. At the southern end of Regent Street, the **Anglican Cathedral** (St John's) and **Government House** nearby are interesting. Both were built in the early 19th century and draw on the romantic and grand memories of colonialism. In the days before the foundation of the Crown Colony, the kings of the Mosquito Coast were crowned in the cathedral, which was built with bricks brought from England as ships' ballast. In the **cathedral** ⓘ *Mon-Fri 0900-1500 and during Sun services, donation requested*, note the 19th-century memorial plaques that give a harrowing account of early deaths from 'country fever' (yellow fever) and other tropical diseases.

In Government House, the **museum** ⓘ *Mon-Fri 0830-1630, US$5*, contains some interesting pictures of colonial times, displays of furniture and silver and glassware, as well as a one showing fishing techniques and model boats. There are pleasant gardens surrounding the museum if you are looking for somewhere quiet.

The **jail building** (1857) in front of the Central Bank on 8 Gabourel Lane has been beautifully renovated and is now the **National Museum of Belize** ⓘ *T223-4524, www.nichbelize.org, Mon-Thu 0830-1700, Fri 0830-1630, US$5*, with exhibits on the history of Belize City and a permanent exhibit on the Maya sites of Belize.

Continuing to the right, pop into the **Image Factory Art Foundation** ⓘ *91 North Front St, www.imagefactorybelize.com, Mon-Fri 0900-1700, free*, for a peek at exhibitions by local artists – more grassroots than the other galleries. Moving towards the end of the peninsula is the **Tourism Village** consisting of souvenir and gift shops and snack bars, along with several handicraft shops. This development caters to tourists arriving from cruise ships. A little further on, at the tip of the peninsula on Marine Parade, is **Memorial Park**, with a small obelisk, two cannon and concrete benches peppered with the holes of land crabs. The views across the bay can be spectacular in the early morning. The park by the **Fort George Lighthouse** has a children's play area and is a popular meeting place. Baron Bliss' tomb is also here. **Belize Zoo** (see page 215) is definitely worth a visit and not far from Belize City. The trip is very easy with buses from Belize City passing the entrance every half hour.

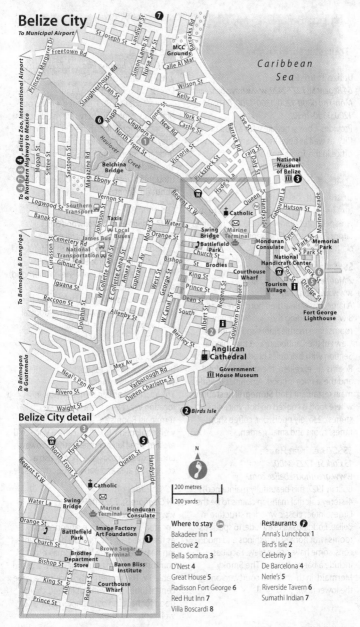

# Belize City

*To Municipal Airport*

Caribbean Sea

## Belize City detail

200 metres
200 yards

**N**

### Where to stay
Bakadeer Inn 1
Belcove 2
Bella Sombra 3
D'Nest 4
Great House 5
Radisson Fort George 6
Red Hut Inn 7
Villa Boscardi 8

### Restaurants
Anna's Lunchbox 1
Bird's Isle 2
Celebrity 3
De Barcelona 4
Nerie's 5
Riverside Tavern 6
Sumathi Indian 7

## Tourist information

**Belize Tourist Board**
*64 Regent St, T227-2420, www.travelbelize.org.*
*Mon-Thu 0800-1200, 1300-1700, Fri 0800-*
*1200, 1300-1630.*
Provides a bus schedule with a map of Belize
City, as well as hotel lists. There's also an
office in the Tourism Village.

## Where to stay

On the north side of the swing-bridge,
turn left up North Front St for some of the
cheaper hotels. Most places can arrange
airport pick-up with advance notice, but
clarify costs carefully.

**$$$$ Radisson Fort George**
*2 Marine Parade, T223-3333,*
*www.radisson.com.*
A large and well-attired hotel spread across
3 wings, including the Club Wing, where
rooms have marble floors and panoramic
views of the Caribbean; and the Colonial
Section with balconies overlooking the sea.
Rooms are excellent, the staff are helpful,
and the service is good. Amenities include a
main restaurant (and **Stonegrill Restaurant**
where food is cooked on hot, volcanic
stones), 2 lovely pools, bar, coffee shop,
fitness room and small garden.

**$$$$ The Great House**
*13 Cork St, T223-3400,*
*www.greathousebelize.com.*
Built in 1927, this beautifully maintained
4-storey colonial mansion claims to be the
largest intact classic wooden structure in
Belize. Lodgings here include 16 spacious
rooms with homey furnishings and mod
cons; some have ocean view. Facilities
include a bar-restaurant, **The Smoky
Mermaid**, in the colonial courtyard on
the lower floor.

**$$$ D'Nest**
*475 Cedar St, Belama Phase II, T223-5416,*
*www.dnestinn.com.*
D'Nest is a very hospitable and
accommodating B&B. Located 3 miles out
of the city centre in a very safe middle class
neighbourhood, it features a selection of
cosy rooms with comfortable king-size
beds and interesting Belizean antiques.
The garden is lush and tranquil and the
thoughtful hosts are very knowledgeable
about the country.

**$$$ Villa Boscardi**
*6043 Manatee Dr, Buttonwood Bay,*
*T223-1691, www.villaboscardi.com.*
Secluded, gracious, friendly and tasteful,
Villa Boscardi is a European-style B&B
situated in a safe residential neighbourhood,
a short distance from downtown. It has 7
spacious rooms fully kitted with large beds,
Wi-Fi, a/c, cable TV and attractive tropical
hardwood furnishings. Pleasant garden,
good cooked breakfast included.

**$$$-$$ Bella Sombra**
*36 Hydes Lane, T223-0223,*
*www.lasbrisasdelmar.net.*
This place has an excellent downtown
location very close to the water taxi
terminals. Rooms are spacious, clean and
well-equipped with Wi-Fi, cable TV, ice cold
a/c and small kitchenettes with microwaves
and fridges (no cookers). There's also a
communal area and parking. Good and safe.

**$$ Bakadeer Inn**
*74 Cleghorn St, T223-0659,*
*www.bakadeerinn.com.*
Located in an area of the city once known
as the Bakadeer, this friendly downtown
inn near the riverside has 12 small but
comfortable rooms with hot water, a/c, and
cable TV. The property also includes a large
central lobby area with tables and chairs,
good for hanging out. Simple, quiet, and
well kept.

## $$ Red Hut Inn
*90 Bella Vista, T223-1907, www.red-hut-inn-belize.50megs.com.*
Located 6 miles from the international airport in a safe residential district, Red Hut Inn is good option for those who don't want to contend with the hustle of downtown Belize City. Rooms are quiet and simple, equipped with cable TV, hot water and Wi-Fi. They also have a deck, hammock and loungers, and can organize connections to the domestic airport and the water taxis.

## $$-$ Belcove Hotel
*9 Regent St West, T227-3054, www.belcove.com.*
Overlooking the waterfront near the swing bridge, the Belcove Hotel is a good, safe downtown option for those on a budget. Rooms are modest, with ($$) or without ($) private bath. Popular with international travellers. There's free coffee in the morning, and it's within easy walking distance of the water taxis.

### Restaurants

It can be difficult to find places to eat between 1500-1800.

## $$$ Riverside Tavern
*2 Mapp St.*
Not a locals' joint, but an upscale American-style bar-restaurant with sports TV, beer, burgers, onion rings and other artery-hardening comfort food. This place will suit those seeking safe shelter or familiar flavours. So-so ambience but the burgers are something special. It's perched on the riverside, as the name suggests.

## $$$-$$ Celebrity
*Marine Parade Blvd, Volta Building, T223-7272, www.celebritybelize.com.*
This reliable middle class restaurant might be considered upmarket for Belize City. It serves local and international food in large portions, including salads, burgers, pastas, meat, and seafood. Popular with families, couples and local businessmen.

## $$$-$$ De Barcelona
*Buttonwood Bay Blvd, T666-4680.*
The best Catalan and Spanish cuisine in town with tasty paella, red tuna, beef tenderloin and tapas. Smart, hip interior and cool outdoor seating under a *palapa*. They also host live regular live music and serve delicious sangria. Excellent, creative and authentic. Recommended for a special evening out.

## $$$-$$ Sumathi Indian
*19 Baymen Av, T223-1172.*
Weary Brits will not be able to resist this authentic curry house. Their menu includes a tempting array of Indian specialities such as chicken, mutton, and shrimp biryani, 4 varieties of naan bread, papadums, chicken tikka and madras, and many more flavourful curries to invigorate even the most jaded taste buds. Good and wholesome, the taste of home.

## $$ Bird's Isle
*90 Albert St.*
Bird's Isle features an open-air deck with panoramic ocean views, ideal for taking in the sunset. Its name refers to the small islet located off the city's southeastern shore. They serve reasonable seafood, salads, burgers, steaks and chicken; you pay for the setting. A great lunch spot; however, take a taxi as the neighbourhood is sketchy.

## $$ Nerie's
*Corner Queen and Daly St, T223-4028, www.neries.bz. Open for breakfast, lunch, and dinner.*
A family-owned business for over 15 years, Nerie's serves up home-cooked Belizean cuisine (including 'the best rice and beans in the country'), along with international fare such as burgers, salads, and fresh fruit juices. They have an extensive menu. At their Douglas Jones St branch there is also a bar.

## $ Anna's Lunchbox
*North Front St. Open for breakfast and lunch.*
Managed by Miss Anna, this friendly locals' place is conveniently located near the San

Pedro Water Taxi, great for a quick bite en route to the island. They serve tasty home-cooked Belizean grub, including fresh Johnny cakes, fry jacks, jerk chicken and, to wash it down, ice-cold Belikin beer.

## Bars and clubs

There are lots of bars, some with jukeboxes, poolrooms and karaoke nights.

Fri night is the most popular night for going out. Clubs often have a cover charge of US$5 and drinks are expensive. Happy hour on Fri starts at 1600 at **Radisson Fort George** and continues at **Biltmore**, Calypso and elsewhere. The best and safest bars are at major hotels: **Fort George, Biltmore Plaza, Bellevue** and **Princess**.

### Club Calypso
*At the Princess Hotel, see Where to stay.* Top bands at weekends.

### The Wet Lizard
*Near the Tourism Village.* Good American/Creole fare, great view.

## Entertainment

### Cinema
**Princess Hotel**, *see Where to stay.* A 2-theatre modern cinema, showing recent movies for US$7.50.

## Shopping

The whole city closes down on Sun except for a few shops open in the morning, eg **Brodies** in the centre of town. Banks and many shops and offices are also closed on Sat afternoons.

### Books
**Brodies**, *Albert St.* Decent selection of books on Belize and some paperback novels. It is now the only bookshop in the city.

### Markets and supermarkets
The market is by the junction of North Front St and Fort St.

**Brodies**. *Closed Sun.* The widest grocery selection, though prices are slightly higher.

### Souvenirs
Handicrafts, woodcarvings and straw items are all good buys. Zericote (or Xericote) wood carvings can be bought at **Brodies**, Central Park end of Regent St (which also sells postcards), the **Fort George Hotel** (see Where to stay, above), or **Egbert Peyrefitte** (11a Cemetery Rd). Such wood carvings are the best buy, but to find a carver rather than buy the tourist fare in shops, ask a taxi driver. The wood sculpture of **Charles Gabb**, who introduced carving into Belize, can be seen at the Art Centre, near Government House. Wood carvers sell their work in front of the main hotels.

**Belize Audubon Society**, *see box, page 212.* A small but good selection of posters, T-shirts, gifts, and jewellery, all locally made in villages, and all at very reasonable prices.

**National Handicraft Center**, *South Park St.* The Belize Chamber of Commerce's showcase promotes craftspeople from all over Belize; come here first for an overview of Belizean art and crafts.

## What to do

### Cultural centres
**Audubon Society**, *see box, page 212.*
**Baron Bliss Institute**, public library, temporary exhibitions and 1 stela and 2 large discs from Caracol on display.
**Belize National Handicraft Center**, *sales room on South Park St.* A good supply of books about Belize culture.
**Programme for Belize**, *1 Eyre St, T227-5616, www.pfbelize.org.* A conservation organization that manages land reserves including Río Bravo.
**Society for the Promotion of Education and Research (SPEAR)**, *5638 Gentle Av, T223-1668, www.spear.org.bz.* A great reference library for everything Belizean.

## Diving

**Hugh Parkey's Belize Dive Connection**, *www.belizediving.com*. Based at the **Radisson's** dock, this is a professional outfit.

## Tour operators

**Discovery Expeditions**, *5916 Manatee Dr, Buttonwood Bay, T223-0748, www.discovery belize.com*. An efficient and professional company offering interesting cultural and adventure tours out of the city and across the country. Recommended.
**Green Dragon**, *based out near Belmopan, but covering most of the country, T822-2124, www.greendragonbelize.com*. Very helpful and will arrange hotel bookings and tours all over Belize.
**Island Expeditions Co**, *Canada-based company, T1-800-667-1630 (Canada/USA), T0800-404 9535 (UK toll-free), www.island expeditions.com*. Adventure and multi-sport wilderness, rainforest and reef trips. Also run **Belize Kayaking**, *www.belizekayaking.com*.
**Maya Travel Services**, *42 Cleghorn St, T223-1623, www.mayatravelservices.com/contact. php*. Gets positive reports.
**S&L Guided Tours**, *91 North Front St, T227-7593, www.sltravelbelize.com*. Recommended group travel (groups of 4 people for most tours, 2 people for Tikal). If booking tours in Belize from abroad it is advisable to check prices and services offered with a reputable tour operator in Belize first.

### Air

International flights arrive at **Phillip Goldson International Airport** on the Northern Highway, Ladyville, T225-2045, www.pgiabelize.com, 10½ miles from Belize City. Taxi to town US$25, 30 mins; see also below. It's a 1½-mile walk to the junction of the Northern Highway where buses pass to the centre (US$1). **Belize City Municipal Airport** for local flights is 2 miles north of the city centre on the seafront, 15 mins' drive away. Taxi to the centre US$5, no bus service.

The international airport has facilities in the check-in area including toilets, a restaurant, internet, bank (daily 0830-1200 and 1230-1800), viewing deck and duty-free shop. There are no facilities on the arrivals side but you can just walk round to the check-in area. If getting a taxi into the centre, be aware that taxi drivers strongly discourage sharing so team up, if need be, before getting outside. Make sure your taxi is legitimate by checking for the green licence plates. Taxis operate on a fixed rate, so you should get the same price quoted by every driver. Ask to see a rate sheet if you have doubts about the price. If transferring direct to or from the islands or elsewhere in Belize with a domestic carrier be sure to stipulate that you would like a connection through the international airport. This will

cost an extra US$20 or so, offset by avoiding an unnecessary transit through Belize City to the municipal airport or boat dock (and an associated US$25 taxi fare).

Domestic services, including the island hops operated by **Maya Island** and **Tropic Air**, arrive at the pocket-sized municipal airstrip, flights every 30 mins, 0700-1630. Flights to and from the islands can be taken from the international airport and companies link their flights to international arrivals and departures; flights from the international airport cost extra (see above). **Maya** and **Tropic** also have services to **Flores**, Guatemala.

## Boat

Boats to **Caye Caulker** continuing to **San Pedro** (Ambergris Caye) and **Chetumal in Mexico** leave from 3 principal boat terminals in Belize City, with sailings at regular times between around 0700 and 1730 each day. As long as you check schedules beforehand you are never more than 30 mins from a boat during the day. The **Water Jets Express** (T226-2194, www.sanpedrowatertaxi.com) dock lies on Bird's Isle at the far end of Albert St in the southside of Belize City, just beyond St John's Cathedral. The company has services 4 times daily to Caye Caulker (US$12 one way, 30-45 mins), San Pedro (US$18 one way, 60-80 mins) and once daily on to Chetumal in Mexico (US$35 from San Pedro and US$40 from Caye Caulker, both one way). The company is also an official agent for Mexican **ADO** buses, and can book tickets from Chetumal or all along the Riviera Maya to Cancún, and connections beyond, including Guatemala.

Belize's other 2 boat terminals both lie on North Front St, about 200 m southeast of the swing bridge in the city centre. Closest to the bridge is the **Marine Terminal**, home to the Caye Caulker Water Taxi Association (T226-0992, www.cayecaulkerwatertaxi.com) also with 4 times daily to Caye Caulker (US$10 one way, 45 mins), San Pedro (US$15 one way, about 90 mins).

A little further on up the same road right next to the cruise ship tourist facility in the **Brown Sugar Terminal**, is the San Pedro Belize Express Water Taxi (Brown Sugar Market Square, 111 North Front St, T223-2225, http://belizewatertaxi.com). They have the same number of sailings to the same destinations as the Caye Caulker Water Taxi Association, for the same price, and once daily, on to Chetumal in Mexico (US$35 from San Pedro and US$40 from Caye Caulker, both one way). Terminals have areas where you can leave a bag and the Caye Caulker Water Taxi Association terminal has a few shops and cafés.

For further information on border crossings to Mexico and Guatemala, see Border crossings box in Practicalities chapter.

## Bus

The main **bus station** is on West Collette Canal St to the west of town, an area that requires some caution. If arriving after dark, arrange for a taxi as walking through this part of town in darkness with luggage can be dangerous; a taxi costs around US$3 to the centre.

Within the city the fare is US$0.50 run by **Belize in Transit** services. They originate next to the taxi stand on Cemetery Rd.

There are bus services to all the main towns. The **National Transportation Co** operates Northern Transport from West Collette Canal St (can store luggage, US$0.50).

**North** to Chetumal (see Southern Mexico chapter), about 15 daily each way, roughly every 30 mins, starting at 0500 until 1800, 3 hrs, US$2.50, express buses from 0600 stopping at **Orange Walk** and **Corozal** only, US$6.50, 2½ hrs. If taking a bus from Chetumal which will arrive in Belize City after dark, decide on a hotel and go there by taxi.

West towards **Guatemala** by bus to **Belmopan** and **San Ignacio**, express bus 0900, US$3, with a/c and refreshments, ordinary bus every 30 mins, Mon-Sat frequent 0600-1900, Sun 0630-1700. The 0600, 0630 and 1015 buses connect at the border with services to **Flores**, Guatemala. To **San Ignacio**, **Benque Viejo** and the **Guatemalan border** via Belmopan, US$2.50 to Belmopan, US$4 to San Ignacio, US$4.50 to Benque, hourly Mon-Sat, 1100-1900. The last possible bus connection to **Flores** leaves the border at 1600, but it is better to get an earlier bus to arrive in daylight. Many buses leave for **Melchor de Mencos**, 0600-1030. To **Flores**, Guatemala, minibuses leave the Marine Terminal on Front St in Belize City; make reservations the previous day. See also Border crossings box in Practicalities chapter.

1st-class express buses from Belize City to **Flores/Tikal** with **Mundo Maya/Línea Dorada**, www.tikalmayanworld.com, leave from Belize City daily at 1000 and 1700, with buses connecting to Guatemala City and beyond. Also with services heading north to **Chetumal**. Check the **Mundo Maya** counter in the Marine Terminal on North Front St.

**South** to **Dangriga**, via Belmopan and the Hummingbird Hwy. **Southern Transport** (T227-3937), from the corner of Vernon and Johnson St near the Belchina Bridge, several daily on the hour 0800-1600, plus Mon 0600, US$5. **James** (T702-2049), to **Punta Gorda** via **Dangriga**, **Cockscomb Basin Wildlife Sanctuary** and **Independence**, every hour from 0515 to 1015 and 1215 to 1515 with the last bus at 1545, 6-8 hrs, US$14.

## Car

**Car hire** Cars start at US$75 plus insurance of around US$15 a day. Most rental firms have offices in Belize City and opposite the international airport terminal building.

**Avis**, T203-4619, avisbelize@btl.net. **Budget**, 2½ miles, Northern Hwy, T223-2435, www.budget-belize.com. **Crystal Auto Rental**, Mile 5 Northern Hwy, T223-1600, www.crystal-belize.com, cheapest deals in town, but not always most reliable, wide selection of vehicles, will release insurance papers for car entry to Guatemala and Mexico. **Hertz**, 11a Cork St, beside Radisson Fort George Hotel, T223-5395, www.hertz belize.com, and International Airport, T225-3300. **Pancho's**, 5747 Lizarraga Av, T224-5554, www.panchosrentalbelize.com, locally owned rental company.

## Taxi

Official cabs have green licence plates (drivers have ID card); within Belize, US$4 for 1 or 2 people; slightly more for 3 or more. There is a taxi stand on Central Park, another on the corner of Collet Canal St and Cemetery Rd, and a number of taxis on Albert St, Queen St and around town. Outside Belize City, US$1.75 per mile, regardless of number of passengers. Belize City to the resorts in Cayo District approximately US$100-125, 1-4 people. No meters, so beware of overcharging and make sure fare is quoted in BZ$ not US$.

# Northern
## cayes

★ The cayes off the coast are attractive, relaxing, slow and very 'Caribbean', an excellent place for diving, sea fishing or just lazing about. Palm trees fringe the coastline, providing day-long shade for resting in your hammock looking out at the stunning azure seas. They are popular destinations, especially in August and between December and May.

There are some 212 sq miles of cayes. The cayes and atolls were home to fishermen and resting points to clean the catch or grow coconuts. But they have always been valued. The Maya built the site of Marco Gonzalez on the southwestern tip of Ambergris Caye, the largest and most populated of the islands.

Nearby Caye Caulker is a popular destination for the budget travellers, while serious divers head for the Turneffe Islands. Other smaller cayes are home to exclusive resorts or remain uninhabited, many being little more than mangrove swamps. St George's Caye, nine miles northeast of Belize, was once the capital and the scene of the battle in 1798 that established British possession.

**Best** for
Birds ▪ Diving ▪ Lazing ▪ Sailing

This island (pronounced Am-*ber*-gris, population 10,445), along with the town of San Pedro, has grown rapidly over the last couple of years, with over 50 hotels and guesthouses on the island. Buildings are still restricted to no more than three storeys in height, and the many wooden structures retain an authentic village atmosphere.

The very helpful **Ambergris tourist information office** ① *Mon-Sat 1000-1300, 1400-1900*, is next to the town hall.

Although sand is in abundance, there are few beach areas around San Pedro town. You cannot, in practice, walk north along the beach from San Pedro to Xcalak, Mexico. The emphasis is on snorkelling on the nearby barrier reef and Hol Chan Marine Park, and the fine scuba diving, sailing, fishing and board sailing. The main boat jetties are on the east (Caribbean Sea) side of San Pedro. It can be dangerous to swim near San Pedro as there have been serious accidents with boats. Boats are restricted to about 5 mph within the line of red buoys about 25 yards offshore, but this is not always adhered to. There is a 'safe' beach in front of the park, just to the south of the government dock. A short distance to the north and south of San Pedro lie miles of deserted beachfront, where picnic barbecues are popular for day-tripping snorkellers and birders who have visited the nearby small cayes hoping to glimpse rosets, spoonbills or white ibis. If you go north you have to cross a small inlet with hand-pulled ferry, US$0.50 for foreigners. **Note** Only very experienced snorkellers should attempt to swim in the cutting between the reef and the open sea.

### Around Ambergris Caye

Just south of Ambergris Caye, and not far from Caye Caulker, is the **Hol Chan Marine Park** ① *US$12 entry fee; the park office (with reef displays and information on Bacalar Chico National Park to the north) is on Caribeña St, T226-2247, www.holchanbelize.org*. This underwater natural park is divided into three zones: Zone A is the reef, where fishing is prohibited; Zone B is the sea grass beds, where fishing can only be done with a special licence (the **Boca Ciega** blue hole is here); Zone C is mangroves where fishing also requires a licence. Only certified scuba divers may dive in the reserve. Fish feeding, although prohibited, takes place at Shark Ray Alley, where about 15 sharks and rays are fed for the entertainment of tourists. Not the most natural of experiences.

**San Pedro** is well known for its diving. Long canyons containing plenty of soft and hard coral formations start at around 50-60 ft going down to 120 ft. Often these have grown into hollow tubes, which make for interesting diving. **Tackle Box**, **Esmeralda**, **Cypress**, **M & Ms** and **Tres Cocos** are only some of the dive sites. The visibility in this area is usually over 100 ft. There is a recompression chamber in San Pedro and a US$1 tax on each tank fill insures treatment throughout the island.

Although offshore, Ambergris Caye airport makes arranging tours to visit places on the mainland very easy (for example, Altun Ha US$60 per person; Lamanai US$125 per person) while still being able to enjoy other water experiences (catamaran sailing, deep-sea fishing, manatee and Coco Solo).

### Where to stay

Accommodation is generally upscale and poor value relative to the mainland.

#### San Pedro

**$$$$ Changes in Latitude**
*36 Coconut Dr, T226-2986, www.changesinlatitudesbelize.com.*
Located 150 m from the sea, this sweet B&B has 6 rooms decorated in retro style. Guests have free use of bikes, a golf cart and the yacht club pool. Local artists occasionally hang out in the courtyard. Lots of good reports, popular, book in advance.

**$$$$ Ramon's Village**
*Coconut Dr, T226-2071, www.ramons.com.*
Nestled amid bougainvillea and hibiscus flowers, this popular dive resort features upscale cabanas styled after the Tahitian cottages on the Polynesian island of Bora Bora. Even if you're not diving it's well worth staying here as there are plenty additional activities of fishing, swimming, boating and snorkelling. Amenities include a pool with a beach-club atmosphere. Highly recommended.

**$$$$ Sun Breeze Hotel**
*Coconut Dr, T226-2191, www.sunbreeze.net.*
The **Sun Breeze** is a modern, villa-style resort with architecture reminiscent of Spain's Costa del Sol. Its dive shop is a branch of Hugh Parkey's (www.belizediving.com), one of the best on the island. Good service and comfortable rooms, nice pool and restaurant. Their sister establishment, Sun Breeze Suites, offer 12 ocean view and 8 ocean front suites with fully equipped kitchen. Recommended.

**$$$$-$$$ Holiday Hotel**
*Barrier Reef Dr, T+1 713 893-3825, www.sanpedroholiday.com.*
This locally owned landmark establishment is built in traditional Caribbean style.

With a convenient central location, it has 16 rooms including suites and a *casita*. Fun atmosphere with good facilities including a bar-grill, spa and tour desk.

**$$$ Conch Shell Inn**
*11 Foreshore St, T226-2062, www.ambergriscaye.com/conchshell.*
Established in 1973, this beachfront favourite has 10 rooms with a shared veranda overlooking the ocean, ideal for chilling out in a hammock. All rooms feature mini-bar, Wi-Fi and slumber-inducing tempurpedic mattresses; some have a full kitchenette. Cheery, friendly, and pink.

**$$$ Mayan Princess**
*Pelican St and seafront, T226-2778, www.mayanprincesshotel.com.*
Right on the beach and close to the heart of the action, the Mayan Princess boasts a great downtown location. Its suites are good value for the island and include a fully equipped kitchen, living area, a/c, cable TV and veranda-balcony. Rooms on the 3rd floor catch the best views and sea breezes. Ask about deals and discounts. Dive packages available with their affiliated shop.

**$$ Hotel San Pedrano**
*T226-2054, sanpedrano@btl.net.*
Modest family-run lodgings, low-key and economical for the island. Rooms are fairly no frills, but they feature a/c, fan, Wi-Fi, private bath and hot water. It's not luxurious, but is adequate for those who intend to spend most of their time on the beach. Friendly, helpful management.

**$$-$ Pedro's Inn**
*Seagrape Dr, T226-3825, www.backpackersbelize.com.*
Starting at US$10 per person per night, this is the only true budget place on the island, aimed squarely at the backpacker market. Their private rooms (**$$**) are fairly good. There's a bar, barbecue and pools.

### $$-$ Ruby's
*On the beach, T226-2063.*
Ramshackle and basic with paper thin walls and an air of decay, Ruby's is fairly typical of cheap Central American lodgings. Its 26 rooms have a/c or fan and private or shared bath. Good views, low prices (for the island) and a central location.

### Outside San Pedro
Several resort-style complexes outside the town offer seclusion and an ambience that borders on paradise.

### $$$$ El Pescador
*On Punta Arena beach 3 miles north of San Pedro, access by boat, T226-2398, www.elpescador.com.*

This award-winning sports fishing lodge offers a range of packages to suit anglers, couples and families. Lodgings include 8 wood-built private villas with all mod cons. There's a restaurant-bar, 3 pools, gym, massage, complimentary kayaks and bicycles and scuba lessons. Good reputation and service.

### $$$$ Mata Chica Resort
*5 miles north of town, T226-5010, www.matachica.com.*

This tasteful, tranquil, European-owned resort features 26 beautiful and stylish stucco cabins with thatched roofs, original art from around the world, mosaic bathrooms, a/c and Matouk and Frette linens. Located on a lovely beach with amenities that include spa treatments, jacuzzi, infinity pool and

the award-winning **Mambo** Restaurant. Romantic and indulgent.

### $$$$ Portofino
*6 miles north, access by boat, T888 240 1923 (toll free), T678-5096, www.portofinobelize.com.*
Overlooking the sea, Portofino offers a series of spacious and very comfortable thatched roof beach cabins gathered around a jewel-like pool. The Belgian owners organize excursions, diving and run one of the best kitchens on the island. Rustic chic and romantic.

### $$$$ Victoria House
*2 miles south of town, T226-2067, T1-800-247-5159 (US toll free), www.victoria-house.com.*
This lavish, crisp-white exclusive resort has received praise from luxury travel media such as Condé Nast. It offers 4 different types of stylishly decorated lodgings, including *casitas*, 'plantation rooms', suites and private villas. Breakfast included. Excellent facilities, including a lovely pool and a good dive shop. Highly recommended.

### $$$$-$$$ Corona del Mar
*Coconut Dr, ½ mile south of San Pedro, T226-2055, www.coronadelmarhotel.com.*
Located within easy walking distance of the town (15 mins), but far enough to enjoy some peace and quiet, the beachfront Corona del Mar offers a variety of accommodation, including standard rooms with ocean, pool or garden views, fully kitted apartments, a master suite and a cottage. A good option for couples, groups or families. Free rum punch all day.

### $$$ The Turtleman's House
*Bacalar Chico Marine Reserve, north end of the island, www.turtlemanshouse.com.*
A Robinson Crusoe-style wooden shack over the water, extremely basic and adventurous. Managed by a marine biologist, Greg Smith, aka the Turtleman, this intriguing accommodation promises up close wilderness encounters with the reef in front

of the cabana and options for excellent turtle, manatee and jungle tours. Something different. Recommended for nature lovers.

### $$$-$$ Ak'bol Yoga Retreat and Eco-Resort
*1 mile north of town past the bridge, T226-2073, www.akbol.com.*
The epitome of rustic chic, this attractive yoga retreat has a range of accommodation, including economical 'village rooms' ($$) and beautiful thatched cabanas ($$$) with mosaic work, carved mahogany sinks and private porches. In addition to yoga, they offer snorkelling, diving, massage and tours.

## Restaurants

### San Pedro

### $$$ Elvi's Kitchen
*www.elviskitchen.com.*
Upmarket restaurant with live music and a roof built around flamboyant tree. It's popular, so can get very busy, and has won international awards.

### $$$ Hidden Treasure
*4088 Sarstoon St, T226-4111, www.hidden treasurebelize.com. Open for dinner only.*
Awarded 'Restaurant of the Year' by the Belize Tourism Board, Hidden Treasure promises a truly magical and romantic dining experience. It serves culinary delights such as roasted lamb chops with wild mushrooms and Madeira wine; fresh snapper fillet seasoned with Mayan spices and cooked in banana leaf; and coconut chicken breast served with orange and ginger sauce. Meals are served in a beautiful garden setting. Highly recommended.

### $$$ Wild Mango's
*South of main strip, T226-2859. Closed Mon.*
Run by Amy Knox, former chef at **Victoria House**, this place is in a rustic setting overlooking the sea. The delicious meals are tastefully presented; try the rum-soaked bacon-wrapped shrimp. Recommended.

### $$$-$$ Blue Water Grill
*At the Sunbreeze Hotel, www. bluewatergrillbelize.com.*
Owned by Kelly McDermott Kanabar, who was born and raised in San Pedro but educated in the US, the popular Blue Water grill overlooks the beach with an open front. They serve an eclectic range of international cuisine including ceviche, buffalo wings, tacos, salads, sandwiches and more. Pizzas are available in the evening and a sushi menu for dinner on Tue and Thu. Recommended.

### $$$-$$ El Fogon
*2 Trigger Fish St, north of Tropic Air Terminal.*
This very presentable and busy restaurant serves delicious Belizean cuisine prepared on a traditional hearth fire. Their seafood is particularly recommended, including dishes such as fish, shrimp and lobster kebabs in mango sauce; lime and garlic shrimp; and conch fritters with honey mustard dipping sauce. A great family place. Recommended.

### $$$-$$ Hurricane's Ceviche Bar and Grill
*Foreshore Beachfront, Coconut Dr.*
Perched at the end of a wooden pier over the waves, this popular seafood restaurant serves very good ceviche, shrimp, conch, lobster and catch of the day. A fine place for quaffing cold beers and rum. Casual and fun, but not cheap; you pay for the ocean views and friendly ambience.

### $$ Estel's Dine by the Sea
*On the beach close to water taxi terminal.*
Good food and 1940s-50s music.

### $$-$ My Secret Deli
*Caribeña St. Open for breakfast and lunch.*
Managed by the amiable Don Oscar from El Salvador, this fantastic locals' joint serves a selection of flavourful daily specials inspired by local recipes and old favourites from the homeland. Offerings include stewed pork with coconut rice and conch soup with corn tortillas. Eat in or take-away. Large

portions, good value and friendly service. Recommended.

### $ Dande's Frozen Custard
*Middle St, www.dande.bz.*
Popular place for an ice cream cone, sorbet or frozen custard.

---

## Outside San Pedro

### $$$ Aji Tapa Bar & Restaurant
*2½ miles north of San Pedro, T226-4047.*
Nestled among palm trees behind a creek, Aji Tapa enjoys prime ocean views from its location on the edge of the beach. They serve tapas and beautifully presented seafood, including good paella, conch ceviche and fish fillets. Candlelit and close to nature with a rustic, romantic atmosphere.

### $$$ Lazy Croc BBQ
*2½ miles north of San Pedro, T226-4015.*
Hidden among the mangroves, this breezy family restaurant with a rustic wooden deck serves good comfort food, hearty platters of barbecue grub, including sweet baby back ribs and succulent pulled pork. Look out for the crocodiles which live in the pond, easy to spot from the bridge and the balcony. A fun place, but not cheap.

### $$$-$$ Palapa Bar and Grill
*1½ miles north of San Pedro.*
This young party place consists of a large wooden *palapa* on the water. They serve hearty grilled grub including smoked barbecue chicken wings, sausage dip, fish platter and a 'kickass humungous hamburger'. They also supply inner tubes so you can float on the water and drink Belikin beers lowered to you in a bucket.

## Bars and clubs

**Big Daddy's Disco**, open evenings but cranks up at midnight. Try also 'Chicken Drop' in Pier Lounge at **Spindrift Hotel** on a Thu night: you bet US$1 on which square the chicken will leave its droppings. **Jaguar's**

Temple and Barefoot Iguana are current popular nightspots.

## Shopping

There are many gift shops in the centre of San Pedro town. It is better to shop around the smaller shops and groceries where prices are clearly marked. When paying check that the bill is correct.

Fidos has Belizean Arts (paintings and prints by local artists) and Ambar Jewelry. Kasbah and Orange sell local crafts and jewellery.

## What to do

### Diving and snorkelling

Park fees are not included in prices quoted. US$10 for Hol Chan, US$30 for Blue Hole, US$10 Half Moon Caye and US$10 for Bacalar Chico. Be clear on what's included. You will likely be charged extra for equipment. Instruction to PADI Open Water level available, from US$350. Local 2-tank dive US$60, Turneffe US$140-160, Blue Hole US$185. Many operators practice chumming to attract fish and sharks; divers should discourage operators from doing this. Accommodation and dive packages at some hotels are very good value. All dive operators offer snorkelling trips from US$25 for Shark Ray Alley to US$125 for the Blue Hole.

   **Note** Check the diving shop's recent safety record before diving.
**Ambergris Divers**, *T226-2634, www.ambergrisdivers.com*. Will collect divers from Caye Caulker for Blue Hole trip. Very good-value dive and accommodation packages with a number of hotels on the island.
**Amigos del Mar**, *opposite Lily's, T226-2706, www.amigosdive.com*. Gets a lot of return customers and has been recommended, but practices chumming at the Blue Hole.
**Ramon's Village**, *T226 2071, www.ramons.com*. A bit more expensive than other operators. Check the diving shop's recent safety record before diving.

### Fishing

**Extreme Reef Adventures**, *office by the dock at Fido's, T226-3513*. Parasailing, banana tubing and other sport tours.
**Sailsports, Holiday Hotel**, *T226-4488, www.sailsportsbelize.com*. Windsurfing, sailing, kitesurfing lessons and rentals.

### Tour operators

**Tanisha Tours**, *T226 2314, www.tanishatours.com*. Trips to the Maya sites on the north of the caye in the Bacalar Chico National Park.
**Travel and Tour Belize**, *in town, T226-2031*. Helpful, all services and can arrange flights, with a request stop at Sarteneja (for the Shipstern Nature Reserve).

## Transport

### Air

**Tropic Air**, T226-2012, and **Maya Island Air**, T226-2435, have flights to/from both **Belize City** airports, many hourly, to **Caye Caulker** and **Corozal**. Charter services are available.

### Bicycle and golf cart

Bicycles US$2.50 per hour, negotiate for long-term rates. Golf carts from US$15 per hour and up to US$300 per week, battery or gas powered, driver's licence needed.

### Boat

More interesting than going by air are the boats. All these call at **Caye Caulker** and San Pedro. **San Pedro Belize Express water taxi**, http://belizewatertaxi.com, to **Caye Caulker** and **Belize City** at 0700 (express to Belize City), 1130, 1430, 1630 and 1800. With **San Pedro Jet Express** at 0600, 1030, 1500 and 1730. Many regular boats to Caye Caulker. Daily services to **Chetumal** in Mexico.

   The *Island Ferry*, T226-3231, from Fido's dock, services the north of the island every 2 hrs from 0700-1700 then hourly 1800-2200. Also at 2400 and 0200 on Wed, Fri and Sat. Returns 0600-2200 every 2 hrs, US$10-25.

On Caye Caulker, a thin line of white sandy beach falls to a sea of blue and green, while the reef can be seen a mile and a half from the shore. By day on this tranquil island, it's diving and snorkelling, sea and sand; at dusk everyone heads up to the Split to watch the sunset. By night it's eating, drinking and dancing. A quiet lobster-fishing island (closed season 15 February to 14 June) until fairly recently, its relaxed atmosphere, gentle climate, postcard-perfect views and the myriad small restaurants and bars have drawn increasing numbers of tourists.

The caye is actually two islands separated by a small channel (the Split); swimming is possible here but beware of fishing and powerboats. All services are on the southern island and, in the north, there is a **marine reserve** ⓘ *free for school parties, tourists are asked for a US$2 donation to help expansion and to increase the work in ecology education.* In the south, next to **Shirley's**, is the **Caye Caulker Mini Reserve**.

Tour operators and hotels on the island have worked hard to improve services for visitors. The atmosphere is friendly and easy-going, but the usual common sense rules apply with regards to personal safety. Drugs are readily available, but they are illegal and you shouldn't expect any sympathy should you get into difficulties. Some think the atmosphere is more relaxed out of high season. Sandflies can be ferocious in season (December to February); take long trousers and a good repellent. Make sure you fix prices before going on trips or hiring equipment and, if you pay the night before, get a receipt.

A walk south along the shore takes you to the airstrip, the Caye Caulker Mini Reserve and to mangroves where the rare black catbird can be seen and its sweet song heard.

### Around Caye Caulker

**Reef trips** are the same as those found on Ambergris Caye; for more details see What to do, above, under San Pedro.

Generally all trips are offered at the same price by agreement between tour operators, eliminating the need to shop around for a good price. Tour operators share clients if numbers are not sufficient. This means that you can be certain there is always a trip, but make sure that the boat operator is reliable. Tour organizers must be licensed by the **Belize Tourist Board** and should have a licence to prove it. To encourage high standards, and for your own safety, insist on seeing proof that your guide is licensed.

Protect against sunburn on reef trips, even while snorkelling. Tours are slightly cheaper from Caye Caulker than Ambergris Caye; see What to do, below.

**Listings** Caye Caulker *map p206*

### Where to stay

In all accommodation, take precautions against theft. The arrival pier is just about in the centre of town, with all the accommodation on or within a 15-min walk of the main street. The southern end of town is slightly quieter and has a smattering of mangrove and bird life, but it's quite a walk from the Split for swimming or snorkelling. Camping on the beach is forbidden.

**$$$$ Iguana Reef Inn**
*Near the football field, T226-0213,*
*www.iguanareefinn.com.*

# Caye Caulker

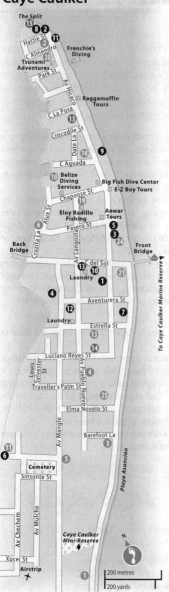

Located near the water's edge, a secluded and upscale resort with rooms that are spacious and decorated with local art and furniture. One of the best places on the island, relaxing and quiet.

### $$$$-$$$ Sea Dreams
*At north end of the island, T226-0602, www.seadreamsbelize.com.*
This popular family-run boutique hotel offers a range of cosy and tastefully attired rooms ($$$) overlooking a lush courtyard with a Banyan tree, as well as lodging in a colourful cabana, modern apartments and a house ($$$$). 10% of profits go to a community school established by co-owner Heidi Curry. Recommended.

### $$$$-$$$ Seaside Cabanas
*First place you reach off the boat, T226-0498, www.seasidecabanas.com.*
Adorned with earthy Moroccan furnishings, **Seaside Cabanas** offers comfortable rooms and cabins designed in Mexican-Belizean style. The best ones have their own roof terraces, kitchenettes, sea views and private hot tubs. Amenities include pool and funky bar. Excellent tours and very helpful.

### $$$ Lazy Iguana
*Southwest side of the island, a block from the cemetery, T226-0350, www.lazyiguana.net.*

| Where to stay | Restaurants |
|---|---|
| Barefoot Beach 3 | Aladdin's 2 |
| Colinda Cabañas 1 | Amor y Cafe 1 |
| Iguana Reef Inn 10 | Caribbean Colors Art Café 3 |
| Lazy Iguana 11 | Chan's Take Out 13 |
| Mara's Place 2 | Glenda's 4 |
| Marin's Guest House 13 | Ice and Beans 5 |
| Maxhapan Cabañas 4 | The Little Kitchen 6 |
| Oasi 5 | Paradiso Café 11 |
| PAW Animal Sanctuary 6 | Pasta per Caso 7 |
| Rainbow 18 | Rainbow 9 |
| Sandy lane 19 | Rose's Bar & Grill 10 |
| Sea Dreams 20 | Syd's 12 |
| Seaside Cabanas 21 | Terry's Grill 8 |
| Tree Tops 25 | |
| Yuma's House 24 | **Bars & clubs** |
| | Herbal Tribes 13 |
| | I & I 14 |
| | Lazy Lizard 15 |

This beautifully designed B&B has a commanding rooftop terrace with 360-degree views, ideal for yoga, sunsets or simply lolling in a hammock. Guestrooms are spacious and homely, and downstairs you'll find 2 communal areas. Also offers onsite massages for guests. Tranquil.

### $$$ Oasi
*9 Av Mangle, T226 0384,
www.oasi-holidaysbelize.com.*
This popular apartment complex has modern, convenient and tastefully decorated units, with fully equipped kitchens, access to verandas with hammocks, Wi-Fi, cable TV and drinking water. Facilities include a bar, barbecue and complimentary use of bikes. A great option for couples and small families, but book in advance.

### $$$ Rainbow Hotel
*T226-0123, www.rainbowhotel-cayecaulker.com.*
This long-standing family-owned hotel enjoys a great central location on a street front facing the beach. Its deluxe suites overlook the ocean and enjoy modern conveniences such as TVs, fridge, a/c and safe. Other options include junior suites, a cabana and a *casita* with 2 apartments. Friendly and helpful.

### $$$ Tree Tops Guesthouse
*T226-0240, www.treetopsbelize.com.*
A long-standing Caye Caulker favourite built in Caribbean-Mediterranean style. This friendly guesthouse offers a range of spotless, spacious boutique rooms and suites, all decorated with intriguing art and craft pieces that reflect the travel experiences of the owners, Terry and Doris Creasy. German spoken, children over 10 only. Recommended.

### $$$-$$ Barefoot Beach
*Playa Asuncion, T226-0205,
www.barefootbeachbelize.com.*
Painted in candy coloured shades of pink, yellow and blue, this cheery and inviting establishment has a range of

accommodation including modern cabanas, cottages, bungalows and oceanfront and ocean-view suites equipped with fridges, cable TV, and a/c. Their most economical lodgings are clean and comfortable 'mini-huts' ($$).

### $$$-$$ Colinda Cabanas
*On the beach facing the reef, T226-0383,
www.colindacabanas.com.*
Enjoying almost constant cool breezes on the east side of the island, these inviting cabanas and suites have a plethora of mod cons including well-equipped kitchens, purified water, Wi-Fi and, most essentially, coffee grinders with Belizean beans. They also have a private pier with a palapa and hammocks, and can supply bicycles at no extra charge.

### $$$-$ Marin's Guest House
*Estrella St, 1½ blocks from the beach at the southern end, T226-0444,
www.marinsguesthouse.com.*
Established in 1970, Marin's is one of the oldest lodgings on the island. The new extension features 4 spacious, simple, comfortable and well-equipped suites in hacienda-style. There are also more economical rooms with private or shared facilities ($) in wooden cabins on stilts. Friendly and hospitable.

### $$$-$ PAW Animal Sanctuary
*1 Pasero St, T624-7076, www.
pawanimalsanctuarybelize.*
Lovers of felines will enjoy staying at the PAW Animal Sanctuary, home to many dozens of cats and a few dogs too. Lodging includes fully equipped self-catering suites ($$$-$$) and rustic beach cabanas ($). Your money goes to a good cause and volunteers get reduced rates. Contact in advance of your stay.

### $$ Mara's Place
*27 Hicaco Av, T600-0080.*
Simple, tidy and good value, this reliable budget hotel has several wood-built duplexes with units on both levels. Each has

their own fridge and porch with a hammock, but no a/c. Located near the Split, guests can also enjoy the private pier and sun loungers, and there's a shared kitchen too. Funky, colourful and fun.

### $$ Maxhapan Cabanas
*55 Av Pueblo Nuevo, T226-0118, maxhapan04@hotmail.com.*
Nestled amid coconut trees in a quiet neighbourhood in the south of the island, Maxhapan is a very hospitable establishment offering tranquil lodging in well-maintained Caribbean-style duplexes. Suites have fridges, cable TV and great private verandas for chilling out. A small, friendly place with lovely management. Recommended.

### $$-$ Sandy Lane
*Corner of Chapoose St and Langosta St, T226-0117.*
Run by Rico and Elma Novelo, an interesting couple who have been active in the local community for decades, **Sandy Lane** offers several simple bungalow-type cabins, clean and economical, and cheapest with shared bathrooms. Their best units feature kitchen and TV for longer stays. Recommended.

### $$-$ Yuma's House
*Playa Asuncion, T206-0019, www.yumashousebelize.com.*
Lots of good reports about this popular backpackers' hostel, one of the cheapest places on the caye and in a great beachfront location. Accommodation includes 6 small dorms ($) and 6 private rooms ($$), or you can sling a hammock. Good amenities, including 2 shared kitchens, chilled-out garden with sitting areas, and a private dock. Arty, funky, and well-maintained. Recommended.

### Restaurants

Beer is sold by the crate at the wholesaler on the dock by the generator; ice for sale at Tropical Paradise.

### $$$ Pasta per Caso
*Av Hicaco.*
Managed by Anna and Armando, this delightful little Italian joint is very low-key, casual and authentic. They make their own pasta by hand and serve a changing menu of delicious home-cooked fare such as spaghetti with calamari, vegetable lasagne and fettuccine with mushroom sauce. There's just a handful of seats out front and they also sell their pasta and sauce in packets to take at home. Great wine and desserts too. Recommended.

### $$$-$$ Aladdin's
*Corner of Front St and Hattie St, just before the Split. Closed Tue.*
Fresh, tasty and fully authentic Lebanese cuisine including falafel, pitta wraps, lamb kebabs, hummus and vegetarian options. A casual joint with just a few picnic tables out front. Friendly, popular and lots of good reports.

### $$$-$$ Paradiso Café
*Av Hicaco.*
Located near the Split where it enjoys ocean breezes, this little café on the seafront serves healthy and hearty breakfasts, good hot and cold coffee (try the frozen cappuccino), smoothies and an array of gourmet sandwiches, including grilled paninis and BLTs. A bit pricey but portions are large. Eat in or take away.

### $$$-$$ Rainbow Bar and Restaurant
*On its own jetty.*
This restaurant has a beautiful view and serves good-value delicious burritos.

### $$$-$$ Syd's Restaurant
*Middle St. Closed Sun.*
Family-run restaurant which is very popular with locals.

### $$$-$$ Terry's Grill
*On the beach by the Split.*
Tempting passersby with its smoky barbecue aromas, this simple beachside grill cooks up a tantalizing array of seafood.

The menu changes with seasons and the fishermen's haul, but often includes lemon and garlic lobster, whole fish or honey mustard fillet, curried conch, shrimp sticks, pork ribs and jerk chicken.

## $$ Amor y Cafe
*Av Hicaco. Tue-Sun 0600-1130.*
Reportedly the best place on the island for breakfast.

## $$ Glenda's
*Back St. Open mornings only.*
An old-time island favourite, serving good breakfast and lunches.

## $$ The Little Kitchen
*Marvin Gainy St, back street on south-western side of the island, ask around.*
Managed by a friendly mother and daughter team, The Little Kitchen serves up a changing menu of home-cooked local fare prepared with love. Offerings include coconut fish fillet, lemon ginger snapper and creole lobster, washed down with fruit juice, rum or Belikin beer.

## $$ Rose's Bar & Grill
*Front St.*
A great grill with good seafood and burgers.

## $$-$ Caribbean Colors Art Café
*Av Hicaco, www.caribbean-colors.com. Open 0700-1500.*
Adorned with vibrant local artwork, this cute little café with an upstairs balcony makes a great breakfast or lunch stop. They serve good-value burritos, pancakes, fruit and granola, tasty bagels and other fresh-baked goodies such as triple chocolate espresso brownies. For lunch there's salads, soups and sushi.

## $ Chan's Take Out
*Corner of Dock and 2nd St. Open late.*
Although it's not much to look at, this hole in the wall is hugely popular with locals and backpackers for its cheap and hearty grub. Offerings include chicken wings, shrimps, pork chops and burgers served with fries. They also do Chinese.

## Coffee shops

### Ice and Beans
*Front St inside the Remax building, www.iceandbeans.com.*
Good coffee, hot or iced, but everyone loves the mini-doughnuts coated in cinnamon, chocolate and sugar. They also do shaved ice and home-made rum balls.

## Bars and clubs

Many of the restaurants become bars in the evenings.

### Herbal Tribes
*Near the north end of the island.*
Bar and restaurant with a good atmosphere.

### I and I Bar.
Used to be the **Swing Bar** and still has the swings. Should be tried later at night.

### Lazy Lizard
*Right at the north tip of the island at the Split.*
An excellent place to watch the sunset.

## Shopping

There are at least 4 small 'markets' on the island where a variety of food can be bought; prices are 20-50% higher than the mainland. There are a couple of gift shops and a gallery in the same building as Coco Loco.

**Chan's Mini Mart**, *Middle St, 1 street back from main street*. Daily including Christmas and New Year's Day.

## What to do

### Diving and snorkelling
Mask and snorkel hire from several dive and tour operators; normally US$2.50 per day.
**Belize Diving Services**, *T226-0143, www. belizedivingservice.com*. A dive shop on the island with similar prices to **Frenchie's**.
**Big Fish Dive Center**, *T226-0450, bigfishdive @btl.net*. Go to the Blue Hole, US$175, Lighthouse Reef and Turneffe. Also does PADI refresher courses and works with **Frenchie's**.

**Frenchie's Diving**, *T226-0234, www. frenchiesdivingbelize.com*. Charges US$310 for a 4-day PADI course, friendly and effective, 2-tank dive US$90, also advanced PADI instruction. Day excursion diving Blue Hole, etc, US$190, snorkellers welcome.

### Fishing

Fishing can be arranged through tour operators or by ringing Eloy Badillo T226-0270.

### Kayaking

Tour agencies on the main street rent kayaks.

### Manatee watching

Available with most tour operators.

### Sailing

See also **Ras Creek** and **E-Z Boy Tours**, below, for their sailing trips.
**Raggamuffin Tours**, *T226-0348, www. raggamuffintours.com*. Do a fun sunset cruise, US$25 per person, with booze and music on a sail boat as well as offering a 3-day all-inclusive sailing tour to Placencia leaving Tue and Fri, US$300 per person, minimum 8 people including all food and 2 nights' camping on Rendezvous Caye and Tobacco Caye. Beats travelling by bus and is an increasingly popular excursion.

### Tour operators

Prices are consistent across all operators, so find someone you connect with and feel you can trust. The main excursion is snorkelling in Hol Chan Marine Park and visiting Shark Ray Alley and San Pedro, US$45, equipment included. Further afield there are other snorkelling trips, river and Maya site tours. Manatees and Goff Caye (a paradise-perfect circular island with good snorkelling around), US$60; fishing trips US$175. Snorkelling excursions to the Turneffe Islands, Half Moon Caye, Bird Sanctuary and Blue Hole on request. **Sunset Tours** are popular with snorkelling until dusk, US$30.

**E-Z Boy Tours**, *on main street, T226-0349*. As well as the usual snorkelling tours, E-Z offers a seahorse, a Maya archaeology and croc-spotting tour.
**Javier Novelo** *at Anwar Tours, T226-0327, www.anwartours.com*. Locally recommended for a range of snorkelling tours.
**Raggamuffin Tours**, *see Sailing, above*. Trips to the Caye Caulker Marine Reserve and Hol Chan. They can also arrange fishing tours with local fishermen, full day, US$275.

**Guides**  Recommended guides include **Ras Creek**, 'a big man with a big heart', in his boat, based at the water taxi dock, US$27.50 including lunch and entrance fee to the Caye Caulker Marine Reserve; seahorse trips, fishing trips, US$37.50; booze cruise, US$10 per person; canoe and snorkel rental. **Neno Rosado**, of Tsunami Adventures, T226-0462, www.tsunamiadventures.com, has been approved by the guide association and is reliable and knowledgeable.

## Transport

### Air

**Maya Island Air** flies to/from **Belize City**, **Corozal** and **San Pedro**, several daily. Also flights with **Tropic Air**, T226-2439.

### Bicycle and golf cart hire

**Island Boy Rentals**, T226-0229. Golf cart rental for US$10 per hr. Bike hire for US$7.50 per day.

### Boat

Boats leave from the main dock in front of **Seaside Cabanas** to **Belize City** with the **Caye Caulker Water Taxi Association** at 0630, 0730, 0830, 1000, 1100, 1200, 1330, 1500, 1600, 1700, 45 mins 1 way (can be 'exciting' if it's rough). To **San Pedro** 0700, 0820, 0845, 0950, 1120, 1250, 1420, 1550 and 1720. **Triple J** leave from the **Rainbow Hotel** dock. Daily services to **Chetumal** in Mexico also available.

Lighthouse Reef is the outermost of the three north–south reef systems off Belize and is some 45 miles to the east of Belize City. Trips out here are not cheap, but if you like diving and have the money, this is well worth the expense. On arrival you must register near the lighthouse with the warden who will provide maps and tell you where you can camp.

There are two cayes of interest: Half Moon Caye (on which the lighthouse stands) and **Long Caye**, where there is accommodation with Huracan Diving (see page 213). Between the two are some of the most pristine coral reefs in the western hemisphere, including the diving shrine of the **Blue Hole** (see below) is found. **Half Moon Caye** is the site of the Red-Footed Booby Sanctuary ① *US$20*, a national reserve. Besides the booby, magnificent frigate birds also nest on the island. The seabirds nest on the western side, which has denser vegetation (the eastern side is covered mainly in coconut palms). Of the 98 other bird species recorded on Half Moon Caye, 77 are migrants. The iguana, the wish willy (smaller than the iguana) and the Anolis allisoni lizard inhabit the caye, and hawksbill and loggerhead turtles lay their eggs on the beaches. The **Belize Audubon Society** in Belize City (see box, page 212) maintains the sanctuary, providing a lookout tower and a trail. The lighthouse on the caye gives fine views of the reef. It was first built in 1820: the present steel tower was added to the brick base in 1931 and nowadays the light is solar powered. Around sunset you can watch the boobies from the lookout as they return from fishing. They land beside their waiting mates at the rate of about 50 a minute, seemingly totally unperturbed by humans.

## ★Blue Hole
*US$20, US$40 to snorkel or dive.*

On Lighthouse Reef is this National Monument, a circular sinkhole which is 1000 ft across and has depths exceeding 400 ft. The crater was probably formed by the collapsed roof of a subterranean cave, and was studied by Jacques Cousteau in 1984. Stalagmites and stalactites can be found and it is rated as one of the best dives in the world. Scuba diving is outstanding at Lighthouse Reef, and includes two walls that descend almost vertically from 30-40 ft to a depth of almost 400 ft.

## Caye Chapel
This was once a small, quiet caye dotted with palms and devoid of sandflies, close to its busier neighbour Caye Caulker, where you could escape to a bit of quiet and solitude. That has all changed, as it is now exclusive as well as secluded.

Conservation is a high priority in Belize. Tourism vies for the top spot as foreign currency earner in the national economy, and is the fastest-growing industry. Nature reserves are supported by a combination of private and public organizations including the **Belize Audubon Society**, the government and international agencies.

The **Belize Audubon Society**, PO Box 1001, 12 Fort Street, Belize City, T223-5004, www.belizeaudubon.org, manages seven protected areas including Half Moon Caye Natural Monument (3929 ha), Cockscomb Basin Wildlife Sanctuary (41,800 ha – the world's only jaguar reserve), Crooked Tree Wildlife Sanctuary (6480 ha – swamp forests and lagoons with wildfowl), Blue Hole National Park (233 ha), Guanacaste National Park (20.25 ha), Tapir Mountain Nature Reserve (formerly known as Society Hall Nature Reserve; 2731 ha – a research area with Maya presence) and the Shipstern Nature Reserve (8910 ha – butterfly breeding, forest, lagoons, mammals and birds, contact BAS or the International Tropical Conservation Foundation, through www.shipstern.org).

The Río Bravo Management and Conservation Area (105,300 ha) bordering Guatemala to the northwest of the country, covers some 4% of the country and is managed by the **Programme for Belize**, PO Box 749, 1 Eyre Street, Belize City, T227-5616, www.pfbelize.org.

Other parks include the Community Baboon Sanctuary at Bermudian Landing, Bladen Nature Reserve (watershed and primary forest) and Hol Chan Marine Reserve (reef ecosystem). More recently designated national parks and reserves include: Five Blue Lakes National Park, based on an unusually deep karst lagoon, and a maze of exotic caves and sinkholes near St Margaret Village on the Hummingbird Highway; Kaax Meen Elijio Panti National Park, at San Antonio Village near the Mountain Pine Ridge Reserve; Vaca Forest Reserve (21,060 ha); and Chiquibul National Park (107,687 ha – containing the Maya ruins of Caracol). There's also Laughing Bird Caye National Park (off Placencia), Glovers Reef Marine Reserve, and Caye Caulker, which now has a marine reserve at its north end.

**Belize Enterprise for Sustained Technology** (BEST), Mile 54 Hummingbird Highway, PO Box 35, Belmopan, T822-3043, www.best.org.bz, is a non-profit organization committed to the sustainable development of Belize's disadvantaged communities and community-based ecotourism, for example Gales Point and Hopkins Village.

On 1 June 1996 a **National Protected Areas Trust Fund** (PACT), www.pactbelize. org, was established to provide finance for the "protection, conservation and enhancement of the natural and cultural treasures of Belize". Funds for PACT come from a US$3.75 conservation fee paid by all foreign visitors on departure by air, land and sea, and from 20% of revenues derived from protected areas entrance fees, cruise ship passenger fees, etc. Visitors pay only one PACT tax every 30 days, so if you go to Tikal for a short trip from Belize, show your receipt to avoid paying twice.

## Where to stay

Many cayes have package deals for a few days or a week.

### $$$$ Blackbird Caye Resort

*Turneffe Islands, T223-2767,*
*www.blackbirdresort.com.*
An ecological resort on this 4000-acre island is used by the **Oceanic Society** and is a potential site for a biosphere reserve underwater project. Weekly packages arranged. Diving or fishing packages available, no bar, take your own alcohol.

### $$$$ Huracan

*Lighthouse Reef, T603 2930,*
*www.huracandiving.com.*
Simple but elegant accommodation in a small chalet with polished wooden floors on a tiny island on the Lighthouse Reef. The sea views from the islands beaches and jetties are unforgettable, with a real sense of remoteness, the diving the best on the reef (this is the only dive operator within 20 mins of the Blue Hole) and the cooking and hospitality from Ruth and her husband Karel warm and welcoming. Prices include transfers from Belize, full board and dives, making this a very good-value option.

### $$$$ Turneffe Flats

*Turneffe Islands, T220-4046, www.tflats.com.*
In a lovely location, offers week-long packages for fishing and scuba; takes 20 guests.

### $$$$ Turneffe Island Resort

*Big Caye Bokel, Turneffe Islands, T532-2990,*
*www.turnefferesort.com.*
Can accommodate 16 guests for week-long fishing and scuba packages.

## What to do

### Diving

The main dive in the Blue Hole is very deep, at least 130 ft; the hole itself is 480 ft deep. Check your own qualifications as the dive operator probably will not; you should be experienced and it is advisable to have at least the Advance Open Water PADI course, although an Open Water qualification is fine if you feel confident and don't have major problems equalizing.

**Huracan Diving**, *T603-2930, www. huracandiving.com.* The only hotel and dive operation on Lighthouse Reef itself. Excellent value (see Where to stay).

Dive operators on Ambergris and on Caye Caulker run trips to Half Moon Caye, the Blue Hole and Turneffe Islands, see above. It's also possible to go from Belize City with:
**Hugh Parkey's Belize Dive Connection**, *based at the Radisson's dock, www.belize diving.com.*
**Sunrise Travel**, *Belize City, T227-2051 or T223-2670.* Helps arrange trips, advance book.

# Belmopan
## & Cayo District

A procession of impressive sights – artificial and natural – line the route from Belize City to Cayo District in Western Belize, starting with Belize Zoo, a pleasant break from the norm. Monkey Bay Wildlife Sanctuary and Guanacaste National Park are both worth a visit. From the bustling town of San Ignacio, there are canoe trips down the Macal River and dramatic cave systems, journeys into the impressive limestone scenery of Mountain Pine Ridge, and the spectacular Maya ruins of Caracol, Xunantunich and Cahal Pech to explore. Day trippers can also cross the border for a quick visit to Tikal in Guatemala. At the heart of the region stands Belmopan, a sterile planned city, business hub and the capital of the nation.

## Belmopan  *Colour map 2, A5.*

quiet and ordered, the planned capital of the nation

As capital of Belize, Belmopan has been the seat of government since 1970. It is 50 miles inland to the west of Belize City, near the junction of the Western Highway and the Hummingbird Highway to Dangriga (Stann Creek Town). Following the devastation caused in Belize City by Hurricane Hattie in 1961, plans were drawn up for a town that could be a centre for government, business and study away from the coast: Belmopan is the result.

The hurricanes of recent years have prompted a renewed interest in plans to develop the Belmopan, and several government organizations are in the process of relocating to the city, injecting a desperately needed 'heart' to this most eerie of capitals. One possible site of interest would be the **Department of Archaeology** in the government plaza, which has a vault containing specimens of the country's artefacts. Unfortunately, the vault is

**Best** for
Adventure ▪ Canoeing ▪ Maya sites ▪ Waterfalls ▪ Wildlife

currently closed and there are no plans to open it in the near future, although there is a small display and plans to build a museum. Part of the collection is displayed in the **National Museum of Belize** in Belize City (see page 190).

Belmopan has the National Assembly building, two blocks of government offices (with broadly Maya-style architecture), the national archives, police headquarters, a hospital, over 700 houses for civil servants, a non-governmental residential district to encourage expansion, and a market. The Western Highway from Belize City is now good (a one-hour drive), continuing to San Ignacio, and there is an airfield (for charter services only).

Travelling from Belize City to Belmopan by road, the Western Highway passes the cemetery, where burial vaults stand elevated above the boggy ground, running through palmetto scrub and savannah landscapes created by 19th-century timber cutting. At Mile 16 is **Hattieville**, originally a temporary settlement for the homeless after Hurricane Hattie in 1961. The highway runs roughly parallel to the Sibun River, once a major trading artery where mahogany logs were floated down to the coast in the rainy season; the place name 'Boom' recalls spots where chains were stretched across rivers to catch logs being floated downstream.

## Around Belmopan

The small but excellent **Belize Zoo** ⓘ *daily 0900-1700, US$7.50, www.belizezoo.org, take any bus from Belize City along the Western Highway (1 hr)*, is at Mile 28½; watch out for the sign or tell the driver where you're going. It is a wonderful collection of local species (originally gathered for a wildlife film), lovingly cared for and displayed in wire-mesh enclosures amid native trees and shady vegetation, including jaguar and smaller cats, pacas (called gibnuts in Belize), snakes, monkeys, parrots, crocodile, tapir (mountain cow), peccary (wari) and much more. Get there early to miss the coach party arrivals. There are tours by enthusiastic guides, and T-shirts and postcards are sold for fundraising. A visit is highly recommended, even for those who hate zoos.

At Mile 31½, the **Monkey Bay Wildlife Sanctuary** ⓘ *www.belizestudyabroad.net*, protects 1070 acres of tropical forest and savannah between the highway and the Sibun River (great swimming and canoeing). Birds are abundant and there is a good chance of seeing mammals.

Forty-seven miles from Belize City, a minor road runs 2 miles north to **Banana Bank Lodge and Jungle Equestrian Adventure** (see Where to stay, below). A mile beyond is the highway junction for Belmopan and Dangriga.

At the confluence of the Belize River and Roaring Creek is the 50-acre **Guanacaste National Park** ⓘ *US$2.50*, protecting a parcel of neotropical rainforest and a huge 100-year-old *guanacaste* (tubroos) tree, which shelters a wide collection of epiphytes including orchids. Many mammals (jaguarundi, kinkajou, agouti etc) and up to 100 species of bird may be seen from the 3 miles of nature trails cut along the river. This is a particularly attractive swimming and picnicking spot at which to stop or break the journey if travelling on to Guatemala. It has a visitor centre, where luggage can be left. To get there, take an early morning bus from Belize City, see the park in a couple of hours, then pick up a bus going to San Ignacio or Dangriga.

Soon after the junction to Belmopan is **Roaring Creek**, once a thriving town but now rather overshadowed by the barely illuminated capital nearby. At Camelote, a dirt road southwards takes you to **Roaring River**. At Teakettle, turn south along a dirt road for 5 miles to **Pook's Hill Reserve** (see Where to stay, below).

The important but unimpressive **Floral Park** archaeological site is just beyond the bridge over **Barton Creek** (Mile 64). Just 2 miles further is **Georgeville**, from where a gravel road runs south into the Mountain Pine Ridge Forest Reserve (see page 224). The highway passes the turn-off at Norland for **Spanish Lookout**, a Mennonite settlement area 6 miles north (B & F Restaurant, Centre Road, by Farmers' Trading Centre, is clean and excellent value). The **Central Farm Agricultural College**, the village of **Esperanza** and other small settlements along the way keep the road interesting until it reaches **Santa Elena**. Formerly only linked by the substantial Hawkesworth suspension bridge to its twin town of San Ignacio, it now has a small, one-lane 'temporary bridge' you must take to cross the river to San Ignacio.

## Listings Belmopan

### Where to stay

Belmopan has been described as a 'disaster' for the budget traveller.

**$$$ Bull Frog Inn**
*25 Half Moon Av, T822-2111,*
*www.bullfroginn.com.*
A 15-min walk east of the market through the parliament complex or a short taxi ride from the bus station. A/c, good, reasonably priced, laundry, karaoke nights on Thu (popular with locals).

**$$ El Rey Inn**
*23 Moho St, T822-3438, www.elreyhotel.com.*
A central, basic place offering big, clean rooms with fan and hot and cold water. Friendly staff, laundry on request.

### Around Belmopan

**$$$$ Pook's Hill Lodge**
*Pook's Hill Reserve, T820-2017,*
*www.pookshilllodge.com.*
A 120-ha nature reserve on Roaring Creek, 6 cabanas, horses and rafting.

**$$$ Orchid Garden Eco-Village Hotel**
*Western Highway Mile 14.5, T225-6991,*
*www.trybelize.com.*
For those who would prefer to give the city a wide berth (or simply wish to be immersed in exuberant natural surroundings), the Orchid Garden boasts wonderfully verdant grounds with nature trails. Located 20 mins outside the city, accommodation is offered as part of all-inclusive packages that include day trips to surrounding natural attractions (contact in advance).

**$$$-$$ Banana Bank Lodge and Jungle Equestrian Adventure**
*Guanacaste National Park, T820-2020,*
*www.bananabank.com.*
Resort accommodation with meals, horse riding along the river and jungle trails, birding and river trips.

**$$ Belize Savanna Guesthouse**
*Pine Savanna Nature Reserve,*
*signed off the Western Highway at*
*Mile 28.5, near Belize Zoo, T822-8005,*
*www.belizesavannaguesthouse.co.*
This down-to-earth and intimate B&B is managed by 2 Emmy-winning natural history film-makers, Carol and Richard Foster, who use their house as a production base and studio. It is some distance from the airport and nearer Belmopan than Belize City, but worth the effort for the unique hospitality and verdant surroundings of the wild savannah. Rooms are cosy and decked with wood in typical Caribbean style. Book in advance. Recommended.

**$ Monkey Bay Wildlife Sanctuary**
*Mile 31 Western Highway, T820-3032,*
*www.belizestudyabroad.net.*
Dorm accommodation or you can camp on a wooden platform with thatched roof; showers are available. You can swim in the river, and meals are eaten with the family.

### Restaurants

Eating options are limited in Belmopan. There are several cheap *comedores* at the back of the market and a couple of bakeries near Constitution Dr Cafés are closed on Sun.

## $$ Caladium
*At Market Square in front of bus terminal.*
Limited fare, moderately priced,
small portions.

## $$ Pasquales Pizza
*Forest Dr and Slim Lane, T822-4663.*
Also serves pasta and hot and
cold sandwiches.

## $$ Perkup Café
*Shopping Center, T822 0001,
www.perkupcoffeeshop.com.*
Good coffee, snacks and ice cream.

### Transport

**Bus**
To **San Ignacio**, hourly on the hour 0500-
2I00, 1 hr, US$2.50. To **Belize City**, Mon-Sat,
every 30 mins, 0600-1900, hourly on Sun,
1 hr, US$3.50. Heading south hourly buses
Mon-Sat 0830-1630 (fewer on Sun) to
**Dangriga**, 1 hr, US$3, **Mango Creek**, 3 hrs,
US$8 and **Punta Gorda**, 4½ hrs, US$9. **James
Bus** leaves for **Belize City** and **Punta Gorda**
from opposite the **National Transportation
Co** bus station. To **Orange Walk** and **Corozal**
take an early bus to Belize City and change.

## San Ignacio and around    Colour map: 2, A5. See also map, page 218.

**an appealing agricultural town, a good base for local trips**

Some 68 miles from Belize City and 10 miles from the border, San Ignacio (locally called Cayo) is the capital of Cayo District and Western Belize's largest town, serving the citrus, cattle and peanut farms of the area, and a good base for excursions into the Mountain Pine Ridge and other places in Western Belize. A convenient town to rest in if coming from Guatemala, it stands amid attractive wooded hills from 200-550 ft and has a pleasant climate.

The town is on the eastern branch of the Old, or Belize, River, known as the Macal. The 180-mile river journey down to Belize City is internationally famous as the route for the annual Ruta Maya Belize River Challenge, a gruelling three-day canoe race held the weekend of Baron Bliss Day, 9 March; see box, page 219.

Dr Rosita Arvigo, a Maya healer, runs the **Ix Chel Wellness Center** ① *25 Burns Av, T804-0264, by appointment only,* offering herbology and traditional Maya healing. She also sells a selection of herbs (the jungle salve, US$5, has been found effective against mosquito bites) and a book on medicinal plants used by the Maya. The herbs and books are also sold in most local gift shops. For local medicines you could also talk to the García sisters (see San Antonio, page 252).

The **San Ignacio Resort Hotel** (see Where to stay, below) houses the **Green Iguana Exhibit and Medicinal Jungle Trail** ① *0700-1600, US$5.45 for a guided tour of the medicinal trail,* where you will learn about the life and habits of this vibrantly coloured reptile. Entrance fees are used to provide scholarships for local pupils. From March to May you're likely to see iguanas in the wild if you take the pleasant half h our walk from San Ignacio to where the Mopan and Macal rivers meet.

A short walk from San Ignacio (800 m from **Hotel San Ignacio**) is **Cahal Pech** ① *daily 0600-1700, US$5,* an interesting Maya site and nature reserve on a wooded hill overlooking the town, with a visitor centre and small museum.

### Around San Ignacio
Four miles west of San Ignacio on a good road is **Bullet Tree Falls**, a pleasant cascade amid relaxing surroundings on the western branch of the Belize River, here in its upper course

known as the Mopan River. On a similarly good road 9 miles southwest of San Ignacio is the tranquil town of **Benque Viejo del Carmen**, near the Guatemalan border. Many of the inhabitants are Maya Mopan. For information on the Benque Viejo–Melchor de Mencos border crossing, see Border crossings box in Practicalities chapter.

Near Benque Viejo is the **Che Chem Ha Cave** ① *T820-4063*, on the private property of the Moralez family on the Vaca Plateau. In contrast to Barton Creek and Actun Tunichil Muknal this is a so-called dry cave, and it has Maya artefacts. The family offers trips into the cave, a 30-minute hike to the entrance, followed by a one- to 1½-hour walk in the cave. The view from the property is stunning and the family serves lunch. Tours start at 0900 and 1300. If you go by private transport be there in time for the tour and call the family in advance or, better still, book a tour with an agency in San Ignacio.

Twelve miles north of San Ignacio is **El Pilar**, an archaeological site that straddles the border with Guatemala. Although it is a large site (about 94 acres), much of it has been left intentionally uncleared so that selected architectural features are exposed within the rainforest. The preserved rainforest here is home to hundreds of species of birds and animals. There are five trails – three archaeological, two nature – the longest of which is 1½ miles. There are more than a dozen pyramids and 25 identified plazas. Unusually for Maya cities in this region, there is an abundance of water (streams and falls). Take the Bullet Tree Road north of San Ignacio, cross the Mopan River Bridge and follow the signs to El Pilar. The reserve is 7 miles from Bullet Tree on an all-weather limestone road. It can be reached by vehicle, horse or mountain bike (hiking is only recommended for the

# San Ignacio

To ② & Branch Mouth Rd

Burns Av

Savannah St

Colective Taxis to Benque de Viejo

David's Adventure Tours

Hospital St

West St

❻

Mayawalk Tours

Galvez

Far West St

❷ Pacz Tours

❸

Savannah Taxi Co-op

Maya St

❶❹

Hudson St

❹

To Bullet Tree Falls

Church St

Far West St

King St

⑤

⑤

Town Hall

To ⑪ , Cahal Pech, Xunantunich, Che Chem Ha Cave,
Benque Viejo del Carmen & Guatemala

Pol

Hawkesworth Bridge

Macal River

To Belize City, San Antonio & Mountain Pine Ridge

N

50 metres
50 yards

**Where to stay** 🛏
Casa Blanca Guesthouse **1**
Hi-Et **3**
Martha's Guest House **4**
Midas Resort **2**

San Ignacio Resort **11**

**Restaurants** 🍴
Eva's Bar **2**
Martha's Kitchen **1**

Mr Greedy's Pizzeria **4**
Serendib **6**

## ON THE ROAD

### Paddling the great Macal River

Time it right and you can paddle down the length of the Macal River taking part in La Ruta Maya canoe race. It's a gruelling three-day open canoe race, starting in San Ignacio covering 180 miles along the river before ending in Belize City on Baron Bliss Day (early March). All food and water is provided for the trip, but you'll need to be fit and healthy. You'll struggle to compete at the racing end of the field unless you're a top athlete and have a canoe of modern design, but plenty of people enter the race for the challenge and with a bit of luck it's possible to turn up, talk with people around town and find yourself a place on a boat. For information, visit www.larutamayabelize.com.

experienced; carry lots of water). The caretakers, who live at the south end of the site in a modern green-roofed house, are happy to show visitors around. The **Cayo Tour Guides Association** works in association with the **Belize River Archaeological Settlement Survey** (BRASS) and can take visitors. See also *Trails of El Pilar: A Guide to the El Pilar Archaeological Reserve for Maya Flora and Fauna*.

South of San Ignacio, halfway between the Clarissa Falls turn-off and Nabitunich, is Chial Road, gateway to adventure. A half-mile down the road is a sharp right turn that takes you through Negroman, the modern site of the ancient Maya city of **Tipu** which has the remains of a Spanish Mission from the 1500s. Across the river from here is **Guacamallo Camp**, a rustic jungle camping and the starting point for canoe trips on the Macal River (see below). Two miles further up, also across the river, is **Ek Tun** (see Where to stay, below). The **Belize Botanic Gardens** ① *T824-3101, www.belizebotanic.org, daily 0700-1700, US$2.50, guided walks 0730-1500, US$7.50*, on 50 acres of rolling hills, is next to the duPlooy's lodge (see Where to stay, below) with hundreds of orchids, dozens of named tree species, ponds and lots of birds. Recommended.

Canoe trips up the **Macal River** are worthwhile. They take about three hours upstream, 1½ hours on return. Hiring a canoe to go upstream without a guide is not recommended unless you are highly proficient as there are Grade II rapids one hour from San Ignacio. Another trip is to **Barton Creek Cave**, a 1½-hour drive followed by a 1½-hour canoe trip in the cave. The cave vault system is vast, the rock formations are beautiful, the silence is eerily comforting and all can be explored for a considerable distance by canoe (US$55 per person, minimum two people). Tours can be arranged at almost every place in San Ignacio.

★**Actun Tunichil Muknal (ATM) Cave** For an adventurous caving tour, you shouldn't leave without going to Actun Tunichil Muknal (ATM) Cave (the Cave of the Stone Sepulchre), a one-hour drive east of San Ignacio to the Tapir Mountain Nature reserve, a 45-minute jungle hike in the reserve and then 3½ hours of adventurous, exhilarating caving, US$75. Besides the beautiful rock formations, this cave is full of Maya artefacts and sacrificial remains. The guides from both **Emilio Awe's Pacz Tours** and **Mayawalk** (see What to do, below) are recommended. Mayawalk also run an overnight ATM tour (US$180); under eights and pregnant women are discouraged from taking this tour.

### Xunantunich *Colour map 2, A5.*
*Daily 0730-1600, US$5; a leaflet on the area is available from the site for US$4. Apart from a small refreshment stand, there are no facilities for visitors, but a museum has been built*

*and a couple of stelae have been put on display in a covered area. It is an extremely hot walk up the hill, with little or no shade, so start early. Last ferry (free) back is at 1630. See also Transport, below.*

At Xunantunich ('Maiden of the Rock') there are Classic Maya remains in beautiful surroundings. The heart of the city was three plazas aligned on a north-south axis, lined with many temples, the remains of a ball court, and surmounted by the Castillo. At 130 ft, this was thought to be the highest artificial structure in Belize until the Sky Palace at Caracol was measured. The impressive view takes in the jungle, the lowlands of Petén and the blue flanks of the Maya Mountains. Maya graffiti can still be seen on the wall of Structure A-16; friezes on the Castillo, some restored in modern plaster, represent astronomical symbols. Extensive excavations took place in 1959-1960 but only limited restoration work has been undertaken.

Just east of the ferry, **Magaña's Art Centre** and the **Xunantunich Women's Group** sell locally made crafts and clothing in a shop on a street off the highway. About 1½ miles further north are the ruins of **Actuncan**, probably a satellite of Xunantunich. Both sites show evidence of earthquake damage.

## Listings San Ignacio and around *map p218*

### Where to stay

Some hotels in town and on Cahal Pech Hill may be noisy at weekends from loud music, and during the day from traffic and buses. In the area surrounding San Ignacio there are many jungle hideaways. Ranging from secluded and exclusive cottages to full activity resorts, and covering a wide range of budgets, these places are normally an adventure on their own. Before going, make sure you know what's included in the price; food is often extra.

**$$$$ San Ignacio Resort Hotel**
*18 Buena Vista Rd, T824-2125,*
*www.sanignacio belize.com.*
At the southern end of town, on the road to Benque Viejo, this hotel has clean rooms with bath, a/c and hot water; some have balconies. Helpful staff, pool, tennis court, tour agency and excellent restaurant. Live music every weekend at the **Stork Club**. The **Green Iguana Exhibit** is on site, see page 217.

**$$$ Martha's Guest House**
*10 West St, T804-3647,*
*www.marthasbelize.com.*

This friendly place has 10 comfortable, clean rooms with TV, a/c, cheaper without; 2 have balconies. There's also a lounge area, a good restaurant and kitchen facilities.

**$$$ Midas Resort**
*Branch Mouth Rd, T824-3172,*
*www.midasbelize.com.*
An attractive 7-acre family-run resort, located on the edge of town, yet with a more remote wilderness feel. Cabana accommodation with Wi-Fi service and access to the river for swims.

**$$$-$$ Casa Blanca Guesthouse**
*10 Burns Av, T824-2080, www.*
*casablancaguesthouse.com.*
A friendly place with 8 clean rooms (2 beds in each), private shower, fan or a/c and TV. Use of kitchenette and free coffee.

**$$-$ Hi-Et**
*12 West St, T824-2828, thehiet@ yahoo.com.*
Lovely, red and cream old wooden building with 10 rooms and private shower, cheaper without. It's reportedly noisy, but it has a nice balcony, and is friendly, helpful and family-run. There are stunning orchids in the patio, and free coffee.

## Around San Ignacio

### $$$$ duPlooy's
*South of San Ignacio, past the Chaa Creek road, then follow (including 1 steep hill) to its end above the Macal River, T824-3101, www.duplooys.com.*
Choices of accommodation and packages are available, enjoy the **Hangover Bar** with cool drinks on the deck overlooking trees and river. The **Belize Botanic Gardens** (see above) is also run by the duPlooy family.

### $$$$ Ek Tun
*South of San Ignacio, T820-3002, in USA T303-4426150, www.ektunbelize.com.*
A 500-acre private jungle retreat on the Macal River, boat access only. There are 2 very private deluxe thatched guest cottages in a spectacular garden setting, and excellent food. It's a great spot for romantic adventurers. Advance reservations only, no drop-ins, adults only and 3-night minimum.

### $$$$ The Lodge at Chaa Creek
*On the Macal River, south of San Ignacio off the Chial Rd, after the turn to Ix Chel Farm, T824-2037, www.chaacreek.com, or hotel office at 56 Burns Av, San Ignacio.*
Upscale accommodation, amenities and tours, with spa, conference centre, butterfly breeding centre, natural history movement and an adventure centre. Strong supporters of environmental groups and projects. Tours and excursions offered.

### $$$ Cahal Pech Village
*South of town, near Cahal Pech, T824-3740, www.cahalpech.com.*
Thatched cabins or a/c rooms, restaurant and bar.

### $$$ Clarissa's Falls
*On Mopan River, down a signed track on the Benque road, around Mile 70, T824-3916, www.clarissafallsresort.aguallos.com.*
Owned by Chena Galvez, thatched cottages on riverbank by a set of rapids, also bunkhouse with hammocks or beds, camping space ($) and hook-ups for RVs, rafting, kayaking and tubing available, wonderful food in the restaurants.

### $$$ Maya Mountain Lodge (Bart and Suzi Mickler)
*¾ mile east of San Ignacio at 9 Cristo Rey Rd, Santa Elena, San Ignacio, T824-2164, www.mayamountain.com.*
Welcoming place offering special weekly, monthly and family rates. There's a restaurant, expensive excursions, a self-guided nature trail and pool. Hiking, riding, canoeing and fishing can be arranged.

### $$$ Windy Hill Resort
*2 miles west of San Ignacio, on Graceland Ranch, T824-2017, www.windyhillresort.com.*
14 cottages, all with bath and dining room. There's also a small pool and nature trails. Horse riding and river trips can be arranged, but they are expensive.

### $$ Aguada Hotel
*Santa Elena, across the river, T804-3609, www.aguadabelize.com.*
Full-service hotel in a quiet part of town with 12 rooms, private baths; a/c costs more. There's a freshwater pond, a heart-shaped pool and an excellent restaurant and bar.

### $$ Parrot Nest
*Near village of Bullet Tree Falls, 3 miles north of San Ignacio, T820-4058, www.parrot-nest.com.*
Family-run with small, comfortable tree houses in beautiful grounds by the river. Breakfast and dinner are available, as well as free tubing. Can arrange local tours.

### $$-$ Cosmos Camping & Cabanas
*Branch Mouth Rd, T824-2116, cosmoscamping@btl.net.*
4 very simple units, or camp on the site alongside the Macal River. Tents for rent, washing and cooking facilities, run by friendly Belizean family, good breakfasts, canoe and bikes for hire. Cabins available ($).

## Camping

### $ Inglewood Camping Grounds
*West of San Ignacio at Mile 68¼, T824-3555, www.inglewoodcampingground.com.*
Palapas, camping, RV hook-ups, hot and cold showers, maintained grounds, some highway noise.

## Restaurants

### $$$ Running W
*In the San Ignacio Resort Hotel (see Where to stay, above).*
One of the best restaurants in town, with live music every 2nd Sat in the hotel bar.

### $$ Eva's Bar
*22 Burns Av, T804-2267. Mon-Sat 0800-1500 and 1800-late.*
Good diner-style restaurant, local dishes, helpful with good local information, bike rental, internet facilities and tours.

### $$ Mr Greedy's Pizzaria
*5 Burns Av. Daily 0600-2100.*
Popular with locals and foreigners. Italian style oven-cooked pizza, beach sand floor and bamboo bar.

### $$ Sanny's Grill
*Several blocks down the hill off the Western Hwy past the Texaco station.*
Serves the 'world's best conch ceviche' and a full dinner menu in a charming setting.

### $$ Serendib
*27 Burns Av, T824-2302. Mon-Sat, 1030-1500 and 1830-1100.*
Good-value excellent Indian-style food, Sri Lankan owners.

### $$-$ Martha's Kitchen
*Below Martha's Guest House (see Where to stay, above).*
Very good breakfasts and Belizean dishes, plus pizzas and burgers, served in a garden patio.

### $ Hode's Place
*Savannah Rd across park, just outside town. Open daily.*
Popular with locals and good value, Belizean food arrives in huge portions, and there's a pleasant yard to sit outside.

### $ Old French Bakery
*JNC building.*
Good pastries for days out exploring.

## Bars and clubs

### Cahal Pech
*www.cahalpech.com, on a hill, with TV station, beside the road to Benque Viejo before the edge of town.*
Music and dancing at weekends, *the* place to be, live bands broadcast on TV and radio. Good views, opposite Cahal Pech archaeological site.

### Culture Club
*Same building as Pitpan, upstairs.*
Live reggae Thu-Sat night, popular with foreigners and the local Rasta crowd.

### Legends 200
*Bullet Tree Rd.*
Disco, popular with locals.

### Pitpan
*Right turn off King St to river. Daily.*
A popular spot with an open-air bar is at the back of the building.

### Stork Club
*San Ignacio Resort Hotel, see Where to stay, above.*
Live music every 2nd Sat in the bar.

## Shopping

There's a fruit and veg market every Fri and Sat morning.

**Black Rock Gift Shop**, *near Flavias, linked to Black Rock Lodge.* Luggage can be left here if canoeing from Black Rock to San Ignacio, arts and crafts, workshop.

**Celina's Supermarket**, *Burns Av, next to the bus station. Mon-Sat 0730-1200, 1300-1600 and 1900-2100.* Not the cheapest but it does have a wide selection.

**Maxim's**, *West St.* Small, cheap supermarket.

**Snooty Fox**, *Waights Av (opposite Martha's).* Book exchange.

## What to do

Many resorts and lodges in this area organize a variety of tours and expeditions. Local tour operators generally offer similar tours at similar prices. Trips to the nearby ruins of Xunantunich (see above) are very easy by bus, with regular traffic going to the Guatemalan border. Tours of Mountain Pine Ridge (see below) are available, but shop around carefully; if you decide to go with a taxi you probably won't get far in the wet season. Trips to Caracol are best arranged from San Ignacio, and if you only want to visit Tikal in Guatemala, you can arrange a day trip that will maximize your time spent at the ruins.

### Body and soul

**Dr Rosita Arvigo**, *see page 217.*

**Therapeutic Massage Studio**, *38 West St, T604-0314. Mon-Fri 0800-1200, 1300-1630. Sat 0830-1200.*

### Tour operators

**David's Adventure Tours**, *near bus terminal, T804-3674.* Recommended for visits to Barton's Creek Cave, US$37, Mountain Pine ridge and Barton, US$67, Caracol, US$75, or guided canoe trips along the Macal River, including the medicinal trail and overnight camping, US$127. Always gets a good report.

**Easy Rider**, *Bullet Tree Rd, T824-3734.* Full-day horse-riding tours for US$40 with lunch.

**Hun Chi'ik Tours**, *Burns Av, T670-0746, www.hunchiiktours.com.* Cave and other tours, specializing in small groups but providing discounts for groups of more than 6 people.

**Maya Mystic Tours**, *Savannah St, T804-0055.* All trips organized including El Pilar, US$45 per person and river canoeing. Shuttles arranged.

**Mayawalk Tours**, *19 Burns Av, T824-3070, www.mayawalk.com.* Has received good recommendations. Similar rates to **Pacz**, also offers overnight rainforest and cave packages if you're looking for some true adventure.

**Pacz Tours**, *30 Burns Av, T824-0536, www.pacztours.net.* Offers great trips to Actun Tunichil Muknal Cave for US$75 including lunch and reserve fee of US$30. Excellent guides. Bob, who runs the bar, is the best starting point for information on any of the trips and is very helpful. Your hotel will also have details and suggestions. Canoe trips on the Macal River, with bird and wildlife watching, medicinal plant trail, good value, US$65; Barton Creek Cave, US$55 for ½-day tour, Mountain Pine Ridge, US$65, Caracol and trip to pools, US$75, Tikal, US$135. Highly recommended.

## Transport

For more information on crossing the border to Guatemala, see Border crossings box in Practicalities chapter.

### Bus

**National Transport Company Bus Station** is on Burns Av. To **Belize City**, Mon-Sat 0430-1800 every hour, Sun hourly 0700-1800, 3½-4 hrs, US$2.50. To **Belmopan**, same schedule as Belize City, 1 hr, US$1.70. To **Benque Viejo**, every 2 hrs, Mon-Sat 0730-2300 (less on Sun), 30 mins, US$0.75. Change at Belmopan for Dangriga and the south. From the bus station at Benque, you need to get a taxi to the immigration post at **Melchor de Mencos**, US$1.25, 2 mins. See also Border crossings box in Practicalities chapter.

    **Minibuses** also run to **Tikal**, making a day trip possible. Organized tours cost about US$70.

### Taxi

Savannah Taxi Drivers' Co-op, T824-2155, T606-7239 (Manuel, 24 hrs). To **Guatemalan border**, US$15 (colectivo US$2.50, on the road, but US$12.50 if you pick them up from their base opposite David's). See also Border crossings box in Practicalities chapter. To **Xunantunich** US$30 return, to **Belize City** US$75, to **Tikal** US$175 return, to **Mountain Pine Ridge**, US$75, **Chaa Creek**, US$30, **Caracol**, US$175 return.

### Xunantunich

### Bus

Bus from San Ignacio towards the border as far as **San José Succotz** (7 miles), US$0.75, where a hand-operated ferry takes visitors and cars across the Mopan River (0800-1600, free); it is then a 20-min walk uphill on an all-weather road. Return buses to San Ignacio pass throughout the afternoon.

## Mountain Pine Ridge   *Colour map 2, A5.*
### undulating landscape of protected forest with waterfalls and limestone caves

Mountain Pine Ridge is a forest reserve that covers 146,000 acres of the northwestern Maya Mountains. It's comprised of a largely undisturbed pine and gallery forest, and valleys of lush hardwood forests filled with orchids, bromeliads and butterflies. The devastation to large swathes of the pine forest first caused by an infestation of the southern pine bark beetle in 2001 continues to impact on the area. Note the frequent changes of colour of the soil and look out for the fascinating insect life. If lucky, you may see deer. There's river scenery to enjoy, high waterfalls, numerous limestone caves and shady picnic sites; it's a popular excursion despite the rough roads.

The easiest way of visiting is on a trip from San Ignacio. Try contacting the Forestry Conservation Officer, T824-3280, who may be able to help. See also Transport, below.

    Two roads lead into the reserve: from Georgeville to the north and up from Santa Elena via Cristo Rey. These meet near **San Antonio**, a Mopan Maya village with many thatched-roof houses and the nearby Pacbitun archaeological site (where stelae and musical instruments have been unearthed). At San Antonio, the García sisters have their workshop, museum and shop where they sell carvings in local slate; this is a regular stop on tours to the Mountain Pine Ridge. The sisters also have a guesthouse ($). You can sample Maya food and learn about the use of medicinal plants. A donation of US$0.50 is requested; US$12.50 is charged to take photos of the sisters at work. There are two buses a day from San Ignacio, 1000 and 1430, from market area; check times of return buses before leaving San Ignacio.

## The falls

The main forest road meanders along rocky spurs, from which unexpected and often breathtaking views emerge of jungle far below and streams plunging hundreds of feet over red-rock canyons. A lookout point (with a small charge) has been provided to view the impressive falls, said to be 1000 ft high (often shrouded in fog October to January). On a clear day you can see Belmopan from this viewpoint. It is quite a long way from the main road and is probably not worth the detour if time is short, particularly in the dry season (February to May) when the flow is restricted. At this time of year, there is an ever-present danger of fire and open fires are strictly prohibited. Eighteen miles into the reserve the road crosses the **Río On**. Here, where the river tumbles into inviting pools over huge granite boulders; is one of Belize's most beautiful picnic and swimming spots. The rocks form little water slides and are fun for children.

## Augustine

Five miles further on is the tiny village of Augustine (also called Douglas D'Silva or **Douglas Forest Station**), the main forest station where there is a shop, accommodation in two houses (bookable through the Forestry Departttment in Belmopan, the Area Forestry Office is in San Antonio) and a **camping ground**, see Where to stay, below. A mile beyond Augustine is a cluster of caves in rich rainforest. The entrance to the **Río Frío Cave** (in fact a tunnel) is over 65 ft high, and there are many spectacular rock formations and sandy beaches where the river flows out. Trees in the parking area and along the Cuevas Gemelas nature trail, which starts one hour from the Río Frío cave, are labelled. It's a beautiful excursion and highly recommended.

Forestry roads continue south further into the mountains, reaching **San Luis** (6 miles), the only other inhabited camp in the area, with a post office, sawmill and forest station, and continuing on over the granite uplands of the Vaca Plateau into the **Chiquibul Forest Reserve** (460,000 acres).

The four forest reserves that cover the Maya Mountains are the responsibility of the Forestry Department, who have only about 20 rangers to patrol over a million acres of heavily forested land. A hunting ban prohibits the carrying of firearms. Legislation, however, allows for controlled logging; all attempts to have some areas declared national parks or biosphere reserves have so far been unsuccessful. You can stay in the area at **Las Cuevas Research Station and Explorers Lodge** (see Where to stay, below).

## ★ Caracol Colour map 2, B5.

About 24 miles south-southwest of Augustine, about one hour by 4WD, Caracol is a rediscovered Maya city. The area is now a National Monument Reservation. Caracol was established about 300 BC and continued well into the Late Classic period (glyphs record a victorious war against Tikal). Why Caracol was built in such a poorly watered region is not known, but Maya engineers showed great ingenuity in constructing reservoirs and terracing the fields. The **Sky Palace** (*Caana*) pyramid, which climbs 138 ft above the site, is being excavated by members of the University of Central Florida. Excavations take place between February and May, but there are year-round caretakers who will show you around. Very knowledgeable guides escort groups around the site twice daily, there's an information centre and an exhibition hall has been built. The road has been improved and is passable for much of the year with normal vehicles and year-round with 4WD. It is an interesting journey as you pass through the Mountain Pine Ridge, then cross the Macal River and immediately enter a broadleaf tropical forest. Take your own food as there is none at the site. Otherwise **Pine Ridge Lodge, Gaia River Lodge** or **Blancaneaux Lodge** are open for lunch (see Where to stay).

## Where to stay

### $$$$ Hidden Valley Inn
*Cooma Cairn Rd, Mountain Pine Ridge, T822-3320, www.hiddenvalleyinn.com.*
This romantic, intimate luxury wilderness lodge has a series of spacious, very comfortable cabins set in a flower-filled garden in one of the remotest and wildest stretches of Mountain Pine Ridge. It offers a broad range of tours and excursions.

### $$$ Mountain Equestrian Trails
*Mile 8, Mountain Pine Ridge Rd (from Georgeville), Central Farm PO, T699 1124, www.metbelize.com.*
Accommodation is in 4 double cabanas with bath, no electricity, hot water and mosquito nets; good food is served in the *cantina*. Half-day, full-day and 4-day adventure tours on horseback in Western Belize, packages, birdwatching tours and other expeditions offered; excellent guides and staff.

## Augustine

### $$$ Las Cuevas Research Station and Explorer's Lodge
*In the Chiquibul Forest, T822-2149, www.lascuevas.org.*
This is a genuine wilderness experience, in an isolated research station open to non-researchers. Rivers, caves and archaeological sites are nearby.

## Camping

### Campsite
*US$1.*
No mattresses (see rangers for all information on the area), keep your receipt, a guard checks it on the way out of Mountain Pine Ridge.

## Caracol

### $$$$ Blancaneaux Lodge
*Mountain Pine Ridge Rd, east of San Ignacio, Central Farm, Cayo District, T824-3878, www.blancaneaux lodge.com.*
Once the mountain retreat of Francis Ford Coppola and his family, now 1 villa and wonderful, huge cabanas decorated in Guatemalan textiles. There's horse riding, croquet, spa, hot pool, overlooking a stream, and a private air strip. Access to Big Rock Falls. Italian restaurant and bar. Recommended.

### $$$$ Gaia River Lodge
*East of San Ignacio, 2½ miles beyond Blancaneaux Lodge, T820-4005, www.gaiariverlodge.com.*
Formerly **Five Sisters Lodge**, rustic cottages lit by oil lamps, with great views and a good-value restaurant. Recommended.

### $$$ Pine Ridge Lodge
*East of San Ignacio, on the road to Augustine, just past turning to Hidden Valley Falls, T606-4557, www.pineridgelodge.com.*
Cabanas in the pinewoods, price includes breakfast.

## Transport

### Taxi
There's no public transport. Apart from tours, the only alternatives are to take a taxi or hire a vehicle or mountain bike. Everything is well signposted. The private pickups that go into San Ignacio from Augustine are usually packed, so hitching is impossible. Taxis charge around US$75-80 for 5 people. Roads are passable but rough Jan-May, but after Jun they are marginal and are impossible in the wet (Sep-Nov). It's essential to seek local advice at the time.

# **North** Belize

North Belize is notable for the agricultural production of sugar, fruit and vegetables and for providing much of the country's food. But among the fields of produce are some well-hidden sights and wildlife magnets. The Maya ruins of Lamanai are just about visible in the spectacular setting of the dense jungle. Wildlife can easily be seen at the Community Baboon Sanctuary, the Crooked Tree Wildlife Sanctuary – home to thousands of beautiful birds – and the wildlife reserve of Shipstern near Sartaneja. The vast Río Bravo Conservation Area nudges up to the Guatemalan border and contains the truly isolated ruins and lodge of Chan Chich.

Heading north out of Belize City, the Northern Highway leads to the Mexican border. You can do the journey in just a few hours, passing through Orange Walk and Corozal, but you won't see a thing. It's definitely worth stopping off if you have time.

**Best** for
Birdwatching ▪ Jungle ruins ▪ Wildlife

## Bermudian Landing

About 15 miles out of Belize City a road heading west leads to the small Creole village of Bermudian Landing (12 miles on a rough road from the turn-off), which has been thrust into the global conservation spotlight. This was once a transfer point for the timber that floated down the Belize River, but now there's a local wildlife museum sponsored by the WWF, and the **Community Baboon Sanctuary** ① *daily 0900-1700, www.howlermonkeys.org, 45- to 60-min guided tours from US$7, including a visit to the small museum; guided wildlife walks are available when booked ahead and simple homestay accommodation is available,* where visitors can see black howler monkeys, many of whom are so used to people that they come very close.

## ★Crooked Tree Wildlife Sanctuary

*US$4; you must register at the visitor centre, drinks are on sale, but take food. There is a helpful, friendly warden, Steve, who will let you sleep on the porch of the visitor centre. It is easy to get a lift to the sanctuary, and someone is usually willing to take visitors back to the main road for a small charge.*

The Northern Highway continues to **Sand Hill**, and a further 12 miles to the turn-off for the Crooked Tree Wildlife Sanctuary, which was set up in 1984 and is a rich area for birds. The network of lagoons and swamps is an internationally protected wetland under the RAMSAR programme, and attracts many migrating birds. The dry season, October to May, is a good time to visit. You may see the huge jabiru stork, the largest flying bird in the western hemisphere at a height of 5 ft and a wingspan of 11-12 ft, which nests here, as well as herons, ducks, vultures, kites, ospreys, hawks, sand pipers, kingfishers, gulls, terns, egrets and swallows. In the forest you can also see and hear howler monkeys. Other animals include coatimundi, crocodiles, iguanas and turtles. Glenn Crawford is a good guide.

The turn-off to the sanctuary is signposted but keep an eye out for the intersection, which is 22 miles from Orange Walk and 33 miles from Belize City. There is another sign further south indicating the sanctuary but this just leads to the park boundary, not to the Wildlife Sanctuary. The mango and cashew trees in the village of Crooked Tree are said to be 100 years old. Birdwatching is best in the early morning but, as buses do not leave Belize City early, for a day trip take an early Corozal bus, get off at the main road (about 1¼ hours from Belize City) and hitch to the sanctuary. The village is tiny and quaint, occupied mostly by Creoles. Boats and guides can be hired for approximately US$80 per boat (maximum four people). It may be worth bargaining as competition is fierce. Trips include a visit to an unexcavated Maya site.

## Altun Ha

*Daily 0900-1700, US$5, insect repellent necessary.*

The Maya remains of Altun Ha, 31 miles north of Belize City and 2 miles off the Old Northern Highway, are worth a visit. Altun Ha was a major ceremonial centre in the Classic period (AD 250-900) and also a trading station linking the Caribbean coast with Maya centres in the interior. There are two central plazas surrounded by 13 partially excavated pyramids and temples. What the visitor sees now is composite, not how the site would have been at any one time in the past. The largest piece of worked Maya jade ever found, a head of the Sun God Kinich Ahau weighing 9½ lb (4.3 kg), was found here in the main temple (B-4) in 1968. It is now in a bank vault in Belize City. Nearby is a large reservoir, now called **Rockstone Road**.

## Where to stay

### Bermudian Landing

**$$$$-$$$ Black Orchid Resort**
*T225 9158, www.blackorchidresort.com.*
Selection of rooms with shared bath
through to luxury villas on the banks of
the Belize River. Restaurant, freshwater
swimming pool, and very good tours along
the Belize River in search of history, howler
monkeys and crocodiles, with friendly
owner Doug Thompson. A great alternative
choice to Belize City or Crooked Tree. Airport
transfers easily arranged.

**$$$ Howler Monkey Resort**
*400 m from museum, T607-1571,*
*www.howlermonkeyresort.bz.*
Cabins with screened windows, fans, shared
bath cheaper. Camping US$5 per person,
bring your own tent. Transport from Belize
City in pickup US$40, 1-4 people, on request.
Breakfast, lunch and dinner, US$5-9. Many
good tours including river tours US$25 per
person, recommended, and night-time
crocodile adventures US$40. Canoe rentals
in Burrell Boom for trips on Belize River to
see birds, howler monkeys, manatee and
other wildlife. Student discount, and TCs,
Visa and MasterCard accepted.

**$ Community Baboon Sanctuary.**
Cabanas are available alongside the visitor
centre, with bath and hot water. Basic
lodging is also available with families in
the village and can be arranged through
the Baboon Sanctuary office.

### Crooked Tree Wildlife Sanctuary

**$$$-$$ Bird's Eye View Lodge**
*T203-2040, www.birdseyeviewbelize.com.*
Owned by the Gillett family. Single and
double rooms, shower, fan, meals available,

boat trips, horse riding, canoe rental,
nature tours with licensed guide. Ask for
information at the **Belize Audubon Society**
(see box, page 212).

**$$$-$$ Crooked Tree Lodge**
*T626 3820, www.crookedtreelodgebelize.com.*
Relaxing birdwatching on the lagoon, and
wildlife- and nature-related tours. Run by
Mick and Angie Webb.

## Transport

### Bermudian Landing
**Bus**
From **Belize City**, Mcfadzean Bus from
corner of Amara Av and Cemetery Rd at
1215 and 1715 Mon-Fri; 1200 and 1400
Sat. **Rancho Bus (Pook's Bus)** from Mosul
St, 1700 Mon-Fri, 1300 Sat, check details,
US$1.50-2, 1 hr. Alternatively, any bus
travelling the Northern Highway can drop
you off at the turn-off to Bermudian Landing
where you can wait for a bus, or hitch a ride.
A day trip giving any meaningful time in the
sanctuary is difficult by public transport, so
it's best to stay the night.

### Crooked Tree Wildlife Sanctuary
**Bus**
Buses from **Belize City** with **JEX** (1035);
return from Crooked Tree at 0600-0700.

### Altun Ha
**Bus**
With little transport on this road, hitching is
not recommended; it's best to go in a private
vehicle or a tour group. Vehicles leave **Belize
City** for the village of **Maskall**, 8 miles north
of Altun Ha, several days a week, but same-
day return is not possible.

The Northern Highway runs to Orange Walk (population 15,990), the centre of a district where Creoles, Mennonites and Maya earn their living from timber, sugar planting and general agriculture. Nearby, the impressive ruins of Lamanai make a good day trip; see below. This is also the departure point for Sarteneja and the Shipstern Peninsula and for the long overland trip to Río Bravo Conservation Area, Chan Chich and Gallon Jug.

There is little to draw the visitor for an extended stay in Orange Walk. The country's second city, it is busy with the comings and goings of a small town. Orange Walk is a truly multicultural centre with inhabitants from all over Central America, making Spanish the predominant language. Originally from Canada, Mennonites live in nearby colonies using the town as their marketing and supply centre. The only battle fought on Belizean soil took place here, during the Yucatecan Caste Wars (1840-1870s): the Maya leader, Marcus Canul, was shot in the fighting in 1872. The **House of Culture** on Main Street shows a history of the town's development.

   Buses plying the route from Belize City to the Mexican border stop on Queen Victoria Avenue, the main street, close to the town hall. While a few pleasant wooden buildings remain on quiet side streets, most are worn out and badly in need of repair. Many have been pulled down and replaced by the standard concrete box affairs, which lack both inspiration and style.

   A toll bridge now spans the New River a few miles south of the town at Tower Hill. There is a market overlooking New River, which is well organized with good food stalls and interesting architecture.

### West and south of Orange Walk

From Orange Walk a road heads west, before turning south, running parallel to the Mexican and then Guatemalan border, where it becomes unpaved. Along this road are several archaeological sites. First is **Cuello**, 4 miles west on San Antonio road, behind Cuello Distillery (ask there for permission to visit); taxi about US$3.50. The site dates back to 1000 BC, but, although it has yielded important discoveries in the study of Maya and pre-Maya cultures, there is little for the layman to appreciate and no facilities for visitors. At **Yo Creek** the road divides, north to San Antonio, and south through miles of cane fields and tiny farming settlements as far as **San Felipe** (20 miles via San Lázaro, Trinidad and August Pine Ridge). At August Pine Ridge there is a daily bus to Orange Walk at 1000. You can camp at the house of Narciso Novelo or 'Chicho' (T323-3019), a little-known secret and a relaxing place to stay set amongst bananas, pine tres, bushes and flowers; no fixed cost, just pay what you think. Chicho will meet you off the bus if you call ahead. At San Felipe, a branch leads southeast to Indian Church/Lamanai, 35 miles from Orange Walk (one hour driving, 4WD needed when wet). Another road heads west to Blue Creek village on the Mexican border (see below).

### Lamanai
*US$5.*

Near Indian Church on the west side of New River Lagoon, 22 miles by river south of Orange Walk, is one of Belize's largest archaeological sites, Lamanai. Difficult to get to and hidden in the jungle, it is a perfect setting to hide the mysteries of the Maya and definitely worth a visit. While the earliest buildings were erected about 700 BC, culminating in the completion of the 112-ft major temple, N10-43, about 100 BC (the tallest known pre-Classic Maya structure), there is evidence the site was occupied as long ago as 1500 BC. As a Maya site, it is believed to have the longest history of continuous occupation and, with the Spanish and British sites mentioned below and the present-day refugee village nearby, Lamanai's history is impressive.

The Maya site has been partially cleared, but covers a large area so a guide is recommended. The views from temple N10-43, dedicated to Chac, are superb; look for the Yin-Yang-like symbol below the throne on one of the other main temples, which also has a 12-ft-tall mask overlooking its plaza. Visitors can wander freely along narrow trails and climb the stairways. There is a very informative museum housing the only known stela found at the site. There is also a fine jungle lodge; see Where to stay, below.

At nearby **Indian Church**, a Spanish mission was built over one of the Maya temples in 1580, and the British established a sugar mill here. The remains of both buildings can still be seen. The archaeological reserve is jungle and howler monkeys are visible in the trees. There are many birds and the best way to see them is to reach Lamanai by boat, easily arranged in Orange Walk or by taking a day trip from Belize City, see Tour operators, page 233. The earlier you go the better, but the trips from Orange Walk all leave at pretty standard times. The mosquitoes are vicious in the wet season (wear trousers and take repellent). The community phone for information on Indian Church, including buses, is T309-3015.

## Blue Creek and around

West of San Felipe is Blue Creek (10 miles), the largest of the Mennonite settlements. Many inhabitants of these close-knit villages arrived in 1959, members of a Canadian colony that had migrated to Chihuahua, Mexico, to escape encroaching modernity. They preserve their Low German dialect, are exempt from military service, and their industry now supplies the country with most of its poultry, eggs, vegetables and furniture. Some settlements, such as Neustadt in the west, have been abandoned because of threats by drug smugglers in the early 1990s.

Belize and Mexico have signed an agreement to build an international bridge from Blue Creek across the river to La Unión, together with a river port close to the bridge. It is not known when work will start; at present there is a canoe-service for foot passengers across the Blue Creek. See also Border crossings box in Practicalities chapter.

A vast area to the south along the **Río Bravo** has been set aside as a conservation area (see box, page 212). Within this, there is a study and accommodation centre near the Maya site of **La Milpa**. The site is at present being excavated by a team from the University of Texas and Boston University, USA.

A good road can be followed 35 miles south to **Gallon Jug**, where a jungle tourism lodge has been built in the **Chan Chich** Maya ruin, see Where to stay, below. The journey to Chan Chich passes through the Río Bravo Conservation Area, is rarely travelled and offers some of the best chances to see wildlife. Chan Chich is believed to have the highest number of jaguar sightings in Belize, and is also a birdwatchers' paradise. Another road has been cut south through Tambos to the main road between Belmopan and San Ignacio, but travel in this region is strictly a dry-weather affair.

## Where to stay

### Orange Walk

Parking for vehicles is very limited at hotels.

#### $$$-$$ Hotel de la Fuente
*14 Main St, T322-2290,*
*www.hoteldelafuente.com.*
Suites of rooms, with kitchenettes, simple
wooden desks and wildlife paintings by a
local artist. Tours to Lamanai available.

#### $$ D'Victoria
*40 Belize Rd (Main St), T322-2518,*
*www.dvictoriabelize.com.*
A reasonably comfortable but somewhat
run-down place with a/c rooms that have
a shower and hot water. There's a pool
and parking.

#### $$ St Christopher's
*12 Main St, T302-1064, www.stchristophers*
*hotelbze.com.*
The best place in town, with beautiful clean
rooms and bathrooms. Highly recommended.

#### $ Akihito Japanese Hotel
*22 Belize Corozal Rd, T302-0185,*
*akihitolee@ hotmail.com.*
An affordable place in the centre of town.

### Lamanai

#### $$$$ Lamanai Outpost Lodge
*At Indian Church, T223-3578,*
*www.lamanai.com.*
Run by the incredibly friendly Howells, this
beautiful lodge is a short walk from Lamanai
ruins, overlooking New River Lagoon. The
thatched wooden cabins have a bath, hot
water, fan and 24-hr electricity. There's also a
restaurant, and day tours with excellent and
well-informed guides. A juvenile crocodile
study is underway and guests are invited
to participate. Package deals are available.

### Camping

Nazario Ku, the site caretaker, permits
camping or hammocks at his house,
opposite path to Lamanai ruins, good value
for backpackers.

### Blue Creek and around

#### $$$$ Chan Chich
*Chiun Chah, T223-4419, www.chanchich.com.*
This beautifully sited lodge is in the midst
of Maya ruins with an extensive trail system
in the grounds and fantastic birdwatching
and wildlife-watching opportunities with
very good guides. Delicious food is served,
and there's a pool. Phone before setting out
for Chan Chich for information on the roads.
Recommended.

#### $$$ La Milpa Field Station
*La Milpa, for information call T323-0011, or*
*contact the Programme for Belize in Belize*
*City (T227-5616, www.pfbelize.org).*
A good base for exploring trails in the region
and birdwatching. The reserve is privately
owned and you will need proof of booking
to pass the various checkpoints. There are
4 spacious and comfortable double cabanas
with a thatched roof overhanging a large
wooden deck, or a dorm sleeping up to 30.
To reach La Milpa, go 6 miles west from Blue
Creek to Tres Leguas, then follow the signs
south towards the Río Bravo Escarpment.

#### $$ Hill Bank Field Station
*On the banks of the New River Lagoon.*
Also a good base for exploring trails in
the region and birdwatching, and with a
dorm sleeping up to 30. See **La Milpa Field
Station** above for contact details.

## Restaurants

### Orange Walk
Most restaurants in town are Chinese.
We've received encouraging reports about
**La Hacienda Steakhouse** and **Marvias**.

**$$ Nahil Mayab**
*www.nahilmayab.com, closed Sun.*
The best in town, serving contemporary
Mexican cuisine, grilled meat and
vegetarian dishes.

**$ Central Plaza Restaurant**
*Behind the main bus terminal.*
A popular choice in a handy location.

**$ Diner**
*Clarke St, behind the hospital.*
Good meals, very friendly; to get
there, take a taxi (US$4) or walk.

## What to do

**Orange Walk**
**Jungle River Tours**, *20 Lovers Lane, T302-
2293, lamanaimayatour@btl.net*. In **Lovers'
Café** on the southeastern corner of the
park. Organize and run trips to Lamanai
(US$40 plus entrance of US$5, including
lunch, departing 0900 returning 1600),
Altun Ha and New River area, regular trips,

*the* specialists on the region and consistently
recommended. They also provide trips to
any destination in Belize with a minimum
of 4 people.

## Transport

**Orange Walk**
**Bus**
The bus station is on street beside the fire
station, on the main road. All buses travelling
from Belize City to Corozal and beyond to
Chetumal stop in Orange Walk; from **Belize**,
US$3. From **Corozal**, US$1.50, 50 mins. For
**Lamanai** take bus to Indian Church (Mon,
Wed, Fri 1600). Buses to **Sarteneja** (which is
40 miles away) outside **Zeta's Store** on Main
St, 5 between 1300 and 1900, US$2.50. Also
to **Progresso** at 1100 and 1130.

**Blue Creek and around**
**Air**
Flights to Chan Chich from **Belize City** can
be chartered.

## North of Orange Walk   Colour map 2, A6.

wildlife reserve, fishing villages and archaeological sites

### Sarteneja and the northeast
From Orange Walk a complex network of roads and tracks converge on **San Estevan** and
Progresso to the north. The Maya ruins near San Estevan have reportedly been flattened
to a large extent and are not very impressive. Ten miles from San Estevan is a road junction;
straight on is **Progresso**, a village picturesquely located on the lagoon of the same name.
The right turn, signposted, runs off to the Mennonite village of **Little Belize** and continues
(in poor condition) to **Chunox**, a village with many Maya houses of pole construction. In
the dry season it is possible to drive from Chunox to the Maya site of Cerros (see below).

Three miles before Sarteneja is the visitor centre for Shipstern Nature Reserve, which
covers 22,000 acres of this northeastern tip of Belize. Hardwood forests, saline lagoon
systems and wide belts of savannah shelter a wide range of mammals (coatis and foxes,
and all the fauna found elsewhere in Belize, except monkeys), reptiles and 200 species of
bird. There are mounds of Maya houses and fields everywhere. The most remote forest,
south of the lagoon, is not accessible to short-term visitors. There is a botanical trail
leading into the forest with trees labelled with Latin and local Yucatec Maya names; a
booklet is available. At the visitor centre is the **Butterfly Breeding Centre** ① *daily 0800-
1700, US$5 including excellent guided tour*. Visit on a sunny day if possible; on dull days the
butterflies hide themselves in the foliage. There is rather poor dormitory accommodation
at the visitor centre, US$10 per person. A day-trip by private car is possible from Sarteneja
or Orange Walk. Mosquito repellent is essential.

Leaving the Northern Highway, a road heads east to **Sarteneja**, a small fishing and former boat-building settlement founded by Yucatán refugees in the 19th century. The main catch is lobster and conch. On Easter Sunday there is a popular regatta, with all types of boat racing, dancing and music. There are the remains of an extensive Maya city scattered throughout the village, and recent discoveries have been made and are currently being explored to the south around the area of Shipstern Lagoon.

## Corozal and around

The Northern Highway continues to Corozal (96 miles from Belize City, population 9110), formerly the centre of the sugar industry, now with a special zone for the clothing industry and garment exports. Much of the old town was destroyed by Hurricane Janet in 1955 and it is now a mixture of modern concrete commercial buildings and Caribbean clapboard seafront houses on stilts. Like Orange Walk it is economically depressed but Corozal is much the safer place. It is open to the sea with a pleasant waterfront where the market is held. There is no beach but you can swim in the sea and lie on the grass. You can check out the local website at www.corozal.com.

Between Orange Walk and Corozal, in San José and San Pablo, is the archaeological site of **Nohmul**, a ceremonial centre whose main acropolis dominates the surrounding cane fields (the name means 'Great Mound'). Permission to visit the site must be obtained from Estevan Itzab, whose house is opposite the water tower.

From Corozal, a road leads 7 miles northeast to **Consejo**, a quiet, seaside fishing village on Chetumal Bay. There's no public transport; a taxi costs about US$10.

Six miles northeast of Corozal, to the right of the road to Chetumal, is **Four Mile Lagoon**, about a quarter of a mile off the road (buses will drop you there). There is clean swimming, better than at Corozal bay, and some food and drinks available; it is often crowded at weekends.

Across the bay to the south of Corozal stand the mounds of **Cerros**, once an active Maya trading port whose central area was reached by canal. Some of the site is flooded but one pyramid, 69-ft-high with stucco masks on its walls, has been partially excavated. Take a boat from Corozal, walk around the bay (a boat is needed to cross the mouth of the New River) or do the dry-season vehicular trail from Progresso and Chunox (see above). Trips can be arranged with **Hotel Maya** and **Hok'Ol K'in Guest House**, from US$60 for a water taxi carrying up to six people.

## Listings North of Orange Walk

### Where to stay

#### Sarteneja

**$ Backpacker's Paradise**
*T423-2016, http://backpackers.blue greenbelize.com, 5 mins from the village.*
Cabins and camping, kitchen and restaurant and a range of activities. Attracts a young and boisterous crowd.

#### Corozal

**$$$ Copa Banana**
*409 Corozal Bay Rd, T422-0284, www.copabanana.bz.*
Newest place in town, with 5 suites all with private bathrooms. US-owned so complimentary coffee each morning. Ask the bus driver to drop you off.

**$$$ Tony's**
*South End, T422-2055, www.tonysinn.com.*
With a/c, clean, comfortable units in
landscaped grounds. Recommended,
but restaurant overpriced.

**$$$-$$ Las Palmas Hotel**
*123, 5th Av South, T422-0196,
www.laspalmashotelbelize.com.*
With bath and fan, OK, *refrescos* available,
good food, lively bar downstairs.

**$$ Hok'Ol K'in Guest House**
*4th Av and 4th St South, T422-3329,
www.corozal.net.*
Immaculate rooms. Runs tours to Cerros.

**$ Caribbean Village Resort**
*South End, T422 2725.*
Hot water, US$5 camping, US$12 trailer
park, restaurant. Recommended.

**Camping**

**Caribbean Motel and Trailer Park**
*See Caribbean Village Resort, above.*
Camping possible (US$4 per person) but
not very safe, shaded sites, restaurant.

**Corozal**
There are many Chinese restaurants in town.

**$$ Cactus Plaza**
*5th Av South.*
A loud bar with lots of fluorescent lighting
and great a/c. Worth trying if you're stuck in
town for the night.

**$ Corozal Garden**
*4th Av, 1 block south.*
Good, quick local food.

**$ Gongora's Pastry**
*Southwest corner of main square.*
Hot pizza pieces, cakes and drinks.

**$ RD's Diner**
*7-4th Av, T422-3796.*
Burgers and American-style food.

**Sartaneja**
**Bus**
Bus from **Belize City** at 1200, US$4.50, from
the corner of Victoria and North Front St.
Buses also leave from **Corozal** (1400), via
Orange Walk (1530).

**Corozal**
**Air**
**Maya Island Air**, daily from Belize City via
Caye Caulker and San Pedro (Ambergris
Caye); **Tropic Air** daily from San Pedro.
Airstrip 3 miles south, taxi US$1.50. Private
charters to **Sartaneja** cost about US$75 for
the 30-min journey (compared with 3 hrs
by road).

**Boat**
To **Orange Walk**, leaving at 1400.

**Bus**
Heading south, buses leave every 30 mins,
starting at 0400 running until 1830. Regular
service 3 hrs, US$2.50, faster express service,
2½ hrs, US$3.50, leaves at 0600, 0700, 1200,
1500 and 1800. If heading north, buses from
**Belize City** continue north to **Chetumal**
terminal, with stopping time to allow for
immigration procedures.

For those coming from Mexico who
are interested in **Tikal** in Guatemala, it is
possible to make the journey border to
border in a day, with a change of bus in
Belize City.

For further information on border
crossings to Mexico and Guatemala, see
Border crossings box in Practicalities chapter.

**Taxi**
**Leslie's Taxi Service**, T422-2377. Transfers
from Corozal to the Mexican border, US$22
for a 4-person taxi. Ask for a quote for other
services. Reliable and professional.

# South Belize
## & the southern cayes

Southern Belize is the most remote part of the country and has poor roads, but it is worth exploring. Dangriga is the largest of several Garífuna settlements that burst into life every year on Settlement Day. The paradise beaches of Hopkins and Placencia are perfect for water sports and relaxing. Cockscomb Basin Wildlife (Jaguar) Sanctuary offers one of the best chances of seeing a big cat in the wild, while the sparsely populated far south around Punta Gorda has many Maya settlements to visit in a region dotted with impressive Maya ruins.

## South to Dangriga *Colour map 2, A6.*

**beautiful verdant route lined with jungle and citrus plantations**

About 2 miles beyond the Belize Zoo on the Western Highway, the Coastal Highway (a good dirt road) runs southeast to Gales Point, a charming fishing village on a peninsula at the south end of Manatee Lagoon, 15 miles north of Dangriga. The villagers are keen to preserve natural resources and there are still significant numbers of the endangered manatee and hawksbill turtles. Boat tours of the lagoon are recommended.

### Along the Hummingbird Highway

The narrow Hummingbird Highway branches off the Western Highway 48 miles west of Belize City, passes Belmopan and heads south. Skirting the eastern edge of Mountain Pine Ridge, the highway meanders through lush scenery of cohune palms, across vast flood plains filled with citrus trees, which provide a spectacular backdrop for the 52-mile journey southeast to Dangriga.

The Hummingbird Highway climbs through rich tropical hardwood forest until reaching Mile 13, where a visitor centre marks a track leading off to **St Herman's Cave**. Two paths, with good birdwatching, lead through shady ferns before descending in steps

**Best** for
Beach life ▪ Big cats ▪ Diving ▪ Maya ruins ▪ Whale sharks

to the cave entrance with its unique microclimate. You can walk for more than a mile underground but it can be slippery if wet; torch and spare batteries essential. There is a 3-mile trail to a campsite from the visitor centre.

Two miles further on is the **Blue Hole National Park** ⓘ *daily 0800-1600, US$4, visitor centre at entrance,* an azure blue swimming hole fringed with vines and ferns, fed by a stream that comes from St Herman's Cave. This is typical karst limestone country with sinkholes, caves and underground streams. After its long journey underground, the water here is deliciously cool until it disappears again into the top of a large underwater cavern. Eventually this joins the Sibun River which enters the sea just south of Belize City. There is a rough 2½-mile trail (good hiking boots are required), through low secondary forest, between St Herman's Cave and the Blue Hole itself. A sign on the roadway warns visitors against thieves; lock your car and leave someone on guard if possible when swimming. An armed guard and more wardens have been hired to prevent further theft and assaults.

The peaks of the mountains dominate the south side of the highway until about Mile 30, when the valley of Stann Creek begins to widen out into Belize's most productive agricultural area, where large citrus groves stretch along the highway.

Canoeing or tubing trips can be organized down Indian Creek, visiting the imaginatively named Caves Five, Four and Three and then Daylight Cave and Darknight Cave, from **Over-the-Top Camp** on the Hummingbird Highway, or **Kingfisher/Belize Adventures** in Placencia. Vehicle support is brought round to meet you on the Coastal Highway near Democracia.

Turn east at Mile 32 for 4 miles along a gravel road to **Tamandua**, a wildlife sanctuary in **Five Blue Lakes National Park** ⓘ *Friends of 5 Blues, PO Box 111, Belmopan, T809-2005, or the warden, Lee Wengrzyn, a local dairy farmer, or else Augustus Palacio.* Follow the track opposite **Over-the-Top Camp**, turning right and crossing the stream for Tamandua, then for another 2 miles or so straight on following the signs for the national park, 1½ miles, where there is camping.

## Listings South to Dangriga

### Where to stay

**$$$$ Caves Branch Jungle Lodge**
*Hummingbird Highway Mile 41.5, T610-3451, www.cavesbranch.com.*
Reached along a ½-mile track, signed on the left, any bus between Belmopan and Dangriga will stop. A secluded spot on the banks of Caves Branch River, comfortable treehouses and cabanas with private baths, delicious meals served buffet style. More than just accommodation, this is very much an activity centre. Great trips through caves, 7-mile underground floats, guided jungle trips, overnight trips as well, tubing, kayaking, mountain biking and rappelling, including

the adrenalin-busting **Black Hole Drop**. Excellent guides, pricey for some budgets but highly recommended.

**$$$$ Sleeping Giant Lodge**
*Hummingbird Highway Mile 36.5, T707-6986, www.sleepinggiantbelize.com.*
Situated on a sloping terrace by the Sibun river, this beautiful rainforest resort enjoys unrivalled views of Sleeping Giant Mountain and the surrounding range. Luxury lodgings include tasteful and tranquil rooms and *casitas* with mahogany woodwork, marble and granite finishes, and hand-crafted furniture. The grounds are lush and leafy and feature a bubbling creek, hot tub and pool. All-inclusive packages available.

## $$ Yamwits
*Hummingbird Highway Mile 35.5,*
*T822-2906, www.yamwits.com.*
Nestled in the fragrant grounds of a citrus orchard, Yamwits is a locally owned, family-run lodging with 6 simple, clean and economical rooms with a wide veranda overlooking the fruit trees and mountains. They serve local cuisine in their restaurant; worth a stop if you're driving through. Friendly hosts, classic Belizean hospitality.

### What to do

There is a wide variety of day and overnight excursions to Gales Point, from US$30 per boat holding 6-8 people. Contact Kevin Andrewin of **Manatee Tour Guides Association** on arrival. Community phone, T02-12031, minimum 48 hrs' notice is advisable, ask for Alice or Josephine.

### Transport

#### Boat
Gales Point can be reached by inland waterways from **Belize City**, but buses have largely superseded boat services.

#### Bus
At least 2 daily **Southern Transport** buses run between **Belize City** and Dangriga on the coastal road.

## Dangriga and around   *Colour map 2, A6.*
### cheerful and busy seafront town with a largely Garífuna population

The chief town of the Stann Creek District, Dangriga (population 11,600) is on the seashore, and has the usual Belizean aspect of wooden clapboard houses elevated on piles. North Stann Creek meets the sea at Dangriga, coming alive with flotillas of boats and fishermen.

There are several petrol stations, a good hospital and an airfield with regular flights. The beach has been considerably cleaned up and extended, being particularly pleasant at the far north of town at the Pelican Beach Hotel, where it is raked and cleaned daily. Palm trees have been planted by Pal's Guest House where the beach has been enlarged. Dangriga means 'standing waters' or 'sweet water' in Garífuna. It's possible to take a boat from Dangriga to Honduras; see Border crossings box in Practicalities chapter.

To understand more about the Garífuna culture, visit the **Gulisi Garífuna Museum** ⓘ *Stann Creek Valley Rd, T502-0639, www.ngcbelize.org, Mon-Fri 1000-1700, Sat 0800-1200, US$5.* The museum includes information about the origins of the Garífuna people, history and customs, with music and a working garden of traditional plants and herbs.

### Cayes near Dangriga
**Tobacco Caye** ⓘ *US$15, 35 mins by speedboat from Dangriga,* is a tiny and quite heavily populated island, but has lots of local flavour and charm and, though becoming a little commercialized, still has an authentic feel. It sits right on the reef and you can snorkel from the sandfly-free beach although there are no large schools of fish; snorkelling gear for rent. Boats go daily, ask at **Riverside Café** ⓘ *US$12-15 per person.*

**South Water Caye**, the focus of a marine reserve, is a lovely palm-fringed tropical island with beautiful beaches, particularly at the south end.

### South of Dangriga
The Southern Highway (now completely paved except for a stretch of a mile or so) connects Dangriga with Punta Gorda in the far south. Six miles inland from Dangriga the

road branches off the Hummingbird Highway and heads south through mixed tropical forests, palmettos and pines along the fringes of the Maya Mountains. West of the road, about 5 miles from the junction with the Hummingbird Highway, a track leads to **Mayflower**, a Maya ruin. Some minimal work has begun on opening it up and some say it will eventually be the biggest archaeological site in southern Belize.

Fifteen miles from Dangriga, a minor road forks off 4 miles east to the Garífuna fishing village of Hopkins. Watch out for sandflies when the weather is calm. The villagers throw household slops into the sea and garbage on to the beach.

Turning east towards the Caribbean just before Kendal a road leads down the Sittee River to **Sittee River Village** and **Possum Point Biological Station**.

### Glover's Reef

Glover's Reef, part of North East Cay and about 45 miles offshore, is an atoll with beautiful diving and has been a **Marine Reserve** ① *US$10*, since 1993. The reef here is pristine and the cayes are generally unspoilt, but yellow blight has hit the area killing most of the existing palm trees, especially on **Long Caye**. The combination of Hurricane Mitch and high water temperatures has damaged the coral, and the snorkelling is not as good as it once was.

## Listings Dangriga and around

### Where to stay

#### Dangriga

**$$$ Pelican Beach**
*Outside town, on the beach north of town, T522-2044, www.pelicanbeachbelize.com.*
This Belizean-owned hotel overlooking the ocean has 20 rooms with private bath, hot water, a/c, veranda, hammocks. Amenities include restaurant, bar, games lounge, gift shop and tours. Friendly and helpful. Take a taxi from town, or it's a 15-min walk from North Stann Creek.

**$$$-$$ Chaleanor**
*35 Magoon St, T522-2587, www.chaleanorhotel.com.*
Managed by Chad and Eleanor Usher, this comfortable guesthouse has fairly large rooms, some with TV and fan and a/c, some with sea views, and a rooftop restaurant.

**$$ Pal's Guest House**
*868 A Magoon St, Dangriga, T522-2095, www.palsbelize.com.*
These 19 units on the beach, all have balconies, sea views, bath, fan and cable TV; cheaper rooms in main building, shared bath downstairs, private upstairs. **Dangriga**

**Dive Centre** runs from next door (see What to do, below).

**$ D's Hostel**
*Corner Mahogany St and Sharp St, T502-3324, www.valsbackpackerhostel.com.*
Formerly Val's place, D's is the only backpacker hostel in town. It's a chilled, friendly place, with a family atmosphere, and has 24 dorm beds, hot and cold water, Wi-Fi (extra), lockers and a book exchange. A waffle breakfast and hot coffee are included.

#### Cayes near Dangriga
#### Tobacco Caye

There is no electricity on the island, but it has a good family atmosphere and is great fun.

**$$$ Reef's End Lodge**
*T522-2419, www.reefsendlodge.com.*
The new Swedish owners have spruced this simple but appealing place up, now probably the best place on the island. Accommodation includes sea view rooms with veranda and wood-built beach cabanas. Minimum 3 nights and rates include full board.

**$ Tobacco Caye Paradise Cabins**
*North Point, T532-2101, www.tobacocayeparadisecabin.com.*
Formerly a holiday lodge belonging to a Belizean family, this accommodation includes 6 simple, rustic, traditionally Caribbean clapboard cabins, suitable for budget travellers. Rates are per person, and meals are available (**$$**).

## South Water Caye

**$$$$ Blue Marlin Lodge**
*T522-2243, www.bluemarlinlodge.com.*
Excellent dive lodge with a host of accommodation include beachside cabins, 'island igloos' and rooms. Offers various packages, small sandy island with snorkelling off the beach, good accommodation and food, runs tours.

**$$$$ Pelican's Beach Resort**
*T522-2044, www.pelicanbeachbelize.com.*
Rooms in a 2-storey colonial building, and 3 secluded cottages. **Pelican University** is ideal for groups housing up to 23 people at US$60 per person per day including 3 meals.

## Other Cayes

**$$$$ Coco Plum Island Resort**
*T1-800-763-7360, www.cocoplumcay.com.*
Set on a private caye, this adults-only private resort would suit couples seeking seclusion and romance. Lodgings include 14 Caribbean-style oceanfront cabanas with well-attired interiors. Various packages available from 'no frills' to 'lover's getaway'. Exclusive and professional.

**$$$$ Thatch Caye Resort**
*T532-2414, www.thatchcayebelize.com.*
Located in the heart of the South Water Caye Marine Reserve, this exclusive private island resort promises access to some great dive and snorkel sites. Lodgings consist of cabanas and *casitas* on the edge of the water. Expensive and rustic-chic.

## South of Dangriga

**$$$$ Hamanasi**
*Sittee Point, T1-877-552-3483, www.hamanasi.com.*
This boutique beachside resort is set in 17-acre gardens bursting with tropical flowers and orchids. Accommodation includes 13 private treehouses on stilts, 2 honeymoon suites and 8 beachfront deluxe rooms. Amenities include pool, kayaks, bikes and a full dive operation.

**$$$$ Jaguar Reef Lodge**
*South of Hopkins, just north of Sittee River, T822-3851, www.jaguarreef.com.*
18 a/c rooms with fridges. Central lodge on sandy beach, pool, diving, snorkelling, kayaking, mountain bikes, birdwatching and wildlife excursions.

**$$$$-$$$ Beaches and Dreams**
*Sittee Point, T523-7259, www.beachesanddreams.com.*
4 extremely well-furnished beachfront rooms. Price includes full breakfast, Dangriga transfer, use of bikes and kayaks.

**$$$ Hopkins Inn**
*On beach south of centre, T523-7283, www.hopkinsinn.com.*
White cabins with private bathroom, very clean and friendly, German spoken. Price includes breakfast, knowledgeable owners.

**$$$-$$ Jungle Jeanie's by the Sea**
*About 1 mile south of Hopkins Village, T533-7047, www.junglebythesea.com.*
Perched between the jungle and the ocean, comfortable wooden beachfront cabanas fully equipped with fan, fridge and coffee-maker. For families there's a beach house and jungle loft. Budget-orientated travellers may prefer the 'mini-cabanas' (**$$**). Simple, natural and pleasant.

**$$ Tipple Tree Beya Inn**
*Just before Sandy Beach Lodge, T520-7006, www.tippletree.com.*
English-American run, 4 rooms in a wooden house and small cabin apartment, camping possible.

### $$-$ Windschief Cabanas
*Hopkins Village, T523-7249,*
*www.windsurfing-belize.com.*
Windschief has 2 simple, wood-built
cabanas. The small one ($) has a double
bed, hot shower, balcony facing the sea, fan,
fridge and coffee-maker. The large one ($$)
has the same facilities but sleeps up to 4.
They also manage a beach bar with Wi-Fi.

### $ The Funky Dodo
*Hopkins Village, T667-0558,*
*www.thefunkydodo.com.*
Accommodation at this funky backpacker
hostel include a 14-bed dorm and 6 private
rooms. Amenities include a small plunge
pool, hammocks, shared kitchen, Wi-Fi and
a treetop bar under a thatched roof. It's cosy
and a bit rustic.

## Glover's Reef

### $$-$ Glover's Atoll Resort
*North East Caye, T532-2916,*
*www.glovers.com.bz.*
8 cabins with wood-burning stoves, you
can also choose dorm or camping. Weekly
rates include round-trip transportation from
Sittee River. Occasional rice and seafood
meals, bring food, some groceries and
drinking water (US$2.50 a gallon) available.
Best to bring everything you will need.
Facilities are very simple and basic. Guests
are sometimes invited to help out.

## Restaurants

### $ Riverside Café
*South bank of river, just east of main road.*
Better inside than it looks from the outside,
good breakfast, good service and food,
best place to get information on boats to
Tobacco Caye.

## Bars and clubs

Listen for local music punta rock, a
Garífuna/African-based Carib sound, now
popular throughout Belize. Home-made
instruments are a Garífuna speciality,
particularly drums. Studios can be visited.

### Local Motion Disco
*Next to Cameleon. Sat-Sun.*
Punta rock, reggae, live music.

### Riviera Club
*Between bridge and Bank of Nova Scotia.*
Popular nightclub at weekends.

## Festivals

**18-19 Nov  Garífuna**, or **Settlement
Day**, celebrating the landing of the Black
Caribs in 1823. Dancing all night and next
day; very popular. Booking advisable for
accommodation. Private homes rent rooms,
though. Boats from Puerto Barrios to Punta
Gorda (see Transport, page 251) tend to
be full, but launches take passengers for
US$10 per person.

## What to do

**Dangriga Dive Centre**, *T522-3262.* Derek
Jones arranges fabulous trips to the cayes.
**Pelican Beach Hotel**, runs tours to
Cockscomb Basin, Gales Point and
citrus factories.
**Rosado's Tours**, *35 Lemon St, T522-2119.*
Government services.
**Treasured Travels**, *64 Commerce St,*
*T522-2578.* Very helpful, run by Diane.

### South of Dangriga
**Second Nature Divers**, *T523-7038, divers@*
*btl.net, or enquire at Hamanasi.* English-
owned, good guides and equipment; a
recommended spot to visit is Sharks' Cave.

### Glover's Reef
**Off The Wall Dive Center**, *Dangriga,*
*T614-6348, www.offthewallbelize.com.*
Offers dive courses. Friendly owners
Jim and Kendra Schofield offer packages
that include transport, accommodation,
meals and diving.

**small seaside community and good base for exploring cayes**

Placencia, a former Creole fishing village 30 miles south of Dangriga, is on a thin sandy peninsula and makes a good jumping-off point for the cayes and their marine life, as well as inland tours. Continuing down the Southern Highway a couple of hotel signs indicate a turning (nothing official, look carefully) to a road that heads east to Riversdale (after 9 miles) turning south to follow the peninsula to Maya Beach, Seine Bight and, eventually, Placencia. The peninsula road is very rough from Riversdale to Seine Bight, with sand mixed with mud; a 4WD is advisable.

Placencia is becoming more popular among people looking for a remote adventure. It's a relaxing combination of chilling out on the beach, fishing, snorkelling and diving. If you time the trip right or get lucky, your visit may coincide with the migrations of the whale shark – the largest fish in the world at up to 55 ft – that passes through local waters from

**Placencia**

| Where to stay 🛏 | | |
|---|---|---|
| Deb & Dave's Last Resort **2** | Seaspray **8** | De Tatch Café **2** |
| Lydia's Guesthouse **5** | Trade Winds **12** | La Dolce Vita **8** |
| Miramar Apartments **15** | Turtle Inn **10** | Omar's Creole Grub **13** |
| Paradise Resort **6** | Yellow House **11** | Pickled Parrot Bar & Grill **7** |
| Ranguana Lodge **7** | | Rumfish **14** |
| Robert's Grove **14** | **Restaurants** 🍴 | Secret Garden **15** |
| Sea Glass Inn **3** | BJ's **1** | Tutti-frutti Ice Cream |
| | Cozy Corner **6** | Parlour **9** |

March to May. And, between January and March, hundreds of scarlet macaws gather at nearby Red Bank. Also worth hitting if you can time it right is the **Lobster Fest** – on the last full weekend in June, with two days of music, dancing and lobster – and the **Sidewalk Arts Festival**, held the weekend before or after Valentine's Day. Placencia is a natural base for one- and two-day trips to **Cockscomb Basin Wildlife Sanctuary**; see page 248. **Big Creek**, on the mainland opposite Placencia, is 3 miles from Mango Creek.

There are no streets, just a network of concrete footpaths connecting the wooden houses that are set among the palms. The main sidewalk through the centre of the village is reported to be in the *Guinness Book of Records* as the world's narrowest street. There is a laid-back atmosphere, with lots of Jamaican music, particularly after the Easter and Christmas celebrations.

The local **Placencia Tourism Center** ⓘ *T523-4045, www.placencia.com, Mon-Fri 0900-1700, closed public holidays, and 1130-1300 during low season,* is in Placencia Village Square, with lots of useful information. It also produces the local monthly newssheet, *Placencia Breeze* (www.placenciabreeze.com).

## Around Placencia

Trips can be made to local cayes and the **Barrier Reef**, approximately 18 miles offshore. Day trips include snorkelling, with a beach barbecue lunch of lobster and conch. Offshore cayes include **Laughing Bird Caye**, **Gladden Spit** and **Silk Cayes Marine Reserve** (reserve fee US$10), also protected by **Friends of Nature**. Whale sharks visit the spit in March, April, May and June for 10 days after the full moon to feed on the spawn of aggregating reef fish.

Several hotels and guide services have kayaks that can be rented to explore some of the nearer islands or the quieter waters of the **Placencia Lagoon**. Those who want to keep their feet dry can go mountain biking on the peninsula or use it as a base for trips to **Cockscomb Basin Wildlife Sanctuary** and Maya ruins.

Day tours by boat south along the coast from Placencia to **Monkey River** and **Monkey River Village** are available. Monkey River tours, US$20 per person, feature howler monkeys, toucans, manatees and iguanas. Monkey River Village can be reached by a rough road, which is not recommended in wet weather. The road ends on the north side of the river and the town is on the south side, so call over for transport. Trips upriver can also be arranged here with locals but kayaking is best organized in Placencia. Trips can be arranged to Red Bank for the scarlet macaws, which gather in their hundreds between January and March. North of Placencia is the Garífuna community of **Seine Bight**.

## Cayes near Placencia

**Ranguana Caye** is a private caye reached from Placencia (US$5). Getting there is free if it fits in with one of the regular trips, otherwise it costs US$150 each way for up to four people. Divers must bring their own scuba equipment. Day trips for diving, snorkelling or just relaxing cost US$45-50, and include lunch. For longer stays, see Where to stay, below.

At the southernmost end of the Mesoamerican Barrier Reef are the **Sapodilla Cayes**, US$10. Tours are arranged from Guatemala (see Río Dulce and Lívingston in Guatemala chapter) or can be made from Placencia. There are settlements on a few of the Cayes including **Hunting Caye**.

The **Silk Cayes**, also known as the **Queen Cayes**, is a small group of tiny, picture-perfect islands, which sits on the outer barrier reef and, together with Gladdens Spit, has become the core zone of the country's newest marine reserve. The Silk Cayes have superb diving, especially on the North Wall. Coral in the deeper areas is in good condition with many tube and barrel sponges and sharks, turtles and rays often seen cruising the reef wall. The

Silk Cayes are a popular destination for Placencia-based dive operators; however, it's not possible to dive in this area during periods of rough weather. The rainy season lasts from June to January.

**Laughing Bird Caye** ⓘ *reserve fee US$4, www.friendsofnaturebelize.org*, used to be the home of the laughing gull (*Larus articilla*) but now is home to other sea birds and has an exciting array of underwater life around its shores.

## Listings Placencia and around *map p242*

### Where to stay

Rooms may be hard to find in the afternoon (after the arrival of the bus from Dangriga). Usually several houses to rent, US$200-550 per week; see the ads at the tourist information centre.

**$$$$ Robert's Grove**
*North of the air strip and Rum Point Inn, T523-3565, www.robertsgrove.com.*
Luxury resort with 2 pools, massage service, boats and jacuzzis set on a white-sand beach shaded by the odd palm. Rooms are spacious, comfortable and quiet and the restaurant serves good, filling food. Entertainment and tours, including PADI diving from its own marina, are organized. Friendly bar staff.

**$$$$ Turtle Inn**
*On beach close to airstrip, T364-3451, www.turtleinn.com.*
Completely destroyed by Hurricane Iris, owner Francis Ford Coppola rebuilt this impressive resort in local and Balinese style set around a circular pool with restaurant and spa.

**$$$$-$$$ Miramar Apartments**
*T523 3658, www.miramarbelize.com.*
Immaculate, fully equipped apartments close to the beach that range from 1-bed studios to 3-bed apartments. Lots of amenities, very comfortable and recommended for families.

**$$$ Paradise Resort**
*Down by the piers, T523-3179, www.paradisevacation belize.com.*
Formerly the **Paradise Vacation Hotel**, Paradise resort has 12 rooms with a/c and private baths. Facilities include pool, restaurant, roof deck with hot tub and views of the harbour. Located on the water at the southern end of Placencia.

**$$$ Ranguana Lodge**
*T523-3112, www.ranguanabelize.com.*
Ranguana Lodge has 5 lovely little wooden cabins, some with sea views. All are well-equipped with hammock, balcony, hot shower, cable TV; those situated in the garden have a full kitchen. Simple, comfortable and very clean. Wi-Fi and barbecue available.

**$$$ Sea Glass Inn**
*Garden Grove, T523-3098, www.seaglassinnbelize.com.*
Formerly known as **Dianni's Guest House**, this affordable boutique hotel has 6 spacious, modern, recently renovated rooms with a/c, hot water and Wi-Fi. There's also a nice balcony with hammocks.

**$$$ Trade Winds Hotel**
*South Point, T523-3122, trdewndpla@btl.net.*
This no-frills place has 9 very colourful cabins in a spacious private plot on the south beach in a great location.

**$$$ The Yellow House**
*T523-3481, www.ctbelize.com.*
A bright yellow building, directly behind **Serenade**, with 4 very comfortable rooms with communicating doors, so excellent for a family or group of friends. Front rooms have microwaves, coffee machines and fridges. They also run several other lodgings in the village.

## $$ Deb and Dave's Last Resort
*T523-3207, www.toadaladventure.com.*
4 very good budget rooms with shared
bathroom and hot water. There's kayak and
bike rental, as well as tours of the local area.
Walk-ins only, no advance reservations.

## $$-$ Lydia's Guesthouse
*T523-3117, www.lydiasguesthouse.com.*
Situated across the sidewalk on a quiet part
of the beach, this simple but very relaxing
place has 8 double rooms with shared toilet
and shower. There are kitchen facilities, free
Wi-Fi and a PC for hire. Recommended.

## $$-$ Seaspray
*T523-3148, www.seasprayhotel.com.*
Very nice, comfortable and friendly, with
good-value rooms for range of prices, from
beachside cabanas to small doubles in the
original building. The popular **De Tatch Café**
is on the beach; see Restaurants, below.

## Camping

### Sea Kunga
*www.seakunga.com.*
Organizes camping tours on the beach.

---

## Around Placencia
## Maya Beach

### $$$$ Green Parrot Beach Houses
*T533-8188, www.greenparrot-belize.com.*
This very chilled place has thatched beach
houses on stilts, all with sea view and
sleeping up to 5, with kitchenettes. There's
also an open-air restaurant and bar.

### $$$$-$$$ Maya Breeze Inn
*T601-9695.*
4 cottages on the beach, 2 with a/c,
restaurant across the road.

### $$$$-$$$ Singing Sands Inn
*T533-3022, www.singingsands.com.*
Set in beautifully landscaped tropical
gardens, Singing Sands has 6 simple,
comfortable thatched cabins with
Guatemalan bedspreads and Mexican
tilework, hot water, fans and an ocean

view. There's snorkelling in front of the
resort at False Caye, and a restaurant and
bar on the beach.

### $$$ Barnacle Bill's
*T533-8110, www.barnaclebills-belize.com.*
Deluxe wood-built cabanas with queen-
sized bed, sleeper/sofa in the living/dining
area, full kitchen, private bath and fans.

## Mango Creek/Independence

### $$ Ursella's Guest House
*T503-2062.*
9 simple rooms with shared or private bath
and TV.

### $ Hotel above People's Restaurant
A very basic place. Ask to borrow a fan and
lamp; the shower is a bucket of water in a
cabin. There's a simple restaurant.

## Cayes near Placencia

### $$$$ Hatchet Caye Resort
*T533-4446, www.hatchetcaye.com.*
Secluded and exclusive, Hatchet Caye is a
luxurious private island resort with a range
of excellent cabanas, all immaculately attired
and very expensive. First class.

### $$$$ Ranguana Caye
*Reservations through Robert's Grove,*
*T523-3565, www.roberts grove.com.*
3 cabanas, each with a double and single
bed, gas stove, private hot showers and
toilet in a separate building. There are
barbecue pits so bring food, but meals
are also available.

## Restaurants

### $$$ La Dolce Vita
*Near Wallen's Market, T523-3115.*
Italian restaurant who claim to have
the best wine selection in town.

### $$$ The Secret Garden
*Near Wallen's Market, T523-3617.*
International cuisine served in a relaxed,
chilled-out atmosphere.

### $$$-$$ Rumfish
*T523-3293, rumfish@btl.net.*
Good-quality restaurant, popular with locals.

### $$ Cozy Corner
*On the beach, T523-3280.*
Very good beachside bar and restaurant.
Good, mid-priced barbecue and
grilled seafood.

### $$ De Tatch Café
*Just before the north end of the sidewalk.*
*Closed Wed.*
Said to be the best coffee in town and it's
certainly hugely popular, with excellent
seafood specials at night and snappy service;
a winner.

### $$ Pickled Parrot Bar and Grill
*Close to Wallen's Market. Closed Sun.*
Good pizza, chicken and seafood.

### $$-$ BJ's Restaurant
*See map, T523-3131.*
Good fried chicken and traditional Creole
food. Owners Percy and Betty offer good
Asian stir-fries and pizza. It's inexpensive
and popular with the locals.

### $ Omar's Creole Grub
*Main St, T624-7168.*
Creole diner.

### $ Tutti-frutti Ice Cream Parlour
*Placencia Village Square.*
Great Italian ice cream, made by real Italians!

---

#### Around Placencia

### $$ Goyo's Inn/Restaurant Independence
*Mango Creek.*
Family-owned, good food.

### $ Lola's Café and Art Gallery
*Sign at south end of Seine Bight.*
For an entertaining evening with dinner,
run by local artist Lola Delgado.

### $ White house with green shutters
*Mango Creek, behind People's.*
Better than at **People's**. Book 2 hrs in
advance if possible.

## Bars and clubs

### Barefoot Beach Bar
*At Tipsy Tuna. Closed Mon.*
A very popular joint on the beach with live
music and a happy hour 1700-1800.

### Tipsy Tuna Sports Bar
*Open from 1900.*
Popular sports and karaoke beachside bar.

## What to do

### Fishing
Fishing, especially saltwater fly-fishing,
is excellent, with recognized world-class
permit fishing. Reputable licensed guides
and tour operators include **Kurt Godfrey**,
T523-3277, and **Earl Godfrey**, T523-3433,
lgodfrey@ btl.net.
**Bruce Leslie**, *from Tutti-frutti, T523-3370.*
Rates for a full day of light tackle and fly
fishing, including lunch, average US$325,
maximum 2 anglers per boat for fly-fishing.
**Destinations Belize**, *T523-4018, www.
destinationsbelize.com.* Offers combination
cayes camping and fishing/snorkelling trips,
plus whale shark interaction tours.

### Kayaking
**Toadal Adventures**, *T523-3207, www.
toadaladventure.com.* A reputable tour
operator for multi-day kayaking trips to
the cayes and Monkey River.

### Scuba-diving and snorkelling
Full PADI scuba-diving courses are available
at most local dive shops for around US$350.
Some dive operators listed below base
themselves out of high-end resorts. Of
the in-town operators **Seahorse**, **Joy
Tours** and **Splash** enjoy solid reputations.
However, environmental standards and
genuine concern for the reef is somewhat
lacking; this could be improved with a little
encouragement. Prices are from about
US$70, plus 9% sales tax, for 2-tank dives,
US$105 to outer reef (gear extra). Snorkel
trips generally cost US$60-70 for a full day

and US$30-45 for a half day, including gear. There is a whale shark and snorkelling fee of US$15 from 1 Mar-3 Jul charged by **Friends of Nature**.

**Joy Tours**, *T651-0464, www.njoybelize.com*. Locally recommended.

**Ocean Motion Guide Service**, *T523-3363, www.oceanmotion placencia.com*. A reputable snorkelling tour operator.

**Seahorse Dive Shop**, *T523-3166, www. belizescuba.com*. Ask for Brian Young. Good selection of gear.

**Splash**, *T523-3058, www.splashbelize.com*. Helpful owners who specialize in dive training and courses.

### Transport

#### Air
Placencia has its own airstrip. **Maya Island Air** and **Tropic Air** (T523-3410) fly several times a day to **Belize City** (international and municipal), also to **Dangriga** and **Punta Gorda**.

#### Boat
The **Hokie Pokie Water Taxi**, T523-2376, www.aguallos.com/hokeypokey. In Placencia leaves from the water taxi fuel station terminal behind the **M'n M** store. In Mango Creek the terminal is across the lagoon to **Independence**. US$5, check website for schedule (regular departures). From here, buses depart for **Punta Gorda** and **Belize City**.

The **Belize–Honduras Boat**, T632-0083, www.belizeferry.com, provides a regular weekly service linking Placencia and **Puerto Cortés** in Honduras. The journey can be quite choppy. From Placencia the boat leaves the dock near the petrol station at 0930 every Fri, passing Big Creek at 1000 to complete immigration formalities. It arrives in Puerto Cortés from1200, US$50. Buy tickets in the Placencia Tourism Center, US$55. Return service leaves Puerto Cortés on Mon at 1100 arriving 1330.

See also Border crossings box in Practicalities chapter.

#### Bus
**Placencia Peninsula Shuttle**, T607-2711, runs from the Placencia dock to the **Zeboz Hotel** 5 times daily each way, US$2.50-5. See the tourist office for schedule. Buses to **Dangriga** direct at 0600, 0630, 1400, 3 hrs, US$5. Express, US$6. Direct bus to to **Punta Gorda**, from Placencia with **Southern Transport** or **James Buses**. Alternatively, take the **Hokie Pokie Water Taxi**, see above, to catch the **James Bus Line** buses from Independence Village, at 0930, 1045, 1500, 1630, 1645, 1½-2½ hrs. For buses to **Dangriga**, 1 hr, **Belmopan**, 2½ hrs and **Belize City**, 3½ hrs, also catch the boat to Independence. Buses leave at 0715, 0815, 1015, 1415 and 1645. Check times and fares at the Placencia tourist centre at the dock next to the **Shell** petrol station.

## Cockscomb Basin Wildlife Sanctuary and around  Colour map 2, B6.

the world's first jaguar sanctuary

★Some 20 miles south of Dangriga, the Southern Highway crosses the Sittee River at the small village of Kendal (ruins nearby). One mile beyond is the village of Maya Centre from where a poor seven-mile track winds west through Cabbage Haul Gap to the Cockscomb Basin Wildlife Sanctuary (21,000 acres, US$5), worth an extended visit if you have two to three days. The sanctuary was created out of the Cockscomb Basin Forest Reserve in 1986 to protect the country's highest recorded density of jaguars (*Panthera onca*), and their smaller cousins the puma (red tiger), the endangered ocelot, the diurnal jaguarundi and that feline cutey, the margay.

Many other mammals share the heavily forested reserve, including coatis, collared peccaries, agoutis, anteaters, Baird's tapirs and tayras (a small weasel-like animal). There are red-eyed tree frogs, boas, iguanas and fer-de-lances, as well as over 290 species of bird, including king vultures and great curassows. The sanctuary is a good place for relaxing, showering under waterfalls, tubing down the river, or listening to birds – hundreds of bird species have been spotted and there are several types of toucan, hummingbirds and scarlet macaws to be seen by early risers. The reserve is sponsored by the Belizean government, the Audubon Society, the Worldwide Fund for Nature and various private firms. Donations are very welcome.

Park HQ is at the former settlement of Quam Bank (whose milpa-farming inhabitants founded the **Maya Centre** outside the reserve). Here there is an informative visitor centre. An 18-mile network of jungle trails spreads out from the centre, ranging in distance from a few hundred yards to 2½ miles. Walkers are unlikely to see any of the big cats as they are nocturnal, but if you fancy a walk in the dark you may be lucky. Note that the guards leave for the day at 1600. You will see birds, frogs, lizards, snakes and spiders. Longer hikes can be planned with the staff.

Nearby is one of Belize's highest summits, **Victoria Peak** (3675 ft), which is an arduous four- or five-day return climb and should not be undertaken lightly. There is virtually no path, a guide is essential; February to May are the best months for the climb. For guides, see What to do, below.

## Listings Cockscomb Basin Wildlife Sanctuary and around

### Where to stay

To guarantee accommodation, contact the Belize Audubon Society; see box, page 212.

**$$$$ Bocawina Rainforest Resort and Adventures**
*T670-8019, T+1-844-894-2311 (international), T1-800-667-1630 (USA toll free), T0800-404 9535 (UK toll free), www.bocawina.com.*
Formerly **Mama Noots Backabush Resort**, this great adventure lodge has traditional cabanas and rooms nestled in the heart of the rainforest. They offer scores of onsite activities including jungle hiking, zip-lining, birdwatching and rappelling. They are ecologically aware, with electricity from solar, wind and hydro systems, and most fruits and veg are grown organically here.

**$$-$ Park HQ**
Purpose-built cabins and dorms ($ per person) with a picnic area. Drinking water is available as are compost toilets, but

you must bring all your own food, drinks, matches, torch, sleeping bag, eating utensils and insect repellent. The nearest shop is at Maya Centre.

## What to do

The **Belize Audubon Society**, see box on page 212, runs the reserve. The most knowledgeable guides to the reserve live in Maya Centre; contact **Julio Saqui**, of Julio's Cultural Tours, T608-4992, www.cockscomb mayatours.com, who runs the village shop and can look after any extra luggage. At Greg's Bar, on the main road in the middle of the village, you can contact **Greg Sho**, an experienced river and mountain guide who can arrange kayak trips.

Full-day Mopan Mayan cultural tours of Maya Centre Village are available including visits to workshops on traditional Mayan cooking, crafts, language and natural tropical medicines. Contact **Liberato** or **Araceli Saqui** at Maya Centre Village. Tour operators in Placencia run day trips for US$65.

## Transport

### Bus

Buses can be booked at time of reservation, or locals will drive you from Maya Centre, otherwise it is a 6-mile, uphill walk from Maya Centre to the reserve – allow 2 hrs for the walk to Maya Centre. If you leave early in the morning going either way you are likely to see quite a lot of wildlife. All buses going south from **Dangriga** go through Maya Centre, 40 mins, US$4; and north from Placencia, return buses from 0700 onwards to Dangriga. If walking, leave all unwanted gear in Dangriga in view of the uphill stretch from Maya Centre, or you can leave luggage at Julio's little store in Maya Centre for a daily fee.

### Taxi

A taxi from **Dangriga** will cost about US$50; it's not difficult to hitch back.

## Punta Gorda and around   Colour map 2, B5.

**culturally diverse market town and fishing port**

The turn-off from the Southern Highway for Mango Creek, Independence and Big Creek comes 15 miles after the Riversdale turn-off, and the road runs 4 miles east through the Savannah Forest Reserve to the mangrove coast opposite Placencia. About 35 miles beyond the junction, 10½ miles north of the T-junction for Punta Gorda, half a mile west of the road, is the Nim Li Punit archaeological site which has a visitor centre and clean spacious housing for the stelae. Nim Li Punit ('The Big Hat') was only discovered in 1974. A score of stelae, 15-20 ft tall, were unearthed, dated AD 700-800, as well as a ball court and several groups of buildings. The site is worth visiting – look for the sign on the highway. Day trips are also offered from Placencia.

Nearby, the highway passes Big Falls Village, almost completely destroyed by Hurricane Iris. Take a short hike back to the hot springs for a swim, camp or sling a hammock, but first seek permission from the landowner, Mr Peter Aleman.

Four miles from Big Falls, the Highway reaches a T-junction, known locally as the 'Dump', marked by a Shell station; the road to San Antonio branches right (west), the main road turns sharp left and runs down through a forest reserve for 13 miles to Punta Gorda. The road is paved from Big Falls to Punta Gorda.

**Punta Gorda** (population 5255) is the southernmost settlement of any size in Belize, with a varied ethnic makeup of Creoles, Q'eqchi', Mopan, Chinese, East Indians and descendants of the many races brought here over the years as labourers in ill-fated settlement attempts. Three miles north of **Toledo** are the remains of the sugar cane settlement founded by Confederate refugees after the American Civil War. The coast, about 10 ft above sea level, is fringed with coconut palms. The seafront is clean and enjoyable – once you get away from Front Street, where the lively and colourful market on Wednesday, Friday and Saturday comes with the associated smells of fish and rotting vegetables. The *Voice of America* has an antenna complex to the south of town.

At **Toledo Visitor Information Center**, also called **Dem Dats Doin** ① *in booth by pier, PO Box 73, T722-2470, demdatsdoin@btl.net, free, irregular opening hours*, Alfredo and Yvonne Villoria provide information on travel, tours, guiding, accommodation with indigenous families (under the Homestay Programme), message service and book exchange, for the whole of Toledo district. The **Tourist Information Centre** ① *Front St, T722-2531, Mon-Sat 0800-1200 and 1300-1700*, provides a wealth of information about the area, including bus schedules to local Maya villages, and can organize flight reservations, hotels, tours and boat trips to Honduras. The **Toledo Ecotourism Association** has an office in the same building, with information on the **Village Guesthouse** and **Ecotrail** programme, and transport to the villages, see also box, page 254.

### Around Punta Gorda

Rainfall in this region is particularly heavy, with more than 170 inches annually, and the vegetation is consequently luxuriant. There are many tours that can be enjoyed on the numerous rivers in the Toledo District. Countless species of birds make their homes along the rivers, as do troops of howler monkeys and other wildlife. Kayaking is a good way to view wildlife on the rivers. There are many white-sand beaches on the cayes off Punta Gorda for the beachcomber, or camper. Fly fishing is becoming a popular sport and sport fishing, snorkelling and scuba-diving are available. Toledo is off the beaten path and has some of the most spectacular views, waterfalls, rainforest, cayes and friendly people.

### Listings Punta Gorda and around

#### Where to stay

knowledgeable owners can organize trips around Toledo.

**$$$$ Cotton Tree Lodge**
*T670-0557, www.cottontreelodge.com.*
11 charming thatched *cabanas* at the woody bank of Moho River, built and run in an eco-friendly manner. Guests can visit local Mayan farmers and have a taste of their culture. The restaurant serves 3 meals a day. Families are welcome.

**$$$ Hickatee**
*T622-4475, www.hickatee.com.*
English breakfast, afternoon tea and wonderful, comfortable accommodation in wooden chalets set in a bird-filled glade in the heart of the rainforest. The helpful and

**$$$ Sea Front Inn**
*4 Front St, T722-2300, www.seafrontinn.com.*
This place offers 14 rooms with private bath hot water, a/c and TV, and a restaurant with great views. **Maya Island Air** and **Tropic Air** agents.

**$$-$ Tate's Guest House**
*34 José María Nuñez St, T722-0147, tatesguesthouse@yahoo.com.*
Friendly guesthouse with clean rooms that have a/c, cheaper without, hot water, bathroom and TV. There's breakfast before 0730, parking and laundry.

### $ Nature's Way Guest House
*65 Front St, T702-2119.*
Clean, friendly place, with good breakfast, and camping gear for rent. Recommended.

### $ St Charles Inn
*23 King St, T722-2149, stcharlespg@btl.net.*
Super-clean, a good budget choice. All rooms are spacious, with bath, fan or a/c, cable TV.

### $ Wahima
*On waterfront, T722-2542.*
Clean and safe, with private bath. The owner Max is friendly and informative. Also rents kitchenettes.

## Restaurants

Several cafés around the market area have good views over the bay.

### $$ Bobby's
*Main St.*
Serves excellent fish dishes. Bobby is a local fishing guide and arranges trips.

### $$ Earth Runnings Café and Bukut Bar
*Main Middle St, T702-2007, bukutbar@hotmail.com. Closed Tue.*
Great, idiosyncratic bar and café with regular live music that also provides tourist information, internet and occasional yoga and therapeutic massage.

### $$ Gomier's
*Behind the Sea Front Inn.*
For vegan meals and soya products.

### $$ Marian's Bayview Restaurant
*76 Front St, T722-0129.*
Serves traditional Belizean and East Indian dishes. Serves good ice cream and food as well.

## What to do

**Green Iguana Eco Adventures**, *T722-2475.* Provides a wide range of tours and services.
**Sun Creek Tours**, *suncreek@hughes.net.*
**Tide Tours**, *Main St, T722-2129, www. tidetours.org.* Organizes ecotours.

## Transport

### Air
Airstrip 5 mins' walk east of town. Daily flights with **Maya Island Air** and **Tropic Air**, T722-2008, from Dangriga, Placencia, Belize City (both airports). Tickets at **Alistair King's** (at Texaco station), **Bob Pennell's** hardware store on Main St, the **Sea Front Inn** on Front St or the offices alongside the airstrip. Advance reservations recommended.

### Boat
**Requena's Charter Services**, T722-2070, leaves Punta Gorda for **Puerto Barrios, Guatemala**, at 0900 every day, US$20, 1 hr, return journey leaves at 1400. Guatemalan operator **Pichilingo** provides a similar service, leaving Puerto Barrios for Punta Gorda at 1000, returning at 1400. See also Border crossings box in Practicalities chapter.

### Bus
**James** bus line to **Belize City** (6½ hrs, longer in heavy rain), daily at 0400, 0500, 0600, 0800, 1000 and 1200. **James** bus returns from Belize City daily, leaving hourly between 0515 and 1015, then 1215, 1315, 1515 and 1545. To **San Antonio** from square, see below; buses to **San Pedro Columbia** and **San José**, Wed and Sat 1200, return Wed and Sat morning. Buses can be delayed in the wet season. For the latest information on schedules, contact the Tourist Information Centre or Dem Dats Doin at the pier by the Customs House.

### San Pedro Columbia

Inland from Punta Gorda there are several interesting villages in the foothills of the Maya Mountains. Take the main road as far as the 'Dump', the road junction with the Southern Highway. Take the road west to San Antonio. After nearly 2 miles, there is a branch to San Pedro Columbia, a Q'eqchi' village where the Maya inhabitants speak the Q'eqchi' language and the women wear colourful costumes, including Guatemalan-style *huipiles*. There are many religious celebrations, at their most intense on **San Luis Rey Day** (5 August).

### Lubaantun

*Daily 0800-1600, beyond San Pedro, continuing left around the church, then right and downhill to the concrete bridge, then left for a mile, a caretaker will point out things of interest. Take refreshments.*

Lubaantun ('Fallen Stones') was the major ceremonial site of southern Belize. The site has a visitor centre and has undergone extensive work to restore a large part of the ruins. It was found to date from AD 800-900, late in the Maya culture and therefore unique. A series of terraced plazas surrounded by temples and palaces ascend along a ridge from south to north. The buildings were constructed with unusual precision and some of the original lime-mortar facings can still be discerned. Excavation revealed whistle figurines, iron pyrite mirrors, obsidian knives, conch shells from Wild Cane Caye, etc. One of the great controversies of the site was the discovery in 1927 of the Crystal Skull by the daughter of the explorer FA Mitchell-Hedges (see box, opposite). This whole region is a network of hilltop sites, mostly unexcavated and unrecognizable to the untrained eye.

### Blue Creek

Blue Creek is another attractive indigenous village which has a marked trail to **Blue Creek Caves** ⓘ *US$12.50 per person, the caretaker is the guide*, and their Maya drawings. The trail leads through forest and along rock-strewn creeks. Swimming nearby is good but choose a spot away from the strong current. Turn off 3 miles before San Antonio at **Roy's Cool Spot** (good restaurant; daily truck and all buses pass here).

### Pusilhá

Pusilhá is one of the most interesting Maya cities, only accessible by boat. Many stelae have been found here dating from AD 573-731, and carvings are similar to those at Quiriguá, Guatemala. Rare features are a walled-in ball court and the abutments remaining from a bridge that once spanned the Moho River. Swimming in the rivers is safe. There are plenty of logging trails and hunters' tracks penetrating the southern faces of the Maya Mountains but if hiking in the forest, do not go alone.

### San Antonio

San Antonio, 21 miles from Punta Gorda, was founded by refugees from San Luis in Guatemala in the late 19th century. Nearby there are Maya ruins of mainly scientific interest. There's a community phone for checking buses and other information, T702-2144. **Dem Dats Doin** in Punta Gorda (see page 250) will also be able to give information. There's a medical centre in the village.

There are no roads to the southern border with Guatemala along the Sarstún River. The **Sarstoon-Temash National Park** is a wilderness of red mangroves and unspoilt rainforest.

## ON THE ROAD

## The Crystal Skull of Lubaantun

In 1927, a young woman by the name of Anna Mitchell-Hedges woke for her 17th birthday. For her it proved more eventful than most as she explored the recently excavated Maya site of Lubaantun to discover a finely crafted crystal skull made of pure quartz – setting off a tale of intrigue that remains to this day.

The size of a small watermelon, the translucent skull of reflected light weighs just over 5 kg. The skull is one of only two ever found in Central America. Its date of manufacture is unknown – but some put it at over 3600 years old – and its purpose is equally curious. Local Maya people gave the skull to Anna's father, the British explorer FA Mitchell-Hedges as a gift, saying it was used for healing and, more sinisterly, for willing death.

Dating the skull precisely is difficult because of the purity of the crystal, but the details of the finding are equally mysterious, with speculation that the skull was 'placed' to make that birthday so special.

There are no visitor facilities at present. At **Barranco**, the only coastal hamlet south of Punta Gorda, there is a village guesthouse (part of TEA, see box, page 254). A dirt road goes to Barranco through the village of Santa Ana, or you can go by boat.

## Listings South of Punta Gorda

### Where to stay

Accommodation is restricted to community-based ecotourism projects where you can stay in the indigenous villages. There are 2 main projects: TEA (Toledo Ecotourism Association), T722-2096, www.teabelize.org, where you can stay in your private accommodation within the village, and the Homestay Programme, where you stay with the family in their house. The Homestay Programme can be arranged via Blue Creek Rainforest Lodge; see below. See also box, page 254.

**$$ Blue Creek Rainforest Lodge**
*www.ize2belize.com.*
Simple wooden bungalows in the middle of the forest and just 15 mins' walk from Blue Creek Village. Pack full with adventure, trekking around the jungle, exploring caves and learning about local culture.

**$ Maya Mountain Research Farm**
*www.mmrfbz.org.*
An organization that promotes forestry research and welcome internship researches and volunteers from a week to a semester. You pay for your accommodation.

### San Antonio

**$ Bol's Hilltop Hotel**
This clean hotel has rooms with showers and toilets. Meals are available.

### Restaurants

#### San Antonio

**$ Theodora or Clara**
*Next to the hotel.*
Both do meals with advance notice. Local specialities are *jippy jappa/kula*, from a local plant, and chicken *caldo*.

## ON THE ROAD

## Guesthouse programme

An interesting alternative to Punta Gorda is to stay in indigenous villages as part of the Guesthouse Programme, run by villagers and the non-competitive cooperative the Toledo Ecotourism Association (TEA).

A number of villages have joined together and developed a visitor scheme. Each has built a well-appointed guesthouse, simple, but clean, with sheets, towels, mosquito nets, oil lamps, ablutions block, and a total of eight bunks in two four-bunk rooms. Visitors stay here, but eat in the villagers' houses on rotation, so each household gains equal income and only has to put up with intrusive foreigners for short periods. Villages taking part include San Miguel, San José (Hawaii), Laguna and Blue Creek. Santa Elena is an isolated village beyond the Dump towards San Ignacio. Medina Bank is more accessible as its location is just off the southern highway. Barranco is a Garífuna village south of Punta Gorda, accessible by boat or poor road.

Local attractions include: San Antonio waterfall; caves at San José (Hawaii); Uxbenka ruins and caves 2½-hour walk from San Antonio (turn right just before Santa Cruz), with commanding view from ruins; and Río Blanco waterfalls, 10 minutes beyond the village. For Uxbenka and Santa Cruz, take Chun's bus on Wednesday and Saturday at 1300 from San Antonio and arrange return time. Do not take Cho's bus, it does not return. Many village men and children speak English. The local indigenous people have been relearning old dances from elderly villagers and are trying to rescue the art of making and playing the harp, violin, marimba and guitar for evening entertainments. Home-made excursions are arranged; these vary from a four-hour

## Transport

### San Antonio
#### Bus and car

From **Punta Gorda**, 1-1½ hrs, US$1.50, Mon, Wed, Fri, Sat 1230, from west side of Central Park, also 1200 on Wed and Sat, continuing to **Santa Cruz**, **Santa Elena** and **Pueblo Viejo** (1 hr from San Antonio). Or, hire a pickup van in **Dangriga**; or get a ride in a truck from the market or rice cooperative's mill in Punta Gorda (1 leaves early afternoon); or go to the road junction at Dump, where the northern branch goes to Independence/Mango Creek, the other to San Antonio; 6 miles, either hitch or walk. Bus from San Antonio to **Punta Gorda**, Mon, Wed, Fri and Sat 0530, also 0500 Wed and Sat (having left Pueblo Viejo at 0400). If going to **Dangriga**, take the 0500, get out at Dump to catch 0530 **Southern Transport** bus going north. This area is full of places to explore and it is worth hiring a vehicle.

trek looking at medicinal plants and explaining agriculture, to seeing very out-of-the-way sights like caves and creeks (take boots, even in dry season). The village tour could be skipped, although by doing this on your own you deprive the 'guide' of income.

One night for two people, with a forest tour and three meals, costs US$43; all profits go direct to the villages, with no outsiders as middlemen. Dorms are US$11 per person. Profits are ploughed back into the villages' infrastructure, schools and other community projects. A US$5 registration fee is payable at the TEA Office at the Tourist Information Center (BTB Building) in Punta Gorda, T722-2096, before visiting the village. The staff provide information about participating villages, key attractions, tours and courses, and take bookings and arrange transport. You may have to arrange your own transport, or a vehicle can be hired. Staff at TEA will be able to advise. Hitching is not recommended as some villages are remote. 'Market' buses leave Punta Gorda every Monday, Wednesday, Friday and Saturday at 1130 or 1200 depending on the village. They come from the villages on the morning of the same days departing early at 0400, 0500 or 0600, depending on the village.

Additionally, there are cultural exchange and tourism programmes operating in several villages that are not part of the TEA co-op, including Na Luum Ca and Aguacate. Accommodation is no frills and there is full immersion in tribal life. Guests sleep with the family in one- or two-room palm-thatch and adobe houses. There's little privacy with shared outhouse 'bathrooms' with no warm water. Meals of corn tortillas, beans and fish or meat are eaten communally. Men are expected to help work the milpa fields and women to grind corn and attend to other traditional duties. See Belize Explorer, www.belizeexplorer.com, a good general guide to community tourism in Belize.

# This is
## Guatemala

Guatemala has a monopoly on colour: from the red lava tongues of volcanoes in the western highlands to the creamy shades of caves in the Petén, and from the white sand of the Caribbean coast near Lívingston to the black sand and orange sunsets over the Pacific.

Completing this work of art are traditional Maya fiestas, where idol worship and Roman Catholicism merge, and jungle temples where ancient ruins tell of long-lost civilizations. Deep in Guatemala's jungle, the majestic cities of the Maya are buried, with temples and plazas, and evidence of human sacrifice and astronomical genius.

Antigua is the colonial centre of the New World. Gracefully ruined after an 18th-century earthquake, its cobbled streets are lined with columned courtyards, toppled church arches, preserved pastel-coloured houses, flowers and fountains galore.

Formed by a volcanic explosion, Lake Atitlán and its three volcanoes are truly breathtaking. Further west, the bustling city of Quetzaltenango makes an excellent base from which to explore volcanoes, markets and villages. In the Verapaces, rivers run through caves stuffed with stalagmites and stalactites. On the humid Pacific coast, Olmec-influenced ruins are buried among coffee bushes and turtles nest on the shore, while on the Caribbean shores, the Garífuna rock to the sound of punta and dolphins frolic in the sea.

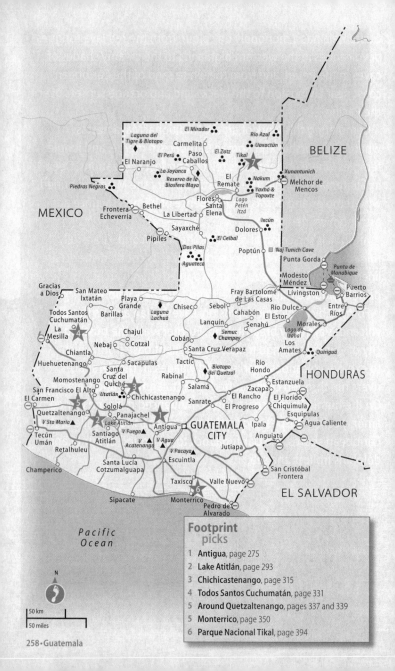

El Mirador

Laguna del
Tigre & Biotopo

Río Azul

Uaxactún

BELIZE

Carmelita

El Perú      Paso      El Zotz      Tikal
El Naranjo      Caballos

La Joyanca      Nakum      Xunantunich

Reserva de la      El      Melchor de
Biosfera Maya      Remate      Mencos

Piedras Negras

MEXICO      Flores      Yaxhá &
Tapoxte

Frontera      Santa      Lago
Echeverría      Bethel      Elena      Petén
La Libertad      Itzá      Ixcún

Sayaxché      Dolores

Pipiles      El Ceibal

Dos Pilas      Poptún      Naj Tunich Cave

Aguateca      Punta Gorda

Modesto      Punta de
Méndez      Manabique

Gracias      San Mateo      Fray Bartolomé      Livingston      Puerto
a Dios      Ixtatán      Playa      de Las Casas      Barrios
Grande      Chisec      Sebol      Río Dulce      Entre
Todos Santos      Barillas      Lanquín      El Estor      Ríos
Cuchumatán      Laguna      Cahabón      Morales
La      Lachuá      Semuc      Senahú      Lago de
Mesilla      Chajul      Champey      Izabal      Quiriguá
Chiantla      Nebaj      Cotzal      Cobán      Los
Huehuetenango      Santa Cruz Verapaz      Amates
Santa      Tactic      Río      HONDURAS
Momostenango      Sacapulas      Hondo
Santa      Rabinal      Biotopo
Cruz del      del Quetzal      Estanzuela
San Francisco El Alto      Quiché      Salamá      Zacapa      El Florido
El Carmen      Utatlán      Chichicastenango      El Rancho      Chiquimula
Quetzaltenango      Sololá      Sanrate      El Progreso      Esquipulas
V Sta Maria      Panajachel      Antigua      Ipala      Agua Caliente
Tecún      Santiago      V Fuego      GUATEMALA      Anguiatú
Umán      Atitlán      V Agua      CITY
Retalhuleu      V Acatenango      V Pacaya      Jutiapa
Santa Lucía      Escuintla      San Cristóbal
Champerico      Cotzumalguapa      Frontera
Valle Nuevo      EL SALVADOR
Taxisco
Sipacate      Monterrico
Pedro de
Alvarado

Pacific
Ocean

N

50 km
50 miles

258 • Guatemala

## Footprint
picks

**1** **Antigua**, page 275
**2** **Lake Atitlán**, page 293
**3** **Chichicastenango**, page 315
**4** **Todos Santos Cuchumatán**, page 331
**5** **Around Quetzaltenango**, pages 337 and 339
**5** **Monterrico**, page 350
**6** **Parque Nacional Tikal**, page 394

Guatemala
City

# Footprint
picks

★ **Antigua**, page 275
Dramatically located at the foot
of three volcanoes.

★ **Lake Atitlán**, page 293
A spectacular and sacred lake protected on all sides by silent volcanic peaks.

★ **Chichicastenango**, page 315
Locals and visitors flock to the twice-weekly frenzy of buying at this
world-famous market town.

★ **Todos Santos Cuchumatán**, page 331
Mountain community known for the distinctive colourful clothes of
its indigenous Mam inhabitants and its All Saints' Day horse race.

★ **Around Quetzaltenango**, pages 337 and 339
Maya villages, hot springs and volcanoes dot the mountains around this
highland town.

★ **Monterrico**, page 350
Boat trips through tangled mangrove swamps to turtle-nesting sites.

★ **Parque Nacional Tikal**, page 394
The jungle-shrouded ruins of Tikal made up the Mayan world's most
enigmatic metropolis.

# Essential Guatemala City

## Finding your feet

Any address not in Zona 1 – and it is absolutely essential to quote zone numbers in addresses – is probably some way from the centre. Addresses themselves, being purely numerical, are usually easy to find. For example, 19 Calle, 4-83 is on 19 Calle between 4 Avenida and 5 Avenida at No 83.

If driving, Avenidas have priority over calles (except in Zona 10, where this rule varies).

## Best places to stay
Posada Belén, page 266
La Inmaculada, page 267
Quetzalroo, page 267

## Getting around

You can walk between the main sights in central Zona 1 but will need to take a bus or taxi to Zonas 9, 10 and 14. Cheap city buses run all day until 2000. Otherwise, take a taxi but for safety reasons make sure it's an official one; see page 274 for more information.

## Safety

As with any big city, take precautions, especially on public transport or in crowded areas such as markets or bus stations. Be vigilant in all zones of the city, even in upmarket areas, and after dark, when it's advisable to take a radio taxi (see also Getting around, above) rather than walk. Avoid withdrawing large sums of money from the bank. Don't wear jewellery or display valuable items such as cameras or phones. It may be best to avoid the Carretera Salvador from the city to the El Salvador border as car-jackings and holdups are becoming increasingly common on that route. To report an incident, contact INGUAT's tourist assistance on T1500, or the police on T110 or T120.

## When to go

Temperatures normally average around the mid-20°Cs, but it can be chilly due to the high altitudes. Wet season is May to October.

## Time required

Two days.

## Best restaurants
Gracia Cocina de Autor, page 268
Hotel Pan American restaurant, page 268
Restaurante Vegetariano Rey Sol, page 268

## Weather Guatemala City

| January | February | March | April | May | June |
|---|---|---|---|---|---|
| 12°C 22°C 0mm | 13°C 23°C 0mm | 14°C 25°C 6mm | 15°C 25°C 12mm | 16°C 25°C 152mm | 16°C 23°C 274mm |

| July | August | September | October | November | December |
|---|---|---|---|---|---|
| 16°C 23°C 203mm | 16°C 23°C 198mm | 16°C 22°C 231mm | 16°C 22°C 173mm | 14°C 22°C 9mm | 13°C 22°C 3mm |

# Guatemala City

Smog-bound and crowded, Guatemala City, known simply as 'Guate', is the commercial and administrative centre of the country. Sketchy in parts and rarely rated by visitors, this is the beating heart of Guatemala and is worth a couple of days if you have time and can bear the noise and pollution in Zona 1. Guatemala City is surrounded by active and dormant volcanoes easily visited on day trips.

## Sights  *Colour map 2, C4.*

*industrial sprawl sprinkled with architectural treasures and urban sculpture*

The old centre of Guatemala City (population 1.2 million, altitude 1500 m) is Zona 1. It is still a busy shopping and commercial area, with some good hotels and restaurants, and many of the cheaper places to stay. However, the main activity of the city has been moving south, first to Zona 4, now to Zonas 9, 10 and 14. With the move have gone commerce, banks, embassies, museums and the best hotels and restaurants. The best residential areas are in the hills to the east, southeast and west.

### Around Zona 1

At the city's heart lies the **Parque Central**. It is intersected by the north–south-running 6 Avenida, the main shopping street. The eastern half has a floodlit fountain; on the west side is **Parque Centenario**, with an acoustic shell in cement used for open-air concerts and public meetings. The Parque Central is popular on Sunday with many *indígenas* selling textiles.

To the east of the plaza is the **cathedral**. It was begun in 1782 and finished in 1815 in classical style with notable blue cupolas and dome. Inside are paintings and statues from ruined Antigua. Solid silver and sacramental reliquary are in the east side chapel of the Sagrario. Next to the cathedral is the colonial mansion of the Archbishop. Aside from the cathedral, the most notable public buildings constructed between 1920 and 1944, after the 1917 earthquake, are the **Palacio Nacional** ① *Mon-Sat 0900-1200 and 1400-1700, entrance and guided tour US$4*, built of light green stone and concealing a lavish interior filled with murals and chandeliers, the police headquarters, the Chamber of Deputies and the post office, which is now home to a small cultural centre. To the west of the cathedral are the Biblioteca Nacional and the Banco del Ejército. Behind the Palacio Nacional is the Presidential Mansion.

## Best for

History ■ Museums ■ Shopping ■ Urban landscapes

# Zona 1

To Cerro del Carmen

Presidential Mansión

Palacio Nacional

La Merced

Parque Central

Biblioteca Nacional

Parque Centenario

Plaza Mayor

Cathedral

Santa Rosa

**Guatemala City maps**
1  Guatemala City: Zona 1, page 262
2  Guatemala City: Zona 9, 10, 13, page 265

Congress

Museo Nacional de Historia

Carmen El Bajo

MUSAC

Las Capuchinas

Santo Domingo

San Francisco

Casa MIMA

ZONA 1

Plaza Bolívar

Line in Use

Teatro Nacional

To Santuario Expiatorio

Disused Line

ZONA 4

To Cuatro Grados Norte & Centro Cívico

300 metres

300 yards

**Where to stay**
Ajau **2** *D2*
Pan American **7** *A2*
Pensión Meza **8** *B3*
Posada Belén **1** *C3*
Theatre International **3** *C2*

**Restaurants**
Altuna **1** *C2*
Café de Imeri **3** *A1*
Helados Marylena **5** *A1*
Rey Sol **7** *A2*

**Bars & clubs**
El Portal **12** *A2*
Europa **4** *B2*
La Bodeguita del Centro **10** *B1*
Las Cien Puertas **14** *A2*

**Transport**
ADN to Santa Elena **5** *C2*
Escobar y Monja Blanca to Cobán **1** *C2*
Fuente del Norte to Río Dulce & Santa Elena/Flores **2** *D2*
Línea Dorada to Río Dulce & Flores **3** *D3*
Marquensita to Quetzaltenango **6** *E1*

Rutas Orientales to Chiquimula & Esquipulas **7** *D3*
Transportes Galgos to Mexico **12** *D2*
Transportes Litegua to Puerto Barrios & Río Dulce **13** *C3*

Museums in Zona 1 include the **Museo Nacional de Historia** ① *9 Calle, 9-70, T2253-6149, www.mcd.gob.gt, Mon-Fri 0900-1700, US$1.50*, which has historical documents and objects from Independence onward. The **Museo de la Universidad de San Carlos de Guatemala (MUSAC)** ① *9 Av, 9-79, T2232-0721, www.musacenlinea.org, Mon, Wed-Fri 0930-1730, Sat 0930-1700, US$1; guided tours at 1000 and 1400*, charts the history of the university. The Salón Mayor is where Guatemala signed its Independence from Mexico in 1823, and in 1826 the Central American Federation, with Guatemala as the seat of power, abolished slavery in the union. Also, Doctor Mariano Gálvez, the country's president from 1831-1838, is buried behind part of the salon wall and a marble bust of him sits outside the door. The Universidad de San Carlos was the first university in Guatemala City. **Casa MIMA** ① *8 Av, 14-12, T2253-6657, casamima@hotmail.com, Mon-Sat 0900-1230, 1400-1500, US$1, no photography*, is the only authentic turn-of-the-19th-century family home open to the public, once owned by the family Ricardo Escobar Vega and Mercedes Fernández Padilla y Abella. It is furnished in European-influenced style with 15th- to mid-20th-century furniture and ornaments.

**Churches**  Most of the churches worth visiting are in Zona 1. **Cerro del Carmen** ① *11 Av y 1 Calle A*, was built as a copy of a hermitage destroyed in 1917-1918, containing a famous image of the Virgen del Carmen. Situated on a hill with good views of the city, it was severely damaged in the earthquake of 1976 and remains in poor shape. **La Merced** ① *11 Av y 5 Calle*, dedicated in 1813, has beautiful altars, organ and pulpit from Antigua as well as jewellery, art treasures and fine statues. **Santo Domingo** ① *12 Av y 10 Calle*, built between 1782 and 1807, is a striking yellow colour, reconstructed after 1917, with an image of Nuestra Señora del Rosario and sculptures. **Sagrado Corazón de Jesús**, or **Santuario Expiatorio** ① *26 Calle y 2 Av*, holds 3000 people; the colourful, exciting modern architecture was by a young Salvadorean architect who had not qualified when he built it. Part of the complex, built in 1963 (church, school and auditorium) is in the shape of a fish. The entrance is a giant arch of multicoloured stained glass, wonderfully illuminated at night. The walls are lined with glass confessionals. **Las Capuchinas** ① *10 Av y 10 Calle*, has a very fine St Anthony altarpiece, and other pieces from Antigua. **Santa Rosa** ① *10 Av y 8 Calle*, was used for 26 years as the cathedral until the present building was ready. The altarpieces are from Antigua (except above the main altar). **San Francisco** ① *6 Av y 13 Calle*, a large yellow and white church that shows earthquake damage outside (1976), has a sculpture of the Sacred Head, originally from Extremadura in Spain. **Carmen El Bajo** ① *8 Av y 10 Calle*, was built in the late 18th century; again the façade was severely damaged in 1976.

## North of the centre
**Parque Minerva** ① *Av Simeón Cañas, Zona 2, www.mapaenrelieve.org, 0900-1700, US$4*, has a huge relief map of the country made in 1905 to a horizontal scale of 1:10,000 and a vertical scale of 1:2,000. The park has basketball and baseball courts, bar and restaurant and a children's playground (unsafe at night). To get there, take bus V21 from 7 Avenida, Zona 4. Just beyond is a popular park, the **Hipódromo,** which is packed on Sundays with bumper cars and mechanical games, and a great little train for kids.

## South of the centre
**Avenida La Reforma**  The modern **Centro Cívico**, which links Zona 1 with Zona 4, includes the Municipalidad, Palacio de Justicia, Ministerio de Finanzas Públicas, Banco de Guatemala, the mortgage bank, the social-security commission and the tourist board. The curious **Teatro Nacional** ① *Mon-Fri 0800-1630 for tours, US$4*, with its blue and white

# BACKGROUND

## Guatemala City

Guatemala City was founded by decree of Carlos III of Spain in 1776 to serve as capital after earthquake damage to the earlier capital, Antigua, in 1773. Almost completely destroyed by earthquakes in 1917-1918, it was rebuilt in modern fashion, or in copied colonial, only to be further damaged by earthquake in 1976. Most of the affected buildings have been restored.

mosaic, dominates the hilltop of the west side of the Centro Cívico. There is an excellent view of the city and surrounding mountains from the roof. An old Spanish fortress provides a backdrop to the open-air theatre adjoining the Teatro Nacional.

**Cuatro Grados Norte**, located on Vía 5 between Ruta 1 and Ruta 2, is a pedestrianized area that has grown up around the IGA theatre and bookshop (a cultural centre, which sometimes has interesting concerts and exhibitions). Cafés and bars have tables on the street and it's safe and fun to wander around at night. The **Centro Cultural de España** is located here with live music, films, exhibitions and conferences, and there is also a branch of **Sophos**, an excellent bookshop. On Saturdays there is a street market with craft and jewellery stalls, often cultural events in the street. On Sundays there are clowns and events for children. It's a strange mix of wealthy Guatemalans strolling with their poodles and alternative street-market types; sit back and enjoy watching the people.

To see the finest residential district go south down 7 Avenida to Ruta 6, which runs diagonally in front of Edificio El Triángulo, past the orange **Capilla de Yurrita** (Ruta 6 y Vía 8). Built as a private chapel in 1928 on the lines of a Russian Orthodox church, it has been described as an example of "opulent 19th-century bizarreness and over-ripe extravagance". There are many woodcarvings, slender white pillars, brown/gold ornamentation and an unusual blue sky window over the altar. Ruta 6 runs into the wide tree-lined Avenida La Reforma.

**Zona 10** To the east, in Zona 10, are some excellent museums. **Museo Ixchel del Traje Indígena** ① *Campus of Universidad Francisco Marroquín, 6 Calle Final, T2331-3623, www.museoixchel.org, Mon-Fri 0900-1700, Sat 0900-1300, US$4.60*, has a collection of indigenous dress. In addition to the clothes there are photos from the early 20th century, paintings and very interesting videos. A shop sells beautiful textiles that aren't available on the tourist market, prices are fixed, and quality costs. **Museo Popol Vuh de Arqueología** ① *6 Calle Final, T2338-7896, www.popolvuh.ufm.edu.gt, Mon-Fri 0900-1700, Sat 0900-1300, US$4.60, US$3 for photos*, has an extensive collection of pre-Columbian and colonial artefacts, as well as a replica of the Dresden Codex, one of the only Maya parchment manuscripts in existence. **Museo de Historia Natural de la USAC y Jardín Botánico** ① *Calle Mcal Cruz 1-56, T2334-6065, Mon-Fri 0800-1600, Sat 0830-1230, US$1.30*, has gardens, stuffed animals and live snakes.

**Zona 13** In **Parque Aurora**, Zona 13, in the southern part of the city, are La Aurora International Airport, the Observatory, racetrack and **Parque Zoológico La Aurora** ① *T2472-0507, www.aurorazoo.org.gt, Tue-Sun 0900-1700, US$3.30*. The newer areas show greater concern for the animals' wellbeing. There are also several museums: the **Museo Nacional de Antropología y Etnología** ① *Salón 5, Parque Aurora, Zona 13, T2475-4406,* *www.munae.gob.gt, Tue-Fri 0900-1600, Sat-Sun 0900-1200, 1330-1600, US$7.90, no photos,* has outstanding Maya pieces including stelae from Piedras Negras and typical Guatemalan dress, as well as good models of Tikal, Quiriguá and Zaculeu. There are sculptures, murals, ceramics, textiles, a collection of masks and an excellent jade collection. Around the corner is the **Museo Nacional de Historia Natural** ① *6 Calle, 7-30, Zona 13, T2472-0468, Mon-Fri 0900-1600, Sat-Sun 0900-1200, 1400-1600, US$6.50,* which houses a collection of national fauna, including stuffed birds, animals, butterflies, geological specimens, etc. Opposite the archaeology museum, the **Museo de Arte Moderno** ① *Salón 6, Parque Aurora, Zona 13, T2472-0467, US$4, Tue-Fri 0900-1600,* has a modest but enjoyable collection. Next door is the **Museo de los Niños** ① *T2475-5076, Tue-Fri 0830-1200, 1300-1630, US$4,* an interactive museum with a gallery of Maya history and the Gallery of Peace which houses the world's largest single standing artificial tree – a *ceiba.*

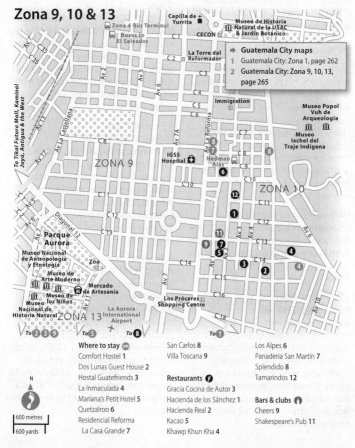

Zona 9, 10 & 13

➡ Guatemala City maps
1 Guatemala City: Zona 1, page 262
2 Guatemala City: Zona 9, 10, 13, page 265

N

600 metres
600 yards

**Where to stay** 🛏
Comfort Hostel 1
Dos Lunas Guest House 2
Hostal Guatefriends 3
La Inmaculada 4
Mariana's Petit Hotel 5
Quetzalroo 6
Residencial Reforma
 La Casa Grande 7
San Carlos 8
Villa Toscana 9

**Restaurants** 🍴
Gracia Cocina de Autor 3
Hacienda de los Sánchez 1
Hacienda Real 2
Kacao 5
Khawp Khun Kha 4
Los Alpes 6
Panaderia San Martín 7
Splendido 8
Tamarindos 12

**Bars & clubs** 🍸
Cheers 9
Shakespeare's Pub 11

## Tourist information

### INGUAT

*7 Av, 1-17, Zona 4 (Centro Cívico), 24 hrs T1801-464-8281, T2421-2800, www. visitguatemala.com. Mon-Fri 0800-1600.*
They are very friendly and English is sometimes spoken. They provide a hotel list, a map of the city, and general information on buses, market days, museums, etc. There is also an office in the airport arrivals hall (T2331-4256, open 0600-2100) where staff are exceptionally helpful and on the ball.

## Where to stay

You can get better prices in the more expensive hotels by booking corporate rates through a travel agent or simply asking at the desk if any lower prices are available. Hotels are often full at Easter and Christmas. At the cheaper hotels, single rooms are not always available. There are many cheap *pensiones* near bus and railway stations and markets; those between Calle 14 and Calle 18 are not very salubrious.

### Hoteles Villas de Guatemala
*Reservations 8 Calle 1-75 Zona 10, T2223-5000, www.villasdeguatemala.com.*
Rents luxury villas throughout Guatemala.

### Zona 1

### $$ Pan American
*9 Calle, 5-63, T2232-6807, www.hotelpanamerican.com.gt.*
This one time art deco jewel of the Centro Histórico is well past its heyday, but worth a look nonetheless. They offer quiet, comfortable, reasonable rooms with TV, but try to avoid those on the main-road side. Award-winning restaurant with good food (see Restaurants, below). Parking, and breakfast included.

### $$ Posada Belén
*13 Calle "A", 10-30, T2232-9226, www.posadabelen.com.*
A colonial-style house run by the friendly Francesca and René Sanchinelli, who speak English. Quiet, comfy rooms with good hot showers. Laundry, email service, luggage store and good meals. Parking. Tours available. A lovely place to stay. Highly recommended.

### $ Ajau
*8 Av, 15-62, T5205-5137, www.hotelajau.com.*
This converted early 20th-century house has 45 simple, adequate, economical rooms set around a central courtyard, with or without private bath. Services include Wi-Fi, internet terminal, airport transfer, laundry and meals. A typical old school cheapie, helpful, secure and no frills.

### $ Pensión Meza
*10 Calle, 10-17, T2232-3177.*
A large ramshackle place with beds in dorms. It's popular with helpful staff and English is spoken. It's sometimes noisy and some rooms are damp. Other rooms are darker than a prison cell, but cheered by graffiti, poetry and paintings. There is table tennis, book exchange, internet at US$8 per hr and or free Wi-Fi.

### $ Theatre International
*8 Av, 14-17, T4202-5112, www.theatreihostel.com.*
Located to the side of the Teatro Abril, this 70-bed party hostel features 2 patios, kitchen, Wi-Fi and complimentary pancake breakfasts. There is a range of accommodation to suit all budgets, include thrifty 8- and 14-bed dorms, and private rooms with or without private bath. One for the whippersnappers and sadly a bit stuck up ("entrance is not allowed for people older than 45").

## South of the centre

### $$$ Comfort Hostel
*17 Calle, 14-35, Zona 10, T2367-0754,*
*www.comforthostel.com.*
This small, secluded and professionally
managed B&B features a very reasonable
restaurant and a small patio where you
can relax or work. Rooms are spacious,
tranquil, tasteful and well equipped with
cable TV, clock radio, Wi-Fi, safety boxes
and sparkling bathrooms with hot water.
Simple but personal.

### $$$ La Inmaculada
*14 calle 7-88, Zona 10, T2314-5100,*
*www.inmaculadahotel.com.*
With Egyptian cotton linens, complimentary
L'Occitane toiletries and slick contemporary
design, La Inmaculada is indeed
immaculately stylish, a great option for
couples or hip young things. Services
include spa treatments and business centre.
Highly tasteful and highly recommended.

### $$$ Residencial Reforma La Casa Grande
*Av La Reforma, 7-67, Zona 10, T2332-0914,*
*www.casagrande-gua.com.*
Near the US embassy, a very attractive
colonial-style house dating to the early
20th century, complete with whitewashed
courtyard and lavish statues. Rooms and
suites are comfortable but also rather simple
and pricey for what you get. Good, small
restaurant, open 0630-2100, also a bar and
internet service.

### $$$ San Carlos
*Av La Reforma, 7-89, Zona 10, T2362-9076,*
*www.hsancarlos.com.*
A small, charming hotel set in a sumptuous
historical property with a small pool and
leafy garden. Rooms are modern, middle-
of-the-road and fully equipped with Wi-Fi
and cable TV; suites and apartments are
more luxurious. Rates includes breakfast
and airport transfer.

### $$ Villa Toscana
*16 Calle 8-20, Zona 13, Aurora I, T2261-2854,*
*www.hostalvillatoscana.com.*
Stylish B&B adorned with tones of gold and
cream. Rooms come with cable TV, Wi-Fi,
handmade hardwood furniture and floral
wall sculptures. The garden, where breakfast
is served under a canopy, features a trim
green lawn and well-tended flowers. Lovely
and relaxing. Airport shuttle included.

### $$-$ Hostal Guatefriends
*16 Calle, 7-40, Zona 13, Aurora I, T5308-3275,*
*www.hostalguatefriends.com.*
Brightly painted hostel accommodation by
the night or the month, including 4-person
dorms ($, but still a bit pricey for Guatemala)
and private rooms ($$) with cable TV and
Wi-Fi. Rates include breakfast and airport
shuttle. Friendly, safe and helpful.

### $$-$ Mariana's Petit Hotel
*20 Calle, 10-17, Zona 13, Aurora II,*
*www.marianaspetithotel.com.*
Located close to the airport with free pickup
and drop-off, this simple and homely B&B
has a range of comfortable, quiet and
unpretentious rooms, all with cable TV and
Wi-Fi. Upstairs there's a lovely roof terrace
where you can soak up the sun. Great
breakfasts. Helpful and hospitable.

### $$-$ Quetzalroo
*6 Av, 7-84, Zona 10, T5746-0830,*
*www.quetzalroo.com.*
This successful Australian/Guatemalteco-
owned youth hostel is recommended as
the best of its kind in the city. The staff
are super-friendly and helpful; rooms are
simple, comfortable and cosy ($$); dorms
are low-key ($). They do a city tours by bike
and a basic breakfast is included. Sociable,
quiet and relaxed.

### $ Dos Lunas Guest House
*21 Calle, 10-92, Zona 13, T2261-4248,*
*www.hoteldoslunas.com.*
Private rooms and dorms in a comfy B&B.
Very close to the airport with free transport
to or from the airport. Storage service, free

breakfast and water and tourist information. Lorena, the landlady, also organizes shuttles and taxis and tours. English spoken. Reservations advisable as often full.

## Restaurants

### Zona 1

There are all kinds of food available in the capital, from the simple national cuisine to French, Chinese and Italian food. There is a plethora of fast-food restaurants and traditional *comedores* where you will get good value for money; a reasonable set meal will cost no more than US$3. The cheapest places to eat are at street stalls and the various markets – take the normal precautions.

### $$$ Altuna
*5 Av, 12-31, www.restaurantealtuna.com.*
This establishment has a beautiful traditional Spanish bar interior and serves tasty Spanish food in huge portions, including paella and seafood. Lobster is available but expensive. Delicious coffee. There is a branch in Zona 10 at 10 Calle, 0-45.

### $$$-$$ Hotel Pan American
*See Where to stay, above.*
Regional and international cuisine served in the central courtyard of this hotel, a faded but distinctive art deco beauty that was once the haunt of the rich and famous. An award-winning establishment with lots of ambience and an affordable lunchtime menu.

### $$-$ Café de Imeri
*6 Calle, 3-34. Closed Sun.*
Sandwiches, salads, soups and pastries in a patio garden. Set lunch and excellent cakes. It's popular with young professional Guatemalans. Try the *pay de queso de elote* (maize cheesecake). Its bakery next door has a rare selection of granary breads, birthday cakes, etc.

### $ Restaurante Vegetariano Rey Sol
*8 Calle, 5-36. Closed Sun.*
A prize vegetarian find – wholesome food and ambience oasis amid the fumes of Zona 1, and popular with the locals. Delicious veggie concoctions at excellent prices served canteen-style by friendly staff. Breakfasts and *licuados* also available. Newer, larger and brighter branch at 11 Calle, 5-51.

### Ice cream parlours

### Helados Marylena
*6 Calle, 2-49. Daily 1000-2200.*
Not quite a meal but almost. This establishment has been serving up the weirdest concoctions for 90 years. From the probably vile – fish, chilli, yucca and cauliflower ice cream – to the heavenly – beer and sputnik (coconut, raisins and pineapple). The *elote* (maize) is good too. This city institution is credited with making children eat their vegetables! Anyone travelling with fussy eaters should stop by here.

### South of the centre
Most of the best restaurants are in the **Zona Viva**, within 10 blocks of the Av La Reforma on the east side, between 6 Calle and 16 Calle in Zona 10. **Zona 9** is just across the other side of Av La Reforma.

There are several options in the area around **Cuatro Grados Norte** providing tapas, sushi, *churros* and chocolate. Lively, especially on Fri and Sat nights.

### $$$ Gracia Cocina de Autor
*14 Calle y 4 Av, Zona 10, T2366 8699.*
Modern and minimalist, Gracia Cocina de Autor serves an eclectic menu of flavourful gourmet dishes by chef Pablo Novales in a stylish setting. Recipes are international fusion with smoked salmon bagels and eggs benedict among the offerings for brunch, lamb chops and roast pork for lunch or dinner. Recommended.

### $$$ Hacienda de los Sánchez
*12 Calle, 2-25, Zona 10.*
Good steaks and local dishes, but seriously crowded at weekends, and so not the most pleasant of settings compared with other steakhouses in the vicinity. Well established and something of a classic on the scene.

### $$$ Hacienda Real
*5 Av 14-67, Zona 10, www.hacienda-real.com.*
An excellent selection of grilled meats with a hint of smokiness. Great ambience, often buzzing, and the candles and palms create a garden-like setting. There's also a nice little bar with Mexican leather chairs on one side.

### $$$ Kacao
*1 Av, 13-51, Zona 10, www.kacao.com.gt.*
A large variety of delicious local and national dishes, which are attractively prepared and served in ample portions. The setting is fantastic: a giant thatched room, *huipiles* for tablecloths and beautiful candle decorations. Some options are expensive.

### $$$ Khawp Khun Kha
*13 Calle A, 7-19, Zona 10, Plaza Tiffany.*
If the flavours of Central America have grown tired and old, try this hip Thai restaurant, serving spicy *panang* and green curries, pad Thai and other specialities sure to liven up your taste buds. Good and tasty, but definitely fusion cuisine and not quite authentically Thai (close enough though).

### $$$ L'Osteria
*Cuatro Grados Norte, Vía 5 between Ruta 1 and Ruta 2.*
Popular Mediterranean restaurant on the corner, complete with a pleasant outdoor terrace. They serve tasty Greek fare, hummous and pitta bread, along with solid Italian favourites such as pizza and lasagne.

### $$$ Splendido
*12 Calle, 4-15, Zona 14, www. restaurantesplendido.com.*
A very presentable bistro-style restaurant with impeccable service and delicious and predominantly French-flavoured fusion

cooking. Main courses include scallops, shrimps, steaks and a selection of pasta. Specialities include sweet chilli tuna, chicken curry, peppered steak and key lime cheesecake.

### $$$ Tamarindos
*11 Calle, 2-19A, Zona 10, T2360-2815.*
Mixed Asian, sushi, Vietnamese rolls, mushrooms stuffed with almonds and crab are some of the tantalizing options at this very smart Asian restaurant with spiral shades and soothing bamboo greens.

### $$ Los Alpes
*10 Calle, 1-09, Zona 10. Closed Mon.*
A Swiss-Austrian place with light meals and a smorgasbord of excellent cakes and chocolates. Popular with Guatemalan families.

### $$-$ Panadería San Martín
*2 Av, Zona 10, www.sanmartinbakery.com.*
San Martín is a very popular bakery with branches across Guatemala and El Salvador. In addition to baked goods, they offer cooked breakfasts and reliable international fare such as pizzas, salads, soups and sandwiches. Not outstanding, but easy and tasty enough.

## Bars and clubs

### Cheers
*13 Calle, 0-40, Zona 10. Mon-Sat 0900-0100, Sun 1300-2400ish.*
A basement sports bar with pool tables, darts and large cable TV. Happy hour until 1800. The awning outside features the logo from the hit TV show.

### El Portal
*Portal del Comercio, 8 Calle, 6-30, Zona 1. Mon-Sat 1000-2200.*
This was a favourite spot of Che Guevara and you can imagine him sitting here holding court at the long wooden bar. A stuffed bull's head now keeps watch over drinkers. To get there, enter the labyrinths of passageways facing the main plaza at No 6-30 where

there is a Coke stand. At the first junction bear round to the left and up on the left you will see its sign. *Comida típica* and marimba music, beer from the barrel.

### Europa
*11 Calle, 5-16, Zona 1. Mon-Sat 0800-0100.*
Popular peace-corps/travellers' hangout. A sports bar, showing videos, with books for sale. They also serve grub.

### La Bodeguita del Centro
*12 Calle, 3-55, Zona 1, T2239-2976.*
The walls of this hip place in an old stockhouse are adorned with posters of Che Guevara, Bob Marley and murdered Salvadorean Archbishop Romero. There's live music Thu-Sat at 2100, talks, plays, films, and exhibitions upstairs. Wooden tables are spread over 2 floors; seriously cheap nachos and soup are on the menu. It's an atmospheric place to spend an evening. Call in to get their *Calendario Cultural* leaflet.

### Las Cien Puertas
*Pasaje Aycinea, 7 Av, 8-44, just south of Plaza Mayor, Zona 1. Daily 1600-2400.*
Has a wonderful atmosphere with political, satirical and love missives covering its walls. There's excellent food and outdoor seating and it's friendly.

### Shakespeare's Pub
*13 Calle, 1-51, Zona 10. Mon-Fri 1100-0100, Sat and Sun 1400-0100.*
English-style basement bar with a good atmosphere, American owner, a favourite with expats and locals, safe for women to drink.

## Entertainment

### Cinema and theatre
There are numerous cinemas and they often show films in English with Spanish subtitles. **Teatro Nacional**, *Centro Cívico, see page 266.* Most programmes are Thu-Sun.

## Shopping

### Bookshops
**Museo Ixchel**, *see page 264.* This museum has a bookshop.
**Museo Popol Vuh bookshop**, *see page 264.* Has a good selection of books on pre-Columbian art, crafts and natural history.

### Maps
Maps can be bought from the **Instituto Geográfico Nacional (IGN)** (Av Las Américas, 5-76, Zona 13, T2332-2611. Mon-Fri 0900-1730). The whole country is covered by about 200 1:50,000 maps available in colour or photocopies of out-of-print sections. None is very up to date. There is, however, an excellent 1996, 1:15,000 map of Guatemala City in 4 sheets. A general *Mapa Turístico* of the country is available here, also at INGUAT, see Tourist information, above.

### Markets
The **Central Market** operates underground behind the cathedral, from 7 to 9 Av, 8 Calle, Zona 1. One floor is dedicated to textiles and crafts, and there is a large, cheap basketware section on the lower floor. Silverware is cheaper at the market than elsewhere in Guatemala City. Other markets include the **Mercado Terminal** in Zona 4, and the **Mercado de Artesanía** in the Parque Aurora, near the airport, which is for tourists. Large shopping centres are good for a wide selection of local crafts, artworks, funky shoes, and clothes. Don't miss the *dulces*, candied fruits and confectionery.

### Shopping centres and supermarkets
The best shopping centres are **Centro Comercial Los Próceres** (18 Calle and 3 Av, Zona 10), the **Centro Comercial La Pradera** (Carretera Roosevelt and Av 26, Zona 10). There is a large **Paiz** supermarket on 18 Calle and 8 Av and a vast shopping mall **Tikal Futura** (at Calzada Roosevelt and 22 Av, Zona 11). *Artesanías* for those who shop with a conscience at the fair-trade outlet **UPAVIM**

(Calle Principal, Col La Esperanza, Mesquital Zona 12, T2479-9061, www.upavim.org, Mon-Fri 0800-1800, Sat 0800-1200).

## What to do

**Clark Tours**, *Plaza Clark, 7 Av 14-76, Zona 9, T2412-4700, www.clarktours.com.gt, and several other locations*. Long-established, very helpful, tours to Copán, Quiriguá, etc.
**Four Directions**, *1 Calle, 30-65, Zona 7, T2439-7715, www.fourdirections.travel*. Recommended for Maya archaeology tours. English spoken.
**Maya Expeditions**, *13 Av, 14-70, Zona 10, T2366-9950, www.mayaexpeditions.com*. Very experienced and helpful, with varied selection of short and longer river/hiking tours, whitewater rafting, bungee jumping, cultural tours, tours to Piedras Negras.
**Trolley Tour**, *T5907-0913, Tue-Sat 1000-1300, Sun 1000*. Pick-ups from Zona 10 hotels for 3-hr city tours, US$20, children US$10.
**Turismo Ek Chuah**, *3 Calle 6-24, Zona 2, T2220-1491, www.ekchuah.com*. Nationwide tours as well as some specialist and tailor-made tours on bicycle and horseback.

## Transport

### Air
The airport is in the south part of the city at La Aurora, 4 km from the Plaza Central, T2331-8392. It has banks, ATMs, internet, bars and restaurants. A taxi to Zona 10 is US$8, Zona 1, US$10, and from Antigua, US$25-30. Shuttles from outside airport to Antigua meet all arriving flights, US$10.

Flights to **Flores** with **Grupo Taca** 0820, 1605 and 1850, and **TAG** at 1630 daily. For the following domestic airlines, phone for schedules: **Aerocharter**, T5401-5893, to **Puerto Barrios**. **Aeródromo**, T5539-9364, to **Huehuetenango**. **Aerolucía**, T5959-7008 to **Quetzaltenango**.

### Bus
#### Local
Buses operate between 0600-2000, after which you'll have to rely on taxis.

In town, US$0.13 per journey on regular buses and on the larger red buses known as *gusanos* (worms) except on Sun and public holidays when they charge US$0.16. One of the most useful bus services is the **101**, which travels down 10 Av, Zona 1, and then cuts across to the 6 Av, Zona 4, and then across Vía 8 and all the way down the Av La Reforma, Zona 10. The **82** also travels from Zona 1 to 10 and can be picked up on the 10 Av, Zona 1 and the 6 Av, Zona 4. Bus **85**, with the same pickup points, goes to the cluster of museums in Zona 13. Buses **37**, **35**, **32** all head for the INGUAT building, which is the large blue and white building in the Centro Cívico complex. **R40** goes from the 6 Av, Zona 4, to the Tikal Futura shopping complex; a good spot to catch the Antigua bus, which pulls up by the bridge to the complex. Buses leaving the 7 Av, Zona 4, just 4 blocks from the Zona 4 bus terminal, for the Plaza Mayor, Zona 1, are *gusano* **V21**, **35**, **36**, **82**, and **101**.

#### Long distance
The Zona 4 chicken bus terminal between 1-4 Av and 7-9 C serves the Occidente (west), the Costa Sur (Pacific coastal plain) and El Salvador. The area of southern Zona 1 contains many bus offices and is the departure point for the Oriente (east), the Caribbean zone, Pacific coast area towards the Mexican border and the north, to Flores and Tikal. 1st-class buses often depart from company offices in Zona 1 (see map, page 262).

There are numerous bus terminals in Guatemala City. The majority of 1st-class buses have their own offices and departure points around Zona 1. Hundreds of chicken buses for the south and west of Guatemala leave the Zona 4 terminal, as well as local city buses. Note that some companies have been moved from Zona 1 and Zona 4 out to Zona 7 and 12. There was a plan, at the time of writing, to redirect all buses for the southern region to leave from Central Sur, Col Villalobos.

International buses (see below) have their offices scattered about the city. (The cheaper Salvador buses leave from near the Zona 4 terminal.) The Zona 4 bus terminal has to be the dirtiest and grimmest public area in the whole of the city.

The main destinations with companies operating from Guatemala City are:

**Antigua**, every 15 mins, 1 hr, US$1, until 2000 from Av 23 and 3 Calle, Zona 3. To **Chimaltenango** and **Los Encuentros**, from 1 Av between 3 y 4. Calle, Zona 7. **Chichicastenango** hourly from 0500-1800, 3 hrs, US$2.20 with **Veloz Quichelense**. **Huehuetenango**, with **Los Halcones**, Calzada Roosevelt, 37-47, Zona 11, T2439-2780, 0700, 1400, 1700, US$7, 5 hrs, and **Transportes Velásquez**, Calzada Roosevelt 9-56, Zona 7, T2440-3316, 0800-1630, every 30 mins, 5 hrs, US$7.

**Panajachel**, with **Transportes Rebulí**, 41 Calle, between 6 y 7 Av, Zona 8, T2230-2748, hourly from 0530-1530, 3 hrs, US$2.20; also to **San Lucas Tolimán** 0530-1530, 3 hrs US$2.10 **San Pedro La Laguna** with **Transportes Méndez**, 41 C, between 6 y and Av, Zona 8, 1300, 4 hrs. **Santiago Atitlán**, with various companies, from 4 C, between 3 y 4 Av, Zona 12, 0400-1700, every 30 mins, 4 hrs, US$4.

**Quetzaltenango** (Xela) and **San Marcos**. 1st-class bus to Xela with **Transportes Alamo**, 12 Av "A", 0-65, Zona 7, T2471-8626, from 0800-1730, 6 daily 4 hrs, US$7. **Líneas Américas**, 2 Av, 18-47, Zona 1, T2232-1432, 0500-1930, 7 daily, US$7. **Galgos**, 7 Av, 19-44, Zona 1, T2232-3661, between 0530-1700, 5 daily, 4 hrs, US$7 to **Tapachula** in Mexico through the El Carmen border; see also

Border crossings box in Practicalities chapter. **Marquensita**, 1 Av, 21-31, Zona 1, T2230-0067. From 0600-1700, 8 a day, US$6.10, to Xela and on to San Marcos. To **Tecpán**, with **Transportes Poaquileña**, 1 Av corner of 3 and 4 Calle, Zona 7, 0530-1900, every 15 mins, 2 hrs, US$1.20.

To **Santa Cruz del Quiché**, Sololá and Totonicapán, buses depart from 41 Calle between 6 and 7 Av, Zona 8.

To **Biotopo del Quetzal** and **Cobán**, 3½ hrs and 4½ hrs respectively, hourly from 0400-1700, US$6 and US$7.50, with **Escobar y Monja Blanca**, 8 Av, 15-16, Zona 1, T2238-1409. **Zacapa**, **Chiquimula** (for **El Florido**, on the Honduran border) and **Esquipulas** with **Rutas Orientales**, 19 Calle, 8-18, Zona 1, T2253-7282, every 30 mins 0430-1800. To **Zacapa**, 3¼ hrs, to **Chiquimula**, 3½ hrs, to **Esquipulas**, 4½ hrs, US$6.

**Puerto Barrios**, with **Transportes Litegua**, 15 Calle, 10-40, Zona 1, T2220-8840, www.litegua.com, 0430-1900, 31 a day, 5 hrs, US$6.80, 1st class US$12 and **Río Dulce**, 0600, 0900, 1130, 5 hrs, US$6.20.

**El Petén** with **Fuente del Norte** (same company as **Líneas Máxima de Petén**), 17 Calle, 8-46, Zona 1, T2251-3817, going to **Río Dulce** and **Santa Elena/Flores**. There are numerous departures 24 hrs; 5 hrs to Río Dulce, US$6.50; to Santa Elena, 9-10 hrs, US$12; buses vary in quality and price, breakdowns not unknown. The 1000 and 2130 departures are a luxury bus **Maya del Oro** with snacks, US$18, the advantage being it doesn't stop at every tree to pick up passengers. **Línea Dorada**, 16 Calle, 10-03, Zona 1, T2220-7990, www.tikalmayan world. com, at 1000, US$16 to **Flores**, 8 hrs and on to **Melchor de Mencos**, 10 hrs. To **Santa Elena ADN**, 8 Av, 16-41, Zona 1, T2251-0050, www.adnautobuses delnorte.com, luxury service, 2100 and 2200, returns at 2100 and 2300, US$19, toilets, TV and snacks.

To **Jalapa** with **Unidos Jalapanecos**, 22 Calle 1-20, Zona 1, T2251-4760, 0430-1830, every 30 mins, 3 hrs, US$2.50 and with **Transportes Melva Nacional**, T2332-6081,

**Tip...**
Watch your bags everywhere, but like a hawk in the Zona 4 terminal.

0415-1715, every 30 mins, 3 hrs 30 mins, US$2.50. Buses also from the Zona 4 terminal. To **San Pedro Pinula** between 0500-1800.

To **Chatia Gomerana**, 4 Calle y 8 Av, Zona 12, to **La Democracia**, every 30 mins from 0600-1630 via Escuintla and Siquinala, 2 hrs. **Transportes Cubanita** to **Reserva Natural de Monterrico** (La Avellana), 4 Calle y 8 Av, Zona 12, at 1030, 1230, 1420, 3 hrs, US$2.50. To **Puerto San José** and **Iztapa**, from the same address, 0430-1645 every 15 mins, 1 hr. To **Retalhuleu** (Reu on bus signs) with **Transportes Fortaleza del Sur**, Calzada Aguilar Batres, 4-15, Zona 12, T22230-3390, between 0010-1910 every 30 mins via Escuintla, Cocales and Mazatenango, 3 hrs, US$6.80. Numerous buses to **Santa Lucía Cotzumalguapa** go from the Zona 4 bus terminal.

## International buses

Reserve the day before if you can. Taking a bus from Guatemala City as far as, say, San José, is tiring and tiresome (the bus company's bureaucracy and the hassle from border officials all take their toll). For crossings to Honduras and El Salvador, see also Border crossings box in Practicalities chapter.

To **Honduras** avoiding El Salvador, take a bus to **Esquipulas**, then a minibus to the border. **Hedman Alas**, 2 Av, 8-73, Zona 10, T2362-5072, www.hedmanalas.com, to **Copán** via El Florido, at 0500 and 0900, 5 hrs, US$30. Also goes on to **San Pedro Sulas**, US$45, and **La Ceiba**, US$52. **Pullmantur** to **Tegucigalpa** daily at 0700 via San Salvador, US$66 and US$94. **Ticabus** to **San Pedro Sula**, US$34 and **Tegucigalpa**, US$34 via San Salvador. **Rutas Orientales**, 19 C, 8-18, T2253-7282 goes to **Honduras** at 0530 via Agua Caliente, 8 hrs, US$28; see also Border crossings box in Practicalities chapter, for more on crossing into Honduras.

To **Mexico** with **Trans Galgos Inter**, 7 Av, 19-44, Zona 1, T2223-3661, www. transgalgosinter.com.gt, to **Tapachula** via **El Carmen**, 0730, 1330, and 1500, 7 hrs; see also Border crossings box in Practicalities

chapter. **Línea Dorada**, address above, to **Tapachula** at 0800, US$24. **Transportes Velásquez**, 20 Calle, 1-37, Zona 1, T2221-1084, 0800-1100, hourly to **La Mesilla**, 7 hrs, US$5. **Transportes Fortaleza del Sur**, Calzada Aguilar Batres, 4-15, Zona 12, T2230-3390 to **Ciudad Tecún Umán**, 0130, 0300, 0330, 0530 via **Retalhuleu**, 5 hrs.

To **Chetumal** via **Belize City**, with **Línea Dorada** change to a minibus in Flores. Leaves 1000, 2100, 2200 and 2230, 2 days, US$42. Journey often takes longer than advertised due to Guatemala–Belize and Belize–Mexico border crossings.

To **El Salvador** via **Valle Nuevo**, border crossing, with **Ticabus**, 0600 and 1300 daily to San Salvador, US$17 1st class, 5 hrs. From **Ticabus** terminal, Calzada Aguilar Batres 22-25, T2473-0633, www.ticabus.com, clean, safe, with waiting area, café, toilets, no luggage deposit.

## Car

**Car hire companies** **Budget**, at the airport; also at 6 Av, 11-24, Zona 9, www. budget.co.uk. **Hertz**, at the airport, T2470-3800, www.hertz.com. **Tabarini**, 2 Calle "A", 7-30, Zona 10, T2331-2643, airport T2331-4755, www.tabarini.com. **Tally**, 7 Av, 14-60, Zona 1, T2232-0421, very competitive, have pickups. Recommended.

**Car and motorcyle repairs** **Mike and Andy Young**, 27 Calle, 13-73, Zona 5, T2331-9263, Mon-Fri 0700-1600. Excellent mechanics for all vehicles, extremely helpful. Honda motorcycle parts from **FA Honda**, Av Bolívar, 31-00, Zona 3, T2471-5232. Some staff speak English. Car and motorcycle parts from **FPK**, 5 Calle, 6-75, Zona 9, T2331-9777. **David González**, 32 Calle, 6-31, Zona 11, T5797-2486, for car, bike and bicycle repairs. Recommended.

## Shuttle

Shuttles are possible between Guatemala City and all other destinations, but reserve in advance. Contact shuttle operators in Antigua (see Antigua Transport, page 289).

Guatemala City to **Antigua**, US$15, **Panajachel** US$30, Chichicastenango US$30, **Copán Ruinas**, US$40, **Cobán**, US$30 and **Quetzaltenango**, US$25.

## Taxi

If possible call a taxi from your hotel or get someone to recommend a reliable driver; there are hundreds of illegal taxis in the city that should be avoided.

There are 3 types of taxis: **Rotativos**, **Estacionarios** and the ones that are metered, called **Taxis Amarillos**. *Rotativos* are everywhere in the city cruising the length and breadth of all zones. You will not wait more than a few minutes for one to come along. They are numbered on their sides and on their back windscreen will be written TR (*Taxi Rotativo*) followed by 4 numbers. Most of them have a company logo stamped on the side as well. *Estacionarios* also have numbers on the sides but are without logo. On their back windscreen they have the letters TE (*Taxi Estacionario*) followed by 4 numbers. They are to be found at bus terminals and outside hotels or in other important places. They will always return to these same waiting points (good to know if you leave something in a taxi). Do not get in a taxi that does not have either of these labels on its back windscreen. *Rotativos* and *Estacionarios* are unmetered, but *Estacionarios* will always charge less than *Rotativos*. The fact that both are unmetered will nearly always work to your advantage because of traffic delays. You will be quoted an inflated price by *Rotativos* by virtue of being a foreigner. *Estacionarios* are fairer. It is about US$8 from the airport to Zona 1. From Zona 1 to 4 is about US$4. The metered *Taxi Amarillo* also moves around but less so than the *Rotativos*, as they are more on call by phone. They only take a couple of minutes to come. **Amarillo Express**, T2332-1515, are available 24 hrs.

# Antigua
## & around

★ Antigua is rightly one of Guatemala's most popular destinations. It overflows with colonial architecture and fine churches on streets that are linked by squat houses, painted in ochre shades and topped with terra-cotta tiles, basking in the fractured light of the setting sun. Antigua is a very attractive city and is the cultural centre of Guatemala; arts flourish here. Maya women sit in their colourful clothes amid the ruins and in the Parque Central. In the late-afternoon light, buildings such as Las Capuchinas are beautiful, and in the evening the cathedral is wonderfully illuminated as if by candlelight.

If the city was not treasure enough, the setting is truly memorable. Volcán Agua (3766 m) is due south and the market is to the west, behind which hang the imposing peaks of Volcán Acatenango (3976 m) and Volcán Fuego (3763 m), which still emits the occasional column of ash as a warning of the latent power within.

Also around Antigua are a cluster of archaeological sites and highland villages to explore.

**Best** for
Art ▪ Learning Spanish ▪ Markets ▪ Semana Santa ▪ Trekking

Avenidas run north to south and calles run from east to west. House numbers do not give any clue about how far from the Parque Central a particular place is.

### Best places to stay

Casa Florencia, page 280
Hostel Tropicana, page 281
Yellow House, page 281

### Safety

Unfortunately, despite its air of tranquillity, Antigua is not without unpleasant incidents. Take care and advice from the tourist office on where to go or not to go. There are numerous tourist police (green uniforms) who are helpful and conspicuous; their office is at 4 Avenida Norte at the side of the Municipal Palace. If you wish to go to Cerro de la Cruz (see page 279), or the cemetery, they will escort you, leaving 1000 and 1500 daily. Antigua is generally safe at night, but it's best to keep to the well-lit area near the centre. Report incidents to police and the tourist office. Tourist assistance 24 hours, T2421-2810.

### Best restaurants

Caffé Mediterráneo, page 282
Hector's, page 282
Micho's Gastropub, page 282
Rainbow Café, page 283
Típico Antigüeño, page 283

## Sights  Colour map 2, C4.
colonial buildings and volcano backdrop

### Parque Central and around

In the centre of the city is the Parque Central, the old Plaza Real, where bullfights and markets were held in the early days. The present park was constructed in the 20th century though the fountain dates back to the 18th century. The **cathedral** ① US$0.40, to the east, dates from 1680 (the first cathedral was demolished in 1669). Much has been destroyed since then and only two of the many original chapels are now in use. The remainder can be visited. The **Palacio de los Capitanes Generales** is to the south. The original building dates from 1558, was virtually destroyed in 1773, was partly restored in the 20th century, and now houses police and government offices. The **Cabildo**, or **Municipal Palace**, is to the north and an arcade of shops to the west. You can climb to the second floor for a great view of the volcanoes (Monday to Friday 0800-1600). The **Museo de Santiago** ① Tue-Fri 0900-1600, Sat-Sun 0900-1200, 1400-1600, US$4, is in the municipal offices to the north of the plaza, as is the **Museo del Libro Antiguo** ① same hours and price, which contains a replica of a 1660 printing press (the original is in Guatemala City), old documents and a collection of 16th- to 18th-century books (1500 volumes in the library). The **Museo de Arte Colonial** ① Tue-Fri 0900-1600, Sat-Sun 0900-1200, 1400-1600, US$6.60, is half a block from Parque Central at Calle 5 Oriente, in the building where the San Carlos University was first housed. It now has mostly 17th- to 18th-century religious art, well laid out in large airy rooms around a colonial patio.

### Hotel Casa Santo Domingo

Hotel Casa Santo Domingo is one of Antigua's most beautiful sights: a converted old Dominican church and also monastery property. Archaeological excavations have turned up some unexpected finds at the site. During the cleaning out of a burial vault in September 1996, one of the greatest finds in

# BACKGROUND
## Antigua

Until it was heavily damaged by an earthquake in 1773, Antigua was the capital city. Founded in 1543, after the destruction of an even earlier capital, Ciudad Vieja, it grew to be the finest city in Central America, with numerous great churches, a university (1676), a printing press (founded 1660), and a population of around 50,000, including many famous sculptors, painters, writers and craftsmen.

Antigua has consistently been damaged by earthquakes. Even when it was the capital, buildings were frequently destroyed and rebuilt, usually in a grander style, until the final cataclysm in 1773. For many years it was abandoned, and most of the accumulated treasures were moved to Guatemala City. Although it slowly repopulated in the 19th century, little was done to prevent further collapse of the main buildings until late in the 20th century when the value of the remaining monuments was finally appreciated. Since 1972, efforts to preserve what was left have gained momentum, and it is now a UNESCO World Heritage Site. The major earthquake of 1976 was a further setback, but you will see many sites that are busy with restoration, preservation or simple clearing.

Antigua's history was unearthed. The vault had been filled with rubble, but care had been taken in placing stones a few feet away from the painted walls. The scene is in the pristine colours of natural red and blue, and depicts Christ, the Virgin Mary, Mary Magdalene and John the Apostle. It was painted in 1683, and was only discovered with the help of ultraviolet light. Within the monastery grounds are the **Colonial Art Museum**, with displays of Guatemalan baroque imagery and silverware and the **Pre-Columbian Art Museum**, **Glass Museum**, **Museum of Guatemalan Apothecary** and the **Popular Art and Handicrafts of Sacatepequez Museum** ① *3 Calle Ote 28, 0900-1700, US$5.25, 1 ticket covers all admissions.*

## Colonial religious buildings

There are many fine religious buildings dating from the colonial era: 22 churches, 14 convents and 11 monasteries, most ruined by earthquakes and in various stages of restoration. Top of the list are the cloisters of the convent of **Las Capuchinas** ① *2 Av Norte y 2 Calle Ote, 0900-1700, US$3.90,* with immensely thick round pillars (1736) adorned with bougainvillea. The church and convent of **San Francisco** ① *1 Av Sur y 7 Calle Ote, 0800-1200, 1400-1700, US$0.40,* with the tomb of Hermano Pedro, is much revered by all the local communities. He was canonized in 2002. The church has been restored and now includes the **Museo de Hermano Pedro** ① *Tue-Sun 0900-1200, 1300-1630, US$0.40.* The convent of **Santa Clara** ① *6 Calle Ote y 2 Av Sur, 0900-1700, US$3.90,* was founded in about 1700 and became one of the biggest in Antigua, until the nuns were forced to move to Guatemala City. The adjoining garden is an oasis of peace. **El Carmen** ① *3 Calle Ote y 3 Av Norte,* has a beautiful façade with strikingly ornate columns, tastefully illuminated at night, but the rest of the complex is in ruins. Likewise **San Agustín** ① *5 Calle Pte y 7 Av Norte,* was once a fine building, but only survived intact from 1761 to 1773; earthquake destruction continued until the final portion of the vault collapsed in 1976, leaving an impressive ruin. **La Compañía de Jesús** ① *3 Calle Pte y 6 Av Norte, 0930-1700,* at one time covered the whole block. The church is today in ruins but the rest of the complex was recently restored by the Spanish government and now houses a cultural centre, **Centro de Formación de la Cooperación**

# Antigua

**To Chimaltenango & Jocotenango**

San Sebastián 6
C de Chajón
C de los Piedra
Nazarenos
Av San Antonio
C de Chajón
Av del Desengaño
C de las Ánimas
Av 7 Norte
Av 6 Norte
C de los Carpinteros
C Camposeco
La Merced
C de la Recolección
La Recolección
San Jerónimo
C 1 Poniente
Santa Teresa
Mayan Spa
Santa Catalina & Arch
Convento de Las Capuchinas
Av 2 Norte
C 2 Poniente
Alameda Santa Lucía
C 2 Oriente
Av 5 Norte
El Carmen
INGUAT
Av 4 Norte
Av 3 Norte
Av de la Recolección
Main Terminal
C 3 Poniente
Sin Fronteras
Tivoli Travel
Busos to Guatemala City
Craft
C 4 Poniente
La Compañía de Jesús
Palacio del Ayuntamiento
Parque Central
Tienda de Doña Gavi
Cathedral
Bus Lane
Supermarket
San Agustín
Supermarket
C 5 Poniente
C 5 Oriente
Av Cementerio
C del Ranchón
C 6 Poniente
San José El Viejo
Palacio de los Capitanes Generales
Museo de Arte Colonial
C 6 Oriente
Av 8 Sur
Av 7 Sur
C 7 Poniente
C 7 Oriente
Ermita Santa Lucía
C 8 Oriente
Av 5 Sur
Av 4 Sur
Av 3 Sur
**To Ciudad Vieja & San Antonio Aguas Calientes**
C 9 Poniente
San José El Viejo
**To**
C 9 Oriente

N
100 metres
100 yards

### Where to stay
Aurora 1 *C4*
Base Camp 7 *D5*
Casa Encantada 31 *E4*
Casa Florencia 6 *A2*
Casa Rustica 2 *D3*
Casa Santo Domingo 8 *C6*
Hostel Tropicana 3 *D3*
Jungle Party Hostal 14 *C3*
Los Encuentros 4 *B2*
Mesón de María 30 *C3*
Posada del Angel 23 *E4*

Posada Juma Ocag 13 *C2*
Posada La Merced 5 *B3*
San Jorge 9 *E4*
Yellow House 28 *B2*

### Restaurants
Bagel Barn 1 *D3*
Café Condesa 3 *D3*
Café Flor 6 *D4*
Caffé Mediterráneo 20 *D3*
Doña Luisa
  Xicoténcatl 10 *C4*

El Sabor del Tiempo 13 *C3*
El Sereno 12 *B4*
Fonda de la Calle Real 14 *C3*
Frida's 15 *B3*
Hector's 5 *B3*
La Antigua Viñería 16 *E3*
La Casserole 41 *C5*
Micho's Gastropub 2 *C4*
Quesos y Vinos 25 *B3*
Rainbow Café &
  Travel Center 26 *D2*
Sabe Rico 8 *D3*

Típico Antigüeño **9** *C2*  
Travel Menu **29** *D3*  
Vivero y Café de  
la Escalonia **31** *E3*

The Snug **7** *D2*

**Bars & clubs**   
Café No Sé **4** *D5*  
Casbah **43** *B3*  
La Chiminea **34** *C3*  
La Sala **45** *D3*  
Ocelot **5** *C4*  
Riki's **19** *C4*

**Española** ⓘ *www.aecid-cf.org.gt, 0900-1800, free*, with occasional exhibitions and workshops. The church and cloisters of **Escuela de Cristo** ⓘ *Calle de los Pasos y de la Cruz*, a small independent monastery (1720-1730), have survived and were restored between 1940 and 1960. The church is simple and has some interesting original artwork. **La Recolección** ⓘ *Calle de la Recolección, 0900-1700, US$5.25*, despite being a late starter (1700), became one of the biggest and finest of Antigua's religious institutions. It is now the most awe-inspiring ruin in the city. **San Jerónimo** ⓘ *Calle de la Recolección, 0900-1700, US$4*, was a school (early 1600s) for La Merced, three blocks away, but later became the local customs house. There is an impressive fountain in the courtyard. **La Merced** ⓘ *1 Calle Pte y 6 Av Norte, 0800-1700*, with its white and yellow façade dominates the surrounding plaza. The church (1767) and cloisters were built with earthquakes in mind and survived better than most. The church remains in use and the **cloisters** ⓘ *US$0.65*, are being further restored. Antigua's finest fountain is in the courtyard. **Santa Teresa** ⓘ *4 Av Norte*, was a modest convent, but the church walls and the lovely west front have survived. It is now the city's men's prison.

Other ruins including **Santa Isabel**, **Santa Cruz**, **La Candelaria**, **San José El Viejo** and **San Sebastián** are to be found round the edges of the city, and there is an interesting set of the Stations of the Cross, each a small chapel, from San Francisco to **El Calvario** church, which was where Pedro de Betancourt (Hermano Pedro) worked as a gardener and planted an esquisuchil tree. He was also the founder of the **Belén Hospital** in 1661, which was destroyed in 1773. However, some years later, his name was given to the **San Pedro Hospital**, which is one block south of the Parque Central.

There is a fabulous panorama from the **Cerro de la Cruz**, which is 15 minutes' walk from the northern end of town along 1 Avenida Norte.

## Tourist information

The monthly magazine *The Revue* is a useful source of tourist information in English with articles, maps, events and advertisements; it's free and widely available in hotels and restaurants.

### INGUAT office

*2a Calle Ote,11 (between Av 2 and Av 3 Norte), T7832-3782, www.visit guatemala.com. Mon-Fri 0800-1700, Sat and Sun 0900-1700.*
Very helpful, with maps and information; occasional exhibitions in rooms around courtyard behind office. Information available about volunteer work. English, Italian and a little German spoken.

## Where to stay

In the better hotels, advance reservations are advised for weekends and Dec-Apr. During Holy Week, hotel prices are significantly higher, sometimes double for the more expensive hotels. In the Jul-Aug period, find your accommodation early in the day.

### $$$$ Casa Santo Domingo
*3 Calle Ote 28, T7820-1220, www.casasantodomingo.com.gt.*
This is a beautifully designed hotel with 126 rooms in the ruins of a 17th-century convent with prehispanic archaeological finds. Good service, beautiful gardens, a magical pool, excellent restaurant with breakfast included. Worth seeing just to dream. See also page 276.

### $$$$ Posada del Angel
*4 Av Sur 24-A, T7832-0260, www.posadadelangel.com.*
Bill Clinton is among the former guests of this famous, sumptuous and award-winning hotel. Lodging is in boutique suites and rooms set around a central courtyard, all with own fireplaces and consistently tasteful

decor. Amenities include dining room, exercise pool and roof terrace. Romantic, exclusive and private.

### $$$ Aurora
*4 Calle Ote 16, T7832-0217, www.hotelauroraantigua.com.*
The oldest hotel in the city with old plumbing (but it works), antique furnishings and 1970s features. Quieter rooms face a colonial patio overflowing with beautiful flowers. Continental breakfast included, English spoken.

### $$$ Casa Encantada
*9 Calle Pte1, esq Av 4 Sur, T7832-7903, www.casaencantada-antigua.com.*
This sweet colonial boutique hotel with 10 rooms is a perfect retreat from the centre of Antigua. It has a small rooftop terrace where breakfast is served and a comfortable sitting room with open fire, books, lilies and textile-lined walls. 2 rooms are accessed by stepping stones in a pond. The suite, with jacuzzi, enjoys views of the 3 volcanoes.

### $$$ Casa Florencia
*7 Av Norte 100, T7832-0261, www.cflorencia.net.*
A sweet little colonial-style hotel enjoying views towards Volcán Agua. They offer 10 pleasant rooms set around a central courtyard with all the usual mod cons including TV, safe and Wi-Fi. The 2nd-floor balcony has *cola de quetzal* plants lining it. Staff are very welcoming. Recommended.

### $$$ Hotel Mesón de María
*3 Calle Pte 8, T7832-6068, www.hotelmesonde maria.com.*
Great little place with a wonderful roof terrace. Their 20 stylish rooms are decorated with local textiles and earthy colours. Free internet and breakfast included at a local restaurant. Friendly and attentive service. Showers have large skylights.

## $$ Hotel Casa Rústica
*6 Av Nte 8, T7832-0694,*
*www.casarusticagt.com.*
Casa Rústica has bright, comfortable
rooms, each equipped with hand-carved
furniture and Guatemalan textiles; cheaper
rooms have shared bath ($). There are good
communal areas, including kitchen, garden
and sun terrace with views. Pleasant, but
on the pricey side. Ask to see a few rooms
before accepting as size and quality vary.

## $$ Hotel Los Encuentros
*7 Av Norte 60, T4114-5400,*
*www.hotelosencuentros.com.*
This guesthouse offers quiet, comfortable
and occasionally quirky rooms with hand-
carved wooden furniture, Guatemalan art,
textiles and antiques. The hostess Irma is
very sweet and helpful. There are cooking
facilities and breakfast is included. Rooms
vary, ask to see a few.

## $$ Hotel San Jorge
*4 Av Sur 13, Calle del Conquistador, T7832-
3132, www.hotelsanjorgeantigua.com.*
Established in 1989, Hotel San Jorge has
lovely green gardens with wide lawns and
flowery beds. Rooms are understated but
have thoughtful touches like wall-to-wall
carpets, There is Talavera tilework, fireplaces,
cable TV and handwoven bedspreads.

## $$ Posada La Merced
*7 Av Nte 43, T7832-3197,*
*www.posadalamercedantigua.com.*
Located 1 block from La Merced church,
this well-established colonial-style
guesthouse features a beautiful patio
with a fountain and plenty of leafy potted
plants. Upstairs, a sun terrace has fine
views. Rooms are smallish and simple, but
comfortable. Quiet, relaxing and central.

## $$-$ Hostel Tropicana
*6 Calle Pte, between Av 4 and 5, T7832-0462,*
*www.tropicanahostel.com.*
This new addition to Antigua's party
hostel scene is a cut above the rest with
its small but refreshing outdoor pool, a

sun deck and a hot tub. There's a well-
stocked bar too, and for chilling out, a leafy
garden framed by ruined colonial walls.
Accommodation includes a range of large
and small dorms ($), and private rooms
($$). Promising and recommended.

## $ Base Camp
*7 Calle Pte 17, T 7832-0468,*
*www.guatemalavolcano.com.*
Nice views of Volcán Agua from the
roof terrace at this fun, young, energetic
hostel marketed to adventure travellers.
Accomodation includes 6 dorm beds and
2 double rooms with lots of shared space
and all the usual hostel facilities. Runs
adventure tours through **Outdoor
Excursions** (see Tour operators, below).

## $ Jungle Party Hostal and Café
*6 Av Norte 20, T7832-0463,*
*www.junglepartyhostal.com.*
Buzzing with backpakers in its onsite bars,
this fun and sociable party hostel enjoys a
great central location and impressive views
of the volcanoes. Accommodation consists
of dorm beds with hot water, lockers, small
patio, TV, hammocks, swings, bean bags,
Wi-Fi, free breakfast and movies. There's
an all-you-can-eat barbecue on Sat.

## $ Posada Juma Ocag
*8 Av Norte 13 (Alameda Santa Lucía),*
*T7832-3109, www.posadajumaocag.com.*
This modest, family-run guesthouse is
small but very clean, and nicely decorated
using local textiles as bedspreads. It has an
enclosed roof terrace and rooms come with
or without private bath. Quiet and friendly
with Wi-Fi, and free coffee in the morning.

## $ Yellow House
*1 Calle Pte 24, T7832-6646,*
*www.guatetravel.com.*
There are 8 clean rooms in this hostel run
by the welcoming Ceci. Breakfast included.
Colonial style, laundry service, free internet.
3 rooms with bath, kitchen, patio, parking.
Recommended.

## Apartments

Look on the notice boards in town. Rooms and apartments are available from about US$25 a week up to US$500 per month. One recommended family is **Estella López** (1 Calle Pte 41A, T7832-1324), who offer board and lodging on a weekly basis. The house is clean, and the family friendly.

## Restaurants

For the cheapest of the cheap go to the stalls on the corner of 4 Calle Pte and 7 Av Norte, and those at the corner of 5 Calle Pte and 4 Av Sur. During the Easter period, the plaza in front of La Merced is transformed into a food market. At all these places you can pick up *elote*, *tortillas*, *tostadas* and *enchiladas*.

### $$$ El Sereno
*4 Av Norte 16, T7832-0501. Open 1200-1500 and 1800-2300.*
International/Italian cuisine. Grand entrance with massive heliconia plants in the courtyard. It has a lovely terrace bar up some stone steps and a cave for romantic dining; it's popular at weekends.

### $$$ La Casserole
*Callejón de Concepción 7, T7832-0219 close to Casa Santo Domingo. Tue-Sat 1200-1500 and 1900-2200, Sun 1200-1500.*
Sophisticated French cooking with fresh fish daily served at tables set in a beautiful courtyard, exclusive. Rigoberta Menchú once dined with Jacques Chirac here.

### $$$ Micho's Gastropub
*4 Calle Ote 10, Edif Jaulon, T7832-3522.*
**Micho's** stands out as one of the city's better establishments with its top-notch international cuisine, creatively prepared and beautifully presented. They serve lunchtime specials, along with breakfast and dinner, good cocktails and wine by the glass. Romantic ambience in the tranquil courtyard. Recommended.

### $$$-$$ Caffé Mediterráneo
*6 Calle Pte 6A, T7832-7180. Wed-Mon 1200-1500 and 1830-2200.*
1 block south of the plaza. Mouth-watering Italian cuisine with great candlelit ambience. Recommended.

### $$$-$$ Fonda de la Calle Real
*5 Av Norte 5 and No 12, T7832 0507, also at 3 Calle Pte 7 (which wins over the others for the setting).*
This place's speciality is *queso fundido*. It also serves local dishes including *pepián* (and a vegetarian version) and *kak-ik*, a Verapaz speciality.

### $$ El Sabor del Tiempo
*Calle del Arco and 3 Calle Poniente, T7832 0516.*
Good steaks, burgers, seafood and pasta in tastefully converted former warehouse, with polished wood and glass cabinets. A bit pricey but full of antiquey character.

### $$ Frida's
*5 Av Norte 29, Calle del Arco, T7832-0504. Daily 1200-0100.*
Ochre and French navy colours decorate this restaurant's tribute to Mexico's famous female artist. It is quite dark inside but Frida memorabilia and colander-like lampshades lighten the interior. Efficient service. 2nd-floor pool table, Wed and Thu ladies' night.

### $$ Hector's
*1 Calle Poniente No 9, T7832-9867.*
Small, busy and welcoming restaurant that serves wonderful food at good prices. Highly recommended.

### $$ La Antigua Viñería
*5 Av Sur 34A, T7832-7370. Mon-Thu 1800-0100, Fri-Sun 1300-0100.*
Owned by Beppe Dángella, next door to San José ruins. Amazing photographic collection of clients in various stages of inebriation, excellent selection of wines and grappa, you name it. Very romantic, feel free to write your comments on the walls, very good food, pop in for a reasonably priced *queso*

*fundido* and glass of wine if you can't afford
the whole hog.

## $$ Quesos y Vinos
*Calle Poniente 1, T7832-7785. Wed-Mon 1200-
1600 and 1800-2200.*
Authentic Italian food and owners, good
selection of wines, wood-fired pizza oven,
sandwiches, popular.

## $$ Sabe Rico
*6 Av Sur No 7, 7832-0648.*
Herb garden restaurant and fine food
deli that serves healthy, organic food
in tranquil surroundings.

## $$-$ Café Flor
*4 Av Sur 1, T7832-5274. Open 1100-2300.*
Full-on delicious Thai/Guatemalan-style
and tandoori food. The stir-fries are delicious,
but a little overpriced. Discounts sometimes
available. Friendly staff.

## $$-$ Rainbow Café
*7 Av Sur, on the corner of 6 Calle Pte.*
Consistently delicious vegetarian food
served in a pleasant courtyard surrounded
by hanging plants, good filling breakfasts,
indulgent crêpes, popular, live music
evenings, good book exchange. Bar at
night with happy hour and ladies' nights.
Recommended.

## $$-$ Travel Menu
*6 Calle Pte 14.*
Buzzing and bohemian, Travel Menu serves
fresh, hearty, reasonably priced international
fare in large portions, including big fat
juicy sandwiches and tofu stir-fry. Candelit
ambience and regular live music. Friendly
and sociable.

## $ Típico Antigüeño
*Alameda Sta Lucía 4, near the PO,
T7832-5995.*
This locally run place offers an absolute
bargain of a *menú del día* (fish, chicken),
which includes soup and sometimes a
drink. It is extremely popular and can get
ridiculously busy, so best to turn up before
1300 for lunch. Recommended.

## Cafés and delis

### Bagel Barn
*5 Calle Pte 2. Open 0600-2200.*
Popular, breakfast, snack deals with bagels
and smoothies, videos shown nightly, free.

### Café Condesa
*5 Av Norte 4. Open 0700-2100.*
West side of the main plaza in a pretty
courtyard, popular, a little pricey for
the portions, breakfast with free coffee
fill-ups, desserts, popular Sun brunches.

### Doña Luisa Xicoténcatl
*4 Calle Ote 12, 1½ blocks east of the plaza.
Daily 0700-2130.*
Popular meeting place with an excellent
bulletin board, serving breakfasts, tasty
ice cream, good coffee, burgers, large
menu, big portions. Good views of Volcán
Agua upstairs. Shop sells good selection
of wholemeal, banana bread, yogurts, etc.
Don't miss the chocolate and orange loaf
if you can get it.

### Vivero y Café de La Escalonia
*5 Av Sur Final 36 Calle, T7832-7074.
Daily 0900-1800.*
This delightful place is well worth the
walk – a café amid a garden centre with
luscious flowers everywhere, including bird
of paradise flowers and tumbergia, a pergola
and classical music. They serve *postres*, herb
breads, salads and cold drinks.

## Bars and clubs

### Café No Sé
*1 Av Sur 11 C, www.cafenose.com.*
Grungy and bohemian, an interesting place
with live music every night, and a range of
high-powered mescal cocktails. Good.

### Casbah
*5 Av Norte 30. Mon-Sat 1800-0100.*
Cover charge includes a drink. Gay night
Thu. Has a medium-sized dance floor with a
podium and plays a mix of good dance and

Latin music, the closest place to a nightclub atmosphere in Antigua.

### La Chimenea
*7 Av Norte 18. Mon-Sat 1700-2430.*
Happy hour every day, seriously cheap, relaxed atmosphere, mixed young crowd, dance floor, salsa, rock.

### La Sala
*6 Calle Pte, T5671-3008.*
One of the most popular salsa dancing and watering holes in town.

### Ocelot
*4 Av Nte 3.*
A splendid watering hole full of interesting characters. They do happy hour, pub quizzes, American grub from the taco cart. Good crowd, popular on the expat scene.

### Riki's Bar
*4 Av Norte 4, inside La Escudilla.*
Usually packed with gringos, but attracts a young Guatemalan crowd as well, and popular with the gay fraternity. Good place to meet people. A good mix of music, including jazz.

### The Snug
*6 Calle Pte 14, next to Travel Menu.*
**The Snug** proves good things do come in small packages. A hit with expats and travellers, this intimate and fully authentic Irish bar does cold beer, rum, occasional live music and interesting conversation. Cosy, friendly and fun.

Entertainment

### Cinemas
Antigua must be the home of the lounge cinema. All show films or videos in English, or with subtitles.
**Café 2000**, *6 Av Sur*. Free films daily and the most popular spot in town to watch movies.
**Cine Sin Ventura**, *5 Av Sur 8*. The only real screen in town, auditorium can get cold, and they need to hit the brightness button.

## Festivals

**Feb** **International Culture Festival**: dance, music and other top-quality performers from around the globe come to Antigua.
**Mar/Apr** **Semana Santa**: see box, opposite.
**21-26 Jul** The feast of **San Santiago**.
**31 Oct-2 Nov** **All Saints** and **All Souls**, in and around Antigua.
**7 Dec** **Quema del Diablo** (burning of the Devil) by lighting fires in front of their houses and burning an effigy of the Devil in the Plazuela de La Concepción at night, thereby starting the Christmas festivities.
**15 Dec** The start of what's known as the **Posadas**, where a group of people leave from each church, dressed as Mary and Joseph, and seek refuge in hotels. They are symbolically refused lodging several times, but are eventually allowed in.

## Shopping

Antigua is a shopper's paradise, with textiles, furniture, candles, fabrics, clothes, sculpture, candies, glass, jade and ceramics on sale. The main municipal market is on Alameda Santa Lucía next to the bus station, where you can buy fruit, clothes and shoes. The *artesanía* market is opposite, next to the bus lane.

### Art
**Galería de Arte Antigua**, *4 Calle Ote 27 y 1 Av. Tue-Sat*. Large art gallery.

### Bookshops
Numerous bookshops sell books in English and Spanish, postcards, posters, maps and guides, including *Footprint Handbooks*.
**Casa del Conde**, *5 Av Norte 4*. Has a full range of books from beautifully illustrated coffee-table books to guides and history books.
**Hamlin and White**, *4 Calle Ote 12A*. Books on Guatemala are cheaper here than at Casa del Conde.
**Rainbow Cafe**, *7 Av Sur 18*. Sells second-hand books.
**Un Poco de Todo**, *near Casa del Conde on the plaza*.

## Semana Santa

This week-long event in Antigua is a spectacular display of religious ritual and floral design. Through billowing clouds of incense, accompanied by music, processions of floats carried by purple-robed men make their way through the town. The cobbled stones are covered in *alfombras* (carpets) of coloured sawdust and flowers.

The day before the processions leave from each church, Holy Vigils (*velaciones*) are held, and the sculpture to be carried is placed before the altar (*retablo*), with a backdrop covering the altar. Floats (*andas*) are topped by colonial sculptures of the cross-carrying Christ. He wears velvet robes of deep blue or green, embroidered with gold and silver threads, and the float is carried on the shoulders by a team of 80 men (*cucuruchos*), who heave and sway their way through the streets for as long as 12 hours. The processions, arranged by a religious brotherhood (*cofradía*), are accompanied by banner and incense carriers, centurions, and a loud brass band.

The largest processions with some of the finest carpets are on Palm Sunday and Good Friday. Not to be missed are: the procession leaving from La Merced on Palm Sunday at 1200-1300; the procession leaving the church of San Francisco on Maundy Thursday; the 0200 sentencing of Jesus and 0600 processions from La Merced on Good Friday; the crucifixion of Christ in front of the cathedral at noon on Good Friday; and the beautiful, candlelit procession of the crucified Christ which passes the Parque Central between 2300 and midnight on Good Friday.

This is the biggest Easter attraction in Latin America so accommodation is booked far ahead. If you plan to be here and haven't reserved a room, arrive a few days before Palm Sunday. If unsuccessful, commuting from Guatemala City is an option. Don't rush; each procession lasts up to 12 hours. The whole week is a fantastic opportunity for photographs – and if you want a decent picture remember the Christ figure always faces right. Arm yourself with a map (available in kiosks in the Parque Central) and follow the processional route before the procession to see all the carpets while they are still intact. (There are also processions into Antigua from surrounding towns every Sunday in Lent.)

**Crafts, textiles, clothes and jewellery**
Many other stores sell textiles, handicrafts, antiques, silver and jade on 5 Av Norte between 1 and 4 Calle Pte and 4 Calle Ote.
**Casa Chicob**, *Callejón de la Concepción 2, www.casachicob.com.* Beautiful textiles, candles and ceramics for sale.
**Casa de Artes**, *4 Av Sur 11, www. casadeartes.com.gt.* For traditional textiles and handicrafts, jewellery, etc, but very expensive.
**Casa de los Gigantes**, *7 Calle Ote 18.* For textiles and handicrafts.

**Diva**, *5 Av Norte 16.* For Western-style clothes and jewellery.
**El Telar**, *Loom Tree, 5 Av Sur 7.* All sorts of coloured tablecloths, napkins, cushion covers and bedspreads are sold here.
**Guate Es**, *4 Calle Ote 10, Edif El Jaulón, www.guate-es.com.* Guate Es has an interesting and attractive stock of clothing, shoes, jewellery and handbags which incorporate colourful Mayan textiles and designs. A new concept, fresh and innovative.
**Huipil market**, *held in the courtyard of La Fuente every Sat 0900-1400.* The display

is very colourful and if the sun is out this is an excellent place for photos.

**Mercado de Artesanías**, *next to the main market at the end of 4 Calle Pte.*

**Nativo's**, *5 Av Norte, 25 "B", T7832-6556.* Sells some beautiful textiles from places like Aguacatán.

**Nim P'ot**, *5 Av Norte 29, T7832-2681, www.nimpot.com.* A mega-warehouse of traditional textiles and crafts brought from around the country. Excellent prices.

**Textura**, *5 Av Norte 33, T7832-5067.* Lots of bedroom accessories.

### Food

**Doña María Gordillo**, *4 Calle Ote 11.* Famous throughout the country. It is impossible to get in the door most days but, if you can, take a peek, to see the *dulces*, as well as the row upon row of yellow wooden owls keeping their beady eyes on the customers.

**La Bodegona**, *5 Calle Pte 32, opposite Posada La Quinta, on 5 Calle Pte and with another entrance on 4 Calle Pte.* Large supermarket.

**Tienda de Doña Gavi**, *3 Av Norte 2, behind the cathedral.* Sells all sorts of lovely potions and herbs, candles and home-made biscuits. Doña Gaviota also sells Guatemala City's most famous ice creams in all sorts of weird and wonderful flavours (see **Helados Marylena**, page 268).

## What to do

### Horse riding

**Ravenscroft Riding Stables**, *2 Av Sur 3, San Juan del Obispo, T7830-6669.* You can also hire horses in Santa María de Jesús.

## Language schools

Footprint has received favourable reports from students for the following language schools:

**Academia Antigüeña de Español**, 1 Pte 10, T7832-7241, www.spanishacademyantiguena.com.

**Alianza Lingüística 'Cano'**, Av El Desengaño 21A, T7832-0370. Private classes are also available.

**Amerispan**, 6 Av Norte 40 and 7 Calle Ote, T7832-0164, www.amerispan.com. In the US, 1334 Walnut St, 6th floor, Philadelphia PA 19107.

**Centro Lingüístico Maya**, 5 Calle Pte 20, T7832-1342, www.clmmaya.com.

**CSA (Christian Spanish Academy)**, 6 Av Norte 15, Aptdo Postal 320, T7832-3922, www.learncsa.com.

**Don Pedro de Alvarado**, 6 Av Norte 39, T5872-2469, www.donpedrospanishschool.com. 25 years' experience.

**Proyecto Bibliotecas Guatemala (PROBIGUA)**, 6 Av Norte 41B, T7832-2998, www.probigua.org. Gives a percentage of profits towards founding and maintaining public libraries in rural towns; frequently recommended.

**Proyecto Lingüístico Francisco Marroquín**, 6 Av Norte, www.plfm-antigua.org.

**Sevilla Academia de Español**, 1 Av Sur 8, T7832-5101, www.sevillantigua. com.

**Tecún Umán**, 6 Calle Pte 34A, T7832-2792, www.tecunuman.centramerica.com.

For private lessons check the ads in Doña Luisa's and others around town and the tourist office. Recommended teachers are: Julia Solís, 5 Calle Pte 36, T7832-5497, julisar@hotmail. com (she lives behind the tailor's shop); and Armalia Jarquín, Av El Desengaño 11 (there are, unbelievably, numerous No 11s on this road), T7832-2377. Armalia's has a sign up and is opposite No 75, which has a tiled plaque.

## ON THE ROAD

Antigua is overrun with language students and so some say it is not the most ideal environment in which to learn Spanish. There are about 70-plus schools, open year round. At any one time there may be 300-600 overseas students in Antigua. Not all schools are officially authorized by INGUAT and the Ministry of Education. INGUAT has a list of authorized schools in its office. Rates depend on the number of hours of tuition per week, and vary from school to school. As a rough guide, the average fee for four hours a day, five days a week is US$120-200, at a reputable school, with homestay, though many are less and some schools offer cheaper classes in the afternoon. You will benefit more from the classes if you have done a bit of study of the basics before you arrive. There are guides who take students around the schools and charge a high commission (make sure this is not added to your account). They may approach tourists arriving on the bus from the capital.

All schools offer one-to-one tuition; if you can meet the teachers in advance, so much the better, but don't let the director's waffle distract you from asking pertinent questions. Paying more does not mean you get better teaching and the standard of teacher varies within schools as well as between schools. Beware of 'hidden extras' and be clear on arrangements for study books. Some schools have an inscription fee. Several schools use a portion of their income to fund social projects and some offer a programme of activities for students such as dance classes, Latin American film, tours, weaving and football. Before making any commitment, find somewhere to stay for a couple of nights and shop around at your leisure. Schools also offer accommodation with local families, but check the place out if possible before you pay a week in advance. Average accommodation rates with a family with three meals a day are US$75-100 per week. In some cases the schools organize group accommodation; if you prefer single, ask for it.

### Spas

**Antigua Spa Resort**, *San Pedro El Panorama, lote 9 and 10 G, T7832-3960. Daily 0900-2100.* Swimming pool, steam baths, sauna, gym, jacuzzi and beauty salon. Reservations advised.
**Mayan Spa**, *Alameda Sta Lucía Norte 20, T7832-3537. Mon-Sat 0900-1800.* Massages and pampering packages, including sauna, steam baths and jacuzzi, are available.

### Swimming

**Porta Hotel Antigua**, non-residents may use the pool for a charge.

**Villas de Antigua**, *Ciudad Vieja exit, T7832-0011-15.* For buffet lunch, swimming and marimba band.

### Tour operators

**Adrenalina Tours**, *3a Calle Poniente, T7882 4147, www.adrenalinatours.com.* Xela's respected tour operator has opened up in Antigua too. As well as shuttles all around Guatemala, there are minibuses to San Cristóbal de las Casas, Mexico, US$55. Also customized packages, weekend trips to Xela and discounted Tikal trips. Recommended.
**Adventure Travel Center Viareal**, *5 Av Norte 25B, T7832-0162.* Daily trips to Guatemalan destinations (including Río Dulce sailing, river

and volcano trips), Monterrico, Quiriguá, El Salvador and Honduras.

**Antigua Tours**, *Casa Santo Domingo, 3 Calle Ote 22, T7832-5821, www.antiguatours.net.* Run by Elizabeth Bell, author of 4 books on Antigua. She offers walking tours of the city (US$20 per person), book in advance, Mon, Thu 1400-1700, Tue, Wed, Fri, Sat 0930-1230. During Lent and Holy Week there are extra tours, giving insight into the processions and carpet making. Highly recommended.

**Aventuras Naturales**, *Col El Naranjo No 53, Antigua, T5381-6615, http://aventuras naturales.tripod.com.* Specialized trips including guided birding tours.

**Aventuras Vacacionales**, *T5306-3584, www.sailing-diving-guatemala.com.* Highly recommended sailing trips on *Las Sirenas* owned by Captain John Clark and sailed by Captain Raúl Hernández (see also under Río Dulce, page 370).

**CA Tours**, *6 Calle Oriente Casa 14, T7832-9638, www.catours.co.uk.* British-run motorbike tour company.

**Eco-Tour Chejo's**, *3 Calle Pte 24, T832-5464, ecotourchejos@hotmail.com.* Well-guarded walks up volcanoes. Interesting tours also available to coffee fincas, flower plantations, etc, shuttle service, horse riding, very helpful.

**Gran Jaguar**, *4 Calle Pte 30, T7832-2712, www. guacalling.com/jaguar/.* Well-organized fun volcano tours with official security. Also shuttles and trips to Tikal and Río Dulce. Very highly recommended for the Pacaya trip.

**Guatemala Reservations.com**, *3 Av Norte 3, T7832-3293, www.guatemalareservations. com. Closed Sun.* A wide range of tours and transport services. Frequently recommended. Also has guidebooks for reference or to buy, along with a water bottle-filling service to encourage recycling. Cheap phone call service. Shuttles and tours.

**Old Town Outfitters**, *5 Av Sur 12 "C", T7832-4171, www.adventureguatemala.com.* Action adventure specialists, with mountain bike tours (½-day tour, US$39), kayak tours hiking and climbing, outdoor equipment on sale, maps, very helpful.

**Outdoor Excursions**, *1 Av Sur 4b, T7832-0074, www.guatemalavolcano.com.* Professional, knowledgeable and fun volcano tour company with private security. Overnight tours to Fuego (US$79), Acatenango (US$79) and Pacaya (US$59).

**Rainbow Travel Center**, *7 Av Sur 8, T7931-7878, www.rainbowtravelcenter.com.* Full local travel service, specialists in student flights and bargain international flights, they will attempt to match any quote. It also sells ISIC, Go25 and teachers' cards. English, French, German and Japanese spoken.

**Sin Fronteras**, *5a Av Norte 15 "A", T7720-4400, www.sinfront.com.* Local tours, shuttles, horse riding, bicycle tours, canopy tours, national and international air tickets including discounts with ISIC and Go25 cards. Also sells travel insurance. Agents for rafting experts **Maya Expeditions**. Reliable and highly recommended.

**Tivoli Travel**, *4 Calle Ote 10, T7832-4274, antigua@tivoli.com.gt. Closed Sun.* Helpful with any travel problem, English, French, Spanish, German, Italian spoken, reconfirm tickets, shuttles, hotel bookings, good-value tours. Useful for organizing independent travel as well as tours.

**ViaVenture**, *2 Calle Ote 2, T7832-2509, www. viaventure.com.* Professional tour operator offering special interest and tailor-made tours.

**Bus**
To **Guatemala City**: buses leave when full between 0530 and 1830, US$1, 1-1½ hrs, depending on the time of day, from the Alameda Santa Lucía near the market, from an exit next to **Pollo Campero** (not from behind the market). All other buses leave from behind the market. To **Chimaltenango**, on the Pan-American Hwy, from 0600-1600, every 15 mins, US$0.65, for connections to **Los Encuentros** (for **Lake Atitlán** and **Chichicastenango**), **Cuatro Caminos** (for **Quetzaltenango**) and **Huehuetenango** (for the Mexican border). It is possible to

get to Chichicastenango and back by bus in a day, especially on Thu and Sun, for the market. Get the bus to Chimaltenango and then change. It's best to leave early. See Chimaltenango for connections. The only direct bus to **Panajachel** is Rebuli, leaving at 0700, from 4 Calle Pte, in front of **La Bodegona** supermarket, US$5, 2½ hrs, returning 1100. Other buses to **Pana** via Chimaltenango with **Rebuli** and **Carrillo y Gonzalez**, 0600-1645, US$2.50. To **Escuintla**, 0530-1600, 1 hr, US$1.25.

To **Ciudad Vieja**, US$0.30, every 30 mins, 20 mins. **San Miguel de las Dueñas**. Take a bus marked 'Dueñas', every 30 mins, 20 mins, US$0.30. To **San Antonio Aguas Calientes**, every 30 mins, 30 mins, US$0.30. To **Santa María de Jesús** every 30 mins, 45 mins, US$0.50.

**International** To **Copán** and other cities in Honduras, including **Tegucigalpa**, with **Hedman Alas**, www.hedmanalas. com, from Posada de Don Rodrigo to its terminal in Guatemala City for a connection to Copán. Leaves at 0330 and 0630 from Antigua, US$41, US$77 return and 0500 and 0900 from Guatemala City, US$35, US$65 return. Return times are 1330 and 1800 to Guatemala City; the earlier bus continues to Antigua. See also Border crossings box in Practicalities chapter.

**Shuttles** Hotels and travel agents run frequent shuttle services to and from **Guatemala City** and the **airport** (1 hr) from 0400 to about 2000 daily, US$10-15 depending on the time of day: details from any agency in town. There are also shuttles to **Chichicastenango**, US$5-18, **Panajachel**, US$5-12, **Quetzaltenango**, US$16, **Monterrico**, US$15, **Flores**, US$20-40, **Copán**, US$8-25 and other destinations, but check for prices and days of travel. **Plus Travel** (www.plustravelguate.com) has some of the best prices and range of destinations, with offices in Antigua (6a Calle Pte No 19, T7832-3147) and Copán Ruinas. Recommended.

former colonial capital, village fiestas and a coffee farm

Ciudad Vieja – the former capital – is 5.5 km southwest of Antigua at the foot of Volcán Agua. Today Ciudad Vieja is itself a suburb of Antigua, but with a handsome church, founded in 1534, and one of the oldest in Central America. There's a fiesta on December 8.

In 1527, Pedro de Alvarado moved his capital, known then as Santiago de Los Caballeros, from Iximché to San Miguel Escobar, now a suburb of Ciudad Vieja. On 11 September 1541, after days of torrential rain, an immense mudslide came down the mountain and swallowed up the city. Alvarado's widow, Doña Beatriz de la Cueva, newly elected governor after his death, was among those drowned.

Between Ciudad Vieja and San Miguel de las Dueñas is the **Valhalla macadamia nut farm** ① T7831-5799, www.exvalhalla.net, free visits and nut tasting, 0800-1700.

About 3 km northwest of Ciudad Vieja is **San Antonio Aguas Calientes**. The hot springs unfortunately disappeared with recent earthquakes, but the village has many small shops selling locally made textiles. **Carolina's Textiles** is recommended for a fine selection, while on the exit road **Alida** has a shop. You can watch the weavers in their homes by the roadside. Local fiestas are 16-21 January, Corpus Christi (a moveable feast celebtrated around June) and 1 November.

Beyond San Juan del Obispo, beside Volcán Agua, is the charming village of **Santa María de Jesús**, with its beautiful view of Antigua. In the early morning there are good views of all three volcanoes from 2 km back down the road towards Antigua. Colourful *huipiles* are worn, made and sold from a couple of stalls, or ask at the shops on the plaza. The local fiesta is on 10 January.

Just north of Antigua is **Jocotenango**. The music museum, **Casa K'ojom** ⓘ *Mon-Fri 0830-1630, Sat 0830-1600, US$4*, is in the **Central Cultural La Azotea**, with displays of traditional Maya and colonial-era instruments. The village also has public saunas at the **Fraternidad Naturista Antigua**.

Five kilometres beyond San Lucas Sacatepéquez, at Km 29.5, Carretera Roosevelt (the Pan-American Highway), is **Santiago Sacatepéquez**, whose fiesta on 1 November, *Día de los Muertos* (All Souls' Day), is characterized by colourful kite-flying (*barriletes*). They also celebrate 25 July. Market days are Wednesday and Friday.

Visiting a **coffee farm** is an interesting short excursion. Tour Finca Los Nietos ⓘ *on the outskirts of Antigua, near the Iglesia San Felipe de Jesús, T7728-0812, www.filadelfiaresort. com*, runs two-hour tours (US$18) three times a day. They are very informative and interesting with expert multilingual guides, in beautiful manicured grounds and restored colonial buildings; also with restaurant and shop.

North of Guatemala City is **Mixco Viejo**, the excavated site of a post-Classic Maya fortress, which spans 14 hilltops, including 12 groups of pyramids. Despite earthquake damage it is worth a visit and is recommended. It was the 16th-century capital of the Pokomam Maya. There are a few buses a day between Mixco Viejo and the Zona 4 terminal, Guatemala City. The bus goes to Pachalum; ask to be dropped at ruins entrance.

## Volcanoes around Antigua

### active volcanoes, lava fields and spectacular views

Each of the four volcanoes that are immediately accessible from Antigua provides a unique set of challenges and rewards. Agua, Fuego and Acatenango volcanoes directly overlook Antigua whilst Volcán Pacaya is about an hour's drive away. All of these volcanoes can be experienced either as part of a day trip (a cheaper and faster option that requires only lightweight packs) or with an overnight excursion (heavier packs making climbing times longer, but with better light conditions for lava viewing and enhancing already spectacular views with beautiful sunset and sunrises).

Whatever option you choose, it is important to prepare properly for the unique features of each volcano (Pacaya is a relatively quick climb in a secure national park, while the three volcanoes on Antigua's perimeter are longer climbs with much greater risk of robberies and attacks). At a minimum, ensure that you have appropriate clothing and footwear (as summits are cold and volcanic ash is sharp bring fleeces and ideally use climbing boots), enough water (very important) and snacks for the trip and make informed decisions about safety. Although you can climb each of these volcanoes independently, you will significantly decrease your risks of getting lost, attacked or not finding shelter by using a professional guiding service; **Outdoor Excursions** (see Tour operators, page 288), which runs trips with expert guides and armed security, is particularly recommended. Remember that altitude takes its toll and for the longer hikes it is important to start early in the morning to allow enough time to ascend and descend in daylight. As a general rule, descents take from a third to a half of the ascent time.

## Volcán Pacaya

*Tours are available for US$6 upwards and are sold by most tour companies in Antigua. The popular and best time for organized trips is to leave Antigua at 1300 and return at 2100. Departures also 0600 returning 1300. There is also a US$3.50 fee to be paid at the entrance to the Volcán Pacaya National Park in San Francisco de Sales (toilets available).*

At 2552 m, the still-active Volcán Pacaya can't be missed and is the most exciting volcano to climb. Pacaya has erupted about 20 times since 1565, but since the mid-1960s it has been continuously active, meaning it can reward climbers with some spectacular lava flows. The cone – now split in two since the most recent eruption, in 2010 – is covered in black basaltic rock, shed from the crater. The rocks get warm and are lethally sharp. One of the results of the eruption is that shallow tunnels have formed, creating natural open-air saunas. They offer quite a spectacular experience, though for obvious safety reasons you should only enter these at the advice of an experience guide.Take a torch/flashlight refreshments and water and – it may sound obvious – wear boots or trainers, not sandals. Walking sticks are also offered at the park entrance – don't be too proud, on the steeper slopes, the crumbly lava screes can be very tricky to climb up or down. If you bring marshmallows to toast on the lava, make sure you have a long stick – lava is (rather unsurprisingly) very hot! Security officers go with the trips and police escorts ensure everyone leaves the area after dark. Check the situation in advance for **camping** (well below the crater lip). Sunrise comes with awesome views over the desolate black lava field to the distant Pacific (airborne dust permitting) and the peaks of Fuego, Acatenango and Agua. And as the sun sets on the horizon, Agua is silhouetted in the distance, a weak orange line streaked behind it.

## Volcán Agua

*Most organized tours with Antigua tour operators are during the day; you should enure that costs include both a guide and security. Trips normally leave Antigua about 0500.*

At 3760 m, Agua is the easiest but least scenic of the three volcanoes overlooking Antiqua. The trail, which can be quite littered, begins at **Santa María de Jesús**. Speak to Aurelio Cuy Chávez at the **Posada El Oasis**, who offers a guide service or take a tour with a reputable agency. You have to register first at the Municipalidad; guides are also available in the main square, about US$50 a day per guide. For Agua's history, see Ciudad Vieja above. The crater has a small shelter (none too clean), which was a shrine, and about 10 antennae. There are great views of Volcán Fuego. It's a three- to five-hour climb if you are fit, and at least two hours down. To get the best views before the clouds cover the summit, it is best to stay at the radio station at the top. Agua can also be climbed from **Alotenango**, a village between Agua and Fuego, south of Ciudad Vieja. It's 9 km from Antigua and its name means 'place surrounded by corn'. Alotenango has a fiesta from 18-20 January.

## Volcán Acatenango

*If you do this climb independently of a tour agency, ask for a guide in La Soledad. However, it is strongly recommended that you use a professional guiding service, ideally with security.*

Acatenango is classified as a dormant volcano and is the third tallest in the country (3975 m) with two peaks to its name. Its first recorded eruption was in 1924. Two other eruptions were reported in 1924-1927 and 1972. The best trail heads south at **La Soledad**, 2300 m (15 km west of Ciudad Vieja), which is 300 m before the road (Route 5) turns right to Acatenango (see Where to stay, below). A small plateau, La Meseta on maps, known locally as **El Conejón**, provides a good camping site half way up (three or four hours). From here it is a further three or four hours' harder going to the top. The views of the nearby (lower) active crater of Fuego are excellent.

## Volcán Fuego
*This is an active volcano with trails that are easy to lose; it is recommended that you use a guiding service and do not venture up to the crater.*

This volcano (3763 m) can be climbed via Volcán Acatenango, sleeping between the two volcanoes, then climbing for a further two to three hours before stopping a safe distance from the crater. This one is for experienced hikers only. Do not underestimate the amount of water needed for the climb. It is a seven-hour ascent with a significant elevation gain; it's a very hard walk, both up and down. There are steep, loose cinder slopes, which are very tedious, in many places. It is possible to camp about three-quarters of the way up in a clearing. Fuego has regular eruptions that shoot massive boulders from its crater, often without warning. Check in Antigua before attempting to climb. If driving down towards the south coast you can see the red volcanic rock it has thrown up.

## Listings Volcanoes

### Where to stay

**$ Pensión**
*Volcán Acatenango.*
Basic, with good cheap meals.

### Transport

**Volcán Agua**
**Bus**
From Antigua to **Alotenango** from 0700-1800, 40 mins.

**Volcán Acatenango**
**Bus**
To reach **La Soledad**, take a bus heading for Yepocapa or Acatenango village and get off at La Soledad.

### Car
**Tabarini**, 6 Av Sur 22, T7832-8107, also at the **Hotel Radisson Villa Antigua**, T7832-7460, www.tabarini.com.

### Horse-drawn carriage
Available at weekends and during fiestas around the plaza.

### Motorcycle hire
**La Ceiba**, 6 Calle Pte 15, T7832-0077.

### Taxi
**Servicio de Taxi 'Antigua'**, Manuel Enrique Gómez, T5417-2180, has been recommended.

### Tuk-tuk
Motorbike taxis with a seat for 2 will whizz you around town for US$1.50.

# Lake Atitlán
## & around

⭐ In the Central Highlands volcano landscapes are dotted with colourful markets and the Maya wearing traditional clothes in the towns and villages. Aldous Huxley called Lake Atitlán "the most beautiful lake in the world" and attractive villages flank its shores. Further north you can explore the streets of Chichicastenango as the town fills with hawkers and vendors at the weekly markets serving tourists and locals alike. North of Chichicastenango, the Quiché and Ixil Triangle regions have small and very traditional hamlets set in beautiful countryside and are easily explored by bus.

## Towards Lake Atitlán  *Colour map 2, C4.*

*beautiful scenery stretching west of the capital*

The Pan-American Highway heads west out of the capital passing through Chimaltenango and on to Los Encuentros where it turns north for Chichicastenango, Santa Cruz del Quiché, Nebaj and the Ixil Triangle, and south for Sololá and the Lake Atitlán region. It continues to the western highland region of Quetzaltenango, Totonicapán, Huehuetenango and the Cuchumatanes Mountains.

### Chimaltenango and around

Chimaltenango is busy with traffic. Here, another road runs south for 20 km to Antigua. This tree-lined road leads to Parramos where it turns sharp left. Straight on through the village, in 1.5 km, is a well known inn and restaurant, **La Posada de Mi Abuelo** (see Where to stay, below). This road continues through mountains to Pastores, Jocotenango and finally to Antigua. Some 6 km south of Chimaltenango, **San Andrés Itzapa** is well worth a visit; there is a very interesting **chapel to Maximón** ① *open till 1800 daily.* Shops by the chapel sell prayer pamphlets and pre-packaged offerings. Beyond Chimaltenango

**Best** for
Lake views ▪ Learning Spanish ▪ Markets ▪ Textiles ▪ Walking

is **Zaragoza**, a former Spanish penal settlement, and beyond that a road leads 13 km north to the interesting village of **Comalapa**. This is the best place to see *naif* painting and there are plenty of galleries. The **tourist information office** ① *Av 3-76, T5766-3874*, is in the house of Andrés Curuchich, a popular artist. There's a colourful market on Monday and Tuesday.

## Routes west: La Mesilla, Tecpán and Los Encuentros

Returning to the Pan-American Highway the road divides 6 km past Zaragoza. The southern branch, the old Pan-American Highway, goes through Patzícia and Patzún (see below) to Lake Atitlán, then north to Los Encuentros. The northern branch, the new Pan-American Highway, which is used by all public transport, goes past Tecpán (see below) and then to Los Encuentros. From Los Encuentros there is only the one road west to San Cristóbal Totonicapán, where it swings northwest to La Mesilla/Ciudad Cuauhtémoc, at the Mexican border; see Border crossings box in Practicalities chapter.

From Zaragoza the Pan-American Highway runs 19 km to near **Tecpán**, which is slightly off the road at 2287 m. It has a particularly fine church with silver altars, carved wooden pillars, odd images and a wonderful ceiling that was severely damaged by the 1976 earthquake. There is accommodation, restaurants and banks. Near Tecpán are

Lake Atitlán

the important Maya ruins of **Iximché** ① *5 km of paved road south of Tecpán, 0800-1700, US$3.25*, once capital and court of the Cakchiqueles. The first capital of Guatemala after its conquest was founded near Iximché; followed in turn by Ciudad Vieja, Antigua and Guatemala City. The ruins are well presented with three plazas, a palace and two ball courts on a promontory surrounded on three sides by steep slopes.

The old and new Pan-American highways rejoin 11 km from Sololá at the **El Cuchillo** junction. About 2 km east is **Los Encuentros**, the junction of the Pan-American Highway and the paved road 18 km northeast to Chichicastenango.

## To Lake Atitlán along the old Pan-American Highway

With amazing views of Lake Atitlán and the surrounding volcanoes, travellers of the southern road from Zaragoza to Lake Atitlán encounter a much more difficult route than the northern option, with several steep hills and many hairpin bends. Nevertheless, if you have both the time and a sturdy vehicle, it is an extremely rewarding trip. Note that there is no police presence whatsoever along the old Pan-American Highway.

The route goes through **Patzicía**, a small Maya village founded in 1545 (no accommodation). Market days are Wednesday and Saturday and the local fiesta is 22-27 July. The famous church, which had a fine altar and beautiful silver, was destroyed by the 1976 earthquake. Beyond is the small town of **Patzún**; its church, dating from 1570, is severely damaged and is not open to the public. There is a Sunday market, which is famous for the silk (and wool) embroidered napkins and for woven *fajas* and striped red cotton cloth; other markets are on Tuesday and Friday and the town fiesta is 17-21 May. For accommodation, ask at the *tiendas*.

The road leaves Patzún and goes south to Xepatán and on to **Godínez**, the highest community overlooking the lake. From Godínez, a good paved road turns off south to the village of San Lucas Tolimán and continues to Santiago Atitlán.

The main (steep, paved) road continues straight on for Panajachel. The high plateau, with vast wheat and maize fields, now breaks off suddenly as though pared by a knife. From a viewpoint here, there is an incomparable view of Lake Atitlán, 600 m below. The very picturesque village of **San Antonio Palopó** is right underneath you, on slopes leading to the water. It is about 12 km from the viewpoint to Panajachel. For the first 6 km you are close to the rim of the old crater and, at the point where the road plunges down to the lakeside, is **San Andrés Semetabaj** which has a beautiful ruined early 17th-century church. Market day is Tuesday. Buses go to Panajachel.

## Sololá

On the road down to Panajachel is Sololá (altitude 2113 m), which has superb views across Lake Atitlán. Outside the world of the tourist, this is the most important town in the area. A fine, modern, white church, with bright stained-glass windows and an attractive clocktower dominates the west side of the plaza. Sololá is even more special for the bustling market that brings the town to life every Tuesday and Friday, when the Maya gather from surrounding commuities to buy and sell local produce. Women and particularly men wear traditional dress. While it is primarily a produce market, there is also a good selection of used *huipiles*. Even if you're not in the market to buy, it is a colourful sight. Markets are mornings only; Friday market gets underway on Thursday. There's a fiesta 11-17 August.

From Sololá the old Pan-American Highway weaves and twists through a 550-m drop in the 8 km to Panajachel. The views are impressive at all times of day, but particularly in the morning. Time allowing, it is quite easy to walk down direct by the road (two hours); you also miss the unnerving bus ride down (US$0.40).

## Where to stay

### Chimaltenango and around

**$$ La Posada de Mi Abuelo**
*Carretera a Yepocapa, Parramos, T7849-5930, see Facebook.*
A delightful inn, formerly a coffee farm, with a good restaurant. Packages with horse riding, biking and meals are available.

**$ Pixcayá**
*0 Av, 1-82, Comalapa, T7849-8260.*
Hot water, parking.

### Sololá

**$ Del Viajero**
*7 Av, 10-45, on Parque Central (also annexe around the corner on Calle 11), T7762-3683.*
Rooms with bath, cheaper without, spacious, clean and friendly, good food in restaurant on the plaza (**El Cafetín**).

**$ El Paisaje**
*9 Calle, 5-41, 2 blocks from Parque Central, T7762-3820.*
Pleasant colonial courtyard, shared baths and toilets, clean, hot water, restaurant, good breakfast, family-run, laundry facilities.

## Transport

### Chimaltenango and around
**Bus**

Any bus heading west from Guatemala City stops at Chimaltenango. To **Antigua** buses leave from the corner of the main road and the road south to Antigua where there is a lime green and blue shop, Auto Repuestos y Frenos Nachma, 45 mins, US$0.34. To **Chichicastenango**, every 30 mins, 0600-1700, 2 hrs, US$2. To **Cuatro Caminos**, 2½ hrs, US$2.50. To **Quetzaltenango**, every 45 mins, 0700-1800, 2½ hrs, US$2.80. To **Tecpán** every 30 mins, 0700-1800, 1 hr.

### Routes west: La Mesilla, Tecpán and Los Encuentros
**Bus**

From Tecpán to **Guatemala City**, 2¼ hrs, buses every hour, US$2.20; easy day trip from **Panajachel** or **Antigua**.

### To Lake Atitlán along the old Pan-American Highway
**Bus**

To and from **Godínez** there are several buses to Panajachel, US$0.45 and 1 bus daily Patzún–Godínez. To **San Andrés Semetabaj**, bus to Panajachel, US$0.40.

### Sololá
**Bus**

To **Chichicastenango**, US$0.50, 1½ hrs; to **Panajachel**, US$0.38, every 30 mins, 20 mins, or 1½-2 hrs' walk. To **Chimaltenango**, US$1.20. To **Quetzaltenango**, US$1.8. Colectivo to **Los Encuentros**, US$0.20. To **Guatemala City** direct US$2.50, 3 hrs.

## Panajachel *Colour map 2, C4.*

**charming old town, busy shopping street and starting point for lake ferries**

The old town of Panajachel is pretty and quiet but the newer development, strung along a main road, is a tucker and trinket emporium. It's busy and stacked cheek by jowl with hundreds of stalls and shops along the principal street. Some of the best bargains are here and textiles and crafts from across the country can be found. Panajachel is a gringo magnet, and if you want to fill up on international cuisine and drink then it's a good place to stay for a few days. There are also stunning views from the lakeshore.

The town centre is the junction of Calle Principal and Calle (or Avenida) Santander. The main bus stop is here, stretching south back down Calle Real, and it marks the junction between the old and the modern towns. It takes about 10 minutes to walk from the junction to the lakeshore. Calle Rancho Grande is sometimes called Calle del Balneario and

# Panajachel

To Market, Godínez, San Lucas Tolimán & Las Trampas
Municipalidad

**Where to stay**
Atitlán 4 *D1*
Dos Mundos 3 *D1*
El Sol 1 *A2*
Jenna's B&B 2 *E2*
Mario's Rooms 15 *D1*
Posada de Don Rodrigo 19 *E1*
Posada de los Volcanes 20 *E1*
Posada Los Encuentros 5 *A2*
Primavera 21 *C1*
Rancho Grande 23 *C2*
Utz Jay 6 *D2*
Villas B'alam Ya 7 *A2*

**Restaurants**
Bombay 2 *D1*
Chez Alex 3 *C1*
Circus Bar 4 *B1*
Crossroads Café 5 *A2*
Deli Llama de Fuego 11 *C1*
El Pájaro Azul 9 *E1*
El Patio 10 *C1*
Guajimbo's 12 *C1*
La Rosticería 1 *B2*
Las Olas 13 *E2*
Los Pumpos 16 *E2*
Maya Pan 6 *C1*
Pana Rock Café 17 *C1*
Sunset Café 18 *E1*
Tocoyal 19 *E2*

**Bars & clubs**
Circus Bar 22 *B1*
Discoteca Chapiteau 20 *B1*
El Aleph 21 *B1*

The original settlement of Panajachel was tucked up against the steep cliffs to the north of the present town, about 1 km from the lake. Virtually all traces of the original Kaqchikel village have disappeared, but the early Spanish impact is evident with the narrow streets, public buildings, plaza and church. The original Franciscan church was founded in 1567 and used as the base for the Christianization of the lake area. Later, the fertile area of the river delta was used for coffee production, orchards and many other crops, some of which are still grown today and can be seen round the back of the tourist streets or incorporated into the gardens of the hotels.

Tourism began here in the early 20th century with several hotels on the waterfront, notably the Tzanjuyú and the Monterrey, the latter originally a wooden building dating from about 1910, rebuilt in 1975. In the 1970s came an influx of young travellers, quite a few of whom stayed on to enjoy the climate and the easy life. Drugs and the hippy element eventually gave Panajachel a bad name, but rising prices and other pressures have encouraged this group to move on, some to San Pedro across the lake. Others joined the commercial scene and still run services today.

other streets have variants. The **tourist information office**, INGUAT ① *Calle Real Principal and Av Los Arboles, T7762-1106, daily 0900-1300 and 1400-1700*, is helpful with information about buses and boats and offer good local knowledge. Also see www.atitlan.com.

**Safety** There have been reports from travellers who have suffered robbery walking around the lake between San Juan and San Pablo and between San Marcos and Tzununá. Seek local advice from **INGUAT**, other travellers and local hotels/hostels before planning a trip.

### Sights

The old town is 1 km from the lake and dominated by the **church**, originally built in 1567, but now restored. It has a fine decorated wooden roof and a mixture of Catholic statues and Maya paintings in the nave. A block up the hill is the daily market, worth a visit on Sunday mornings especially for embroideries. The local fiesta runs from 1-7 October; the main days are at the weekend and on 4 October.

In contrast, the modern town, almost entirely devoted to tourism, spreads out towards the lake. Calle Santander is the principal street, leading directly to the short but attractive **promenade** and boat docks. The section between Calle Santander and Calle Rancho Grande has been turned into a park, which delightfully frames the traditional view across the lake to the volcanoes. Near the promenade, at the **Hotel Posada de Don Rodrigo**, is the **Museo Lacustre Atitlán** ① *daily 0900-1200, 1400-1800, US$4.40*, created by Roberto Samayoa, a prominent local diver and archaeologist, to house some of the many items found in the lake. The geological history is explained and there is a fine display of Maya classical pottery and ceremonial artefacts classified by period. A submerged village has been found at a depth of 20 m, which is being investigated. It has been named **Samabaj** in honour of Don Roberto. For those interested in local art, visit **La Galería** (near **Rancho Grande Hotel**), where Nan Cuz, an indigenous painter, sells her pictures evoking the spirit of village life. She has been painting since 1958 and has achieved international recognition.

On the road past the entrance to **Hotel Atitlán** is the **Reserva Natural Atitlán** ① *T7762-2565, www.atitlanreserva.com, daily 0800-1800, US$8.30 entrance, US$29-45 zipline (including entrance),* a reserve with a bird refuge, butterfly collection, monkeys and native mammals in natural surroundings, with a picnic area, herb garden, waterfall, visitor centre, café, ziplines and access to the lakeside beach. Camping and lodging are available ($).

## Listings Panajachel *map p297.*

### Where to stay

**$$$$ Villas B'alam Ya**
*Outside Panajachel, Carretera a Catarina Palopó Km 2, T7762-2522, www.panzaverde.com.*
The sister property of the swish Meson Panza Verde in Antigua, Villas B'alam Ya includes 4 luxury villas on the hillside and lakeshore, all tastefully attired and equipped with all mod cons. Guests can enjoy plentiful services and facilities including kayaks, gourmet room service, tours and yoga classes. Very peaceful, secluded and romantic.

**$$$ Atitlán**
*1 km west of centre on lake, 2nd turning off the road to Sololá, T7762-1441, www.hotelatitlan.com.*
Full board available, colonial style, excellent rooms and service, beautiful gardens with views across lake, pool, private beach and top-class restaurant.

**$$$ Posada de Don Rodrigo**
*Final Calle Santander, overlooks the lake, T7762-2326, www.posadadedonrodrigo.com.*
Pool, sauna, terrace, gardens, good restaurant, excellent food and service, comfortable and luxurious bathrooms, and fireplaces.

**$$$ Rancho Grande**
*Calle Rancho Grande, Centro, T7762-1554, www.ranchogrande inn.com.*
Cottages in charming setting, 4 blocks from beach, popular for long stay, good, including breakfast with pancakes. Pool with café in spacious gardens which have good children's play equipment. Staff are helpful. Recommended.

**$$$-$$ Jenna's B&B**
*Casa Loma, Calle Rancho Grande, T5458-1984, www.jennasriver bedandbreakfast.com.*
This quirky B&B has 7 cosy guest rooms decorated with local antiques, Guatemalan art and textiles. There is also a basement apartment available by the week or month and, for those seeking something different, a yurt ($$$). Amenities include garden, TV, Wi-Fi, living room and full bar. Breakfast included, additional meals on request.

**$$ Dos Mundos**
*Calle Santander 4-72, Centro, T7762-2078, www.hoteldosmundos.com.*
Pool, cable TV, some rooms surround pool, good Italian restaurant (**La Lanterna**). Breakfast included.

**$$ Posada de los Volcanes**
*Calle Santander, 5-51, Centro, T7762-0244, www.posadadelosvolcanes.com.*
12 rooms with bath, hot water, clean, comfortable, quiet, friendly owners, Julio and Jeanette Parajón.

**$$ Posada Los Encuentros**
*Barrio Jucany, a 15-min walk from town, T7762-1603, www.losencuentros.com.*
Off-the-beaten track in Panajachel, Los Encuentros boasts a lovely medicinal herb garden, wood-fuelled sauna, thermally heated mineral pool, and a well-equipped fitness centre. They have links to local healers and offer Mayan cultural tours. Accommodation includes 7 pleasant rooms.

**$$ Primavera**
*Calle Santander, Centro, T7762-2052, www.primaveratitlan.com.*

Clean, bright rooms, with TV, cypress wood furniture, gorgeous showers, washing machine available, friendly. Recommended. **Chez Alex** next door serves French food in a lovely patio setting at the back. Don't get a room overlooking the street at weekends.

### $$ Utz Jay
*5 Calle, 2-50, Zona 2, T7762-0217, www.hotelutzjay.com.*
This small hotel has 13 rooms overlooking a lush tropical garden replete with leafy foliage and birds. Rooms are clean and tranquil, equipped with hot water and decorated with Mayan textiles. Services available at extra cost include breakfast, laundry, sauna, jacuzzi and packed lunch.

### $ Hotel El Sol
*Barrio Jucanya, a 15-min walk from town, T7762-6090, www.hotelelsolpanajachel.com.*
Hotel El Sol is a Japanese-owned hostel, which is quiet, good value, economical and suitable for backpackers or families. Lodgings include immaculately clean private rooms and an 8-bed dorm. There is a small garden outside and a sun terrace with views of the hills. Inside there is a restaurant and lounges for watching DVDs. Pleasant and restful.

### $ Mario's Rooms
*Calle Santander esq Calle 14 de Febrero, Centro, T7762-1313.*
Cheaper without bath, with garden, clean, bright rooms, hot showers, good breakfast, but not included, popular and friendly.

## Apartments
Ask around for houses to rent; available from US$125 a month for a basic place, to US$200, but almost impossible to find in Nov and Dec. Break-ins and robberies of tourist houses are not uncommon. Water supply is variable. **Apartamentos Bohemia**, Callejón Chinimaya, rents furnished bungalows.

## Camping
Possible in the grounds of **Hotel Visión Azul** and **Tzanjuyú**.

### $$$ Chez Alex
*Calle Santander, centre, T7762-0172. Open 1200-1500 and 1800-2000.*
French menu, good quality, mainly tourists, credit cards accepted.

### $$$ Tocoyal
*Annexe to Hotel del Lago.*
A/c, groups welcome, buffet on request but tourist prices.

### $$ Circus Bar
*Av Los Arboles 0-62, T7762-2056. Open 1200-2400.*
Italian dishes including delicious pasta and pizzas, good coffee, popular. Live music from 2030, excellent atmosphere. Recommended.

### $$ Crossroads Café
*Calle de Campanario 0-27. Tue-Sat 0900-1300 and 1500-1900.*
Global choice of quality coffee, but you can't go wrong with Guatemalan! Excellent cakes.

### $$ El Patio
*Calle Santander.*
Good food, very good large breakfasts, quiet atmosphere but perfect for people-watching from the garden. Try the amaretto coffee.

### $$ Guajimbo's
*Calle Santander.*
Good atmosphere, excellent steaks, fast service, popular, live music some evenings. Recommended.

### $$ La Rosticería
*Av Los Arboles 0-42, T7762-2063. Daily 0700-2300.*
Good food, try eggs 'McChisme' for breakfast, good fresh pasta, excellent banana cake, good atmosphere, popular, a bit pricey. Live piano music at weekends, friendly service.

### $$ Los Pumpos
*Calle del Lago.*
Varied menu, bar, good fish and seafood dishes.

## $$ Pana Rock Café
*With Pana Arte upstairs, Calle Santander 3-72.*
Buzzing around happy hour (2 for 1), salsa music, very popular, international food, pizza.

## $$ Sunset Café
*Superb location on the lake. Open 1100-2400.*
Excellent for drinks, light meals and main dishes, live music evenings, but you pay for the view.

## $$-$ Bombay
*Calle Santander near Calle 15 Febrero, T7762-0611. Open 1100-2130.*
Vegetarian recipes, including spicy curries, German beer, Mexican food, good food and wines, set lunch popular, good service. Very highly recommended.

## $$-$ El Pájaro Azul
*Calle Santander 2-75, T7762-2596. Open 1000-2200.*
Café, bar, crêperie with gorgeous stuffed sweet or savoury crêpes, cakes and pies. Vegetarian options available. Reasonable prices, good for late breakfasts. Recommended.

## $ Deli Llama de Fuego
*Calle Santander, T7762-2586. Thu-Tue 0700-2200.*
Sweet little café with a giant cheese plant as its focus. Breakfasts, muffins, bagels, pizzas, pasta, Mexican food and vegetarian sandwiches.

## $ Restaurante Las Olas
*Overlooking the lake at the end of Calle Santander, down by the dock.*
Serves the absolute best nachos, great for just before catching the boat.

### Bakeries

## Maya Pan
*Calle Santander 1-61.*
Excellent wholemeal breads and pastries, banana bread comes out of the oven at 0930, wonderful, cinnamon rolls and internet too. Recommended.

## Bars and clubs

## Circus Bar
*Av los Arboles. Daily 1200-0200.*
Good live music from 2030.

## Discoteca Chapiteau
*Av los Arboles 0-69.*
Nightclub Thu-Sat 1900-0100.

## El Aleph
*Av los Arboles. Thu-Sat 1900-0300.*
One of a number of bars.

## Shopping

Bartering is the norm. There are better bargains here than in Chichicastenango. The main tourist shops are on Calle Santander.

**Librería del Lago**, *Calle Santander Local A-8, T7762-2788. Daily 0900-1800.* Great bookshop selling a good range of quality English-language and Spanish books.
**Tinamit Maya Shopping Centre**, *Calle Santander.* Bargain for good prices. Maya sell their wares cheaply on the lakeside; varied selection, bargaining is easy/expected.

## What to do

### Cycling
There are several rental agencies on Calle Santander, eg **Maco Cycle Rental** and **Tono Cycle Rental**. Also **Alquiler de Bicicletas Emanuel**, on Calle 14 de Febrero. Prices start at US$2 per hr or about US$10 for a day.

### Diving
**ATI Divers**, *round the back of El Patio, Calle Santander, T5706-4117, www.laiguana perdida. com.* A range of options including PADI Open Water US$220, fun dive US$30, 2 for US$50. PADI Rescue and Dive Master also available. Altitude speciality, US$80. Dives are made off Santa Cruz La Laguna and are of special interest to those looking for altitude diving. Here there are spectacular walls that drop off, rock formations you can swim through, trees underwater and, because of its volcanic

nature, hot spots, which leaves the lake bottom sediment boiling to touch. Take advice on visibility before you opt for a dive.

### Fishing

Lake fishing can be arranged, black bass (*mojarra*) up to 4 kg can be caught. Boats for up to 5 people can be hired for about US$15. Check with INGUAT, see page 298, for latest information.

### Hang-gliding

**Rogelio**, *contactable through America's Tours, Calle Santander, and other agencies will make arrangements, at least 24 hrs' notice is required.* Jumps are made from San Jorge La Laguna or from above Santa Catarina, depending on weather conditions.

### Kayaking and canoing

Kayak hire is around US$2 per hr. Ask at the hotels, INGUAT and at lakeshore. Watch out for strong winds that occasionally blow up quickly across the lake; these are potentially dangerous in small boats.
**Diversiones Acuáticos Balán**, *in a small red and white tower on the lakeshore.* Rent out kayaks.

### Tour operators

All offer shuttle services to Chichicastenango, Antigua, the Mexican borders, etc, and some to San Cristóbal de las Casas (see Transport, below) and can arrange most activities on and around the lake. There are a number of tour operators on Calle Santander, including those listed below.
**America's Tours**, *T7762-2021.*
**Centroamericana Tourist Service**, *T7832-5032.*
**Tierra Maya**, *T7725-7320.* Friendly and reliable tour operator, which runs shuttles to San Cristóbal de las Casas as well as within Guatemala.
**Toliman Travel**, *T7762-1275.*

### Waterskiing

Arrangements can be made with **ATI Divers** at **Iguana Perdida** in Santa Cruz.

Transport

### Boat

There are 2 types of transport – the scheduled ferry service to Santiago Atitlán and the *lanchas* to all the other villages. The tourist office has the latest information on boats. The boat service to **Santiago Atitlán** runs from the dock at the end of Calle Rancho Grande (Muelle Público) from 0600-1630, 8 daily, 20 mins in launch, US$3.10, 1 hr in the large **Naviera Santiago** ferry, T7762-0309 or 20-35 mins in the fast *lanchas*. Some *lanchas* to all the other villages leave from here, but most from the dock at the end of Calle Embarcadero run by **Tzanjuyú** from 0630-1700 every 45 mins or when full (minimum 10 people). If you set off from the main dock the *lancha* will pull in at the Calle Embarcadero dock as well. These *lanchas* call in at **Santa Cruz**, **Jaibalito**, **Tzununá**, **San Marcos**, **San Pablo**, **San Juan** and **San Pedro**, US$1.20 to US$2.50 to **San Marcos** and beyond. To **San Pedro** US$3.10. There are no regular boats to Santa Catarina, San Antonio or San Lucas: pickups and buses serve these communities, or charter a *lancha*, US$30 return to Santa Catarina and San Antonio.

The 1st boat of the day is at 0700. If there is a demand, there will almost always be a boatman willing to run a service but non-official boats can charge what they like. Virtually all the dozen or so communities round the lake have docks, and you can take a regular boat to any of those round the western side. The only reliable services back to Panajachel are from **Santiago** or **San Pedro** up to about 1600. If you wait on the smaller docks round the western side up to this time, you can get a ride back to Panajachel, flag them down in case they don't see you, but they usually pull in if it's the last service of the day.

Note that, officially, locals pay less. Only buy tickets on the boat; if you buy them from the numerous ticket touts on the dockside, you will be overcharged. Bad weather can, of course, affect the boat services. Crossings are generally rougher in the afternoons, worth bearing in mind if you suffer from sea-sickness.

**Boat hire and tours** *Lanchas* can be hired to go anywhere round the lake, about US$100 for 5 people for a full day. For round trips to **San Pedro** and **Santiago** and possibly **San Antonio Palopó**, with stopovers, go early to the lakefront and bargain. Trip takes a full day, eg 0830-1530, with stops of 1 hr or so at each, around US$6-7, if the boat is full. If on a tour, be careful not to miss the boat at each stage; if you do, you will have to pay again.

**Bus**

**Rebuli** buses leave from opposite Hotel Fonda del Sol on Calle Real, otherwise, the main stop is where Calle Santander meets Calle Real. **Rebuli** to **Guatemala City**, 3½ hrs, US$3.30, crowded, hourly between 0500 and 1500. To **Guatemala City** via **Escuintla** south coast, 8 a day plus 3 **Pullman** a day. Direct bus to **Quetzaltenango**, 7 a day between 0530 and 1415, US$2.70, 2½ hrs. There are direct buses to **Los Encuentros** on the Pan-American Hwy (US$0.75). To **Chichicastenango** direct, Thu and Sun, 0645, 0700, 0730 and then hourly to 1530. Other days between 0700-1500, US$2, 1½ hrs. There are 4 daily direct buses to **Cuatro Caminos**, US$1.60 from 0530, for connections to Totonicapán,

Quetzaltenango, Huehuetenango, etc. To **Antigua** take a bus up to Los Encuentros through Sololá. Change for a bus to **Chimaltenango** US$3.10, and change there for Antigua. There is also a direct bus (**Rebuli**) to **Antigua** leaving 1030-1100, daily, US$4.40. To **Sololá**, US$0.40, 20 mins, every 30 mins. You can wait for through buses by the market on Calle Real. The fastest way to southern **Mexico** is probably by bus south to Cocales, 2½ hrs, 5 buses between 0600 and 1400, then many buses along the Pacific Highway to **Tapachula** on the border. For **La Mesilla**, take a bus up to Los Encuentros, change west for Cuatro Caminos. Here catch a bus north to La Mesilla; see also Border crossings box in Practicalities chapter. Some travel agencies go direct to **San Cristóbal de las Casas** via La Mesilla, daily at 0600. See Tour operators, above.

**Shuttles** Services are run jointly by travel agencies, to **Guatemala City**, **Antigua**, **Quetzaltenango**, **Chichi** and more. Around 4 a day. **Antigua**, US$14, **Chichicastenango**, on market days, US$15, **Quetzaltenango** US$20 and the **Mexican border** US$40. **Atitrans**, Calle Santander, next to Hotel Regis, T7762-0146, is recommended.

**Motorcycle**

**Motorcycle hire** About US$6 per hour, plus fuel and US$100 deposit. Try **Maco Cycle** near the junction of Calle Santander and 14 de Febrero, T7762-0883.

**Motorcycle parts** David's Store, opposite Hotel Maya Kanek, has good prices and also does repairs.

Villages around the lake are connected to Panajachel by boat services. Some are served by buses. Travelling round the lake is the best way to enjoy the stunning scenery and the effect of changing light and wind on the mood of the area. The slower you travel the better, and walking round the lake gives some fantastic views (but take advice on safety). With accommodation at towns and villages on the way, there is no problem finding somewhere to bed down for the night if you want to make a complete circuit. The lake is 50 km in circumference and you can walk on or near the shore for most of it. Here and there the cliffs are too steep to allow for easy walking and private properties elsewhere force you to move up 'inland'.

For boat information see Transport, page 302. At almost any time of year, but especially between January and March, strong winds (*El Xocomil*) occasionally blow up quickly across the lake. This can be dangerous for small boats.

## Santa Catarina Palopó
The town, within easy walking distance (4 km) of Panajachel, has an attractive adobe church. Reed mats are made here, and you can buy *huipiles* (beautiful, green, blue and yellow) and men's shirts. Watch weaving at **Artesanías Carolina** on the way out towards San Antonio. Bargaining is normal. There are hot springs close to the town and an art gallery. Houses can be rented and there is at least one superb hotel (see Where to stay, below). The town fiesta is 25 November.

## San Antonio Palopó
Six kilometres beyond Santa Catarina, San Antonio Palopó has another fine 16th-century church. Climbing the hill from the dock, it lies in an amphitheatre created by the mountains behind. Up above there are hot springs and a cave in the rocks used for local ceremonies. The village is noted for the clothes and head dresses of the men, and *huipiles* and shirts are cheaper than in Santa Catarina. A good hike is to take the bus from Panajachel to Godínez; take the path toward the lake 500 m south along the road to Cocales, walk on down from there to San Antonio Palopó (one hour) and then along the road back to Panajachel via Santa Catarina Palopó (three hours). You can walk on round the lake from San Antonio, but you must eventually climb steeply up to the road at Agua Escondida. The local fiesta is 12-14 June.

## San Lucas Tolimán
San Lucas is at the southeastern tip of the lake and is not as attractive as other towns. It is known for its fiestas and markets especially Holy Week with processions, arches and carpets on the Thursday and Friday, and 15-20 October. Market days are Tuesday, Friday and Sunday (the best). There are two banks and an internet centre. **Comité Campesino del Altiplano** ⓘ *T5804-9451, www.ccda.galeon.com*, is based in the small village of Quixaya, 10 minutes from San Lucas. This Campesino Cooperative now produces fairtrade organic coffee buying from small farmers. You can visit its organic processing plant on a small coffee finca and learn about its *café justicia,* and political work. Long-term volunteers welcome, Spanish required.

## Volcán Atitlán and Volcán Tolimán

*Ask Father Gregorio at the Parroquia church, 2 blocks from the Central Plaza, or at the Municipalidad for information and for available guides in San Lucas. Father Greg has worked in the area for more than 40 years so has a vested interest in recommending safe and good guides. One guide is Carlos Huberto Alinan Chicoj, leaving at 2400 with torches to arrive at the summit by 0630 to avoid early cloud cover.*

From San Lucas the cones of **Atitlán**, 3535 m, and **Tolimán**, 3158 m, can be climbed. The route leaves from the south end of town and makes for the saddle (known as Los Planes, or Chanán) between the two volcanoes. From there it is south to Atitlán and north to the double cone (they are 1 km apart) and crater of Tolimán. Though straightforward, each climb is complicated by many working paths and thick cover above 2600 m. If you are fit, either can be climbed in seven hours, five hours down. Cloud on the volcano is common, but least likely from November to March. There have been reports of robbery so consider taking a guide, and ask local advice before setting out.

## Santiago Atitlán

Santiago is a fascinating town, as much for the stunningly beautiful embroidered clothing of the locals, as for the history and character of the place with its mix of Roman Catholic, evangelical and Maximón worship. There are 35 evangelical temples in town as well as the house of the revered idol Maximón. The Easter celebrations here rival Antigua's for interest and colour. These are some of the most curious and reverential ceremonies in the world. If you only visit Guatemala once in your lifetime and it's at Easter and you can't bear to leave Antigua, come to Santiago at least for Good Friday. Commemorative events last all week and include Maximón as well as Christ.

You will be taken to the house of Maximón for a small fee. The fine church, with a wide nave decorated with colourful statues, was founded in 1547. The original roof was lost to earthquakes. There is a plaque dedicated to priest Father Francis Aplas Rother who was assassinated by the government in the church on 28 August 1981. At certain times of the year, the square is decked with streamers gently flapping in the breeze. The Tz'utujil women wear fine clothes and the men wear striped, half-length embroidered trousers (the most beautiful in Guatemala). There is a daily market, best on Friday and all sorts of artwork and crafts can be bought. **Asociación Cojol ya weaving centre** ① *T5499-5717, Mon-Fri 0900-1600, Sat 0900-1300, free, weaving tours also.* As well as Holy Week, the local fiesta takes place 23-27 July.

Near town is the hill, **Cerro de Oro**, with a small village of that name on the lake. The summit (1892 m) can be reached from the village in 45 minutes.

For more information on the **Lake Atitlán Medical project** and volunteer opportunities, see www.puebloapueblo.org.

## San Pedro La Laguna

San Pedro is a small town set on a tiny promontory with coffee bushes threaded around tracks lined with hostels and restaurants on the lakeside fringes. The tourists and long-term gringos have colonized the lakeside while the Tz'utujil Maya dominate the main part of the town up a very steep hill behind. San Pedro is now the favourite spot to hang out in for a couple of days or longer. It's a place to relax, to soak in hot baths, learn a bit of Spanish, horse ride and trek up Nariz de Maya. Some of the semi-permanent gringo inhabitants run bars and cafés or sell home-made jewellery and the like. The cobbled road from the dock facing Panajachel (known as the *muelle*) climbs up to the centre and another goes down, more or less at right angles, to the other dock (known as the *playa* or beach) facing Santiago with the town arranged around. There's a mazy network of *callejones* and paths that fringe the shoreline between the two ferries. Market days are Thursday and Sunday (better) and there's a fiesta 27-30 June with traditional dances.

# San Pedro La Laguna

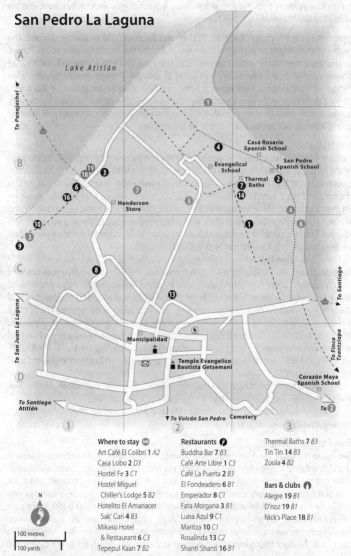

### Where to stay

Art Café El Colibri **1** A2
Casa Lobo **2** D3
Hostel Fe **3** C1
Hostel Miguel
  Chiller's Lodge **5** B2
Hotelito El Amanacer
  Sak' Cari **4** B3
Mikaso Hotel
  & Restaurant **6** C3
Tepepul Kaan **7** B2

### Restaurants

Buddha Bar **7** B3
Café Arte Libre **1** C3
Café La Puerta **2** B3
El Fondeadero **6** B1
Emperador **8** C1
Fata Morgana **3** B1
Luna Azul **9** C1
Maritza **10** C1
Rosalinda **13** C2
Shanti Shanti **16** B1

Thermal Baths **7** B3
Tin Tin **14** B3
Zoola **4** B2

### Bars & clubs

Alegre **19** B1
D'noz **19** B1
Nick's Place **18** B1

The town lies at the foot of the **Volcán San Pedro** (3020 m), which can be climbed in four to five hours, three hours down. It is now in the Parque Ecológico Volcán San Pedro, and the US$15 entrances includes the services of a guide. **Politur** also work in the park and there have been no incidents of robbery since the park's inauguration. Camping is possible. Go early (0530) for the view, because after 1000 the top is usually smothered in cloud; also you will be in the shade all the way up and part of the way down.

**Descubre San Pedro** has set up a museum of local culture and coffee, with natural medicine and Maya cosmovision tours.

Evangelical churches are well represented in San Pedro, and you can hardly miss the yellow and white **Templo Evangélico Bautista Getsemaní** in the centre. A visit to the rug-making cooperative on the beach is of interest and backstrap weaving is taught at some places. A session at the **thermal baths** ① *about US$10, Mon-Sat 0800-1900, best to reserve in advance*, is a relaxing experience. Note that the water is solar heated, not chemical hot springs. Massage is also available, US$10.

Canoes are made in San Pedro and hire is possible.

## San Juan La Laguna and Santa Clara La Laguna

The road north from San Pedro passes around a headland to San Juan La Laguna (2 km), a traditional lakeside town. Look for **Los Artesanos de San Juan** ① *8 Av, 6-20, Zona 2, T5963-9803*, and another image of Maximón displayed in the house opposite the Municipalidad. **Rupalaj Kistalin** ① *close to the textile store, LEMA, T5964-0040, daily 0800-1700*, is a highly recommended organization run by local guides. **LEMA** ① *T2425-9441, lema@sanjuanlalaguna.com*, the women weavers' association that uses natural dyes in their textiles, is also in town. Weaving classes (T7759-9126) are possible too. On the road towards San Pablo there's a good viewpoint from the hilltop with the cross; a popular walk. A more substantial walk, about three hours, is up behind the village to Santa Clara La Laguna, 2100 m, passing the village of **Cerro Cristalino** with its attractive, white church with images of saints around the walls.

## Santa María Visitación and San Pablo La Laguna

A short distance (500 m) to the west, separated by a gully, is a smaller village, Santa María Visitación. As with Santa Clara La Laguna, this is a typical highland village, and unspoilt by tourism. San Juan is connected to San Pablo by the lakeshore road, an attractive 4-km stretch mainly through coffee plantations. San Pablo, a busy village set 80 m above the lake, is known for rope making from *cantala* (maguey) fibres, which are also used for bags and fabric weaving.

## San Marcos La Laguna

San Marcos' location is deceptive with the main part of the community 'hidden' up the hill. The quiet village centre is set at the upper end of a gentle slope that runs 300 m through coffee and fruit trees down to the lake, reached by two paved walkways. If arriving by boat and staying in San Marcos, ask to be dropped at the Schumann or the Pirámides dock. The village has grown rapidly in the last few years with a focus on the spiritual and energy; there is a lot of massage, yoga, and all sorts of other therapies. It is the ideal place to be pampered. Beyond the centre 300 m to the east is the main dock of the village down a cobbled road. Down the two main pathways are the hotels; some with waterfront sites have their own docks. There is a slanting trail leaving the village up through dramatic scenery over to Santa Lucía Utatlán, passing close to Cerro San Marcos, 2918 m, the highest point in the region apart from the volcanoes.

## San Marcos to Santa Cruz

From the end of San Marcos where the stone track goes down to the dock, a rough track leads to **Tzununá**, passable for small trucks and 4WD vehicles, with views across the lake all the way. The village of Tzununá is along the tree-lined road through coffee plantations with a few houses up the valley behind. There is also a hotel with wonderful views (see Where to stay, below). There is a dock on the lakeside but no facilities. From here to Panajachel there are no roads or vehicular tracks and the villages can only be reached by boat, on horse or on foot. Also from here are some of the most spectacular views of the lake and the southern volcanoes. **Jaibalito** is smaller still than Tzununá, and hemmed in by the mountains with wonderful accommodation (see Where to stay, below). Arguably the best walk in the Atitlán area is from Jaibalito to Santa Cruz.

## Santa Cruz La Laguna

Santa Cruz village is set in the most dramatic scenery of the lake. Three deep ravines come down to the bay separating two spurs. A stone roadway climbs up the left-hand spur, picks up the main walking route from Jaibalito and crosses over a deep ravine (unfortunately used as a rubbish tip) to the plaza, on the only flat section of the right spur, about 120 m above the lake. The communal life of the village centres on the plaza. The hotels, one of them overflowing with flowers, are on the lakeshore. Behind the village are steep, rocky forested peaks, many too steep even for the locals to cultivate. The fiesta takes place 7-11 May.

There is good walking here. Apart from the lake route, strenuous hikes inland eventually lead to the Santa Lucía Utatlán–Sololá road. From the left-hand (west) ravine reached from the path that runs behind the lakeshore section, a trail goes through fields to an impossible looking gorge, eventually climbing up to Chaquijchoy, **Finca María Linda** and a trail to San José Chacayá (about four hours). In the reverse direction, the path southwest from San José leads to the Finca María Linda, which is close to the crater rim from where due south is a track to Jaibalito, to the left (east) round to the trail to Santa Cruz. Others follow the ridges towards San José and the road. These are for experienced hikers, and a compass (you are travelling due north) is essential if the cloud descends and there is no one to ask. From Santa Cruz to Panajachel along the coast is difficult, steep and unconsolidated, with few definitive paths. If you do get to the delta of the Río Quiscab, you may find private land is barred. The alternatives are either to go up to Sololá, about 6 km and 800 m up, or get a boat.

**Listings** Around Lake Atitlán *map p306.*

## Where to stay

### Santa Catarina Palopó

You can stay in private houses (ask around) or rent rooms (take a sleeping bag).

**$$$$ Casa Colibri**
*Carretera a San Antonio Palopó Km 6.7, entrada a Tzampoc Casa 4, T5353-5823, www.lacasacolibri.com.*

Beautifully designed and decorated, this plush vacation rental boasts an extravagant infinity pool overlooking the lake, sauna, fireplaces, and 5 luxurious guestrooms, all with en suite bathrooms. Tasteful and tranquil with space for 12 people.

**$$$$ Casa Palopó**
*Carretera a San Antonio Palopó, Km 6.8, less than 1 km beyond Santa Catarina, on the left up a steep hill, T5773-7777, www.casapalopo.com.*

One of the finest hotels in the country, 9 beautiful rooms all richly furnished, flowers on arrival, excellent service, heated pool, spa, gym and a top-class restaurant overlooking the lake. Reservations necessary.

### $$$$ Tzam Poc Resort
*Vía Rural Km 6.5, T7762-2680, www.atitlanresort.com.*
Resort on the slopes above Santa Catarina with an amazing infinity pool. Lovely villas and spa. There's also an archery range.

### $$$ Villa Santa Catarina
*T7762-1291, www.villasdeguatemala.com.*
36 comfortable rooms with balconies around the pool, most with view of the lake. Good restaurant.

### $$ Hotel Terrazas del Lago
*T7762-0157, www.hotelterrazasdellago.com.*
On the lake with view, bath, clean, restaurant, a unique hotel built up over the past 30 plus years.

## San Lucas Tolimán

### $$$ Toliman
*Av 6, 1 block from the lake, T7722-0033.*
18 rooms and suites in colonial style washed in terracotta colours with some lovely dark wood furniture. Suite No 1 is very romantic with lit steps to a sunken bath, good but expensive restaurant (reservations), fine gardens, pool, partial lake views. Recommended.

### $ Casa Cruz Inn
*Av 5 4-78, a couple of blocks from the park.*
Clean, comfortable beds, run by an elderly couple, garden, quiet, good value.

### $ Hotel y Restaurante Don Pedro
*Av 6, on lakeside, T7722-0028.*
An unattractive building in a sort of clumsy rustic style, a little rough around the edges, with 12 rooms, restaurant, bar.

### $ La Cascada de María
*Calle 6, 6-80, T7722-0136.*
With bath, TV, parking, garden, restaurant, good.

## Santiago Atitlán
Book ahead for Holy Week.

### $$$$ Lake Villa Guatemala
*Between Santiago and Cerro de Oro, 5 km from Santiago Atitlán, T5050-0767, www.lakevillaguatemala.com.*
This private villa with just 2 cosy guestrooms would particularly suit those seeking a spiritual retreat. With hilltop and lakeside views, the property offers numerous meditation spaces, including rooms, terraces and gardens. The food is gourmet vegan and the owners can arrange Mayan ceremonies and consultations with local healers. Minimum 2-night stay.

### $$$-$$ Posada de Santiago
*1.5 km south of town, T7721-7366, www.posadade santiago.com.*
Relaxing lakeside lodge with comfortable stone cottages (some cheaper accommodation), restaurant with home-grown produce and delicious food, tours and a pool. Massage and language classes arranged. Friendly and amusing management – David, Susie and his mum, Bonnie – quite a trio. Has its own dock or walk from town. Highly recommended.

### $$ Bambú
*On the lakeside, 500 m by road towards San Lucas, T7721-7332, www.ecobambu.com.*
10 rooms, 2 bungalows and 1 *casita* in an attractive setting with beautifully tended gardens, restaurant, a secluded pool, a few minutes by *lancha* from the dock. Kayaks available.

### $$ Mystical Yoga Farm
*Bahia de Atitlán, a 5-min boat ride from Santiago, T4860-9538, www.mysticalyogafarm.com.*
There are surely few better places to practice asanas than on the shores of Lake Atitlán.

Part of the **School Yoga Institute**, which has properties and yoga schools all over the world, the Mystical Yoga Farm offers all-inclusive packages which cover lodging, food, meditation, workshops, ceremonies and more. 3-night minimum stay.

### $ Chi-Nim-Ya
*Walk up from the dock, take the 1st left, walk 50 m and it's there on the left, T7721-7131.*
Clean, comfortable and friendly, cheaper without bath, good value, good café, cheap, large helpings.

### $ Tzutuhil
*On left up the road from the dock to centre, above Ferretería La Esquina, T7721-7174.*
With bath and TV, cheaper without, restaurant, great views, good.

### Camping
Camping is possible near **Bambú**.

## San Pedro La Laguna
Accommodation is mostly cheap and laid back; it's worth bringing your own sleeping bag.

### $$$ Casa Lobo
*6 Av, Callejon B, on the lakeshore, 200 m after Villa Cuba, 15 mins' walk out of town, www.casalobo.org.*
Set in verdant grounds overlooking the lake, German-owned Casa Lobo is a secluded colonial-style property with a range of bungalows, apartments and houses, all tastefully furnished and fully equipped with Wi-Fi, stove, fridge and cable TV. 2-night minimum stay.

### $$-$ Mikaso Hotel Resto
*Callejon A, I-82, T7721-8232, www.mikasohotel.com.*
Owned and managed by a family from Quebec, **Mikaso** has great lake views and a good restaurant serving wood-fired pizzas and crêpes. Private rooms are clean and cosy ($$) and for the thrifty there's 6 and 8-bed dorms ($). Facilities include a hot tub,

roof terrace, pool table, shared kitchen and Swedish massage. Occasional live music.

### $ Art Café El Colibri
*Behind Colegio Bethel, in front of the museum Tzununya, T7721-8378, www.colibrisanpedro.com.*
Colibri offers Spanish and painting classes and is also home to an art gallery, restaurant-cafe and a small B&B with 3 quiet, no-frills rooms, all equipped with hot showers. Owned by a local artist, very chilled place, simple and down to earth, lovely atmosphere complete with friendly dogs.

### $ Hostel Fe
*Calle Principal, turn right from the boat dock, then 60 m along the lake on the left, T3486-7027, www.hostelfe.com.*
If you're in San Pedro to party, try Hostel Fe. Perched on the edge of the water, their restaurant-bar is buzzing with action every most evening; Tue is Ladies' Night, Fri is quiz night. Other sources of entertainment include a diving platform, board games, darts and live music. Accommodation is in basic dorms and private rooms.

### $ Hostel Miguel Chiller's Lodge
*Opposite Yo Mama Hostel.*
Managed by the friendly Miguel and his family, this quiet, low-key hostel has a handful of simple private rooms and dorm accommodation. Amenities include Wi-Fi, shared kitchen, lounge and barbecue. There are great views of San Pedro volcano from the roof terrace. Relaxed and hospitable. Good breakfast included.

### $ Hotelito El Amanacer Sak' Cari
*T7721-8096, www.hotelsakcari.com.*
With bath, hot water, lovely rooms with great garden, ask for those with fabulous lake views. Extremely good value. Recommended.

### $ Tepepul Kaan
*6 Calle 5-10, take the 2nd left heading up from the Pana boat dock, T4301-2271, www.hoteltepepulkaan.com.*

This ultra-economical hotel offers basic rooms with bath for about US$10 a night and donates 25% of the rates to scholarship funds for local students. Facilities include kitchen, hammocks, lawn and lake view. They claim to offer the 'best deal' in San Pedro and they may be right.

## San Juan La Laguna

### $$$-$$ Hotel Uxlabil
*T5990-6016/2366-9555 (in Guatemala City),*
*www.uxlabil.com.*
This is an eco-hotel set up on the hill with its own dock (flooded, like all the village shore, in 2010), a short walk from the town centre. It's run by very friendly people with a small restaurant, and beautiful views from its rooftop terrace. It is a perfect, relaxing getaway, with a Maya sauna and tended gardens, in this most unassuming and interesting of towns. It has links with the ecotourism association in town. Recommended.

## San Marcos La Laguna

### $$$-$$ Aaculaax
*Las Pirámides dock, on a path from the Centro Holístico, T5287-0521, www.aaculaax.com.*
A Hansel-and-Gretel affair on the lakeshore, run by German Niels. It is a blend of cave work with Gaudí-type influence from the stained-glass work down to the sculptures and lamp shades. A corner of artistic nirvana on Lake Atitlán. Each of the 7 rooms with private bathroom is different, with quirky decor. It is run on an eco-basis, with compost toilets and all. There is a restaurant, bar, bakery and massage room, as well as glass and papier mâché workshops. Highly recommended.

### $$ Posada del Bosque Encantado
*Barrio 3, T4146-1050, www.hotel posadaencantado.com.*
Rustic and arty, this colonial-style guesthouse features spacious, earthy, brick-built rooms with solid wood doors, red tile roofs, terracotta floors, Mayan textiles and

stonework. The garden is so verdant and lush it is like a mini-jungle. Their restaurant serves *comida típica*.

### $ Hotel Jinava
*2nd dock, left at the top of 1st pathway, T5299-3311, www.hoteljinava.com.*
This is heaven on a hill. With fabulous views, this German-owned place clings to a steep slope with lovely rooms, restaurants, terraces and a patio. There are books and games or solitude if you want it. It's close to the lakeshore with its own dock where launches will drop you. There are only 5 rooms, breakfast included. Recommended.

### $ Hotel Paco Real
*Barrio 3, T4688-3715,*
*www.pacorealatitlan.com.*
Located 50 m from the lake, Paco Real has simple but comfortable rooms inside wood and stone-built *cabañas*, with or without private bath. Also on site is a *temazcal* sauna, lush garden, Wi-Fi, bar-restaurant, movie projector and book exchange.

### $ Las Pirámides del Ka
*Las Pirámides dock,*
*www.laspiramidesdelka.com.*
A residential meditation centre.
See also What to do, below.

### $ Unicornio
*Las Pirámides dock, 2nd pathway.*
With self-catering, bungalows, shared kitchen and bathrooms. It also has a little post office.

## San Marcos to Santa Cruz

### $$$ Lomas de Tzununá
*Tzununá, T7820-4060,*
*www.lomasdetzununa.com.*
This hotel enjoys a spectacular position high up above the lake. The views from the restaurant terrace are magnificent. The 10 spacious rooms, decorated with local textiles, have 2 beds each with lake views and a balcony. The hotel, run by a friendly Belgian family, offers walking, biking,

kayaking and cultural tours. The restaurant ($$-$) uses home-made ingredients, the hotel is run on solar energy and the pool does not use chlorine. Board games, internet, bar and giant chess available. The family are reforesting a hill. Breakfast and taxes included.

### $$ La Casa del Mundo
*Jaibalito, T5218-5332,*
*www.lacasadelmundo.com.*
Enjoys one of the most spectacular positions on the entire lake. Room No 15 has the best view followed by room No 1. Cheaper rooms have shared bathrooms. Many facilities, standard family-style dinner, lakeside hot tub, a memorable place with fantastic views. Repeatedly recommended.

## Santa Cruz La Laguna

### $$$$ Laguna Lodge
*1 Tzantizotz, Santa Cruz La Laguna,*
*T4066-8135, www.thelagunalodge.com.*
Overlooking the lake, this luxury boutique hotel features tasteful suites beautifully decorated with handmade furniture and antiques. A stunning setting, exquisite design and impeccably executed. Spa services available. Romantic and restful. Recommended.

### $$$ La Fortuna
*Patzisotz Bay, between Panajachel and Santa Cruz, T5203-1033, www.lafortunaatitlan.com.*
A truly green venture with solar energy and all natural building materials, this self-described 'nano boutique hotel' is a very romantic option with its 4 luxury bungalows set in beautifully landscaped grounds. Secluded and tranquil, the perfect getaway.

### $$$-$$ Villa Sumaya
*Paxanax, beyond the dock, about 15 mins' walk, T5810-7199, www.villasumaya.com.*
With its own dock, this comfortable, peaceful place has a sauna, massage and healing therapies and yoga. Rates include breakfast.

### $$-$ Arca de Noé
*To the left of the dock, T5515-3712.*
Bungalows, cheaper rooms with shared bathrooms, good restaurant, barbecue, lake activities arranged, nice atmosphere, veranda overlooking a really beautiful flower-filled gardens and the lake. Low-voltage solar power.

### $$-$ La Casa Rosa
*To the right as you face the dock from the water, along a path, T5416-1251, www.atitlanlacasarosa.com.*
Bungalows and rooms, with bath, cheaper without, home-made meals, attractive garden, sauna. Candlelit dinners at weekends.

### $$-$ La Iguana Perdida
*Opposite dock, T5706-4117,*
*www.laiguanaperdida.com.*
Rooms with and without bathroom and dorm ($ per person) with shared bath, lively, especially weekends, delicious vegetarian food, barbecue, popular, friendly, great atmosphere. **ATI Divers** centre (see What to do, below), waterskiing; kayaks and snorkelling. Bring a torch.

## Restaurants

### San Lucas Tolimán

### $ La Pizza de Sam
*Av 7, 1 block down from the plaza towards the lake.*
Pizzas and spaghetti.

### $ Restaurant Jardín
*Orange building on corner of plaza.*
*Comida típica* and *licuados*.

### Santiago Atitlán
There are many cheap *comedores* near the centre. The best restaurants are at the hotels.

### $$$ El Pescador
*On corner 1 block before Tzutuhil.*
Full menu, good but expensive.

**\$\$\$ Posada de Santiago**
*1.5 km south of town, T7721-7167.*
Delicious, wholesome food and
excellent service in lovely surroundings.
Highly recommended.

**\$ Restaurant Wach'alal**
*Close to Gran Sol. Daily 0800-2000.*
A small yellow-painted café serving
breakfasts, snacks and cakes. Airy
and pleasant.

## San Pedro La Laguna
Be careful of drinking water in San Pedro;
both cholera and dysentery exist here.

**\$\$-\$ Café Arte Libre**
*Up the hill from Hotel San Pedro.*
All meals, vegetarian dishes, good value.

**\$\$-\$ Luna Azul**
*Along shore.*
Popular for breakfast and lunch,
good omelettes.

**\$\$-\$ Restaurant Maritza**
With commanding views over lake. Chilled
place to hang out with reggae music. Service
is slow though. 5 rooms also to rent with
shared bath (\$).

**\$\$-\$ Tin Tin**
Good value. Thai food, delightful garden.
Recommended.

**\$ Buddha Bar**
Shows movies every night and has a rooftop
and sports bar.

**\$ Café La Puerta**
*On the north shore coastal path.*
*Daily 0800-1700.*
Cheap, tasty dishes, with tables in a quirky
garden, or looking out over the lake.
Beautiful setting.

**\$ Comedor Sta Elena**
*Near Nick's Italian.*
Seriously cheap and filling breakfasts.

**\$ El Fondeadero**
Good food, lovely terraced gardens,
reasonable prices.

**\$ Emperador**
*Up the hill.*
*Comedor* serving good local dishes.

**\$ Fata Morgana**
*Near the Panajachel dock.*
Great focaccia bread sandwiches, with pizza
and fine coffee too.

**\$ Rosalinda**
*Near centre of village.*
Friendly, breakfasts (eg *mosh*), local fish and
good for banana and chocolate cakes.

**\$ Thermal Baths**
*Along shore from playa.*
Good vegetarian food and coffee, but
it's expensive.

**\$ Zoola**
*Close to the north shore. Open 0900-2100.*
A quiet, hideaway with pleasant garden.
A great spot.

## San Marcos La Laguna
All hotels and hostels offer food.

**\$\$-\$ Il Giardino**
*Up the 2nd pathway.*
Attractive garden, Italian owners,
good breakfasts.

## Bars and clubs

### San Pedro La Laguna
**Nick's Place**, overlooking the main dock, is
popular, and well frequented in the evening.
Nearby are **Bar Alegre**, a sports bar (www.
thealegrepub.com) and **D'noz**. **Ti Kaaj** is
another popular spot.

## What to do

### Santiago Atitlán
**Aventura en Atitlán**, *Jim and Nancy Matison,
Finca San Santiago, T7811-5516. 10 km outside
Santiago.* Riding and hiking tours.

**Francisco Tizná** *from the Asociación de Guías de Turismo, T7721-7558*. Extremely informative. Ask for him at the dock or at any of the hotels. Payment is by way of donation.

## San Pedro La Laguna

There is a growing list of activities available in San Pedro, from hiking up the Nariz de Maya (5 hrs, US$13) and other local trips, through to local crafts. Yoga for all levels is available down towards the shore (US$5 for 1½ hrs).

### Language schools

San Pedro is a popular place for learning Spanish. Students may make their own accommodation arrangements but homestays are possible.

**Casa Rosario**, *www.casarosario.com*. Offers classes from US$70 a week for 20 hrs' tuition.

**Corazón Maya**, *T7721-8160, www. corazonmaya.com*. Classes from US$49 a week. Tz'utujil classes also. Run by the welcoming Marta Navichoc.

**San Pedro**, *T5715-4604, www.sanpedro spanishschool.org*. Classes from US$75 per week. The school has a great location with gardens close to the lakeshore.

### San Juan La Laguna

**Rupalaj Kistalin**, *T5964-0040, rupalajkistalin@yahoo.es*. Offers interesting cultural tours of the town visiting painters, weavers, *cofradías* and traditional healers. As well as this cultural circuit there is an adventure circuit taking in Panan forest and a canopy tour at Park Chuiraxamolo' or a nature circuit taking in a climb up the Rostro de Maya and fishing and kayaking. Some of the local guides speak English. Highly recommended.

### San Marcos La Laguna

**Body and soul**

**Casa Azul Eco Resort**, *T5070-7101, www. casa-azul-ecoresort.com*. A gorgeous little place offering yoga and reiki, among other therapies and writers' workshops hosted by Joyce Maynard. There's also a sauna, campfire and café/restaurant serving vegetarian food. You can reach it from the first dock, or from the centre of the village.

**Kaivalya Yoga and Ashram**, *50 m on the left after the Lion's gate at the entrance to San Marcos, T3199-1344, www. yogaretreatguatemala.com*. Spiritual seekers may find illumination at this interesting ashram which offers everything from yoga and meditation classes to 'dark retreats'.

**Las Pirámides del Ka**, *www.laspiramides delka.com*. The month-long course costs US$420, or US$15 by the day if you stay for shorter periods, accommodation included. Courses are also available for non-residents. In the grounds are a sauna, a vegetarian restaurant with freshly baked bread and a library. This is a relaxing, peaceful place.

**San Marcos Holistic Centre**, *up the 2nd pathway, beyond Unicornio, www. sanmholisticcentre.com*. Mon-Sat 1000-1700. Offers iridology, acupuncture, kinesiology, Indian head massage, reflexology and massage. Classes in various techniques can also be taken.

## Transport

### Santa Catarina Palopó

There are frequent pickups from Panajachel and boat services.

### San Antonio Palopó

Frequent pickups from Panajachel. Enquire about boats.

### San Lucas Tolimán

**Boat**

Enquire about boats. Private *lancha*, US$35.

**Bus**

To **Santiago Atitlán**, hourly and to **Guatemala City** via **Panajachel**.

## Santiago Atitlán

### Boat

4 sailings daily to Pana with *Naviera*, 1¼ hrs, US$1.80, or by *lancha* when full, 20-35 mins, US$1.30-2. To **San Pedro** by *lancha* several a day, enquire at the dock for times, 45 mins, US$1.80.

### Bus

To **Guatemala City**, US$2.60 (5 a day, first at 0300). 2 **Pullmans** a day, US$3.40. To **Panajachel**, 0600, 2 hrs, or take any bus and change on main road south of San Lucas.

## San Pedro La Laguna

### Boat

Up to 10 *lanchas* to **Panajachel**. To **Santiago**, leave when full (45 mins, US$2.50). To **San Marcos**, every 2 hrs. Private *lanchas* (10 people at US$2 each).

### Bus

There are daily buses to **Guatemala City**, several leave in the early morning and early afternoon, 4 hrs, US$4.50, to **Antigua** and to **Quetzaltenango**, in the morning, 3½ hrs, US$3.

## San Marcos La Laguna

### Boat

Service roughly every ½ hr to **Panajachel** and to **San Pedro**. Wait on any dock. Fare US$1.80 to either.

### Bus

San Pedro to Pan-American Hwy can be boarded at San Pablo. **Pickup** Frequent pickups from the village centre and anywhere along the main road. To **San Pedro**, US$0.50, less to villages en route.

## Chichicastenango  *Colour map 2, C4.*

*famous for its market where hundreds come for a bargain*

★Chichicastenango (altitude 2071 m) is a curious blend of mysticism and commercialism. On market mornings the steps of the church are blanketed in flowers as the women, in traditional dress, fluff up their skirts, amid baskets of lilies, roses and blackberries. But, with its mixture of Catholic and indigenous religion readily visible, it is more than just a shopping trolley stop. On a hilltop peppered with pine, villagers worship at a Mayan shrine; in town, a time-honoured tradition of brotherhoods focuses on saint worship. Coupled with the mist that encircles the valley in the late afternoon, you can sense an air of intrigue.

A large plaza is the focus of the town, with two white churches facing one another: **Santo Tomás** the parish church and **Calvario**. Santo Tomás, founded in 1540, is open to visitors, although photography is not allowed, and visitors are asked to be discreet and enter by a side door (through an arch to the right). Next to Santo Tomás are the cloisters of the Dominican monastery (1542). Here the famous *Popol Vuh* manuscript of the Maya creation story was found. A human skull wedged behind a carved stone face, found in Sacapulas, can be seen at the **Museo Arqueológico Regional** ① *main plaza, Tue, Wed, Fri, Sat 0800-1200, 1400-1600, Thu 0800-1600, Sun 0800-1400, closed Mon, US$0.70, photographs and video camera not permitted.* There's also a jade collection once owned by 1926-1944 parish priest Father Rossbach. The **tourist office** ① *5 Av and Teatro Municipalidad, 1 block from church, T7756-2022, daily 0800-2000*, is helpful and provides a free leaflet with map, and local tour information.

The Sunday and Thursday markets are both very touristy, and bargains are harder to come by once shuttle-loads of people arrive mid-morning. Articles from all over the Highlands are available: rugs, carpets and bedspreads; walk one or two streets away from the main congregation of stalls for more realistic prices, but prices are cheaper in Panajachel for the same items and you won't find anything here that you can't find in Panajachel.

The idol, **Pascual Abaj**, a god of fertility, is a large black stone with human features on a hill overlooking the town. Crosses in the ground surrounding the shrine are prayed in front of for the health of men, women and children, and for the dead. Fires burn and the wax of a thousand candles, flowers and sugar cover the shrine. One ceremony you may see is that of a girl from the town requesting a good and sober husband. If you wish to undergo a ceremony to plead for a partner, or to secure safety from robbery or misfortune, you may ask the *curandero* (US$7 including photographs). To reach the deity, walk along 5 Avenida, turn right on 9 Calle, down the hill, cross the stream and take the second track from the left going steepest uphill, which passes directly through a farmhouse and buildings. The farm now belongs to a mask-maker whom you can visit and buy masks from. Follow the path to the top of the pine-topped hill where you may well see a Maya ceremony in progress. It's about 30 minutes' walk. The site can be easily visited independently (in a small group), or an INGUAT-approved guide arranged through the local tourist committee can take you there and explain its history and significance (US$6.50, one or two hours, identified by a license in town).

# Chichicastenango

*To Santa Cruz del Quiché*

Arco
Gucumatz

Buses to Quiché
& Ixil Triangle

Cemetery

Calvario    Plaza

Museo
Arqueológico
Regional    Alcaldía

Maya
Chichi Van

Dominican
Monastery    Santo
Tomás

*Mask Factory & Pascual Abaj*    *To ❶❷❻, Guatemala City & Los Encuentros*

| Where to stay | Salvador 6 | La Villa de los Cofrades 4 |
| N | Chalet House 3 | Santo Tomás 11 | Las Brasas Steak House 5 |
| | Chugüilá 4 | Tuttos 2 | Tu Café 3 |
| | Mayan Inn 8 | | Tziguan Tinamit 6 |
| | Pensión Girón 9 | **Restaurants** | |
| 200 metres | Posada Belén 1 | La Fonda de Tzijolaj 4 | |
| 200 yards | Posada El Arco 5 | La Parrillada 2 | |

## BACKGROUND

### Chichicastenango

Often called 'Chichi' but also known as Santo Tomás, Chichicastenango is the hub of the Maya-K'iche' highlands. The name derives from the *chichicaste*, a prickly purple plant-like a nettle, which grows profusely, and *tenango*, meaning 'place of'. Today the locals call the town 'Siguan Tinamit' meaning 'place surrounded by ravines'. The townsfolk are also known as Masheños, which comes from the word Max, also meaning Tomás. About 1000 ladinos live in the town, but 20,000 Maya live in the hills nearby and flood the town for the Thursday and Sunday markets. The town itself has winding streets of white houses roofed with bright red tiles, which wander over a little knoll in the centre of a cup-shaped valley surrounded by high mountains.

The men's traditional outfit is a short-waisted embroidered jacket and knee breeches of black cloth, a woven sash and an embroidered kerchief around the head. The cost of this outfit, now over US$200, means that fewer and fewer men are wearing it. Women wear *huipiles* with red embroidery against black or brown and their *cortes* skirts have dark blue stripes.

## Listings Chichicastenango *map p316*

### Where to stay

You won't find accommodation easily on Sat evening, when prices are increased. As soon as you get off the bus, boys will swamp you and insist on taking you to certain hotels.

**$$$ Mayan Inn**
*Corner of 8 Calle, 1-91, T7756-1176, www.mayaninn.com.gt.*
A classic, colonial-style courtyard hotel, filled with plants, polished antique furniture, beautiful dining room and bar with fireplaces. Gas-heated showers and internet. The staff are very friendly and wear traditional dress. Secure parking.

**$$$ Santo Tomás**
*7 Av, 5-32, T7756-1061.*
A very attractive building with beautiful colonial furnishings and parrots in patios. There's a pool, sauna, good restaurant and bar. It is often full at weekends. Buffet lunch

(US$14) is served on market days in the stylish dining room, with attendants in traditional dress.

**$$ Posada El Arco**
*4 Calle, 4-36, T7756-1255.*
Clean, very pretty, small, friendly, garden, washing facilities, negotiate lower rates for stays longer than a night, some large rooms, good view, parking, English spoken.

**$$-$ Chalet House**
*3 Calle, 7-44, T7756-1360, www.chalethotelguatemala. com.* A clean, guesthouse with family atmosphere, hot water. Don't be put off by the dingy street.

**$ Chugüilá**
*5 Av, 5-24, T7756-1134, hotelchuguila@yahoo.com.*
Some rooms have fireplaces. Avoid the front rooms, which are noisy. There's also a restaurant.

## $ Pensión Girón
*Edif Girón on 6 Calle, 4-52, T7756-1156.*
Clean rooms with bath, cheaper without,
hot water, parking.

## $ Posada Belén
*12 Calle, 5-55, T7756-1244.*
With bath, cheaper without, hot water, clean,
will do laundry, fine views from balconies
and hummingbirds in attractive garden,
good value. Recommended.

## $ Salvador
*10 Calle, 4-47.*
Large rooms with bath, a few with fireplaces
(you can buy wood in the market), good
views over town, parking. Cheaper, smaller
rooms without bath available.

## $ Tuttos
*12 Calle, near Posada Belén, T7756-7540.*
Reasonable rooms.

## Restaurants

The best food is in the top hotels, but is
expensive. On market days there are plenty
of good food stalls and *comedores* in the
centre of the plaza that offer chicken in
different guises or a set lunch for US$1.50.

There are several good restaurants in
the Centro Comercial Santo Tomás, on the
north side of the plaza (market).

## $$ La Fonda de Tzijolaj
*On the plaza.*
Great view of the market below, good meals,
pizza, prompt service, reasonable prices.

## $$ Las Brasas Steak House
*6 Calle 4-52, T7756-2226.*
Nice atmosphere, good steak menu, accepts
credit cards.

## $$-$ La Villa de los Cofrades
*On the plaza.*
Café downstairs, breakfasts, cappuccinos,
espressos, good value. There is a 2nd
restaurant 2 blocks up the street towards
Arco Gucumatz, which is more expensive

but has a great people-watching upstairs
location. An escape during market days,
and popular for breakfast.

## $$-$ Tziguan Tinamit
*On the corner of 5 Av, esq 6 Calle.*
Some local dishes, steaks, tasty pizzas,
breakfasts, good pies but a little more
expensive than most places, good.

## $ Caffé Tuttos
*See Where to stay. Daily 0700-2200.*
Good breakfast deals, pizzas, and
*menú del día*, reasonable prices.

## $ La Parrillada
*6 C 5-37, Interior Comercial Turkaj.*
Escape the market bustle, courtyard,
reasonable prices, breakfast available.

## $ Tu Café
*5 Av 6-44, on market place, Santo Tomás side.*
*Open 0730-2000.*
Snacks, budget breakfast, sandwiches,
set lunch, good value.

## Festivals

**1 Jan** Padre Eterno.
**20 Jan** San Sebastián.
**19 Mar** San José.
**Feb/Apr** Jesús Nazareno and María de
Dolores (both Fri in Lent).
**Mar/Apr** Semana Santa (Holy Week).
**29 Apr** San Pedro Mártir.
**3 May** Santa Cruz.
**29 Jun** Corpus Christi.
**18 Aug** Virgen de la Coronación.
**14 Sep** Santa Cruz.
**29 Sep** San Miguel.
**30 Sep** San Jerónimo Doctor.
**1st Sun of Oct** Virgen del Rosario.
**2nd Sun in Oct** Virgen de Concepción.
**1 Nov** San Miguel.
**13-22 Dec** Santo Tomás, with 21 Dec
being the main day. There are processions,
traditional dances, the *Palo Volador* (19, 20,
21 Dec) marimba music, well worth a visit –
very crowded.

# ON THE ROAD

## Markets

Market days in Guatemala are alive with colour and each community is characterized by unique clothes and crafts. Simply wandering through the labyrinthine stalls amid the frenetic throng of colour, noise, aromas and movement is a potent and memorable experience.

Markets run the gamut from low-key indoor bazaars to massive, sprawling outdoor events that draw traders from across the country. The most famous takes place in the town of **Chichicastenango**, an hour north of Lake Atitlán, where Maya and visitors converge in a twice-weekly frenzy of produce and textile shopping. It is a superb venue for souvenir purchases and the quintessential Guatemala market experience. **Sololá**, 20 minutes from Panajachel, hosts a Friday market that is always crowded with locals but rarely visited by foreigners, so it's an authentic slice of Mayan culture. For sheer size and scope, don't miss the Friday market at **San Francicso de Alto**, the largest, busiest and best stocked open-air market in Central America.

When shopping, bartering is the norm and almost expected; sometimes, unbelievable discounts can be obtained. You won't do better anywhere else in Central America, but getting the discount is less important than paying a fair price. Woven goods are normally cheapest bought in the town of origin. Try to avoid middlemen and buy direct from the weaver. Guatemalan coffee is highly recommended, although the best is exported; coffee sold locally is not vacuum-packed.

### Shopping

Chichicastenango's markets are on Sun and Thu. See box, above.

**Ut'z Bat'z**, *5a Avenida and 5a Calle, T5008-5193*. Women's Fair Trade weaving workshop, with free demonstrations; high-quality clothes and bags for sale.

### What to do

**Chichicastenango**
**Maya Chichi Van**, *6 Av, 6-45, T7756-2187, mayachichivan@yahoo.com*. Shuttles and tours ranging from US$10-650.

### Transport

**Bus**
Buses passing through Chichi all stop at 5 Av/5 Calle by the **Hotel Chugüilá**, where there are always police and bus personnel

to give information. To **Guatemala City**, every 15 mins 0200-1730, 3 hrs, US$3.70. To **Santa Cruz del Quiché**, every ½ hr 0600-2000, US$0.70, 30 mins or 20 mins, if the bus driver is aiming for honours in the graduation from the School of Kamikaze Bus Tactics. To **Panajachel**, ½ hr, US$2, several until early afternoon or take any bus heading south and change at Los Encuentros. Same goes for **Antigua**, where you need to change at Chimaltenango. To **Quetzaltenango**, 5 between 0430-0830, 2½ hrs, US$3.80. To **Mexico**, and all points west, take any bus to Los Encuentros and change. To **Escuintla** via Santa Lucía Cotzumalguapa, between 0300 and 1700, 3 hrs, US$2.80. There are additional buses to local villages especially on market days.

**Shuttles** These operate to **Guatemala City**, **Xela**, **Panajachel**, **Huehuetenango** and **Mexican border**. See Maya Chichi Van, in What to do, above.

Santa Cruz del Quiché (population 7750, altitude 2000 m), often simply called Quiché, attracts few tourists here and prices are consequently reasonable. Its main attraction is Utatlán, the remains of the Maya K'iche' capital. The large Parque Central has a military garrison on the east side with a jail on the lower floor and a sinister military museum with reminders of recent conflicts above. The date of the town's fiesta varies around the Assumption but is usually held around 14-20 August.

Three kilometres away are the remains of temples and other structures of the former Quiché capital, **Gumarcaj**, sometimes spelt **K'umarkaaj**, and now generally called **Utatlán** ① *0800-1700, US$1.30, from the bus station, walk west along 10 Calle for 40 mins until you reach a small junction with a blue sign (SECP), take the right lane up through gates to the site.* The city was largely destroyed by the Spaniards, but the stonework of the original buildings can be seen in the ruins, which can be reached on foot; the setting is very attractive and well maintained. There are two subterranean burial chambers (take a torch, as there are unexpected drops) still used by the Maya for worship and chicken sacrifices. The seven plazas, many temples, ball court, gladiator's archway and other features are marked.

There is a paved road east from Quiché to (8 km) **Santo Tomás Chiché**, a picturesque village with a fine, rarely visited Saturday market (fiesta 25-28 December). There is also a road to this village from Chichicastenango. Although it is a short-cut, it is rough and virtually impassable in any vehicle. It makes a good, three- to four-hour walk, however. Further east (45 km) from Chiché is **Zacualpa**, where beautiful woollen bags are woven. The church has a remarkably fine façade and there is an unnamed *pensión* near the plaza. Market days are Sunday and Thursday.

At **Joyabaj** women weave fascinating *huipiles* and there is a colourful Sunday market, followed by a procession at about noon from the church led by the elders with drums and pipes. This was a stopping place on the old route from Mexico to Antigua. There is good walking in the wooded hills around, for example north to Chorraxaj (two hours), or across the Río Cocol south to Piedras Blancas to see blankets being woven. During fiesta week (9-15 August) Joyabaj has a *Palo Volador* and other traditional dances. There is a restaurant next to the Esso station on the Santa Cruz end of the plaza with a bank opposite (will change US dollars cash).

### The road east to Cobán

The road east from **Sacapulas** is one of the most beautiful mountain roads in all Guatemala, with magnificent scenery in the narrow valleys. There is accommodation in **Uspantán** and this is the place to stay for the night enroute to Cobán. The road is not paved beyond Uspantán.

It's a five-hour walk from Uspantán south to **Chimul**, the birthplace of **Rigoberta Menchú**, Nobel Peace Prize winner in 1992. The village was virtually wiped out during the 1980s, but the settlement is coming to life again. Only pickups go to the village.

## Where to stay

There are several very basic options around the bus arrival/departure area.

**$ Rey K'iché**
*8 Calle, 0-9, 2 blocks from bus terminal.*
Clean, comfortable, hot water, parking, restaurant, TV.

**$ San Pascual**
*7 Calle, 0-43, 2 blocks south of the central plaza, T5555-1107.*
Good location, with bath, cheaper without, quiet, locked parking.

### The road east to Cobán

There are a couple of *hospedajes* in Uspantán.

**$ Galindo**
*4 blocks east of the Parque Central.*
Clean, friendly, recommended.

## Restaurants

Try *sincronizadas*, hot tortillas baked with cubed ham, spiced chicken and cheese.

**$ La Cabañita Café**
*1 Av, 1-17.*
Charming, small café with pinewood furniture, home-made pies and cakes, excellent breakfasts (pancakes, cereals, etc), eggs any way you want 'em, and great snacks, such as *sincronizadas*.

**$ La Toscan**
*1 Av just north of the church, same road as La Cabañita.*
A little pizza and *pastelería* with checked cloth-covered tables. Lasagne lunch a bargain with garlic bread and pizza by the slice also.

## Transport

### Bus

Terminal at 10 Calle y 1 Av, Zona 5.
To **Guatemala City**, passing through **Chichicastenango**, at 0300 until 1700, 3 hrs, US$4.50. To **Nebaj** and **Cotzal**, 8 a day, US$3.20, 2 hrs. Buses leave, passing through Sacapulas (1 hr, US$2.50), roughly every hour from 0800-2100. To **Uspantán**, via **Sacapulas**, for **Cobán** and **San Pedro Carchá** every hour, 2 hrs, US$3.90. To **Joyabaj**, several daily, via Chiché and Zacualpa, US$1.80, 1½ hrs. 1st at 0800 with buses going on to the capital. Last bus back to Quiché at 1600. It is possible to get to **Huehuetenango** in a day via Sacapulas, then pickup from bridge to **Aguacatán** and bus from there to Huehuetenango. Last bus to Huehue from Aguacatán, 1600. Daily buses also to **Quetzaltenango**, **San Marcos**, and to **Panajachel**. To **Joyabaj**, Joyita bus from Guatemala City, 10 a day between 0200 and 1600, 5 hrs, US$1.80. There are buses from Quiché to **San Andrés Sajcabaja**.

### The road east to Cobán
### Bus and truck

Several trucks to Cobán, daily in the morning from **Sacapulas**; 7 hrs if you're lucky, usually much longer. Start very early if you wish to make it to Cobán the same day. **Transportes Mejía** from Aguacatán to **Cobán** stops in Sacapulas on Tue and Sat mornings. Also possible to take Quiché–Uspantán buses (0930, 1300, 1500), passing Sacapulas at about 1030, 1400, 1600. Then take the early morning buses at 0300 and 0500 from Uspantán to Cobán or the **Transportes Mejía** buses. After that, pickups leave when full. Hitchhiking to Cobán is also possible. Buses to **Quiché** 0300, 2200, other early morning departures.

The Ixil Triangle is made of up of the highland communities of Nebaj, Chajul and Cotzal set in the beautiful Cuchumatanes mountains, although sadly, out of local necessity, many of the slopes have been badly deforested and the wood burnt for fires. The traditional dress of the Nebaj women – an explosion of primary colours – is spectacular. Much of this area was decimated during the Civil War and then repopulated with the introduction of 'model villages' established by the government. Evidence of wartime activities can still be seen and more remote Maya Ixil-speaking villages are gradually opening up to visitors with the introduction of hostel and trekking facilities.

## Nebaj and around

The town of Nebaj is high in the Cuchumatanes Mountains and its green slopes are often layered with mist. It is coloured by the beautiful dress worn by the local women, in an extravaganza of predominantly green, with red, yellow, orange, white and purple. The *corte* is mainly maroon with vertical stripes of black and yellow; some are bright red, and the *huipil* is of a geometric design. The women also wear a headdress with colourful bushy pom-poms on them. The men hardly ever wear the traditional costume; their jacket is red and embroidered in black designs. The main plaza is dominated by a large, simple white church. At the edge of the plaza there are weaving cooperatives selling *cortes*, *huipiles* and handicrafts from the town and the surrounding area – bargaining is possible. When you arrive, boys will meet you from incoming buses and will guide you to a *hospedaje* – they expect a tip. Nebaj has Sunday and Thursday markets and a fiesta on 12-15 August with traditional dancing. There is an excellent website for Nebaj, www.nebaj.com, run by Solidaridad Internacional, with useful phrases in Ixil and your daily Maya horoscope. There's a **tourist office**ⓘ *6a Av and 8a Calle Cantón Vitzal, T7755-8337.*

La Tumba de la Indígena Maya is a shrine a 15-minute walk outside Nebaj where some of those massacred during the war were buried. Take the same route as to Ak'Tzumbal, but at the bottom of the very steep hill, immediately after the bridge over the river, take a left, walk straight on over a paved road, then you come to a small junction – carry straight on until you see a minor crossroads on a path with an orange house gate to your left. Look up and you will see a small building. This is the shrine. Walk to your right where you will see a steep set of stairs leading to the shrine.

There is a walk to **Ak'Tzumbal**, through fields with rabbits, and through long, thin earth tunnels used by the military and guerrillas during the war. You need a guide to walk this cross-country route. Alternatively, you can take the road to Ak'Tzumbal, where the new houses still display signs warning of the danger of land mines. Walk down 15 Avenida de Septiembre away from the church, and take a left just before **El Triangulo** gas station past **El Viajero Hospedaje**, then left and then right down a very steep hill and keep walking (1½ hours). When you reach a small yellow tower just before a fork take the right (the left goes to Salquil Grande) to reach the model village. Above the village of Ak'Tzumbal is **La Pista**, an airstrip used during the war. Next to it bomb craters scar the landscape. Only a few avocado trees, between the bomb holes, survive, and the *gasolinera* to refuel planes, is still there, although it is now covered in corrugated iron. Ask around for directions.

## Chajul and Cotzal

Chajul, the second largest village in the Ixil Triangle, is known for its part in the Civil War, where Rigoberta Menchú's brother was killed in the plaza, as relayed in her book *I, Rigoberta Menchú*. According to the Nobel Peace Prize winner, on 9 September 1979 her 16-year-old brother Petrocinio was kidnapped after being turned in for 15 quetzales. He was tortured in the plaza by the army along with numerous others. Villagers were forced to watch the torture under threat of being branded communists. People were set on fire, but the onlookers had weapons and looked ready to fight. This caused the army to withdraw. Chajul's main fiesta is the second Friday in Lent. There is also a pilgrimage to Christ of Golgotha on the second Friday in Lent, beginning the Wednesday before (the image is escorted by 'Romans' in blue police uniforms). Market day is Tuesday and Friday. It is possible to walk from Chajul to Cotzal. It's a six-hour walk from Nebaj to Chajul.

Cotzal is spread over a large area on a number of steep hills. The village's fiesta is 22-25 June, peaking on the day of St John the Baptist (24 June). Market days are Wednesday and Saturday. You can hire bikes from **Maya Tour** on the plaza next to the church. Nebaj to Cotzal is a pleasant four-hour walk. There's no accommodation or restaurants in other small villages and it is difficult to specify what transport is available in this area as trucks and the occasional pickup or commercial van are affected by road and weather conditions. For this reason, be prepared to have to spend the night in villages.

## Listings The Ixil Triangle

### Where to stay

**$ Solidaridad Internacional**
Supports 6 hostels in the villages of **Xexocom**, **Chortiz**, **Xeo**, **Cocop**, **Cotzol** and **Párramos Grande** where there is room for 5 people. Contact them at the PRODONT-IXIL office, Av 15 de Septiembre, Nebaj.

### Nebaj and around

**$$-$ Hotel Turansa**
*1 block from plaza down 5 Calle, T7755-8219.*
Tiny rooms, but very clean, soap, towels, 2nd-floor rooms are nicer, cable TV and parking, little shop in entrance, phone service.

**$ Hospedaje Esperanza**
*6 Av, 2-36.*
Very friendly, clean, hot showers in shared bathroom, noisy when evangelical churches nearby have activities, hotel is cleaner than it looks from the outside.

**$ Hostal Ixil Don Juan**
*0 Av A, 1 Calle B, Canton Simocol. Take Av 15 de Septiembre and take a left at Comedor*

*Sarita, opposite grey office of PRODONT-IXIL, then it's 100 m to the right, on the right, T7755-4014/1529.*
Part of **Programa Quiché**, run with the support of the EU, there are 6 beds in 2 rooms, each bed with a locked strongbox, and hot showers. The colonial building has a traditional sauna, *chuj*.

**$ Hotel Mayan Ixil**
*On north side of main square, T7755-8168.*
Just 5 rooms with private bath and gas hot water. Small restaurant overlooking the plaza, internet service downstairs.

**$ Ilebal Tenam**
*Cantón Simecal, bottom of Av 15 de Septiembre, road to Chajul, T7755-8039.*
Hot water, shared and private bath, very clean, friendly, parking inside, attractive decor.

**$ Media Luna MediaSol**
*T5749-7450, www.nebaj.com/hostel.htm.*
A backpackers' hostel close to **El Descanso** restaurant with dorms and private rooms. The hostel's also got a little kitchenette, DVD player and Wi-Fi.

## Chajul

There are a couple of very basic *hospedajes* in town.

## Cotzal

### $ Hostal Doña Teresa

Has a sauna, patio and honey products for sale.

## Restaurants

### Nebaj and around

*Boxboles* are squash leaves rolled tightly with *masa* and chopped meat or chicken, boiled and served with salsa and fresh orange juice.

### $ El Descanso

Popular volunteer hang-out, good food and useful information about their other community-based projects (see www.nebaj.com).

### $ Maya Ixil

*On the Parque Central.*

Substantial food, local and international dishes, pleasant family atmosphere.

### $ Pizza del César

*Daily 0730-2100.*

Breakfasts, mouth-wateringly good strawberry cake, and hamburgers as well as pizzas.

## Cotzal

### $ Comedor and Hospedaje El Maguey

Bland meals, but a decent size, plus drink, are served up for for US$1.70. Don't stay here though, unless you're desperate.

## What to do

### Nebaj and around

**Guías Ixiles** *(El Descanso Restaurant), www. nebaj.com.* ½- to 3-day hikes, bike rental. There's also a 3-day hike to Todos Santos.

**Solidaridad Internacional**, *Av 15 de Septiembre, www.nebaj.org. Inside the PRODONT-IXIL (Proyecto de Promoción de Infraestructuras y Ecoturismo) office, in a grey building on the right 1 block after the Gasolinera El Triángulo on the road to Chajul.* For further information call in to see the director Pascual, who is very helpful. 2-, 3- and 4-day hikes, horses available. Options to stay in community *posadas*, with packages available, from 1 to 4 days, full board, from about US$100-200 per person.

### Chajul and Cotzal

Ask Teresa at **Hostal Doña Teresa** about trips from the Cotzal or ask for Sebastián Xel Rivera who leads 1-day camping trips.

## Transport

### Nebaj and around
#### Bus

The bus ride to Quiché is full of fabulous views and hair-raising bends but the road is now fully paved. Buses to **Quiché** (US$3.20, 2½ hrs) passing through **Sacapulas** (1¾ hrs from Nebaj, US$1.30) leave hourly from 0500-1530. Bus to **Cobán** leaves Gazolinera Quetzal at 0500, 4-5 hrs, US$6.50. Cobán to Nebaj at 1300. Alternatively get to Sacapulas on the main road, and wait for a bus.

### Chajul and Cotzal
#### Bus

Buses to Chajul and Cotzal do not run on a set schedule. It is best to ask the day before you want to travel, at the bus station. There are buses and numerous pickups on Sun when villagers come to Nebaj for its market, which would be a good day to visit the villages. Alternatively, bargain with a local pickup driver to take you on a trip.

# **Western** highlands

Just before the volcanic highlands reach their highest peaks, this part of the western highlands takes the form of scores of small market towns and villages, each with its own character: the loud animal market at San Francisco El Alto, the extra-planetary landscape at Momostenango, and its Maya cosmovision centre, and the dancing extravaganzas at Totonicapán. The modern *ladino* town of Huehuetenango sits at the gateway to the Sierra de los Cuchumatanes, within which hides, in a cold gash in a sky-hugging valley, the indigenous town and weaving centre of Todos Santos Cuchumatán.

## North to Huehuetenango *Colour map 2, B3/C3.*

**highland Mayan towns with colourful markets**

### Nahualá and Cuatro Caminos

Before the major four-way junction of Cuatro Caminos, the Pan-American Highway runs past Nahualá, a Maya village at 2470 m. The traditional *traje* is distinctive and best seen on market days on Thursday and Sunday, when finely embroidered cuffs and collars are sold, as well as very popular *huipiles*. The **Fiesta de Santa Catalina** is on 23-26 November (25th is the main day).

There is an unpaved all-weather road a little to the north and 16 km longer, from Los Encuentros (on the Pan-American Highway) through Totonicapán (40 km) to San Cristóbal Totonicapán. The route from Chichicastenango to Quiché, Xecajá and Totonicapán takes a day by car or motorcycle, but is well worth taking and recommended by cyclists. There are no buses. There is also a scenic road from Totonicapán to Santa Cruz del Quiché via San Antonio Ilotenango. It takes one hour by car or motorcycle and two hours by pickup truck. There are no buses on this route either.

Cuatro Caminos is a busy junction with roads, east to Totonicapán, west to Los Encuentros, north to Huehuetenango and south to Quetzaltenango. Buses stop here every few seconds so you will never have to wait long for a connection. There is a petrol station and lots of vendors to keep you fed and watered. Just north of Cuatro Caminos is **San Cristóbal Totonicapán**, noted for its *huipiles*.

**Best** for
Festivals ▪ Hiking ▪ Markets ▪ Textiles

## Totonicapán

The route to San Miguel Totonicapán (altitude 2500 m), the capital of its department, passes through pine-forested hillsides, pretty red-tiled roofs and *milpas* of maize on the roadside. The 18th-century beige church stands on one of the main squares, unfortunately now a car park, at 6 y 7 Avenida between 3 and 4 Calle. The market is considered by Guatemalans to be one of the cheapest, and it is certainly very colourful. Saturday is the main market noted for ceramics and cloth, with a small gathering on Tuesdays. There is a traditional dance fiesta on 12-13 August, music concerts and a chance to see *cofradía* rituals. The annual **feria** is on 24-30 September in celebration of the Archangel San Miguel, with the main fiesta on 29 September. The **Casa de Cultura** ⓘ *8 Av, 2-17, T5630-0554, www.larutamayaonline.com/aventura.html*, run by Carlos Humberto Molina, displays an excellent collection of fiesta masks, made on site at the mask factory, and for sale. It has a cultural programme with a number of tour options, cultural activities and bicycle adventures. You need to reserve in advance.

## San Francisco El Alto

San Francisco stands high on a great big mound in the cold mountains at 2640 m above the great valley in which lie Totonicapán, San Cristóbal and Quetzaltenango. It is famous for its market, which is stuffed to capacity, and for the animal market held above town, where creatures from piglets to kittens to budgies are for sale. The town's fiesta is on 1-6 October, in honour of St Francis of Assisi.

The market is packed to bursting point on Fridays with locals buying all sorts, including woollen blankets for resale throughout the country. It's an excellent place for buying woven and embroidered textiles of good quality, but beware of pickpockets. Go early to see as much action as possible. Climb up through the town for 10 minutes to see the animal market (ask for directions all the time as it's hard to see 5 m ahead, the place is so packed).

The **church** on the main square is magnificent; notice the double-headed Hapsburg eagle. It is often full on market days with locals lighting candles, and their live purchases ignoring the 'Silencio' posters. The white west front of the church complements the bright colours of the rest of the plaza, especially the vivid green and pink of the Municipalidad.

## Momostenango

Momostenango is set in a valley with ribbons of houses climbing higgledy-piggledy out of the valley floor. Momostenango, at 2220 m, represents *Shol Mumus* in K'iche', meaning 'among the hills', and on its outlying hills are numerous altars and a hilltop image of a Maya god. Some 300 medicine men are said to practise in the town. Their insignia of office is a little bag containing beans and quartz crystals. Momostenango is the chief blanket-weaving centre in the country, and locals can be seen beating the blankets (*chamarras*) on stones, to shrink them. There are also weird stone peaks known as the *riscos* – eroded fluted columns and draperies formed of volcanic ash – on the outskirts of town.

The town is quiet except on Wednesday and Sunday market days, the latter being larger and good for weaving, especially the blankets. On non-market days try **Tienda Manuel de Jesús Agancel** ⓘ *1 Av, 1-50, Zona 4, near bank*, for good bargains, especially blankets and carpets. There is also **Artesanía Paclom** ⓘ *corner of 1 Calle and 3 Av, Zona 2*, just five minutes along the road to Xela. This family have the weaving looms in their back yard and will show you how it's all done if you ask.

The **Feast of Wajshakib Batz' Oj** (pronounced 'washakip'), is celebrated by hundreds of *Aj Kij* (Maya priests) who come for ceremonies. New priests are initiated on this first day of the ritual new year; the initiation lasting the year. The town's very popular fiesta is between 21 July and 4 August, with the town's patron saint of Santiago Apóstol celebrated on 25 July. The **Baile de Convites** is held in December with other dances on 8, 12 and 31 December and 1 January. At **Takilibén Maya Misión** ① *3 Av 'A', 6-85, Zona 3, T7736-5537, wajshakibbatz13@yahoo.es*, just after the Texaco garage on the right on the way in from Xela, Chuch Kajaw (day keeper/senior priest) Rigoberto Itzep welcomes all interested in learning more about Maya culture and cosmology. He offers courses in culture and does Maya horoscope readings. He also has a **Maya sauna** (*Tuj*).

Just outside town are three sets of *riscos* (eroded columns of sandstone with embedded quartz particles), creating a strange eerie landscape of pinnacles that look like rocket lollipop ice creams. To get there, take the 2 Calle, Zona 2, which is the one to the right of the church, for five minutes until you see a sign on a building pointing to the left. Follow the signs until you reach the earth structures (five to 10 minutes).

## Listings North to Huehuetenango

### Where to stay

**Totonicapán**

**$ Hospedaje San Miguel**
*3 Calle, 7-49, Zona 1, T7766-1452.*
Rooms with or without bath, hot water, communal TV.

**$ Pensión Blanquita**
*13 Av and 4 Calle.*
20 rooms, hot showers, good. Opposite this *pensión* is a Shell station.

**San Francisco El Alto**

**$ Hotel Vásquez**
*4 Av, 11-53, T7738-4003.*
Rooms all with private bathroom. Parking.

**$ Vista Hermosa**
*2 Calle, 2-23, T7738-4010.*
36 rooms, cheaper without bathroom, hot water, TV.

**Momostenango**

**$ Estiver Ixcel**
*1 Calle, 4-15, Zona 4, downhill away from plaza, T7736-5036.*
12 rooms, hot water, cheaper without bath, clean.

**$ Hospedaje y Comedor Paclom**
*Close to central plaza, at 1 Calle, 1-71, Zona 4.*

Pretty inner courtyard with caged birds and plants, hot water in shared bathrooms.

**$ La Villa**
*1 Av, 1-13, Zona 1, below bank, T7736-5108.*
6 rooms, warm water only, clean and nicely presented.

### Restaurants

**Totonicapán**

**$ Comedor Brenda 2**
*9 Av, 3-31.*
Good, serving local food.

**$ Comedor Letty**
*3 Calle, 8-18.*
Typical Guatemalan fare.

**Momostenango**

**$ Comedor Santa Isabel**
*Next door to Hospedaje y Comedor Paclom.*
Friendly, cheap and good breakfasts.

**$ Flipper**
*1 Calle y 2 Av A.*
Good *licuados* and a range of fruit juices.

**$ Hospedaje y Comedor Paclom**
*Close to the central plaza and where buses arrive from Xela, 1 Calle, 1-71, Zona 4.*
Cheap meals, including snacks in a pretty inner courtyard.

## Transport

### Totonicapán
**Bus** Every 15 mins to **Quetzaltenango**, US$0.40, 45 mins. To **Los Encuentros**, US$2.20. To **Cuatro Caminos**, 30 mins, US$0.30.

### San Francisco El Alto
**Bus** 2 km along the Pan-American Hwy heading north from Cuatro Caminos is a paved road, which runs to San Francisco El Alto (3 km) and then to Momostenango (19 km). Bus from **Quetzaltenango**, 50 mins on Fri, US$0.75. The last bus back is at 1800.

### Momostenango
**Bus** From **Cuatro Caminos** (US$0.50) and **Quetzaltenango**, 1-1½ hrs. Buses to **Xela** every 30 mins from 0430-1600.

## Huehuetenango and around  *Colour map 2, B3.*

**a pleasant, large town and a busy transport hub**

Huehuetenango (altitude 1905 m) – colloquially known as Huehue – offers little to detain you. However, it is an important transport centre serving the Cuchumatanes Mountains and the Mexican border. Its bus terminal, 2 km from town, is one of the busiest in the country. There are Maya ruins near the town, which were badly restored by the infamous United Fruit Company, and new adventure tourism opportunities opening up nearby. Trips, including horse rides, to more remote spots in the Huehuetenango region to see forests, haciendas and lakes are organized by Unicornio Azul. A useful website is www.interhuehue.com.

**Huehuetenango**

To El Calvario & Buses to Chiantla, El Mirador & Todos Santos

To Chiantla & Todos Santos Cuchumatán

Mercado Municipal

Supermarket

Plaza

Cathedral

Taxis

Buses to Zaculeu

Bus to Terminal

Taxis

To Zaculeu

Los Halcones to Guatemala City

To Telgua (El Triángulo), Bus Station, Pan-American Highway & Guatemala City

N

200 metres
200 yards

**Where to stay**
Casa Blanca **1**
Cascata **2**
Mary **3**
Todos Santos Inn **4**

**Restaurants**
Café Bugambilias **1**

La Cabaña del Café **3**
La Fonda de Don Juan **4**
Mi Tierra Café **5**

The neoclassical **cathedral** was built between 1867 and 1874, destroyed by earthquake in 1902, and took 10 years to repair. In 1956, the image of the patron saint, the Virgen de la Concepción was burnt in a fire. Then, during the 1976 earthquake, 80% of it was damaged, save the bells, façade and cupola. The skyline to the north of the city is dominated by the Sierrra de los Cuchumatanes, the largest area over 3000 m in Central America.

The ruins of **Zaculeu** ① *0800-1800, US$6.40*, the old capital of the Mam Maya, are 5 km west of Huehuetenango on top of a rise with steep drops on three sides – a site chosen because of these natural defence measures. Its original name in Mam was *Xinabajul*, meaning 'between ravines'. In K'iche' it means 'white earth'. It was first settled in the Early Classic period (AD 250-600), but it flourished during the late post-Classic (AD 1200-1530). In July 1525, Gonzalo de Alvarado, the brother of Guatemala's conqueror, Pedro de Alvarado, set out for Zaculeu with 80 Spaniards, 40 horses and 2000 indigenous fighters, passing Mazatenango and Totonicapán on the way. The battle lasted four months, during which time the soldiers and residents of Zaculeu were dying of hunger, and eating their dead neighbours. The weakened Kaibil Balam, the Zaculeu *cacique* (chief), called for a meeting with Gonzalo. Gonzalo told the Mam chief that peace was not on the cards. Negotiations followed with the outcome being that Kaibil Balam be instructed in Christianity, obey the Spanish king and leave the city, whereupon Gonzalo de Alvarado would take possession of the Mam kingdom settlement in the name of the Spanish crown.

## Aguacatán

The women of Aguacatán (altitude 1670 m) wear the most stunning headdresses in the country. On sale in *tiendas* in town, they are a long, slim belt of woven threads using many colours. The women also wear beautiful clothes: the *cortes* are dark with horizontal stripes of yellow, pink, blue and green. The town fiesta is 40 days after Holy Week, Virgen de la Encarnación.

## Towards Todos Santos Cuchumatán

To get to Todos Santos, you have to climb the front range of the Cuchumatanes Mountains above Chiantla by a steep road from Huehuetenango. **Chiantla** has the Luna Café with art gallery and the nearby paleontological site of **El Mamutz**. Looking down on a clear day the cathedral at Huehuetenango resembles a blob of orange blancmange on the plain. At the summit, at about 3300 m, there is **El Mirador**.

The paved road continues over bleak moorland to Paquix where the road divides. The unpaved road to the north continues to Soloma. The other to the west goes through Aldea Chiabel, noted for its outhouses, more obvious than the small dwellings they serve. Here, giant agave plants appear to have large pom-poms attached, reminiscent of the baubles on Gaudí's Sagrada Familia in Barcelona. On this journey you often pass through cloud layer, eventually surfacing above it. On cloudier days you will be completely submerged until descending again to Huehuetenango. The road crosses a pass at 3394 m before a difficult long descent to Todos Santos, about 50 km from Huehuetenango.

The walk northwest from Chiantla to Todos Santos Cuchumatanes can be done in around 12-14 hours, or better, two days, staying overnight at **El Potrillo** in the barn owned by Rigoberto Alva. This route crosses one of the highest parts of the sierra at over 3500 m. Alternatively, cycle the 40-km part-gravel road, which is steep in places, but very rewarding.

## Where to stay

### Huehuetenango

**$$ Casa Blanca**
*7 Av, 3-41, T7769-0777.*
Comfortable, good restaurant in a pleasant garden, buffet breakfast, set lunch, very popular and good value, parking.

**$$ Cascata**
*Lote 4, 42, Zona 5, Col Alvarado, Calzada Kaibil Balam, close to the bus station, T7769-0795, www.hotelcascata.ya.st.*
Newish hotel with 16 rooms with Wi-Fi and private bathrooms. It is owned by Dutch, French and English folk and the service is excellent.

**$ Mary**
*2 Calle, 3-52, T7764-1618.*
With bath, cheaper without, good beds, hot water, cable TV, parking, clean, quiet, safe, well-maintained, good value. Recommended.

**$ Todos Santos Inn**
*2 Calle, 6-74, T7764-1241.*
Shared bath and private bath available, hot water, TV, helpful, clean, laundry, some rooms a bit damp, luggage stored. Recommended.

## Restaurants

### Huehuetenango

**$$-$ La Cabaña del Café**
*2 Calle, 6-50.*
Log cabin café with to-die-for cappuccino, snack food and good *chapín* breakfasts, good atmosphere. Recommended.

**$ Café Bugambilias**
*5 Av 3-59, on the plaza.*
Large, unusual 4-storey building, most of which is a popular, cheap, restaurant, very good breakfasts, *almuerzos*, sandwiches. Recommended.

**$ La Fonda de Don Juan**
*2 Calle, 5-35.*
Italian restaurant and bar (try the *cavatini*), sandwiches, big choice of desserts, *licuados*, coffees, good pizzas, also *comida típica*, with reasonable prices all served in a bright environment with red and white checked tablecloths.

**$ Mi Tierra Café**
*4 Calle, 6-46, T7764-1473.*
Good drinks and light meals, Mexican offerings; try the *fajitas*, nice setting, popular with locals and travellers. Recommended.

## What to do

**Unicornio Azul**, *based in Chancol, T5205-9328, www.unicornioazul.com.* Horse-riding trips, trekking, mountain biking and birdwatching in the Cuchumatanes.

## Transport

### Huehuetenango
**Bus and taxi**
**Local** From the terminal to town, take 'Centro' minibus, which pulls up at cathedral, 5 mins. Taxis from behind the covered market. Walking takes 20-25 mins. Bus leaves Salvador Osorio School, final Calle 2, every 30 mins, 15 mins, to **Zaculeu**, last return 1830. Taxi, US$8, including waiting time. To walk takes about 1 hr; either take 6 Av north, cross the river and follow the road to the left, through Zaculeu modern village to the ruins, or go past the school and turn right beyond the river. The signs are barely visible.

**Long distance** To **Guatemala City**, 5 hrs, US$11, Los Halcones, 7 Av, 3-62, Zona 1 (they do not leave from the terminal) at 0430, 0700, 1400, reliable. From the bus terminal there are numerous services daily to the capital from 0215-1600 via **Chimaltenango**, 5 hrs, US$4. Via **Mazatenango** there are 5 daily.

**North** To **Todos Santos Cuchumatán**, 10 daily until 1630, 2-3 hrs, US$3.60. To **Barillas**, via **San Juan Ixcoy** (2½ hrs), **Soloma** (3 hrs), and **San Mateo Ixtatan** (7 hrs), 10 daily from 0200-2330, US$7. There are also buses to **San Rafael la Independencia** passing through Soloma and **Sta Eulalia**.

**Northwest** To **La Mesilla** for Mexico, frequent buses between 0530-1800, US$3.50, 2½ hrs, last bus returning to Huehue, 1800. To **Nentón**, via La Mesilla twice a day. To **Gracias a Dios**, several times a day.

**South** To **Quetzaltenango**, 13 a day from 0600-1600, US$3, 2-2¼ hrs. To **Cuatro Caminos**, US$2, 2 hrs. To **Los Encuentros**, for Lake Atitlán and Chichicastenango, 3 hrs.

**East** To **Aguacatán**, 12 daily, 0600-1900, 1 hr 10 mins, US$1.20. To **Nebaj** you have to get to Sacapulas via Aguacatán. To **Sacapulas**, 1130, 1245. To **Cobán**, take the earliest bus/pickup to Aguacatán and then Sacapulas and continue to Uspantán to change for Cobán.

## Aguacatán
### Bus
From **Huehue**, 1 hr 10 mins. It is 26 km east of Huehuetenango on a semi-paved route (good views). Returning between 0445 and 1600. Buses and pickups for **Sacapulas** and for onward connections to Nebaj and Cobán leave from the main street going out of town. Wait anywhere along there to catch your ride. It is 1½ hrs from Aguacatán to Sacapulas. To **Guatemala City** at 0300, 1100.

## Todos Santos Cuchumatán and around   Colour map 2, B3.
### indigenous village in a spectacular mountain setting

★High in the Cuchumatanes, the Mam-speaking Todos Santeros maintain a traditional way of life with their striking, bright, indigenous dress and their adherence to the 260-day Tzolkin calendar. Todos Santos (altitude 2470 m) is hemmed in by 3800-m-high mountains either side that squeeze it into one long, 2-km street down the valley. The town is famous for its weaving, and even more famous for the horse race, see box, page 332.

Some of Guatemala's best weaving is done in Todo Santos. Fine *huipiles* may be bought in the cooperative on the main street and direct from the makers. The men wear the famous red-and-white striped trousers. Some wear a black wool over-trouser piece. Their jackets are white, pink, purple and red-striped with beautifully coloured, and intricately embroidered, collars and cuffs. Their straw hat is wrapped with a blue band. You can buy the embroidered cuffs and collars for men's shirts, the red trousers, and gorgeous colourful crocheted bags made by the men. The women wear navy blue *cortes* with thin, light blue, vertical stripes.

There is a colourful Saturday market and a smaller one on Wednesday. The **church** near the park was built in 1580.

### Around Todos Santos
The closest walk is to **Las Letras**, where the words 'Todos Santos' are spelt out in white stone on a hillside above the town. The walk takes an hour. To get there take the path down the side of **Restaurant Cuchumatlán**. The highest point of the Cuchumatanes, and the highest non-volcanic peak in the country, **La Torre** at 3837 m, is to the northeast of Todos Santos and can be reached from the village of **Tzichem** on the road to Concepción Huista. When clear, it's possible to see the top of Volcán Santa María, one of the highest volcanoes in Guatemala. The hike takes about five hours. The best way to do it is to start in the afternoon and spend the night near the top. It is convenient for camping, with wood but no water. A compass is essential in case of mist.

## ON THE ROAD

### Todos Santos festival

The horse racing festival of Todos Santos is one of the most celebrated and spectacular in Central America – it is also a frenzied day that usually degenerates into a drunken mess. Quite simply riders race between two points, having a drink at each turn until they fall off.

According to Professor Margarito Calmo Cruz, the origins of the fiesta lie in the 15th or 16th century with the arrival of the conquistadores to Todos Santos. They arrived on horses wearing large, colourful clothes with bright scarves flowing down their backs and feathers in their hats. The locals experimented, imitating them, enjoyed it and the tradition was born.

When the day begins, the men are pretty tipsy, but sprightly and clean. The race is frantic and colourful with scarves flying out the backs of the men. As the day wears on, they get completely smashed, riding with arms outstretched – whip in one hand and beer bottle in the other. They are mudspattered, dishevelled and are moaning and groaning from the enjoyment and the alcohol which must easily have reached near comatose level. At times the riders fall, and look pretty lifeless. They are dragged by the scruff of the neck, regardless of serious injury or death, to the edge of the fence as quickly as possible, to avoid trampling.

The men guzzle gallons of beer and the aim is to continue racing all day. A fall means instant dismissal from the race. There are wardens on the side lines with batons, whose primary job is the welfare of the horses, changing them when they see necessary. But they also deal with protesting fallen riders, who try and clamber back onto their horses. By the end of the day the spectacle is pretty grotesque. The horses are drenched with sweat and wild-eyed with fear. The men look hideous and are paralytic from booze. The edge of the course and the town is littered with bodies.

The race takes place on the road that winds its way out of town, not the incoming road from Huehue. It starts at 0800. There are about 15 riders on the course at any one time. It continues until noon, stops for *cerveza* guzzling and begins again at 1400, ending at 1700.

From Todos Santos, you can also hike south to **San Juan Atitán**, four to five hours, where the locals wear an interesting *traje típico*. Market days are on Mondays and Thursdays. From there you can hike to the Pan-American Highway; it's a one day walk. The local fiesta is 22-26 June.

### Jacaltenango to the Mexican border

The road from Todos Santos continues northwest through **Concepción Huista**. Here the women wear towels as shawls and Jacalteco is spoken. The fiesta, 29 January-3 February, has fireworks and dancing. The hatmaker in Canton Pilar supplies the hats for Todos Santos, he welcomes viewers and will make a hat to your specifications (but if you want a typical Todos Santos leather *cincho*, buy it there).

Beyond Jacaltenango is **Nentón**, and **Gracias a Dios** at the Mexican border. When the road north out of Huehue splits at Paquix, the right fork goes to **San Mateo Ixtatán**, with ruins nearby. The road from Paquix crosses the roof of the Cuchumatanes, before descending to **San Juan Ixcoy, Soloma** and **Santa Eulalia**, where the people speak O'anjob'al as they do in Soloma. East along a scenic route is **Barillas**. There are several *pensiones* in these places and regular buses from Huehue.

## Where to stay

Reservations are necessary in the week before the Nov horse race, but even if the town is full, locals offer their homes.

### $ Casa Familiar
*Up the hill, close to central park, T7783-0656.*
Run by the friendly family of Santiaga Mendoza Pablo. Hot shower, sauna, breakfast, dinner, delicious banana bread, spectacular view, popular. The Mendoza family give weaving lessons.

### $ Hotel La Paz
Friendly, great view of the main street from balconies, excellent spot for the 1 Nov fiesta, shared showers not great, enclosed parking.

### $ Hotel Mam
*Above the central park, next to Hotelito Todos Santos.*
Friendly, clean, hot water, but needs 1 hr to warm up, not too cold in the rooms as an open fire warms the building, good value.

### $ Hotelito Todos Santos
*Above the central park.*
Hot water, clean, small café, but beware of boys taking you to the hotel quoting one price, and then on arrival, finding the price has mysteriously gone up.

### Around Todos Santos

### $ Hospedaje San Diego
*San Juan Atitán.*
Only 3 beds, basic, friendly, clean, food available.

## Restaurants

There are *comedores* on the 2nd floor of the market selling very cheap meals.

### $ Comedor Katy
Will prepare vegetarian meals on request, good-value *menú del día*.

### $ Cuchumatlán
Has sandwiches, pizza and pancakes, and is popular at night.

## Festivals

**1 Nov  Horse race**. The festival begins on 21 Oct. See box, opposite.
**2 Nov  Day of the Dead**, when locals visit the cemetery and leave flowers and food.

## Shopping

The following shops all sell bags, trousers, shirts, *huipiles*, jackets and clothes. The best bargains are at **Tienda Maribel**, up the hill from Casa Familiar, and **Cooperativa Estrella de Occidente**, on the main street. **Casa Mendoza**, just beyond Tienda Maribel, is where Telésforo Mendoza makes clothes to measure. **Domingo Calmo** also makes clothes to measure. His large, brown house with tin roof is on the main road to the Ruinas (5 mins); follow the road up from Casa Familiar. Ask for **Casa de Domingo**.

## Transport

### Bus
To **Huehuetenango**, 2-3 hrs, crowded Mon and Fri, 0400, 0500, 0600, 0615-0630, 1145, 1230, 1300. Possible changes on Sat so ask beforehand. For petrol, ask at **El Molino**.

### Jacaltenango to the Mexican border
### Bus
From **Huehuetenango** at 0330, 0500, returning at 1130 and 1400; also pickups.

# Quetzaltenango
## & around

Quetzaltenango (commonly known as Xela, pronounced 'shayla') is the most important city in western Guatemala. It is set among a group of high mountains and volcanoes, one of which, Santa María, caused much death and destruction after an eruption in 1902. The bulk of the city is modern, but its 19th-century downtown revamp and its narrow streets give the centre more of a historic feel. There is a pleasant park with its beautifully restored façade of the colonial church. It is an excellent base from which to visit nearby hot springs, religious idols, volcanoes and market towns.

## Quetzaltenango  Colour map 2, C3.

**Guatemala's second city, with a colonial cathedral and breathtaking views**

The central park, Parque Centro América, is the focus of Quezaltenango (altitude 2335 m). It is surrounded by the cathedral, with its beautifully restored original colonial façade, and a number of elegant neoclassical buildings, constructed during the late 19th and early 20th century.

The modern cathedral, **Catedral de la Diócesis de los Altos**, was constructed in 1899 and is set back behind the original. The surviving façade of the 1535 **Catedral del Espíritu Santo** is beautiful, intricately carved and with restored portions of murals on its right side. On the south side of the park is the **Casa de la Cultura**. Inside are the **Museo de la Marimba** with exhibits and documents relating to the 1871 Liberal Revolution. On the right-hand side of the building is the totally curious **Museo de Historia Natural** ① *Mon-Fri 0800-1200, 1400-1800, US$0.90*. Deformed stuffed animals are cheek by jowl with pre-Columbian pottery, sports memorabilia, fizzy drink bottles, a lightning-damaged mirror and dinosaur remains. It satisfies the most morbid of curiosities with displays of a two-headed calf, Siamese twin pigs, an eight-legged goat, and a strange sea creature

**Best** for
Textiles ▪ Thermal baths ▪ Religious architecture

### Getting around

The town centre is compact and all sites and most services are within walking distance. The Santa Fe city bus goes between the terminal, the rotonda and the town centre. Out of town destination buses stop at the rotonda and it is quicker to get here from the town centre than to the Minerva Terminal. City buses for the terminal leave from 4 Calle and 13 Avenida, Zona 1, and those straight for the rotonda leave from 11 Avenida and 10 Calle, Zona 1, US$0.15.

A taxi within Zona 1, or from Zona 1 to a closer part of Zona 3, is about US$3.20.

that looks like an alien, known as *Diabillo del Mar* (little sea devil). On the park's southwest side is the **Museo de Arte**, with a collection of contemporary Guatemalan art, and the **Museo del Ferrocarril Nacional de los Altos** ⓘ *7 Calle and 12 Av, Mon-Fri 0800-1200, 1400-1800, US$0.90*, recounting the story of an electric railway between Xela and the Pacific slope. The **Banco de Occidente**, founded in 1881, and the first bank to opened in Guatemala, dominates the northern edge of the park. The overly wired-up **Municipalidad** straddles the eastern edge of the park with its neoclassical columns. Its first building blocks were laid in 1881, but it wasn't completed until 1897.

The stately **Teatro Municipal** (1892-1896) is on 14 Avenida and 1 Calle and can be visited outside of performance hours. Restored at a cost of four million quetzales, it has an imposing presence. To its left, on Avenida 14 "A", is the **Teatro Roma**. Building began in 1898, but was not completed until 1931, when it became the first cinema to open in Guatemala. It was restored in 2000 as a theatre with a capacity for 1400 and is open for performances.

There is a sickly green modern church, the **Sagrado Corazón**, on the Parque Benito Juárez near the market. Inside is a gigantic, freestanding, Chagall-influenced painting with swooping angels, and Christ in a glass box, built into the picture. The church of **La Transfiguración** ⓘ *near the corner of 11 Calle and 5 Av, Zona 1*, houses the largest crucified Christ figure (San Salvador del Mundo) to be found in Central America – it is almost 3 m in height and now housed behind glass. At 20 Avenida and 4 Calle is the city's **Cementerio** ⓘ *0700-1900*. Inside are the remains of the Quetzalteco President, Estrada Cabrera (1898-1920) in a small cream neoclassical temple. Behind his tomb are the unmarked graves of a large number of cholera victims wiped out in a 19th-century epidemic. Manuel Lisandra Barillas (Guatemalan President 1885-1892) is also entombed here. There is a small patio area known as Colonia Alemana lined with graves of German residents; a large area where those that died as martyrs in the civil war lie; and a memorial to those that perished in the September Revolution of 1897. The town's fiestas are 9-17 September, Holy Week and the October fiesta of La Virgen del Rosario.

# Quetzaltenango

**To Estado Mario Camposeco & Olintepeque**

**To Transportes Alamo**

Calzado Rodolfo Robles

La Democracia Market & Sagrado Corazón

Parque Gabriel Pinillos

C 0a

To ⑫, Transportes Galgos, Mont Blanc Shopping Centre, Templo de Minerva, Market & Minerva Bus Terminal

Teatro Roma

ZONA 1

Teatro Municipal

C 0C

Agencia de Viajes SAB

C 1

To Líneas América Buses, La Rotonda, Cuatro Caminos & Guatemala City

Vrisa

Museo de Ferrocarril Nacional de los Altos & Museo de Arte

Despensa Familiar Supermarket

Parque Centro América

Municipalidad

Cathedral

Casa de la Cultura

Centro Comercial Municipal

Buses to Almolonga & Zunil

Cine

100 metres
100 yards

N

**Where to stay**
7 Orejas Hostal **1** *A1*
Black Cat Hostel **10** *B2*
Casa Doña Mercedes **4** *C1*
Casa Mañen **6** *C3*
Casa Renaissance **5** *D2*
Casa San Bartolomé **14** *C3*

Casa Seibel **7** *D3*
Casa Xelajú **8** *D1*
Hostel Nim Sut **9** *B3*
Kiktem-Ja **11** *C2*
Modelo **12** *B1*
Villa del Centro **13** *B2*

**Restaurants**
Asados Puente **17** *C2*
Bakeshop **12** *A1*
Blue Angel Café **2** *C1*
Café Baviera **1** *C2*

Café y Chocolate
La Luna **8** *C3*
Cardinali **20** *B2*
Chocolate Doña
Pancha **18** *D1*
El Apaste **4** *C2*
El Deli Crepe **5** *B2*
La Chatia Artesana **3** *C1*
Las Calas **9** *B1*
Royal París & Guatemaya
Intercultural Travel
Agency **10** *B1*

Sabor de India **7** *B1*
Salón Tecún **16** *C2*
Tertulianos Villas Lesbia **6** *B2*
Ut'z Hua **11** *B2*

**Bars & clubs**
El Duende **14** *A1*
El Zaguán **13** *A1*
La Taberna de Don
Rodrigo **15** *A2*
Ojalá **19** *B1*

# BACKGROUND

## Quetzaltenango

The most important battle of the Spanish conquest took place near Quetzaltenango when the great K'iche' warrior Tecún Umán was slain. In October 1902 the Volcán Santa María erupted, showering the city with half a metre of dust. An ash cloud soared 8.6 km into the air and some 1500 people were killed by volcanic fallout and gas. A further 3000 people died a short while later from malaria due to plagues of mosquitoes which had not been wiped out by the blast. Some 20 years on, a new volcano, born after the 1902 eruption, began to erupt. This smaller volcano, Santiaguito, spews clouds of dust and ash on a daily basis and is considered one of the most dangerous volcanoes in the world. The city's prosperity, as seen by the grand neoclassical architecture in the centre, was built on the back of the success of the coffee fincas on the nearby coastal plain. This led to the country's first bank being established here.

## ★North of Quetzaltenango

Between Quetzaltenango and Cuatro Caminos is the small *ladino* town of **Salcajá**, where *jaspé* skirt material has been woven since 1861. If you fancy a taste or a whiff of some potent liquor before bracing yourself for an entry into Quetzaltenango, then this is the place to halt. It is worth a visit not only for the booze but its famous church – the oldest in Central America – and for its textiles, often seen being produced in the streets. In 1524 the first church in Central America was founded by the conquering Spaniards. **San Jacinto** is a small church on 6 Avenida y 2 Calle; it may not always be open. *Caldo de frutas*, a highly alcoholic drink with quite a kick, is not openly sold but is made in the town and drunk on festive occasions. It is illegal to drink it in public places. It is a concoction of nances, cherries, peaches, apples and quinces and is left to ferment in rum. There is also *rompope*, a drink made with eggs. Salcajá is a town that also revolves around textiles, with shops on every street. Yarn is tied and dyed, untied, and wraps are then stretched around telephone poles along the road or on the riverside. One of these can be seen outside San Jacinto church. Market day is Tuesday.

**San Andrés Xecul** is a small village in stunning surroundings with an extraordinarily lurid-coloured church, 8 km north of Xela. Painted a deep-mustard yellow in 1900, its figurines, including angels, have been given blue wings and pastel-pink skirts. Climb the hill a bit above the town and catch a glimpse of the fantastic dome – mulitcoloured like a beach ball. With your back to the church climb the cobbled street leading up the right-hand side of the plaza to a yellow and maroon chapel peering out across the valley. The view from here is spectacular. Market day is Thursday, opposite the church. The town's fiestas are on 21 November, 30 November and 1 December.

## ★South of Quetzaltenango

Souteast of Xela is Cantel which has the largest and oldest textile factory in the country. Sunday is market day and the town's fiesta is 12-18 August (main day 15 August). At Easter a passion play is performed. A little further on, on the outskirts of town, on the right-hand side (one minute on the bus), is the white **Copavic glass factory** ① *T7763-8038*, *www.copavic.com, Mon-Fri 0500-1300, Sat 0500-1200*, where you can watch and photograph the workers blow the recycled glass.

**Zunil** Pinned in by a very steep-sided valley is the town of Zunil, 9 km from Quetzaltenango. It is visited for the nearby hot thermal baths that many come to wallow in, and for its worship of its well-dressed idol San Simón (Maximón). The market is held on Mondays. The town's fiesta is 22-26 November (main day 25) and there is a very colourful Holy Week. The **church** is striking both inside and out. It has a large decorated altarpiece and a small shrine to murdered Bishop Gerardi at the altar. The façade is white with serpentine columns wrapped in carved ivy.

**San Simón** (Maximón) is worshipped in the town and is often dressed in different clothes at different times. A small charge is made for the upkeep and to take photos; ask anyone in the town to escort you to his house. To the left of the church is the **Santa Ana Cooperative**, which sells beautiful *huipiles*, shirt and skirt materials, as well as bags and bookmarks.

The nearby extinct **Volcán Pico Zunil**, rises to 3542 m to the southeast of the town. On its slopes are the **thermal baths of Fuentes Georginas** ⓘ *0700-1900, US$2.70*, which you'll know you're approaching by the wafts of sulphurous fumes that come your way. There are several different-sized pools set into the mountainside surrounded by thick, luscious vegetation and enveloped in the steam that continuously rises up in wafts from the hot pools. There are spectacular views on the way to the baths.

The thermal baths of **Aguas Amargas** ⓘ *0800-1700, US$2, children, US$1.30*, are on Zunil Mountain below Fuentes Georginas. They are reached by following the road south and heading east (left) by Estancia de La Cruz. This road passes fields of flowers and would make a great trip on a bike.

**El Viejo Palmar** This is Guatemala's Pompeii. The river that cuts through here flows directly down from the active Santiaguito volcanic cone following a series of serious lahars (mudflows of water and volcanic material) that took place in the 1990s. The small town of 10,000 was evacuated, leaving an extraordinary legacy. In August 1998, the whole south end of the ghost town was destroyed by a massive lahar that crushed the church. This also shifted the course of the Río Nimá I, which began to flow directly through the centre of the church remains. Very heavy erosion since has left the west front and the altar separated by a 30-m-deep ravine – an unbelievable sight.

**Volcán Santa María and Santiaguito** Santiaguito's mother, Santa María (3772 m), is a rough 5½-hour climb (1500 m). You can see Santiaguito (2488 m) below, erupting mostly with ash blasts and sometimes lava flows from a mirador. It is possible to camp at the summit of Santa María, or on the saddle west of the summit, but it is cold and windy, but worth it because dawn provides views of the entire country's volcanic chain and an almighty shadow is cast across the area by Santa Maria's form. Santiaguito is a fairly new volcano that formed after the eruption of Santa María out of its crater. Do not attempt to climb Santiaguito: it erupts continuously on a daily basis throwing up ash and is considered one of the most dangerous volcanoes in the world. To see it erupting you need to climb Santa María, where you can look down on this smaller volcano. See Tour operators, page 343.

**Laguna Chicabal** **San Martín rangers' station** ⓘ *0700-1800, US$2*, is where the two-hour climb to Laguna Chicabal starts. This is a lime-green lake, at 2712 m, in the crater of the extinct volcano (2900 m) of the same name, with wild white lilies, known as *cartucho*, growing at the edges. The Maya believe the waters are sacred and it is thought that if you swim in the lake you will become ill. The highlight of a trip here is the sight of the clouds tumbling down over the circle of trees that surround the lake, and then appearing to bounce on the surface before dispersing. Ceremonies of Maya initiation are held at the lake in early May, known as *Jueves de la Ascensión*. The walk from San Martín takes about two hours.

## ★ West of Quetzaltenango

It takes 30 minutes to reach **San Juan Ostuncalco**, 15 km away. It's a pleasant, prosperous town with a big white church noted for its good weekly market on Sunday and beautiful sashes worn by men. Its fiesta, Virgen de la Candelaria, is held on 29 January to 2 February. The road, which is paved, switchbacks 37 km down valleys and over pine-clad mountains to a plateau looking over the valley in which are San Pedro and San Marcos. **San Marcos** has a few places to stay and eat. It is a transport hub with little to see. **San Pedro Sacatepéquez** has a huge market on Thursday. The Maya women wear golden and purple skirts.

The extinct **Volcán Tajumulco**, at 4220 m, is the highest in Central America. Start very early in the day if you plan to return to San Marcos by nightfall. It's about a five-hour climb and a three-hour descent. Once you have reached the ridge on Tajumulco, turn right along the top of it; there are two peaks, the higher is on the right. The peak on the left (4100 m) is used for shamanistic rituals.

Dormant **Volcán Tacaná** (4093 m) on the Mexican border may be climbed from the village of Sibinal. Its last eruption was 1949, but there was activity in 2001, so check before climbing. It is the second highest volcano in Guatemala with a 400-m-wide crater and fumaroles on its flanks. Take a bus to Sibinal from San Marcos. It is a six-hour difficult climb to the summit and it's recommended that you ask for a guide in the village. About 15 km west of San Marcos the road begins its descent from 2500 m to the lowlands. In 53 km to **Malacatán** it drops to 366 m. It is a winding ride with continuous bends, but the scenery is attractive. There is accommodation.

The road to the coastal plain from San Juan Ostuncalco is the most attractive of all the routes down from the highlands, bypassing most of the small towns through quickly changing scenery as you lose height. After San Juan, go south for 1.5 km to **Concepción Chiquirichapa**, with a bright blue and yellow church, which is one of the wealthiest villages in the country. It has a small market early every Thursday morning and a fiesta on 5-9 December. About 6 km beyond is **San Martín Sacatepéquez**, which used to be known as San Martín Chile Verde, and is famous for its hot chillies. This village appears in Miguel Angel Asturias' *Mulata de Tal*. It stands in a windy, cold gash in the mountains. The slopes are superbly steep and farmed, giving fantastic vistas on the climb up and down from Laguna Chicabal (see above). The men wear very striking long red and white striped tunics, beautifully embroidered around the hem. Market day is Sunday. The fiesta runs from 7-12 November (main day 11 November).

## Tourist information

General information can be found at
www.xelapages.com and www.xela
who.com, which has good listings.

### INGUAT
*7 Calle, 11-35, on the park, T7761-4931.
Mon-Fri 0900-1600, Sat 0900-1300.*
Not recommended. Try the recommended
tour operators (see What to do, below) for
information instead.

## Where to stay

At Easter, 12-18 Sep and Christmas, rooms
need to be booked well in advance.

### $$ Casa Mañen
*9a Av, 4-11, Zona 1, T7765-0786.*
Reports are consistently good, serves great
breakfasts and friendly staff offer a very
warm welcome. Room 2 is a great option
with a bed on a mezzanine. Some rooms
have microwave, fridge and TV. All are
comfortable, and furnished with attractive
wooden accessories. There is a small, pretty
courtyard area and secure parking.

### $$ Casa San Bartolomé
*2 Av, 71-17, T7761-9511,
www.casasanbartolome.com.*
Located in a historical neighbourhood near
the Parque Central, Casa San Bartolomé
is a colonial-style B&B with 7 simple and
unpretentious rooms, all equipped with
Wi-Fi, cable TV, hot water and heating.
There's a small garden and mountain views
from the shared balcony. Breakfast included.

### $$ Hotel Modelo
*14 Av A, 2-31, T7761-2529,
www.hotelmodelo1892.com.*
This comfortable colonial-style option
enjoys a convenient central location and a
handsome interior furnished with antiques
and abundant potted plants. They offer

19 spacious rooms complete with hot
water, cable TV, private bath and Wi-Fi.

### $$-$ 7 Orejas Hostal
*2 Calle, 16-92, T7768-3218, www.7orejas.com.*
Set in a handsome colonial building, this
hotel is well maintained and professionally
managed. They offer simple but attractive
rooms with cable TV, private bath, and solid
hand-carved furniture, as well as a cheaper
option in their 8-bed dorm. Upstairs you
can enjoy breakfast (US$4) on their pleasant
open-air terrace. There are also furnished
apartments for long stays. Recommended.

### $$-$ Casa Doña Mercedes
*6 Calle y 14 Av, 13-42, T5687-3305,
www.hostalcasadonamercedes.com.gt.*
Good value, hospitable and affordable, this
modest little guesthouse has a range of tidy,
spacious and pleasant rooms with hot water
and cable TV. There's also a fully equipped
kitchen and cheery communal areas.

### $$-$ Villa del Centro
*12 Av, 3-61, T7761-1767,
www.hotelvilladelcentro.com.*
Quiet, clean and friendly, Villa del Centro has
a great central location less than a block from
the Parque Central. It offers simple, pleasant,
recently renovated rooms with firm beds,
Wi-Fi and TV.

### $ Black Cat Hostel
*13 Av, 3-33, Zona 1, T7761-2091,
www.blackcathostels.net.*
A hostel in the old Casa Kaehler. Dorms and
private rooms all with shared bathrooms.
Breakfast included.

### $ Casa Renaissance
*9 Calle, 11-26, T3121-6315,
www.casarenaissance.com.*
Bright, cosy, and full of character, Casa
Renaissance is a colonial-style guesthouse
that is over a century old. It boasts lots of
homey enclaves including 2 patios with

hammocks and a living room with sofas and a TV. Rooms are simple but comfortable. Additional facilities include Wi-Fi, kitchen, free coffee and tea.

### $ Casa Seibel
*9 Av, 8-10, T5958-7529, www.casaseibel.com.*
Featuring wooden floors, 2 leafy courtyards and an old piano, this charming hostel and guesthouse has lots of character and history. Accommodation includes simple dorms and spacious rooms and there are dining rooms, communal lounges and an open kitchen. Friendly hostess. Economical and recommended.

### $ Casa Xelajú
*Callejón 15, Diagonal 13-02, T7761-5954, www.casaxelaju.com.*
Part of a Spanish school but also available to non-students, Casa Xelajú has several nice little 1-bed apartments complete with fully equipped kitchens, Wi-Fi, cable TV, hot water and bath tubs. Very quiet and comfortable, a great deal if you're in town for a while. Weekly or monthly rental. Recommended.

### $ Hostel Nim Sut
*4 Calle, 9-42, T7761-3083, www.hostelnim sutquetzaltenango.weebly.com.*
A nice little hostel with a pleasant courtyard and good mountain views from the roof terrace. They have economical private rooms and dorms, with or without private bath. Rates include drinking water, Wi-Fi, use of kitchen, but breakfast is extra.

### $ Kiktem-Ja
*13 Av, 7-18, Zona 1, T7761-4304.*
A central location with 16 colonial-style rooms, nicely furnished, locally made blankets on the beds, wooden floors, all with bath, hot water, open fires, car parking inside gates.

## Zunil

### $$$-$$ Las Cumbres Eco-Saunas y Gastronomía
*T5399-0029, www.las cumbres.com.gt. Daily 0700-1800.*

Beyond Zunil on the left-hand side of the road heading to the coast (Km 210). This is the place for some R&R with saunas emitting natural steam from the geothermal activity nearby. There are 12 rooms with sauna, cheaper without, and separate saunas and jacuzzis for day visitors (US$2.50 per hr) and a restaurant serving good regional food and natural juices. Highly recommended. See Transport, below, for transfers.

### $ Turicentro Fuentes Georginas.
6 cold bungalows with 2 double beds and 2 bungalows with 3 single beds. They have cold showers, fireplaces with wood, electricity 1700-2200 and barbecue grills for guests' use near the baths. Guests can use the baths after public closing times. Reasonably priced restaurant with breakfasts, snacks and drinks, 0800-1800.

## Restaurants

### $$$-$$ Cardinali
*14 Av, 3-25, Zona 1.*
Owned by Benito, a NY Italian, great Italian food, including large pizzas with 31 varieties: 2 for 1 on Tue and Thu; tasty pastas of 20 varieties, extensive wine list. Recommended. Also does home delivery in 30 mins (T7761-0924).

### $$$-$ Las Calas
*14 Av "A", 3-21, Zona 1. Mon-Sat.*
Breakfasts, salads, soups, paella and pastas served around a courtyard with changing art hanging from walls. The food is tasty with delicious bread to accompany, but small portions are served. The breakfast service is far too slow. Adjoining bar.

### $$$-$ Restaurante Royal París
*14 Av "A", 3-06, Zona 1.*
Delicious food (try the fish in a creamy mushroom sauce), excellent choices, including vegetarian. Also cheap options. Run by Stéphane and Emmanuelle. Recommended. Live music from 2000 on Fri.

### $$$-$ Restaurante Tertulianos Villa Lesbia
*14 Av, 5-26, Zona 3, T7767-4666.*
Gourmet quality, specializing in meat, cheese and chocolate fondues, and scrumptious desserts. Recommended.

### $$ El Apaste
*5 Calle, 14-48, Zona 3, T7776-6249.*
Local Xela cuisine, rich stews and meats, traditionally served in the eponymous *apaste* (terracotta dish).

### $$ Sabor de India
*15 Avenida, 3-64.*
Don't miss this fully authentic Indian restaurant. It serves wholesome, flavourful, good value curries complete with naan bread. Lovely sweet mango lassis, good service and relaxed ambience. Recommended.

### $$ Ut'z Hua
*Av 12, 3-02, Zona 1.*
This prettily decorated restaurant with purple tablecloths does typical food, which is always very good and filling. Ask for the *pollo con mole* or fish. Recommended.

### $$-$ Asados Puente
*7 Calle, 13-29.*
Lots of veggie dishes with tofu and tempeh. Also ceviche. Popular with expats. Run by Ken Cielatka and Eva Melgar. Some profits go towards helping ill children.

### $$-$ Salón Tecún
*Pasaje Enríquez, off the park at 12 Av y 4 Calle, Zona 1.*
Bar, local food, breakfasts also, TV. Always popular with gringos and locals.

### $ El Deli Crepe
*14 Av, 3-15, Zona 1.*
Good tacos, *almuerzo* with soup, great milkshakes, savoury and sweet crêpes, juicy *fajitas* that arrive steaming.

## Cafés and bakeries

### Bakeshop at 18 Av
*1-40, Zona 3. Tue and Fri 0900-1800.*
Mennonite bakery that is Xela's answer to *dulce* heaven. They bake a whole range of cookies, muffins, breads and cakes and sells fresh yoghurt and cheeses. Get there early as the goodies go really fast.

### Blue Angel Café
*7 Calle, 15-79, Zona 1.*
Great salads, light meals, service a little slow though, movies shown on a monthly rotation, useful noticeboard.

### Café Baviera
*5 Calle, 13-14, Zona 1. Open 0700-2000.*
Good cheap meals and excellent pies, huge cake portions (try the carrot cake) and coffee in large premises, with walls lined from ceiling to floor with old photos and posters. Good for breakfasts, but a little on the expensive side. Popular, but lacks warmth.

### Café y Chocolate La Luna
*8 Av, 4-11, Zona 1.*
Delicious hot chocolate with or without added luxuries, good cheap snacks, also top chocolates and *pasteles* (the strawberry and cream pie is recommended), pleasant atmosphere in a colonial house decorated with moon symbols, fairy lights, and old photos; a good meeting place.

### Chocolate Doña Pancha
*10a Calle 16-67 Zona 1, T7761-9700.*
High-quality chocolate factory, with great range of drinks, cakes and pastries, also chocolate products to take away.

### La Chatia Artesana
*7 Calle, 15-18, www.lachatia-artesana.com.*
This wonderful café-restaurant serves superb gourmet sandwiches, such as chicken teriyaki and portobello mushrooms, on a variety of artisanal breads. There's also delicious cookies, brownies and other snacks, along with fresh coffee and juice. Lovely outdoor courtyard. Recommended.

## Bars and clubs

### El Duende
*14 Av 'A,' 1-42, Zona 1. Open 1800-2330.*
Popular café-bar. A favourite among Guatemalans and gringos.

### El Zaguán
*14 Av 'A', A-70, Zona 1. Wed, Thu 1900-2430, Fri, Sat 2100-2430.*
A disco-bar, US$3.25, drink included; plays salsa music.

### La Taberna de Don Rodrigo
*14 Av, Calle C-47, Zona 1.*
Cosy bar, reasonable food served in dark wood atmosphere, draught beer.

### Ojalá
*15 Av 'A', 3-33.*
An entertainment venue, popular with both locals and gringos, which also shows films.

## Entertainment

See also **Blue Angel Café** and **Ojalá** in Cafés and bakeries and Bars and clubs, above.

### Cinemas
**Cine Sofía**, *7 Calle 15-18. Mon-Fri 1800.*
**La Pradera**, *in shopping mall in Zona 3, next to bus terminal.* 5 screens, latest releases.

### Dance
**Trópica Latina**, *5 Calle 12-24, Zona 1, T5892-8861, tropicalatina@xelawho.com.* Classes Mon-Sat.

### Theatre
**Teatro Municipal**, *14 Av and 1 Calle.* Main season May-Nov, theatre, opera, etc.

## Shopping

### Bookshops
**Vrisa**, *15 Av, 3-64, T7761-3237.* A good range of English-language second-hand books.

## Markets
The **main market** is at Templo de Minerva on the western edge of town (take the local bus, US$0.10); at the southeast corner of Parque Centro América is the **Centro Comercial Municipal**, a shopping centre with craft and textile shops on the upper levels, food, clothes, etc below. There is another **market** at 2 Calle y 16 Av, Zona 3, south of Parque Benito Juárez, known as La Democracia. Every first Sun of the month there also is an art and handicrafts market, around Parque Centro América.

## Supermarkets
**Centro Comercial Mont Blanc**, *Paiz, 4 Calle between 18-19 Av, Zona 3.*
**Despensa Familiar**, *13 Av, 6-94.*
**La Pradera**, *near the Minerva Terminal.*

### North of Quetzaltenango
The smallest bottle of bright yellow *rompope* is sold in various shops around Salcajá, including the **Fábrica de Pénjamo** (2 Av, 4-03, Zona 1, US$1.55), and it slips down the throat very nicely!

## What to do

When climbing the volcanoes make sure your guides stay with you all the time; it can get dangerous when the cloud rolls down.
**Adrenalina Tours**, *inside Pasaje Enríquez, T7761-4509, www.adrenalinatours.com.* Numerous tours are on offer including bike, fishing, rafting, horse riding, rock climbing and volcano tours as well as packages to Belize, Honduras and the Petén and trips to Huehue and Todos Santos. Specializes in hikes and treks all over Guatemala. Highly recommended.
**Agencia de Viajes SAB**, *1 Calle, 12-35, T7761-6402.* Good for cheap flights.
**Guatemaya Intercultural Travel Agency**, *14 Av "A", 3-06, T7765-0040.* Very helpful.
**Mayaexplor**, *T7761-5057, www.mayaexplor. com.* Run by Thierry Roquet, who arranges a variety of trips around Xela and around

the country. He can also arrange excursions into Mexico, Belize and Honduras and treks, eg Nebaj–Todos Santos. French-speaking. His website offers useful info for travellers. A proportion of funds goes towards local development projects. Recommended.

**Quetzaltrekkers**, *based inside Casa Argentina at Diagonal 12, 8-37, T7765-5895, www.quetzaltrekkers.com.* This recommended, established, non-profit agency is known for its 3-day hike (Sat morning to Mon afternoon) from Xela across to Lake Atitlán. Proceeds go to the **Escuela de la Calle School** for children at risk, and a dorm for homeless kids. Also offers trek from Nebaj–Todos Santos, 6 days, full-moon hike up Santa María and others. Hiking volunteers are also needed for a 3-month minimum period: hiking experience and reasonable Spanish required.

**Tranvia de los Altos**, *www.tranviadelos altos.com.* Provides daytime and nighttime walking tours in Xela as well as excursions. Guided city tour is only US$4. Recommended.

## Zunil

See **Las Cumbres Eco-Saunas y Gastronomía**, T5399-0029, under Where to stay, above.

## Language schools

See also box, page 287. Many of Xela's schools can be found at www.xelapages.com/schools.htm. There are many schools offering individual tuition, accommodation with families, extra-curricular activities and excursions. Some also offer Mayan languages. Several schools fund community-development projects, and students are invited to participate with voluntary work. Some schools are non-profit making; enquire carefully. Extra-curricular activities are generally better organized at the larger schools. Prices start from US$130 per week including accommodation, but rise in June-August to US$150 and up. The following have been recommended:

**Centro de Estudios de Español Pop Wuj**, 1 Calle, 17-72, T7761-8286, www.pop-wuj.org.
**Guatemalensis**, 19 Av, 2-14, Zona 1, T7765-1384, www.geocities.com/spanland/.
**Sol Latino**, Diagonal 12, 6-58, Zona 1, T5613-7222, www.spanishschoollatino.com.
**Instituto Central América (ICA)**, 19 Av, 1-47 Calle, Zona 1, T7763-1871.
**INEPAS (Instituto de Estudios Español y Participación en Ayuda Social)**, 15 Av, 4-59, T7765-1308, www.inepas. org. Keen on social projects and has already founded a primary school in a Maya village, extremely welcoming.
**Juan Sisay Spanish School**, 15 Av, 8-38, Zona 1, T7761-1586, www.juansisay.com.
**Kie-Balam**, Diagonal 12, 4-46, Zona 1, T7761-1636, kie_balam@hotmail.com. Offers conversation classes in the afternoon in addition to regular hours.
**La Paz**, Diagonal 11, 7-36, T7761-2159, xela.escuela lapaz@gmail.com.
**Minerva Spanish School**, 24 Av, 4-39, Zona 3, T7767-4427, www.minervaspanishschool.com.
**Proyecto Lingüístico Quetzalteco de Español**, 5 Calle, 2-40, Zona 1, T7765-2140, hermandad@plqe.org. Recommended.
**Proyecto Lingüístico 'Santa María'**, 14 Av "A", 1-26, T7765-1262. Volunteer opportunities and free internet access.
**Sakribal**, 6 C, 7-42, Zona 1, T7763-0717, www.sakribal.com. Community projects are available.
**Ulew Tinimit**, 4 C, 15-23, Zona 1, T7761-6242, www.spanish guatemala.org. Utatlán, 12 Av, 14-32, Pasaje Enríquez, Zona 1, T7763-0446, utatlan_xela@hotmail.com. Voluntary work opportunities, one of the cheaper schools.

## Bus

Most visitors arrive by bus, a 30-min (14.5 km) journey southwest of Cuatro Caminos. Buses pull into the Zona 3 Minerva Terminal. To get a bus into the city centre, take a path through the market at its far left or its far right, which brings you out in front of the Minerva Temple. Watch out for very clever pickpockets walking through this market. Buses for the town centre face away (left) from the temple. All Santa Fe services go to Parque Centro América, US$0.15. Alternatively take a taxi.

**Local** City buses run between 0600 and 1900. Between the town centre and Minerva Terminal, bus No 6, Santa Fe, US$0.20, 15-30 mins, depending on traffic. Catch the bus at the corner of 4 Calle and 13 Av by Pasaje Enríquez. Buses to the Rotonda leave from the corner of 11 Av and 10 Calle, US$0.20, or catch bus No 6, 10 or 13, from Av 12 y 3 Calle as they come down to the park, 15 mins. To catch buses to **San Francisco El Alto**, **Momostenango**, the **south coast** and **Zunil**, get off the local bus at the Rotonda, then walk a couple of steps away from the road to step into a feeder road where they all line up.

**Long distance** To **Guatemala City**, **Galgos**, Calle Rodolfo Robles, 17-43, Zona 1, T7761-2248, 1st-class buses, at 0400, 1230, 1500, US$5, 4 hrs, will carry bicycles; **Marquensita** several a day (office in the capital 21 Calle, 1-56, Zona 1), leaves from the Minerva Terminal, US$4.60, comfortable, 4 hrs. **Líneas América**, from 7 Av, 3-33, Zona 2, T7761-2063, US$5, 4 hrs, between 0515-2000, 6 daily. **Línea Dorada**, 12 Av and 5 C, Zona 3, T7767-5198, 0400 and 1530, US$9. **Transportes Alamo** from 14 Av, 5-15, Zona 3, T7763-5044, between 0430 and 1430, 7 a day, US$5, 4 hrs.

The following destinations are served by buses leaving from the Minerva Terminal, Zona 3 and the Rotonda. For **Antigua**, change at Chimaltenango by either taking a chicken bus or Pullman. To **Almolonga**, via **Cantel**, every 30 mins, US$0.50, 10 mins. (Buses to Almolonga and Zunil not via Cantel, leave from the corner of 10 Av and 10 Calle, Zona 1.) To **Chichicastenango** with **Transportes Veloz Quichelense de Hilda Esperanza**, several from 0500 to 1530, US$3.80, 2½ hrs. To **Cuatro Caminos** US$0.50, 30 mins. To **Huehuetenango** with **Transportes Velásquez**, every 30 mins 0500-1730, US$2.50, 2½ hrs. To **La Mesilla** at 0500, 0600, 0700, 0800, 1300, 1400 with **Transportes Unión Fronteriza**, US$3.60, 4 hrs. To **Los Encuentros**, US$2.20. To **Malacatán**, US$3.60, 5 hrs. To **Momostenango**, US$1.20, 1½ hrs. To **Panajachel**, with **Transportes Morales**, at 0500, 0600, 1000, 1200, 1500, US$3.20, 2½-3 hrs. To **Retalhuleu**, US$1.20, 1½ hrs. To **Salcajá**, every 30 mins, US$0.40, 15 mins. To **San Andrés Xecul** every 2 hrs, US$0.60, 30 mins. To **San Cristóbal Totonicapán**, every 30 mins, US$0.40, 20 mins. To **San Francisco El Alto**, US$0.70. **San Marcos**, every 30 mins, US$1, 1 hr. **San Martín Sacatepéquez/San Martín Chile Verde**, US$0.70, 1 hr. **Santiago Atitlán**, with **Ninfa de Atitlán** at 0800, 1100, 1230, 1630, 4½ hrs. To **Ciudad Tecún Umán** every 30 mins, 0500-1400, US$3.60, 4 hrs. To **Totonicapán**, every 20 mins, US$1.20, 1 hr. To **Zunil**, every 30 mins, US$0.70, 20-30 mins.

**Shuttle** Adrenalina Tours, see Tour operators, above, runs shuttles. To **Cobán**, US$45, Panajachel, US$20 and Antigua, US$25. Adrenalina also runs a shuttle to and from **San Cristóbal de las Casas**, Mexico, US$35.

## Car

**Car hire** Tabarini Renta Autos, 9 Calle, 9-21, Zona 1, T7763-0418.

**Mechanic** José Ramiro Muñoz R, 1 Calle, 19-11, Zona 1, T7761-8204. Also **Goodyear Taller** at the Rotonda and for motorbikes **Moto Servicio Rudy**, 2 Av, 3-48, Zona 1, T7765-5433.

### Taxi
Found all over town, notably lined up along Parque Centro América.
**Taxis Xelaju**, T7761-4456.

## North of Quetzaltenango
### Bus
All buses heading to Quetzaltenango from Cuatro Caminos pass through **Salcajá**, 10 mins. From Xela to **San Andrés Xecul**, US$0.60, 30 mins. Or take any bus heading to Cuatro Caminos and getting off at the Esso station on the left-hand side, and then almost doubling back on yourself to take the San Andrés road. There are pickups from here.

## South of Quetzaltenango
### Bus
**Cantel** is 10-15 mins by bus (11 km), and US$0.24 from Xela on the way to Zunil, but you need to take the bus marked for Cantel Fábrica and Zunil, not Almolonga and Zunil. From **Zunil** to Xela via Almolonga leaves from the bridge. Walk down the left-hand side of the church to the bottom of the hill, take a left and you'll see the buses the other side of the bridge, US$0.60. **Fuentes Georginas** is reached either by walking the 8 km uphill just to the south of Zunil, 2 hrs (300-m ascent; take the right fork after 4 km, but be careful as robbery has occurred here), by pickup truck in 15 mins (US$10 return with a 1-hr wait), or hitch. If you come by bus to Zunil and are walking to the Fuentes, don't go down into town with the bus, but get off on the main road at the Pepsi stand and walk to the entrance road, which is visible 100 m away on the left. See also Shuttles, above, for transfer to the thermal pools.

## El Viejo Palmar
### Bus
Just before San Felipe, and just before the Puente Samalá III, if you're heading south, is the turn to the right for El Viejo Palmar. Take any bus heading to the south coast, and asked to be dropped off at the entrance and walk. Or, take a pickup from San Felipe park. Ask for Beto or Brígido.

### Taxi
From Xela round trip is US$25, or take a tour from town.

## Volcán Santa María and Santiaguito
### Bus
To reach the volcano take the bus to **Llano del Pinal**, 7 km away, from the Minerva Terminal (every 30 mins, last bus back 1800). Get off at the crossroads and follow the dirt road towards the right side of the volcano until it sweeps up the right (about 40 mins), take the footpath to the left (where it is marked for some distance); bear right at the saddle where another path comes in from the left, but look carefully as it is easily missed.

## Laguna Chicabal
### Bus/car
The last bus to **Quetzaltenango** leaves at 1900, 1 hr. Parking at the entrance, US$2. It is a 40-min walk from the car park (and you'll need a sturdy vehicle if you attempt the steep first ascent in a car).

## West of Quetzaltenango
### Bus
Volcán Tajumulco can be reached by getting to the village of **San Sebastián** from San Marcos, which takes about 2 hrs.

# Southern
## Guatemala

The southern coastal plain of Guatemala supports many plantations of coffee, sugar and tropical fruit trees and its climate is unbearably hot and humid. Amid the fincas some of the most curious archaeological finds have been unearthed, a mixture of monument styles such as Maya and Olmec, including Abaj Takalik, the cane field stones at Santa Lucía Cotzumalguapa and the big 'Buddhas' of Monte Alto.

On the coast are the black-sand beaches and nature reserves of the popular and laid-back Monterrico and Sipacate resorts, where nesting turtles burrow in the sand and masses of birds take to the skies around. Casting a shadow over the coast, the Central Highland volcanoes of Lake Atitlán, and the Antigua trio of Fuego, Acatenango and Agua, look spectacular, looming on the horizon above the lowlands.

**Best** for
Fishing ▪ Pre-Colombian sites ▪ Turtles ▪ Views

## Routes to El Salvador

Three routes pass through Southern Guatemala to El Salvador. The main towns are busy but scruffy with little to attract the visitor. See also Border crossings box in Practicalities chapter, for more information on crossing into El Salvador.

**Route 1   The Pan-American Highway**: The first route heads directly south along the paved Pan-American Highway from Guatemala City (CA1) to the border at **San Cristóbal Frontera**. **Cuilapa**, the capital of Santa Rosa Department, is 65 km along the Highway. About 9 km beyond Los Esclavos is the El Molino junction. Further east, just off the Pan-American Highway, is the village of **El Progreso**, dominated by the imposing Volcán Suchitán, at 2042 m, now part of the Parque Regional Volcán Suchitán run by La Fundación de la Naturaleza. There is accommodation. The town fiesta with horse racing is from 10-16 November. From El Progreso, a good paved road goes north 43 km to Jalapa through open, mostly dry country, with volcanoes always in view. There are several crater lakes including **Laguna del Hoyo** near Monjas that are worth visiting. The higher ground is forested. Beyond Jutiapa and El Progreso the Pan-American Highway heads east and then south to Asunción Mita. Here there is a turning left to Lago de Güija. Before reaching the border at **San Cristóbal Frontera**, the Pan-American Highway dips and skirts the shores (right) of **Lago Atescatempa**, with several islands set in heavy forest.

**Route 2   Via Jalpatagua**: The second, quicker way of getting to San Salvador is to take a highway that cuts off right from the first route at El Molino junction, about 7 km beyond the Esclavos bridge. This cut-off goes through El Oratorio and Jalpatagua to the border at **Valle Nuevo**, continuing then to Ahuachapán and San Salvador.

**Route 3   El Salvador (La) via the border at Ciudad Pedro de Alvarado**: This coastal route goes from **Escuintla** (see below) to the border bridge over the Río Paz at La Hachadura (El Salvador). It takes two hours from Escuintla to the border. At **Taxisco**, there is a white church with a curious hearts and holly design on the façade. Further east is Guazacapán, which merges into **Chiquimulilla**, 3 km to the north, the most important town of the area, with good-quality leather goods available. There is accommodation available. A side excursion can be made from Chiquimulilla up the winding CA 16 through coffee fincas and farmland. About 20 km along there is a turning to the left down a 2- to 3-km steep, narrow, dirt road that goes to **Laguna de Ixpaco**, an impressive, greenish-yellow lake that is 350 m in diameter. It is boiling in some places, emitting sulphurous fumes and set in dense forest. This trip can also be made by heading south off the Pan-American Highway after Cuilapa (just before Los Esclavos) towards Chiquimulilla on the CA 16, with old trees on either side, some with orchids in them, where you will reach the sign to Ixpaco, after 20 km. Thirty kilometres beyond on the Pacific Highway is **Ciudad Pedro de Alvarado** on the border.

## Guatemala City to the Pacific coast   Colour map 2, C4.

tranquil lake and Pacific ports

### Amatitlán

Heading south from the capital on Highway CA19, the town of Amatitlán is perched on the banks of a lake of the same name. Sadly, the lake is too polluted for swimming, but rowing boats ply its waters, US$5 per hour. Less demanding is the **teleférico** ① *Fri-Sun 0900-1700, US$2 return*, climbing from its station on the lakeshore to supply commanding views of the surroundings. The main reason for coming to Amatitlán, however, is the **Day of the Cross** on 3 May, when the Christ figure is removed from the church and floated out of a boat amid candles and decorations. South of Amatitlán, the village of **Palín** has a Sunday market in a plaza under an enormous ceiba tree. The textiles are exceptional, but are increasingly difficult to find. There are great views of Pacaya to the east as you head down to the coast, Volcán Agua to the northwest, and the Pacific lowlands to the west.

## Escuintla

Highway CA19 from Guatemala City and Highway 14 from Antigua converge in Escuintla: a large, unattractive provincial centre set in a rich tropical valley. This town acts a major transport hub for the Pacific slope with connections to all the main ports, as well as the international borders with Mexico and El Salvador via Highway CA2, which runs east–west through the region. There are cheap lodgings if you get stuck. For entertainment, you could head 25 km southeast to admire the beasts at the **Autosafari Chapín** ① *Carretera a Taxisco Km 87.5, www.autosafarichapin.com, Tue-Sun, 0900-1730, US$8.* Any bus to Taxisco should be able to drop you at the entrance.

## Puerto San José, Chulamar and Iztapa

South of Escuintla, a fast paved highway heads to Puerto San José, which first opened for business (especially the coffee trade) in 1853 and was once upon a time the country's second largest port. The climate is hot, the streets and most of the beaches are dirty, and at weekends the town fills up with people from the capital. There are swimming beaches nearby, but beware of the strong undercurrent. One of the more popular ones is Chulamar, some 5 km to the west. Iztapa, 12 km east of Puerto San José, is world renowned for deep-sea fishing. Sail fish, bill fish, marlin, tuna, dorado, roosterfish, yellowfin and snapper are to be found in large numbers here. The **Chiquimulilla Canal** runs either side of Puerto San José parallel to the coast for close to 100 km.

## Listings Guatemala City to the Pacific coast

### Where to stay

**Puerto San José, Chulamar and Iztapa**
There are a number of *comedores* in town.

**$$$$ Soleil Pacífico**
*Chulamar, T7879-4444, www. hotelessoleilguatemala.com.*
Set in rambling landscaped grounds, this large all-inclusive resort is the only accommodation of its type in the area. It boasts luxury rooms, suites and bungalows in addition to all the usual luxuries, including 2 jacuzzis, pools, volleyball courts, football fields, restaurants and lounges. There have been a few mixed reports and maintenance issues.

**$$$ Hotel y Turicentro Eden Pacific**
*Barrio El Laberinto, Puerto San José, T7881-1605, www.hoteledenpacific.com.*
Overlooking the beach, a family-run hotel with a self-contained chalet for 12 guests and 35 reasonable a/c rooms with TV. Facilities include pool and restaurant. Various packages are available.

**$$-$ Hotel Club Sol y Playa Tropical**
*1 Calle, 5-48, on the canal, Iztapa, T7881-4365.*
Adequate lodgings with restaurant, pool, friendly staff and fair standard rooms with fans.

## Transport

### Bus

To and from Guatemala City to **Amatitlán** (every 30 mins, US$0.50) from 0700-2045 from 14 Av, between 3 y 4 Calle, Zona 1, Guatemala City. From **Escuintla** (1½ hrs) to the capital from 8 Calle and 2 Av, Zona 1, near the corner of the plaza in Escuintla. Buses that have come along the Pacific Highway and are going on to the capital pull up at the main bus terminal on 4 Av. From the terminal there are buses direct to **Antigua** every 30 mins, 1-1½ hrs, US$1.20. To **Taxisco** from Escuintla, every 30 mins, 0700-1700, 40 mins, for connections onwards (hourly) to La Avellana, for boats to Monterrico. Frequent buses to **Iztapa** with the last bus departing at 2030.

If you are changing in Escuintla for **Santa Lucía Cotzumalguapa** to the west, you need to take a left out of the bus terminal along the 4 Av up a slight incline towards the police fortress and take a left here on its corner, 9 Calle, through the market. Head for 3 blocks straight, passing the Cinammon Pastelería y Panadería on the right at 9 Calle and 2 Av. At the end here are buses heading to Santa Lucía and further west along the Pacific Highway. It is a 5- to 10-min walk. Buses leave here every 5 mins. To **Santa Lucía Cotzumalguapa** (the bus *ayudantes* shout 'Santa'), 35 mins, US$1.20. On the return, buses pull up at the corner of the 8 Calle and 2 Av, where Guatemala City buses also pass.

### Puerto San José, Chulamar and Iztapa

### Bus

Regular buses from the capital passing through **Escuintla**, 2-3 hrs. If you are heading further east by road from Iztapa along the coast to **Monterrico** (past loofah plantations), see page 352.

## Monterrico  *Colour map 2, C4.*

**a small black-sand resort backed by languid mangroves**

★Monterrico is a beachside village where the sunsets are a rich orange and the waves crash spectacularly on to the shore. Due to powerful riptides even strong swimmers can get into trouble here, so take care. The village itself is hot and sleepy during the week, but increasingly popular at the weekends. If you are in the area between September and January, thanks to the efforts of local hatcheries, you can sponsor a baby turtle's waddle to freedom.

The landing stage is 10 minutes' walk from the ocean front, where you'll find the main restaurants and places to stay. When you step off the dock take the first left, and keep left, which heads directly to the main cluster of beach hotels. This road is known as Calle del Proyecto or Calle del Muelle. Walking straight on from the dock takes you to the main drag in town. When you get to the main drag and want to walk to the main group of hotels, take a left along the beach or take the sandy path to the left one block back from the beach where the sand is a tiny bit easier to walk on.

Although Monterrico's popularity is growing fast, its views are undisturbed by high-rise blocks. All the hotels, mostly rustic and laid-back, are lined up along the beach, and there are a few shops and *comedores* not linked to hotels, in this village of just 1500 people. The village is surrounded by canals carpeted in aquatic plants and mangrove swamps with bird and turtle reserves in their midst. These areas make up the **Biotopo Monterrico-Hawaii** (also known as the **Monterrico Nature Reserve**), which can be explored by *lancha* with the turtle hatchery (see below), around US$10 per person for a one- to two-hour tour. Anteater, armadillo, racoon and weasel live in the area, but it is worth taking the boat trip at sunrise or sunset to see migratory North and South American birds, including flamingo.

However, the real stars in this patch are the olive ridleys *Parlama blanca* and *Parlama negra* turtles, which lay eggs between July and October, and the Baule turtle, which lays between between October and February. There is a turtle hatchery in the village, the **Tortugario Monterrico** ⓘ *daily 0800-1200, 1400-1700, US$6.50*, which offers night tours and volunteer opportunities. Just behind the hatchery there are 300 breeding crocodiles, 150 turtles and iguanas. The turtle liberation event takes place every Saturday night between October and February. Around 8 km east of Monterrico is another hatchery, also offering tours and volunteering. It is run by **Arcas Guatemala** ⓘ *inside Parque Hawaii, T4743-4655, www.arcasguatemala.com; buses from Monterrico every 1-2 hrs, 30 mins, US$0.65.*

## Listings Monterrico

### Where to stay

Most hotels are fully booked by Sat midday and prices rise at weekends so book beforehand.

**$$$$-$$$ Isleta de Gaia**
*East of Monterrico on a small island near Las Lisas, T7885-0044, www.isleta-de-gaia.com.*
Managed by a French-American team, an exclusive boutique hotel located on a private island between the Chiquimulilla Canal and the Pacific ocean. Accommodation is in tasteful, traditional bungalows. A great hideaway and the most interesting lodging for miles, but accessible only by private *lancha*; contact in advance to organize transport. Rustic-chic. Recommended.

**$$$ Atelie del Mar**
*Just off the beach, west of Calle Principal, 5752-5528, www.hotelateliedelmar.com.*
This personable boutique hotel has a secluded, colourful, well-tended garden, an art gallery featuring work by the owner, Violeta Marroquín, a restaurant and 2 pools. Accommodation includes 16 rooms of different sizes, all equipped with a/c, TV, and private bath. Rates include breakfast and Wi-Fi. Hospitable and helpful. Good service.

**$$$ Dos Mundos**
*8901 Monterrico Rd, east of Calle Principal, T7823-0820, www.hotelsdosmundos.com.*
One of Monterrico's more upmarket options, The resort-style Dos Mundos boasts

14 well-attired bungalows with a/c and a rather beautiful infinity pool overlooking the ocean. Other amenities include restaurant, bar, and tours. Breakfast included.

**$$$-$ Café del Sol**
*250 m west of Calle Principal, T5810-0821, www.cafe-del-sol.com.*
Quiet, simple and comfortable beachside lodgings, including 13 pleasant rooms. The newest ones are the most comfortable ($$$); those across the road in an annexe are much more spartan ($). There is also a bar area, pool, jacuzzi and restaurant. Part of their profits go to Eternal Spring Foundation, a sustainable development organization. Recommended.

**$$ Hotel Pez de Oro**
*At the end of main strip to the east, T2368-3684, www.pezdeoro.com.*
18 spacious bungalows with traditional thatched roofs, terraces, and hammocks, all attractively set around a pool. All rooms have private bathroom, mosquito lamps, hand-woven bedspreads, pretty bedside lights and fan; some have a/c. Secluded and tranquil. Recommended.

**$$ Hotel Restaurante Dulce y Salado**
*Some way away from the main cluster of hotels and a 500-m hard walk east through sand if you are on foot, T4154-0252, www.dulceysaladoguatemala.com.*
The sea breezes and uninterrupted view of the highland volcanoes at this secluded hotel

are fantastic. Set around a pool, the thatched cabins are nice and clean, with bath, fans and mosquito nets. Run by a friendly Italian couple, Fulvio and Graziella. Breakfast included, good Italian food in the restaurant.

### $$-$ Johnny's Place
*Main strip, T4369-6900,*
*www.johnnysplacehotel.com.*
Very popular with locals and gringos, Johnny's Place is a buzzing social space (especially at weekends) with a wide range of accommodation including bungalows ($$$), rooms ($$), suites, economy 'backpacker' rooms with shared bath, and for the very thrifty, dorms ($). There is internet, table tennis, pools and a beachside restaurant with free coffee fill-ups. A good place for groups. Recommended.

### $ El Delfín
*On the beachfront, 20 m from Calle Principal,*
*T4661-9255, www.hotel-el-delfin.com.*
Lots of good reports about this cheery no-frills option, popular with backpackers and families. Accommodation includes a range of good value bungalows and rooms with deals sometimes available if staying more than 3 nights. The restaurant and bar overlook the beach and serve vegetarian food. Organizes shuttles at any hour. Relaxing and recommended.

## Restaurants

Be careful, especially with *ceviche*. There are lots of seafood joints and local *comedores* along Calle Principal, which leads to the beach. The best and most popular of the bunch appears to be:

### $$$-$$ Taberna El Pelicano
*On the seafront past Johnny's Place. Wed-Sat.*
Named after a rescued pelican called Pancho, this relaxed and well-established haunt offers a diverse and creative menu of steaks, pastas, salads and seafood, all very fresh and prepared according to flavourful Swiss and Italian recipes. Try the catch of the day or the toasted camembert salad. Recommended.

## Bars and clubs

For drinking and dancing, try **Johnny's Place** (see Where to stay, above), thronging with party-loving Guatemaltecos on Fri and Sat nights. Also worth a look is **Mañanitas Beach Lounge**, overlooking the beach at the end of Calle Principal.

## What to do

### Tour operators
Those preferring to stay on land can rent horses for a jaunt on the beach. *Lancha* and turtle-searching tours are operated by a couple of agencies in town.

## Transport

### Bus and boat
There are 3 ways of getting to Monterrico: 2 by public transport and 1 by shuttle.

The **1st route** to Monterrico involves heading direct to the Pacific coast by taking a bus from the capital to **Puerto San José**, 1 hr, and changing for a bus to **Iztapa**. Or take a direct bus from Escuintla to Iztapa. Then cross river by the toll bridge to **Pueblo Viejo** for US$1.60 per vehicle (buses excluded), or US$0.80 per foot passenger, 5 mins. The buses now continue to Monterrico, about 25 km east, 1 hr. Buses run to and from Iztapa between 0600-1500, from the corner of main street and the road to Pueblo Viejo to the left, 3 blocks north of the beach, just past the Catholic church on the right.

The **2nd route** involves getting to Taxisco first and then La Avellana. There are also direct buses to La Avellana from Guatemala City, see page 273. If you are coming from Antigua, take a bus to **Escuintla** 1-1½ hrs. From there, there are regular departures to **Taxisco**, 40 mins. From Taxisco to La Avellana, buses leave hourly until 1800, US$1, 20 mins. If you take an international bus from Escuintla (45 mins), it will drop you off just past the Taxisco town turn-off, just before a bridge with a slip road. Walk up the road (5 mins) and veer to the right where you'll see the bus stop for **La Avellana**. At La Avellana take the **motor boats** through mangrove swamps, 20-30 mins, US$0.60 for foot passengers, from 0630 and then hourly until 1800. The journey via this route from Antigua to Monterrico takes about 3¼ hrs if your connections are good. Return boats to La Avellana leave at 0330, 0530, 0700, 0800, 0900, 1030, 1200, 1300, 1430, 1600. Buses leave La Avellana for Taxisco hourly until 1800. Buses pull up near the **Banco Nor-Oriente** where numerous buses heading to Guatemala and Escuintla pass.

**Shuttles** Alternatively, numerous travel agencies in **Antigua** run shuttles, US$10-12 one way. You can book a return shuttle journey in Monterrico by going to the language school on the road that leads to the dock. There are also mini buses operating from Monterrico to **Iztapa** and vice-versa.

Amid the sugar-cane fields and fincas of this coastal town lie an extraordinary range of carved stones and images with influences from pre-Maya civilizations, believed mostly to be ancient Mexican cultures, including the Izapa civilization from the Pacific coast area of Mexico near the Guatemalan border.

Four main points of interest entice visitors to the area: Bilbao, El Baúl, Finca El Baúl and the **Museo de Cultura Cotzumalguapa**. The town is just north of the Pacific Highway, where some of the hotels and banks are.

### Bilbao, El Baúl, Finca El Baúl and Museo de Cultura Cotzumalguapa
*You can visit all the sites on foot. However, you are advised not to go wandering in and out of the cane fields at the Bilbao site as there have been numerous assaults in the past. You can walk along the tarmacked road north to the El Baúl sites (6 km and 8 km respectively from town), but there is no shade, so take lots of water. Ask for directions. There is an occasional 'Río Santiago' bus, which goes as far as Colonia Maya, close to the El Baúl hilltop. Only workers' buses go to Finca El Baúl in the morning, returning at night. Alternatively, take a taxi from town (next to the plaza) and negotiate a trip to all 4 areas. They will charge around US$20. Note Do not believe any taxi driver who tells you that Las Piedras (the stones) have been moved from the cane fields to the museum because of the increasing assaults.*

There is considerable confusion about who carved the range of monuments and stelae scattered around the town. It is safe to say that the style of the monuments found in the last 150 years is a blend of a number of pre-Columbian styles. Some believe the prominent influence is Toltec, the ancestors of the Maya K'iche', Kaqchikel, Tz'utujil and Pipiles. It is thought the Tolteca-Pipil had been influenced in turn by the Classic culture from Teotihuacán, a massive urban state northeast of the present Mexico City, which had its zenith in the seventh century AD. However, some experts say that there is no concrete evidence to suggest that the Pipiles migrated as early as AD 400 or that they were influenced by Teotihuacán. All in all, the cultural make-up of this corner of Guatemala may never be known.

The remnants at **Bilbao**, first re-discovered in 1860, are mainly buried beneath the sugar cane but monuments found above ground show pre-Maya influences. It is thought that the city was inhabited 1200 BC-AD 800. There are four large boulders – known as Las Piedras – in sugar-cane fields, which can be reached on foot from the tracks leading from the end of 4 Avenida in town. **El Baúl** is a Late Classic ceremonial centre, 6 km north of Santa Lucía, with two carved stone pieces to see; most of its monuments were built between AD 600 and 900. **Finca El Baúl** has a collection of sculptures and stelae gathered from the large area of the finca grounds.

The **Museo de Cultura Cotzumalguapa** ① *Finca Las Ilusiones, Mon-Fri 0800-1600, Sat 0800-1200, US$1.30, less than 1 km east of town, ask the person in charge for the key,* displays numerous artefacts collected from the finca and a copy of the famous Bilbao Monument 21 from the cane fields. To get to the museum, walk east along the Pacific Highway and take a left turn into the finca site.

## Santa Lucía Cotzumalguapa to the Mexican border

Beyond Santa Lucía Cotzumalguapa is **Cocales**, where a good road north leads to Patulul and after 30 km, to Lake Atitlán at San Lucas Tolimán. The Pacific Highway continues through San Antonio Suchitepéquez to **Mazatenango** (where just beyond are the crossroads for Retalhueleu and Champerico) and on to Coatepeque and Ciudad Tecún Umán for the Mexican border; see Border crossings box in Practicalities chapter. Mazatenango is the chief town of the Costa Grande zone. While not especially attractive, the Parque Central is very pleasant with many fine trees providing shade. There is a huge fiesta in the last week of February, when hotels are full and double their prices. At that time, beware of children carrying (and throwing) flour.

## Retalhuleu and around

Retalhuleu, normally referred to as 'Reu' (pronounced 'Ray-oo') is the capital of the department. The entrance to the town is grand with a string of royal palms lining the route, known as Calzada Las Palmas. It serves a large number of coffee and sugar estates and much of its population is wealthy. The original colonial church of **San Antonio de Padua** is in the central plaza. Bordering the plaza to the east is the neoclassical **Palacio del Gobierno**, with a giant quetzal sculpture on top. The **Museo de Arqueología y Etnología** ① *Tue-Sat 0830-1300, 1400-1800, Sun 0900-1230, US$1.30, next to the palacio,* is small. Downstairs are exhibits of Maya ceramics.

If you fancy cooling off, near Reu are the **Parque Acuático Xocomil** ① *Km 180.5 on the road from Xela to Champerio, T7722-9400, www.irtra.org.gt, Thu-Sun 0900-1700, US$9.60.* Nearby is the enormous theme park with giant pyramids of **Xetulul** ① *T7722-9450, www. irtra.org.gt, Thu-Sun 100-1800, US$26.*

## Abaj Takalik

*Daily 0700-1700, US$3.25, guides are volunteers so tips are welcomed.*

One of the best ancient sites to visit outside El Petén is Abaj Takalik, a ruined city that lies, sweltering, on the southern plain. Its name means 'standing stone' in K'iche'. The site was discovered in 1888 by botanist Doctor Gustav Brühl. It is believed to have flourished in the late pre-Classic period of 300 BC to AD 250 strategically placed to control commerce between the highlands and the Pacific coast. There are some 239 monuments, which include 68 stelae, 32 altars and some 71 buildings, all set in peaceful surroundings. The environment is loved by birds and butterflies, including blue morphos, and by orchids, which flower magnificently between January and March. The main temple buildings are mostly up to 12 m high, suggesting an early date before techniques were available to build Tikal-sized structures.

## Towards the Mexican border

The main road runs 21 km east off the Pacific Highway to **Coatepeque**, one of the richest coffee zones in the country. There is a bright, modern church in the leafy Plaza Central. The local fiesta takes place from 11-19 March. There are several hotels, *hospedajes* and restaurants. **Colomba**, an attractive typical village east of Coatepeque in the lowlands, has a basic *hospedaje*.

## Listings Santa Lucía Cotzumalguapa and around

### Where to stay

#### Santa Lucía Cotzumalguapa

**$$ Santiaguito**
*Pacific Highway at Km 90.4, T7882-5435,*
*hsantiaguito@yahoo.com.mx.*
Located on the highway on the west side of Santa Lucía, probably the best option in town (which isn't saying much). Rooms have a/c, TV and hot and cold water. Nice leafy grounds with a pool and restaurant. Non-guests can use the pool for US$2.60.

**$$-$ Hotel El Camino**
*Diagonally opposite Santiaguito across the highway at Km 90.5, T7882-5316.*
Large if fairly simple rooms with bath, TV, tepid water and fan. Some have a/c (more expensive). Restaurant attached.

**$ Hospedaje La Reforma**
*A stone's throw from the park on 4 Av, 4-71, T7882-1731.*
Lots of dark box rooms and dark shared showers, ask to see before accepting. Clean, ultra-cheap and basic, would suit budget travellers with modest needs.

#### Retalhuleu and around

**$$ Astor**
*5 Calle 4-60, T7957-8300,*
*www.hotelastorguatemala.com.*
Constructed in the late 19th century and converted to a hotel in 1923 by the Ruiz Javalois family, this handsome colonial-style lodging offers 27 clean, comfortable rooms set around a pretty courtyard. Amenities include a pool, jacuzzi, parking, bar and restaurant. Non-guests can use the pool (better than the one at **Posada de Don José**) for a fee. A good option, recommended.

**$$ La Colonia**
*1.5 km to the north at Km 180.5,*
*T7772-2048, www.hlacoloniareu.com.*
This good value highway lodging boasts a relaxing garden space and patio with leafy tropical plants and pools for adults and children. The lodgings encompass a variety of rooms equipped with a/c and cable TV; ask to see a few. Good food is served in the restaurant.

**$$ Posada de Don José**
*5 Calle, 3-67, T7962-2900,*
*www.posadadonjose.com.*
Don Jose's is a well-established colonial-style option with 2 floors of comfortable, spacious well-attired rooms overlooking a central courtyard with a pool; some are newer than others, ask to see a few. The restaurant is possibly the best in town, serving such mouth-watering temptations as lobster sautéed in cognac. Non-guests can use the pool for a small fee.

**$$ Siboney**
*5 km northwest of Reu in San Sebastián,*
*Km 180.5, T7772-2174, www.hotelsiboney.com.*
A very reasonable 3-star option on the highway, motel-style with comfortable rooms set around pool. There's a water slide for the kids and a jacuzzi for the adults. Try the *caldo de mariscos* or *paella* in the excellent restaurant. Non-guests can pay to use the pool.

## Restaurants

### Retalhuleu and around
There are lots of pizzerias and a few fast food joints in town. For a quality dining experience, head to **Hotel Astor** or **Posada de Don José** (see Where to stay, above). Alternatively, for something cheap and low-key, try:

**$$ Restaurante La Luna**
*8a Av and 5a Calle, a block from the main plaza.*
Well established and popular, La Luna is the place for good value, hearty, home-cooked *típico* meals.

## Transport

### Santa Lucía Cotzumalguapa
**Bus**
Regular departures to the capital. Buses plying the Pacific Highway also pass through, so if you are coming from Reu in the west or Escuintla in the east you can get off here.

**Car**
If you are driving, there are a glut of 24-hr **Esso** and **Texaco** gas stations here. See under Guatemala City to the Pacific coast, page 350, for catching transport from **Escuintla**.

### Santa Lucía Cotzumalguapa to the Mexican border
**Bus**
5 a day **Cocales-Panajachel**, between 0600 and 1400, 2½ hrs. Frequent buses to **Mazatenango** from Guatemala City, US$5. To the border at **Ciudad Tecún Umán**, US$2.10, an irregular service with Fortaleza del Sur.

### Retalhuleu and around
**Bus**
Services along the Pacific Highway to Mexico leave from the main bus terminal, which is beyond the city limits at 5 Av 'A'. To **Coatepeque** (0600-1800), **Malacatán**, **Mazatenango** and **Champerico** (0500-1800). Buses also leave from here to **El Asintal**, for Abaj Takalik, 30 mins, every 30 mins from 0600-1830, last bus back to Reu 1800. Or catch them before that from the corner of 5 Av 'A' and the Esso gas station as they turn to head for the village. Leaving from a smaller terminal at 7 Av/10 Calle, there are regular buses to **Ciudad Tecún Umán**, **Talismán** and **Guatemala City** via the Pacific route, and to **Xela** (1¾ hrs, every hour 0500-1800).

### Abaj Takalik
**Bus**
Take a bus to El from **Retalhuleu** and walk the hot 4 km to the site entrance. Or, take any bus heading along the Pacific Highway and get off at the **El Asintal** crossroads. Take a pickup from here to El Asintal; then a pickup from the town square to Abaj Takalik. As there are only fincas along this road, you will probably be on your own, in which case it is US$5 to the site or US$10 round trip, including waiting time. Bargain hard.

**Taxi and tour**
A taxi from central plaza in Reu to the site and back including waiting time is US$13. Alternatively, take a tour from Xela.

### Towards the Mexican border
**Bus**
From Quetzaltenango to **Coatepeque**, catch any bus heading to Ciudad Tecún Umán from Reu.

# Guatemala City
## to the Caribbean

From the capital to the Caribbean, the main road passes through the Río Motagua Valley, punctuated by cacti and bordered by the Sierra de Las Minas mountains rising abruptly in the west. Dinosaur remains, the black Christ and the Maya ruins of Quiriguá can be found on or close to the highway. The banana port of Puerto Barrios is a large transport and commercial hub and jumping-off point for the Garífuna town of Lívingston. Trips down the lush gorge of the Río Dulce are a highlight; nearby are some great places to see and stay on its banks, as well as accommodation around Lago de Izabal.

The Carretera al Atlántico, or Atlantic Highway, stretches from Guatemala City all the way to Puerto Barrios on the Caribbean coast in the department of Izabal. Most worthwhile places to visit are off this fast main road, along the Río Motagua valley, where cactus, bramble, willow and acacia grow. There are numerous buses plying the route.

**Best** for
Boat trips ▪ Caribbean lifestyle ▪ Wildlife

## Along the Atlantic Highway

Before Teculután is **El Rancho** at Km 85, the jumping-off point for a trip north to Cobán (see page 376). There are a few places to stay here. Geologists will be interested in the **Motagua fault** near Santa Cruz, between Teculután and Río Hondo. Just before Río Hondo (Km 138), a paved road runs south towards Estanzuela. Shortly before this town you pass a monument on the right commemorating the 1976 earthquake, which activated a fault line that cut across the road. It can still be seen in the fields on either side of the road. The epicentre of this massive earthquake, which measured 7.5 on the Richter scale, and killed 23,000 people, was at **Los Amates**, 65 km further down the valley towards Puerto Barrios.

### Estanzuela

Estanzuela is a small town fronting the highway. Its **Museo de Palaeontología, Arqueología y Geología** ① *daily 0800-1700, free,* displays the incredible reconstructed skeletal remains of a 4-m prehistoric giant sloth found in Zone 6, Guatemala City and a giant armadillo, among others. To get there, either take a **Rutas Orientales** bus from Guatemala City to Zacapa (every 30 minutes 0430-1800, 2¾ to three hours), or take a minibus south from Río Hondo and ask to be dropped at the first entrance to the town on the right. Then walk right, into the town, and continue for 600 m to the museum, 10 minutes. When you reach the school, walk to the right and you will see the museum. Moving on to Esquipulas, take the same Rutas Orientales service that continues from Zacapa, US$6, 1½ hours.

## Chiquimula, Volcán de Ipala and the Honduran border *Colour map 2, C5.*

### volcanic lake and impressive Mayan site

Chiquimula is a stop-off point for travellers who stay here on their way to or from Copán Ruinas, Honduras, if they can't make the connection in one day. The town's fiesta, which includes bullfighting, is from 11-18 August.

An alternative route to Chiquimula and Esquipulas is from the southeast corner of Guatemala City (Zona 10), where the Pan-American Highway heads towards the Salvadorean border. After a few kilometres there is a turning to **San José Pinula** (fiesta: 16-20 March). After San José, an unpaved branch road continues for 203 km through fine scenery to **Mataquescuintla**, **Jalapa** (several *hospedajes*, good bus connections; fiesta: 2-5 May), **San Pedro Pinula**, **San Luis Jilotepeque** and **Ipala** to Chiquimula.

Southwest of Chiquimula, the extinct Volcán de Ipala (1650 m) can be visited. The crater lake is cool and good for swimming. To get here, take an early bus to **Ipala** from Chiquimula; stay on the bus and ask the driver to let you off at Aldea El Chaparroncito (10 minutes after Ipala). From here it's a 1½-hour ascent, following red arrows every now and then. Another ascent goes via Municipio Agua Blanca. Take a minibus to **Agua Blanca** from Ipala and get out at the small village of El Sauce, where the trail starts. The last bus from Ipala to Chiquimula is 1700.

At **Vado Hondo**, 10 km south of Chiquimula on the road to Esquipulas, a smooth dirt road branches east to the Honduran border (48 km) and a further 11 km to the great Maya ruins of Copán. The border is 1 km after the village. For more on crossing to Honduras, see Border crossings box in Practicalities chapter.

## Esquipulas

Esquipulas is dominated by a large, white basilica, which attracts millions of pilgrims from across Central America to view the image of a Black Christ. The town has pulled out the stops for visitors, who, as well as a religious fill, will lack nothing in the way of food, drink and some of the best kitsch souvenirs on the market. If it's possible, stop at the mirador, 1 km from the town, for a spectacular view on the way in of the basilica, which sits at the end of a 1.5-km main avenue. The history of the famous *Cristo Negro* records that in 1735 Father Pedro Pardo de Figueroa, suffering from an incurable chronic illness, stood in front of the image to pray, and was cured. A few years later, after becoming Archbishop of Guatemala he ordered a new church to be built to house the sculpture. The **basilica** ① *open until 2000*, was completed in 1758 and the *Cristo Negro* was transferred from the parish church shortly after that. Inside the basilica, the Black Christ is on a gold cross, elaborately engraved with vines and grapes. It was carved by Quirio Cataño in dark balsam wood in 1595. The image attracts over 1,000,000 visitors per year, some crawling on their hands and knees to pay homage. The main pilgrimage periods are 1-15 January (with 15 January being the busiest day), during Lent, Holy Week and 21-27 July.

## Quiriguá *Colour map 3, B5.*

*Daily 0730-1630, US$4. Take insect repellent. There are toilets, a restaurant, a museum and a jade store and you can store your luggage with the guards. There is no accommodation at the site (yet). The site is reached by a paved road from the Atlantic Highway. The village of Quiriguá is about halfway between Zacapa and Puerto Barrios on the highway, and about 3 km from the entrance road to the ruins.*

The remarkable Late Classic ruins of Quiriguá include the tallest stelae found in the Maya world. The UNESCO World Heritage Site is small, with an excavated acropolis to see, but the highlight of a visit is the sight of the ornately carved tall stelae and the zoomorphic altars. The Maya here were very industrious, producing monuments every five years between AD 751 and 806, coinciding with the height of their prosperity and confident rule. The earliest recorded monument dates from AD 480.

It is believed that Quiriguá was an important trading post between Tikal and Copán, inhabited since the second century, but principally it was a ceremonial centre. The Kings of Quiriguá were involved in the rivalries, wars and changing alliances between Tikal, Copán and Calakmul. It rose to prominence in the middle of the eighth century, around the time of Cauac Sky who ascended to the throne in AD 724. Cauac Sky was appointed to the position by 18 Rabbit, powerful ruler of Copán (now in Honduras), and its surrounding settlements. It seems that he was fed up with being a subordinate under the domination of Copán, and during his reign, Quiriguá attacked Copán and captured 18 Rabbit. One of the stelae tells of the beheading of the Copán King in the plaza at Quiriguá as a sacrifice after the AD 738 battle. After this event 18 Rabbit disappears from the official chronicle and a 20-year hiatus follows in the historical record of Copán. Following this victory, Quiriguá became an independent kingdom and gained control of the Motagua Valley, enriching itself in the process. And, from AD 751, a monument was carved and erected every five years for the next 55 years.

The tallest stelae at Quiriguá is **Stelae E**, which is 10.66 m high with another 2.5 m or so buried beneath. It is 1.52 m wide and weighs 65 tonnes. One of its dates corresponds with the enthronement of Cauac Sky, in AD 724, but it's thought to date from AD 771. All of the stelae, in parkland surrounded by ceiba trees and palms, have shelters, which makes photography difficult. Some monuments have been carved in the shape of animals, some mythical, all of symbolic importance to the Maya.

Thirteen kilometres from Quiriguá is the turn-off for **Mariscos** and Lago de Izabal (see page 368). A further 28 km on are the very hot twin towns of Bananera/Morales. From Bananera there are buses to Río Dulce, Puerto Barrios and the Petén.

## Puerto Barrios *Colour map 2, B6.*

Puerto Barrios, on the Caribbean coast, is a hot and dusty port town, still a central banana point, but now largely superseded as a port by Santo Tomás. The launch to the Garífuna town of Lívingston leaves from the municipal dock here. While not an unpleasant town, it is not a destination in itself, but rather a launch pad to more beautiful and happening spots in Guatemala. It's also the departure point for the Honduran Caribbean. On the way into town, note the cemetery on the right-hand side, where you will pass a small Indian mausoleum with elephant carvings. During the 19th century, *culi* (coolies) of Hindu origin migrated from Jamaica to Guatemala to work on the plantations. The fiesta is 16-22 July.

## Listings Chiquimula, Volcán de Ipala and the Honduran border

### Where to stay

#### Chiquimula

**$$-$ Posada Perla del Oriente**
*2 Calle between 11 and 12 Av, T7942-0014.*
Near the bus station, this quiet place has plain but spacious rooms with TV and fan ($); some have a/c ($$). There is parking, a restaurant and a pool; grounds are verdant and tranquil. A good deal. Recommended.

**$ Hernández**
*3 Calle, 7-41, T7942-0708.*
Enjoying a convenient central location, this reliable cheapie offers basic, spartan rooms with fan or a/c, cheaper with shared bath. A pool adds to its attraction. Family-run (the owner, Henry, speaks fluent English), quiet and friendly.

**$ Hotel Posada Don Adán**
*8 Av, 4-30, T7942-0549.*
A good, cheap option. **Don Adán** has tidy little rooms with private bath, fan, a/c, TV. Run by a friendly, older couple.

#### Esquipulas

There are plenty of cheap hotels, *hospedajes* and *comedores* all over town, especially in and around 11 Calle, also known as Doble Vía Quirio Cataño. Prices tend to double before the Jan feast day. They also rise at Easter and at weekends. When quiet, midweek, bargain for lower room prices.

**$$$ Hotel El Gran Chortí**
*On the outskirts of town at Km 222, T6685-9696, www.realgranchorti.com.*
Rack rates are on the pricey side, but the grounds are lovely. Rooms are dated, restful and OK. They come complete with cable TV, Wi-Fi, a/c, phone and *frigobar*. There is also a great pool with slides, a restaurant serving meat, pasta and seafood dishes, and a bar.

**$$$ Legendario**
*3 Av and 9 Calle, T7943-1824, www.hotellegendario.com.*
The most expensive place in town, comfortable enough but not great value. Rooms are simple, fine, well equipped and unremarkable. The real draw is the leafy garden and the massive pool, but check it is open before checking in.

**$$$ Payaquí**
*2 Av, 11-26, T7943-1143, www.hotelpayaqui.com.*
The 40 rooms are fair and fine (the suites are comfortable too, if a bit grandiose), with *frigobars*, full of beers for the pilgrims to guzzle, hot-water showers and free drinking water. Facilities include a pool, jacuzzi, spa services, business centre, parking, restaurant

and bar. Credit cards, Honduran lempiras and US dollars accepted.

## $$ Hotel El Peregrino
*2 Av, 11-94, T7943-1054,*
*www.elperegrinoesquipulas.com.*
A small, quiet, comfortable hotel, nothing fancy but quite adequate. Their unique selling point is the rooftop terrace with a small pool and unobstructed views of the basilica. Ask to see rooms before accepting.

## $$ Hotel Real Santa María
*2 Av y 10a Calle, 20-1, T7943-0214,*
*www.hotelrealsantamaria.com.*
Situated a block from the basilica with fine views from its terrace, Real Santa María boasts sumptuous antiques and elaborate wood carved panels in the reception area. Rooms are simple and pleasant. They feature the usual conveniences including Wi-Fi, a/c, and hot water, but avoid those facing the street. There is also a pool and parking area.

## $ Hotel Real Esquipulas
*10a Calle, 3-25, T7943-3293,*
*www.realesquipulashotel.com.*
This uninspired cheapie has plain windowless rooms with hot water, cable TV and a/c. Not really royal, but perfectly adequate for thrifty sorts.

## Quiriguá

## $$ Hotel Restaurante Santa Mónica
*In Los Amates, 2 km south of Quiriguá village on the highway, T7947-3838.*
17 rooms all with private bath, TV and fan, pool, restaurant. It is opposite a 24-hr Texaco gas station and convenient if you don't want to walk the 10-15 mins into Quiriguá village. There are a couple of shops, banks, and *comedores* here.

## $$-$ Posada de Quiriguá
*Km 204, Barrio Toltec, Aldea Quiriguá,*
*Los Amates, T5349-5817,*
*www.geocities.jp/masaki_quirigua.*
Designed and managed by Masaki Kuwada from Japan, Posada de Quiriguá is an attractive guesthouse with a lovely tropical garden and a range of simple but restful rooms, easily the best place to stay in the area. The restaurant serves hearty Guatemalan breakfasts and authentic sushi for dinner. Recommended, but tricky to find – ask around town.

## $ Hotel y Restaurante Royal
*T7947-3639.*
Basic budget lodgings with a restaurant attached. Rooms have bath, cheaper without, clean, mosquito netting on all windows. A good place to meet other travellers.

## Puerto Barrios
There is not much reason to stay and good options are thin on the ground. The following are OK for a night:

## $$ El Reformador
*16 Calle and 7 Av 159, T7948-5489.*
Set around shaded patios, 51 rooms with bathroom, fan and TV, some with a/c, restaurant, laundry service, clean, quiet, accepts credit cards. The same management run the **Oguatour** travel agency across the road. OK.

## $$-$ Hotel del Norte
*At the end of 7 Calle, T7948-2116.*
A rickety, old wooden structure with sloping landings on the seafront side. All rooms have bath, some with a/c. There's a pool and expensive restaurant, but worth it for the English colonial tearoom atmosphere, no credit cards, but will change dollars. Ask to see a few different rooms, some have great views. The newest are the most comfortable, but lack the dilapidated style that makes this hotel an attraction.

## $ Hotel Europa 2
*3a Av, between 11a and 12a Calle,*
*T7948-1292.*
Located in a quiet neighbourhood near the dock, acceptable budget lodgings with clean, simple rooms with brick walls, wandering chickens in the grounds.

Recommended chiefly for its friendly and helpful Cuban management.

## Restaurants

### Chiquimula

**$ Magic**
*Corner of 8 Av and 3 Calle.*
A good place from which to watch the world go by, and most of what's on offer is seriously cheap. Sandwiches, *licuados* and burgers.

**$ Pastelería Las Violetas**
*7 Av, 4-80, and another near Hotel Victoria.*
An excellent cake shop with a fine spread, good-value sandwiches too, plus great cappuccino, and a/c. Next door is its bakery.

### Esquipulas
There are plenty of restaurants, but prices are high for Guatemala.

**$$$ La Hacienda**
*2 Av, 10-20.*
Delicious barbecued chicken and steaks. Kids' menu available, breakfasts available. One of the smartest restaurants in town.

**$$ Restaurante Payaquí**
*2 Av, 11-26, inside the hotel of the same name.*
Specialities include turkey in *pipián*, also lunches and breakfasts. A poolside restaurant makes a pleasant change.

**$ Café Pistachos**
*Close to Hotel Calle Real.*
Clean, cheap snack bar with burgers, hotdogs, etc.

### Puerto Barrios

**$$$-$$ Restaurante Safari**
*At the north end of 5 Av and 1 Calle, overlooking the bay with views all around.*
Basically serving up oceans of fish, including whole fish, *ceviche* and fishburgers.

**$$ La Fonda de Quique**
*An orange and white wooden building at 5 Av and corner of 12 Calle.*

Nicely a/c with hand-made wooden furniture, serving lobster, fish and meats, plus snacks.

## Bars and clubs

### Puerto Barrios

**Mariscos de Izabal**
*Open until 0100.*
One of the most popular spots in Puerto Barrios, this thatched bar is mostly a drinking den but also has tacos, tortillas and burgers served amid beating Latin rhythms.

**The Container**
*Just past the Hotel del Norte overlooking the sea. Open 0700-2300.*
An unusual bar constructed from the front half of an old ship equipped with portholes, and a number of banana containers from the massive banana businesses just up the road.

## Transport

### Chiquimula
**Bus**
There are 3 terminals in Chiquimula, all within 50 m of each other. To **Guatemala City**, **Transportes Guerra** and **Rutas Orientales**, hourly, US$4, 3¼-3½ hrs, leave from 11 Av between 1 and 2 Calle, as do buses for **Puerto Barrios**, several companies, every 30 mins, between 0300-1500, 4 hrs, US$6.50. To **Quiriguá**, US$3.20, 1 hr 50 mins. Take any Puerto Barrios-bound bus. On to **Río Dulce** take the Barrios bus and get off at La Ruidosa junction and change, or change at Bananera/Morales. To **Flores** with **Transportes María Elena**, 8 hrs, 0400, 0800, 1300. Buses to **Ipala** and **Jalapa** also leave from here; 4 buses daily to Jalapa between 0500-1230, 4½ hrs, US$5.80; to Ipala, US$2.20. Supplemented by minibuses 0600-1715 to Ipala. To **Zacapa**, 25 mins, from the terminal inside the market at 10 Av between 1 and 2 Calle. Same for those to **Esquipulas**, every 10 mins, US$2.70, until 1900. To and from **Cobán** via El Rancho (where a change must be made). Buses to **El Florido** (on the

Honduras border) leave with **Transportes Vilma** from inside the market at 1 Calle, between 10 and 11 Av, T7942-2253, between 0530-1630, US$2.70, 1½ hrs. Buses return from the border at 0530, 0630 and then hourly 0700-1700. For more on crossing to Honduras, see Border crossings box in Practicalities chapter.

### Esquipulas
#### Bus
**Rutas Orientales**. Leaving Esquipulas, 1 Av "A" and 11 Calle, T7943-1366, for **Guatemala City** every 30 mins from 0200-1700, 4½ hrs, US$8.50. To **Chiquimula** by minibus, every 30 mins, 0430-1830, US$1.40.

### Quiriguá
#### Bus
Emphasize to the bus driver if you want Quiriguá *pueblo* and not the *ruinas*. Countless travellers have found themselves left at the ruins and having to make a return journey to the village for accommodation.

To get to the **ruins** directly, take any bus heading along the highway towards Puerto Barrios and ask to be let off at the *ruinas*. At this ruins crossroads, take a pickup (very regular), 10 mins, US$0.50, or bus (much slower and less regular) to the ruins 4 km away. The last bus back to the highway is at 1700. You can walk, but take lots of water, as it's hot and dusty with little shade.

To get to the **village** of Quiriguá, 3 km south from the ruins entrance road, it is only a 10-min walk to the **Hotel Royal**. Keep to the paved road, round a left-hand bend, and it's 100 m up on the left. Or take a local bus heading from the highway into the village. The **Hotel Edén** is a further 5 mins down the hill. There is a frequent daily bus service that runs a circular route between Los Amates, Quiriguá village and then on to the entrance road to the ruins. You can also walk through the banana plantations from Quiriguá village to the ruins as well. From **Hotel Royal** walk past the church towards the old train station and the **Hotel Edén**, and follow the tracks branching to the right, through the plantation to the ruins.

### Puerto Barrios
#### Boat
It's a 10-min walk to the municipal dock at the end of Calle 12, from the **Litegua** bus station. Ferries *(barca)* leave for **Lívingston** at 1030 and 0500 (1½ hrs, US$2.50). *Lanchas* also leave when a minimum of 12 people are ready to go, 30 mins, US$3.80. The only scheduled *lanchas* leave at 0630, 0730, 0900 and 1100, and the last will leave, if there are enough people, at 1800. **Transportes El Chato**, 1 Av, between 10 and 11 Calle, T7948-5525, pichilingo2000@yahoo.com, also does trips from here to **Punta de Manabique**, and other places near and far.

**To Belize** *Lanchas* leave for **Punta Gorda** at 1000 with **Transportes El Chato**, address above, returning at 1400, 1 hr 20 mins, US$22. Also services with **Requena** to Punta Gorda at 1400, returning at 0900. See also Border crossings box in Practicalities chapter.

#### Bus
To **Guatemala City**, with Litegua, 6 Av between 9 and 10 Calle, T7948-1002, www. litegua.com. 18 a day, 5 hrs, US$11-7.50. Bus to **El Rancho** (turn-off for Biotopo del Quetzal and Cobán), 4 hrs, take any bus to Guatemala City. To **Quiriguá**, 2 hrs, take any capital-bound bus. To **Chiquimula**, operated by Carmencita, 4 hrs. Alternatively, catch a bus to Guatemala City, getting off at Río Hondo, and catch a colectivo or any bus heading to Chiquimula. For **Río Dulce**, take any bus heading for Guatemala City and change at **La Ruidosa** (15 mins). For minibuses to **Entre Ríos**, for the El Cinchado border crossing to **Honduras** (**Corinto**), with connections to **Omoa**, **Puerto Cortés** and **La Ceiba**. See also Border crossings box in Practicalities chapter, for more information on crossing into Honduras.

Lívingston, or La Buga, is populated mostly by Garífuna, who bring a colourful flavour to this corner of Guatemala. With its tropical sounds and smells, it is a good place to hang out for a few days, sitting on the dock of the bay, or larging it up with the locals, *punta*-style.

*Coco pan* and *cocado* (a coconut, sugar and ginger *dulce*) and locally made jewellery are sold in the streets. The town is the centre of fishing and shrimping in the Bay of Amatique and only accessible by boat. It is nearly 23 km by sea from Puerto Barrios and there are regular daily boat runs that take 35 minutes in a fast *lancha*.

The bulk of the town is up a small steep slope leading straight from the dock, which is at the mouth of the Río Dulce estuary. The other part of town is a linear spread along the river estuary, just north of the dock and then first left. The town is small and everything is within walking distance. The Caribbean beach is pretty dirty nearer the river estuary end, but a little further up the coast, it is cleaner, with palm trees and accommodation. Closer to the town are a couple of bars and weekend beach discos. The town's **Centro Cultural Garífuna-Q'eqchi** is perched on a hillock, and has the best views in the whole of Lívingston. The town's fiestas are 24-31 December, in honour of the Virgen del Rosario, with dancing including the *punta*, and Garífuna Day, 26 November. The small but helpful **tourist office** ① *on the east side of the Parque Municipal, www.livingston.com.gt, daily 0600-1800*, with a café and exhibition space behind.

## Around Lívingston

Northwest along the coastline towards the Río Sarstún, on the border with Belize (where manatee can be seen), is the **Río Blanco beach** (45 minutes by *lancha* from Lívingston), followed by **Playa Quehueche** (also spelt Keueche). Beyond Quehueche, about 6 km (1½ hours) from Lívingston, are **Los Siete Altares**, a set of small waterfalls and pools hidden in the greenery. They are at their best during the rainy season when the water cascades down to the sea. In the drier seasons much of the water is channelled down small, eroded grooves on large slabs of grey rock, where you can stretch out and enjoy the sun. Early *Tarzan* movies were filmed here. Don't stroll on the beach after dark and be careful of your belongings at the Siete Altares end. Police occasionally accompany tourists to the falls; check on arrival what the security situation is. Boats can be hired in Lívingston to visit beaches along the coast towards San Juan and the Río Sarstún.

For one of the best trips in Guatemala take a boat up the **Río Dulce** through the sheer-sided canyon towards El Golfete, where the river broadens. Trees and vegetation cling to the canyon walls, their roots plunging into the waters for a long drink below. The scenery here is gorgeous, especially in the mornings, when the waters are unshaken. Tours can be arranged from Lívingston for US$12. You can also paddle up the Río Dulce gorge on *cayucos*, which can be hired from some of the hotels in Lívingston.

The **Biotopo Chocón Machacas** ① *0700-1600, US$2.50 (private hire at US$125 is the only transport option)*, is one place where the elusive manatee (sea cow) hangs out, but you are unlikely to see him munching his way across the lake bottom, as he is very shy and retreats at the sound of a boat motor. The manatee is an aquatic herbivore, which can be up to 4 m long when adult, and weigh more than 450 kg. It eats for six to eight hours daily and can consume more than 10% of its body weight in a 24-hour period. Administered by CECON, the reserve is a mangrove zone, halfway between Río Dulce town and

Lívingston, on the northern shore of **El Golfete**, an area where the Río Dulce broadens into a lake 5 km across. Four Q'eqchi' communities of 400 people live on land within the 6245-ha reserve. Within the reserve are carpets of water lilies, dragonflies, blue morpho butterflies, pelicans and cormorants. On land, spot army ants, crabs, mahogany trees and the *labios rojos* ('hot lips') flower.

**Proyecto Ak' Tenamit** ① www.aktenamit.org, meaning 'new village' in Q'eqchi', is 15 minutes upriver from Lívingston. It was set up to help 7000 Q'eqchi' Maya displaced by the civil war. Volunteers are needed for a minimum of a month's work (board and transport are available, and volunteers get weekends off). A working knowledge of Spanish is required. There's also a shop and restaurant, with excursions, run by locally trained volunteer guides. Near here is the **Río Tatín tributary** the wonderfully sited **Finca Tatín** and **Hotelito Perdido**; see Where to stay, below. **Reserva Ecológica Cerro San Gil**, with its natural pools, karstic caves and biostation, can be visited from here, or from Río Dulce. Contact **FUNDAECO** ① www.fundaeco.org.gt.

## Punta de Manabique

Punta de Manabique is a fine, finger-shaped peninsula northeast of Puerto Barrios and just visible across the bay from Lívingston, coated in a beach of white sand on its eastern side, and by mangrove on the other. Travelling north to the point of the peninsula, you pass the Bahía de Graciosa, where dolphins frolic and manatees silently graze under the surface. In its virgin tropical forest live howler monkeys, parrots, snakes, pizote, tapirs and peccary and, on its beaches, turtles. There is a visitor centre, scientific station and a hotel. For more information contact the **Fundación Mario Dary** ① www.guate.net/fundary manabique/fundacion.htm, which operates conservation, health, education and ecotourism projects.

## Listings Lívingston and around

### Where to stay

#### $$$ Hotel Villa Caribe
*Up Calle Principal from the dock on the right,*
*T7947-0072, www.villasdeguatemala.com.*
Part of an upscale Guatemalan hotel chain, Villa Caribe enjoys a privileged vantage from its hillside perch. All rooms have views of the Río Dulce or the Caribbean, there is also a pool (available to non-guests when the hotel is not busy for US$6.50), bar and a large restaurant. The best in town, popular with tour groups, but needs some maintenance.

#### $$ Posada El Delfín
*T7947-0976, www.posadaeldelfin.com.*
Located at the mouth of the Río Dulce on a long pier that juts out into the sea, El Delfín promises tranquil views of the local wildlife and boat traffic. They offer 24 reasonable

rooms and suites, chill-out areas with hammocks, and a restaurant. Tours available.

#### $$ Vecchia Toscana
*Barrio Paris, T7947-0884,*
*www.livingston-vecchiatoscana.com.*
This Italian-owned lodging on the beach features a leafy garden with a refreshing pool, breezy rooftop terraces, private pier and a decent Italian restaurant with sea views. Accommodation is in a variety of simple, tranquil, comfortable and occasionally brightly painted rooms, most of them equipped with a/c.

#### $ Casa de la Iguana
*Calle Marcos Sánchez Díaz,*
*5 mins from the dock, T7947-0064,*
*www.casadelaiguana.com.*
A very cool party hostel with ultra-cheap dorms, private rooms with shared bath, and economical 'jungle huts' set around

well-tended garden, as well as space for tents and hammocks. Hot showers, Wi-Fi, bar, daily happy hour and a pub quiz on Sun; what more could you need?

### $ Casa Nostra
*Near the river, T7947-0842, www.casanostralivingston.com.*
Rooms at this simple little bed and breakfast are clean, cheap and colourful. It is recommended chiefly for its friendly host, Stuart Winand, and for its good food, which includes excellent pizza and fresh seafood prepared with international flavours. Very hospitable, good reports.

### $ Casa Rosada
*600 m from the dock, T7947-0303, www.hotelcasarosada.com.*
This pastel-pink house set on the waterfront offers 10 bungalows furnished with attractive hand-painted furniture. The room upstairs overlooks the bay. Meals are set for the day, ranging from pasta to delicious shrimps bathed in garlic. Good, friendly and chilled out, but reservations advisable.

### $ Flowas
*Barrio Compoamor, on the beach, T7947-0376, infoflowas@gmail.com.*
Rustic beach bungalows for those who like to be up close to the lapping ocean. Each unit has a porch and hammock. Tranquil and secluded with a hippy backpacker vibe.

### $ Hotel Ríos Tropicales
*T7947-0158, www.mctropic.webs.com.*
This place has some nice touches to distinguish it from the majority of other places in town, like terracotta-tiled floors. They offer 11 rooms, with fans, 5 with private bath, book exchange and the **McTropic** restaurant up the road with internet and a tour operator.

## Around Lívingston

### $$-$ Q'ana Itz'am
*Lagunita Salvador, T5992-1853, www.lagunitasalvador.com.*
This excellent Q'eqchi community tourism project includes an ecolodge with rustic wooden cabins and a lovely jungle setting. Activities include kayaking, hiking, nature observation and traditional dances. Advance reservation absolutely necessary. Highly recommended.

### $ Finca Tatín
*Río Tatín tributary, with great dock space to hang out on, T5902-0831, www.fincatatin. centroamerica.com.*
This lovely, rustic, wood-built B&B offers a range of Robinson Crusoe lodgings including dorms, private rooms and simple bungalows nestled in the jungle. The Casa Grande (main house) is the focal point for evening gatherings where you can enjoy games, books, table tennis and music. Tours and kayak rental available.

### $ Hotel Ecológico Salvador Gaviota
*Along the coast, towards Siete Altares, beyond Hotel Ecológico Siete Altares, T7947-0874, www.hotelsalvadorgaviota.com.*
The beach here is lovely, hummingbirds flit about and the owner Lisette is friendly. Rooms have shared bath, but the bungalows for 2 or 4 people have private bath. Rooms available for monthly rent, all set in lush surroundings. There is a bar and restaurant (0730-2200), and free *lancha* service; ring beforehand. Tours available. Highly recommended.

### $ Hotelito Perdido
*On the Río Lampara, can be dropped off on the Lívingston–Río Dulce boat service, T5725-1576, www.hotelitoperdido.com.*
This quiet, rustic very attractive hideaway is located across the river from the mineral hot springs. Grounds include tropical gardens, winding pathways, bar-restaurant and 5 types of wood-built jungle lodgings. They also rent kayaks and wooden *cayucos*. Ecologically oriented with solar power, recycling and organic vegetable plots. Recommended.

## $ The Roundhouse
*La Pintada, 20 mins by boat from Livingston, T4294-9730, www. roundhouseguatemala.com.*
The Roundhouse is a popular party hostel with a great setting on the riverbank. It has an environmentally aware ethos with solar hot water, a natural feed water system and bio-sand purification. Accommodation is in dorms or private rooms, both very affordable.

## Restaurants

Fresh fish is available everywhere; in restaurants ask for *tapado*, a rich soup with various types of seafood, banana and coconut. Women sell *pan de coco* on the streets.

### $$ Bahía Azul
*Calle Principal.*
Serving excellent breakfasts but dreadful coffee, this place specializes in salsas, *camarones* and *langosta*. There You can sit at tables on the street or in the dining room. There is also a tourist service and the **Exotic Travel Agency**.

### $$ Buga Mama
An excellent example of an innovative development project and well worth checking out. Local Mayan young people staff this large restaurant located next to the water as part of their training with the Ak'Tenamit project (www.aktenamit.org). The food is OK, the service excellent, and it's in a great spot too.

### $$ El Malecón
*50 m from the dock on the left.*
Serves *chapín* and Western-style breakfasts, seafood and chicken *fajitas*, all in a large, airy wooden dining area.

### $$ Happy Fish
*Just along from the Hotel Río Dulce.*
A popular restaurant with an internet café. Serves a truckload of fish (not quite so happy now) with good coffee. Occasional live music at weekends.

## $ McTropic
*Opposite the Hotel Río Dulce.*
This popular place offers great breakfasts and cocktails at street tables, with good service.

## $ Rasta Mesa Restaurant
*In Barrio Nevago, just past the cemetery, www.site.rasta mesa.com.*
Garífuna cultural centre and restaurant with music, history, and classes in cooking and drumming. A great place to hang out.

## $ Tiburón Gato
*Far end of Calle Principal.*
A simple open-fronted place, serving a good range of fish, seafood and pasta. It's open for breakfasts too.

## Bars and clubs

### Lugudi Barana
*Sun 1500-0100 only.*
A disco that's also on the beach and popular with visitors and locals.

## Festivals

**26 Nov  Garífuna Day**.
**24-31 Dec**  In honour of the **Virgen del Rosario**, with traditional dancing.

## What to do

### Tour operators
**Captain Eric**, *located at the Pitchi Mango snack bar on the main street, T4265-5278*. Will arrange 1- to 2-day boat tours for groups of up to 5 people to the surrounding region.

You can also contract any of the *lancheros* at the dock to take you to Río Dulce, Playa Blanca and Siete Altares.

## Transport

### Boat
Ferry to **Puerto Barrios** to (22.5 km), 1½ hrs, US$1.60 at 0500 and 1400 Mon-Sat. Private *lanchas* taking 16-25 people also sail this route, 30 mins, US$4. They leave at 0630 and 0730 each day and at 0900 and 1100

Mon-Sat to Puerto Barrios and then when full. Lívingston to **Río Dulce**, with short stops at **Aguas Calientes** and the **Biotopo Chacón Machacas**, US$15.50 1 way. *Lanchas* definitely leave at 0900 and 1430 for **Río Dulce**, but these make no stops. To **Honduras** (Omoa, Puerto Cortés, La Ceiba), *lanchas* can be organized at the dock or through tour operators, see above. See also Border crossings box in Practicalities chapter. To **Belize** (Punta Gorda, Placencia, Cayos Zapotillos), check with tour operators,

see above, about boats to Belize. Anyone who takes you must have a manifest with passengers' names, stamped and signed at the immigration office. On Tue and Fri fast *lanchas* make the trip to Punta Gorda (US$22). Enquire at the dock and negotiate a fare with the *lanchero* association. See also Border crossings box in Practicalities chapter, for more information on crossing into Belize. Boats to Placencia and the Zapotilla cayes can also be arranged.

## Lago de Izabal   Colour map 2, B5.

**beautiful riverside and lakeside places to stay**

The vast Lago de Izabal, the largest lake in Guatemala at 717 sq km, narrows to form a neck at the town of Fronteras. Better known as Río Dulce, it is famed for its riverside setting. Just south of Río Dulce on the lake is the restored Castillo de San Felipe, while on the northern shore of the lake is the town of El Estor, and on its southern shore the smaller town of Mariscos. Further east, beyond Río Dulce, the river broadens out to El Golfete, where there is the Biotopo Chacón Machacas, see above. It then narrows into one of the finest gorges in the world, and opens out at its estuary, with Lívingston at its head. This area can be wet in the rainy season, but it experiences a lull in July, known as the *canícula*.

### Fronteras/Río Dulce and around

Río Dulce is a good place to stop and kick back for a couple of days. Allow yourself to be tempted to laze on a boat for the afternoon, walk in the nearby jungle, or eat and drink at one of several dockside restaurants. Río Dulce, www.mayaparadise.com, is 23 km upstream from Lívingston at the entrance to Lago de Izabal, is easily accessible from Puerto Barrios by road, and is the last major stop before the Petén. It's also a good place to collect information about the area stretching from El Estor to Lívingston.

On the shore of Lago de Izabal is **Casa Guatemala** ① *14 Calle, 10-63, Zona 1, Guatemala City, T2231-9408, www.casa-guatemala.org* (also known as **Hotel Backpacker's**), an orphanage where you can work in exchange for basic accommodation and food. At the entrance to Lago de Izabal, 2 km upstream, is the old Spanish fort of **Castillo de San Felipe** ① *0800-1700, US$3.30.* The fortification was first built in 1643 to defend the coast against attacks from pirates; it has been well preserved and in lovely grounds; great views from the battlements. Between Río Dulce and El Estor is **Finca El Paraíso**, a hot waterfall with waters that plunge into a cool-water pool below.

### El Estor and around

Strung along the northwest shore of Lago de Izabal, backed by the Santa Cruz mountain range and facing the Sierra de las Minas, El Estor enjoys one of the most beautiful vistas in Guatemala. It's a great place to relax, swim (down a nearby canyon), go fishing and spot manatee. Some businesses are expecting the new road to bring a surge of tourist visitors.

For the next few years though you'll still have the place mostly to yourself. The town dates back to the days when the Europeans living in the Atlantic area got their provisions from a store situated at this spot, now the **Hotel Vista al Lago**. Briton Skinner and Dutchman Klee supplied the region from *el store* 1815-1850. Nickel mining began just outside town in 1978, but was suspended at the **Exmibal plant** after the oil crisis of 1982, because the process depended on cheap sources of energy.

You can hire a boat from Río Dulce to El Estor, passing near the hot waterfall, inland at Finca El Paraíso, which can be reached by a good trail in about 40 minutes. The Río Sauce cuts through the impressive **Cañon El Boquerón**, where you can swim with the current all the way down the canyon, which is brilliant fun. It's a deep canyon with lots of old man's beard hanging down, strange rock formations and otters and troops of howler monkeys whooping about. One of the locals will paddle you upstream for about 800 m (US$1). Exploring the Río Zarco, closer to town, also makes for a good trip, with cold swimming. The **Refugio de Vida Silvestre Bocas del Polochic** (Bocas del Polochic Wildlife Reserve) is a 23,000-ha protected area on the western shores of the lake. Howler monkeys are commonly seen. In addition to over 350 bird species, there are iguanas, turtles and the chance of sighting crocodiles and manatees. The NGO **Defensores de la Naturaleza** ⓘ *2 Calle and 5 Av, El Estor, T2440-8138 in the capital, www.defensores.org.gt*, has a research station at Selempim with bunk beds ($ per person), food, showers and kitchen. It's a two- or three-hour boat ride from El Estor to Ensenada Los Lagartos. Tours are available from town for US$30 for two people. Contact the office in El Estor or ask at a hotel about boat services.

**Mariscos** is on the southern shore of Lago de Izabal. The best reason to come here is the nearby **Denny's Beach**; see Where to stay, below.

## Where to stay

### Fronteras/Río Dulce and around
All the establishments below are located out of town on the water. If you need to stay in the less attractive locale of Río Dulce itself, try **Hotel Vista al Río** ($), just past **Bruno's** under the bridge, T7930-5665, www.hotelvistario.com.

### $$$-$$ Hacienda Tijax
*T7930-5505, www.tijax.com. 2 mins by lancha from the dock, yacht moorings available.*
There is a beautiful jungle trail with canopy walkway at the tranquil Hacienda Tijax, also a rubber plantation, bird sanctuary, pool with whirlpool and jacuzzi, and natural swimming pools. Activities include horse riding, kayaking, sailing and rowboat hire and a medicine trail. Accommodation is in well-built wooden cabins with mod cons, including a/c. There is excellent food in the riverside bar and restaurant. Highly recommended.

### $$-$ Tortugal Hotel and Marina
*T5306-6432, www.tortugal.com.*
Beautifully presented bungalows with gorgeous soft rugs on the floor and various other types of accommodation including open-air ranchos and a *casita*. There is plentiful hot water. Also here is a riverside restaurant and bar, pool table in a cool upstairs attic room with books, satellite TV, internet, phone and fax service. Very highly recommended.

### $ Hotel Backpacker's
*Just out of town by the bridge on the south bank of the river, T7930-5169, www.hotelbackpackers.com.*
Profits of Hotel Backpacker's go to the Casa Guatemala Orphanage and guests have the option of working for their lodging as

part of a volunteer holiday. There are basic dorms with lockers and simple private rooms with bathroom, as well as a restaurant and bar, and internet and telephone service. Recommended.

### $ Hotel Kangaroo
*On the Río La Colocha, T5363-6716, www.hotelkangaroo.com.*
Perched on the water's edge, this Mexican-Australian owned river lodge has rustic wood-built rooms, dorms and bungalows, all very simple and close to nature. There's a bar-restaurant on the decking serving Aussie and Mexican grub, and an unheated jacuzzi.

### El Estor and around
### $$$-$$ Denny's Beach
*T5398-0908, www.dennysbeach.com.*
This remote place offers resort-style lodgings with a gorgeous lakeside location, accessible by *lancha* from Río Dulce (minimum fee US$41), or free from Mariscos if you call ahead. Tours, wake boarding and horse riding can be arranged. Internet service.

### $ Hotel Vista al Lago
*6 Av, 1-13, T7949-7205.*
21 clean rooms with private bath and fan. Ask for the lakeview rooms, where there is a pleasant wooden balcony on which to sit. Friendly owner Oscar Paz will take you fishing, and runs ecological and cultural tours.

### $ Villela
*6 Av, 2-06, T7949-7214.*
With a flower-filled garden with chairs to sit out in, this place has 9 big, clean rooms with bath, although some are quite dark. Recommended.

## Restaurants

### Fronteras/Río Dulce and around
There are restaurants in the hotels and a couple along the main road.

### $$-$ Ranchón Mary
*El Relleno, T7930-5103.*
Thatch-roofed waterfront deck with tables, serving delicious fish and seafood and ice-cold beer.

### $$-$ Rosita's Restaurant
*San Felipe de Lara, T5054-3541.*
Lovely waterfront location with open deck, overlooking the bridge, 5 mins by *lancha* from Río Dulce. Great seafood, nachos and home-made banana pie.

### El Estor and around
### $ Dorita
Popular with the locals, this *comedor* serves good seafood meals which are excellent value.

### $ Marisabela
*8 Av and 1 Calle.*
Good and cheap spaghetti, as well as fish and chicken, with lake views.

### $ Restaurant del Lago
*West side of main square.*
This popular restaurant overlooks the main square and offers local dishes.

### $ Restaurant Elsita
*2 blocks north of the market on 8 Av.*
This is a great people-watching place with a large menu and good food.

## What to do

### Fronteras/Río Dulce
### Sailing
**Captain John Clark**'s sailing trips on his 46-ft Polynesian catamaran, *Las Sirenas*, are highly recommended. Food, taxes, snorkelling and fishing gear, and windsurf boards included. Contact **Aventuras Vacacionales SA**, Antigua, www.sailing-diving-guatemala.com; see page 288.

**Coastguard** For emergencies, call Guarda Costa on VHF channel 16, T4040-4971.

## Tour operators

**Atitrans Tours**, *on the little road heading to the dockside*. To **Finca Paraíso** for US$20.
**Otiturs**, *opposite Tijax Express*, T5219-4520. Run by the friendly and helpful Otto Archila. Offers a minibus service as well as tours to local sites, internal flights and boat trips.
**Tijax Express**, *opposite Atitrans*, T7930-5505, info@tijax.com. Agent for Hacienda Tijax (over the river).

*Lancheros* offer trips on the river and on Lago de Izabal. They can be contacted at the *muelle principal*, under the bridge. Ask for Cesár Mendez, T5819-7436, or ask at **Atitrans** for collection.

## Transport

### Fronteras/Río Dulce and around

**Boat**
*Lanchas colectivas* leave for **Lívingston** at 0930 and 1300, US$15.50. Private *lanchas* can be arranged at the dock to any of the river or lakeside hotels.

**Bus**
**Local** To get to **Castillo de San Felipe**, take a boat from Río Dulce, or *camioneta* from the corner of the main road to Tikal, and the first turning left after the bridge by **Pollandia**, 5 mins, or a 5-km walk. From Río Dulce to **Finca El Paraíso**, take the same road, 45 mins, US$1.70. Buses to Río Dulce pass the finca between 40 and 50 mins past the hour. To **El Estor**, from the same Pollandia turn-off, US$2.50, 1½ hrs on a paved road, 0500-1600, hourly, returning 0500-1600. To **Puerto Barrios**, take any bus to **La Ruidosa** and change, 35 mins to junction then a further 35 mins to Puerto Barrios.

**Long-distance** To **Guatemala City** and **Flores**: through buses stop at Río Dulce. To

**Guatemala City** with **Litegua**, T7930-5251, www.litegua.com, 7 a day between 0300 and 1515, US$7.54, 6 hrs. **Fuente del Norte**, T5692-1988, 23 services daily, US$6.30. Luxury service 1300, 1700 and 2400, US$13. **Línea Dorada**, at 1300, luxury service, 5 hrs, US$13. To **Flores** from 0630-0300, 25 buses daily, 4½ hrs with **Fuente del Norte**, US$8. Luxury service, 1430, US$13. This bus also stops at **Finca Ixobel** and **Poptún**, US$3.90. **Línea Dorada**, to Flores, 1500, 3 hrs, luxury service with a/c, TV and snacks, US$13, and on to **Melchor de Mencos** for Belize; see also Border crossings box in Practicalities chapter, for more information on crossing into Belize. **Fuente del Norte**, also to **Melchor de Mencos**, at 1300, 2130 and 2330, 6 hrs, US$12.50. Also to, **Sayaxché** at 2200 and one to **Naranjo** at 2100.

**Shuttles** Atitrans, T7930-5111, www.atitrans.com, runs shuttles to **Antigua**, **Flores**, **Copán Ruinas** and **Guatemala City**.

### El Estor and around

**Bus** The ferry from Mariscos no longer runs, but a private *lancha* can be contracted.

To **Río Dulce**, 0500-1600, hourly, 1 hr, US$2.20. Direct bus to **Cobán**, at 1300, 7 hrs, US$5.60. Also via either Panzós and Tactic, or Cahabón and Lanquín. For the **Cañón El Boquerón**, take the Río Dulce bus and ask to be dropped at the entrance. Or hire a bike from town (8 km) or a taxi, US$6.50, including waiting time.

To **Cobán**, with **Transportes Valenciana**, 1200, 0200, 0400 and 0800, 8 long and dusty hrs, with no proper stop. To **Guatemala City**, 0100 direct, via Río Dulce, 7 hrs, US$6.30, or go to Río Dulce and catch one. At 2400 and 0300 via Río Polochic Valley. For **Santa Elena, Petén** take a bus to Río Dulce and pick on up from there.

# **The** Verapaces

Propped up on a massive limestone table eroded over thousands of years, the plateau of the Verapaz region is riddled with caves, underground tunnels, stalagtites and stalagmites. Cavernous labyrinths used by the Maya for worship, in their belief that caves are the entrances to the underworld, are also now visited by travellers who marvel at the natural interior design of these subterranean spaces.

Nature has performed its work above ground too. At Semuc Champey, pools of tranquil, turquoise-green water span a monumental limestone bridge; beneath the bridge a river thunders violently through. The quetzal reserve also provides the opportunity to witness a feather flash of red or green of the elusive bird, and dead insects provide curious interest in Rabinal, where their body parts end up on ornamental gourds.

The centre of this region – the imperial city of Cobán – provides respite for the traveller with a clutch of museums honouring the Maya, coffee and orchid, and a fantastic entertainment spectacle at the end of July with a whirlwind of traditional dances and a Maya beauty contest.

**Best** for
Caves ▪ Coffee fincas ▪ Orchids ▪ Quetzals

Baja Verapaz region is made up of a handful of Achi'-Maya speaking towns, namely Salamá, Rabinal, San Jerónimo and Cubulco. The department is known for the quetzal reserve, the large Dominican finca and aqueduct, and the weird decorative technique of the crafts in Rabinal.

### Sierra de las Minas Biosphere Reserve
*To visit, get a permit in San Augustín from the office of La Fundación de Defensores de la Naturaleza, Barrio San Sebastián, 1 block before the Municipalidad, T7936-0681, ctot@defensores.org.gt, www.defensores.org.gt. The contact is César Tot. Alternatively, contact the Fundación offices in Santa Elena, Petén, at 5 Calle, 3 Av "A", Zona 2, T7926-3095, lacandon@defensores.org.gt, or in the capital at 7 Av, 7-09, Zona 13, T2440-8138.*

Just north of El Rancho, in the Department of El Progreso, is **San Agustín Acasaguastlán**, an entrance for the Sierra de las Minas Biosphere Reserve, one of Guatemala's largest conservation areas with peaks topping 3000 m and home to the quetzal, harpy eagle and peregrine falcon, puma, jaguar, spider monkey, howler monkey, tapir and pizote.

### Biotopo del Quetzal
*Daily 0700-1600, US$2.60, parking, disabled entrance. Run by Centro de Estudios Conservacionistas (CECON), Av Reforma, 0-63, Zona 10, Guatemala City, T2331-0904, cecon@usac.edu.gt.*

The Biotopo del Quetzal, or **Biosphere Mario Dary Rivera**, is between Cobán and Guatemala City at Km 160.5, 4 km south of Purulhá and 53 km from Cobán. There are two trails. Increasing numbers of quetzals have been reported in the Biotopo, but they are still very elusive. Ask for advice from the rangers. The area around the Biotopo has been protected as a **Corredor Biológico Bosque Nuboso**, with numerous privately run reserves and restaurants by the roadside offering birdwatching trails, waterfalls, natural swimming holes and caves. For more information, see www.bosquenuboso.com.gt.

### Salamá, Rabinal and Cubulco
Just before Salamá is **San Jerónimo**, with a Dominican church and convent, from where friars tended vineyards, exported wine and cultivated sugar. There is an old sugar mill (*trapiche*) on display at the finca and a huge aqueduct of 124 arches to transport water to the sugar cane fields and the town. Salamá sits in a valley with a colonial cathedral, containing carved gilt altarpieces as its centrepiece. The town also has one of a few remaining **Templos de Minerva** in the country, built in 1916. Behind the Calvario church is the hill Cerro de la Santa Cruz, from where a view of the valley can be seen. Market day is Monday and is worth a visit.

The village of **Rabinal** was founded in 1537 by Fray Bartolomé de las Casas. It has a 16th-century church, and a busy Sunday market, where lacquered gourds, beautiful *huipiles* and embroidered napkins are sold. The glossy lacquer of the gourd is made from the body oil of a farmed scaly insect called the *niij*. The male *niij* is boiled in water to release its oil, which is then mixed with soot powder to create the lacquer. The **Museo Rabinal Achí** ⓘ *2 Calle y 4 Av, Zona 3, T5311-1536, museoachi@hotmail.com,* displays historical exhibits and has produced bilingual books about the Achí culture.

West of Rabinal, set amid maize fields and peach trees, Cubulco is known for its tradition of performing the pole dance, *Palo Volador*, which takes place every 20-25 July. Men,

# BACKGROUND

## The Verapaces

Before the Spanish conquest of the region, Las Verapaces had a notorious reputation; it was known as Tezulutlán (land of war) for its aggressive warlike residents, who fought repeated battles with their neighbours and rivals, the K'iche' Maya. These warring locals were not going to be a pushover for the Spanish conquerors and they strongly resisted when their land was invaded. The Spanish eventually retreated and the weapon replaced with the cross. Thus, Carlos V of Spain gave the area the title of Verdadera Paz (true peace) in 1548.

The region's modern history saw it converted into a massive coffee- and cardamom-growing region. German coffee fincas were established from the 1830s until the Second World War, when the Germans were invited over to plough the earth by the Guatemalan government. Many of the fincas were expropriated during the war, but some were saved from this fate by naming a Guatemalan as the owner of the property. The area still produces some of Guatemala's finest coffee – served up with some of the finest cakes. The Germans also introduced cardamom to the Verapaces, when a *finquero* requested some seeds for use in biscuits. Guatemala is now the world's largest producer of cardamom.

attached by rope, have to leap from the top of the pole and spiral down, accompanied by marimba music. There are three basic *hospedajes* in town.

## Listings Baja Verapaz

### Where to stay

#### Biotopo del Quetzal

**$$ Posada Montaña del Quetzal**
*At Km 156, T7823-9636,*
*www.hposadaquetzal.com.*
Rustic and remote, this tranquil highland *posada* offers modest bungalows or rooms with spartan furnishings, private bathrooms and hot water; try to get one with a fireplace so you can get good and toasty after dark. There's also café, bar, pool and gardens. Simple, romantic and rugged.

**$$ Ram Tzul**
*Km 158, T5908-4066, www.ramtzul.com.*
Set in rambling 100-ha grounds, the wood-built cabins at Ram Tzul are very beautiful and creatively rendered, some of them featuring stained-glass windows, lovely stonework and superb views of the forested hills. The restaurant is equally interesting and serves hearty *comida típica*. Dozens of excursions can be arranged. Recommended.

**$ Hospedaje Ranchitos del Quetzal**
*Km 160.8, T7823-5860.*
Conveniently located just 200 m from the Biotopo entrance, this economical place has clean and simple rooms in old and new buildings, with shared or private bathrooms and hot water. There's also a *comedor*. It's good for early morning foray.

### Transport

#### Biotopo del Quetzal
**Bus**
From **Guatemala City**, take a Cobán bus with **Escobar-Monja Blanca** and ask to be let out at the Biotopo, hourly from 0400-1700, 3½ hrs, US$3.50. From **Cobán**, 1 hr, US$0.80, take any capital-bound bus

or a minibus from Campo 2 near football stadium every 20 mins, US$0.80. From **El Rancho**–Biotopo, 1¼ hrs. Cobán–Purulhá, local buses ply this route between 0645-2000 returning until 1730, 1 hr 20 mins.

## Salamá, Rabinal and Cubulco
### Bus
Salamá–Rabinal, 1-1½ hrs. Rabinal is reached by travelling west from Salamá on a paved road. From **Guatemala City**, 5½ hrs, a beautiful, occasionally heart-stopping ride, or via El Progreso, and then Salamá by bus. Buses leave 0330-1600 to Guatemala City via Salamá from Cubulco. There is a bus between Rabinal and Cubulco, supplemented by pickup rides.

---

# Alta Verapaz
### mountainous limestone region with caves and a mystical lake

The region of Alta Verapaz is based on a gigantic mountain, Sierra de Chamá. Dinosaurs roamed the area more than 65 million years ago before it was engulfed by sea. It later emerged, covered with limestone rock, which over millions of years has left the area riddled with caves, and dotted with small hills. In the far northwest of the department are the emerald-green waters of Laguna Lachuá.

### Santa Cruz Verapaz and around *Colour map 2, B4.*
Santa Cruz Verapaz has a fine white 16th-century church with a fiesta between 1-4 May when you can see the wonderful Danza de los Guacamayos (scarlet macaws). This **Poqomchi' Maya** village is 15 km northwest of Tactic, at the junction with the road to Uspantán. To get there, take the San Cristóbal Verapaz bus, 25 minutes, or take a bus heading to the capital, get off at the junction and walk 200 m into town. The local fiestas are 15, 20 January, 21-26 July with the *Palo Volador*. The devil-burning dance can be seen on 8 December. Six kilometres west towards Uspantán is **San Cristóbal Verapaz**, which has a large, white, colonial church. From the church, a 1-km long, straight, road (Calle del Calvario) slopes down and then curves upwards to a hilltop **Calvario Church**. At Easter, the whole road is carpeted in flowers that rival those on display in Antigua at this time of year. There is **Museo Katinamit** ⓘ *T7950-4039, cecep@intelnet. net.gt, Mon-Fri 0900-1200, 1500-1700, run by the Centro Comunitario Educativo Poqomchi'*, dedicated to the preservation and learning of the Poqomchi' culture.

## Listings Alta Verapaz

### Where to stay

#### $$$-$$ Casa Kirvá
*Km 204.4, Tontem village, T4693-4800, www.casakirva.com.*
Perched on a hill, Casa Kirvá is a reasonably new, beautifully constructed lodge with fine stone and woodwork, wonderful landscaped grounds and a striking architectural design that successfully blends contemporary and colonial styles. Rooms veer toward comfort and simplicity rather than ostentatiousness.

#### $$$-$$ Hotel Park
*Km 196, on the main road south of the junction to the Poqomchi' Maya village, Santa Cruz, T7955-3600, www.parkhotelresort.com.*
This Italian-owned resort on the highway has a lavish and immaculately landscaped

garden, restaurants, gym, tennis court, heated pool, convention centre, wildlife rescue centre and, should you require it for a dramatic entrance or exit, a helipad. Accommodation includes 158 rooms and *casitas* spread across 7 complexes.

### $ Eco Hotel Chi' Ixim
*Km 182.5, just beyond Tactic, T7953-9198.*
Simple and rustic, Chi' Ixim offers economical rooms and cabins with private bath, hot water and fireplaces. There is also a restaurant, garden and lots of wandering livestock.

### $ Hotel El Portón Real
*4 Av, 1-44, Zona 1, Santa Cruz Verapaz, T7950-4604.*
This hotel may look dreary from the outside, but inside it's lovely, with lots of wood furnishings and run by a very friendly *señora*.

There are rooms with bath, cheaper without, as well as hot water and free drinking water. The hotel closes its doors at 2130.

## Transport

### Bus
From **Cobán** between 0600-1915 every 15 mins, US$0.700, 40 mins. All capital-bound buses from Cobán run through **Tactic**, or take a local bus between 0645-2000, returning between 0500-1730, 40 mins, US$0.80. Bus from Cobán to **Senahú**, 6 hrs, from opposite INJAV building, from 0600-1400, 4 daily, US$2.90. If you are coming from El Estor, get off at the Senahú turn-off, hitch or wait for the buses from Cobán. Trucks take this road, but there is little traffic, so you have to be at the junction very early to be in luck.

## Cobán and around   *Colour map 2, B4.*

**attractive colonial town surrounded by coffee plantations**

The cathedral and centre of the Imperial City of Cobán (www.cobanav.net, altitude 1320 m), is perched on a long, thin plateau with exceptionally steep roads climbing down from the plaza. To the south the roads are filled with the odd, well-preserved colonial building and a coffee finca.

There is year-round soft rainfall, known as *chipi-chipi*, which is a godsend to the coffee and cardamom plants growing nearby. Most visitors use the city as a base for visiting sights in the surrounding area, trips to Semuc Champey, Languin and as a stepping-off point for rafting trips on the Río Cahabón. English is spoken at the **city tourist office** ⓘ *Parque Central*, where they have lots of information and can help organize tours. The **INGUAT office** ⓘ *7 Av 1-17, in Los Arcos shopping centre, T7951-0216, Mon-Fri 0800-1600, Sat 0900-1300*, is very helpful with leaflets and maps on the whole Verapaz region. For online information on northern Alta Verapaz and the southern Petén, check www.puertamundomaya.com.

The **cathedral** is on the east side of the Parque Central and dates from the middle of the 16th century. The chapel of **El Calvario**, in the northwest, has its original façade still intact. On the way up to the church are altars used by worshippers who freely blend Maya and Roman Catholic beliefs. It's worth climbing the 142 steps to get a bird's-eye view of Cobán. The **Museo El Príncipe Maya** ⓘ *6 Av, 4-26, Zona 3, Mon-Sat 0900-1300, 1400-1800, US$1.30*, is a private museum of pre-Columbian artefacts. The **Parque Nacional Las Victorias** ⓘ *just west of El Calvario, daily 0700-1800, US$0.80*, has two little lagoons in its 84 ha. There are paths and you can picnic and camp, toilets but no showers, but check with the tourist office about safety before going. The daily market is near the bus terminal.

Starbucks coffee fans can check out where their mug of the old bean comes from, direct from **Finca Santa Margarita** ⓘ *on the edge of town, 3 Calle, 4-12, Zona 2, T7951-3067, Mon-Fri 0800-1230, 1330-1700, Sat 0800-1200, 45-min tour with English/Spanish-speaking* *guides, US$2.50.* Don't miss a visit to the flower-filled world of **Vivero Verapaz** ① *2.5 km southwest of town, 40-min walk, or taxi ride, 0900-1200, 1400-1700 daily, US$1.30; US$1.30 for guided tour*, an orchid farm with more than 23,000 specimens, mostly flowering from December to February – the best time to go – with the majority flowering in January.

## Around Cobán

Southeast of Cobán (8 km) is **San Juan Chamelco** with an old colonial church. A one-hour walk from here is **Aldea Chajaneb** (see Where to stay, below). Along this road are the caves of **Grutas Rey Marcos** ① *US$1.30*, and **Balneario Cecilinda** ① *0800-1700*. **San Pedro Carchá** is 5 km east of Cobán on the main road and used to be famous for its pottery, textiles, wooden masks and silver, but only the pottery and silver are available now. The local food speciality here is *kaq Ik*, a turkey broth.

## Parque Nacional Laguna Lachuá *Colour map 2, B4.*
*T5704 1509 to hire a guide for the day, US$4, main entrance, US$5.20, Mon-Sat 0900-1700.*

Near **Playa Grande**, northwest of Cobán, is Parque Nacional Laguna Lachuá. The deep velvet-green lake, formed by a meteor impact, is 5 sq km and 220 m deep in places. It is surrounded by virtually unspoilt dense jungle, and the chances of seeing wildlife at dawn and dusk are high. There is a guided nature trail and camping and a basic guesthouse. In this area is the **Río Ikbolay**, a green river that runs underground through caves. When it

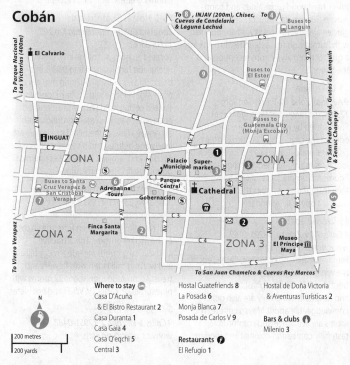

Cobán

**Where to stay** 🛏
Casa D'Acuña
 & El Bistro Restaurant **2**
Casa Duranta **1**
Casa Gaia **4**
Casa Q'eqchi **5**
Central **3**
Hostal Guatefriends **8**
La Posada **6**
Monja Blanca **7**
Posada de Carlos V **9**

**Restaurants** 🍴
El Refugio **1**

Hostal de Doña Victoria
 & Aventuras Turísticas **2**

**Bars & clubs** 🍸
Milenio **3**

emerges the other side it is blue. The river has changed its course over time leaving some of its run-through caves empty, making it possible to walk through them. The **Proyecto Ecológico Quetzal**, see page 380, runs jungle hikes in this area.

## Listings Cobán and around *map p377*

### Where to stay

Accommodation is extremely hard to find on the Fri and Sat of Rabin Ajau (last week of Jul) and in Aug. For Rabin Ajau you need to be in town a few days beforehand to secure a room, or ring and reserve.

#### $$ Casa Duranta
*3 Calle, 4-46, Zona 3, T7951-4188, www.casaduranta.com.*
With a convenient central location near the plaza, Casa Duranta has 10 large, simple rooms with hot water, cable TV, Wi-Fi, hardwood furnishings and hand-woven Guatemalan bedspreads. The leafy garden and interior courtyard are popular with hummingbirds, a definite plus. Ask for a quieter room away from reception and the street.

#### $$ Casa Gaia
*9 Av Final, Zona 10, Barrio San Jorge, T7941-7021, www.hotelcasagaia.com.*
Surrounded by native pine forests on the edge of the city, 14 blocks from central park (20 mins' walk), Casa Gaia is a lovely secluded lodge set in well-tended 10-ha grounds. Rooms are simple, tasteful and tranquil, and their restaurant overlooks the trees with a pleasant open-air veranda.

#### $$ Casa Q'eqchi
*4 Calle, 7-29, Zona 3, T3295-9169, www.hotelencoban.com.*
Family-owned and operated, Casa Q'eqchi is a very helpful, friendly and personable boutique B&B. The emphasis is on service and hospitality, and they are also quite knowledgeable about Mayan culture. The rooms are attractive and comfortable, tastefully combining colonial and modern

styles. There is a pleasant courtyard too. Recommended.

#### $$ La Posada
*1 Calle, 4-12, Zone 2, T7952-1495, www.laposadacoban.com.gt.*
One of Cobán's best, this handsome colonial hotel offers 16 atmospheric rooms decorated with popular and religious art, antique furnishings, tiled bathrooms and fireplaces. The gardens are flourishing and well-kept. Featuring a terrace and fireplace, the restaurant is stylish too; stop by for a drink, if nothing else. Credit cards accepted.

#### $$-$ Hostal Guatefriends
*Carretera Cobán-Guatemala Km 205, T4715-3508.*
Located 10 mins out of the city, this very restful and highly appealing B&B is in a beautiful and unusual building reminiscent of an Alpine lodge with its fine stonework, slanted ceilings and cosy wood-panelled enclaves. It's set in verdant grounds, with expansive views of the hills. The owners are lovely and helpful, and it's a great choice for couples and families. There are economical dorms too ($). Recommended.

#### $$-$ Posada de Carlos V
*1 Av, 3-44, Zona 1, T7951 3501, www.hotelcarlosvcoban.com.*
This is a calm oasis hidden from the chaos of the market outside. The attractive landscaped grounds include a rocky hillside and walking trail laden with flowers and trees. Accommodation spans 22 rooms with pine furniture, cable TV, Wi-Fi and hot water.

#### $ Casa D'Acuña
*4 Calle, 3-11, Zona 2, T7951-0482, www.casadeacuna.com.*

Housed by a fine colonial edifice, Casa D'Acuña is a decent hostel with 4 small dorms and 2 private rooms, shared ultra-clean bathrooms with hot water, laundry service, internet, excellent meals, tempting goodies and coffee in El Bistro restaurant, which overlooks a pretty courtyard (see Restaurants, below). The owners also run a tourist office, shop and tours. Recommended.

### $ Central
*1 Calle, 1-79, T7952-1442.*
A stone's throw from the cathedral in a great location, Hotel Central has 15 very clean large rooms with hot shower, all set around a central patio. Rooms with TV cost a little extra. A good budget option.

### $ Monja Blanca
*2 Calle, 6-30 Zona 2, T7952-1712.*
The peaceful, simple, comfortable place is run by a slightly eccentric *señora* and looks shut from the outside. Once inside, all rooms are set around a tranquil leafy courtyard, which is great for chilling out. There is also an old-fashioned dining room serving good value breakfast. Recommended.

## Restaurants

### $$$-$$ El Bistro
*In Casa D'Acuña, see Where to stay, above.*
Excellent menu and massive portions. Try the blueberry pancakes. There's also great yogurt, and don't walk through the restaurant without putting your nose into the cake cabinet! Recommended.

### $$ El Refugio
*2 Av, 2-28, Zona 4, T7952-1338.*
*Open 1030-2300.*
Excellent service and substantial portions at good-value prices of steaks, fish, chicken and snacks, as well as set lunch. There are also cocktails, a big screen TV and a bar.

### $$ Hostal de Doña Victoria
*See Where to stay, above.*
Serves breakfast, lunch and supper in a semi-open area with a pleasant, quiet ambience.

Good Italian food, including vegetarian options, is the speciality of the house. There is also a mini cellar bar.

## Cafés

### Café Fantasia
*1 Calle, 3-13, western end of the main park.*
A handy spot open for breakfast.

### Café La Posada
*Part of La Posada (see Where to stay).*
*Open afternoons.*
Divine brownies and ice cream, sofas with a view of the Parque Central.

## Bars and clubs

### Milenio
*3 Av 1-11, Zona 4.*
A popular place with a mature crowd and 5 rooms, a dance floor, live music weekends, beer by the jug, pool table and big screen TV. There's a minimum consumption of US$3 at weekends.

## Entertainment

### Cinema
**Plaza Magdalena**, *a few blocks west of town.*
Multi-screen cinema usually showing the latest releases.

## Festivals

Mar/Apr **Holy Week**.
Last week of Jul **Rabin Ajau**, the election of the Maya Beauty Queen. Around this time the **Paa banc** is also performed, when the chiefs of brotherhoods are elected for the year.
1-6 Aug **Santo Domingo**, the town's fiesta in honour of its patron.

## What to do

**Adrenalina Tours**, *west of the main square.* Reliable tour operator, with a national presence.

## ON THE ROAD

### Nature tourism

The majority of tour operators listed in this guide will offer nature-oriented tours. There are several national parks, biotopes and protected areas in Guatemala, each with their highlights. CECON (Centro de Estudios Conservacionistas) and INGUAT have set up conservation areas for the protection of Guatemalan wildlife (the quetzal, manatee, jaguar, etc) and their habitats. Several other national parks (some including Maya archaeological sites) and forest reserves have been set up or are planned. For wildlife volunteering opportunities, see Volunteering, Guatemala, in the Practicalities chapter.

CONAP (Consejo Nacional de Areas Protegidas), T2238-0000, http://conap.online.fr, is the national parks and protected areas authority.

Proyecto Ecológico Quetzal, T7952-1047, www.ecoquetzal.org, a non-profit-making project, is another useful organization. It offers ecotourism stays with indigenous families in remote areas.

**Aventuras Turísticas**, *3 Calle, 2-38, Zona 3, T7952-2213, www.aventurasturisticas.com.* Also offers tourist information.
**Proyecto Ecológico Quetzal**, *2 Calle, 14-36, Zona 1, Cobán, T7952-1047, www. ecoquetzal.org.* Contact David Unger. Trips are organized to the multicoloured Río Ikbolay, northwest of Cobán, see page 377, and the mountain community of Chicacnab.

### Transport

#### Bus
The central bus terminal has attempted to group the multitude of bus stations into one place. While many now depart from this bus terminal, there are still a number of departure points scattered around town. Seek local advice for updates or changes.

To **Guatemala City** with **Transportes Escobar-Monja Blanca**, T7951-3571, every 30 mins from 0200-1600, 4-5 hrs, US$7, from its own offices near the terminal. **El Estor**, 4 daily from Av 5, Calle 4, 1st at 0830, and

mostly morning departures, but check in the terminal beforehand, 7 hrs, US$5.60.

To **Fray Bartolomé de las Casas**, 0600-1600 by bus, pickup and trucks, every 30 mins. Route **Raxrujá–Sayaxché–Flores** there are minibuses **Micro buses del Norte** that leave from the terminal del norte near INJAV 0530 and 0630, 5 hrs, US$7.20. In Sayaxché you take a passenger canoe across the river (there is also a car ferry) where minibuses will whisk you to Flores on a tarmacked road in 45 mins. To **Uspantán**, 1000 and 1200, 5 hrs, US$2 from 1 Calle and 7 Av, Zona 2. Cobán can be reached from **Santa Cruz del Quiché** via Sacapulas and Uspantán, and from **Huehuetenango** via Aguacatán, Sacapulas and Uspantán.

### Around Cobán
#### Bus
Every 20 mins from Cobán to **San Juan Chamelco**, US$0.25, 20 mins from Wasen Bridge, Diagonal 15, Zona 7 To **San Pedro Carchá**, every 15 mins, US$0.25, 20 mins from 2 Calle and 4 Av, Zona 4.

Lanquín is surrounded by mountainous scenery reminiscent of an Alpine landscape. It nestles in the bottom of a valley, where a river runs. With this mountain ambience, caves and the clear water pools at Semuc Champey, it is worth kicking back for a few days and inhaling the high-altitude air.

Lanquín is 56 km east of Cobán, 10 km from the Pajal junction. Just before the town are the **Grutas de Lanquín** ① *0800-1600, US$3, 30-min walk from town*. The caves are lit for 200 m and strange stalactite shapes are given names, but it's worth taking a torch. The cave, whose ceiling hangs with thousands of stalactites, is dangerously slippery from guano mud, although handrails will help you out. The sight of the bats flying out at dusk is impressive. Outside the cave you can swim in the river and camp for free.

From Lanquín you can visit the natural bridge of **Semuc Champey** ① *0600-1800, US$6, parking available*, a liquid paradise stretching 60 m across the Cahabón Gorge. The limestone bridge is covered in stepped, glowing blue and green water pools which span the length and breadth of it. Upstream you can see the water being channelled under the bridge. As it thunders through, it is spectacular. At its voluminous exit you can climb down from the bridge and see it cascading. You can swim in all the pools and little hot flows pour into some of them. Tours of Semuc Champey from Cobán cost around US$31.

## Listings Lanquín and Semuc Champey

### Where to stay

**Semuc Champey**

**$$-$ Greengo's**
*400 m from Semuc Champey, T3020-8016, www.greengoshotel.com.*
A good Israeli-run hostel in a natural setting and a convenient location near the pools. There are simple dorms, rooms and brightly painted wooden cabins with slanted roofs. The interiors are very rustic, but feature comfy enough beds and an electrical socket. Facilities include a volleyball court, table football, Wi-Fi, backgammon and a shared kitchen.

**$$-$ Utopia**
*By the river, 11 km from Lanquín and 3 km from Semuc Champey, T3135-8329, www.utopiaecohotel.com.*
In great natural surrroundings a 30- to 60-min hike to the pools, this relaxed, rustic eco-hotel has a friendly and sociable atmosphere. It offers a wide range of

accommodation including riverside *cabañas* with stone walls and floors ($$), simple wood-built cabins ($), semi-private 'nooks' in the dormitory loft, bunk beds and hammocks. There is also a restaurant-bar and Spanish school.

**$ El Muro**
*Calle Principal, Lanquín, T5413-6442, www.elmurolanquin.com.*
Although not exactly a party hostel, this place has a bar, and sometimes can get lively. Accommodation includes simple rooms, dorms, and for the ultra-thrifty, open-air hammocks. There is an attractive porch overlooking the jungle foliage. It's conveniently located for early morning or late night transport connections in Lanquín, or any other amenities you might need in town.

**$ El Portal de Champey**
*At the entrance to Semuc Champey, T4091-7878, www.elportaldechampey.com.*
Built from local materials on the banks of the Río Cahabón, this is the closest

accommodation to Semuc Champey itself and located at the end of the road. Accommodation include very simple and rustic cabins and dorms. Like many other places in the area, electricity is limited. There's no hot water and you'll need insect repellent.

### $ El Retiro
*5 mins from Lanquín on the road to Cahabón, T3225 9251, www.elretirolanquin.com.*
Campsite, *cabañas*, rooms, dorms and restaurant, all in a gorgeous riverside location. There's an open fire for cooking, hammocks to chill out in, a sauna for detoxing, and inner tubes for floating on the river. A fun, relaxing, sociable place which is very popular, with a summer camp feel. To get there don't get off in town, continue for 5 mins and ask to be dropped off. Recommended.

### $ Hostal Oasis
*Just outside Lanquín by the river, a 5-min tuk-tuk ride, T5870-9739, www.carlosmeza2.wix.com/hostaloasis.*
Recommended as one of the few locally owned lodgings in the area and a friendly, low-key alternative to the party places. Like most other hostels around Lanquín, it has rustic dorms and *cabañas*, and offers filling fare at its restaurant, along with very occasional evening shindigs. The guys running the place are great and stand out for their helpfulness. Located steps from the river, you can go inner tubing too.

## Transport

### Lanquín and Semuc Champey
**Bus**
From **Cobán** there are minibuses that leave from the 3 Av, 5-6 Calle, 9 a day 0730-1745, US$3.80. From Lanquín to Semuc Champey hire a pickup, see below. From Lanquín to **Flores**, take a Cobán-bound bus to **Pajal**, 1 hr, then any passing bus or vehicle to **Sebol**, 2-2½ hrs (there are Las Casas–Cobán buses passing hourly in the morning only) and then pickup, hitch or bus to Sayaxché and then Flores.

Semuc Champey is a 10-km walk to the south from Lanquín, 3 hrs' walking along the road, which is quite tough for the first hour as the road climbs very steeply out of Lanquín. If planning to return to Lanquín the same day, start very early to avoid the midday heat. To get there in a pickup start early (0630), US$0.85, or ask around for a private lift (US$13 return). Transport is very irregular so it's best to start walking and keep your fingers crossed. By 1200-1300 there are usually people returning to town to hitch a lift with. If you are on your own and out of season, it would be wise to arrange a lift back.

### Car
There is a petrol station in Lanquín near the church.

**Car hire** Inque Renta Autos, T7952-1431, **Tabarini**, T7952-1504.

### Parque Nacional Laguna Lachuá
Heading for **Playa Grande** from Cobán, also known as **Ixcán Grande**, ask the bus driver to let you off before Playa Grande at 'la entrada del parque', from where it's a 4.2-km (1-hr) walk to the park entrance. Minibuses leave Cobán every 30 mins via Chisec, 4 hrs, US$8 opposite INJAV.

About 100 km northeast of Cobán is Sebol, reached via Chisec and unappealing Raxrujá. From here roads go north to Sayaxché and east to Modesto Méndez via Fray Bartolomé de las Casas.

West of Raxrujá are the **Grutas de Candelaria** ① *US$5.35 including a guided tour*, an extensive cavern system with stalagmites. Tubing is available. Take the road to Raxrujá and look for the Candelaria Camposanto village at Km 310 between Chisec and Raxrujá or look for a sign saying 'Escuela de Autogestión Muqbilbe' and enter here to get to the caves and eco-hotel. Camping is possible. Both points of access offer activities for visitors. North of Raxrujá is the Maya site of **Cancuén** ① *www.puertamundomaya.com, ask in Cobán about tours*, reached by *lancha* in 30 minutes (US$40 for one to 12 people), from the village of La Unión (camping and meals are available at the site). Ten kilometres east of Sebol, and 15 minutes by bus, is **Fray Bartolomé de las Casas**, a town that is just a stop-off for travellers on the long run between Poptún and Cobán or Sayaxché. A road (that is nearly all tarmacked) links Fray Bartolomé de las Casas, Sebol and Sayaxché via Raxrujá. The scenery is beautiful with luscious palms, solitary sheer-sided hills and thatched-roofed homes.

## Listings North of Cobán and southern Petén crossroads

### Where to stay

**$$$-$$ Complejo Cultural y Ecoturístico Cuevas de Candelaria**
*T7861-2203, www.cuevasdecandelaria.com.*
Set in 40 ha of grounds, including pleasant walking paths where you can admire the tropical flora and fauna, accommodation in La Candelaria includes very comfortable thatched *cabañas* and private rooms. There's a good restaurant and café on site. Full board is available.

**$ Las Diamelas**
*Fray Bartolomé de las Casas, just off park, T5810-1785.*
This place offers the cleanest rooms in town. The restaurant food is OK and cheap.

**$ Rancho Ríos Escondidos**
*Near Grutas de Candelaria, on the main road.*
Camping is possible at this farmhouse. Ask for Doña América.

### Transport

**Bus**
Local transport in the form of minibuses and pickups connects most of the towns in this section before nightfall.

Bus to **Poptún** from Fray Bartolomé de las Casas leaves at 0300 from the central park, 5¾ hrs, US$5.10. This road is extremely rough and the journey is a bone-bashing, coccyx-crushing one. Buses to **Cobán** at 0400 until 1100 on the hour. However, do not be surprised if one does not turn up and you have to wait for the next one. To **Flores** via Sebol, Raxrujá and Sayaxché at 0700 (3½ hrs) a further 30 mins to 1 hr to Flores. The road from **Raxrujá** via Chisec to Cobán is very steep and rocky. **Chisec** to Cobán, 1½ hrs. The Sayaxché–Cobán bus arrives at Fray Bartolomé de las Casas for breakfast and continues between 0800 and 0900. You can also go from here to Sebol to Modesto Méndez to join the highway to **Flores**, but it is a very slow, a killer of a journey. Buses leave from Cobán for Chisec from Campo 2 at 0500, 0800, 0900.

# El Petén

Deep in the lush lowland jungles of the Petén lie the lost worlds of Maya cities, pyramids and ceremonial centres, where layers of ancient dust speak ancient tales. At Tikal, where battles and burials are recorded in intricately carved stone, temples push through the tree canopy, wrapped in a mystical shroud.

Although all human life has vanished from these once-powerful centres, the forest is humming with the latter-day lords of the jungle: the howler monkeys that roar day and night. There are also toucans, hummingbirds, spider monkeys, wild pig and coatimundi. Jaguar, god of the underworld in Maya religion, stalks the jungle but remains elusive, as does the puma and tapir.

Further into the undergrowth away from Tikal, the adventurous traveller can visit El Mirador, the largest Maya stronghold, as well as El Zotz, El Perú, El Ceibal and Uaxactún by river, on foot and on horseback.

**Best** for
Jungle ▪ Tikal ▪ Wildlife

## Poptún   *Colour map 2, B5.*

### a rural backdoor to the Petén

Poptún is best known for its association with Finca Ixobel; see Where to stay, below. Otherwise, it is just a staging-post between Río Dulce and Flores, or a stop-off to switch buses for the ride west to Cobán.

## Listings Poptún

### Where to stay

**$$-$ Finca Ixobel**
*T5410-4307, www.fincaixobel.com.*
A working farm owned by Carole Devine, widowed after the assassination of her husband in 1990. This highly acclaimed 'paradise' has become the victim of its own reputation and is frequently crowded especially at weekends. However, you can still camp peacefully and there are great treehouses, dorm beds, private rooms and bungalows. One of the highlights is the food. The finca offers a range of trips that could keep you there for days. Recommended.

### Transport

#### Bus

Take any **Fuente del Norte** bus or any bus heading to the capital from **Flores**, 2 hrs. To Flores catch any Flores-bound bus from the capital. To **Río Dulce**, 2 hrs. Buses will drop you at the driveway to **Finca Ixobel** if that's your destination, just ask. From there it's a 15-min walk. Or, get off at the main bus stop and arrange a taxi there or through **Finca Ixobel**. To **Guatemala City** there are plenty daily, 7-8 hrs, US$10-13. The only bus that continues to **Fray Bartolomé de las Casas** (Las Casas on the bus sign) leaves at 1030, 5¾ hrs, US$8.

## Essential El Petén

### When to go

The dry season and wet season offer different advantages and disadvantages. In the months of November through to early May, access to all sites is possible as tracks are bone-dry. There are also fewer mosquitoes and if you are a bird lover, the mating season falls in this period. In the rainy winter months, from May to November, tracks become muddy quagmires making many of them impassable, also bringing greater humidity and mosquitoes. Take plenty of repellent, and reapply frequently. It's also fiercely hot and humid at all times in these parts so lots of sun screen and drinking water are essential.

### Safety

Roadside robbery used to be a problem on the road to Tikal and to Yaxhá. Get independent, up-to-date advice before visiting these places and leave all valuables at your hotel. Asistur, see Safety in Practicalities chapter, can assist and have a base at Tikal.

### Best places to stay

**Finca Ixobel**, Poptún, see left column
**Flores Hotel Boutique**, Flores, page 388
**Hostal Los Amigos**, Flores, page 389
**La Lancha**, Lake Petén Itzá, page 390
**Posada del Cerro**, near El Remate, page 390

# BACKGROUND

## El Petén

Predominantly covered in jungle, the Petén is the largest department of Guatemala although it has the smallest number of inhabitants. This jungle region was settled by the Maya Itzá Kanek in about AD 600, with their seat then known as La Isla de Tah Itzá (Tayasal in Spanish), now modern-day Flores. The northern area was so impenetrable that the Itzás were untouched by Spanish inroads into Guatemala until the Mexican conquistador Hernán Cortés and Spanish chronicler Bernal Díaz del Castillo dropped by in 1525 on their way from Mexico to Honduras. In 1697 Martín Urzua y Arismendi, the governor of the Yucatán, fought the first battle of the Itzás, crossing Lake Petén Itzá in a galley killing 100 indigenous people in the ensuing battle, and capturing King Canek. He and his men destroyed the temples and palaces of Tayasal and so finished off the last independent Maya state.

In 1990, 21,487 sq km of the north of the Petén was declared a Reserva de la Biósfera Maya (Maya Biosphere Reserve), by CONAP, the National Council for Protected Areas. It became the largest protected tropical forest area in Central America. Inside the boundaries of the biosphere are the Parque Nacional Tikal, Parque Nacional Mirador–Río Azul and Parque Nacional Laguna del Tigre.

## Flores and Santa Elena  Colour map 2, B4/B5.

*a colourful island town and its less elegant mainland counterpart*

Flores is perched on a tiny island in Lake Petén Itzá. Red roofs and palm trees jostle for position as they spread up the small hill, which is topped by the white twin-towered cathedral. Some of the streets of the town are lined with houses and restaurants that have been given lashings of colourful paint, giving Flores a Caribbean flavour. A pleasant new lakeshore *malecón* has been built around the island, with benches, street lamps and jetties for swimming. *Lanchas*, drifting among the lilies and dragonflies, are pinned to the lake edges.

Santa Elena is the dustier and noisier twin town on the mainland where the cheapest hotels, banking services and bus terminal can be found.

### Sights

The **cathedral**, Nuestra Señora de los Remedios y San Pablo del Itzá, is plain inside, and houses a Cristo Negro, part of a chain of Black Christs that stretches across Central America, with the focus of worship at Esquipulas. **Paraíso Escondido** is home to the **zoo** ① *US$2.70*. A dugout to the island costs US$16 round trip. Near the zoo is ARCAS (Asociación de Rescate y Conservación de Vida Silvestre) ① *T5208-0968, www.arcasguatemala.com, US$2*, where they care for rescued animals and release them back into the wild. Volunteers are welcome. There is a centre and interactive trails at the site. Boat tours of the lake depart from the end of the causeway in Flores, around US$20 for one hour, but it's worth bargaining. There is also a longer tour that costs around U$50 for three to four hours, calling at the zoo and **El Mirador** on the Maya ruin of **Tayasal** ① *US$2.70*.

**Actún Kan caves** ① *0800-1700, US$2.70*, are a fascinating labyrinth of tunnels where, legend has it, a large serpent lived. They are 3 km south of Santa Elena and a 30- to

45-minute walk. To get there take the 6 Avenida out of Santa Elena to its end, turn left at a small hill, then take the first road to the right where it is well marked. South of Santa Elena at Km 468 is **Parque Natural Ixpanpajul** ① *T2336-0576, www.ixpanpajul.com*, where forest canopy Tarzan tours, zip-wire, night safari, birdwatching and horse riding and more are on offer. Local fiestas include 12-15 January, the Petén *feria*, and 11-12 December in honour of the Virgen de Guadalupe.

## Around Lake Petén Itzá

**San Andrés**, 16 km by road from Santa Elena, enjoys sweeping views of Lake Petén Itzá, and its houses climb steeply down to the lakeshore. There is a language school, **Eco-Escuela Español** ① *T5940-1235, www.ecoescuelaespanol.org*, which offers 20 hours of classes, homestay and extra-curricular activities for a week, US$150. Adonis, a villager, takes good-value tours to El Zotz and El Mirador and has been recommended. Ask

# Flores

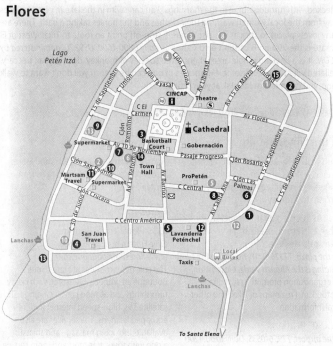

N

50 metres
50 yards

**Where to stay** 🛏
Casa Amelia **13**
Casazul **3**
Flores Hotel Boutique **1**
Hospedaje Doña Goya **4**
Hostal Los Amigos **5**
Isla de Flores **6**
La Casona de la Isla **2**
Sabana **8**
Santana **10**
Villa del Lago **12**

**Restaurants** 🍴
Café Arqueológico Yax-há **1**
Café Uka **12**
Capitán Tortuga **11**
Cool Beans **2**
El Mirador **3**
Hacienda del Rey **4**
La Albahaca **10**
La Canoa **5**

La Galería del Zotz **6**
La Luna **7**
Las Puertas Café Bar **8**
La Villa del Chef **9**
Mayan Princess Restaurant
  Café Bar & Cinema **14**
Raíces **13**
Suica **15**

around for him; his house is close to the shoreline. You can also volunteer in the village with **Volunteer Petén** ⓘ *Parque Nueva Juventud, T5711-0040, www.volunteerpeten.com*, a conservation and community project.

The attractive village of **San José**, a traditional Maya Itzá village, where efforts are being made to preserve the Itzá language and revive old traditions, is 2 km further northeast on the lake from San Andrés. Its painted and thatched homes huddling steeply on the lakeshore make it a much better day trip than San Andrés. It also has a Spanish school, the **Escuela Bio-Itzá** ⓘ *www.ecobioitza.org*, which offers classes, homestay and camping for US$150 a week. Some 4 km beyond the village a signed track leads to the Classic period site of **Motul**, with 33 plazas, tall pyramids and some stelae depicting Maya kings. It takes 20 minutes to walk between the two villages. On 1 November San José hosts the **Holy Skull Procession**.

At the eastern side of Lake Petén Itzá is **El Remate**. The sunsets are superb and the lake is flecked with turquoise blue in the mornings. You can swim in the lake in certain places away from the local women washing their clothes and the horses taking a bath. There are many lovely places to stay, as it is also a handy stop-off point en route to Tikal. West of El Remate is the 700-ha **Biotopo Cerro Cahuí** ⓘ *daily 0800-1600, US$2.70, administered by CECON*. It is a lowland jungle area where three species of monkey, deer, jaguar, peccary, ocellated wild turkey and some 450 species of bird can be seen. If you don't want to walk alone, you can hire a guide. Ask at your *posada*.

## Listings Flores and Santa Elena *map p387*

### Tourist information

If you wish to make trips independently to remote Maya sites, check with ProPetén to see if they have vehicles making the journey.

**CINCAP (Centro de Información sobre la Naturaleza Cultura y Artesanía de Petén**
*On the plaza, T7926-0718, housed in the same building is the Alianza Verde. Closed Mon.*
An organization promoting sustainable ecotourism. Free maps of Tikal, and other local information.

**INGUAT**
*In the airport, T7956-0533. Daily 0700-1200 and 1500-1800.*

**ProPetén**
*Calle Central, T7867-5155, www.propeten.org.*
Associated with Conservation International.

### Where to stay

There are hotels in Santa Elena and Flores across the causeway (10 to 15 mins from Santa Elena).

#### Flores

**$$$$ Flores Hotel Boutique**
*Calle Fraternidad, T7867-7568,*
*www.floreshotelboutique.com.*
The chic modern suites at Flores Hotel Boutique are impeccably attired with classy furnishings and all mod cons including LCD satellite TVs, high-speed internet and fully equipped kitchens. Spa services are also available, including massage and shiatsu, along with tours, transport and room service. Attentive and hospitable: the best luxury option on the island.

**$$$ Isla de Flores**
*Av La Reforma, T7867-5176,*
*www.hotelisladeflores.com.*
Bright, young and stylish, Hotel Isla de Flores partly occupies a traditional island

townhouse, recently renovated with several extensions and tasteful modern decor. Amenities include wooden sun deck and jacuzzi overlooking the lake and a restaurant downstairs. Rooms are comfortable, airy and tranquil.

## $$ Hotel Casa Amelia
*Calle La Unión, T7867-5430, www.hotelcasamelia.com.*
Cheerful and friendly hotel with 15 comfortable, a/c rooms, 6 of which have lake views. There's also a terrace and a pool table.

## $$ Hotel Casazul
*Calle Fraternindad, T7867-5451, www.hotelesdepeten.com.*
The 9 rooms are all blue and most have a lakeside view. All come with cable TV, a/c and fan.

## $$ Hotel Santana
*Calle 30 de Junio, T7867-5123, www.santanapeten.com.*
Clean rooms, all with their own terrace a/c, and TV. There's also a lakeside restaurant and a pool.

## $$ La Casona de la Isla
*Callejón San Pedrito, on the lake, T7867-5163, www.hotelesdepeten.com.*
This friendly place has elegant, clean rooms with fans and TV. Good restaurant, nice breakfasts, bar, garden and pool.

## $$ Sabana
*Calle La Unión, T7867-5100, www.hotelsabana.com.*
Huge, airy rooms, good service, clean, pleasant, with funky green wavy paintwork in lobby. Good views, lakeside pool and restaurant. Caters for European package tours.

## $$ Villa del Lago
*Calle 15 de Septiembre, T7867-5181, www.hotelvilladelago.com.gt.*
Very clean rooms with a/c and fan, cheaper with shared bath, some rooms have a lake view and balcony. Breakfast is served on a terrace overlooking the lake, but the service is excruciatingly slow. Breakfast is open to non-guests, but avoid it in high season unless you don't mind a long wait.

## $ Chal Tun Ha Hostel
*San Miguel peninsula, 3 mins by boat from Flores, T4219-0851, www.chaltunhahostel.com.*
This family-owned hostel offers cheap dorm beds and a variety of basic wooden *cabañas* on stilts, each with screens and private porch, and surrounded by trees. There is a restaurant-bar with fine views and refreshing breezes. Overlooking the lake, the garden has sun loungers, hammocks and a small pool. There is a sister hostel, Chal Tun Ha Hostel Flores Island, on the island but it's not quite as good as this one.

## $ Hospedaje Doña Goya
*Calle Unión, T7926-3538, http://hospedajedonagoya.weebly.com.*
A friendly, family-run place with 6 basic but clean rooms, 3 with private bath (cheaper without), 3 with balcony. The terrace has superb views, and there's internet, a book exchange, kitchen and hammocks on a thatched roof terrace.

## $ Hostal Los Amigos
*Calle Central and Av Barrios, T7867-5075, www.amigoshostel.com.*
This hostal is very popular with backpackers but can be crowded and noisy. There's a choice of a private rooms, dorms with 20 beds, luxury dorms and hammocks with a funky courtyard. Good, cheap restaurant; bar and internet available. Staff are very helpful and friendly. Highly recommended. It also rents out hammocks and mosquito nets for tours to Tikal.

## Santa Elena

## $$$$ Hotel Casona del Lago
*Overlooking the lake, T7952-8700, www.hotelesde peten.com.*
32 spacious rooms, some with balcony, in this lovely duck-egg blue and white hotel. Pool, restaurant, internet and travel agency.

### $ San Juan
*Calle 2, close to the Catholic church, T7926-0562, sanjuanttravel@hotmail.com.gt.*
Full of budget travellers in the older rooms, cheaper with shared bath, but not always spotless. Some remodelled rooms have a/c and TV. Exchanges US dollars and Mexican pesos and buys Belizean dollars. It's not the best place to stay but it's safe, and there's a public phone inside and parking. Note that the Tikal minibuses leave from 0500 so you will probably be woken early.

## Around Lake Petén Itzá
To reach the lodgings along the north shore of the lake can be up to a 2-km walk from El Remate centre, depending on where you stay (turn left, west on the Flores–Tikal main road). There is street light up to the Biotopo entrance until 2200.

### $$$$ Bahía Taitzá Hotel and Restaurant
*Barrio El Porvenir, San José, T7928-8125, www.taitza.com.*
The 8 lovely rooms are decorated with local furnishings and set behind a beautiful lawn that sweeps down to the lakeshore. Rates include breakfast and transfer, and there's a restaurant on site.

### $$$$-$$$ La Lancha
*T7928-8331, www.blancaneaux.com.*
Francis Ford Coppola's attractive, small hotel is quiet and friendly, and in a lovely setting. It has 10 rooms which have been tastefully furnished and are decorated using local arts and crafts. 4 rooms have lake views from their balconies. There's a pool and the terrace restaurant serves excellent local cuisine. Horse riding and kayaking trips are available.

### $$$ El Sombrero
*Laguna Yax-Ha, T4215-8777, www.ecolodgeelsombrero.com.*
Hidden in the jungle on the shores of Yaxhá lagoon, El Sombrero is a well-established and family-run ecolodge, Italian owned with a good social and ethical philosophy. Accommodation is in simple but comfortable stone cabins with their own porches. Expect the usual jungle facilities, including limited electricity.

### $$$ Hotel Ni'tun
*2 km from San Andrés on the Santa Elena road, T5201-0759, www.nitun.com.*
These luxury *cabañas* on a wooded hillside above the lake are run by a friendly couple, Bernie and Lore, who cook fantastic vegetarian meals and organize expeditions to remote sites.

### $$$-$$ Posada del Cerro
*Just west of El Remate near the entrance of the Biotopo Cerro Cahui, T5376-8722, www.posadadelcerro.com.*
The epitome of rustic chic, Posada del Cerro incorporates contemporary decor, furnishings and finishes with traditional rancho architecture. Their cosy apartments ($$$) feature a double bed, a sofa bed and a fully equipped kitchen. Rooms ($$) include attractive stonework, hardwood furniture and thatched roofs. Very relaxing, comfortable, natural and ecologically aware.

### $$ La Mansión del Pajaro Serpiente
*El Remate, T5967-9816, www.30minutesfromtikal.com.*
Set in lush tropical grounds replete with palms, orchids, peacocks and walking trails, this traditional B&B features very reasonable stone-built cabins with mahogany furniture, hand-woven bedspreads and views of the lake; some have a/c. There's a large pool with a waterfall, tours and a dining room. A secluded natural retreat perched on a hilltop.

### $ Hotel y Restaurante Mon Ami
*On the El Remate side, T7928-8413, www.hotelmon ami.com.*
Lovely bungalows, dorms and hammocks for sleeping. The conservationist owner organizes guided tours to Yaxhá and Nakum. English, French and Spanish are spoken. The restaurant (0700-2130) serves seriously cheap chicken, pasta and other dishes, and offers a selection of wines.

### $ La Casa de Don David
*20 m from the main road, on
the El Remate side, T7928-8469,
www.lacasadedondavid.com.*
Clean and comfortable; all rooms with
private bath and some with a/c. There's a
great view from the terrace restaurant, which
serves cheap food. Transport to Tikal and
other tours are available and there's free bike
hire. They have a wealth of information and
can offer helpful advice.

### $ Las Gardenias
*El Remate, T5936-6984,
www.hotelasgardenias.com.*
A quiet family-run guesthouse on the way
to Tikal. Rooms are simple, clean, airy, bright,
and fully equipped with hot shower, TV and
a/c. They have a restaurant serving breakfast,
*comida típica* and an à la carte menu, and
the communal terrace has hammocks and
views of Lake Petén Itza. Shuttles and tours
can be arranged. There's limited internet in
the lobby.

### $ Sun Breeze Hotel
*Exactly on the corner, on the El Remate side,
T7928-8044.*
Run by the very friendly Humberto Castro,
this place has little wooden rooms with
views over the lake. Fans and *mosquiteros* are
in each room, and 2 rooms have a private
bathroom. Humberto runs a daily service to
Tikal, as well as other trips.

## Restaurants

### Flores

### $$$-$$ Raíces
*T5521-1843, raicesrestaurante@gmail.com.*
Excellent waterfront restaurant beside the
*lanchas* near the far west end of Calle Sur.
Specialities include *parillas* and kebabs.
Great seafood.

### $$ La Villa Del Chef
*T4366-3822, lavilladelchefguatemala@
yahoo.com.*
Friendly German-owned restaurant at the
south end of Calle Unión that specializes in
*pescado blanco.* It has a happy hour and also
rents canoes for lake tours. Recommended.

### $$ Mayan Princess Restaurant Café Bar and Cinema
*Reforma and 10 de Noviembre. Closed Sun.*
Has the most adventurous menu on the
island including daily specials, many with
an Asian flavour, relaxed atmosphere, with
bright coloured textile cloths on the tables.
Internet and free films.

### $$-$ Café Arqueológico Yax-há
*Calle 15 de Septiembre, T5830-2060,
www.cafeyaxha.com.*
Cheap daily soups, Maya specialities, such as
chicken in tamarind sauce, great smoothies,
and home-made nachos. German owner
Dieter (who speaks English too) offers tours
to little-known Maya sites and works with
local communities to protect them.

### $$-$ Capitán Tortuga
*Calle 30 de junio.*
Pizzas, pasta and bar snacks, with dayglo
painted walls and lakeside terrace.

### $$-$ Hacienda del Rey
*Calle Sur.*
Expensive Argentine steaks are on the menu,
but the breakfasts are seriously cheap.

### $$-$ La Albahaca
*Calle 30 de Junio.*
First-class home-made pasta and
chocolate cake.

### $$-$ La Galería del Zotz
*15 de Septiembre.*
A wide range of food, delicious pizzas, good
service and presentation, popular with locals.

### $$-$ La Luna
*Av 10 de Noviembre. Closed Sun.*
Refreshing natural lemonade, range of
fish, meat and vegetarian dishes. The
restaurant has a beautiful courtyard
with blue paintwork set under lush
pink bougainvillea. Recommended.

### $$-$ Las Puertas Café Bar
*Av Santa Ana and Calle Central, T7867-5242.*
*Closes at 2300 for food and 2400 completely.*
*Closed Sun.*
Cheap breakfasts, huge menu, good, large
pasta portions. It's popular at night with
locals and travellers and is in an airy building,
chilled atmosphere, games available.

### $ Café Uka
*Calle Centro América. Open from 0600.*
Filling breakfasts and meals.

### $ Cool Beans
*Calle Fraternidad, T5571-9240,*
*coolbeans@itelgua.com.*
Cheap food with home-made bread
and pastries.

### $ El Mirador
*Overlooking the lake but view obscured by*
*restaurant wall.*
Seriously cheap food and snacks but service
is slow.

### $ La Canoa
*Calle Centro América.*
Good breakfasts (try the pancakes), dinners
start at US$1.50, with good *comida típica*,
very friendly owners.

### $ Suica
*Calle Fraternidad. Mon-Sat 1200-1900.*
Small place serving an unusual mix of sushi,
tempura and curries.

## Santa Elena

### $$ El Rodeo
*1 Calle.*
Excellent restaurant serving reasonably priced
food. Plays classical music and sometimes
there's impromptu singing performances.

### $ El Petenchel
*Calle 2.*
Vegetarian food served here as well as
conventional meats and meals. Excellent
breakfasts and a good-value *menú del día*.
Music played, prompt service.

### $ Restaurante Mijaro
*Calle 2 and Av 8.*
Great filling breakfasts and a bargain
*menú del día* at US$1.70, all in a thatched-
roofed roadside location.

## What to do

### Tour operators
Beware 'helpful' touts, especially those on
buses, and don't be pressured into buying
tours, transport or accommodation; there's
plenty to choose from in Flores.
**Martsam Travel**, *Calle 30 de Junio, Flores,*
*T7867-5377, www.martsam.com.* Guided tours
to Tikal, El Zotz, El Mirador, El Perú, Yaxhá,
Nakum, Aguateca, Ceibal and Uaxactún.
Guides with wildlife and ornithological
knowledge in addition to archaeological
knowledge. Highly recommended.
**Mayan Adventure**, *Calle 15 de Septiembre,*
*Flores, T5830-2060, www.the-mayan-*
*adventure.com.* Led by German archaeologist
Dieter Richter, this company offers insightful
expeditions and tours to a range of sites
under excavation. An insider look at the
scientific work of archaeology.
**San Juan Travel Agency**, *T7926-0042.*
Offers transport (US$7.50 return) to Tikal and
excursions to Ceibal, Uaxactún, and Yaxhá
(US$80). Mixed reports, not a first choice.
**Tikal Connection**, *international airport,*
*T7926-1537, www.tikalcnx.com.* Runs tours to
El Perú, El Mirador, Nakbé, El Zotz, Yaxhá, Dos
Aguadas, Uaxactún. It also sells bus tickets.

## Transport

### Air
Flores is 2 km from the international airport
on the outskirts of Santa Elena. A taxi from
the airport into Santa Elena or Flores costs
US$1.30 and takes 5 mins, but bargain hard.

Be early for flights, as overbooking is
common. The airport departures hall
has an internet place. Tour operator and
hotel representatives are based in the
arrival halls. The cost of a return flight is

between US$180-220, shop around. **Grupo Taca**, T2470-8222, www.taca.com, leaves **Guatemala City** daily at 0645, 0955, 1725, 1 hr, returns 0820, 1605 and 1850. **Tag**, T2360-3038, www.tag.com.gt, flies at 0630 returning 1630. To **Cancún**, **Grupo Taca**. To **Belize City**, **Tropic Air**, www.tropicair.com.

## Boat
*Lanchas* moor along Calle Sur, Flores; behind the **Hotel Santana**; from the dock behind **Hotel Casona de Isla**; and beside the arch on the causeway.

## Bus
If you arrive by long-distance bus from Guatemala City, Mexico or Belize, the terminal is 10 blocks south of the causeway, which links Flores and Santa Elena. Chicken buses run between the two, US$0.35. Tuk-tuks charge US$0.90 for journeys between them.

**Local** Local buses (chicken buses), US$0.26, Flores to Santa Elena, leave from the end of the causeway in Flores.

**Long distance** All long-distance buses leave from the relocated bus terminal, 6 blocks south of the Calle Principal in Santa Elena. It has a snack bar, toilets, seating and ATM. Opposite are restaurants, *comedores*, and a bakery. Banrural is down the side. To **Guatemala City**, **Línea Dorada**, daily office hours 0500-2200, www.tikalmayan world.com, leaves 1000, 2100, 1st class, US$30; 2200, US$16, 8 hrs. **Autobuses del Norte (ADN)**, T7924-8131, www.adnauto busesdelnorte.com, luxury service, 1000, 2100, 2300, US$23. **Fuente del Norte**, T7926-0666, office open 24 hrs, buses every 45 mins-1 hr, 0330-2230, US$12, 9 hrs. At 1000, 1400, 2100, 2200, US$20, 7-8 hrs. 2nd-class buses, **Rosita**, T7926-5178 and **Rápidos del Sur**, T7924-8072, also go to the capital, US$13. If you are going only to **Poptún**, 2 hrs, or **Río Dulce**, 3½-4 hrs, make sure you do not pay the full fare to Guatemala City. To **Sayaxché** with **Pinita**, T9926-0726, at 1100,

returns next day at 0600, US$2.50. With **Fuente del Norte** at 0600, US$1.70, returning 0600. Colectivos also leave every 15 mins 0530-1700, US$2.40. Buses run around the lake to **San Andrés**, with one at 1200 with **Pinita** continuing to **Cruce dos Aguadas**, US$2.90 and **Carmelita**, US$3.30 for access to El Mirador. Returning from Carmelita at 0500 the next day. Minibuses also run to San Andrés. To **Chiquimula**, take **Transportes María Elena**, T5550-4190, at 0400, 0800, 1300, US$3. The **María Elena** bus continues onto **Esquipulas**, 9 hrs, US$12. **Fuente del Norte** to **Cobán**, 0530, 0630, 1230, 1330, 5 hrs, US$8. Or take a minibus to Sayaxché and change. Shuttle transfers may also be possible. To **Jutiapa**, 0500, 0530, 7 hrs, returning 0900, US$10-12.

**International** To **Melchor de Mencos** at the Belize border, 0500, 0600, 1630, 2300, 1½ hrs, US$3.30. Returning 0200, 0500, 0600, 1630, 2300. See also Border crossings box in Practicalities chapter, for more information on crossing into Belize. Also with **Línea Dorada** and on to **Chetumal**, **Mexico.** See also Border crossings box in Practicalities chapter.

To **Copán Ruinas**, **Honduras**, take **Transportes María Elena**, T5550-4190, to Chiquimula at 0400, 0800, 1300, US$13 then from Chiquimula to El Florido and finally on to Copán Ruinas. Alternatively, take any bus to the capital and change at Río Hondo. See also Border crossings box in Practicalities chapter, for more on crossing to Honduras. To **San Salvador**, 0600, 8 hrs, US$26.70; see also Border crossings box in Practicalities chapter, for crossing into El Salvador.

## Car
There are plenty of agencies at the airport, mostly Suzuki jeeps, which cost about US$65-80 per day. **Hertz**, at the airport, T7926-0332. **Garrido** at Sac-Nicte Hotel, Calle 1, Santa Elena, T7926-1732.

**Petrol** Available in Santa Elena at the 24-hr Texaco garage on the way to the airport.

**Boat**

Public *lanchas* from San Benito have virtually come to a stop. Visitors can still charter a *lancha* from Flores for about US$10.

**Bus**

There's a bus ticket and internet office opposite the turning to El Remate. Any bus/ shuttle heading for Tikal can stop at El Remate, US$2.50, last bus around 1600; taxi around US$10. Returning to **Flores**, pick up any shuttle heading south (this is a lot easier after 1300 when tourists are returning). There is a bus service heading to **Flores** from El Remate at 0600, 0700, 0830, 0930, 1300 and 1400. Shuttles leave every 30 mins for San Andrés, US$0.70, 30 mins and go on to San José.

## Parque Nacional Tikal  *Colour map 2, A5.*

**Mayan skyscrapers pushing up through the jungle canopy**

★Tikal will have you transfixed. Its steep-sided temples for the mighty dead, stelae commemorating the powerful rulers, inscriptions recording the noble deeds and the passing of time, and burials that were stuffed with jade and bone funerary offerings, make up the greatest Mayan city in this tropical pocket of Guatemala.

**The ruins** *Numbers in brackets refer to the map, page 396.*

The **Great Plaza (3)** is a four-layered plaza with its earliest foundations laid around 150 BC and its latest around AD 700. It is dwarfed by its two principal temples – Temples I and II. On the north side of the plaza between these two temples are two rows of monuments. It includes Stela 29, erected in AD 292, which depicts Tikal's emblem glyph – the symbol of a Mayan city – and the third century AD ruler Scroll Ahau Jaguar, who is bearing a two-headed ceremonial bar.

**Temple I (Temple of the Great Jaguar) (1)**, on the east side of the Great Plaza, rises to 44 m in height with nine stepped terraces. It was ordered to be built by the ruler Ah Cacao, who ruled between AD 682 to around AD 720-724, who probably planned it for use as his shrine. His tomb, the magnificent Burial 116, was discovered beneath Temple I in 1962 with a wealth of burial goods on and around his skeleton. The display is reconstructed in the Museo Cerámico/Tikal.

**Temple II (Temple of the Masks) (2)** faces Temple I on the Great Plaza and rises to 38 m, although with its roof comb it would have been higher. It's thought Ah Cacao ordered its construction as well. The lintel on the doorway here depicted a woman wearing a cape, and experts have suggested that this could be his wife.

## ON THE ROAD

### Wildlife

Tikal is a fantastic place for seeing animal and bird life of the jungle. Wildlife includes spider monkeys, howler monkeys, three species of toucan (most prominent being the keel-billed toucan), deer, foxes and many other birds and insects. Pumas have been seen on quieter paths and coatimundis (pizotes), in large family groups, are often seen rummaging through the bins. The ocellated turkeys with their sky-blue heads with orange baubles attached are seen in abundance at the entrance, and at El Mundo Perdido.

## Getting there

From Flores, it's possible to visit Tikal in a day. San Juan Travel Agency minibuses leave hourly between 0500 and 1000, one at 1400 and return at 1230 and hourly between 1400 and 1700 (though on the way back from Tikal, buses are likely to leave 10-15 minutes before scheduled), one hour, US$7.50 return. Several other companies also run trips such as Línea Dorada at 0500, 0830, 1530, returning 1400 and 1700. If you have not bought a return ticket you can often get a discounted seat on a returning bus if it's not full. Minibuses also meet Guatemala City–Flores flights. A taxi to Tikal costs US$60 one way. You can also visit Tikal with a one-day or two-day package tour from Guatemala City or Antigua.

## Opening times and entry fee

Daily 0600-1800, US$20 per day, payable at the national park entrance, 18 km from the ruins (park administration, T7920-0025).

## Time required

An overall impression of the ruins may be gained in five hours, but you need at least two days to see them properly. If you enter after 1600 your ticket is valid for the following day. To enter the site before or after closing time costs US$13 and you must be accompanied by a guide. If you stay the night in the park hotels, you can enter at 0500 once the police have scoured the grounds. This gives you at least a two-hour head start on visitors coming in from Flores.

## Tourist information

A guide is highly recommended as outlying structures can otherwise be missed. The official Tourist Guide Association offers tours of varying natures and in different languages, US$40 for four people plus US$5 for each additional person, just turn up at the visitor centre. A private guide can be hired for US$60 or you can join up with a group for US$15 per person. Tours are available in Spanish, English, Italian, German and French. The guidebook *Tikal*, by WR Coe, in several languages, has an excellent map; or you can buy a reasonable leaflet/map at the entrance, US$2.50. Free transport around the site is available for elderly and disabled visitors, in an adapted pickup truck, with wheelchair access.

## Facilities

At the park's visitor centre there is a post office, which stores luggage, a tourist guide service (see under Tourist information), exchange facilities, toilets, a restaurant and a few shops that sell relevant guidebooks.

## When to go

Try to visit the ruins after 1400, or before 0900, as there are fewer visitors. From April to December it rains every day for a while; it is busiest November to January, during the Easter and summer holidays and most weekends. The best time for birdwatching tours is December to April, with November to February being the mating season. Mosquitoes can be a real problem even during the day if straying away from open spaces.

## What to take

Bring a hat, mosquito repellent, water and snacks with you as it's extremely hot, drinks at the site aren't cheap and there's a lot of legwork involved.

The **North Acropolis (4)** contains some 100 buildings piled on top of earlier structures in a 1-ha area and is the burial ground of all of Tikal's rulers until the break with royal practice made by Ah Cacao. In 1960, the prized Stelae 31, now in the Museo Cerámico/Tikal, see below, was found under the Acropolis. It was dedicated in AD 445. Its base was deliberately burnt by the Maya and buried under Acropolis buildings in the eighth century. This burning was thought to be like a 'killing', where the burning ritual would 'kill' the power of the ruler depicted on the monument, say, after death. It's thought to depict the ruler Siyah Chan K'awil (Stormy Sky), who died sometime around AD 457 having succeeded to the throne in AD 411. Yax Moch Xok (Great Scaffold Shark) is thought to be entombed in the first century

# Tikal

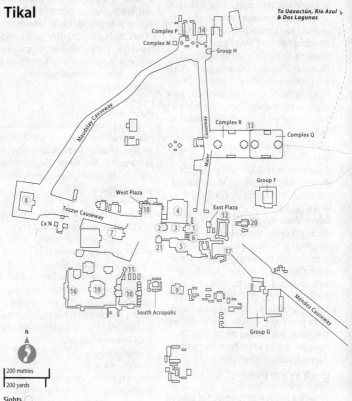

**To Uaxactún, Río Azul & Dos Lagunas**

Complex P

Complex M

Group H

Maudslay Causeway

Maler Causeway

Complex R

Complex Q

Group F

West Plaza

Tozzer Causeway

Cx N

East Plaza

Group G

South Acropolis

Méndez Causeway

N

200 metres
200 yards

## Sights ○

Temple I (Temple of the
Great Jaguar) **1**
Temple II (Temple of the
Masks) **2**
Great Plaza **3**
North Acropolis **4**
Central Acropolis **5**

Ball Court **6**
Temple III (Temple of the
Jaguar Priest) **7**
Temple IV (Temple of the
Double-Headed Serpent) **8**
Temple V **9**

Plaza of the Seven
Temples **10**
Triple Ball Court **11**
Market **12**
Twin Pyramid Complexes
Q & R **13**

North Group **14**
Temple VI (Temple of
Inscriptions) **15**
El Mundo Perdido (Lost
World) **16**

AD grave, Burial 85. Surrounding the headless male body were burial objects and a mask bearing the royal head band. Under a building directly in the centre of this acropolis Burial 22 – that of ruler Great Jaguar Paw, who reigned in the fourth century, and died around AD 379 – was discovered. Also found here was Burial 10, thought to be the tomb of Nun Yax Ayin I (Curl Nose), who succeeded to the throne in AD 379 after Great Jaguar Paw. Inside were the remains of nine sacrificed servants as well as turtles and crocodile remains and a plethora of pottery pieces. The pottery laid out in this tomb had Teotihuacán artistic influences, demonstrating Tikal's links to the powers of Teotihuacán and Teotihuacán-influenced Kaminal Juyú. Burial 48 is thought to be the tomb of Curl Nose's son, Siyah Chan K'awil (Stormy Sky).

**Central Acropolis (5)** is made up of a complex of courts connected by passages and stairways, which have expanded over the centuries to cover 1.6 ha. Most of the building work carried out took place between AD 550-900 in the late-Classic era. The **East Plaza** behind Temple I is the centre of the highway junctions of the Maler Causeway in the north, and the Méndez Causeway heading southeast.

On the western side of the **West Plaza** is structure 5D II under which Burial 77 was brought to light. The skeleton was adorned with a jade pendant, which was stolen from the site museum in the 1980s.

**Temple III (Temple of the Jaguar Priest) (7)** is so called because of the scene of a figure in a glamorous jaguar pelt on a lintel found on the temple. Some experts believe this figure is Ah Chitam (Nun Yax Ayin II, Ruler C), son of Yax Kin, and grandson of the great Ah Cacao, and so propose that this is his shrine, although there has been no confirmation of this. Temple III was constructed around AD 810 and is 55 m tall.

**Temple IV (Temple of the Double-Headed Serpent) (8)** is the highest building in Tikal at 70 m. It was built in the late-Classic period around AD 741, as proven by hieroglyphic inscriptions and carbon dating. It's thought it was built to honour Yax Kin, the son of Ah Cacao, who became ruler in AD 734. A date on the lintel is AD 741, the same year that Temple I was dedicated.

**Temple V (9)**, constructed between AD 700-750 during the reign of Yax Kin, is 58 m high. It is the mortuary temple of an unknown ruler.

Museo Cerámico **1**
Park Administration **2**
Disused Airfield **3**
Minibus Park

Entrance & Tickets

Museo Lítico
Visitor Centre

Comedores

Entrance

To Flores

# BACKGROUND

## Tikal

At its height, the total 'urban' area of Tikal was more than 100 sq km, with the population somewhere between 50,000 and 100,000. The low-lying hill site of Tikal was first occupied around 600 BC during the pre-Classic era, but its buildings date from 300 BC. It became an important Maya centre from AD 300 onwards, which coincided with the decline of the mega power to the north, El Mirador. It was governed by a powerful dynasty of 30-plus rulers between about the first century AD until about AD 869, with the last known named ruler being Hasaw Chan K'awill II.

Tikal's main structures, which cover 2.5 sq km, were constructed from AD 550 to 900 during the late-Classic period. These include the towering mega structures of temples – shrines to the glorious dead – whose roof combs were once decorated with coloured stucco figures of Tikal lords. Doorways on the temple rooms were intricately carved – using the termite-resistant wood of the sapodilla tree – with figures and symbols, known as lintels.

Tikal's stelae tell of kings and accessions and war and death. Its oldest stela dates from AD 292. Many Central Mexican influences have been found on the stelae imagery, in burial sites at Tikal and in decorative architectural technique, which led archaeologists to conclude that the city was heavily influenced from the west by forces from the great enclave of Teotihuacán, now just outside Mexico City. This war-like state bred a cult of war and sacrifice and seemed intent on spreading its culture. After the collapse of Teotihuacán in AD 600, a renaissance at Tikal was achieved by the ruler Ah Cacao (Lord Cocoa, Ruler A, Moon Double Comb, Hasaw Chan K'awil I, Sky Rain) who succeeded to the throne in AD 682 and died sometime in the 720s.

However, in the latter part of the eighth century the fortunes of Tikal declined. The last date recorded on a stela is AD 889. The site was finally abandoned in the 10th century. Most archaeologists now agree the collapse was due to warfare with neighbouring states, overpopulation, which resulted in environmental destruction, and drought. Tikal's existence was first reported by Spanish monk Andrés de Avendaño, but its official discovery is attributed to Modesto Méndez, commissioner of the Petén, and Ambrosio Tut, governor of the Petén, in 1848. They were both accompanied by the artist Eusebio Lara.

**El Mundo Perdido (The Lost World) (16)**. The **Great Pyramid** is at the centre of this lost world. At 30 m high, it is the largest pyramid at Tikal. It is flat topped and its stairways are flanked by masks. From the top a great view over the canopy to the tops of other temples can be enjoyed. Together with other buildings to the west, it forms part of an astronomical complex. The Lost World pyramid is a pre-Classic structure, but was improved upon in the Early Classic. East of El Mundo Perdido is the **Plaza of the Seven Temples (10)**, constructed during the Late Classic period (AD 600-800). There is a triple ball court lying at its northern edge.

**Temple VI (Temple of the Inscriptions) (15)** was discovered in 1951. The 12-m-high roof comb is covered on both sides in hieroglyphic text and is the longest hieroglyphic recording to date. It was carved in AD 766, but the temple was built under the rule of Yax Kin some years before. Altar 9 is at the base of the temple as is Stela 21, said to depict the sculptured foot of the ruler Yax Kin to mark his accession as ruler in AD 734. Unfortunately because of the location of this temple away from the rest of the main structures it has become a hideout for robbers and worse. Some guides no longer take people there. Take advice before going, if at all.

The **North Group** has several twin pyramid complexes, including Complexes Q and R, marking the passing of the *katun* – a Maya 20-year period.

The **Museo Cerámico (Museo Tikal)** ⓘ *near the Jungle Lodge, Mon-Fri 0900-1700, Sat and Sun, 0900-1600, US$1.30,* has a collection of Maya ceramics, but its prize exhibits are Stela 31 with its still clear carvings, and the reconstruction of the tomb of Tikal's great ruler, Ah Cacao. In the **Museo Lítico** ⓘ *inside the visitor centre, Mon-Fri 0900-1700, Sat and Sun, 0900-1600,* there are stelae and great photographs of the temples as they were originally found, and of their reconstruction, including the 1968 rebuild of the Temple II steps. **Note** Photography is no longer permitted in either of these museums.

## Listings Parque Nacional Tikal *map p396*

### Where to stay

You are advised to book when you arrive; in high season, book in advance. Take a torch: 24-hr electricity is not normally available.

#### $$$-$$ Jungle Lodge
*T5361-4098, www.quik.guate.com/jltikal/ index.html.*
These spacious, comfortable bungalows have bath, 24-hr hot water and a fan (electricity 0700-2100); it's cheaper without bath. There's also a pool and they can cash TCs. Full board is available (although we've had consistent reports of unsatisfactory food, slow service and small portions). Jungle Lodge's Tikal tours have been recommended.

#### $$$-$$ Tikal Inn
*T7926-1917.*
This place has bungalows and rooms, hot water 1800-1900, electricity 0900-1600 and 1800-2200, and helpful staff. The beautiful pool is for guest use only. Natural history tours at 0930 for US$10 for a minimum 2 people.

#### $$ Jaguar Inn
*T7926-0002, www.jaguartikal.com.*
Full board is available, less without food. There is also a dorm with 6 beds, hammocks with mosquito nets, and lockers. Electricity is available 1800-2200 and there's hot water in the morning or on request Mar-Oct and Nov-Feb, 0600-2100. They will provide a picnic lunch and can store luggage.

### Camping

#### $ Camping Tikal
*Run by the Restaurante del Parque, reservations T2370-8140, or at the Petén Espléndido, T7926-0880.*
If you have your own tent or hammock it's US$5; if you need to rent the gear it's US$8. There are also *cabañas* with mattresses and mosquito nets for US$7 per person. It also does deals that include breakfast, lunch and dinner ranging from US$15-30 for a double. Communal showers available. Take your own water as the supply is very variable.

There are literally hundreds of Mayan sites in the Petén. Below is a handful of sites, whose ruins have been explored, and of whose histories something is known.

### Uaxactún *Colour map 2, A5.*

In the village of Uaxactún (pronounced Waash-ak-tún) are ruins, famous for the oldest complete Maya astronomical complex found, and a stuccoed temple with serpent and jaguar head decoration. The village itself is little more than a row of houses either side of a disused airstrip. The site is 24 km north of Tikal on an unpaved road. It is in fairly good condition taking less than one hour in any vehicle.

Uaxactún is one of the longest-occupied Mayan sites. Its origins lie in the middle pre-Classic (1000-300 BC) and its decline came by the early post-Classic (AD 925-1200) like many of its neighbouring powers. Its final stelae, dated AD 889, is one of the last to be found in the region. The site is named after a stela, which corresponds to Baktun 8 (8 x 400 Maya years), carved in AD 889; *uaxac* means 8, *tun* means stone.

South of the remains of a ball court, in **Group B**, a turtle carving can be seen, and Stela 5, which marks the takeover of the city, launched from Tikal. Next door to this stela under Temple B-VIII were found the remains of two adults, including a pregnant woman, a girl of about 15 and a baby. It is believed this may have been the governor and his family who were sacrificed in AD 378. From Group B, take the causeway to **Group A**. In Group A, Structure A-V had 90 rooms and there were many tombs to be seen. The highest structure in the complex is Palace A-XVIII, where red paint can still be seen on the walls. In **Group E** the oldest observatory (E-VII-sub) ever found faces structures in which the equinoxes and solstices were observed. When the pyramid (E-VII) covering this sub-structure was removed, fairly well preserved stucco masks of jaguar and serpent heads were found flanking the stairways of the sub-structure.

The ruins lie either side of the village, the main groups (**Group A** and **Group B**) are to the northwest (take a left just before **Hotel El Chiclero** and follow the road round on a continuous left to reach this group). A smaller group (**Group E**) with the observatory is to the southwest (take any track, right off the airstrip, and ask. This group is 400 m away.

### El Zotz *Colour map 2, A5.*

El Zotz, meaning bat in Q'eqchi', is so called because of the nightly flight from a nearby cave of thousands of bats. There is an alternative hiking route as well (see below). Incredibly, from Temple IV, the highest in the complex at 75 m, it is possible to see in the distance, some 30 km away, Temple IV at Tikal. The wooden lintel from Temple I (dated AD 500-550) is to be found in the Museo Nacional de Arqueología y Etnología in the capital. Each evening at about 1850 the sky is darkened for 10 minutes by the fantastic spectacle of tens of thousands of bats flying out of a cave near the camp. The 200-m-high cave pock-marked with holes is a 30-minute walk from the camp. If you are at the cave you'll see the flight above you and get doused in falling excrement. If you remain at the campsite you will see them streaking the dark blue sky with black in straight columns. It's also accessible via Uaxactún. There is some basic infrastructure for the guards, and you can camp.

One of the best trips you can do in the Petén is a three-day hike to El Zotz and on through the jungle to Tikal. The journey, although long, is not arduous, and is accompanied by birds, blue morpho butterflies and spider monkeys chucking branches at you all the way.

## El Perú and the Estación Biológica Guacamayo *Colour map 2, A4.*

A visit to El Perú is included in the **Scarlet Macaw Trail**, a two- to five-day trip into the **Parque Nacional Laguna del Tigre**, through the main breeding area of the scarlet macaw. There is little to see at the Mayan site, but the journey to it is worthwhile. In 2004 the 1200-year-old tomb and skeleton of a Maya queen were found. A more direct trip involves getting to the isolated Q'eqchi'-speaking community of **Paso Caballos** (1¾ hours). Here, the **Comité de Turismo** can organize transport by *lancha* along the Río San Pedro. From Paso Caballos it is one hour by *lancha* to the El Perú campsite and path.

It's possible to stop off at the **Estación Biológica Guacamayo** ① *US$1.30, volunteers may be needed, contact Propeten, www.propeten.org,* where there is an ongoing programme to study the wild scarlet macaws (*ara macao*). The chances of seeing endangered scarlet macaws during March, April and May in this area is high because that's when they are reproducing.

A couple of minutes upriver is the landing stage, from where it's a 30-minute walk to the campsite of El Perú: howler monkeys, hummingbirds, oropendola birds and fireflies abound. From there, it is a two-hour walk to the El Perú ruins. Small coral snakes slither about, howler monkeys roar, spider monkeys chuck branches down on the path. White-lipped peccaries, nesting white turtles, eagles, fox and kingfishers have also been seen. The trip may be impossible between June and August because of rising rivers during the rainy season and because the unpaved road to Paso Caballos may not be passable. Doing it on your own is possible, although you may have to wait for connections and you will need a guide, about US$20 per day.

## El Mirador, El Tintal and Nakbé *Colour map 2, A5.*

El Mirador is the largest Mayan site in the country. It dates from the late pre-Classic period (300 BC-AD 250) and is thought to have sustained a population of tens of thousands. It takes five days to get to El Mirador. From Flores it is 2½ to three hours to the village of Carmelita by bus or truck, from where it is seven hours walking, or part horse riding to El Mirador. It can be done in four days – two days to get there and two days to return. The route is difficult and the mosquitoes and ticks and the relentless heat can make it a trying trip. Organized tours are arranged by travel agents in Flores; get reassurance that your guides have enough food and water. If you opt to go to El Mirador independently, ask in Carmelita for the **Comité de Turismo**, which will arrange mules and guides. Take water, food, tents and torches.

It is about 25 km to El Tintal, a camp where you can sling a hammock, or another 10 km to El Arroyo, where there is a little river for a swim near a *chiclero* camp. It takes another day to El Mirador, or longer, if you detour via Nakbé. You will pass *chiclero* camps on the way, which are very hospitable, but very poor. In May, June and July there is no mud, but there is little chance of seeing wildlife or flora. In July to December, when the rains come, the chances of glimpsing wildlife is much greater and there are lots of flowers. It is a lot fresher, but there can be tonnes of mud, sometimes making the route impassable. The mosquitos are also in a frenzy during the rainy season. Think carefully about going on the trip (one reader called it "purgatory").

The site, which is part of the Parque Nacional Mirador-Río Azul, is divided into two parts with the **El Tigre Pyramid** and complex in the western part, and the **La Danta** complex, the largest in the Maya world, in the east, 2 km away. The larger of two huge pyramids – La Danta – is 70 m high; stucco masks of jaguars and birds flank the stairways of the temple complex. The other, El Tigre, is 55 m in height and is a wonderful place to be on top of at night, with a view of endless jungle and other sites, including Calakmul, in Mexico. In **Carmelita** ask around for space to sling your hammock or camp. There is a basic *comedor*. **El Tintal**, a day's hike from El Mirador, is said to be the second largest site in Petén, connected by a causeway to El Mirador, with great views from the top of the pyramids. **Nakbé**, 10 km southeast of El Mirador, is the earliest known lowland Maya site (1000-400 BC), with the earliest examples of carved monuments.

### Río Azul and Kinal *Colour map 2, A5.*

From Uaxactún a dirt road leads north to the *campamento* of **Dos Lagunas**. It's a lovely place to camp, with few mosquitoes, but swimming will certainly attract crocodiles. The guards' camp at **Ixcán Río**, on the far bank of the Río Azul, can be reached in one long day's walk, crossing by canoe if the water is high. If low enough to cross by vehicle you can drive to the Río Azul site, a further 6 km on a wide, shady track. It is also possible to continue into Mexico if your paperwork is OK. A barely passable side track to the east from the camp leads to the ruins of Kinal. The big attraction at Río Azul are the famous black and red painted tombs, technically off limits to visitors without special permission, but visits have been known.

### Yaxhá, Topoxte, Nakum and Melchor de Mencos *Colour map 2, A5.*
*T7861-0250, www.conap.com.gt. Yaxhá is open 0800-1700. Entry to each site US$9.*

This group of sites has been designated as a national park. About 65 km from Flores, on the Belize road ending at Melchor de Mencos, is a turning left, a dry weather road, which brings you in 8.5 km to Laguna Yaxhá. On the northern shore is the site of Yaxhá (meaning Green Water), the third largest known Classic Maya site in the country, accessible by causeway. This untouristy site is good for birdwatching and the views from the temples of the milky green lake are outstanding. The tallest structure, **Templo de las Manos Rojas**, is 30 m high. In the lake is the unusual Late post-Classic site (AD120-1530) of Topoxte. (The island is accessible by boat from Yaxhá, 15 minutes.) About 20 km further north of Yaxhá lies Nakum, which is thought to have been both a trading and ceremonial centre. You will need a guide and your own transport if you have not come on a tour.

### Northwest Petén and the Mexican border *Colour map 2, A4.*

An unpaved road runs 151 km west from Flores to **El Naranjo** on the Río San Pedro, near the Mexican border. Close by is **La Joyanca**, a site where the chance of wildlife spotting is high. You can camp at the *cruce* with the guards.

### Parque Nacional Laguna del Tigre and Biotopo *Colour map 2, A4.*

The park and biotope is a vast area of jungle and wetlands north of El Naranjo. The best place to stay is the CECON camp, across the river below the ferry. This is where the guards live and they will let you stay in the bunk house and use their kitchen. Getting into the reserve is not easy and you will need to be fully equipped, but a few people go up the Río Escondido. The lagoons abound in wildlife, including enormous crocodiles and spectacular bird life. Contact **CECON** ⓘ *Centro de Estudios Conservacionistas (CECON), Av Reforma, 0-63, Zona 10, Guatemala City, T2331-0904, cecon@usac.edu.gt,* for more information.

### Sayaxché *Colour map 2, B4.*

Sayaxché, south of Flores on the road to Cobán, has a frontier town feel to it as its focus is on a bend on the Río de la Pasión. It is a good base for visiting the southern Petén including a number of archaeological sites, namely El Ceibal. You can change US dollar bills and traveller's cheques at **Banoro**.

## El Ceibal *Colour map 2, B4.*

This major ceremonial site is reached by a 45-minute *lancha* ride up the Río de la Pasión from Sayaxché. It is about 1.5 km from the left bank of Río de la Pasión hidden in vegetation and extending for 1.5 sq km. The height of activity at the site was from 800 BC to the first century AD. Archaeologists agree that it appears to have been abandoned in between about AD 500 and AD 690 and then repopulated at a later stage when there was an era of stelae production between AD 771 and 889. It later declined during the early decades of the 10th century and was abandoned. You can sling a hammock at El Ceibal and use the guard's fire for making coffee if you ask politely – a mosquito net is advisable, and take repellent for walking in the jungle surroundings. Tours can be arranged in Flores for a day trip to Sayaxché and El Ceibal (around US$65) but there is limited time to see the site. From Sayaxché the ruins of the **Altar de los Sacrificios** at the confluence of the Ríos de la Pasión and Usumacinta can also be reached. It was one of the earliest sites in the Péten, with a founding date earlier than that of Tikal. Most of its monuments are not in good condition. Also within reach of Sayaxché is **Itzán**, discovered in 1968.

## Piedras Negras *Colour map 2, A3.*

Still further down the Río Usumacinta in the west of Petén is Piedras Negras, a huge Classic period site. In the 1930s Tatiana Proskouriakoff first recognized the periods of time inscribed on stelae here coincided with human life spans or reigns, and so began the task of deciphering the meaning of Maya glyphs. Advance arrangements are necessary with a rafting company to reach Piedras Negras. **Maya Expeditions** (see page 271) run expeditions, taking in Piedras Negras, Bonampak, Yaxchilán and Palenque. This trip is a real adventure. The riverbanks are covered in the best remaining tropical forest in Guatemala, inhabited by elusive wildlife and hiding more ruins. Once you've rafted down to Piedras Negras, you have to raft out. Though most of the river is fairly placid, there are the 30-m **Busilhá Falls**, where a crystal-clear tributary cascades over limestone terraces and two deep canyons, with impressive rapids to negotiate, before reaching the take-out two days later.

## Petexbatún

From Sayaxché, the Río de la Pasión is a good route to visit other Maya ruins. From **Laguna Petexbatún** (16 km), a fisherman's paradise can be reached by outboard canoe from Sayaxché. Excursions can be made from here to unexcavated ruins that are generally grouped together under the title Petexbatún. These include **Arroyo de la Piedra**, Dos Pilas and Aguateca. **Dos Pilas** has many well-preserved stelae, and an important tomb of a king was found here in 1991 – that of its Ruler 2, who died in AD 726. Dos Pilas flourished in the Classic period when as many as 10,000 lived in the city. There are many carved monuments and hieroglyphic stairways at the site, which record the important events of city life. **Aguateca**, where the ruins are so far little excavated, gives a feeling of authenticity. The city was abandoned in the early ninth century for unknown reasons. Again, a tour is advisable. It's a boat trip and a short walk away. The site was found with numerous walls (it's known the city was attacked in AD 790) and a chasm actually splits the site in two. The natural limestone bridge connects a large plaza with platforms and buildings in the west with an area of a series of smaller plazas in the east. These places are off the beaten track and an adventure to get to.

### Uaxactún

**$ Aldana's Lodge**
*T5801-2588, edeniaa@ yahoo.com.*
Run by a friendly family, Aldana's Lodge has small, white, clean *casitas*, as well as tent and hammock space behind **El Chiclero**. Just before **El Chiclero** take a left on the road to the ruins and then take the 1st right until you see a whitewashed *casita* on the right (2 mins).

**$ El Chiclero**
*T7926-1095.*
Neat and clean, hammocks and rooms in a garden, also good food by arrangement.

### Sayaxché

**$ Guayacán**
*Close to ferry, T7928-6111.*
Owner Julio Godoy is a good source of information.

**$ Hotel Posada Segura**
*Turn right from the dock area and then 1st left, T7928-6162.*
One of the best options in town, clean, and some rooms have a bath and TV.

### Petexbatún

**$$$ Chiminos Island Lodge**
*T2335-3506, www.chiminosisland.com.*
Remote, small ecolodge close to a Maya site on a peninsula on the river, in a great for exploring local sites, fishing and wildlife spotting. Rates includes all food.

**$$$ Posada Caribe**
*T7928-6117.*
Comfortable *cabañas* with bathroom and shower. They offer trips to **Aguateca** by launch and a guide for excursions. Rates include 3 meals.

### Camping
Camping is possible at Escobado, on the lakeside.

### Restaurants

### Uaxactún

**$ Comedor Imperial**
*At the village entrance.*
Bargain *comida típica* for US$1.30.

### Sayaxché

**$$$ El Botanero Café Restaurante and Bar**
*Straight up from the dock and 2nd left.*
A funky wooden bar with logs and seats carved from tree trunks.

**$ Restaurant La Montaña**
*Near dock.*
Cheap food, local information given.

**$ Yakín**
*Near dock.*
Cheap, good food; try the *licuados*.

### What to do

### Uaxactún
For guided walks around the ruins ask for one of the trained guides, US$10. For expeditions further afield, contact Elfido Aldana at **Posada Aldana**. Neria Baldizón at **El Chiclero** has high-clearance pickups and plenty of experience in organizing both vehicle and mule trips to any site. She charges US$200 per person to go to Río Azul.

### Sayaxché
**Viajes Don Pedro**, *on the river front near the dock, T7928-6109.* Runs launches to El Ceibal (US$35 for up to 3), Petexbatún and Aguateca (US$60 for up to 5), Dos Pilas (US$50 for small group). Trip possible by jeep in the dry season, Altar de los Sacrificios (US$100 minimum 2 people) and round trips to Yaxchilán for 3 days (US$400). Mon-Sat 0700-1800, Sun 0700-1200.

### Uaxactún
**Bus**

To Uaxactún from **Santa Elena** at 1200 arriving between 1600-1700, US$2.60, returning 0500 with **Transportes Pinita**. Foreigners have to pay US$2 to pass through Parque Nacional Tikal on their way to Uaxactún, payable at the main entrance to Tikal.

### El Mirador, El Tintal and Nakbé
**Bus**

1 bus daily with **Transportes Pinita** to **Carmelita**. See Flores for information.

### Northwest Petén and the Mexican border
**Boat and bus**

To **El Naranjo** at 0500 and 1000, returning at 0500, 1100 and 1300, US$4. Or hire a *lancha* from Paso Caballos.

### Sayaxché
**Bus**

There are buses to **Flores**, 0600, 0700, 1-2 hrs, and microbuses every 30 mins. To **Raxrujá** and on to **Cobán** via **Chisec** at 0400, US$.80, 6½ hrs direct to Cobán. There are pickups after that hourly and some further buses direct and not via Chisec. For **Lanquín** take the bus to Raxrujá, then a pickup to Sebol, and then a pickup to Lanquín, or the Lanquín *cruce* at Pajal, and wait for onward transport. If you are heading to **Guatemala City** from here it could be quicker to head north to Flores rather than take the long road down to Cobán. However, this road has now been entirely tarmacked.

### Petexbatún
**Boat**

It is 30-40 mins in *lancha* from Sayaxché to the stop for **Dos Pilas** to hire horses. It's 50 mins-1 hr to **Chiminos** lodge and 1 hr 20 mins to the **Aguateca** site. To Dos Pilas and Aguateca from Chiminos, US$27 return to each site.

# This is
## El Salvador

El Salvador is a lively country and the people are just as friendly – some say more so – than in the rest of Central America. Ornately painted and colourful buses bump from place to place, just as they do in Guatemala and Honduras, but El Salvador has better roads and the quality of the buses is superior to that of neighbouring countries. While the rest of Central America relies on tortillas, Salvadoreans fill them with beans, cheese or meat and call them *pupusas*. Pinning it down is difficult but there's a slightly different feel here from neighbouring countries.

Guidebooks tend to urge caution, but in reality El Salvador is no more dangerous than other Central American countries. During the civil war, Salvadoreans sought refuge abroad; now they're returning, bringing with them a gang culture and other less-than-favourable imports from the United States, although as a tourist you are rarely subjected to any of these social problems. Despite the high rate of gang-related crime, frequent natural disasters and a tourist infrastructure less developed than its neighbouring countries, there are some compelling reasons why you should visit El Salvador: dramatic volcanic landscapes, blue-green lagoons, horizon-filling panoramas and golden beaches.

In the northern hills around El Poy and Perquín the trekking is divine, with far-reaching views across staggered horizons. The stark cinder cone of Volcán Izalco offers a challenging but rewarding trek from the slopes of Cerro Verde, while El Imposible National Park provides the chance to visit a forest. Along the coast, choose from surfing, diving or simply lazing around and watching the endless display of Pacific sunsets.

PINTURITAS · 2013

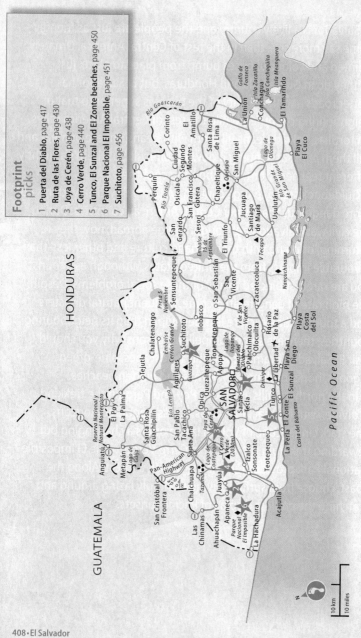

## Footprint picks

1 **Puerta del Diablo**, page 417
2 **Ruta de las Flores**, page 430
3 **Joya de Cerén**, page 438
4 **Cerro Verde**, page 440
5 **Tunco, El Sunzal and El Zonte beaches**, page 450
6 **Parque Nacional El Imposible**, page 451
7 **Suchitoto**, page 456

# Footprint
## picks

★ **Puerta del Diablo**, page 417

Two huge rocks framing a stunning view of Volcán San Vicente.

★ **Ruta de las Flores**, page 430

Soak up the warmth, colour and disarming rural charm of El Salvador's Route of Flowers.

★ **Joya de Cerén**, page 438

An intimate glimpse of daily life in the ancient Mayan world.

★ **Cerro Verde**, page 440

Volcanic peak with spectacular views of Lago Coatepeque and Volcán Santa Ana, and great trekking, wildlife and flowers.

★ **Tunco, El Sunzal and El Zonte beaches**, page 450

Happening towns on the Costa del Bálsamo with black-sand beaches and excellent surf breaks.

★ **Parque Nacional El Imposible**, page 451

An impressive park rich in flora and fauna.

★ **Suchitoto**, page 456

On the shore of the vast Cerrón Grande reservoir is this culturally rich colonial town, a must-see in northern El Salvador.

# Essential San Salvador

## Finding your feet

Four broad streets meet at the city centre: Avenida Cuscatlán and its continuation Avenida España run south to north; Calle Delgado and its continuation Calle Arce, with a slight blip, from east to west. This principle is retained throughout: the *avenidas* run north to south and the *calles* east to west. The even-numbered *avenidas* are east of the central *avenidas*, odd numbers west; north of the central *calles*, they are dubbed Norte, south of the central *calles* Sur. The even-numbered *calles* are south of the two central *calles*, the odd numbers north. East of the central *avenidas* they are dubbed Oriente (Ote), west of the central *avenidas* Poniente (Pte). Sounding more complicated than it is, the system is straightforward and quickly grasped.

## Getting around

The main focal points of the city are the historical centre, the commercial district some 3 km to the west around Boulevard de los Héroes, and the residential and commercial districts of Escalón and Zona Rosa another 2 km further west. City buses and taxis are needed to get between the three (see page 425).

## Safety

The city centre is considered by many to be dangerous after dark. San Benito, Maquilishuat, La Gran Vía and Multiplaza are considered safer areas than others, but you should still take care. As a general rule, stay out of poorly lit areas and keep to main roads where there are more people around. At night, taxis are strongly recommended if you don't know exactly where you're going.

Armed security personnel are commonplace. There is a heightened atmosphere of tension in some areas. In downtown areas, especially at markets, don't carry cameras, wear watches or jewellery, or flash money around. Be vigilant when withdrawing cash from ATMs. See also www.gov.uk/foreign-travel-advice/el-salvador.

## When to go

The climate is semi-tropical. The average for San Salvador is 28°C with a variation of only about 3°C. Days are often hot, especially in the dry season, but the temperature drops in the late afternoon and nights are usually pleasantly mild.

## Weather San Salvador

| January | February | March | April | May | June |
|---|---|---|---|---|---|
| 18°C | 18°C | 19°C | 21°C | 21°C | 21°C |
| 28°C | 29°C | 30°C | 30°C | 28°C | 27°C |
| 10mm | 0mm | 10mm | 30mm | 130mm | 310mm |

| July | August | September | October | November | December |
|---|---|---|---|---|---|
| 20°C | 20°C | 20°C | 20°C | 19°C | 18°C |
| 28°C | 28°C | 27°C | 27°C | 27°C | 27°C |
| 280mm | 330mm | 330mm | 210mm | 30mm | 0mm |

# San Salvador
## & around

Surrounded by a ring of mountains in a highly seismic valley known as 'Valle de las Hamacas', San Salvador toils under the threat of earthquakes. As one of the largest cities in Central America, a sprawling, relentless and busy place, San Salvador can at times seem almost heartless. Do not be deceived. Beneath its hard urban exterior are some sensitive cultural inclinations and a slew of intriguing museums dedicated to art, anthropology and history. There are green zones too, including city parks, a botanical garden and a zoo. San Salvador also retains the charm of the Spanish era, thanks to being one of the first European cities in the New World.

From the nouveau riche to the urban poor, its human geography is framed by its great wealth disparities. In the downtown area, crumbling buildings await renovation and restoration. More prosperous neighbourhoods to the west have since risen to glory, with their gleaming shopping malls and designer suburbs.

Beyond the outskirts, western El Salvador is a verdant, compact and easy to explore region with good transport links.

**Best** for
Colonial charm ▪ Museums ▪ Spectacular viewpoint

The Centro Histórico in San Salvador (altitude 680-1000 m, population 2,297,282 including suburbs) is laid out in a classic colonial grid but few colonial buildings have survived history's devastating tremors. Instead, the downtown core is complemented by a trove of fascinating 20th-century architecture: art deco, futurist, neo-Gothic, modernist and populuxe works are all on display.

## San Salvador

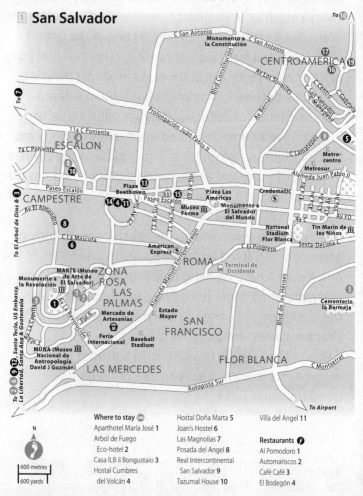

| Where to stay | Hostal Doña Marta **5** | Villa del Angel **11** |
|---|---|---|
| Aparthotel María José **1** | Joan's Hostel **6** | |
| Arbol de Fuego | Las Magnolias **7** | **Restaurants** |
| Eco-hotel **2** | Posada del Angel **8** | Al Pomodoro **1** |
| Casa ILB il Bongustaio **3** | Real Intercontinental | Automariscos **2** |
| Hostal Cumbres | San Salvador **9** | Café Café **3** |
| del Volcán **4** | Tazumal House **10** | El Bodegón **4** |

600 metres
600 yards

N

At the intersection of Avenida Cuscatlán and Calle Rubén Darío is the **Plaza Barrios**, the heart of the Centro Histórico. A fine equestrian statue looks west towards the renaissance-style **Palacio Nacional** ① *Mon-Fri 0800-1600, free.* Built 1904-1911 to replace an earlier structure, it contains a wealth of antique furnishings spread across 105 rooms and four main salons in red, yellow, pink and blue.

To the north is the **Catedral Metropolitana**, which was left unfinished for several years after Archbishop Romero suspended its construction to use the money to reduce poverty. Work was resumed in 1990 and completed in 1999, the last consecration of a cathedral

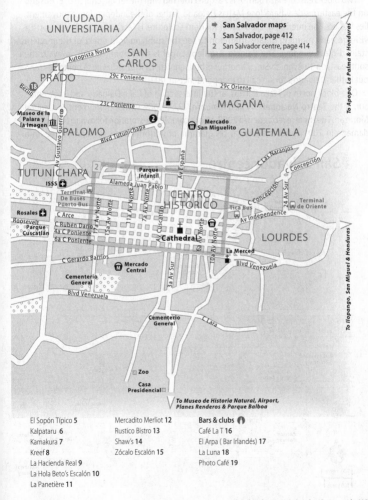

El Sopón Típico **5**
Kalpataru **6**
Kamakura **7**
Kreef **8**
La Hacienda Real **9**
La Hola Beto's Escalón **10**
La Panetière **11**

Mercadito Merliot **12**
Rustico Bistro **13**
Shaw's **14**
Zócalo Escalón **15**

**Bars & clubs** 🌶
Café La T **16**
El Arpa ( Bar Irlandés) **17**
La Luna **18**
Photo Café **19**

of the millennium. It now stands as a beacon of tranquillity amid the dirt and noise of the downtown capital. It commands a striking presence, gleaming white and modern, its façade flanked by two giant murals vividly splashed with the colourful work of the country's most famous artist, **Fernando Llort**. Inside it is quite bare, but for the fabulous circular stained-glass window of a dove surrounded by a hundred shards of brilliant yellow glass, which in turn is framed by yellow stars set in deep lapis lazuli-blue glass. Beneath the cathedral, a new chapel has been created to house the tomb of assassinated **Archbishop Oscar Romero**.

Two blocks east of Plaza Barrios is **Parque Libertad** with the rebuilt church of **El Rosario** on the eastern side where José Matías Delgado, father of the Independence movement, lies buried. The interior, decked out in modern sculpture, is fascinating and well worth a visit; go early morning or late afternoon to see the stunning light effect of the modern stained-glass window. The **Palacio Arquiepiscopal** is next door. Not far away to the southeast, on 10 Avenida Sur, is another rebuilt church, **La Merced**, whose belltower rang out Father Delgado's tocsin call to Independence in 1811.

One block north of Plaza Barrios, at the intersection of Calle Delgado and 2a Avenida Sur, is the **Teatro Nacional** ① *Plaza Morazán, T2222-5689*, with a monument to General Morazán. The theatre reopened in 2008, after a complete restoration following earthquake damage in 2001; it hosts a regular programme of performances, sometimes free, in a

sumptuous auditorium with red velvet seats. Heading east three blocks along Delgado is the **Mercado Ex-Cuartel**, and the expected confusion of sounds and smells that besiege the senses. Nearby are some of the cheapest (and most insalubrious) hotels in the city.

## West of the Centro Histórico
### commercial district with worthwhile museums, slick shopping centres and restaurants

Running west from the Teatro Nacional, Calle Delgado changes its name to Calle Arce and passes the great church of El Sagrado Corazón de Jesús on 13 Avenida Norte, worth seeing for its stained-glass windows. Turn left (south) one block and you come to Parque Bolívar, perched between the national printing office and the Department of Health. Running along its north side is Calle Rubén Darío (2a Calle Poniente), which becomes Alameda Roosevelt, then Paseo General Escalón as it leads through the commercial and residential districts west of the centre.

Five blocks west of Parque Bolívar on Alameda Roosevelt is **Parque Cuscatlán** with its green lawns and shady trees, always a hit with families on Sundays. Here you'll find the sombre **Monumento a la Memoria y la Verdad** ① www.memoriayverdad.org, which contains the engraved names of 30,000 victims of El Salvador's civil war. For something lighter, head to the **Tin Marín Museo de los Niños** ① 6-10 Calle Pte, entre Gimnasio Nacional y Parque Cuscatlán, www.tinmarin.org, Tue-Sun 0900-1715, US$3, a colourful children's museum that includes a butterfly reserve and planetarium. Heading north from the park on 25 Avenida Norte takes you in the direction of the University. Turn left at 27 Avenida Norte for the **Museo de la Palara y la Imagen (MUPI)** ① 27 Av Norte 1140, between 19 y 21 Calle Pte, T2564-7005, www.museo.com.sv, Mon-Fri 0800-1200 and 1400-1700, Sat 0800-1200, US$1. Dedicated to preserving memories of the civil war, its collection includes a movie, photo and audio archive, and a social science library.

Continuing west on Alameda Roosevelt, there is a major junction at 49 Avenida: to the south, the avenue passes the national stadium, **Estadio Olímpico Flor Blanca**, before becoming the main highway to the international airport. To the north, it crosses Alameda Juan Pablo II, beyond which it changes name to **Bulevar de los Héroes**, home to the fashionable shopping centres, Metrocentro and the newer Metrosur,

> ➡ **San Salvador maps**
> 1 San Salvador, page 412
> 2 San Salvador centre, page 414

the **Hotel Real Intercontinental**, some of the city's better restaurants and a glut of fast-food places, which is a busy area at all times, especially at night. At the petrol station by Metrocentro, mariachis and other musicians gather each evening, waiting to be hired; others wander around the restaurants, playing to diners.

The next big landmark on Alameda Roosevelt at the Plaza Las Américas is the **Monumento al Salvador del Mundo**, a statue of Jesus standing on the Earth atop a column. From this junction the Pan-American Highway heads southwest to Santa Tecla. Straight ahead is **Paseo General Escalón**, Parque Beethoven and an area with many restaurants, shops, and the Colonia Escalón residential district. Hidden behind the towering office blocks and flanking the Salvador monument on the southwest is the **Museo Forma** ① *Av Manuel Enrique Araujo, T2298-4269, Mon-Fri 1000-1700, Sat 1000-1300, US$3*, a small modern art gallery housed in a neocolonial-style castle. It hosts an interesting collection of paintings and sculpture by Salvadorean artists.

## Zona Rosa and Colonia San Benito

### refreshingly leafy residential and entertainment quarters

Accessed from either the Pan-American Highway or Escalón are the Zona Rosa and Colonia San Benito, home to some of the city's most elegant restaurants and upscale hotels.

This area also has many art galleries such as **Galería Espacio** ① *Av La Capilla*, **Galería 1-2-3** ① *Calle La Reforma*, and **La Pinacoteca** ① *Blv Hipódromo*, to name a few. See local press for details of exhibitions.

The **Museo Nacional de Antropología David J Guzman (MUNA)** ① *Feria Internacional, Av de la Revolución y Cra a Santa Tecla, T2243-3750, Tue-Sun 1000-1800, US$3*, is a modern museum worth visiting, showcasing exhibits on the country's archaeological and historical past as well as numerous cultural events; descriptions in Spanish only, but free guided tours available in afternoons with English-speaking guides (check at the desk as they only operate if enough visitors). Just north of the museum at the end of Avenida Revolución is the **Museo de Arte de El Salvador (MARTE)** ① *T2243-6099, www.marte.org.sv, Tue-Sun 1000-1800, US$1.50 (free on Sun), café and shop (both closed Sun) in lobby*. This privately run modern arts museum has permanent exhibits depicting the history of Salvadorean painters with temporary exhibits of artists from Latin America and other parts of the world.

For a refreshing stroll in pleasant landscaped gardens, take the No 44 bus southwest of the Zona Rosa and ask the driver to drop you at the turn-off for the **Jardín Botánico La Laguna** ① *Antiguo Cuscatlan, www.jardinbotanico.org.sv, Sat-Sun 0900-1730*.

North of Zona Rosa is **El Arbol de Dios** ① *Av Masferrer 575, opposite Kreef, T2263-9206, www.fernando-llort.com, Mon-Fri 0800-1900, Sat 0900-1800*, an arts and crafts shop, restaurant, museum and garden, operated by the famed Salvadorean artist Fernando Llort, who designed the façade of the Metropolitan Cathedral and is known for his naïf-style wood paintings. The display here also includes the work of other artists.

**Tip...**
Foreigners are advised not to be out in the city centre after dark.

If the crush of humanity become too much in the capital, many places can be visited in a day from San Salvador either on the frequent bus services or by car. There are potential day trips to nearby volcanoes, crater lakes and beauty spots, such as Los Planes de Renderos, the Puerta del Diablo and San Salvador's own volcano, Boquerón, which has a paved road all the way to the top.

To the south is the indigenous village of **Panchimalco**, heading east are the beautiful setting and views around **Lago de Ilopango**; and to the southwest the crater of **Volcán San Salvador** (see page 418). Heading west towards Santa Ana, but still manageable in a day, are the archaeological sites of **Joya de Cerén**, El Salvador's Pompeii, **San Andrés** (see page 438) and the peaks of **Volcán Izalco** and **Cerro Verde** (see page 439) with the deep blue waters of **Lago de Coatepeque** in the crater below.

The limits of a comfortable weekend trip will take you to the garden park of **Ichanmichen**, which is restful (see page 476), and the pyramid of **Tazumal** (west of Santa Ana) is also worth a visit (see page 442). At weekends the coast around La Libertad (see page 447) is very popular. Bus No 495 from the Terminal del Occidente goes to the seaside resort of **Costa del Sol** (see page 475).

## South of the Centro Histórico

Lasting most of the day by bus (No 12), or two to three hours by car, a good sightseeing tour heads south of the Centro Histórico. Starting a few blocks southwest of the main square on the eastern side of the Mercado Central, it includes the **San Salvador Zoo** ① *Calle Modelo, T2270-0828, Wed-Sun 0900-1600, US$1*, which, although small, is quiet and attractive. Southeast of the zoo, the **Museo Militar de las Fuerzas Armadas** ① *behind the presidential palace of San Jacinto at the former Cuartel El Zapote, 10 Av Sur y Calle Capitán Alberto Sánchez, T2250-0000, daily 0800-1200 and 1400-1700, free,* has a collection of exhibits of weapons, uniforms and decorations of the armed forces, and weapons captured from FMLN guerrillas. Several blocks away inside Parque Saburo Hirao is the small **Museo de Historia Natural (MUHNES)** ① *Final Calle Los Viveros, Wed-Sun 0900-1600, US$0.75,* with interesting displays on prehistoric findings and a herbal medicine garden. Coninuing south on winding highway RN 6S takes you into a residential district in the mountain range of **Planes de Renderos**. This place is crowned by the beautiful **Parque Balboa** ① *daily 0800-1800, see under Puerta de Diablo below for how to get there,* and there's a good view of the city from El Mirador at the foot of the park. Parque Balboa is a Turicentro, with cycle paths, playground and gardens.

## ★Puerta del Diablo

*Bus No 12 from eastern side of Mercado Central and No 12-MC marked 'Mil Cumbres' run almost hourly to Puerta del Diablo and Parque Balboa. Bus No 17 goes from the same location to Panchimalco through Los Planes de Renderos so you can get off at the junction there and take the No 12 to Parque Puerta del Diablo and Parque Balboa.*

From the **Parque Balboa** a scenic road runs to the summit of **Cerro Chulo**, from which the view, seen through the Puerta del Diablo (Devil's Door), is even better.

The Puerta del Diablo consists of two enormous, nearly vertical rocks which frame a magnificent view of the Volcán San Vicente. The rocks are very steep but the sides can be climbed on reasonable paths for an even better view. A little beyond the car park and drinks stands at the Puerta del Diablo is a path climbing up a further summit, from which there are 360-degree views: to the coast, Lago Ilopango, the capital and volcanoes, including San Salvador, Izalco and Cerro Verde and San Vicente.

At the foot of Cerro Chulo is **Panchimalco** (see below). The route to Panchimalco (No 17 from Mercado Central) and the coast branches off the road to Parque Balboa at the village of **Los Planes**, a few kilometres before the park.

## Panchimalco

*Bus No 17 from Mercado Central at 12 Calle Poniente, San Salvador, every 45 mins (45 mins), or minibus from near Mercado Central, very crowded but quicker (30 mins), and cheaper (US$0.80).*

This small town and the surrounding area are home to the **Pancho**, descendants of the Pipil tribes, one of the region's dominant indigenous groups prior to conquest. This is one of the few places in El Salvador where you can still see indigenous people in traditional dress. Streets of large cobbles, with low adobe houses, thread their way between huge boulders at the foot of Cerro Chulo. A very fine baroque colonial church, Santa Cruz, has a white façade with statues of eight saints. Inside are splendid woodcarvings and wooden columns, altars, ceilings and benches. There is a bell inscribed with the cipher and titles of the Holy Roman Emperor Charles V, and a colourful cemetery. The Casa de La Cultura in the main street has frequent cultural events and crafts stores. The **Fiesta de Santa Cruz de Roma** is held on 12-14 September, with music and traditional dances; on 3 May (or the second Sunday of the month) there is the procession of **Las Palmas**.

## Lago de Ilopango

*Bus No 15, marked Apulo, runs from the bus stop on Parque Hula Hula in San Salvador to the lake (via the airport), 1¼ hrs, US$1. Entrance to the Turicentro camping site costs US$0.60.*

Beyond the four-lane highway to Ilopango airport (14.5 km east) lie the deep waters of Lago de Ilopango. Surrounded by mountains, the views around El Salvador's largest and deepest crater lake are impressive. Before the conquest local people used to appease the harvest gods by drowning four virgins here every year. Private chalets make access to the lake difficult, except at clubs and the **Turicentro Apulo**, but it is well worth a visit. The eastern shore is less polluted and is reached from Cojutepeque. There are a number of lakeside cafés and bathing clubs, some of which hire dug-outs by the hour. The cafés are busy in the dry season (try **Teresa's** for fish dishes), but often closed in the middle of the year. **Hotel Vista del Lago** ① *3 km from Apulo turn-off on the highway,* is on a hill top.

## Volcán San Salvador

*Buses leave a block from Plaza Merliot in San Salvador. By car you turn right just after the Plaza Merliot Mall and continue to the end of the road where a paved road takes you up the volcano.*

This large massif at 1839 m has an impressive crater, more than 1.5 km wide and 543 m deep, known as **El Boquerón**. About 2 km to the east is the equally dramatic peak of **El Picacho** (1960 m), which dominates the capital. A walk clockwise round the crater takes about two hours; the first half is easy, the second half rough. The views are magnificent, if somewhat spoilt by TV and radio towers. The area by Boquerón is now a park administrated by the Ministry of Tourism. The area is closed off, with guards during opening hours (daily 0800-1500). **La Laguna** botanical garden is near the summit. The inner slopes of the crater are covered with trees, and at the bottom is a smaller cone from the eruption of 1917.

You can follow the road north and then turn right through extensive coffee plantations and forest to reach the summit of **El Picacho**. This also makes an excellent climb from the Escalón suburb of San Salvador, in the early morning preferably, which takes about three to four hours return trip (take a guide). The easy access, great views and fresh climate has made the Volcán San Salvador a popular destination for people in the capital and, as a result, new restaurants have opened their doors in recent years. See Restaurants, page 421.

Another access to the volcano from the city side is by **Ecoparque El Espino** ① *run by El Espino Cooperative T2289-0749/69, US$1.50.* The entrance is by the Polideportivo in Ciudad Merliot, take bus No 42 Calle especial and walk 100 m. They have several trails, bike rental and small cafeterias. The trails end at a mirador with a panoramic view of the city.

## Listings San Salvador *maps p412 and p414*

### Tourist information

**Corporación Salvadoreña de Turismo (Corsatur)**
*Edif Carbonel No 1, Col Roma Alameda Dr Manuel Enrique Araujo Pasaje Carbonel San Salvador, T2243-7835, www.elsalvador.travel. Mon-Fri 0800-1230 and 1330-1730.*
Good information on buses, archaeological sites, beaches and national parks. Texaco and Esso sell good maps at some of their service stations.

**Instituto Geográfico Nacional**
*1 Calle Pte y 43 Av Norte 02310, Col Flor Blanca, T2260-8000.*
The best maps of the city and country.

**Instituto Salvadoreño de Turismo (ISTU)**
*41 Av Norte y Alameda Roosevelt 115, T2260-9249, www.istu.gob.sv.*
Has useful information about the 13 government-run Turicentros recreation and water parks in the country and on Cerro Verde and Walter T Deininger national parks.

### Where to stay

In the downtown area, some hotels lock their doors very early. Many cheap *hospedajes* near Terminal de Oriente are of dubious safety and not recommended for single women. 13% VAT (IVA) is added to bills at major hotels. Most of the cheaper hotels are around the Centro Histórico. Be careful in this area, particularly at night.

**$$$$ Casa ILB il Bongustaio**
*Blv del Hipódromo 605, Colonia San Benito, T2528-4200, www.casailb.com.*
This upscale boutique lodging has 5 stylish, contemporary, minimalist suites with crisp tones and generous floor space. Each is equipped with cable TV, Wi-Fi, minibar and plush furnishings. Facilities include a bar, restaurant and parking. An attractive option. Recommended.

**$$$$ Hotel Real Intercontinental San Salvador**
*Blv de los Héroes and Av Sisimiles, in front of the Metrocentro, T2211-3333, www.grupo real.com.*

A useful landmark, smart, formal atmosphere (popular with business visitors), **Avis** car hire, **Taca** desk, and a shop selling souvenirs, postcards, US papers and magazines.

### $$$ Aparthotel María José
*Av La Capilla 223, Zona Rosa, Colonia San Benito, T2263-4790, www.aparthotelmariajose.com.*
These cosy, modern apartments have fully equipped kitchens (with fridge, toaster-oven, and coffee machine), dining room, bedroom, and living room with cable TV and sofa bed. Wi-Fi and parking.

### $$$ Villa del Angel
*71 Av Norte 219, Colonia Escalón, T2223-7171, www.villadelangelhotel.com.*
This villa-style guesthouse has simple, modern, minimalist rooms with a trendy lime green colour scheme and all mod cons including super-efficient a/c, Wi-Fi, hot water and cable TV. There's also a small garden. Conveniently located next to Escalón mall.

### $$$-$$ Posada del Angel
*85 Av Norte 321, Colonia Escalón, T2556-1172, www.hotellaposadadelangel.com.*
Featuring tasteful and down-to-earth decor, rooms at the Posada del Angel are quiet, calming and cosy. Breakfast is served in the garden, which is well maintained with lavish plant life. Good value, accommodating and professionally managed.

### $$ Arbol de Fuego Eco-hotel
*Av Antiguo Cuscatlan 11C, Colonia La Sultana, T2557-3601, www.arboldefuego.com.*
With numerous accolades and international recommendations for its sustainable practices, this attractive eco-hotel offers cosy rooms with typical Salvadoran decor, including locally sourced textiles and artwork, as well as all the usual amenities including Wi-Fi, cable TV, a/c and hot water. An oasis in the urban jungle. Breakfast included. Recommended.

### $$ Hotel Tazumal House
*Final 35 Av Norte 3, Reparto Santa Fe, T2235-2506, www.hoteltazumalhouse.com.*
Located near the university, Tazumal house offers simple, modern, comfortable rooms with all the usual conveniences including cable TV, a/c, Wi-Fi and hot water. There's a pleasant garden out back where you can rest, relax, or take breakfast in the morning. Friendly, homely, hospitable and good value.

### $$ Las Magnolias
*Av Las Magnolias 226, Col. San Benito, T2528-6500, www.lasmagnolias.com.sv.*
This unassuming hotel with 2 wings, old and new, is situated in a quiet residential street within walking distance of bars and restaurants. It has spacious rooms and suites decorated with earthy tones and solid furniture. There's a pleasant garden filled with tropical foliage, breakfast included, and coffee refills all day.

### $ Hostal Cumbres del Volcán
*85 Av Norte 637, Col Escalón, T2207-3705, www.cumbresdelvolcan.com.*
This pleasant, down-to-earth hostel in a safe neighbourhood opened its doors in 2010 and continues to receive a stream of budget travellers. Accommodation includes shared dorms and private rooms, with or without private bath and a/c. There is laundry, Wi-Fi and parking, but no kitchen.

### $ Hostal Doña Marta
*Pasaje Maracaibo 1-B, Urbanizacion Venezuela, T2301-3006, www.hostal donamarta.blogspot.co.uk.*
This low-key, economical, family-run hostel is safely nestled in a gated community. It's a little out of the way with few facilities in the neighbourhood, but there is a bus stop nearby. The owners are friendly and helpful and can organize airport pick-up for a fee. All rooms have shared bath.

## $ Joan's Hostel
*Calle del Mediterráneo 12, Colonia Jardines de Guadalupe, Antiguo Cuscatlán, T7860-7157, www.joanshostal.blogspot.co.uk.*
A safe, clean hostel in a quiet residential area that would suit couples or older travellers. Accommodation includes dorms and private rooms and there's a kitchen for self-catering. Note there are no signs outside so the hostel can be tricky to find. The hostess, Ana, is friendly and helpful.

### Restaurants

In the older downtown area few places are open to eat after 1830. Restaurants are open later in the western sections of the city. Along Blv Hipódromo, San Benito, restaurants are generally very good, but expensive. On Blv de los Héroes there are many restaurants, including US-style fast-food places. The strip along Calle San Antonio Abad has several local eateries.

## $$$ Al Pomodoro
*Av La Revolución y Calle Circunvalación 184, Col San Benito, T2243-7888, www.alpomodoro.com.sv.*
Nestled in the Zona Rosa next to the Sheraton hotel, this upscale and tastefully presented Italian eatery serves a variety of pastas, pizzas, seafood and meat dishes. Attentive service and they keep a good stock of wine too. Popular and reliable.

## $$$ Café Café
*Calle El Tanque 130, 99 Av Norte y 7 y 9 Calle Pte bis 130, T2263-4034, www.cafecafe.com.sv.*
Café Café serves excellent Peruvian cuisine. Specialities include fillet of salmon with honey and orange sauce, tuna with scallop sauce, and a seafood platter with a mix of fresh prawns, octopus, and crab in a white wine sauce. Not cheap, but recommended.

## $$$ El Bodegón
*Paseo Escalón 3956 and 77 Av Norte, T2263-5283.*
El Bodeón is a rather sober and formal San Salvador institution with very classic airs. They serve fine traditional Spanish cuisine, such as paella and *crema catalana*. Not trendy, but romantic and dependable.

## $$$ Kamakura
*93 Av Norte 617, Col Escalón T2263-2401, www.restaurantekamakura.com.*
Kamakura is an authentic Japanese restaurant set inside a residential home and it serves the best sushi in town. Rolls are perfectly fresh and generously sized (try the *sashimi botánico*) with soups, green tea and vegetable tempura also available. Good traditional flavours; a taste of Tokyo.

## $$$ La Hacienda Real
*Just opposite of La Gran Vía Mall T, Km 8, Cra Panamericana, next to Air Force offices, T2243-8567, www.hacienda-real.com.*
Without a doubt some of the best steaks in El Salvador, excellent service, prime beef cuts and finger-licking food. Part of an international chain with branches in Guatemala and Honduras.

## $$$ La Hola Beto's Escalón
*Pasaje Dordelly 4352 between 85 and 87 Av Norte (above Paseo Escalón), www.laholabetos.com.*
This long-established seafood joint has branches across the city. The ceviche and seafood soup are very good and they also serve Italian and steaks. Fresh food, great service, parking. Recommended.

## $$ Automariscos
*Located next to roundabout by the Don Rua church, 5a Av Norte, Blv Tutunichapa, T2226-5363, also outlet in San Benito, Av Revolución No 179 (between Pizza Hut and Anthropological museum), T2243-3653.*

A family business more than 15 years in operation, Automariscos serves out-of-the-ordinary seafood and huge portions. Offerings include ceviches, soups and shrimp cocktails.

### $$ El Sopón Típico
*71 Av Norte and 1 Calle Pte 3702, Col Escalón, T2298-3008 and Blv de Los Héroes, Pasaje Las Palmeras 130, Urbanización Florida T2260-2671, www.elsopontipico.com.*

A very relaxed and down-to-earth eatery serving typical Salvadorean soups and other dishes, including *gallo en chicha* (chicken in maize wine) and *mariscada* (seafood chowder).

### $$ Kalpataru
*Calle La Mascota 928 and Calle Maquilishuat, just below Arbol de Dios, www.kalpataru.com.sv. Open until 2230.*

Full restaurant service and lunch buffet, good atmosphere. Best vegetarian place in town. They also offer reasonably priced yoga classes.

### $$ Rustico Bistro
*3a Calle Pte y Pasaje Los Pinos 3877, Col Escalón.*

This place serves the best gourmet burgers in town: thick, flavourful, and cooked to taste. They also do a mean beef panini and a formidable hot dog, all with a side of Cajun-spiced fries. Awesome and highly recommended.

### $$ Zócalo Escalón
*71 Av Norte, T2257-6851, next to Galerías mall.*

Excellent Mexican food in small, casual place, with outdoor tables; other branches around city, including Zona Rosa, San Benito and Santa Elena.

### $$-$ Mercadito Merliot
*Antiguo Cuscatlán.*

Famous food market with fresh seafood dishes (among others).

## Cafés and delís

There are numerous cafeterías serving cheap traditional meals such as *tamales*, *pupusas*, *frijoles*, rice with vegetables, etc. Often these places can be found around the major hotels.

### Kreef
*Plaza Kreef, 87 Av Sur and Av los Almendros Block G, Zona 11, Urbanización Maquilishuat T2264-7094, www.kreef.com.*

Restaurant and deli, specialities meat and juicy chicken fillets, imported cheese, beer and wine. Live music at weekends.

### La Panetière
*Plaza Villaviciencio, locales 34-35, Paseo Escalón, www.lapanetiere.com.sv.*

Delicious French pastry, crêpes, cappuccinos, salads, and breakfasts. Popular with foreigners, a bit pricey but worth it.

### Shaw's
*Paseo Escalón, 1 block west of Plaza Beethoven, Zona Rosa and at Metrocentro.*

Pricey but good coffee and chocolates, also sell US magazines, a few English-language books and greetings cards.

## Bars and clubs

Check for gigs in *La Prensa Gráfica* and *El Diario de Hoy*. All big hotels have their own nightclub. All discos have ladies' night on Wed and Thu when women enter free and get a discount on drinks; go in a group.

Zona Rosa, Col San Benito, has many bars/discos/open-air cafés in a well-lit area, crowded Fri-Sat nights (cover charge US$10), take bus No 30 B from near Esso/Texaco/Mundo Feliz on Blv de los Héroes before 2000, taxi thereafter. Just beyond Zona Rosa, Multiplaza and La Gran Vía malls are favourite places for going out; both have clubs, cafés and bars where young people gather at weekends. The most popular spots in Multiplaza are **Envy**, **Stanza** and **La Cueva**.

### Café La T
*Opposite Centro Comercial San Luis*
Run by German Anne, also has a fairtrade gift shop.

### El Arpa Irlandés
*Av A 137 Col San José.*
Run by Gerry from Ireland.

### La Luna
*Calle Berlín 228, off Blv de los Héroes, Urbanización Buenos Aires 3, T2260-2921. Wed-Sun.*
Great food and atmosphere, live music some nights, decor and furniture designed by local artists. Popular and fashionable place to hang out. Reasonably priced drinks and snacks; take a taxi late at night.

### Photo Café
*Col El Roble, Pje 2 21, T2100-2469, near the National University.*
An artsy place run by photojournalists.

## Entertainment

### Cinema
A few older-style cinemas in the centre are being overshadowed by the multiplexes along the Blv de los Héroes; most screenings are in English with Spanish sub-titles. Look in local press for listings. Arthouse films are shown at **La Luna** and **Café La T** (see above) for free. See schedules for events. **Alliance Française** arranges film seasons, T2223-8084.

### Music, dance and theatre
Ballet and theatre at the **Teatro Nacional de Bellas Artes**, see page 414, and music or plays at the **Teatro Cámera**.

### Spectator sports
Check *La Prensa Gráfica* and *El Diario de Hoy.*
**Baseball** On the field opposite Mercado Nacional de Artesanías, Tue-Fri 1700, Cuban and US coaches, local teams, entrance US$1.25.

**Boat racing** Club Náutico (at the Estero de Jaltepeque), is famous for its boat races across the mud flats at low tide.
**Football** Sun and Thu at the Cuscatlán and/or Flor Blanca stadiums.
**Motor racing** At the El Jabalí autodrome on lava fields near Quetzaltepeque.

## Festivals

**Mar/Apr** Holy Week.
**Jul/Aug** Celebrations of **El Salvador del Mundo** are held the fortnight preceding 6 Aug. As a climax, colourful floats wend their way up the Campo de Marte (the park encompasssing Parque Infantil and Palacio de Deportes; 9 Calle Pte and Av España). On 5 Aug, an ancient image of the Saviour is borne before the large procession, before church services the next day, celebrating the **Feast of the Transfiguration**.
**12 Dec** Día del Indígena; there are colourful processions honouring the **Virgen de Guadalupe** (take bus No 101 to the Basílica de Guadalupe, on the Cra a Santa Tecla).

## Shopping

Visa and MasterCard are accepted in most shops.

### Bookshops
Magazines and newspapers in English can be bought at leading hotels and many shops sell US magazines. **Cervantes** (9 Av Sur 114 in the Centre and Edif El Paseo 3, Paseo Escalón); **Clásicos Roxsil** (6 Av Sur 1-6, Santa Tecla, T2228-1212); **Editorial Piedra Santa** (Av Olímpica 3428, Av 65-67 Sur, T2223-5502); **Etc Ediciones** (in Centro Comercial Basilea, San Benito). Some English books at **Librería Cultural Salvadoreña** in Metrosur. **Olivos**, *also café and restaurant, just below Hotel Princess, Zona Rosa, T2245-4221, www.olivoscafe.com.* Has a wide selection of books, specializing in alternative medicine and health.

## Crafts

You can buy fairtrade arts and crafts at **Café La T** (see under Bars and clubs above, Calle San Antonio Abad), and **Nahanché**. Metrocentro, Centro Comercial Basilea and Multiplaza have a great selection of handicrafts from all over the country.

**El Arbol de Dios**, *La Mascota y Av Masferrer, T2224-6200, see page 416.*

**Mercado Ex-Cuartel**, *8 Av Norte, 1 Calle Ote.* Crafts market, a few blocks east of the Teatro Nacional, rebuilt after a fire in 1995.

**Mercado Nacional de Artesanías**, *opposite the Estado Mayor on the road to Santa Tecla (buses 101A, B or C, 42B, 79, 34, 30B), at prices similar to the Mercado Ex-Cuartel, daily 0800-1800.* A one-stop craft shop with a good cross-section of items even if they are not that well presented. Some of the cheapest prices around.

## Shopping malls

**Metrocentro** (large shopping mall on the Blv de los Héroes, northwest of the city centre). Together with **Metrosur** this is the largest shopping mall in Central America. Another shopping centre, **Villas Españolas** (on the Paseo Escalón, 1 block south of the Redondel Masferrer); is more exclusive, with expensive boutiques. **Galerías Escalón** (Col Escalón), has department stores and cybercafés. **El Paseo** (just at the corner of 79 Av, Escalón), is the newish mall. The area west of Zona Rosa has 3 newer malls named **Multiplaza**, **Hiper Mall Cascadas** and **La Gran Vía**.

What to do

## Diving

**El Salvador Divers**, *Paseo Escalón 3 Calle Pte 5020, Col Escalón, T2264-0961, www.elsalvadordivers.com.* Offer weekly excursions and classes. Located behind the Villavicencio Mall.

## Language schools

**Centro de Intercambio y Solidaridad**, *Av Bolívar 103, Colonia Libertad, T2235-1330, www.cis-elsalvador.org.* Spanish school in the mornings 0800-1200, English school in the afternoons 1700-1900 (volunteer English teachers needed for 10-week sessions).

## Tour operators

**Inter Tours**, *Balam Quitze mall in Paseo Escalon, T2263-6188, www.viajero.com.sv.* One of the most recognized travel agencies in the capital. They have excellent service and can track down that special rate you need.

**OTEC Turismo Joven**, *Centro Comercial El Partenope, local 2, Paseo Escalón, T2264-0200.* Official ISIC office in El Salvador and STA Travel representative, offering travel assistance, reissue of lost tickets, changes and rerouting. Special prices for students, teachers and young people with an ISIC card.

**Pullmantur**, *Av La Revolución, T2243-1300.* Luxury bus service to Guatemala and excellent package tours to Antigua.

**Salva Natura**, *33 Av Sur 640, Col Flor Blanca, T2279-1515, www.salvanatura.org.* For information about Parque Nacional El Imposible in the southwest, near Tacuba and Ataco.

**Tour In El Salvador**, *T2207-4155, www.tour inelsalvador.com.* Minibus tours around the country and to Guatemala and Honduras; experienced and very knowledgeable guide Jorge Martínez. Highly recommended.

Transport

## Air

The international airport, Monseñor Óscar Arnulfo Romero (**SAL**), T2339-9455, www.aeropuertoelsalvador.gob.sv, at Comalapa is 62 km southeast from San Salvador towards Costa del Sol beach, reached by a 4-lane, toll highway. **Acacya** minibus to airport, from 3 Calle Pte y 19 Av Norte,

T2271-4937, airport T2339-9182, at 0600, 0700, 1000, 1400 (be there 15 mins before), US$3 one-way (leaves from airport when full, on right as you go out). **Acacya** also has a taxi service, US$25, the same as other radio taxi companies; ordinary taxis charge US$20. Taxi to **La Libertad** beach US$30. To **Costa del Sol** US$50. There is a post office, a tourist office, 2 exchange desks (including Citi Bank) and duty-free shopping for both departures and arrivals.

The old airport is at Ilopango, 13 km east of the city and is primarily used by the air force and for some domestic flights.

## Bus

**Local** Most buses stop running at 2100. City buses charge US$0.20 and microbuses charges US$0.25 within the city; make sure you have the right change or a small bill to hand. Most run 0500-2000, after which time use taxis.

**Some useful routes**: No 29 from Terminal de Oriente to Metrocentro via downtown; **No 30** Mercado Central to Metrocentro; **No 30B** from Mundo Feliz (100 m up from Esso station on Blv de los Héroes) to Escalón, 79 Av Norte, Zona Rosa (San Benito), Alameda Roosevelt and back to Metrocentro along 49 Av; **No 34** San Benito–Mercado de Artesanías–Terminal de Occidente–Mercado Central–Terminal Oriente; **No 52** 'Paseo' Parque Infantil–Metrocentro–Plaza Las Américas– Paseo Escalón–Plaza Masferrer; **No 52** 'Hotel' Parque Infantil–Metrocentro–Hotel Copa Airlines–Plaza Masferrer. Route **No 101** buses to/from Santa Tecla are blue and white for either class of service.

**Long distance and international** Domestic services go from **Terminal de Occidente**, off Blv Venezuela, T2223-3784 (take city buses 4, 7C, 27, 44 or 34); **Terminal de Oriente**, end of Avenida Peralta in Centro Urbano Lourdes (take city buses No 29 from Metrocentro, 42 from Alameda, or No 4, from 7 C), T2281-3086, very crowded with buses and passengers, keep your eyes open for the bus you want; and **Terminal Sur**, San Marcos, Zona Franca, about 9 km from the city (take city bus No 26 from Universidad Nacional area or Avenida España downtown, take taxi to city after 1830). Terminal de Sonsonate, located just outside city centre, by main road to Acajutla T2450-4625. Terminal de Santa Ana T2440-0938. Routes and fares are given under destinations. For La Libertad and beaches west to Playa El Zonte, plenty of buses go from opposite Iglesia Ceiba Guadalupe, a short taxi ride from centre: Bus No 102 to La Libertad and Nos 107 or 192 to Playa El Zonte, approx 1 hr, US$1.

**Heading south**: Recognized international bus company **Ticabus** departs from Hotel San Carlos, Calle Concepción 121, T2222-4808, www.ticabus.com. Also with an office in Blv del Hipódromo, Zona Rosa, T2243-9764. To **Tapachula** 0600 and 1200 noon, 11 hrs, US$30. To **Guatemala**, 0600 and 1300, 5 hrs, US$15. To **Tegucigalpa**, 1200, 7 hrs, US$15. To **Managua**, 0500, 12 hrs, US$30. To **San José**, 33 hrs including overnight in Managua, US$50. To **Panama City**, depart 0500, arriving 1700 next day, US$75. They now have an executive coach service to **Nicaragua** for US$44, and **Costa Rica** US$58 (both depart 0300) and to **Panama** at 0500, US$93. **King Quality**, Puerto Bus Terminal, Alameda Juan Pablo II y 19 Av Norte, T2241-8704; in Zona Rosa T2271-1361, www.king-qualityca.com. You can walk there from city centre, but it's not advisable with luggage; take bus 101D from Metrocentro, or bus 29, 52 to 21 Av Norte, 2 blocks south of terminal (city buses don't permit heavy luggage). The terminal has a *casa de cambio* (good rates) and a restaurant. They have departures to Central America and Mexico. Departure times from

Puerto Bus station (check office for times from Zona Rosa).

**Service to Guatemala** with domestic carriers includes **Pezzarossi**, **Taca**, **Transesmer**, **Melva**, and **Vencedora**. All operate services to **Guatemala City** more or less hourly (5½ hrs, US$13). Departures between 0500 and 1600. **Confortlines** (sister company of **King Quality**) has departures to Guatemala at 0800 and 1400 for US$30 – higher-class bus than the regular service but no meals. **Pullmantur**, T2243-1300, runs a 0700 service Mon-Sat, a 0830 Sun, and a daily luxury 1500 service from Hotel Marriott Presidente in Zona Rosa for US$35, with a/c, film, drinks and meals.

**Service to Mexico** also from Terminal de Occidente, **El Cóndor** goes to **Talismán**, Mexico via Sonsonate, La Hachadura and Escuintla, US$12, 0330, 9½ hrs, also 0700-0800 to Guatemala City. **Transgalgos** has direct departures to Mexico from Puerto Bus.

**Car**

**Car hire**  Local insurance (about US$10-15 per day plus a deductible US$1000 deposit) is mandatory and 13% IVA applies. **Avis**, 43 Av Sur 137, Colonia Flor Blanca www.avis.com.sv, T2500-2847; **Budget**, Hotel Sheraton Presidente, Col San Benito T2283-2908 and Calle Mirador and 85 Av Norte 648, Col Escalón, T2264-3888, www.budget.com; **Euro Rent-Cars**, 29 Calle Pte and 7 Av Norte 1622, T2235-5232, chamba_r@hotmail.com, cheap daily rates from US$10; **Hertz**, corner of 91 Av Nte and 9 Calle Pte, T2264-2818, www.hertz.com; **Sandoval & Co**, T2235-4405, sub-compact late-model cars from US$10 per day, English spoken.

**Car repairs**  Modern service centres of **Record** and **Impressa**, are found throughout the capital. Good source of spare parts found at **Super Repuestos**, T2221-4440.

**Insurance**  **Asesuiza** is widely used for car insurance, T2209-5025, as is **La Centroamericana**, T2298-6666.

**Car papers**  Ministerio de Hacienda, T2226-1900, 'Tres Torres', turn left on Blv de los Héroes, 300 m past Texaco station.

**Taxi**

Plenty (all yellow), don't have meters, ask fare before getting in. Trips within San Salvador will have a minimun cost of US$4 and most trips will be between US$4 and US$7. Airport is approximately US$25. Few drivers speak English. They will charge more in the rain. More expensive radio taxis may be hired through **Acacya**, T2271-4937.

# Western
## El Salvador

West of San Salvador, lush green hills and rolling cattle pastures are punctuated by indigenous and colonial villages on the approach to Sonosante, an important agricultural centre basking in volcanic shadows.

Beyond it, the Ruta de las Flores is one of El Salvador's prime attractions. Disarming cobblestone streets, colonial airs, craft traditions, culinary highlights, vibrant festivals and a thriving art scene make the communities on this 40-km-long route a popular weekend getaway. Steeped in tranquil coffee fincas and arresting mountain views, the surrounding countryside is ideal for hiking and horse riding too.

North of the Ruta de las Flores, little indigenous villages and pre-Columbian ruins contrast with the vibrancy of Santa Ana, El Salvador's second largest city. The big attractions here are Lago de Coatepeque and the wilderness of Parque Nacional Cerro Verde, home to the peak of Volcán Santa Ana. Three routes lead to Guatemala, the northernmost passing close to Metapán and the impressive cloudforests of Parque Nacional Montecristo on the border with Honduras.

**Best** for
Archaeology ▪ Festivals ▪ Flowers ▪ Volcanoes

From the junction with the Pan-American Highway, just west of Colón, route CA 8 heads west, past Armenia, to the town of Izalco (population 70,959) at the foot of Izalco volcano (8 km from Sonsonate, bus 53C). The town has evolved from the gradual merging of the *ladino* village of Dolores Izalco and the indigenous village of Asunción Izalco. In colonial times this was an important trading centre and in 1932 it experienced a communist rebellion. Today the town is enjoying a tourist revival thanks to its colonial architecture, its prominent and active indigenous population, and its rich heritage of religious imagery which blends indigenous and Roman Catholic beliefs.

A week-long festival celebrating El Salvador del Mundo runs 8-15 August and there is also a local celebration from 24 November to 10 December. The Feast of John the Baptist runs from 17-24 June.

**Tip...**
The town of Izalco and Izalco volcano are not directly connected by road. A paved road branches off the Pan-American Highway 14 km before the turning for Izalco town and goes up towards Volcán Izalco.

### Sonsonate

Sonsonate (altitude 225 m, population 71,541), 64 km from the capital, is the country's chief cattle-raising region. It also produces sugar, tobacco, rice, tropical fruits, hides and balsam. The city was founded in 1552 and is hot, dirty and crowded, but worth checking out for its colonial architecture in the city centre. The beautiful **El Pilar** church (1723) is strongly reminiscent of the church of El Pilar in San Vicente. The **cathedral** has many cupolas (the largest covered with white porcelain) and was badly damaged in the 2001 earthquake but is now fully restored. The old church of **San Antonio del Monte** (completed 1861), 1 km from the city, draws pilgrims from afar (fiesta 22-26 August). There is a small **railway museum**, look for the locomotive at the entrance to the city on the highway from San Salvador (Km 65). An important market is held each Sunday. In the northern outskirts of the city there is a waterfall on the Río Sensunapán. Legend has it that an indigenous princess drowned there, and on the anniversary of her death a gold casket appears below the falls.

The main annual event is **Feria de la Candelaria** in February. Easter Week processions are celebrated with particular fervour and are probably the most impressive in the whole country. On Easter Thursday and Holy Friday the streets are filled with thousands of members of the *cofradías* (brotherhoods).

### Around Sonsonate

There are several **waterfalls** and other sites of natural beauty in the Sonsonate district. To the west, near the village of **Santo Domingo de Guzmán** (bus No 246 from Sonsonate), are the falls of **El Escuco** (2 km north), **Tepechapa** (1.5 km further) and **La Quebrada** (further still up the Río Tepechapa), all within walking distance of both Santo Domingo and each other. Walk through the town then follow the river; there are several spots to swim. Santo Domingo de Guzmán is also known for its *alfarería* (pottery) of *comales*, clay plates used to create tortillas and *pupusas* over the open fire, and its many Náhuatl-speaking habitants. There's a festival in Santo Domingo, 24-25 December.

A short distance north is **San Pedro Puxtla** (bus No 246), with a modern church built on the remains of an 18th-century edifice. From here you can visit the **Tequendama Falls** on the Río Sihuapán. Bus No 219 goes east to **Cuisnahuat** (with an 18th-century baroque church), where the Fiesta de San Judas takes place 23-29 November. From there it is 2 km south to the Río Apancoyo, or 4 km north to **Peñón El Escalón** (covered in balsam trees) and **El Istucal Cave**, at the foot of the Escalón hill, where indigenous rites are celebrated in November.

## Listings Izalco to Sonsonate

## Where to stay

### Izalco

**$$ La Casona de Los Vega**
*2a Av Norte 24, in the centre, T2453-5951, www.lacasonadelosvega.com.sv.*
An atmospheric colonial home converted into a comfortable hotel and restaurant. Pleasant garden and good views. Tours available.

**$ El Chele**
*Final Av Roberto Carillas, Calle La Violeta, Caserío Texcalito, T2453-6740. Ricardo Salazar, T7798-8079.*
Located some 800 m north of Izalco at a finca surrounded by forest, this place has a great view of Volcán Izalco. Escorted hikes and horse rides available to Cerro Verde and its surrounding slopes and Izalco with visits to 2 pre-Columbian ruins nearby. Free transport available, call to arrange. English spoken.

### Sonsonate

**$$ Agape**
*Km 63 on outskirts of town, take old road through Sonsonate, the hotel is on the exit street to San Salvador, just before the main roundabout on the right side, T2451-2667, www.hotelagape.com.sv.*
Adequate suites and rooms with a/c or fan, safe parking, restaurant, gardens, cable TV, pool and laundry service.

## Restaurants

### Izalco

There are several *comedores* in town.

**$$ Casa de Campo**
*Across from Turicentro Atecozol, T2453-6530. Open weekends only.*
The old *casco* of the finca **Cuyancúa** has been restored with beautiful gardens, making it a good spot for a meal. The fish raised in the artificial lake is served in the restaurant. Horses are available for hire.

**$ Mariona**
*In the centre, T2453-6580.*
This *comedor* serves a 55-year-old recipe for *sopa de gallina* (Creole chicken soup) which is famous all over Izalco.

**$ Restaurante El Cheles**
*In the centre of Izalco with another branch out of town at Final Av Roberto Carillas, Calle La Violeta, Caserío Texcalito, T2453-5392.*
Owner Ricardo Salazar speaks English and can arrange escorted hikes and horse riding to Cerro Verde.

### Sonsonate

**$$ Doña Laura**
*Inside Hotel Agape (see Where to stay, above). Open 0730-2100.*
Highly recommended.

## Sonsonate

**Bus** No 248 to **Santa Ana**, US$1.50 along Carr 12 north, 39 km, a beautiful journey. To **Ahuachapán**, bus No 249, 2 hrs, slow, best to go early in the day. To Ataco, via Juayúa and Ahuachapán, No 23, US$1, 1½ hrs To **Barra de Santiago**, bus No 285. To **Los Cobanos** bus No 259. Take care at the bus terminal and on rural routes (eg in Nahuizalco area). From **San Salvador** to Sonsonate by bus No 530, US$0.80, 1½ hrs, very frequent.

## Ruta de las Flores   *Colour map 2, C5.*

### flower-festooned villages filled with culture and tradition

★Steeped in fragrant coffee groves and bucolic highland scenery, El Salvador's legendary Ruta de las Flores climbs northwest towards Ahuachapán, gently wending on Route CA 8.

Driving at leisure is the best way to explore the region, but frequent buses from Sonsonate (bus 249 and 285, two hours) also cover the 40-km stretch. It is also possible to access the Ruta de las Flores from Santa Ana in the opposite direction.

### Nahuizalco

The route begins just beyond the indigenous village of Nahuizalco (population 49,081). Some of the older women here still wear the *refajo* (a doubled length of cloth made of tie-dyed threads worn over a wrap-round skirt), and various crafts are still made, including wood and rattan furniture. Although use of the indigenous language is dying out, you do still encounter people who speak Náhuatl. The night market, unique in El Salvador, opens at dusk and has traditional local food on sale. There's a religious festival 19-25 June, with music, **Danza de los Historiantes** and art exhibitions; also 24-25 December, with music and **Danza de los Pastores**. Take bus 53 D from Sonsonate.

### Salcoatitán and Juayúa

Further up the mountainside at Km 82 is **Salcoatitán** (population 5484) at 1045 m above sea level, a colonial village with a beautiful park in front of the colonial church. This cosy village used to be only a drive-through on the way to Juayúa or Apaneca but has experienced a tourist revival lately with several new restaurants, art galleries and artisan shops.

Further along, the road branches off to Juayúa 2 km further north and the same bus from Sonsonate takes a detour into the village and back. **Juayúa** is the largest city on the Ruta de Las Flores – the name means 'River of Purple Orchids' in the local Náhuatl dialect – and sits nestled in a valley dominated by volcanoes. It's a peaceful spot where you can watch people at work and kids playing in the semi-cobbled street. The surrounding region is blanketed in coffee groves; the bean was introduced to the area in 1838 and today the town produces about 10% of the coffee exported from El Salvador. Its church houses an image of the **Cristo Negro** (Black Christ) carved by Quirio Cataño at the end of the 16th century. **Tourist information** is available from Jaime Salgado, at **Juayutur** ① *T2469-2310, juayutur@ navegante.com.sv*. He can provide good information about the activities available in the region, which include rappelling waterfalls, the hike of the seven waterfalls and the mountain lagoon with wild horses. Guides are trained local youngsters. Also check out the

**Casa de la Cultura**, on the corner next to the park for information on Juayúa. Gaby and Julio Vega, the owners of **Akwaterra Tours**ⓘ *www.aventuraelsalvador.com*, run a mountain cabin at Finca Portezuelo named **La Escondida**; also a camping site with ready made-up tents on decks under covers. They're fluent in English and offer a wide range of activites at **Portezuelo Adventure Park** such as hiking, mountain biking, horseback riding, zip-wire circuit, ATVs and paragliding.

There are a number of excursions you can do in the area to see wildlife, including river otters, toucans, butterflies and many other animals. In the dry season **Laguna de las Ranas** (Laguna Seca) dries up, attracting numerous reptiles as it shrinks. There are also trips to the 30-m-high waterfall at **Salto el Talquezal**, the 50-m-high **Salto de la Lagunilla Azul** and several other waterfalls in the region (seven in one day if you take a tour), with swimming and picnics on the way (see below). Every weekend Juayúa celebrates the Feria Gastronómica, an opportunity to try a variety of traditional dishes, often accompanied by local events, music and shows.

The **Feria Gastrónomica Internacional** is in January and celebrates with dishes from all over the world; other festivals include **Día de los Canchules** (31 October), when people ask for candies and **Día de las Mercedes** (17 September), when the houses are decorated with branches and candles leading up to the procession of the Virgen de la Merced. Another local attraction is the **Museo del Café**, of the coffee cooperative **La Majada**ⓘ *T2467-9008 ext 1451, www.cafemajadaoro.com.sv*, located in **San José La Majada**, just outside Juayua on the road to Los Naranjos. Tours include information on coffee processing and a trip to the processing plant. A coffee shop offers local brews and iced coffee.

## Apaneca

Between Ahuachapán and Sonsonate, 91 km from San Salvador and 29 km from Las Chinamas on the border, is Apaneca (altitude 1450 m, population 8383), an extremely peaceful town (and the highest town in the country), with small cobbled streets, marking the summit of the **Ruta de las Flores**. Founded by Pedro de Alvarado in 1543, Apaneca is known for its cool climate and winds – *apaneca* means 'rivers of wind' in Náhuatl.

The town has a colonial centre, a traditional *parque* and a municipal market selling fruit, flowers and handicrafts. One of the oldest parochial churches in the country used to corner the central park but was demolished after damage caused by the 2001 earthquake. It has been partially reconstructed, with a modern twist. The artisan market is a great place to see the local arts and crafts. Other local industries include coffee, flowers for export and furniture. Have a look at the topiary creations outside the police station and check out the **Casa de la Cultura** in the centre of town.

There are two small lakes nearby to the north, **Laguna Verde** and **Laguna Las Ninfas**, whose crater-like walls are clothed in tropical forest and cypress trees. It is possible to swim in the former, but the latter is too shallow and reedy. According to local legend, a swim is meant to be very beneficial to your health and the lakes are very popular with tourists. This is the Cordillera de Apaneca, part of the narrow highland belt running southeast of Ahuachapán.

South of Apaneca is the **Cascada del Río Cauta**. To get there, take bus No 216 from Ahuachapán towards Jujutla, alight 3 km after the turn-off to Apaneca, then walk 300 m along the trail to the waterfall.

In the grounds of Finca Santa Leticia lies an **archaeological site** ⓘ *US$2; 2-hr coffee tour US$20; both combined US$35, www.hotelsantaleticia.com, bus No 249 from Juayúa (10 mins)*. It is believed to be 2600 years old and was rediscovered in 1968 by the farm owner. Three huge monuments are buried among the coffee groves and you feel like a first-time discoverer as you travel the winding route to get there. There are three stone spheres with human characteristics weighing between 6000 and 11,000 kg.

## Ataco

Concepción de Ataco, to give the town its full name, located just below Apaneca, is now a favourite on the Ruta de Las Flores. The village has undergone a complete renovation, and now has cobbled streets, old-fashioned benches and streetlights, and a popular weekend festival with food, flowers, and arts and crafts. Some excellent coffee shops and restaurants, offering cuisine from Mexico to France, continue to open up, mainly for weekends only, making Ataco one of the most visited villages in the area, and well worth a weekend trip.

Look for the *marimba* and the traditional dances in the main square and drop by **Diconte & Axul**, an artsy café that offers anything from delicious home-made pies to original arts and crafts that are giving La Palma art a run for their money. The **House of Coffee** has an espresso machine and serves the excellent world-class coffee grown in Ataco at their own finca for five generations.

## Ahuachapán

Coffee is the main export of Ahuachapán (altitude 785 m, population 110,511), a quiet town with low and simple houses. One of the most popular local sights is the geothermal field of **Los Ausoles**, 3 km road from Ahuachapan and marked on the road out of town to Apaneca as 'Planta Geotérmica'. You can't go into the plant, but when you arrive take the road to the right where, just a little way up the hill on the left, you come to a little house, geysers of boiling mud with plumes of steam and strong whiffs of sulphur. The *ausoles* are used for generating 30% of the country's electricity. For a small tip the house owner will take you into his back garden to see the fumaroles and boiling pools.

Taking the northern road from Ahuachapán, 9 km west of town near the village of **Los Toles** are the **Tehuasilla Falls**, where the Río El Molino falls 60 m (take bus No 293 from Ahuachapán to Los Toles, then walk 1 km). The road continues northwest through the treeless **Llano del Espino**, with its small lake, and across the Río Paz into Guatemala.

## Around Ahuachapán

Tacuba (population 29,585) is an indigenous town, around 850 m above sea level, and 15 km west of Ahuachapán. Tacuba means 'the village of the football game', probably relating to the *juego de pelota* of the Maya, and the existence of many pre-Columbian mounds in the surrounding area suggest the region was heavily populated in the past. At the entrance to the town are the largest colonial church ruins in El Salvador, torn down by the earthquake of Santa Marta, the same tremors that ruined large parts of Antigua, Guatemala, in 1773. You can also visit the Casa de la Cultura office, Concultura ⓘ *3 km on main st north, daily 0900-1230 and 1330-1600*, to see an interesting display of photos. The town is near the northern entrance of Parque Nacional El Imposible (see page 451), which is accessed by hiking or 4WD in the dry season.

The surrounding area offers a wide range of opportunities including waterfalls, pristine rivers, mountain hikes and panoramic views. **Ceiba de los Pericos**, 15 minutes out of Tacuba by car, is a 600-year-old ceiba tree where thousands of parrots flock together at dusk to sleep in its branches, ending the day with a deafening noise before resting for the night. In Tacuba centre the **Ceiba de las Garzas** is the rendezvous of hundreds of *garzas* (herons).

Local tour company **El Imposible Tours**, led by Tacuba native Manolo González, provide tours of the Tacuba area and to Parque Nacional El Imposible (see page 437). The dirt road leading from Tacuba to the cordillera is steep and spectacular and provides impressive views; it is recommended although a 4WD is required.

## Listings Ruta de las Flores

### Where to stay

#### Salcoatitán and Juayúa
Check www.juayua.com for a complete list of hotels and restaurants in this area.

#### $$$-$ La Escondida
*6 km north of Juayúa at Finca El Portezuelo, T7888-4552, www.akwa terra.com.*
B&B in an exceptionally beautiful location, in a coffee plantation cradled between Laguna Verde and forest-clad mountains, with a view over to Ahuachapán to the north. Cosily furnished rooms, with fireplace, DVD, equipped kitchen. Contact Julio and Gaby (English spoken). They also offer coffee decks – a tent protected by a roofed wooden structure – and camping.

#### $$ Hotel Juayúa
*Urb Esmeralda, Final 6a Av Norte, Juayúa, T2469-2109, www.hoteljuayua.net.*
A rustic and intimate little guesthouse with fine views from the garden and a pool. Rooms are cosy, tranquil and comfortable. Rates include breakfast and internet.

#### $$-$ El Mirador
*A block from the park, Juayúa, T2452-2432, www.hotelelmiradorjuayua.blogspot.co.uk.*
A 3-storey building with restaurant on top. Rooms include cable TV, fan, private

bath with hot water. There is a cheap backpackers' dorm too. Best option for low rates and central location.

#### $ Anahuac
*1 Calle Pte and 5 Av Norte, Juayúa, T2469-2401, www.hotelanahuac.com.*
Dorms and private rooms for backpackers and tours, with garden, hammocks and a book exchange. The very friendly owner Cesar also runs nearby **Café Cadejo** (live music at weekends); extremely popular and highly recommended.

#### $ Doña Mercedes
*29 Av Sur, 6 Calle Oriente 3-6, Juayúa, 1 block south of Farmacia Don Bosco, T2452-2287.*
Spotless accommodation and very attentive, grandmotherly service. Discounts for longer stays. A welcoming family. Recommended.

#### $ Hostal Casa Mazeta
*4 blocks from main square opposite the church, Juayúa, T2406-3403, www.casamazeta.com.*
Great backpackers' hostel in former family home, cosy rooms, dorm and covered hammock space, with garden, kitchen, Wi-Fi and lounge area with DVD library. French owner, also speaks English, German and Spanish. Tours, parking space and laundry. Recommended.

## Apaneca

### $$$ Santa Leticia
*Cra Sonsonate Km 86.5, south of Apaneca, T2433-0357, www.hotelsantaleticia.com.*
Nestled inside the Santa Leticia coffee finca, this mountain resort features comfortable double rooms decorated in locally carved wood, a solar-heated pool, gardens, and tranquil highland views. There is also a restaurant with live music on Sun. Offers access to Santa Leticia archaeological site.

### $$ Las Cabañas de Apaneca
*T2433-0500, Cra Sonsonate Km 90, south of Apaneca, www.cabanasapaneca.com.*
Las Cabañas de Apaneca offers 17 simple but comfortable rooms set in a well-tended garden with views. Each has their own terrace with seats, hot water and cable TV. More expensive with full board.

### $$-$ Hostal Rural las Orquídeas
*Av Central Sur 4, T2433-0061.*
This centrally located option promises clean, simple rooms and accessible prices. Also offer accommodation in a family home.

## Laguna Verde

### $$ Hotel Laguna Verde Guest House
*T7859-2865.*
A nice small house and a wood cabin located at the rim of a deep secondary crater with a spectacular view. Located 250 m from Laguna Verde and 3 km from Apaneca, a perfect departure point for hiking in the area. Microbuses serve the area several times a day; check current schedules.

## Ataco

### $$$ Alicante Montaña
*Cra Sonsonate Km 93.5, between Apaneca and Ataco, T2433-0175, www.alicanteapaneca.com.*
26 very clean log cabin rooms with hot water, cable TV. Huge, barn-like restaurant,

attentive service and good value meals, pool, spa and jacuzzi; attractive grounds with aviary. Very friendly and helpful. Recommended.

### $$$ Casa Degraciela
*1a Calle Ote y 2a Av Nte 2, Barrio El Centro, T7546-7124, www.casadegraciela.com.*
A beautiful boutique option set in an authentic, historical, colonial-style building complete with a sumptuous garden. Rooms are handsomely attired with antique furnishings and earthy tones. The building has been in the family for 150 years. Recommended.

### $$$ El Carmen Estate
*Km 97 Cra Sonsonate, on the edge of town, T2243-0304, www.elcarmenestate.com.*
The Carmen Coffee estate has 2 types of accommodation, both very tasteful and intriguing lodgings. The **Casona** is the original plantation house, over 100 years old but renovated for modern use, while the **Quinta** is a country villa, suitable for a family or group (it's also possible to rent single rooms here). Recommended.

### $$$ Hotel Misión de Angeles
*Final 4a Av Norte, on the edge of town on a hill, T2404-1800, www.misiondeangeles.com.*
The 10 boutique rooms at the Misión de Angeles are stylish and simple. They feature solid wood furniture, tasteful local artwork, muted tones and wood beams; some have balconies with mountain views. Great restaurant overlooking the countryside.

### $$$-$$ Los Portones de Ataco
*2a Av Sur 2, T6114-8030, www.losportonesdeataco.webstudio503.com.*
Los Portones is a new *hostal*. It offers comfortable, simple, homely rooms with cable TV, hot water and internet. The on-site café serves good food and local coffee. Rates negotiable.

## $$ El Jardín de Celeste
*Cra Sononate Km 94, between Apaneca and Ataco, T2433-0277, www.eljardindeceleste.com.*
10 rustic cabins with local flair located in a coffee grove and surrounded by colourful plants. The restaurant has capacity for larger parties and conventions. Beautifully decorated throughout the place with antiques, orchids, plants and arts and crafts.

## $$ La Posada de Don Oli
*1a Av Sur, entre 2 and 4 Calle Pte, T2450-5155, oogomezduarte@yahoo.com.mx.*
Hotel and restaurant in a colonial setting, owned by the local mayor, Oscar Gómez. Guides available for visits to the local sights. Simple, no-frills, family-run digs.

## Ahuachapán

### $$$$-$$ Termales de Santa Teresa
*Beneficio Bendix, Cra hacia Ataco, frente a Ciudadela, southeast of Ahuachapán (see website for directions), T7696-4647, www. termalesdesantateresa.com.*
Mineral-rich hot springs, channelled into various bathing pools, are the unique selling point of this affordable resort. Lodgings consist of 4 bungalows, all well-attired. The best is 'Emabajada de Japón', complete with its own private pool and tasteful, traditional furnishings. Great low-season and mid-week discounts.

## $$ Casa Blanca
*2 Av Norte y Calle Gerardo Barrios, T2443-1505.*
A simple, no-frills and charming little hotel with spotless rooms overlooking a courtyard. Good central location, breakfast included. Recommended.

## $$-$ La Casa de Mamapán
*Pasaje La Concordia, T2413-2507, www.lacasademamapan.com.*

Nestled in the Centro Histórico near the church, Casa de Mamapán is a comfortable, colonial-style, well-renovated historic building and family-run choice with 10 rooms, all equipped with a/c, fan, Wi-Fi, hot water and cable TV. Don't miss the colourful mural on the outside wall, the work of 2 local brothers.

## Around Ahuachapán

### $$ La Cabaña de Tacuba
*Tacuba, 50 m west of Alcaldía, T2417-4332.*
Nice hotel with large park grounds, access to river and swimming pools, a/c, cable TV. Great food at the restaurant.

### $ Hostal de Mama y Papa
*Tacuba, Barrio El Calvario, 1 Calle 1, T2417-4268, www.imposibletours.com.*
Home of the delightful González family, dorm and private rooms with private bath available; roof terrace, DVDs, Wi-Fi access, crazy ducks guard the garden. Excellent, cheap food. The son, Manolo, runs **El Imposible Tours**, one of the most adventurous and expert outfits in the country; see What to do, page 437.

## Restaurants

## Salcoatitán and Juayúa
Each weekend the whole central plaza of Juayua is invaded by the Gastronomical Food Fair; grab a chair and a table if you can, the event attracts folks from far and near. During the week there are several other options.

### $$ El Cadejo Café
*Calle Monseñor Romero.*
This excellent bohemian café-bar has a pleasant outdoor patio and hosts occasional live music. They serve great pub grub and snacks, including wholesome sandwiches, as well as beer and iced coffee. Good vibe, especially after dark.

## $$ Restaurante R&R
*Calle Merceditas Careres 1-2, T2452-2083.*
The best restaurant in town serves excellent grilled chicken and meat, including steak rubbed in coffee. There are also vegetarian options. Filling and flavourful comfort food from a Salvadorean chef trained in Canada. Recommended.

## $ Comedor Laura's
*1 block from the park on 1 Av Sur, Juayúa, T2452-2098. Daily 0700-2000.*
'The best in town' according to one reader, serving *comida a la vista*.

## $ Parque Restaurante La Colina
*Km 82 on the turn-off between Juayúa and Salcoatitán, T2452-2916.*
Old timer in the region, popular with families, also has hammocks for relaxation after the meal as well as cabins and horse rides for the kids.

## $ Taquería La Guadalupana
*Av Daniel Cordón Sur and 2a Calle Ote, Juayúa T2452-2195.*
Authentic Mexican grub including hearty tacos. Popular with the local youth.

## Cafés

### Pastelería y Cafetería Festival
*4 Calle Pte and 1 Av Sur, T2452-2269.*
Bakery and coffee shop – try the *pastelitos de ciruela* (plum pie) or the traditional *semita*. Good view overlooking the park.

## Apaneca
Stalls in the municipal market offer cheap meals and typical dishes. Try the *budín* at the middle stall on the right side of market entrance (might be the best in El Salvador). A definite must for those on a budget or for experiencing local food.

## $$$-$$ La Cocina de Mi Abuela
*2 Calle Pte y 1 Av Sur, T2433-0100. Weekends; and Cabañas de Apaneca.*
The 2 largest restaurants, and the most popular spots. Attract people from far and wide.

## $$ El Rosario
*By the turn-off at Km 95 Cra Sonsonate, between Apaneca and Ataco, T2433-0205.*
Offers different grilled dishes, from regular *churrascos* to *pelibuey* (a mix between goat and sheep), *jaripeo* (Salvadorean version of rodeo), horse shows and musical entertainments weekends.

## $$ Entre Nubes
*Km 93.5 Cra Sonsonate, T2433-0345, www.entrenubescafe.com.*
Exceptionally beautiful nursery plants surround this fine coffee shop (open weekends) and open-air restaurant. They serve *comida típica* in addition to great desserts and varieties of coffee.

## $$ Parque Ecoturístico Las Cascadas de Don Juan
*T2273-1380, lascascadasdedonjuan@yahoo.com.*
Serving typical dishes and also offer hikes to the waterfalls, freshwater springs as well as a camping area.

## $ Laguna Verde Restaurant
*Km 3.5 Carr El Caserío by La Laguna Verde, T2261-0167. Only open weekends.*
A cosy and rustic spot serving typical dishes of the region.

## Ataco

### $$-$ The House of Coffee
*T2450-5353, thoc@hotmail.com. Tue-Sun.*
A must visit, the café has the only professional espresso machine in town. Home-made cakes and steaming hot 'Cup of Excellence' award-winning coffee is available here.

## $$-$ Tayua
*T7233-6508.*
A gem of a place 2 blocks uphill from the plaza, run by English-speaking and trained chef Veronica, and her husband. Wide range of dishes usually using home-produced organic veg from the restaurant's own garden. Antique decor and background jazz. They also have a bakery, producing the best bread and pastries in town.

### Ahuachapán
There are a handful of restaurants with lake views by Laguna del Espino just outside Ahuachapán.

## $$ Restaurant El Paseo, Restaurant Tanya and El Parador
*On the Las Chinamas road.*
All serve good meals.

## What to do

### Apaneca
**Apaneca Aventura**, *Calle Los Platanares 2, T2433-0470, apanecaaventura@yahoo.com.* Specialize in off-road buggy rides around the mountains and forests, including to Laguna Verde and Ausole de Santa Teresa geysers and thermal baths. English manager Becky, and with English-speaking guides. Highly recommended.

### Tacuba
**El Imposible Tours**, *see Hostal de Mama y Papa, page 435.* Range of activities including mountain biking, canyoning and hiking; overnight trips combining tour of Barra de Santiago and mangroves. Highly recommended.

## Transport

### Apaneca
**Bus** Local buses stop by the plaza, others pass on the main road, a few blocks north, leaving you with a fairly long walk. Laguna Verde can be reached on foot from Apaneca to Cantón Palo Verde and Hoyo de Cuajuste, then a further 1 km from where the road ends.

### Ahuachapán
**Bus** Ahuachapán is 100 km from **San Salvador** by bus 202, US$0.90, every 20 mins, 0430-1830 to the capital, 2 hrs via Santa Ana. Microbuses to **border** from northwest corner of the Parque, US$0.45, 25 mins, slower buses same price; see also Border crossings box in Practicalities chapter for El Salvador– Guatemala. Bus No 210 to **Santa Ana** 1 hr, US$0.50. Bus No 235 El Express to **Metapán** 1¼ hrs, US$0.90. Frequent buses and minivans to the border at Km 117.

### Tacuba
**Bus** Buses leave the terminal in **Ahuachapán** every 30 mins, 0500-1530, return 1630-1700, via **Ataco**; US$0.60, 45 mins, rough road.

The new Pan-American Highway parallels the old one, continuing northwest to the border with Guatemala at San Cristóbal. Santa Ana, acting as a transport hub, has routes out to Ahuachapán to the west and the border at Las Chinamas, as well as north to Metapán and beyond to the border crossing of Anguiatú. See Border crossings box in Practicalities chapter.

Fifteen kilometres from Santa Tecla, 7 km beyond the junction with the Sonsonate road, there is a junction to the right. This road forks immediately, right to **Quezaltepeque**, left (at **Joya de Cerén** café) to **San Juan Opico**. After a few kilometres on the San Juan road, you cross the railway by the Kimberley-Clark factory.

### ★Joya de Cerén

*T2401-5782, www.fundar.org.sv/joyadeceren, Tue-Sun 0900-1600, US$3, parking US$1. See Transport, page 440.*

After the girder bridge crossing the Río Sucio there is a grain store beside which is Joya de Cerén (32 km from the capital). This is a major archaeological site and on the World Heritage List of UNESCO (the only one in El Salvador), not for spectacular temples, but because this is the only known site where ordinary Maya houses have been preserved having been buried by the ash from the nearby Laguna Caldera volcano in about AD 600. Buildings and construction methods can be clearly seen; a painted book and household objects have been found. All the structures are covered with protective roofing. The site has a small but good museum, café, toilets and car park. Official tours are in Spanish but English-language tours are available upon request.

### San Andrés

*Tue-Sun 0900-1600, US$3, popular for weekend picnics, otherwise it's quiet. Has a café. Take bus No 201 from Terminal de Occidente, US$1.50 (same bus from Santa Ana) T2319-3220, www.fundar.org.sv/sanandre.*

Back on the main road, heading west is the excavated archaeological site of San Andrés, halfway between Santa Tecla and Coatepeque on the estate of the same name (its full name is La Campana de San Andrés). It is located at Km 32.5 on the Pan-American Highway, just after the Hilasal towel factory. A **museum** at the site displays some of the ceramics found (others can be seen at the Museo Nacional de Antropología David J Guzmán – MUNA – in San Salvador, see page 416). The museum also features a special indigo section with information about this natural dye. El Salvador was the number one producer of indigo in the world during the colonial era. A large indigo *obraje* (processing basin) – probably the largest found in Latin America – was found at San Andrés during an archaeological excavation and has been preserved. There are good views of the nearby hills.

## ON THE ROAD

### Climbing Izalco

Izalco, as can be seen from the lack of vegetation, is a geologically young volcano. Historical records show that activity began in the 17th century as a sulphurous smoke vent but, in February 1770, violent eruptions formed a cone that was more or less in constant activity until 1957. There was a small eruption in 1966 through a blowhole on the southeast slope testified by two 1000-m lava flows. Since that time, it has been quiescent.

A path leads off the road (signposted) just below the car park on Cerro Verde. In 20-30 minutes, descend to the saddle between Cerro Verde and Izalco, then it's one to 1½ hours up (steep but manageable). The contrast between the green forest of Cerro Verde and the coal-black lava around Izalco is impressive. The climb is three hours from base. Beware of falling rocks when climbing. There's a spectacular view from the top so try to ensure that low cloud is not expected before planning to go. For a quick descent, find a rivulet of soft volcanic sand and half-slide, half-walk down in 15 minutes, then it's about one hour back up the saddle. This 'cinder running' requires care, strong shoes and consideration for those below.

If you wish to climb the volcano you need to take the first bus to Cerro Verde, as the park rangers wait for the passengers from this bus before they start the guided climb to the volcano at 1100.

### Lago de Coatepeque

At El Congo, 13 km before Santa Ana, a branch road leads south to the northern shore of the beautiful Lago de Coatepeque, a favourite weekend resort, with good sailing, watersports and fishing, near the foot of Santa Ana volcano. Many weekend homes line the north and east shores, making access to the water difficult, but there are public *balnearios*. The lakeside hotels are a good option for having a meal and to use their infrastructure for the day. You can also get boat rides on the lake through the hotels or by independent fishermen. There are *aguas termales* (hot springs) on the opposite side of the lake. A ride is between US$15 and US$45. There are two islands in the lake – **Anteojos** which is close to the hotels, and **Teopán** on the far side. The local Fiesta del Santo Niño de Atocha runs from 25-29 June.

### Cerro Verde, Volcán Izalco and Volcán Santa Ana

*Park entrance US$1, passport or photocopy required, car park US$0.70. Guided tour to the summit of Izalco or Santa Ana is included, leaving from the entrance daily 1100. The guided tour through the nature trail around the Cerro Verde Summit is US$0.25 per person and is led by local trained guides. The Turicentro Cerro Verde (the summit of Cerro Verde with its trails, the car park and departure point for the hikes to the volcano) is run by the Ministry of Tourism, for information T2222-8000, www.elsalvador.travel. The whole area covering the volcanoes Santa Ana, Cerro Verde and Izalco and surrounding area are part of the Parque Nacional de los Volcanes, which is administrated by Salvanatura, T2279-1515, www. salvanatura.org. To access Cerro Verde, take bus No 208 from Santa Ana at 0800, passing El Congo at 0815 to catch the 1100 departure. If you come from Sonsonate side, take the No 209 bus from Sonsonate to Cerro Verde.*

**★Parque Nacional Cerro Verde** From El Congo a road runs south, around the east shore of Lago Coatepeque. This road is locally known as Carretera Panorámica, due to the fantastic view of Coatepeque on one side and the mountains and valleys beyond the ridge. After reaching the summit, the paved road branches right, climbing above the south end of the lake to Parque Nacional Cerro Verde (2030 m) with its fine and surprising views of the Izalco volcano (1910 m), and Santa Ana volcano (2381 m), the highest volcano in the country. In October 2005, Santa Ana erupted for the first time in more than 100 years. The road up to Cerro Verde is lined with beautiful flowers and halfway up there is a mirador with a great view of Lago Coatepeque. Cerro Verde is probably one of the most beautiful places in El Salvador due to the special flora and fauna, breathtaking views and fine volcano trekking.

**Tip...**
For the best view of Izalco, go in the morning, although the afternoon clouds around the cone can be enchanting.

A 30-minute walk along a nature trail leads you around the crater ridge, to a series of miradors with views of Lago Coatepeque and Santa Ana volcano. For information on climbing Volcán Izalco, see box, page 439.

The old hotel and its volcano-view terrace were destroyed in the 2001 earthquake but you can still go there for an amazing view over Izalco volcanic crater. There are now a couple of cabins available for US$35-55. For information call the **Turicentro** ① *T7949-2751*.

## Listings Santa Tecla to Santa Ana

### Where to stay

#### Lago de Coatepeque

**$ Amacuilco**
*300 m from Telecom, T7822-4061.*
This place has 6 basic but clean and airy rooms, some with lake view, and hammocks. Discounts for longer stays, *marimba* classes, Spanish and Náhuatl lessons, and an art gallery. All meals available, pool, great view with jetty over the lake, secure, boat excursions on lake, tours arranged from US$30-40 per day, kayaks and bikes for rent. Run by a very helpful manager called Sandra. Recommended.

### Restaurants

#### Lago de Coatepeque

**$$$-$$ Rancho Alegre**
*Eastern shore of the lake near Santa Catarina church, T2441-6071, www. restauranteranchoalegresv.com.*

The Rancho's offerings include a variety of *comida típica* with meat fare, such as grilled steak or rabbit in tomato sauce; soups; chicken; and seafood, including breaded shrimps or fillet. A great setting on the lake and they offer accommodation too (**$$**).

### Transport

#### Joya de Cerén

**Bus** No 108 from **San Salvador** Terminal de Occidente to San Juan; US$0.45, 1 hr. Bus No 201 from **Santa Ana**, US$0.60, 1 hr, ask the bus driver to drop you at Desvío Opico from where you can catch another bus to Joya de Cerén.

#### Lago de Coatepeque

**Bus** From **Santa Ana**, bus No 220 'El Lago' to the lake every 30 mins, US$0.35. From **San Salvador**; bus No 201 to El Congo (bridge at Km 50) on Pan-American Hwy, US$1, then pick up the No 220 bus to the lake, US$0.45.

Other buses to **Guatemala** may also stop at El Congo, so it's worth checking.

**Taxi** From **Santa Ana,** US$10.

### Cerro Verde and Volcán Izalco

**Bus** From **Santa Ana**, bus No 248 goes to Santa Ana and Cerro Verde via El Congo. If you come from San Salvador wait for the bus at the other side of the main road, near the turn-off to Lake Coatepeque. The departures from Santa Ana are 0800, 1000 1100 and 1300. The bus arrives approximately 30 mins later at El Congo. The return bus leaves Cerro Verde at 1100, 1200, 1300, 1500, 1600 and 1730. The latest bus stops at El Congo and does not go all the way to Santa Ana. The journey between Cerro Verde at El Congo takes approximately 1 hr.

If you travel from **San Salvador** take the bus towards Santa Ana (No 205). Get off at the Shell petrol station at El Congo, cross the bridge that goes over the highway and catch the No 248 at the junction from Santa Ana. If you come from the west take the bus from Esso petrol station beween Izalco and Ateos that leads to Santa Ana and get off at junction 14 km below Cerro Verde summit and wait for No 248 that comes from El Congo.

## Santa Ana and around  *Colour map 2, C5.*

El Salvador's second city

Santa Ana (altitude 776 m, population 245,421) is 55 km from San Salvador and capital of its department. The basin of the Santa Ana volcano is exceptionally fertile, producing large amounts of coffee, with sugar cane coming a close second. The city, named Santa Ana La Grande by Fray Bernardino Villapando in 1567, is the business centre of western El Salvador.

There are some fine buildings: the neo-Gothic **cathedral**, and several other churches, especially **El Calvario**, in neoclassical style. Of special interest is the classical **Teatro de Santa Ana** ⓘ *on the north side of the plaza, a guide (small charge) will show you round on weekdays, refer to the local press for performances,* originally completed in 1910, now in the latter stages of interior restoration and one of the finest theatres in Central America. The Fiestas Julias take place from 1-26 July.

### Los Naranjos and around

Moving northeast of Juayúa, swirling up a scenic mountain road connecting Juayúa with Santa Ana, you arrive at Los Naranjos, a small traditional coffee village located at the mountain pass between Santa Ana and the Pilón volcanoes. The lines of wind-breaking trees preventing damage to coffee trees are particularly beautiful, while the high altitude makes the climate cool with the scent of cypress forests. A series of restaurants and small cabins for lodging has popped up in recent years and is an excellent option for cool climate and countryside relaxation.

At Km 82 on the Carretera Salcoatitán to Juayúa is **Parque y Restaurante La Colina** ⓘ *T2452-2916, www.lacolinajuayua.com,* with hammocks, arts and crafts, and horse riding available. **Apaneca** is a short distance uphill from Sonsonate, see page 431.

### Chalchuapa

About 16 km west of Santa Ana, on the road to Ahuachapán, lies Chalchuapa (altitude 640 m, population 96,727). President Barrios of Guatemala was killed in battle here in

1885, while trying to reunite Central America by force. There are some good colonial-style domestic buildings. The church of Santiago Apóstol is particularly striking; almost the only one in El Salvador which shows strong indigenous influences (restored 1997-1998). Fiestas are on 18-21 July, Santiago Apóstol, and 12-16 August, San Roque.

**Tazumal** ruins next to the cemetery in Chalchuapa, are the tallest and probably the most impressive in El Salvador. They were built about AD 980 by the Pipil, with a 14-step pyramid. In 2004 the ruins suffered a partial collapse of the main pyramid due to the filtration of water which led to extensive excavations and application of new preservation techniques (getting rid of the old concrete) and many new discoveries were made. The excavations concluded in 2006. The site has been occupied since 5000 BC and in the **Museo Stanley H Boggs** ⓘ *Tue-Sun 0900-1600, T2408-4295*, you find artefacts found in Tazumal since the first excavations in the 1950s.

**Casa Blanca Archaeological Site** ⓘ *Km 78 Pan-American Hwy, T2408-4641, Tue-Sun 0900-1600, US$1*, just outside Chalchuapa, has several pyramids, ongoing excavations, and a museum that provides an insight into the archaeology of the area and information on indigo (*añil*) production. If you want to participate in the indigo workshop the cost is US$3. It's very interesting, educational and you can keep the products produced. Recommended.

# Santa Ana

**Where to stay**
Casa Frolaz 5
Casa Verde 6
Casa Vieja 7
El Faro 1
Sahara 4
Villa Napoli 8

**Restaurants**
Expresión 1
Los Horcones 2
Lover's Steak House 3
Talitunal 4

200 metres
200 yards

## Atiquizaya

The road continues 12 km west to Atiquizaya, a small, quiet town with one *hospedaje*, several good *pupuserías* (1600-2100) and **Restaurante Atiquizaya**, which can be found at the intersection with the main highway to Ahuachapán. At **Cataratas del Río Malacachupán** there is a beautiful 50-m-high waterfall cascading into a lagoon; it's a 1-km hike to get there. Nearby is **Volcán Chingo** on the Guatemalan border. Another attraction is **Aguas Calientes**, a hot spring that runs into the river and is excellent for a relaxing bath and for enjoying nature. It's a short ride from Atiquizaya, but bring a local guide.

## Metapán

**Texistepeque**, 17 km north of Santa Ana on the road to Metapán, has an 18th-century baroque church, with fiestas on 23-27 December and 15 January. The town was one of the main areas for indigo production, and colonial processing plants known as *obrajes* exist all around the area. Visit the indigo workshop and museum of **Licenciado Marroquín** just out of town.

**Metapán** is about 10 km northeast of Lago de Güija and 32 km north of Santa Ana. Its colonial baroque **Catedral de San Pedro**, completed by 1743, is one of the very few to have survived in El Salvador. The altarpieces have some very good silver work, and the façade is splendid. The Fiesta de San Pedro Apóstol runs from 25-29 June. There are lots of easy walks with good views towards **Lago de Metapán** and, further on, **Lago de Güija**. If planning to walk in the hills near Metapán, seek local advice and do not walk alone.

**Parque Acuático Apuzunga** ① *20 mins' drive from Metapán towards Santa Ana, T2483-8952, www.apuzunga.com*, is an adventure park by the Río Guajoyo, with fun pools, slides, zip-wires and a range of activities, including whitewater rafting and kayaking. There's a restaurant overlooking the river offering great views of the rafts shooting the rapids and the zip-wire over the water.

## Reserva Nacional y Natural Montecristo

A mountain track from Metapán gives access to El Salvador's last remaining cloudforest, where there is an abundance of protected wildlife. It now forms part of El Trifinio, or the International Biosphere 'La Fraternidad', administered jointly by Guatemala, Honduras and El Salvador. The summit of **Cerro Montecristo** (2418 m) is the point where the three borders meet. At the Casco Colonial, a former finca, is a visitor centre, with a small museum and wildlife exhibits. Nearby is an **orchid garden** with over 100 species (the best time to see them in flower is early spring), an orchard and a camping ground in the forest. The views are stunning, as is the change seen in flora and fauna with the altitude. This highest elevated part is closed for visitors during the mating and reproduction season of the animals (31 May to 31 October).

**Park information** 20 km from Metapán to the park. Park employees (*guardabosques*) escort visitors and a permit is obtained (via fax or email) through MARN (Ministry of Environment) in San Salvador, T2267-6259 (with Patrimonio Natural and ask for Solicitud de Ingreso a Parque Nacional Montecristo). You need to fill out a form and pay US$6 per person. A 4WD is necessary in the wet season (mid-May to mid-October). To hire a 4WD and driver, contact Sr Francisco Xavier Monterosa, Calle 15 de Septiembre Casa 40, T2402-2805/T7350-1111 (mobile). The trails to the summit take four hours. Camping is permitted, with three campsites inside the park, spacious and clean, under the pine trees, with toilets, barbecue grills and picnic benches and tables. An overnight stay is needed if you want to reach the summit; worthwhile to fully appreciate the dramatic changes in vegetation as you climb from 800-2400 m above sea level.

## Listings Santa Ana and around *map p442*

### Where to stay

#### Santa Ana

Many hotels close their doors from 2000, so arrive early if you can.

#### $$$-$$ Villa Napoli
*Quinta 'del Moral', Km 62-63 Cra Antigua a Santa Ana, T7808-0831, www.villanapoli-elsalvador.com.*
As the name suggests, this hospitable and highly recommended B&B is Italian-owned. Service is warm and typically Mediterranean with an emphasis on client satisfaction. Rooms are simple, homely and comfortable, complete with local artwork, cable TV, a/c, and Wi-Fi; some have special discount rates for multiple nights. There is also a pool.

#### $$ Sahara
*3 Calle Pte y 10 Av Sur, T2447-8865.*
This older hotel has adequate and comfortable rooms with good service, but it's a little overpriced. Popular for receptions and other events.

#### $$-$ Casa Verde
*7a Calle Pte, entre 8 y 10 Av Sur, 25 Santa Ana, T7840-4896, www.hostalcasaverde.com.*
An interesting 1940s house converted to a hostel. Rooms are clean and spacious and boast gallons of hot water. Dorms feature sturdy beds and unisex bathrooms. There are 2 kitchens with free coffee and water, Wi-Fi, lounge room with wide-screen TV and movies, 3 courtyards and a grill. As if that wasn't enough, there's a large pool and a roof terrace with panoramic views. Highly recommended.

#### $ Casa Frolaz
*29 Calle Pte 42-B between 8 and 10 Av Sur, T2440-5302, www.casafrolaz.blog.com.*
Beautiful and clean hostel with art, paintings, history books and a friendly reception, hot showers, tropical garden with hammocks and barbecue. Very popular with backpackers, constantly recommended.

#### $ Casa Vieja
*9a Av Sur 10, T7757-1145.*
This humble guesthouse has a patio, Wi-Fi and shared kitchen. Rooms are definitely no frills, but clean, spacious and comfortable, and the chilled out family atmosphere is definitely a winner. The owner Luis is very helpful and friendly.

#### $ El Faro I
*14 Av Sur 9 entre 9 y 11 Calle Pte, T2447-7787, www.hoteleselfaro.com.*
El Faro has 14 simple, economical rooms equipped with cable TV. Part of a local hospitality empire that includes 5 different establishments throughout the region, including lakeside accommodation; see their website for more details.

### Los Naranjos and around

#### $$$ Los Naranjos Town Houses
*Av 3, T7771-1484, losnaranjostownhouses@gmail.com.*
Nestled among the trees and built from wood and stone, 4 unique and cosy countryside houses. Each has their own kitchen, cable TV and access to the tropical garden. Some enjoy great mountain views from their balconies.

### $$$-$ Paso del Alaska Resort
*Cra Santa Ana-Sonsonate Km 83,*
*Vía Los Naranjos, T7731-7030,*
*www.pasodelaalaska.com.*
A great option for families and lovers of the
outdoors, Paso de Alaska is an adventure
tourism centre offering a host of activities
including climbing walls, canopy tours,
horse riding and hiking. Lodging includes
comfortable cabins, apartments and tents.
Their restaurant is reasonably popular too.
Day-trippers welcome.

## Metapán and around

### $$$ Villa Limón
*T2442-0149, www.hostalvillalimonmetapan.*
*com. 30 mins' drive up very rough road (4WD*
*only) northwest of Metapán.*
Cosy, clean rooms in wooden *cabañas*, and a
campsite in beautiful mountainside location,
with huge zip-wires over the pine forests.
Amazing views over Metapán, to lakes and
volcanoes beyond. Full board, or bring your
own food, advanced reservation essential;
guided walks to nearby waterfalls, and horse
riding available. Recommended.

### $$$-$$ Copa Cabana Aventura
*Lotificación Loma Linda, T2402-0750,*
*www.copacabanametapan.com.*
Enjoying fine vistas from its hilltop
perch above Metapán, Copa Cabana
offers comfortable rooms with shared
balconies and a pool. Their restaurant
serves *comida típica*.

### $$ San José
*Cra Internacional Km 113, Metapán,*
*near bus station, T2442-0556,*
*www.hoteleselsalvador.com.*
This modern option has generic quarters
with a/c, cable TV, safe parking and
a restaurant.

## Restaurants

Restaurants close quite early, between
2000 and 2100. *Comedores* are usually
cheap and good value or try the food
stalls beside the plaza or in front of the
cathedral. Look for excellent pineapples
in season.

### $$ Los Horcones
*On main plaza next to the cathedral.*
Like a jungle lodge inside, with pleasant
balcony dining and good cheap meals.

### $$ Lover's Steak House
*21 Calle Ote, entre Av Independencia y*
*3a Av Sur, Barrio San Miguelito.*
A very popular and long-standing place.
Great value, recommended.

### $$ Talitunal
*5 Av Sur 6. Mon-Sat 0900-1900.*
Vegetarian, attractive, good lunch, owner
is a doctor and expert on medicinal plants.

### $ Expresión
*11 Calle Pte 20, between Av 6 and 8,*
*T2440-1410, www.expresioncultural.org.*
A great little coffee bar, restaurant,
bookshop and internet café, with occasional
art exhibitions. The owner, Angel, speaks
English. An obligatory stop. Recommended.

### Chalchuapa
Several cheap and informal eateries with
good-quality meals can be found around
charming Parque Central.

### $$ Los Antojitos
*Calle Ramón Flores 6.*
Good meals.

### Metapán
Just before entering Metapán, 50 m off
the highway, at the rim of the Lagunita
Metapán, there are a couple of places
with an international menu offering good
fish from the lake, including **La Cocina de**

**Metapán**, T2423-0014, which also has a pool and terrace. Both have a/c.

**$$-$ Balompie**
*Opposite church on main square, T2402-3567.*
Upstairs restaurant, nice balcony, serves good-value mix of meat, seafood, pasta and snacks. Also serves the football stadium behind.

## Transport

**Bus** No 201 from Terminal del Occidente, **San Salvador**, US$1-1.25, 1 hr, every 10-15 mins, 0400-1830. To **La Libertad**, take 'autopista' route bus to San Salvador and change buses in Nueva San Salvador. Buses (**Melva**, **Pezzarossi** and others) leave frequently from 25 Calle Pte y 8 Av Sur, T2440-3606, for **Guatemala City**, full fare as from San Salvador, 4-4½ hrs including border stops. Alternatively, there are local buses to the border for US$0.45; they leave from the market. Frequent buses to **Metapán** and border at **Anguiatú**. No 238 follows a beautiful route to **Juayúa**; see also Border crossings box in Practicalities chapter.

### Atiquizaya

**Bus** There are frequent buses to the river from the central park in Atiquizaya; buses No 202 and 456 from Terminal Occidente in **San Salvador**, 2 hrs, US$0.90. From **Santa Ana**, 45 mins, US$0.40. All Ahuachapán buses stop in the Parque Central.

### Metapán

**Bus and car** From **Santa Ana** bus No 235, US$0.80, 1 hr. If driving **San Salvador**–Metapán, a bypass skirts Santa Ana. Bus No 211 to border at **Anguiatú**; see also Border crossings box in Practicalities chapter.

# Western Pacific coast

South of the capital, the seamy, steamy, rough-and-ready port town and low-key resort of La Libertad is the gateway to El Salvador's western Pacific coast, including the famous Costa del Bálsamo, which takes its name from pain-relieving balsam, once a major export of the region. On the steep slopes of the departments of Sonsonate and La Libertad, scattered balsam trees are still tapped for their aromatic juices, but the region is better known for its epic surf. A string of fishing villages turned low-key beach towns invite casual exploration with their blend of quiet beaches, private resorts, rustic digs and crashing Pacific waves. Buses travel along the coast as far as the border with Nicaragua and the journey offers stunning views of the rugged volcanic landscape.

## La Libertad   *Colour map 2, C5.*

### a popular, laid-back seaside resort, with great surf nearby

Just before Santa Tecla, a branch road turns south for 24 km to the fishing port of La Libertad (population 35,997), 34 km from San Salvador and just 25 minutes from the Comalapa International Airport. Despite its reputation for sketchiness, and being none too clean, this is a busy resort and the whole area has been remodelled. It now has an amphitheatre, soccer and basketball courts, and a Complejo Turístico where the old naval building once stood, with a *malecón* and several restaurants.

The pier is worth seeing for the fish market awnings and, when the fleet is in, for the boats hauled up out of the water along its length. The cemetery by the beach has tombstones painted in the national colours, blue and white. On the seafront are several hotels and restaurants. At a small plaza, by the **Punta Roca** restaurant, the road curves left to the point, offering fine views of La Libertad bay and along the coast. The market street is two blocks inland across from the central church. The coast to the east and west has good

**Best** for
Beaches ■ Diving ■ Surfing ■ Wildlife

fishing, surfing and bathing. The beaches are black volcanic sand (which can get very hot).

**Tip...**
La Libertad gets very crowded at weekends and holidays. For overnight stays the beaches to the west of La Libertad are better.

Dedicated surfers may wish to stay for a while, as the breaks at Punta Roca in Puerto La Libertad are rated among the best in the world. The season runs from November to April and the surf is excellent. Watch your belongings on the beach and don't stay out alone late at night.

The town holds an annual **Gastronomic Festival** in early December and has resurrected the tradition of *lunadas* (full-moon parties) in the dry season. Bonfires are lit on the beach, restaurants stay open late offering *comida típica*, and some places provide live music and themed nights.

### Around La Libertad

Just a few kilometres east of La Libertad on the Carretera Litoral is **Parque Nacional Walter Deininger** ① *run by the Ministry of Tourism, T2243-7835, www.elsalvador.travel, for more information contact ISTU on T2222-8000, www.istu.gob.sv, US$3.* There are rivers and caves, and the park is great for hiking. There is even a seed bank for endangered tree species, an array of medicinal plants and a nursery. The views are fantastic and it's a good way to learn more about the flora and fauna, guides are available upon request.

## Listings La Libertad

### Tourist information

There's a **tourist kiosk** (T2346-1634, Mon-Fri 0800-1600, Sat and Sun 0900-1300) in the modern white complex opposite the fish market pier. You can also find local information in Spanish at www.puertolalibertad.com.

### Where to stay

**$$$ AST Surf Hotel**
*Calle Principal Malecón, Punta Roca, T2312-5143, www.astsurfhotel.com.*
Overlooking the break at Punta Roca, AST is one of El Salvador's finest surf lodges. It has 7 boutique rooms with Wi-Fi, satellite TV, a/c and large beds; 4 of them have ocean views. Various packages are available. Built by surfers for surfers.

**$$ Pacific Sunrise**
*Calle Obispo, entrance of La Libertad, T2346-2000, www.hoteleselsalvador.com.*
Hotel with pool, restaurant and rooms over-looking the Obispo beach, which can be accessed via an ingenious pedestrian overpass. Good rates if more people share the rooms.

**$$ Rick**
*Behind Punta Roca.*
A well-established and well-worn old cheapie. It has clean, basic rooms with bath. Friendly, good value. Also has a restaurant.

### Restaurants

There are cheap restaurants near the pier, in the market, and around Playa La Paz, Playa El Obispo and El Sunzal. An area with new buildings located where the old Marina used to be close to the pier now hosts a series of great seafood eateries.

## $$ El Nuevo Altamar
*4 Calle Pte, Playa La Paz, T2335-3235.*
Good for seafood, steaks and bird.

## $$ La Curva de Don Gere
*East of the Faro mall at the entrance to*
*La Libertad, T2335-34360.*
Legendary place run by Geremias Alvarado
with several outlets in El Salvador (and the
US). One of the trademarks is their seafood
cream chowder in huge sizes including king
crab legs and other goodies.

## $$ La Dolce Vita
*Playa Las Flores, 200 m east of the Shell petrol
station, T2335-3592.*
Excellent seafood and pasta restaurant.

## $$ Mariscos Freddy and La Marea
*On the beach at Playa Obispo.*
Good-value seafood restaurants.

## $$-$ Punta Roca
*5 Av Sur, T2335-3261. Mon-Fri 0800-2000,
Sat and Sun 0800-2300.*
Try the shrimp soup. Owned by American
ex-pat Robert Rotherham, father of the
national surf champion Jimmy Rotherham.

## What to do

### Surfing
Look for board rentals and surf lessons
at hostels on the coast west of Puerto La
Libertad. Also look at www.sunzal.com,
which offers great surfing tours combined
with photography by local photographer,
El Vaquero.

### Punta Roca
*Restaurant in La Libertad, T2335-3261,
www.puntarocarockets.com.*
Owner Robert Rotherham (father of
Surf Champion Jimmy Rotherham) runs
surfboard rental, including boards for both
pros and beginners (see website for details).
He also arranges excursions including deep-
sea fishing for up to 3 people, see www.
puntaroca.com.sv (which features webcam
of area, surf and weather report) for more
information. English spoken. Recommended.

## Transport

**Bus** The station for buses going down to
Puerto La Libertad is now located at the
17th Av Sur at the intersection of Blv Venezuela
by the general cemetery in San Salvador. The
buses going to San Salvador from Puerto
La Libertad leave from the terminal at the
entrance of the city centre by the ball courts.
Departures from Puerto La Libertad along
the coast to **Sonsonate** at 0600.

For beaches around Acajutla and west,
take the direct bus from Terminal de
Occidente to Sonsonate and then on: No 285
to **Barra de Santiago**, No 28 to **Cara Sucia**
and the border and No 252 to **Acajutla**.

For **Costa del Sol**, **Zacatecoluca** and
connections toward eastern beaches go
from Terminal del Sur by San Marcos in
San Salvador.

---

## Costa del Bálsamo *Colour map 2, C5.*
**rugged black-sand beaches, rocky outcrops and hidden coves**

The Costa del Bálsamo unfolds between the ports of La Libertad and Acajutla. Playa
Conchalío, 3 km west of La Libertad, is the first in the series of sandy stretches,
closely followed by Playa El Cocal and Playa San Blas, which both cater to surfers,
and Playa El Majahual, which also has good waves but is not very clean or safe. All
of these beaches tend to be inundated with daytrippers at the weekend and during
national holidays.

★**Playa El Tunco** One of the most popular beaches for foreigners is Playa El Tunco. Offering easy access to two decent breaks – El Sunzal and La Bocana – it is renowned as one of the best surf spots in the area but is not so attractive for bathing. To get here take bus No 80 from La Libertad and get off at the turn-off where all the surfer hotels signs are posted (**Roca Sunzal** is the most visible one). It is then a short walk (a couple of blocks) to the seafront. **Club Salvadoreño** ⓘ *www.clubsalvadoreno.com*, and **Club Tecleño** ⓘ *www.clubtecleno.com*, both have their beach premises here and El Tunco itself has several hotels and restaurants. The nightlife can be buzzing, if decidedly low-key.

★**El Sunzal** Further up the road at Km 43.5 is El Sunzal. Although the breaks are amazing at Sunzal, there have been reports of theft on the beach at dusk, so choose your accommodation carefully (such as the upmarket Casa de Mar, see Where to stay, below) or stay at El Tunco instead.

★**Playa El Zonte** At Km 49.5 is **Playa Palmarcito**. This tiny and inviting beach is great for escaping the crowds and is good for novice surfers, as the breaks are not as violent as on other beaches. At Km 53.5 is Playa El Zonte, is another favourite among foreign tourists. It's a bit safer and quieter than El Tunco, being further away from La Libertad. The top-notch surf breaks has made El Zonte a place people stay longer than anticipated, and there are several well-established hotels with restaurant service. There are also several informal, cheap cafés and room rentals down at the beach.

The Carretera Litoral continues for a further 40 km or so to Acajutla past rocky bays, remote black-sand beaches and through tunnels. Take great care if you bathe along this coast, as it can be dangerous.

## Acajutla and around

At the junction of San Julián, a short journey south from Sonsonate, the coastal road heads south to the lowland city of Acajutla (population 52,359), El Salvador's main port serving the western and central areas, 85 km from San Salvador (the port is 8 km south of the Coastal Highway). It is a popular seaside resort during the summer for Salvadoreans, but lodging in the village is not considered safe for foreigners. There are some good seafood restaurants with panoramic views.

The rocky beach of **Los Cóbanos** (14 km south of Acajutla via San Julián, bus from Sonsonate) is very popular with weekending Salvadoreans and has one of only two coral reefs along the entire Central American Pacific coast, making it a popular dive spot. Fishermen arrange boat trips; negotiate a price. José Roberto Suárez at **Los Cobanos Village Lodge** ⓘ *T2420-5248, sas_tun@hotmail.com*, speaks English and rents boats and diving equipment.

The paved coastal road heads west running along the coast for 43 km before reaching the Guatemalan frontier at **La Hachadura**.

The black-sand beaches northwest of Acajutla at **Metalío** and Costa Azul (mostly full of private beach houses) and **Barra de Santiago** are recommended, although there are few public facilities. Barra de Santiago is a peninsula, 30 km west of Acajutla, and the beach is reached along a 7 km compact dirt road or across a beautiful lagoon. The entire area is a protected natural area in the process of being declared an ecological reserve to protect endangered species, including turtles, crocodiles and sea falcons. The *garza azul* (blue heron) is one of the amazing rare birds only found here. The mangrove is the third largest in El Salvador. This beach has an island named **El Cajete,** which has an archaeological site dating back to around AD 900. There are several pyramids but the area has not been excavated. **El Capricho Beach House** is a beautiful beachfront hotel here (see Where to stay, page 453).

★**Parque Nacional El Imposible** *Colour map 2, C5.*
*Park entrance is US$6, payable at the gate. For more information contact Salvanatura office, 33 Av Sur 640, Col Flor Blanca, San Salvador, T2279-1515, www.salvanatura.org. Voluntary donation of US$4-5 a day. To get to the park, take the San Salvador–Sonsonate bus, and then bus No 259 to Cara Sucia. Pickups leave for the park at 1100 and 1400. From Guatemala and the border, regular buses heading for San Salvador pass through Cara Sucia from where you catch the 1100 and 1400 pickups.*

So called because of the difficulty of transporting coffee through its ravines and down to the coast, today this 'impossibility' has helped preserve some of the last vestiges of El Salvador's flora and fauna on the rocky slopes and forests of the coastal **Cordillera de Apaneca**. Mule trains used to travel through the region, navigating the steep passes from which the park takes its name.

Among the mammals are puma, ocelot, agouti and ant bear; the birds include black-crested eagle, white hawk and other birds of prey, black and white owls, and woodpeckers. There is also a wide variety of reptiles, amphibians and insects, the greatest diversity in the country. There are eight different strata of forest, and over 300 species of tree have been identified. There is a small visitor centre, and rivers and natural pools to swim in. Trained naturalist guides from the nearby community of San Miguelito accompany visitors into the park, helping to identify season specific trails and routes, and pointing out interesting plants, animals and other attractions along the way.

## Listings Costa del Bálsamo

### Where to stay

#### Playa El Cocal

**$$$ Punta Roca Surf Resort**
*T2300-0474, www.puntaroca.com.sv.*
Owned by National Champion Jimmy Rotherham, Punta Roca is a solid option for surfers. Accommodation includes simple rooms and bungalows.

#### Playa San Blas

**$$$ Sabas Beach Resort**
*Cra Litoral Km 39, T2346-0029, www.sabasbeachresort.com.*
Nestled on the beach with easy access to Punta Roca and El Sunzal, Sabas resort is aimed squarely at surfers. Rooms enjoy

beach, ocean or mountain views. There's a pool, bar and open-air seafood restaurant.

#### Playa El Majahual

**$$ Hotel y Restaurante Santa Fe**
*Cra Litoral Km 40.5, at the entrance to Majahual beach, T2310-6508.*
Safe, relaxed and functional place with a pool and restaurant. Popular with Salvadoreans.

#### Playa El Tunco

**$$$ Tekuani Kal**
*Cra Litoral Km 42, T2355-6500, www.tekuanikal.com.*
Tekuani Kal is a modern boutique option. With commanding ocean views from

their private balconies, rooms are bright, colourful, spacious and well attired. There is also a pool, bar and a fairly decent restaurant overlooking the waves.

### $$ Roca Sunzal
*Km 42, T2389-6126, www.rocasunzal.com.*
One of the best hotels in El Tunco, beautifully located in front of the beach. Great views, pool, good food in restaurant. The suites have artsy and original decor. Great value and good service. Recommended.

### $$-$ Hotel Mopelia
*T2389-6265,*
*www.hotelmopelia-salvador.com.*
Owned by Frenchman Gilles, Hotel Mopelia is a popular spot, with a bar and pizzeria **Tunco Veloz**; see Restaurants below. Accommodation includes economical 'backpacker' rooms with shared bath and more pricey 'suites' with a/c. There is a pool.

### $ La Guitarra
*Cra Litoral Km42, T2389-6390,*
*www.surfingeltunco.com.*
Fun place with a rocking beach bar. Accommodation includes 18 rooms with and without a/c, discounts for longer stays, Wi-Fi.

### $ Papayas Lodge
*T2389-6231, www.papayalodge.com.*
Family-run surf hostel. Clean rooms with fans, use of kitchen and safe. Owned by Salvadorean surf legend, Papaya. Board sales and repair and surf classes. Recommended.

### $ Sol Bohemio
*Cra Litoral Km39, T7262-0497,*
*www.solbohemio.com.*
Offer reasonable rates, as do a couple of the smaller hostels, such as **Barriles**. They have a pool.

### Playa El Sunzal

### $$$$ B Boutique
*Cra Litoral Km 45.9, Tamanique, T7210-9258,*
*www.bboutiquehotel.com.*

Crisp, classy, chic and minimalist, B Boutique enjoys unrivalled ocean views from its enviable cliff side perch. Rooms are calming, spacious and unbeatably stylish. When not admiring the sunset, guests can enjoy a private infinity pool, terrace and solarium. Recommended.

### $$$$-$$$ Casa de Mar
*www.casademarhotel.com.*
This luxury hotel, located just in front of the breaks, is a good option if you want a splurge or to dine in their gourmet seafood restaurant, **Café Sunzal**, which has great food and panoramic views. Breakfast and Wi-Fi included.

### $$$ Cielo Vista Hotel and Spa
*Cra Litoral Km 43, T2374-2236,*
*www.cielovistahotel.com.*
Secluded and tranquil, Cielo Vista is a very special and romantic lodging set in beautiful lush grounds. It offers 5 luxury suites with individual themes, all impeccably furnished with 4-poster beds, private patios and jacuzzis. Spa treatments are available at extra cost. Stylish, luxurious and extravagant. Rates are per person. Recommended.

### $$$-$$ Kayu Resort
*Cra Litoral Km 43.5, T2389-6289,*
*www.kayuelsalvador.com.*
Perched above the beach, Kayu resort is an exclusive surf lodge with 7 cheery rooms, including 'economical' and 'luxury' options. There's an infinity pool and jacuzzi, both with calming ocean views. Breakfast included and tours available.

### $$ Hostal Los Almendros
*Cra Litoral Km 44.5, T7727 3194,*
*www.go2losalmendros.com.*
This cosy little surf hostel offers 8 reasonable, affordable rooms with fan and private bath. Food and tours are available and you can also enjoy ocean views and/or hammock time on the upper terrace.

## $ Sunzal Point

*Cra Litoral Km 44, T7327-9869,*
*www.sunzalpoint.com.*

Sunzal Point claims to be the oldest surf
lodge in El Salvador, originally opened
by the Angulo family in 1961. It has been
renovated several times since then but
remains a solid option for youthful travellers.
It offers basic dorms and rooms, hammocks,
kitchen, board rental, yoga classes, a party
atmosphere and budget-friendly rates.

### Playa Palmarcito

## $$$ Atami Escape Resort

*Km 49.5, T2355-7923, www.atami.com.sv.*
Perched atop a cliff next to Palmarcito in
2-ha grounds is this beautiful place with
its own beach, 4 pools, plus saltwater pools
and a water slide. Good rooms with a/c,
cable TV and Wi-Fi. There's an expensive
seafood restaurant, 2 bars and gardens.
Day visitors US$20.

## $ El Palmarcito

*Km 50, T7942-4879, www.elpalmarcito.com.*
This beachfront hotel offer surf lessons and
board rental. There's also a restaurant.

### Playa El Zonte

## $ Esencia Nativa

*T7737-8879, www.esencianativa.com.*
Run by surfer Alex Novoa, with cheap
rooms, dorm and pool. Popular restaurant
serves range of options, including great
veggie food and is busy at weekends.
Surfing lessons and board rentals available.
Popular with surfers.

## $ Horizonte Surf Camp

*T2323-0099, saburosurfcamp@hotmail.com.*
Simple bungalows, some with a/c, set in
attractive gardens with a pool, beachfront
restaurant offering good food, and board
rental. Clean, good service. Good choice
for surfers. Room for up to 6 people on
3rd floor. Great view.

## $ La Casa de Frida Hotel

*T2302-6068, www.lacasadefrida.com.*
Lodging in cabins behind restaurant
with beachfront garden. Cosy place
with hammocks.

## Acajutla and around

## $$$$ La Cocotera Resort & Ecolodge

*Barra de Santiago, T2245-3691,*
*www.lacocoteraresort.com.*
Rates per person are fully inclusive – full-
board and airport transfers. Small luxurious
resort with thatched bungalows on the
beach and with mangroves behind; pool,
kayaks, and tours available. Very peaceful.
Recommended.

## $$ Los Cóbanos Village Lodge

*Cra Acajutla, turn right at*
*Restaurant Marsolie, T2420-5248,*
*www.loscobanos.com.sv.*
Beachfront cabins with pool and restaurant.
Scuba diving, surfing, fishing on offer. TV
and internet available.

## $$-$ El Capricho Beach House

*Barra de Santiago (same owners as*
*Ximena's), take direct bus No 285 to La Barra*
*de Santiago, which departs twice daily*
*from Sonsonate, or bus towards border and*
*pickup from turn-off, T2260-2481, www.*
*ximenasguesthouse.com (under Capricho).*
Beautiful beach and located in a wildlife
reserve, close to mangroves and the tip of the
peninsula. Clean rooms with bath and a/c,
cabin with dorms and ceiling fan. Tours of the
mangroves, fishing, surf lessons and board
rental all available. Transport from the capital
and tours to Parque Nacional El Imposible
available. A safe place. Recommended.

## Parque Nacional El Imposible

### $$ Hostal El Imposible
*T2411-5484.*
With restaurant/bar area, pool and small trail. 5 cabins sleeping 2-6 people have private bath, hot water and small terrace, also restaurant service. Information from **Salvanatura** in San Salvador, T2279-1515. www.salvanatura.org.

### Restaurants

### El Sunzal
Around the Sunzal area are several very good restaurants, such **Hola Beto's**, **Las Pamas Mirador** and **La Curva de Don Gere**. All have beautiful vistas along the coast.

### $$ Café Sunzal
*Km 43.5 Cra, T2389-6019, www.cafesunzal.com.*
Great seafood and steak house, exquisite international cuisine. Excellent views over El Sunzal beach.

### Playa Palmarcito

### $ Restaurante Las Palmas
*Just in front of the beach.*
Great meals and low prices.

### Playa San Blas and Playa El Tunco
Tunco is on the rise and new places keep popping up.

### $$ Hotel and Restaurante Roca Sunzal
Delicious seafood and a very good bar. All with an excellent beachfront location. Recommended.

### $$ Hotel Mopelia
*See Where to stay, above.*
This place has a pizzeria and their well-stocked bar is open all week.

### $$-$ La Bocana
*In front of the Tunco (pig).*
Owned and operated by Luis who's very friendly. Beachfront, offering great view from 2nd storey. Good seafood, great value.

### $ Dale Dale Café
*Behind Roca Sunzal.*
Coffee shop serving delicious brownies, muffins and coffee to go with it.

### $ Erika
*T2389-6054.*
Run by owner Amelia Hernández. Very popular with the locals. 2nd-storey palm thatched place with great atmosphere.

### El Zonte

### $ Esencia Nativa
*See Where to stay, above.*
Run by charismatic Alex Novoa, Esencia Nativa has an innovative menu, including good veggie options and pizzas, served at the poolside. Folks in the know come down from the capital just to get a bite.

### $ Horizonte Surf Resort
An attractive restaurant at the beachfront run by Japanese Saburo. The view from 2nd floor is especially lovely. Good value.

### $ La Casa de Frida
*El Zonte, T2253-2949, www.lacasadefrida.com.*
A great restaurant located in a large beachfront garden dotted with tables and hammocks.

### Transport

**Acajutla and around**
58 km from **Santa Ana**.

**Bus** No 207 from Terminal Occidente, **San Salvador** (US$2.80), or No 252 from **Sonsonate** (US$0.30).

# Northern
## El Salvador

The obscure archaeological site of Cihuatán may appeal to diehard ruin-seekers, but bohemian Suchitoto is the undisputed highlight of northern El Salvador. The town itself is a tranquil place to unwind and the surrounding countryside, punctuated by highland waterfalls and the vast blue expanse of Cerrón Grande reservoir, is worth exploring too. Towards the Honduran border, La Palma is framed by fragrant pine forests and the country's highest peak, El Pital. On the other side of the reservoir, Chalatenango is the gateway to some fairly remote and bucolic communities. From here, a backdoor route leads all the way to Perquín and the Honduran border in the east (see page 470).

**Best** for
Arts ▪ Birds ▪ Crafts ▪ Suchitoto

The old highway, Troncal del Norte (CA 4) used to be the only acess to the north from the capital, but has been replaced with a modern highway. This can be accessed from Boulevard de la Constitución, in the northeastern part of San Salvador, and swirls west around the Volcán de San Salvador towards the Pan-American Highway and branches out to Nejapa, Quezaltepeque and Apopa to the north. It is 2½ hours by car from San Salvador to La Palma, then 11 km to the border at El Poy; see page 461.

## Apopa and Tonacatepeque

*Bus 38 B from San Salvador to Apopa, US$0.35.*

Marking the junction with the road to Quetzaltepeque (12 km), Apopa has been subsumed into San Salvador's metropolitan sprawl and few travellers stop here. A paved road runs east from here to Tonacatepeque, an attractive small town on a high plateau. It has a small textile industry and is in an agricultural setting; check out the charming park and the colonial church. There has been some archaeological exploration of the town's original site, 5 km away. A paved road from Tonacatepeque runs 13 km south to the Pan-American Highway, some 5 km from the capital. At the same junction, a highway runs north from the Pan-American Highway to Suchitoto.

## Aguilares

From Apopa, it's 21 km to Aguilares, 4 km beyond which are the ruins of **Cihuatán** ① *Tue-Sun 0900-1600.* The name means 'place of women' and was presided over by female royalty. This was the largest city in Mesoamerica during the Toltec period, when the city was surrounded by extended fortification measuring more than 10 sq km. The biggest archaeological site in the country has several tall pyramids, ball courts and *temazcales* (ritual saunas). For more information about the site, contact chief archaeologist Paul Amaroli at FUNDAR in San Salvador, T2235-9453, www.fundar.org.sv.

A road goes from Aguilares heading east to Suchitoto. If heading north, see page 460.

## ★Suchitoto

*See also www.gaesuchitoto.com and www.suchitoto-el-salvador.com. For information in English, contact US citizen Roberto Broz who runs Hostel and Restaurant El Gringo; see Restaurants, below.*

Suchitoto (population 24,786), meaning 'the place of birds and flowers' in Náhuatl, was founded by the Pipil more than 1000 years ago. In 1528 the capital was moved to Suchitoto for 15 years as the villa of San Salvador suffered attacks from local tribes. In 1853 an earthquake destroyed much of San Salvador and many affluent families moved to Suchitoto leaving a lasting impression on the town.

Today it is a small, very attractive colonial town with cobbled streets, balconied houses and an interesting church. It is one of the favourite tourist spots in the country, with cultural traditions kept alive by the many artists living and working there. Several hotels and restaurants offer fantastic views towards Suchitlán and Volcán Guazapa. More than 200 species of bird have been identified in the area, and white-tailed deer inhabit the local woods.

The town was almost completely deserted in the early 1990s after 12 years of civil war which severely affected the region – 90% of the population left, leaving Suchitoto a virtual ghost town. However, a cultural revival has stimulated a range of activities and events, and the town is now considered the cultural capital of the country. Life centres on the main plaza which every evening becomes a bustle of people wandering the streets. Suchitoto's telegraph poles have been decorated by artist Paulo Rusconi, and Parque San Martín, to the west of town, is dotted with modern sculptures, some made using materials left over from the war. Arts and cultural festivals with internationally renowned artists take place every February. Another local festivity is the *Palo Encebado*, a competition involving attempts to clamber to the top of long greasy poles, and the *cerdo encebado* where a pig smeared with lard is chased through town and is kept by the first person who manages to grab it.

The **Teatro de Las Ruinas** is almost fully restored and hosts concerts and events. Contact Sra Chávez, T2335-1086, for more information. **Iglesia de Santa Lucía** ① *Mon-Sat 0800-1200 and 1400-1600, all day Sun*, built in 1858 with wooden and hollow columns, has also been restored with a lot of stencil work inside. There is a splendid view from the church tower. **Casa Museo de Alejandro Cotto** ① *daily 0900-1200 and 1400-1600, US$4, guided tour in Spanish (T2335-1140)*, home of movie director Alejandro Cotto, is an interesting museum with more than 132 paintings of El Salvador's most renowned artists, collections of books and music instruments.

**Suchitoto**

100 metres
100 yards

**Where to stay**
El Gringo Hostel 2
El Tejado 5
Hostel Los Sánchez 7
Los Almendros de
San Lorenzo 1
Posada Alta Vista 3

Posada de Suchitlán 4
Posada Blanca Luna 8
Villa Balanza 6

**Restaurants**
Café El Obraje 1
El Dorado 6

El Gringo 2
Los Almendros de
San Lorenzo 4
Lupita del Portal 3
Villa Balanza 8

## Around Suchitoto

A 30-minute walk north of town leads to the **Embalse Cerrón Grande** (also known as **Lago de Suchitlán**). **Proyecto Turístico Pesquero Puerto San Juan** is a harbour with boat shuttle services and a complex of restaurants, craft shops and cafés on the lake shore. This is the departure point for boat excursions across to remote areas in neighbouring Chalatenango, ask around and negotiate prices. Trips are available to five islands including **Isla de Los Pájaros**, which makes an interesting trip (one to 1½ hours).

Ferries cross the Embalse Cerrón Grande for San Luis del Carmen (25 minutes to San Luis, frequent departures all day), where there is **Comedor Carmen**, and buses to Chalatenango. The ferry also makes a stop at the small village of **San Francisco Lempa**.

**Los Tercios**, a waterfall with striking, gigantic, black, hexagonal-shaped basaltic columns, can be reached by car, foot and by *lancha*. It is at its most impressive in the wet season when the full force of nature is on show. Walk 10-15 minutes from town down the very steep road towards the lake known as Calle al Lago de Suchitlán. Lifts are available for about US$2-3 if you can't face the steep climb back to town afterwards, ask around. At the lake shore, where there are *comedores*, ask for a *lanchero*. A *lancha* to the base of the trail to Los Tercios is US$5-6 (negotiable) and takes 10 minutes (ask the *lanchero* to point out the trail).

**La Ciudad Vieja**, one-time site of the capital, is 10 km from Suchitoto. An original Pipil town, it was taken over by the Spanish who made it their central base for 17 years before electrical storms, lack of water, and cholera forced them to flee. It is a private site but can be visited. There are plans for a museum and a café.

Boat trips go to lakeside villages associated with the FMLN in the civil war. On the road to Aguilares, 12 km away, a **Bosque de la Reconciliación** is being developed at the foot of Cerro de Guazapa. Contact **CESTA** ① *T2213-1400, www.cesta-foe.org*, in San Salvador, or contact the park directly on T2213-1403 and speak to Jesús Arriola. Also, 3 km along this road is **Aguacayo** and a large church, badly damaged during the war.

## Listings North of San Salvador *map p457*

### Tourist information

#### Suchitoto

**MITUR tourist office**
*Parque Centenario, T2335-1835. Mon-Fri 0800-1700, Sat-Sun 0800-1600.*

**Muncipal tourist office**
*Calle Francisco Morazán 7, next to the telephone office, T2335-1782, www. suchitoto-el-salvador.com. Daily 0800-1700.*
Daily tours of the city centre, to Los Tercios waterfall and to Lake Suchitlán.

### Where to stay

#### Suchitoto

**$$$$ Los Almendros de San Lorenzo**
*4 Calle Pte, next to police station, T2335-1200, www.hotelsalvador.com.*
In a restored colonial house with exclusive rooms, suites and delightful gardens. Delicious meals in the restaurant (see Restaurants below); people come from the capital to lunch here at weekends. Art gallery **Pascal**, across the street, has great exhibits, textiles and handicrafts (same French owner).

### $$$$-$$$ Posada de Suchitlán
*Final 4 Calle Pte, at the western end of town, T2335-1064, www.laposada.com.sv.*
Colonial-style, beautifully tiled and decorated, excellent hotel and restaurant, including local speciality, *gallo a chichi* (chicken cooked in maize wine); stunning lake views.

### $$$ El Tejado
*3 Av Norte 58, Barrio Concepción, T2335-1769, www.eltejado suchitoto.net.*
Beautifully restored colonial house with attractively furnished and spotless rooms, some with balcony; pool and gorgeous view of Lake Suchitlán. Pretty terrace restaurant.

### $$ Hacienda La Bermuda
*Km 34.8 Cra a Suchitoto, T2226-1839, www.labermuda.com.*
Hotel and restaurant (see below) with frequent cultural activities, located just outside Suchitoto. Very atmospheric and full of history.

### $$ Villa Balanza
*North edge of Parque San Martín, T2335-1408. On the street behind the restaurant of the same name and 250 m to the right down the hill.*
Small rooms but nicely furnished, with lovely views of lake from the hotel balcony.

### $$-$ Posada Alta Vista
*Av 15 de Septiembre 8, near the square, T2335-1645, www.hotelposadaaltavista.com.*
Good rooms, although the cheaper ones can be hot. Helpful, friendly staff. Rooftop terrace with great view of the town.

### $ El Gringo Hostel
*Calle Francisco Morazán 27, T2327-2351, www.elgringosuchitoto.com.*
A small and cosy hostel with just 2 private rooms and 1 shared dorm. There's a simple shared kitchen, book exchange, chill out patio and Wi-Fi. Simple, economical, and

definitely no frills. American-owned, as the name might suggest.

### $ Hostal Los Sánchez
*4a Calle Pte.*
The Sanchez brothers have received lots of good reports for their kindness and hospitality. The rooms here are clean, simple, very spacious, and economical, and there's a good rooftop terrace with views over the town. Cable TV but no Wi-Fi.

### $ Posada Blanca Luna
*1a Av Sur y 1a Calle Ote 7, a block south of the church, T2335-1661, www.blancaluna.comoj.com.*
This tranquil and slightly bohemian guesthouse has simple, economical rooms set around a small patio adorned with a hammock, tables and chairs. There is a small but functional communal kitchen, free drinking water and Wi-Fi at extra cost.

## Restaurants

### Suchitoto
Local specialities include *salporitas* (made of corn meal) and *chachamachas*. Try the *pupusas* in the market. Several eating options around the main plaza; many restaurants only open weekend evenings, especially during off season.

### $$$ Los Almendros de San Lorenzo
*4 Calle Pte, next to police station, Barrio El Centro (see Where to stay, above), T2335-1200, plebailly@hotel elsalvador.com.*
Best restaurant in Suchitoto. Has a French chef, serves succulent meals and visitors come from San Salvador on weekends to dine here.

### $$ El Dorado
*By Lake Suchitlán, T2225-5103, www.gaesuchitoto.com.*
Bar and restaurant that hosts frequent concerts.

## $$ Hacienda La Bermuda
*See Where to stay, above.*
Colonial-style restaurant with pool and cultural events.

## $$ Lupita del Portal
*Parque Centenario, T2335-1679.*
*Open until midnight.*
The current hot spot. Serves gourmet *pupusas* with home-grown herbs, Salvadorean specialities and natural teas. Owner René Barbón also runs **Suchitoto Adventure Outfitters** from here, an excellent tour operator (see What to do, below).

## $$ Villa Balanza
*Parque San Martín, T2335-1408, www.villabalanzarestaurante.com.*
Rustic farm decor and antique bric-a-brac, serving excellent local cuisine, steaks and fish, and home-made fruit preserves.

## $ Café El Obraje
*Next to Santa Lucía church, T2335-1173.*
*Closed Tue.*
Clean and reasonably priced, with good breakfast variety.

## $ Restaurant El Gringo
*See Where to stay, above.*
*Mon-Sat 0800-2000.*
Serves *pupusas* (normal and gourmet), Tex/Mex and typical Salvadorean foods. Famous for veggie burritos.

## What to do

### Suchitoto
**Suchitoto Adventure Outfitters**, *Calle San Martín 4b, T7921-4216.* Excellent local tours, including 5-hr horse-riding trip up Volcán Guazapa to former guerrilla camp, fascinating insights on war history (US$35). Owner René Barbón speaks excellent English and is extremely knowledgeable and helpful.

## Transport

### Suchitoto
**Bus** To **Aguilares**, No 163 every 30 mins, 0500-1800, 30 mins. Regular buses (No 129) from Terminal Oriente, **San Salvador**, beginning at 0330. The bus stops at the market and leaves town for the capital from 3 Av Norte. To **Ilobasco** by dirt road, 0800 and 1000, returning 1230 and 1430.

**Ferry** Cross the Embalse Cerrón Grande (Lago de Suchitlán) for **San Luis del Carmen** (25 mins to San Luis, frequent departures throughout the day, will leave whenever full, cars US$8, foot passengers US$1) where there is **Comedor Carmen**, and buses linking to **Chalatenango**. Small *lanchas* also make the short crossing from San Juan to San Francisco Lempa on the north shore, with onward buses to Chalatenango, US$5 for the whole boat (up to approximately 10 passengers).

## Chalatenango *Colour map 2, C5.*

### a delightful little town

Highway 4 continues north from Aguilares, passing the western extremity of the Cerrón Grande reservoir. A branch to the east skirts the northern side of the reservoir to Chalatenango (population 30,808, altitude 450 m), capital of the department of the same name.

It is the centre of an important region of traditional livestock farms. It has a good market and several craft shops; for example, **Artesanías Chalateca**, for bags and hammocks. The weekly horse fairs, where horses, saddles and other equipment are for sale, are very popular. The town's annual fairs and fiestas are on 24 June and 1-2 November.

Rural Chalatenango is mainly agricultural and has many remote villages; there are a number of non-governmental organizations working in the area.

## Listings Chalatenango

### Where to stay

**$ La Ceiba**
*1a Calle Pte, near 5a Av Norte, behind the military fort, Barrio Las Flores, T2301-1080.*
Basic rooms with shower and bath and a/c in a quiet corner of town.

### Restaurants

There are several restaurants to choose from including:

**$$$-$ Rinconcito El Nuevo**
*Next to the military fort.*
Good restaurant with an à la carte menu as well as *pupusas*. Check out bizarre collection of old sewing machines, irons, typewriters and other knick-knacks on display in the adjacent colonnade.

### Transport

**Bus** No 125 from Oriente terminal, **San Salvador**, US$2, 2½ hrs.

## La Palma and around  Colour map 2, C5.

**charming village in pine-clad mountains, and well worth a visit**

The main road continues north through Tejutla to La Palma (altitude 1100 m, population 12,235). It is famous for its local crafts, particularly brightly painted wood carvings and hand-embroidered tapestries. Also produced are handicrafts made from clay, metal, cane and seeds. There are a number of workshops in La Palma where you can see handicrafts being made and buy some (see box, page 463). The Fiesta del Dulce Nombre de María takes place mid- or late February.

The picturesque village of **San Ignacio**, 6 km north of La Palma, has two or three small *talleres* producing handicrafts (20 minutes by bus, US$0.10 each way).

San Ignacio is the departure point for buses ascending a safe but steep road leading up to the highest mountain of El Salvador, El Pital (2730 m). As you reach the pass below the mountain top, the road branches to **Las Pilas** to the left and **Miramundo** to the right. Both Miramundo and Las Pilas have small agricultural communities, specializing in organic crops. The extensive cabbage fields combined with the pine-clad mountains make for beautiful vistas.

If you take the road from the summit to the right, you end up in Miramundo which gives a view of pretty much all El Salvador. On clear days you can see almost all the volcanoes in the country, including Volcán Pacaya and Volcán Agua in Guatemala. This is no doubt the best view in the country.

### Border with western Honduras

The road continues north to the border at **El Poy**, for western Honduras; see Border crossings box in Practicalities chapter. From Citalá, there is a small town with a colonial church and a potent war history (you still see bullet holes in the walls of the houses on street corners). One kilometre west off the highway just before El Poy, an adventurous road leads to Metapán. Two buses daily take three hours to travel the 40 km, a rough but beautiful journey.

## Where to stay

**$$$$-$$$ El Pital Highland**
*East of San Ignacio at the edge of the Reserva Biologica El Pital, T2221-6954, www.elpital.com.sv.*
Suitable for adventurous couples or families, El Pital Highland has 3 highland *cabañas* of various sizes, all equipped with chimneys for those chilly nights (do bring warm clothing too). There are also cheaper rooms. Rates include 3 meals. It's best to contact the lodge in advance of your visit.

**$$$ Entre Pinos**
*San Ignacio, T2335-9312, www.entrepinosresortandspa.com.*
1st-class resort complex, a/c, pool, cable TV, sauna and small shop.

**$$$-$$ Hostal El Pital Lecho de Flores**
*Cantón Río Chiquito, southern edge of the Reserva Biological El Pital, T2313-5470, www.elpitallechodeflores.com.*
Hostal El Pital has 6 *cabañas* built from stone or wood, each suitable for up to 4-6. There is a restaurant and various packages to cover costs of lodging, food and guides.

**$$ Hotel La Palma**
*Troncal del Norte, 84 km Cra, La Palma, T2335-9012, www.hotellapalma.com.sv.*
32 large rooms, clean, with bath. Friendly, with good restaurant, beautiful gardens, good pool, ceramics workshop, parking and petrol station. Also runs guided walks around local trails, including El Tecomate, Río Nunuapa and Los Pozos. Recommended.

**$ Casa de Huéspedes Las Orquídeas**
*Las Pilas.*
Run by a local farming family. Ask for a guided trip to the mountain top nearby, for an unrivalled panoramic view and free peaches.

**$ Hostal Miramundo**
*Miramundo, T2219-6251, www.hotelmiramundo.com.*
Nice rooms with hot water. A restaurant, great food and great views. Recommended.

**$ Las Praderas de San Ignacio**
*San Ignacio, a few kilometres before the border, T2350-9330, www.hotelpraderasdesanignacio.com.*
Cabins, beautiful gardens and an inexpensive restaurant.

## Restaurants

In Ignacio, there are many local *comedores*, including Comedor Elisabeth, which offer delicious *comida a la vista* including fresh milk, cheese and cream.

**$ El Poyetón**
*Barrio San Antonio, 1 block from church, La Palma.*
Reliable, serves simple dishes.

**$ La Estancia**
*Calle Principal, La Palma, T2335-9049. Open 0800-2000.*
Good menu, useful bulletin board.

## Shopping

**Handicrafts**
There are more than 80 arts and crafts workshops in La Palma; www.lapalma elsalvador.com, provides a complete list

## ON THE ROAD

## Handicrafts of El Salvador

The artists' village of **La Palma**, in a pine-covered valley under Miramundo mountain, is 84 km north of the capital 10 km south of the Honduran frontier. Here, in 1971, the artist **Fernando Llort** 'planted a seed' known as the *copinol* (a species of the locust tree) from which sprang the first artists' cooperative, now called **La Semilla de Dios** (Seed of God). The copinol seed is firm and round; on it the artisans base a spiritual motif that emanates from their land and soul.

The town and its craftspeople are now famous for their work in wood, including exotically carved *cofres* (adorned wooden chests), and traditional Christmas *muñecas de barro* (clay dolls) and ornamental angels. Wood carvings, other crafts and the designs of the original paintings by Llort, are all produced and exported from La Palma to the rest of El Salvador and thence worldwide.

In 1971 the area was almost exclusively agricultural. Today 75% of the population of La Palma and neighbouring San Ignacio are engaged directly or indirectly in producing handicrafts. The painter **Alfredo Linares** (born 1957 in Santa Ana, arrived in La Palma 1981 after studying in Guatemala and Florence) has a gallery in La Palma, employing and assisting local artists. His paintings and miniatures are marketed abroad, yet you will often find him working in the family pharmacy next to the gallery. Many of La Palma's images are displayed on the famous Hilasal towels. If you cannot get to La Palma, visit the shop/gallery/workshop of Fernando Llort in San Salvador, **Arbol de Dios**.

Twenty kilometres from the capital is the indigenous town of **Panchimalco**, where weaving on the loom and other traditional crafts are being revived. Many Náhuatl traditions, customs, dances and the language survived here as the original indigenous people hid from the Spanish conquistadors in the valley beneath the Puerta del Diablo (now in Parque Balboa). In 1996 the painter Eddie Alberto Orantes and his family opened the **Centro de Arte y Cultura Tunatiuh**, named after a Náhuatl deity who is depicted as a human face rising as a sun over a pyramid. The project employs local youths (from broken homes, or former addicts) in the production of weavings, paintings and ceramics.

In the mountains of western El Salvador, villages in the coffee zone, such as **Nahuizalco**, specialize in weaving henequen, bamboo and reed into table mats and wicker furniture. There are also local artists like Maya sculptor **Ahtzic Selis**, who works with clay and jade. East of the capital, at **Ilobasco** (60 km), many ceramic workshops produce items including the famous *sorpresas*, miniature figures enclosed in an egg shell. In the capital there are craft markets, and throughout the country, outlets range from the elegant to the rustic. Everywhere, artists and artisans welcome visitors into their workshops.

of all the workshops and how to contact them. Many workshops have come together and formed a **Placita Artesanal**, an artisan market, which is located by the Catholic church on the central plaza.

**Cooperativa La Semilla de Dios**, *Plaza San Antonio*. The original cooperative founded by Fernando Llort in 1971. It has a huge selection of crafts and paintings and is helpful.

**Gallery Alfredo Linares**, *Sr Linares' house (if gallery is unattended, ask in the pharmacy)*, *T2335-9049. Daily 0900-1800.* Friendly well-known artist whose paintings sell for US$18-75. Recommended.

**Palma City**, *Calle Principal behind church.* Sra Alicia Mata is very helpful and will help find objects, whether she stocks them or not (wood, ceramics, *telas*, etc).

## Transport

**Bus** From **San Salvador**, Terminal de Oriente, No 119, US$2.25, 3 hrs, last bus at 1630. To La Palma from Amayo, crossroads with Troncal del Norte (main highway to San Salvador), and E-W road to **Chalatenango**, bus No 119 every 30 mins, US$1.35.

# Eastern
## El Salvador

The towns of eastern El Salvador maintain a rich festival life and strong craft traditions: Ilobasco is a pottery centre and San Sebastián specializes in textiles. The ancient town of San Vincente has history and colonial airs whilst San Miguel is a small, hot, rapidly growing city and transport hub. To the north, don't miss Perquín, a special little mountain town steeped in arresting scenery and legends of the revolution. To the south, on the coast, the port town of La Unión is not a destination in itself, but the jumping-off point for the mellow pirate isles of Meanguera, Zacatillo and Conchagüita.

### East from San Salvador  *Colour map 2, C5/C6.*

> towards El Salvador's rural heartland

There are two roads to the port of La Unión (formerly known as Cutuco) on the Gulf of Fonseca: the Pan-American Highway, 185 km through Cojutepeque and San Miguel (see page 467); and the coastal highway, also paved, running through Santo Tomás, Olocuilta, Zacatecoluca and Usulután.

The Pan-American Highway is dual carriageway out of the city, but becomes single carriageway for several kilometres either side of Cojutepeque – sections that are twisty, rough and seem to induce some very bad driving.

At San Martín, 18 km from the capital, a paved road heads north to Suchitoto, 25 km on the southern shore of the Embalse Cerrón Grande, also known as Lago de Suchitlán. At Km 34.8 is **Hacienda La Bermuda**, see page 459.

#### Cojutepeque

The capital of the Department of Cuscatlán, Cojutepeque (population 50,315) is 34 km from San Salvador and the first town on the Pan-American Highway encountered when

**Best** for
Crafts ■ Festivals ■ Revolutionary memories

heading east. There is a good weekly market. The town is famous for cigars, smoked sausages, *quesadillas* and tongue, and its annual feria on 29 August has fruits and sweets, saddlery, leather goods, pottery and headwear on sale from neighbouring villages, and sisal hammocks, ropes, bags and hats from the small factories of Cacaopera (Department of Morazán). There is also a **sugar cane festival** on 12-20 January. Lago de Ilopango is a short trip to the southwest.

**Cerro de las Pavas**, a conical hill near Cojutepeque, dominates **Lago de Ilopango** and offers splendid views of wide valleys and tall mountains. Its shrine of **Our Lady of Fátima** draws many pilgrims every year (religious ceremonies take place here on 13 May).

## Ilobasco

From **San Rafael Cedros**, 6 km east of Cojutepeque, a 16-km paved road north to Ilobasco (population 61,510) has a branch road east to Sensuntepeque at about Km 13. The surrounding area, devoted to cattle, coffee, sugar and indigo, is exceptionally beautiful. Many of Ilobasco's population are workers in clay; although some of its decorated pottery is now mass-produced and has lost much of its charm, this is definitely the best place to buy pottery in El Salvador. Check out miniature *sorpresas*, delicately shaped microscopic sceneries the size of an egg (don't miss the naughty ones). Try **Hermanos López** ① *entrance to town*, or José y Víctor Antino Herrera ① *Av Carlos Bonilla 61, T2332-2324, look for the 'Kiko' sign*, where there are fine miniatures for sale. The annual fiesta is on 29 September.

## San Sebastián

Four kilometres from the turning to Ilobasco, further south along the Pan-American Highway at **Santo Domingo** (Km 44 from San Salvador), a paved road leads for 5 km to San Sebastián (population 14,411), where colourfully patterned cloth hammocks and bedspreads are made. You can watch them being woven on complex looms of wood and string. Behind **Funeraria Durán** there is a weaving workshop. Sr Durán will take you past the caskets to see the weavers. The **Casa de Cultura**, about 50 m from the plaza, will direct you to weaving centres and give information on handicrafts. Before buying, check prices and beware of overcharging. Market day is on Monday.

## San Vicente

Founded in 1635, San Vicente (population 53,213) is 61 km from the capital and lies a little southeast of the Highway on the Río Alcahuapa, at the foot of the double-peaked **Volcán San Vicente** (or **Chinchontepec**), with very fine views of the Jiboa valley to the west. The town has a lovely setting and is a peaceful place to spend a night or two. Its pride and joy is **El Pilar** (1762-1769), the most original church in the country. It was here that the local chief, **Anastasio Aquino**, took the crown from the statue of San José and crowned himself King of the Nonualcos during the rebellion of 1832.

El Pilar stands on a small square 1½ blocks south of the Parque Central. On the latter is the **cathedral**, whose nave is draped with golden curtains. In the middle of the main plaza is a tall, open-work **clock tower**, quite a landmark when descending the hill into the city. Three blocks east of the main plaza is the *tempisque* tree under which the city's foundation charter was drawn up. The tree was decreed a national monument on 26 April 1984. There's an extensive market area a few blocks west of the centre and hammock sellers are on nearby streets. An army barracks takes up an entire block in the centre.

There's a small **war museum**; ask the FMLN office here or in San Salvador. Carnival day is 1 November.

## Around San Vicente

Three kilometres southeast of the town is the **Balneario Amapulapa** ① *T2393-0412, US$0.80 entry and US$0.90 parking charges, a Turicentro.* There are three pools at different levels in a wooded setting. The tourist police patrols here and lately it's been considered a safe place for tourists, although women should not walk to the area alone. It's reached by bus No 177 from Zacatecoluca bus station, and by pickup from the San Vicente bus station.

**Laguna de Apastepeque** ① *T2389-7172,* near San Vicente off the Pan-American Highway, is small but picturesque. Take bus No 156 from San Vicente, or No 499 from San Salvador. Ask in San Vicente for guides for climbing the San Vicente volcano.

## San Miguel

Set at the foot of the Volcán San Miguel (Chaparrastique), which last erupted in 1976 but has shown activity ever since, San Miguel (population 218,410) is the third largest city in El Salvador, 136 km from San Salvador. Apart from its huge carnival (see below), San Miguel is not a place you're likely to want to linger; there are traffic-clogged streets, stinking gutters, a hot, sticky climate and few conventional tourist attractions.

The capital of its department, the town was founded in 1530 as a military fortress by Don Luis de Moscoso. It now has one of the fastest growing economies in Central America, thanks partly to *remesas* (money received from family members who have emigrated to the US), as this part of the country experienced heavy migration both during and after the

**San Vicente**

*To Pan American Highway & San Salvador*

5 C Pte

1 Av Norte

5 C Ote/Domingo Santos

Cambio León

F A Figueroa/3 C Pte

Av Canónigo R Lazo/2 Av Nte

Dr A J Cañas

Tempisque Tree

Clock Tower

Cathedral

Lic Hernán Miranda

Daniel Díaz

Bus to Apasteque

Alcaldía

Army Barracks

Av María de los Angeles

Av José María Cornejo

Gobernación

1 de Julio 1823

Av Inocente Marín

Av F C Cañadas

Av Max Ramírez

Av Pres M A Molina y Cañasco

Av Ana Guerra de Jesús

Av Cayetano Molino Quiroz

Lic Basilio Meriño

Alberto de Merino

El Pilar

N

Indalecio Miranda

Juan C Segovia

200 metres
200 yards

**Where to stay** ⊖
Central Park 1

civil war. The town has two shady plazas: **Parque David J Guzmán**, containing the bare 18th-century cathedral, and the adjacent **Plaza Barrios**, flanked by overflowing market stalls. The city's **theatre** dates from 1909 and has been reopened in all its original glory.

The **Fiesta de la Virgen de la Paz** is on the last Saturday in November, and one of the biggest carnivals in Central America, known as **El Carnaval de San Miguel**, also takes place here. The free festival features parades and marching bands filing down Avenida Roosevelt to the city centre, from 1900 until late. For more information contact the **Comite de Festejos** ⓘ *T2660-1326*.

**Listings** East from San Salvador *maps p467 and p468*

### Where to stay

**San Vicente**

**$ Central Park**
*On Parque Central, T2393-0383.*
Good, clean rooms, with bath, a/c and phone. Cheaper with fan, cheaper still without TV. Café and restaurant downstairs.

**San Miguel**
Most hotels are on the entrance roads, although there are plenty of cheap places near the bus station.

**$$ Trópico Inn**
*Av Roosevelt Sur 303, T2682-1082, www.tropicoinn.com.sv.*

Clean and comfortable, with reasonable restaurant, swimming pool, garden and safe parking for motorbikes. Recommended.

**$ King Palace**
*Opposite the bus station.*
Good breakfast.

### Restaurants

**Ilobasco**
There are 2 pizzerias, several local *comedores*, a **Pollo Campero** and a **Taco Hut**.

**$$ Restaurante Ricky**
*3 Av Sur.*
The town's only real restaurant with à la carte dining.

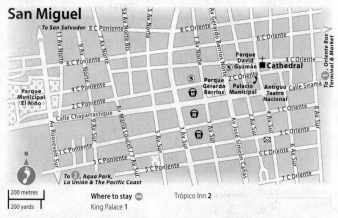

San Miguel

Where to stay 
King Palace 1    Trópico Inn 2

## San Vicente

The San Vicente Gastronomical festival is held on the last Sat of the month at the central park. Close to Hotel Central Park are **Pops** and **La Nevería**, for good ice cream.

## San Miguel

Try *bocadillos de totopostes*, maize balls with either chilli or cheese; and *tustacos*, which are like small tortillas with sugar or honey. Both are delicious and traditional.

**$ El Gran Tejano**
*4 Calle Pte, near the cathedral.*
Great steaks.

**$ Restaurant Perkin Lenca**
*Km 205.5 Cra a Perquín, T2680-4080, www.perkinlenca.com. Daily 0700-2000.*
Part of the hotel of the same name, this restaurant serves traditional food.

## Transport

### Cojutepeque

**Bus** No 113 from Oriente terminal in **San Salvador** (US$0.80); buses leave from Cojutepeque on the corner of the plaza, 2 blocks from the main plaza.

### San Sebastián

**Bus** No 110 from the Oriente terminal runs from **San Salvador** to San Sebastián (1½ hrs, US$1). There are also buses from **Cojutepeque**.

### San Vicente

**Bus** No 116 from Oriente terminal, **San Salvador**, every 10 mins or so (1½ hrs, US$0.90). Returning to the capital, catch bus from the bus station, Av Victoriano Rodríguez y Juan Crisóstomo Segovia; outside the cathedral; or on the road out of town. To **Zacatecoluca**, No 177 (US$0.50) from bus station. Buses to some local destinations leave from the street that runs west to east through the market. You have to take 2 buses to get to **San Miguel** (see below), the first to the Pan-American Hwy, where there is a bus and food stop, then another on to San Miguel (US$1.50 total).

### San Miguel

**Bus** Nos 301, 306 and 346 from Oriente terminal, **San Salvador** US$2.50, every 30 mins from 0500 to 1630, 2½ hrs. There are also 3 comfortable express buses daily, 2 hrs, US$5.

There are frequent buses to the Honduran border at **El Amatillo**, US$1; see also Border crossings box in Practicalities chapter. 4 buses, No 332A, daily to **Perquín**, from 0600-1240, 2¾ hrs, US$1.60. Direct to Tegucigalpa, with **King Quality Bus**, T2271-0307, www.kingqualityca.com, daily at 0830 and 1630, 6 hrs, US$35.

Several routes radiate outwards from San Miguel. A paved road runs south to the Pacific Highway. Go south along it for 12 km, where a road leads to Playa El Cuco (bus No 320 from San Miguel, US$1.50). A mainly paved, reasonable road goes to west to San Jorge and Usulután: leave the Pan-American Highway 5 km west of San Miguel, where the road passes hills and coffee plantations with good views of the San Miguel volcano.

Another route heads northeast to the small town of Jocorro, where the road splits with options to Honduras. Heading north, San Francisco Gotera leads to the Perquín crossing; east of Jocorro the road leads to the border crossing at El Amatillo (see Border crossings box in Practicalities chapter); and directly east from San Miguel lies La Unión, with connections north to El Amatillo.

## San Francisco Gotera and around

The capital of Morazán Department can be reached directly from the Oriente terminal in San Salvador, or from San Miguel (bus No 328). There are places to stay (see Where to stay, below).

Beyond San Francisco, the road runs to **Jocaitique** (there is a bus) from where an unpaved road climbs into the mountains through pine forests to **Sabanetas**, near the Honduran border; see Border crossings box in Practicalities chapter. Accommodation is available at Jocaitique and Sabanetas.

Northeast of San Francisco is **Corinto** ⓘ *20 mins north of the village on foot, just east of the path to the Cantón Coretito, open daily,* which has two rock overhangs showing faint evidence of pre-Columbian wall paintings. To get there take an early bus, No 327, from San Miguel, US$1.

## Ciudad Segundo Montes and around

Eight kilometres north of San Francisco Gotera is Ciudad Segundo Montes, a group of villages housing 8500 repatriated Salvadorean refugees (the community is named after one of the six Jesuit priests murdered at the Central American University in 1989). Schafic Vive is a small museum with information on the community. If you wish to visit contact PRODETUR ⓘ *T2680-4086,* for information. No formal accommodation is available.

Fourteen kilometres north of San Francisco is **Delicias de la Concepción**, where fine decorated hammocks and ceramics are made. The prices are good and the people are helpful; worth a visit. Buses every 20 minutes from San Francisco.

## Perquín and around

Perquín (altitude 1200 m, population 3158) – meaning 'Road of the Hot Coals'– is 205 km from San Salvador and was the guerrillas' 'capital', and the scene of much military activity. War damage used to be visible around the town, but all is now peaceful and the scenery is very beautiful, surrounded by pine-topped mountains. There is a small central square with a Casa de la Cultura, and post office. Opposite is the plain Iglesia Católica Universal Progresista, next to which is POLITUR, the very helpful and friendly police station. The tourist office is jointly run by PRODETUR and **Perkin Tours travel agency** ⓘ *Final del Calle Principal, T2680-4086, www.prodeturperquin.tripod.com, Mon-Fri 0800-1700.*

The **Museo de la Revolución** ⓘ *T7942-3721, daily 0800-1700, US$1.20, no photos or filming allowed, guided tours in Spanish, camping permitted, US$1,* clearly signposted from the plaza, has temporary exhibits as well as one on Archbishop Romero and all the gory details of his murder – nothing is spared. The museum, run by ex-guerrillas, is badly lit, but fascinating with photographs, propaganda posters, explanations, objects, pictures of the missing, and military paraphernalia. In the garden is the wreckage of an American-made helicopter, shot down by guerrillas in 1984. Sprawled like a piece of modern art, it would look at home in a contemporary art gallery. There is also a room where a recreated cabin shows the place from where the clandestine radio *Venceremos* broadcast their programmes during the war.

Behind the town is the **Cerro de Perquín** ⓘ *US$0.25 to climb, it is advisable to bring a guide.* The views are fantastic with the town below nestling in the tropical scenery, green parrots flying through the pine trees, and the mountains stretching towards the border with Honduras. The **Festival de Invierno**, 1-6 August, is a mixture of music, exhibitions and film. Book accommodation in advance if you're planning to come for the festival. The **Festival de San Sebastián** is on 21-22 January, and the celebration of the **Virgen del Tránsito**, the patron saint of the church, takes place 14-15 August.

Nearby villages such as Arambala and El Mozote can be visited, or you can take a walking tour. At **El Mozote** is a memorial to a massacre that took place in 1981, during which more than 800 people, among them children and babies, were brutally murdered. Five kilometres west of Perquín is **Arambala**, which is slowly being rebuilt. Locals will give you a tour (free, but tips appreciated) of the town and church, which has been largely rebuilt since being destroyed by fire in the 1980s; a sad and deeply moving experience, well worth the effort. Opposite the church is a small crafts shop run by a local women's cooperative, some of whom are also guides. Near Perquín, turn-off 2 km south, are the park and trails of **Cerro Pelón**. Nearby is **El Llano del Muerto**, a tourist area of naturally heated pools and wells. North of Perquín, straddling the border with Honduras, is one of the few unpolluted rivers in the country. The people of Morazán are more reserved with strangers than in the rest of El Salvador. If travelling on your own, 4WD is advised.

**Ruta de Paz** run by **Perkin Tours** ⓘ *T2680-4086, perkintours@yahoo.es, daily 0800-1700, 0800-2100 during the winter festival,* provides walks, culture and adventure tourism, and can organize accommodation. Tours last for between 25 minutes and two days, and are for one to 10 people. Ask for Serafín Gómez, who is in charge of the tours.

## Santa Rosa de Lima

The shortest route from San Miguel to the Honduran border takes the Ruta Militar northeast through Santa Rosa de Lima (population 27,693) to the Goascarán bridge at El Amatillo, a total of 58 km on paved road; see Border crossings box in Practicalities chapter.

Santa Rosa is a charming little place with a wonderful colonial church set in the hillside. There are gold and silver mines, a market on Wednesday, and a curiously large number of pharmacies and shoe shops. The FMLN office has details about the **Codelum Project**, a refugee camp in Monte Barrios. The fiesta is on 22-31 August.

## Where to stay

### San Francisco Gotera

**$$-$ Hospedaje San Francisco**
*Av Morazán 29, T2654-0066.*
Nice garden and hammocks.

### Perquín and around

**$$ Hotel Perkin Lenca**
*Km 205.5 Cra a Perquín, T2680-4080,*
*www.perkinlenca.com.*
Cosy Swiss cabins with piping hot showers
and thick blankets. Excellent meals in
restaurant **La Cocina de Ma'Anita**, with
panoramic terrace overlooking forested hills,
daily 0700-1900. US owner Ronald organizes
tours to El Mozote with former guerrilla
guides, a bit grim but very moving.

**$ Cocina Mama Toya y Mama Juana**
*At the entrance of Perquin village,*
*T2680-4045.*
Small rooms with 3 beds and
shared bath. Parking.

**$ La Posada de Don Manuel**
*5 mins from Perquín at the bottom of the hill,*
*CTE Perquín T2680-4037.*
Previously called **El Gigante**, countless
partitioned rooms that would probably be
noisy if full, but rarely are. Clean, with cold
showers and meals. They have a highly
recommended restaurant and organize
tours with guides. Friendly.

### Camping

It's possible to camp in the grounds of the
**Museo de la Revolución**, near a crater
formed by a 227-kg bomb dropped in 1981.
Ask in the nearby *tiendas*.

Near the Río Zapo, **PRODETUR** (T2680-
4311, prodeturperquin.tripod.com), has a
great campsite with facilities, and there are

guides who can give you a tour of the area.
Good for both trekking and hiking. There is
also a simple cabin for rent here.

### Santa Rosa de Lima

**$ Hospedaje Mundial**
*Near the market.*
Basic rooms with fan. Friendly, lots
of parking.

**$ Recreo**
*2 blocks from town centre in front of police*
*station and Telecom, 4 Av Norte, Barrio el*
*Recreo, T2641-2126.*
Basic fan rooms, noisy but friendly.
Recommended.

## Restaurants

### Perquín and around

**$ Antojitos Marisol**
*T2680-4063, near the church on the south*
*side of the plaza. Open late.*
Simple food.

**$ La Cocina de Mi Abuela**
*At the entrance to town. T2502-2630.*
Popular with locals with good, local dishes.

### Santa Rosa de Lima

**$$ Martina**
*Near the bridge.*
Good food including *sopa de apretadores*
for US$7.

## Transport

### Perquín and around
**Bus** From **San Miguel**, bus No 332A
(2¾ hrs, US$1.50). The bus from Terminal
Oriente in **San Salvador** (4½ hrs) is very
crowded, luggage a hindrance. Bus or truck

from **Cd Segundo Montes**. Transport back to Cd Segundo Montes or San Miguel may be difficult in the afternoons.

**Car**
If you're driving fill your tank before getting to Perquín because the last petrol station is 20 mins from the city and closes at 1700.

**Santa Rosa de Lima**
**Bus** To the Honduran border every 15 mins, US$0.50; see also Border crossings box in Practicalities chapter. Direct buses also to **San Salvador**, No 306, from 0400 until 1400, US$3.25, 3½ hrs.

## La Unión  *Colour map 2, C6.*

launching pad for remote Pacific islands

It is another 42 km from San Miguel to the port of La Unión (population 34,045), on the Gulf of Fonseca. The spectacular setting on the west shore of the gulf does little to offset the heat and the faded glory of this port town which handles half the country's trade. Shortly before entering the town, the Pan-American Highway turns north for 33 km to the Goascarán bridge at El Amatillo on the border with Honduras (see Border crossings box in Practicalities chapter). The huge project of the modern port of La Unión includes numerous foreign investments, such as a large Spanish tuna fish processing plant, with supporting infrastructure including new roads, hotels and a school running training in logistics and tourism.

### Around la Unión
**Conchagua** is worth visiting to see one of the few old colonial churches in the country, and there is a good bus service from La Unión (No 382, US$0.10). The church was begun in 1693, after the original Conchagua had been moved to its present site following repeated attacks on the island settlements by the English. There are fiestas on 18-21 January and 24 July.

There is also **Volcán Conchagua** (1243 m) which can be climbed but is a hard walk, particularly near the top where protective clothing is useful against the vegetation. It's about four hours up and two hours down, but you will be rewarded with superb views over Volcán San Miguel to the west and the Gulf of Fonseca, which is bordered by El Salvador, Honduras and Nicaragua (where the Cosigüina volcano is prominent) to the east. Alternatively, you can drive up via the community of Conchagita (4WD only).

In the Gulf of Fonseca are the Salvadorean islands of **Isla Zacatillo**, **Isla Conchagüita** and the largest, **Isla Meanguera** (about 4 km by 7 km). English and Spanish pirates occupied Isla Meanguera in the late 1600s, and international claims remained until the International Court of Justice in The Hague awarded the island to El Salvador in 1992, in preference to claims from Honduras and Nicaragua.

A *lancha* leaves La Unión for the town of **Meanguera del Golfo**, on Meanguera. The journey across the gulf is beautiful, with tranquil waters, fishing boats and views to the surrounding mountains. The island has secluded beaches with good bathing; for example, Majahual (a 45-minute walk), fringed with palm trees. About 2400 people live on this carefree island, where painted boats float in the cove surrounded by small *tiendas* and *comedores* that serve fish, shark and prawns. The highest point on the island is **Cerro de Evaristo** at 512 m. Launches leave La Unión daily at 1000, or private boats may leave earlier when full; the journey takes 45 minutes, US$2-3. It's possible to arrange transport with a local boatman to Coyolito (Honduras), Isla Amapala, or for day trips around the gulf (about US$80), but make sure the price is agreed beforehand. You can travel to Honduras or Nicaragua if you have visited immigration in La Unión first to get the necessary paperwork.

## Listings La Unión

### Where to stay

**$ San Francisco**
*Calle General Menéndez 6-3, Barrio Concepción, T2604-4159.*
Clean and friendly, some rooms with hammocks and fan. Noisy and has some water supply problems, but OK. Safe parking.

### Around La Unión

**$$$ Hotel Joya del Golfo**
*Isla de Meanguera, T2648-0072.*
Wonderfully relaxing hotel in the next bay beyond the harbour (ask the *lancha* from La Unión to drop you off), run by an extremely hospitable US-Salvadorean family. There are 4 lovely rooms, beautifully furnished, with 4-poster beds, a/c, cable TV and balcony. Excellent food in cosy family lounge, with books, games and DVDs. Kayaks for guests and boat to nearby beaches (US$10), plus hikes around island. Reservations essential. Highly recommended.

**$ Hotel Paraíso**
*Meanguera del Golfo.*
Has rooms with TV, private bath and hot water. Recommended.

### Restaurants

Bottled water is hard to find, but *agua helada* from clean sources is sold (US$0.25 a bag). There are several cheap *comedores* to choose from; try **Comedores Gallego ($)** and **Rosita ($)**, recommended. **Comedor Tere ($)**, Av General Menéndez 2.2, is also good.

**$$ Amanecer Marino**
*On the waterfront.*
Beautiful view of the bay and good for watching the world go by. Serves seafood.

**$ Las Lunas**
*3 blocks from the central park.*
Nice atmosphere. Very popular among locals.

**$ Restaurante Puerto Viejo**
*Located in front of El Dragón.*
Big portions, cheap. Best seafood in town; try *tazón de sopa de pescado*.

### Transport

**Bus** The terminal is at 3 Calle Pte (block 3). To **San Salvador**, bus 304, US$2, 2-3 hrs, many daily, direct or via San Miguel, 1 passes the harbour at 0300. Bus 324 to **San Miguel**, US$1. Bus to Honduran border at **El Amatillo**, No 353, US$1.80; see also Border crossings box in Practicalities chapter.

# Eastern
## Pacific coast

As yet unexploited, the Pacific shoreline east of San Salvador does not boast the big resorts and surf enclaves of the west, although it does have the Costa del Sol, the most developed tourist destination in the region. For those willing to get off the beaten track, there are more tranquil and intriguing possibilities, including isolated beaches, teeming mangroves and lagoons filled with marine life. For many travellers, the region presents an adventurous route to the Nicaraguan border and the Gulf of Fonseca, whose cut-off islands present special appeal.

## East of La Libertad  Colour map 2, C5/C6.
### remote beaches and tangled mangroves

The road to La Unión runs east through the southern cotton lands. It begins on a four-lane motorway to the airport at Comalapa. The first place of any importance is at Km 13, Santo Tomás where there are prehispanic ruins at Cushululitán, a short distance north. A road to the east, rising to 1000 m, runs south of Lago de Ilopango to join the Pan-American Highway beyond Cojutepeque.

From Santo Tomás it's 10 km on to **Olocuilta**, an old town famed for its church and known worldwide for its rice dough *pupusas*. It hosts a colourful market on Sundays under a great tree. Both Santo Tomás and Olocuilta can be reached by bus 133 from San Salvador. The highway to the airport crosses the Carretera Litoral (CA 2) near the towns of San Luis Talpa and Comalapa. The coastal road goes east, through Rosario de la Paz, across Río Jiboa and on to Zacatecoluca.

### Costa del Sol
Just after Rosario, a branch road to the south leads to **La Herradura** (bus 153 from Terminal del Sur to La Herradura, US$1.25, 1½ hours) and the Playa Costa del Sol on the Pacific,

**Best** for
Boat trips ■ Marine life ■ Remote beaches

which is being developed as a tourist resort. The beach is on a narrow peninsula, along the length of which are private houses which prevent access to the sand until you reach the **Turicentro** ⓘ *0800-1800*. Here, *cabañas* can be rented for the day or for 24 hours, but they are not suitable for sleeping. Playa Costa del Sol is crowded at weekends and holidays, as there are extensive sandy beaches. However, the sea has a mild undertow; so go carefully until you are sure. Expensive hotels are continuously popping up and prices are a bit over the top; budget travellers might choose some of the smaller hotels by **Playa Los Blancos**. On the road to Costa del Sol, there is also a great water park, **Atlantis Water Park** ⓘ *Km 51, carretera Costa del Sol, T2211-4103, www.atlantis.com.sv, US$10; children US$6, on bus routes No 495 and 143 (every 15 mins)*. Options from San Salvador include hotel pickup, small lunch and entrance from US$15-20.

## Isla Tasajera

At the southeast end of the Costa del Sol road, near the **Pacific Paradise** hotel, a ferry (US$1.75) leaves for Isla Tasajera in the Estero de Jaltepeque (tidal lagoon). For boat excursions, take the Costa del Sol bus to the last stop at La Puntilla and negotiate with the local boatmen. Boat hire for the day costs US$75, including pilot. It's a great trip into the lagoon, with mangroves, dolphin watching and trips up to the river mouth of the Río Lempa (the longest river in the country).

## Zacatecoluca

The capital of La Paz Department is 56 km from San Salvador by road and 19 km south of San Vicente. Zacatecoluca (altitude 201 m, population 65,826) is a good place to buy hammocks (for example nylon 'doubles', US$13). José Simeón Cañas, who abolished slavery in Central America, was born here. There is a cathedral in the Moorish style and an excellent art gallery as well as a mall with a supermarket and several stores.

## Ichanmichen

*Admission and car parking US$0.75 per person, bungalow rental US$4.*

Near the town is the park and Turicentro of Ichanmichen ('the place of the little fish'). It is crossed by canals and decorated with natural spring pools where you can swim. It is very hot but there is plenty of shade.

## Usulután, Playa El Espino and Laguna El Jocotal

About 110 km from the capital is Usulután, capital of its department. It's a large, dirty and unsafe place, and only useful as a transit point (bus No 302 from San Salvador, US$1.40). The coastal highway goes direct from Usulután to La Unión.

Playa El Espino can be reached from Usulután, by car (4WD), pickup or slow bus; it is very remote but lovely. Some small hotels and restaurants operate, but most only at weekends. To visit the reserve, enquire at the entrance; hire a boat to see more.

Beyond Usulután, the impressive silhouette of **Volcán Chaparrasque** rises out of the flat coastal plain. Two roads go northeast to San Miguel, the first from 10 km along at El Tránsito, the second a further 5 km east, which keeps to the low ground south and east of Volcán San Miguel. Two kilometres beyond this turning on the Carretera Litoral is a short road to the right leading to Laguna El Jocotal, a national nature reserve supported by the World Wildlife Fund, which has an abundance of birds and snakes.

## Playa El Cuco and around
*Bus No 320 to San Miguel, US$0.45, 1 hr, last bus 1600.*

About 12 km from the junction for San Miguel there is a turning to the right leading in 7 km to Playa El Cuco, a popular beach with several cheap places to stay near the bus station. The main beach is liable to get crowded and dirty at weekends and holidays, but is deserted mid-week. Single women should take care here; locals warn against walking along the beach after sunset. Cases of malaria have also been reported. Another popular beach, **El Tamarindo**, is reached by following the coastal road a little further before taking a right turn.

## Listings East of La Libertad

### Where to stay

**Costa del Sol**
Cheaper accommodation can be found 1 km east at Playa Los Blancos and in La Herradura.

**$$ Izalco Cabaña Club**
30 rooms and a pool. Good value, seafood is a speciality.

**$ Miny Hotel y Restaurant Mila**
*Km 66, opposite police station.*
Very friendly, owner Marcos speaks English. Clean, simple, fan, pool, good food, beach access. Take bus No 495 from Terminal Sur, San Salvador; buses are very crowded at weekends, but the resort is quiet during the week.

**Playa El Cuco and around**

**$$ Trópico Club**
*2.5 km along the coast from Playa El Cuco, T2682-1073, tropicoinn@yahoo.com.*
Several cabins, pool and open-air dining. Leads directly to the beach. Run by the **Trópico Inn** in San Miguel (T2661-1800); see page 70.

**$ Los Leones Marinos**
*El Cuco, T2619-9015.*
Clean and tidy with bath.

**Playa Las Flores**

**$$$$-$$$ Las Flores Surf Resort**
*Close to Playa El Cuco, T2619-9118, www.lasfloresresort.com.*

Run by surf expert Rodrigo Barraza, this boutique hotel caters mostly for foreign tourists, making an excellent choice for an upscale budget.

**Playa Torola**

**$$ Torola Cabaña Club**
*Km 175, T2681-5528.*
This friendly place with a welcoming owner has a pool looking out to sea and a great open-air bar/restaurant. Recommended.

### Restaurants

**Costa del Sol**

**$ Restaurante Kenny Mar**
*Km 60, Cra Costa del Sol, Playa San Marcelino, T2338-2578.*
Delicious seafood with beachfront view.

### Transport

**Zacatecoluca**
**Bus** No 133 from Terminal Sur, **San Salvador**. Direct bus to **La Libertad** 1540 (US$0.85), or take San Salvador bus, change at Comalapa, 2 hrs.

**Playa El Cuco and around**
**Boat** Boat from El Tamarindo across the bay leads to a short cut to **La Unión**.

**Bus** From **La Unión**, 20 mins.

# This is
# Honduras

Sliced, spliced and spread across a mountainous interior, Honduras is a pleasantly challenging surprise that has developed in curiously disconnected zones. In the heart of the mountains Tegucigalpa epitomizes the Latin city – a chaotic celebration of colonial architecture divided by steeply sloping cobbled streets. By contrast, the republic's second and more modern city, San Pedro Sula, on the coastal lowland plain, has a neat matrix of *calles* and *avenidas* that seem rather dull by comparison.

A world away, the Bay Islands bask under sunny skies. Utila thrives on a throw-it-together-and-see-if-it-works existence. It's easily the cheapest place to learn to dive in the western hemisphere.

Honduras is the second largest Central American republic after Nicaragua, but its population is smaller than that of neighbouring El Salvador, the smallest country. Bordered by Nicaragua, Guatemala, El Salvador and a narrow coastal Pacific strip, it is the northern Caribbean coast and beautiful Bay Islands that are a natural focus and a prime destination for visitors.

Inland, the mountainous terrain creates natural obstacles to easy, direct travel around the country. It also means that, for trekking and hiking, there are great swathes of beautiful hillside, much of which is dotted with small communities, largely disinterested in the comings and goings of the few travellers who venture so far off the beaten track.

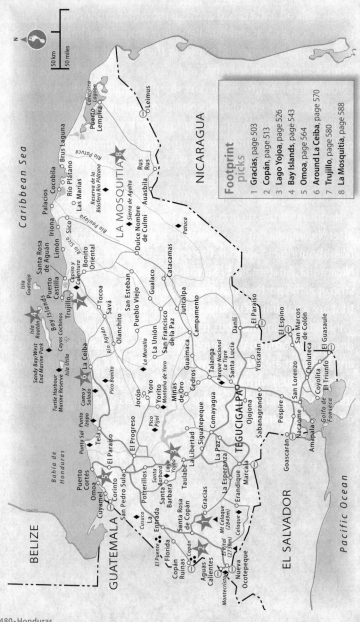

Caribbean Sea

BELIZE

GUATEMALA

NICARAGUA

EL SALVADOR

Pacific Ocean

Bahía de Honduras

Golfo de Fonseca

**TEGUCIGALPA**

LA MOSQUITIA 8

Reserva de la Biosfera Río Plátano

N

50 km
50 miles

Puerto Lempira · Caratasca Lagoon · Leimus · Brus Laguna · Cocobila · Río Plátano · Palacios · Las Marías · Rus Rus · Auasbila · Sierra de Agalta · Dulce Nombre de Culmí · Patuca · Río Patuca · Río Paulaya · Río Sico · Capiro y Calentura · Santa Rosa de Aguán · Limón · Bonito Oriental · Irióna · Sicó · Catacamas · San Esteban · Gualaco · Juticalpa · Campamento · La Unión · San Francisco de la Paz · Pueblo Viejo · Guaimaca · Talanga · Parque Nacional La Tigre · Santa Lucía · Cedros · Yuscarán · Danlí · El Paraíso · El Espino · San Marcos de Colón · Choluteca · El Guasaule · El Triunfo · Coyolito · Nacaome · San Lorenzo · Amapala · Goascarán · Pespire · Sabanagrande · Ojojona · La Paz · Marcala · La Esperanza · Taulabé · Siguatepeque · Comayagua · La Libertad · Erandique · Celaque · Mt Celaque (2849m) · Gracias · Santa Rosa de Copán · Nueva Ocotepeque · Aguas Calientes · Copán Ruinas · Copán · Florida · El Puente · Montecristo · El Pital (2730m) · La Entrada · San Pedro Sula · Potterillos · Santa Bárbara · Lago Yojoa · Pico Pijol · El Progreso · Tela · Punta Sal · Puerto Cortés · Corinto · Cuyamel · Omoa · Cusuco · Jocón · Yoro · Yorito · Montaña de Yoro · Minas de Oro · Pico Bonito · La Muralla · Olanchito · Río Aguán · Savá · Tocoa · Trujillo · Puerto Castilla · Isla Guanaja · Isla Roatán · B & V Islands · Sandy Bay/West End Marine Park · Cayos Cochinos · Isla Utila · Turtle Harbour Marine Reserve · La Ceiba · Cuero y Salado · Punta Izopo

480·Honduras

# Footprint picks

★ **Gracias**, page 503

Don your hiking boots for the mountains around Gracias, including
Las Minas, the highest peak in Honduras.

★ **Copán**, page 513

The haunting Mayan ruins guard some fascinating sculptures and statues.

★ **Lago Yojoa**, page 526

Lake Yojoa is surrounded by rambling nature reserves and coffee fincas.

★ **Bay Islands**, page 543

Languid beaches and a kaleidoscope of coral reefs.

★ **Omoa**, page 564

Stunning beach backed by jungle-clad mountains.

★ **Around La Ceiba**, page 570

Garífuna communities, tranquil beaches and Parque Nacional Pico Bonito.

★ **Trujillo**, page 580

Laid-back beach town and good base for surrounding activities.

★ **La Mosquitia**, page 588

One of Central America's most remote destinations.

# Essential Tegucigalpa

## Finding your feet

The winding of streets in the city means that moving around in the first few days is as much about instinct as following any map. The Tegucigalpa section of the city uses both names and numbers for streets, but names are used more commonly. In Comayagüela, streets designated by number are the norm. Addresses tend not to be very precise, especially in the *colonias* around Boulevard Morazán east and south of the centre of Tegucigalpa.

## Best places to stay

**Humuya Inn**, page 487
**Minister Business Hotel**, page 487
**Nuevo Boston**, page 488
**Granada 2 and Granada 3**, page 488

## Getting around

There are cheap buses, but for safety it is better to use taxis.

## Tip...

On arrival it is very much easier – and recommended for safety – to take a taxi to your hotel until you get to know the city.

## Best restaurants

**Hacienda Real**, page 489
**La Cumbre**, page 489
**Rojo, Verde y Ajo**, page 489
**El Patio**, page 489
**Don Pepe's Terraza**, page 489

## Safety

Generally speaking, Tegucigalpa is cleaner and safer (especially at night) than Comayagüela. If you have anything stolen, report it to **Dirección de Investigación Criminal (DGIC)**, 5 Avenida, 7-8 Calle (next to Edificio Palermo), T2237-4799.

## Tip...

For good restaurants, take a walk down the pedestrianized stretch of Avenida Paz Barahona. In the evening, take a taxi to Boulevard Morazón.

## When to go

The city's altitude gives it a reliable climate: temperate during the rainy season from May to October; warm, with cool nights in March and April; and cool and dry with cool nights from November to April.

## Weather Tegucigalpa

| January | February | March | April | May | June |
|---------|----------|-------|-------|-----|------|
| 15°C | 15°C | 16°C | 18°C | 18°C | 18°C |
| 6°C | 26°C | 28°C | 29°C | 29°C | 27°C |
| 0mm | 0mm | 0mm | 30mm | 150mm | 160mm |

| July | August | September | October | November | December |
|------|--------|----------|---------|----------|----------|
| 18°C | 18°C | 18°C | 17°C | 16°C | 16°C |
| 27°C | 27°C | 27°C | 26°C | 25°C | 24°C |
| 80mm | 80mm | 180mm | 130mm | 30mm | 10mm |

# Tegucigalpa
## & around

Built on the region's mineral wealth, Tegucigalpa, the capital of Honduras, is a relentless urban dynamo, neither beautiful nor compelling, but as a hub of business and transport, essential and unavoidable.

The chaotic Tegucigalpa – or Tegus as it is called by locals – is cramped and crowded, but still somehow retains a degree of charm in what remains of the colonial centre. If you can bear to stay away from the Caribbean for a few days, it has much more history and charisma than its rival San Pedro Sula, to the north.

Surrounded by sharp, high peaks on three sides, the city is built on the lower slopes of El Picacho. Its smattering of Spanish colonial plazas, churches and townhouses contrast with much newer structures – high-rise office blocks, condos and shopping malls – which are signs of the city's growing, if unevenly distributed, wealth and commercialism. The commercial centre is around Boulevard Morazán, an area known as 'zona viva', full of cafés, restaurants and shops. For contrast to the modern functional city, you can visit some of the centuries-old mining settlements set in forested valleys among the nearby mountains that are ideal for hiking.

**Best** for
Hiking ▪ Markets ▪ Museums

## Sights *Colour map 3, C2.*

Crossing the river in Tegucigalpa (altitude 1000 m, population 1.1 million) from Comayagüela by the colonial Mallol bridge, on the left is the old **Casa Presidencial** (1919), home to the National Archive. When this was a museum, visitors could see the president's office and the Salón Azul state room. Try asking – you may be lucky. (The new Palacio Presidencial is a modern building on Boulevard Juan Pablo II in Colonia Lomas del Mayab.)

Calle Bolívar leads to the Congress building and the former site of the University, founded in 1847. The site adjoining the church in Plaza La Merced is now the **Galería Nacional de Arte** ① *Tue-Fri 0900-1600, Sat 0900-1200, US$1.50*, a beautifully restored

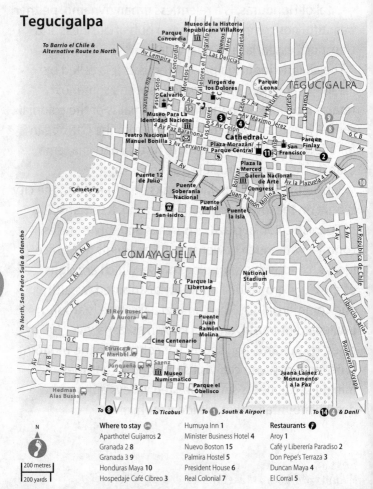

# Tegucigalpa

**N**

200 metres
200 yards

| Where to stay | | Humuya Inn 1 | Restaurants |
|---|---|---|---|
| Aparthotel Guijarros 2 | | Minister Business Hotel 4 | Aroy 1 |
| Granada 2 8 | | Nuevo Boston 15 | Café y Librería Paradiso 2 |
| Granada 3 9 | | Palmira Hostel 5 | Don Pepe's Terraza 3 |
| Honduras Maya 10 | | President House 6 | Duncan Maya 4 |
| Hospedaje Café Cibreo 3 | | Real Colonial 7 | El Corral 5 |

17th-century building, housing a very fine collection of Honduran modern and colonial art, prehistoric rock carvings and some remarkable pre-Colombian ceramic pieces. There are useful descriptions of exhibits, and explanations of the mythology embodied in the prehistoric and pre-Colombian art.

Calle Bolívar leads to the main square, Plaza Morazán (commonly known as Parque Central). On the eastern side of the square is the **Palacio del Distrito Central**, and the domed and double-towered **cathedral**, built in the late 18th century but which have had a complete facelift. See the gilt colonial altarpiece, the fine examples of Spanish colonial art, the cloisters and, in Holy Week, the ceremony of the Descent from the Cross.

Avenida Miguel Paz Barahona, running through the north side of the square, is a key venue. To the east is the church of **San Francisco**, with its clangorous bells, and, on 3 Calle, called Avenida Cervantes, the old **Spanish Mint** (1770), now the national printing works.

From Plaza Morazán, heading west towards the river to Avenida Miguel Paz Barahona, opposite the post office is the **Museo Para La Identidad Nacional** ⓘ *T2238-7412, www.min.hn, Tue-Sat 0900-1700, Sun 1100-1700, US$3.30*, a museum that is unashamedly about Honduras for Hondurans. There is a good multimedia presentation (with an audioguide, in Spanish only), and a well-thought-out trip through Honduran history, from plate tectonics to the present day. Its star attraction is 'Virtual Copán' – a wide-screen CGI recreation of the Maya ruins, entrance US$1.65; there are also occasional temporary exhibitions. It offers just enough detail without getting heavy; every capital city in Central America should have a museum like this.

Heading east a block, then left (north) along 5 Calle (Calle Los Dolores), is the 18th-century church of **Iglesia de Nuestra Señora de los Dolores**. Two blocks north and three blocks west of the church is the beautiful Parque Concordia with good copies of Maya sculpture and temples. On a hilltop one block above Parque Concordia, on Calle Morelos 3A, is the **Museo de la Historia Republicana Villa Roy**, the former site of the Museo Nacional and, in 1936, home of the former president,

To El Picacho & Parque las Naciones Unidas

San Pablo Ⓜ

COLONIA VIERA

COLONIA REFORMA

COLONIA MATAMOROS

Gutemberg

Av La Paz

To Valle de Angeles

Plaza San Martín

COLONIA PALMIRA

Boulevard Morazán

C Venezia

Lloyds Ⓢ

Centro Comercial Los Castaños

To 6

To 10 2 6

C Ruben Dario

COLONIA RUBEN DARIO

C Realle de Minas

To 5 8 9

El Patio **6**
Gino's Pasta Café **7**
Hacienda Real **8**
La Cacerola **9**
Marjaba Café **10**
Merendero El Buen Gusto **11**

Rojo, Verde y Ajo **12**
Tony's Mar **14**

# BACKGROUND

## Tegucigalpa

Founded as a silver and gold mining camp in 1578, Tegucigalpa means silver hill in the original indigenous tongue; miners first discovered gold at the north end of the current Soberanía bridge. The present city is comprised of the two former towns of Comayagüela and Tegucigalpa which, although divided by the steeply banked Río Choluteca, became the capital in 1880 and are now united administratively as the Distrito Central.

Being off the main earthquake fault line, Tegucigalpa has not been subjected to disasters by fire or earthquake, unlike many of its Central American neighbours, so it has retained many traditional features. The stuccoed houses, with a single, heavily barred entrance leading to a central patio, are often attractively coloured. However, the old low skyline of the city has been punctuated by several modern tall buildings, and much of the old landscape changed with the arrival of Hurricane Mitch.

The rains of Hurricane Mitch in October 1998 had a devastating effect on the Distrito Central. But the damage caused by the Choluteca bursting its banks is hard to see these days, with the exception of the first avenue of Comayagüela, where abandoned homes and buildings remain empty. Bridges washed away by the floodwaters have now been replaced, power supplies are back and, in some respects, traffic is actually better now, since many routes were diverted from the heart of downtown. Today, Hurricane Mitch lives on as painful memory.

Julio Lozano. Sadly, the building sustained severe structural damage from landslides in 2014 and at the time of research the museum was closed for the foreseeable future. It may or may not reopen; check with the tourist office for the latest news.

Back on Avenida Miguel Paz Barahona, and further west, are the **Teatro Nacional Manuel Bonilla**, with a rather grand interior (1915) inspired by the Athenée Theatre in Paris and, across the square, the beautiful old church of **El Calvario**. Built in elegant colonial style, El Calvario's roof is supported by 14 pillars.

In Colonia Palmira, to the southeast of the city, is Boulevard Morazán, with shopping and business complexes, embassies, banks, restaurants, *cafeterías* and bars. You can get a fine view of the city from the **Monumento a La Paz** ⓘ *open till 1700*, on Juana Laínez hill, near the Estadio Nacional (National Stadium), but don't walk up alone.

The backdrop to Tegucigalpa is the summit of **El Picacho**, with the Cristo del Picacho statue looming up to the north (see Valle de Angeles, below), although this can be hard to see at times. From Plaza Morazán go up 7 Calle and the Calle de la Leona to **Parque La Leona**, a small handsome park with a railed walk overlooking the city and safer than Monumento a La Paz.

Higher still is the reservoir in El Picacho, also known as the **United Nations Park**, which can be reached by a special bus from the No 9 bus stop, behind Los Dolores church (in front of Farmacia Santa Bárbara, Sunday only, US$0.15); alternatively, take a bus to El Piligüin or Corralitos (daily at 0600) from the north side of Parque Herrera in front of the Teatro Nacional Manuel Bonilla.

## Comayagüela

Crossing the bridge of 12 de Julio (quite near the Teatro Nacional Manuel Bonilla, see above) you can visit Comayagüela's market of San Isidro. In the Edificio del Banco Central, is the **Pinacoteca Arturo H Medrano** ⓘ *12 Calle entre 5 y 6 Av*, which houses approximately 500 works by five Honduran artists, and the **Museo Numismático** ⓘ *Mon-Fri 0900-1200, 1300-1600*, which has a collection of coins and banknotes.

## Listings Tegucigalpa *map p484*

### Tourist information

**Instituto Hondureño de Turismo**
*Edif Europa, Av Ramón E Cruz and Calle República de México, 3rd floor, Col San Carlos, T2222-2124; also at Toncontín Airport, open 0830-1530.*
Tourist offices provide lists of hotels and sell posters and postcards. Information on cultural events around the country from **Teatro Nacional Manuel Bonilla** is better than at regional tourist offices.

### Where to stay

There is a 4% tax on hotel bills, plus 12% sales tax: check if it is included in the price.

**$$$ Aparthotel Guijarros**
*Col Lomas del Guijarro, Calle Roma 3929, T2235-6851, www.guijarros.com.*
Enjoying a good location in a safe residential neighbourhood, Aparthotel Guijarros offers a range of modern rooms, suites, and apartments, all fully kitted with 32 inch screens, microwave, mini-fridge, Wi-Fi, hair-dryers and more. Offerings in the restaurant include home-grown organic produce. A decent and reliable option with very accommodating staff.

**$$$ Honduras Maya**
*Av República de Chile, Col Palmira, T2280-5000, www.hotelhondurasmaya.hn.*
Spacious rooms and apartments, dated decor, casino and pool, **Bar Mirador** with nightly happy hour 1700-1900, *cafeterías,*

restaurant, very good buffet breakfast, conference hall and convention facilities for 1300, view over the city from upper rooms. Excellent travel agency in the basement. Expensive internet access.

**$$$ Humuya Inn**
*Col Humuya 1150, 5 mins from airport, T2239-2206, www.humuyainn.com.*
Helpful, homey and professionally run lodgings with lots of good reports. Accommodation includes rooms and service apartments, US owner. Quiet family atmosphere and nice views from the rooftop terrace. Recommended.

**$$$ Minister Business Hotel**
*Col Florencia Norte, Blv Suyapa 2340, T2280-6464, www.ministerbusiness.com.*
This swish business hotel boasts stylish contemporary decor and a superb rooftop bar with 360-degree views of the city. Rooms are smallish but well-attired with plush fixtures and modern amenities, including cable TV, high-speed Wi-Fi and coffee machine. A very comfortable and presentable option. Recommended.

**$$$ President House Hotel**
*Col Lomas del Guijarro, Av Enrique Tierno Galvan, T2231-0431, www. presidenthousehotel.com.*
Well-situated in a quiet residential neighbourhood, this refurbished colonial-style townhouse was originally built for Honduran ex-president Ramón Ernesto Cruz. Perched on a hill, it offers airy

terraces with a restaurant and coffeehouse. Accommodation is in comfortable rooms with a/c, cable TV, hot water, safe box and Wi-Fi. A good deal for single travellers ($).

### $$$-$$ Real Colonial Hotel
*Col Palmira, Calzada San Martín 458, T2220-7497, www.realcolonialhotel.hn.*
The Real Colonial is a cosy, 6-storey hotel with attentive service, bright murals and a small outdoor patio where you can enjoy breakfast. Rooms are simple, comfortable and modern, featuring all the usual amenities including high-speed Wi-Fi, a/c, and 32" screen. Nestled in an exclusive neighbourhood.

### $$ Hospedaje Café Cibreo
*Col Palmira, Calzada San Martín 452, T2220-5323, www.hospedajecafecibreo. cdvhotels.com.*
Formerly Leslie's Place, this homely and well-established B&B has a restaurant-café serving Mediterranean-style cooking in an open-air courtyard. Rooms have high-speed Wi-Fi, hot water, cable TV and a/c. Close to bars and restaurants. Down-to-earth and pleasant.

### $$ Nuevo Boston
*Av Máximo Jerez 321, T2237-9411.*
In a central location, this well-run, simple place has spotless rooms with good beds, and hot water. Rooms on the street side are noisy. Good value, no credit cards, free coffee, mineral water and cookies in lounge, stores luggage. Recommended.

### $ Granada 2 and $ Granada 3
*T238-4438 and T2237-0843, on the street leading uphill (to Barrio Casamate) from northeast corner of Parque Finlay.*
Good beds, hot water and safe parking. It can be noisy from passing traffic so try to get a room at the back. Recommended.

### $ Palmira Hostel
*Av Juan Lindo, T2236-9143, www.palmirahostel.com.*
A cheap, comfortable, reliable hostel located in a safe part of town opposite the French embassy and around the corner from the US embassy. They offer well-kept dorms and private rooms, clean and spartan. There is a small outdoor terrace and indoor communal areas, including a kitchen. Wi-Fi included.

---

## Comayagüela

Comayagüela is convenient for buses to the north and west and there are many cheap *pensiones* and rooms. It is noisier and dirtier than Tegucigalpa and many places are unsuitable for travellers. If you are carrying luggage, take a taxi.

## Restaurants

Most places close on Sun.

### $$$ El Corral
*4a Av, opposite Hotel Clarión, Col Alameda, T2232-5066.*
Big, brash steakhouse, with excellent grilled meats and decent wine list. Lively at weekends, with live music, karaoke and dancing.

### $$$ Gino's Pasta Café
*Distrito Hotelero San Martín, Col Palmira, www.ginos-pastacafe.com.*
Gino serves some of the best home-cooked Italian food in Honduras, fresh, simple, and flavourful, the way good Italian food should be. Soups, salads, pastas and pizza are among the authentic offerings at this cosy and popular eatery.

### Tip...
There are good Chinese restaurants on Calle del Telégrafo in the centre; they offer huge servings at reasonable prices.

### $$$ Hacienda Real
*Plaza Colprosumah and Blv Juan Pablo II,*
*west side of Hotel Marriot, T2239-6860,*
*www.hacienda-real.com.*
One of the finest steakhouses in Honduras,
set in a handsome colonial-style building
and part of a high-end international
franchise with branches in Guatemala and El
Salvador. Prices are steep, but not by western
standards. Popular for business lunches.

### $$$ La Cumbre
*Northeast of the city, El Hatillo Km 7.5,*
*T2211-9000, www.lacumbrehn.com.*
La Cumbre promises a memorable fine
dining experience with its disarming hill-top
setting and expansive views over the valley
and city below. Prices for its pasta, steaks
and seafood aren't cheap, but the cuisine
and service are exceptional. Romantic and
intimate, one of the best.

### $$$ Rojo
*Verde y Ajo, Av República de*
*Argentina 1930, Col Palmira, T2232-*
*5653, www.rojoverdeyajo.com.*
A very stylish and well-executed restaurant
with diverse international offerings such as
beef medallions in cognac sauce and shrimp
with champagne butter. Occasional live
music, guest chefs and wine-tasting events.
Warm and convivial. Recommended.

### $$ Aroy
*Blv Morazán, T9481-9095,*
*www.aroyhn.wix.com/aroy.*
Aroy serves authentic Thai cuisine with a
tempting menu of delectable delights such
as summer rolls, stuffed cucumber, chicken
satay, Thai coco soup, and green papaya
salad. Wholesome home-cooking and a
pleasant interior.

### $$ Duncan Maya
*Av Colón 618, opposite central Pizza Hut.*
This popular locals' haunt is a lively place
and it occasionally hosts live music. Food is

filling and reasonably priced fare, including
mostly national staples.

### $$ Marjaba Café
*Av República Dominicana 3641, T8880-*
*7358, www.marjabacafe.com. Tue-Sun for*
*lunch only.*
Wholesome, tasty, affordable and fully
authentic Middle Eastern fare, and occasional
belly dancers. For lunch, the buffet-style
*menú del día* includes a meat dish, 5 sides
and a drink. Friendly service and vegetarian
options too.

### $$ Tony's Mar
*Col Florencia, Blv Suyapa, T2232-5266,*
*www.tonysmarrestaurante.com.*
This reliable seafood joint has been serving
up fish, prawns and ceviche for 25 years.
Large servings, fresh, tasty, wholesome and
reasonably priced. The current menu has lots
of variety, including octopus and conch.

### $$-$ El Patio
*Easternmost end of Blv Morazán, T2221-3842,*
*www.elpatiohn.com.*
Traditional food served in a large casual
dining hall bedecked with old photos and
fairy lights. Good service and atmosphere,
and generous portions. A long-standing
Tegus favourite. Recommended.

### $ Don Pepe's Terraza
*Av Colón 530, upstairs, T2222-1084.*
Central, cheap, live music, but typical
Honduran atmosphere. Heaty locals' joint
with hearty grub. Recommended.

### $ La Cacerola
*Col Lomas del Mayab, Av República de Costa*
*Rica 1692.*
This chilled out little eatery specializes in
*comida típica*, of which its hot soups are
particularly renowned; the *sopa de caracol*
(conch soup), a national favourite, is not to
be missed. Sandwiches and wraps are also
available. A light, cosy, friendly place, good
for an inexpensive lunch.

**$ Merendero El Buen Gusto**
*Calle Hipolito Matute, behind the cathedral.*
An unpretentious downtown joint where
you can rub shoulders with the locals and
wolf down some hearty home-cooked grub.
Convenient, but not fine dining.

### Cafés and bakeries

**Café y Librería Paradiso**
*Av Paz Barahona 1351.*
Excellent coffee and snacks, good library,
paintings and photos to enjoy, and
newspapers and magazines on sale. A good
meeting place with a bohemian atmosphere.

**Salman's**
*Blv Morazán, next to Centro Comercial Maya,
www.pansalmans.com.*
Several outlets. Good bread/pastries,
including baguettes and doughnuts.

## Bars and clubs

In front of the Universidad Nacional on Blv
Suyapa is La Peña, where every Fri at 2100
there is live music, singing and dancing,
entrance US$1.40.

Blv Morazán has plenty of choice in nightlife
including **Taco Taco**, a good bar, sometimes
with live mariachi music; next door **Tequila**,
a popular drinking place only open at
weekends. **Tobacco Road Tavern**, a popular
gringo hang-out, in the downtown area
on Calle Matute. **Iguana Rana Bar** is very
popular with locals and visitors, similarly **La
Puerta del Alcalá**, 3½ blocks down from
Taca office on Blv Morazán, Col Castaño Sur.
Pleasant open setting.

**Tierra Libre**
*Calle Casa de las Naciones Unidas 2118,
5 mins' walk from Plaza San Martín in Col
Palmira, T3232-8923. Mon-Sat, 1700-2400.*
Arty cinephile café/bar, with occasional
screenings, small and friendly, with good
cocktails and snacks.

## Entertainment

### Cinemas

**Plazas 1 to 5** (in Centro Comercial Plaza
Miraflores on Blv Miraflores). **Regis**, **Real**,
**Opera**, and **Sagitario** (at Centro Comercial
Centroamérica, Blv Miraflores), for good US
films. **Multiplaza** (Col Lomas del Mayab),
6 screens. In the city centre, **Lido Palace**,
**Variedades** and **Aries** (200 m up Av
Gutemberg leading from Parque Finlay
to Col Reforma).

## Shopping

### Bookshops

**Editorial Guaymuras**, *Av Miguel
Cervantes 1055.*
**Librería Paradiso**, *see under Cafés and
bakeries, above.* Books in Spanish.
**Mercado San Isidro**, *6 Av y 2 Calle,
Comayagüela.* Second-hand
bookstalls, cheap.
**Metromedia**, *Edif Casa Real, Av San Carlos,
behind Centro Comercial Los Castaños,
Blv Morazán.* English books, new and
second-hand, for sale or exchange.

### Markets

**Mercado de Artesanías**, *3 Av, 15 Calle,
next to Parque El Soldado.* Good value.
**Mercado San Isidro**, *6 Av at 1 Calle,
Comayagüela.* Many fascinating things,
but filthy; do not buy food here. Sat is
busiest day.
　　Good supermarkets: **La Colonia** (in
Blv Morazón); **Más y Menos** (in Av de la
Paz). Also on Calle Salvador, 1 block south
of Peatonal.

## What to do

**Explore Honduras Tour Service**, *Col Zerón
21-23 Av, 10 Calle NO, San Pedro Sula, T2552-
6242, www.explorehonduras.com.* Copán and
Bay Islands tours.

## Air

**Toncontín Airport (TGU)**, www.
interairports.hn, is 6.5 km south of the
centre in a narrow valley creating difficult
landing conditions: morning fog or bad
weather can cause it to close. The airport
opens at 0530. Check in at least 2 hrs before
departure; there are snacks, souvenir shops,
several duty-free stores and internet. Buses
to airport from Comayagüela, on 4 Av
between 6 and 7 Calle, or from Av Máximo
Jerez in downtown Tegucigalpa; into town
US$0.19, every 20 mins from left-hand side
outside the airport; official airport taxis
(recommended) to the centre cost US$12-15;
street cabs cost around US$5-6.

## Bus

**Local** Fares are US$0.08-0.12; stops are
official but unmarked.

**Long distance** There is no central bus
station and bus companies have offices
throughout Comayagüela. To **San Pedro
Sula** on Northern Hwy, 3¼-4 hrs depending
on service. Several companies, including:
**Sáenz**, Centro Comercial Perisur, Blv Unión
Europea, T2233-4229, and **Hedman
Alas**, 11 Av, 13-14 Calle, Comayagüela,
T2237-7143, www.hedmanalas.com,
US$18; both recommended; **El Rey**, 6 Av,
9 Calle, Comayagüela, T2237-6609; **Viajes
Nacionales** (Viana), terminal on Blv de
Las Fuerzas Armadas, T2235-8185. To
**Tela** and **La Ceiba**, **Viana Clase Oro**, and
**Etrusca**, 8 Av, 12 y 13 Calle, T2222-6881. To
**Choluteca**, **Mi Esperanza**, 6 Av, 23-24 Calle,
Comayagüela, T2225-1502. To **Trujillo**,
**Cotraibal**, 7 Av, 10-11 Calle, Comayagüela,
T2237-1666. To **La Esperanza**, **Empresa
Joelito**, 4 Calle, No 834, Comayagüela. To
**Comayagua**, most going to San Pedro
Sula and **Transportes Catrachos**, Col
Torocagua, Blv del Norte, Comayagüela.
To **Valle de Angeles** and **Santa Lucía**,

from stop on Av La Paz (near filling station
opposite hospital). To **Juticalpa** and
**Catacamas**, **Empresa Aurora**, 8 Calle,
6-7 Av, Comayagüela, T2237-3647. For **Danlí**
and **El Paraíso**, for the Nicaraguan border
at Las Manos, see page 541, and Border
crossings box in Practicalities chapter.

For travellers leaving Tegucigalpa, take
the Tiloarque bus on Av Máximo Jerez, by
Calle Palace, and get off in Comayagüela
at Cine Centenario (Av 6) for nearby
**Empresa Aurora** buses (for **Olancho**)
and **El Rey** buses (for **San Pedro Sula**).
3 blocks northwest is Cine Lux, near which
are **Empresas Unidas** and **Maribel** (8 Av,
11-12 Calle, T2237-3032) for **Siguatepeque**.
Tiloarque bus continues to Mi Esperanza bus
terminal (for **Choluteca** and **Nicaraguan
border**). Take a 'Carrizal' or 'Santa Fe' bus
ascending Belén (9 Calle) for **Hedman
Alas** buses to **San Pedro Sula** and for
Comayagua buses. The **Norteño** bus line
to San Pedro Sula is alongside Mamachepa
market, from where there are also buses
for **Nacaome** and **El Amatillo** border with
El Salvador.

**International** **Ticabus**, Centro Comercial
Plaza Toncontin, Entrada Principal de Lomas
de Toncontin, Calle Hacia El IPM, south of
the airport, T2291-0022, www.ticabus.com,
to **Managua** (US$23, 8 hrs), **San José**
(US$65), **San Salvador** (US$21), **Guatemala
City** (US$21, 12 hrs) and **Panama** (US$173)
daily. Note: fares listed above are one-way
'executive' class. Make sure you reserve
several days ahead. **Hedman Alas** have a
service to **Guatemala City** and **Antigua** that
leaves Tegucigalpa for San Pedro Sula, 0545,
12 hrs, US$52. Alternatively to **Nicaragua**,
take **Mi Esperanza** bus to San Marcos de
Colón, then taxi or local bus to El Espino on
border. To **San Marcos**, 4 daily from 0730,
direct to border at 0400, US$2.50, 5 hrs
(0730 is the latest one that will get you into
Nicaragua the same day). Or **Mi Esperanza**

bus to Río Guasaule border, several daily, 4 hrs, US$2. To **San Salvador**, Cruceros del Golfo, Barrio Guacerique, Blv Comunidad Económica Europea, Comayagüela, T2233-7415, US$18, at 0600 and 1300, 6 hrs travelling, 1 hr or more at border. Connections to **Guatemala** and **Mexico**; direct bus to border at El Amatillo, US$2.50, 3 hrs, several daily; alternatively from San Pedro Sula via Nueva Ocotepeque and El Poy. To **San Salvador** and **Guatemala**, with **King Quality** from Tegucigalpa (T2225-5415) from **Cruceros del Golfo** terminal, 0600 and 1300 and San Pedro Sula (T2553-4547) at 0630. Alternatively, to Guatemala go to San Pedro Sula and take **Escobar, Impala** or **Congolón** to Nueva Ocotepeque and the border at **Agua Caliente**, or via **Copán** (see page 520 and Border crossings box in Practicalities chapter).

**Car**

**Car hire** Avis, Edif Palmira and airport, T2232-0088. **Budget**, Blv Suyapa and airport, T2235-9531. **Hertz**, Centro Comercial Villa Real, Col Palmira, T2239-0772. **Maya**, Av República de Chile 202, Col Palmira, T2232-0992. **Molinari**, 1 Av, 2 Calle, Comayagüela and airport, T2237-5335. **Thrifty**, Col Prados Universitarios, T2235-6077. **Toyota**, T2235-6694.

**Car repairs** Metal Mecánica, 1 block south of Av de los Próceres, Col Lara. Volkswagen dealer near Parque Concordia, good.

**Taxi**
About US$4-6 per person, but you can often bargain down to around US$3 for short distances within the city. More after 2200, cheaper on designated routes, eg Miraflores to centre.

## Around Tegucigalpa

*ancient mining towns steeped in aromatic highland pine forests*

Heading north out of Tegucigalpa on the Olancho road, you come to Talanga, with a post office and Hondutel near the market on the main road. From Talanga it is a short trip to the historic and beautiful settlements of Cedros and Minas de Oro. From the Parque Central an unpaved road leads south to the Tegucigalpa–Danlí road making a triangular route possible back to the capital.

### Cedros *Colour map 3, B3.*
Cedros (altitude 1034 m), 77 km north of Tegucigalpa, is one of Honduras' earliest settlements, dating from Pedro de Alvarado's mining operations of 1536. It is an outstanding colonial mining town with cobbled streets, perched high on an eminence amid forests. The festival of El Señor del Buen Fin takes place in the first two weeks of January. Buses to Talanga, Cedros and nearby San Ignacio leave from Reynita de San Ignacio in Mercado Zonal Belén, Comayagüela, T224-0066, five daily.

### Santa Lucía *Colour map 3, B3.*
About 14 km northeast of Tegucigalpa, on the way to Valle de Angeles, a right turn goes to the quaint old mining village of Santa Lucía (altitude 1400-1600 m) which is perched precariously on a steep, pine forested mountainside overlooking the valley with Tegucigalpa below. The town has a colonial church with a Christ statue given by King Felipe II of Spain in 1592. There is a charming legend of the Black Christ, which the authorities ordered to be taken down to Tegucigalpa when Santa Lucía lost its former

importance as a mining centre. Every step it was carried away from Santa Lucía it became heavier. When it was impossible to carry it any further they turned round, and by the time they were back in Santa Lucía, it was as light as a feather.

The town is lively with parties on Saturday night, and there is a festival in the second and third weeks of January, celebrating the 15 January Día de Cristo de las Mercedes. There are souvenir shops in the town, including **Cerámicas Ucles** just past the lagoon, second street on left, and another ceramics shop at the entrance on your right. On the way into the town from the capital the road is lined with many nurseries, selling flowers and plants for which the region is famous. There are good walks up the mountain on various trails, with fine views of Tegucigalpa.

A good circuit is to descend east from the mountain towards **San Juan del Rancho** through lovely landscapes on a good dirt road, then connect with the paved road to **El Zamorano**. From there continue either to El Zamorano, or return to Tegucigalpa (see below for the opposite direction).

## Valle de Angeles
About 30 minutes' drive from Tegucigalpa, Valle de Angeles (altitude 1310 m) is on a plain below **Monte San Juan**, with **Cerro El Picacho** (2270 m) and **Cerro La Tigra** nearby. It is a popular spot for trips from the city, with a cool climate year round, and is surrounded by pine forests. The town's shady little main plaza is decorated with brightly painted benches and bandstand, a pretty little twin-domed church and fringed by several restaurants with outdoor tables. The **tourist office** ① *Sat, Sun 0900-1200, 1330-1800*, is helpful but has limited information. There are tracks going through the forests, old mines to explore, a picnic area and a swimming pool; it gets crowded on Sundays. At the top of Cerro El Picacho there is a stunning view of the city and a **zoo** ① *daily, 0800-1500, US$0.20*, of mostly indigenous animals including jaguar, spider monkeys and other animals and birds.

## Parque Nacional La Tigra *Colour map 3, B3.*
*Open 0800-1600, US$10 entry. There are 2 visitor centres. To reach the Jutiapa centre, 24 km from the capital, take a bus from Parque Herrera opposite the Teatro Nacional and exit at Aldea El Chaparro, from where it is a 20-min walk. To reach the El Rosario visitor centre, take a bus from to San Juancito from the Gasolinera San Felipe, opposite the San Felipe Hospital, from where it is a 45-min walk to the entrance. Lodging and maps are available at both centres. There are hiking trails of varying difficulty and single hikers must have a guide, US$10-20 per trail. For more information, see Where to stay and Transport, below.*

Only 11 km from Tegucigalpa, this cloudforest covers 238 sq km and is considered one of the richest habitats in the world with a great diversity of flora and fauna: bromeliads, orchids, arborescent ferns and over 200 species of bird. There are good climbs to the heights of Picacho and excellent hikes in the park. Crumbling remains of the old mine buildings are dotted around the hillsides, some abandoned, others inhabited. Local resident Miguel Angel Sierra (T964-8334) has some fascinating remnants, including an original gold mould and old photographs, all of which he is happy to show to visitors. The small **Pulpería-Cafetería El Rosario** sells snacks, coffee and groceries, which are useful if you're hiking in the park, and has lovely views from its tiny terrace and balcony.

A recommended hike is the **Sendero La Esperanza**, which leads to the road; turn right then take the **Sendero Bosque Nublado** on your left. The whole circuit takes about one hour 20 minutes. A few quetzal birds survive here, but you will need a good eye. In the rainy season (June, July, October and November) there is a spectacular 100-m waterfall (**Cascada de la Gloria**), which falls on a vast igneous rock. Do not leave paths when walking as there are steep drops. Also get advice about personal safety, as robberies have occurred.

At Km 24 on the road to Danlí, there are climbs to the highest peak through the Uyuca rainforest. Information is available from the Escuela Agrícola Panamericana in the breathtaking **Valle del Zamorano**, or from the **Amitigra office** ① *Col Palmira dos calles al sur (de la Nunciatura Apostólica), Av Santa Sede casa 210, Tegucigalpa, T2231-3641*. The school has rooms for visitors. Visits to the school are organized by some tour operators. On the northwest flank of Uyuca is the picturesque village of **Tatumbla**.

## Suyapa

East of Tegucigalpa, the village of Suyapa attracts pilgrims to its big basilica, home to a tiny wooden image of the Virgin, about 8 cm high, set into the altar. A fiesta is held 1-4 February, see Festivals section in Planning chapter. Take a bus to the University or to Suyapa from 'La Isla', one block northwest of the city stadium.

## Sabanagrande *Colour map 3, C2.*

To the south (40 km) is Sabanagrande, just off the main highway. This typical colonial town, complete with cobbled streets, is a good day trip from Tegucigalpa. There is an interesting colonial church (1809), **Nuestra Señora del Rosario 'Apa Kun Ka'** (the place of water for washing), with the fiesta of La Virgen de la Candelaria from 1-11 February. At 1000 m, it has a mild climate, beautiful scenery with pleasant walks, including views to the Pacific and the Gulf of Fonseca. The town is famous for its *rosquillas* (a type of biscuit).

## Ojojona

Ojojona (altitude 1400 m) is another quaint and completely unspoiled old village about 30 minutes (24 km) south of Tegucigalpa; turn right off the Southern Highway. The village pottery is interesting but make your selection carefully as some of it is reported to be of poor quality. **La Casona del Pueblo** offers the best handicrafts in town, including fine rustic ceramics. The local fiesta is 18-20 January. There are two well-preserved colonial churches in Ojojona, with fine paintings, plus two more in nearby **Santa Ana**, which is passed on the way from Tegucigalpa.

## Listings Around Tegucigalpa

### Where to stay

#### Santa Lucía

**$$ Hotel Santa Lucía Resort**
*1.2 km before Santa Lucía, T2779-0540, www.hotelsantaluciaresort.com.*
Set among pine trees dripping with moss (*rigil*). Spacious and comfy log cabins, with cable TV, lounge area, and balcony; pleasant grounds and ample parking space.

**$$ La Posada de Doña Estefana**
*T2779-0441, meeb@yahoo.com.*
Overlooking the church in the heart of the well-preserved colonial town, this place has pretty rooms with cable TV and great views from balcony. There is a lounge and a pool; breakfast is included.

## $$ Texas Guesthouse
*1.5 km from the entrance to town, located right off the main street, T9891-2374, www.texasguesthousehn.com.*
The Texas Guesthouse offers 14 cosy, comfortable and presentable rooms with hot water, minibar, a/c, TV and Wi-Fi. There is secure parking, laundry service and exercise machines. Helpful, well kept and down-to-earth. Recommended.

### Valle de Angeles

**$$ Hotel y Restaurante Posada del Angel**
*Northeast of centre, T2766-2233, hotelposada delangel@yahoo.com.*
Swimming pool, indifferent service, moderate prices.

**$$-$ Villas del Valle**
*500 m north of town, T766-2534, www.villasdelvalle.com.*
Selection of rooms, cabins and suites. Honduran and European food in the restaurant.

### Parque Nacional La Tigra
Basic guesthouse accommodation ($) is also an option in San Juancito if you're stuck.

**$ Eco-Albergue El Rosario**
Accommodation for 30 which includes bathrooms and a cafeteria.

**$ Eco-Albergue Jutiapa**
6 triple rooms and a cabin for 3 people, each with bath. Camping is available.

## Restaurants

### Santa Lucía

**$$$-$$ La Placita de Susy**
*Barrio Lodo Prieto, 1 km after the turning for the highway, www.laplacitadsusy.com.*
This popular family restaurant has a lovely rural setting with green lawns, good views and homely wood-built architecture. Food

is international with a particular emphasis on Argentine meat dishes, which are also their best offerings.

**$$ Miluska**
A Czech restaurant serving Czech and Honduran food. Recommended.

### Valle de Angeles

**$$$-$$ Los 4 Vientos**
*Valle de Angeles Km 20, T9473-4711.*
This secluded rural retreat has beautiful rambling grounds filled with trees and immaculately landscaped flower beds. They serve a diverse range of international fare, including burgers, pizzas, seafood, and vegetarian dishes. Relaxed alfresco dining, good for families.

**$$ Epocas**
*Calle Mineral, opposite the Town Hall on the main plaza, T9636-1235.*
A wonderful ramshackle place, full of antiques and bric-a-brac, from old French horns to vintage cash registers (some items for sale); mixed menu of steak, chicken and fish as well as *típicos*; cheerfully talkative parrots in the backyard.

**$$ La Casa de las Abuelas**
*1 block north of Parque Central, T2766-2626.*
Pleasant courtyard with wine bar, café, library, satellite TV, email, phone, information and art gallery.

**$$ Las Tejas**
*Opposite the Centro Turístico La Florida.*
A Dutch-owned restaurant, serving traditional mix of meat and *típico* dishes.

**$ Restaurante Turístico de Valle de Angeles**
*T2766-2148.*
On the top of the hill overlooking town, with rustic decor, cartwheel table tops and lovely views over the forested valley. Good meat and fish dishes but slow service.

### Cafés

#### Café La Estancia
*Calle Principal, frente al Salón Comunal.*
A superb coffeehouse set in a very appealing colonial building with wooden platforms, open-air balconies and arresting antique flourishes. Lots of character.

### Parque Nacional La Tigra

#### $ Grocery store
*Next door to Hotelito San Juan, San Juancito.*
Sells fuel, drinks and can prepare *comida corriente*; same owners as hotel, T2766-2237.

## Festivals

#### Suyapa
1-4 Feb **Fiesta**, with a televised *alborada* with singers, music and fireworks, from 2000-2400 on the 2nd evening.

#### Sabanagrande
1-11 Feb **Fiesta** of La Virgen de la Candelaria.

#### Ojojona
18-20 Jan **Fiesta**.

## Transport

#### Santa Lucía
**Bus** To Santa Lucía from Mercado San Pablo, **Tegucigalpa**, Bus 101, every 45 mins, US$0.50, past the statue of Simón Bolívar by the Esso station, Av de los Próceres.

#### Valle de Angeles
**Bus** To **Valle de Angeles** every 45 mins, US$0.50, 1 hr, leaves from San Felipe, near the hospital. To **San Juan de Flores** 1000, 1230, 1530.

#### Parque Nacional La Tigra
**Bus** Buses to the **Jutiapa visitor centre** leave from Parque Herrera, Mon-Fri 0700, 0900, 1400, 1600, 1700; Sat-Sun 0800, 1000, 1200, 1300, 1500, 1 hr, US$1.10; exit at Aldea El Chaparro and walk for 20 mins. Return buses to Tegucigalpa depart every 1-2 hrs 0530-1500; check with the visitor centre for specific times. Buses to **El Rosario visitor centre** depart from the Gasolinera San Felipe, opposite the San Felipe Hospital, 1400, 1500 and 1700, 1 hr, US$1.10; exit at San Juancito and walk for 45 mins. Return buses at 0530, 0630 and 0800.

#### Ojojona
**Bus** Buses leave **Comayagüela** every 15-30 mins from Calle 4, Av 6, near San Isidro market, US$0.50, 1 hr. From same location, buses go west to **Lepaterique** ('place of the jaguar'), another colonial village, over 1-hr drive through rugged, forested terrain. Distant view of Pacific on fine days from heights above village.

# Tegucigalpa
## to Copán

Treasured for its exceptional artistry, the serene ruins of Copán are Honduras' big Maya attraction. Located close to the Guatemalan border, the city once marked the eastern extent of Mayan civilization, a network of competing city-states which reached as far west as Chiapas in Mexico. The journey to Copán from Tegucigalpa involves traversing some highly convoluted countryside. Rising and falling with sublime mountain vistas, the road connects a procession of indigenous and mining communities steeped in age-old legends, lore, tradition and crafts.

The town of Gracias is one of the country's most historical settlements, popular with adventurers for the nearby mountain of Celaque, the highest peak in Honduras. Further north, Santa Rosa de Copán is rich in colonial heritage, while Copán itself is situated near the colonial town of Copán Ruinas with its bonus of nearby hot springs and flocks of gregarious macaws.

**Best** for
Colonial towns ▪ Hiking ▪ Macaws ▪ Maya ruins ▪ Mountain scenery

Highway CA5, also known as the Carretera del Norte (Northern Highway), leaves the capital at Comayagüela and enters the vast valley of Támara, with the village of the same name. A turning leads to the San Matías waterfall, in a delightful area for walking in cool forested mountains.

The road climbs to the forested heights of **Parque Aventuras** ⓘ *open at weekends*, at Km 33, good food, swimming pools, horses, bikes, then to **Zambrano** (altitude 1450 m) at Km 34 and, at Km 36, midway between Tegucigalpa and Comayagua, **Parque Aurora** ⓘ *T9990-3338, camping US$0.50 per person, admission US$0.70, food supplies nearby*. It has a small zoo, good swimming pools and a picnic area among pine-covered hills, a lake with rowing boats (hire US$1 per hour), a snack bar and lovely scenery. The birdwatching is good too.

Before descending to the Comayagua Valley, the Northern Highway reaches another forested mountainous escarpment. Stalls selling home-made honey and garish chunky pottery line the roadside. A track leads off to the right (ask for directions), with about 30 minutes' climb on foot to a tableland and the natural fortress of **Tenampua**, where the indigenous inhabitants put up their last resistance to the *conquistadores*, even after the death of Lempira. It has an interesting wall and entrance portal.

## Listings Támara and Zambrano

### Where to stay

#### Támara

**$ Posada Don Willy**
*500 m southwest of the toll station near Balneario San Francisco.*
With bath (electric shower), clean, quiet, fan, excellent value.

#### Zambrano

**$$$ Caserío Valuz**
*1.5 km from the highway, 20 mins' walk on the road to Catarata Escondida, T9996-4294 (mob), www.caseriovaluz.wordpress.com.*

This charming country inn has 15 rooms with bath, most with balconies, 1- to 3-night packages including meals, also rooms for backpackers, with use of kitchen, volunteer work in exchange for room and board possible, a great place to relax, hike, read and paint.

**$$$-$ Casitas Primavera**
*Barrio La Primavera, 1.5 km west of main road, T2898-26625/ T2239-2328.*
Cosy houses, lovely setting, sleeps 6 (arrangements can be made for 1-2 people, $).

On Highway CA5, approximately 34 km after Zambrano, westbound Highway CA7 branches off towards Marcala (altitude 1300 m), 77 km away in the Department of La Paz. The region's staggered hills and mountains enjoy comfortable temperatures during the day and cool temperatures at the night, making them a particularly good place to escape the lowlands during the sweltering months of March to May.

It's ideal hiking country with beautiful scenery and dramatic waterfalls in the surrounding area. Marcala is also a good base from which to visit Yarula, Santa Elena, Opatoro, San José and Guajiquiro. The region is one of the finest coffee-producing areas of Honduras and a visit to Comarca, at the entrance to town, gives an idea of how coffee is processed. Semana Santa is celebrated with a large procession through the main street and there is a fiesta in honour of San Miguel Arcángel in the last week of September.

## Around Marcala

**Balneario El Manzanal** ① *3 km on the road to La Esperanza, open weekends only*, has a restaurant, two swimming pools and a boating lake. For panoramic views high above Marcala, follow this hike (one hour): head north past **Hotel Medina**, turn right (east) after the hotel and follow the road up into hills. After 2 km the road branches. Take the left branch and immediately on the left is a football field. A small path leaves from this field on the west side taking you through a small area of pine trees then out onto a ridge for excellent views. The track continues down from the ridge back to town, passing an unusual cemetery on a hill.

**Musula** There are caves nearby on Musula mountain, the Cueva de las Animas in Guamizales and Cueva de El Gigante and El León near La Estanzuela with a high waterfall close by. Other waterfalls are El Chiflador, 67 m high, Las Golondrinas, La Chorrera and Santa Rosita. Transport goes to La Florida where there is good walking to the village of **Opatoro** and climbing **Cerro Guajiquiro**. Between Opatoro and Guajiquiro is the **Reserva las Trancas**, a heavily forested mountain where quetzales have been seen.

**Yarula and Santa Elena** These are two tiny municipalities, the latter about 40 km from Marcala, with beautiful views (bus Marcala–Santa Elena 1230 returns 0500 next day, 2¾ hours, enquire at Gámez bus office opposite market; truck daily 0830 returns from Santa Elena at 1300). Sometimes meals are available at *comedores* in Yarula and Santa Elena. The dirt road from Marcala gradually deteriorates, the last 20 km being terrible, high clearance essential, 4WD recommended. In **La Cueva Pintada**, south of Santa Elena, there are pre-Columbian cave paintings (*pinturas rupestres*) of snakes, men and dogs; ask for a guide in Santa Elena. Ask also in this village about the *Danza de los Negritos*, performed at the annual **Fiesta de Santiago**, 24-25 March, in front of the church. A special performance may be organized, the dancers wearing their old wooden masks, if suitable payment is offered.

The village of **San José** (altitude 1700 m) is a Lenca community where the climate can be cool and windy even in the hottest months. The scenery is superb, there's good hill walking (see box, page 508, for two examples; there are many others) and also rivers for swimming. Frequent pickups from Marcala, and two daily minibuses at about 0815 and 0900; from San José to Marcala minibuses depart at 0615 and 0645, one hour, US$1.

## Listings Marcala and around

### Where to stay

**$ Medina**
*On main road, T2898-1866.*
The most comfortable, clean, modern with bath, *cafetería*, free purified water. Highly recommended.

**$ Unnamed hotel**
*San José.*
Run by Brit Nigel Potter ('Nayo'). Basic but comfortable and clean, with meals. He also takes groups to stay in Lenca villages, US$5 per person plus US$10 per person for accommodation in a village; ask for the house of Doña Gloria, Profe Vinda, Nayo or Ruth. At least one of these will be present to meet visitors.

### Restaurants

**$$ Riviera Linda**
*Opposite Hotel Medina.*
Pleasant atmosphere and spacious restaurant. It's a little pricey but serves good food.

**$ Café Express**
*Beside Esso.*
Good breakfast and *comida corrida*. Recommended.

**$ Darwin**
*Main street in centre.*
Cheap breakfasts from 0700. Recommended.

**$ El Mirador**
*On entering town by petrol station.*
Nice views from veranda, good food. Recommended.

**Around Marcala**
**$ Comedor**
*500 m before plaza on main road.*
Good, clean and cheap.

### What to do

For trips to visit Lenca villages see the unnamed hotel in San José, Where to stay, above.

### Transport

**Bus**  To **Tegucigalpa** 0500, 0915 and 1000 daily via La Paz, 4 hrs, US$2.40 (bus from Tegucigalpa at 0800 and 1400, **Empresa Lila**, 4-5 Av, 7 Calle, No 418 Comayagüela, opposite Hispano cinema); bus to **La Paz** only, 0700, 2 hrs, US$1; several minibuses a day, 1½ hrs, US$1.50. Bus also from Comayagua. Pickup truck to **San José** at around 1000 from market, ask for drivers, Don Santos, Torencio, or Gustavo. Bus to **La Esperanza** at about 0830, unreliable, check with driver, Don Pincho, at the supermarket next to where the bus is parked (same street as Hotel Medina), 1½-2 hrs, otherwise hitching possible, going rate US$1.20. Bus to **San Miguel**, El Salvador, Transportes Wendy Patricia, 0500, 1200, 7 hrs, US$3.50.

North of Marcala, Highway CA11A connects with La Esperanza (altitude 1485 m) 30 km away, an old colonial town in a pleasant valley. It has an attractive church in front of the park and there is a grotto carved out of the mountainside west of the town centre, a site of religious festivals. There is a market on Thursdays and Sundays when the Lenca from nearby villages sell wares and food, but no handicrafts. Nearby is the indigenous village of Yaramanguila.

The surroundings include forested hills with lakes and waterfalls, great for walking although they are very cold in December and January. One option is to hike to **Cerro de Ojos**, a hill to the northwest and visible from La Esperanza. It is forested with a clearing on top littered with many strange cylindrical holes; no one knows how they were formed. The turning to this hill is on the La Esperanza to San Juan road. Ask for directions.

### Erandique

It is 45 km from La Esperanza to **San Juan del Caite** on Highway CA11A (a few *hospedajes*, **Lempira**, **Sánchez**, and the comfortable **Hacienda**, two restaurants nearby, helpful people and Peace Corps workers). From here a dirt road runs 26 km south to the small town of Erandique. Founded in 1560 and set high in pine-clad mountains not far from the border with El Salvador, it is a friendly town, and very beautiful. Lempira was born nearby, and was killed a few kilometres away. The third weekend in January is the local **Fiesta de San Sebastián**. The best time to visit is at the weekend and market days are Friday and Sunday. Each of the three barrios has a handsome colonial church.

There are lakes, rivers, waterfalls, springs and bathing ponds in the vicinity; ask around for directions. Nearby is **San Antonio** where fine opals (not cut gems, but stones encased in rock) are mined and may be purchased. The many hamlets in the surrounding mountains are reached by roads that have been either resurfaced or rebuilt and the landscapes are magnificent.

There are several roads radiating from Erandique, including one to **Mapulaca** and the border with El Salvador (no immigration or customs or bridge here, at the Río Lempa), a road to San Andrés and another to Piraera (all passable in a car).

## Listings  La Esperanza and around

### Where to stay

#### La Esperanza
There are several simple but pleasant pensiones around town.

#### $$ Casa Arroyo
*Northwest of town past Supermercado Melissa (see website for map), T2783-1721, www.casadelarroyohn.com.*

Surrounded by nature and highland views, this tranquil B&B enjoys a lovely hacienda setting in the hills. Accommodation includes clean, cosy and homely rooms and cabins with cable TV and hot water. Quiet and romantic, would suit couples or families.

#### $$-$ Posada Papa Chepe
*Frente al Parque López, T2783-0443, http://posadapapachepe.cdvhotels.com.*

Conveniently located in the centre of town, Papa Chepe's is a solid colonial-style option with simple, good value rooms and a tranquil garden-courtyard overflowing with leafy plants. There's a restaurant on-site and all the usual amenities including cable TV and Wi-Fi.

## Restaurants

### La Esperanza

#### $$ Casa Vieja
*Opposite Parque López.*
Set in a well-renovated colonial townhouse, Casa Vieja boasts a great atmosphere with its spacious dining hall and high wood-beam ceilings. They do very tasty burgers and other filling international fare. The best place in town, a good spot for a drink too. Recommended.

#### $$ Papá Chepe
*Opposite Parque López. Open for breakfast, lunch and dinner.*
Papá Chepe serves wholesome home-cooked grub including national staples and solid international fare: chicken and rice, pancakes, grilled meats are among the offerings. Pleasant, clean, café-style interior.

#### $ Café El Ecológico
*Corner of Parque Central.*
Home-made cakes and pastries, fruit drinks, and delicious home-made jams.

## Festivals

### La Esperanza
**3rd week in Jul** Festival de la Papa.
**8 Dec** Fiesta de la Virgen de la Concepción.

## Transport

### La Esperanza
#### Bus
To **Tegucigalpa** several daily, 3½ hrs, US$5 (**Cobramil**, also to **San Pedro Sula**, and **Joelito**, 4 hrs, US$2.60). To **Siguatepeque** 0700, 0900, last at 1000, US$1.50, 1 hrs; also to **Siguatepeque**, **Comayagua** at 0600; and to the **Salvadorean border**; bus stops by market. Hourly minibuses to **Yaramanguila**, 30 mins. Daily bus to **Marcala**, 2 hrs at 1230 (but check), US$0.80 (truck, US$1.20, 2¼ hrs). Minibus service at 1130, US$1.50. Daily minibus service to **San Juan**, departs between 1030-1200 from a parking space midway between the 2 bus stops, 2½ hrs, pickups also do this journey, very crowded; for **Erandique**, alight at Erandique turn-off, 1 km before San Juan and wait for truck to pass (*comedor* plus basic *hospedaje* at intersection). If going to Gracias, stay on the La Esperanza–San Juan bus until the end of the line where a pickup collects passengers 15 mins or so later, 1 hr San Juan–Gracias. Buses to **Lake Yojoa** (see page 526), 2 hrs, US$2.50.

### Erandique
#### Bus
There are minibuses to Erandique from the bridge on the road to La Esperanza, 1100 daily, although most people go by truck from Gracias (there is sometimes a van service as far as San Juan) or La Esperanza (change trucks at San Juan intersection, very dusty). Return minibus to Gracias at 0500 daily, which connects with the bus to La Esperanza in San Juan. Trucks leave Erandique 0700 daily, but sometimes earlier, and occasionally a 2nd one leaves around 0800 for Gracias, otherwise be prepared for a long wait for a pickup.

colonial treasure set beneath mountain giants

★One of the oldest settlements in Honduras, dominated by Montañas de Celaque, Puca and Opulaca – the country's highest peaks – Gracias (altitude 765 m) is a charming, friendly town. Just 50 km from Santa Rosa, both the town and the surrounding countryside are worth a visit.

Gracias was the centre from which Francisco de Montejo, thrice governor of Honduras, put down the great indigenous revolt of 1537-1538. Alonso de Cáceres, his lieutenant, besieged Lempira the indigenous leader in his impregnable mountain-top fortress at Cerquín, finally luring him out under a flag of truce, ambushed him and treacherously killed him. When the Audiencia de los Confines was formed in 1544, Gracias became the administrative centre of Central America.

There are three colonial churches, **San Sebastián**, **Las Mercedes** and **San Marcos** (a fourth, Santa Lucía, is southwest of Gracias), and a restored fort, with two fine Spanish cannon, on a hill five minutes' walk west of the centre. The fort, **El Castillo San Cristóbal**, has been well restored, and at the foot of the northern ramparts is the tomb of Juan Lindo, president of Honduras 1847-1852, who introduced free education through a system of state schools.

## Balneario Aguas Termales
*Daily 0600-2000, US$2.50, rental of towels, hammock, inner tube, restaurant/bar.*

Some 6 km from Gracias along the road to Esperanza (side road signposted), are hot, mineral-rich, communal thermal pools in the forest for swimming and soaking. It takes an hour to walk there via a path, and 1½ hours by road. To find the path, walk 2 km beyond the bridge over Río Arcagual to a second bridge before which turn right by a white house. Climb the hill and take the first path on the left (no sign), cross the river and continue for about 15 minutes to the pools. The Balneario is a good place to have a barbecue and rest your weary limbs after hiking.

## Parque Nacional Celaque
This protected park is home to **Monte Celaque**, which at 2849 m, is the highest point in Honduras. It takes at least a day to climb from Gracias to the summit but most people allow two days to enjoy the trip.

The Parque Nacional Celaque visitor centre (1400 m) is 8 km from Gracias, or two hours' walk. There are several intersections, so it's best to ask at each. Not much of the 8-km road from Gracias to the park is passable when wet, without a high-clearance or 4WD vehicle. Behind the visitor centre is a trail going down to the river where a crystal-clear pool and waterfall make for wonderful bathing.

The trail to the summit begins from behind the visitor centre. Along the trail the trees are marked with ribbons. It takes at least six hours to reach the summit from the visitor centre and it's four hours down. The first three hours of ascent are easy, to a campsite at 2000 m (**Campamento Don Tomás**) where there is small hut. A

**Tip...**
A helpful tourist office in the Parque Central can store luggage and arrange transport to Parque Nacional Celaque.

better campsite if you can make it is **Campamento Naranjo**, with water, at about 2500 m – but you'll need a tent. Between these two sites, the climb is particularly steep and in cloudforest. Look out for spider monkeys. Above 2600 m quetzals have been seen. Many hikers don't bother with the summit as it is forested and enclosed. There is a trail westward from the summit to Belén Gualcho which is steep towards Belén. It takes a couple of days and a guide might be a good idea.

You can also enjoy a day walk to **Mirador La Cascada** ① *entry fee US$3 plus US$3 per night camping in the mountain*, about three hours from the visitor centre, 1½ hours downhill going back. Transport can be arranged with the tourist office in the Plaza Central (US$10 per vehicle for up to four people).

For guides, contact **Dona Mercedes' Comedor** in Villa Verde (T2994-96681), **Don Luis Melgar**, or **Don Cándido** (T299715114), or one of their brothers; all recommended. Ask the guide the exact way or pay US$6 for the guide. There is a warden, Miguel, living nearby who can supply food and beer but it is safer to take supplies from Gracias. Contact **Cohdefor** or CIPANAC in Gracias before leaving for full information.

Don't forget good hiking boots, warm clothing, insect repellent and, given the dense forest and possibility of heavy cloud, a compass is also recommended for safety. Also, beware of snakes.

Visiting the other peaks around Gracias is more complicated but interesting.

## Listings Gracias *map p504*

### Where to stay

**$$$ Posada de Don Juan**
*Calle Principal opposite Banco de Occidente, T2656-1020, www. posadadedonjuanhotel.com.*
An attractive colonial-style lodging with a pleasant garden, refreshing pool and 42 rooms. Good beds, great hot showers, nice big towels, cotton sheets, Wi-Fi and cable TV.

### Gracias

To Santa Rosa de Copán

Río Arcagual

Cohdefor

C Principal

Las Mercedes

Palacio Municipal

Parque Central

San Marcos

Av Eleuterio Galeano Trejo

Av Principal Dr Juan Lindo

To ① & Castillo San Cristóbal

To Santa Lucía & Celaque

San Sebástian

To La Campa

To ②

N

200 metres
200 yards

To La Esperanza & Aguas Termales

**Where to stay**
El Trapiche **1**
Finca El Capitán **2**
Guancascos **3**
María Rosa **4**
Posada de Don Juan **5**
Real Camino Lenca **6**

**Restaurants** 🍴
Café-Bar El Gran Cogolon **1**
El Señorial **2**
Kandil Kafe and Pizzeria **3**
Rinconcito Graciano **4**

### $$$-$$ Real Camino Lenca
*Av Juan Lindo y Calle Jeremia Cisneros, T2656-1712, www.realcaminolencahotel.com.*
Set in a converted colonial mansion, the centrally located Real Camino Lenca is one of the town's more upscale options. Rooms are spotless and well-attired, but the hotel's unique selling point is the breezy rooftop bar with a modern lounge ambience and panoramic views. There's a great restaurant too. Recommended.

### $$ Guancascos
*At the west end of Hondutel road, T2656-1219, www.guancascos.com.*
A lovely little colonial guesthouse set on a former coffee farm on a hillside. Rooms are simple, clean and tranquil; also rents 2-room cabin at Villa Verde adjacent to Monte Celaque visitor centre. Strong green and sustainable ethos and lots of local community connections. Recommended.

### $ Finca El Capitán
*1 km from the centre of town, T2656-1659, www.hotelfincaelcapitan.galeon.com.*
Simple *cabaña*-style lodgings set around a leafy garden, adobe-built and each with their own hammock, cable TV and hot water. There is a restaurant on site and a small pool for cooling off. A pleasant, good value option with natural surroundings, but you may need a moto-taxi to get into town.

### $ Hotel El Trapiche
*Next to the Terminal de buses Celaque Gracias, T3158-6102.*
This motel-style option is set in pleasant verdant grounds and is a good option for drivers. Accommodation includes 14 rooms with cable TV, hot water and a/c.

### $ María Rosa
*Av José María Medina, 150 m south of the Central Park, Barrio El Rosario.*
Another colonial option, this is a low-key and economical place. Rooms overlook a small courtyard with a dipping pool. Restaurant. Helpful, English-speaking staff. Unpretentious and reliable.

## Parque Nacional Celaque

### $ Visitor centre
There are 7 beds, shower and cooking facilities, drinks available, well maintained. There is another cabin nearby with 10 beds. Take a torch and sleeping bag.

## Restaurants

For breakfast, try the *comedores* near the market or, better, the restaurant at Hotel Iris (good *comida corriente* too) or Guancascos.

### $$$ Cafe-Bar El Gran Cogolon
*Inside the Hotel Real Camino Lenca, Av Juan Lindo y Calle Jeremia Cisneros, www.realcaminolencahotel.com.*
This elegant bar-restaurant enjoys commanding views of the town from its rooftop perch. They have a wine list and an array of cocktails. Pastas are their speciality. Lounge-style ambience, good for a drink.

### $$$-$$ Kandil Kafe & Pizzeria
*Av José María Medina 34, Barrio La Merced.*
Set in a cosy colonial townhouse, this lovely little eatery offers an eclectic range of international food from nachos to chicken wings. Pizzas are what they do best, however. There's seating indoors and out with a pleasant garden-patio at the back. Good atmosphere. Recommended.

### $$ Guancascos
*See Where to stay, above.*
The popular Guanascos has pleasant views of the town from its terrace and it offers an array of local and international fare including spaghetti bolognese, black bean soup, Mexican tacos and Honduran breakfasts. Relaxing space. Recommended.

**$$ Rinconcito Graciano**
*2½ blocks south of the Mercado Municipal, Av San Sebastián.*
This well-established Graciano haunt serves a variety of local and international fare, including *nacatamales* with chicken or pork, sandwiches, soups and vegetarian dishes. Uses lots of local produce. Rustic and earthy ambience.

**$ El Señorial**
*Main street.*
Simple meals and snacks, once house of former president Dr Juan Lindo.

---

**Parque Nacional Celaque**

**$ Comedor Doña Alejandrina**
*Just before the visitor centre.*
Provides excellent breakfasts.

## What to do

**Tour operators**
**Guancascos Tourist Centre**, *at the Guancascos Hotel, see Where to stay, above.* Arranges tours and expeditions to Monte Celaque Parque Nacional, local villages and other attractions.

## Transport

**Bus**
A bus goes to **La Esperanza** at 0530 and 0730, or take bus to Erandique (they leave when full from La Planta) get off at San Juan from where frequent buses goes to La Esperanza (1 hr, US$2). There is a bus service to **Santa Rosa de Copán**, US$1.30, from 0530 to 1630, 5 times a day, 1½ hrs; beautiful journey through majestic scenery. Also to **San Pedro Sula** at 0500, 0800 and 0900, US$3, 4 hrs. Daily bus service to **Lepaera** 1400, 1½ hrs, US$1.50; daily bus to **San Manuel de Colohuete** at 1300. **Cotral** bus ticket office is 1 block north of Parque Central. **Torito** bus, a few metres from the main terminal, has buses to the Guatemalan border at **Agua Caliente**, one at 1000, change buses at Nueva Ocotepeque; see also Border crossings box in Practicalities chapter.

---

## Santa Rosa de Copán and around  *Colour map 3, B1.*

*a storehouse of colonial heritage*

Santa Rosa (altitude 1160 m) is an important regional town with a colonial atmosphere of cobbled streets and some of the best architecture in Honduras. The town is set in some of the best scenery in Honduras and the fine weather makes it ideal for hiking, horses and mountain biking.

Originally known as Los Llanos, Santa Rosa was made a municipality in 1812 and became capital of the Department of Copán when it was split from Gracias (now Lempira). Santa Rosa owes its wealth to the fact that it's an agricultural and cattle-raising area. Maize and tobacco are grown here, and visitors can see traditional hand-rolling at the Flor de **Copán cigar factory** ① *3 blocks east of the bus terminal, T2662 0185, Mon-Fri until 1700, closed 1130-1300, tours in Spanish at 1000 and 1400, US$2 per person; ask the guard at the gate.* The central plaza and church are perched on a hilltop. There is a quieter plaza, the **Parque Infantil** ① *Calle Real Centenario y 6 Av SO*, a fenced playground and a pleasant place to relax. The main **market** ① *1 Calle and 3 Av NE*, has good leather items. **Farmers' markets** are held daily in Barrio Santa Teresa (take 4 Calle SE past 5 Avenida SE), and at 4 Calle SE and 5 Avenida SE on Sunday 0500 to 1000. For further information, visit www.visitesantarosadecopan.com.

## Around Santa Rosa de Copán

Taking time to explore some of the forested hills around Santa Rosa will lead you through spectacular scenery and give an insight into the life of agricultural Honduras.

There are buses from Santa Rosa west to the small town of **Dulce Nombre de Copán** (US$0.55). There are rooms available next to the Hondutel office. Hikers heading for Copán and the border can continue west through the mountains to stay at **San Agustín** (buses and pickups from Santa Rosa), take a hammock or sleeping bag, continuing next day through Mirasol to reach the Ruinas road at El Jaral, 11 km east of Copán ruins.

South of Santa Rosa, buses pass through **Cucuyagua**, with a scenic river, good swimming and camping on its banks, and **San Pedro de Copán**, an attractive village and an entry point into the Parque Nacional Celaque, see page 503.

A mule trail (see box, page 508) connects **Belén Gualcho**, a Lenca village in the mountains and a good base for exploring the surrounding area, with **San Manuel de Colohuete** (1500 m), which has a magnificent colonial church whose façade is sculpted with figures of saints. Buses go to San Manuel from Gracias at 1300, four hours, and there's usually a pickup returning in the evening. There are no hotels so you must ask villagers about places to stay. There is an equally fine colonial church 30 minutes by 4WD vehicle to the southwest at **San Sebastián Colosuca** (1550 m). The village has a mild climate (two *hospedajes*; or try Don Rubilio; food at Doña Clementina García or Doña

## Santa Rosa de Copán

**Where to stay** 🛏
Casa Real **1**
Elvir **2**
Hospedaje Calle Real **3**
Posada de Juan B&B **4**
San Jorge **5**

**Restaurants** 🍴
El Café de las Velas **1**
El Rodeo **2**
Flamingos **3**
Jireth Delicias
 Alimentarias **4**
Kaldi's Koffee **5**
Las Haciendas **6**
Lenca Maya **7**
Weekends Pizza **8**

100 metres
100 yards

## ON THE ROAD
## Walking from San Manuel Colohuete to Belén Gualcho

There is a well-defined, well-used and easy-to-follow mule trail linking these two villages, which makes a good one- or two-day hike. Maps are not essential as there are communities at many points along the way where advice can be sought.

As the local security situation is constantly changing, it is absolutely essential to check on the feasibility of this journey before setting out.

The path leading away from the village leaves from opposite the *pulpería* and *comedor* where the bus drops you, heading west and downhill into a valley. The path is used by 4WD vehicles and continues to San Sebastián. Just after the community of San José, after passing the last house, the path to Belén branches off. A smaller path leaves the 4WD track and climbs steeply up to your right and more northwest.

**One hour** Just after Peña Blanca, the path direction becomes unclear after it crosses an area of white chalky rocks. There are several other paths here. The main path heads north and steeply downhill at this point.

**Two hours** There is water all the year round in the Quebrada de Rogán.

**Three hours** All year round water in Río Gualmite, a short descent. After this there is a longish, steep ascent.

**Four hours** Just after this point the path branches on a large flat grassy area. Both paths lead to Belén Gualcho. The one to the left drops and crosses the river and then you are faced with a long, arduous and very steep ascent. We would recommend taking the path to the right, which exits to the far right of a grassy area by three small houses.

**Five hours** The path climbs as it skirts around the Cerro Capitán. Just after passing the steepest part, a small landslide forces the path into a descent almost to the river. From here, only 2 m above the river, you can walk steeply down off the path to the river bank where there is the most perfect campsite. Flat sandy soil in some shade on the edge of a coffee plantation and 2 m from the river.

**Six hours** From the camping site there is a long, continuous climb before dropping down sharply to cross the river. It is possible, but difficult, to cross the river at the point the path meets it. Take a small path off to the right just before the river, which leads to a suspension bridge. From the river it is a long continuous climb, not especially steep, to Belén Gualcho. It is between two small peaks that can be seen clearly after crossing the river. There are more houses after crossing the river and the odd *pulpería* where you can buy *refrescos* or food.

Alicia Molina). The **Feria de San Sebastián** is on 20 January. An hour's walk away is the Cueva del Diablo and 6 km away is Cerro El Alta with a lagoon at the top. From San Sebastián, a mule trail goes via the heights of **Agua Fría** to reach the route near the border at **Tomalá**.

## Where to stay

### Santa Rosa de Copán

#### $$$ Elvir
*Calle Real Centenario SO, 3 Av SO, T2662-0805, www.hotelelvir.com.*
A stylish, comfortable lodging with 41 rooms and 2 suites. It's safe, clean and quiet, and all rooms have their own bath, TV, hot water and drinking water. Free internet is in the lobby and good but pricey meals are served in the cafetería or restaurant. There's also a gym and rooftop pool and bar.

#### $$ Casa Real
*2 Calle entre 3 y 4 Av NE, next to the Instituto María Auxiliadora, Barrio El Carmen, T2662-0801, www.hotelcasarealsrc.com.*
One of the larger hotels in town, a bit dated and definitely geared to nationals, but reasonable. Rooms have LCD TVs, Wi-Fi and hot water, and suites come with jacuzzi. There is also a restaurant, gym, pool and business centre on site.

#### $$ Posada de Juan B&B
*Barrio El Carmen, half a block east of the Catholic university, T2662-0254, www.laposadadejuan.com.*
This homely and pleasant B&B has cosy enclaves and a tranquil garden space where you can relax, read and have breakfast. There are just 5 rooms, each equipped with cable TV, hot water, a/c and Wi-Fi. Good value and very hospitable. Recommended.

#### $$-$ Hotel San Jorge
*2 Av SO, entre Calle 1 y 2, T2662-0254, www.hotelsanjorgehn.com.*
This attentive family-run hotel sometimes provides lodging for Canadian Habitat for Humanity groups. Rooms are large, clean, and unpretentious and all come with cable TV, Wi-Fi, hot water, fan or a/c. Simple, solid and economical.

#### $ Hospedaje Calle Real
*Real Centenario y 6 Av NE.*
A clean, quiet and friendly place, the best of the cheaper accommodation but sometimes there are water failures.

### Around Santa Rosa de Copán
In Belén Gualcho hotels fill up quickly on Sat as traders arrive for the Sun market.

#### $ Hotelito El Carmen
*Belén Gualcho, 2 blocks east down from the church in the plaza.*
Friendly, clean, good views. Recommended.

#### $ Pensión
*Corquín.*
Good *pensión* with a charming garden. Recommended.

## Restaurants

### Santa Rosa de Copán
Carnivores are well served here.

#### $$ El Rodeo
*1 Av SE.*
El Rodeo is a well-established restaurant and one of the better ones in Santa Rosa, although it's pricey. It specializes in succulent steak slabs and grilled beef. Good atmosphere, with plenty of dead animals on the walls. Things get jaunty at weekends with live ranchero music.

#### $$ Flamingos
*1 Av SE, off main plaza, T2662-0654.*
Popular and long-serving place that specializes in seafood. They also do reasonably priced and good pasta and chop suey; upstairs there's a lounge bar with painted flamingos on walls.

## $$ Las Haciendas
*1 Av Calle SE.*
This colonial-style family restaurant dishes up generous portions of hearty grub. Steak and seafood, varied menu, filling *comida corriente*, and an attractive patio bar. Recommended.

## $$ Restaurante Lenca Maya
*Barrio Santa Teresa, 1 block south of Casa Bueso, T2662-1243.*
Set in a cosy colonial townhouse complete with solid wood tables and a romantic outdoor patio (recommended), Restaurante Lenca Maya serves Honduran-style barbecued meat and soups. Hearty and comforting, a good spot for families, couples or friends.

## $ Weekends Pizza
*3 Av SO and 3C, T2662-4221.*
*Wed-Sun 0900-2100.*
Downhill on edge of town but worth the walk for good-value pizzas, pasta and unusual extras like cheese straws; bright and colourful with lime green and marigold yellow walls. Home-made bread, local honey and coffee for sale. Recommended.

## Cafés

### El Café de las Velas
*Barrio El Carmen, half a block northeast of Hotel Elvir, www.elcafedelasvelas.com.*
So-called for its staggering variety of candles, this elegant coffee shop grows its own Arabica beans. They also do superb smoothies and cooked breakfasts.

### Jireth Delicias Alimentarias
*3 Calle, 3 Av, Barrio Santa Teresa, www.jireth.com.*
Jireth sells tasty artisanal breads, cakes, and hot coffee, as well as full plates of pasta.

### Kaldi's Koffee Shop
*South side of the cathedral, opposite Deporticentro Edwin.*

Located next to the church, a cosy little coffee house serving delicious caffeinated fare and sweet treats.

## Around Santa Rosa de Copán
In Belén Gualcho there are 2 *comedores* on south side of plaza and east side on corner with store.

## $ Comedor Mery
*Belén Gualcho.*
1 block northwest of plaza. Good food in a welcoming family atmosphere.

## Bars and clubs

### Santa Rosa de Copán

**Extasis**
Shows videos Mon-Thu night.

**Luna Jaguar**
*at 3 Av, between 1 Calle SE and Calle Real Centenario.*
The hottest disco in town, but proper dress required.

**Manzanitas**
*On the corner of 3 Av SE and Calle Real Centenario.*
A good place if you fancy singing your heart out to a little karaoke.

## Entertainment

### Santa Rosa de Copán
#### Cinema
Plaza Saavedra, opposite Blanca Nieves. Films shown nightly at 1900.

## Festivals

### Santa Rosa de Copán
**21-31 Aug  Festival de Santa Rosa de Lima;** the 'Tobacco Queen' is crowned at the end of the week.

## Shopping

### Santa Rosa de Copán
**Supermercado Manzanitaz**, *Calle Centenario*.

## What to do

### Santa Rosa de Copán
**Tour operators**
**Lenca Land Trails**, *at Hotel Elvir, T2662-1375*.
Run by Max Elvir, who organizes cultural
tours of the Lenca mountain villages in
western Honduras, hiking, mountain biking,
the lot; including a fascinating visit to a
*purería* (cigar workshop), pilgrimage shrine
and archaeological site at Quezailica, a
village 38 km north of Santa Rosa. Excellent
source of information about the region.
Highly recommended.

## Transport

### Santa Rosa de Copán
**Bus** Buses depart from the city bus station
on Carretera Internacional.
   **Local** 'El Urbano' bus to centre from bus
station (on Carretera Internacional, 2 km
below town, opposite Hotel Mayaland),
US$0.15,15 mins; taxi US$1.40.
   **Long distance** If coming from the
Guatemalan border at Nueva Ocotepeque,
the bus will stop at the end of town near

Av Centenario, 2 km below town, opposite
Hotel Mayaland. To **Tegucigalpa**, **Toritos**
leaves at 0400 from terminal Mon-Sat 0400
and 1000 Sun, US$6, 10 hrs; also **Empresa
de Transportes la Sultana** (T2662-0940)
has departures at 0500, 0700, and 0900.
Alternatively, take an express bus to San
Pedro Sula and an express bus on to
Tegucigalpa (US$5, 6 hrs). To **Gracias**,
**Transportes Lempira**, several 0630-1800,
1½ hrs, US$1.30. To **San Pedro Sula**,
US$2.50, 4 hrs, every 45 mins 0400-1730,
express service daily 2½ hrs, US$3.50
(**Empresa Torito**). Bus to **La Entrada**, 1 hr,
US$1. To **Copán Ruinas**, 4 hrs on good
road, US$2.90, several direct daily 1100,
1230 and 1400. Alternatively, take any bus
to La Entrada, 1 hr, US$1, and transfer to a
Copán Ruinas bus. South on paved road to
**Nueva Ocotepeque**, 6 daily, US$1.80, 2 hrs.
There you change buses for El Salvador and
Guatemala (1 hr to border, US$1, bus leaves
hourly until 1700).

### Around Santa Rosa de Copán
**Bus** Numerous buses head south daily
from Santa Rosa to **Corquín** (US$0.75, 2 hrs).
**Belén Gualcho** to **Santa Rosa** daily at 0430
(Sun at 0930). To **Gracias** from main plaza at
0400, 0500 and 1330.

## Nueva Ocotepeque *Colour map 3, B/C1.*
**cloudforest hiking near the international borders**

Heading south from Santa Rosa, Nueva Ocotepeque gives access to good hiking
and leads to the borders with Guatemala and El Salvador. The old colonial church of
La Vieja (or La Antigua) between Nueva Ocotepeque and the border is in the village
of Antigua Ocotepeque, which was founded in the 1540s, but destroyed by a flood
from Cerro El Pital in 1934.

**El Pital,** 30 km east of Nueva Ocotepeque, at 2730 m is the third highest point in Honduras
with several square kilometres of cloudforest. The **Guisayote Biological Reserve** protects
35 sq km of cloudforest, about 50% virgin and is reached from the Western Highway,
where there are trails and good hiking. Access is from El Portillo, the name of the pass
on the main road north. El Portillo to El Sillón, the park's southern entrance, is three to

five hours. There's a twice-daily bus from El Sillón to Ocotepeque. The park has not been developed for tourism.

The **Parque Nacional Montecristo** forms part of the Trifinio/La Fraternidad project, administered jointly by Honduras, Guatemala and El Salvador. The park is quite remote from the Honduran side, two to three days to the summit, but there are easy-to-follow trails. Access is best from Metapán in El Salvador. From the lookout point at the peak you can see about 90% of El Salvador and 20% of Honduras on a clear day. The natural resources office, for information, is opposite Texaco, two blocks from Hotel y Comedor Congolón at the south end of town. Raymond J Sabella of the US Peace Corps has written a very thorough description of the natural and historical attractions of the Department, including hikes, waterfalls and caves.

## Listings Nueva Ocotepeque

### Where to stay

**$$ Maya Chortis**
*Barrio San José, 4 Calle, 3 Av NE, T2653-3377.*
Good-value nice rooms with bath, double beds, hot water, fan, TV, minibar and phone. The quieter rooms are at back. There is also room service and a good restaurant. Breakfast included.

**$$ Sandoval**
*Opposite Hondutel, T2653-3098.*
Rooms and suites with private bath, hot water, cable TV, minibar, phone and room service; there's a good-value restaurant. Breakfast included.

**$ Gran**
*About 250 m from town at the junction of the roads for El Salvador and Guatemala, just north of town, at Sinuapa.*
Pleasant, clean place with bath and cold water, single beds only.

### Restaurants

**Comedor Nora** ($), Parque Central, and **Merendera Ruth** ($), 2 Calle NE, just off Parque Central, both offer economical *comida corriente*, preferable to *comedores* around bus terminal.

**$$ Sandoval and Don Chepe**
*At Maya Chortis.*
The best options. Excellent food, small wine lists, good value. Recommended.

### Transport

**Bus** Transportes Escobar daily service **Tegucigalpa** to Nueva Ocotepeque/ Agua Caliente, via La Entrada and Santa Rosa de Copán (12 Av entre 8 y 9 C, Barrio Concepción, Comayagüela, T2237-4897; **Hotel Sandoval**, T2653-3098, Nueva Ocotepeque). Buses to **San Pedro Sula** stop at La Entrada (US$1.70), 1st at 0030, for connections to Copán. There are splendid mountain views. From **San Pedro Sula** there are regular buses via Santa Rosa south (6 hrs, US$4.50); road is well paved.

★A charming town set in the hills just to the east of the border with Guatemala, Copán Ruinas (www.copanhonduras.org)– to give the town its full name – thrives and survives on visitors passing through to visit the nearby ruins (see page 521). Nevertheless, it is arguably the best-preserved and one of the most pleasant towns in Honduras. For those arriving from nearby Guatemala, it's a good place to stop for a few days before heading straight to San Pedro Sula (172 km) and the Bay Islands or Tegucigalpa (395 km). In addition to the enigmatic ruins of Copán, the town offers good hotels and restaurants, coffee plantation tours, hiking, caving, hot springs, horse riding, language schools and volunteer opportunities.

The **Museo de Arqueología** ⓘ *on the town square, Mon-Sat 0800-1600, US$2*, has explanations in Spanish of the Maya empire and stelae. The exhibits are on the dusty side, but there is an interesting selection of artefacts, a burial site and a tomb that was unearthed during a road-building project. The completely restored Old Cuartel now houses the **Casa K'inich Interactive Children's Museum** ⓘ *Up the hill from Hotel Marina Copán, www.asociacioncopan.org, US$1.10, Wed-Fri 1400-1700*, an interesting museum

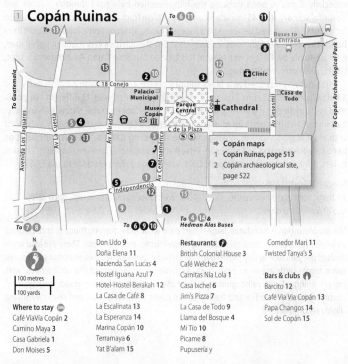

# Copán Ruinas

**Where to stay** 🛏
Café VíaVía Copán **2**
Camino Maya **3**
Casa Gabriela **1**
Don Moises **5**
Don Udo **9**
Doña Elena **11**
Hacienda San Lucas **4**
Hostel Iguana Azul **7**
Hotel-Hostel Berakah **12**
La Casa de Café **8**
La Escalinata **13**
La Esperanza **14**
Marina Copán **10**
Terramaya **6**
Yat B'alam **15**

**Restaurants** 🍴
British Colonial House **3**
Café Welchez **2**
Carnitas Nía Lola **1**
Casa Ixchel **6**
Jim's Pizza **7**
La Casa de Todo **9**
Llama del Bosque **4**
Mi Tío **10**
Picame **8**
Pupusería y
Comedor Mari **11**
Twisted Tanya's **5**

**Bars & clubs** 🍸
Barcito **12**
Café Via Via Copán **13**
Papa Changos **14**
Sol de Copán **15**

➡ **Copán maps**
1 Copán Ruinas, page 513
2 Copán archaeological site, page 522

for everyone, not just for kids, and in a nice spot with great views of the town from towers in the perimeter wall. An excellent permanent **photography exhibition** ⓘ *Mon-Fri, 0800-1600, free*, has opened at the Municipalidad on the main plaza. There are rare period photos and documentation from the first archaeological expedition to Copán at the turn of the 20th century, donated by Harvard University's Peabody Museum and archaeologists Barbara and Bill Fash.

## Around Copán Ruinas

There are many caves around Copán to visit; some of which have unearthed Maya artefacts; ask locally. Also here, and in the neighbouring part of Guatemala, are a few remaining Chorti indigenous villages, such as La Pintada, surrounded by cornfields and forests, which is great countryside for hiking and horse-riding (see What to do, page 519). The villages are particularly interesting to visit on 1 November, Día de Los Muertos, when there are family and communal ceremonies for the dead. Nine kilometres east of Copán is **Santa Rita**, a small colonial town on the Copán River with cobblestones and red roofs.

## Luna Jaguar Spa

*20 km north from Copán, T2651-4746, www.lunajaguarspa.com, daily 0900-2100.*

The mineral-rich hot springs at Luna Jaguar Spa are a great place to rest and unwind, especially if you've been trekking the hills. Reached by a road through villages and beautiful scenery, it's a 45-minute journey by vehicle from Copán; pickups sometimes go for about US$25, shared between passengers. The cheapest option is local transport from beside the soccer field (three buses daily, US$1.50), though it's a very rough unpaved road, only advisable by 4WD in wet season. It is best to use **Base Camp Adventures** for trips, US$15, plus entry to hot springs.

Imaginatively designed as a Maya spiritual centre, complete with a tunnel entry to a Xibalba 'underworld', Luna Jaguar offers a hedonistic treat, with 13 different hot pools, mud bath, hydrotherapy warm shower, DIY hot stone foot massage, nature trail and river bathing (US$10, plus extra for massage treatments), all set among the steamy lush forest with aloof Maya sculptures looking over the simmering bathers. There is a therapist on hand for advice; snacks and drinks are served at the poolside. There are changing facilities, toilets, drinks and snacks in the park. Cold water pools before entrance to spa, US$3.

## Macaw Mountain

*10 mins from the town centre, T2651-4245, www.macawmountain.org, open 0900-1700, US$10 (valid for 3 days).*

Macaw Mountain is Honduras' largest bird park with 130+ parrots, toucans and macaws, all locally rescued or donated, including some injured and sick birds. There are also some birds of prey, including tiny pigmy owls, all lovingly cared for in clean, spacious enclosures; some tamer birds are in an open area. Activities include tours of the coffee *finca*, with expert bilingual naturalist guides; a riverside restaurant serving good, hearty food, including excellent coffee and freshly baked cakes; a visitor centre; and river swimming. Highly recommended.

## La Entrada: Copán to San Pedro Sula

Approximately 60 km east of Copán Ruinas on Highway CA11, the hot, dusty town of La Entrada marks the junction with Highway CA4, also known as the Western Highway. The town offers bus connections with Santa Rosa (see page 506) to the south and San Pedro Sula 115 km away to the northeast, but due to the risk of highway robbery, it is recommended that you take a direct non-stop service from Copán.

**El Puente** ① *daily 0800-1600, US$5*, is a national archaeological park reached by taking a turn-off, 4.5 km west from La Entrada on the Copán road, then turning right on a well-signposted paved road, 6 km to the visitor centre. It is near the confluence of the Chamelecón and Chinamito rivers and is thought to have been a regional centre between AD 600 and 900.

## Listings Copán Ruinas *map p513*

### Where to stay

#### $$$$ Hacienda San Lucas
*Couth out of town, T2651-4495,*
*www.haciendasanlucas.com.*
This renovated hacienda home has lovely views of Copán river valley and is a great spot for calm and tranquillity. Accommodation and amenities include 8 rooms with hot water bath, Wi-Fi, restaurant and hiking trails. Secluded and romantic.

#### $$$ Camino Maya
*Corner of main plaza, T2651-4646,*
*www.caminomayahotel.com.*
Another solid colonial-style option. Rooms are bright and airy; some have balconies, but those on the courtyard are quieter than those facing the street. Facilities include a good restaurant, cable TV, a/c and Wi-Fi. English spoken.

#### $$$ La Casa de Café
*4½ blocks west of plaza, T2651-4620,*
*www.casadecafecopan.com.*
Renovated colonial home with beautifully designed garden and lovely views over the valley. Rates include breakfast, coffee all day, library and expert local information. Friendly and interesting hosts, English spoken. It's popular so it's best to reserve in advance. Protected parking. The **Bamboo**

Patio massage pavilion offers 1-hr relaxation massage. Wi-Fi. Recommended.

#### $$$ Terramaya
*2 blocks uphill from main plaza, T2651-4623,*
*www.terramayacopan.com.*
The town's first boutique-style hotel with 6 small but tasteful rooms, glorious countryside views from those upstairs, leafy little garden with massage area and outdoor shower; lounge areas and library. Breakfast included. Same owners as La Casa del Café (see above), very helpful and knowledgeable for local tours and activities.

#### $$$-$$ Casa Gabriela
*Calle Independencia, 1 block south of the*
*Parque Central, Barrio El Centro, T2651-4436,*
*www.hotelcasagabriela.com.*
A well-attired boutique option whose rooms combine airy simplicity, earthy tones and solid wood furniture to relaxing effect. Rooms have semi-orthopaedic beds, LCD TVs, cotton sheets, a/c and Wi-Fi. The colonial patio has leafy plants and a restaurant.

#### $$$-$$ La Esperanza
*South of town on the banks of*
*the Copán river, T2651-4676,*
*www.haciendalaesperanza.org.*
The delightfully secluded setting of La Esperanza, a colonial-style B&B just a short

walk out of town, encompasses verdant landscaped grounds filled with green lawns, fountains, tropical trees and patios. Accommodation includes 4 fully appointed rooms with modern amenities and a touch of rustic chic. 100% of proceeds go to **Paramedics for Children**.

### $$$-$$ Marina Copán
*On the plaza occupying almost an entire block, T2651-4070, www.hotelmarinacopan.com.*
A long-established colonial favourite with a pool, sauna, restaurant, bar, live marimba music at weekends; also caters for tour groups. Rooms and suites are tasteful and spacious with hand-crafted furniture and balconies overlooking the plaza. Friendly atmosphere. Recommended.

### $$$-$$ Yat B'alam
*Calle Independencia, Barrio El Centro, T2651-4388, www.yatbalam.com.*
Offering an array of atmospheric boutique rooms, this handsome colonial townhouse retains its old school charm with cobblestone enclaves, terracotta tiles, wooden rocking chairs, wrought iron beds and other traditional touches. Modern amenities include Wi-Fi, a/c, fridge, cable TV and DVD player.

### $$ Don Udo
*Av Mirador, Barrio El Centro, T2651-4533, www.donudos.com.*
This colonial-style, family-run B&B features a calming breakfast patio surrounded by abundant plants. Accommodation includes 14 rooms overlooking the central courtyard. There is transport, tours, Wi-Fi, massage, sauna, sun deck, laundry services and a fully stocked international bar with a daily happy hour.

### $$ Doña Elena
*Av Centroamérica, Barrio El Calvario, T2651-4029, www.casadonaelena.com.*

Founded in 1998 by Doña Elena and her last son, Nery, this homely *hospedaje* prides itself on hospitality. They don't promise luxury, but rooms are comfortable and reasonably priced, all fully kitted with TVs, a/c, Wi-Fi, hot water and panoramic views of the gardens or mountains. Solid, helpful and reliable.

### $$ La Escalinata
*Av La Cuesta, Barrio Buena Vista, www.hotellaescalinata.com.*
La Escalinata is a dependable guesthouse with 9 simple but well-equipped rooms: facilities include Wi-Fi, hot water and semi-orthopaedic beds. The inn's unique selling point is its view of the mountains and treetops, yours to enjoy if you snag a room with a private balcony.

### $$-$ Don Moises
*Calle de la Plaza, T2651-4543, www.hoteldonmoisescopan.com.*
Don Moises offers simple budget rooms equipped with Wi-Fi, fan or a/c, hot water, and cable TV. There's also a shared kitchen, lockers, laundry and relaxing sun terrace with hammocks. Kind, helpful and hospitable; a good choice for thrifty wanderers.

### $ Café Via Via Copán
*T2651-4652, www.viaviacafe.com.*
Great rooms, part of a worldwide Belgian network of cafés, breakfast US$2.75, special price for students with card and discounts for more than 1 night, hot water, good beds, bar and great vegetarian food.

### $ Hostel Iguana Azul
*Next to La Casa de Café and under same ownership, T2651-4620, www.iguanaazulcopan.com.*
Good for backpackers, this clean, comfortable hostel with colonial decor offers dorm-style bunk beds in 2 rooms, with shared bath; also 3 more private double rooms. There is hot water, free purified water, lockers, laundry facilities, garden

patio, common area, books, magazines, travel guides (including Footprint), maps, garden, fans and a safe box. English spoken.

### $ Hotel-Hostel Berakah
*1 block north of Parque Central, T9828-9827, www.hotelberakahcopan.hostel.com.*
This pleasant and centrally located hotel-hostel has some of the cheapest dorm beds in town, which come complete with quality mattresses and useful amenities like Wi-Fi, a pool table, kitchen and hammocks. Intimate, friendly and affordable. There are a few private rooms too.

## Apartments

### Casa Jaguar Rental Home
*Just 5 blocks from Parque Central, T2651-4620, www.casajaguarcopan.com.*
Comfortable village residence with 2 double bedrooms with a/c, fully equipped for self-catering. Available for the night, week or month. Contact **La Casa de Café**, see above.

### La Entrada
There are several other cheapies and no-frills guesthouses in town.

### $$-$ San Carlos
*T2661-2228, www.hotelelsancarlos.com.*
Reliable and economical with very adequate rooms, all with a/c and cable TV. There's also a pool, bar and a restaurant. Excellent value.

## Restaurants

### $$$ Hacienda San Lucas
*South out of town, T2651-4495, www.haciendasanlucas.com.*
Using traditional recipes and old world cooking techniques, Hacienda San Lucas has developed an interesting style of Mayan fusion cuisine. Reservations are required for lunch (1200-1400) and dinner; drop-ins for groups of less than 4 welcome for

breakfast. A great place for a special meal. Recommended.

### $$$ Twisted Tanya's
*Calle Independencia and Av La Cuesta, T2651-4182, www.twistedtanya.com. Mon-Sat 1500-2200.*
Happy hour 1600-1800. Fine dining and quirky retro decor (ie mirror balls). The menu includes rich and creative international cuisine such as seasonal fish with a cream loroco flower bud sauce, tequila shrimp and slow-roasted pork with sage and onion stuffing. Lovely open-air setting on the 2nd floor.

### $$$-$$ British Colonial House
*Av Copán y Calle 18 Conejo, Parque Central.*
This popular British-run gastropub serves a diverse range of international fare in generous portions including Thai curries, chicken tikka masala, steaks and much more. For the homesick, there's 'pub grub' and comfort food straight from old Blighty, including shepherd's pie.

### $$$-$$ Casa Ixchel
*Approximately 25 mins out of town by car, shuttles offered for spa users, T2651-4515, www.spaixchel.com.*
Casa Ixchel is a day spa and coffee finca. Its restaurant is set in a peaceful outdoor patio filled with potted palms and dazzling bougainvillea and their menu includes cooked breakfasts, light meals and international café fare, such as pancakes, burgers and pastas, all accompanied by seasonal fruit juices, medicinal tea and locally sourced coffee. A tranquil healing space.

### $$$-$$ Mi Tío
*Av Centroamericano, 1½ blocks south of the Parque Central, T9791-6572, www.mitiocopan.com.*
This family-run Uruguayan restaurant serves hearty platters of beef, chicken and pork straight off the *parillada*, along with a few

fish and vegetarian dishes, sandwiches and light snacks. Lots of flavour, recommended for carnivores.

### $$ Café Via Via Copán
*See Where to stay, above.*
Via Via serves an eclectic range of international grub from hamburgers to lasagne to *comida típica*. Can be hit-and-miss but breakfasts are fairly reliable. A pleasant space and a popular evening nightspot with the traveller crowd.

### $$ Jim's Pizza
*½ a block from Hotel Camino Maya.*
Jim's Pizza claims to be the first and most authentic pizza joint in western Honduras with thin-crust pizzas prepared according to traditional family recipes. They also serve burgers, lasagne and subs and, at weekends, rotisserie chicken. A friendly, casual place, popular with tourists and expats.

### $$ La Casa de Todo
*1 block from Parque Central, www. casadetodo.com. Open 0700-2100.*
In a pleasant garden setting, this restaurant has internet, a craft shop and book exchange. They often host NGOs and other community groups.

### $$ Llama del Bosque
*2 blocks west of plaza. Open for breakfast, lunch and dinner.*
This attractive place offers large portions of reasonable food; try their *carnitas típicas*. Recommended.

### $ Carnitas Nía Lola
*2 blocks south of Parque Central, at the end of the road. Daily 0700-2200.*
A busy bar with *comida típica* served in a relaxed atmosphere. Also has a book exchange.

### $ Pupusería y Comedor Mari
*Av Sesesmil.*
The best cheap, typical food in town, with daily specials like seafood soup. Clean, decent service, and very popular with locals at lunchtime. Food is fresh, cheap and plentiful.

## Cafés
### Café Welchez
*Next to Hotel Marina Copán, www.cafehonduras.com.*
They serve their own gourmet coffee, good cakes and desserts, including coconut flan, but it's on the pricey side. There's a pleasant upstairs terrace.

### Santa Rita
Unnamed outdoor restaurant, off the main road next to the Esso station. Speciality *tajadas*, huge portions, cheap. Recommended.

## Bars and clubs

### Barcito
*1 block down from SW corner of main square.*
Small, cosy, laid-back bar on an upstairs open terrace. Happy hour is 1700-1900. They also serve great and inexpensive gourmet snacks and tapas.

### Café Via Via Copán
*See Where to stay, above. Open every night till 2400.*
European chill-out lounge vibe, comfortable and popular, food until 2100.

### Papa Changos
*Located a few blocks from downtown.*
After hours spot, popular with young locals and traveller crowd. Gets going at midnight on Fri and Sat. The place to let loose and party till dawn.

## Sol de Copán

*Calle El Mirador, Barrio Buena Vista, look for the turret.*

Managed by Tomas from Munich, the Sol de Copán is a bona fide German microbrewery with some excellent nectar on tap, undoubtedly the best German brews in Honduras. If all that authentic Bavarian beer leaves you peckish, order some bratwurst to soak it up. Recommended.

## Shopping

Selling all sorts of local crafts are **La Casa de Todo** (down the street from **Banco de Occidente**), one of Copán's best crafts shop, with a popular café for light meals and snacks (see Restaurants, above); **Yax Kuk Mo** (the southwest corner of plaza), has biggest selection; **Mayan Connection** (opposite **Barcito**, see Bars and clubs, above), is a bit more expensive but offers better than average quality.

**La Casa del Jade**, *1 block uphill from Hotel Marina Copán (with another branch in lobby).* Specializes in high-class designer jewellery.

## What to do

### Language schools

**Academia de Español Guacamaya**, T2651-4360, www.guacamaya.com. Classes US$160 a week, plus homestay US$60. Recommended.

**Ixbalanque**, T2651-4432, www.ixbalanque. com. This school offers one-to-one teaching plus board and lodging with a local family, US$300 for classes and a 7-day homestay.

### Birdwatching and wildlife observation

**Alexander Alvarado**, *based in Copán Ruinas, T9751-1680, www.honduranbirds.com.* Alexander Alvarado also leads birdwatching and hiking tours around the country; he knows his stuff and speaks good English.

**Bob Gallardo**, *T2651-4133, www.birdsof honduras.com.* A birding guide and naturalist, Bob Gallardo is an expert on Honduras flora and fauna. He leads birding trips, natural history tours, orchid and serpent tours around Copán and other parts of Honduras, including La Mosquitia.

### Canopy tours

**Canopy Copán Ruinas**, *2 km from downtown on the road to the hot springs, T9330-2024.* One of the best canopy tours in the country with 16 high-speed cables; the longest runs for a staggering 1 km. Stunning views of the countryside and rainforest. Contact the canopy directly or via a tour operator in town (around US$45 per person).

### Coffee tours

**Copán Coffee Tour**, *Finca Santa Isabel, 40 mins' drive from Copán Ruinas, T2651-4202, www.cafehonduras.com.* Run by family producers of high-quality Welchez coffee for 3 generations. The 3- to 4-hr tour of grounds shows the whole production process in a lovely hillside setting, with expert multilingual guides; US$25-30. There is also a terrace restaurant overlooking river. Horse riding is available, through countryside rich with flora and fauna, including some 80 bird species and medicinal plants. The best tour of its kind in the area. Highly recommended.

### Horse riding

You will probably be approached with offers of horse hire, which is a good way of getting to nearby attractions. Riding trips are available to Los Sapos and Las Sepulturas, US$15 for 3 hrs. Watch out for taxi and on the street recommendations as the quality and price can be poor.

**Finca El Cisne**, *T2651-4695, www.fincaelcisne. com.* Full-day tours to the coffee plantation high in the mountains including horse riding, lunch and transport, US$82 per person with overnight accommodation available for an extra US$13. Also trips to hot springs on this working hacienda.

## Tour operators

**Base Camp Adventures**, *T2651-4695, www.basecampcopan.wordpress.com.* Nature hikes US$10, treks, motocross tours US$40, horse riding US$15, expedition hikes US$20 and transport including shuttles to Guatemala City, Antigua US$20.

**Copán Connections**, *T2651-4182, www.copanconnections.com.* Tours, hotels, transport, specializing in Copán and Bay Islands. Run by Tanya of **Twisted Tanya** fame.

**MC Tours**, *Av Centroamérica, T2651 4154, www.mctours-honduras.com.* Local and countrywide tours.

**Transport**

### Bus

Heading inland you normally have to go to San Pedro Sula before heading for the coast or south to the capital.

There is a 1st-class direct service to **San Pedro Sula** with connections to **Tegucigalpa** and **La Ceiba** with **Hedman Alas** (T2651-4037, www.hedmanalas.com), 3 a day, 3 hrs to San Pedro. US$16, at 1030 and 1430, with connections in San Pedro for Tegucigalpa and La Ceiba. Also 0515 daily connection to **Tela**, 8 hrs, US$22 and **San Pedro Sula Airport**, US$21. To **Guatemala City** (US$35) and **Antigua** (US$42) at 1420 and 1800. To **San Pedro Sula Casasola Express** for San Pedro Sula (T2651-4078) at 0400, 0500, 0600, 0700 and 1400. Both services are comfortable, efficient, good value and with reclining seats.

If heading for **Santa Rosa de Copán** or **Gracias** get a bus to the junction at La Entrada and change there. Buses for **La Entrada** leave Copán Ruinas every 30 mins, 1 hr, US$1.80.

**Plus+ Agency** daily shuttle bus service (www.plustravelguate.com, T2651-4088), main office in Copán Ruinas, Comercial Handal, Calle Independencia, to many destinations around Honduras and to Guatemala City and Antigua (US$8). If travelling in a group, private express minibuses can be hired to **San Pedro Sula**, **Tela**, **La Ceiba**, and airport from **Hotel Patty** and **Yaragua Tours** – US$120 regardless of number of people. Numerous boys greet you on arrival to carry bags or offer directions for a small fee; while most are good kids, some will tell you hotels are closed when they aren't.

### Tuk-tuk

As in much of Honduras, tuk-tuks have arrived, providing cheap, easy transport. Short trips around town cost US$0.50, **Macaw Mountain Bird Park** US$1.10, **ruins** US$0.80, **Hedman Alas** terminal US$1.10.

## Copán archaeological site *Colour map 3, B1.*

#### a Classic-era Mayan centre with astounding statues and sculptures

★The magnificent ruins of Copán are one of Central America's major Maya sites, certainly the most significant in Honduras, and they mark the southeastern limit of Maya dominance.

Just 1 km from the village, there is a path beside the road from Copán to the ruins which passes two stelae en route.

Photographs of the excavation work and a maquette of the site are located in a small exhibition room at the visitor centre. There is a cafetería by the entrance to the ruins, and also a handicrafts shop, in the Parque Arqueológico, next to the bookshop, with local and country maps, and a Spanish/English guidebook for the ruins, which is rather generalized. Useful books are: *Scribes, Warriors and Kings: City of Copán*, by William and Barbara Fash, and *History Carved in Stone, a guide to Copán*, by William Fash and Ricardo Argucía, published locally and available at the site. Luggage can be left for free.

### Museo de Escultura Maya
*US$7, ticket from the main ticket office not at the museum.*

It is essential to visit the museum before the ruins. The impressive and huge two-storey Museum of Maya Sculpture and sculpture park houses the recently excavated carvings and has good explanations in Spanish and English. In the middle of the museum is an open-air courtyard with a full-size reproduction of the Rosalila temple, found intact buried under Temple 16 with its original paint and carvings (see below). A reproduction of the doorway to Temple 16 is on the upper floor. The museum houses the original stelae to prevent weather damage, while copies will be placed on site. More than 2000 other objects found at Copán are also in the museum. The exit leads to the ruins via the nature trail.

### Archaeological site

The ruins were engulfed in jungle when John Lloyd Stephens and Frederick Catherwood examined them in 1839. Stephens, a lawyer, and Catherwood, an architect, were the first English-speaking travellers to explore the regions originally settled by the Maya. They are credited with recording the existence of many of the ruins in the Maya area. Some of the finest examples of sculpture from Copán are now in London and Boston.

In the 1930s, the Carnegie Institute cleared the ground and rebuilt the

> ### Essential Copán archaeological site
>
> #### Site information
>
> Daily 0800-1600, US$15 entrance to ruins and Las Sepulturas, admission valid for one day. To explore the tunnels is a pricey and unnecessary, US$15. Bilingual guided tours available (US$25, two hours), recommended. The Copán Guide Association has a kiosk in the parking area where qualified bilingual guides can be hired at a fixed rate.
>
> #### Tip...
>
> Get to the ruins as early as possible, or stay late in the day so you have a chance to be there without hordes of people.

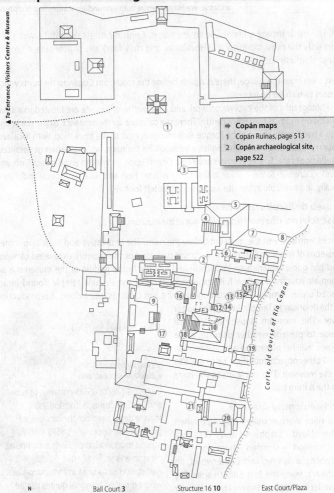

> ➡ **Copán maps**
> 1 Copán Ruinas, page 513
> 2 Copán archaeological site, page 522

Corte, old course of Río Copan

N

50 metres
50 yards

Main Plaza with Stelae **1**
Acrópolis **2**

Ball Court **3**
Hieroglyphic Stairway **4**
Structure 26 **5**
Council House,
  Temple 22A **6**
Temple of Meditation/
  Temple 22 **7**
House of Knives **8**
Structure 13 **9**

Structure 16 **10**
Altar Q **11**
Rosalila Building
  (within Structure 16) **12**
Entrance to Rosalila &
  Jaguar tunnels **13**
Hunal Building
  (beneath Rosalila)
  & Tomb of Founder **14**

East Court/Plaza
  de los Jaguares **15**
Plaza Occidental **16**
Altar I **17**
Altar H **18**
Temple 18 **19**
Structure 32 **20**
Zona Residencial **21**

Hieroglyphic Stairway, and since then the ruins have been maintained by the government. Some of the most complex carvings are found on the 21 **stelae**, or 3-m columns of stones on which the passage of time was originally believed to have been recorded. Under many of the stelae was a vault; some have been excavated. The stelae are deeply incised and carved with faces, figures and animals. There are royal portraits with inscriptions recording deeds and the lineage of those portrayed as well as dates of birth, marriage and death. Ball courts were revealed during excavation, and one of them has been fully restored. The **Hieroglyphic Stairway** leads up a pyramid; its upper level supported a temple. Its other sides are still under excavation. The stairway is covered for protection, but a good view can be gained from the foot and there is access to the top via the adjacent plaza.

After Hurricane Mitch, the **Rosalila Temple**, in Temple 16, was opened to the public, as were other previously restricted excavations, in an effort to attract more visitors. The Rosalila and Jaguar tunnels below the site are now open to visitors at an additional cost (see above). Much fascinating excavation work is now in progress, stacks of labelled carved stones have been placed under shelters, and the site looks like it is becoming even more interesting as new buildings are revealed.

The most atmospheric buildings are those still half-buried under roots and soil. The last stela was set up in Copán between AD 800 and 820, after less than five centuries of civilized existence. The nearby river has been diverted to prevent it encroaching on the site when in flood.

Also near the ruins is a *sendero natural* (nature trail) through the jungle to the minor ball court; take mosquito repellent. The trail takes 30 minutes and has a few signposts explaining the plants, animals and spirituality of the forest to the Maya. After 1600 is the best time to see animals on the *sendero natural*, which is open until 1700. About 4 km from the main centre is the ceremonial site known as **Los Sapos** ① *entry US$2* (The Toads), a pre-Classic site with early stone carvings. The toad was a Maya symbol of fertility. East of the main ruins near Los Sapos is a stone, **Estela 12**, which lines up with another, **Estela 10**, on the other side of the valley at sunrise and sunset on 12 April every year.

One kilometre beyond the main ruins, along the road to San Pedro Sula, or connected by a stone path from the main site, is an area called **Las Sepulturas** ① *entrance is almost 2 km from the main site, entry to this site is included in the main Copán ticket*, a residential area where ceramics dating back to 1000 BC have been found. Exhibits from the site are on display in the Copán Museum. It is a delightful site, beautifully excavated and well maintained, peaceful and in lovely surroundings.

# Tegucigalpa
## to San Pedro Sula

Like the capital, San Pedro Sula is a rapidly developing and largely unappealing destination; a sweltering business and transport hub as much forged by North American commercial appetites as by the illicit cocaine trade. Most travellers pass through on their way to the Caribbean coast. For those seeking access to the languid shores of the Bay Islands, the Northern Highway from the capital to San Pedro remains the fastest option, but it is worth pausing en route to enjoy the fine colonial heritage of Comayagua, the entrancing mountain beauty spots of Lago Yojoa and Pulhapanzak waterfall, and the intriguing craft villages of Santa Bárbara department.

## Comayagua and around   *Colour map 3, B2.*
### a historic colonial city and the former capital of Honduras

Founded on 7 December 1537 as Villa Santa María de Comayagua on the site of an indigenous village by Alonzo de Cáceres. Located on the rich Comayagua plain, 1½ hours' drive (93 km) north of the capital, Comayagua (altitude 550 m) has many old colonial buildings, reflecting the importance of Honduras' first capital after Independence in 1821. The centre has had an impressive makeover recently, and is worth a visit for the handsome colonial architecture in and around the main square, Plaza León Alvarado.

On 3 September 1543, it was designated the Seat of the Audiencia de los Confines by King Felipe II of Spain. President Marco Aurelio Soto transferred the capital to Tegucigalpa in 1880. Comayagua was declared a city in 1557, 20 years after its founding. Within a couple of centuries a rash of civic and religious buildings were constructed. The former university, the first in Central America, was founded in 1632 and closed in 1842 (it was located in

**Best** for
Colonial architecture ▪ Crafts ▪ Lakes & waterfalls

the Casa Cural, Bishop's Palace, where the bishops have lived since 1558). Others include the churches of **La Merced** (1550-1588) and **La Caridad** (1730), **San Francisco** (1574) and **San Sebastián** (1575). **San Juan de Dios** (1590 but destroyed by earthquake in 1750), the church where the Inquisition sat, is now the site of the Hospital Santa Teresa. **El Carmen** was built in 1785.

The wealth of colonial heritage has attracted funds for renovation, which have produced a slow transformation in the town. The most interesting building is the **cathedral** ① *daily 0700-1900*, in the Parque Central, inaugurated in 1711, with its plain square tower and façade decorated with sculpted figures of the saints, which contains some of the finest examples of colonial art in Honduras. Of the 16 original hand-carved and gilded altars, just four survive today. The clock in the tower was originally made over 800 years ago in Spain and is the oldest working clock in the Americas. It was given to Comayagua by Felipe II in 1582. At first it was in La Merced when that was the cathedral, but it was moved to the new cathedral in 1715. You can climb the tower to see the clock and the old bells, with tour guides on hand in the cathedral (Ever Villanueva, T2994-77551, is knowledgeable and friendly). A huge floor mosaic of the cathedral façade has been built on the square, best seen from the tower.

Half a block north of the cathedral is the **Ecclesiastical Museum** ① *daily 0930-1200, 1400-1700, US$0.60*. One block south of the cathedral, the **Museo de Arqueología** ① *at the corner of 6 Calle and 1 Av NO, Wed-Fri 0800-1600, Sat and Sun 0900-1200, 1300-1600, US$1.70*, housed in the former Palacio de Gobernación, is small scale but fascinating, with six rooms each devoted to a different period. Much of the collection came from digs in the El Cajón region, 47 km north of Comayagua, before the area was flooded for the hydroelectricity project. The **Casa Cultural** on a corner of the plaza, left of the cathedral, has permanent and temporary exhibitions of the city history and art.

There are two colonial plazas shaded by trees and shrubs. A stone portal and a portion of the façade of **Casa Real** (the viceroy's residence) still survive. Built in 1739-1741, it was damaged by an earthquake in 1750 and destroyed by tremors in 1856. The army still uses a quaint old fortress built when Comayagua was the capital. There is a lively market area.

**Parque Nacional Montaña de Comayagua** is only 13 km from Comayagua, reached from the villages of San José de la Mora (4WD necessary) or San Jerónimo and Río Negro (usually passable). Contact **Fundación Ecosimco** ① *0 Calle y 1 Av NO in Comayagua, T772-4681*, for further information about the trails which lead through the cloudforest to waterfalls. The mountain (2407 m) has 6000 ha of cloudforest and is a major watershed for the area.

## Siguatepeque

The Northern Highway crosses the Comayagua plain, part of the gap in the mountains which stretches from the Gulf of Fonseca to the Ulúa lowlands. Set in forested highlands 32 km northwest of Comayagua is the town of Siguatepeque (altitude 1150 m), which has a cool climate. It is the site of the Escuela Nacional de Ciencias Forestales (which is worth a visit) and, being exactly halfway between Tegucigalpa and San Pedro Sula (128 km), is a collection point for the produce of the Intibucá, Comayagua and Lempira departments. The Cerro and Bosque de Calanterique, behind the Evangelical Hospital, is a 45-minute walk from the town centre. The Parque Central is pleasant, shaded by tall trees with the church of San Pablo on the north side on the east.

Southwest from Siguatepeque, the route to La Esperanza is a beautiful paved road through lovely forested mountainous country, via **Jesús de Otoro**, where there are two basic *hospedajes* and **Balneario San Juan de Quelala** ① *US$0.30*, which has a *cafetería* and picnic sites. North from Siguatepeque, the highway goes over the forested escarpment of the continental divide, before descending towards Lago Yojoa. Just south of Taulabé on the highway are the illuminated **Caves of Taulabé** ① *daily, US$0.40, guides available*, with both stalactites and bats. North of Taulabé, and 16 km south of the lake is the turn-off northwest of a paved road to Santa Bárbara.

## ★Lago Yojoa

*For local information contact Enrique Campos or his son at Hotel Agua Azul (see Where to stay, below). For more information, contact Proyecto Humuya, behind Iglesia Betel, 21 de Agosto, Siguatepeque, T2773-2426.*

Sitting pretty among the mountains is the impressive Lake Yojoa (altitude 635 m), which is 22.5 km long and 10 km wide. To the west rise the Montañas de Santa Bárbara which include the country's second highest peak and the **Parque Nacional de Santa Bárbara** (see page 527). To the east is the **Parque Nacional Montaña Cerro Azul-Meámbar**. Pumas, jaguars and other animals live in the forests, pine-clad slopes and the cloudforest forming part of the reservoir of the Lago Yojoa basin. The national parks also have many waterfalls. The 50-sq-km Azul-Meámbar park is 30 km north of Siguatepeque and its highest point is 2047 m.

To get to any of the entry points (Meámbar, the main one, Jardines, Bacadia, Monte Verde or San Isidro) a 4WD is necessary. A local ecological group, **Ecolago** ① *Edif Midence Soto, Parque Central (Tegucigalpa), T2237 9659*, has marked out the area and can offer guided tours. **Ecolago** has guides who are expert in spotting regional birds; at least 373 species have been identified around the lake. At one time the lake was full of bass, but overfishing and pollution have decimated the stocks. Tilapia farming is now very important.

The Northern Highway follows the eastern margin to the lake's southern tip at **Pito Solo**, where sailing and motor boats can be hired. Frustratingly, there is no public access to the lakeshore, which is fenced off by farms and private properties. Lake excursions are also available at several of the waterfront hotels and restaurants (see Listings, below), which also offer the best views.

On the northern shore of Lago Yojoa is a complex of pre-Columbian settlements called **Los Naranjos** ① *US$5*, which are believed to have had a population of several thousand. It is considered to be the country's third most important archaeological site spanning the period from 1000 BC to AD 1000, and includes two ball courts. The site is slowly being developed for tourism by the Institute of Anthropology and History and has a visitor centre, small museum and coffee shop and a number of forest walking trails. Excavation work is currently in progress. The local office of the institute (T2557-8197) is at the **Hotel Brisas de Lago**. From the lake it is 37 km down to the hot Ulúa lowlands.

A paved road skirts the lake's northern shore for 12 km via Peña Blanca. A road heads southwest to **El Mochito**, Honduras' most important mining centre. A bus from 2 Avenida in San Pedro Sula goes to Las Vegas-El Mochito mine for walks along the west side of Lago Yojoa. Buses will generally stop anywhere along the east side of the lake. Another road heads north from the northern shore, through Río Lindo, to **Caracol** on the Northern

Highway. This road gives access to the Pulhapanzak waterfall, with some unexcavated ceremonial mounds adjacent, and to Ojo de Agua, a pretty bathing spot near Caracol. **Peña Blanca** is, according to one reader, a "very ugly town" on the north side of the lake.

## Pulhapanzak waterfall
*T3319-7282, www.pulhahn.com, daily 0600-1800, US$2.80. The caretaker allows camping for US$0.85; cabins are also available ($$$).*

The impressive 42-m-high waterfall at Pulhapanzak is on the Río Lindo. The waterfall is beautiful during, or just after the rainy season, and in sunshine there is a rainbow over the gorge. A path leads down to the foot of the falls, thick with spray, and is very slippery; you can swim in the river just before the edge – if you dare! There is a picnic area, a small *cafetería* and a good *comedor* 15 minutes' walk away down in the village, but the site does get crowded at weekends and holidays. River tubing is a seasonal option and there is also a large zip-wire course inside the grounds, with 13 sections, including one breathtaking stretch over the falls (US$25).

## Santa Bárbara and around
Santa Bárbara (altitude: 290 m), surrounded by high mountains, forested hills and rivers, lies in a hot lowland valley 32 km west of Lago Yojoa. One of the nicest main towns in Honduras, it has little of architectural or historical interest compared with Gracias, Ojojona or Yuscarán, but it is here that you will find Panama hats and other goods made from junco palm. The majority of the population is fair-skinned (some redheads).

In addition to being a pleasant place to stay, Santa Bárbara is also a good base for visiting villages throughout the Santa Bárbara Department. Nearby, the ruined colonial city of **Tencoa** has been rediscovered. A short local trek behind the town climbs the hills to the ruined site of **Castillo Bogran**, with fine views across the valley and the town. Heading south out of Santa Bárbara, the paved road joins the Northern Highway south of Lago Yojoa.

The Department of Santa Bárbara is called the Cuna de los Artesanos (cradle of artisans), with over 10,000 craftspeople involved in the manufacture of handicrafts. The main products come from the small junco palm; for example, fine hats and baskets. The main towns for junco items are **La Arada**, 25 minutes from Santa Bárbara on the road to San Nicolás, and then branching off south, and **Ceguaca**, on a side road off the road to Tegucigalpa. Flowers and dolls from corn husks are made in Nueva Celilac. Mezcal is used to make carpets, rugs and hammocks, which are easy to find in towns such as **Ilama**, on the road to San Pedro Sula, which has one of the best small colonial churches in Honduras (no accommodation). People here also make *petates* (rugs) and purses.

Between Santa Bárbara and Lago Yojoa is the **Parque Nacional de Santa Bárbara** which contains the country's second highest peak, Montaña de Santa Bárbara at 2744 m. The rock is principally limestone with many subterranean caves. There is little tourist development as yet, with just one trail, and you can track down a guide in Los Andes, a village above Peña Blanca and Las Vegas. The best time to visit is the dry season, January to June. For information contact **Asociación Ecológica Corazón Verde** ① *Palacio Municipal, Santa Bárbara.* There is a **Cohdefor** office just below the market (look for the sign) but they are not helpful.

## Tourist information

### Casa Cultural
*Near the cathedral, Parque Central,*
*T2772-2028. Tue-Thu 0900-1700, Fri*
*and Sat 0900-2100, Sun 0900-1200.*
Tourist information is available here,
including city map for sale, US$1.20. City
tours are available in an open-topped tram
from outside the Casa Cultural, daily every
30 mins, US$1.50.

## Where to stay

### Comayagua

#### $$$ Santa María
*Km 82 on the Tegucigalpa highway,*
*T2772-7872, www.hotelsmc.com.*
The best in town, although not in the centre.
Rooms are comfortable, if generic. Amenities
include spacious grounds with lawns and a
large pool.

#### $$ Casa Grande
*Barrio Abajo, ½ a block to the east of Cine*
*Valladolid, T2772-0772.*
This good-looking and well-restored
19th-century colonial-style *casa* has lots of
attractive touches: solid antique furniture,
clay tiles, wood beams, terracotta tones and
a courtyard filled with tropical plants. It's an
intimate and romantic place to stay with lots
of character.

#### $$ Hotel Antigua Comayagua
*6a Calle NO, T2772-0816, www.*
*hotelantiguacomayagua.com.*
The Antigua has a great central location just
50 m from the Parque Central. Its rooms
are spacious and presentable and have hot
water, a/c, mini-fridge, Wi-Fi and cable TV.
The real draw, however, is the well-kept
garden and sizeable pool.

#### $$ Posada de mi Viejo
*Barrio San Sebastian, opposite Iglesia*
*San Sebastian, T2771-9312, www.*
*hotellaposadademiviejo.com.*
Set around a central courtyard with a small
pool, this reliable *posada* has 22 spacious,
modern, down-to-earth rooms with hot
water, Wi-Fi and cable TV. Safe and spotless.
Breakfast included.

### Siguatepeque

#### $$ Park Place
*Parque Central, T2773-9212.*
An unbeatable central location opposite the
main plaza. Rooms are on the small side, but
reasonable and recently renovated. There's
a pool on the roof and views over the town.
Comfortable and attentive. Good reports.

#### $$ Vuestra Casa
*Blv Morazán, Barrio Abajo, T2773-0885.*
This comfortable B&B has a range of decent,
modern rooms with all the usual amenities;
the suites are particularly appealing and
come with fireplaces. Safe, secure, friendly
place with leafy grounds, pool and views of
the mountains.

### Lago Yojoa

#### $$$$ Gualiqueme
*Cottage at edge of lake, for information*
*contact Richard Joint at Honduyate,*
*T2882-3129.*
Has 4 bedrooms in main house, 2 in annexe.
Daily, weekly, monthly rental, weekend
packages include ferry and fishing boat.

#### $$ Brisas del Lago
*Close to Peña Blanca at the northern*
*end of the lake, T2608-7229,*
*www.hotelbrisasdellago.com.*
Large, 1960s concrete hotel now looking
a bit dated and mildewed, but with

spacious rooms with a/c, cable TV and balcony, good value family suites; great lake views from gardens and pool. Good restaurant but overpriced, launches for hire and horse riding.

### $$-$ D&D Brewery and Guesthouse
*T2994-9719, www.ddbrewery.com.*
Probably the best place on the lake, complete with 3 spacious cabins, 11 private rooms, 2 mixed dorms and 4 campsites. There is a pool and a restaurant but the real draw is the craft beer on tap. Recommended.

### $$-$ Los Remos
*Pito Solo, at the south end of the lake, T2557-8054.*
Has cabins and camping facilities. Clean, beautiful setting, good food, nice for breakfasts, no beach but swimming pool and boat trips. Parking US$3.

### $ Boarding House Moderno
*Barrio Arriba, T643-2203.*
Quiet place offering rooms with a hot shower; those with a fan are better value than with a/c. Parking. Recommended.

### $ Gran Hotel Colonial
*1½ blocks from Parque Central, T2643-2665.*
Friendly hotel with sparsely furnished rooms, some with a/c, cold water. There's a good view from the roof. Recommended.

### $ Hotel Agua Azul
*At north end of lake, about 3 km west from junction at Km 166, T2991-7244.*

Set in beautiful gardens, basic clean cabins for 2 or more people, meals for non-residents, but the food and service in restaurant is poor. There's a swimming pool, fishing, horse riding and boating, launches, kayaks and pedalos for hire, around US$6 for 30 mins; mosquito coils. The manager speaks English and there's a good reduction in low season. Recommended (except when loud karaoke is in full swing).

## Santa Bárbara and around

### $ Ruth
*Calle La Libertad, T2643-2632.*
Rooms without windows, fan.

## Restaurants

### Comayagua

#### $$$-$$ El Torito
*Colonia San Miguel, on the Tegucigalpa road, opposite Polaris.*
This local steakhouse is one of Comayagua's better joints. They serve succulent and locally sourced beef cuts along with chicken, shrimp and fish dishes. Hearty, good value and authentically Hondureño.

#### $$ La Gota de Limón
*5a Calle NO. Sun-Wed 1030-1900; Thu-Sat 1030-0200.*
A hit with pretty young things, La Gota de Limón serves economical *comida típica* by day and spins Latin favourites by night; don your dancing shoes and rock up to the rooftop terrace.

San Pedro Sula is the second largest and most industrialized city in the country and a centre for the banana, coffee, sugar and timber trades. It is a distribution hub for northern and western Honduras with good road links. Its business community is mainly of Arab origin, and it is considered one of the fastest-growing cities between Mexico and Panama. By Central American standards, San Pedro Sula is a well-planned, modern city, but it's not a city you'll be inclined to stay in for long.

San Pedro Sula (altitude 60-150 m, population 900,000) was founded in 1536 by Pedro de Alvarado in the lush and fertile valley of the Ulúa (Sula) River, beneath the forested slopes of the Merendón mountains. There are many banana plantations. In recent years, the city has gained international notoriety as one of the most violent places on earth. On average, there are three homicides per day in San Pedro Sula, a sprawling urban powerhouse ingloriously dubbed the 'murder capital of the world'. Like Ciudad Juárez in Mexico, its

**Where to stay** 🛏
Casa del Arbol Galerias **1**
Casa El Mesón B&B **2**
Dos Molinos B&B **3**
Ejecutivo **4**
Guaras Hostal **5**
Isabella Boutique **6**
La Madrugada Hostel **7**
La Posada B&B **8**
Real Intercontinental
 San Pedro Sula **9**

**Restaurants** 🍴
Baranda **1**
Comidas Casas Viejas **2**
Entre Pisco y Nazca **3**
Garden Bistro **4**
Orange Deli and Burgers **5**
Pamplona **6**
Pat's Steakhouse **7**
Trattoria Bel Paese **8**

**Bars & clubs** 🍸
La Musa Gastropub **9**

problems are at least partly a consequence of its strategic location on international drug trafficking routes.

The city is divided into four quadrants: Noreste (Northeast, NE), Noroeste (Northwest, NO), Sudeste (Southeast, SE) and Sudoeste (Southwest, SO), where most of the hotels are located, although newer hotels, shopping malls and restaurant chains are in the Noroeste.

Although pleasant in the cooler season from November to February, temperatures are very high for the rest of the year. It is, nevertheless, a relatively clean city and the traffic is not too bad. The higher and cooler suburb of Bella Vista, with its fine views over the city, provides relief from the intense heat of the centre.

**Safety** San Pedro Sula has a fearsome reputation, but it is also an important business centre that welcomes scores of international travellers annually. The vast majority of violent crime is gang-related; provided you follow big city rules and do not stray into outlying barrios, you are unlikely to encounter any problems. Stay alert at all times and avoid areas without a police presence (or armed security). San Pedro Sula is not a great city for pedestrians but do not use urban buses; instead use radio taxis to get around (ask your hotel to call one). Do not walk the streets at night.

## Sights

The large neocolonial-style **cathedral** was completed in the 1950s. **Museo de Antropología e Historia** ① *3 Av, 4 Calle NO, Mon, Wed-Sat 0900-1600, Sun 0900-1500, US$0.75, 1st Sun of the month is free*, has displays of the cultures that once inhabited the Ulúa Valley up to Spanish colonization and, on the first floor, local history since colonization. There is a museum café in the adjacent garden with fine stelae and a good set lunch.

### Parque Nacional Cusuco *Colour map 3, B1.*

*Entrance is US$15, which includes a guided trip; you cannot go on your own. Contact the HRPF at 5 Av, 1 Calle NO, San Pedro Sula, T552-1014. Also contact Cohdefor, 10 Av, 5 Calle NO, Barrio Guamilito, San Pedro Sula, T553-4959, or Cambio CA, who run tours. Permission from HRPF is required to walk through the park to Tegucigalpita on the coast. There is a visitor centre but bring your own food. You cannot stay or camp in the park, but camping is possible outside. Access by dirt road from Cofradía (Cafetería Negro, 1 block northwest of plaza, good food), on the road to Santa Rosa de Copán, then to Buenos Aires: 2 hrs by car from San Pedro Sula, 4WD recommended.*

Parque Nacional Cusuco, 20 km west of San Pedro Sula, offers some excellent hikes, trails and birdwatching in cloudforest. Now managed by the Fundación Ecológica Héctor Rodrigo Pastor Fasquelle (HRPF), the park was exploited for lumber until the 1950s. It was declared a protected area in 1959 when the Venezuelan ecologist, Geraldo Budowski, reported the pine trees there were the highest in Central America. Cutting was stopped and the lumber company abandoned the site.

Parque Nacional Cusuco is a splendid location and well worth the effort. The area includes tropical rainforest and cloudforest with all the associated flora and fauna. It includes **Cerro Jilinco**, 2242 m, and **Cerro San Ildefonso**, 2228 m. There are four trails, ranging from 30 minutes to two days. They use old logging roads traversing forested ridges with good views. HRPF produces a bird checklist that includes the quetzal.

## Where to stay

### $$$$ Real Intercontinental San Pedro Sula
*Blv del Sur at Centro Comercial Multiplaza, T2545-2500, www.ichotelsgroup.com.*
A long-established favourite among business travellers. Reliable, secure and predictably comfortable. One of the best.

### $$$ Casa del Arbol Galerías
*Intersection of 7ma Calle, Colonia Jardines del Valle y 1ra Av de la Colonia Villas del Sol, near the Galerias mall, T2566-4201, www.hotelcasadelarbol.com.*
This environmentally aware hotel has solar panels and a tree growing through it. Clean, modern, minimalist rooms with crisp white sheets and all the usual comforts including cable TV, a/c and Wi-Fi. They have a second facility downtown. Continental breakfast included.

### $$$ Casa El Mesón B&B
*Bloque 10 Casa 8, Colonia Tara, T2551-3303, www.casaelmeson.com.*
Super-friendly and hospitable, this cosy B&B is managed by Jimmy and Sandra Pinell, who have 20 years of experience working in hospitality as tour guides and restauranteurs. Homely accommodation with attentive service in tranquil surroundings.

### $$$ Ejecutivo
*2 Calle 10 Av SO, T2552-4289, www.hotel-ejecutivo.com.*
A solid if uninspired business class option. They offer simple, reasonable, generic rooms with a/c, cable TV, hot water and Wi-Fi. Also have their own generator in case of grid problems.

### $$$ Isabella Boutique Hotel
*8 Calle NO, T2550-9191, www.hotel isabellaboutique.directotels.com.*

Decked in swish contemporary decor, the Isabella Boutique is one of San Pedro Sula's more stylish options. They have 12 attractive rooms with cable TVs, coffee-makers, a/c and fridges. Facilities include a pool, business centre, airport pickup and lounge-bar.

### $$ La Posada B&B
*Colonia Universidad, 21 Calle "A" 9 y 11 Av, Casa 172, T2566-3312, www.laposadahn.com.*
Located within walking distance of the Galerias mall, the Posada B&B has simple, clean, comfortable rooms kitted with Wi-Fi, a/c and hot water. There is a small pool in the garden and some hammocks for chilling out. They also offer free bus station pickup and drop off (one trip per booking). Breakfast and local calls included. Good, quiet, reliable place.

### $$-$ Dos Molinos B&B
*Barrio Paz Barahona, 13 Calle 8 y 9 Av 34, T2550-5926, www.dosmolinos.hostel.com.*
Dos Molinos is a favourite with Peace Corps volunteers whenever they're in town. A simple, safe, economical place with no-frills rooms and friendly, helpful service. They can pick you up from the bus terminal and provide information.

### $$-$ La Madrugada Hostel
*8 Calle 8 y 9 Av NO, T2540-1309, www.lamadrugadahostel.com.*
A pleasant new place, clean and tidy, with a youthful vibe that will appeal to backpackers. Dorms are on the pricey side, but worth it for the good looks and comfort. Rooms have 42 inch TVs. The adjoining bar-restaurant is a good place for a cool beer. Creatively rendered, with lots of potential.

### $$-$ The Guaras Hostal
*Colonia Andalucía, 13 Calle and 13 Av NE 6, T9650-4431, www.theguarashostal.com.*

A very clean and secure hostel located in a gated community. Dorms (**$**) are cosy and well kept. Rooms have a/c, cable TV and Wi-Fi, with (**$$**) or without private bath (**$**). Relaxed, homely place, family-run and hospitable. Bus terminal pickup/drop-off included.

## Restaurants

There are international restaurants in all the top hotels.

### $$$ Baranda
*20 Av, entre 1-2 calle NO, Colonia Moderna.*
Drawing influence from Southeast Asia, Japan, India, France and Italy, Baranda serves intriguing international fusion cuisine, expertly prepared by Chef Ana María Selgado Pellman. Spicy Thai curries are among the recommended offerings.

### $$$ Pamplona
*On plaza, opposite Gran Hotel Sula.*
Pleasant decor, good food, strong coffee and excellent service. Spanish-owned, as the name might suggest.

### $$$ Pat's Steak house
*5 Calle SO, Barrio Rio de Piedras, 1½ blocks uphill from Blv Circunvalación.*
Along with tempting Caribbean seafood, Pat's steakhouse serves the best beef cuts in town and has a good wine list too. One of the oldest restaurants in San Pedro Sula and still great. Consistent and reliable, an old favourite. Recommended.

### $$$ Trattoria Bel Paese
*5 Calle A, entre 13-14 Av, Barrio Los Andes.*
Fettuccini with mushrooms and seafood ravioli are among the home-cooked treats cooked up Piero and his wife at this authentic Italian trattoria, claimed by many to be the best in town. A great place for friends and family. Don't miss the desserts!

### $$$-$$ Garden Bistro
*10 Calle 17 Av, next to the Hilton Princess Hotel.*
Cosy and stylish, this smart little place has distinctly European airs, unsurprisingly given the English ownership. Their menu features an eclectic range of international favourites, British fish and chips, American turkey sandwiches, Spanish tapas, Italian pasta and Indian tikka masala included. Good reports.

### $$$-$$ Orange Deli and Burgers
*5 Calle, entre 18-19 Av, Barrio Rio de Piedras.*
Delicious gourmet burgers cooked to taste; try the 'True Blue', which comes with blue cheese, or the 'Fidel Burger' with pulled pork. A friendly, fun, cosy place that serves good mojitos too.

### $$ Entre Pisco y Nazca
*3 Calle y 19 Avenida NO, Colonia Moderna, www.entrepiscoynazca.com.*
Gourmet Peruvian good, including traditional ceviches and contemporary interpretations of old classics; order a selection and share. Don't miss the pisco sour.

### $$-$ Comidas Casas Viejas
*10 Calle, 10 Av, Barrio Los Andes, T2516-1472. Daily 0600-2200.*
Hearty *comida típica* served indoors or outside on the terrace. Offerings include chicken soup, leg of pork and grilled meat, all served with tasty handmade tortillas. Authentic, casual and affordable.

## Bars and clubs

A thriving nightlife exists beyond the casinos.

### La Musa Gastropub
*5 Calle, entre 17-18 Av, Barrio Río de Piedras.*
A very hip and handsome place that serves tempting tapas and delicious cocktails, including mouth-watering margaritas, mojitos, piña coladas, lemon frappe daikiris and sangrias. Good for a meal, a drink, or both.

## Entertainment

### Cinemas

There are 8 cinemas, all showing Hollywood movies; look in local press for details.

### Theatre

**Centro Cultural Sampedrano**. Stages productions.
**Proyecto Teatral Futuro**, is a semi-professional company presenting contemporary theatre of Latin American countries and translations of European playwrights, as well as ballet, children's theatre, and workshops. Offices and studio-theatre at 4 Calle 3-4 Av NO, Edif INMOSA, 3rd floor, T2552-3074.

## Festivals

End Jun **Feria Juniana**, the city's main festival.

## Shopping

### Handicrafts

Large artisan market, **Mercado Guamilito Artesanía** (*6 Calle 7-8 Av NO, daily 0800-1700*), typical Honduran handicrafts, cigars and 'gifiti' – local moonshine, at good prices (bargain), with a few imported goods from Guatemala and Ecuador; also good for fruit and vegetables, and *baleada comedores*. **Danilo's Pura Piel** (*factory and shop 18 Av B/9 Calle SO*). **Honduras Souvenirs** (*Calle Peatonal No 7*), mahogany woodcraft. The **IMAPRO Handicraft School** in El Progreso has a retail outlet at 1 Calle 4-5 Av SE, well worth visiting, fixed prices, good value, good mahogany carvings. The **Museum Gift Shop**, at the Museo de Antropología e Historia has lots of cheap *artesanía* gifts open during museum visiting hours.

## What to do

### Tour operators

**Maya Temple**, www.mayatempletours.com. Also offers travel services.

## Transport

**Air** San Pedro Sula is a more important international gateway than Tegucigalpa. Its airport, **Ramón Villeda Morales (SAP)** is 15 km from the city centre along a good 4-lane highway; for safety, use an authorised yellow airport taxi to get into town, US$20. Taxis to the airport costs US$12, but bargain hard. There are free airport shuttle from the big hotels. Buses and colectivos do not go to the airport terminal itself; you have to walk the final 1 km from the La Lima road. At the airport is a duty free shop, Global One phones, banks and a restaurant on the 2nd floor. Flights to **Tegucigalpa** (35 mins), **La Ceiba**, **Utila** and to **Roatán**. See Getting there in Practicalities chapter for international flights.

**Bus Local** Local buses cost US$0.10, smaller minibuses cost US$0.20.
**Long distance** The Gran Central Metropolitana is clean, safe and a short US$3 taxi from the centre of San Pedro Sula. **Heading south**, buses pass **Lago Yojoa** for **Tegucigalpa**, very regular service provided by several companies, 4½ hrs, 250 km by paved road. Main bus services with comfortable coaches in the town centre are **Hedman Alas**, T2516-2273, 0830, 1330 and 1730, US$18; **Transportes Sáenz**, T2553-4969, US$7; **El Rey**, T2553-4264, or **Express**, T2557-8355; **Transportes Norteños**, T2552-2145, last bus at 1900; **Viana**, T2556-9261.
**Heading west** from San Pedro the road leads to **Puerto Cortés**, a pleasant 45-min journey down the lush river valley. With **Empresa Impala**, T2553-3111, from 0430 until 2200, US$1, or **Citul**, and also on to **Omoa** from 0600.

Heading east buses go to **La Lima**, **El Progreso**, **Tela** and **La Ceiba** (**Tupsa** and **Catisa**, very regular to El Progreso, hourly to La Ceiba from 0600 and 1800, 3 hrs, US$3), some with a change in El Progreso, others direct. Also 1st class to La Ceiba with **Viana** at 1030 and 1730, and with **Hedman Alas** at 0600, 1030, 1520 and 1820. US$16 To **Trujillo**, 3 per day, 6 hrs, US$5, comfortable.

**Heading southwest** buses go to **Santa Rosa de Copán** through the Department of Ocotepeque, with superb mountain scenery, to the **Guatemalan border**. Congolón, and **Empresa Toritos y Copanecos**, serve **Nueva Ocotepeque** (US$8) and **Agua Caliente** on the Guatemalan border with 7 buses a day; **Congolón**, T2553-1174. For more information on Guatemala–Honduras border crossings, see Border crossings box in Practicalities chapter.

To **Santa Rosa de Copán**, with connections at La Entrada for **Copán Ruinas**, with **Empresa Toritos y Copanecos**, T2563-4930, leaving every 20 mins, 0345-1715, 3 hrs, US$3.70. Take a bus to the junction of La Entrada and change for connection to Copán Ruinas if you're not going direct. 1st-class bus to **Copán Ruinas** with **Hedman**

**Alas**, T2516-2273, daily at 1030 and 1500, 3 hrs, US$16 with a/c, movie and bathrooms. Also direct service with **Casasola-Cheny Express** at 0800, 1300 and 1400.

**International** Services available from **Ticabus** covering the whole of Central America from Mexico to Panama.

**Car Car rentals** Avis, 1 Calle, 6 Av NE, T2553-0888; **Blitz**, Hotel Sula and airport (T2552-2405 or 668-3171); **Budget**, 1 Calle 7 Av NO, T2552-2295, airport T2668-3179; **Maya Eco Tours**, 3 Av NO, 7-8 Calle, and airport (T2552-2670 or 2668-3168); **Molinari**, Hotel Sula and airport (T2553-2639 or 2668-6178); **Toyota**, 3 Av 5 y 6 Calle NO, T2557-2666 or airport T2668-3174.

**Car repairs** Invanal, 13 Calle, 5 y 6 Av NE, T2552-7083. Excellent service from Víctor Mora.

---

**Parque Nacional Cusuco**

**Bus** San Pedro Sula–Cofradía, 1 hr, US$0.15, from 5 Av, 11 Calle SO (buses drop you at turn-off 1 km from town); pickup Cofradía-Buenos Aires 1½ hrs, US$1.75, best on Mon at 1400 (wait at small shop on outskirts of town on Buenos Aires road); the park is 12 km from Buenos Aires.

# Tegucigalpa
## to the Pacific

From the capital to the Golfo de Fonseca the route twists through mountain valleys down to the volcanic islands and Honduras' Pacific ports of San Lorenzo and Amapala. Near the coast the Pan-American Highway leads west to El Salvador and east though the hot plains of Choluteca to the quiet but popular beaches of Cedeña and Ratón and ultimately to Nicaragua. An alternative route to Nicaragua heads east, through the agricultural town of Danlí, to the border at Las Manos. Short detours from the highway lead to picturesque colonial villages and old mining centres in the hills.

## The road to the Pacific  *Colour map 3, C2.*

steamy Pacific ports and lesser-visited beaches

### Tegucigalpa to Goascarán

From the capital a paved road runs south through fine scenery. Beyond Sabanagrande (see page 494) is **Pespire**, a picturesque colonial village with the beautiful church of San Francisco, which has triple domes. Pespire produces small, delicious mangoes. At **Jícaro Galán** (92 km) the road joins the Pan-American Highway, which heads west through **Nacaome**, where there is a colonial church, to the border with El Salvador at **Goascarán**; see also Border crossings box in Practicalities chapter. At Jícaro Galán, Ticabus and other international buses from San Salvador, Tegucigalpa and Managua meet and exchange passengers.

### San Lorenzo

The Pan-American Highway continues south from Jícaro Galán, to the Pacific coast (46 km) at San Lorenzo, a dirty town on the shores of the Gulf of Fonseca. The climate on the Pacific litoral is very hot.

**Best** for
Aguardiente ▪ Fishing ▪ Tropical flowers ▪ Volcanic islands

## Amapala

A 31-km road leaves the Pan-American Highway 2 km west of San Lorenzo, signed to Coyolito. It passes through scrub and mangrove swamps before crossing a causeway to a hilly island, around which it winds to the jetty at **Coyolito** (no *hospedajes* but a *comedor* and *refrescarías*).

The Pacific port of Amapala, on Isla del Tigre, has been replaced by Puerto de Henecán in San Lorenzo, and is reached by a road which leaves the Pan-American Highway at the eastern edge of San Lorenzo. The **Isla del Tigre** is yet another place reputed to be the site of hidden pirate treasure. In the 16th century it was visited by a number of pirates, including Sir Francis Drake. Amapala was capital of Honduras for a brief period in 1876 when Marco Aurelio Soto was president. Today, in addition to a naval base, Amapala is a charming, decaying backwater. The 783-m extinct Amapala volcano has a road to the summit where there is a US army unit and a DEA contingent. You can walk round the island in half a day. There is a ferry service from Coyolito, but fishermen will take you to San Lorenzo for a small fee, not by motor launch, and the trip takes half a day. The deep-sea fishing in the gulf is good; it's possible to charter boats to La Unión in El Salvador.

## Listings Tegucigalpa to the Pacific

### Where to stay

**Tegucigalpa to Goascarán**
There are very basic hotels with restaurants at the border in Goascarán.

**$$ Oasis Colonial**
*Jícaro Galán, T2881-2220.*
Nice rooms, good restaurant and pool and an unnamed basic guesthouse.

**San Lorenzo**

**$$ Miramar**
*Barrio Plaza Marina, T2781-2039.*
Has 26 rooms, 4 with a/c, good restaurant, overpriced. As it's located in a rough dockside area it's best not to walk there.

**$ Perla del Pacífico**
*On main street, T2781-3025.*
In a central location, this friendly, charming place offers comfortable rooms with a fan and bath. Recommended.

**Amapala**
Ask for **Doña Marianita**, who rents the 1st floor of her house.

**$$ Hotel Villas Playa Negra**
*Aldea Playa Negra, T2898-8534.*
In an isolated lovely setting, this hotel has 7 rooms with a/c and 7 with fan, as well as a pool, beach and a restaurant.

**$ Al Mar**
*Above Playa Grande.*
With a lovely view of the mountains and sunset, Al Mar offers rooms with fans.

### Restaurants

**San Lorenzo**

**$$ Restaurant-Bar Henecán**
*Parque Central.*
A/c, good food and service, not cheap but worth it.

**Amapala**

**$ Mercado Municipal**
Several clean *comedores*.

**$ Restaurant-Bar Miramar**
*By the harbour.*
Overlooking the sea, this is a pleasant restaurant with very friendly staff, good

meals, including hamburgers and *boquitas*, and you can hang your hammock.

### Transport

#### San Lorenzo
**Bus** Frequent *busitos* from **Tegucigalpa** to San Lorenzo (US$1) and **Choluteca** (US$1.50).

### Amapala
**Boat** Motorized *lanchas* run between **Coyolito** and Amapala, US$0.35 per person when launch is full (about 10 passengers), about US$4 to hire a launch (but you will probably have to pay for the return trip as well). 1st boat leaves Amapala at 0700 to connect with 1st Coyolito–San Lorenzo bus at 0800; next bus from Coyolito at 0900.

## Choluteca and around  Colour map 3, C3.

*a trade hub with a colonial core*

Choluteca is expanding rapidly on the back of the local industries of coffee, cotton and cattle which flourish despite the hot climate. Founded in 1535, the town was one of the earliest settlements in Honduras, and still has a colonial centre.

The church of **La Merced** (1643) is being renovated and is due to be reconsecrated. The **Casa de la Cultura** and **Biblioteca Municipal** are in the colonial house of José Cecilio del Valle on the corner of the Parque Central. A fine steel suspension bridge crosses the broad river at the entrance into Choluteca from the north (it was built in 1937). The social centre of San José Obrero ① *3 Calle SO*, is where handicrafts, in particular carved wood and chairs, can be bought. The **Mercado Municipal** ① *7 Av SO, 3 Calle SO*, is on outskirts of town.

Cedeño beach, on the eastern side of the Gulf of Fonseca 40 km from Choluteca, is a lovely though primitive spot, with clean sand stretching for miles and often thundering surf. Avoid public holidays, weekend crowds and take a good insect repellent. There are spectacular views and sunsets over the Gulf of Fonseca south to Nicaragua and west to El Salvador, and of the volcanic islands in the bay. There's an hourly bus from Choluteca (US$0.60, 1½ hours). A turn-off leads from the Choluteca–Cedeño road to Ratón beach, which is more pleasant than Cedeño. There's a bus from Choluteca at 1130, returning next morning.

### Listings Choluteca and around

#### Where to stay

**$$ Camino Real**
*Road to Guasaule, T2882-0610.*
Long-established place with a pool, and good steaks in restaurant. Recommended.

**$$ La Fuente**
*Cra Panamericana, past bridge, T2782-0253.*
Reasonable highway pitstop with bath, swimming pool, Wi-Fi in the rooms, a/c and meals.

**$ Hibueras**
*Av Bojórquez, Barrio El Centro, T2882-0512.*
With bath and fan, clean, purified water, *comedor* attached, good value.

**$ Pacífico**
*Near Mi Esperanza terminal, outside the city.*
Quiet place with clean, cool rooms, with fan and cable TV. Hammocks, safe parking, fresh drinking water, and breakfast US$1.50.

## $ Pierre

*Av Valle y Calle Williams, T2882-0676.*
Central place offering rooms with bath (ants in the taps), a/c or fan and TV. There's free protected parking and the *cafetería* serves good breakfasts. Credit cards accepted. Recommended.

## $ Santa Rosa

*3 Calle NO, in the centre, just west of market, T2882-0355.*
Some rooms with bath, pleasant patio, laundry facilities, clean, friendly. Recommended.

### Restaurants

## $$ Alondra

*Parque Central. Open Fri-Sun only.*
Old colonial house.

## $ Comedor Central

*Parque Central.*
*Comida corriente* daily specials, *licuados*, sandwiches, good for breakfast. Local specialities are the drinks *posole* and *horchata de morro*.

## $ El Burrito

*Blv Choluteca between 4 and 5 Av N.*
With good-value meals and fast service.

## $ El Conquistador

*On Pan-American, opposite La Fuente.*
Steaks etc, outdoor seating but you have to eat inside, good but slow service. Will change money for customers. Recommended.

### Festivals

**8 Dec** The feast day of the **Virgen de la Concepción**, a week of festivities, followed by the **Festival del Sur**, 'Ferisur'.

### Transport

**Bus** To **El Espino** (Nicaraguan border) from Choluteca, US$1.15, 1 hr, 1st at 0700, last at 1400; see also Border crossings box in Practicalities chapter. Also frequent minibuses to **El Amatillo** (El Salvador border) via San Lorenzo, US$1, from bus stop at bridge; see also Border crossings box in Practicalities chapter. Buses to Choluteca from Tegucigalpa with **Mi Esperanza**, **Bonanza** and **El Dandy**; **Bonanza** continues to San Marcos and departs Tegucigalpa hourly from 0530, 4 hrs to Choluteca, US$1.90. The municipal bus terminal is about 10 blocks from the municipal market, about 8 blocks from cathedral/Parque Central; **Mi Esperanza** has its own terminal 1 block from municipal terminal.

## East of Tegucigalpa  *Colour map 3, C3.*

#### former mining towns and tobacco plantations

A good paved road runs east from Tegucigalpa through the hills to Danlí, 92 km away in the Department of El Paraíso. There are no signs when leaving Tegucigalpa, so ask for directions. Some 40 km along, in the Zambrano Valley (see page 498), is the Escuela Agrícola Panamericana, which is run for all students of the Americas with US help: it has a fine collection of tropical flowers (book visits in advance at the office in Tegucigalpa).

### Yuscarán

At Km 47.5, a paved road branches south to Yuscarán (altitude 1070 m), set in rolling pineland country preserved by the **Reserva Biológica de Yuscarán**, which protects much of the land around Montserrat mountain. The climate here is semi-tropical. Yuscarán was an important mining centre in colonial days and is a picturesque village, with cobbled streets and houses on a steep hillside. Ask to see the museum near the town plaza; you have to ask around to find the person who has the key, antiques and photographs are displayed in a restored mansion which belonged to a mining family. There is a **Casa de Cultura** ① *in the former Casa Fortín, open Mon-Sat*. The Yuscarán **distilleries** ① *one in the centre, the other on the outskirts, tours possible*, are considered by many to produce the best *aguardiente* in Honduras. The Montserrat mountain that looms over Yuscarán is riddled with mines. The old **Guavias mine** is close to Yuscarán, some 4 km along the road to Agua Fría. About 10 km further along, a narrow, winding road climbs steeply through pine woods to the summit of **Pico Montserrat** (1891 m).

## Danlí

Danlí (altitude 760 m), 102 km from Tegucigalpa, is noted for sugar and coffee production, a large meat-packing company (Orinsa), and is a centre of the tobacco industry. There are four cigar factories. The **Honduras-América SA factory** ① *right-hand side of Cine Aladino, Mon-Fri 0800-1200 and 1300-1700, Sat 0800-1200*, produces export-quality cigars at good prices. At **Placencia Tabacos**, on the road to Tegucigalpa, you can watch cigar-making. Prices are better than at Santa Rosa. From Danlí to the north are **Cerro San Cristóbal** and the beautiful **Lago San Julián**.

## El Paraíso

A paved road goes south 18 km to El Paraíso, and beyond to the Nicaraguan border at Las Manos/Ocotal; see Border crossings box in Practicalities chapter. El Paraíso is a pretty town in an area producing coffee, bananas and rice.

## Listings East of Tegucigalpa

### Where to stay

#### Yuscarán

**$ Hotel**
*T2892-7213.*
Owned by Dutch man Freek de Haan and his Honduran wife and daughter, private or dormitory rooms, with beautiful views of Nicaraguan mountains in the distance.

**$ Hotel Carol**
Set in an annex to the owner's fine colonial house, this small, safe hotel with a family atmosphere has 6 modern, good-value rooms with bath and hot water.

#### Danlí

**$$-$ Gran Hotel Granada**
*T2883-2499.*
Bar, cable TV, accepts Visa. Restaurant and swimming pool, locals pay half price.

**$ La Esperanza**
*Gabriela Mistral, next to Esso station, T2883-2106.*
Friendly place offering rooms with bath, hot water, fan (more expensive with a/c), TV and drinking water. Parking.

#### El Paraíso

**$ 5a Av Hotel y Restaurant**
*5 Av y 10 Calle, T2893-4298.*
Rooms with bath and hot water. The restaurant specializes in Mexican-American food. Parking.

## Restaurants

### Yuscarán

**$ Cafetería Colonial**
*Opposite Banco de Occidente.*
Serves excellent *desayuno típico* and
*comida corriente*.

### Danlí

**$ Comedor Claudio**
Serves tasty *comida corriente* and you
can pick up some good information
from the locals.

## Festivals

### Danlí

**3rd week Aug** **Fiesta del Maíz** lasts all
week, with cultural and sporting events,
all-night street party on the Sat; it gets very
crowded with people from Tegucigalpa.

## Transport

### Yuscarán

**Bus** Frequent buses to **Zamorano** and
**Tegucigalpa**; from the capital buses leave

from Mercado Jacaleapa. For information, ask
anyone in the Parque Central in Yuscarán.

### Danlí

**Bus** From **Tegucigalpa**, US$2, from
Blv Miraflores near Mercado Jacaleapa
(from left-hand side of market as you face
it), Col Kennedy, Tegucigalpa, hourly, 2 hrs,
arrive 1½ hrs before you want to leave, long
queues for tickets (take 'Kennedy' bus from
C La Isla near the football stadium in central
Tegucigalpa, or taxi, US$1.20, to Mercado
Jacaleapa). **Express** bus from Col Kennedy,
0830, 1230 and 1700, US$2. One road goes
east from Danlí to **Santa María** (several
buses daily), over a mountain range with
great views.

### El Paraíso

**Bus** Minibuses from **Danlí** terminal to
El Paraíso, frequent (0600 to 1740), US$0.40,
30 mins, don't believe taxi drivers who
say there are no minibuses. **Emtra Oriente**,
Av 6, Calle 6-7, runs 4 times a day from
**Tegucigalpa** to El Paraíso, 2½ hrs, US$1.50.
Buses from El Paraíso to **Las Manos**, about
every 1½ hrs, US$0.35, 30 mins, or taxi US$4,
15 mins.

# **Bay** Islands

★ A string of beautiful islands of white sandy beaches, coconut palms and gentle sea breezes, off the northern coast of Honduras, the Bay Islands (Islas de la Bahía) are the country's most popular tourist attraction.

Located some 32 km north of La Ceiba, the three main islands are Utila, Guanaja and, the largest and most developed, Roatán. At the eastern end of Roatán are three smaller islands: Morat, Santa Elena, and Barbareta, with many islets and cayes to explore.

The rich and extensive underwater environment is one of the main attractions; reefs surround the islands, often within swimming distance of the shore. The warm, clear Caribbean waters provide excellent diving, which is some of the cheapest in the Caribbean. Equally enjoyable are the magnificent beaches, tropical sunsets and the relaxed atmosphere which positively encourages you to take to your hammock, lie back and relax.

The culture is far less Latino than on the mainland. English is spoken by many and there are still Black Carib – Garífuna – descendants of those deported from St Vincent in 1797.

**Best** for
Beaches ▪ Diving ▪ Jungle ▪ Relaxing

# BACKGROUND

## Bay Islands

English-speaking blacks constitute the majority of the population, particularly on Roatán. Utila has a population that is about half black and half white, the latter of British descent mainly from the settlers from Grand Cayman who arrived in 1830. Columbus anchored here in 1502, during his fourth voyage. In the 18th century the islands were the base for English, French and Dutch buccaneers. They were in British hands for over a century, but were finally ceded to Honduras in 1859. Latin Hondurans have been moving to the islands from the mainland in recent years

The traditional industry is fishing, mostly shellfish, with fleets based at French Harbour; but the supporting boat-building is a dying industry. Tourism is now a major source of income, particularly because of the scuba-diving attractions.

## Utila  *Colour map 3, B3.*

**the cheapest and least developed of the islands**

With a a laid-back ambience, Utila (area 41 sq km) is only 32 km from La Ceiba and is low lying, with just two hills, Pumpkin and the smaller Stewarts, either side of the town known as East Harbour.

The first inhabitants were the Paya and there is scant archaeological evidence of their culture. Later the island was used by pirates; Henry Morgan is reputed to have hidden booty in the caves. The population now is descended from Black Caribs and white Cayman Islanders with a recent influx from mainland Honduras. Independence Day (15 September) festivities, including boxing and climbing greased poles, are worth staying for.

## Utila

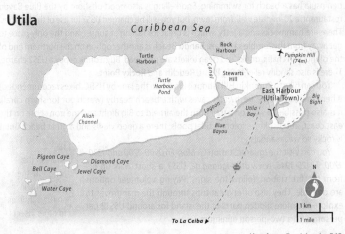

## Bay Island diving

Underwater, caves and caverns are a common feature, with a wide variety of sponges and the best collection of pillar coral in the Caribbean. There are many protected areas including the marine parks of Turtle Harbour on Utila, and Sandy Bay/West End on Roatán, which has permanent mooring buoys at the popular dive sites to avoid damage from anchors. Several other areas have been proposed as marine reserves by the Asociación Hondureña de Ecología: the Santuario Marino de Utila, Parque Nacional Marino Barbareta and Parque Nacional Marino Guanaja. The Bay Islands have their own conservation association (see under Roatán, page 553). Basic etiquette for snorkelling and diving applies. Snorkellers and divers should not stand on or touch the coral reefs; any contact, even the turbulence from a fin, will kill the delicate organisms.

### Utila's dive sites

There are currently around 50 dive sites around Utila, where permanent moorings have been established to minimize damage to the coral reef. Although the reef is colourful and varied, there are not a lot of fish, and lobster have almost disappeared. The dive sites are close to shore at about 20 m depth but they are all boat dives. Diving off the north coast is more spectacular, with drop-offs, canyons and caves. Fish are more numerous, helped by the establishment of the Turtle Harbour Marine Reserve and Wildlife Refuge.

## Around Utila

There are no big resorts on the island, although a couple of small, lodge-style, upmarket places have opened; otherwise the accommodation is rather basic. Sunbathing and swimming is not particularly good; people come for the diving. **Jack Neal Beach** has white sand with good snorkelling and swimming. **Chepee's White Hole** at the end of Blue Bayou peninsula has a beach for swimming. Snorkelling is also good offshore by the Blue Bayou restaurant, a 20-minute walk from town, but you will be charged US$1 for use of the facilities. There are hammocks and a jetty, which is great for fishing at sunset, and the only place to get away from the terrible sandflies. **Bandu Beach** is another option on the northern end of the island. Sun chairs, drinks and clean toilets are provided. Buy a drink or pay a US$2 charge. There is also sandfly relief at **Big Bight**, **Redcliff** and **Rocky Point**.

You can hike to **Pumpkin Hill** (about 4 km down the lane by HSBC, bikes recommended) where there are some freshwater caves with a beach nearby (watch out for sharp coral). It is also possible to walk on a trail from the airfield to Big Bight and the iron shore on the east coast, about 2 km, exploring tidal pools; there a good views and a great beach but it is rocky so wear sandals.

You can visit the **Iguana Station** ⓘ *Mon-Fri 0900-1200 and 1330-1700, T2425-3946, www.utila-iguana.de, US$3*, a short walk up hill from the fire station; follow the signs. Paying volunteer options are possible. They also offer great trips through the mangroves to explore the more hidden parts of the island for around US$12 per person, with a two-person minimum.

**Tip...**
Beware of the strong sun (the locals bathe in T-shirts), sandflies and other insects.

## Utila's cayes

A 20-minute motorboat ride from East Harbour are the cayes, a chain of small islands populated by fisherfolk off the southwest coast of Utila, which are known as the Cayitos de Utila. **Jewel Caye** and **Pigeon Caye** are connected by a bridge and are inhabited by a fishing community, which reportedly settled there to get away from the sandflies on Utila. Basic accommodation and food is available. **Diamond Caye** is privately owned and the snorkelling offshore here is excellent. **Water Caye** is a coconut island with 'white hole' sandy areas and with wonderful bathing in the afternoons. It is the only place where you can camp, sling a hammock or, in an emergency, sleep in or under the house of the caretaker; take food and fresh water, or rent the caretaker's canoe and get supplies from Jewel Caye.

## Listings Utila map p543

### Tourist information

See the island's official website, www.aboututila.com, for details of hotels, restaurants and diving.

### Where to stay

**$$$$ Utila Lodge**
*On Utila Bay, west of the main dock, T1-855-846-3483 (US), www.utilalodge.com.*
Set on a large pier over the water, this wood-built diving lodge offers spacious, calming, comfortable rooms with cable TV, Wi-Fi, porch, sun-deck, hammock, and ocean views. Amenities include restaurant-bar and a hyperbaric chamber which serves the local community. Various scuba packages are available. The divers' mecca.

**$$$$ Utopia Village**
*Southwest coast, resort will arrange transport, T512-333-1684 (US), www.utopiautila.com.*
Utopia Village is, for those who can afford it, the swanky resort option, complete with infinity pool, gym, library lounge, massage room, dive shop, beach bar and *palapas*. Secluded on a hard-to-reach part of the island, it has an exclusive feel, but it is still relatively small, intimate and low-key. Rooms are modern and impeccably attired.

**$$$$-$$$ Laguna Beach Resort**
*On the point opposite Blue Bayou, T2668-68452, www.utila.com.*
A comfortable lodge, with bungalows each with their own jetty. The 8-day package includes meals and diving for US$970, non-diver US$840. Fishing is offered, and they can accommodate a maximum of 40.

**$$$ Jade Seahorse**
*T2425-3270, www.jadeseahorse.com.*
5 great cabins, artistic, unusual and very funky, restaurant, bar, fantastic artistic gardens. Recommended.

**$$$-$$ Lazy Daze on the Bay**
*The Point, T2425-3170, www.myutilahotel.com.*
This small hotel on the waterfront is set in a converted family compound. It has down-to-earth and well-equipped rooms complete with a/c, fan, cable TV, Wi-Fi, coffee-maker, toaster, microwave, fridge and hot water. Their apartments, however, are much larger and better value. There is also a boat house.

**$$$-$$ Mango Inn**
*The Point, T2425-3326, www.mango-inn.com.*
Spotless rooms with bath, cheaper without, and fan. Helpful staff, and there's a pool

and a roof terrace. Reduction for students with **Utila Dive Centre**. **Mango Café** and **La Dolce Vita Pizzeria** for brick-oven pizzas on the premises. Recommended.

### $$$-$$ The Lighthouse
*Eastern Harbour, T2425-3164,*
*www.utilalighthouse.com.*
Perched over the water, the Lighthouse is a Caribbean colonial-style 2-storey hotel with wraparound balconies and panoramic views of the water and harbour. Rooms are simple but comfortable and have their own hammocks and the sound of relaxing rhythms of the waves. Good central location and lots of recommendations.

### $$$-$$ Trudy's
*5 mins from airport, T2425-3103.*
Rooms with a/c and hot water. Also **Trudy's Suites**, with colour TV, fridge and microwave. **Underwater Vision** dive shop on site. Recommended.

### $$-$ Pirate's Bay Inn
*On Utila Bay, T2425-3818,*
*www.piratesbayinn.com.*
This dynamic dive lodge caters to mid-range and budget travellers with 5 a/c private rooms and 3 shared dorms, all equipped with hot water and Wi-Fi. There's also a shared balcony overlooking the bay complete with hammocks. Best rates for divers with Captain Morgan's Dive Centre.

### $ Cooper's Inn
*Main St, towards the Point, T2425-3184.*
This helpful, hospitable, family-run guesthouse features unpretentious rooms with a/c, private bathroom and kitchenette. Cheap, clean, tidy and chilled.

### $ Rubi's Inn
*Main St, towards the Point, T2425-3240.*
Rubi's is a spotless and economical 2-storey guesthouse with tranquil, wood-built rooms equipped with fridges and hot water. There is a shared kitchen. Locally owned,

central, convenient, and a good choice for budget travellers.

### Utila's cayes
All hotels are small family-run affairs ($).

### $ Hotel Kayla
*www.utilacaysdiving.com.*
Free accommodation at Jewell Cay with PADI courses. Jewell Cay and Pigeon Cay are linked by a bridge.
   You can rent out **Little Cay** and **Sandy Cay** completely, details available from cayosutila@hotmail.com.

## Restaurants

Menus are often ruled by the supply boat: on Tue and Fri restaurants have everything, by the weekend some drinks run out.
For more recommendations, see www.utilaguide.com.

### $$$ Jade Seahorse
*Fri-Wed 1100-2200.*
A variety of home-made seafood dishes and *licuados*, with the coolest decor in town. It includes the very popular **Treetanic** bar; see Bars and clubs, below.

### $$$-$$ Mango Inn Bar and Grill
*Rocky Hill Rd, near the crossroads*
*and the Banco Atlántida, www.*
*mangoinnbarandgrill.com.*
Breakfast burritos, buttermilk pancakes, French toast and yogurt with granola are among the morning options; choose from burgers, burritos, beer-battered shrimp, sandwiches, salads and pizzas (recommended) for lunch or dinner. Lovely setting and atmosphere.

### $$ Babalu Bar and Grill
*Main St, Barrio La Punta.*
Babalu is the oldest dock bar in Utila, hosts to popular open mic nights and live music on Monday. They serve mostly tapas and Italian, including almond and olive pesto

on home-made focaccia, baked pasta with sweet pepper sauce and *salame di cioccolato*.

## $$ Driftwood Café
Texan barbecue-style place with good burgers and grilled seafood. Wood-built with a deck and an open-air setting above the water. Fun place, popular with expats and often buzzing.

## $$ El Picante
*Up towards Mango Inn.*
Upscale Mexican restaurant in a good location. Good nachos and tasty margaritas. A fine view from the balcony.

## $$ Foo King Wok
*Main St, opposite Tranquila Bar.*
*Mon, Wed and Fri 1800-2200.*
The name may be tongue-in-cheek, but the changing menu of authentic Asian cuisine is definitely a winner. Offerings include flavourful delights such as steamed dumplings, Thai curries, Vietnamese spring rolls and Szechuan fare.

## $$ Jungle Café
*At the end of Iguana Station road, www.utilaguru.com.*
The Jungle Café's changing set menu and daily specials usually include a variety of seafood, meat and vegetarian options, all prepared with love (some roasted dishes can up to 48 hrs to get ready!). Possibilities include paprika lamb goulash, Thai coconut calamari rings and filet mignon.

## $$ La Piccola
Upscale yet relaxed atmosphere offering lunch and dinner; one of the best places in town. Dishes include pasta, garlic bread, fish and pizza; great service.

## $$-$ Che Pancho
*Main St, under the cinema, 5 mins east of the centre.*
Che Pancho is a casual little eatery with outdoor tables. They serve light meals, snacks and café fare, including Spanish omelette, sandwiches, crepes, fried eggs, catch of the day and French fries. Good drinks – try the mango *licuado*, papaya smoothie or iced coffee.

## $ Big Mamas
Lovely little place serving authentic home-cooked grub and café fare, including *comida típica*, shrimp burger, wraps. The prettiest restaurant on Utila. Friendly and relaxed.

## $ RJ's BBQ and Grill House
*Wed, Fri, Sun 1730-2200.*
Great Caribbean-style barbecue dishes, including steaks and fresh seafood. Very popular, busy, buzzing, and fills up fast. Recommended.

## $ Skidrow Bar and Restaurant
*In front of Ecomarine Dive shop.*
Great burritos, popular with expats. Mon night is pub quiz night.

# Cafés

## Rio Coco Café
*Main St, between Utila Dive Center and Free Dive Utila, www.riococobeans.com.*
Rich, tasty, sustainably sourced coffee from the headwaters of the Río Coco. Great cakes and sweet treats too. Fun place, Wi-Fi included.

## Utila Tea Cup
*Cola del Mico road, inside the museum.*
Refreshing herbal infusions to wash down sweet and savoury treats, including quiche, apple French toast and pineapple coconut pie.

---

## Utila's cayes
There are a few restaurants, a Sat night disco and little else.

# ESSENTIAL
## Diving off Utila

Dive with care for yourself and the reef at all times; www.roatanet.com has plenty of information about Utila and its dive sites.

Utila is a very popular dive training centre. Learning to dive is cheaper here than anywhere else in the Caribbean, especially if you include the low living expenses. It is best to do a course of some sort; students come first in line for places on boats and recreational divers have to fit in. In recent years, Utila has developed a reputation for poor safety and there have been some accidents requiring emergency treatment in the recompression chamber on Roatán. Serious attempts have been made to change this by the diving community of Utila. The three or four accidents that happen annually are a result of cowboy divers and drug or alcohol abuse.

**Instructors** Choose an instructor who you get on with, and one who has small classes and cares about safety; follow the rules on alcohol/drug abuse and pay attention to the dive tables. There is a rapid turnover of instructors; many stay only a season to earn money to continue their travels, and some have a lax attitude towards diving regulations and diving tables. Check that equipment looks in good condition and well maintained. Boats vary; you may find it difficult to climb into a dory if there are waves. While a dive shop has a responsibility to set standards of safety, you also have a responsibility to know about diving times. If you don't, or are a beginner, ask.

**Price** There is broad price agreement across dive shops in Utila. Out of the revenues the Utila Dive Supporters' Association can budget for spending, facilities and

## Bars and clubs

### Bar in the Bush
*100 m beyond the Mango Inn, Wed 1800-2330, Fri (Ladies' Night) and Sun 1800-0300.*
Bar in the Bush is the place to go, very popular, lots of dancing and always packed.

### Coco Loco
*On the jetty at the harbour front near Tranquila Bar.*
Very popular with young divers, together these 2 places are the anchors and reigning kings of late-night Utila nightlife.

### La Pirata Bar
*At the dock.*
High up, breezy, with great views.

### Treetanic Bar
*Inside Jade Seahorse; see Restaurants, above. Open 1700-2400.*
High up in the trees; a hot spot on the island.

## Entertainment

### Cinema
**Reef Cinema**, *opposite Bay Islands Originals shop.* Shows films at 1930 every night, at US$3 per person. Popcorn, hotdogs, a/c, comfortable seats, big screen. Also inside the cinema is **Funkytown Books and Music**, an excellent bookshop to trade, sell and rent. Stock up here before you travel anywhere else. Also trades MP3s.

**Utila Centre for Marine Ecology**, *opposite Trudy's, www.utilaecology.org.* Offers free presentations on Tropical Marine Ecology, the 1st and 3rd Mon of each month, 1830-1930.

eventually conservation. Whatever you may think of the idea, one benefit, is greater safety and better organized protection of the reef. Whether this works remains to be seen, but the price of saving a few dollars could end up costing lives. Dive insurance at US$3 per day for fun divers, US$9 for students (Advanced, or Open Water), US$30 for divemasters is compulsory and is available from the BICA office. It covers air ambulance to Roatán and the recompression chamber. Treat any cuts from the coral seriously, they do not heal easily.

**PADI courses**  A PADI Open Water course costs from around US$260 (including certificate) with four dives, an Advanced course costs US$260 with five dives, slightly less if you do the Open Water course with the dive shop first. You can work your way up through the courses with rescue diver (US$260) and dive master (US$800). The Open Water usually comes with two free fun dives. Credit cards, if accepted, are 6% extra. Not permitted by credit cards but as all companies on the island do it you can't go elsewhere. Competition is fierce with over 15 dive shops looking for business, so you can pick and choose. Once qualified, fun dives are US$50 for two tanks. Dive shops offer free basic accommodation with packages. Most schools offer instruction in English or German; French and Spanish are usually available somewhere, while tuition handbooks are provided in numerous languages including Japanese. A variety of courses is available up to instructor level. If planning to do a diving course, it is helpful but not essential to take passport-sized photographs with you for the PADI card. Many dive shops have affiliated hotels or hostels where they may offer discounts or all-inclusive packages if you decide to take a course.

## Festivals

**Aug** **Sun Jam** on Water Caye at a weekend at the beginning of Aug, www.sunjam utila. com. Look out for details locally. They charge a US$2.50 entrance fee to the island; bring your own tent/hammock, food and water.

## Shopping

### Arts and crafts
**Bay Islands Original Shop**. *Mon-Fri 0900-1200 and 1300-1800, Sat and Sun 0900-1200.* Sells T-shirts, sarongs, coffee, hats, etc.
**Gunter Kordovsky**. A painter and sculptor with a gallery at his house, with a good map of Utila, paintings, cards and wood carving.
**Utila Lodge Gift Shop.** Also worth trying.

## What to do

The **Utila Snorkel Center**, for all those who do not want to dive, organizes trips. Inside Mango Tree Business building. See also box, above.

### Dive operators
**Altons Dive Center**, *T2425-3704, www.diveinutila.com.* Offers NAUI and PADI certification, weekly fish talk, popular, owned by the mayor of Utila. Recommended,
**Bay Islands College of Diving**, *on main street close to Hondutel tower,* T425-3291, *www.dive-utila.com.* 5-star PADI facility, experienced and well-qualified staff, good boats ranging from 50 ft, for large parties to skiff for smaller ones, environmentally sound. Only dive shop on the island with in-house pool and hot tub. The trauma centre

and recompression chamber, shared by all dive shops, is located here. 5-star facility.

**Captain Morgan's**, *T2425-3349, www. divingutila.com.* Has been recommended for small classes, good equipment, friendly staff. The only dive shop that offers accommodation on nearby Pigeon Key. Popular with travelling couples.

**Deep Blue Divers**, *T2425-3211, www.deep blueutila.com.* One of the newer operators on the island. The friendly owners are getting good feedback through word of mouth.

**Gunter's Ecomarine Dive Shop**, *T2425-3350, http://ecomarinegunters.blogspot. co.uk.* Dive school with 4 divers per group maximum, 7 languages spoken. Most laid-back dive shop and the only dive school that does not hassle divers arriving at the ferry dock.

**Underwater Vision Dive Center**, *Trudy's, T2425-3103, www.utilascubadiving.com.* With accommodation. Very nice location at the Bay.

**Utila Dive Centre**, *Mango Inn, PADI CDC, T2425-3326, www.utiladivecentre.com.* Well-maintained equipment, daily trips to north coast in fast dory, recommended. All boats covered and custom-built, surface interval on cayes.

**Utila Watersports**, *T2425-3264, run by Troy Bodden.* 4 students per class. Troy also hires out snorkelling gear, photographic and video equipment and takes boat trips. Good reports.

**Whale Shark & Oceanic Research Centre** (**WSORC**), *T2425-3760, www.wsorc.com.* A professional scientific organization committed to education and preserving Utila's oceans, offers speciality courses including whale shark research, naturalist courses, research diver, fish ID, Coral ID. Free presentation 1930 Sun nights about whale sharks.

## Transport

**Air** Utila receives flights from **Tegucigalpa**, **La Ceiba** and **Roatán**. Domestic airlines serving the Bay Islands include **Aerocaribe**, **Aerolineas Sosa**, **CM Airlines**, **Isleña/ Sansa Regional**, **Island Air** and **Lanhsa**. International airlines include **American Airlines**, **United**, **Delta**, **Sunwing** and **Taca** (for more information, see page 560).

**Boat** Services to/from Utila with the Utila Princess, T2408-5163, www.utilaprincess. com, **La Ceiba–Utila** 0930 and 1600; **Utila–La Ceiba**, 0620 and 1400, US$25. Daily sailings Utila–**Roatán**, on Captain Vern's catamaran *Nina Elisabeth II*, T3346-2600 (mob), or ask at **Gunter's Dive Shop** on Utila and **Coconut Divers**, Half Moon Bay, Roatán. US$55 one way, no fixed schedule. Dock fee required when leaving Utila (US$1)

**Cycling** Bike hire about US$5 per day. Try **Delco Bike**.

Despite its size and development, Roatán (area 127 sq km) has managed to retain its idyllic charm, and quiet beaches are often just a short walk away. There is a paved road running from West End through to French Harbour, almost to Oak Ridge, continuing unpaved to Punta Gorda and Wilkes Point, as well as other unmade roads.

### Coxen Hole

The capital and administrative centre of the department, Coxen Hole, or **Roatán City**, is on the southwest shore. Planes land and boats dock here and you can get transport to other parts of the island. It is a colourfully scruffy little town with not much of tourist interest but some souvenir shops are opening.

Besides being the seat of the local government, it has immigration, customs and the law courts. There is a post office, supermarket, handicraft shops, restaurants, banks, travel agents, a bookshop and various other stores. Buses leave from outside the supermarket. All public transport starts or ends here. If taxis are shared, they are colectivos and charge the same as buses. A huge, swanky cruise-liner dock has opened outside the western end of town, with the Town Center shopping mall, offering pricey cafés, gift shops, duty-free stores, and – probably unique on the island – free and spotless public toilets.

### Sandy Bay

A short journey from Coxen Hole, en route to West End, is Sandy Bay, one of the quieter towns on the island. The **Carambola Botanical Gardens** ① *opposite Anthony's Key Resort, www.carambolagardens.com, daily 0800-1700, US$10, guided tours (US$5) or self-guided nature trails*, created in 1985, contain many flowering plants, ferns and varieties of trees which can be explored on a network of trails; it is well worth a visit. The **Roatán Museum** ① *T2445-3003, US$4*, has displays covering the history of the island, with plenty of information about the pirates who called Roatán home, and a collection of artefacts.

# Roatán

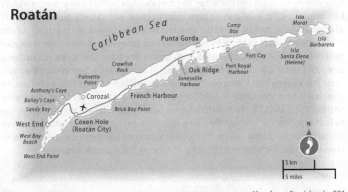

*Caribbean Sea*

Isla Morat · Isla Barbareta · Camp Bay · Punta Gorda · Fort Cay · Port Royal Harbour · Isla Santa Elena (Helene) · Crawfish Rock · Oak Ridge · Jonesville Harbour · Palmetto Point · Anthony's Caye · Bailey's Caye · Corozal · French Harbour · Sandy Bay · Brick Bay Point · West End · Coxen Hole (Roatán City) · West Bay Beach · West End Point

5 km
5 miles

N

## West End

Five minutes by road beyond Sandy Bay, the popular community of West End, at the western tip of the island, is the most popular place to stay. It's a narrow beach on a palm-fringed bay with a distinctly laid-back atmosphere. The **Sandy Bay/West End Marine Park** protects marine life in the area and large numbers of fish have flourished along the coast creating spectacular snorkelling. There are numerous good foreign and local restaurants with lots of pizza/pasta places, as well as hotels, *cabañas* and rooms to rent for all budgets. It is a stiff walk from Coxen Hole over the hills (three hours) to West End, or take the bus on the paved road (US$1; 20 minutes). See www.roatanmarinepark.com for more details.

## West Bay

A beautiful clean beach with excellent snorkelling on the reef, particularly at the west end, where the reef is only 10-20 m offshore and the water is shallow right up to where the wall drops off 50-75 m out and scuba-diving begins. Biting sandflies – *jejenes* – can be a pest here at dusk, but since the hotel staff started raking the beach every day, which exposes their eggs to the sun and kills them, they are no longer such a nuisance. Developers have discovered the delights of West Bay and the atmosphere is changing fast. Apartments, hotels, bars and restaurants are springing up, though mostly low-rise, and hidden behind the palm trees, so it's still pretty quiet here during the week.

## East of Coxen Hole

**French Harbour**, on the south coast, with its shrimping and lobster fleet, is the main fishing port of Roatán. There is no beach and there are two seafood-packing plants. The road passes Coleman's (Midway) Bakery, where you can buy freshly baked products. The bay is protected by the reef and small cayes, which provide safe anchorage. Roatan Dive and Yacht Club and Romeos Marina (at Brick Bay) offer services for visiting yachts. Several charter yachts are based here. There are a few cheap, clean places to stay, as well as expensive hotels and dive resorts. Eldon's Supermarket is open daily and has a range of imported US food.

## Across the island

The main road goes across the mountain ridge along the island with side roads to Jonesville, Punta Gorda and Oak Ridge. You can take a bus on this route to see the island's hilly interior, with beautiful views from coast to coast. Alternatively, hire a small 4WD, which is almost as cheap if shared between four people and allows you to explore the dirt roads and empty bays along the island's northern tip. **Jonesville** is known for its mangrove canal, which is best reached by hiring a taxi boat in Oak Ridge. **Oak Ridge**, situated on a caye (US$1 crossing in a dory from the bus stop), is built around a deep inlet on the south coast. It is a sleepy little fishing port, with rows of dwellings built on stilts on the water's edge (a bus from Coxen Hole to Oak Ridge takes about one and a half hours, depending on passengers, US$1.70). Much of the town has been rebuilt after widespread destruction by Hurricane Mitch in 1998, but the new buildings have retained the same traditional stilt design and pastel colours. Boatmen offer tours around the bay and through mangroves to caves allegedly used by pirates; US$20 for 45 minutes, but it's worth bargaining.

## Tourist information

Local information maps are available from Librería Casi Todo, West End. The Voice Book is a useful online directory of island services and businesses, as well as local news and reviews; a monthly magazine edition is available in most hotels: www.bayislandsvoice.com.

**Bay Islands Conservation Association (BICA)**
*Casa Brady, 1st floor, Sandy Bay, 200 m off road to Anthony's Key Resort, T2445-3117, www.bicaroatan.com.*
Irma Brady, director of BICA, which manages the Sandy Bay/West End Marine National Park and Port Royal National Park in the eastern tip of island, has lots of information about the reef and its conservation work; volunteers are welcome.

## Where to stay

### Coxen Hole

There are a few basic options if stuck, but nothing great. Try:

**$$ Cay View**
*Calle Principal, T2445-1202.*
A/c, bath, TV, phone, laundry, restaurant, bar, dingy rooms, one with seaview, no breakfast, overpriced, but just about adequate if you're desperate.

### Sandy Bay

**$$$$-$$$ Anthony Key Resort**
*Off Sandy Bay on Anthony Key, T800-227-3483 (from USA), www.anthonyskey.com.*
Secluded and intimate, the far-flung island hideaway of Anthony Key offers very comfortable bungalows with hard wood floors, elevated decking, hammocks, and spectacular ocean views. Various dive packages are available.

**$$$ Hobbies Hideaway**
*T9929-4720, www.hobbies-hideaway.com.*
With a tranquil and secluded location, Hobbies Hideaway has clean, comfortable, ocean-view apartments with fully equipped kitchens, a/c, and orthopaedic beds. Lots of activities on offer from fishing to island tours. Helpful and hospitable hosts.

**$$$ Tranquilesas EcoLodge and Dive Center**
*Cra Principal, T9958-4719, www.tranquilseas.com.*
Set among lush landscaped tropical gardens, this PADI dive resort has a range of luxury wood-built *cabañas* some with ocean views. Also a restaurant overlooking the water and free use of kayaks. Packages available. Rustic chic.

**$$$-$ Roatan Backpackers' Hostel**
*T9714-0413, www.roatanbackpackers.com.*
One of the island's better economical options, this low-key hostel offers simple dorms with wooden bunks, each with their own fan. Communal facilities include Wi-Fi, book exchange, kitchen, shaded porch and pool. *Casitas* and apartments are also available ($$$).

### West End

**$$$$ The Beach House**
*At the entrance to West End, T515-4266, www.thebeachhouseroatan.com.*
Constructed in typical Caribbean colonial style, this wood-built hotel overlooks the waves with a breezy veranda and a bar on the upper deck. It offers a range of rooms, all very tastefully attired with classy modern furnishings, some with beachside views. Suites boast a full kitchen. Continental breakfast included.

### $$$ Half Moon Bay Cabins
*Half Moon Bay, T445-4242.*
Bungalows and cabins with bath, and a restaurant with excellent seafood.

### $$$ The Lily Pond House Hotel
*T3265-0220, www.lilypondroatan.com.*
The Lily Pond claims to be the most luxurious boutique accommodation in Roatan's West End. Set on 3 levels, its rooms are comfortable and stylish, with tasteful hardwood furniture and flooring, cable TV, private entrances, a/c and 4-poster beds. Their restaurant serves good seafood in a garden setting.

### $$$ Mariposa Lodge
*T8983-7259, www.mariposa-lodge.com.*
An intimate little lodging nestled among gardens about 100 m from the beach. Accommodation includes rooms and apartments with a/c and use of an upper deck with hammocks. Dive and stay packages available. Good hosts and attentive service.

### $$$ Splash Inn Dive Resort
*T9626-7919, www.roatansplashinn.com.*
Set in leafy grounds by the beach, Splash Inn Dive has simple, cool, whitewashed rooms with a/c, cable TV and Wi-Fi. Amenities include a dive shop and international restaurant. The generator ensures there are no power outages. Personable service and lots of good reports.

### $$ Posada Arco Iris
*Half Moon Bay, T2445-4264, www.roatanposada.com.*
Apartments with kitchen, hot water, fan and large balcony, with friendly owners. There's a restaurant specializing in grilled meats. Highly recommended.

### $$ Roatan Bed and Breakfast apartments
*T8990 3887, www.roatan-bed-and-breakfast.com.*
Roatán Bed and Breakfast is a lovely property in a secluded location on a hill a short distance from the tourist hub of West End. Its 3 rooms are tranquil, wood-built and environmentally friendly, and each has Wi-Fi, cable TV, fan and ocean views. There are also 2 self-catering apartments with full kitchen and garden access. Recommended.

### $$ Sea Breeze
*North of West End, T2445-4026, www.seabreezeroatan.com.*
Nice rooms, hot water, baths, a/c optional, suites and studios available with kitchens. Windsurfers and kayaks for rent.

### $$ Seagrape Plantation Resort
*Half Moon Bay, T2445-4428, www.seagraperoatan.com.*
In a good location on a rocky promontory, this resort offers cabins and rooms with private bath and hot water. There's a friendly, family atmosphere, no beach, but snorkelling possible, a full-service restaurant and bar. Fun dives for US$35 with equipment. Inclusive packages available; Visa accepted.

### $$-$ Chillies
*Half Moon Bay, T2445-4003, www.nativesonsroatan.com/chillies.htm.*
Double rooms and dorm, clean, fully equipped kitchen, lounge, big balcony, camping and hammocks available. Excellent value for money.

### $ Buena Onda
*Next to the gas station, Cra Principal, T9770-0158, www.hbuenaonda.com.*
Buena Onda is the dream project of a long-term traveller who understands what makes a good backpacker hostel tick. It is a youthful, sociable place with 3 dorms and a private room, weekly barbecue and cinema, roof terrace, kitchen, hot showers, DVD player and hammocks.

## West Bay

### $$$$ Island Pearl
*On the beach, T2445-5005,*
*www.roatanpearl.com.*
Double-storey well-decorated apartments
with hand-painted furniture, a/c, hot water
and a tiled kitchen.

### $$$$ Las Sirenas
*Midway along the beach, T2445-5009,*
*www.hmresorts.com.*
Rooms, suites and enormous apartments,
with a/c, cable TV and kitchen; small
swimming pool. Full board and shared
amenities with adjacent HM resorts:
**Henry Morgan**, **Mayan Princess** and
**Paradise Beach**. Quiet, clean and well run.
Recommended.

### $$$$ Xbalanque Resort
*Tamarind Dr, T9719-5282,*
*www.xbalanque-roatan.com.*
With impeccable contemporary design,
Xbalanque is a stylish luxury resort
overlooking the ocean. It offers beautiful
suites and beachfront villas, a suave rooftop
bar, infinity pool, lounge and gym. Set it
in 3 ha of grounds, there are also many
tranquil walking trails. Recommended, if
you can afford it.

### $$$ West Bay B&B
*T2445-5080, www.westbay*
*bedandbreakfast.com.*
Managed by Glen from San Diego, the
hospitable West Bay B&B offers a range
of clean, comfortable, well-appointed
rooms equipped with fridge, a/c, DVD
player and satellite TV. General amenities
include backup generator, internet café,
DVD collection, laundry, snorkel gear,
book exchange and home-cooked food.
Discounts for stays of over 5 nights. Just
2 mins from the beach and good value for
the area.

### $$$-$$ Bananarama
*Centre of West Bay beach, T2992-9679.*
Good-value rooms with bath, hot water
and fan. PADI dive courses available;
breakfast included. Recommended.

### $$$-$$ Las Rocas
*Next to Bite on the Beach, T2445-1841,*
*www.lasrocasresort.com.*
Duplex *cabañas*, very close together, hot
water, balcony, smaller cabins sleep 3, larger
ones sleep 6. Free boat transport to West
End and back, and there's a dive shop and
a restaurant.

## East of Coxen Hole

### $$$$ Reef House Resort
*Oak Ridge, T2435-1482,*
*www.reefhouseresort.com.*
Meals and various packages, including diving.
Wooden cabins with sea-view balconies, and
a seaside bar a private natural pool. Dock
facilities, and good snorkelling from the shore.

### $$$$-$$$ Mango Creek
*Port Royal, boat access, T8916-8704,*
*www.mangocreeklodge.com.*
Spacious, calming, wood-built and fully
equipped with an open-air deck and
hammock where you can chill out to the
sounds of the ocean, accommodation
at Mango Creek consists of 6 wonderful
over-the-water *cabañas*. There are cheaper,
less exotic rooms in the main lodge too.
Packages are available.

### $$$-$ Marble Hill Farms
*Less than 1 km past Oak Ridge, T3335-5409,*
*www.marblehillfarms.com.*
Marble Hill Farms offers a wide range of
accommodation including well-furnished
sea view rooms complete with sofa, DVD,
a/c and kitchenette; island-style 'adventurer
casitas' with private bedrooms, kitchenettes
and enclosed decking; 'explorer treehouses',
which consist of yurt-style thatch roof

cabins on elevated decking; and backpacker dorms ($).

## Restaurants

Evening meals cost US$4-10. There is a good seafood restaurant on Osgood Caye a few mins by free water taxi from the wharf.

### Coxen Hole

#### $$ Le Bistro
*10 mins' walk along seafront between Coxen Hole and West Bay, T9527-3136.*
Perched on a rocky outcrop on the beach. Thai and Vietnamese cuisine, with spicy seafood and curries. Beautiful spot with deck overlooking the sea. French owner François also takes snorkelling trips.

#### $ Madah's Kitchen
*Main St. Open for breakfast and lunch.*
Founded by Deenie Edania Webster, better known as Madah (Mother), this authentic locals' joint serves wholesome home-cooked Caribbean fare, including fresh seafood and barbecue chicken.

#### $ Tacos al Pastor
*Main St, west of the dock.*
Cheap and easy eats close to the dock. As the name suggests, fully authentic Mexican fare. Friendly and casual.

### Sandy Bay

#### $$$-$$ Blue Bahia Beach Grill
*Inside the Blue Bahia Resort, www.beachgrillroatan.com.*
Dependable international fare in a resort setting. Weekly specials include: bottomless mimosas on Sun; all-you-can-eat pasta on Mon; steak night on Tue; barbecue on Wed; 2-for-1 on rum on Thu; all-you-can-eat lionfish on Fri; burgers on Sat. Great location by the waves and views of the sunset.

#### $$$-$$ Blue Parrot
*Sandy Bay Rd.*
This low-key Jamaican eatery serves jerk pork and chicken. A fun and friendly place with typical Caribbean hospitality. Popular with the expats, a lively scene.

### West End

#### $$$ Half Moon Bay Restaurant
*Half Moon Bay.*
Lovely location sitting on the terrace overlooking sea, with excellent food. But it's more expensive than most and service can be very slow.

#### $$$ Tong
Restaurant in a good location serving Asian and Middle East specialities, with a salad buffet. It's expensive but worth it.

#### $$$-$$ Roatan Oasis
*Carretera Principal, at the entrance to the village, www.roatanoasis.com. Mon-Fri 1700-2300.*
The popular Roatan Oasis cooks up a diverse range of international cuisine: American, Asian fusion, Mediterranean, Italian, Moroccan, Thai and vegetarian, to name a few. Past offerings include Jack Daniels chicken wings, Korean barbecue ribs, and duck and blue cheese salad. Live music and menu changes every Mon. Recommended.

#### $$ Café Escondido
*West End Rd, www.cafeescondido.com.*
A relaxed and sociable place, open-air and overlooking the water. They serve cooked breakfasts, café snacks and international fare, with a special emphasis on Chinese, including rice bowls and noodles. Beverages include ice coffees, smoothies, cocktails, local and imported beers. A popular watering hole.

#### $$ Cindy's Place
*Next to Sunset Inn.*
Local family breakfast, lunches and dinner in garden, serving fish caught the same

morning, as well as also lobster and king crab. Recommended.

## $$ Monkey Island Beach Café
*West End Rd, near the entrance to West End.*
This Tex Mex and seafood restaurant has found an innovative solution to the region's invasive lion fish problem – turn them into fish tacos! Other good grub includes pig roast and barbecued chicken in a beer can. A fun place with live music during the week.

## $$ Por Qué No
*Between Eagle Ray and Fosters.*
A friendly German-owned café serving good coffee and reasonable breakfasts. Evening menu includes 'Wiener Art' schnitzel and Jagerschnitzel. For dessert, try the crêpe in rum-orange sauce.

## $$-$ C Level Café and Bar
*Next to Reef Glider's Dive Center.*
A casual little open-air bar-restaurant, friendly and popular with divers. They serve café fare, including cooked breakfasts and subs, but most people come for the evening pizza (Mon-Fri, slices only on Wed). A good place to sip beer. 'Build your own Bloody Mary' may suit those seeking hair of the dog.

## $ Anthony's Chicken and more
*West End Rd, in front of Beach House.*
A low-key locals' joint. Their home-cooked fare includes roast chicken, fried fish, jerk chicken, chicken burrito and grilled pork. Tasty and great value. A good lunch spot.

## $ Creole Rotisserie Chicken
*West End Rd.*
As the name might suggest, wholesome home-cooked rotisserie chicken served with rice and beans. If you get there for lunch, there's usually some cinnamon rolls on offer too. A classic locals' joint managed by Dola.

## West Bay

### $$$ Bite on the Beach
*On the point over West Bay.*
Excellent place offering Wed-Sun brunch, served on a huge deck in a gorgeous position; fresh food and great fruit punch. Nightly feeding of moray eels, which swim – or wriggle – up to the edge of the dock. A fun place, very friendly, and very much what Roatán is about. Recommended.

### $$$ Nice 'N Spicy
*Behind the mall in the side road to the beach.*
A cosy little restaurant serving reliable Asian grub. Choose from noodles with beef, pork, chicken, shrimp or vegetables served with a variety of Chinese, Malaysian and Thai sauces, among others. Traditionalists may enjoy the Indian or Thai curry.

### $$$ Vintage Pearl Restaurant and Wine Cellar
*Cra Principal, www.roatanpearl.com.*
Gourmet offerings at the Vintage Pearl include succulent steak and fresh seafood. There's also a selection of fine wine. Intimate and extravagant, the place for gourmands and lovers. Fixed price 3-course meals available.

### $$$-$$ Beachers
*West Bay Beach.*
This open-air restaurant by the waves serves typical Caribbean seafood, including coconut shrimp and catch-of-the-day with your choice of French fries or rice. There's international fare too (when in stock) including BLTs and burgers. Good service and impeccable views. Occasional live music.

### $$ Pizzarama
*Inside Bananarama dive resort, www.bananarama.com.*
The stone-baked pizzas at this fun beachside restaurant can't be faulted for their tasty toppings and Italian-style crusts. Go on a Mon night and get 2 for 1 on large ones.

### East of Coxen Hole

There is a *taquería* close to HSBC on the main road in French Harbour serving good tacos, burritos and hamburgers.

### $$$ Gios
*French Harbour.*
Top-quality seafood, with king crab a speciality.

### $$$ Roatan Dive and Yacht Club
*French Harbour.*
Daily specials, pizza, salads, sandwiches, usually very good.

### $$ BJ's Backyard Restaurant
*Oak Ridge, at the harbour.*
Island cooking, with fishburgers and smoked foods, all at reasonable prices. There is a pizzeria and, next door, a supermarket.

### $$ Romeo's
*French Harbour.*
Romeo, who is Honduran-Italian, serves good seafood, and continental cuisine.

## Entertainment

Most clubs come alive about midnight, play reggae, salsa, *punta* and some rock.

### Coxen Hole

**Harbour View**. *Open Thu-Sun nights late.* Hot, atmospheric and very local. There are usually no problems with visitors, but avoid getting involved in disputes. US$0.50 entrance.

### West End

**Bahía Azul**. Fri is party night, with DJs and dancing.
**C-bar**. In a fantastic location on the beachfront near Seagrape Plantation.
**Foster's**. The late night hotspot, with dance music Thu night as well as band nights.
**Lone's Bar**, *Mermaid Beach*. Nightly barbecue, with reggae music.

**Sundowners Bar**. Popular bar with a happy hour from 1700-1900 and a Sun quiz followed by a barbecue.

### East of Coxen Hole

**Al's**, *Barrio Las Fuertes, before French Harbour. Closed Sat night.* Salsa and plenty of *punta*.

## Shopping

### Supermarkets

It's best to buy supplies in Coxen Hole; **Coconut Tree** at West End is expensive. **Woods** is cheaper. **Eldon** in French Harbour is also expensive. **Ezekiel**, West End, opposite church, sells fruit and veg. **Mall Megaplaza**, French Harbour. New shopping mall by roadside east of town, with fast-food outlets.

## What to do

### Boat trips

Kayak rentals and tours from **Seablades**, contact Alex at **Casi Todo**, 3- to 7-day kayak tours, US$150-250. Full and ½-day rental US$20 and US$12 (with instruction), kayaks available at **Tyll's**. From Rick's American Café, **Casablanca** charters on yacht *Defiance III*, sunset cruises, party trips, full-day snorkelling, also can be arranged through **Casi Todo**. At West Bay beach is a glass-bottomed boat, **Caribbean Reef Explorer**, US$20 per 1½ hrs, unfortunately includes fish feeding, which upsets the reef's ecological balance. Glass-bottomed boat and 3-person submarine tours from the dock at Half Moon Bay, US$25 per person.

### Diving

If you don't want to dive, the snorkelling is normally excellent. The creation of the Sandy Bay/West End Marine Park along 4 km of coast from Lawson Rock around the southwest tip to Key Hole has encouraged the return of large numbers of fish in that area and there are several interesting dive sites. Lobsters are still rare, but large grouper are now common and curious about divers. If the sea is rough off **West End** try diving around **French Harbour** (or vice versa) where the cayes provide some protection. There are more mangroves on this side, which attract the fish. **Flowers Bay** on the south side has some spectacular wall dives, but not many fish, and it is calm during the 'Northers' which blow in Dec-Feb. Few people dive the east end except the live-aboards (**Bay Islands Aggressor**, **The Aggressor Fleet**, **Romeo Tower**, French Harbour, T2445-1518) and people on camping trips to Pigeon Cay, so it is relatively unspoilt. Because fishing is allowed to the east, tropical fish are scarce and the reef is damaged in places. In addition to a few stormy days from Dec to Feb, you can also expect stinging hydroids in the top few feet of water around Mar and Apr which bother people who are sensitive to stings. Vinegar is the local remedy.

**Courses** As on Utila, the dive operators concentrate on instruction but prices vary (the municipal government sets minimum prices). You can normally find a course starting within 1 or 2 days. There is more on offer than in Utila; not everyone teaches only PADI courses. Prices for courses and diving vary with the season. In low season good deals abound. Open Water US$320, advanced US$280, fun dives US$40 (2-9 dives are US$35 each, 10+ US$30 each). Despite the huge number of dive students, Roatán has a good safety record but it still pays to shop around and find an instructor you feel confident with at a dive shop which is well organized with well-maintained equipment. As in other 'adventure' sports, the cheapest is not always the best. Dive insurance is US$2 per day, and is sometimes included in the course price. If you do not have dive insurance and need their services, the hyperbaric chamber charges a minimum of US$800.

### Dive operators
**Anthony's Key Resort**, *Sandy Bay, T2445-3049, www.anthonyskey.com*. Mostly hotel package diving, also swim and dive with dolphins.

**Bananarama**, *West Bay, in centre of beach, next to Cabaña Roatana, T2445-5005*. Small, friendly dive shop, run by young German family, boat and shore diving.

**Native Son's Water Sports**, *next to Mermaid cabins, West End, T2445-4003*. Run by Alvin, local instructor, PADI and PDSI courses and fun dives.

**Ocean Connections** at Sunset Inn, *West End, T3327-0935, www.ocean-connections. com*. Run by Carol and Phil Stevens with emphasis on safety and fun, good equipment, multilingual instructors, PADI courses, BSAC, the only shop with nitrox instruction, fast boats, also rooms and restaurant, dive/accommodation packages available. Recommended. Also at West Bay, entrance through Paradise Beach Resort – though not attached to the resort – one of the few independent operators, T2445-5017. Very friendly and highly recommended.

**Scuba Romance**, *Dixon Cove*. Shop and equipment, large diesel boat and compressor, diving the south wall and the reef at Mary's Place, overnight trips to Barbareta, 6 dives, US$80, sleeping on the boat, work with Palm Cove Resort, cabin-style accommodation, home cooking.

**Sueño del Mar Divers**, *T2445-4343*. Good, inexpensive, American-style operation, which tends to dive the sites closest to home.

**Tyll's Dive**, *West End, T9698-0416, www.tyllsdive.com*. Multilingual instructors, PADI, SSI courses. Accommodation also available.

**West End Divers**, *West End, T2445-4289, www.westendivers.com*. Italian owned, competent bilingual instructors, PADI Dive Centre.

## Fishing

Trips can be arranged through Eddie, contact at **Cindy's** next to Ocean Divers, West End, small dory, local expert, good results, US$30 per hr, but prices can vary. Alternatively, go fishing in style from French Harbour, **Hot Rods** (T445-1862)sports fisher, US$500 per day charter. Contact **Casi Todo** (T2445-1347), for fishing tours, ½- and full day. Fishing trips also available on **Flame** (contact Darson or Bernadette, T445-1616), US$20 per hr.

## Submarine trips

Karl Stanley offers a probably unique opportunity with deep-sea submarine trips down to 2000 ft. At US$600 per person, a little on the pricey side, but then it's not an everyday option. **Stanley Submarines**, www.stanleysubmarines.com.

## Tour operators

The airport travel agency has information on hotels, and will make bookings, with no commission. **Bay Islands Tour and Travel Center**, in Coxen Hole (Suite 208, Cooper Building, T2445-1585) and French Harbour. **Casi Todo 1** in West End or **Casi Todo 2** in Coxen Hole can arrange tours, locally and on the mainland, including fishing, kayaking, island tours, trips to Barbareta and Copán. Local and international air tickets also sold here as well as new and second-hand books, Mon-Sat, 0900-1630. **Columbia Tours** (Barrio El Centro, T2445-1160), good prices for international travel, very helpful. **Carlos Hinds**, T2445-1446, has a van for trips, reasonable and dependable.

At **Belvedere's Lodge** on the headland at Half Moon Bay, Dennis runs snorkelling trips to secluded bays beyond Antony's Key in a glass-bottomed yacht. He also takes charters and sunset cruises all along the coast. Horse riding available from **Keifitos** or **Jimmy's** in West End. Alex does day trips to Punta Gorda and 2- to 3-day trips in his sailboat *Adventure Girl*, which is moored at **Ocean Divers** dock, contact here or at **Tyll's**. **Far Tortugas** charters, trimaran *Genesis*, does sailing trips with snorkelling and reef drag (snorkellers towed behind slow-moving boat), US$45 per day, US$25 per ½ day, contact **Casi Todo** (West End, T2445-1347). **Coconut Tree** have a rainforest tour to Pico Bonito, US$112 (guide, transport, lunch and snorkelling).

## Zip-wire

High-wire canopy tour circuits are the latest craze on Roatán, with half a dozen sites strung around the island, including **Pirates of the Caribbean** (T2455-7576), **Mayan Jungle Canopy** (www.boddentours.com), and **South Shore Canopy Tour** (on West Bay Rd, T9967-1381, www.southshorezipline.com).

## Transport

**Air** The airport is 20 mins' walk from Coxen Hole, or you can catch a taxi from outside the airport for US$1.50. There is a hotel reservation desk in the airport, T2445-1930. Change in Coxen Hole for taxis to West End. US$1 per person for colectivos to West End, US$2 to Oak Ridge. If you take a taxi from the airport they charge US$10 per taxi; if you pick one up on the main road you may be able to bargain down to US$5. Domestic airlines serving the Bay Islands include **Aerocaribe**, www.aerocaribehn.com; **Aerolineas Sosa**, www.aerolineasosahn.com, CM Airlines, **www.cmairlines.com**; **Isleña/Sansa Regional**, www.flyislena.com, and **Lanhsa**, www.lanhsa.com. Always buy your ticket in advance (none on sale at airport), as reservations are not always honoured.

**Boat** Services to/from Roatán with Roatán Ferry, T2445-1795 (La Ceiba), www.roatanferry.com, **La Ceiba–Roatán**, 0930 and 1630, **Roatán–La Ceiba**, 0700 and 1400, US$31 regular class, US$36 1st class. No sailings in bad weather. At times the crossing can be rough, seasickness pills available at ticket counter, and steward gives out sick bags; smart modern ship, with café, and 2 decks, comfortable seating. Irregular boats from **Puerto Cortés** and **Utila**. Cruise ships visit from time to time, mostly visiting **Tabayana Resort** on West Bay.

**Bus** From Coxen Hole to Sandy Bay is a 2-hr walk, or a US$1.70 bus ride, every 30 mins 0600-1700 from market, a couple of blocks in from Calle Principal. **Ticabus** buses go to French Harbour, Oak Ridge and Punta Gorda, daily every 45 mins from 0600-1630, US$1.75; from parking lot opposite Centro Médico Euceda east end of Calle Principal.

**Car rental** **Captain Van**, West End, vans, also mopeds and bicycles, good information about the islands; **Roatan Rentals**, West End, range of vehicles, pickups and vans for rent; **Sandy Bay Rent-A-Car**, US$42 per day

all inclusive, jeep rental, T2445-1710, agency also in West End outside Sunset Inn; **Toyota**, opposite airport, have pickups, US$46, 4WD, US$65, Starlets US$35 per day, also 12-seater bus, US$56 per day, T2445-1166.

**Cycling and mopeds** Captain Van's Rentals, West End; also from **Ole Rentavan**, T445-1819.

**Taxi** If you take a private taxi, *privado*, negotiate the price in advance. The official rate from the airport to Sandy Bay/West End is US$15 per taxi regardless of the number of passengers; from ferry dock to West End is US$20. Luis (waiter at **Bite on the Beach** restaurant West End), runs taxi tours, very informative and knowledgeable, T9892-9846. Water taxis from West End to West Bay, every few minutes depending on passengers, US$3, from jetty next to **Foster's Bar**.

## Isla Guanaja  Colour map 3, A3.

a forest reserve and national marine park

Columbus called Guanaja (area 56 sq km) the Island of Pines, but Hurricane Mitch swept most of them away. Since then, a great replanting effort has been completed and, until the pines have regrown, flowering and fruiting plants thrive on the island. Good (but sweaty) clambering on the island gives splendid views of the jungle and the sea and there are several attractive waterfalls, which can be visited on the hills rising to the summit of 415 m.

The first English settler was Robert Haylock, who arrived in 1856 with a land title to part of the island, the two cayes that now form the main settlement of Bonacca and some of the Mosquito coast. He was followed in 1866 by John Kirkconnell who purchased Hog Caye, where the Haylocks raised pigs away from the sandflies. These two families became sailors, boat builders and landowners, and formed the basis of the present population.

Much of Guanaja town, locally known as **Bonacca** and covering a small caye off the coast, is built on stilts above sea water, with boardwalks and concrete pathways, hence its nickname: the 'Venice of Honduras'. There are three small villages, **Mangrove Bight**, **Savannah Bight** and **North East Bight**, on the main island. Much of the accommodation is in all-inclusive resorts, but you can visit independently as well. Sandflies and mosquitoes cannot be escaped on the island, and none of the beaches offer respite (coconut oil, baby oil or any oily suntan lotion will help to ward off sandflies). The cayes are better, including Guanaja town. South West Caye is especially recommended.

## Where to stay

**$ Harry Carter**
*T2455-4303, ask for fan.*
Rooms are clean.

**$ Miss Melba**
*Just before Hotel Alexander sign on left,*
*house with flowers.*
Run by a friendly old lady with lots of island
information, 3 rooms in boarding house,
with shared bathroom and cold water.
Great porch and gardens.

## Restaurants

**$$ Harbour Light**
*Through Mountain View nightclub.*
Good food, reasonably priced for the island.

## What to do

### Diving and sailing

The most famous dive site off Guanaja is
the wreck of the *Jado Trader*, sunk in 1987
in about 30 m on a flat bottom surrounded
by some large coral pinnacles which rise to
about 15 m. Big black groupers and moray
eels live here, as does a large shy jewfish
and many other fish and crustaceans.

**End of The World**, *next to Bayman Bay Club*,
*T2402-3016*. Diving instruction, beachfront
bar, restaurant, cabins, kayaks, canoes, hobie
cats, white-sand beach, fishing. Highly
recommended resort.
**Jado Divers**, *beside Melba's, T2453-4326*.
US$26 for 2 dives, run by Matthew from US.
Preston Borden will take snorkellers out for
US$25 per boat load (4-6 people), larger
parties accommodated with larger boat, or
for customized excursions, very flexible.

## Transport

**Air** The airport is on Guanaja but you have
to get a water taxi from there to wherever
you are staying; there are no roads or cars;
**Sosa** and **Isleña** (T2453-4208) fly daily from
**La Ceiba**, 30 mins. Other non-scheduled
flights available.

**Boat** The *Suyapa* sails between Guanaja,
**La Ceiba** and **Puerto Cortés**. The *Miss
Sheila* also does this run and on to **George
Town** (**Grand Cayman**). *Cable Doly Zapata*,
Guanaja, for monthly sailing dates to Grand
Cayman (US$75 1 way). Irregular sailings
from Guanaja to **Trujillo**, 5 hrs.

# North
## coast

Along the Caribbean lowlands are a mix of banana-exporting ports, historic towns and Garífuna villages. As the historic base for the United Fruit Company, the region claims kudos as the symbolic birthplace of the world's first banana republic. Throughout the early 20th century, the influx of plantation labourers from Jamaica and other English-speaking colonies infused the coast with a distinctive African-Caribbean culture that takes great pride in its unique forms of music, dance and cooking.

Steeped in steamy rainforests, brackish swamps and tangled mangroves, the coast has abundant exotic flora and fauna too. In between the main towns of interest – Omoa, Puerto Cortés, Tela, La Ceiba and Trujillo – you will find isolated beaches and resorts, and national parks like Pico Bonito, which are perfect for hiking and whitewater rafting. Close to the shore and accessible from La Ceiba, are the small, palm-fringed Hog Islands, more attractively known as Cayos Cochinos (see page 572).

Running parallel to the coast, a route from El Progreso leads to rarely visited national parks, pristine cloudforest and an alternative route to La Ceiba.

**Best** for
Ecotourism ▪ Hiking ▪ Whitewater rafting ▪ Wildlife

**rough-and-ready port town contrasts with lush fishing village**

## Puerto Cortés

Stuck out on the northwestern coast of the country and backed by the large bay of Laguna de Alvarado, Puerto Cortés is hot, tempered by sea breezes and close to many beautiful palm-fringed beaches. However, most people find little in Puerto Cortés to detain them and instead head straight to the infinitely more attractive village of Omoa.

The economic success of the place is due to its location and the fact that most Honduran trade passes through the port, which is just 58 km from San Pedro Sula by road and rail, and 333 km from Tegucigalpa. It has a small oil refinery, a free zone and, being two days' voyage from New Orleans, is one of the most important ports in Central America.

The Parque Central contains many fine trees but focuses on a huge Indian poplar, planted as a sapling in 1941, in the centre that provides an extensive canopy.

## ★Omoa

Omoa, 18 km from Puerto Cortés, is set in the beautiful Bahía de Omoa where the mountains, lusciously carpeted in jungle, tumble towards the sea. You can watch fine purple sunsets from the quiet laid-back bars on the beach and, if you're lucky, see dolphins in the bay. It has an 18th-century castle, **Fortaleza de San Fernando**, now renovated and worth a visit. It was built by the Spaniards in 1759 to protect the coast and shipments of silver, gold and cacao from British pirates. There is a **visitor centre** and a small, interesting **museum** ⓘ *Mon-Sun 0900-1600, US$1.40, tickets on sale at gate, guides available.*

During the week Omoa is a quiet, friendly fishing village, but at weekends it gets a little busier with Hondurans from San Pedro and the place becomes littered, followed by a grand clean-up on the Monday morning. Near Omoa are two waterfalls (**Los Chorros**), with lovely walks to each, and good hiking in attractive scenery both along the coast and inland.

It's a fair walk from the main road. Get a tuk-tuk for US$0.50 to the beach. Note: there are no ATMs in Omoa.

## Listings  Puerto Cortés and Omoa

### Where to stay

#### Puerto Cortés

Avoid 4 Calle between 1 and 2 Av and the area on 1 Av opposite the dockyards; it is unpleasant by day and dangerous at night.

#### $$$ Costa Azul
*Playa El Faro, T2665-5215,*
*www.hotelcostazul.net.*
One of the town's better places, with restaurant, disco-bar, billiards, table tennis, pool, horse riding, volley ball. Good value.

#### $$ Villa del Sol
*Barrio El Porvenir, in front of the municipal beach, T2665-4939, www.villadelsolhn.com.*
In an interesting location by the beach, Villa del Sol has very reasonable guestrooms, which are spacious but simple. Each is fully equipped with a/c, hot water, private balcony, cable TV and phone. There's a restaurant and helpful staff. Safe and secure. Recommended.

#### $ Formosa
*3 Av 2 Calle E.*
Good-value, clean rooms with fan, bath (some without), no towel, but with soap and toilet paper. Friendly Chinese owner.

## Omoa

### $$ Sueño de Mar
*T2658-9047, www.suenosdemar.com.*
Chilled out hotel at the quiet end of
the beach with a handful of rooms of
differing sizes, run by Canadian couple
Karen and Mark. A great spot, offering
Canadian breakfasts, laundry and Wi-Fi.
Recommended.

### $ Roli's Place
*T2658-9082, http://yaxpactours.com.*
Located 80 m from beach, this great place
has clean rooms with private bath and hot
water, and good information of the region.
It offers bikes and kayaks for guests' use,
games, a shady garden and a campground.
Roli will change TCs, quetzals, euros and
dollars. As it's quiet after 2200 it's not a
party place.

## Restaurants

### Puerto Cortés

### $$$-$$ Restaurante La Ola
*Inside Hotel Villa del Sol, Barrio El Porvenir,*
*opposite the municipal beaches, T2665-4939,*
*www.villadelsolhn.com.*
La Ola serves typical Honduran fare from
*steak típico* to a host of fresh seafood such as
prawns, conch, king crab (when in season)
and fish fillet. Solid and reliable.

### $$ Pekín
*2 Av, 6-7 Calle.*
Excellent Chinese, with a/c and good
service. It's a bit pricey but recommended.
**Supermercado Pekín** is next door.

### Omoa

### $$-$ Family Restaurant
*Mila 2, 7 km before Omoa on the highway*
*to Guatemala.*
Perched on the seafront, this modest eatery
serves wholesome home-cooked fare and is

often crowded with loyal patrons. Fresh and
economical. Try the seafood soup.

### $ Fisherman's Hut
*200 m to right of pier.*
Clean, good food, seafood, recommended.
Don't expect early Sun breakfasts after the
partying the night before.

## Festivals

### Puerto Cortés
**Aug** **Noche Veneciana** on 3rd Sat.

## Shopping

### Puerto Cortés
There is a souvenir shop, **Marthita's**, in the
customs administration building (opposite
Hondutel). The market in the town centre
is worth a visit, 3 Calle between 2 and 3 Av.
**Supertienda Paico** is on the Parque.

## Transport

### Puerto Cortés
**Boat To Guatemala** Information from
**Ocean Travel** at 3 Av, 2 blocks west of
plaza. See also Border crossings box in
Practicalities chapter.

**To Belize** Boats connecting to Belize
leave from beside the bridge over the
lagoon (Barra La Laguna), at the Muelle de
Mariscos, next to El Delfín restaurant (also
known as the 'Pescaderia'). The **D-Express,**
**www.belizeferry.com,** leaves Puerto Cortés
on Mon at 1100, for **Mango Creek** and on
to **Placencia,** 4 hrs arriving around 1340,
US$65. The *Pride of Belize* also departs Mon
at 1100 and calls at Dangriga and Belize City.
Check-in closes 15 mins prior to departure,
though it is best to get on the passenger list
as early as possible.

Remember to get your exit stamp from
the Immigration office, located next to the
D-Express ticket office at the Muelle de
Mariscos. If arriving from Belize and heading

on straight away you don't need to go into town to catch a bus. Get on to the bridge, cross over the other side and keep walking 200 m to the main road. Buses going past are going to San Pedro Sula and beyond.

**Bus** Virtually all buses now arrive and leave from 4 Av 2-4 Calle. Bus service at least hourly to **San Pedro Sula**, US$2.30, 45 mins, **Citul** (4 Av between 3 and 4 Calle) and **Impala** (4 Av y 3 Calle, T2255-0606). **Expresos del Caribe**, **Expresos de Citul** and **Expresos del Atlantic** all have minibuses to **San Pedro Sula**. Bus to **Omoa** and **Tegucigalpita** from 4 Av, old school bus, loud music, very full; guard your belongings.

**Citral Costeños** go to the Guatemalan border, 4-5 Av, 3Calle E. Regular buses leave for **Omoa** (US$0.70) at 0730 to get to **Corinto** at the Guatemalan border. See also Border crossings box in Practicalities chapter.

### Omoa

**Boat** Boats leave for **Lívingston**, Guatemala, on Tue and Fri around 1000. Ask around to confirm. Ask at **Fisherman's Hut** for Sr Juan Ramón Menjivar.

**Bus** Frequent buses to the Guatemalan border at 1000, 1400 and 1700. See Border crossings box in Practicalities chapter for information.

## East of San Pedro Sula   *Colour map 3, B2.*
### a former United Fruit outpost enveloped in remote beaches and humid wetlands

### Tela

Tela used to be an important banana port before the pier was partly destroyed by fire. Easily reached from San Pedro Sula with a bus service via El Progreso, it is pleasantly laid out with a sandy but dirty beach.

Tela Viejo to the east is the original city joined by a bridge to Tela Nuevo, the residential area built for the executives of the American banana and farming company **Chiquita**. There is a pleasant walk along the beach east to Ensenada, or west to San Juan. More information is available at www.telahonduras.com. **Note** Make sure you take a cab after midnight; US$1.50 per person at night.

### Around Tela

Local buses and trucks from the corner just east of the market go east to the Garífuna village of **Triunfo de la Cruz**, which is set in a beautiful bay. Site of the first Spanish settlement on the mainland, a sea battle between Cristóbal de Olid and Francisco de Las Casas (two of Cortés' lieutenants) was fought here in 1524.

Beyond Triunfo de la Cruz is an interesting coastal area that includes the cape, **Parque Nacional Punta Izopo** (1½-hour walk along the beach, take water; 12 km from Tela) and the mouth of the Río León. This, and its immediate hinterland, is a good place to see parrots, toucans, turtles, alligators and monkeys as well as the first landing point of the Spanish conqueror Cristóbal de Olid. For information, contact **Prolansate** (see box, opposite). To get right into the forest and enjoy the wildlife, it is best to take an organized tour (see What to do, page 569). A trip to Punta Izopo involves kayaking through mangrove swamps up the Río Plátano, Indiana Jones style.

## ON THE ROAD

### Environmental challenge

The **Fundación Para la Protección de Lancetilla, Punta Sal y Texiguat (Prolansate)** is a non-governmental, non-profit organization based in Tela. Originally set up by Peace Corps volunteers, it is now operated by local personnel and is involved in environmental programmes to protect and educate in conjunction with community development and ecotourism. It manages four protected areas: Parque Nacional 'Jeannette Kawas' (Punta Sal), Jardín Botánico Lancetilla, Refugio de Vida Silvestre Texiguat and Refugio de Vida Silvestre Punta Izopo. The Prolansate visitor centre, Calle 9 Avenida 2-3 NE, Tela, T2448-2042, www.prolansate.org, organizes trips to Punta Sal, Punta Izopo and Lancetilla, with guides, and provides information about other national parks, wildlife refuges and bird sanctuaries.

### Parque Nacional Punta Sal 'Jeannette Kawas'

*US$2, daily 0800-1500. It is recommended that you contact Prolansate for more information, www.prolansate.org.*

Encompassing 80,000 ha of sublime palm-fringed shoreline, the Parque Nacional Punta Sal 'Jeannette Kawas' is one of the most important parks in Honduras. It has two parts: the peninsula and the lagoon. During the dry season some 350 species of bird live within the lagoon, surrounded by forest, mangroves and wetlands.

Once inhabited only by Garífuna, the area has suffered from the immigration of cattle farmers who have cleared the forest, causing erosion, and from a palm oil extraction plant on the Río San Alejo, which has dumped waste in the river and contaminated the lagoons. Conservation and environmental protection programmes are now underway. To get there you will need a motor boat, or take a bus (three a day) to Tornabé and hitch a ride 12 km, or take the crab truck at 1300 for US$0.40 (back at 1700), on to Miami, a small, all-thatched fishing village (two hours' walk along beach from Tornabé), beer on ice available, and walk the remaining 10 km along the beach. There are also pickups from Punta Sal to Miami, contact Prolansate for information.

### Lancetilla Jardín Botánico

*T2448-1740, www.jblancetilla.esnacifor.hn. It's not well signposted; a guide is recommended, ask at the Cohdefor office. Guide services daily 0800-1530, US$8. Good maps are available in English or Spanish US$0.30. Simple cabin accommodation is available ($). To get here, take a taxi from Tela, US$4, but there are few in the park for the return journey in the afternoon, so organize collection in advance.*

Located 5 km inland, the Lancetilla Jardín Botánico was founded in 1926 by the United Fruit Company as a plant research station. Today, it is the second largest botanical garden in the world. It has more than 1000 varieties of plant and over 200 bird species have been identified in its grounds. It has fruit trees from every continent, the most extensive collection of Asiatic fruit trees in the western hemisphere, an orchid garden, and plantations of mahogany and teak alongside a 1200-ha virgin tropical rainforest. But be warned, there are many mosquitoes.

## Where to stay

### Tela

During Easter week, the town is packed; room rates double and advance booking is essential.

### $$$ Capitán Beach
*Calle 9, T 3233-8182, www.hotelcapitanbeach.com.*
Located 6 blocks from the main plaza and right across from the beach, this is a relatively recent edition to Tela's hotel scene. They have 10 clean, comfortable rooms with cable TV, Wi-Fi and a/c, all overlooking a tempting pool, and a well-stocked restaurant-bar upstairs with views of the ocean. Good choice.

### $$$ Gran Central
*Just south of the centre of town, T448-1099, www.hotelgran central.com.*
This French-owned, beautifully restored historic banana-port-era hotel has 1 suite, kitchen, hot water, cable TV, a/c, security and a safe box in each room. Local excursions available. Highly recommended.

### $$$ Posada Las Iguanas
*Barrio Buena Vista, near Escuela Luis Landa, T2448-4625, www.posadaslasiguanas.biz.*
Set inside a former United Fruit Company property, Posada Las Iguanas is a stylish boutique option with lots of character and comfort. Accommodation includes a range of handsome villas, suites and rooms, all kitted out with the usual amenities. Grounds are verdant and tranquil and there's also a sauna and pool to keep you entertained. Recommended.

### $$$-$$ Hotel Marsol
*Calle del Comercio, Av Nicaragua, T2448-1782, www.hotelmarsoltela.com.*
Located 200 m from the beach, Hotel Marsol is chiefly recommended for its attached dive centre. Even if you're not planning any underwater forays, it's a very reasonable lodging with 23 smart rooms and breakfast included.

### $$$-$$ Maya Vista
*Top of hill, steep flight of steps starting opposite Preluna, T2448-1497, www.mayavista.com.*
Canadian-owned, this place has fantastic views and a restaurant serving delicious French-Canadian cuisine. Rooms have bath, hot water and a/c. French and English spoken. Very highly recommended.

### $$ Coco Cabaña
*Playa Barrio El Tigre, Triunfo de la Cruz, T3335-4599, www.hotelcaraibe.com.*
These 'eco-cabins' were thoughtfully constructed using waste plastic bottles. Each unit has Wi-Fi, a kitchenette and a private terrace with hammocks. No frills, unpretentious and on the rustic side, as all beach lodgings should be.

### $$ Ejecutivos Aparthotel
*Av 4, Contiguo a Hondutel, T2448-1076, www.ejecutivosah.com.*
Marketed to nationals, this down-to-earth downtown lodging offers a range of comfortable and reliable rooms and apartments. Simple, solid place with the usual amenities, including cable TV, Wi-Fi, hot water and some a/c.

### $ Sara
*11 Calle, 6 Av, behind the restaurant Tiburón Playa, T2448-1477.*
Basic in a rickety old building, with bath, or without, poor sanitation. Cheapest in town, popular with backpackers, friendly, noisy especially at weekends from all-night discos.

### Around Tela

There are cheap houses and *cabañas* for rent in Triunfo de la Cruz. There is a small hotel in Río Tinto, near Parque Nacional Punta Sal; accommodation is available in private houses.

### $$$-$$ Caribbean Coral Inn
*Triunfo de la Cruz, T9957-8605, www.caribbeancoralinns.com.*
Simple, homely rooms and bungalows with hammock, terrace, Wi-Fi and garden or sea views.

### $$$-$$ The Last Resort
*Tornabé, T2984-3964.*
Has 8 bungalows for rent, some a/c, some fan, hot water, with breakfast. There are several cabins for different sized groups.

## Restaurants

### Tela
The best eating is in the hotel restaurants.

### $$$ Casa Azul
*Barrio El Centro. Open till 2300.*
Run by Mark from Texas, subs, dinner specials, book exchange. Helpful.

### $$ César Mariscos
*Open from 0700.*
Attractive location on the beach, serves good seafood and has a very good breakfast menu.

### $$ Luces del Norte
*Of Doña Mercedes, 11 Calle, 2 Av NE, towards beach from Parque Central, next to Hotel Puerto Rico.*
Very popular place serving delicious seafood and good typical breakfasts. Also has good information and a book exchange.

### $$ Maya Vista
*In hotel (see Where to stay, above).*
Run by Québécois Pierre, serving fine cuisine; one of the best in Tela. Highly recommended.

### $$-$ Bungalow
*Calle Cabañas, Barrio El Centro.*
Kitsch and ramshackle, Bungalow is a typical Caribbean eatery serving typical Caribbean grub, such as fried chicken and whole fish. Creaky wooden floorboards and chequered table cloths. The owner Norman is larger than life.

### $ Bella Italia
*www.pizzeriabellaitalia.weebly.com.*
Italian-owned restaurant serving pizza, on the walkway by the beach.

## Festivals

### Tela
**Jun** Fiesta de San Antonio.

## What to do

### Tela
**Garífuna Tours**, *southwest corner of Parque Central, T2448-2904, www.garifunatours.com.*
Knowledgeable and helpful with mountain bike hire, US$5 per day. Day trips to Punta Sal (US$31, meals extra), Los Micos lagoon (US$31) and Punta Izopo (US$24). La Ceiba–Cayos Cochinos (US$39), La Ceiba–Cuero Salado (US$68), Pico Bonito (US$33). Also trips further afield to La Ceiba, Mosquitia (4 days, US$499) and a shuttle service between San Pedro Sula and La Ceiba, US$18 per person. Also La Ceiba–Copán, US$45. Good value. Highly recommended.

### Language schools
**Mango Café Spanish School**, T2448-0338, www.mangocafe.net. Mon-Fri 4 hrs' tuition a day, US$115, with a local tour on Sat.

## Transport

### Tela

**Bike** Hire from **Garífuna Tours**, 9 Calle y Parque Central (see What to do, above), and from **Hotel Mango**.

**Bus** Catisa or Tupsa lines from San Pedro Sula to **El Progreso** (US$0.50) where you must change to go on to **Tela** (3 hrs in total) and **La Ceiba** (last bus at 2030 with **Transportes Cristina**). On **Catisa** bus ask to be let off at the petrol station on the main road, then take a taxi to the beach, US$0.50. Also 1st-class service with **Hedman Alas** at 1010, 1415 and 1810.

Bus from Tela to **El Progreso** every 25 mins; last bus at 1830, US$1.50. To **La Ceiba**, every 30 mins, from 0410 until 1800, 2 hrs, US$2.

Direct to **Tegucigalpa**, **Traliasa**, 1 a day from Hotel Los Arcos, US$4.50, same bus to **La Ceiba** (this service avoids San Pedro Sula; 6 a day with **Transportes Cristinas** (US$9.20). To **Copán**, leave by 0700 via El Progreso and San Pedro Sula; to arrive same day. To **San Pedro Sula**, 1130 and 1715 with **Diana Express** (US$2.50), or 8 a day with **Transportes Tela Express**, last bus at 1700 (US$3). To **Trujillo** through Savá, Tocoa and Corocito.

**Shuttle** Garífuna Tours, see page 569, offers a shuttle service direct to **San Pedro**, US$18 and **Copán Ruinas**, US$45.

### Around Tela

**Bus** To **Triunfo de la Cruz**, US$0.40 (about 5 km, if no return bus, walk to main road where buses pass).

## La Ceiba and around   Colour map 3, B3.

once the country's busiest port, now upcoming ecotourism centre

La Ceiba, the capital of Atlántida Department and the third largest city in Honduras, stands on the narrow coastal plain between the Caribbean and the rugged Nombre de Dios mountain range crowned by the spectacular Pico Bonito (2435 m), see page 573. The climate is hot, but tempered by sea winds. Maritime trade has now passed to Puerto Cortés and Puerto Castilla, but there is still some activity in the city's port.

The close proximity to Pico Bonito National park, Cuero y Salado Wildlife Refuge and the Cayos Cochinos Marine Reserve gives the city the ambitious target of becoming an important hub for ecotourism. While the opportunities aren't immediately obvious, there is definitely a buzz about town – watch out for developments. The main plaza is worth walking around to see statues of various famous Hondurans including Lempira and a couple of ponds.

A **butterfly and insect museum** ① Col El Sauce, 2a Etapa Casa G-12, T2442-2874, http://butterflywebsite.com, Mon-Fri 0800-1600, closed Wed afternoon, Sat and Sun for groups only with advance reservation, US$1.20, student reductions, has a collection of over 10,000 butterflies, roughly 2000 other insects and snakes. It's good for all ages; there's a 25-minute video in both Spanish and English and Robert and Myriam Lehman guide visitors expertly through the life of the butterfly. There is also a **Butterfly Farm** ① daily 0800-1530, entry US$6, on the grounds of **The Lodge** at Pico Bonito.

### ★Around La Ceiba

There are scores of small, rewarding attractions around La Ceiba. **Jutiapa** is a small dusty town with a pretty little colonial church. Contact Standard Fruit Company, Dole office in La Ceiba (off main plaza) to visit a local pineapple plantation. **Corozal** is an interesting

Garífuna village near La Ceiba, at Km 209.5, with a beach, Playas de Sambrano and a hotel. **Sambo Creek**, another Garífuna village, has nice beaches, a few good hotels, a canopy tour and hot springs. It is an increasingly popular destination with foreign travellers and well worth checking out (see What to do, below). Near the towns of **Esparta** and **El Porvenir**, thousands of crabs come out of the sea in July and August and travel long distances inland. The **Catarata El Bejuco** is a waterfall 7 km along the old dirt road to **Olanchito** (11 km from La Ceiba). Follow a path signposted to Balneario Los Lobos to the waterfall about 1 km upriver through the jungle. There is good swimming from a pebbly

**La Ceiba**

Caribbean Sea

N

200 metres
200 yards

**Where to stay** 🛏
Casa de España 1
Casa de Nery 2
El Estadio 3
Gran Hotel París 6
Quinta Real 8

Rainbow Village 4

**Restaurants** 🍴
Café Ki'Bok 1
Cafetería Cobel 4
El Guapo's 3

El Jardín de Susana 5
Expatriates Bar, Grill &
  Cigar Emporium 2
La Palapa 6
Paty's 7
Ponderosa 8

beach where the river broadens. Along this road is **El Naranjo** near **Omega Tours Jungle Lodge and Adventure Company**.

**Yaruca**, 20 km down the old road to Olanchito, is easily reached by bus and offers good views of Pico Bonito. **Eco-Zona Río María**, 5 km along the Trujillo highway (signposted path up to the foothills of the Cordillera Nombre de Dios), is a beautiful walk through the lush countryside of a protected area. Just beyond Río María is **Balneario Los Chorros** (signposted), a series of small waterfalls through giant boulders into a deep rock pool that is great for swimming (with refreshments nearby). Upstream there is some beautiful scenery and you can continue walking through the forest and in the river, where there are more pools. Another bathing place, Agua Azul, with restaurant is a short distance away. The active can get on the **Río Cangrejal** for the exhilarating rush of Grade II, III and IV **whitewater rapids**, which can be combined with treks in to the wilderness of **Parque Nacional Pico Bonito** (see below).

## Beaches around La Ceiba

Beaches in and near La Ceiba include **Playa Miramar** (which is dirty and not recommended), **La Barra** (a better option), **Perú** (across the Río Cangrejal at Km 205.5, better still, quiet except at weekends, deserted tourist complex, restaurant, access by road to Tocoa, 10 km, then signposted side road 1.5 km, or along the beach 6 km from La Ceiba) and **La Ensenada** (close to Corozal).

The beaches near the fishing villages of Río Esteban and Balfate are very special and are near Cayos Cochinos (Hog Islands) where the snorkelling and diving is spectacular.

## Cayos Cochinos

The Hog Islands, 17 km northeast of La Ceiba, constitute two small islands and 13 palm-fringed cayes. **Cochino Grande** is the larger island, rising to an altitude of just 143 m, and **Cochino Pequeño** is the smaller. Both have lush tropical vegetation with primeval hardwood forests and there are fewer biting insects than in the Bay Islands. As part of a National Marine Reserve, Cayos Cochinos and the surrounding waters are protected and filled with sealife. There is a fee to enter parts of the islands of US$10. There are Garífuna fishing villages of palm-thatched huts at Chachauate on Lower Monitor Cay, where you can organize basic accommodation, and East End Village on Cochino Grande.

Transport to the Hog Islands can be sought on the supply *cayuco* from Nueva Armenia, or by boat from La Ceiba, Sambo Creek or Roatán. However, for safety, it is recommended

**Cayos Cochinos (Hog Islands)**

you use an insured tour operator with a good seaworthy vessel and life jackets; the extra cost is negligible. There is a small dirt airstrip and dug-out canoes are the local form of transport. The islands are privately owned and access to most of the cayes is limited, being occupied only by caretakers. Take whatever you need with you as there is almost nothing on the smaller cayes. However, the Garífuna are going to and fro all the time.

## Parque Nacional Pico Bonito

*Entrance US$7; children US$4. For further information on the park contact FUPNAPIB, on the La Ceiba–Tela highway, T2442-3044. Take care if you enter the forest: tracks are not yet developed, a compass is advisable. Tour companies in La Ceiba arrange trips to the park.*

Parque Nacional Pico Bonito (674 sq km) is the largest national park in Honduras and is home to Pico Bonito (2435 m). The Río Cangrejal, a mecca for whitewater rafting, marks the eastern border of the park. It has deep tropical hardwood forests that shelter, among other animals, jaguars and three species of monkey, deep canyons and tumbling streams and waterfalls (including Las Gemelas, which fall vertically for some 200 m).

The park has two areas open for tourism. The first is the Río Zacate area, located past the community of El Pino, 10 km west of La Ceiba; the second is on the Río Cangrejal, near the community of El Naranjo, about 7.5 km from the paved highway.

A hanging bridge over the Río Cangrejal provides access to the visitor centre and the **El Mapache Trail** up to the top of **El Bejuco** waterfall. Further up the road in **Las Mangas**, Guaruma (T2442-2693) there is a very nice trail with beautiful swimming holes in a pristine creek. The trail is well maintained and local guides are available.

For the Río Zacate area, access is just past the dry stream (*quebrada seca*) bridge on the main La Ceiba to Tela highway from where the road leads to the entrance through pineapple plantations to a steep trail leading up to the Río Zacate waterfall, about one hour 20 minutes' hiking. A good price range of accommodation is available in both areas.

### Cuero y Salado Wildlife Reserve

*Open 0600-1800, US$10 to enter the reserve, which you can pay at Fucsa; keep the receipt. It's an extra US$5 per person for accommodation. The reserve is managed by the Fundación Cuero y Salado (Fucsa) Refugio de Vida Silvestre, 1 block north and 3 blocks west of Parque Central to the left of the Standard Fruit Company, La Ceiba, T2443-0329, www.fucsa.blogspot.co.uk. The foundation is open to volunteers, preferably those who speak English and Spanish.*

## Essential Cuero y Salado Wildlife Reserve

### Getting there

Take a bus to La Unión (every hour, 0600 until 1500 from La Ceiba terminus, 1½ hours, ask to get off at the railway line, ferrocarril, or Km 17), an interesting journey through pineapple fields. There are several ways of getting into the park from La Unión. Walking takes 1½ hours. Groups usually take a *motocarro*, a dilapidated train that also transports the coconut crop; there are definite departures at 0700 and 0800. From near Doña Tina's house (meals available), take a *burra*, a flat-bed railcar propelled by two men with poles (a great way to see the countryside) to the community on the banks of the Río Salado. To return to La Unión, it is another *burra* ride or a two-hour walk along the railway, then, either wait for a La Ceiba bus (last one at 1500), or ask for the short cut through grapefruit groves, 20 minutes, which leads to the main La Ceiba–Tela road, where there are many more buses back to town.

Encompassing 13,225 ha of rainforest and wetlands between the Cuero and Salado rivers, 27 km west of La Ceiba, is the Cuero y Salado Wildlife Reserve, which has a great variety of flora and fauna, including manatee, jaguar, monkeys and a large population of local and migratory birds.

Nilmo, a knowledgeable biologist who acts as a guide, takes morning and evening boat trips for those staying overnight, either through the canal dug by Standard Fruit, parallel to the beach between the palms and the mangroves, or down to the Salado lagoon. Five kayaks are available for visitors' use. In the reserve are spider and capuchin monkeys, iguanas, jaguar, tapirs, crocodiles, manatee, hummingbirds, toucans, ospreys, eagles and vultures. A five-hour trip will take you to Barra de Colorado to see the manatees. Fucsa's administration centre, on the banks of the Río Salado, has photos, charts, maps, radio and a two-room visitors' house. There is also a visitor centre, with a full-service cafeteria and bilingual guides.

## Listings La Ceiba and around *map p571*

### Where to stay

#### La Ceiba

**$$$ Casa de Nery**
*Primera Calle, Este Barrio La Isla, La Zona Viva, www.hotellacasadenery.com.*
A good option for families, the green lawns of the resort-style Casa de Nery overlook the ocean and include a large pool, volleyball and basketball court. Amenities include Wi-Fi, a/c, cable TV and minibar. There are just 10 rooms and one smart little bungalow suitable for a couple.

**$$$ Quinta Real**
*Zona Viva, on the beach, T2440-3311, www.quintarealhotel.com.*
Popular place with big, well-furnished rooms that have a/c and cable TV. There's a pool, beach, restaurant and bars and free internet. (Taxi drivers sometimes confuse it with the **Hotel Quinta** opposite the Golf Club on the Tela–La Ceiba road, which is not as nice).

**$$$-$$ Gran Hotel Paris**
*Parque Central, T2440-1414, www.granhotelparisonline.com.*
Located in the heart of La Ceiba, this is the oldest hotel in town, established 1915. It

has 84 comfortable if unadventurous rooms with a/c, cable TV and Wi-Fi. The grounds include a pleasant pool, bar and a restaurant.

**$$ Casa de España**
*Av 14 de Julio, entre Tercera y Cuarta Calle, T2454-0210, www.hotelcasadeespana.com.*
Simple, reliable, neat, quiet and economical accommodation with a decent restaurant and roof terrace serving meat, seafood and tapas. Lovely, helpful, English-speaking owners and good reports.

**$$ Hotel Rainbow Village**
*Colonia Confite, 2 mins from the airport, T2408-5696, www.hotel-rainbow-village.com.*
This cute hotel is called the Rainbow Village for its multicoloured bungalows. Amenities include a pleasant garden with hammocks, bar and pool. Barbara, the owner, is an excellent chef.

**$ El Estadio**
*Calle Estero, next to the football stadium, T3187-6027.*
Simple and basic, but all you need, this budget hotel would suit backpackers. The owner Peter is very friendly, helpful and English-speaking. Good Wi-Fi connections and there are cheap dorms too.

## $ Tornabé Hostel
*Bloque 4 No 13, Colonia Monteverde,*
*T9813-8998, www.tornabe.com.*
Dorm beds at this jolly little backpacker
hostel are just US$7 when you book a shuttle
to/from Guatemala or Nicaragua. Facilities
include Wi-Fi, movies and a/c. A new place,
intimate, helpful and accommodating.

## Around La Ceiba

### $$$ Diving Pelican Inn
*Sambo Creek, on Playa Helen, T3369-2208,*
*www.divingpelicaninn.com.*
Perched on the edge of the beach, Diving
Pelican Inn is a villa-style B&B with 2 rooms
and a detached apartment, all with lock
boxes and private entrances, as well as a
wealth of mod cons such as DVD player,
coffee-maker, a/c and purified water. There's
a pool with a waterfall, sun deck, honesty
bar, fire pit and DVD library. Low-key and
quiet, a good option for couples.

### $$ Hotel Canadien
*Sambo Creek, T2440-2099,*
*www.hotelcanadien.com.*
Long-standing and hospitable
accommodation, including double suites.
They can arrange trips to the Hog Islands
for US$80 per boat.

### $$ La Delphina Bed and Breakfast
*Sambo Creek, T2405-1557,*
*www.ladelphina.net.*
A chilled out and intimate B&B option right
on the edge of the beach. Rooms are simple
but comfortable and amenities include bar,
restaurant and pool. A variety of excursions
and activities can be arranged. Attentive
service and good reports.

### $$ Paradise Found
*Sambo Creek, Playa Helen, 1 block past the*
*bus stop, near Hotel Canadian, T9808-8888,*
*www.paradisefoundlaceiba.com.*

Managed by Dante and Kristina, this down-
to-earth B&B offers tidy, homely, no-frills
lodgings with Wi-Fi and a/c; one room is
wheelchair accessible. Good restaurant
overlooking the waves (Dante is the chef),
bike rentals and a variety of excursions are
available. Good reports. Recommended.

### $$ Villa Helen's Hotel
*Sambo Creek, look for the signs*
*from the main road, T2408-1137,*
*www.villahelens.com.*
Intimate and affordable, Villa Helen offers
4 beachfront rooms with cable TV and a/c,
2 suites with ocean views and 6 low-key
cabins with a/c, hot water, living room and
mountain views. Amenities include a leafy
garden with a hexagonal jacuzzi, a poolside
bar-restaurant, and massage services.
Friendly and welcoming.

## Cayos Cochinos

### $$ Turtle Bay Eco-Resort
*Cochino Grande, T9842-3231,*
*www.turtlebayecoresort.com.*
Rustic cabins on the hillside, with hot water
and fans. There's diving offshore, yacht
moorings, and a music festival at the end
of Jul, with local bands and dancers. For view
over the cayes to the mainland, there's a
good steep walk up to lighthouse.

## Parque Nacional Pico Bonito
## Río Cangrejo area

### $$$$ Las Cascadas Lodge
*El Naranjo, T9923-6237,*
*www.lascascadaslodge.com.*
Named after the 5 waterfalls cascading
through the grounds, this luxurious jungle
lodge was designed by award-winning
architect David Sellon. It is a singularly
beautiful property with boutique cabins and
suites nestled on the banks of the Cangrejal
river. A very special, romantic place.

#### $$$$-$$$ Villas Pico Bonito
*7.5 km Carretera de Yaruca, T2416-5007,*
*www.villaspicobonito.com.*
An upscale jungle resort with a range of
luxurious villas that would suit families or
groups. Each unit is unique, some are more
rustic and simple than others, but all enjoy
tidy furnishings and forest views. The lovely
landscaped grounds feature an infinity pool
and restaurant.

#### $$$ Casa Cangrejal
*Km 10 Río Cangrejal road, T2416-5046,*
*www.casacangrejal.com.*
This charming stone-built B&B backs
onto verdant forests with restful patios
and chill-out hammocks. Perfect for
post-hike relaxation, a nearby creek has
been channelled into small bathing pools,
continually refreshed with highland water.
All rooms have Wi-Fi and the usual mod
cons. Natural and tranquil.

#### $$$ La Villa de Soledad
*Look for the turn-off approximately 150 m*
*south of the visitor centre, T9967-4548,*
*www.lavilladesoledad.com.*
A lot of love and care has gone into the Villa
de Soledad, the best B&B in the Pico Bonito
area. Hosts John and Soledad are warm
and attentive and know the surrounding
countryside intimately; rafting, hiking and
canopy tours can all be arranged. Steeped
in verdant tropical gardens, accommodation
includes tranquil, light, cosy and well-ventilated
rooms which open onto their own terraces,
all with hammocks. Highly recommended.

#### $$-$ Jungle River Lodge
*On Río Cangrejal overlooking Pico Bonito,*
*T2440-1268, www.jungleriverlodge.com.*
Private rooms and dorms, natural pools,
restaurant and breathtaking views. Rafting,
canopy tours, zip-wires, hiking and
mountain biking tours available. Activities
include a free night's accommodation. Take
Yaruka bus from main bus terminal, get off

at Km 7; a blue kayak marks the entrance
on the river side of the road, call to arrange
transport or join a tour.

#### $$-$ Omega Tours Jungle Lodge and Adventure Company
*El Naranjo, T9631-0295,*
*www.omegatours.info.*
With wide range of options from simple
rooms to comfortable *cabañas* and good
food. Rafting and kayaking are available on
the Río Cangrejal and trips to La Mosquitia
(see page 588).

### Río Zacate area

#### $$$$ The Lodge
*Pico Bonito, 15 mins' drive west of La Ceiba,*
*T2440-0388, T1-888-428-0221 (USA),*
*www.picobonito.com.*
Honduras' first world-class ecolodge at the
base of Parque Nacional Pico Bonito. Luxury
wooden cabins – with no TV, very peaceful –
in 160 ha of grounds. There are forest trails,
with lookout towers, natural swimming
holes and waterfalls; nature guides and
tours, very popular with birders; butterfly
farm and serpentarium; swimming pool and
gourmet restaurant. Highly recommended.

#### $ Natural View Ecoturism Center
*In El Pino, T2386-9678.*
Very rustic cabins with access to trails in
the vicinity. Cabins are built of adobe walls
and thatched room, with a private bath,
mosquito screens, but no power. Set in
the middle of a plant nursery with a good
restaurant on premises. Efraín can help
arrange several good trips nearby including
a boat trip down the lower Río Zacate
through mangroves to a farm located next
to the beach, adjacent to Cuero y Salado.

#### $ Posada del Buen Pastor
*T2950-3404.*
Has 4 rustic rooms on the upper storey of
a private home with private bath, cable TV
and fan.

## Cuero y Salado Wildlife Reserve

### $ Refuge
*T2443-0329, www.fucsa.blogspot.co.uk.*
Fucsa's administration centre, on the banks of the Río Salado. Has photos, charts, maps, radio and a 2-room visitor house, sleeping 4 in basic bunks, electricity 1800-2100. There are no mosquito nets, so avoid Sep and Oct if you can. Don't wear open footwear as snakes and yellow scorpions can be found here. Food is available. There's also tent space for camping at the refuge. Book in advance.

## Restaurants

### La Ceiba

#### $$ Cafetería Cobel
*7 Calle between Av Atlántida and 14 de Julio, 2 blocks from Parque Central.*
This could be the best *cafetería* in the entire country; unmissable. Very popular with locals, it's always crowded, and serves good fresh food, with daily specials. Highly recommended.

#### $$ El Guapo's
*Corner of 14 de Julio and 14 Calle.*
*Open daily for dinner.*
US-Honduran owned, good combination of international and typical Honduran cuisine.

#### $$ El Jardín de Susana
*Off Av Morazán and Calle 15, a bit hidden, ask around.*
A new venture by Susana, the owner of the locally revered Mango Tango (now closed). They serve grilled fish, salads, home-made breads, fresh fruit juices, soups, pasta and other home-cooked fare. As the name might suggest, it also promises a pleasant garden setting. A bit pricey for La Ceiba, but worth it.

#### $$ La Palapa
*Av Víctor Hugo, next to Hotel Quinta Real.*
Giant, palm-roofed, wood-beamed *palapa*, serving juicy steaks, grills, fish, seafood and burgers; also a sports bar with half a dozen TV screens, and serving ice-cold beer. Good value for money though indifferent service.

#### $$ Ponderosa
*Av 14 de Julio, ½ a block from Calle 17, www.restaurantelaponderosalaceiba honduras.blogspot.co.uk.*
A great rancho-style bar-restaurant with authentic *comida típica*, rum and beer; all served at plastic tables. They specialize in grilled meats, all served with a side of *frijoles* and fried *plátano*. Hearty locals' joint with good prices, generous portions and live music and dancing at the weekends.

#### $$-$ Café Ki'Bok
*4a Av, entre Calles 8a-9a.*
This chilled-out bohemian café has a great stock of paperbacks to keep you entertained; take one, leave one behind. They serve coffee, cooked breakfasts and *comida típica*. Cosy, friendly and informal, with free Wi-Fi.

#### $ Expatriates Bar, Grill and Cigar Emporium
*Final de Calle 12, above Refricón, 3 blocks south, 3 blocks east of Parque Central.*
*Thu-Tue 1600-2400.*
Honduran-American owners, very affordable food, including good steak and shrimps. Free internet. Also have a branch at the Cangrejal River, Km 9.

#### $ Paty's
*Av 14 de Julio between 6 and 7 Calle.*
Clean place offering milkshakes, wheatgerm, cereals, doughnuts, etc, and purified water. Opposite is an excellent pastry shop. There are 2 more **Paty's**, at 8 Calle E and the bus terminal.

### Around La Ceiba

#### $$ Kabasa
*Sambo Creek.*
Seafood Garífuna-style, bar, in a delightful location.

## $$ Paradise Found Bar and Grill
*1 block past Sambo Creek bus stop, near Hotel Canadian, www.paradisefoundlaceiba.com.*
A superb setting by the beach with an open-air veranda overlooking the waves. Offerings include massive hamburgers, home-made lasagne, brick-oven pizza, fresh seafood, and barbecue ribs, in addition to vegan and vegetarian options. You're in good hands as the chef is Italian.

### Festivals

#### La Ceiba
**15-28 May San Isidro** La Ceiba's patron saint's celebrations continue for 2 weeks, the highlight being the international carnival on the 3rd Sat in May, when La Ceiba parties long and hard to the Afro-Caribbean beat of *punta* rock.

### Shopping

#### La Ceiba
**Carrion Department Store** (Av San Isidro with 7A Calle). **Deli Mart** late-night corner store on 14 de Julio, round the corner from the internet café, shuts at 2300. **El Regalito**, good-quality souvenirs at reasonable prices in small passage by large Carrión store.
**T Boot**, store for hiking boots, Calle 1, east of Av San Isidro, T2443-2499. **Supermarket Super Ceibena** (2 on Av 14 de Julio and 6A Calle).

### What to do

#### La Ceiba
**Adventure tourism**
Hiking, kayaking and whitewater rafting are all popular and many tour operators also maintain jungle lodges (see Where to stay, above). Ask around to find a tour that suits your needs and to verify credentials.

**La Moskitia Eco Aventuras**, *Av 14 de Julio at Parque Manuel Bonilla, T2442-0104, www.lamoskitia.hn*. Eco-adventure tours, run by Jorge Salaverri, an extremely knowledgeable nature guide, who is enthusiastic and flexible. Specializes in trips to Mosquitia, including week-long expeditions to Las Marias and hikes up Pico Baltimore and Pico Dama. Highly recommended.
**Omega Tours**, *T2440-0334, www.omegatours.info*. Runs rafting and kayaking trips on the Río Cangrejal, jungle hikes, and own hotel 30 mins upstream. Also tours to La Mosquitia ranging from easy adventure tours of 4 days to up to 13-day expeditions. Prices drop dramatically with more than 2 people.

**Canopy tours**
There are 2 modest canopy tours in La Ceiba, one in Pico Bonito National Park, US$40 per person; the other in Sambo Creek Spa, US$45 per person (see Spas below). Any tour operator in La Ceiba should be able to organize tickets and transport.

**Diving**
**Pirate Islands Divers**, *T3228-0009, www.pirateislandsdivers.com*. Pirate Islands Divers specializes in Cayos Cochinos diving with trips leaving Sambo Creek every day at 0700, weather permitting. They also offer PADI certification, from Open Water to Dive Master.

**Language schools**
It's best to do some research and look at the options. The following are worth considering:
**Central America Spanish School**, *Av San Isidro No 110, Calle 12 y 13, next to Foto Indio, T2440-1707, www.ca-spanish.com*. US$150 for the week, homestay also an option adding US$70, also have branches on Utila and Roatan.
**Centro Internacional de Idiomas**, *T2440-1557, www.hondurasspanish.com*. Provides a range of classes 5 days for US$150, with hotel option US$290, with branches in Utila and Roatán.

## Spas

**Sambo Creek Canopy Tour and Spa**, *main highway, 500 m east of the turn-off for Hotel Canadien, T3355-6481.* Services include a mud bath, massage and mineral-rich hot springs, all in a beautiful natural setting. Entrance US$25. Recommended.

## Tour operators

**Garífuna Tours**, *Av San Isidro 1 Calle, T2440-3252, www.garifunatours.com.* Day trips into Pico Bonito National Park (US$34 per person), Cuero y Salado (US$49), rafting on the Cangrejal (US$34), trips out to Cayos Cochinos (US$49) and a shuttle service to Tela (US$1).

**Reservaciones La Ceiba**, *Col El Sauce, 4th floor, Block W, House 3, T2443-6536, www. reservacioneslaceiba.com.* A community-led tour operator, sustainable, co-operative and ecologically aware. They offer a broad range of natural and cultural tours including hiking in Pico Bonito, wildlife observation, visits to fincas, community tourism and rafting. Recommended.

**Tourist Options**, *Av La República, T9982-7534, www.hondurastouristoptions.com.* A wide range of regional and national tours, including birding trips, tours of Copán, Roatán, Cuero y Saldo Wildlife reserve and the Cayos Cochinos.

## Cuero y Salado Wildlife Reserve

Although it is possible to go to the Salado and hire a villager and his boat, a qualified guide will show you much more. It is essential to bring a hat and sun lotion with you. Travel agencies in La Ceiba run tours there, but **Fucsa** arranges visits and owns the only accommodation in the reserve. Before going, check with **Fucsa** in La Ceiba. Although the office only has basic information, the people are helpful and there are displays and books about the flora and fauna to be found in the park. A guide and kayak for a 1-hr trip costs about US$10.

Boatmen charge about US$20 for a 2-hr trip or US$40 for 5 hrs (6-7 persons maximum), US$6-7 for the guide.

## Transport

**Air** For La Mosquitia see page 593.

**Aeropuerto Internacional Golosón** (LCE) is 10 km out of town. See Getting there in Practicalities chapter, for international services. For details of flights to Bay Islands, see page 550. One-way fares to Roatán start at around US$50. At weekends there are some charter flights that may be better than scheduled flights. Taxi to town US$8 per person or walk 200 m to the main road and share for US$2 with other passengers, also buses from bus station near Cric Cric Burger at end 3 Av, US$0.15. Intercity buses pass by the entrance.

**Boat** Ferry schedules from the Muelle de Cabotaje as follows: Services to/from Utila with the Utila Princess, T2408-5163, www. utilaprincess.com, **La Ceiba–Utila** 0930 and 1600; **Utila–La Ceiba**, 0620 and 1400, US$25. Services to/from Roatán with Roatán Ferry, T2445-1795, www.roatanferry.com, **La Ceiba–Roatán**, 0930 and 1630, **Roatán–La Ceiba**, 0700 and 1400, US$31 regular class, US$36 first class. It is too far to walk to the pier, about 15-min taxi ride from town, US$2-3 per person if sharing with 4 people, buses available from centre of town.

Trips to the **Hog Islands** can be arranged, call T441-5987 or through **Garífuna Tours** (see What to do, page 569), US$65 for a boat load.

**Bus** Taxis from centre to bus terminal, which is a little way west of town (follow Blv 15 de Septiembre), cost US$1 per person, or there are buses from Parque Central. Most buses leave from here. **Traliasa**, **Etrusca** and **Cristina** bus service to **Tegucigalpa** via Tela several daily, US$6, avoiding San Pedro Sula (US$1 to Tela, 2 hrs); also hourly service to **San Pedro Sula**, US$2 (3-4 hrs). **Empresa**

Tupsa direct to **San Pedro Sula** almost hourly from 0530 until 1800. Also 1st class with **Hedman Alas** – take taxi to separate terminal. To **Trujillo**, 3 hrs direct, 4½ hrs local (very slow), every 1½ hrs or so, US$3; daily bus La Ceiba– Trujillo–Santa Rosa de Aguán. To **Olanchito**, US$1, 3 hrs; also regular buses to **Sonaguera**, **Tocoa**, **Balfate**, **Isletas**, **San Esteban** and other regional locations.

**Car  Car rental**  Dino's Rent-a-Car, Hotel Partenon Beach, T2443-0404. **Maya Rent-a-Car**, Hotel La Quinta, T2443-3071. **Molinari** in Hotel París on Parque Central, T2443-0055.

**Beaches around La Ceiba**

**Bus**  To **Nueva Armenia** from La Ceiba at 1100, US$0.75, 2½ hrs. At the bus stop is the office where boat trips are arranged to **Cayos Cochinos**, US$10, trips start at 0700.

## Trujillo and around  *Colour map 3, B3.*

### historic banana port surrounded by mangroves and Garífuna villages

★Once a major port and the former capital, Trujillo (www.trujillohonduras.com) sits on the southern shore of the palm-fringed Bay of Trujillo. It is a quiet, pleasant town with clean beaches nearby and calm water that is ideal for swimming.

Christopher Columbus landed close to the area on his fourth voyage to the Americas and the town was later founded in 1525 by Juan de Medina, making it the oldest town in Honduras. Hernán Cortés arrived here after his famous march overland from Yucatán in pursuit of his usurping lieutenant, Olid. Filibuster William Walker was shot near here in 1860; a commemorative stone marks the spot in the rear garden of the hospital, one block east of the Parque Central, and the old cemetery (near Hotel Trujillo) is his final resting place.

**Fortaleza Santa Bárbara** ① *US$1*, a ruined Spanish fortress overlooking the bay, is worth a visit. Most of the relics found there have been moved to the museum of Rufino Galán, but there are still a few rusty muskets and cannon balls. Twenty minutes' walk from Trujillo plaza is the **Museo y Piscina Rufino Galán Cáceres** ① *US$1, US$0.50 to swim*, which has a swimming pool filled from the Río Cristales with changing rooms and picnic facilities. Close by, the wreckage of a US C-80 aircraft that crashed in 1985 forms part of Sr Galán's museum. The rest of the collection is a mass of curios, some very interesting. The cemetery is rather overgrown, with collapsed and open tombs, but it does give a feel of the origins of early residents. The **Fiesta de San Juan Bautista** is in June, with participation from surrounding Garífuna settlements.

West of Trujillo, just past the football field on the Santa Fe road, is the **Río Grande**, which has lovely pools and waterfalls for river bathing, best during the rainy season. Take the path on the far side of river, after about 10 minutes cut down to the rocks and follow the river upstream along the boulders.

### Beaches

Good beaches are found both on the peninsula and around Trujillo Bay. Before setting out ask which beaches are safe. Take a bus from near the Parque Central towards Puerto Castilla and ask the driver to let you off at the path about 1 km beyond the bridge over the lagoon. Other beaches around Puerto Castilla are separated by mangroves, are littered and have sandflies. The beaches in town tend to be less clean. If you're tempted to walk to find a cleaner stretch of sand don't walk alone; tourists here have been assaulted and robbed.

## West of Trujillo

There are interesting Garífuna villages west of Trujillo. The road is rough, often impassable in wet weather, and jeeps are needed even in the dry season. **Santa Fe**, 10 km west of Trujillo, is a friendly place with several good Garífuna restaurants; for example, **Comedor Caballero** and **Las Brisas de Santa Fe**, on the endless white sandy beach. The bus service continues to **San Antonio** (with a good restaurant behind the beach) and **Guadalupe**. Walk in the morning along the beach to Santa Fe and then get a bus back to Trujillo, taking plenty of water and sun block. This stretch of beach is outstanding, but watch out for *marea roja*, a sea organism that colours the water pink and can give irritating skin rashes to bathers. Also, be warned, local people consider this walk unsafe. It's best to go in a large group.

## Santa Rosa de Aguán

One of the largest Garífuna communities, Santa Rosa de Aguán is an interesting coastal town, some 40 km east of Trujillo, with 7000 hospitable English- and Spanish-speaking inhabitants. The spreading settlement lies at the mouth of the Río Aguán, the greater part on the east of the bay. A white-sand beach stretches all the way to Limón, and the thundering surf is an impressive sight. Take drinking water, insect repellent, mosquito coils and high-factor sun screen.

If driving from Trujillo, turn left at Km 343, 20 km along the highway, where a good gravel road runs another 20 km to Santa Rosa. From where the road ends at the west bank, take a canoe ferry across to the east side.

## Parque Nacional Capiro y Calentura

The Parque Nacional Capiro y Calentura encompasses these two mountains over looking Trujillo. The four- to six-hour walk to the summit gives spectacular views and on a clear day Isla Roatán can be seen in the distance. The walk is best done early in the morning when the forest is alive with the sounds of birds, monkeys and other wildlife. The path can be reached by walking (or taking a taxi) up the hill past the **Villa Brinkley Hotel**. The road to the summit is in poor condition from the entrance of the park and can only be driven in a 4WD. Insect repellent is needed if you pause. As with all walks in this area, it's safest to go in a group. The park is run by the **Fundación Capiro Calentura Guaimoreto** (**FUCAGUA**) ① *Parque Central, T434-429, Trujillo, open Mon-Fri.* They have information on all the reserves in the area and also on hiking and tours. Until a new office is built in the park, entry tickets must be bought here before going to Capiro y Calentura. They are opening up trails, improving old ones and organizing guided tours through parts of the forest. The hike along the Sendero de la Culebrina uses the remnants of a colonial stone road used to transport gold from the mines in the Valle de Aguán. Halfway up the **Cerro de las Cuevas**, 7 km beyond Cuyamel, are impressive caves showing traces of occupation by pre-Columbian Pech people.

## Refugio de Vida Silvestre Laguna de Guaimoreto (RVSLG)

FUCAGUA, see above, also administers the Refugio de Vida Silvestre, Laguna de Guaimoreto (RVSLG), northeast of Trujillo, where there is a bird island (Isla de los Pájaros), monkeys and good fishing. To visit, either arrange a trip with Fucagua, a tour agency such as Turtle Tours, or take a bus from Trujillo towards Puerto Castilla, get off just after the bridge which crosses the lagoon, then walk away from the lagoon for about 200 m to a dirt track on the left. Follow this and cross a low bridge and on the left is the house of a man who rents dug-out canoes. The Isla de los Pájaros is about 3 km up the lagoon, a bit too far for a dug-out. Another alternative is to go down to the wharf and hire out a motorized canoe or launch (price depends on the number of passengers and length of trip). There are no roads, paths or facilities in the area.

## Listings Trujillo and around

### Where to stay

**$$$ Tranquility Bay Beach Retreat**
*5 km west of Trujillo next to the Campa Vista development, T9928-2095, www.tranquilitybayhonduras.com.*
Managed by Larry and Linda from Vancouver, Tranquility Bay Beach Retreat is as relaxing as it promises to be. Their 5 *cabañas* are spacious and well-ventilated, have tropical views and sea breezes, and each one has a hammock too. The grounds are tidy, green and well-groomed.

**$$$-$$ Christopher Columbus Beach Resort**
*Outside town along the beach, drive across airstrip, T2434-4966.*
Has 72 rooms and suites, a/c, cable TV, pool, restaurant, watersports, tennis; it's painted bright turquoise.

**$$ Hotel Casa Alemania**
*Barrio Río Negro, 20 mins from the centre of Trujillo, T2434-4466.*
Managed by Gunter and Paula, this pleasant and hospitable B&B is a great place to chill out, especially in the bar in the evenings. Rooms are clean, cool, and comfortable. Good food and company.

**$$ Hotel y Restaurante Campamento**
*4 km west of Trujillo on the road to Santa Fe.*
This family-owned hotel-farm by the beach is a cosy, affordable, low-key spot and there are lots of nice animals on the property.

Accommodation includes simple but well-kitted *cabañas*. A great local option, very welcoming and hospitable.

**$$ O'Glynn**
*3 blocks south of the plaza, T2434-4592.*
Smart, clean place, with good rooms and bathrooms, a/c, TV and fridge in some rooms. Highly recommended.

**$ Mar de Plata**
*Up street west, T2434-4174.*
Upstairs rooms are best, with a beautiful view, bath and fan. Friendly and helpful staff.

### Restaurants

Don't miss the coconut bread, a speciality of the Garífuna.

**$$ Chico's Place**
*On the beach.*
Friendly and fun, Chico's Place is a typical open-air Caribbean beach restaurant with a thatched roof and ocean views. They serve whole fish and Salva Vida beer, so you can't go wrong. Take a walk through town to get there.

**$$ El Delfín**
*On the beach.*
Another good beachside option, El Delfín is a 3-storey structure that catches cool ocean breezes. They serve good chicken and seafood, including grilled shrimp, lobster and fish with a butter sauce.

## $$ Oasis

*Opposite HSBC.*
Canadian-owned restaurant and bar serving good food with outdoor seating. A good meeting place, with an information board, local tours, English books for sale and a book exchange.

## $ Bahía Bar

*T2434-4770, on the beach by the landing strip next to Christopher Columbus.*
Popular with expats, also Hondurans at weekends, serving vegetarian food. Also has showers and toilets.

### Cafés

**Ares Coffee**
*On the road to the beach, next to the national police just of the Parque Central, www.arescoffee.com.*
A local coffee franchise with good strong brews, a/c and free Wi-Fi.

### Bars and clubs

Head to **Rincón de los Amigos** or **Rogue's** if you're looking for drink at the end of the day. Also try the **Gringo Bar** and **Bahía Bar**. In **Barrio Cristales** at weekends there's *punta* music and lively atmosphere. Recommended.

### Entertainment

The cinema shows current US releases (most in English with subtitles).

### Shopping

**Garí-Arte Souvenir**, *T2434-4207, daily.* In the centre of Barrio Cristales, is recommended for authentic Garífuna souvenirs. Owned by Ricardo Lacayo.
**Tienda Souvenir Artesanía**, *next to Hotel Emperador.* Handicrafts, hand-painted toys.
3 supermarkets in the town centre.

### Transport

**Boat** Cargo boats leave for **Mosquitia** (ask all captains at the dock, wait up to 3 days, see page 588), the **Bay Islands** (very difficult) and Honduran ports to the west. Ask at the jetty. The trip to **Puerta Lempira** costs about US$15.

**Bus** Trujillo can be reached by bus from **San Pedro Sula**, **Tela** and **La Ceiba** by a paved road through Savá, Tocoa and Corocito. From **La Ceiba** it is 3 hrs by direct bus, 4 hrs by local. 3 direct **Cotraibal** buses in early morning from Trujillo. Bus from **Tegucigalpa** (Comayagüela) with **Cotraibal**, 7 Av between 10 and 11 Calle, US$6, 9 hrs; some buses to the capital go via La Unión, which is not as safe a route as via San Pedro Sula. To **San Pedro Sula**, 5 daily 0200-0800, US$5. Public transport also to **San Esteban** and **Juticalpa** (leave from in front of church at 0400, but check locally, arriving 1130, US$5.20). Bus to **Santa Fe** at 0930, US$0.40, leaves from outside **Glenny's Super Tienda**. To **Santa Rosa de Aguán** and **Limón** daily.

## El Progreso and east  *Colour map 3, B2.*

### a highland beauty off the beaten track

El Progreso, an important but unattractive agricultural and commercial centre on the Río Ulúa, is 30 minutes' drive on the paved highway southeast of San Pedro Sula, en route to Tela. While most people make straight for the coast at Tela, heading east from El Progreso leads through mountain scenery up to the small town of Yoro, beyond to Olanchito and a link to La Ceiba. With everyone else rushing to the Bay Islands, you could well have the place to yourself.

## Parque Nacional Pico Pijol

This park protects the 2282-m summit of primary cloudforest that is home to many quetzales. It is 32 km from the town of **Morazán** in the Yoro Department, which is 41 km from Progreso (bus from Progreso or Santa Rita). In Morazán are **Hospedaje El Corazón Sagrado**, several restaurants and a disco. The lower slopes of Pico Pijol have been heavily farmed. Access by vehicle is possible as far as Subirana. A guide is needed from there to a large cave nearby; access is difficult. Another trail to the summit (2282 m) starts at **Nueva Esperanza** village (bus from Morazán, Parque Central); ask for the correct trail. The first day is tough, all uphill with no shade; the second is tougher and requires a lot of clearing. Take a compass and topographical map. Also in the park is the waterfall at **Las Piratas** (bus Morazán–Los Murillos and then walk to El Ocotillo; ask for Las Piratas).

## Yoro and around

The paved highway to the prosperous little town of Yoro passes through pleasant countryside surrounded by mountains and dotted with ranches and farms. The **Parque Nacional Montaña de Yoro** is 8 km to the southeast (access from Marale), comprising 257 sq km of cloudforest, home to the Tolupanes people, also known as Xicaques. The **Asociación Ecológica Amigos de la Montaña de Yoro** has an office in the Parque Central in Yoro. From Yoro a dirt road continues to **Olanchito** via **Jocón**, through attractive country as the road snakes along the pine-forested slopes of Montaña Piedra Blanca and Montaña de la Bellota, with fine views of the surrounding valleys and distant mountain ranges.

## Listings El Progreso and east

### Where to stay

**Yoro and around**

**$ Aníbal**
*Corner of Parque Central, Yoro.*
Excellent value and clean, pleasant rooms with private or shared bath and a wide balcony. There's also a restaurant.

**$ Nelson**
*Yoro.*
Comfortable rooms with bath, fan, modern, good restaurant/bar and good outdoor swimming pool on 3rd floor, bar/disco on roof with marvellous views. Warmly recommended.

**$ Valle Aguán y Chabelito**
*1 block north of Parque Central, Olanchito, T2446-6718 (same management as Hotel Olanchito).*
Single rooms with a/c, doubles with fan, all rooms with cable TV. The best in town, with the best restaurant.

### Transport

**Yoro and around**
**Bus**
Hourly bus service to **El Progreso**, several daily to **Sulaco**.

Accessible only by air or sea, the Mosquitia coast is a vast expanse of rivers and swamps, coastal lagoons and tropical forests filled with wildlife but with few people.

From February to May you can taste the *vino de coyol*, which is extracted from a palm (a hole is made at the top of the trunk and the sap that flows out is drunk neat). With sugar added it ferments and becomes alcoholic (*chichi*); it is so strong it is called *patada de burro* (mule kick).

The Carretera de Olancho runs from the capital northeast to the Caribbean coast. It passes through Guaimaca and San Diego, Campamento, 127 km, a small, friendly village (with a few basic *hospedajes*) surrounded by pine forests, and on to the Río Guayape, 143 km.

By the river crossing at **Los Limones** is an unpaved road north to **La Unión** (56 km), deep in the northern moutains passing through beautiful forests and lush green countryside. To the north is the **Refugio de Vida Silvestre La Muralla-Los Higuerales** ⓘ *US$1*, where quetzales and emerald toucanettes can be seen between March and May in the cloud forest. For those that have made the effort to get to this spot, if you're camping you may experience the frissonic pleasure of jaguars 'screaming' during the night. The park comprises the three peaks of **La Muralla**, 1981 m, **Las Parras**, 2064 m, and **Los Higuerales**, 1985 m. Cohdefor has an office on the main plaza for information, closed weekends. You are now required to take a guide with you on the trail. Cost is US$4, arrange in La Unión. Four trails range from 1-10 km and are recommended. There are two campsites in the forest (contact Cohdefor on T2222-1027 for prior arrangements), or there is accommodation for one or two at the visitor centre.

## Juticalpa

The main road continues another 50 km from Los Limones to Juticalpa (altitude 420 m), the capital of Olancho department, in a rich agricultural area for herding cattle and growing cereals and sugar cane. There is a paved road northeast through the cattle land of Catacamas, continuing to just beyond Dulce Nombre de Culmí.

## Catacamas and around

Catacamas (altitude 400 m) lies at the foot of Agalta mountain in the Río Guayape valley in the Department of Olancho, 210 km from Tegucigalpa. The Río Guayape (named after an indigenous dress, *guayapis*) is famous for its gold nuggets.

The town was established by the Spaniards and the colonial church dates from the early 18th century. It is an agricultural and cattle-raising district. The National School of Agriculture (ENA) is based here; ask if you wish to visit their agricultural demonstration plots in the Guayape valley, 5 km south of the town.

Hiking in the mountains behind Catacamas is beautiful. From Murmullo there are trails to coffee farms. **Río Talgua**, 4 km east of Catacamas, is interesting with caves in which significant pre-Columbian remains have been found. The area and caves are worth a visit. Hiking to **El Boquerón**, stop off at the main road near Punuare, 17 km west of Catacamas, and walk up **Río Olancho**, which has nice limestone cliffs and a pretty river canyon. Through much of the canyon the stream flows underground.

Beyond Catacamas, a rough road continues northeast up the Río Tinto Valley to **Dulce Nombre de Culmí**. Further on is **Paya** where the road becomes a mule track but, in three to four days in the dry season, a route can be made over the divide (Cerro de Will) and down the Río Paulaya to Mosquitia (see below). Local police say that there is a path in the dry season from Dulce Nombre to San Esteban (about 30 km).

## Juticalpa to Trujillo

There is a fine scenic road from Juticalpa to Trujillo. From Juticalpa head northeast and turn left where the paved road ends, to **San Francisco de la Paz**. Beyond San Francisco is **Gualaco**, which has an interesting colonial church (there are several places to stay; see Where to stay, below).

The town of **San Esteban** is 23 km from Gualaco. On the way you pass Agalta mountain, and some of the highest points in Honduras, as well as several waterfalls on the Río Babilonia.

After San Esteban the road continues to **Bonito Oriental** (via El Carbón, a mahogany collection point with the Paya communities in the vicinity). There are four hotels here. The final 38 km from Bonito Oriental to Trujillo are paved, through Corocito. There are many dirt roads between San Francisco and Trujillo. If driving, ask directions if in any doubt. Fuel is available in the larger villages but there is none between San Esteban and Bonito Oriental.

## Parque Nacional Sierra de Agalta

Between the roads Juticalpa–Gualaco–San Esteban and Juticalpa–Catacamas–Dulce Nombre de Culmí lies the cloudforest of the Parque Nacional Sierra de Agalta, extending over 1200 ha and reaching a height of 2590 m at **Monte de Babilonia**, a massif with a number of interesting mountains. Several different ecosystems have been found with a wide variety of fauna and flora: 200 species of bird have been identified so far. There are several points of entry. Contact **Cohdefor** in Juticalpa, Culmí, Gualaco, San Esteban or Catacamas for information on access, maps, guides, mules and lodging. There is no infrastructure in the park, but a base camp is being built. A good trail leads to **La Picucha** mountain (2354 m). Access is from El Pacayal, 750 m, a short distance towards San Esteban from Gualaco (bus at 0700 which goes on to Tocoa). There are two campsites on the trail; the first at 1060 m is just short of **La Chorrera** waterfall, which has a colony of white-collared swifts that nest in the cave behind the falls. Four to six hours' walk above is the second campsite at 1900 m. The final section is mainly dwarf forest with low undergrowth on the summit. There is much wildlife to be seen and a good viewpoint 1 km beyond at the site of two abandoned radio towers. Hiking time is two days.

## Where to stay

**$ Hospedaje San Carlos**
*La Unión.*
Serves good vegetarian food.

**$ Hotel**
*On plaza, Guaimaca, above restaurant Las Cascadas.*
Good value, clean rooms, and friendly staff.

### Juticalpa

**$ El Paso**
*1 Av NE y 6 Calle NO, 6 blocks south of Parque (on way to highway), T2885-2311.*
Quiet place offering clean rooms with bath and fan. Laundry facilities. Highly recommended.

**$ Familiar**
*1 Calle NO between Parque and Antúñez.*
Basic but clean rooms with bath. Recommended.

### Catacamas and around

**$ Juan Carlos**
*Barrio José Trinidad Reyes, T2899-4212.*
Good restaurant. Recommended.

**$ La Colina**
*T2899-4488.*
Rooms with bath, hot water, fan and TV. Parking.

### Juticalpa to Trujillo

**$ Calle Real**
*Gualaco, near Parque Central.*
Friendly place with basic rooms, will store luggage.

**$ Centro**
*San Esteban.*
The best place to stay, with spotless rooms and run by a nice family.

## Restaurants

### Juticalpa

**$ Casa Blanca**
*1 Calle SE.*
Quite a smart restaurant with a good cheap menu; try the paella.

**$ El Rancho**
*2 Av NE.*
Pleasant place which specializes in meat dishes and has lots of choice on its menu.

### Cafés

**La Galera**
*2 Av NE.*
Specializes in *pinchos*.

**Tropical Juices**
*Blv de los Poetas.*
Good fruit juices.

### Catacamas and around

In **Dulce Nombre de Culmí**, there are several *comedores* on the main plaza.

**$ As de Oro**
*Catacamas.*
Good beef dishes, served in Wild West–style surroundings.

**$ Continental**
*Catacamas.*
Chicken dishes and pizza, which you can wash down with a US beer.

### Juticalpa to Trujillo

There are 3 nice *comedores* in **San Esteban** near the Hotel San Esteban.

## Bars and clubs

### Catacamas and around
Fernandos and Extasis Montefresco are bars outside town towards Tegucigalpa, with pool (US$1.20) and live music 2 evenings a week.

## Entertainment

### Catacamas and around
Cine Maya, Barrio El Centro, cinema.

## Shopping

### Juticalpa
From 0600 on Sat, the market in Parque Central has a good selection of food, fruit, vegetables and souvenirs, said to be the best outdoor market in Olancho.

## Transport

Bus From Comayagüela to La Unión, daily, take 4 hrs. To get to the park, hire a truck from La Unión for about US$18. There's little traffic so it's difficult to hitchhike. If driving from San Pedro Sula, take the road east through Yoro and Mangulile; from La Ceiba, take the Savá– Olanchito road and turn south 13 km before Olanchito.

### Juticalpa
Bus Bus station is on 1 Av NE, 1 km southeast of Parque Central, taxis US$0.50. Hourly to Tegucigalpa from 0330 to 1800; to San Esteban from opposite Aurora bus terminal at 0800, 6 hrs, US$2.25. To Trujillo 0400, 9 hrs, US$5.20. To Tocoa at 0500.

### Catcamas and around
Bus From Tegucigalpa to Juticalpa/Catacamas, Empresa Aurora, 8 Calle 6-7 Av, Comayagüela, T237-3647, hourly 0400-1700, 3¼ hrs, US$2 to Juticalpa, 4 hrs US$2.75 to Catacamas. Juticalpa–Catacamas, 40 mins, US$0.60. To Dulce Nombre de Culmí (see above), 3 hrs, US$1.35, several daily.

### Juticalpa to Trujillo
Bus To Juticalpa and to the north coast (Tocoa and Trujillo) buses are fairly frequent.

# La Mosquitia  *Colour map 3, B5.*

the Miskito heartland

★Forested, swampy and almost uninhabited, Mosquitia is well worth visiting if you have the time and energy. In the the Central American Little Amazon, you can hope to see rainforest wildlife including monkeys and incredible birdlife as you drift through the varied habitat that includes lowland tropical rainforest, coastal lagoons, undisturbed beaches, mangroves, grasslands and patches of pine savannah. Home to members of the Miskito and Pech tribes as well as the Garífuna ethnic group who live in small communities on the coast and along the major rivers. The Río Plátano Biosphere Reserve, a UNESCO World Heritage Site, covers an area over 5200 sq km, one of the largest protected areas in Central America.

## Coastal villages
A narrow strand of land divides the inland waterway and Ibans lagoon from the Caribbean. Along this pleasant setting lie a number of small native villages starting with the Garífuna village of Plaplaya and continuing through the Miskito villages of Ibans, Cocobila, Raistá, Belén, Nueva Jerusalem and Kuri. Trails connect all of these villages making exploration

# Essential La Mosquitia

## Access

While certainly a challenging environment, many backpackers visit the reserve either alone or with professional guides. For those travelling alone, as long as you have basic Spanish and are a reasonably confident traveller this is the cheapest option.

## Tourist information

**Mosquitia Pawisa (MOPAWI)**, head office in Puerto Lempira, T898-7460, www.mopawi.org, another office in Tegucigalpa, Residencias Tres Caminos 4b, lote 67, T235-8659, plus offices in several other villages, is the best source of information about the indigenous communities in Mosquitia. It is a non-profit-making, non-sectarian organization dedicated to the development of the region and the conservation of the biodiversity of its flora and fauna; volunteer opportunities are available.

MOPAWI is concerned with the protection of natural and human resources throughout Mosquitia and the Department of Gracias a Dios. Among its programmes is the conservation of marine turtles and the green iguana. The Reserva Biósfera Río Plátano (525,100 ha) with the Reserva Antropólogica Tawahka, the Reserva Nacional Patuca and together with Mosquitia Nicaragüense, constitute one of the largest forest reserves north of the Amazon.

## What to take

It's a tough environment and you should go prepared. Take a mosquito net and repellent, clothing for rain and also for cooler temperatures at night, good walking shoes and a first-aid kit. Also enough cash in small denominations for your stay (there are no banks in the area) and plastic bags to keep things dry.

## Medical services

Alas de Socorro operates from Ahuas to collect sick people from villages to take them to Ahuas hospital. Contact the Moravian church (in Puerto Lempira Reverend Stanley Goff, otherwise local pastors will help).

## When to go

With access by air, sea and road, you can visit any time of the year but it is usually best to avoid the heavy rains from November to January. The driest months are March to May and August to October.

---

easy with vast expanses of unspoiled, white-sand beaches providing an easy route for getting from place to place, with the sea providing a wonderful way to cool off during the heat of the day.

Apart from generally relaxing in the slow-paced life along the coast there are several interesting things to do in the area. In **Plaplaya**, a community-run Sea Turtle Project aims to protect the leatherback and loggerhead turtles that nest along the coast. Each night during the breeding season (March-June) members of the village patrol the beaches to find nesting turtles, carefully gathering the eggs and re-burying them in a guarded area where they are watched over until they hatch. The newborn turtles are then released into the sea. Visitors can accompany the beach patrols for a small donation to the program. There are two traditional dance groups in Plaplaya that can provide an interesting evening's entertainment for visitors.

The Miskito village of **Kuri**, 1½ hours along the beach from Belén, is worth a visit. Here the traditional wooden and thatch houses sit behind the beach, sheltered from the sea breezes by the 'Beach Grape' and palm trees along the sand dunes.

## Reserva de la Biósfera Río Plátano

The reserve was established by the Honduran government in 1980 to protect the outstanding natural and cultural resources of the Río Plátano valley and its environs. In 1982 UNESCO declared the reserve a World Heritage Site. The

> **Tip...**
> Several commercial guides organize trips into the Río Plátano Biosphere Reserve and may be a good option for those with limited Spanish.

tropical jungles here shelter a number of endangered birds, mammals and fish, among them **scarlet macaws** and **harpy eagles**, **jaguars** and **tapirs**, and the **cuyamel**, a prized food fish fast becoming extinct throughout Honduras. In addition, there are a number of **archaeological sites** about which little is known, although archaeologists finally managed to locate the fabled lost White City of the Maya in 2015, hidden in an isolated valley, in an undisclosed location, deep in the thick jungles of the Plátano headwaters.

The Miskito and the Pech living along the lower Plátano cultivate yuca, bananas, rice, corn and beans, and also feed themselves by hunting and fishing. The upper (southern) portion of the Plátano watershed is being quickly populated by mestizo immigrants from the poverty-stricken south of Honduras. These new settlers are cutting down the forest to plant crops and raise cattle, hunting wildlife mercilessly and dynamite-fishing. The government's intention officially to allow settlers into the Sico and Paulaya valleys, on the western edge of the reserve, was roundly criticized. It was feared that the agrarian reform programme would lead to the desertification of the Río Plátano. Added to the damage being done by the settlers, there are now disturbing reports that drug smugglers are cutting landing strips deep in the jungle. Given the pressure the reserve is under, it is recommended to visit it sooner rather than later.

## Along the Río Plátano

For those in search of a little more rugged adventure you should find a boat to take you up the Río Plátano to Las Marías, a small Miskito and Pech village that is the last outpost of civilization in this part of the reserve. Local boatman are trying to organize themselves with a view to regulating minimum standards, a fair price for the passage and a rotation system to ensure the work is shared more evenly between them.

Most people stay the night in Raistá before and after visiting Las Marías. Fuel is very expensive in La Mosquitia and this is reflected in the high cost of transportation. The ride to Las Marías costs about US$130 so put together a group of four or five people to share the cost. That price should get you a boat and boatman for three days to take you on the round trip (four to six hours each way) from the coast with a day in Las Marías to look around. If you stay longer you should negotiate a fair price with the boatman to cover his extra time. Bring food and water for the trip as well as other jungle gear. The journey upstream to Las Marías, although beautiful, can become very tedious and uncomfortable. Birdwatching can provide a diversion; there are three species of toucan as well as several species of parrot, tanagers, herons, kingfishers, vultures, hawk eagles and oropendolas. If you are lucky you might see crocodiles, turtles or iguanas. On arrival in Las Marías, arrange return at once.

An alternative route to Las Marías is by boat across Ibans Lagoon, 45 minutes by tuk-tuk, then 6½ hours' walk through jungle (rough path, hot, mosquitoes, take lots of water and insect repellent, and wear good hiking boots). This is only recommended for fit walkers in drier weather. Expect to pay around US$30 for the guide, and if returning from Las Marías by boat you'll probably still have to pay the return fare even if you're only travelling one way.

## Las Marías

This Miskito-Pech village is the furthest limit of upstream settlement. Once in Las Marías you're normally met by a member of the *saca guía*, a representative of the Las Marías Ecotourism Committee who will let you know what trips are available in the area and help make arrangements on a rotation system that shares the work among the community. This group was set up with the help of MOPAWI and Peace Corps with the aim of developing and coordinating a system of ecotourism that benefits the local people, protects the reserve and also offers extraordinary experiences to tourists. A number of guides have been trained in Las Marías to deal with international visitors. They are coordinated by the Committee, have a set price structure with prices and rules posted on the walls of all the *hospedajes*.

Typical guided trips include day hiking on trails around the village, a three-day hike to scenic **Pico Dama** (very strenuous), a day trip by *pipante* upriver to see the **petroglyphs** at **Walpulbansirpi** left by the ancestors of the Pech or multi-day trips upriver to visit other petroglyph sites and view wildlife in the heart of the reserve. Note that it's harder to advance upriver during the rainy season from June to December.

## Brus Laguna

It is a 15-minute scenic flight from Puerto Lempira (see below) above Caratasca Lagoon and grassy, pine-covered savannahs to **Ahuas**, one-hour walk from the Patuca River (fabled for gold). There is a hospital here, four missions, some basic accommodation and a generally improving atmosphere. Irregular *cayucos* sail down to Brus Laguna for US$2.50, at the mouth of the Río Patuca, or US$12.50 (15 minutes) scenic flight in the mission plane. The airstrip is 4 km from the village; take a lift for US$1. There is a disco at the riverside to the left of the bridge. The village is plagued by mosquitoes throughout summer and autumn.

## Puerto Lempira

Puerto Lempira is on the large Caratasca Lagoon. The main office of MOPAWI (see page 589) is here. The airstrip is only five minutes' walk from town. Regular tuk-tuks (motorized canoes) cross the lagoon to **Kaukira**, US$1.20 (a nice place, but there's nothing there), **Yagurabila** and **Palkaka**. The tuk-tuks leave Kaukira daily except Sunday at 0500, returning during the morning. In the afternoon the lagoon is usually too rough to cross.

Inland by road from Puerto Lempira are **Mocorón** and **Rus Rus**, which may be visited with difficulty (there is no public transport but any vehicle will give a lift) and is a beautiful, quiet village (accommodation at Friends of America hospital's house; meals from Capi's next door, ask Friends about transport out). A branch off this road leads southeast to **Leimus** on the Río Coco and the border with Nicaragua. Ask for Evaristo López (at whose house you can get breakfast) who can arrange transport to Leimus, most days, three to four hours for about US$3.50. He is also knowledgeable about area safety.

The road continues south to the small town of **Ahuashbila** on the upper river of the Río Coco, which marks the border with Nicaragua.

### Where to stay

#### Coastal villages
**Plaplaya**

**$ Basilia**
*15 mins west of centre.*
Traditional and the cheapest.

**$ Doña Sede**
*East of village centre.*
Good meals.

#### Raistá and Belén
Choose between **Eddie and Elma Bodden**
($) on the lagoon and **Doña Cecilia Bodden**
($), just up from the lagoon towards the sea.
Try the food at **Elma's Kitchen** ($) in Raistá,
thought by some to be the best on the
coast. Near the lagoon between Raistá and
Belén is **Doña Exe** ($), and in Belén there is
**Doña Mendilia** ($), near the grass airstrip.

#### Las Marías
Balancing the benefits of tourism is difficult
in such a sensitive area. Sharing the benefits
is one way of offsetting the negative impact
of tourism and, whenever possible, the
Ecotourism Committee tries to share tourists
between the 4 basic but clean *hospedajes* (all
$) of **Ovidio**, **Justa**, **Tinglas** or **Diana**, with
meals available for US$3. Very friendly and
with wonderful community atmosphere,
highly recommended (no electricity after
about 1900, so bring a torch).

#### Brus Laguna

**$ Estancia and Paradise**
*T2433-8043 and T2433-8039.*
Rooms with a fan and optional private bath.

#### Puerto Lempira

**$ Gran Hotel Flores**
Some rooms with bath. Recommended.

**$ Pensión Moderno**
Good, friendly place, with electricity
from 1800-2230.

**$ Villas Caratascas**
Huts with bath. There is also a restaurant
and a disco here.

### Restaurants

#### Puerto Lempira

**$ Delmy**
*3 blocks north of main street.*
Noisy restaurant serving chicken and
other dishes.

**$ Doña Aida**
*North side of main road to landing bridge.*
Fresh orange juice.

**$ La Mosquitia**
*Centro Comercial Segovia in main street.*
Breakfasts and cheap fish.

### What to do

All-inclusive packages range from 3-14 days
and cost about US$100 per day. In order to
support ecotourism in the reserve you are
encouraged to check the tour operator you
are considering works with local people.
For other options, see under What to do,
Tela (page 569) and La Ceiba (page 578).

**Bob 'The Butterfly, Bird and Bug
Guy' Gallardo**, *based in Copán Ruinas,*
*rgallardo32@hotmail.com.* Highly regarded
birding and other specialized nature trips
to La Mosquitia.
**La Moskitia Eco Aventuras**, *with Jorge
Salaverri, office in La Ceiba, T2442-0104,*

*www.lamoskitia.hn*. Specializing in trips to La Mosquitia, this excellent company is possibly the best and most knowledgeable wildlife guide in all Central America. **Mesoamerica Travel** (Col Juan Lindo, No 709, 8 Calle and 32 Av NO, San Pedro Sula, T2558-6447, www.mesoamerica-travel.com) and **Fundación Patuca** (Hauke Hoops) (T236-9910), also specialize in travel in this region. **Mesoamerica** is the only company to run tours to the Zona Arriba of the Río Patuca (5 or 10 days).

## Las Marías

The services of the *saca guía* are US$3.50. Guides are required even for day hikes due to the possibility of getting lost or injured on the faint jungle trails. The cost for a guide is US$6 per day for groups up to 5. Overnight hikes require 2 guides. River trips in a *pipante*, a shallow dug-out canoe manoeuvered with poles (*palancas*) and paddles (*canaletes*), require 3 guides plus US$4.20 for the canoe. 2 visitors and their gear will fit in each boat with the guides.

## Transport

### La Mosquitia

**Air** Alas de Socorro fly to **Ahuas**, T2233-7025. This company charters planes for US$565, but per person it is US$60 1 way to Ahuas. **SAMi** flies to various villages from Puerto Lempira, eg **Ahuas**, **Brus Laguna**, **Belén**. There are expensive express flights to places like **Auka**, **Raya**, **Kaukira**.

**Boat** Coastal supply vessels run between **La Ceiba** and the coastal villages of La Mosquitia. The *Corazón* and *Mr Jim* make the trip weekly and their captains can be found at the harbour east of La Ceiba. Prices vary (US$10-20); be prepared for basic conditions. There are no passenger facilities such as beds or toilets on board and the journey takes a good 24 hrs.

Rivers, lagoons and inland waterways are the highways in the reserve and dug-out canoes provide the public transportation. Once in Palacios, you can catch colectivo boat transport at the landing near the **Río Tinto Hotel** to travel along the inland passage to coastal villages in the reserve such as Plaplaya, Raistá and Belén (about US$3.50 for a 1 or 2-hr trip). There is usually a boat to meet the planes that arrive in the morning and information on prices to different locations is posted in the airline offices. If you miss the colectivo you will usually have to pay extra for a special trip (about US$20).

**Road** An upgraded road is the cheapest and most favoured route by locals. Take a bus from **La Ceiba** to Tocoa (US$2). From the market in Tocoa take a series of pickups (US$16 per person) along the beach to Batalla, crossing the various creeks that block the way in launches that wait to meet the cars. The journey to **Batalla** takes about 5½ hrs. From Batalla cross the lagoon in a boat to **Palacios** (US$0.70) and continue from there. The trip is not possible in the wetter months of the year (Jul, Oct and Nov).

**Note** Some may suggest the possibility of catching a truck from Limón to Sangrilaya then walking along the beach and wading across rivers for 1-2 days to get to Batalla. While this is possible it is not recommended because of the heat, bugs and general safety issues.

# This is
## Nicaragua

Nicaragua is a land born out of poetry, fire and brazen revolutionary spirit; few countries can boast such an authentic character. The 1979 Sandinista Revolution, more than other historical episode, is indelibly etched on the Nicaraguan psyche. As a moment of self-realization, it continues to inspire great national pride and endless passionate discourse.

Sadly, over a decade of civil war left its mark too, with broken infrastructure, poverty, unemployment and a lingering negative image. Fortunately, those dark days are gone, and Nicaragua is at lasting peace and very much on its way up. Burgeoning foreign investment, including a bold new transoceanic canal project, signal dramatic transformations for this long overlooked Central American nation, but head off the beaten track and development is patchy: power cuts are common, many towns lack paved roads, horses and carts are still widely used and wood remains the principal source of fuel.

Despite Nicaragua's hardships, the nation's cultural life is among the most sophisticated in Central America. The country revels in unique forms of dance, music and festivals, many of them with prehispanic roots. But most of all Nicaragua breathes poetry, the unrivalled national passion. It has produced some of the most important poets in the history of the Spanish language.

Nicaragua's expressive and tempestuous national temperament runs in striking parallel to its volatile geological scenery. A rugged spine of more than 50 volcanoes runs from the northwest Pacific to the watery expanse of Lake Nicaragua. Elsewhere, nearly 20% of the country's land mass is an officially protected area. These diverse ecosystems include rainforests, cloud forests, and wetlands, which guard 10% of the earth's biodiversity.

For those willing to take the plunge, Nicaragua's ethereal natural beauty and anarchic charms tend to leave lasting impressions. Through it all, the people, eternally warm and good humoured, are the country's finest asset.

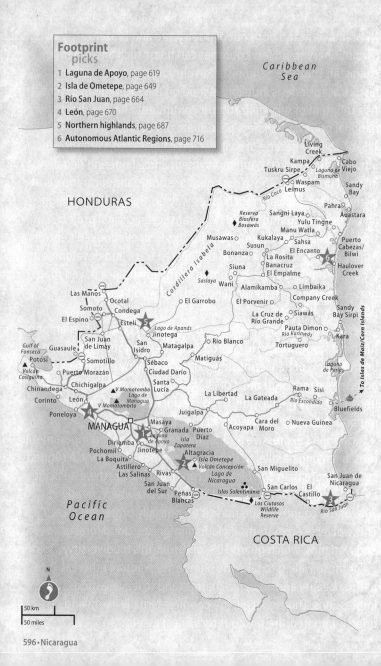

## Footprint picks

*Caribbean Sea*

HONDURAS

Living Creek
Kampa
Tuskru Sirpe
Waspam
Leimus
*Laguna de Bismuna*
Cabo Viejo
Sandy Bay
Pahra
Auastara
*Río Coco*

Reserva Biosfera Bosawás
Sangni Laya
Yulu Tingne
Manu Watla
Kukalaya
Sahsa
El Encanto
Puerto Cabezas/ Bilwi
Musawas
Susun
Bonanza
La Rosita
Banacruz
El Empalme
Haulover Creek

*Cordillera Isabela*

*Saslaya*
Siuna
Wani
Alamikamba
Limbaika

Las Manos
Ocotal
Somoto
Condega
El Espino
Estelí
El Garrobo
El Porvenir
Company Creek

San Juan de Limay
Lago de Apanás
Jinotega
La Cruz de Río Grande
Siawás
Sandy Bay Sirpi

*Gulf of Fonseca*
Guasaule
San Isidro
Matagalpa
Río Blanco
Pauta Dimon
*Río Kurinwás*
Kara

Potosí
*Volcán Cosigüina*
Somotillo
Puerto Morazán
Sébaco
Ciudad Darío
Matiguás
Tortuguero
*Laguna de Perlas*

Chichigalpa
Santa Lucía
La Libertad
Rama
Sisi
*Río Escondido*

Chinandega
León
*V Momotombo*
*Lago de Managua*
*V Momotombito*
Juigalpa
La Gateada
Bluefields

Corinto
Poneloya
MANAGUA
Masaya
Granada
Puerto Díaz
Acoyapa
Cara del Moro
Nueva Guinea

Diriamba
*Laguna de Apoyo*
*Isla Zapatera*

Pochomil
Jinotepe
Altagracia
*Isla Ometepe*
*Volcán Concepción*
San Miguelito

La Boquita
Astillero
Rivas
*Lago de Nicaragua*
San Carlos
El Castillo
San Juan de Nicaragua

Las Salinas
San Juan del Sur
Peñas Blancas
*Islas Solentiname*
*Los Ciutasos Wildlife Reserve*
*Río San Juan*

*To Islas de Maíz/Corn Islands*

*Pacific Ocean*

COSTA RICA

N

50 km
50 miles

Managua

# Footprint
## picks

★ **Laguna de Apoyo**,
page 619
The most stunning of Nicaragua's
15 crater lakes changes through
azure, turquoise and navy blue.

★ **Isla de Ometepe**, page 649
A bastion of peace, tranquillity and numinous volcanic beauty on
Central America's largest lake, Lago Nicaragua.

★ **Río San Juan**, page 664
Navigate the remote Río San Juan with excellent wildlife spotting.

★ **León**, page 670
Talk politics, party hard, then conquer a volcano.

★ **Northern highlands**, page 687
A chain of volcanoes lie in the rugged northern highlands where
*campesino* culture predominates.

★ **Autonomous Atlantic Regions**, page 716
Discover lost-in-time Miskito and Afro-Caribbean communities on
this isolated coast.

# Essential Managua

## Getting around

Managua has nothing that even remotely resembles a city grid and walking is a challenge and unsafe for those who are not familiar with the city. The best bet is to get to Metrocentro and not travel more than five blocks on foot (see Safety, below). Local buses are confusing, crowded and not recommended due to thieves. Taxi is the preferred method of transport for newcomers. Unfortunately, hiring a Managua taxi is not as safe or straightforward as you might hope, but once mastered it is an efficient way to explore Managua. Negotiate the fare before getting in by asking *¿por cuánto me lleva?* It is cheaper to ride *colectivo* (shared), but not recommended due to safety concerns (see below).

## Best restaurants

**La Casa de Los Mejía Godoy**, page 607
**Rancho Tiscapa**, page 607
**El Churrasco**, page 607
**A La Vista Buffet**, page 607
**El Muelle**, page 608

## Orientation

In Managua, directions are based around the lake, so it is essential to know where the lake is and keep a bird's eye view of the city in your mind. With the location of Lake Managua you have north (*al lago*); away from the lake is south (*al sur*). Then you need to use basic Spanish and the sun. Where the sun comes up (*arriba*) is east and where it goes down (*abajo*) is west. City blocks are *cuadras* (abbreviated in this book as 'c'), and metres are better known here by their old Spanish approximation – *varas* (vrs). The key element once you fix your compass is the landmark from which directions begin. Once you find the landmark, getting to your ultimate destination is simple. For example, take **El Caramanchel** bar, Plaza Inter, 2 c sur, 15 varas abajo: to sip Nicaraguan rum here first you need to locate Plaza Inter, then go two blocks south and continue 15 m west.

## Safety

Like most capitals, Managua suffers from a healthy criminal population, so be sure to take all the usual precautions. At night, do not walk more than a few blocks anywhere, as the streets are deserted and there are almost no police. The Metrocentro area is relatively safe, but it's still best not to walk alone after dark. Parts of Martha Quezada are now unsafe at all hours, particularly on the roads between the Ticabus terminal and Plaza Inter; ask locally about the situation before setting out. Do not ride in unlicensed taxis, especially with helpful local 'friends' you have just met, as you risk being kidnapped and robbed. Always ask to see the driver's ID and check the license plate number matches the one on the taxi door.

## Weather Managua

| January | February | March | April | May | June |
|---|---|---|---|---|---|
| ☀ 31°C 21°C 2mm | ☀ 32°C 21°C 2mm | ☀ 33°C 22°C 3mm | ☀ 33°C 23°C 9mm | ⛅ 33°C 24°C 66mm | ⛅ 31°C 23°C 78mm |

| July | August | September | October | November | December |
|---|---|---|---|---|---|
| 🌧 30°C 23°C 30mm | 🌧 31°C 23°C 60mm | 🌧 30°C 23°C 99mm | 🌧 30°C 22°C 90mm | ☀ 31°C 22°C 36mm | ☀ 30°C 21°C 3mm |

# Managua
## & around

If, as the local saying goes, Nicaragua is the country where 'lead floats and cork sinks', Managua is its perfect capital. It's certainly hard to make any sense of a lakefront city which ignores its lake and where you can drive around for hours without ever seeing any water. Managua has 20% of the country's population, yet there is little overcrowding; it has no centre and lots of trees (from the air you can see more trees than buildings); it is a place where parks are concrete, not green, spaces – there are too many of those already; and where, when directions are given, they refer to buildings that haven't existed for over 30 years. Managua is the capital without a city, a massive suburb of over a million people (there was a downtown once but it was swept away in the 1972 earthquake). And yet, despite having no centre, no skyline and no logic, Managua is still a good place to start your visit. It is full of energy and is the heartbeat of the Nicaraguan economy and psyche.

**Best** for
Ancient footprints ▪ Birdwatching in the sierras ▪ Museums

## Lakefront and the old centre

### new waterside developments contrast with weary historical edifices

From the *malecón* in Managua (altitude 40-200 m), the Península Chiltepe can be seen jutting out into Lake Managua, part of an ancient volcanic complex that includes two crater lakes, Apoyeque and Xiloá.

The *malecón* is the site of a popular touristic development with a parade of rancho-style eateries, **Puerto Salvador Allende** ⓘ *www.epn.com.ni*. Boat tours depart from the pier for nearby **Isla de Amor** ⓘ *Tue-Sun 1100, 1300, 1500, 1700; 45 mins; US$3, top-floor 'VIP' rate US$4 children US$1.25*. The stage with the giant acoustic shell right next to the *malecón* is used for concerts, political speeches and rallies.

Southeast of the malecón stands the **Teatro Rubén Darío or Teatro Nacional** ⓘ *T2222-7426, www.tnrubendario.gob.ni, US$1.50-20, depending on show, most programmes Thu-Sun*, a project of the last Somoza's wife, which survived the earthquake of 1972 and provides the only quality stage in Managua for plays, concerts and dance productions. Just south of the theatre is the Parque Rubén Darío, a small park with a 1933 monument sculpted from Italian marble by Nicaraguan architect Mario Favilli, said to be the aesthetic symbol of modernism. In front of the statue is the Parque Central. Now central to almost nothing, it was once surrounded by three- to five-storey buildings and narrow streets that made up the pre-1972 Managua.

**Managua**

| Where to stay | Camino Real 2 | Bars & clubs |
|---|---|---|
| Best Western Las Mercedes 1 | | La Cavanga 3 |

Next to the park is a dancing, musical fountain and the garish **Casa Presidencial** that has been described (generously) as 'post-modernist eclectic'. Directly opposite is the neoclassical Palacio Nacional de la Cultura, finished in 1935 after the original was destroyed in an earthquake in 1931. The elegant interior houses two gardens, the national archive, the national library, and the **Museo Nacional de Nicaragua** ⓘ *T2222-4820, Tue-Sat 0900-1600, Sun 0900-1500, US$2 (guided tour only, sometimes available in English), US$2.50, extra charge to video, US$1 to photograph*, with a fine pre-Columbian collection and historical expositions. Next to the Palacio de la Cultura is the Catedral Vieja (Old Cathedral), partially destroyed in the 1972 earthquake. There is something romantic about this old and sad cathedral in ruins; a monument to what Managua might have been.

The **Centro Cultural Managua** ⓘ *on the south side of the Palacio de la Cultura, T2222-5921*, was built out of the ruins of the Gran Hotel de Managua, the best hotel in town from the 1940s to 1960s. Now, as a cultural centre, it has a selection of before-and-after photos of quake-struck Managua in 1972, art exhibits and temporary antique and craft shops. Across the Carretera Norte from the Centro Cultural Managua, the Parque de Paz (Peace Park) is a graveyard for a few dozen truckloads of AK-47s and other weapons which were buried here as a monument to the end of the Contra War; some can be seen sticking out of the cement. Sadly, the park is now unsafe to visit; check with a taxi driver about the current situation. Heading south from the old centre down the Avenida Bolívar is the Asemblea Nacional (parliamentary building) and the **Arboretum Nacional**, which houses 180 species of plant including Nicaragua's national flower, the *sacuanjoche* (*Plumeria rubra*).

## Martha Quezada and Bolonia
### low-key barrio and Managua's finest residential district

Two blocks south of the government offices is the historic pyramid-shaped Intercontinental building, now home to the Hotel Crowne Plaza.

West of here, the streets descend to the district of Martha Quezada, also known as 'Ticabus', where you'll find a concentration of budget accommodation and two of the international bus stations. **Note** It is unsafe to walk from the Intercontinental building to the barrio.

South of Martha Quezada, Bolonia is home to all Nicaragua's major television networks, most of its embassies, some decent art galleries and several good eating and sleeping options.

## Laguna de Tiscapa and around

crater lake set in a protected area

The Parque Nacional de la Loma de Tiscapa (Tuesday-Sunday 0900-1730, US$1 admission for pedestrians, US$2 admission for cars) has a fabulous panoramic view of Managua and is great for photographing the city. It is reached by the small road that runs directly behind the Crowne Plaza Hotel. At the top, a giant black silhouette of Augusto C Sandino looks out over the city and Laguna de Tiscapa on the south side of the hill. This park is also the site of the former presidential palace (ruined by the earthquake in 1972). Sandino signed a peace treaty here in 1933 and, after dining here with the then President Sacasa one year later, was abducted and shot under orders of the first Somoza, who would push Sacasa out of office in 1936 and found a 43-year family dynasty. Both father and son dictators used part of the palace to hold and torture dissidents. **Note** Avoid taking photographs until you're at the top of the hill, as the access road to the park passes Nicaragua's national military headquarters.

Some 500 m south of the Laguna de Tiscapa is the Catedral Metropolitana de la Purísima Concepción de María, designed by the Mexican architect Ricardo Legorreta, who has said his inspiration was found in an ancient temple in Cholula, Mexico. Begun in 1991 and finished in September 1993, it is popularly known as La Catedral Nueva (New Cathedral). This mosque-like Catholic church is basically a squat, anti-seismic box with a beehive roof. The stark concrete interior has a post-nuclear feel with a modern altar reminiscent of a UN Security Council setting.

### ② Martha Quezada & Bolonia

**Where to stay** 🛏
Crowne Plaza **16**
Europeo **6**
Hostal Dulce Sueño **5**
La Posada del Angel **19**
Los Cisneros **20**
Los Felipe **21**
Mansión Teodolinda **1**
Posadita de Bolonia **11**

**Restaurants** 🍴
A La Vista Buffet **15**
Ananda **11**
El Churrasco **1**
La Casa de Los Mejía Godoy **2**
Mirna's **7**
Rancho Tiscapa **3**

**Bars & clubs** 🍸
Shannon Bar Irlandés **10**

South of the bizarre New Cathedral stands the big fountains of Rotonda Rubén Darío (Rubén Darío roundabout), right next to the cloistered Metrocentro shopping centre. From here, the Carretera a Masaya runs south to the Rotonda Centroamérica, thereafter passing the Camino de Oriente shopping centre and the upmarket Galerías Santo Domingo mall, finally exiting the city to connect with Nindirí, Masaya and Granada. The web of streets surrounding the northern section of the Carretera are home to middle-class residences, restaurants, bars, and galleries. The Universidad Centroamericana (UCA), where express buses to Granada and León depart, lies some 300 m west of Metrocentro.

3 **Metrocentro**

**Where to stay** 🛏
Aloha Bed & Breakfast **6**
Colibrí **8**
El Almendro **1**
Elements Boutique Hotel **11**
Los Robles **2**
Managua Backpackers'
  Inn **3**
Real Intercontinental
  Metrocentro **4**

**Restaurants** 🍴
Casa de Café **1**
Casa de las Nogueras **2**
Don Cándido **14**
Don Parrillón **15**
El Guapinol **16**
El Muelle **3**
El Tercer Ojo **11**
La Cocina de Doña
  Haydeé **6**

La Hora del Taco **7**
Terraza Cevichería **5**

**Bars & clubs** 🍸
Chamán **35**
Hipa Hipa **4**
Santera **12**

## Museo Las Huellas de Acahualinca

*Along the lake, 2 km due west of the Museo Nacional, T2266-5774, Tue-Fri 0900-1600, Sat-Sun 0900-1500, US$4 with an additional US$2 charged to take photographs and US$3 to use video cameras. Taxi recommended as it is hard to find.*

In 1874, during digging for quarry stone near the shores of Lake Managua, one of the oldest known evidences of human presence in Central America was found: footprints of men, women and children left in petrified subsoil. Radiocarbon-dated to 4000 BC, the tracks were imprinted in fresh volcanic mud, the product of a burning cloud eruption. What were these ancient ancestors doing when they made these perfectly preserved footprints? After numerous theories, studies have now determined that they were made by 10 different people walking upright, some weighed down, perhaps with children or supplies. The footprints were undoubtedly covered in volcanic sand shortly afterwards, preserving an ancient passage and a modern enigma. This small but interesting museum was created around the original excavation site of the so-called Huellas de Acahualinca ('footprints in the land of sunflowers').

## Las Sierras de Managua

Behind the suburban sprawl of Managua, Las Sierras rise 950 m above sea level into a broad area of forest and mountains. The region is home to two important nature reserves, including one of the Pacific basin's best birdwatching destinations, the **Reserva Privada Silvestre Montibelli** ① *Km 19, Carretera a Ticuantepe, T2220-9801, www.montibelli.com, Tue-Sun, turn right at the sign for the reserve and follow signs for 2.5 km, by reservation 3 days in advance only*. The 162-ha family-owned finca is home to more than 100 avian species including toucans, parrots, mot-mots, trogons, manikins and hummingbirds. Guided trekking costs US$15 per person (minimum two); a birdwatching or a butterfly tour with a local guide is US$45 per person with breakfast. Birders might also find inspiration in the 184-ha **Reserva Natural El Chocoyero** ① *Km 21.5, Carretera a Ticuantepe, turn right at the sign for the reserve and then follow signs for 7 km, T2276-7810, US$4, the rangers act as guides*. Pacific parakeets (*Aratinga strenua*) nest here in staggering numbers –there are around 700-900 couples – and the best place to see them is at the El Chocoyero waterfall where the cliffs are dotted with tiny holes that they use for nesting.

To get to Montibelli or El Chocoyero on public transport, take a bus from Mercado Israel Lewites (or La UCA, Managua's University bus terminal) to La Concepción or San Marcos and tell the driver you want to get off at the entrance; it is then a long dusty or muddy walk depending on the season. Taxis can be hired for US$40-60 return trip with a wait.

## Tourist information

**Nicaraguan Institute of Tourism (INTUR)**
(1 block south and 1 block west of the
Crowne Plaza Hotel (the old Intercontinental,
T2254-5191, www.visitanicaragua.com, Mon-
Fri 0800-1300). They have maps, flyers and
free brochures in English, but are generally
not geared up for public visits. The airport
INTUR is just past the immigration check.
Information on nature reserves and parks
can be found at the **Ministerio de Medio
Ambiente y Recursos Naturales (MARENA)**
(Km 12.5, Carretera Norte, T2263-2617,
www.marena.gob.ni, Mon-Fri 0800-1300).

## Where to stay

### Managua Airport

**$$$ Best Western Las Mercedes**
*Km 11 Carretera Norte, directly across from
international terminal of airport, T2255-9910,
www.lasmercedes.com.ni.*
Conveniently located for flight connections.
Rooms are generic and comfortable enough,
but poor value.

**$$$ Camino Real**
*Km 9.5 Carretera Norte, T2255-5888,
www.caminoreal.com.ni.*
A popular option for delayed passengers or
those en route to other destinations. Rooms
are comfortable, modern and well equipped,
but those close to the pool are often noisy
(early-risers take note).

### Martha Quezada

Commonly known as Ticabus after the
international bus terminal, Martha Quezada
has plentiful budget lodgings, most of
them very basic and grungy. The streets are
increasingly unsafe for wandering and you
should stay alert at all times.

**$$$$-$$$ Hotel Crowne Plaza**
*'El viejo Hotel Inter', in front of the Plaza
Inter shopping centre, T2228-3530,
www.crowneplaza.com.*
This is one of the most historic buildings
in Managua, home to the foreign press for
more than a decade and the new Sandinista
government briefly in the early 1980s. Some
rooms have lake views but are generally
small for the price.

**$$$ Mansión Teodolinda**
*INTUR, 1 c al sur, 1 c abajo, T2228-1050,
www.teodolinda.com.ni.*
This hotel, popular with business people, has
good quality, unpretentious rooms, all with
Wi-Fi and kitchenettes. There's also a pool,
bar, restaurant, gym, vehicle rental agency,
transport to/from the airport and laundry
service. Recommended.

**$$-$ Los Cisneros**
*Ticabus, 1 c al norte, 1½ c abajo, T2222-3535,
www.hotelloscisneros.com.*
Comfortable apartments and rooms
overlooking a lush garden with hammock
space. All have cable TV, a/c and Wi-Fi (at
extra cost), but only the apartments have hot
water. Rooms and apartments are cheaper
with fan. Los Cisneros can organize transit to
the airport and tours all over the country.

**$ Hostal Dulce Sueño**
*Ticabus, ½ c arriba, T2228-4195,
www.hostaldulcesueno.com.*
A stone's throw from the Ticabus terminal,
this budget hotel has clean, reasonable rooms
with fan and private bath (some have TV), and
a relaxing patio with rocking chairs. Simple,
family-run and economical. Kitchen and
laundry service, cooked breakfast on request.

**$ Los Felipe**
*Ticabus, 1½ c abajo, T2222-6501,
www.hotellosfelipe.com.ni.*
This hotel has a lovely garden, pool, cats and
many brightly coloured parrots, sadly caged

and in desperate need of stimulation. The 28 small, basic rooms have private bath, cable TV, Wi-Fi and telephone; cheaper with fan. A good deal for budget travellers, but can't be recommended due to the caged birds.

## Bolonia

### $$$ Hotel Europeo
*Canal 2, 75 vrs abajo, T2268-2130, www.hoteleuropeo.com.ni.*
Each room is different and some have interesting furnishings. The rooms out back are best. Restaurant, bar, business centre, secure parking, laundry service, guard and pool. Price includes continental breakfast. Staff are friendly and helpful. A quiet location.

### $$$ La Posada del Angel
*opposite Iglesia San Francisco, T2268-7228.*
This hotel, filled with interesting art work and antique furniture, has lots of personality. Good, clean rooms have private cable TV, a/c, minibar, Wi-Fi and telephone. There's also a pool, restaurant, office centre and laundry service. Breakfast is included. Book in advance.

### $$ Posadita de Bolonia
*Canal 2, 3 c abajo, 75 m al sur, casa 12, T2268-6692, www.posaditadebolonia.com.*
This intimate hotel has 8 rooms with private bath, a/c, cable TV, telephone and Wi-Fi. It's in a quiet area, close to several galleries, and operates as a **Costeña** agent. The friendly owner speaks English and is helpful. Breakfast included. Recommended.

## Metrocentro

### $$$$ Real Intercontinental Metrocentro
*Metrocentro shopping plaza, T2276-8989, www.realhotelsandresorts.com.*
Nicaragua's finest international hotel, popular with business travellers. It has 157 well-attired rooms, pool, restaurant, bar and secretary service. Special weekend and multi-day rates with some tour operators.

### $$$$-$$$ Elements Boutique Hotel
*Colonial Los Robles, contiguo a Plaza Cuba, T2277-0718, www.elements-hb.com.*
Stylish and tasteful, this smart place has slick rooms and suites, bar-lounge, garden, pool, gym and all modern amenities. Breakfast included.

### $$$ Hotel Los Robles
*Restaurante La Marseillaise, 30 vrs al sur, T2267-3008, www.hotellosrobles.com.*
Managua's best B&B offers 14 comfortable rooms with classy furnishings, cable TV, Wi-Fi and luxurious bathtubs. The beautiful colonial interior is complemented by a lush, cool garden, complete with bubbling fountain. Book in advance. Recommended.

### $$$-$$ Aloha Bed and Breakfast
*McDonald's Metrocentro, 1 c abajo, 2 c norte, T2277-0251, www.hotelalohanicaragua.com.*
Nestled in a quiet residential cul-de-sac, **Aloha** has comfortable rooms (some are a bit dark, ask to see before accepting) with good solid wooden furniture, cable TV, safe boxes and Wi-Fi. The lobby is clean and secure. Attentive service.

### $$$-$$ Hotel El Almendro
*Rotonda Rubén Darío, 1 c sur, 3 c abajo (behind big wall, ring bell), T2270-1260, www.hotelelalmendro.com.*
2 blocks from La UCA (the university), this private, secure hotel has good, comfortable rooms, pool, pleasant garden space, private parking and studio apartments (**$$$**) with kitchenettes. It's a decent choice. Breakfast included.

### $$ Colibrí
*Monte de los Olivos, 1 c al lago, 1½ c abajo, T2252-4300, www.colibrihotelmanagua.com.*
A clean, decent, well-kept hotel with a pleasant little garden. Rooms are small and simple, comfortable and well attired and include cable TV, a/c, safe and Wi-Fi. Breakfast also included. Tranquil, secure and good access to a few nearby restaurants.

### $$-$ Managua Backpackers' Inn
*Monte Los Olivos, 1 c al lago, 1 c abajo,
½ c al lago, Casa 55, T2267-0006,
www.managuahostel.com.*
The only budget hostel in the Metrocentro
area is kitted out with thrifty dorms ($)
and simple private rooms ($$-$). There's
also a pool, hammocks and shared kitchen.
They offer tourist information and are happy
to help.

## Restaurants

The Metrocentro shopping centre has
several good restaurants ($) in its food
court on the bottom level, including
cheaper versions of good Nicaraguan
restaurants. Lunch buffets are not all-you-
can-eat: rather, you are charged for what
you ask to be put on your plate, but this is
still the most economical way to eat a big
meal in Managua.

### Martha Quezada

### $$ Ananda
*Estatua de Montoya 10 vrs arriba,
T2228-4140. Daily 0700-2100.*
Nicaragua's original non-meat eatery and
still one of the best. They serve wholesome
vegetarian food, juices, smoothies, breakfasts
and soups.

### $$ La Casa de Los Mejía Godoy
*Costado oeste del Hotel Crowne Plaza,
T2222-6110, www.losmejiagodoy.com.
Mon-Tue 0800-1630, Wed-Sat 0800-1300.*
This famous terraced restaurant regularly
hosts nationally renowned live music acts.
They serve Nicaraguan cuisine, wholesome
breakfasts and good, cheap lunch buffets
(Mon-Fri only). Very popular. Recommended.

### $$ Rancho Tiscapa
*Gate at Military Hospital, 300 vrs sur,
T2268-4290.*
Laid-back ranch-style eatery and bar. They
serve traditional dishes like *indio viejo, gallo
pinto* and *cuajada con tortilla*. Good food and

a great, breezy view of new Managua and
Las Sierras. Recommended.

### $ Mirna's
*Near Pensión Norma. Open 0700-1500.*
Good-value breakfasts and *comidas*,
lunch buffet 1200-1500 popular with
travellers and Nicaraguans, friendly service.
Recommended.

### Bolonia

### $$$ El Churrasco
*Rotonda El Güegüence, T2266-6661,
www.restauranteelchurrasco.com.*
This is where the Nicaraguan president and
parliamentary members decide the country's
future over a big steak. Try the restaurant's
namesake which is an Argentine-style
cut with garlic and parsley sauce.
Recommended.

### $ A La Vista Buffet
*Canal 2, 2 c abajo, ½ c lago (next to Pulpería
América). Lunch only 1130-1430.*
Nicaragua's best lunch buffet. They do
a staggering and inexpensive variety of
pork, chicken, beef, rice dishes, salads and
vegetable mixers, plantains, potato crêpes
and fruit drinks. Popular with local television
crews and reporters, as well as local office
workers, who are often queueing down the
street at midday. Highly recommended.

### Metrocentro

### $$$ Casa de las Nogueras
*Av Principal Los Robles No R 17, T2278-2506.*
A popular and often-recommended high-
class dining establishment. They serve fine
international and Mediterranean cuisine
on a pleasant colonial patio. The interior,
meanwhile, boasts sumptuous and ornate
decoration. A Managua institution.

### $$$ Don Cándido
*Where El Chamán used to be, 75 vrs sur, T2277-
2485, www.restaurantedoncandido.com.*
The place to enjoy a good grilled steak.
Carnivores will delight at the array of

well-presented options, including cuts of *churrasco*, tenderloin, rib-eye, fillet, New York and many others. All meat is certified 100% Aberdeen Angus.

### $$$-$$ Don Parrillón
*Zona Hippos, 2 c sur, T2270-0471.*
Another meat and grill option conveniently located in the heart of Managua's Zona Rosa. Look for the little chimney chugging away on the street.

### $$ El Muelle
*Intercontinental Metrocentro, 1½ c arriba, T2278-0056.*
Managua's best seafood. There's excellent *pargo al vapor* (steamed red snapper), *dorado a la parrilla*, *cocktail de pulpo* (octopus) and great ceviche. It's a crowded, informal setting with outdoor seating. Highly recommended.

### $$ El Tercer Ojo
*Hotel Seminole, 2½ c sur, T2277-4787, el.com.ni. Daily 1500-0200.*
'The Third Eye' strives for fusion cuisine with mixed success. The interior is imaginative and interesting. Good DJs on some nights.

### $$ La Cocina de Doña Haydée
*Opposite Pastelería Aurami, Planes de Altamira, T2270-6100, www.lacocina.com.ni. Mon-Sun 0730-2230.*
Once a popular family kitchen eatery that has gone upscale. They serve traditional Nicaraguan food; try the *surtido* dish for 2, the *nacatamales* and traditional *Pío V* dessert, a sumptuous rum cake. Popular with foreign residents.

### $$ La Hora del Taco
*Monte de los Olivos, 1 c al lago, on Calle Los Robles, T2277-5074.*
Good Mexican dishes including fajitas and burritos. A warm, relaxed atmosphere.

### $ El Guapinol
*www.restauranteelguapinol.com. From 1000 daily.*
The best of the food court eateries with excellent grilled meat dishes, chicken, fish and a hearty veggie dish (US$5). Try *copinol*, a dish with grilled beef, avocado, fried cheese, salad and tortilla and *gallo pinto*, US$4.

### $ Terraza Cevichería
*Monte de los Olivos, 1 c al lago, 1 c abajo.*
A simple little restaurant serving good-value, tasty, fresh ceviche, seafood and cold beer. Their shrimp and octopus salad claims to be the best in town. There's an open-air seating area, always packed at lunchtime.

## Cafés

### Casa de Café
*Lacmiel, 1 c arriba, 1½ c sur, T2278-0605. Mon-Sun 0700-2200.*
The mother of all cafés in Managua, with an airy upstairs seating area that makes the average coffee taste much better. Good turkey sandwiches, desserts, pies and *empanadas*. There's another branch on the 2nd level of the Metrocentro shopping plaza, but it lacks the charm and fresh air. Popular and recommended.

## Bars and clubs

The biggest rage in Nicaragua dancing is *reggaeton*, a Spanish language rap-reggae. Dancing is an integral part of Nicaraguan life, at any age, and the line between *el bar* and *la discoteca* is not very well defined. Generally, people over 30 dance at bars and the discos are for 18-30 years.

### Bar Chamán
*Universidad Nacional de Ingeniería (UNI), 1½ c norte, T2272-1873, www.chamanbar.com.*
US$3 entrance which includes US$1.50 drinks coupon. A young, devout dancing crowd sweats it out to salsa, rock and reggaeton.

### Hipa Hipa
*Km 7.5 Carretera a Masaya, Plaza Familiar, www.elhipa.com.*
Dress smartly for this popular disco, a favourite among Managua's rich kids. The best action is on Wed, Fri and Sat night; cover includes a few drinks.

## Santera

*de Pizza Valenti, 80 m al Norte, T2278-8585.*
In addition to live poetry, theatre and music performances, Santera features an eclectic mix of musical genres, including jazz, pop, reggae and salsa. Relaxed, bohemian and friendly. Snacks and national beers are served.

## Shannon Bar Irlandés

*Ticabus, 1 c arriba, 1 c sur.*
Fabled Irish pub serving fast food, whisky and expensive Guinness. A Managua institution and popular with an international crowd.

## Entertainment

### Cinema

If possible, see a comedy; the unrestrained laughter of the Nicaraguan audience is sure to make the movie much funnier. You'll find screens at all the city's big shopping malls (see Shopping, below). Alternatively, try: **Alianza Francesa**, *Altamira, Mexican Embassy, ½ c norte, T2267-2811, www. alianzafrancesa.org.ni.* French films every Wed and Sat at 2000, free admission, art exhibits during the day.

### Dance and theatre

Managua has no regular dance and theatre performances so it will take a bit of research to time your visit to coincide with a live show. To find out what's on the cultural and musical calendar for the weekend in Managua, Granada and León, check the *La Prensa* supplement *Viernes Chiquito* every Thu.

## Festivals

**19 Jul 19 de Julio** is the anniversary of the fall of the last Somoza in 1979, a Sandinista party in front of the stage with the big acoustic shell at the *malecón*. The party attracts around 100,000 plus from all over the country; don't forget to wear the Sandinista colours of black and red.
**1-10 Aug** On 1 Aug a statue of **Santo Domingo**, Managua's patron saint and Nicaragua's most diminutive saint, is brought from his hilltop church in Santo Domingo in the southern outskirts of Managua, in a crowded and heavily guarded (by riot police) procession to central Managua.
**7 Dec La Purísima**, celebrating the purity of the Virgin countrywide and particularly in Managua in the more than 600 barrios of the city. Private altars are erected to the Virgin Mary and food gifts are given to those who arrive to sing to the altars, with some families serving up as many as 5000 *nacatamales* in a night.

## Shopping

### Handicrafts

The best place for handicrafts in Managua is the **Mercado Central Roberto Huembes**, where there's an ample selection from most of the country artisans. **Note** All the markets have some crafts, but avoid the **Mercado Oriental**. Possibly the biggest informal market in Latin America, this is the heart of darkness in Managua and unsafe for casual exploration. The most complete of the non-market artisan shops is **Galería Códice** (Colonial Los Robles, Hotel Colón, 1 c sur, 2½ c arriba, No 15, T2267-2635, www. galeriacodice.com, Mon-Sat 0900-1830), whose selection includes rarely found items like rosewood carvings from the Caribbean coast and ceramic dolls from Somoto.

### Shopping malls

The 3 big shopping malls, in order of increasing social exclusivity, are the Plaza Inter, Metrocentro and Galerías Santo Domingo. The cinemas are better in Santo Domingo and Plaza Inter, but the food court is much better in Metrocentro.

### Supermarkets

3 big chains are represented in Managua, **Supermercado La Colonia** being the best. It is located in Plaza España and at the roundabout in the Centroamérica neighbourhood. **Supermercado La Unión**, on Carretera a Masaya, is similar

to La Colonia. **Supermercados Pali**, branches of which can be found scattered around the city, is the cheapest, with goods still in their shipping boxes.

## What to do

### Baseball
The national sport and passion is baseball, which has been established in Nicaragua for more than 100 years. Games in Managua are on Sun mornings at the national stadium, **Estadio Denis Martínez**, just north of the Barrio Martha Quezada. Check the local newspapers for the game schedule. Seats cost US$1-5 per person.

### Language schools
**Academia Europea**, *Hotel Princess, 1 c abajo, ½ c sur, T2278-0829*. The best school in Managua, with structured classes of varying lengths and qualified instructors.
**Universidad Centroamericana**, *better known as La UCA, T2278-3923 and T2267-0352, www.uca.edu.ni*. Runs Spanish courses that are cheaper than some private institutions, but with larger classes.

### Tour operators
See also local tour operators throughout the book.
**Careli Tours**, *Planes de Altamira, opposite the Colegio Pedagógico La Salle, T2278-6919, www. carelitours.com*. One of Nicaragua's oldest tour operators with a professional service, very good English speaking guides and traditional tours to all parts of Nicaragua.
**Solentiname Tours**, *Apartado Postal 1388, T2270-9981, www.solentiname.com*. Eco-friendly tours of the lake, Caribbean coast, colonial cities and Río San Juan. Spanish, English, German, French and Russian spoken.
**Tours Nicaragua**, *Centro Richardson, contiguo al Banco Central de Nicaragua, T2265-3095, www.toursnicaragua.com*. One of the best, offering captivating and personalized tours with a cultural, historical or ecological emphasis. Guides, transfers, accommodation and admission costs are included in the price. English speaking, helpful, professional and highly recommended. All tours are private and pre-booked; no walk-ins please.

## Transport

### Air
**Managua International Airport** is on the eastern outskirts of Managua. Upon landing you must pay US$10 at the immigration counter. Taxis to Metrocentro, Bolonia or Martha Quezada should cost US$5-10, but airport taxis may try to charge double; journey time is 20-30 mins in good traffic. Be sure to have precise directions in Spanish and use licensed vehicles only. A taxi hailed on the highway outside will charge US$5-6, but these are less secure and should be avoided if arriving after dark.

**Domestic flights** Nicaragua's sole domestic airline is **La Costeña**, T2263-2142, www.lacostena.com.ni, which operates a small fleet of single-prop Cessna Caravans and 2-prop Short 360s. In the Cessnas there is no room for overhead lockers, so pack light and check in all you can. For checked luggage on all flights there is a 15-kg weight limit per person for one-way flight, 25 kg for round-trip tickets; any excess is payable on check-in. There is a US$2 exit tax on domestic flights.

Tickets can be bought at the domestic terminal, which is located just west of the exit for arriving international passengers, or from travel agents or tour operators.

Fuel and ticket prices are rising and schedules are subject to change at any time.

To **Bilwi**, 0630, 1030, 1400 (Mon-Sat only), US$97 one-way, US$148 return, 1½ hrs. To **Bluefields**, 0615, 0900 (Mon-Sat only), 1430, US$83 one-way, US$128 return, 1 hr. To **Corn Islands**, 0615, 1430, US$107 one-way, US$165 return, 1½ hrs.

To **Minas**, 0900, US$92 one-way, US$139 return, 1 hr. To **San Carlos**, Thu and Sun, 1200, US$82 one-way, US$120 return, 1 hr. To **San Juan de Nicaragua**, Thu and Sun,

1200, US$102 one-way, US$140 return. Flights to Waspam were suspended at the time of research. For return times see individual destinations.

**International flights** You should reconfirm your flight out of Nicaragua 48 hrs in advance by calling the local airline office during business hours Mon-Sat. Most good hotels will provide this service. There's a US$35 exit tax on all international flights, sometimes included in the price of your ticket.

## Bus

International bus companies provide comfortable transportation from all capitals of Central America. The 2 main ones are **Transnica**, near Metrocentro, and **Ticabus** in Martha Quezada district. Taxis wait at the bus stations; transfers to central hotels are normally around US$4-5.

**Intercity buses** *Bus Expresos* are dramatically faster than regular routes. Payment is often required in advance and seat reservations are becoming more common.

The microbuses at **La UCA** (pronounced 'La OO-ka'), close to the Metrocentro and opposite the University, are highly recommended if travelling to Granada, León or Masaya. To **Granada**, every 15 mins or when full, 0530-2100, US$1.25, 1 hr. To **Diriamba**, every 30 mins or when full, 0530-2000, US$1.15, 45 mins. To **Jinotepe**, 0530-2000, every 20 mins or when full, US$1.15, 1 hr. To **León**, every 30 mins, 0730-2100, US$2.75, 1½ hrs. To **Masaya**, every 15 mins or when full, 0530-2000, US$0.75, 40 mins.

**Mercado Roberto Huembes**, also called Mercado Central, is used for destinations southwest. To **Granada**, every 15 mins, 0520-2200, Sun 0610-2100, US$0.75, 1½ hrs. To **Masaya**, every 20 mins, 0625-1930, Sun until 1600, US$0.50, 50 mins. To **Peñas Blancas**, every 30 mins or when full, US$3.50, 2½ hrs; or go to Rivas for connections. To **Rivas**, every 30 mins, 0600-1900, US$2, 1¾ hrs. To **San**

**Juan del Sur**, 1000 and 1600, US$3.25, 2½ hrs; or go to Rivas for connections To **San Jorge** (ferry to Ometepe), every 30 mins, 0600-2100, US$2.20, 2 hrs; or go to Rivas for connections.

**Mercado Mayoreo**, for destinations east and then north or south. To **Boaco**, every 20 mins, 0500-1800, US$2, 3hrs. To **Camoapa**, every 40 mins, 0630-1700, US$2.20, 3 hrs. To **El Rama**, 5 daily, 0500-2200, US$7.50, 6-7 hrs; express bus 1400, 1800, 2200, US$9, 5-6 hrs. To **Estelí**, express bus, hourly 0545-1730, US$3, 2½ hrs. To **Jinotega**, hourly, 0400-1730, US$3.50, 4 hrs; or go to Matagalpa for connections. To **Juigalpa**, every 20 mins, 0500-1730, US$2.50, 4 hrs. To **Matagalpa**, express bus, hourly, 0330-1800, US$2.10, 2½ hrs. To **Ocotal**, express buses, 12 daily, 0545-1745, US$4.50, 3½ hrs. To **San Rafael del Norte**, express bus, 1500, US$5, 4 hrs. To **San Carlos**, 0500, 0600, 0700, 1300, US$8, 7-10 hrs. To **Somoto**, 8 daily, US$4, 4 hrs.

**Mercado Israel Lewites**, also called Mercado Boer, for destinations west and northwest. Some microbuses leave from here too. To **Chinandega**, express buses, every 30 mins, 0600-1915, US$3, 2½ hrs. To **Corinto**, every hour, 0500-1715, US$3.50, 3 hrs. To **Diriamba**, every 20 mins, 0530-1930, US$1.10, 1 hr 15 mins. To **El Sauce**, express buses, 0730, 1430, 1600, US$3.25, 3½ hrs. To **Guasaule**, 0430, 0530, 1530, US$3.25, 4 hrs. To **Jinotepe**, every 20 mins, 0530-1930, US$0.50, 1 hr 30 mins. To **León**, every 30 mins, 0545-1645, US$1.50, 2½ hrs; express buses, every 30 mins, 0500-1645, US$1.85, 2 hrs; microbuses, every 30 mins or when full, 0600-1700, US$2.75, 1½ hrs. To **Pochomil**, every 20 mins, 0600-1920, US$1.10, 2 hrs.

**International buses** If time isn't a critical issue, international buses are a cheap and efficient way to travel between Nicaragua and other Central American countries. When leaving Managua you will need to check in 1 hr in advance with passport and ticket. Several companies operate the international routes, but **Ticabus** is the most popular.

## Car

From the south, the Carretera a Masaya leads directly to Managua's new centre, Metrocentro; try to avoid arriving from this direction from 0700-0900 when the entrance to the city is heavily congested. The Pan-American Highway (Carretera Panamericana) enters Managua at the international airport and skirts the eastern shores of Lake Managua. Stay on this highway until you reach the old centre before attempting to turn south in search of the new one. Avenida Bolívar runs south from the old centre past the Plaza Inter shopping centre and into the heart of new Managua; turn east onto the Pista de la Resistencia to reach the Metrocentro shopping mall. If arriving from León and the northwest you need to head east from Km 7 of Carretera Sur to find new Managua.

**Car hire** All agencies have rental desks at the international airport arrivals terminal. It is not a good idea to rent a car for getting around Managua, as it is a confusing city, fender benders are common and an accident could see you end up in jail (even if you are not at fault). Outside the capital, main roads are better marked and a rental car means you can get around more freely.

For good service and 24-hr roadside assistance, the best rental agency is **Budget**, with rental cars at the airport, T2263-1222, and Holiday Inn, T2270-9669. Their main office is just off Carretera Sur, Estatua de Montoya, 1 c al sur, 1 c arriba, T2255-0001. Approximate cost of a small Toyota is US$50 per day while a 4WD (a good idea if exploring) is around US$100 per day with insurance and 200 km a day included; 4WD weekly rental rates range from US$600-750.

## Taxi

Taxis without red licence plates are *piratas* (unregistered); avoid them. Taxis can be flagged down in the street. Find out the fare before you board the vehicle. Fares are always per person, not per car. Taxis hired from the airport or shopping malls are more expensive but secure.

**Radio taxis** pick you up and do not stop for other passengers; they are much more secure for this reason and cost twice as much: **Cooperativa 25 de Febrero**, T2222-4728; **Cooperativa 2 de Agosto**, T2263-1512; **Cooperativa René Chávez**, T2222-3293; **Cooperativa Mario Lizano**, T2268-7669. Get a quote on the phone and reconfirm agreed cost when the taxi arrives.

# Masaya
## & around

Overlooked by ancient volcanoes and home to communities still rooted in their distant indigenous past, Masaya and the surrounding *pueblos blancos* are distinguished by archaic folklore and vibrant craftwork. Irresistibly sleepy until fiesta time, these ancient settlements play host to bustling workshops, Nicaragua's best *artesanía* market and a famously hospitable population who are directly descended from the Chorotega peoples. Among their attributes is a fierce and indomitable spirit that has been roused time and again during difficult periods. It was here that the legendary chief Dirangén fought against the Spaniards; here that bloody rebellions erupted against Somoza; and here that the nation made a final stand against US invader William Walker. It is no surprise then that the region also spawned Augusto Sandino, Nicaragua's most celebrated revolutionary.

**Best** for
Crafts ■ Crater lakes ■ Hiking ■ Volcanic views

Nearly every barrio in Masaya (altitude 234 m, population 140,000) has its own little church, but two dominate the city. In Masaya's leafy Parque Central is La Parroquia de Nuestra Señora de la Asunción, a late baroque church that dates from 1750. The clean lines and simple elegance of its interior make it one of the most attractive churches in Nicaragua and well worth a visit.

San Jerónimo, though not on Parque Central, is the spiritual heart of Masaya. This attractive domed church, visible from miles around, is home to the city's patron Saint Jerome and a focal point for his more than two-month-long festival. The celebration begins on 30 September and continues until early December, making it by far the longest

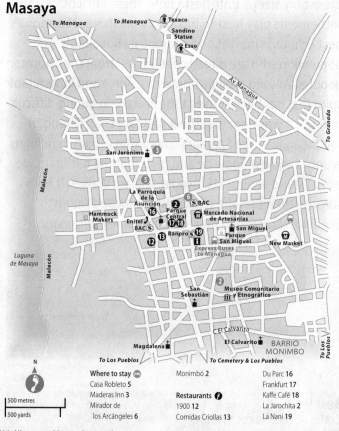

**Masaya**

*To Managua*    *To Managua*   Texaco

Sandino Statue

Esso

*Av Managua*

*To Granada*

*Malecón*

San Jerónimo **3**

**5**

La Parroquia de la Asunción

**6** BAC

Hammock Makers

Enitel
BAC **16** Parque Central **2**

**17 18** Banpro **19**

**13**

**12**

Mercado Nacional de Artesanías

San Miguel

Parque San Miguel

New Market

Express Buses to Managua

*Laguna de Masaya*

*Malecón*

San Sebastián **2**

Museo Comunitario y Etnográfico

C El Calvarito

Magdalena

El Calvarito

BARRIO MONIMBÓ

*To Los Pueblos*

*To Los Pueblos*

*To Cemetery & Los Pueblos*

*To Los Pueblos*

**N**

500 metres
500 yards

**Where to stay**
Casa Robleto **5**
Maderas Inn **3**
Mirador de los Arcángeles **6**

Monimbó **2**

**Restaurants**
1900 **12**
Comidas Criollas **13**

Du Parc **16**
Frankfurt **17**
Kaffe Café **18**
La Jarochita **2**
La Nani **19**

patron saint festival in Nicaragua and perhaps in Latin America. The downtown area can be explored on foot.

## Mercado Nacional de Artesanías
*Southeast corner of Parque Central, 1 c arriba, daily 0900-1800; folkloric performances Thu 1900-2200. There is a DHL office open daily 1000-1700 inside the market in case you end up buying more than you can carry.*

Most people come to Masaya to shop and the country's best craft market is here in the 19th-century Mercado Nacional de Artesanías. The late Gothic walls of the original market were damaged by shelling and the inside of the market burned during the 1978-1979 Revolution. After two decades of sitting in ruins it is today dedicated exclusively to handmade crafts.

There are 80 exhibition booths and several restaurants inside the market. Leather, ceramics, cigars, hammocks, soapstone sculptures, masks, textiles and primitivista paintings are just some of the goods on offer. Every Thursday night from 1900 to 2200 there is a live performance on the market's stage. These usually include one of Masaya's many folkloric dance groups with beautifully costumed performers and live marimba music accompaniment.

A **folkloric museum** ① *US$2*, located inside the market near the administrative offices, features photographic exhibitions, costumes, musical instruments and crafts from Masaya and around.

## Laguna de Masaya and El Malecón
The best view of the deep blue 27-sq-km Laguna de Masaya and the Masaya volcanic complex is from the *malecón*, or waterfront, often frequented by romantic couples. The lake is 300 m below, sadly polluted and unfit for swimming. Before the pump was installed in the late 19th century, all of the town's water was brought up from the lake in ceramic vases on women's heads: a 24-hour-a-day activity according to British naturalist Thomas Belt who marvelled at the ease with which the Masaya women dropped down into the crater and glided back out with a full load of water. There are more than 200 petroglyphs on the walls of the descent, but no official guides to take you; try the INTUR office or ask around locally.

## Comunidad Indígena de Monimbó
The famous indigenous barrio of Monimbó is the heart and soul of Masaya. The Council of Elders, a surviving form of native government, still exists here and the beating of drums of deerskin stretched over an avocado trunk still calls people to festival and meetings and, in times of trouble, to war. In 1978, the people of Monimbó rebelled against Somoza's repressive Guardia Nacional, holding the barrio for one week using home-made contact bombs and other revolutionary handicrafts. This and other proud moments in Monimbó's revolutionary past are documented in the flag-draped **Museo Comunitario y Etnográfico La Insurrección de Monimbó** ① *Damas Salesianas 1½ c arriba, orlancabrera@hotmail.com, Mon-Fri 0900-1600, US$0.50.*

The neighbourhood is also famous for its industrious artisan workshops, which export their output all over Central America. They can be toured independently, but it is much easier to enlist a local guide. The highest concentration of workshops is located between the unattractive Iglesia Magdalena and the cemetery.

## Fortaleza de Coyotepe

*Carretera Masaya Km 28. Daily 0900-1600, US$2. Bring a torch/flashlight, or offer the guide US$2 to show you the cells below. The access road is a steep but short climb from the Carretera a Masaya, parking U$1.*

Just outside Masaya city limits is the extinct volcanic cone of Coyotepe (Coyote Hill) and a post-colonial fortress. The fortress was built in 1893 by the Liberal president José Santos Zelaya to defend his control of Masaya and Managua from the Conservatives of Granada. In 1912, it saw action as the Liberals battled the US Marines and lost. Though donated to the Boy Scouts of Masaya during the 1960s, the fortress was used by the second General Somoza as a political prison. There are 43 cells on two floors that can be visited; people have reported hearing the distant echo of screams. The top deck offers a splendid 360-degree view of Masaya, Laguna de Masaya and the Masaya volcanoes, and on to Granada and its Volcán Mombacho.

## Listings Masaya *map p614*

### Tourist information

**INTUR**
*Banpro, ½ c sur, just south of the artisan market, T2522-7615, masaya@intur.gob.ni. Mon-Fri 0800-1300.*
INTUR has a branch office in Masaya. They have maps of the city, flyers and information on events, but are otherwise not very useful.

### Where to stay

Quality lodging in Masaya is very limited due to its proximity to Managua and Granada.

**$$ Hotel Monimbó**
*Plaza Pedro Joaquín Chomorro, 1 c arriba, 1½ c norte, T2522-6867, hotelmonimbo04@hotmail.com.*
The best place in town, situated in the barrio of Monimbó. 7 clean, quiet, comfortable, well-attired rooms with private bath, pleasant patio and garden space with relaxing hammocks. Breakfast included. Recommended.

**$$-$ Casa Robleto**
*Av San Jerónimo, Parque San Jerónimo, 1½ c sur.*
A traditional Nicaraguan guesthouse in an attractive colonial building, ably operated by the hospitable Don Frank and his family. Clean, simple, restful rooms overlook the interior courtyard while the lobby features elegant finishes and antique furniture.

**$$-$ Maderas Inn**
*Bomberos, 2 c sur, T2522-5825, www.hotelmaderasinn.com.*
A friendly little place with a pleasant family ambience and a variety of basic, slightly grungy rooms kitted out with private bath, a/c, cable TV. Several other economical options on the same street.

**$$-$ Mirador del los Arcángeles**
*Mercado de Artesanías, 1½ c norte, T2522-3796, sirdi.16@hotmail.com.*
A grand old building built at the turn of the 20th century. Rooms are on 2 floors and include cold-water showers and cable TV. Those with a/c cost more (**$$**). Do not leave valuable items unattended in the room. Wi-Fi available.

### Restaurants

**$$$-$ Frankfurt**
*East side of the Parque Central, same building as Kaffe Café.*
A clean, airy restaurant serving tasty sausages with sauerkraut (**$**), including German, Italian and Spanish varieties, as well

heartier and more elaborate *platos fuertes*
($$$), such as red snapper, meat platters
and steak in Béarnaise sauce. 'Beer and
bratwurst'. Good.

### $$ La Jarochita
*East side of the Parque Central, 50 vrs norte,
T2522-2186. Daily 1100-2200.*
The best Mexican in Nicaragua; some drive
from Managua just to eat here. Try *sopa
de tortilla* and chicken *enchiladas* in *mole*
sauce, *chimichangas* and Mexican beer.
Recommended.

### $$-$ 1900
*Palí Central, ½ c sur. Closed Mon.*
A well-presented restaurant with huge
wooden gates and an outdoor patio with
a small performance stage. They serve
steaks, seafood, crêpes, sandwiches,
coffee and wine. A good-value executive
menu ($) is available for lunch Tue-Fri.

### $$-$ Du Parc
*North side of the Parque Central.*
A French-style café-restaurant serving
wholesome international fare. Offerings
include paninis, crêpes, burgers and pork
chops. Indoor and outdoor seating is
available, including a small terrace on the
pavement, good for people-watching.

### $ Comidas Criollas
*South side of Parque Central.*
This large, clean, buffet restaurant serves
up healthy portions of Nica fare.

### Cafés and bakeries

#### Kaffe Café
*East side of the Parque Central.*
Good strong coffees, cappuccinos,
lattes and frappés. Food available from the
German restaurant next door. Patio seating
inside or outdoors overlooking the park.

#### La Nani
*Opposite the southern entrance of the
artesanía market.*
A clean, modern coffee shop serving good
brews, bread, pastries and typical café fare,
including sandwiches.

## Transport

There are frequent bus services from
Managua's Roberto Huembes market and
La UCA bus station, as well as Granada's bus
terminals. Many buses (including those with
final destinations other than Masaya) do not
pass through the city centre, but drop you
at the traffic lights on the highway, several
blocks north of the Parque Central.

**Bus** Most buses depart from the regular
market or Mercado Municipal, 4 blocks
east of the south side of the artisan
market. Express bus to **Managua** (Roberto
Huembes), every 20 mins, 0500-1900,
US$0.60, 50 mins. To **Jinotepe**, every
20 mins, 0500-1800, US$0.80, 1½ hrs. To
**Granada**, every 30 mins, 0600-1800, US$0.50,
45 mins. To **Matagalpa**, 0600, 0700, US$2.75,
4 hrs (schedule subject to change).

From Parque San Miguelito, between
the artisan and regular markets on Calle
San Miguel, express buses leave for La UCA
in **Managua**, every 30 mins, 0530-1900,
US$0.60, 40 mins. You can also board any bus
on the Carretera a Masaya to **Managua** or
towards **Granada**. Note the sign above front
windscreen for destination and flag it down.
For **Parque Nacional Volcán Masaya** take
any Managua bus and ask to step down at
park entrance. Buses to **Valle de Apoyo** leave
twice daily, 1000, 1530, 45 mins, US$0.70, then
walk down the road that drops into the crater.

**Taxi** Fares around town are US$0.40 per
person anywhere in the city. Approximate
taxi fares to: **Granada** US$15, **Laguna de
Apoyo**, US$7, **Managua** US$20, **airport**
US$25. Horse-drawn carriages (*coches*) are
for local transport inside Masaya, US$0.50.

Masaya's intriguing cultural assets are complemented by vivid physical landscapes, including the area around Volcán Masaya, which has been threatening cataclysm for centuries. Hiking trails snake up and around the angry giant, promising unforgettable olfactory encounters and stirring views.

Nearby, the infinitely more sedate Laguna Apoyo is the country's most alluring crater lake, with eternally warm, soothing waters heated by underwater vents. This is a special, peaceful place that is largely unspoiled (although increasingly threatened) by human activities. The surrounding *mesa* of highland villages, known as Los Pueblos Blancos, with their historic churches and spirited festivals, extends all the way from Laguna de Apoyo to the Pacific coast.

## Parque Nacional Volcán Masaya
*T2528-1444, pvmasaya@ideay.net.ni, 0900-1645, US$4, including entrance to the museum. Any bus that runs between Masaya and Managua can drop you at the park entrance, Km 23, Carretera a Masaya, but the long, hot, uphill walk to the visitor centre, 1.5km away, make a hired taxi (US$1.50), tour company or private car a valuable asset. Hitching is possible, as are guided hikes, US$0.70-3 per person payable at the museum before you set out.*

The heavily smoking Volcán Masaya complex is one of the most unusual volcanoes in the Americas and reported to be one of only four on earth that maintain a constant pool of lava (neither receding nor discharging) in its open crater. It is a place of eerie beauty with its rugged lunar landscapes punctuated by delicate plant life. The main attraction, the smoldering Santiago crater, seems almost peaceful – until one recalls that it is an open vent to the centre of the earth and prone to sudden acts of geological violence.

The complex was called Popogatepe ('burning mountain') by the Chorotega people. In 1529, the Spanish chronicler Oviedo wrote that there were many ceremonies at the base of the mountain, including the supposed sacrifice of young women and boys to appease Chacitutique, the goddess of fire. In the adjacent village of Nindirí, Chief Tenderí told Oviedo about a magical fortune-teller who lived inside the crater: a very ugly old woman, naked, with black teeth, wrinkled skin and tangled hair. Oviedo became convinced that she was the Devil. Around the same time Friar Francisco de Bobadilla hiked to the summit to perform an exorcism and place a large wooden cross above the lava pool to keep the door to Hell (the lava pool) shut.

As it appears today, the Santiago crater, 500 m in circumference and 250 m deep, was created after a violent eruption in 1853. It erupted again in 1858 and fell silent until the 20th century, when it erupted in 1902, 1918, 1921, 1924, 1925, 1947, 1953 and 1965, before collapsing in 1985. In early 2001 the crater's gaseous output came almost to a complete stop and on 23 April 2001 the resulting pressure created a minor eruption. Debris pelted the parking area at the summit (during visiting hours) with hundreds of flaming rocks. Exactly 10 minutes later the crater shot some tubes of lava on to the hillside just east of the parking area, setting it ablaze. Miraculously there were only minor injuries but several vehicles were badly damaged by falling stones. There have been no major explosions since then, but volcanologists noted significant episodes of gas and ash emission, as well as visible incandescence from the crater, in the years 2003 to 2006 and 2008. In 2012, the volcano spat out some hot rocks and began making ominous groaning noises; the park was temporarily closed to visitors, reopening several days later.

During your visit, watch out for any significant change in smoke colour, or any persistent rumbling, which may indicate a pending eruption. Do not spend more than 20 minutes at the crater's edge, especially with children, as the steam and smoke are very toxic. Asthmatics may want to avoid the area altogether (or should at least pack the appropriate inhalers). The park boasts 20 km of trails and the rangers at the visitor centre can tell you which ones are open. **Night tours** provide your best chance to see the red hot lava simmering beneath the earth's surface. They depart daily, 1700, US$10, with a minimum of six people, 2½ hours, book at least one day in advance. The real heroes of the park are the bright green parakeets that nest in the truly toxic environment of the active Santiago crater. They can be spotted late in the afternoon returning to their nests, chattering and soaring happily through the suffocating clouds of hydrochloric acid and sulphur dioxide.

## ★ Reserva Natural Laguna de Apoyo

Heated by thermal vents, Nicaragua's most beautiful crater lake, Laguna de Apoyo, is clean, clear, comfortably warm, and rich in minerals. Swimming here is a rejuvenating experience, but many come just to gaze at the changing colours of the lake's hypnotic surface. Created by a massive volcanic explosion some 23,000 years ago, the drop from the crater's edge to the lake is more than 400 m. The lake itself is 6 km in diameter. Access to the inside of the crater is from two cobbled roads, one that starts near Monimbó and the other from the Carretera a Granada at Km 37.5. Both end in a tiny settlement called Valle de Apoyo that sits at the crater's north rim. From there, a steep road slices down the northern wall to the lake shore, where you'll find hotels and hostels offering day use of their facilities. It's easiest to go by car, but infrequent buses do run. There are daily departures to Valle de Apoyo from Masaya, or regular buses between Masaya and Granada; get off at Km 37.5 and walk up the 5-km access road. Hitchhiking is possible though traffic is sparse on weekdays. In Granada, several hostels including the **Bearded Monkey**, **Oasis** and **La Libertad** offer daily transfers to Apoyo; they depart around 1000-1100, US$6 round-trip (does not include day use of facilities at the lake). The other alternative is a taxi from Granada (US$10-15) or Masaya (US$5-7) or Managua (US$20-25).

## Los Pueblos Blancos

Los Pueblos Blancos are politically divided by the provinces of Masaya, Granada and Carazo, but they are really one continuous settlement. This area, like Monimbó and Nindirí, is the land of the Chorotegas, and the local people have a very quiet but firm pride in their pre-Conquest history and culture.

Popular with day trippers from Granada, the attractive hillside village of **Catarina** has a simple church built and an obvious love of potted plants. The town climbs up the extinct cone of Volcán Apoyo until overlooking its deep blue lagoon with a mirador and complex of restaurants. Across the highway from Catarina is the traditional Chorotega village of **San Juan de Oriente**, famous for its elegant ceramic earthenware. At least 80% of the villagers are involved in some aspect of pottery production and sales. To buy direct from the source or to see the artisans at work, you can visit the artisans' co-operative, **Cooperativa Quetzal-Coatl** ① *25 m inside the first entrance to the town, T2558-0337, www.cooperativaquetzalcoatl.wordpress.com, daily 0800-1700.*

Heading south towards the Mombacho Volcano, on the highway between Catarina and San Juan de Oriente, you'll find the historic twin villages of **Diriá** and **Diriomo**. Once the seat of power of the fierce chief Diriangén, who ruled when the Spanish arrived to impose their dominance, Diriá is today one of the sleepiest of the highland *pueblos*, only really coming to life during festivals. Occupying part of the upper rim of Laguna de Apoyo, its mirador is in some ways more spectacular than the complex at Catarina. Neighbouring Diriomo is a farming centre famous for its sorcery and its traditional sweets known as *cajetas*. The most popular of the sweet houses is **La Casa de las Cajetas** ① *Parque Central, opposite the church, T2557-0015, cajeta@datatex.com.ni, tours available, call ahead.* Diriomo's **Iglesia Santuario de Nuestra Señora de Candelaria**, built over the course of over 100 years from 1795 using a mixture of stone and brick, is one of the most visually pleasing structures in Nicaragua.

Best known for its famous son, the nationalist rebel General Augusto C Sandino, **Niquinohomo** is a quiet colonial village founded in 1548 by the Spanish. Tellingly, the name Niquinohomo is Chorotega for 'Valley of the Warriors'. The rebel general's childhood home is today the **public library** ① *Parque Central, opposite the gigantic cross that guards the church, Mon-Fri 0900-1200 and 1400-1800,* and it houses a small display on his life. **Nandasmo** is several kilometres west of Niquinohomo and borders the south side of Laguna de Masaya. The village itself sees few outsiders and feels neglected. Past its entrance, the highway leads to Masatepe and becomes an endless roadside furniture market. Eight kilometres west of Masatepe, the Pueblos highway enters the coffee-growing department of Carazo and the university town of **San Marcos**. In 2005, the oldest evidence of organized settlement was unearthed here in an archaeological excavation by the National Museum with ceramic and human remains dating from 2500 BC.

South from San Marcos is the highway to the highland town of **Jinotepe**, which has a coffee- and agriculture-based economy and some pretty, older homes. In comparison with many other *pueblos* on the *mesa*, nearby **Diriamba** is a slightly grungy, disorganized place. It was here that the late 17th-century anti-establishment comedy and focal point of Nicaraguan culture, *El Güegüence*, is thought to have originated, and it is performed during the town's patron saint festival for San Sebastián. One of the grandest of the Pueblos churches can be found in front of Diriamba's tired-looking Parque Central.

## Listings Around Masaya

### Where to stay

#### Reserva Natural Laguna de Apoyo

**$$ San Simian**
*South of Norome Resort, T8850-8101, www.sansimian.com.*
A peaceful spot with 5 great *cabañas* with Balinese-style outdoor shower or bathtubs – perfect for a soak under the starry sky. Facilities include restaurant, bar, dock, hammocks, kayaks and a catamaran (US$25 per hr). Day use US$5. Yoga, massage, Spanish classes and manicure/pedicure can be arranged. Recommended.

**$$-$ Hostel Paradiso**
*West side of the lake, T8187-4542, www.hostelparadiso.com.*
Formerly **Crater's Edge** hostel, this excellent lakeside lodging has comfortable dorms and rooms, full bar and restaurant, direct access to the water, sun loungers, floating dock, Wi-Fi and stunning views. If you don't want to stay overnight, you can make use of the facilities, US$7 per person per day, excluding transport from **Hostel Oasis** in Granada. Advance booking recommended.

**$ Estación Biológica Laguna de Apoyo (FUNDECI-GAIA)**
*North shore of lake, follow signs for Apoyo Spanish School, T8882-3992, www.gaianicaragua.org.*
Friendly, low-key lodging managed by biologist Dr Jeffry McCrary, an expert on the laguna's ecology. Accommodation is in rustic dorms and rooms with tasty home-cooked meals served 3 times daily. Activities include reforestation (volunteers receive discounts), Spanish school, diving, kayaking and birdwatching. The research station also offers biology courses and is a great place to learn about conservation. It's close to the lake and walking trails and is highly recommended.

**$ The Peace Project**
*50 m from the Ranchos, T8266-8404, www.thepeaceprojectnicaragua.org.*
A socially aware community project working primarily in education and environment. Their hostel has good, clean dorms and rooms with a range of activities on offer. Friendly and easy-going. Pleasant environment.

### What to do

**Reserva Natural Laguna de Apoyo**
**Diving**
**Estación Biológica Laguna de Apoyo (FUNDECI-GAIA)**, *north shore, T8882-3992,* *www.gaianicaragua.org.* Visibility is generally good and native species include rainbow bass, freshwater turtles and a few endemic species which you may be asked to record for the purposes of scientific research. A 2-tank dive with the project costs US$60; PADI open water certification around US$305, prior arrangement essential.

### Language schools

**Apoyo Intensive Spanish School**, *inside Estación Ecológica (FUNDECI-GAIA), T8882-3992, www.gaianicaragua.org.* Nicaragua's oldest Spanish school and still one of the best. In the Reserva Natural Laguna de Apoyo, this school offers one-to-one instruction with complete immersion, 1 week US$240, 2 weeks US$460, 3 weeks US$670, 4 weeks US$870; all rates include meals and lodging, native instructors and three excursions per week. Excellent tutors.

### Transport

**Reserva Natural Laguna de Apoyo**
**Buses** to **Masaya**, 0630, 1130, 1630, 1 hr, US$0.50. To **Granada**, take a Masaya bus, exit on the highway and catch a Granada-bound bus. **Shuttles** to **Granada** depart daily from Hostel Paradiso and the Monkey Hut, around 1600, 30 mins, US$6 (return). **Taxi** to **Granada** costs US$15, to **Masaya** US$5.

# Granada
## & around

Set against the expansive landscape of Lake Nicaragua and Volcán Mombacho, Granada is Nicaragua's most handsome and romantic city, an endlessly photogenic place that blends wistful colonial grandeur with vibrant local street life. Centuries of attacks by marauding pirates and North American filibusters mean that many of the city's elegant Spanish houses and thronging public squares are reconstructions of earlier structures, but fortunately Granada, a bastion of old money and conservatism, has remained largely faithful to its original design.

Today, despite its numerous reinventions, the city has maintained its colonial good looks and earned its place as a major tourist hub. Weary travellers will delight in its well-developed infrastructure, its reputable hotels and restaurants, and its abundance of helpful tour operators. Others may complain that Granada – Nicaragua's most visited destination – is in danger of losing itself under the swell of foreign interest. For better or worse, the expat crowd is now an established force in the city, but scenes of visceral local colour continue to enliven its streets, plazas, markets and others public spaces.

**Best** for
Colonial grandeur ▪ Lake Nicaragua ▪ Religious architecture

Despite the repeated ransackings, Granada (altitude 60 m, population, 111,500) has maintained an unmistakable colonial appeal. The architectural style has been described as a mixture of Nicaraguan baroque and neoclassical: a fascinating visual mix of Spanish adobe tile roof structures and Italian-inspired homes with ornate ceiling work and balconies.

Granada's city centre is small and manageable on foot. Parque Central is the best reference point and the cathedral is visible from most of the city. Much of Granada's beauty can be appreciated within an area of five blocks around the centre.

The centre of Granada is generally safe, but it can become very empty after 2100 and some thefts have been reported. Police presence is almost non-existent on weekday nights so take precautions. Avoid walking alone late at night and don't go to the barrios outside the centre. Take care along the waterfront at any time of day and avoid it completely after dark.

## Parque Central

The Parque Central is officially called Parque Colón (Columbus Park), though no one uses that name. Its tall trees and benches make it a good place to while away some time and observe local life. On its east side, the Catedral has become a symbol for Granada, last rebuilt and extended after William Walker's flaming departure in November 1856. The original church was erected in 1583 and rebuilt in 1633 and 1751. Reconstruction began again on the cathedral after Walker was shot and buried in 1860, but was held up by lack of funds in 1891. The work in progress was later demolished and restarted to become today's church, finally opened in 1915. It has neoclassic and Gothic touches and its impressive size and towers make it a beautiful backdrop to the city, but the interior is plain.

## Calle Real Xalteva

The most attractive of the Granada churches is **Iglesia La Merced**, which can be seen as part of an interesting walk down Calle Real Xalteva. Built between 1751 and 1781 and also damaged by William Walker, La Merced has maintained much of its colonial charm and part of the original façade. You can ascend the bell tower for great views over the city, recommended at dusk (US$1). One block south and two blocks west of La Merced is the **Casa Natal Sor María Romero** ① *Tue-Sun 0800-1200, 1400-1700, free*, a small chapel and humble collection of artefacts and books from the life of María Romero Meneses (born in Granada 1902, died in Las Peñitas, León 1977), who became a Salesian nun at 28 and spent the rest of her life caring for the poor and ill; her beatification was approved in Rome on 14 April 2002 by Pope John Paul II.

Further down the Calle Real Xalteva is the **Plaza de Xalteva**, which has unusual stone lanterns and walls, said to be a tribute to ancient Indian constructions. Granada no longer has an indigenous barrio of any kind, but you can see the remains of the walls from the colonial period that separated the Spanish and indigenous sectors marked by a small tile plaque. The church on the plaza, **Iglesia Xalteva**, was yet another victim of William Walker. The current version is reminiscent of a New England church – a bit lacking in flair. Continuing further west along the Calle Real Xalteva you'll arrive at the little **Capilla María Auxiliadora** with its interesting façade and the lovely detail work inside. At the end of the street is the 18th-century fort and ammunitions hold, **Fortaleza**

**de la Pólvora** ⓘ *open during daylight hours, US$1-2 donation to the caretaker.* The fort was built in 1749 and used primarily as an ammunitions hold, then as a military base and finally a prison. You can climb up inside the southeastern turret on a flimsy ladder for views down the street.

# Granada

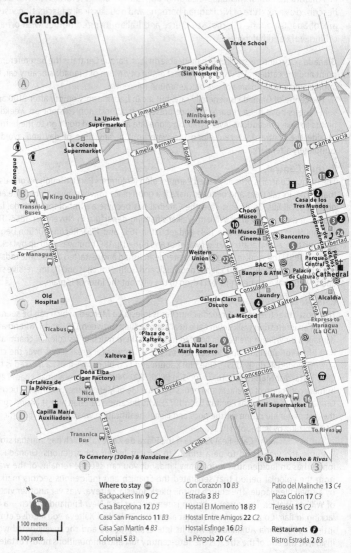

**Where to stay** 🛏
Backpackers Inn **9** *C2*
Casa Barcelona **12** *D3*
Casa San Francisco **11** *B3*
Casa San Martín **4** *B3*
Colonial **5** *B3*

Con Corazón **10** *B3*
Estrada **3** *B3*
Hostal El Momento **18** *B3*
Hostal Entre Amigos **22** *C2*
Hostal Esfinge **16** *D3*
La Pérgola **20** *C4*

Patio del Malinche **13** *C4*
Plaza Colón **17** *C3*
Terrasol **15** *C2*

**Restaurants** 🍴
Bistro Estrada **2** *B3*

## Calle Atravesada

There are a few sights of interest along the Calle Atravesada. Dating from 1886 and beautifully restored, the **old train station**, at the far northern end of the street, is now a trade school. Several blocks south and opposite Calle Arsenal is **Mi Museo**

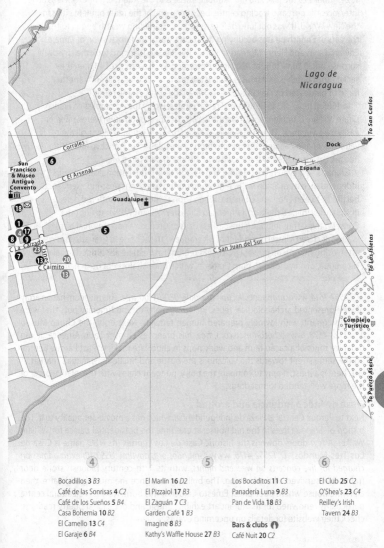

Bocadillos **3** *B3*
Café de las Sonrisas **4** *C2*
Café de los Sueños **5** *B4*
Casa Bohemia **10** *B2*
El Camello **13** *C4*
El Garaje **6** *B4*

El Marlín **16** *D2*
El Pizzaiol **17** *B3*
El Zaguán **7** *C3*
Garden Café **1** *B3*
Imagine **8** *B3*
Kathy's Waffle House **27** *B3*

Los Bocaditos **11** *C3*
Panadería Luna **9** *B3*
Pan de Vida **18** *B3*

**Bars & clubs** 🎵
Café Nuit **20** *C2*

El Club **25** *C2*
O'Shea's **23** *C4*
Reilley's Irish
Tavern **24** *B3*

# BACKGROUND
## Granada

Granada was founded by Captain Francisco Hernández de Córdoba around 21 April 1524. Thanks to the lake and Río San Juan's access to the Atlantic, it flourished as an inter-oceanic port and trading centre, becoming one of the most opulent cities in the New World. It was not long before reports of Granadino wealth began to reach the ears of English pirates occupying the recently acquired possession of Jamaica. Edward Davis and Henry Morgan sailed up the Río San Juan and took the city by surprise on 29 June 1665 at 0200 in the morning. With a group of 40 men they sacked the churches and houses before escaping to Las Isletas. In 1670 another band of pirates led by Gallardillo sacked Granada via the same route.

In 1685, a force of 345 British and French pirates, led by the accomplished French pirate William Dampier, came from the Pacific. The local population were armed but easily overwhelmed. They had, however, taken the precaution of hiding all their valuables on Isla Zapatera. The pirates burned the Iglesia San Francisco and 18 big houses, then retreated to the Pacific with the loss of only three men.

Granada saw even more burning and destruction in the nationalist uprisings for Independence from Spain in 1811-1812 and during persistent post-Independence battles between León and Granada. When León's Liberal Party suffered defeat in 1854 they invited the North American filibuster William Walker to fight the Conservatives, thus initiating the darkest days of Granada's post-colonial history. Walker declared himself president of Nicaragua with the cede in Granada, but after losing his grip on power (which was regional at best) he absconded to Lake Nicaragua, giving orders to burn Granada, which once again went up in flames.

ⓘ T2552-7614, www.granadacollection.org, daily 0800-1700, free. This museum has an array of well-presented archaeological relics, including many rotund funerary pots that were once 'pregnant' with lovingly prepared human remains. Next door, the **Choco Museo** ⓘ T2552-4678, www.chocomuseo.com, free, has branches all over Latin America; it can organize tours of a cacao farm and workshops in chocolate making. Past Parque Central on the same street towards the volcano is the bustle and hustle of Granada's **market**. A visit here is a must, if only to compare the noisy, pungent chaos with the relative order of the more well-tended tourist drags.

### Plaza de Independencia and around

Next to Parque Central is Plaza de Independencia, which has a movie-set quality to it. The bishop of Granada lives in the red house, at one time the presidential palace for William Walker. A few doors down is the historic **Casa de Los Leones** (its NGO name is **Casa de Los Tres Mundos**) ⓘ T2552-4176, www.c3mundos.org, daytime US$0.40; extra admission charged for live concerts on weekend nights, with its 17th-century Moorish stone door frame that survived all the burning. The building was once the municipal theatre, then a private house where poet-priest Ernesto Cardenal was born. Now it is a cultural centre particularly renowned for its vibrant art exhibits, music and occasional poetry readings; check their website for details on upcoming events.

One block east from the northeast corner of Plaza de la Independencia is the white **Iglesia San Francisco** (1524), Nicaragua's oldest standing church with original steps. It was burnt down in 1685 by William Dampier, rebuilt, then modified in 1836 before being reduced to flames in 1856 on Walker's departure. It was finally rebuilt in 1868 with a fine restoration of the interior and a controversial decoration of the façade; some complain that it now looks like a birthday cake. Connected to the church is the **Museo Antiguo Convento de San Francisco** ① *T2552-5535, Mon-Fri 0800-1700, Sat-Sun 0900-1600, US$2, US$2.50 extra to photograph*. Originally founded as a convent in 1529, the interior garden is dominated by towering 100-year-old palms, often full of squawking parakeets. In the east wing of the building is one of the country's most interesting pre-Columbian museums, housing large religious sculptures from the island of Zapatera in Lake Nicaragua (see page 635). The sculptures date from AD 800-1200; of particular note are the double standing or seated figures bearing huge animals, or doubles, on their heads and shoulders.

## Calle Calzada

East from the Parque Central, the brightly coloured and well-manicured Calle Calzada contains the city's highest concentration of restaurants and foreign tourists. This is the place for people-watching and enjoying a good cold beer. The parade of gringo eateries peters out about halfway towards the lake, where you'll find the **Iglesia Guadalupe**. This church has seen plenty of action, thanks to its location near the water. Walker's forces used it as a final stronghold before escaping to the lake where Walker was keeping well away from the fighting, on a steamship. Originally constructed in 1626, its exterior has a melancholy, rustic charm, although the post-Walker interior lacks character. Beyond the church you'll pass the red cross and a baseball field before arriving at the lake and ferry port. Head south along the shore and you'll reach the fortress-like gates of the **Complejo Turístico**, a large recreation area of restaurants, discos and cafés, popular with the locals, particularly over Christmas, Easter and New Year.

## Listings Granada *map p624*

### Tourist information

**INTUR**
*Calle Corrales, Catedral, 2 c norte, 20 vrs abajo, T2552-6858, www. visitanicaragua.com. Mon-Fri 0800-1700.*
Flyers, maps and brochures and, if you're lucky, English-speaking staff.

Elsewhere, good sources of local information are the tourist directory, *Anda Ya*, www. andayanicaragua.com, and the quarterly colour magazine *Qué Pasa Granada*, www. quepasagranada.com, available in hotels and restaurants throughout town.

### Where to stay

**$$$ Casa San Francisco**
*Corrales 207, T2552-8235, www.hotelcasasanfrancisco.com.*
Professionally managed and tastefully decorated, Casa San Francisco is a well-established Granada favourite. They have 8 luxury rooms and 1 suite, complete with excellent mattresses and cotton linen. Recommended.

**$$$ Hotel Colonial**
*Calle La Libertad, Parque Central, 25 vrs al norte, T2552-7299, www.hotelcolonialgranada.com.*
This centrally located, colonial-style hotel has a range of pleasant, comfortable lodgings,

including 27 heavily decorated rooms with 4-poster beds and 10 luxury suites with jacuzzi. There are 2 pools, a conference centre, a tour agency and a restaurant that serves breakfast only.

### $$$ Hotel Estrada
*Calle El Arsenal, Iglesia San Francisco, ½ c abajo, T2552-7393, www.hotelestrada.com.*
A tranquil, tastefully restored colonial house with a charming leafy courtyard and 7 pleasant, well-lit rooms complete with 4-poster beds. English, German, Spanish and French are spoken, and prices include breakfast and a welcome drink.

### $$$ Patio del Malinche
*Calle El Caimito, de Alcaldía, 2½ c al lago, T2552-2235, www.patiodelmalinche.com.*
This beautiful and tastefully restored colonial building has 16 clean, comfortable rooms overlooking an attractive garden and pool. There's a bar and tranquil patio space in which you can have breakfast or simply relax. Tidy and elegant.

### $$$ Plaza Colón
*Frente al Parque Central, T2552-8489, www.hotelplazacolon.com.*
Atmospheric colonial grandeur at this long-established hotel on the plaza. Rooms have all the usual luxury amenities, but those with balconies also have fantastic views over the square. There's a pool, restaurant and a small army of staff to care for your needs. Recommended.

### $$ Casa San Martín
*Calle La Calzada, catedral, 1 c lago, T2552-6185, www.hcasasanmartin.com.*
An authentic Granadino guesthouse and beautiful home with 8 clean, cool, spacious rooms. Nice decor and garden terrace. Good service and central location, staff speak English.

### $$ Hotel Casa Barcelona
*Puente Palmira, 1 c al lago, 1 c sur y 25 vrs al lago, T2552-7438, www.hotelcasabarcelona.com.*

Secluded and excellent-value lodging, a 10-min walk from the centre. Simple, clean, comfortable rooms in little *casitas* in the garden. Friendly, helpful owners.

### $$ Hotel Con Corazón
*Calle Santa Lucía 141, T2552-8852, www.hotelconcorazon.com.*
As the name suggests, this 'hotel with heart' strives to be ethical and donates its profits to social causes. Rooms are simple, minimalist and comfortable; all are fitted with a/c, cable TV and fan. There's a pleasant colonial patio, bar, pool, hammocks and a restaurant serving international food (**$$**). Often recommended.

### $$ La Pérgola
*Calle el Caimito, de la Alcaldía, 3 c al lago, T2552-4221, www.lapergola.com.ni.*
Originally a 19th-century colonial home, with 11 comfortable rooms set around a leafy courtyard from where you can see Volcán Mombacho. Hotel services include parking, tours, transfers, Wi-Fi and bar. Clean, tidy and professional. Breakfast included.

### $$ Terrasol
*Av Barricada, T2552-8825, www.hotelterrasol.com.*
Rooms are comfortable, modern and adorned with good artwork. Each has cable TV, private bath and a/c (cheaper with fan). Some have balconies with views of the street. The restaurant downstairs has had good reports, thanks to the managers who have a background in the food industry.

### $$-$ Backpackers Inn
*Esquina Calle Real Xalteva y Av Barricada, 25 m sur, T2552-4609, www.backpackers-inn.com.*
A very clean and attractive hostel for independent travellers with small but well-attired rooms and dorms. There's a colonial courtyard, traditional art work, good hammocks, well-tended garden, café, business centre and restaurant. Recommended.

### $ Hostal El Momento
*Calle El Arsenal 104, T2552-2811, www.hostelgranadanicaragua.com.*

Clean, bright hostel in a small colonial house with colourful decor. Amenities include chilled out garden space, dorms and private rooms, TV lounge with DVD and movie nights. A relaxed place with a mixed crowd of young and old. Recommended.

### $ Hostal Entre Amigos
*Calle 14 de Septiembre, de la Iglesia Merced, 2½ c al norte, T2552-3966.*
A quiet, friendly, hospitable hostel with simple dorms and rooms, kitchen, common area, DVDs, new beds, Wi-Fi and free salsa classes daily. Laid back and sociable, but not a party hostel. Helpful owner.

### $ Hostal Esfinge
*Opposite market, T2552-4826, www.hospedajeesfinge.com.*
Lots of character at this friendly old hotel near the market. They offer a variety of simple rooms, including those with bath, shared bath and a/c (**$$**). There's a shared kitchen, washing area, ping-pong table, lockers, fridge and a leafy garden with pleasant hammocks and seating. Nica-owned and recommended for down-to-earth budget travellers.

## Restaurants

### $$$ Bistro Estrada
*Calle El Arsenal, www.bistroestrada.com.*
The place for a special occasion, the Bistro Estrada serves high-quality international cuisine. Starters include Italian salad and seafood soup. Mains include sirloin béarnaise, lamb chops and red snapper. Excellent presentation and a good wine list.

### $$$ Imagine
*Calle La Libertad, del Parque Central, 1 c al lago, T8842-2587, www.imagine restaurantandbar.com.*
A very decent and creative restaurant that utilizes fresh and organic ingredients to produce dishes like seared sushi tuna, 100% grain-fed lamb chops, flaming breast of duck and mango bread with chocolate fondue. Recommended.

### $$$-$$ Bocadillos
*Calle Corrales 207, inside Casa San Francisco (see Where to stay, above).*
Managed by Shaun and Karina, Bocadillas serves tasty tapas-style dishes that draw inspiration from a range of international sources – try the hoisin ribs, Venezuelan *arepas* and chicken *tamales*. Lovely intimate dining on the roof terrace, friendly efficient service and good cocktails.

### $$$-$$ El Zaguán
*On road behind cathedral (east side), T2552-2522. Mon-Fri 1200-1500 and 1800-2200, Sat and Sun 1200-2200.*
Incredible, succulent grilled meats and steaks, cooked on a wood fire and served impeccably. Undoubtedly the best beef cuts in Granada, if not Nicaragua. Meat-lovers should not miss this place. Highly recommended.

### $$ Café de los Sueños
*Calle Calzada, Catedral, 3½ c al lago.*
A great little café with some terrace seating on the Calzada as well as inside on a colonial patio. They serve big, fresh crunchy salads, sandwiches, crêpes, good coffee, smoothies, quiches, paninis, lasagne, soup, key lime pie and more. Service with a smile. Recommended.

### $$ Casa Bohemia
*Calle Corrales, next to the Bomberos (fire station). Tue-Sat 0600-0000.*
A little off the beaten track, Casa Bohemia serves tasty and reasonably priced local and international fare, including chilli con carne, ginger chicken, *churrasco* and vegetable burrito. Relaxed low-key ambience and an attractive colonial setting. Friendly owner and good vibe.

### $$ El Camello
*Calle El Caimito, del Parque Central 2 c al lago. Closed Tue.*
El Camello serves wholesome home-made Mediterranean, Moroccan and Middle Eastern cuisine, including kebabs, curries, falafels, Greek salads and tagines, and

weekend specials of lamb and pork. Casual dining and drinking, lots of good reports.

## $$ El Garaje
*Calle Corrales, del Convento de San Francisco, 2½ c al lago, T8651-7412. Mon-Fri 1130-1830.*
A wonderful Canadian-owned restaurant and undoubtedly one of Granada's best options. The menu changes weekly and includes tasty specials like chickpea curry, Italian sausage sandwich, Mediterranean salad and Szechuan steak wrap. Fresh, healthy, beautifully presented home-cooking. Good vegetarian options too. Highly recommended.

## $$ El Marlín
*Calle la Hoyada, Iglesia de Xalteva, 1 c al sur y 30 vrs al lago.*
Excellent, fresh Peruvian seafood, including sumptuous shrimps, fillets and lobster tail. Pleasant interior and a garden, good presentation and service. The place for an intimate evening meal. Large servings and friendly owners.

## $$ El Pizzaiol
*Calle La Libertad, Parque Central, 1 c al lago.*
An authentic Italian restaurant with a stylish interior and open-air seating in the garden. They serve good pastas and the best stone-baked pizzas in Granada. Friendly service, take-away available.

## $$ Garden Café
*Calle Libertad and Av Cervantes, Parque Central, 1 c al lago, www.gardencafegranada.com.*
A very relaxed, breezy and well-presented café with a lovely leafy garden and patio space. They do good breakfasts, sandwiches, wraps, coffees, muffins, smoothies and cookies. There's an excellent book collection and Wi-Fi. Friendly and pleasant. Recommended.

## $$ Kathy's Waffle House
*Opposite Iglesia San Francisco. Open 0730-1400.*
The best breakfasts in Granada. It's always busy here in the morning, especially at weekends. You'll find everything from waffles and pancakes to *huevos rancheros*, all with free coffee refills. Highly recommended.

## $ Café de las Sonrisas
*Iglesia Merced, ½ c al lago, www.tioantonio.org.*
An excellent social project run by Tío Antonio and attached to the hammock shop next door, Café de las Sonrisas only employs people who are hearing and speech impaired. They serve unpretentious Nica fare, breakfasts and snacks; menus include illustrations to help with sign language. Recommended.

## $ Los Bocaditos
*Calle El Comercio. Mon-Sat 0800-2200, Sun 0800-1600.*
A bustling, but clean, locals' joint with buffet from 1100-1500, breakfast and dinner menu.

## Cafés and bakeries

### Panadería Luna
*Calle Calzada, Parque Central, 1 c al lago.*
A selection of European-style white and brown bread, cookies, cakes and other treats. They serve sandwiches and coffee too, as well as juices and fresh fruit smoothies in the establishment next door.

### Pan de Vida
*Calle El Arsenal, Costado Sur del Iglesia San Francisco. Mon-Wed.*
Delicious artisan bread and baked treats cooked in a wood-fired oven. Occasional cook-your-own pizza dinners.

## Bars and clubs

The action tends to gravitate towards Calle La Calzada with a kind of thronging carnivalesque atmosphere Fri-Sun evenings. Sit outside to watch the wandering street performers, including mariachis and break dancers, some of them quite good.

### Café Nuit
*Calle La Libertad, Parque Central, 2½ c abajo.*
A well-established dance and live music venue, well known for its salsa nights.

### El Club
*Calle de la Libertad, Parque Central, T2552-4245.*
A modern bar with a European ambience, pumping dance music and a mixture of locals and foreigners. Stylish and a cut above the rest. Most popular Thu-Sat, when parties run late into the night.

### O'Shea's
*Calle La Calzada, Parque Central, 2 c al lago.*
A very popular 'Irish' pub on the Calzada, complete with authentic Nicaraguan staff. They serve Guinness and pub grub, including good fish and chips.

### Reilley's Irish Tavern
*Calle La Libertad, del Parque Central 1 c abajo.*
A sociable Irish pub, probably the best and most genuine in Nicaragua, with English roast on Sun afternoons and Guinness on tap. Serves grub, including wings and burgers. Recommended.

## Entertainment

### Cinema
**Cine Karawala**, *Calle Atravezada, behind Hotel Alhambra, T2552-2442.* 2-screen cinema that only seems to open Fri-Sun.

### Theatre
**La Escuela de Comedia y Mimo**, *Calle Calzada, T2552-8310, www.escueladecomedia. org.* A grassroots theatre school that teaches acting, mime, clowning and circus skills to disadvantaged local children. Check their website for upcoming performances.

## Festivals

**Feb Poetry Festival**, a captivating and popular literary festival that draws national and international crowds, check website for dates, www.festivalpoesianicaragua.com.
**Mar Folklore, Artesanía and Food Festival** for 3 days in Mar (check locally for dates).
**Aug** 1st weekend in August is **El Tope de los Toros** with bulls released and then caught one at a time, much tamer than Pamplona, though occasionally the bulls

get away sending everyone running for cover. **Assumption of the Virgin** (14-30).
**Dec** Celebrations for the **Virgin Mary,** with numerous parades and firecrackers leading up to **Christmas**.

## Shopping

### Books
**Lucha Libro Books**, *Av Cervantes, between Calle Calzada and La Libertad, www. luchalibrobooks.com.* An excellent stock of interesting books including novels and non-fiction, natural and social history, *Footprint* travel guides, beautifully bound cult classics from *Black Sparrow Press*, works by Louis Ferdinand Céline and much more. Recommended.

### Cigars
There is some rolling done in Granada although most of the wrap and filler are brought from Estelí where the best cigars are made outside Cuba (see Estelí, page 696).
**Doña Elba Cigars**, *Calle Real, Iglesia Xalteva, ½ c abajo, T2552-7348, elbacigar@yahoo.com. mx.* A long-established factory where you can learn more about cigar making or just pick up some fresh *puros*.
**Mombacho Cigars**, *422 Calle La Calzada, www.mombachocigars.com.* A swish Canadian outfit offering rolling demonstrations from their elegant headquarters on the Calzada.

### Markets
**El Mercado de Granada**, *Parque Central, 1 c abajo, then south on Calle Atravesada.* A large green building surrounded by many street stalls. It's dark, dirty and packed and there have been plans to move it for years but for now it remains in its claustrophobic location.
**La Colonia**, *on the highway to Masaya.* Next door, **La Unión** is also reasonably well-stocked.
**Supermercado Palí**, *just west of the market.* Dark and dirty, with a selection of low-priced goods.

## Boating and kayaking

**NicarAgua Dulce**, *Marina Cocibola, Bahía de Asese, T2552-8827, www.nicaraguadulce-ecotourism.com; bookings through Granada Mía on the Parque Central*. An ecologically aware outfit that contributes to local communities. They offer kayak rental by the hour or day to explore the lesser-visited Asese Bay, which can be done with or without a guide, or additional bicycle rental if you wish to explore the peninsula by land. Boat tours of the Isletas are offered, as well as tours to their idyllic private island, Zopango, where you can chill out in a hammock, swim or stroll along the botanical track. Taxi to the marina is supplied when you book a 3-hr tour or more.

## Body and soul

**Pure Natural Health and Fitness Center**, *Calle Corrales, from Convento San Francisco, 1½ c al lago, T8481-3264, www.purenica. com*. A range of well-priced packages and therapies including excellent massage, acupuncture and beauty treatments. Classes include meditation, yoga, kick-boxing and aerobics. Weights and cross-trainers available in the gym. If you visit, be sure to meet Snoopy, the giant African tortoise!

## Butterfly observation

**Nicaragua Butterfly Reserve**, *3 km west from Granada cemetery, check website for directions, T8863-2943, www. nicaraguabutterflyreserve.wordpress.com*. Open 0800-1600, US$5. Private reserve on a 4-ha property, home to 20 species of butterfly endangered by loss of habitat. Tours are self-guided or with a resident butterfly expert.

## Canopy tours

Canopy tours can be booked through tour operators in town or directly with the providers. Costs are US$35-40 per person excluding transport.

**Miravalle Canopy Tour**, *T8872-2555, www.miravallecanopytour.blogspot.com*. Works with many tour operators in Granada. Costs are lower the larger the group.
**Mombacho Canopy Tour**, *located on the road up to the Mombacho cloudforest reserve, T8997-5846, www.mombacho.org. Daily 0900-1700 (book at least 24 hrs in advance)*. It combines well with a visit to the cloudforest reserve which is on this side of the volcano. Managed by the Cocibolca Foundation.
**Mombotour**, *Empalme Guanacaste Diriomo, 4 km hacia la Reserva Natural Volcán Mombacho, T8388-2734, www.cafelasflores. com*. Now part of a coffee farm, **Café Las Flores**, with its main office in Managua, but you can also book through their website. Many other options available, including kayaking, hiking on Mombacho, tour of coffee plantation, etc.

## Cycling

Cycling is a great way to explore the area, particularly the Península de Asese. Many agencies rent out bikes, but the following are specialists:
**Detour**, *see Tour operators, below. Good bicycles with shock absorbers, locks, maps, helmets, tips and repair kit at US$2 per hr, US$3 for 2 hrs, US$4 for 3-4 hrs, US$5 for 6 hrs, US$8 for a full 24 hrs*. They also offer excellent and adventurous cycling tours along the old railway lines around Granada, advance booking necessary. Recommended.

## Language schools

The following schools are well-established and proven:
**APC Spanish School**, *Calle Vega, T8866-4581, www.spanishgranada.com*. Flexible immersion classes in this centrally located language school. There are volunteer opportunities with local NGOs.
**Casa Xalteva**, *Calle Real Xalteva 103, Iglesia Xalteva, ½ c al norte, T2552-2436, www. casaxalteva.org*. Small Spanish classes for beginners and advanced students, 1 week to several months. Homestays

arranged and voluntary work with children. Recommended.

**Nicaragua Mía**, *Calle Caimito, de Alcaldía, 3½ c al lago, T2552-0347, www.spanishschool nicaraguamia.com*. All teachers are professional university graduates or university professors, knowledgeable about Nicaraguan culture, history and politics.

**One on One**, *Calle La Calzada 450, T8442-6299, www.spanish1on1.net*. One on One uses a unique teaching system where each student has 4 different tutors, thus encouraging greater aural comprehension. Instruction is flexible, by the hour or week, with homestay, volunteering and activities available.

**Tour operators**

**Detour**, *Calle Corrales, Alcaldía, 150 vrs al lago, T2552-0155, www.detour-nicaragua.com*. Detour works with community co-ops, indigenous and women's organizations to offers a range of very interesting cultural and historical tours in 6 parts of the country, including adventurous trips to the gold mines of Chontales, rural tourism on Isla Ometepe and the Atlantic coast, visits to Rama communities, turtle watching, tours of the rural llano, including an overnight stay in a historic house and extensive horse-trekking expeditions. Advance booking necessary.

**Oro Travel**, *Calle Corrales, Convento San Francisco, ½ c abajo, T2552-4568, www. orotravel.com*. Granada's best tour operator offers quality personalized tours and trips to every part of the country, as well as transfers, package deals and more. Owner Pascal speaks French, English and German. Friendly and helpful. Highly recommended.

**Tierra Tour**, *Calle la Calzada, catedral, 2 c lago, T2552-8273, www.tierratour.com*. This well-established Dutch/Nicaraguan agency offers a wide range of affordable services including good-value trips to Las Isletas, night tours of Masaya, cloudforest tours, birding expeditions and shuttles. Helpful and friendly.

**UCA Tierra y Agua**, *Gasolinera UNO Palmira, 75 vrs abajo, T2552-0238, www.ucatierrayagua. org. Daily 0900-1600*. This organization will help you arrange a visit to rural communities around Granada. Very interesting and highly recommended for a perspective on local life and the land.

**Va Pues**, *Parque Central, blue house next to the cathedral, T2552-4835, www.vapues.com*. This award-winning agency offers canopy tours, turtle expeditions, Zapatera cultural heritage tours, car rental, domestic flights and a 'romantic getaway' tour to a private island. They work closely with a sister company, **Agua Trails**, *www.aguatrails.com*, which operates out of Costa Rica and specializes in the Río San Juan region on the border.

**Volunteering**

Several good organizations in Granada are working to improve the lives of local children, including:

**La Esperanza Granada**, *Calle Libertad 307, Parque Central, 1½ c arriba, T8913-8946, www. la-esperanza-granada.org*. This reputable NGO works with local schools to improve literacy, numeracy and IT skills.

**The Girls' Home**, *T+44 (0)207 923-2078, www.hogardeninasmadrealbertina.com*. Directed by London-based Rachel Collingwood, a home for orphaned and abused girls, seeking volunteers for a minimum 3-month commitment.

## Transport

**Boat and ferry** For short expeditions, you can easily find boats by the lakeside *malecón* and in the Complejo Turístico. Otherwise try: **Marina Cocibolca**, *www.marinacocibolca.net*. Check the Marina's administrative offices for information on costs and schedules for visits to the Isletas, Zapatera and nearby private reserves.

For long-distance ferry trips, services depart from the *malecón* and schedules are subject to change and delay, *www.epn.ni*. The ferry to **San Carlos**, a challenging 12- to 14-hr journey on Río San Juan across Lake Nicaragua, leaves the main dock on Mon and Thu at 1400, and stops at **Altagracia**, **Ometepe** after 4 hrs

(US$4.25 1st class, US$2 2nd class), **Morrito** (8 hrs, US$5 1st class, US$3, 2nd class), **San Miguelito** (10 hrs, US$5.50 1st class, US$3 2nd class) and finally **San Carlos** (14 hrs, US$9 1st class, US$3.75 2nd class). Take your own food and water, hammock, pillow and sleeping bag if you have them. Although you'll still be sleeping on a hard bench or floor, the 1st-class deck is much more comfortable than the crowded and noisy 2nd-class deck below – worth the extra dollars. The ferry returns from San Carlos on Tue and Fri at 1400, following the same route. For Isla Ometepe it usually works out faster to go overland to **San Jorge** and catch a 1-hr ferry; see San Jorge, page 640, for more details.

**Bus** Overland, there are express buses from Managua's UCA terminal (recommended) and slow buses from Roberto Huembes market, as well as services from Masaya and Rivas. Several international bus companies, including **Transnica** and **Ticabus**, stop in Granada on routes north from Costa Rica.

**Intercity bus** For the border with **Costa Rica** use **Rivas** bus to connect to **Peñas Blancas** service or use international buses; see also Nicaragua–Costa Rica border box in the Practicalities chapter.

Express minibuses to La UCA in **Managua** from a small car park just south of Parque Central on Calle Vega, every 20 mins, 0500-2000, 45 mins, US$1. Another express service departs from a different terminal, shell station, 1 c abajo, 1 c norte, which goes to the sketchy Mercado Oriental, US$1. Either can drop you on the highway exit to **Masaya**, US$0.60, from where it's a 20-min walk or 5-min taxi ride to the centre. Buses to Mercado Roberto Huembes, Managua, US$0.60, also leave from a station near the old hospital in Granada, west of centre, but they're slower and only marginally cheaper.

Leaving from the Shell station, Mercado, 1 c al lago: to **Rivas**, 7 daily, 0540-1510, 1½ hrs, US$1.50, most depart before midday; to Nandaime, every 20 mins, 0500-1800, 20 mins, US0.70; to **Niquinohomo**, every

30 mins, 0550-1800, 45 mins, US$1, use this bus for visits to **Diriá**, **Diriomo**, **San Juan de Oriente**, **Catarina**; to **Jinotepe**, 0550, 0610, 0830, 1110, 1210 and 1710, 1½ hrs, US$0.80, for visits to **Los Pueblos**, including **Masatepe** and **San Marcos**. There's a second terminal nearby, Shell station, 1 c abajo, 1 c norte, serving **Masaya**, every 30 mins, 0500-1800, 40 mins, US$0.50.

**International bus** To **San José**, Costa Rica, daily, US$29. See individual offices for schedules: **Ticabus**, Av Arellano, from the old hospital, 1½ c al sur, T2552-8535, www.ticabus.com; **Transnica**, Calle El Tamarindo, T2552-6619, www.transnica.com; 2nd branch north on the same street. Also try **Nica Express** or **Central Line**, both on Av Arellano.

A shuttle to **Laguna Apoyo** leaves daily from the **Bearded Monkey Hostel**, Calle 14 de Septiembre, dropping passengers at the **Monkey Hut** by the lake shore, 1000-1100, 30 mins, US$6 round-trip (plus US$6 for use of the facilities). They return at 1600-1700. Several other hotels offer shuttle services, including **Hostel Oasis**, Calle Estrada, which drop you at the **Paradiso**.

Many companies and tour operators offer shuttle services to other parts of the country, including **Tierra Tours on the Calzada.** Approximate one-way fares: to **Managua** airport, US$12; **León**, US$20; **San Juan del Sur**, US$18; and **San Jorge**, US$15.

**Horse-drawn carriage** *Coches* are for hire and are used as taxis here, as in Masaya, Rivas and Chinandega. Normal rate for a trip to the market or bus station should be no more than US$1.50. The drivers are also happy to take foreigners around the city and actually make very good and willing guides if you can decipher their Spanish. Rates are normally US$5 for 30 mins, US$10 for 1 hr.

**Taxi** Granada taxi drivers are useful for finding places away from the centre, fares to anywhere within the city are US$0.50 per person during the day, US$1 at night. To **Managua** US$25, but check taxi looks strong enough to make the journey. Overcharging is rife.

Granada is not just a pretty face; beyond its disarming aesthetic charms, you'll find scores of enticing outdoor attractions. The expansive waters of Central America's largest freshwater lake, Lake Nicaragua (or Lago Cocibolca, as it's known locally), are home to hundreds of scattered isles and enclaves, many of them occupied by lost-in-time fishing communities.

Volcán Mombacho, looming darkly to the south, is home to Nicaragua's best-managed wildlife reserve, boasting well-tended hiking trails, commanding views, diverse flora and fauna and, for those seeking adrenalin-charged encounters with the arboreal canopy, high-speed ziplines (see What to do, in Granada section, above).

### Las Isletas

Scattered across the surface of Lake Nicaragua, Las Isletas are a chain of 354 islands created by a massive eruption of Mombacho volcano. Birdlife in the archipelago is rich, with plenty of egrets, cormorants, ospreys, magpie jays, kingfishers, Montezuma oropendulas and various species of swallow, flycatcher, parrot and parakeet, as well as the occasional mot-mot. The islands' population consists mainly of humble fishermen and boatmen, though many of the islands are now privately owned by wealthy Nicaraguans who use them for weekend and holiday escapes. The school, cemetery, restaurants and bars are all on different islands and the locals commute by rowing boat or by hitching rides from the tour boats that circulate in the calm waters. The peninsula that juts out between the islands has small docks and restaurants on both sides.

The immediate (north) side of the islands is accessed by the road that runs through the tourist centre of Granada and finishes at the malecón and docks. This is the more popular side and boat rides are cheaper from here (US$20 per boat for two hours). In addition to the many luxurious homes on this part of the islands is the tiny, late 17th-century Spanish fort, **San Pablo**, on the extreme northeast of the chain. Some 3 km from downtown on the southern side of the peninsula lies **Bahía de Asese**, where boats also offer one-hour rides around the islands. Despite the fact that there are fewer canals here you will have a better chance to see normal island life since this southern part of the archipelago is populated by more locals, some of them quite impoverished. Two hours on this side is normally US$40 with both sides charging US$1.50 for parking. A taxi to the docks costs US$4 or less.

### Parque Nacional Archipiélago Zapatera

Although the most important relics have been taken to museums, this archipelago of 11 islands remains one of the country's most interesting pre-Columbian sites. Isla Zapatera, the centrepiece and Lake Nicaragua's second largest island, is a very old and extinct volcano that has been eroded over the centuries and is now covered in forest. It has both tropical dry and wet forest ecosystems depending on elevation, which reaches a maximum height of 625 m. It is a beautiful island for hiking, with varied wildlife and an accessible crater lake, close to the northwest shore of the island.

There are conflicting reports on the island's indigenous name, ranging from Xomotename (duck village) to Mazagalpan (the houses with nets). Archaeological evidence dating from 500 BC to AD 1515 has been documented from more than 20 sites on the island, including massive basalt images attributed to the Chorotega people (now housed by the Museo Convento San Francisco in Granada and the Museo Nacional in

Managua). The island system is 40 km south of Granada, one hour by *panga* (skiff), more if there are lake swells. Several Granada tour companies offer one-day trips that include lunch, boat and guide, including **Oro Travel** and **Detour**, page 633. **Tours Nicaragua** in Managua, page 610, offers a visit to Zapatera as part of a sophisticated week-long archaeological trip guided by a National Museum archaeologist.

## Reserva Natural Volcán Mombacho

*T2552-5858, www.mombacho.org, Fri-Sun 0800-1700, US$16, children US$8, including transfer to the reserve from the parking area. If walking (not recommended), entrance is US$3. Tickets are sold at the parking area at the base. It is possible to stay overnight in the research station; cost per person with meals and a night tour is US$40. To get to the reserve, take a bus between Nandaime or Rivas and Granada or Masaya. Get off at the Empalme Guanacaste and walk (or take a taxi) 1 km to the car park. From here you can take a truck to the top of the volcano (great view), 25 mins; they leave from the parking area (Fri-Sun 0800, 1000, 1300, 1500) or try hitching with one of the park rangers.*

Mombacho volcano, 10 km outside Granada, is home to one of only two cloudforests found in Nicaragua's Pacific lowlands. Protected as a nature reserve and administered by the non-profit **Cocibolca Foundation**, it is home to many species of butterfly and the famous Mombacho salamander (*Bolitoglossa mombachoensis*), which is found nowhere else in the world. It also has terrific views of extinct craters and, if cloud cover permits, of Granada, Lake Nicaragua and Las Isletas. Most visitors opt for a leisurely one- or two-hour stroll along the **Sendero Cráter**, an easy trail that leads through magnificent cloudforest full of ferns, bromeliads and orchids. An optional guide costs US$7 per group. The **Sendero El Tigrillo** is a short but tough hike to views of the main crater, two hours, guided only, US$12 per group. The **Sendero El Puma** is only 4 km in length but takes around four hours to cover because of the elevation changes. This is the best walk for seeing wildlife, which can be very elusive during the daytime. A guide is obligatory and they charge US$17 per group. English-speaking guides are available for all trails at an additional cost of US$5.

## Listings Around Granada

### Where to stay

#### Las Isletas

**$$$$ Jicaro Island Eco-lodge**
*On Jicaro island, T2552-6353,*
*www.jicarolodge.com.*
An upscale nature resort with 9 beautifully presented *casitas* and a secluded setting – a fine spot for honeymoons or romantic getaways. Massage and yoga treatments are available, as well as a range of soft adventure tours.

#### Isla Zapatera

**$$$-$$ Santa María (Managua office)**
*Frente al Colegio Centroamérica,*
*Tienda DCO Mediterráneo, T277-5299,*
*www.islazapatera.com.*
A new ecolodge located in the bay of Santa María on Zapatera. They offer 6 pleasant rooms with capacity for 4 people in each, night fishing, bar and deck. Rates are listed for a group of 8, not including transport.

## Reserva Natural Volcán Mombacho

**$$$ Mombacho Lodge**
*Halfway up to the coffee finca
from the park office, T8499-1029,
www.mombacholodge.com.*
Spacious wooden cabins in the jungle with
hot water, verandas and access to **Finca Café
Las Flores**. Open to visitors, the restaurant
serves fresh international food. 3 meals for
the day, US$30.

**$ Treehouse Poste Rojo**
*Pozo de Oro, 10 km outside Granada
on the road to Nandaime, T8903-4563,
www.posterojo.com.*
Known affectionately as the **Tree House
Hostel**, it has attractive and rustic wooden
lodgings connected by Robinson Crusoe
walkways. Activities include volunteering
and full-moon parties. Buzzing and sociable.

# Southern
## Pacific coast

Empty wave-swept beaches, isolated surf spots and a prime position just off the Panamerican Highway – it's no surprise that Nicaragua's southern Pacific coast is enjoying a special prosperity and burgeoning international interest.

Geographically speaking, this is the youngest part of the country. It forms the outer fringe of the tapering isthmus of Rivas, which separates the ocean from the freshwater expanse of Lake Nicaragua with swathes of ultra-fertile lowlands. The dry season here is very parched and brown, but during the rest of the year the landscape is flushed green and dotted with flower-festooned gardens. Roadside stalls, shaded by rows of mango trees, offer a bounty of fresh fruit: watermelon, mango, *níspero* and some of the biggest papaya you'll see anywhere.

San Juan del Sur, an hour from the Costa Rican border, has become the region's big tourist mecca. It is one of Central America's big expat towns, but has not entirely lost its small-town fishing village feel with a fleet of little boats anchored off its golden sands. The many kilometres of Pacific shoreline north and south of San Juan's sweeping half-moon bay are prettier, but the real attractions are the olive ridley turtles that have been coming to this stretch of coast for thousands of years.

**Best** for
Beaches ▪ Boat trips ▪ Fishing ▪ Turtles

For the filibuster William Walker, who fought and lost three battles here, Rivas was never a very happy place. Today, as a provincial capital, founded in 1720, and transport hub, it provides connections south to San Juan del Sur and the Costa Rican border, east to Isla Ometepe, and north to Granada and Managua.

The town has a few modest sights but nothing to detain you: the **Templo Parroquial de San Pedro** (1863) on Parque Central has a design reminiscent of the cathedral in León; the **Museo de Antropología e Historia** ① *Escuela International de Agricultura, 1 c arriba, 1½ c norte, Mon-Fri 0900-1200, 1400-1700, Sat 0900-1200, US$2,* maintains a dwindling but precious collection of archaeological pieces.

It may seem like an extension of Rivas, but San Jorge, where ferries depart to Isla Ometepe, is actually a separate town (see Transport, below). South of Rivas on the Pan-American Highway, at the turning for San Juan del Sur (see below), the little windswept village of La Virgen has a stunning view of the big lake and Ometepe. It is here that the distance between the waters of Lake Nicaragua and the Pacific Ocean is shortest, only 18 km. South of La Virgen, the Panamerican highway passes the coastal town of **Sapoá** before arriving at **Peñas Blancas** and the Costa Rican border; see also Nicaragua–Costa Rica border box in the Practicalities chapter.

## Listings Rivas to Costa Rica

### Where to stay

**Rivas**

**$$ Nicarao Inn Hotel**
*Rivas, northwest corner of Parque Central, 2 c abajo, T2563-3836, www.hotelnicaraoinn.com.ni.*
The finest hotel in town has 18 tastefully decorated, comfortable rooms, all with a/c, cable TV, hot water and Wi-Fi. Services include laundry, car rental, conference centre, restaurant and bar. Polite and professional. Breakfast included.

### Transport

**Rivas**
**Bus** The main bus terminal is at the market. **Managua**, every 30 mins, 0630-1700, US$2, 2½ hrs; express buses, US$2.50. To **Granada**, every 45 mins, 0530-1625, US$1.50, 1¾ hrs. To **Jinotepe**, every 30 mins, 0540-1710, US$1.50, 1¾ hrs. To **San Jorge**, every 30 mins, US$0.30, 20 mins. To **San Juan del Sur**, every 30 mins, 0600-1830, US$1, 45 mins. To destinations south of San Juan del Sur, including **Playa el Coco**, **La Flor** and **Ostional**, 3 daily, 1100, 1500, 1630, US$2.60, 2-3 hrs. To **Peñas Blancas**, every 30 mins, 0500-1600, US$0.75, 1 hr.

**International bus** Ticabus, de la UNO, 1½ c norte, T8847-1407, www.ticabus.com, and **Transnica**, UNO, 1½ c norte, T8898-5195, www.transnica.com, have buses bound for **Costa Rica** and **Honduras** stopping at the UNO station on the highway.

**Taxi** From the centre of Rivas to the dock at **San Jorge**, US$1 colectivo (US$4 private). To **San Juan del Sur**, US$1.75 colectivo (US$7.50 private). To **Peñas Blancas**, US$2 colectivo (US$8 private). In all cases beware of overcharging and avoid 'helpful' characters (see Border crossings box in Practicalities chapter). Colectivos depart from the corner opposite the bus station.

## San Jorge

**Boat and ferry** Ferries and boats depart from San Jorge to the main port of **Moyogalpa** on Isla Ometepe and to the smaller pier at **San José del Sur**. The ferries are the larger and more comfortable option. Services are subject to random and seasonal change, but you won't have to wait more than an hour for a departure. To **Moyogalpa**, 8 ferries daily, 5 in the morning, 3 in the afternoon, 0700-1730, US$3, 6 boats daily, US$1.50-2, 1 hr. To **San José del Sur**,

0930, 1400, 1700, ferry US$3, boat US$2, 1 hr. Reduced services on Sun. If you have a high-clearance 4WD you may want to take it across on the ferry (US$20 each way). Arrive at least 1 hr before the ferry departure to reserve a spot (if possible call the day before, T2278-8190, to make an initial reservation). You will need to fill out some paperwork and buy a boarding ticket for each person travelling. Make sure you reserve your spot as close to the ferry ramp as possible, but leave room for trucks and cars coming off the ferry.

## San Juan del Sur  Colour map 4, A2.

a magnet for property developers, US retirees and international surfers

Not long ago this was a special, secret place – a tiny coastal paradise on Nicaragua's Pacific coast. In recent years, however, this little town on a big bay has become very popular. Today, cruise ships anchor in its deeper waters and tourists have arrived in quantity. No more the precious enclave, San Juan del Sur (population 14,621) is a buzzing party town and its transformation into the type of gringo pleasure resort that is so common in Costa Rica is nearly complete. Although San Juan del Sur is no longer the place to experience a country off the beaten path, it is fun and convenient, and there are still many empty beaches along local coastline, one of the most beautiful stretches in Central America.

You are strongly advised to check the current safety situation on the beaches before heading out. Under no circumstances walk to Playa Yankee or Playa Remanso, north of San Juan del Sur, as this road is a haunt of thieves. Don't linger on the sand after dark in San Juan del Sur.

### Sights

San Juan is a natural bay of light-brown sand, clear waters and 200-m-high cliffs that mark its borders. The sunsets are placed perfectly out over the Pacific, framed by fishing boats bobbing in the water. In 1866, Mark Twain described San Juan as "a few tumble-down frame shanties" and said it was "crowded with horses, mules and ambulances (horse carriages) and half-clad yellow natives". Today there are plenty of half-clad people, though fewer and fewer are natives, and most are enjoying the sun and sea. What makes San Juan del Sur really different from other Nicaraguan beach towns is the growing expat crowd. Today, for better or worse, the town plays host to scores of rum-soaked gringo bars, thronging party hostels, high-rise condos, boutique hotels and scores of seafood restaurants offering the catch of the day. As ever, intrepid wave-seekers can climb in a boat, escape the crowds and find very good breaks along a coastline that has a year-round offshore breeze. See What to do, below.

## BACKGROUND

### San Juan del Sur

The sleepy fishing village of San Juan del Sur began working as a commercial port in 1827 and in 1830 took the name Puerto Independencia. Its claim to fame came during the California gold rush when thousands of North Americans, anxious to reach California, would travel by boat from the Caribbean up the Río San Juan, across Lake Nicaragua, overland for 18 km from La Virgen, and then by boat again from San Juan to California. It is estimated that some 84,880 passengers passed through the town en route to the Golden State and some 75,000 on their way to New York. As soon as the transcontinental railway in the USA was completed, the trip through Central America was no longer necessary. The final crossing was made on 8 May 1868.

**Listings** San Juan del Sur *map p642*

### Where to stay

Many hotels in the region of San Juan del Sur double and triple their rates for Semana Santa and around Christmas and New Year.

#### $$$$ Pelican Eyes Resort
*Parroquia, 1½ c arriba, T2563-7000, www.pelicaneyesresort.com.*
Beautiful, peaceful, luxurious houses and hotel suites with private bath, a/c, cable TV, sitting area, great furnishings and views of the bay. Sailing trips on the *Pelican Eyes* boat can be arranged. The best in town with a plethora of comforts and amenities.

#### $$$$-$$$ Victoriano
*Paseo Marítimo, costado norte Enitel, T2568-2005, www.hotelvictoriano.com.*
This gorgeous clapboard mansion is actually a restored English Victorian-era family house. Rooms are simple, stylish and elegant with a/c, cable TV, DVD, Wi-Fi and all the usual amenities. Great restaurant-bar, pool and garden. One of the best in town and a place to be seen.

#### $$$ Hotel Alcazar
*Calle el Paseo del Rey, opposite the Eskimo, T2568-2075, www.hotelalcazarnicaragua.com.*
Crisp, stylish and contemporary rooms at this boutique hotel on the seafront, each immaculately furnished with tasteful

hardwood furniture and their own balcony overlooking the waves. Wi-Fi, pool, cable TV and a/c. Recommended.

#### $$$ La Posada Azul
*BDF, ½ c arriba, T2568-2698, www.laposadaazul.com.*
La Posada Azul is a tranquil and intimate lodging with just a handful of comfortable, well-furnished rooms. A beautiful wooden building with lots of history and character. There's a lush garden, self-service bar and a modest pool. A/c, private bath, hot water and Wi-Fi. Full breakfast included. Recommended.

#### $$$ Villa Isabella
*Across from the northeast corner of the church, T2568-2568, www.villaisabellasjds.com.*
This lovely, well-decorated wooden house has 17 clean rooms with private bath, a/c, disabled access, ample windows and light. There's a pool, garage parking, Wi-Fi, free calls to USA, video library and breakfast included in the price. English spoken, very helpful. Discounts for groups.

#### $$ Casa Ariki
*Mercado Municipal, 2½ c sur, www.casaariki.com.*
A laid-back little downtown guesthouse with friendly hosts, Sarah and Baldo.

Common area with board games, books, magazines and free morning coffee. They have 4 clean, simple, spacious rooms with fan and cable TV, a/c at extra cost (US$10); one has private bath. Surf, yoga and Spanish packages in the pipeline.

**\$\$ El Puerto**
*UNO, 1 c al mar, T2568-2661,*
*hotel-el-puerto@gmx.net.*

Simple, comfortable, economical rooms with private bath and a/c (cheaper with fan). Good value, friendly and clean. There's also Wi-Fi and free coffee in the morning.

**\$\$ Hotel Azul Pitahaya**
*Mercado, 1 c al mar, T2568-2294,*
*www.hotelazulsanjuan.com.*
Comfortable rooms with good mattresses, hot water, cable TV and a/c. There's Wi-Fi in

# San Juan del Sur

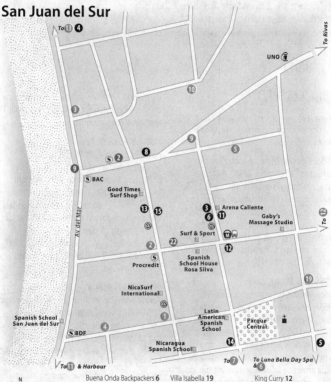

To ⑬ ④
To Rivas
UNO 🛒
⑩
③
⑨
Ⓢ ②
⑧
⑤
⑨
Ⓢ BAC
Good Times Surf Shop ▪
⑬ ⑮
③ ▪ Arena Caliente
⑥ ⑪
Gaby's Massage Studio
Av del Mar
@
Surf & Sport ▪
Ⓜ 🚗
②
㉒
⑫
Ⓢ
Procredit
Spanish School House Rosa Silva
NicaSurf International ▪
@
⑲
Spanish School San Juan del Sur ▪
Latin American Spanish School ▪
Ⓢ BDF
④
①
Parque Central ✝
Nicaragua Spanish School ▪
⑭
⑤
To ⑪ & Harbour
To ⑦
To Luna Bella Day Spa ⑤ & ⑥

N

50 metres
50 yards

**Where to stay** 🛏
Alcazar **3**
Azul Pitahaya **2**

Buena Onda Backpackers **6**
Casa Ariki **7**
Casa Oro Youth Hostel **1**
El Puerto **16**
La Dolce Vita **9**
La Posada Azul **4**
Maracuyá **10**
Pelican Eyes Resort **12**
Secret Cove Inn **5**
Victoriano **11**

Villa Isabella **19**
Yajure Surf Hostel **13**

**Restaurants** 🍴
Bambú Beach Club **4**
Café Mediterráneo **6**
Cha Cha Cha **11**
Comedor Margarita **3**
El Colibrí **5**
Gato Negro **8**

King Curry **12**
Nacho Libre **13**
Pizzería San Juan **14**
Simon Says **15**

**Bars & clubs** 🍸
Big Wave Dave's **2**
Iguana Bar **9**
Republika **22**

the café downstairs, which serves familiar gringo food. Tours, surf board rental and transportation available. Breakfast included.

## $$ Hotel Maracuyá
*Gato Negro, 1 c norte, 1 c este, on the hill, T2568-2002, www.hotelmaracuya.com.*
A cheerful, locally owned B&B with an elevated terrace-bar that enjoys expansive ocean views and sunset vistas. Rooms are pleasant, simple, colourful and unpretentious, all equipped with fan, cable TV, Wi-Fi (a/c costs US$18 extra). Relaxing hammocks in the garden.

## $$ La Dolce Vita
*Gasolinera UNO, 1 c oeste, T2568-2649, ladolcevita.sjs@gmail.com.*
A historic building on the corner converted to a friendly family-run guesthouse and fine Italian restaurant. Rooms are simple and cosy with comfortable beds and private bath, a/c is US$10 extra. There's a small patio with hammock for chilling out. Breakfast included.

## $$-$ Yajure Surf Hostel
*Barrio la Talangera, next to the bridge, T2568-2105, www.yajuresurfhostel.com.*
Popular with 20-somethings and surfers, fun and sociable, but not a party hostel. Common areas are good and spacious, complete with hammocks, TV, sofas and table tennis; there's a great pool and a shared kitchen too. 3 dorms ($) and 2 private rooms ($$) available. Options for surf lessons and tours.

## $ Buena Onda Backpackers
*Barrio Frente Sur, 50 m on the left-hand side past the Casa de Dragón, T8743-2769, sanjuandelsurbackpackers.com.*
A bit of a climb to get there, but you'll be rewarded with unrivalled views of the bay at this great new backpacker hostel. Private rooms are simple and spartan; amenities include shared kitchen and bar. Superb social areas are comprised of multi-level open-air terraces with very inviting hammocks.

## $ Casa Oro Youth Hostel
*Hotel Colonial, 20 vrs sur, T2568-2415, www.casaeloro.com.*
A very popular hostel with clean, economical dorms (the ones upstairs are better), simple but pleasant private rooms and a plethora of services including Wi-Fi, computer terminals, shuttles, tours and surf lessons. They also have a self-service kitchen, daily surf reports and a breezy bar-terrace that's great for evening drinks. Breakfast served 3 times a week. Youthful, fun and buzzing.

## $ Secret Cove Inn
*Mercado, 2 c sur, ½ c abajo, T8672-3013, www.thesecretcovenicaragua.com.*
Intimate and friendly B&B lodging with a handful of clean, comfortable, well-appointed rooms. They offer tours and information, use of kitchen, hammocks, Wi-Fi and a relaxed communal area. Very welcoming and helpful. Nice owners. Recommended.

## Restaurants

There are many popular, but overpriced, restaurants lining the beach, where your tourist dollars buy excellent sea views and mediocre food. Only the better ones are included below. For budget dining you can't beat the market.

## $$$ Bambú Beach Club
*Malecón Norte, 200 m from the bridge, www.thebambu beachclub.com.*
Conceived and executed by a German-Austrian-Italian trio, the Bambú Beach Club is one of San Juan's finest dining options and often recommended. Mediterranean-inspired seafood with a hint of Nica.

## $$$-$$ El Colibrí
*Mercado, 1 c este, 2½ c sur.*
The best restaurant in town, with an excellent and eclectic Mediterranean menu, great decor and ambience, fine wines and really good food, much of it organic. Pleasant, hospitable and highly recommended.

## $$ Café Mediterránaeo

*In front of the market.*

An intimate little Italian restaurant, casual and low-key. Their Italian chef reputedly does the best pasta in town and their menu also includes Mediterranean-style chicken and fish, as well as light snacks, including paninis. Doubles up as a café in the day when you can pick up a good espresso or cappuccino.

## $$ Cha Cha Cha

*Av Gaspar García Laviana y Callejón del Sindicato, 10 m north of the market.*

A fun, friendly little restaurant, good for a cold beer and a chat. They serve wholesome international comfort food, including potato salad, burritos, nachos, jerk chicken in rum sauce, 3-bean vegetarian casserole and, on Fri (not to be missed), beer-battered fish and chips and Guinness.

## $$ King Curry

*At the bus stop, opposite the Mercado Municipal.*

The perfect antidote to weary taste buds, King Curry serves up feisty and flavourful Asian cuisine, spicy curries with a Central American twist. Owned by a trained German chef, Marcus, who lived in India. Often packed in the evenings. Recommended.

## $$ Nacho Libre

*Mercado Municipal, 1 c al oeste, ½ c al norte. Closed Mon.*

An awesome array of gourmet beef and veggie burgers, the best in town, all served with tasty home-cut fries. Other options include ceviche and 'Mexican pizza'. Casual and sociable, laid-back ambience. Recommended.

## $$ Pizzería San Juan

*Southwest corner of Parque Central, ½ c al mar. Tue-Sun 1700-2130.*

Often buzzing with expats and visitors, this restaurant serves excellent and authentic Italian pizzas, large enough to satisfy 2 people. Recommended, but perhaps not for a romantic evening meal.

## $ Comedor Margarita

*Mercado, ½ c norte.*

*Comida típica* and other cheap fare. Unpretentious, wholesome and good-value daily specials. A nice change. Recommended.

### Cafés and juice bars

#### Gato Negro

*Mercado, 1 c al mar, 1 c norte.*

Popular gringo café with good, if slightly pricey, coffee, a reading space, breakfasts and snacks. This is also one of the best bookshops in the country, with the largest collection of English-language books on Nicaragua, and plenty of fiction too. Chocolate chip and banana pancakes are great for those with a sweet tooth. Recommended.

#### Simon Says

*Av Vanderbilt, Gato Negro, 60 m sur.*

Bohemian little café with good artwork and a host of board games. They serve a variety of nutritious fruit smoothies, wraps, sandwiches, coffee and cooked breakfasts. Chilled ambience. Recommended.

### Bars and clubs

#### Big Wave Dave's

*UNO, 200 m al mar, T2568-2203, www. bigwavedaves.net. Tue-Sun 0830-0000.*

Popular with foreigners out to party and hook up with others. Wholesome pub food and a busy, boozy atmosphere.

#### Iguana Bar

*Malecón, next door to Timón, www.iguanabeachbar.com.*

Also known as **Henry's Iguana**, a very popular hang-out with tourists, often buzzing and a good place to knock back rum and beer. They also do food, including sandwiches, burgers, beer and cheese-drenched nachos. Various happy hours and events, check the website for the latest.

### Republika

*Mercado, ½ c al mar.*
Intimate café-style bar, low-key, with a friendly crowd and occasional live music and barbecue.

## What to do

### Diving

The waters around San Juan del Sur are home to a wrecked Russian trawler and a plethora of sea creatures including rays, turtles and eels.
**Neptune Watersports**, *T2568-2752, www. neptunenicadiving.com*. This PADI centre offers 2-tank dives. Open water certification and training to Dive Master level. They also do fishing and snorkelling tours.

### Fishing

Depending on the season, the waters around San Juan harbour all kinds of game fish, including marlin, jack and dorado. Many hotels and surf shops offer fishing packages, including **Gran Océano**. Otherwise try:
**Super Fly Sport Fishing**, *advance reservation only, T8884-8444, www.nicafishing.com*. Fly fishing and light tackle, deep-sea fishing, Captain Gabriel Fernández, fluent in English with lots of experience, also fishes north Pacific coast and Lake Nicaragua.

### Language schools

**APC**, *BDF, 20 vrs sur, T8678-7839*. One-to-one classes, homestays, activities.
**Nicaragua Language School**, *southwest corner of Parque Central, ½ c al mar, T2568-2142, www.nicaspanish.com*. One-to-one immersion classes, volunteer opportunities and customized classes. Free internet.
**Spanish School House Rosa Silva**, *mercado, 50 m al mar, T8682-2938*. 20 hrs of 'dynamic' classes cost US$120, student accommodation or homestay are extra. Activities include swimming, hiking and cooking. All teachers are English-speaking. Teaching by the hour, US$7.
**Spanish School San Juan del Sur**, *T2568-2432, www.sjdsspanish.com*. Regular morning classes, tutoring with flexible hours.

**Spanish Ya**, *UNO, 100 vrs norte T8898-5036, www.learnspanishya.com*. One-to-one classes, accommodation, activities and volunteer opportunities. DELE courses and diplomas.

### Sailing

**Pelican Eyes Sailing Adventures**, *Parroquia 1½ c arriba, T2563-7000, www.pelicaneyes resort.com*. Sails to the beach at Brasilito, US$90 per person full day, US$60 per person half day, discount for hotel guests, minimum 10 people, leaves San Juan at 0900.

### Surfing

The coast north and south of San Juan del Sur is among the best in Central America for surfing, access to the best areas are by boat or long treks in 4WD. Board rental costs US$10 per day; lessons US$30 per hr. The best shop in town is:
**Good Times Surf Shop**, *Malecón, next to Iguana Bar, T8675-1621, www.goodtimes surfshop.com*. Also known as 'Outer Reef S.A.', This well-established and professional surf shop specializes in quality and customized surfboard rentals, lessons and tours. Tours include day trips as well as multi-day and boat trips to surf hard-to-reach waves. Friendly, helpful and highly recommended. Dave claims he "will never piss on your leg and tell you it's raining". Recommended.

## Transport

Buses and shared taxis leave from Rivas bus station. If coming from the Costa Rican border, take any bus towards Rivas and step down at the entrance to the Carretera a San Juan del Sur in La Virgen. If you are visiting outlying beaches you can arrange private transport with local hotels or use one of the converted cattle trucks that shuttle tourists north and south. For the wilder and truly untamed stretches further away from town you will need a decent 4WD (see below) and/or a boat.

**Bus** To **Managua** express bus 0500, 0530, 0600, 1730, US$3.50, 2½ hrs, ordinary bus every hour 0500-1530, US$2.50, 3½ hrs. Or take a bus/taxi to Rivas and change here. To **Rivas**, every 30 mins, 0500-1700, US$1, 40 mins. For **La Flor** or **Playa El Coco** use bus to **El Ostional**, 1600, 1700, US$ 0.70, 1½ hrs. Return from El Coco at 0600, 0730 and 1630.

**Shuttles** Several companies run shuttles to the beaches north and south of San Juan del Sur, including **Casa Oro Youth Hostel**. Several daily departures to **Los Playones**, next to Maderas, and 1 daily departure to **Remanso**, US$5. Note schedules are affected by tides and may not operate in inclement weather.

**4WD** You can usually find a 4WD pick-up to make trips to outlying beaches or to go surfing. You should plan a day in advance and ask for some help from your hotel. Prices range from US$20-75 depending on the trip and time. You can also hire 4WDs, contact **Alamo Rent a Car**, inside hotel Casa Blanca, T2277-1117, www.alamonicaragua.com.

**Taxi** Taxi Colectivo is a very feasible way to get to Rivas and slightly quicker than the bus. They depart from the market, US$1.75 per person, or US$7.50 for the whole taxi, but tourist rates are often double.

## North of San Juan del Sur  *Colour map 4, A1/2.*

**spectacular beaches with white sand and rugged forested hillsides**

There is an unpaved access road to beaches north of San Juan del Sur at the entrance to the town. It is possible to travel the entire length of the coast to Chacocente from here, though it is quite a trip as the road does not follow the shoreline but moves inland to Tola (west of Rivas) and then back to the ocean. The surface is changeable from hard-packed dirt to sand, stone and mud; in the rainy season a 4WD or sturdy horse is needed.

**Playa Marsella** has plenty of signs that mark the exit to the beach. It is a slow-growing destination set on pleasant sands, but not one of the most impressive in the region. North of here, **Los Playones** is playing host to growing crowds of surfers with a scruffy beer shack and hordes of daily shuttle trucks. The waves are good for beginners, but often overcrowded. **Maderas** is the next beach along, where many shuttles claim to take you (they don't, they drop you at the car park at Los Playones). This is a pleasant, tranquil spot, good for swimming and host to some affordable lodgings (book in advance). **Bahía Majagual** is the next bay north, a lovely white-sand beach tucked into a cove. On the road to Majagual is the private entrance to **Morgan's Rock**, a multi-million dollar private nature reserve and ecolodge, beautiful but costly. To the north are yet more pristine beaches, like **Manzanillo** and **El Gigante**, and all have development projects. Notable is the legendary surf spot **Popoyo**. The surf here is very big with a good swell and it still has waves when the rest of the ocean is as calm as a swimming pool. One of the prettiest beaches on the northern Rivas coast is **Playa Conejo**, now taken over by **Hotel Punta Teonoste**. This is the nearest decent accommodation to Chacocente Wildlife Refuge, 7 km north of the hotel (see below) with year-round access via the highway from Ochomogo.

### Refugio de Vida Silvestre Río Escalante Chacocente

*www.chacocente-nicaragua.com. There is a US$5 entrance fee. There is no public transport to the park and a 4WD is necessary during the turtle-laying season from Aug to Nov. There are 2 entrances to the area, one from Santa Teresa south of Jinotepe. Follow that road until the pavement ends and then turn left to the coast. Before you reach the bay of Astillero you will see a turning to the right with a sign for Chacocente. Alternatively, at Km 80 on the Pan-American*

*Highway, on the south side of the bridge over the Río Ochomogo, a rough dirt road runs west to the Pacific Ocean. This is a 40-km journey through small friendly settlements to the same turning for the reserve.*

This is one of the four most important sea turtle nesting sites on the entire Pacific seaboard of the American continent. The park is also a critical tropical dry forest reserve and a good place to see giant iguanas and varied birdlife. The beach itself is lovely, with a long open stretch of sand that runs back into the forest, perfect for stringing up a hammock. Camping is permitted – this may well be the most beautiful camping spot along the coast – but no facilities are provided and you will need to come well stocked with water and supplies. The Nicaraguan environmental protection agency **MARENA** has built attractive cabins for park rangers and scientists and it is possible that they will rent them to visitors in the future. Nesting turtles can also be observed at La Flor wildlife refuge (see page 648).

## Listings North of San Juan del Sur

### Where to stay

**$$$$ Morgan's Rock Hacienda & Ecolodge**
*Playa Ocotal, reservations T8670-7676, www.morgansrock.com.*
Famous ecolodge with precious wood bungalows and unrivalled views of the ocean and forest. The cabins are built on a high bluff above the beach and are connected to the restaurant and pool by a suspension bridge. The food, included in the price, has received mixed reports; the hotel has rave reviews. Highly recommended if you've got the dosh.

**$$$$-$$$ Two Brothers Surf Resort**
*T8877-7501, Playa Popoyo, www.twobrotherssurf.com.*
Stylish whitewashed self-catering *cabañas* and villas set in well-groomed grounds, all different and tastefully attired with hand-carved Indonesian temple doors and arches. The interiors are spacious, comfortable and equipped with cafetière, fridge, microwave, stove, hot water and Wi-Fi. Prices are per villa not per person; surf packages available. Advance reservation essential.

**$$$ Buena Vista Surf Club**
*Playa Maderas, T8863-4180, www.buenavistasurfclub.com.*
The Buena Vista boasts several attractive luxury tree houses up on the cliffs, each with private bath, fan and mosquito nets. The communal 'rancho', where guests gather to eat and drink, has superb views of the ocean. Breakfast and dinner included; minimum 2-night stay. Board rental and tours available.

**$$$ El Empalme a Las Playas**
*At the fork in the road between Playa Marsella and Playa Maderas, T8803-7280, www.playa marsella.com.*
A friendly, personable lodging just minutes from the beach and surf. Accommodation is in rustic cane and thatch *cabañas*; each is equipped with a private bath and fan. Lots of pleasant greenery and wildlife around. Breakfast included. Often recommended.

**$$$ Hotel Punta Teonoste**
*Playa Conejo, Las Salinas, reservations in Managua at Hotel Los Robles, T2563-9001, www.punta teonoste.com.*
Charming cabins overlooking a lovely beach. The bathroom and shower outside units are in a private open-air area, there's weak water pressure, unusual decor, private decks with hammock and circular bar at beach. All meals included. Avoid windy months from Dec-Mar.

**$$$-$ Hotel Magnific Rock**
*End of the road to Playa Popoyo, T8916-6916, www.magnificrockpopoyo.com.*
A wood and brick built surf and yoga retreat with panoramic views of the ocean

and close to some lesser-known breaks. Accommodation includes luxury self-contained apartments and suites (**$$$**) and more modest hostel-style accommodation in shared *cabañas* (**$**).

**$$ Casa Maderas Ecolodge**
*Playa Maderas road, 200 m from the junction, 10 mins from the beach, T8786-4897, www.casamaderas.com.*
Resort-style lodging with 16 white *cabañas* (**$$**), artistically adorned with colourful

tropical-themed murals. Yoga, pool, restaurant and massage. One cabin serves as a shared dorm (**$**).

**$ Los Tres Hermanos**
*Los Playones, T8879-5272.*
Scruffy little shack popular with surfers and budget travellers, conveniently located next to the shuttle drop-off. There are just 10 dorm beds, usually full, and you can pitch a tent for US$2. Beer, water and *comida típica* available. A bit of a dive.

## South of San Juan del Sur   *Colour map 4, B2.*

**surf beaches and nesting sea turtles**

A paved road runs south from the bridge at the entrance to San Juan del Sur towards El Ostional. There are signs for Playa Remanso, the first and most accessible beach south of San Juan, very popular with surfers. Further on is Playa Hermosa, accessible from a 4-km dirt road roughly 6 km along the Ostional road. After Hermosa, isolated Playa Yankee is also renowned for its waves. Continuing south, the beautifully scenic country road has many elevation changes and ocean vistas. Playa El Coco is a long copper-coloured beach with strong surf most of the year. Beyond El Coco, the road passes El Ostional near the Costa Rican border, a tiny fishing village that's now being sought out by wave hunters.

### Refugio de Vida Silvestre La Flor
*US$10, US$2.50 student discount, access by 4WD or on foot.*

Just past Playa El Coco and 18 km from the highway at San Juan del Sur, La Flor Wildlife Refuge protects tropical dry forest, mangroves, estuary and 800 m of beachfront. This beautiful sweeping cove with light tan sand is an important site for nesting sea turtles. The best time to come is between August and November. Rangers protect the multitudinous arrivals during high season and are very happy to explain, in Spanish, about the animals' reproductive habits. Sometimes turtles arrive in their thousands (as many as 20,000), usually over a period of four days. Camping can be provided (although there is a limited number of tents) during the season, US$25 per night. Bring a hammock and mosquito netting, as insects are vicious at dusk.

## Listings South of San Juan del Sur

### Where to stay

**$$$$-$$$ Parque Marítimo El Coco**
*18 km south of San Juan del Sur, T8999-8069, www.playael coco.com.ni.*
Apartments and houses right on the sand and close to La Flor Wildlife Refuge. Suits

4-10 people, most have a/c, all have baths, TV and cleaning service included. There's a general store and restaurant in the complex. The beach, backed by forest, can have strong waves. Rates vary according to season, weekday nights are less expensive. Interesting rural excursions are offered.

# **Isla** de Ometepe

★ Rising dream-like from the waters of Lake Nicaragua, the ethereal isle of Ometepe is composed of two prehistoric volcanoes. Volcán Concepción is the larger of the two: geologically active, temperamental and prone to outbursts of smoke and ash. Now extinct, Volcán Maderas is tranquil and verdant, its fertile slopes cloaked in misty cloudforests.

The ancient Nahuas of Mexico were guided to Ometepe by the gods, so the legend goes, after many years of fruitless wandering. Today, the island's pre-Columbian heritage survives in the form of cryptic petroglyphs and enigmatic statues depicting shamans and animal spirits. Directly descended from those ancient cultures, Ometepe's inhabitants are mostly fisherfolk and farmers and some of Nicaragua's kindest people.

This is a fine place for volunteering or learning about organic farming. The rich volcanic soil means agriculture here has always been organic, but a wave of foreigners are introducing more sophisticated and ecologically aware permaculture techniques. Thus far, tourist development has kept within the style and scale of the island, a UNESCO Biosphere Reserve since 2010, although there are now murmurings of larger, less sympathetic construction projects.

**Best** for
Island life ▪ Petroglyphs ▪ Volcanoes ▪ Wildlife

The port of entry for arrivals from San Jorge, this place is an increasingly popular stopover, particularly with those leaving on an early boat or climbing Concepción from the western route. The name translates as the 'place of mosquitoes', but there aren't really any more here than there are elsewhere in the region.

One interesting excursion from Moyogalpa (in the dry season only) is to walk or rent a bicycle to visit **Punta Jesús María**, 4-5 km away, with a good beach and a panoramic view of the island. It is well signposted from the Altagracia road; just before Esquipulas head straight towards the lake.

### Moyogalpa to Altagracia

There are two roads from Moyogalpa to Altagracia. The northern route is very rough but also very natural and scenic; it runs through the tiny villages of **La Concepción**, **La Flor** and **San Mateo**. There are commanding views of the volcano with its forests and 1957 lava flow beyond rock-strewn pasture and highland banana plantations, but it is a tough slog by bicycle and impossible by car without 4WD. Most transport uses the southern route to Altagracia, which is completely paved.

## Ometepe

**Where to stay** 🛏

Albergue Ecológico
  Porvenir **22**
American & Café **14**
Caballito Mar **4**
Central **5**
Charco Verde Inn **6**
Chico Largo Hostel **19**
Costa Azul **18**

El Encanto **20**
Finca del Sol **8**
Finca Ecológica El
  Zopilote **23**
Finca Magdalena **13**
Finca Playa Venecia **15**
Finca Santo Domingo **2**
Hacienda Mérida **7**
Hospedaje Ortiz **9**

Island Landing **10**
Istiam **1**
Little Morgan's **11**
Totoco **12**
Villa Paraíso **3**

Petroglyphs ⁙

## ON THE ROAD
### Climbing the volcanoes

**Volcán Concepción** There are two main trails leading up to the summit. One of the paths is best accessed from Moyogalpa, where there is lots of accommodation. The other is from Altagracia. Climbing the volcano without a local guide is not advised under any circumstances and can be very dangerous; a climber died here in 2004 after falling into a ravine. Ask your hotel about recommended tour guides; many of the locals know the trail well but that does not make them reliable guides; use extreme caution if contacting a guide not recommended by a tour operator or well-known hotel. The view from Concepción is breathtaking. The cone is very steep near the summit and loose footing and high winds are common. Follow the guide's advice if winds are deemed too strong for the summit. From Moyogalpa the trail begins near the village of La Flor and the north side of the active cone. You should allow eight hours for the climb. Bring plenty of water and breathable, strong and flexible hiking shoes. From Altagracia the hike starts 2 km away and travels through a cinder gully, between forested slopes and a lava flow. The ascent takes five hours, 3½ hours if you are very fit. Take water and sunscreen. Tropical dry and wet forest, heat from the crater and howler monkeys are added attractions.

**Volcán Maderas** Three trails ascend Maderas. One departs from Hotel La Omaja near Mérida, another from Finca El Porvenir near Santa Cruz, and the last from Finca Magdalena near Balgües. Presently, the trail from Finca Magdelena is the only one fit enough to follow, but check locally. You should allow five hours up and three hours down, although relatively dry trail conditions could cut down hiking time considerably. Expect to get very muddy in any case. Ropes are necessary if you want to climb down into the Laguna de Maderas after reaching the summit. Swimming in the laguna is not recommended; one tourist got stuck in the mud after jumping in and, rather farcically, had to be pulled out with a rope made of the tour group's trousers. Hiking Maderas can no longer be done without a guide, following the deaths of British and American hikers who apparently either got lost or tried to descend the west face of the volcano and fell. While some hikers still seem reluctant to pay a local guide, it is a cheap life insurance policy and helps the very humble local economy. Guides are also useful in pointing out animals and petroglyphs that outsiders may miss. There is an entrance fee of US$2 to climb Maderas. The trail leads through farms, fences and gets steeper and rockier with elevation. The forest changes with altitude from tropical dry, to tropical wet and finally cloud forest, with howler monkeys accompanying your journey. Guides can be found for this climb in Moyogalpa, Altagracia and Santo Domingo or at Finca Magdelena where the hike begins.

The southern road passes the town of **Esquipulas**, where it is rumoured that the great Chief Niqueragua may have been buried, and the village of **Los Angeles**, which has some of the oldest known evidence of ancient settlement. Before the next community, San José del Sur, a turning leads to the **Museo El Ceibo** ① *El Sacremento, T-15, www.elceibomuseos.com, daily 0800-1700, US$8 to view both pre-Columbian and numismatic collections or US$4 each,* which has the best collection of pre-Columbian artefacts on the island along with a fine

## BACKGROUND

## Isla de Ometepe

Ceramic evidence shows that the island has been inhabited for at least 3500 years, although some believe this figure could be 12,000 years or more. Little is known about the pre-Conquest cultures. From ceramic analysis carried out by US archaeologist Frederick W Lange (published in 1992), it appears the people of 1500 BC came from South America as part of a northern immigration that continued to Mexico, settling in what is today the town of Los Angeles. In the mid-1990s, a six-year survey revealed 73 pre-Columbian sites with 1700 petroglyph panels, and that is just the tip of the iceberg. One of the most interesting and easily accessible archaeological finds is in the grounds of Albergue Ecológico Porvenir (see Where to stay, page 657), which has a sundial, and what some believe to be an alien being and a representation of the god of death.

collection of antique notes and coins, many dating to the beginning of the Republic. Just past San José del Sur is the rough, narrow access road to **Charco Verde**, a big pond with a popular legend of a wicked sorcerer, Chico Largo, who was said to have shape-shifting powers and whose discarnate spirit guards the pond.

**Listings** Moyogalpa and *around map p650*

### Where to stay

#### Moyogalpa

**$$ The Corner House**
*Main street, 200 m up from the port, T2569-4177, www.thecornerhouseometepe.com.*
A pleasant little guesthouse on the main drag with 4 brick rooms and wooden furniture, views of Concepción, tranquil hammocks and Wi-Fi. Often full and bookings not accepted. Breakfast or takeaway lunch included and a great restaurant downstairs.

**$$-$ American Café and Hotel**
*Muelle Municipal, 100 vrs arriba, a white building on the right, T8650-4069, www.americancafeandhotel.com.*
Excellent value, handsome, comfortable, spacious, well-furnished and immaculately clean rooms. All have good mattresses, attractive fixtures and hot water (a/c available, $$). Hosts Bob and Simone are very friendly and hospitable. Italian, German, Spanish and English spoken. Recommended.

**$$-$ Hospedaje Soma**
*Opposite Instituto Smith, up the hill from the port, left at the church and straight on for 250 m, a 10-min walk, T2569-4310, www.hospedajesoma.com.*
A tranquil spot offering a mix of dorms ($), private rooms ($ with shared bath, $$ without), and cabins ($$). There's a large leafy garden, hammock space, open porch dining area, barbecue and fire pit. Full breakfast included.

**$$-$ The Landing**
*Muelle Municipal, 20 vrs arriba, almost next to the port, T2569-4113, www.thelandinghotel.com.*
A comfortable hostel-hotel with a range of options. For the impoverished there are hammocks and dorms; for the better off there are small private rooms, well-equipped apartments and comfortable *casitas* with open-air kitchen and dining space. Awesome chill-out spaces with breezy views of the lake. Friendly and hospitable.

## $ Yogi's Hostel
*The port, 3 blocks up, 2 blocks to the right,*
*T8691-5044.*
Low-key, relaxed hostel with a friendly and
helpful owner, Robinson. They have 2 mixed
dorms (double beds available for an extra
US$1) and 6 private rooms (3 with private
bath). Amenities include Wi-Fi, communal
kitchen, hammocks, volcano tours, bike and
moped rental. *Tranquilo.*

## Moyogalpa to Altagracia

### $$ Hotel Charco Verde Inn
*Almost next to the lagoon, San José del Sur,*
*T8887-9302, www.charcoverde.com.ni.*
Pleasant *cabañas* with private bath, a/c,
terrace and doubles with private bath
and fan. Services include restaurant, bar,
Wi-Fi, tours, kayaks, bicycles, horses and
transportation. An Ometepe favourite with
good reports.

### $$-$ Finca Playa Venecia
*250 m from the main road, San José del Sur,*
*T8887-0191, www.fincavenecia.com.*
Very chilled, comfortable lodgings and a
lovely lakeside garden. They have 4 rooms
($) and 15 *cabañas* ($$) of different sizes,
some with lake view and some cheaper ones
with fan. There's a good restaurant in the
grounds, Wi-Fi, horses, tours, motorcycles,
transportation and English-speaking guides.
Recommended.

## Restaurants

### Moyogalpa
Almost all lodges serve meals; see Where to
stay, above.

### $$ Los Ranchitos
*Muelle Municipal, 2 c arriba, ½ c sur,*
*T2569-4112.*
One of the best in town, with a dirt floor and
thatched roof. They serve fish, vegetarian
pasta, vegetable soup, chicken in garlic
butter, steak, pork and other hearty meat
dishes, all served in the usual Nica way, with
rice, beans, plantain and salad.

### $$ Pizzeria Buon Appetito
*Main street, 100 m up from the port.*
A well-presented Italian restaurant, the
smartest place in town, great ambience
and reasonable service. The menu of
pizza and pasta is a little pricey and not
consistently good, but the food is filling
and it's a pleasant place to unwind after
a long day hiking volcanoes.

### $$-$ The American Café
*The pier, 100 vrs arriba.*
Had enough of *gallo pinto*? This is the place for
home-made food with flavour, including chilli
con carne, *huevos rancheros*, cream cheese
bagels, pancakes and waffles. Very tasty and
good value. They also have a small second-
hand book collection. Recommended.

### $$-$ The Corner House
*Muelle Municipal, 200 vrs arriba, opposite the*
*petrol station.*
A bustling café-restaurant offering decent
coffee and espresso, sandwiches, creative
salads and tasty breakfasts, like eggs
Benedict. All ingredients are sourced locally.
Friendly owners. Recommended.

### $ The Chicken Lady
*The port, 3 blocks up, 2 blocks to the right,*
*2 doors from Yogi's Hostel.*
Budget travellers will delight in the generous
and ultra-cheap portions of chicken and
fried yucca at this informal evening *fritanga*;
US$1.50 gets you a plate.

## Festivals

### Moyogalpa
Dates for some of the festivities vary
according to the solar cycle.
**Jul** The town's patron saint festival (**Santa
Ana**) is a very lively affair. Processions begin
on **23 Jul** in the barrio La Paloma and
continue for several days. On **25 Jul** there is a
lovely dance with girls dressed in indigenous
costume and on **26 Jul** there's a huge party
with bullfights at a ring north of the church.
**Dec** 2nd week of Dec, an impressive
**marathon** takes endurance runners up

Concepción (25 km), Maderas (50 km) or both (100 km).

## What to do

### Moyogalpa
#### ATVs, biking and motorbiking

Bikes and motorbikes are now ubiquitous on Isla Ometepe and are a great way to get around. Most hotels rent them and charge US$5-7 per day for bicycles, US$20-30 for motorbikes or mopeds. Ask at the shops near the dock, or try **Robinson**, who has cycles, motorbikes and a few ATVs (US$80 per day); find him at **Yogi's Hostel** (T8691-5044, robinson170884@gmail.com). Ensure your vehicle is robust if aiming to cross the rough roads on the north side of Concepción or the east side of Maderas. Some tourists have been in nasty and expensive accidents with motorbike rentals. Clarify all insurance details before hiring and, if you've never ridden before, understand that a quick jaunt up and down a football pitch does not qualify you to ride on the roads.

## Transport

All times are Mon-Sat and subject to change; on Sun there are very few buses. Always confirm times if planning a long journey involving connections. Hitching is possible.

Most of the island is linked by a bus service, otherwise trucks are used. The road is paved almost as far as Balgüe; it remains unpaved and in poor condition towards Mérida. There is a slow ferry from San Carlos on the Río San Juan. The ferry from Granada is not recommended; it is quicker to go via San Jorge.

### Moyogalpa
**Boat and ferry**  Schedules are always subject to change. To **San Jorge**, hourly, 0500-1730, ferry US$3, boat US$2, 1 hr. Reduced service on Sun. See also San Jorge transport, page 640.

**Bus**  Buses wait for the boats in Moyogalpa and run to **Altagracia** Mon-Sat, every 1-2 hrs, 0530-1830, US$1, 1 hr; Sun, several from 0530-1830. To **San Ramón** Mon-Sat, 0830, 0930, US$1.25, 3 hrs. To **Mérida**, Mon-Sat, 1445, 1630, US$2, 2 hrs; Sun 1245. To **Balgües**, Mon-Sat, 1030, 1530, US$2, 2 hrs; Sun 1020. For **Charco Verde** and San José del Sur, take any bus to Altagracia and ask the driver where to get out. For **Playa Santo Domingo** or **Santa Cruz**, take any bus bound for Balgües, San Ramón or Mérida; or go to the Santo Domingo turn-off before Altagracia and get a connection there.

**Taxi**  Pick-up and van taxis wait for the ferry, along with a handful of spiffy new tuk-tuks. Price is per journey not per person, some have room for 4 passengers, others 2, the rest go in the back, which has a far better view, but is dusty in dry season. To **Altagracia** US$12-15, to **Santo Domingo** US$20-25, to **Mérida** US$30. Try **Transporte Ometepe**, T8695-9905, robertometeour@yahoo.es, or ask a hotel to arrange pickup.

### Moyogalpa to Altagracia
**Boat and ferry**  Boats depart from San José del Sur to **San Jorge**, 0540, 0730, 1330, 1520, ferry US$3, boat US$2, 1 hr. Reduced service on Sun.

## Altagracia

calm, unpretentious town, the most important on the island

Altagracia hides its population of around 20,000 well, except at weekends when there is usually dancing and drinking, not to mention the odd fight among the local cowboys. The town predates the arrival of the Spanish and was once home to two tribes who named their villages Aztagalpa (egrets' nest) and Cosonigalpa.

Next to Altagracia's crumbling old church is a **sculpture park** ⓘ *daily 0900-1700, US$1.50*, containing intriguing pre-Columbian statues. They are estimated to date from AD 800 and represent human forms and their alter egos or animal protectors. On the plaza, the **Museo de Ometepe** ⓘ *Tue-Sun 0900-1200, 1400-1600, US$2*, has displays of archaeology and covers local ethnographic and environmental themes (in Spanish only).

## Listings Altagracia

### Where to stay

**$ Hospedaje y Restaurante Ortiz**
*Del Hotel Central, 1 c arriba, ½ c al sur, follow signs near the entrance to town, T8923-1628.*
A very friendly, relaxed hotel managed by the hospitable Don Mario. An amiable family atmosphere. Highly recommended for budget travellers, but bear in mind it's very basic. Noisy neighbourhood dogs, bring earplugs.

**$ Hotel Central**
*Iglesia, 2 c sur, T2552-8770, doscarflores@yahoo.es.*
19 rooms and 6 *cabañas*, most with private bath and fan. There's a restaurant and bar, bicycle rental, tours, laundry service, parking and hammocks to rest your weary bones. Dominoes and chess to keep you entertained in the evening.

### Festivals

**Oct-Nov** The town's patron saint, **San Diego de Alcalá**, is celebrated from 28 Oct to 18 Nov with many dances and traditions, particularly the **Baile del Zompopo** (the dance of the leaf-cutter ant), which is famous throughout the country.
**Dec** The **Purísima** celebrations to the Virgin Mary on 7 Dec are a marathon affair here of singing to a large, heavily decorated image of Santa María on the back of a pick-up truck in what is truly a Fellini-esque setting.

### What to do

**Archaeology**
Professor Hamilton Silva, north side of the Catholic church, or ask at the museum, T8905-3744, is a resident expert on Ometepe's history and archaeology. He speaks a little English and leads interesting good-value tours to the island's petroglyph sites.

### Transport

**Bus** For **Playa Santo Domingo** use any bus to San Ramón, Mérida or Balgües. To **Moyogalpa**, Mon-Sat every 1-2 hrs, 0430-0530, US$1, 1hr; Sun several daily, 0430-1700. To **Balgües**, Mon-Sat, 8 daily, 0430-1700, US$1, 1 hr; Sun 1040. To **Mérida**, Mon-Sat, 6 daily, 0730-1600, US$1, 2 hrs. To **San Ramón**, Mon-Sat, 1030, 1400, US$1.30, 3 hrs.

**Ferry** The port of Altagracia is called **San Antonio** and is 2 km north of the town; pick-up trucks meet the boat that passes between Granada and San Carlos. To **San Carlos**, Mon and Thu 1800-1900, upper deck (1st class) US$7, lower deck US$2.50, 11 hrs. To **Granada**, Tue and Fri, 2300-0000, upper deck (1st class) US$4.50, lower deck US$2, 3½ hrs. You strongly advised to travel on the upper deck and wear warm clothes. A sleeping bag, pillow and anti-sickness tablets are useful too.

**sweeping sandy beach overlooked by Volcán Maderas**

Santo Domingo lies on the narrow isthmus between Concepción and Maderas. The coastline of Santo Domingo is one of the prettiest freshwater beaches in Nicaragua and, with the forest-covered Volcán Maderas looming at the beach's end, truly exotic. The warm water, gentle waves and gradual shelf make it a great swimming beach.

It is reached via a paved road which begins near Altagracia's southern exit and after 2 km, passes **El Ojo de Agua**① *0700-1800, US$1*, where you'll find refreshing man-made swimming pools, a small ranch and some gentle walking trails.

On this side of the island the trade winds blow nearly all year round and keep the heat and insects at bay. At times the wind is too strong for some visitors. There are many magpie jays, parrots, vultures, ospreys and hawks around Santo Domingo.

### Santa Cruz

The diminutive settlement of Santa Cruz lies at the foot of Volcán Maderas, just south of Santo Domingo. The road forks here – one route goes north towards Balgüe, the other heads south to Mérida and San Ramón – making it a good base for exploring both sides of Maderas.

Several hikers have fallen to their deaths trying to reach the summits of Ometepe's volcanoes unguided. Always use professional and qualified guides and beware of local scammers.

### Balgüe and around

The road to Balgüe is now paved. The village itself is a little sad in appearance, but the people are warm and friendly. Balgüe is the entrance to the trailhead for the climb to the summit of Maderas (see box, page 651). There are several interesting **organic farms** in the area, including the famous Finca Magdalena, Finca Campestre and Bona Fide farm, where you can study permaculture techniques.

## Listings Playa Santo Domingo and around

### Where to stay

#### Playa Santo Domingo

**$$$-$$ Villa Paraíso**
*Beachfront, T2569-4859,*
*www.villaparaiso.com.ni.*
One of Ometepe's longest established and most pleasant lodgings. It has a beautiful, peaceful setting with 25 stone *cabañas* **$$$** ) and 5 rooms **$$** ). Most have a/c, private bath, hot water, cable TV, minibar and internet. Some of the cabins have a patio and lake view. Often fully booked, best to reserve in advance.

**$$$-$ Xalli**
*Playa Santo Domingo, T2569-4876,*
*www.ometepebeachhotel.com.*

An elegantly refurbished beachfront hotel with 7 modern rooms, including 'value rooms' **$** ) for the budget traveller, 'deluxe' rooms and suites **$$$** ). Service includes restaurant and bar serving locally sourced organic food and drink, Wi-Fi and tours. Sustainably operated and community-orientated. Recommended.

#### Santa Cruz

**$$ Finca del Sol**
*From the fork in the road, 200 m*
*towards Balgües, T8364-6394,*
*www.hotelfincadelsol.com.*
A lovely natural place with comfortable and ecologically designed *cabañas*. All are equipped with solar power, orthopaedic mattresses, TV, DVD player, shower and

compost toilet. They grow their own organic fruit and vegetables and also keep sheep. A maximum of 8 guests are permitted; book in advance. Highly recommended.

### $ Albergue Ecológico Porvenir
*T8447-9466, www.porvenirometepe. blogspot.com.*
Stunning views at this tranquil lodge at the foot of Maderas. Rooms are clean, simple, comfortable and tidy, with private bath and fan. Scores of petroglyphs are scattered throughout the grounds. Good value. Recommended.

### $ Finca Ecológica El Zopilote
*From the fork in the road, 300 m towards Balgües, T8369-0644, www.ometepezopilote.com.*
El Zopilote is a funky organic finca that's popular with backpackers, hippies and eco-warrior types. They offer dorm beds, hammocks and *cabañas*. Tranquil and alternative.

### $ Little Morgan's
*From the fork in the road, 200 m towards Balgües, T8949-7074, www.littlemorgans.com.*
Little Morgan's is a fun, popular, youthful place with hospitable Irish management, a pool table and a well-stocked bar. They offer rustic dorms, hammocks and 2 *casitas*, as well as guided tours and kayaks (there's access to a good sheltered bay). Some of the hotel's structures are artfully reminiscent of *Lord of the Rings*.

## Balgüe and around

### $$$ Totoco Eco-Lodge
*Balgües, sign from the road, 1.5-km steep climb uphill, T8358-7718, www.totoco.com.ni.*
Totoco is an ethically oriented and ecologically aware project that includes a permaculture farm, ecolodge and development centre. They have several comfortable custom-designed *cabañas* with solar-powered hot showers. There's a great restaurant with superb views, a lovely pool and they offer a range of excellent tours. Highly recommended.

### $$-$ Finca Magdalena
*Balgües, signs from the road, 1.5-km steep climb uphill, T8498-1683, www.fincamagdalena.com.*
Famous co-operative farm run by 26 families, with accommodation in cottages, *cabañas* ($$), doubles ($), singles, dorms and hammocks. Also camping. Stunning views across lake and to Concepción. Friendly, basic and often jammed to the rafters with backpackers. Good meals served for around US$2-3. You can work in exchange for lodging, 1 month minimum.

## Restaurants

### Playa Santo Domingo

### $$ Natural
*Playa Santo Domingo, on the edge of the strip.*
Charming little hippy shack on the beach. Serves vegetarian food that's reasonably tasty but not good value. OK.

### Santa Cruz

### $ Comedor Santa Cruz
*From the fork in the road, 50 m towards Balgües.*
Home cooking from the irrepressible Doña Pilar, who serves up the usual hearty Nica meat, fish and chicken fare. Service is achingly slow, so bring a book or a deck of cards.

### Balgüe

### $$ Café Campestre
Roadside café-restaurant that serves one of the best curries in Nicaragua (hot, spicy and highly recommended). There's tamer fare too, including burritos, burgers, sandwiches and other tasty, well-prepared creations that are sure to please the gringo palate. Juices, coffee and breakfast offered too. Recommended.

## What to do

### Balgüe
**Organic farming**
**Bona Fide**, *www.projectbonafide.com.* Also known as Michael's farm, Bona Fide offers innovative courses in permaculture as well as volunteer opportunities.

From the fork at Santa Cruz, the road goes south past small homes and ranches and through the village of Mérida, in an area that was once a farm belonging to the Somoza family. It's possible to hire kayaks from Caballitos Mar (see Where to stay, below) if you wish to explore the nearby Río Istiam, an attractive waterway replete with birds, mammals and caiman.

### San Ramón

Further along the eastern shores of Maderas is the affluent town San Ramón. The 'biological station' is the starting point for a hike up the west face of Maderas Volcano to a stunning 40-m cascade, also called **San Ramón**. Sadly the walk has lost some of its charm due to the biological station's bad land management. As well as heavily planting the area with cash crops, they have installed a guard who you will need to pay to pass, US$5. Transport is not as frequent on this side of the island and you may have a long walk if you are not on a tour.

## Listings Mérida and around

### Where to stay

#### Mérida

**$$-$ Finca Mystica**
*El Congo, 550 m norte, T8751-9653,*
*www.fincamystica.com.*
Artistically designed round cabins ($$) set on a 10-ha farm. All building materials were locally sourced and the cabins constructed using cob, an organic adobe-like material composed of soil, sand, manure and rice straw. The overall effect is very organic and relaxing. There is a communal cabin too, for budget travellers ($).

**$$-$ Hacienda Mérida**
*El Puerto Viejo de Somoza, T8868-8973,*
*www.hmerida.com.*
Popular hostel with a beautiful setting by the lake. Lodgings have wheelchair access and include a mixture of dorms and rooms, some with views ($$). There's a children's school on site where you can volunteer, also kayak rental, good quality mountain bikes, internet and a range of tours available.

**$ Caballitos Mar**
*Follow signs from the road, T8842-6120,*
*www.caballitosmar.com.*
Ultra-cheap Mérida alternative that has the best access to the Río Istiam and good kayaks for day or night tours. Fernando, the Spanish owner, is friendly and helpful and cooks up a very decent paella. Rooms are very basic and rustic.

### What to do

#### Mérida
#### Kayaking
**Caballitos Mar**, *follow signs from the road, T8842-6120, www.caballitosmar.com.* The best starting point for kayak excursions down the Río Istiam, where you might spot caiman and turtles. Rentals are available for US$5 per hr, negotiable. Dawn is the best time for wildlife viewing, pack sunscreen and check lake conditions before setting out. There are also night tours.

# Río San Juan
## & the Archipiélago Solentiname

A natural canal between the Pacific and Atlantic oceans, the Río San Juan has long drawn enterprising factions keen to exploit its commercial and military potential: the British navy, Napoleon III and the US government among them. Fortunately they all failed, and today the river remains one of Central America's great natural attractions: a mini Amazonas where the evening symphony of tropical birds, high-pitched cicadas, ardent tree frogs, and vociferous howler monkeys hints at the multitude of strange creatures inhabiting the darkened rainforests on its banks.

Part of this remote region encompasses the southeastern sector of Lake Nicaragua, including the fabled Solentiname archipelago, a chain of pretty, drowsy islands that were once the site of an intriguing social experiment. In 1965, the poet-priest Ernesto Cardenal came here to preach liberation theology and instruct the locals in artistic methods. His dream was a kind of radical Christian-Communist utopia that combined religion and revolution, spiritual love and community conscience. The result was a school of primitivist art whose vivid output is internationally renowned.

**Best** for
Art ▪ Birdwatching ▪ Boat travel ▪ Island life

Perched like a ragged vulture between the San Juan river and Lake Nicaragua, San Carlos is a major crossroads, jungle gateway, border crossing (to Costa Rica, south along the Río Frío), as well as the capital of the isolated Río San Juan province. It has a sultry 'last outpost' feel: this is where the last buses arrive from the outside world after a lengthy journey through forests and wetlands, the big boat from Granada docks here after 15 or so hours on the lake, and, once a day, the single-propeller Cessna buzzes the rusting tin roofs as it arrives from Managua onto San Carlos' landing strip.

The locals are philosophical about the future of their town, which stands in contrast to the sublime natural beauty in the surrounding countryside. Los Guatuzos Wildlife Reserve is alive with nature on the southern shores of Lake Nicaragua and the soporific Solentiname archipelago is the place where life finds itself in the lively colours and brush strokes of painted canvases.

### Sights
Since the so-called 'discovery' of the Río San Juan by the Spanish Captain Ruy Díaz in 1525, San Carlos has had strategic importance. Its location means controlling San Carlos means controlling the water passages from north to south and east to west. The town was first founded in 1526, but it did not officially become a port until 1542. The town (and a fortress that has not survived) were abandoned for an unknown length of time and were re-founded as San Carlos during the 17th century. A new fortress was built but was sacked by pirates in 1670; part of it survives today as a small **museum** ⓘ *0900-1200, 1400-1700, free*, and the town's principal tourist attraction. Today, San Carlos acts as a trading centre and as a staging post for Nicaraguan migrant workers and for a small but growing number of tourists. The city is small and easily navigated on foot. You are advised to bring as much cash as you'll need to the region due to the possible failure of the ATM in San Carlos.

### San Carlos to Costa Rica
South of San Carlos, the Río Frío connects Lake Nicaragua and the Río San Juan to Los Chiles in northern Costa Rica. Formalities must be completed in San Carlos before crossing the border; see also Nicaragua–Costa Rica border box in the Practicalities chapter. The river passes through the superb **Refugio de Vida Silvestre Los Guatuzos** (see below) and the east bank is home to a small nature reserve called **Esperanza Verde** (see page 689). The limits of Nicaraguan territory are marked by a little green guard house. Although the river is used mainly as a commuter route, there is some beautiful wildlife and vegetation and it is rare not to see at least one clan of howler monkeys along the banks or even swimming.

### Refugio de Vida Silvestre Los Guatuzos
Nicaraguan biologists consider Los Guatuzos Wildlife Refuge the cradle of life for the lake, because of its importance as a bird-nesting site and its infinite links in the area's complex ecological chain. More than a dozen rivers run through the reserve, the most popular for wildlife viewing being the **Río Papaturro**. The ecosystems are diverse with tropical dry forest, tropical wet forest, rainforest and extensive wetlands. Best of all are the many narrow rivers lined with gallery forest, the ideal setting for viewing wildlife. The vegetation here is stunning with over 315 species of plants, including some primary

forest trees over 35 m in height, and 130 species of orchid. The most impressive aspect of the reserve, however, is the density of its birdlife. As well as the many elegant egrets and herons, there are five species of kingfisher, countless jacanas, the pretty purple gallinule, wood storks, the roseate spoonbill, jabiru, osprey, laughing falcon, scarlet-rumped tanagers, trogons, bellbirds and six species of parrot.

Some local residents have become involved in the research and protection of the reserve at the **Centro Ecológico de Los Guatuzos** ① *Managua office T2270-5434, www. losguatuzos.com, US$6 including tour of the grounds and projects; canopy bridge US$10 extra.* The ecological centre has over 100 species of orchid on display, a turtle hatchery and a caiman breeding centre. There is also a system of wobbly canopy bridges to allow visitors to observe wildlife from high up in the trees. If you don't suffer from vertigo, this is a wonderful experience allowing you to get right up close to the wildlife.

## Archipiélago Solentiname

The Solentiname archipelago is a protected national monument and one of the most scenic parts of Lake Nicaragua. It is made up of 36 islands, all very remote, sparsely populated, without roads, telephones, electricity or running water. This is Nicaragua as it was two centuries ago, with only the outboard motorboat as a reminder of the modern world. There is plenty to keep you occupied on the islands, including visits to local artists, boating, swimming and nature walks. The main problem is the lack of public boats; services from San Carlos depart just twice a week (although plans are underway to establish a daily express service). This means you will have to hire a boat or use a tour operator to organize your trip or allow plenty of time to find transport when you're out there.

**Isla Mancarrón** is the biggest island in the chain and has the highest elevation at 250 m. It derives its name from the indigenous word for the coyol palm tree, which is used to make a sweet palm wine. The famous revolutionary/poet/sculptor/Catholic priest/ Minister of Culture, Ernesto Cardenal, made his name here by founding a primitivista school of painting, poetry and sculpture, and even decorating the local parish church in naïve art. The church is open and there is a museum just behind the altar (ask permission to visit). It contains the first oil painting ever made on Solentiname, a bird's eye view of the island, and many other curiosities. Mancarrón is good for walking and it is home to many parrots and Montezuma oropendolas. Ask in the village for a guide to show you the way to the mirador, which has super views of the archipelago.

Named for its once-plentiful population of deer, **La Venada** (also known as Isla Donald Guevara) is a long narrow island that is home to many artists, including Rodolfo Arellano who lives on the southwestern side of the island. He and his wife are among the islands' original painters and his family welcome visitors to see and purchase their work. On the north side of the island is a series of semi-submerged caves with some of the best examples of petroglyphs which are attributed to the Guatuzo people. The cave can be visited by boat, though the entrance is dangerous if the lake is rough. Isla San Fernando, also known as Elvis Chavarría, is also famous for its artisan work and painting. It has some of the prettiest houses in the archipelago and is home to the famous Pineda artist family. On a hill, the **Museo Archipiélago Solentiname** ① *T2583-0095 (in San Carlos), US$2,* has a small pre-Columbian collection, with some interesting explanations of local culture and ecology. It also has a fabulous view of the islands, not to be missed at sunset. **Mancarroncito** is a big, wild, mountainous island with primary forest. There is some good hiking in the forest, although the terrain is steep. Ask at your guesthouse for a recommended guide.

## Tourist information

### Tourist office
*On the waterfront malecón, T2583-0301.*
*Mon-Fri 0800-1200, 1400-1700.*
They have a selection of maps and flyers.
They're helpful, but speak Spanish only.

## Where to stay

### San Carlos

### $$ Gran Lago Hotel
*Caruna, 25 vrs al lago, T2583-0075,*
*hotelgrandlago.rsj@gmail.com.*
Has views of the lake and serves fruit
breakfast in the mornings. The rooms are
comfortable, with private bath, a/c, cable TV,
Wi-Fi and 24-hr water. Purified water
and coffee available throughout the day.

### $$-$ Cabinas Leyko
*Policía Nacional, 2 c abajo, T2583-0354,*
*leyko@ibw.com.ni.*
One of the better places in town, with clean,
comfortable wooden cabins overlooking the
wetlands, good mattresses, Wi-Fi, private bath
and a/c. There are some not-so-good rooms
too ($), cheaper with fan and shared bath.

### $ Carelhy's Hotel
*Iglesia Católica, ½ c sur, T2583-0389.*
15 clean and simple rooms, a bit tired; 5 have
a/c. Each room has 2 beds and can sleep 3
people. Can help arrange tours or transport.
Discount for longer stays or groups.

### Refugio de Vida Silvestre Los Guatuzos

### $$ Esperanza Verde
*Río Frío, 4 km from San Carlos, T2583-0127,*
*fundeverde@yahoo.es.*
In a beautiful area rich in wildlife, these
280 ha of private reserve inside the Los
Guatuzos Wildlife Refuge have good nature
trails for birdwatching. There are 20 rooms
with single beds, fan, shared bath. Prices
include 3 meals per day.

### $$ La Esquina del Lago
*At the mouth of the Río Frío, T8849-0600,*
*www.riosanjuan.info.*
Surrounded by vegetation and visited
by 61 species of bird, this tranquil and
hospitable fishing lodge on the water is
owned by former newspaper man Philippe
Tisseaux. A range of tours are available,
including birdwatching and world-class
sports fishing. Excellent food, which uses
fresh fish and home-grown herbs. Free use of
kayak and free transport from San Carlos,
a 5-min ride away.

### $ Centro Ecológico de Los Guatuzos
*Río Papaturro, T2270-3561,*
*www.losguatuzos.com.*
An attractive research station on the
riverfront. Lodging is in wooden rooms with
bunk beds, 1 with private bath. Meals for
guests from US$5, served in a local house.
Guided visits to forest trails, excursions to
others rivers in the reserve. Night caiman
tours by boat. Private boat to and from San
Carlos can be arranged. All tours in Spanish
only, some Managua tour operators arrange
programmes with an English-speaking guide
(see page 610).

### Archipiélago Solentiname

### $$ Cabañas Paraíso
*Isla San Fernando, T2583-9015,*
*www.hcp.nicaragua-info.com.*
The lack of trees means that the views are
spectacular and the sun hot. Rooms are very
clean, bright and crowded, with private bath.
Feels a bit Miami, but friendly. Excursions in
very fine boats are offered.

### $$ Hotel Celentiname or Doña María
*Isla San Fernando, T2276-1910,*
*www.hotelcelentiname.blogspot.com.*
This laid-back place is the most traditional
of the hotels here. It has a lovely location
facing another island and a lush garden
filled with big trees, hummingbirds, iguanas

and, at night, fishing bats. The rustic cabins have private bath and nice decks. Sad dorm rooms are not much cheaper with shared baths. Generated power, all meals included. Friendly owners. Recommended.

## $$ Hotel Mancarrón
*Isla Mancarrón, up the hill from the cement dock and church, T2270-9981, www.hotelmancarron.com.*
Great birdwatching around this hotel that has access to the artisan village. Rooms are airy, screened, equipped with mosquito netting and private bath. The managers are personal and friendly. Prices include 3 great home-cooked meals per day. Recommended.

## $ Hospedaje Reynaldo Ucarte
*Isla Mancarrón, main village.*
4 decent but basic rooms with shared baths. Meals available on request. Friendly, nice area with lots of children and trees.

## Restaurants

### San Carlos

#### $$$-$$ Granadino
*Opposite Alejandro Granja playing field, T2583-0386. Daily 0900-0200.*
Considered the best in town, with a relaxed ambience and pleasant river views. *Camarones en salsa*, steak and hamburgers. Not cheap.

#### $$-$ Kaoma
*Across from Western Union, T2583-0293. Daily from 0900 until the last customer collapses in a pool of rum.*
Nautically themed and also decorated with dozens of oropendola nests. There's fresh fish caught by the owner, good *camarones de río* (freshwater prawns) and dancing when the locals are inspired. Views of the river from the wooden deck and occasionally refreshing breezes. Recommended.

#### $ El Mirador
*Iglesia Católica, 1½ c sur, T2583-0367. Daily 0700-2000.*
Superb view from patio of Lake Nicaragua, Solentiname, Río Frío and Río San Juan and the jumbled roofs of the city. Decent chicken, fish and beef dishes starting at US$3 with friendly service. Recommended, though it closes if the *chayules* (mosquitoes) are in town.

#### $ Soda Comedor San Carlos
*Muelle Principal, 100 m sur.*
One of many cheap and popular places in the area serving economical Nica food.

## Shopping

### San Carlos
Stock up on purified water and food for a long journey. The market is a cramped nightmare, but in front of immigration there are stalls to buy goods. High-top rubber boots or wellingtons are standard equipment in these parts, perfect for jungle treks (hiking boots are not recommended) and cost US$5-10.

## What to do

### San Carlos
**Tour operators**
**San Carlos Sport Fishing**, *La Esquina del Lago hotel, at the mouth of the Río Frío, T8849-0600, www.riosanjuan.info.* Operated by Phillipe Tisseaux, who has many years of experience fishing the Río San Juan, where plenty of tarpon, snook and rainbow bass can be caught. He also offers birdwatching, kayaking and cultural tours. Recommended.

## Transport

### San Carlos
**Air** La Costeña has twice-weekly flights from San Carlos to **Managua**, Thu and Sun, 1415, US$82 one-way, US$120 return, 1 hr (subject to seasonal changes; see page 610 for outgoing schedules). A taxi from the airport should cost around US$1, otherwise it's a 30-min walk to the centre of town. Arrive 1 hr before departure. Note: overbooking is common. There are no reserved seats and only 5 seats with a decent view, all on the left. There are also twice-weekly flights from San Carlos to the

new airport in **San Juan de Nicaragua**, Thu and Sun 1255, US$55 one-way, US$85 return, 30 mins.

**Airline office** La Costeña, Fortaleza San Carlos, 1 c sur, 2 c arriba, T583-0271.

**Bus** From San Carlos to **Managua**, 8 daily, US$7, 5-6 hrs; to **Juigalpa**, 4 daily, 1000-1330, US$4, 4 hrs; to **El Rama**, 0900, US$7, 7 hrs.

**Motorboat** Small motor boats are called *pangas*; long, narrow ones are *botes* and big broad ones are known as *planos*.

**Public** Arrive at least 30 mins in advance to ensure a seat on a short ride; allow 1 hr or more for long trips. All schedules are subject to random and/or seasonal changes; check locally before setting out. To **Solentiname**, Tue, Fri, 1300, US$4, 2½ hrs, stopping at islands **La Venada**, **San Fernando**, **Mancarrón**. At the time of research, there was talk of express services starting soon, enquire locally for the latest information. To **Los Guatuzos**, stopping at **Papaturro**, Tue, Wed, Fri, 0900, US$5, 3½ hrs. To **Los Chiles**, Costa Rica, daily 1030, 1300, 1500, US$8, 2 hrs; see also Nicaragua–Costa Rica border box in the Practicalities chapter. To **El Castillo** (and **Sábalos**), Mon-Sat (express) 0630, 1030, 1630; (slow) 0800, 1200, 1430, 1530; Sun (slow) 1330. Avoid the slow boat if you can, it's a gruelling 6-hr ride. To **San Juan de Nicaragua**, Tue, Thu, Fri 0600, 12-14 hrs, US$14; express services run in the wet season only, Tue 0600, Wed 1000, Fri 0600, and Sun 1000, 6 hrs, US$30. The ferry to **Granada** leaves from main dock in San Carlos, Tue and Fri 1400, 1st class US$9.50, 2nd class US$4, 14 hrs. 1st class has a TV, better seats and is usually less crowded; it's worth the extra money. Bring a hammock if you can and expect a challenging journey.

**Private** Motorboats are available for hire; they are expensive but afford freedom to view wildlife. They are also faster, leave when you want and allow you to check out different hotels. Beyond El Castillo downriver there are only 2 boats per week, so private transport is the only other option. Ask at tourism office for recommendations.

**Taxi** Taxis wait for arriving flights at the landing strip; if you miss them you will have to walk to town (30 mins). To get to the landing strip, taxis can be found in town between the market and *muelle flotante*. All fares are US$1, exact change is essential. Drivers are helpful.

**Archipiélago Solentiname**
**Boat** Solentiname to **San Carlos**, Tue, Fri 0430, US$4, 2½ hrs. **Los Guatuzos** and **Río Papaturro** to **San Carlos**, Mon, Tue, Thu 0600, US$5, 3½ hrs.

## Along the Río San Juan  *Colour map 4, A3/B3.*

**vast and extraordinarily beautiful river**

★ The Río San Juan is Lake Nicaragua's sole outlet to the sea. Three major rivers that originate in Costa Rica and more than 17 smaller tributaries also feed this mighty river, which is up to 350 m wide at points. At San Carlos, enough water enters the river in a 24-hour period in the dry season to supply water to all of Central America for one year – a gigantic resource that Nicaragua has yet to exploit. For the visitor, it is an opportunity to experience the rainforest and to journey from Central America's biggest lake all the way to the thundering surf of Nicaragua's eastern seaboard. Travel is only possible by boat, with a regular daily service to El Castillo and sparse public boat operations downriver. To really explore, private boat hire is necessary, though expensive.

## Río Sábalo

Outside the limits of San Carlos, the river is lined with wetlands, providing good opportunities for birdwatching. Deforestation in this section of the river (until El Castillo) is getting increasingly worse, however. The Río Sábalo is an important tributary named after the large fish found in this region, the *sábalo* (tarpon). The town at its mouth, **Boca de Sábalos**, is melancholy, muddy and friendly. There are decent lodges in the area (see Where to stay, below) and the people of Sábalo seem happy to see outsiders. There are some small rapids just past the river's drainage into the Río San Juan. The fishing for *sábalo real* (giant tarpon) is quite good here. They can reach up to 2.5 m and weigh in at 150 kg. Another popular sport fish is *robalo* (snook) and much better to eat than tarpon.

## El Castillo

The peaceful village of El Castillo, 60 km from San Carlos, is an attractive riverfront settlement backed by the 17th-century Fortaleza de la Inmaculada Concepción (Fortress of the Immaculate Conception). Construction of the fort began in 1673 after British pirate Henry Morgan made off down the Río San Juan with £500,000 of loot plundered from the city of Granada. From its hilltop vantage the fort enjoys long views to the east, where it came under attack by the British several times in the 18th century, most notably by Admiral Nelson, who managed to capture it briefly before being forced to abandon by a Central American counter offensive. Inside the fortress you'll find a **library** and **museum** ⓘ *0900-1200, 1400-1700, US$2*; the views alone are worth the price of admission. There is also an educational museum behind the fortress, **Centro de Interpretación de la Naturaleza**, with displays and explanations of local wildlife and vegetation as well as a butterfly farm. There are no banks here so bring all the cash you need before setting out.

## Reserva Biológica Indio Maíz

A few kilometres downstream is the Río Bartola and the beginning of the Reserva Biológica Indio Maíz, 3000 sq km of mostly primary rainforest and home to more than 600 species of bird, 300 species of reptile and 200 species of mammal including many big cats and howler, white-faced and spider monkeys. Sleeping is possible in **Refugio Bartola**, a research station and training ground for biologists; it has a labyrinth of well-mapped trails behind the lodge. The hotel guides are very knowledgeable. They will also take you down the Río Bartola in a canoe for great wildlife viewing and birding. Neglect in recent years has made turning up without booking a bit of a gamble, so do book in advance. Camping is possible; ask the park ranger (his house is across the Río Bartola from the **Refugio Bartola** lodge).

## Río Bartola to the Caribbean

The river past **Bartola** becomes more beautiful and the Costa Rican border reaches to the south bank of the river. The Costa Rican side is partially deforested; the Nicaraguan side with the Indio Maíz Reserve is almost entirely intact. Watch out for turtles, birds and crocodiles. Two hours downriver is the **Río Sarapiquí** and immigration checkpoints for both Costa Rica and Nicaragua (no stamps available though). If coming from the Río San Juan to Río Sarapiquí you will need to check in with the Costa Rican guard station if you want to spend the night, or even if you want to pick up something at the store. If continuing down the river without stopping you only need to check in at the Nicaraguan station on the Río San Juan. See also the Nicaragua–Costa Rica border box in the Practicalities chapter.

Past the Sarapiquí, the San Juan branches north, and both sides of the river (heavily forested) become part of Nicaragua again as the Río Colorado heads into Costa Rica.

Two hours or so later, the San Juan reaches the Caribbean via a series of magnificent forest-wrapped lagoons.

## San Juan de Nicaragua *Colour map 4, A3.*

One of the wettest places on the American continent with more than 5000 mm of rain each year, San Juan de Nicaragua (formerly known as San Juan del Norte) is also one of the most beautiful, with primary rainforest, lagoons, rivers and the desolate surf of the Caribbean Sea. The end-of-the-world feeling is not lost in this little village of winding paths, homes on stilts, and flooded yards.

It is settled by a small population (estimated at 275), though it was once a boom town in the 19th century, when the American industrialist Cornelius Vanderbilt was running his steamship line between New York and San Francisco. Then called Greytown, San Juan de Nicaragua was the pick-up point for the steamship journey to the Pacific via the Río San Juan, Lake Nicaragua to La Virgen and then by mule overland to San Juan del Sur. If in your own boat (chartered), a trip down the **Río Indio** is recommended, with lots of wildlife, virgin forest and Rama (please respect their culture and privacy). A visit to the ruins of old **Greytown** is also interesting, but much of its haunting ambience has been lost with the construction of a new airport in its vicinity.

Edgar 'Rasta' Coulson is the best guide in town, and a good cook too; he waits for new arrivals and owns **Cabinas El Escondite** (see Where to stay, below). There are no banks and the most common currency is Costa Rican colones thanks to the (relatively) easy access to El Limón, Costa Rica. You can pay in córdobas or dollars, but expect change in colones. There is a Nicaraguan customs and immigration at San Juan de Nicaragua, but officially entrance and exit stamps for international travel cannot be obtained here.

## Listings Along the Río San Juan

### Where to stay

### Río Sábalo

**$$$ Monte Cristo River Resort**
*2 km downriver from Boca de Sábalos,*
*T2583-0197, www.montecristoriver.com.*
A well-established ecolodge and resort set inside its own rambling private nature reserve. It has comfortable cabins with private bath, dance floor and **Mark Twain Bar**. Sometimes loud weekend parties arrive from El Castillo to use the dance hall. Rate covers 3 meals and all activities, including kayaking, fishing and horses. Recommended.

**$$ Hotel Sábalos**
*On confluence of San Juan and Sábalo rivers,*
*T2271-7424, www.hotelsabalos.com.ni.*
This simple and friendly wooden hotel has a good location, with views up and down the river, great for watching locals pass in canoes.

9 wooden rooms have private bath and fan. The best resting spot on upper San Juan. Recommended.

**$$ Sábalos Lodge**
*In front of El Toro rapids, just downriver*
*from Río Sábalo, T2278-1405 (Managua),*
*www.sabaloslodge.com.*
Funky and attractive mix of huts, cabins, shacks, some with bath inside, and hammocks. One nice unit on the river has a sitting room and deck, all open to the outside with mosquito netting. Beautiful grounds but not much forest around.

**$ Hotel Grand River Lodge**
*Between San Carlos and Boca de Sabalos,*
*3 km from the community of Esperanza,*
*T8366-6187, www.hotelgrandriverlodge.com.*
Simple wooden cabins with private toilet. They offer a plethora of activities including

horse riding, kayaking, community tours and hiking. Friendly, hospitable owners.

## El Castillo

### $$ Hotel Victoria
*El muelle, 400 vrs arriba, at the end of the end road, T2583-0188, www.hotelvictoriaelcastillo.com.*
This friendly and hospitable hotel has 9 wood-panelled rooms with cable TV, a/c and private bath ($ with shared bath). Downstairs there's a pleasant restaurant overlooking the water and a nearby stream filled with turtles and caimans. Tours with accredited guides include horse-riding and night tours. The best place in town. Recommended.

### $ Albergue El Castillo
*Next to fortress above city dock, T8924-5608.*
Comfortable, if simple, wooden rooms and great views from a shared balcony overlooking the river. Only 1 room has a private bath; for extra side ventilation, the best rooms are Nos 1 and 10, but you have noisy bats for company in No 10. Also noisy early morning as the public boats warm up (0500) motors. Breakfast and 25 mins of internet included.

### $ Hotel Tropical
*Calle Principal, del muelle, 130 m sur, T8699-8883.*
A fantastic location overlooking the river, Hotel Tropical has a smart wooden balcony for chilling out and a handful of clean, comfortable rooms with private bath, some with a/c. The restaurant downstairs isn't bad either.

### $ Nena Lodge
*El muelle, 350 vrs arriba, T8821-2135, www.nenalodge.com.*
This hotel has a range of simple budget rooms equipped with mosquito nets, soap and towels. Many of them open onto a communal balcony slung with hammocks. There is a tour agency on site, running trips to **Finca Los Cocos**, **Sendero Bartola** and **Sendero Aguas Frescas**, among others.

## Río Bartola to the Caribbean

### $$$$ Río Indio Lodge
*Between Indio and San Juan rivers, near San Juan de Nicaragua, T506-2231-4299, www.therioindiolodge.com.*
Multi-million dollar lodge, designed for upscale fishing packages but excellent for wildlife safaris, birdwatching and rainforest walks. Named one of the top 10 jungle lodges in the world.

### $$$ Basecamp Bartola
*Community of Bartola, on the Río Bartola, T8913-8215.*
A new sustainable tourism project organized and led on a co-operative basis by the community of Bartola. Lodging is in tents on wooden platforms with all-inclusive packets covering transport, meals and guided tours of the rainforest. Contact in advance of visit as you will need guides to locate the camp.

### $$ Refugio Bartola
*Confluence of Río San Juan and Río Bartola, T8376-6979, www.refugiobartola.com.*
Simple wooden rooms with private bath, high ceilings and solid beds. Prices include 3 meals, juice and coffee, bats in roof and frogs in toilet at no extra charge. There's a research station on site, with lots of creepy creatures in jars, including what could be the world's largest cockroach. Recommended.

## San Juan de Nicaragua

### $ Cabinas El Escondite
*Behind the military base north of the pier, ask for Rasta, T8414-9761.*
Spacious wooden *cabinas* with bunk beds, private bath and a pleasant garden. The owner, Rasta, speaks English and cooks the best Caribbean food in town ($$-$). Great host and relaxed vibe. Recommended.

### $ Hotelito Evo
*Proyecto habitacional, Grupo 'Bed and Breakfast', Casa 18, west of the pier, ask around for Enrique's place, T2583-9019.*

This cosy B&B has a relaxed family atmosphere and 7 simple rooms, most with private bath. The owner, Enrique, is friendly and knows the history of the town. Breakfast included and other meals available.

## Restaurants

### El Castillo
Eating is good here; the freshwater prawns (*camarones de río*) and snook (*robalo*) are both excellent.

### $$$-$$ Bar Cofalito
*On the jetty.*
Has a great view upstairs overlooking the river and serves excellent *camarones de río*, considered by many the best in town, with fresh fish most evenings.

### $$$-$$ Borders Coffee
*Next to the dock.*
Good but pricey pasta in organic tomato sauce, vegetarian fare, curries, shrimps and fresh organic cappuccinos at this friendly little café. Nice views of the river and a good place to wait for your boat. They can also arrange stays at a nearby finca.

### $ Vanessa's
*El muelle, 1 c arriba.*
Great spot by the rapids, with fish and river shrimp. Can be hit and miss; check the catch is fresh before ordering.

What to do

## What to do

### El Castillo
**Tour operators**
**First Step Adventure and Eco-Tours**,
*inside Bar Cofalito's, next to the dock, T8432-8441.* Kayaking, fishing, hiking and custom-made adventures. Miguel is an English-speaking native who has spent some 18 years exploring the Río San Juan area. Fun and recommended.

## Transport

### El Castillo
All schedules are subject to change; confirm times locally.

To **San Carlos**; Mon-Sat (express) 0530, 1130, 1530; (slow) 0530, 1130, 1530; (slow) 0500, 0700, 1400, US$3.75 express, US$2 slow boat, 1½-2½ hrs. To **San Juan de Nicaragua**, Tue, Thu, Fri 0900, US$12.50, 8-9 hrs. In the west season, express services run Tue and Fri 0800, 5-6 hrs, US$25.

### San Juan de Nicaragua
**Air** The new airport on the edge of Greytown receives 2 weekly flights from **Managua** via San Carlos, Thu and Sun, 1200, US$55 (return US$85), 1½ hrs; they return at 1330. There are no roads from the airport to the town so it is best to organize a water taxi with your chosen lodging before arrival, around US$10. Note there is no ticket office at the airport; buy return portion in advance.

**Boat** All schedules are subject to change; check times locally.

To **San Carlos**, stopping at **El Castillo**, Thu and Sun 0430, US$12.50 (US$25 express). A service between San Juan de Nicaragua and **Bluefields** usually leaves once a week, but days change and it is very inconsistent. The ride is 3-4 hrs and extremely wet and bumpy, not advised for those with back problems.

# León & around

León is the artistic and intellectual heart of the country, the spiritual home of Nicaragua's greatest poets, and, since 1979, a hotbed of Sandinista activity. A wealth of satirical murals, bombed-out ruins and bullet-marked buildings are evidence of the city's turbulent revolutionary past, whilst its student population lends it a vibrant nightlife.

After a day exploring León, you can relax in one of its many bars, share a few rounds of Flor de Caña and take in a rousing performance of live folk music.

If the heat and frenetic activity of the downtown area prove too much, the Pacific coastline beyond León is accented by beaches, barrier islands and coastal lagoons. An excursion to the sleepy shores of Poneloya and Las Peñitas, 20 minutes west, is always refreshing and welcome, but the bucolic retreat of Jiquilillo, perched on the remote and less-visited coast of the Cosegüina Peninsula, is the place for serious hammock time. Equally, if you're seeking serious adventure, León is the gateway to some immense and extraordinary panoramas. Home to one of the most densely active volcanic chains in the world, the Cordillera Los Maribios, this is a land born of scorched skies and violently shifting geological tempers. Smoking craters, steaming pools, tranquil lakes and stark, rolling, black-sand slopes perfect for high-speed boarding all await exploration.

**Best** for
Adventure tours ▪ Cathedral ▪ Music ▪ Turtles ▪ Volcanoes

**youthful university town with appealing colonial churches and museums**

★ Though taxis are cheap, the simplest and richest pleasure in León (altitude 109 m, population 155,000) is walking its historic streets, noting the infinite variety of elaborate doors, ceiling work and window ironwork, as well as sneaking peeks inside the grand houses to see their lush interior gardens. Each barrio supports its own unique church and beautiful colonial homes.

The city is laid out in the classic Spanish colonial grid system, based around a central plaza, commonly referred to as Parque Central. The majestic León Cathedral faces west and sits on the park's east side. Roads running east–west are *calles* and those running north–south *avenidas*. Calle Rubén Darío runs directly west from Parque Central, through Sutiava and all the way to the Pacific Ocean.

### Cathedral of León
*It's possible to climb the cathedral for commanding views of the city and countryside, US$1.*

The Cathedral of León, officially the **Basílica de la Asunción**, is the pride of both city and country. This impressive structure – a UNESCO World Heritage Site since 2011 – is the work of 113 years of labour (1747-1860). Legend has it that the plans for the cathedrals of Lima in Peru and León were switched by mistake, but there is no evidence to support that charming excuse for such a big church in such a little country. The design was conceived by Guatemalan architect Diego de Porres and has been described as Central American baroque. Its squat towers and super-thick walls stem from the experience gained in building in the seismically active valley of Ciudad Antigua. Inside, the cathedral houses a very fine **ivory Christ**, the consecrated **Altar of Sacrifices** and the **Choir of Córdoba**. The **tomb of Rubén Darío**, Nicaragua's greatest poet, is guarded by a sorrowing lion.

### West of the cathedral
There are several interesting and historic buildings on **Parque Central**, including the **archbishop's house** opposite the south side of the cathedral, and the historic **Seminario de San Ramón**, founded in 1680, which today houses a primary school. Next door, the Gothic **Colegio de Asunción** (primary and secondary school) is often mistaken for a church.

The grand old Palacio Municipal stands on the southwest corner of Parque Central, a 1930s structure that has been decaying since its Somoza-era heyday. Today it houses the pro-Sandinista **Museo de la Revolución** ⓘ *daily 0800-1800, US$1.50*, where visitors can learn about the 1979 revolution and hear gripping war stories from former FSLN fighters. Your visit concludes with a trip to the roof for great views over the plaza. One block south of the Palacio Municipal is the beautifully restored **Teatro Municipal José de la Cruz Mena** ⓘ *Mon-Fri 0800-1230 and 1400-1700, plays and concerts from US$1-15*, built in the 19th century and named after León's greatest classical composer.

Two blocks west of Parque Central is the **Convento y Iglesia San Francisco**. The church was damaged in 1979 during fighting in the Revolution but maintains much of its ancient charm. It was the city's first convent when founded in 1639 and has now been converted into a hotel called **El Convento** (see Where to stay, below). On the corner opposite the church stands the **Museo de Arte Fundación Ortiz-Guardián** ⓘ *T2277-2627, www.fundacionortizguardian.org, Tue-Sun 1030-1800 entrance US$2*, a lovely colonial home that doubles as an excellent art museum with work from Europe, Latin America and Nicaragua.

## BACKGROUND

### León

León served the capital of Nicaragua for 242 years until it was moved to Managua. The present city was founded in 1610 after the abandonment of its cursed original location, known today as León Viejo (see page 681). The site was chosen to be close to the large indigenous settlement of Sutiava and to the Pacific.

In the 1960s and 70s, León became a hotbed for the Frente Sandinista de Liberación Nacional (FSLN) Marxist underground. Fighting against Somoza Debayle (the son of Somoza García) was fierce in León, with much damage suffered by the old city, some of which can still be seen today. After a final brutal battle which lasted from 3 June to 9 July 1979 and was won by the rebels, the FSLN, led by female Comandante Dora María Tellez, succeeded. The city is still strongly Sandinista, with every mayor since 1979 coming from the FSLN party.

One block west on Calle Central is the **Museo-Archivo Rubén Darío** ① *Calle Central, Iglesia San Francisco, 1 c abajo, T2311-2388, Tue-Sat 0800-1200, 1400-1700, Sun 0800-1200, US$1*, which has an interesting collection of the national hero's personal possessions, photographs, portraits and a library with poetry books in Spanish, English and French. Its other claim to fame is that the great metaphysical poet Alfonso Cortés lost his mind here.

### East of the cathedral

On Calle Central, three blocks east of the cathedral, is the **Iglesia El Calvario**. Built in the mid-1700s, it was restored in 2000, the towering Momotombo Volcano in the background supplying a dramatic setting. Two blocks north of the church is the **Museo Entomológico** ① *ENEL, 30 vrs arriba, opposite Western Union, T2311-6586, www.bio-nica.info, daily 0900-1200, 1400-1600, US$0.50*, home to the amazing insect collection of Nicaragua's foremost entomologist, Dr Jean-Michel Maes.

### North of the cathedral

Two blocks north of Parque Central is the lovely **Iglesia La Merced**, built in the late 1700s. This is León's second most important church and home of the patron saint of León, the Virgen de las Mercedes. In the early 19th century there was a fire in the main altar that holds the image and legend has it that a local black slave rushed into the flames to rescue it. In gratitude for his heroism he was granted his freedom. The interior of the church is arguably the most ornately decorated in Nicaragua.

One and half blocks west of the La Merced, is the **Centro Popular de la Cultura**, which has occasional exhibitions and events (see schedule on bulletin board in front lobby). Three blocks west and one block north, the **Iglesia de Zaragoza** was built from 1884 to 1934 and has two octagonal turrets and an arched doorway with tower above.

Two blocks north of the cathedral's lions on Avenida Central is the **Iglesia La Recolección**, with a beautiful baroque Mexican façade that tells the entire story of the Passion of Christ. Two blocks north and one block east is the simple yet handsome **Iglesia San Juan Bautista**, which sits on the east side of the Parque San Juan, otherwise known as the *parquecito*. Three blocks west and two blocks north, the **Iglesia San Felipe** was built in the late 16th century for the religious services of the city's black and mulatto population.

## South of the cathedral

Three blocks south and half a block west of the cathedral is the **Museo de Leyendas y Tradiciones** ⓘ *T2311-2886, www.museoleyendasytradiciones.com, Tue-Sat 0800-1200, 1400-1700, Sun 0800-1200, US$2.* This project of Doña Carmen Toruño is a physical demonstration of some of the many legends that populate the bedtime stories of Nicaraguan children.

Three blocks west of the museum, the **Iglesia de San Nicolás de Laborío**, founded in 1618 for the local indigenous population, is the most modest of the León churches, constructed of wood and tiles over adobe walls with a simple façade and altar.

# León

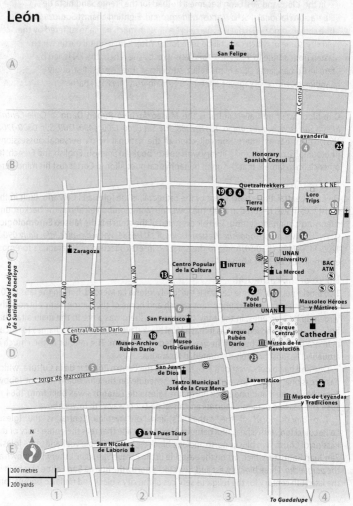

Four blocks east of the museum is the **Centro Iniciativa Medio Ambiental (CIMAC)**
ⓘ *Iglesia de San Sebastián, 4 c arriba, Mon-Fri 0800-1200, 1400-1730, US$1*, an ecological
garden with a broad range of local flora on show, including plenty of shady fruit trees, and
a gentle interpretive trail that takes no more than 30 minutes to traverse.

## Comunidad Indígena de Sutiava

Like Monimbó in Masaya, Sutiava is the one of the remaining examples of indigenous
urban living. The Sutiavans have a fiercely independent culture and a language that survived

**Where to stay** 🛏
Azul 2 *B4*
Bigfoot Hostel 17 *C5*
Cacique Adiact 4 *B4*
Casa de Huéspedes
  El Nancite 15 *C5*
El Albergue de León 1 *B5*
El Convento 6 *D2*
Hostal Calle de
  los Poetas 7 *D1*
Hostel Colibrí 10 *B4*
La Casona Colonial 14 *B4*
La Perla 11 *C3*
Lazybones Hostel 3 *C3*
Posada Fuente
  Castalia 18 *A4*
Real 19 *C5*
Tortuga Booluda 5 *D1*
Via Via 20 *C5*

**Restaurants** 🍴
Al Carbón 2 *C3*
Café Nicaragüita 8 *B3*
Carnívoro 9 *C4*
Cocinarte 5 *E2*
Comedor Lucía 11 *C5*
El Desayunazo 19 *B3*
El Mississippi 12 *D6*
La Casa Vieja 13 *C2*
La Mexicana 4 *B3*
Le Turon 17 *C5*
Libélula 18 *D2*
Manhattan 22 *C3*
Pan y Paz 7 *C5*
Pizzería Antonino 24 *B3*
Porky's House 25 *B4*

**Bars & clubs** 🍸
Café Taquezal 23 *D3*
Camaleón 14 *C4*
El Mirador 10 *C3*
Olla Quemada 15 *D1*
Via Via 1 *C5*

## ON THE ROAD

## Rubén Darío: the prince of Spanish letters

The great Chilean poet Pablo Neruda called him 'one of the most creative poets in the Spanish language' when, together with the immortal Spanish poet Federico García Lorca, he paid tribute to Rubén Darío in Buenos Aires in 1933. In front of more than 100 Argentine writers, Lorca and Neruda delivered the tribute to the poet they called 'then and forever unequalled'.

Darío is without a doubt the most famous Nicaraguan. He is one of the greatest poets in the history of the Spanish language and the country's supreme hero. Born Felix Rubén García Sarmiento in Metapa, Nicaragua in 1867, Rubén Darío was raised in León and had learnt to read by the age of four. By the time he was 10, little Rubén had read Don Quixote, The Bible, 1001 Arabian Nights and the works of Cicero. When he was 11, he studied the Latin classics in depth with Jesuits at the school of La Iglesia de La Recolección. In 1879, at the age of 12, his first verses were published in the León daily newspaper El Termómetro. Two years later he was preparing his first book. Later, he became the founder of the Modernist movement in poetry, which crossed the Atlantic and became popular in Spain. His most noted work, Azul, revolutionized Spanish literature, establishing a new mode of poetic expression.

As well as being a poet, Darío was a diplomat and a journalist. He wrote for numerous publications in Argentina, the US, Spain and France. In 1916 he returned to the city of León, and, despite several attempts at surgery, died of cirrhosis on the night of 6 February. After a week of tributes he was buried in the Cathedral of León.

Ox that I saw in my childhood, as you steamed
in the burning gold of the Nicaraguan sun,
there on the rich plantation filled with tropical
harmonies; woodland dove, of the woods that sang
with the sound of the wind, of axes, of birds and wild bulls:
I salute you both, because you are both my life.

You, heavy ox, evoke the gentle dawn
that signalled it was time to milk the cow,
when my existence was all white and rose;
and you, sweet mountain dove, cooing and calling,
you signify all that my own springtime, now
so far away, possessed of the Divine Springtime.

*'Far Away'*, Rubén Darío. From Selected Poems by Rubén Darío, translated by Lysander Kemp, University of Texas, Austin, 1988.

despite being surrounded by the numerically superior Chorotega culture in pre-Columbian times and later by the Spanish. Celebrations for Holy week, or **Semana Santa**, in Sutiava showcase spectacular sawdust street paintings made on *Viernes Santo* (Good Friday).

The entrance to the community is marked by the change of Calle Rubén Darío into a two-lane road with a central divider full of plants. Sutiava's **Iglesia Parroquial de San Juan Bautista de Sutiava** (1698-1710) is one of the most authentic representations of

Nicaraguan baroque and features a representation of the Maribio Sun God on the ceiling; the definitive icon for indigenous pride. Two blocks north of the San Juan church is the community-run **Museo de la Comunidad Indígena de Sutiava** or **Museo Adiact** ⓘ *T2311-5371, Mon-Fri 0800-1200 and 1400-1700, Sat 0800-1200, donations greatly appreciated,* marked by a fading mural. The museum is named after the last great leader, Adiac, who was hanged by the Spanish in an old tamarind tree still standing three blocks south and two blocks west of the San Juan church.

## Listings León *map p672*

### Tourist information

**Nicaraguan Institute of Tourism (INTUR)**
*Parque Rubén Darío, 1½ c norte, T2311-3682.*
They have limited information and flyers; staff speak Spanish only.

**UNAN**
*Next to Restaurante El Sesteo, on Parque Central.*
A small office run by the tourism students of the university.

### Where to stay

There's no shortage of cheap beds in León with new hostels and backpacker hotels springing up all the time; dorms cost US$5-10 per night. If you plan on staying in the city a month or more, many houses rent student rooms at competitive rates (US$100-150 per month).

**$$$ Hotel El Convento**
*Connected to Iglesia San Francisco, T2311-7053, www.elconventonicaragua.com.*
Housed in an old colonial convent, this beautiful, intriguing hotel is decorated with antique art, including an impressive gold-leaf altar and sombre religious icons. Recommended.

**$$$ La Perla**
*Iglesia La Merced, 1½ c norte, T2311 2279, www.laperlaleon.com.*
This handsome old 19th-century building has been carefully remodelled and now boasts elegant a/c rooms, some with bath tubs, several suites, a bar, restaurant, casino and pool. Spacious and grand.

**$$$-$$ Cacique Adiact**
*Costado noreste de UNAN, 1½ c norte, T2311-0303, www.hotelcaciqueadiact.com.*
A Danish/Nicaraguan-owned 'eco-hotel' that uses solar panels and rainwater recycling systems. The building consists of a tastefully restored 2-floor colonial house overlooking a large pool. Lodgings are crisp, clean and comfortable, including 11 apartments ($$$) and 6 rooms ($$). Recommended.

**$$ Hotel Azul**
*Catedral, 2½ c norte, T2315-4519, www.hotelazulleon.com.*
Hotel Azul is a stylish addition to León's burgeoning hotel scene. Housed in a converted colonial building, it has a small pool and a good restaurant. Rooms are simple and minimalist. Triples are much more spacious than doubles.

**$$ Hotel Real**
*Iglesia La Recolección, 150 m arriba, T2311-2606, www.hotelrealdeleon.net.*
A pleasant and tranquil guesthouse with a leafy inner courtyard and antique furniture. The rooftop terrace has refreshing breezes and views of the churches. Continental breakfast included. Good reports.

**$$ Posada Fuente Castalia**
*Iglesia La Recolección, 250 m norte, T2311-4645, www.posadafuentecastalia.com.*
A homely guesthouse with traditional Nicaraguan decor, hospitable family ambience and a flowery inner courtyard. Prices include continental breakfast.

### $$-$ Casa de Huéspedes El Nancite
*Iglesia El Calvario, 1½ c norte, T2315-4323,*
*www.guesthouseelnancite.com.*
Tranquil, tasteful and comfortable. This
orange-themed guesthouse has a handful
of good-value rooms set around a lush
courtyard. Good for couples. Recommended.

### $$-$ La Casona Colonial
*Parque San Juan, ½ c abajo, T2311-3178,*
*www.casonacolonialguest.com.*
This pleasant colonial house has 7 good-
value, homely rooms with attractive antique.
Management is friendly and hospitable, and
there's a lovely green garden too. Cheaper
with fan ($). Recommended.

### $ Bigfoot Hostel
*Banco ProCredit, ½ c sur, T8917-8832,*
*www.bigfootnicaragua.com.*
Sociable, buzzing and popular with the
whipper-snappers. This hip backpackers'
joint has lots of economical dorm space,
a handful of private rooms, TV, pool table,
bar, lockers and a popular restaurant. Their
*mojitos* are famous and well worth a taste –
happy hour runs 1800-2000.

### $ El Albergue de León
*Gasolinera Petronic, ½ c abajo, T8894-1787,*
*www.hostalelalberguedeleon.com.*
A brightly coloured, laid-back, friendly,
cheerful, helpful and knowledgeable
hostel with a shady plant-filled courtyard,
revolutionary art, ultra-cheap dorms and
basic private rooms. Funky and alternative.
Recommended.

### $ Hostal Calle de los Poetas
*Calle Rubén Darío, Museo Darío, 1½ c abajo,*
*T2311-3306, www.journeynicaragua.org.*
This comfortable, good-value guesthouse
has a relaxed home ambience, 3 spacious
rooms with private and shared bath, a
beautiful garden and friendly hosts. Often
full, so arrive early. Discounts for longer stays.
Recommended.

### $ Hostel Colibrí
*Iglesia La Recolección, ½ c norte, T2311-3858,*
*www.hostelcolibri.com.*
A relaxed and sociable hostel with a good
ambiance. They have 9 private rooms and
2 dorms, some with private bath. Visited
by hummingbirds, the garden has a quiet,
tranquil rancho slung with hammocks.
Bilingual staff; Dutch/Nicaraguan-owned.
Full breakfast included.

### $ Lazybones Hostel
*Parque de los Poetas, 2½ c norte, T2311-3472,*
*www.lazyboneshostelnicaragua.com.*
An efficient, helpful, friendly hostel with a
refreshing pool and extras including free
coffee and tea, Wi-Fi and DVD rental. Clean
dorms and private rooms; some have private
bath, cheaper without. Check out the mural
by one of Managua's best graffiti artists.

### $ Tortuga Booluda
*Southwest corner of Parque Central, 3½ c*
*abajo, T2311-4653, www.tortugabooluda.com.*
A very pleasant, friendly hostel with clean
dorms ($), private rooms ($) and an a/c
'suite' with views ($$). Wi-Fi, pancake
breakfast, organic coffee, kitchen, pool table,
guitars, book exchange, tours and Spanish
classes available. Discounts for peace corps
volunteers and long-term rentals in low
season. Relaxed and recommended.

### $ Via Via
*Banco ProCredit, ½ c sur, T2311-6142,*
*www.viaviacafe.com.*
Part of a worldwide network of Belgian cafés,
this excellent and professionally managed
hostel offers clean dorm beds and a range
of private rooms, some with TV. There's a
tranquil garden and popular restaurant-bar.
In the manager's words, "a meeting place for
cultures". Recommended.

## $$$-$$ Le Turon
*Iglesia La Recolección, 1 c arriba, 20 vrs sur.*
An elegant bistro-style restaurant with a verdant inner courtyard and balcony. French-flavoured gastronomic offerings including seafood mains like lobster, octopus and *corvina* in basil and cream sauce, filet mignon, beef bourguignon, chicken cordon bleu and a range of rich desserts, such as mango and lime panna cotta. Good presentation, a great place for a romantic dinner.

## $$ Al Carbón
*Iglesia La Merced, 25 vrs abajo.*
A well-presented grillhouse with good ambience and tables set around a cool inner courtyard. Carnivores will delight in the meat platters, steaks, chicken and ribs, but there are a few vegetarian options too. Large servings and great service. Tasty and filling, but not gourmet. A good stock of wine. Recommended.

## $$ Carnívoro
*Iglesia La Recolección, 1 c abajo, 20 m norte. Closed Mon.*
A good steakhouse with a stylish interior and a diverse menu of Middle Eastern, North American and even Thai dishes. Offerings include meat kebabs, grilled platters, burgers and a few good vegetarian and seafood options. Their best and most reliable dishes are the tender Aberdeen Angus beef steaks.

## $$ Cocinarte
*Costado norte Iglesia de Laborío.*
Laid-back vegetarian restaurant with an intriguing international menu of mainly Eastern, Middle Eastern and Nicaraguan cuisine. Starters include squash soup, pitta bread with hummus and tortilla chips. Mains include Indian curry, falafels, Moroccan tagine, chop suey, pasta, Greek and Caesar salads. They use a lot of fresh and organic produce and serve delicious fruit juices. Friendly service and pleasant ambience. Recommended.

## $$ La Casa Vieja
*Hotel El Convento, 1½ c abajo. Mon-Sat 1600-2300.*
Lovely, intimate restaurant-bar with a rustic feel. Serves reasonably tasty meat and chicken dishes, beer and delicious home-made lemonade. Popular with Nicas.

## $$ Manhattan
*Iglesia la Merced, 75 vrs norte, opposite Hotel La Perla. Closed Sun-Mon.*
Chilled-out lounge bar and restaurant serving fresh sushi tapas and crisp *mojitos*, a refreshing change from Nica fare, although some items may not always be in stock. Clean, modern place with good service.

## $$-$ Pizzeria Antonino
*Parque de los Poetas, 2½ c norte. Wed-Mon for lunch and dinner.*
A casual pizzeria serving US-style pizzas, beer and soft drinks. Quite cheesy, a bit greasy, but good; probably the best pizzas in town.

## $$-$ Porky's House
*Iglesia La Recolección, 2 c norte, www.porkyshouse.com.*
As the name suggests, for lovers of pork, smoked and grilled. They serve a variety of chops and steaks, burgers, sandwiches and tacos, sides of fries and guacamole, and cold beer.

## $ Café Nicaragüita
*Iglesia de la Merced, 2 c norte, 90 vrs abajo. Open for breakfast, lunch, dinner.*
Bohemian little eatery serving economical Nica fare, wraps, sandwiches, pasta, crêpes and *brochetas*. There's a relaxed reading room and a stock of books.

## $ Comedor Lucía
*Banco ProCredit, ½ c sur. Mon-Sat.*
Reputable *comedor* serving good and reliable *comida típica* and buffet food, popular with locals. Dinner is much simpler and cheaper than lunch.

### $ El Desayunazo
*Parque de las Poetas, 3 c norte.*
*Open 0600-1200.*
A great breakfast spot where you can enjoy blueberry pancakes, fruit salad, waffles and *huevos rancheros*, among others. Friendly, speedy service.

### $ El Mississippi
*Southeast corner of the cathedral,*
*1 c sur, 2½ c arriba.*
Also known as **La Cucaracha**, everyone raves about the bean soup here. Simple, unpretentious dining at this locals' haunt. Tasty, energizing and highly recommended.

### $ La Mexicana
*La Iglesia Merced, 2 c norte, ½ c abajo.*
Economical, no-frills Mexican grub, but tasty and completely authentic. The *chilaquiles* and *burritos de res* are the best offerings, particularly after a cold beer or 2. Popular with the locals, greasy and recommended, in spite of the sullen service.

### Cafés and bakeries

### Libélula
*Iglesia San Francisco, 75 vrs abajo.*
A very popular coffeehouse with an indoor patio, artistically prepared cappuccinos, cakes, snacks and breakfast. The best coffeeshop in town. Wi-Fi.

### Pan y Paz
*Northeast corner of the cathedral, 1 c norte, 1½ c arriba, www.panypaz.com.*
This excellent French bakery serves what is probably the best bread in Nicaragua. They also offer great-value sandwiches, delicious quiches and scintillating fresh fruit juices. Highly recommended.

## Bars and clubs

León has a vibrant nightlife, thanks to its large student population. The action moves between different places throughout the week.

### Café Taquezal
*Southwest corner of Parque Central, ½ c abajo, T311-7282. Mon-Sat 1800-0200.*
Pleasant atmosphere with good live folk music on Thu nights. Classic León decor. Food served.

### Camaleón
*Iglesia La Recolección, 35 vrs abajo.*
Camaleón is a hot and sweaty after-party place and something of a León institution. It's best enjoyed in a state of absolute inebriation. So wrong it's almost right.

### El Mirador
*Opposite Parque La Merced, behind Don Señor.*
Rooftop bar that's popular with Nicas and travellers. Cool and breezy. The door is unmarked, accessible from the basketball court.

### Olla Quemada
*Museo Rubén Darío, ½ c abajo.*
Popular on Wed nights with live music acts and lots of beer; salsa on Thu. Great place, friendly atmosphere.

### Via Via
*See Where to stay, ½ c sur.*
Good on most nights, but best on Fri when there's live music. Good, warm atmosphere. Popular with foreigners and Nicas and often praised.

## Entertainment

### Cinema
There is a cinema with 3 screens in the Plaza Nuevo Siglo, next to the La Unión supermarket. It shows mostly US movies with Spanish subtitles, US$2.50.

## Festivals

**Feb Rubén Darío's** birthday celebrations.
**Mar/Apr** León is famed for the beauty of its religious festivals, particularly **Semana Santa** (Holy Week). Starting on **Domingo de Ramos** (Palm Sun) the cathedral has a procession every day of the week and the Parish church of Sutiava has many

events (see page 673), as do all of the other churches of León. (A program of processions and events can be obtained from the Nicaraguan Institute of Tourism, INTUR.)

**14 Aug  Gritería Chiquita** (see Gritería, below) was instituted in 1947 to protect León during a violent eruption of the nearby Cerro Negro volcano.

**24 Sep**  Patron saint of León, **La Virgin de las Mercedes**.

**7-8 Dec  La Purísima** or **Gritería** (the Virgin Mary's conception of Jesus), like Semana Santa, is celebrated throughout the country, but is best in León, as this is where the tradition began. Altars are built in front of private residences and outside churches during the day.

## Shopping

### Bookshops
**Búho Books**, *Hostal Calle de los Poetas, Museo Rubén Darío, 1½ c abajo, T2311-3306, www. journeynicaragua.org. Closed Sun-Mon.* Well-stocked with new and second-hand titles, in English, Spanish, Dutch, German and more.

### Crafts and markets
If you're looking for crafts, try the street markets on the north side of the cathedral. Additionally, **Flor de Luna** (*Iglesia San Fransisco, 75 vrs abajo, Mon-Sat 0900-1900*), stocks Nicaraguan *artesanías*, whilst **Kamañ** (*southwest corner of the Parque Central, 20 vrs abajo*), sells an assortment of handicrafts, bags and simple jewellery.

### Supermarkets
**La Unión**, *Catedral, 1 c norte, 2 c arriba.* Modern and well stocked.

## What to do

### Cultural and community tourism
**Nicasí Tours**, *La Merced, 2 c norte, ½ c abajo, T2311-2289, www.nicasitours.com.* The best cultural and community tours in town. Nicasí offers a diverse range of activities including rooster fights, cooking, cowboy, city and

historical tours. Promises unique insights into the Nica way of life. Recommended.

### Language schools
**León Spanish School**, *Casa de Cultura, Iglesia La Merced, 1½ c abajo, T2311-2116, www. leonspanishschool.org.* Flexible weekly or hourly one-on-one tuition with activities, volunteering and homestay options. Pleasant location inside the Casa de Cultura.

**Metropolis Academy**, *northwest corner of the cathedral, ½ c norte, T8932-6686, www.metropolisspanish.com.* A range of programmes from simple hourly tuition to full-time courses with daily activities and family homestay.

**UP Spanish School**, *Parque Central, 3½ c norte, T8878-3345, www.upspanishschoolleon. com.* Flexible one-on-one classes with experienced and dedicated teachers. Options include homestay, volunteering and activities. Good reports and highly recommended.

### Tour operators
**Green Pathways**, *Banco ProCredit, ½ c sur, T2315-0964, www.greenpathways.com.* Green pathways aspires to carbon-neutral sustainability and donates proceeds to environmental projects. They offer the usual range of local tours, but also specialize in alternative 'adventure in nature' trips further afield. These include whale-watching expeditions, tours of the Atlantic coast, birdwatching and tours of the northern highlands.

**Loro Trips**, *Catedral, 3 c norte, 10 m arriba, T2311-7151, www.lorotrips.com.* A socially and ecologically aware tour operator that uses local guides and contributes to local communities. Their tours take in cultural and natural attractions, including trips to the volcanoes, cooking tours, neighbourhood tours and Rubén Darío tours. They also offer personalized tours to destinations further afield and can arrange good volunteer work thanks to their ties with the city.

**Tierra Tours**, *La Merced, 1½ c norte, T2315-4278, www.tierratour.com*. This Nicaragua travel specialist is Dutch/Nicaraguan-owned. They offer good information and affordable tours of León, the Maribios volcanoes and Isla Juan Venado reserve. Also domestic flights, multi-day packages and tailor-made trips all over the country, as well as shuttles direct to Granada and other places. Well established and reliable with helpful tri-lingual staff.

**Va Pues**, *north side of El Laborio Church, inside Cocinarte restaurant, T2315-4099, www.vapues.com*. Popular tours include sandboarding on Cerro Negro, cultural trips to León Viejo, night turtle tours, kayaking, mangrove tours, tours of Sutiava's workshops, horse riding, visits to San Jacinto's mud fields or Pacific coast salt factories and city tours. English, French, Dutch and Spanish spoken. They have an office in Granada and can organize trips all over the country. Well established and professional.

### Trekking

**Journey Nicaragua**, *Calle Rubén Darío, 1½ c abajo, inside Hostal Calle de Los Poetas, T2311-3306, www.journeynicaragua.org*. Kayaking in Juan Venado and Laguna El Tigre, volcano expeditions, poetry tours. Rigo Sampson, the director of Journey Nicaragua, comes from a family of devout hikers and climbers and is Nicaragua's foremost expert on climbing the Los Maribios volcanoes. He also works closely with educational organizations. Professional and highly recommended.

**Quetzaltrekkers**, *Mercantil, ½ c abajo, next to La Mexicana restaurant, T2311-7388, www.quetzaltrekkers.com*. An ethical non-profit organization with proceeds going to street kids. Multi-day hikes to Los Maribios US$20-US$70 including transport, food, water, camping equipment. Quetzaltrekkers is volunteer-led and the team is always looking for new additions. They prefer a 3-month commitment and will train you as a guide. Nice guys and recommended.

**Sonati Tours**, *northeast corner of the cathedral, 3 c norte, ½ c arriba, T8591-9601, www.sonati.org*. Affiliated to an environmental education NGO, Sonati offers ecology-focused tours of the volcanoes, forests, mangroves and nature reserves. There is particular emphasis on flora and fauna. Birdwatching in dry forest and mangrove swamps is also offered.

## Transport

**Bus** The bus terminal is in the far eastern part of town, a long walk (20-30 mins) or short taxi ride from the centre. Small trucks also ferry people between the bus terminal and town for US$0.25.

Note express buses to Estelí and Matagalpa leave only if there are enough passengers; travel on Fri if possible, or simply go to San Isidro for connections. To **Managua**, express bus to La UCA, every 30 mins, 0400-1900, US$2, 1 hr 45 mins. To **Chinandega**, express bus, every 15 mins, 0500-1800, US$1, 1 hr 45 mins. To **Corinto**, every 30 mins, 0500-1800, US$1.25, 2 hrs. To **Chichigalpa**, every 15 mins, 0400-1800, US$0.75, 1 hr. To **Estelí**, express bus, 0520, 1245, 1415, 1530, US$2.50, 3 hrs; or go to San Isidro and change. To **Matagalpa**, express bus, 0420, 0730, 1445, US$2.50, 3 hrs; or go to San Isidro and change. To **San Isidro**, every 30 mins, 0420-1730, US$2.25, 2½ hrs. To **El Sauce**, hourly, 0800-1600, US$2.50, 2½ hrs. To **El Guasaule**, 0500, US$2, 2½ hrs. To **Salinas Grandes**, 0600,1200, US$0.80, 1½ hrs.

Buses and trucks for **Poneloya** and **Las Peñitas** leave from Sutiava market, every hour, 0530-1735, US$0.75, 25 mins. Service can be irregular so check to see when last bus will return. There are more buses on weekends.

**Domestic and international shuttles** A number of tour operators, including **Tierra Tours**, offer shuttles to the destinations of **Granada** and **Managua** airport. Additionally, some companies now offer comfortable connections to **El Salvador** and **Guatemala**, US$60-80.

**International buses** Contact individual agencies for schedules and costs;

**Ticabus**, San Juan church, 2 c norte, in the Viajes Cumbia travel agency, T2311-6153, www.ticabus.com. **Nica Expresso**, Agencia Benitours, north side of Iglesia San Juan, 25 vrs norte, T2312-4082.

**Taxi** Daytime fares are cheap: US$0.75 per person to any destination in the city. They cost US$1 at night. Taxis can also be hired to visit **Poneloya** beach and the fumaroles at **San Jacinto** (see page 682). Rates for longer trips vary greatly, with a trip to **San Jacinto** normally costing US$15-20 plus US$1 for every 15 mins of waiting or a higher flat rate for the taxi to wait as long as you wish. Trips outside must be negotiated in advance.

## Around León  *Colour map 4, A1.*
Pacific beaches, historic ruins and the legendary Maribios volcano chain

The Pacific beaches of Las Peñitas and Poneloya lie only 21 km from León down a paved highway; regular buses depart from Sutiava and there is a US$1 entrance fee if you come by car on the weekend. Poneloya is the most popular with Nicas, but Las Peñitas, further on, tends to be a little cleaner and less crowded. The beaches themselves boast wide swathes of sand, warm water and pelicans. Swimming is not recommended however; the currents are deceptively strong and foreigners die here every year assuming that strong swimming skills will keep them out of trouble.

At Km 74 on the Carretera Vieja a León is a scenic dirt track that leads through pleasant pastures to the Nicaraguan Pacific and the long wave-swept beach of Salinas Grandes, known to intrepid surfers. The oil and fishing port of Puerto Sandino, also accessible via a paved road off the Carretera Vieja a León, is gaining popularity too thanks to its world-class breaks; **Miramar Beach**, 6 km south of the town, is reportedly the best. Roughly 17 km south of Sandino on a coast road, the fishing hamlet of El Tránsito has a more remote and rustic setting with a crescent-shaped cove and access to reliable surf.

### Reserva Natural Isla Juan Venado
Accessible from Las Peñitas, the Reserva Natural Isla Juan Venado is a 22-km-long island and turtle-nesting site (August to December), home to mangroves, crocodiles, crabs, iguanas and a healthy aquatic birdlife. To explore the canal that runs behind it, you should allow about four hours in a motorboat, US$50-60, or about US$20 for a short trip; touring needs to be timed with high tide. Kayaking is also offered here at the **Hostel Barca de Oro** and local tour operators in León, one of which, **Journey Nicaragua** (see page 680), has a house in Salinas Grandes and offers a rewarding circuit traversing the entire wildlife refuge, US$25-75 per person depending on group size. Night tours are useful for spotting crocodiles and sea turtles laying eggs, but take plenty of insect repellent.

### León Viejo
*Daily 0800-1700. US$2, including parking and a Spanish-speaking guide; ask questions first to gauge the depth of the guide's knowledge. The sun is brutally strong here so avoid 1100-1430.*

At Km 54 on the Carretera Nueva a Managua is the exit for the 12-km access road to the quiet lakeside village of Puerto Momotombo and the adjoining archaeological site of León Viejo, a UNESCO World Heritage Site and a must for anyone interested in colonial history. At first sight, it consists of nothing more than a few old foundations, but this unfinished excavation site is all that remains of one of the most tragic of Spanish settlements, one which witnessed some of the most brutal acts of the Conquest and was ultimately destroyed by a series of earthquakes and volcanic eruptions between 1580 and 1610.

## Los Volcanes Maribios

A scintillating landscape of sulphurous craters, steaming black sand slopes, simmering pools and imminent eruptions, Los Maribios, a rocky 60-km spine made up of 21 volcanoes, five of which are active, are reason enough to visit Nicaragua's northwest provinces. The cones rise from just above sea level to an average height of 1000 m, filling every vista with earthen pyramids. Most have unpaved road access, though some can only be reached on foot or horseback. It is strongly recommended that you climb with a guide from León or use someone from the local communities at the base of each volcano.

**Volcán Momotombo** At the southern tip of the Maribios range, the symmetrical cone of Volcán Momotombo (1260 m) towers over the shores of Lake Managua, an inspiration to poets over the centuries. The climb to the summit is a long one, normally taking two days, and it is best to go with a León tour operator who can supply a guide and camping gear. The view from the smoking summit is exceptional.

**Cerro Negro** This is a fierce little volcano, the newest in the western hemisphere and the most violent of the Maribios range. In 1850, what was a flat cornfield came to life with 10 days of violent eruption, leaving a hill 70 m high. In the short period since, it has grown to a height of 450 m with persistently violent eruptions shooting magma and ashes up to 8000 m in the air. Fortunately, most of the eruptions have come with ample seismic warning; have a look at www.ineter.gob.ni before climbing. As its name suggests, Cerro Negro is jet-black, made up of black gravel, solidified black lava flows and massive black sand dunes that inspire the local past-time of high-speed volcano boarding; almost any tour operator in León offers this adrenalin-charged thrill, but **Tierra Tour** and **Bigfoot Hostel** are particularly recommended (hint: sitting on the board is more fun than standing).

**Volcán Santa Clara** At the base of Volcán Santa Clara, 15 km from the highway between León and Chinandega, is the entrance to the town of **San Jacinto**, marked by a big sign that says 'Los Hervideros de San Jacinto'. The land drops off behind the village to a field of smoking, bubbling and hissing micro-craters; the Maribios range in miniature and the result of the water table leaking onto a magma vein of nearby Volcán Telica (see below). Entrance is US$2 and local children act as guides; choose one and heed instructions as to where it is safe to walk (avoid treading on the crystallized white sulphur and to listen for hissing). Increased caution is required after rains when the ground is prone to collapse.

**Volcán Telica** Highly active Volcán Telica (1061 m) is part of a 9088-ha tropical dry forest. It last erupted on 25 September 2013 when it exploded violently and produced a 1.5-km ash column. There is a long but rewarding hike that starts from just off the highway to Chinandega before the entrance to the village of **Quezalguaque**, following an ox-cart trail up the north shoulder of the cone, around to its east face and then up to the summit. The hike can take three to five hours round trip, or you can continue to San Jacinto. This hike takes six to eight hours and involves three ascents. Local guides are available if you start the climb from San Jacinto or, for the northeast route, use a León tour operator (see page 679).

**Volcán San Cristóbal** (1745 m)  This is another of Los Maribios' very active volcanoes and the highest in Nicaragua. It has had almost constant activity since 1999, with the last recorded eruption in September 2012, when 1500 people living in its immediate vicinity were evacuated to safety. One of the most symmetrical and handsome of the Maribios volcano range, San Cristóbal is a difficult climb that should only be attempted with a guide and by hikers who are physically fit. Avoid the windy months (November to March).

## Listings Around León

### Where to stay

#### Pacific beaches

**$$$-$$ Miramar Surf Camp**
*Punta Miramar, Puerto Sandino, T8945-1785, www.miramarsurfcamp.net.*
Chilled-out surf lodge with 2 large brick-built compounds and 13 simple rooms equipped with a/c. Parking, pool, restaurant, games area and hammocks are among the amenities. Quiet and secluded with great access to local breaks.

**$$$-$$ Rise Up Surf Camp**
*Salinas Grande, T8125-0990, www.riseupsurftoursnicaragua.com.*
A comfortable and professionally maintained surf camp some 30 mins from León. Good access to the world-class waves of Puerto Sandino. Meals, tours, yoga and massage available. Book beds and transport through **Green Pathways** in León (see page 679).

**$$ Solid Surf Tours and Lodging**
*El Tránsito, T8447-0143, www.solidsurfadventure.com.*
On beachfront with 5 decent a/c rooms and access to some 18 breaks. Seafood and Nica fare, available as part of packages. Beach bonfires, volunteering, surf photography and a host of outdoor activities. Bilingual staff.

**$$-$ Surfing Turtle Lodge**
*Isla Los Brasiles, transport from Poneloya, T8640-0644, www.surfingturtlelodge.com.*
This solar-powered surfers' lodge is located right on the beach. It has simple wooden cabins ($$), double rooms ($$) and an economical dorm ($). Options include surf lessons, board rental, massage, Spanish lessons, fishing and salsa. Protects the turtles that visit the island.

**$ Barca de Oro**
*Las Peñitas, at the end of the beach facing Isla Juan Venado Wildlife Refuge, www.barcadeoro.com, T2317-0275.*
Friendly, funky hotel and day trip hangout with dorm beds and private rooms. Bamboo 'eco-cabañas' sleeping 4 are also available, kitted with solar lighting and water recycling. Services include kayaking, horse riding, body boarding, turtle watching, restaurant and more. The hotel is the departure point for many trips to Isla Juan Venado.

**$ The Lazy Turtle**
*Overlooking the bay, Las Peñitas, T8546-7403, www.thelazyturtle.com.*
Canadian-owned guesthouse with a handful of simple, comfortable rooms, all with good mattresses. Their breezy restaurant serves Tex-Mex, burgers, comfort food and a host of specials depending on what's in season. Friendly and welcoming hosts, the best place in Las Peñitas. Recommended.

### Transport

#### Pacific beaches
Buses pass through **Mateare**, **Nagarote** and **La Paz Centro** on the Carretera every 15 mins between **León** and **Managua**.

#### Poneloya and Las Peñitas
Buses to León pass hourly, 0530-1730, 20 mins, US$0.60.

#### Salinas Grandes
Buses to **León** daily at 0900 and 1500.

**Puerto Sandino**

Buses to **León** hourly, US$0.75, 30 mins.
To **Managua**, hourly, US$1.75, 1 hr.

**El Tránsito**

To **Managua**, 0500, 0600, 0700, US$1, 1½ hrs. To **León**, take a pickup to the Carretera Vieja and catch a passing bus from there, US$1, 30 mins.

**León Viejo**

Buses between Puerto Momotombo (León Viejo) and **La Paz Centro** every 1½ hrs, from 0400-1600, US$0.40. Taxi or hired car can be used as roads are good.

## Chinandega and around   *Colour map 4, A1.*

**grungy and super-hot city**

Chinandega sits in the middle of the most extensive plain of volcanic soil in Nicaragua, which some believe to be the most fertile valley in all of Central America. The locals are very welcoming and the city has two pretty churches that act as bookends for the downtown area.

South of Chinandega, Chichigalpa is a bustling agricultural centre that is best known for its Flor de Caña distillery, which produces what many believe to be the finest rum in the world; tour operators in León can arrange guided visits to its vaults.

## Listings Chinandega and around

### Where to stay

#### Chinandega

**$$ Los Balcones**
*Esquina de los bancos, 75 vrs norte, T2341-8994, www.hotelbalcones.com.*
Same owners as the reputable Los Balcones in León. 18 clean, comfortable rooms with cable TV, hot water and a/c. Wi-Fi and breakfast included. Good.

**$ Don Mario's**
*Enitel, 170 vrs norte, T2341-4054.*
Great-value rooms and friendly hosts at this homely lodging. Rooms have a/c, private bath and cable TV; cheaper with fan. Chill-out space and tables overlook the plant-filled courtyard and the kitchen is available if you wish. The owners speak excellent English, "anything you want, just ask". Relaxed family atmosphere and highly recommended.

### Restaurants

#### Chinandega

**$$ Buenos Aires**
*Plaza Colonial, 2½ c sur.*
A good place for an evening meal. This jaunty, brightly coloured restaurant serves meat, chicken and fish dishes under a thatched palapa roof. Specialities include a range of enchiladas, beef steaks and breaded shrimp dishes. Not bad.

**$$ El Paraíso**
*Plaza Colonial, 3 c arriba, on the Guasaule highway.*
A large outdoor restaurant with a vast palapa roof. Serving the usual meat, chicken and fish fare. A favourite of lunchtime businessmen and moneyed Nicaraguans.

**$ Las Tejitas**
*Parque Central, 7 c arriba.*
Cheap and cheerful. They serve buffet food, grilled meats and *comida típica*.

Very popular and always packed out. A Chinandega institution.

**Chinandega**
**Bus** Most buses leave from the new market at southeast edge of town. To **Corinto**, buses and microbuses, every 20 mins, 0430-1800, US$0.50, 30 mins. To **Somotillo**, every 3 hrs, 0900-1500, US$2, 2 hrs. To **Guasaule**, every 30 mins, 0400-1700, US$2, 2 hrs.

To **Managua**, every 30 mins, 0430-1700, US$2.50, 3 hrs. To **León**, frequent buses 0430-1800, US$1, 1 hr.

Buses for **Potosí**, **El Viejo**, Jiquilillo and **Puerto Morazán** leave from the Santa Ana Mercadito northwest of town. A bus links Terminal, Mercado and Mercadito. To El Viejo, every 20 mins, US$0.60, 10 mins. To **Jiquilillo** and **Reserva Natural Estero Padre Ramos**, 0630, 1000, 1130, 1500, 1630, US$1, ½ hrs. To **Potosí**, 0930 and 1030, US$1.50, 3½ hrs.

## Cosigüina Peninsula  *Colour map 3, C2.*

### region with a forgotten end-of-the-earth feel

El Viejo, 5 km from Chinandega, is a slightly run-down but peaceful place. The 70-cm-tall image in its church of the Immaculate Conception of the Virgin Mary, called La Virgen del Trono, is the patron saint of Nicaragua and one of the most venerated images in all of Central America.

From El Viejo, it is a scenic drive or bumpy bus ride to the Cosigüina Peninsula, which should be done in public bus or 4WD only. If driving, it is essential to buy purified water and fill up with fuel before leaving El Viejo; there are no petrol stations on the peninsula.

There are some long empty beaches on the peninsula's coast. The first section of the highway is paved and passes gigantic ranches. Before the pavement ends, there are two turnings that lead to the desolate beaches of Nicaragua's extreme northwest. The first leads to the sweeping coastline of Aposentillo and the second to Jiquilillo, a quiet, friendly, laid-back community that is now receiving a steady stream of backpackers. Reached by another long, winding dirt and rock path off the highway is the upscale yachters' resort of **Marina Puesta del Sol**, located between Aposentillo and the tiny fishing village of **Los Aserradores**. North of the Playa Aposentillo is the remote coastal estuary reserve of Padre Ramos, named after a priest from El Viejo who drowned here. Access is best from the highway to Jiquilillo, as the ranger station is located at the southern part of the estuary. It is possible to camp here and hire a boat and local guide through the park staff's contacts.

At the northwesternmost point of Nicaragua, Volcán Cosigüina has some unique wildlife and 13,168 ha of protected tropical dry forest. The success of the reserve is that it is the last remaining Nicaragua Pacific coast habitat for the **scarlet macaw**. The view from the summit is why most hikers come to Cosigüina: a sweeping panorama that includes the islands in the Gulf of Fonseca and El Salvador to the north, Honduras to the east, and the emerald crater lake 700 m below the summit. Ascents are best arranged with a tour operator in León.

Arriving in Potosí is much like arriving at any remote place. Although it is only 60 km from Chinandega, the rocky road, searing heat and chocolate-brown waters of the prehistoric bay of **Golfo de Fonseca** are other-worldly. From the solitary dock in Potosí, it is only 15 minutes by boat to a commercial shipping port in Honduras and two hours to La Unión in El Salvador (see Nicaragua–El Savador box in the Practicalities chapter).

## Where to stay

**$$$$ Marina Puesta del Sol**
*Los Aserradores, T8883-0781,*
*www.marinapuestadelsol.com.*
19 suites overlooking the bay and marina,
all spacious and modern with generic decor
and patios. Some have jacuzzi and the
higher-level suites have a great view of bay
and volcanoes.

**$$$-$$ Thunderbomb Surf Camp**
*Playa Santa María del Mar, T8478-0070,*
*www.thunderbombsurf.com.*
A small surf resort and Dutch-Nicaraguan
enterprise with comfortable lodging (rooms
include a/c, TV and private bath) dorms,
Tiki loft, hammocks, yoga platform and a
restaurant. They can provide transport and
offer a range of all-inclusive packages.

**$$$-$ Monty's Surf Camp**
*Jiquilillo, where Bar Los Gemelos*
*used to be, 150 m sur, T8424-4087,*
*www.montysbeachlodge.com.*
This rustic surf lodge on the beach has a
variety of private rooms, some with private
bath ($$$), some without ($$), and a dorm
($). Various 'stay and play' packages available,
as well as surf school, kayaks, volcano tours
and horse riding.

**$ Rancho Esperanza**
*Jiquilillo, 200 m behind Disco ONVI, T8879-*
*1795, www.rancho-esperanza.com.*
This friendly and relaxed 'low-impact' rancho
has a good location on the beach. Various
bamboo *cabañas* are available, as well as
dorms, campground or hammocks for the
thrifty. 3 meals a day cost around US$13.
Activities include surfing, kayaking, hiking and
community tours. Volunteer opportunities
are also available. Good reports.

**$ Rancho Tranquilo**
*Near Pulpería Tina Mata, Los Zorros,*
*10 mins from Jiquilillo, T8968-2290,*
*www.ranchotranquilo.wordpress.com.*
For people looking to escape the gringo trail,
**Rancho Tranquilo** is a relaxed backpacker
place with cabins and ultra-cheap dorms.
There are also hammocks, vegetarian food
and volunteer opportunities. Managed by
Tina, a friendly lady from California.

## What to do

**Tour operators**
**Ecodetur**, *IRO INATEC, 1 c norte, 1 c abajo,*
*T2344-2381, www.ecodetur.com.* Ecotouristic
NGO and co-op with knowledgeable local
guides offering interesting packages that
include hikes to the summit of Cosigüina,
community visits, tours of mangrove forests
and hot springs.

# Northern
## highlands

★ Nicaragua's ruggedly beautiful northern mountains and valleys have staged much of the history that has given the country its war-torn international reputation. It was here that indigenous cultures attacked Spanish mining operations in the 16th century and, in the 19th century, fought confiscation of communal lands that were to go to German immigrants for coffee growing. This is where Sandino fought the US Marines' occupation of Nicaragua and where the rebel Sandinistas launched their first attacks against the Somoza administration in the 1960s. Then, in the 1980s, the Contras waged war against the Sandinista Government in these mountains.

Today, most visitors would be hard pressed to see where all this aggression came from, or that it existed at all. Most of the northern ranges and plains are full of sleepy villages with ancient churches, rustic cowboys and smiling children. This is where the soil and the homes blend into a single palette: the red-brown clay earth reflected in the brown adobe walls and red-tiled roofs. Nothing is rushed here and many of the region's villages are evidence that time travel is indeed possible, with the 21st century in no danger of showing itself around here anytime soon, at least not until the 20th century arrives.

**Best** for
Birds ▪ Cigars ▪ Coffee fincas ▪ Ecolodges ▪ Whitewater rafting

Set in a broad valley encircled by green mountains, including the handsome Cerro de Apante at 1442 m, Matagalpa (altitude 682 m, population 98,000) is the Nicaraguan capital of coffee production, an industry started in the 1870s by German and other European immigrants. The town appears quite attractive from a distance, but less so close up: its streets are narrow, noisy and vaguely claustrophobic, and a circular sprawl of scruffy barrios climb the surrounding hills, threatening to one day enclose the city in concrete.

But beyond Matagalpa's rough-and-ready façade you'll find the city is an excellent base for exploring the region's arresting mountain scenery, its nature reserves, ecolodges, farming communities and coffee fincas, among the best in the world.

Inexpensive taxis are plentiful around the city, but the downtown area is also easy to walk around and safe. The barrios on the outskirts should be avoided. There are two main streets that run south from the main plaza, Parque Morazán, to the little Parque Darío, where it is a bit more peaceful; of these, Avenida José Benito Escobar is the principal commercial drag.

### Sights

Although the main attraction of Matagalpa is the sublime beauty that lies just outside it, the **Catedral de San Pedro de Matagalpa** (1897) on Parque Morazán is worth a visit. There are two other churches that are also pleasant: the late 19th-century **Templo de San José de Laborio** in front of the Parque Darío and the primitive Nicaraguan baroque **Iglesia de Molagüina**, which is the oldest church in Matagalpa, believed to date from 1751. East of Parque Darío is the **Museo Casa Carlos Fonseca** ① *Parque Darío, 1 c este, T2772-2932, Mon-Fri 0830-1200 and 1400-1700*, a memorial to the principal intellectual and founder of the FSLN, who was shot by the National Guard less than three years before the success of the Revolution. The **Coffee Museum** ① *on the main avenue, Parque Morazán, 1½ c sur, T2772-0587, Mon-Fri 0800-1730, Sat 0800-1200*, houses the town's **cultural centre**, offering music and painting classes and displays on the history of local coffee production.

### Around Matagalpa

Located within the **Reserva Apante** ① *US$1*, a few kilometres southeast of Matagalpa, Cerro Apante offers commanding views of Matagalpa and the surrounding countryside. It takes two hours to reach the summit on the main trail. In the west of Matagalpa, the **Mirador El Calvario** ① *US$0.20*, also offers astounding panoramic views, as well as a very modest canopy line, US$4. It is unsafe to walk; take a taxi (US$4). Salto Santa Emilia, also known as Cascada Blanca, is an invigorating waterfall located 15 km outside Matagalpa, near the town of Santa Emilia. There is a pleasant hotel with a mirador overlooking its crashing waters, **Eco-lodge Cascada Blanca**, which serves food to day-trippers. To get the *cascada*, take a bus north on the El Tuma–La Daila highway, pass through Santa Emilia and exit just after the second bridge, where the path to the waterfall leads off to the right. **Note** Due to toxic run-off, do not swim in the crash pools or river during coffee season, late November to late January.

## Esperanza Verde

*Office in San Ramón, Iglesia Católica, 1½ c este, T8775-5338, www.fincaesperanzaverde.com.*

East of Matagalpa is the largely indigenous town of **San Ramón** founded by a friar from León, José Ramón de Jesús María, in 1800. Beyond San Ramón is **Yucul**, home to the well-managed ecolodge and private nature reserve of Esperanza Verde, located 3.5 km from the village. This award-winning reserve has a butterfly breeding project, organic shade-grown coffee cultivation, five hiking trails, five waterfalls and great views to the mountains

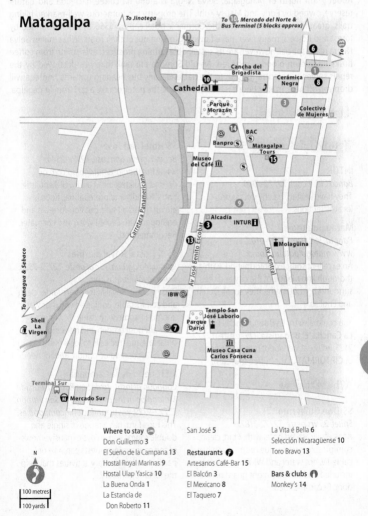

Matagalpa

To Jinotega

To ⑩, Mercado del Norte &
Bus Terminal (5 blocks approx)

Cancha del
Brigadista

Cerámica
Negra

Cathedral ⑩

Parque
Morazán

Colectivo
de Mujeres

BAC

Banpro ⑭ Matagalpa
Tours

Museo
del Café

Carretera Panamericana

To Managua & Sebaco

Alcadía ③ INTUR

Av. José Benito Escobar

Molagüina

Av. Central

IBW

Shell
La Virgen

Templo San
José Laborío
Parque
Darío ⑦ ⑤

Museo Casa Cuna
Carlos Fonseca

Terminal Sur

Mercado Sur

N

100 metres
100 yards

**Where to stay** 🛏
Don Guillermo 3
El Sueño de la Campana 13
Hostal Royal Marinas 9
Hostal Ulap Yasica 10
La Buena Onda 1
La Estancia de
    Don Roberto 11

San José 5

**Restaurants** 🍴
Artesanos Café-Bar 15
El Balcón 3
El Mexicano 8
El Taquero 7

La Vita é Bella 6
Selección Nicaragüense 10
Toro Bravo 13

**Bars & clubs** 🍸
Monkey's 14

of the region. There are few finer places in Nicaragua for birdwatching and enjoying the nature of the northern mountains. Accommodation is in rustic but comfortable wood and brick built cabins ($$$) with contemplative views of the hills. Buses run to Yucul from Matagalpa's north terminal and there are signs for the reserve from San Ramón.

## Selva Negra
*Carretera a Jinotega Km 139.5, T2772-3883, www.selvanegra.com.*

About 7 km north of Matagalpa, Selva Negra is a 600-ha coffee hacienda and nature reserve, owned by Eddy and Mausy Kuhl. The property has numerous well-marked hiking trails, great for birdwatching, and the Germanic hotel cabins ($$$$-$) are surrounded by forest and flowers; many even have flowers growing out of their roofs. What makes Selva Negra really special, however, are its sustainable farming practices: everything from coffee husks to chicken blood is recycled. An old Somoza-era tank that was destroyed by the rebels serves as an entrance sign to the hacienda; any bus heading towards Jinotega will drop you off here, from where it is a 1.5-km walk to the hotel; or take a taxi from Matagalpa.

## Listings Matagalpa *map p689*

### Tourist information

**INTUR**
*Banco Citi, 1 c sur, T2772-7060.*
They have limited, patchy details on local attractions.

**Matagalpa tours**
*Banpro, ½ c este, T2772-0108, www.matagalpatours.com.*
An excellent source of information, with a thorough knowledge of the city and the surrounding mountains; they speak Dutch and English.

You could also try **La Buena Onda Hostel La Cancha 'El Brigadista'** (2½ c este, T2772-2135, www.labuenaondamatagalpa.com), or **CIPTURMAT** in the coffee museum.

### Where to stay

**$$ Don Guillermo**
*Enitel, 25 vrs oeste, T2772-3182.*
A tastefully attired hotel with 7 big, clean, comfortable, good-value rooms. Each has cable TV, hot water and Wi-Fi. Breakfast is included and there's a night guard on the door. Recommended.

**$$ Hotel San José**
*Behind Iglesia San José, T2772-2544, www.hotelsanjosematagalpa.com.ni.*
An immaculately clean and well-kept little hotel, friendly and professional. Rooms are on the small side, but comfortable and equipped with cable TV, fan and hot water. Recommended.

**$$-$ Hostal Royal Marinas**
*Iglesia Molagüina, ½ c al oeste, T2772-7525, www.royalmarinas.com.*
Rooms at the Royal Marinas are large, clean and comfortable, equipped with hot water and Wi-Fi, some with cable TV. There's a pleasant front garden and rates include breakfast and free calls to local numbers and the US. A good-value option. Recommended.

**$ El Sueño de la Campana**
*Contiguo al Instituto de San Ramón, outside Matagalpa in the community of San Ramón, T2772-9729, www.fundacionlacampana.es.*
This rural farm has a range of single and double rooms and enjoys expansive views of the countryside. Guests can hike or participate in voluntary activities that help the local community.

### $ Hostal Ulap Yasica
*Carretera a La Dalia Km 133, 10 mins from the centre, take a taxi, US$1, T2772-6443, www.hostalulapyasica.com.*
The grounds are verdant and restful at this low-impact hostel built with wood and solar powered. It has simple dorms and rooms and a restaurant serving light meals. Laundry service, Wi-Fi, common areas and free organic coffee produced on site. Good reports.

### $ La Buena Onda
*Cancha el Brigadista, 2½ c este, T2772-2135, www.hostelmatagalpa.com.*
An excellent friendly, chilled-out hostel with 2 clean, comfortable dorms, each with private bath and large lockers. There are also some spacious private rooms, book exchange, TV room, DVDs, free coffee, laundry service, shared kitchen and more. Knowledgeable and helpful with good connections to **Matagalpa Tours** (page 693). Recommended.

### $ La Estancia de Don Roberto
*Catedral San Pedro 2 c al norte, 1 c al oeste, ½ c al norte, T2772-3814, www.laestanciadedonroberto.com.ni.*
A quiet, clean, good-value and hospitable family-run hotel with lots of bright artwork on the walls and spacious rooms with hot water, cable TV, fridge, Wi-Fi; laundry service and breakfast at extra cost. Apartments are also available.

### Restaurants

### $$$-$$ Toro Bravo
*Casa de la Novia, 1 c al oeste, 10 vrs al sur, www.restaurantetorobravo.com.*
Overlooking the Matagalpa river, Toro Bravo is a smart steakhouse, the most upmarket and elegant restaurant in town. They serve an array of succulent and reasonably priced beef cuts, including T-bone, rib eye, filet mignon and New York steak. There's also seafood, pork, chicken, burgers and wings.

### $$ Artesanos Café-Bar
*Banpro, ½ c este.*
This pleasant café-bar has a wooden, rancho-style interior. They do breakfasts, light lunches and hot and cold drinks including *licuados*, iced coffee and excellent cappuccinos. Popular with locals and tourists.

### $$ La Vita é Bella
*Col Lainez 10, from Buena Onda, ½ c north, then right down an alleyway to an unmarked house, T2772-5476.*
An Italian-run restaurant, which has received strong praise from several readers, but perhaps not as great as it once was. Pleasant outdoor seating on a patio.

### $$-$ El Balcón
*Alcadía Municipal, 25 m al sur.*
El Balcón serves reasonable to good Nica and international fare, including *pollo a la plancha*, brochetas, steaks, burgers, quesadillas and fish. Served Mon-Sat, the lunchtime *menú ejecutivo* is very good value and recommended ($). Pleasant interior with the airy upstairs balcony overlooking Matagalpa's main street. A reliable option for breakfast, lunch and dinner.

### $ El Mexicano
*Brigadista, 2½ c este. Mon-Sat 1100-2100.*
Brightly painted Mexican eatery offering a range of affordable dishes including fajitas, nachos and burritos. Friendly and casual. Recommended for budget travellers.

### $ El Taquero
*Parque Darío, 1 c al sur, ½ c al oeste. Open 1800-0100.*
El Taquero plies a roaring trade in the evening as local families gather to enjoy its mouth-watering flame-grilled meat dishes, including Nica and Mexican staples such as tacos, burritos, *churrasco*, steaks and enchiladas. Takeaway available. Recommended.

## Cafés

### Selección Nicaragüense
*Catedral, ½ c al norte.*
The best coffee shop in town with excellent hot and cold coffee, including cappuccino, iced coffee and americanos. The interior is contemporary and laid back, and often buzzing with students in the evening. A small selection of snacks, including cakes, paninis and pies available. Good staff. Wi-Fi.

## Bars and clubs

### Artesanos Café-Bar
*See Restaurants, above.*
A popular place that draws a diverse crowd of locals and expats. Cocktails, rum and beer, in addition to coffee. Recommended.

### Monkey's
*South side of the Parque Central.*
Built from wood and occupying a commanding position on Parque Morazán, Monkey's is an open-air structure with several breezy decks. They host live music on Wed and Sat, including salsa and merengue; a friendly spot to knock back a few beers.

## Shopping

### Crafts
**Artesanías La Alforja Matagalpa**, *Cancha el Brigadista, 2½ c al este, inside La Buena Onda Hostel. Mon-Sat 0900-1800.* A broad range of local crafts, including jewellery from San Ramón, hand-woven textiles, black pottery, coffee, chocolate and wood-carvings.
**Cerámica Negra**, *Parque Darío.* This kiosk, open irregularly, sells black pottery in the northern tradition, a style found only in parts of Chile, Nicaragua and Mexico. There is evidence that this school of ceramics dates back to 1500 BC in this region of Nicaragua. For more information contact Estela Rodríguez, T2772-4812.
**Colectivos de Mujeres de Matagalpa**, *Banco Uno, 2½ c este, T2772-4462. Mon-Fri 0800-1200, 1400-1730, Sat 0800-1200.*

Native fabrics, leather goods, ceramics and an orange and coffee liqueur made by women's cooperatives in El Chile, Molino Norte and Malinche.
**Telares Indígenas Nicaragua**, *Semáforos Parque Morazán, 1 c al sur, ½ c al este, same building as Matagalpa Tours, T8654-4824.* Fair-trade textiles produced by the indigenous community of El Chile, including purses, backpacks, wallets and carpets, all handmade using organic cotton.

## What to do

### Coffee tours
The **Coffee Museum, INTUR, Hostal La Buena Onda** or **Matagalpa Tours** can help you arrange trips to the many coffee fincas in the area. Outside the season, late-Nov to late-Jan, you will not see workers picking in the plantations. **Selva Negra** and **Esperanza Verde** are both interesting coffee fincas (see pages 689 and 690) that can be visited independently. Other options include:
**Monkey's Coffee and Cacao Workshop**, *southwest corner of Parque Morazán, inside Restaurante Monkey's. Tue-Sun 1000-1200 and 1500-1900.* A fun 2-hr workshop in artisan coffee production where participants toast, grind and pack their own coffee to drink and to take away. Also includes instruction in tasting techniques, an overview of the cultural context of coffee production and an explanation of cacao processing.
**UCA San Ramón**, *opposite the Parque Municipal, San Ramón, T2772-5247, www. ucasanramon.com.* This organization can arrange a 'hands-on' experience of coffee production, where you meet farming communities and participate in the process.

### Language schools
**Colibrí Spanish School**, *Banpro, ½ c este, T2772-0108, www.colibrispanishschool.com, next to Matagalpa Tours.* They offer packages of 15, 20 and 30 hrs one-on-one with options for homestays (meals included) or lodging in an apartment. Courses include all materials

and various sociocultural activities including visits to local attractions, social events, cooking and dance classes, films and tours of the city. Costs US$7-10 per hr.

## Tour operators

**Matagalpa Tours**, *Banpro, ½ c este, T2772-0108, www.matagalpatours.com*. This reputable agency explores the north of Nicaragua from a different point of view. Trekking, hiking, birdwatching and rural community tours are among their well-established repertoire, now supplemented by exciting whitewater rafting trips down the Río Tuma (May-Jan, Class II-IV), the first of their kind in the country. Another of their most interesting options involves visiting Mayagna communities and working mines in the remote northeast of the country. Also offers excellent mountain-bike tours, from 2 hrs to several days. Dutch- and English-speaking, helpful and friendly. The best agency in town for all your adventuring needs. Highly recommended.

**Northward Nicaragua Tours**, *Parque Rubén Darío, 2½ c oeste, T2772-0605, www. adventure-nicaragua.com*. Founded by Nicaraguan tour guide and outdoors enthusiast Alvaro Rodríguez, who offers a range of custom-made tours throughout the Nicaraguan countryside. Recommended for hardcore adventurers and adrenalin junkies.

Transport

**Bus** Terminal Sur (Cotransur) is near Mercado del Sur and used for all destinations outside the department of Matagalpa.

To **Jinotega**, every 30 mins, 0500-1900, US$1, 1½ hrs (buses are packed on Sun, avoid). To **Managua**, every 30 mins, 0335-1805, US$2.40, 3-4 hrs; express buses (recommended), every hr, 0520-1720, US$2.90, 2½ hrs. To **Estelí**, every 30 mins, 0515-1745, US$1.20, 2-3 hrs. Express bus to **León** (subject to change), 0600, 1500, 1600, US$2.90, 2½ hrs, departs only if there is sufficient demand, otherwise take an Estelí bus to the junction (*empalme*) south of San Isidro and change. Express bus to **Masaya**, 1400, 1530, US$2.90, 4 hrs. Infrequent services run to **Chinandega**.

Terminal Norte, by Mercado del Norte (Guanuca), is for all destinations within the province of Matagalpa including **San Ramón** and **El Tuma**. Taxi between terminals US$0.50.

**Taxi** Matagalpa taxis are helpful and cheap. Average fare inside the city is US$0.50. Fare to **Selva Negra** US$4-5 per person.

## Jinotega *Colour map 4, A1.*

### coffee city with a refreshing climate and a relaxed atmosphere

Jinotega (altitude 1004 m, population 33,000) is the diminutive capital of a sprawling province that has almost no infrastructure to date and remains one of the poorest and least developed parts of the country. Like Matagalpa, it is an important area for the nation's coffee industry and subject to the whim of international coffee prices. Nestled in a valley of green mountains and shaded from the tropical sun, Jinotega's helpful and charming people are its greatest assets. Jinotega is easy to walk around, but avoid walking after 2200 at the weekend.

## Sights

Jinotega is not visited by many foreigners, except for those working on international projects. The city has grown rapidly to the east of the centre in recent years, which means that the central park is actually now in the west of town. The area around the main plaza and the very attractive cathedral, **El Templo Parroquial** (1805), is full of broad streets and has a tranquil, small-town feel. The Gothic cathedral has an interior that reflects the local climate, with a lovely clean, cool, whitewashed simplicity. The city's symbol is the cross-topped mountain, **Cerro La Peña Cruz**, to the west of central park. Every 3 May more than 5000 pilgrims walk to the top to take part in a Mass at the summit at 0900. (The hike to the summit takes just over an hour.)

## Around Jinotega

The beautiful **Lago de Apanás**, 8 km east of Jinotega, was created by the damming of the Río Tuma in 1964 to form a 54-sq-km shiny blue body of water. To visit the lake take a bus from Jinotega bound for Austurias–Pantasma (hourly 0700-1500, one hour, US$2). You can go out on the lake with one of the members of the fishing co-operative **La Unión del Norte** who charge US$10 per hour for an excursion by motorboat and US$6 per hour by rowing boat. Ask at El Portillo de Apanás.

Protected since 2002, the **Reserva Natural Datanlí-Diablo** ① www.exploredatanli.com, encompasses a sprawling massif between Matagalpa and Jinotega, concluding at Lago de Apanás in the north. Rising to a height of 1680 m at the challenging peak of El Diablo, the area is punctuated by misty cloudforests and rugged hills, rolling coffee fincas and somnambulant villages. The southern side of the reserve can be accessed by a turning marked 'Fundadora' on the Matagalpa–Jinotega highway; from there, it is 6 km on a dirt road to the **Eco-Albergue La Fundadora** ① T8855-2573, www.fundadora.org, which has brick cabins ($), camping space, a simple restaurant and tour guides (if walking, it is just 3 km from the turning of Las Latas to the Eco-Albergue). On the northern side of the reserve, the best facilities can be found at **Finca La Bastilla** ① T2782-4335, www.bastillaecolodge. com, which boasts excellent ecologically sound wooden cabins overlooking the landscape ($$-$). Northeast of La Bastilla, a hiking trail connects to the community of **Gobiado**, which has rustic lodging, food and guides. To get to La Bastilla, 20 km northeast of Jinotega, take the road towards Pantasma and look for the second turning on the right after the Jigüina bridge; it is 5 km along a dirt road from here (4WD only). Those using public transport can call ahead for pick-up; or take a taxi from Jinotega, US$20.

Just 25 km northwest from Jinotega is the tiny village of **San Rafael**, a pleasant, authentic mountain town with a gigantic church and a rich history. **La Iglesia Parroquial** was first built in 1887 and its most famous feature is a mural next to the entrance depicting the temptation of Christ; the devil's face is said to resemble the Sandinista leader Daniel Ortega. The festival for San Rafael usually lasts eight days and takes place around 29 September.

## Listings Jinotega

### Tourist information

INTUR
*Del Parque Otto Casco, 1 c al norte,*
*T2782-4552, jinotega@intur.gob.ni.*
*Mon-Fri 0800-1200 and 1400-1600.*
One of the country's better tourist offices. The well-informed staff have good information on the town and surrounding areas.

### Where to stay

**$$ La Estancia de Don Francisco**
*UNO Central 250 m al norte, T2782-2309,*
*www.estanciadedonfrancisco.com.*
A family-run bed and breakfast with just 5 rooms, all different, decent and tastefully furnished. Patio, garden, bar, Wi-Fi and cable TV. Comfortable beds and attentive service. Recommended.

## $$ La Quinta
*Parque Central, 7 c norte, over the bridge,*
*T2782-2522, becquerfernandez@yahoo.ca.*
This Nicaraguan mini-resort has a pleasant
setting among the pine trees. There's a range
of include Wi-Fi, parking, pool, restaurant,
karaoke bar and disco. Recommended.

## $ Hotel Sollentuna Hem
*Gasolinera Puma, 1 c arriba, 2½ c norte,*
*T2782-2334, hotelsollentuna@gmail.com.*
This clean, safe, family hotel has 16 rooms,
all with private bath, cable TV, fan and hot
water. The owner, who lived in Sweden
for many years, offers a range of beauty
treatments, including massage and pedicure.
Breakfast and dinner are served, and coffee
tours are available. Pleasant and professional.

## $ La Biósfera Reserve and Retreat
*Km 158 Carretera Matagalpa–Jinotega, T8698-*
*1439, www.hijuela.com, 3 km outside Jinotega.*
La Biósfera is a socially and ecologically
aware lodging committed to green energy,
permaculture and 'interpersonal harmony'.
Lodging is in spartan rustic cabins and
dorms, with opportunities for hiking, star-
gazing, alternative therapies and workshops.

## Restaurants

## $$ La Perrera
*Km 158 Carretera Matagalpa–Jinotega,*
*www.restaurantelaperrera.com.*
Oft-praised restaurant 3 km out of town,
serving international fare and seafood.
Offerings include steak and chips, fajitas, pork
chops in barbecue sauce and fried fish fillet.

## $$-$ Restaurante El Tico
*Across from La Salle athletic field, T782-2530.*
*Daily 0800-2200.*
44-year-old establishment in a very modern
location, popular with couples, moderately
priced dishes, try surf and turf (*mar y tierra*)
or *pollo a la plancha*, also cheap dishes and
sandwiches. Recommended.

## $$-$ Soda Buffet El Tico
*Gasolinera Puma, 2½ c sur. Open for*
*breakfast, lunch and dinner.*
Reasonable buffet restaurant serving typical
Nicaraguan food. Clean, reliable and popular
with tourists. Best to get there early when
the food is fresh.

## Cafés

## Flor de Jinotega
*Ferretería Blandón Moreno, 1 c abajo,*
*www.soppexcca.org/en.*
The best coffee in town, produced
by an environmentally aware and
progressive cooperative, **Soppexcca**.
Highly recommended.

## What to do

## Tour operators
**Apanás Tours**, *opposite the bus station,*
*T8403-4617, infoapanastours@gmail.com.*
A new local outfit offering a range of cultural
and adventure tours including trips to
the Lago Apanás, San Rafael del Norte, El
Castillo chocolate factory and various nature
reserves. Hiking and kayaking are among the
options; bilingual guides available.
**UCA Soppexcca**, *Ferretería Blandón Moreno,*
*1 c abajo, www.soppexcca.org/en.* This great
organization comprises 15 organic coffee
cooperatives who offer tours to see how
their award-winning beans are cultivated
and prepared for export.

## Around Jinotega
## Canopy tours
**Canopy Tour La Brellera**, *Carretera San*
*Rafael–Yalí Km 5, T2784-2356.* Located just
outside San Rafael del Norte, La Brellera is
a new canopy tour with 1.5 km of ziplines.
Costs per person US$15, open 0800-1800. To
get there, take a bus towards Yalí from the
Mercado Municipal in Jinotega and ask to get
off at La Brellera, US$1; or go to San Rafael del
Norte and take a taxi.

## Transport

Most destinations will require a change of bus in Matagalpa. To **Matagalpa**, every 30 mins, 0500-1800, US$1.50, 1½ hrs. Express bus to **Managua**, 11 daily, 0400-1600, US$3.20, 3½ hrs. To **San Rafael del Norte**, departing from the Mercado, 10 daily, 0600-1730 US$1, 1 hr. Taxis in Jinotega are available for local transport, average fare US$.50.

## Estelí  *Colour map 4, A1.*

### unpretentious university town surrounded by highland villages and national parks

At first glance, Estelí (altitude 844 m, population 107,458) appears to be a jumbled unattractive place, but this is one of the most lively and industrious towns in Nicaragua. It is known nationally as one of the biggest commercial centres in the north and internationally as the cigar capital of Central America and, like Matagalpa and Jinotega, it is set in an area of bucolic villages and verdant countryside. The Sandinistas remain a force to be reckoned with in Estelí and the party colours of black and red can be seen all around town.

The city centre lies to the west of the highway, with the focus of its life and commerce on two avenues that bear south from the Parque Central. Taxis are cheap in the town and walking is safe in the daytime. Exercise caution at night and don't wander around the barrios.

### Sights

Estelí was founded in 1711 by Spanish colonists who abruptly left Nueva Segovia, now Ciudad Antigua (see page 702), to escape joint Miskito-British attacks on the old city. Sadly the town was razed in 1978-1979 by Somoza's National Guard, which used aerial bombing and tanks to put down repeated uprisings by the population spurred on by the FSLN. To learn more about the city's revolutionary past, head to the **Galería de Héroes y Mártires** ⓘ *Casa de Cultura, ½ c al norte, T2714-0942, www.galleryofheroesandmartyrs.blogspot.com, Tue-Fri 0900-1630, free,* which has photographic exhibitions and artefacts highlighting the struggle and sacrifice of the city's fallen comrades. Estelí is known as the capital of **cigars**, with the finest tobacco in Central America grown in the surrounding mountains. Most of the city's factories were founded by exiled Cubans, who brought their seeds and expertise with them in the 1960s. If you would like to see the production process, a handful of local guides and tour operators lead tours to selected manufacturers; see What to do, below.

### Around Estelí

The **Reserva Natural Meseta Tisey-Estanzuela** ⓘ *managed by Fundación Fider, Petronic El Carmen, 1½ c abajo, Estelí, T713-3918, fiderest@ibw.com.ni,* is home to rugged mountain scenery quite different from the landscape of Nicaragua's Pacific Basin: there are pine and oak forests, moss-covered granite boulders, rivers and cascades. The biggest attraction is the lovely **Estanzuela waterfall**, accessed by a signed 5 km dirt road just south of Estelí.

North of Estelí, a very poor dirt road runs west to the rural village of **San Juan de Limay**, famous across Nicaragua for the beautiful soapstone (*marmolina*) carvings produced by more than 50 carvers who work in the area. It can take up to two hours to travel the 44 km, but it's worth it for those who like remote villages and crafts.

On the east side of the Pan-American highway, about 25 km north of Estelí, is the sleepy village of **Condega**, another vehemently Sandinista town. Above the cemetery there is a park with an old aeroplane from Somoza's National Guard, downed by FSLN rebels in 1979

# Estelí

To Cigar Factory (Segovia Cigars)

To Somoto & Honduras

Crafts

Parque Central

Cathedral

Gran Vía Bolívar

Artesanía Sorpresa

Amnlae Women's Centre

Supermercado Palí

El Salvador Cooperative

Ministry of Health Information Centre

Cenac Language School

Craft

Parque Infantil

Carretera Panamericana

Bus Station North

Gran Vía Bolívar

To Somoto & Honduras

C 14 NE

C 2 NE

C 1 NE

C Perú

C 1 SE

C 2 SE

C 3 SE

C 5 SE

C 7 SE

C 9 SE

C 11 SE

To Buses South & Managua

N

100 metres
200 yards

**Where to stay**
Casa Nicarao 7
Cuallitlan 8
Hostal Sonati 9
Hostal Tomabú 5
Los Arcos 12
Luna International Hostel 4
Puro Estelí 11

Cafetería El Rincón
Pinareño 7
Casa Vecchia 12
Cohifer 3
El Quesito 15
La Casita 10
Pullaso's Olé 4
Tipiscayan 14

**Restaurants**
Ananda 1
Café Don Luis 11
Café Luz 2

**Bars & clubs**
Cigarzone 11
Semáforo Rancho 16

and now rusting like a dinosaur carcass. The name Condega means 'land of potters' and the local artisans make traditional, red-clay pottery that is both attractive and functional.

## Reserva Natural Miraflor
*T2713-2971, www.ucamiraflor.com, US$2.*

Northeast of Estelí, this reserve is full of diverse wildlife and vegetation and offers opportunities to visit and stay in local communities. The ecosystem changes with altitude from tropical savannah to tropical dry forest, then to pine forest and finally cloudforest at its highest elevations. The legendary quetzal lives here, along with trogons, magpie jays, the turquoise-browed mot-mot, many birds of prey, howler monkeys, mountain lions, ocelots, deer, sloths, river otters, racoons and tree frogs. The reserve also has some gallery forest, ideal for viewing wildlife, a variety of orchids and a 60-m-high waterfall that flows during the rainy season. For unbiased information on lodging and excursions inside the reserve, visit **Miraflor Ecotours and Adventure** ⓘ *east side of the cathedral, 1 c norte, T8496-7449, www.cafeluzyluna.com*, inside the Treehuggers tourism office. You are strongly advised to arrange guides and/ or accommodation prior to setting out.

## Listings Estelí map p697

### Tourist information

#### INTUR
*Southwest corner of the Parque Central, ½ c oeste, 2nd floor of the red building, T2713-6799.*
This office has information on local attractions including nature reserves, cigar factories and Spanish schools.

#### Treehuggers tourism office
*East side of the cathedral, 1 c norte, T8496-7449, www.cafeluzyluna.com. Open 0800-2000.*
Managed by Luna International Hostel across the street, this place is a great source of English-language information.

## Where to stay

### $$ Hotel Cuallitlan
*Restaurante El Sopón (Km 146.5) 4 c este, 1 c norte, 400 m from the Panamericana, T2713-2446, www.hotelcuallitlan.com.*
A secluded and tranquil hideaway with 13 comfortable wooden cabins and a ranch-style restaurant. The grounds encompass a pleasant garden with shady trees, hammocks and patios. Hospitable and helpful. Rustic-chic.

### $$ Hotel Los Arcos
*Northeast corner of the cathedral, ½ c norte, T2713-3830, www.hotelosarcosesteli.com.*
This brightly painted, professionally managed and comfortable hotel has 32 clean, spacious rooms with private bath, a/c or fan and cable TV. There's also parking, laundry service and Wi-Fi. The attached restaurant, **Vuela Vuela**, is also reputable and profits go to social projects. Breakfast included.

### $ Casa Hotel Nicarao
*Parque Central, 1½ c sur, T2713-2490.*
9 clean, basic rooms with fan and private bath, all set around a relaxing, sociable courtyard filled with plants, paintings and sitting space. Friendly with a good atmosphere, but the walls are thin and you'll hear everything going on inside and out. There are cheaper rooms without bath.

### $ Hostal Sonati
*Northeast corner of Parque Central, 3 c este, T2713-6043, www.sonati.org.*
A cheerful new backpacker hostel and NGO dedicated to social and environmental responsibility. They have 4 rooms and 3 dorms, all with hot water. Services including laundry, bag storage, book exchange, kitchen, Wi-Fi, free coffee, tourist information, guitar, hammocks and tours (see What to do, below). Helpful and friendly.

### $ Hostal Tomabú
*Opposite the Parque Infantil, T2713-3783, www.hostaltomabu.com. Friendly, family-run hotel whose name means 'place of the sun'.*

15 good, clean rooms with hot water, fan and cable TV, most with Wi-Fi. Bright colours and potted flowers. Lots of connections with tour operators and professional, personal attention. Shared kitchen, lending library and common areas. Recommended.

### $ Hotel Puro Estelí
*Costado noreste de la Catedral, 1 c norte, 75 vrs este, T2713-6404, www.hotelpuroesteli.com.*
Owned by a major cigar manufacturer, **Drew Estate**, this hotel has a large *humidor* in the lobby where you can stock up on *puros*. Rooms are simple, comfortable and economical, and tastefully adorned with bright artwork. It has the usual amenities. Good value.

### $ Luna International Hostel
*Catedral, 1 c al norte, 1 c arriba, T8441-8466, www.cafeluzyluna.com.*
This popular hostel is part of an excellent non-profit social enterprise. Facilities include 4 dorms, 3 private rooms, hammock space, an activities board, tourist information, lockers, hot water, Wi-Fi, tours, free organic coffee and drinking water. Volunteer work in Miraflor can be arranged here; 3 months' commitment and Spanish speakers preferred. Discounts for longer stays and groups. Highly recommended.

## Restaurants

### $$$ Pullaso's Olé
*Autolote del norte, 1 c oeste, www.pullasosole.com.*
A superb steakhouse and the best restaurant in town. They serve certified Angus beef and a range of sumptuous cuts including sirloin, T-bone, rib eye and porterhouse steaks. Attentive service, a good wine list and outdoor seating on a patio. The place for a special evening meal. Recommended.

### $$$-$$ Cohifer
*Catedral, 1 c este, ½ c al sur.*
A well-established Nicaraguan restaurant, considered 'upmarket' for Estelí and popular

with business people at lunchtime. They serve the usual steak, chicken, fish and pork dishes, as well as lighter economical fare. Nothing extraordinary, but service is good and the food is generally tasty and reliable.

### $$ Tipiscayan
*Northeast corner of Parque Central, 2 c norte, 2½ c arriba.*
A relaxing space with lots of interesting artwork and a good balcony upstairs. They serve a range of meat and chicken dishes in *jalapeño* and other sauces.

### $$-$ Café Luz
*Catedral, 1 c al norte, 1 c arriba.*
This English-owned café is part of a non-profit enterprise that supports communities in Miraflor. All salads, herbs and vegetables are locally sourced and organic. They serve a range of wholesome lunches, dinners and breakfasts, including fruit salads with home-made yogurt and granola, pancakes with honey, and *nacatamales*. Beverages include local coffee and tasty fresh fruit juices with no added sugar. Recommended.

### $$-$ Cafetería El Rincón Pinareño
*Enitel, ½ c sur.*
Nicaraguan dishes and home-made pastries, try *vaca frita* (shredded fried beef with onions and bell peppers) and *sandwich cubano*. Good service and food, crowded for lunch.

### $$-$ Casa Vecchia
*Southwest corner of the Parque Central, 2 c sur, 1 c oeste.*
A low-key Italian restaurant serving decent pasta dishes, including lasagne. Intimate and casual setting.

### $ El Quesito
*Northeast corner of the Parque Central, 2 c este. Closed Sun.*
A little locals' joint with rustic furniture and the usual hearty Nica fare, economical and filling. Often full at breakfast time.

## Cafés, bakeries and juice bars

### Ananda
*Enitel, 10 vrs abajo.*
Chilled-out yoga centre full of happy-looking plants. They serve delicious and healthy fresh fruit *licuados*, the perfect nutrient boost. Highly recommended.

### Café Don Luis
*Bancentro, 25 vrs al norte.*
A buzzing little café on the corner with tables outside, ideal for people-watching. They serve paninis, sweet snacks, coffee, espresso, cappuccino and excellent cheesecake. Wi-Fi.

### La Casita
*Opposite la Barranca, at south entrance to Estelí on Panamericana, T2713-4917, casita@sdnnic.org.ni.*
Nicaragua's best home-made yogurt in tropical fruit flavours. Very cute place with pleasant outdoor seating underneath trees on back patio. Recommended.

## Bars and clubs

### Café Luz
*See Restaurants, above.*
Most evenings at **Café Luz** see an eclectic mix of expats, Nicas, volunteers and travellers gathering to drink beer, coffee or rum, or otherwise engage in relaxed conversation.

### Cigarszone
*Carretera Panamericana, southern entrance to the city.*
Estelí's most modern and popular disco. Also features live music and boisterous young things.

### Semáforo Rancho Bar
*Hospital San Juan de Dios, 400 m sur.*
Don your dancing shoes for Estelí's quintessential night spot. It hosts some of the best live music in the country, with nationally and internationally renowned acts performing regularly.

## What to do

### Cigar making

Estelí's famous cigar factories can be toured with independent guides or agencies. For aficionados, **Drew Estates** (www.cigarsafari. com, contactable through Hotel Puro Estelí), offer 'cigar safari' tours. Also recommended are **Treehuggers Tours** (see below). Alternatively, you can contact the factories directly (a comprehensive list is available from **INTUR**), although not all of them offer tours.

### Language schools

**CENAC, Centro Nicaragüense de Aprendizaje y Cultura**, *250 m north of the UNO gas station, T2713-5437, www.spanish schoolcenac.com*. 20 hrs of Spanish classes, living with a family, full board, trips to countryside, meetings and seminars, opportunities to work on community projects, US$185 per week. Also teaches English to Nicaraguans and others and welcomes volunteer tutors.

**Horizonte Nica**, *INISER, 2 c arriba, ½ c al norte, T2713-4117*. Intensive Spanish courses with a programme of activities and homestay. They offer excursions and voluntary work and aim to educate you about local communities as well as the language.

**Spanish Conversation School**, *Costado del Cine Nancy, ½ c al oeste, T2714-2237, www. spanishconversation.net*. Full immersion and non-immersion courses with options for homestay and activities. They also offer classes via Skype.

### Tour operators

**Sonati Tours**, *northeast corner of the Parque Central, 3 c este, T2713-6043, www.sonati.org*. An environmental education organization and youth hostel offering culture and nature tours of communities and nature reserves in the north of Nicaragua, including Somoto Canyon. **Treehuggers tourism office**, *east side of the cathedral, 1 c norte, T8496-74498405-8919, www.cafeluzyluna.com*. In addition to Miraflores excursions, Treehuggers offers tours of Estelí and its murals, cigar factories, Somoto Canyon and beyond. They also run 'extreme hikes' and night hikes to observe nocturnal birds. Good.

## Transport

**Bus** Estelí is a transport hub with express bus services from Managua, Matagalpa and León. Regular buses connect it with Somoto and Ocotal, both of which connect to the Honduran border; see Nicaragua–Honduras border box in the Practicalities chapter.

Buses enter and leave Estelí via 2 terminals, both on the Pan-American highway. The north terminal deals with northern destinations like Somoto and Ocotal. The south terminal, a short distance away, deals with southern destinations like Managua. A handful of Managua express buses also stop at the Shell station, east of the centre on the Pan-American highway.

**North station**: to **Somoto**, every hour, 0530-1810, US$1.10, 2½ hrs, use this service to connect to El Espino border bus. To **Ocotal**, every hour, 0600-1730, US$1.40, 2 hrs, use this for bus to Las Manos crossing. To **Jinotega**, 5 daily, US$2, 2 hrs. To **El Sauce**, 0900, US$1.25, 3 hrs. To **San Juan de Limay**, 7 daily, US$2, 3 hrs. To **Miraflor**, take a bus heading towards **San Sebastián de Yalí** (not one that goes to Condega first), 3 daily 0600, 1200, 1600, US$2, 1½ hrs. Return bus passes at 0700, 1100 and 1620.

**South station**: express bus to **León**, 1500, US$2.75, 3 hrs. To **Managua**, every 30 mins, 0330-1800, US$2, 3 hrs; express buses, roughly 30 mins, 0545-1515, US$3, 2 hrs. To **Matagalpa**, every 30 mins, 0520-1650, US$1.40, 2 hrs; express buses, 0805, 1435, US$1.50, 1½ hrs.

**Taxi** Taxis are common on the Carretera Panamericana in Estelí, at the bus stations and in the town proper. Fares per person, inside the city centre US$0.50, from the bus stations to centre US$1. Night fares are higher and trips to the dance clubs on the outskirts cost US$2-3. As always, agree on fare before long rides; in town just get in.

## Towards Honduras: Madriz and Nueva Segovia   Colour map 3, C3.

stop off for a rosquilla in one of the seemingly forgotten towns

Rolling north from Estelí, the Pan-American Highway enters the fragrant pine forests and rugged mountains of Madriz, where everything happens in its own time. West of Somoto, the provincial capital, the international crossing at El Espino provides rapid access to southern Honduras and El Salvador; see also Nicaragua–Honduras border box in the Practicalities chapter. The most direct route to Tegucigalpa, however, is through the neighbouring department of Nueva Segovia, a deeply rural region and early colonial mining centre. Local buses are slow and dusty; for serious exploration of the region's hidden attractions, 4WD is recommended.

### Somoto

The sleepy town of Somoto is celebrated for its world-famous sons, the folk musicians Carlos and Luis Enrique Mejía Godoy, and for its superb *rosquillas* (baked corn and cheese biscuits) which are practically a religion. No one seems sure when *rosquillas* became a tradition, but the oldest residents recall that they were already popular in the 1920s. The most famous baker could be **Betty Espinoza** ① *Enitel, 3 c norte, T2722-2173, Mon-Sat 0500-1000*, who is happy for visitors to watch the process of butter, corn, eggs, milk, sugar and Nicaraguan feta cheese being made into *rosquillas*; her seven employees and big wood-burning ovens crank out 3000 of them per day. For the border crossing to Honduras, see Nicaragua–Honduras border box in the Practicalities chapter.

### Somoto Canyon

*To get to the canyon, follow the highway about 15 km north of Somoto, where you'll find a signposted dirt track at the bridge over the Tapacalí River; it is a 20-min walk from here. Follow the track 3 km to the end where you will meet guides with a boat who will ferry you to the canyon. Take care on the slippery rocks. A taxi here costs around US$5.*

Known locally as Namancambre, Somoto Canyon soars above crystal-clear waters at the source of the great Río Coco, which runs for more than 750 km to the Caribbean Sea. A walk in the 3-km-long canyon is both a contemplative and adventurous experience, requiring careful hiking over slippery rocks that hug the 100-m-high walls. You can swim or tube in the river during dry season, but it can be very dangerous in the rainy season (June to November) and even if not swimming, as the river is prone to flash floods and the currents are very strong. There are various hikes you can undertake in the area lasting anything from three to 12 hours. A cooperative of guides works near the entrance of the canyon, offering its services for around US$25 per day, depending on your requirements, as well as the option of rustic lodging in their community; contact Henri Soriano, T8610-7642.

### Comunidad Indígena de Totogalpa

Arriving in Totogalpa, a seemingly forgotten town with red-clay streets and lightly crumbling adobe homes, feels like arriving at the very end of the earth. The original settlement dates back more than 1600 years and is located in the community of San José, northeast of the current village, on the banks of the Río Coco. The remains of circular stone houses and ceramics suggest that this was a large settlement AD 400-600.

## Ocotal

Named after the ocotl species of pine tree, Ocotal has the dubious distinction of being the first town in the world to be bombed by a fleet of military planes in combat circumstances, courtesy of the US Marines in July 1927. Today, this little city is the financial and trading centre of Nueva Segovia. It has little to offer visitors, but it is a useful base for exploring the region, or to rest before or after the border crossing at Las Manos; see Nicaragua–Honduras border box in the Practicalities chapter. Its main attraction is **Parque Las Madres**, a lush tropical garden designed by the ex-mayor of Ocotal and tropical plant expert, Don Fausto Sánchez.

## Ciudad Antigua

Nestled in a valley of rolling hills, the Ciudad Antigua of today is truly in the middle of nowhere, but that was not always the case. Originally called Nueva Ciudad Segovia, it was founded in 1611 by Spanish colonists who hurriedly abandoned the first Ciudad Segovia settlement (founded between 1541 and 1543 near present day Quilalí) as a result of continued attacks by the indigenous population. In the late 1600s, the city was attacked by pirates and most of the population fled to found Ocotal, or further south to found Estelí. The village has not changed much for the last few centuries, providing an excellent opportunity to step back in time. Its 17th-century **church** features a whitewashed adobe interior with an ornate gold leaf altar bearing a famous image of Jesus or El Señor de los Milagros, said to have been brought to Ciudad Antigua, along with the heavy altar, via a Caribbean port in Honduras by manpower alone.

## Listings Towards Honduras: Madriz and Nueva Segovia

### Where to stay

#### Somoto

**$$ Hotel Colonial**
*Iglesia, ½ c sur, T2722-2040.*
A well-established hotel with an attractive lobby and exterior, but only so-so rooms; all have private bath, cable TV and fan. Popular with businessmen and NGOs, but not as good as it once was; ask to see a few rooms (some are big, others not) and check mattresses before accepting.

**$ Hotel El Rosario**
*Claro, 1 c este, 2722-2083, www.hotelelrosario.webs.com.*
Your best option for value and hospitality. El Rosario is a basic, family-run hotel with 13 clean rooms, all equipped with small flatscreen TVs, private bath, cold water and fast Wi-Fi; a/c is US$10 extra.

#### Ocotal

**$$ Hotel Frontera**
*Behind the Shell station on the highway to Las Manos, T2732-2668, hosfrosa@turbonett.com.*
The best hotel in town, even if it looks like a prison compound from outside. It has an inviting pool, bar, restaurant and events room.

**$$-$ Casa Huésped 'Llamarada del Bosque'**
*Parque Central, T2732-2643, llamaradadelbosque@hotmail.com.*
Conveniently located, this reasonably priced hotel has a wide range of rooms, but those upstairs are more spacious, modern and comfortable. They also own the popular restaurant on the corner of the plaza.

### Transport

#### Somoto

Buses to **El Espino** and the Honduran border (see Nicaragua–Honduras border box in the

Practicalities chapter), every hour, 0515-1715, US$0.50, 40 mins. To **Estelí**, every hour, 0520-1700, US$1.25, 2½ hrs; express buses are Managua-bound, US$1.65, 1½ hrs, they will drop you off at the Shell station, just east of central Estelí. Express bus to **Managua**, Mon-Sat, 0345, 0500, 0615, 0730, 1400, 1515, Sun 1400, 1515, US$4, 3½ hrs. To **Ocotal**, every 45 mins, 0345-1635, US$0.75, 1½ hrs.

## Comunidad Indígena de Totogalpa

Buses pass the village on the highway, every 15 mins for **Ocotal**, US$0.40, and **Estelí**, US$0.80.

## Ocotal

**Bus** The bus station for Ocotal is on the highway, 1 km south of the town centre, 15-20 mins' walk from Parque Central. Buses to **Las Manos/Honduras border** (see Nicaragua–Honduras border box in the Practicalities chapter) every 30 mins, 0500-1645, US$0.80, 45 mins. To **Somoto**, every 45 mins, 0545-1830, US$0.75, 2½ hrs. Express bus to **Managua**, 10 daily, 0400-1530, US$4.50, 4 hrs. To **Ciudad Antigua**, 0500, 1200, US$1.25, 1½ hrs. To **Estelí**, leaves the city market every hour, 0445-1800, US$1.30, 2½ hrs; express buses are Managua-bound, 2 hrs, US$1.65, they will drop you off at the Shell station, just east of central Estelí.

**Taxi** Ocotal taxis are cheap, with rides within town costing about US$0.40. A ride to **Las Manos** and the border with Honduras (see Nicaragua–Honduras border box in the Practicalities chapter) will cost US$7-9.

## Ciudad Antigua

There is 1 bus per day to **Ocotal** at 1400, 1½ hrs, US$1.50.

# Caribbean coast

A world away from its Pacific cousin, Nicaragua's Caribbean coast (or Costa Atlántica, as it is also known) revels in its feisty multicultural heritage. British buccaneers, Jamaican labourers, Chinese immigrants, African-descendent Garífunas, indigenous Miskitos, Mayagnas and Ramas have all contributed to the region's exotic flavours. Lilting Creole English, not Spanish, is the traditional lingua franca. The reason why the coast has developed along its own unique trajectory becomes clear if you fly over the region for a bird's eye view: an unrelenting carpet of green tree tops, meandering toffee-coloured rivers and swollen lagoons separate it from the rest of Nicaragua and few roads – or Spanish colonists – have ever penetrated this inhospitable wilderness of rainforest and swamp.

The Corn Islands are the region's principal attraction: two dazzling offshore atolls with white-sand beaches, scintillating coral reefs and turquoise waters. Little Corn is a low-key dive centre, while Big Corn is home to diverse fishing communities and a good place to sample authentic Caribbean life, as long as it lasts. On the mainland, the city of Bluefields, a decaying and shambolic spectre, is ripe with all the sights, sounds and smells of any bustling tropical port. This is the place to drink rum and watch the tropical storms roll in.

**Best** for
Beaches ▪ Diving ▪ Isolation ▪ Reggae

*the heart and soul of Nicaragua's Caribbean world*

★ Dirty and chaotic but curiously inviting, Bluefields (altitude 20 m, population 48,000) is the capital of Southern Atlantic Autonomous Region, known by its acronym RAAS. It is located at the mouth of the Río Escondido, which opens into Bluefields Bay in front of the town. The majority of the population is mestizo, with African-Caribbean Creole a close second. The other four ethnic groups of the region are represented and the main attraction of the town is its ethnic diversity and west Caribbean demeanour. The main church is Moravian, the language is Creole English and the music is country and reggae.

Most of Bluefields can be seen on foot, though taxis are recommended at night. All visits to surrounding attractions are by boat. Do not go wandering in the barrios. If desperate for cash **BanPro** in Barrio Central opposite the Moravian church (T2822-2261) has two ATMs. Another ATM can be found at the **LaFise Bancentro** just a block up on the Calle Commercial.

Bluefields is a good jumping-off point to visit Pearl Lagoon and other less explored areas of the wide-open region.

### Sights
Lacking any conventional tourist attractions, the appeal of Bluefields lies in getting to know its people; anyone willing to scratch the city's surface will find no shortage of strange stories and colourful characters. A good place to learn about the city's swashbuckling past is the CIDCA-BICU **Historical Museum of the Atlantic Coast** ① *Barrio Punta Fría, Mon-Fri 0900-1700, US$2*, where you'll find an intriguing collection of artefacts including a photo collection showing Bluefields before it was destroyed by Hurricane Joan in 1988. Downstairs there is a very good cultural library. Within Nicaragua, Bluefields is best known for its dancing, best seen during the exuberant annual Maypole (**Palo de Mayo**) celebrations (also known as **Mayo Ya**).

### Around Bluefields
El Bluff is a peninsula that separates the sea from the Bay of Bluefields. In happier days it was a busy port, but now a fleet of rusting shrimping boats evidence the town's decline. Its beach is the nearest stretch of sand to Bluefields: long, wide and a little bit dirty, but OK for an afternoon; bring repellent for the sand flies. Boats to El Bluff leave from the southern dock in Bluefields next to the market. The boat costs US$3 and leaves when full, 0730-1730.

In the bay of Bluefields, the tiny island of **Rama Cay** is home to one of the last tribes of the Rama, calm and friendly people who are renowned for their shyness, generosity, and linguistic skills. They are fairly accustomed to visitors but sadly this is the least studied group of all the indigenous peoples in Nicaragua and the most likely to lose its own language. A boat ride to the island, 20-30 minutes, costs US$15-50 depending on the number of passengers. Check at the dock next to the market to see if any boats are going; if you hitch a ride, returning could be a problem.

### Laguna de Perlas
This oval-shaped coastal lagoon, 80 km north of Bluefields, covers 518 sq km and is fed principally by the jungle-lined Río Kurinwás, but also by the rivers Wawashán, Patch,

## BACKGROUND

### Bluefields

Bluefields is named after the Dutch pirate Henry Bluefeldt (or Blauvedlt) who hid in the bay's waters in 1610. The native Kukra were hired by Dutch and British pirates to help them with boat repairs and small time trade began with the Europeans. The first permanent European settlers arrived in the late 18th century and the ethnic mix of the area began to change. The 19th century saw a healthy trade in bananas and an influx of African-Caribbeans from Jamaica to work in the plantations. Today, the indigenous and Creole populations have become marginalized with Spanish-speaking settlers from the Pacific dominating the city's economic sphere.

Orinoco and Ñari. Pearl Lagoon's shores range from pine forests and mangroves to savannah and rainforest.

The village of Laguna de Perlas, in the far southwest of the estuary, is the most developed place in the region and a good place to start your explorations. The local community is predominantly African-Caribbean but there are also plenty of Miskito and mestizo inhabitants. You'll find the best accommodation in the entire region here (see Where to stay, below) and there are boat services to Bluefields three times a day. There are no banks or ATMs in Pearl Lagoon so bring all the cash you need. If you get really stuck there's a **Western Union** office opposite the dock.

Pearl Lagoon is the point of departure for the Pearl Cays, a dazzling white-sand archipelago around 1½ hours away by high-speed *panga*. The cays – composed of numerous small islands – are tranquil and idyllic, but tourism here is uncontrolled and their ownership by wealthy foreigners is fiercely disputed; **Kabu Tours** are recommended as the sustainable option (see What to do, below).

On the north shore of the lagoon, the community of **Orinoco** is home to Nicaragua's largest population of Garífuna people, who are descended from escaped shipwrecked slaves. In a mixture of old African and indigenous influences, many of their dances and culinary customs remain intact. **Hostal Garífuna** has lodging and can organize wildlife tours and cultural presentations, including spectacular drumming. Orinoco has an annual cultural festival from 17-19 November.

## Listings Bluefields and around

### Tourist information

**INTUR**
*Opposite the police station, Barrio Punta Fría, T2572-0221, raas@intur.gob.ni.*
*Mon-Fri 0800-1700.*
This tourist office has Spanish-speaking staff and very limited information on local attractions. Also see the entertaining *Right Side Guide*, www.rightsideguide.com.

### Where to stay

**Bluefields**
Many hotels in Bluefields are quite basic and grim. Check rooms before accepting.

**$$ Caribbean Dream**
*Barrio Punta Fría, Pescafrito, ½ c sur, T2572-1943.*
27 clean rooms with private bath, a/c or fan, and cable TV. Services include restaurant with home cooking and à la carte menu, Wi-Fi

(US$2 per day) and laundry. Clean and often fully booked, call ahead. Owners helpful.

## $$ South Atlantic II
*Barrio Central, next to petrol station Levy, T2572-2265.*

Upstairs are clean rooms with reasonable mattresses, private bath, cable TV and a/c. Downstairs you'll find the economy quarters ($), which all have a fan and private bath but are also quite damp and dingy. There's a sports bar-restaurant that's good for a beer. Friendly.

## $ Hostal Doña Vero
*Barrio Central, opposite Mercadito Mas x Menos, T2572-2166.*

New, clean, well-attended budget lodgings and without doubt the best deal in town. Rooms on the top floor are large, comfortable and great value. Those downstairs are smaller. Some ultra-cheap quarters have shared bath. Recommended.

### Rama Cay
A handful of families offer lodgings to visitors, including that of the Moravian pastor. Enquire at the GTRK office located 2 blocks south of the park in Bluefields.

### Laguna de Perlas

## $$-$ Casa Blanca
*In May 4 sector, T2572-0508.*

One of the best hotels in town, with a range of clean, light, comfortable rooms; 5 have private bath, 6 have shared bath. The owners, Sven and Miss Dell, are very hospitable and friendly, and offer fishing expeditions, trips to the cays, general information and community tours. They're happy to answer questions by email, and prefer reservations in advance. Restaurant attached and internet available. A good family house, recommended.

## $ Hostal Garífuna
*In Orinoco, 50 m from the dock, T8937-0123, www.hostalgarifuna.net.*

Owned and managed by Kensy Sambola, a respected Garífuna anthropologist, Hostal

Garífuna is your one-stop shop for cultural information and tours. Rooms are clean and comfortable with shared bath and there's also a pleasant garden slung with hammocks. Meals are served. Highly recommended.

## $ Hotel Slilma
*Entel tower, 50 vrs sur, 75 vrs arriba on the left-hand turn, T2572-0523, rondownleiva@hotmail.com.*

Also known by its Spanish name, **Las Estrellas**, Hotel Slilma is a friendly, helpful lodging, recommended for budget travellers. They have 20 rooms, most with shared bath, cable TV and fan, but a few new ones also have private bath and a/c. Various hammocks and porches for chilling out.

## Restaurants

### Bluefields

## $$$-$$ Chez Marcel
*Alcaldía, 1 c sur, ½ c abajo, T2572-2347.*

The fading red curtains speak of better days, but the food is still OK and the service attentive. As you may be the only customers, the atmosphere can be a bit lifeless. Dishes include filet mignon, shrimp in garlic butter and grilled lobster.

## $$ El Flotante
*Barrio Punta Fría, T2572-2988. Daily 1000-2200.*

Built over the water at the end of the main street with a great view of the fishing boats and islets. They serve good shrimp and lobster, but service is slow. Dancing at weekends.

## $$ Pelican
*Barrio Pointeen, La Punta, at the end of the road.*

Evenings here are often buzzing with drinkers and diners. Great breezes from the balcony, comfortable interior, friendly service and average food, including seafood and meat. Not a bad place to have a few drinks in the evening.

## $$ Salmar
*Alcaldía, 1 c sur, ½ c abajo, T2572-2128. Daily 1600-2400.*

If you're bored of seafood and rice, this long-running restaurant serves reasonable (but not fantastic) Tex Mex, including burritos, as well as the usual local fare. Attentive service. The best place in town at last check.

## $ Comedor Vera Blanca
*Barrio Central, opposite ADEPHCA.*
A simple *comedor* offering high-carb food, including the obligatory chicken and fish dishes. Often packed with locals for lunch and dinner.

### Laguna de Perlas

## $$ Casa Ulrich
*Muelle Principal, 300 vrs norte, www.casaulrich.com.*
Local owner Fred Ulrich was trained as a chef in Switzerland and you will be hard pressed to find better food in town. It is possibly the best restaurant on the coast. Give them a half-day notice and order the rundown. The restaurant is upstairs facing the lagoon. They have good rooms too.

## $$ Queen Lobster
*Muelle Principal, 200 vrs norte, T8662-3393, www.queenlobster.com.*
Owned by Nuria Dixon Curtis, this restaurant ranks highly. This ranch-style eatery on the water's edge serves good seafood, including lobster and crab in red or coconut sauce. Order 'Mr Snapper' and you'll get a whole pound of fish. Good views and recommended.

## $ Comedor Eva
*Across the street from Green Lodge, 20 m down towards the water.*
All plates including fish, shrimp and lobster for US$4. And Miss Eva is an excellent cook.

## Bars and clubs

### Bluefields
The action starts at **La La**, moves to **Cima** and ends during the early hours at **Four Brothers**.

### Cima Club
*Banpro, 1 c abajo.*
It's hard to miss this centrally located dance hall with 2 floors and a large sign. Popular and often recommended by locals.

### Four Brothers
*Cotton tree, from Alcaldía, 1 c al mar, 4½ c sur.*
The best reggae spot in Nicaragua, a big ranch full of great dancing. Usually open Tue-Sun but Fri and Sat nights can be dancing room only. Admission US$1.

### La La Place
*Barrio Pointeen.*
This wooden construction on the water's edge is popular with the city's Creole population, especially on Fri, Sat and Sun night. They play reggae, country and dancehall through very large speakers.

## What to do

### Laguna de Perlas
**Tour operators**
Many restaurants hoteliers are able to arrange guides, tours, or transport; **Casa Blanca** and **Queen Lobster** are highly recommended. For turtle-watching, try: **Kabu Tours**, *WCS office, 75 vrs south of the muelle, T8714-5196, kabutours.com.* Kabu is a new initiative from the Wildlife Conservation Society that has trained former sea turtle fisherman to be conservationists and guides. They offer day and overnight trips to the cays, turtle-viewing expeditions and snorkelling trips with new equipment (including a portable toilet). This is the highest-quality tour you will find and the price reflects it, but it all goes to a good conservationist cause. Recommended.

## Transport

### Bluefields
The new highway from Managua to Bluefields via Nueva Guinea is scheduled to open sometime in 2015; check locally for the latest news. Until then, overland travellers must take a bus from Managua to El Rama and from there a boat down the Río Escondido. Alternatively, **La Costeña** flies to Bluefields 3 times daily from Managua's domestic terminal, twice daily from the Corn Islands and 3 times a week from Bilwi.

**Air** The airport is 3 km south of the city centre, either walk (30 mins) or take a taxi US$0.75 per person. **La Costeña** office, inside the terminal, T2572-2500. All schedules are subject to random and seasonal changes. It's best to get your name on the list several days in advance, if possible, and especially if travelling to Bilwi.

To **Managua**, daily 0815, 1110, 1600, US$83 one-way, US$128 return, 1 hr. To **Corn Islands**, daily 0730, 1510, US$64 one-way, US$99 return, 20 mins. To **Bilwi**, Mon, Wed, Fri, 1110, US$96 one-way, US$148 return, 1 hr.

**Boat** The motorboats (*pangas*) from **El Rama** to Bluefields depart when full, several daily, 0530-1600, US$10, 2 hrs. *Pangas* departing earlier in the day are more reliable, and services on Sun are restricted. The ferry is slightly cheaper and much slower, departing Mon and Thu around 0800 when the bus has arrived, US$8, 8 hrs.

Note that all schedules (especially Corn Island boats) are subject to change; confirm departure times at the port well in advance of your trip. Pregnant women or those with back problems should think twice before taking long *panga* trips. Use heavy-duty plastic bags to protect your luggage. If the Corn Island ferry is grounded no replacement will be made available.

To **Laguna de Perlas**, 0900, 1200, 1600, US$7.50, 45 mins. To **El Rama**, 0530-1600, several daily, US$10, 2 hrs. To **Orinoco**, Mon, Tue, Sun 0730, US$11, 2 hrs. To **San Juan de Nicaragua**, usually 1 a week, days change, enquire at the port. To **Corn Islands**, US$10-12. *Río Escondido*, Wed, 0900-1200; *Captain D*, Wed, 1200, stopping in El Bluff until 1700; *Island Express*, Fri, leaves directly from El Bluff 0200-0400; *Humberto C*, Fri, leaves directly from El Bluff, 0500; *Genesis*, Sun, leaves directly from El Bluff, 0800. To **El Bluff**, several daily, depart when full from the dock near the market, 0630-1730, US$1.50, 15 mins.

**Bus** Buses from El Rama to **Managua** depart roughly every hour, US$8, 9 hrs; express bus (recommended), 0900, US$9.50, 7 hrs. A bus also goes from El Rama to **Pearl Lagoon**, 1600, US$7.50, 3 hrs.

**Taxi** Taxi rides anywhere in the city are US$0.50 per person (US$0.75 to the airport or at night).

## Laguna de Perlas

To **Bluefields**, *panga* leaves at 0600, 0700 and 1300. US$7.50, 45 mins, Get to the dock the day before to get your name on the passenger list. Services are restricted on Sun. Bus to **El Rama**, 0600, US$7.50, 3 hrs. To **Managua**, it's possible to drive all the way, but the roads are rough. A strong 4WD can get you there in 8 hrs, on a good day.

**low-key island retreats, home to colourful clapboard houses and idyllic beaches**

Seventy kilometres off the mainland of Nicaragua, the Corn Islands (population 6370) are a portrait of Caribbean indolence, with languid palm trees and easy, rum-soaked dilapidation. Divorced from the mainland by 70 km of turquoise sea, many islanders are incurable eccentrics. Few, if any, pay much mind to the world outside, concerning themselves only with the friendships, feuds and often entertaining gossip that is the staple diet of island life.

Sadly, a burgeoning tourist trade and Colombian 'business interests' mean the islands are no longer the place to experience the authentic Caribbean life of days gone by. Outsiders are steadily infiltrating, bringing tourists, foreign-owned hotels and crime. But like everything else here, the pace of change has been slow. Scratch the surface and you'll discover that many things are as they have always been: rains come and go, mangoes fall, and waves lap the sugar-white beaches in perpetuity.

**Safety** Paradise has a dark side and you should use common sense at all times. Avoid walking at night on the island anywhere, always use a taxi to get between bars and your hotel. There is now a police force on Little Corn, but they may be hard to find. It's better not to walk alone in the bush, and avoid walking around late at night. Don't go out with locals unless recommended by your hotel; thieves, known as 'pirates', sometimes pose as informal tour guides.

### Big Corn

Big Corn does not offer the natural beauty of Little Corn, but it is more lively and those who bore easily or are not interested in snorkelling or diving might prefer the big island. Most of the island's social life, however, is concentrated in the built-up community around Brig Bay. The beaches on the west and southern side of the island are best for swimming. Walking around the island takes about three hours.

Around Waula Point is **Picnic Centre**, a fine beach for swimming and sunbathing. On the sparsely populated southeastern part of the island is the long and tranquil **Long Beach** in Long Bay. With Quinn Hill rising above the western part of the bay it is also very scenic – climb the hill to see an interesting pyramid art sculpture, the **Soul of the World**, www.souloftheworld.com, part of a global installation with counterparts in Botswana, Argentina, New Zealand and other far-off destinations. The most interesting nature is to be found beneath the water, with beautiful reefs and rich marine life. There are also several ancient cannons belonging to a sunken Spanish galleon. Snorkelling is best on the northern coast of Big Corn, just west of **Sally Peachy**.

The eastern side of the island is the most rustic and quieter. Facing the Atlantic, it has good waves for most of the year and plenty of rocks. There is also a lovely community here called **South End**, the most idyllic example of Afro-Caribbean culture on the islands.

There are numerous estuaries and wetlands all around the island, containing a startling amount of fresh water. Birdlife is generally disappointing.

The island celebrates the abolition of slavery with a Crab Soup festival on 27-29 August.

Big Corn has a good landing strip, airport terminal and quite a few decent hotels. 'Bucks' are córdobas in island speak. There is a **Banpro** with a working ATM, Brig Bay; however, it has been known to break down, so bring cash reserves in case of complications. Traveller's cheques are not accepted or changed anywhere, but dollars are widely used. If stuck, you might get a credit card advance at the airport or **Desideri Café** on Little Corn.

## Little Corn

Little Corn is more relaxed and less developed than its larger neighbour, although it now suffers from low-level crime and sees huge numbers of visitors in the high season. The locals on the island are keenly aware of the beauty of their home and are learning to adapt to its growing popularity. The small island has some of the finest coral reefs in Nicaragua and is a superb place for snorkelling and diving. (*National Geographic Explorer* gave the reefs nine out of 10.)

The island also has good opportunities for walking, with the north end of the island a mixture of scrub forest and grazing land leading down to the brilliant turquoise sea. The prettiest side of the island is also the windward side; visiting during a windy period can be disappointing for snorkellers but helps calm mosquitoes and the heat. The most developed areas are along the western shores of the narrow southern part of the island, separated from the windswept east coast by a large swamp. This is where the boats arrive and there are numerous options for sleeping and eating. The water is calm and good for swimming and there is a good sense of community spirit here.

There are lovely highlands at both ends of the island. The highlands of the southeast have two small but superb beaches just past **Casa Iguana** (see Where to stay, below); the northern ones also have great beaches and but fewer visitors. East beach is south of an attractive Asian-style lodge called **Derek's Place** (see Where to stay, below), where you will find a spectacular stretch of sand that runs the entire length of the island, broken only by some small rocky points. Near the end of this beach there are good places to eat right on the sand and several lodges. All the beaches have white sand, although it disappears at high tide in places.

## Listings Corn Islands

### Tourist information

There is an official tourist office at the wharf that is closed more often than not. Your best bet is to chat to locals. Good online sources of information are www.bigcornisland.com and www.rightsideguide.com.

### Where to stay

**Big Corn**

**$$$ Casa Canada**
*South End, T8644-0925,*
*www.casa-canada.com.*
Sophisticated, luxurious rooms with ocean views. Each is splendidly equipped with a DVD player, minibar, coffee-maker, leather chairs and mahogany furniture. There's free Wi-Fi for guests and a beautiful infinity pool

overlooks the waves. Friendly and hospitable management. Recommended.

**$$$ Sea Star Spa**
*Long Bay, www.seastarspa.net.*
The island's 1st full-service spa hotel caters to those who like to be pampered. The 4 rooms face the sea and there are plenty of amenities, including a 24-hr concierge buzzer. A good choice if you don't mind seeing the caged jungle 'pets' on the premises.

**$$$-$$ Hotel Paraíso**
*Brig Bay, T2575-5111, www.paraisoclub.com.*
A professional, friendly hotel, managed by 2 Dutchmen, Mike and Ton, who contribute to local social projects. They have 9 doubles (**$$**) and 5 bungalows (**$$$**). **The hotel** is next to the beach, and there's good snorkelling at the wreck offshore.

Tours, massages and fishing trips can be arranged; ask Mike about seeing the reefs or touring the island in a golf cart. Prices include breakfast at their restaurant. Highly recommended.

### $$$-$$ Princesa de la Isla
*Waula Point, T8854-2403,*
*www.laprincesadelaisla.com.*
The Princess' setting on a windswept point is eternally romantic. They have 2 bungalows ($$$) – often reserved for honeymooners – and a handful of rooms ($$), all with hot water, hammocks and unusual furnishings. The friendly Italian owners also offer good coffee, wine and Italian food ($$$) – call 3-4 hrs in advance to get the pasta cooking. Wi-Fi available.

### $$ Los Escapados
*By the well, Sally Peachy, T8511-7038.*
This new little place is hidden up a steep dirt road and offers 3 'glamping-style' *cabañas* with a great view over the sea. Beds are semi-orthopedic kings that split to singles, and breakfast and Wi-Fi are included.

### $$ Vientos del Norte
*North End, T2575-5112, www.bigcornisland.*
*com/vientosdelnorte.html.*
Also known as Ike's place, Vientos del Norte offers a range of well-equipped quarters with fridge, coffee machine, microwave and toaster. Those overlooking the ocean or with a/c cost slightly more. They also have an annex with well-furnished family-sized lodgings and some economy rooms. Friendly, recommended.

### $ G&G Hotel/Hostal
*Brig Bay, www.gandghotelbigcornisland.com.*
More hotel than *hostal*, G&G offer large rooms with private bathrooms, TV, a/c or fan. There is a pretty good bar/restaurant on site with the constant low drone of reggae music. Wi-Fi is available in both the hotel and restaurant.

### $ May Flowers
*Brig Bay, on the beach, T8821-8749.*
This guesthouse on the beach has 4 good, clean, straightforward rooms with private bath and fan. A good option for budget travellers and couples. Quiet and peaceful but just a short walk from the action on Brig Bay.

### $ Silver Sand
*Sally Peachy, south of rocky point, T8948-1436.*
Managed by the colourful Ira Gómez, who could well be a character from a *Pirates of the Caribbean* movie. His rustic fishermen's cabins have seen better days, but their secluded setting near the beach is tranquil and pleasant. Ira can organize fishing trips, and cook up the catch in his bar-restaurant on the beach. Look out for the feisty turkeys and pack insect repellent.

## Little Corn
The north end is the greenest, wildest area, but somewhat isolated and difficult to reach at night. The cheapest lodgings are clustered on the south side of the island.

### $$$$ Yemaya
*North end of the island,*
*www.littlecornhotel.com.*
Treat yourself to spa, massage and yoga in this self-proclaimed eco-hotel and wellness centre. Or just stay in one of the 16 posh *cabañas* overlooking one of the best beaches on the island. In fact, there is no better place to stay anywhere on the Corn Islands.

### $$$ Farm Peace and Love
*North end of the island,*
*www.farmpeacelove.com.*
Not a hotel, Farm Peace and Love has a cottage and a 'suite', both with fully equipped kitchens and enough space for 3 adults, or 2 adults and 2 children under 10 (sharing a bed). This is the place for people who wish to self-cater and get away from it all. Book your stay well in advance, as they are often full.

### $$$-$$ Casa Iguana
*On southeastern bluff, www.casaiguana.net.*
This is a famous, popular lodging, beautifully located with stunning views of the beaches. They have 4 'economy' *cabañas* with shared bath ($$), 9 *casitas* with private bath ($$$), and 2 'luxury' *casitas* ($$$). They grow their own food in lush, attractive gardens, offer great breakfasts and sociable dining. An interesting outfit, if something of a tourist summer camp. Book in advance, especially in high season.

### $$$-$$ Little Corn Beach and Bungalow
*On the east beach, T8333-0956, www.littlecornbb.com.*
The most popular place on the beach with a mixture of smart bunkhouses ($$), rooms ($$) and bungalows ($$$). All come with fan and sleep up to 4 (US$5 extra for each additional person). The bungalows are particularly comfortable and have good views, wooden floors and decent showers. Restaurant attached.

### $$ Derek's Place
*At northeastern tip, www.dereksplace littlecorn.com.*
Attractive wooden cabins on stilts, faintly reminiscent of Southeast Asia. All are equipped with renewable energy, mosquito nets, quality mattresses, hammocks, porches, sea views and private bathrooms. The restaurant serves flavourful and interesting food, including fresh fruit juices and various coconut-based dishes, including curries. They also operate the **Little Dive Shack by the Sea**.

### $$ Sunrise Paradise
*On east coast just north of Grace Cool Spot (see below), T8414-4074.*
Also known as **Carlito's** and managed by the head of the island's informal security service, who is a real gentleman. They offer a range of simple cabins all with fan and electricity. Those with shared bath are cheaper, but the facilities are inadequate for the number of guests sharing. They also have food, beer and hammocks.

### $ Elsa's
*North along beach from Casa Iguana (see above).*
The long-established Elsa's offers simple wooden cabins with sea views and own bath, as well as cheaper lodgings without either. The restaurant serves lobster, fish and vegetarian food for US$6-10 a plate. Snorkels, tours, hammocks and beer available. Hospitable, friendly, safe and relaxed.

### $ Three Brothers
*20 m south of the triangle.*
This is the go-to place for most backpackers. Centrally located, shared bathrooms and kitchen and 2 of the friendliest island owners you will meet. Recommended.

## Restaurants

### Big Corn

### $$$-$$ The Buccaneer
*Brig Bay, inside Hotel Paraíso, see Where to stay, above. Open for breakfast, lunch and dinner.*
Clean, friendly and presentable restaurant with a thatched palm roof. They serve seafood and meat dishes, including lobster, shrimp, filet mignon and hamburgers.

### $$ Fisher's Cave
*See Where to stay.*
This great little seafood restaurant overlooks the water and fishing boats. Usually a relaxing spot, although it's sometimes loud with inebriated fishermen. Good for a coffee or beer whilst awaiting the boat to Little Corn. Check out the pools filled with live fish.

### $$-$ Island Style
*Long Beach. Open lunch and dinner.*
This beach restaurant-bar is earning a reputation as a cool dining and drinking spot. Open air, with loud music and authentic local vibe with occasional concerts.

### $$-$ Marlene's Food Place
*South End. Open lunch and dinner.*
Friendly, low-key place with outdoor tables and chairs. A good budget option for

standard Nica fare, they also serve seafood and have a good selection of juices.

## $$-$ Seva's Place
*in Sally Peachy neighborhood.*
One of the island's best and longest-established restaurants. They serve great seafood, meat and chicken from a fine location with rooftop seats and ocean views. Try the lobster *a la plancha*.

## $$-$ Spekito's Place
*Next door to Nico's Bar, Sally Peachy. Open lunch and dinner.*
The reggae music thumping through the palm-leaf hut restaurant right over the water makes their typical seafood dishes taste even better. The service may leave something to be desired, but then again this is the Caribbean.

### Ice cream parlours

#### Relax
*South End. Open 0800-2000.*
Also known as Virgil's Place, they do the best ice cream on the island and some light meals too, including fried chicken.

### Little Corn

#### $$$-$$ Habana Libre
*Just north of boat landing.*
Really tasty, flavourful dishes including succulent veal, fish and lobster served with interesting sauces. There's terraced seating, good music and amiable staff. Cuban specialities are available on request and in advance. Be sure to try a *mojito*; they're outstanding.

#### $$ Desideri's
*80 m south from the wharf.*
A relaxing alternative to the louder crowd that gather at some of the other restaurants, you can consider this your living room away from home. The menu is international but specializes in Italian cuisine with lobster thermidor and lasagne as two of their signature dishes. They also

offer a variety of fresh juices, wines and coffees. Wi-Fi available.

#### $$ Tranquilo Café
*100 m south of the wharf. Open from 0930.*
A range of full meals and light dishes, including smoked ribs, pork bruschetta, ceviche, burgers, chicken fillets, fish tacos, home-made ice cream and cookies. Very popular and quite tasty. Seating is outdoors on a wooden veranda with weekly bonfire parties and cultural presentations. Slow island Wi-Fi available. Gift shop attached.

#### $$-$ Doña Rosa's
*The port, 175 m south, 100 m east, on the path to Casa Iguana.*
Reasonably priced for the island, you can get a 3-course meal for US$6 or so, including fish and shrimp dishes. The portions are on the small side though.

#### $$-$ Miss Bridgette's
*The dock, 20 m south, then slightly east, off the path.*
A lovely little *comedor* serving wholesome, home-cooked fare. Service is very Caribbean, so be prepared to wait.

### Bars and clubs

#### Big Corn
After dark, always use taxis to get between your hotel and the bars, even if they're close to each other.

#### Bamboolay
*South End. Open 1900-0200.*
This is one of the newest and most popular bars on the island. Better for drinking and socializing than dancing, though the dedicated dance room still fills up when the popular songs are on spin. Reggae, dancehall and soul all weekend long.

#### Nico's
*South End. Open 1900-0200.*
The action kicks off on Sun, with wall-to-wall drinking and dancing by the waves. They serve beef soup when you need perking up. Thu features country and western.

### Xtasis
*Brig Bay. Open 1900-0200.*
Same thumping music but a somewhat rougher local crowd. 'Professional' women and the occasional fight are par for the course here.

## What to do

### Big Corn
### Bicycles, golf carts and motorbikes
**Corn Island Car Rental**, *Southwest Bay, next to Arenas, T8643-9881, also available at Sunrise Hotel, South End.* A range of **golf carts** available, US$50 for 6 hrs; US$82 for 24 hrs (4 people). **Scooters** US$40 for 6 hrs; US$60 for 24 hrs. **Bicycles** US$15 for 6 hrs; US$25 for 24 hrs.

### Diving
**Nautilus Resort & Dive Centre**, *Brig Bay, T2575-5077, www.nautilus-dive-nicaragua. com.* Diving and snorkelling tours to see the cannons of the old Spanish galleon, Blowing Rock and coral reefs, as well as trips further afield. PADI Open Water certification from US$300, advanced certification from US$250, night dives and 2-tank dives US$670 per person (Little Corn and Blowing Rock, US$95), snorkelling trips and glass-bottom boat tours at US$20 per person.

### Fishing
**Ira Gómez**, *Silver Sand hotel, Sally Peachy, south of rocky point, T8948-1436.* One of those irresistible local characters, Ira is an enthusiastic fishing man.

### Little Corn
### Diving
Little Corn Island is one of the best and cheapest places in the world to get diving qualifications. Excluding manuals, an Open Water certificate costs approximately US$305; Advanced Open Water US$240. A 1-tank dive cost US$35; 2-tanks US$65.
**Dive Little Corn**, *boat landing in village, T8823-1154, www.divelittlecorn.com.* There's

a strong PADI ethos at this 5-star, Gold Palm centre, with training right up to assistant instructor level. They also offer night dives, single and 2-tank dives, snorkelling tours, and 5- or 10-dive packages; trips leave several times daily. There's a 10% discount if you stay with **Casa Iguana**; consult their website for more details.
**Dolphin Dive**, *in the village, south of the dock, T8690-0225, www.dolphindive littlecorn. com.* Dolphin Dive offers PADI instruction to Dive Master level, and a range of customized trips for diving, fishing or snorkelling. Underwater digital camera rental costs US$15 including a CD. Various dive packages are available, including discounts at **Hotel Delfines** next door.
**Little Dive Shack By The Sea**, *Derek's Place, dereksplace@gmail.com.* If you are looking for a more personalized and exclusive dive trip, this is it. Groups are capped at 4 people. US$350 for Open Water course taught by a certified PADI instructor all the way down to US$35 1-tank dive or US$70 discovery dive.

### Tour operators
**Radio Carib**, *behind the new Culture Centre, T8232-2661, radiocarib@yahoo.com.* The operators of the local radio station offer **Little Island History Tours** by appointment. It's a great opportunity to learn of the island's pre-Columbian, pirate and natural history.

## Transport

Big Corn is 13 sq km and Little Corn is 3.5 sq km. About 11 km of Caribbean Sea separates them. Big Corn has a paved road that does a lap of the island with 1 bus and nearly 100 taxis. Little Corn has no roads; walking or boating are the only ways of getting around.

**Air** **La Costeña** flies from Big Corn to **Managua** with a stop in **Bluefields**, daily at 0810 and 1540, US$107 one-way, US$165 return, 1½ hrs. Re-confirm seats 1-2 days before travelling or you might be moved to a later flight. **La Costeña** office is at the airport on Big Corn, T2575-5131.

**Boat  Inter-island boats**  Big Corn to Little Corn, daily 1000, 1630, US$6, 30 mins. Little Corn to Big Corn, daily 0630, 1330, US$6, 30 mins. Boats leave from main dock, first come, first served. The open-hull *pangas* with two big outboards run on Sun, Tue, Wed, Fri and Sat, the 100-seat yacht runs on Mon and Thu. If on the *panga*, buy big plastic bags at shop across from dock entrance to keep luggage dry. Sit near the back for a smoother ride, near the front centre, as it's drier, but you can expect to get bounced around quite a bit.

**Mainland boats**  Schedules are always changing, check locally for the latest; 5 boats travel between Corn Islands and **Bluefields**, US$10-12 one-way, including: *Genesis*, Mon, 1800; *Río Escondido*, Thu, 0900; *Captain D*, Sat, 0000; *Island Express*, Sun, 1700; *Humberto C*, Sun, 1700. One service per month Corn Islands to Bilwi, *Captain D*, usually Fri, 1700, US$25.

**Bus**  A bus circles the paved island road on Big Corn every 30 mins, US$0.50.

**Taxi**  Taxis charge US$1-2 for trips to and from the airport or any trip after 2000. The usual fare to most destinations is US$0.75. Hourly taxi rates are US$6 per hr, poor value, as there are many taxis and trip fares are cheap.

## The Northern Atlantic Autonomous Region (RAAN)  Colour map 3, B6.
### Nicaragua's fabled Miskito heartland

★ The RAAN is one of the most isolated and intriguing destinations in Central America, a land steeped in fishing, farming, folklore and magic, accessible only by a treacherous unpaved highway from Managua, or by plane.

Christopher Columbus was the first European to make contact, arriving in the midst of a storm and finding refuge in the bay at the mouth of the Río Coco; he named it Cabo Gracias a Dios (Cape Thank God). In the early 1600s, the British started trading with the coast people and made allies out of the Miskitos, who went on to dominate the region with British help. Various shipwrecks, from pirates to slave ships, brought new cultural influences, as did Moravian missions, international loggers and banana plantations.

### Bilwi (Puerto Cabezas)
Principally a large Miskito town, Bilwi, or Puerto Cabezas as it has been known for the last century, is the capital of the RAAN and has a distinct atmosphere from Bluefields. Waspam on the Río Coco is the heart and soul of the Miskito world, but it is here that the Miskito political party Yatama became the first indigenous party to assume control of a provincial capital in the country's modern history. The town itself may not win any beauty contests, but it does have an end-of-the-earth feel and a 730-m-long pier that stretches into the Caribbean Sea. For the truly intrepid, the Miskito communities around Bilwi offer some of the most interesting and adventurous community tourism in Central America. The **Asociación de Mujeres Indígenas de la Costa Atlántica (AMICA)** ⓘ *Barrio La Libertad, Bilwi, T2792-2219, asociacionamica@yahoo.es*, can connect you with guides.

### Waspam (Wangki)  Colour map 3, B5.
Waspam is considered the capital of the Río Coco, a transport hub and trading centre for the 116 Miskito communities that line the great waterway. Most travel is by motorized canoes dug out of a single tree (*cayucos*). In the dry season they are punted using long poles. From Waspam, you can travel up or down stream, but careful planning and a trustworthy guide are essential; speak to **La Casa de la Rose** (see Where to stay, below). The road from Bilwi

to Waspam is only open during the dry season. It is a 130-km trip that takes at least three hours by 4WD and six to eight hours by public bus (see Transport, below). This trip will take you through pine forests, red earth plains and several Miskito villages. If you have good maps and experience with wilderness navigation, the dirt tracks between Waspam and Bilwi are great for mountain biking. It's also possible to cross to Leimus in Honduras from Waspam; see Nicaragua–Honduras box in the Practicalities chapter.

## Listings The Northern Atlantic Autonomous Region (RAAN)

### Where to stay

#### Bilwi

**$ Casa Museo**
*Next to Centro de Computación Ansell, T2792-2225.*
Also known as Miss Judy's, this lovely house has lots of interesting art and artefacts in the attached museum and gallery. Rooms are spacious and comfortable and have private bath, TV and a/c (cheaper with fan). Friendly and interesting, with lots of family history. Restaurant attached, excellent value and highly recommended.

#### Waspam

**$ La Casa de la Rose**
*Almost next to the airport, roseck@ibw.com.ni.*
This comfortable wooden hotel has rooms with private bath, hammocks and screened windows. Tasty home-cooked meals are available, as well as internet access. Look out for the red macaws. Recommended.

### Transport

#### Bilwi
**Air** The airport is 3 km north of town, from where taxis charge US$2 to anywhere in Bilwi. If flying to Bluefields, try to get your name on the list several days in advance. To **Bluefields**, Mon, Wed, Fri, 1210, US$96 one-way, US$148 return, 1 hr. To **Managua**, **La Costeña**, daily 0820, 1220, 1610, US$97 one-way, US$148 round-trip;

   **Note** Bring your passport as there are immigration checks by the police in Bilwi and sometimes in the waiting lounge in Managua.

**Bus** The bus station is a few kilometres out of town; take a taxi, US$0.50. To **Managua**, 1100, 1300, US$21, 18-24 hrs. To **Waspam**, 0600, US$6, 6 hrs. All these journeys require a strong back and stomach.

# This is
## Costa Rica

A beacon of neutral democratic ideals, Costa Rica stands out in a turbulent region; as far back as the 1930s one commentator called it the 'Switzerland of Central America'. Whatever its political credentials and claims to neutrality, this country is undeniably a nature-lovers' paradise: you'll find moss-draped cloudforest on the slopes of Monteverde, where the red and green sacred quetzal bird hides in the treetops and hummingbirds busy round drinking nectar, there's rainforest wilderness on the Osa Peninsula and remote turtle-nesting beaches on the north Atlantic and Pacific coasts. The country's volcanic peaks range from the gentle steaming lagoons of Irazú and Poás to the explosive Arenal, just outside La Fortuna, where red-hot lava lights up the night sky.

Travellers looking to combine nature and comfort should head to the endless sand and surf beaches of the Nicoya Peninsula, Quepos and Parque Nacional Manuel Antonio, or to the off-beat strands of the Caribbean. For adrenalin junkies there's whitewater rafting, trekking and coast-to-coast mountain biking, and the chance to climb the barren *páramo* savannahs to the peak of Cerro Chirripó.

Historically Costa Rica has avoided the extremes of external influences. The Spanish found no mineral wealth here or compliant indigenous labour to work the land. Hard conditions and poverty forced both conquerors and conquered to work and live side by side. It was only with the arrival of wealth from the magic coffee bean in the central highlands that a landed gentry arose to conflict with the interests of a liberal merchant class. As a result, Costa Rica's architectural highlights are somewhat limited compared to much of the region, concentrated in the churches that dot the central highlands. But, just like the country's natural nuances that host incredible diversity, the architectural differences are subtle. And just like the natural wonders, you'll have to look harder to truly appreciate them.

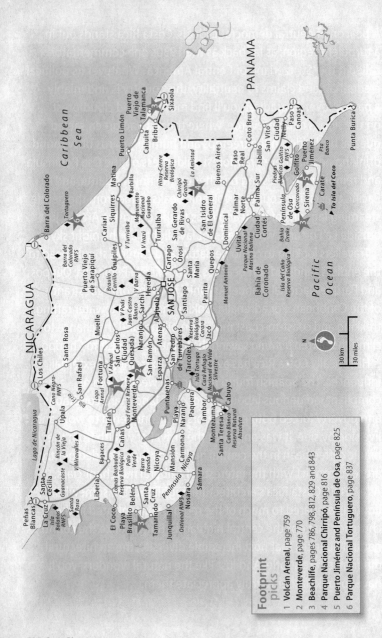

## Footprint picks

1 **Volcán Arenal**, page 759
2 **Monteverde**, page 770
3 **Beachlife**, pages 786, 798, 812, 829 and 843
4 **Parque Nacional Chirripó**, page 816
5 **Puerto Jiménez and Península de Osa**, page 825
6 **Parque Nacional Tortuguero**, page 837

# Footprint picks

★ **Volcán Arenal**, page 759

Hike through diverse ecosystems at the foot of this perfect volcanic cone, then bask in hot springs.

★ **Monteverde**, page 770

Soar through the spectacular cloudforest canopy on a high-speed zip-line.

★ **Beachlife**, pages 786, 798, 812, 829 and 843

See of the best sunsets on the planet from rainforest-fringed beaches.

★ **Parque Nacional Chirripó**, page 816

Scale the country's highest peak at the heart of the continental divide.

★ **Puerto Jiménez and Península de Osa**, page 825

Encounter sublime rainforest fauna on this remote Pacific peninsula.

★ **Parque Nacional Tortuguero**, page 837

Watch prehistoric turtles lumber out of the surf to nest.

# Essential San José

## Finding your feet

Most of the city conforms to a grid layout – *avenidas* run east–west; *calles* north–south. Avenidas to the north of Avenida Central are given odd numbers; those to the south even numbers. Calles to the west of Calle Central are even-numbered; those to the east are odd-numbered. Despite this semblance of order, neither *avenidas* nor *calles* are very well-marked beyond the downtown area and many locals give directions based on archaic points of reference (eg 'three blocks south of the gas station'). The length of a single city block is usually given as *'cien metros'* (100 m), regardless of its actual measurement.

## Getting around

Walking is the best way to get around downtown San José with an increasing number of streets now fully or partly pedestrianized. Driving in San José is not recommended. Rush hour is officially 0700-0900 and 1700-1900, but the streets are often congested at all waking hours. If you do decide to drive, note that restrictions are in place for all local vehicles, including rental cars. The last digit of your licence plate assigns a no-drive day, applicable 0600-1900: 1 and 2 Monday; 3 and 4 Tuesday; 5 and 6 Wednesday; 7 and 8 Thursday; 9 and 0 Friday. Taxis can be ordered by phone or hailed in the street. They are red and are legally required to have and use meters (known as *marías*). Commuter trains now link the city centre with some of the suburbs and a few cities in the Meseta Central (see Transport, page 738).

## Safety

The downtown area is generally safe in the day, but big city rules apply. As ever, speak to your hotelier about the safety of the local area. Most of the bus stations are in dicey neighbourhoods and you should use taxis to get in and out, especially at night. If you run into any trouble at all, tourist police are available. Note some taxi drivers are looking to make commissions from hotels and may try to deceive you about the safety or availability of your chosen lodging.

## Immigration

The immigration office is on the airport highway, opposite Hospital México. You need to go here for visas extensions, etc. Queues can take all day. To get there, take bus No 10 or 10A Uruca, marked 'México', then cross over highway at the bridge and walk 200 m along highway – just look for the queue or ask the driver. Better to find a travel agent who can obtain what you need for a fee, say US$5. Make sure you get a receipt if you give up your passport.

## Weather San José

| | January | February | March | April | May | June |
|---|---|---|---|---|---|---|
| | 23°C | 24°C | 26°C | 26°C | 26°C | 26°C |
| | 14°C | 14°C | 15°C | 16°C | 16°C | 16°C |
| | 10mm | 0mm | 20mm | 40mm | 220mm | 240mm |

| | July | August | September | October | November | December |
|---|---|---|---|---|---|---|
| | 25°C | 25°C | 26°C | 25°C | 25°C | 23°C |
| | 16°C | 16°C | 16°C | 15°C | 15°C | 14°C |
| | 210mm | 240mm | 300mm | 290mm | 140mm | 40mm |

# San José
## & around

Home to one-third of the country's population, San José is the gritty capital of Costa Rica: a modern, sprawling, high-charged city jammed with traffic and frenetic crowds of pedestrians. It is not so much aesthetic as intriguing – the place to see a nation on the move.

The city was founded in 1737 with the expansion of lucrative tobacco plantations in the fertile valley of Aserrí. In 1823, it emerged as the capital of a newly independent Costa Rica after turbulent wars with the competing regional powers of Alajuela, Heredia and Cartago. Earthquakes have since destroyed much of the city's original architecture, but a smattering of historic mansions and churches remain.

Although it fails to charm most visitors, San José is one of the most friendly and accessible capitals in Central America, home to a thriving arts scene, fine restaurants, galleries, museums and nightclubs, as well as numerous shady plazas and parks, which are oases from the overheated mayhem outside.

**Best** for
Galleries ▪ Markets ▪ Parks ▪ Restaurants

### Around Avenida Central and Calle Central

Many of the most interesting public buildings in San José (altitude 1150 m) are near the intersection of Avenida Central and Calle Central. The **Teatro Nacional** ① *just off Av 2, on Calle 3, T2010-1100, Mon-Sat 0900-1800, www.teatronacional.go.cr, from US$5,* built in 1897, has marble staircases, statues, frescoes and foyer decorated in gold with Venetian plate mirrors. Nearby is **Plaza de la Cultura** ① *Av Central, Calle 3-5,* which, in addition to being a great place for people-watching, hosts occasional public concerts. The **Museo de Oro Precolombino** ① *entrance is off Calle 5, T2243-4221, www.museosdelbancocentral.org, daily 0915-1700, US$10,* has a booty of golden treasure buried beneath the Plaza de la Cultura. Fine golden figures of frogs, spiders, raptors and other creatures glisten in this spectacular pre-Columbian gold museum sponsored by the **Banco Central**.

Four blocks east of the plaza, it's worth checking out the **Museo del Jade y Arte Precolombino** ① *Av Central and Calle 13, T2287 6034, www.portal.ins-cr.com, daily 1000-1700, US$10,* which hosts the largest collection of jade carvings in Central America, as well as pre-Columbian pottery and sculpture.

Also east from the Plaza de la Cultura, the **Museo Nacional** ① *Calle 17, Av Central-2, T2257-1433, www.museocostarica.go.cr, Tue-Sat 0830-1630, Sun 0900-1630, US$8, children*

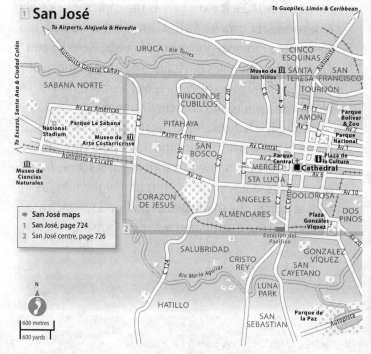

San José maps
1  San José, page 724
2  San José centre, page 726

*and students with ID free*, has interesting displays on archaeology, anthropology, and national history. Facing it is the **Plaza de la Democracia**, a concrete cascade built to mark the November 1989 centenary of Costa Rican democracy. The **Palacio Nacional** ① *Av Central, Calle 15*, is home of the Legislative Assembly; any visitor can attend debates, sessions start at 1600.

Two blocks north of the Museo Nacional is the **Parque Nacional**, with a grandiloquent bronze monument representing the five Central American republics ousting the filibuster William Walker (see Nicaragua section in Background chapter). To the north of the park is the **Biblioteca Nacional**. In the old liquor factory west of the Biblioteca Nacional, now the Centro Nacional de la Cultura, is the **Museo de Arte y Diseño Contemporáneo** ① *Av 3, Calle 15-17, T2257-7202, www. ww.madc.cr, Mon-Sat 0930-1700, US$3, students with ID US$1*.

Along Calle Central, west of the Teatro Nacional, is **Parque Central**, with a bandstand among trees. East of the park is the monumental architecture of the **Catedral Metropolitana**; to the north is the **Teatro Melico Salazar** ① *see press for details or call T2295-6000, www. teatromelico.go.cr*, which has a good mix of performances throughout the year.

Further west, in **Parque Braulio Carrillo**, opposite the eclectic neo-Gothic design of **La Merced** church, is a huge carved granite ball brought from the Diquis archaeological site near Palmar Norte. There are other such designs at the entrance to the Museo de Ciencias Naturales.

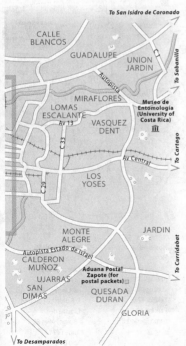

## Parque La Sabana

At the end of Paseo Colón, at Calle 42, **Parque La Sabana** was converted from the former city airport in the 1950s; the old airport building on the east side is now the **Museo de Arte Costarricense** ① *T2256-1281, Tue-Sun 0900-1600, www.musarco. go.cr, free*, with a small but interesting display of paintings and sculptures. At the west end of the park is the **Estadio Nacional**, with seating for 20,000 spectators at (mainly) football matches.

Opposite the southwest corner of Parque Sabana are the impressive natural displays of the **Museo de Ciencias Naturales** ① *Colegio La Salle, T2232-5179, www.lasalle. ed.cr, Mon-Sat 0730-1600, Sun 0900-1700, US$1.50, children US$1*, next to the Ministry of Agriculture; take 'Sabana Estadio' bus from Avenida 2, Calle 1 to the gate.

## North of Avenida Central

On Calle 2, is the **Unión Club**, the principal social centre of the country. Opposite is the **Correo Central**, general post and telegraph office which also houses an internet café, pastry shop and the **Museo Postal, Telegráfico y Filatélico** ① *upstairs, Mon-Fri 0800-1700, free*.

A couple of blocks to the west is the hustle and bustle of the **Mercado Central**, dating back to 1881, rich with the shouts, cries, smells and chaos of a fresh produce market. Good cheap meals for sale as well as some interesting nick-nacks for the passing tourist. Often crowded; watch for thieves.

## ② San José centre

➡ San José maps
1  San José, page 724
2  San José centre, page 726

**Where to stay** 🛏
Aranjuez 2 *A6*
Casa 69 3 *C6*
Casa Alfi 4 *C4*
Casa Ridgway 9 *C6*
Costa Rica Guesthouse 5 *C6*
Del Rey 14 *B5*
Don Carlos 17 *B5*
El Presidente 6 *B5*
Grano de Oro 26 *B2*
Hostel Bekuo 7 *C6*
Hostel Casa del Parque 8 *B6*
Hostel Van Gogh 10 *B5*
In & Basic Hostel
  Lounge 11 *C6*
Kekoldi 12 *B5*
Park Inn 13 *C2*
Santo Tomás 1 *B5*

**Restaurants** 🍴
Alma de Café 1 *B5*
Café de los Deseos 2 *A6*
Corner Pizzeria
  & Cafeteria 3 *B2*
El Balcón de Europa 4 *B5*
Esquina de
  Buenos Aires 5 *C5*
Jurgen's 7 *C6*
Kalú 8 *A5*

The Disneyesque building on the horizon to the north of the city is the **Centro Costarricense de Ciencias y Cultura** (Scientific and Cultural Centre) in the old city penitentiary with the **Galería Nacional, Biblioteca Carlos Luis Sáenz**, the **Auditorio Nacional** and **Museo de Los Niños** ① *Calle 4, Av 9, T2258-4929, www.museocr.org, Tue-*

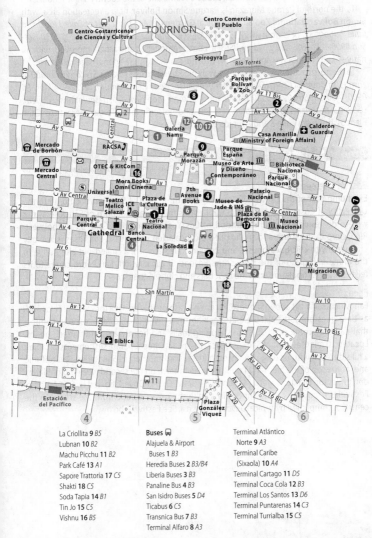

| | | |
|---|---|---|
| La Criollita **9** *B5* | **Buses** 🚌 | Terminal Atlántico |
| Lubnan **10** *B2* | Alajuela & Airport | Norte **9** *A3* |
| Machu Picchu **11** *B2* | Buses **1** *B3* | Terminal Caribe |
| Park Café **13** *A1* | Heredia Buses **2** *B3/B4* | (Sixaola) **10** *A4* |
| Sapore Trattoria **17** *C5* | Liberia Buses **3** *B3* | Terminal Cartago **11** *D5* |
| Shakti **18** *C5* | Panaline Bus **4** *B3* | Terminal Coca Cola **12** *B3* |
| Soda Tapia **14** *B1* | San Isidro Buses **5** *D4* | Terminal Los Santos **13** *D6* |
| Tin Jo **15** *C5* | Ticabus **6** *C5* | Terminal Puntarenas **14** *C3* |
| Vishnu **16** *B5* | Transnica Bus **7** *B3* | Terminal Turrialba **15** *C5* |
| | Terminal Alfaro **8** *A3* | |

*Fri 0800-1630, Sat-Sun 0930-1700, US$3, children US$2.50.* Interesting as much for the well-restored building as for the exhibits using former prison cells and spaces to good effect.

Along Avenida 3, north of the Plaza de la Cultura, are the four gardens of the remodelled **Parque Morazán**. A little to the northeast, **Parque España**, cool, quiet and intimate, is home to the **Casa Amarilla** (Yellow House), seat of the Ministry of Foreign Affairs, and the **Edificio Metálico**, imported from Europe to become one of the country's first schools.

To the north of Parque Morazán is **Parque Simón Bolívar**, now a recreation area, with **Simón Bolívar National Zoo and Botanical Gardens** ⓘ *Av 11, just east of Calle 7 (go down Calle 7 about 3 blocks from Av 7), T2233-6701, www.fundazoo.org, Mon-Fri 0800-1530, Sat-Sun 0900-1630, US$4.30, children US$3.* It's been remodelled and much improved, with all native plants numbered and listed in a brochure; although the animal cages are small.

To the north of the city, a reasonable walk or a short taxi ride away, is **Spirogyra** ⓘ *100 m east, 150 m south of Centro Comercial El Pueblo (near Hotel Villa Tournón), T2222-937, Mon-Fri 0900-1400, Sat-Sun 0900-1500, guided tours for more than 10 people (reservations required), US$8, US$6 students, US$4 children*, a fascinating butterfly farm. To get there, take 'Calle Blancos' bus from Calle 3 and Avenida 5 to El Pueblo.

## Around San José

*fashionable, relaxed well-heeled suburbs*

### East of the centre

Extending east of the downtown core, the youthful town of **San Pedro** is home to the University of Costa Rica. Avenida Central enters this de facto suburb of San José at the well-to-do residential neighbourhood of **Los Yoses**, framed by Calle 33 in the west, Río Ocloro in the south and traffic-plied Cicunvalación in the east. Los Yoses is liberally endowed with chic guesthouses and bohemian restaurants, a chilled-out alternative to the grime and grind of the city centre. Beyond Circunvalación, San Pedro caters to its feisty student population with the best bars and clubs in the city.

### Escazú

Fancying itself a cut above San José, Escazú is a fashionable enclave for wealthy Ticos and, as time goes on, soft-bellied expats seeking the convenience, cleanliness and comfort that can only come with US-style shopping malls and heavily air-conditioned condos. Located 20 minutes west of San José, Escazú is in fact three separate settlements climbing a hillside, each with its own church, each increasingly authentic: San Rafael, San Antonio and, at the top of the hill, San Miguel. If you're in town on the second weekend of March, don't miss the **Día del Boyero** (National Day of the Oxcart Driver), hosted by San Antonio. Festivities culminate on the Sunday in a colourful oxcart parade from the school to the centre, accompanied by typical *payasos* (clowns). See Festivals, below.

## Tourist information

**Instituto Costarricense de Turismo (ICT)**
*East side of Juan Pablo II Bridge, over the General Cañas Highway, T2299-5800, www.visitcostarica.com. Mon-Fri 0700-1500.*
The central offices of ICT are inconveniently located in the northwest of the city. Instead, the helpful downtown branch (Av Central, between Calles 1 and 3, T2222-1090), is recommended for casual enquiries. An **ICT kiosk** can also be found at Juan Santamaría airport.

## Where to stay

**Central San José**
For hotels near the airport, see Alajuela, page 743.

**$$$$-$$$ Grano de Oro**
*Calle 30, Av 2-4, T2255-3322, www.hotelgrano deoro.com.*
A sumptuous converted early 20th-century tropical mansion with 40 rooms and suites, beautiful terrace gardens, renowned restaurant, jacuzzi and massage services. A stylish blend of tradition and modernity. Recommended.

**$$$$-$$$ Park Inn**
*Av 6 y Calle 28, T2257-1011, www.parkinn.com/hotel-sanjose.*
A business hotel from Radisson, the Park Inn boasts 117 rooms and all modern amenities including pool, gym, business centre, meeting rooms, and bar-restaurant. Decor is sleek and contemporary. Good service, reliable.

**$$$ Don Carlos**
*Calle 9, Av 7-9, T2221-6707, www.doncarloshotel.com.*
A slightly eccentric traditional city house adorned with interesting artwork, antiques, and statuary. They offer a variety of tasteful rooms and suites, free coffee, sun deck, Wi-Fi,

gift shop, airport shuttle, car hire and tours. Breakfast included.

**$$$ El Presidente**
*Av Central, Calle 7, T2010-0000, www.hotel-presidente.com.*
A landmark business hotel with 91 plush rooms and suites, stylish contemporary furnishings, and all modern amenities including LCD TVs with premium channels, Wi-Fi, safes, gym, spa, casino, restaurant, jacuzzi and business services.

**$$$ Hotel del Rey**
*Av 1, Calle 9, T2257-7800, www.hoteldelrey.com.*
At the heart of the upmarket red-light district, the landmark Hotel del Rey is home to the most famous (legal) brothel in Costa Rica, the **Blue Marlin** bar. It's an interesting place for people-watching, popular with couples out for a drink as much as lonely 'Sexpats' in search of company. The rooms are quite comfortable, but the walls are a bit thin. There's also a restaurant and casino.

**$$$ Santo Tomás**
*Av 7, Calle 3-5, T2255-0448, www.hotelsantotomas.com.*
Don't be put off by the plain exterior, Santo Tomás is a well-recommended boutique lodging set in a converted French Victorian mansion. It boasts 20 comfortable rooms, restful and enticing common areas, and helpful, friendly, professional staff. Amenities include garden, pool, jacuzzi, Wi-Fi, secure parking and restaurant. Tours available.

**$$ Casa 69**
*Calle 25bis No 69, T2256-8879, www.casa69.com.*
An award-winning B&B, centrally located with an emphasis on hospitality and service. Rooms are comfortable and stylish; common areas include living room, dining room, sundeck and a leafy courtyard. Lots of bars on the same street. Recommended.

## $$ Casa Alfi
*Calle 3 No 459, Av 4-6, T2221-2102,*
*www.casaalfihotel.com.*
Near the Teatro Nacional, an old-school
B&B with no-frills single rooms, spacious
standards and suites, all fully equipped with
orthopaedic mattresses, hot water, Wi-Fi and
cable TV. 1 wheelchair-accessible room is
also available. Friendly, comfortable, simple
and quiet.

## $$ Costa Rica Guesthouse
*Av 6, Calles 21-23, T2223-7034,*
*www.costa-rica-guesthouse.com.*
A restored 1904 Victorian townhouse with
23 private rooms (cheaper with shared bath),
each with TV, Wi-Fi and semi-orthopaedic
mattress. Amenities include parking, bar-
lounge, disabled access, free tea and coffee.
Decor is simple, tasteful and calm.

## $$ Hotel Aranjuez
*Calle 19, Av 11-13, T2256-1825,*
*www.hotelaranjuez.com.*
A well-established wood-built hotel
composed of 9 houses faithful to their
1930s architectural heritage. Rooms are
comfortable and cosy with lots of original
details like double doors, French windows,
clapboard walls and wooden floors. Studios
and apartments are also available for weekly
or monthly rental. Recommended.

## $$ Hotel Kekoldi
*Av 9, Calle 5-7, T2248-0804, www.kekoldi.com.*
A 1920s art deco building nestled among
the former mansions of coffee barons in the
historic Barrio Amón. They have 10 well-
appointed rooms and a shady garden replete
with tropical plants and birds. Clean, friendly,
bright and comfortable. Recommended.

## $$-$ Casa Ridgway
*Calle 15, Av 6-8, T2233-6168,*
*www.casaridgwayhostel.com.*
A friendly non-profit guesthouse run
by the Quaker Peace Center. They offer
dorms ($) and private rooms ($$) with

or without bath, all named after peace
activists like Mother Teresa and Gandhi.
A good place to engage with others on
human rights and social justice issues.
Group rates and facilities available.

## $$-$ Hostel Casa del Parque
*Calle 19, Av 1-3, T2233-3437,*
*www.hostelcasadelparque.com.*
A very clean and presentable family-run
hostel, not a party place, complete with a
pleasant patio, shared kitchen, common
areas, free coffee, Wi-Fi, a 10-bed dorm
and 4 private rooms, all with orthopaedic
mattresses. Relaxed and friendly.
Recommended.

## $$-$ Hostel Van Gogh
*Calle 7, Av 7-9, 150 m from Parque Morazán,*
*T8399-3879, www.hostelvangogh.hostel.com.*
Small, friendly, helpful hostel with dorms ($)
and private rooms ($$). Amenities include
Wi-Fi, pool table, shared kitchen (basic), book
exchange, satellite TV, DVDs and garden.
Relaxed place, hospitable, professional,
well maintained and recommended.

---

## East of the centre

## $$-$ Hostel Bekuo
*325 m west of Spoon, Los Yoses, T2234-1091,*
*www.hostelbekuo.com.*
An intimate, laid-back, friendly, homely
hostel with a range of private rooms ($$) and
dorms ($), as well as a small garden complete
with a rabbit. Services include Wi-Fi, kitchen,
movies, luggage store, phone, info.

## $$-$ In & Basic Hostel Lounge
*200 m south and 75 m west of Spoon, north*
*side of Fatima's chuch, Los Yoses, T2232-2998,*
*www.inbasic.com.*
A very hip and stylish hostel with glamorous
1950s decor. They have 8 private rooms ($$)
and dorm beds ($), a fully equipped kitchen,
3 lounge areas, a backyard and a barbecue
area. Recommended.

## Escazú

### $$$ Tierra Mágica
*Calle San Miguel, T2289-9154,*
*www.tierramagica-costarica.com.*
Doubling up as the art studio of Barbara
Odio Ygelsias, Tierra Mágica is a very cosy
and beautifully presented B&B with great
tile work, artistic concrete floors and a lush
garden. Rooms are spacious and relaxing.
Art workshops are also available here.

### $$$-$$ Costa Verde Inn
*300 m south of the 2nd San Antonio*
*de Escazú cemetery, T2228-4080,*
*www.costaverdeinn.com.*
A secluded and charming country home
with 14 imaginatively decorated rooms – a
popular choice away from the town centre.

Restaurants

### Central San José
At lunchtime, cheaper restaurants offer a set
meal called a *casado*, US$5-10, which is often
good value.

### $$$ El Balcón de Europa
*Calle 9, between Av Central and Av 1,*
*25 m al norte de Chelles, T2221-4841.*
This old-school Italian trattoria is a
convenient and reliable dinner spot in the
heart of the downtown area. They serve
good home-cooked pasta, lasagne, soups,
and seafood. A cosy interior adorned with
historic photos of the neighbourhood.

### $$$ Esquina de Buenos Aires
*Calle 11 esquina Av 4, T2223-1909,*
*www.laesquinadebuenosaires.com.*
Highly popular and full of character, this
stylish Argentine steak house cooks up
some of the most flavourful cuts in the city,
including succulent rib eye, striploin and
tenderloin steak. Vegetarians can enjoy a
range of home-made pastas.

### $$$ Kalú
*Calle 7 y Av 11, 300 m al norte del Parque*
*Morazán, Barrio Amón, T2221-2081,*
*www.kalu.co.cr.*
Kalú is a young and trendy place, a welcome
oasis in the urban grind. The owner, Chef
Camille Ratton, was trained in France and
offers an eclectic range of international
dishes including Thai chicken, falafels,
gourmet sandwiches and burgers.

### $$$ Lubnan
*Paseo Colón, Calle 22-24, T2257-6071,*
*www.lubnancr.com.*
A long-standing Lebanese restaurant serving
authentic cuisine from the homeland,
including shwarma, kafta and shish kebab.
Vegetarian selections too, including falafel
and hummus, great service, and belly
dancing on Thu.

### $$$ Park Café
*Sabana Norte, 75 m north of Rosti Pollos,*
*T2290-6324, www.parkcafecostarica.*
*blogspot.com. Tue-Sat 1730-2100.*
Chef Richard Neat has won multiple Michelin
stars in Europe and now brings his culinary
mastery to Costa Rica with this prestigious
restaurant set in the garden of an intriguing
antique store. Dress code applies, no small
children, reservations a must.

### $$$ Tin Jo
*Calle 11, Av 6-8, T2221-7605, www.tinjo.com.*
Established more than 3 decades ago,
Tin Jo is a San José institution. It serves
probably the best Asian cuisine in town with
authentic dishes from China, India, Japan,
Thailand, Vietnam and the Philippines. Great
setting in a converted historic mansion.
Recommended.

### $$$-$$ The Corner Pizzeria and Cafeteria
*Calle 28 y Av 2, T2255-3333.*
A casual joint serving tasty artisan-style
pizzas with traditional Italian crusts. Friendly
staff, good ambience and occasional live
music on Fri night. A great option for couples
and families.

### $$$-$$ Machu Picchu
*Calle 32, Av 1-3, T2222-7384,*
*www.restaurantemachu picchu.com.*
*Mon-Sat 1000-2200, Sun 1100-1800.*

As the name might suggest, excellent Peruvian food, including tasty ceviche starters and succulent seafood mains such as spicy prawns, garlic octopus, and lemon sea bass. Good service and a homely atmosphere.

### $$$-$$ Sapore Trattoria
*Av 2a, 75 m west of Plaza de la Democracia, T2222-8906.*
A small but graceful Italian restaurant serving home-made pastas, pizzas and other traditional dishes, all lovingly made with genuine Italian ingredients. Good wines and desserts.

### $$-$ La Criollita
*Av 7, Calle 7-9, T2256-6511.*
If you're hankering after a wholesome plate of good old-fashioned *comida típica*, La Criollita is a classic downtown option. At lunchtime they dish up massive and reasonably priced *casados*, hugely popular with local business men. Recommended.

### $$-$ Shakti
*Av 8 y Calle 13, T2222-4475, www.restauranteshakti.com.*
A host of health-conscious options including tasty salads, pastas, soups, soya burgers and fruit juices are on the menu at this bright and airy vegetarian restaurant, established in 1987.

### $$-$ Vishnu
*Av 1, Calle 1-3, also on Calle 14, Av 2. Daily 0800-2000.*
Best known vegetarian place in town, always bustling at lunchtime. Try their cheap and good *plato del día*, their soya cheese sandwiches and ice cream, or their wholemeal bread.

### $ Soda Tapia
*Calle 42, Av 2-4, east side of Parque Sabana, www.sodatapia.com.*
On the park, a classic stopping place for Josefinos. They serve wholesome *comida típica*. Cheap, cheerful, and quick.

## Cafés

### Alma de Café
*Av 2, Calle 3-5, in foyer of National Theatre, www.almadecafe.net. Mon-Sat.*
This stylish café inside the national theatre is reminiscent of old Europe with its lofty ceiling and marble floor. In addition to good coffee, they serve crêpes, sandwiches and quiches. Pricey but worth it for the sheer style and sophistication of the belle époque interior.

### Café de los Deseos
*Calle 15, Av 11, T2222-0496, www. cafedelosdeseos.com. Closed Mon.*
Buzzing and bohemian, Café de los Deseos is a fun place to hang out, popular with local hipsters. In addition to coffee and craft beer, they serve international comfort food like fish tacos, chicken wings, pizza, quesadillas and burgers.

### East of the centre

### $$$ Jurgen's
*Calle 41 and Paseo Rubén Darío, Barrio Dent in Los Yoses, T2224-2455. Closed Sun.*
Adjoining **Boutique Hotel** Jade, Jurgen's is a smart and sophisticated place, good for a business lunch or a romantic evening meal. It boasts an excellent and creative international menu. First-class service.

## Bars and clubs

### Central San José
There are dark and interesting bars around Parque Morazán, many of them populated by wastrel gringo expats and ladies of ill repute. The **Centro Comercial El Pueblo**, north of town in Barrio Tournón, is a mall with a cluster of restaurants, bars and discos. This is where many young Ticos party the night away until dawn, but it is now in decline, increasingly insalubrious and unsafe; better entertainment can be had in San Pedro (see below).

## East of the centre

North of Av Central, Calle de la Armagua (aka Calle 3) is the swinging epicentre of the student drinking scene, home to scores of bars and nightclubs, a great place to wander in a group. The action really gets going after 2300 and one of the most popular joints is **Terra U** (www.terrau.com). For live music, you could try:

### Jazz Café

*Paralela a la Autopista Próspero Fernández 1st exit after the toll, next to Comfort Suizo, opposite Hospital Cima, www.jazzcafecostarica.com.* As the name suggests, this is the place to soak up some syncopated rhythms. Check the website for the live music schedule. Also a branch in Escazú.

## Entertainment

### Cinemas

Modern cinemas showing latest releases are located throughout the metropolitan area, see *La Nación* for listings.

**Cine Universitario**, *at the UCR's Abelardo Bonilla law school auditorium in San Pedro, T2511-5323, www. accionsocial.ucr.ac.cr/web/ ec/cine-universitario.* Shows good films Thu-Fri, 1830, US$5.

**Sala Garbo**, *Av 2, Calle 28, T2222-1034, www. salagarbocr.com.* Shows independent art house movies.

**Variedades**, *Calle 5, Av Central-1, T2222-6108.* Others can be found in **Los Yoses** (T2223-0085), **San Pedro** (T2283-5716), **Rohrmoser** (T2232-3271) and **Heredia** (T2293-3300).

### Theatre

More than 20 theatres offer live productions in the San José area; check the *Tiempo Libre* entertainment supplement every Thu in *La Nación* for show times, mostly weekends.

**Teatro del Angel**, *Av Central, Calle 13-15, T2222-8258.* Has 3 modern dance companies.

**Teatro Melico Salazar**, *Parque Central, T2295-6000, www.teatromelico.go.cr.* For popular, folkloric shows.

**Teatro Nacional**, *Av 2, Calle 3-5, T2221-5341, T2010-1100, www.teatronacional.go.cr.* Recommended for the productions, the architecture and the bar/café. Behind it is La Plaza de la Cultura, a large complex.

## Festivals

**Dec-Jan** **Christmas/New Year**. Festivities last from mid-Dec to the 1st week of Jan, with dances, horse shows and much confetti throwing in the crowded streets. The annual **El Tope** horse parade starts at noon on 26 Dec and travels along the principal avenues of San José with a **carnival** the next day.

**Mar** The **International Festival of Culture** assembles musicians from throughout Central America in a week of performances in the Plaza de la Cultura around the 2nd week of Mar, although concern over the future of the event exists due to lack of funding.

**2nd weekend in Mar** **Día del Boyero** (Day of the Oxcart Driver) is celebrated in San Antonio de Escazú. Parades of ox-drawn carts, with music, dancing and blessings from the priesthood. Festivities culminate on the Sun in a colourful oxcart parade. Dancing in the evening to marimba music.

**Mar/Apr** Street parades during **Easter week**.

**Sep 15** **Independence Day**. Bands and dance troupes move through the streets, although activities start to kick-off the night before with the traditional nationwide singing of the National Anthem at 1800.

## Shopping

### Crafts and markets

**Canapi**, *Calle 11, Av 1.* An *artesanía* cooperative, cheaper than most.

**Centro Comercial El Pueblo**, *near the Villa Tournón Hotel.* Has a number of stalls but is mainly upmarket, built in a traditional *pueblo* style.

**La Casona**, *Calle Central, Av Central-1. Daily 0900-1900.* A market of small *artesanía* shops, full of interesting little stalls.

**Galería Namu**, *opposite the Alianza Francesa building on Av 7 and Calle 5-7, T2256-3412,*

*www.galerianamu.com. Mon-Sat 0900-1630.*
The best one-stop shop for home-grown
and indigenous art, with the distinctly
bright-coloured ceramics of Cecilia Figueres.
Items can be shipped if required and online
shopping is possible.

**Mercado Nacional de Artesanía**, *Calle 11,
Av 4, T2221-5012. Mon-Fri 0900-1800, Sat 0900-
1700.* A good one-stop shop with a wide
variety of goods.

**Plaza de la Democracia**, *in front of the
National Museum.* Tented stalls run the
length of a city block, a great place to buy
hammocks, arts and crafts at competitive
prices. Don't be afraid to negotiate.

## What to do

### Bungee jumping
After Rafael Iglesias Bridge (Río Colorado),
continue on Pan-American Highway 1.5 km,
turn right at Salón Los Alfaro, down the track
to Puente Colorado.

**Tropical Bungee**, *T2248-2212, www.bungee.
co.cr.* Operates daily 0900-1600 in high
season, US$75 1st jump, US$45 for the 2nd
(same day only) includes transport from
San José, reservations required.

### Cycling
**Coast to Coast Adventures**, *T2280-8054,
www.ctocadventures.com.* Run trips in the
local area.

### Language schools
The number of schools has increased
rapidly. Listed below are just a selection
recommended by readers. Generally,
schools offer tuition in groups of 2-5 for
2-4 weeks. Lectures, films, outings and
social occasions are usually included
and accommodation with families is
encouraged. Many schools are linked to
the university and can offer credits towards
a US course. Rates, including lodging, are
around US$1000-1100 a month.

**Academia Tica de Español**, *in San Rafael de
Coronado, 10 km north of San José,
T2229-0013, www.academiatica.com.*

**AmeriSpan**, *1334 Walnut St, 6th floor,
Philadelphia, PA 19107, T215-751-1100,
www.amerispan.com.* Has affiliated
schools in Alajuela, Heredia, San José
and 6 others locations.

**Costa Rican Language Academy**, *Barrio
California, T2280-5834, www.spanishand
more.com.* Run by Aída Chávez, offers
language study and accommodation
with local families, and instruction in
Latin American music and dancing as well.

**Costa Rica Spanish Institute**, *Zapote in
San Pedro district, T2234-1001, www.cosi.co.cr.*
Also branch in Manuel Antonio.

**Universal de Idiomas**, *in Moravia, T2223-
9662, www.universal-edu.com.* Emphasis is
on conversational Spanish.

**LEARN SPANISH**
in Costa Rica
City & Beachfront Campuses

all ages / nationalities

Free activities and tours

www.interculturacostarica.com
spanish@interculturacostarica.com
Tel.: (506) 2260 8480 **Heredia City Campus**
Tel.: (506) 2656 3000 **Samara Beach Campus**

## Nature tours

**ACTUAR**, *T2290-7514, www.actuarcosta rica.com*. An association of 26 community-based rural tourism groups.

**Aguas Bravas**, *T2292-2072, www.aguas-bravas.co.cr*. Whitewater rafting on rivers around the Central Valley, also horse riding, biking, hiking and camping.

**Bay Island Cruises**, *Paseo Colón, 275 m north of Pizza Hut, opposite Policía Municipal, T2258-3536, www.bayislandcruises.com*. One of several companies focusing on trips to Tortuga Island. Daily tours (US$115) include lunch and transport from San José area.

**Costa Rica Expeditions**, *Av 3, Calles 25 y 29, T2521-6099, www.costaricaexpeditions. com*. Upmarket wildlife adventures include whitewater rafting (US$99-169 for 1-day trip on Río Pacuare, includes lunch and transport) and further options. They own **Tortuga Lodge**, **Corcovado Lodge Tent Camp** and **Monteverde Lodge**. Daily trips, highly recommended.

**Ecole Travel**, *Barrio Escalante, del Centro Cultural Costarricense Norteamericano, 50 m norte y 25 m oeste, T2253-8884, www.ecole travel.com*. Chilean-Dutch, highly recommended for budget tours to Tortuguero, Corcovado and tailor-made excursions off the beaten track.

**Horizontes**, *Calle 28, Av 1-3, T2222-2022, www.horizontes.com*. A big operator in Costa Rica, high standards, educational and special interest, advice given and arrangements made for groups and individuals.

**Ríos Tropicales**, *Calle 38, between Paseo Colón and Av 2, 50 m south of Subway, T2233-6455, www.riostropicales.com*. Specialists in whitewater rafting and kayaking, good selection, careful to assess your abilities, good food, excellent guides, from US$225 for 2-day trip on Río Pacuare, waterfalls, rapids, including camping and food. Many other options throughout the country.

## Night tours

**Costa Rican Nights Tour**, *La Uruca, T2242-9200, www.puebloantiguo.co.cr*. Takes place Wed, Fri, Sat 1900-2200. This 3-hr dinner show incorporates fireworks, marimba music, a show and a guided tour through San José in Pueblo Antiguo.

## Tour operators

**Aventuras Naturales**, *Av 5, Calle 33-35, T2225-3939, www.adventurecostarica.com*. Specialists in whitewater rafting with their own lodge on the Pacuare, which has a canopy adventure tour. Also several other trips.

**COOPRENA (Simbiosis Tours)**, *San José, T2290-8646, www.turismorural.com*. A group supporting small farmers, broadly working to the principle of sustainable tourism. Offers tours and accommodation around the country.

**Costa Rican Trails**, *325 Curridabat de la Pops, 300 m al sur y 250 m al este, T1 888-803-3344 (USA), T1866-865-7013 (Canada), www. costaricantrails.com*. Travel agency and tour operator, offering 1-day and multi-day tours and packages, selected and resorts, reliable local ground and air transport.

**Swiss Travel Service**, *T2282-4898, www.swisstravelcr.com*. One of the biggest tour operators with branches in many of the smarter hotels. Can provide any standard tour, plus several specialist tours for birdwatchers. Good guides and warmly recommended.

## Transport

### San José

### Air

The **Aeropuerto Internacional Juan Santamaría (SJO)**, T2437-2400, www. fly2sanjose.com, is at El Coco, 16 km from San José along the Autopista General Cañas. All international departures are subject to US$29 departure tax, payable at the **Bancrédito** counter prior to check-in. A 2nd airport, **Aeropuerto Tobias Bolaños**, 8 km west of San José, in Pavas, is a hub for charter and some domestic flights.

Efficient **Tuasa** buses to city centre from the highway outside the ground-floor terminal, every 10 mins, 35 mins, US$1; also services to **Alajuela**, every 15 mins, 15 mins, US$1; and **Heredia**, every 20 mins, 20 mins, US$1. In San José, buses to **airport** (continuing on to Alajuela) leave from Av Central-2, Calle 10, every 10 mins from 0500-2100; 45 mins, US$1 (good service, plenty of luggage space).

Bright orange airport taxis (T2222-6865, www.taxiaeropuerto.com) cost around US$25, tickets available from pre-payment kiosks. Taxis run all night from the main square. For early flights you can reserve a taxi from any San José hotel the night before. All taxi companies run a 24-hr service.

**Domestic flights** 2 airlines operate domestic flights: **Sansa**, T2290-4400, www.flysansa.com, and **Nature Air**, T2299-6000, www.natureair.com. The Sansa terminal is next to the main terminal at SJO and they run a free bus service for passengers. If you made reservations before arriving in Costa Rica, confirm and collect tickets as soon as possible after arrival. Book ahead, especially for the beaches. In Feb and Mar, planes can be fully booked 3 weeks ahead. On all internal scheduled and charter flights there is a baggage allowance of 1 checked and 1 carry-on bag, 7-18 kg depending on carrier and fare class; fees for excess weight approximately US$2-3 per kg. Oversized items such as surfboards or bicycles are charged at US$30 if there is room in the cargo hold. Departure and arrival taxes applicable if travelling to Arenal, Quepos and Tambor; total US$5-14. For more information, see Getting around in Practicalities chapter.

**Bus**
**Local** Urban routes in San José cost US$0.50 or less. A cheap tour of San José can be made on the bus marked *periférico* from Paseo Colón in front of the Cine Colón, or at La Sabana bus stop, a 45-min circuit of the city. A smaller circuit is made by the 'Sabana/Cementerio' bus; pick it up at Av 2, Calle 8-10.

**Long distance** Buses have their terminals scattered round town (see map, page 726) but the majority are close to the Coca Cola Terminal, in the central west of the city.

There are several shuttle bus companies including **Interbus**, T2283-5573, www.interbusonline.com, and **Fantasy Tours/GrayLine**, T2220-2126, www.graylinecostarica.com, offer transport from the capital to dozens of beach and tourism destinations in comfortable a/c minibuses, with bilingual drivers and hotel pickup. Tickets US$30-80 one-way, with a good weekly pass.

**Meseta Central** To the **Aeropuerto Internacional Juan Santamaría** and onwards to **Alajuela**, every 10 mins, 0400-2200, 20-40 mins, US$1, departing from the TUASA Terminal, Av 2, Calle 12-14. To **Cartago**, every 10 mins, 0500-0000, 45 mins, US$1.10, departing from Calle 5 and Av 10 with **Empresa Lumaca**, T2537-2320. To **Heredia**, every 10 mins, 0500-2300, 30 mins, US$0.90, departing from Calle 1, Av 7-9. To **Turrialba**, hourly (direct service), 0500-2100, 2 hrs, US$2.90, departing from the Transtusa terminal, Calle 13 and Av 6, T2222-4464, indirect services are slower but more frequent. To **Volcán Irazú**, 2 daily, 0800, 1230, 2hrs, US$4.20, departing from Av 2, Calle 1-3.

**Northern Costa Rica** To **Ciudad Quesada** (**San Carlos**), every 40 mins (direct service), 0730-1730, 2-3 hrs, US$3.60; to **La Fortuna**, 3 daily, 0615, 0840, 1130, 5 hrs, US$4.50; to **Los Chiles**, 2 daily, 0530, 1500, 5 hrs, US$5.40; all departing from the San Carlos Terminal, Calle 12, Av 7-9 with **Autotransportes San José-San Carlos**, T2255-0567. To **Tilarán**, 5 daily, 0730-1830, 4 hrs, US$7.20, departing from Calle 20 y Av 3, T2695-5611. To **Cañas**, 5 daily, 3½ hrs, US$5.40, departing from Calle 14, Av 1-3 with **Empresa La Cañera**, T2258-5792. To **Liberia**, hourly, 0600-2000, 4½ hrs, US$6, departing from Calle 24, Av 5-7, Pulmitan de Liberia, T2222-1650. To **Monteverde/Santa Elena**,

2 daily, 0630, 1430, 5 hrs, US$5.10, departing from Calle 12, Av 7-9, with **Transportes Tilarán**, T2222-3854. To **Peñas Blancas** on the Nicaraguan border, hourly, 0330-1900, 6 hrs, US$8.40, departing from Calle 14, Av 3-5, 1 block north of the Coca Cola Terminal with **Transportes Deldú**, T2256-9072; for more on the crossing to Nicaragua, see Nicaragua–Costa Rica box in the Practicalities chapter. To **Puntarenas**, hourly (direct), 0600-1900, 2½ hrs, US$3, departing from Calle 16 y Av 12 with **Empresarios Unidos**, T2222-8231.

**Península de Nicoya** To **Montezuma** and **Malpaís**, 2 daily, 0600, 1400, 5 hrs, US$9.20, including ferry connection; to **Playa Bejuco**, 2 daily, 0530, 1400, 4 hrs, US$10; all departing from the San Carlos Terminal, Calle 12, Av 7-9, T2221-7479. To **Nicoya**, 6 daily, 0530-1700, 5 hrs, US$5; to **Playa Sámara**, 2 daily, 1200, 1700 (only in high season), 5 hrs, US$8.10; to **Playa Tamarindo**, 2 daily, 1130 via Liberia, 1530 via Tempisque, 5½ hrs, US$10.20; to **Santa Cruz**, 7 daily, 0700-1900, 5 hrs, US$5.20, all departing from the Alfaro Terminal, Calle 14, Av 5, T2222-2666. To **Playa del Coco**, 3 daily, 0800, 1400, 1600, 5 hrs, US$7.50, departing from Calle 24, Av 5-7, Pulmitan, T2222-0458. To **Playa Flamingo**, 3 daily, 0800, 1030, 1500, 6 hrs, US$11, departing from Calle 20, Av 1-3, with **Tralapa**, T2221-7202.

**Central Pacific Coast** To **Dominical** and **Uvita**, 2 daily, 0600, 1500, 7 hrs, US$9.50; to **Quepos** and **Manuel Antonio**, 6 daily, 0600-1930, 4 hrs, US$6.30, all departing from the Terminal Tracopa, Calle 5, Av 18-20, T2221-4214. To **Jacó**, 7 daily, 0600-1900, 1½ hrs, US$4.30, departing from the Terminal Coca-Cola, Calle 16, Av 1-3, T2290-7920.

**Southern Costa Rica** To **Ciudad Neily**, 4 daily, 0500-1830, 8 hrs, US$13.30; to **Golfito**, 3 daily, 0700, 1530, 2215, 8 hrs, US$13.30; to **Palmar Norte**, 8 daily, 0500-1630, 7 hrs, US$10.50; to **Paso Canoas**, 8 daily, 0500-2200, 7 hrs, US$13.40; to **San Isidro**, 14 daily, 0500-1830, 3 hrs, US$6.30; to **San**

**Vito**, 4 daily, 0600-1600, 7½ hrs, US$12.70; all departing from the Tracopa terminal, Calle 5, Av 18-20, T2221-4214. To **Puerto Jiménez**, 2 daily, 0800, 1200, 8 hrs, US$13.60, departing from Calle 14, Av 9-11 with **Transportes Blanco**, T2257-4121.

**Caribbean coast** To **Cahuita**, 4 daily, 0600-1600, 4 hrs, US$8.50; to **Puerto Viejo de Talamanca**, 4 daily, 0600-1600, 4½ hrs, US$9.90; and to **Sixaola** (on the Panamanian border), 4 daily, 0600-1600, 6 hrs, US$12.10, all departing from Terminal Atlántico Norte (also known as Terminal San Carlos), Calle 12, Av 7-9, T2750-0023; for more on crossing the border to Panama, see Costa Rica–Panama box in the Practicalities chapter. To **Cariari**, 9 daily, 0630-2030, 2 hrs, US$4; to **Puerto Limón**, hourly, 0500-1900, 3 hrs, US$5.75; to **Puerto Viejo de Sarapiquí**, 10 daily, 0630-1830, 2 hrs, US$5; and to **Siquirres**, 11 daily, 0630-1800, 1½ hrs, US$3.45, all departing from the Terminal del Caribe, Calle Central and Av 15, with **Transporte Caribeños**, T2222-0610.

**International** In Dec and Jan, buses are often booked 2 weeks ahead. Before departure, have your ticket confirmed on arrival at the terminal. When buying and confirming your ticket, you must show your passport. If luggage is light, it is often faster to hop between local buses and cross the border on foot.

Ticabus terminal at Paseo Colón, 200 m north and 100 m west of Torre Mercedes, T2221-0006, www.ticabus.com; downtown ticket agent at Calle 9-11, Av 4, T2221-8954, office open Mon-Sun 0600-1700. **Ticabus** to **Guatemala City**, 3 daily, 60 hrs, US$78 tourist class, US$99 tourist-executive class, with overnight stay in Managua and San Salvador. To **Tegucigalpa**, 3 daily, 48 hrs, US$48 tourist class, US$61 tourist-executive class, overnight in Managua. To **Managua** 3 daily, US$27 tourist class, US$40 executive class, 10 hrs including 1 hr at Costa Rican side of border and up to another 2 hrs on Nicaraguan side while they search bags.

To **Panama City** 1200 daily, US$42 tourist class, US$58 executive class, 18 hrs (book in advance). **Transnica**, Calle 22, Av 3-5, T2223-4242, www.transnica.com, runs buses with TV, video, a/c, snacks, toilet, to **Managua** 4 daily, US$27. **Expreso Panaline** goes to **Panama City** daily at 1200 from the Terminal de Empresarios Unidos de Puntarenas Calle 16, Av 10-12, T2221-7694, www.expresopanama.com, US$40 1 way, US$80 return, reduction for students, arrives 0300; a/c, payment by Visa/MasterCard accepted. A bus to **Changuinola** via the Sixaola– Guabito border post leaves San José at 1000 daily, 8 hrs, from opposite Terminal Alfaro, T2556-1432 for info, best to arrive 1 hr before departure; the bus goes via Siquirres and is the quick route to **Limón**. For more on crossing the border to Panama, see also Costa Rica–Panama border crossing box in the Practicalities chapter.

### Car hire

Most local agencies are on or close to Paseo Colón, with a branch or drop-off site at or close to the airport and other locations around the country.

International companies with services include **Adobe**, **Alamo**, **Avis**, **Budget**, **Dollar**, **Economy**, **Hertz**, **Hola**, **National**, **Payless**, **Thrifty**, **Toyota** and **Tricolor**.

**Rent-a-car Costa Rica**, T2442-6000, www. rentacarcostarica.com, is a local company with several offices around town including Hostal Toruma, most competitively priced in town; **Wild Rider Motorcycles**, also rents cheap 4WD vehicles (see below).

### Cycle repairs

**Cyclo Quiros**, Apartado 1366, Pavas, 300 m west of US Embassy. The brothers Quiros have been repairing bikes for 25 years, highly recommended.

### Motorcycle and bike rental

**Wild Rider Motorcycles**, Paseo Colón, Calle 32 diagonal Kentucky, next to **Aventuras Backpackers**, T2258-4604, www. wild-rider.com, Honda XR250s, Yamaha XT600s and Suzuki DR650SE available for rent from US$55-80 a day, US$700-1200 deposit required. 4WD vehicles also available, US$240-410 per week, monthly discounts.

### Taxi

Minimum fare US$1 for 1 km, US$1.10 additional kilometre. Taxis used to charge more after 2200, but that rule has been rescinded. Taxis are red and have electronic meters called *marías*, if yours doesn't, get out and take another cab. For journeys over 12 km, price should be negotiated between driver and passenger. Radio cabs can be booked in advance. To order a taxi, call **Coopeguaria**, T2226-1366, **Coopeirazu**, T2254-3211, **Coopemoravia**, T2229-8882, **Coopetaxi**, T2235-9966, **Taxi San Jorge**, T2221-3434, **Taxis Guaria**, T2226-1366, **Taxis Unidos SA**, which are the official taxis of the Juan Santamaría International Airport and are orange instead of red, T2222-6865.

### Train

Costa Rica has revived its train services between the capital and some nearby destinations in the Meseta Central, although they are intended more for commuters than tourists. The Terminal Atlántico, Av 3 and Calle 21, serves **Cartago** and **Heredia** with departures every 30-45 mins, Mon-Fri, in the early morning and early evening only. For more information, see www.trenurbano.co.cr.

# Meseta Central

Hilly and fertile with a temperate climate, the Meseta Central is a major coffee-growing area where fairly heavily populated, picturesque and prosperous settlements sit in the shadows of active volcanoes. Exploring the towns and villages of the region – each with its own character and style – gives a good insight into the very heart of Costa Rica. Although it's easier to explore the region in a private vehicle, frequent public buses and short journeys make hopping between towns fairly straightforward. If stepping out from San José it's probably worth dumping most of your luggage in the city and travelling light.

## Alajuela and around  Colour map 4, B3.

relaxed provincial capital famous for its flowers and market days

Despite being the second largest city in the country, Alajuela is a mild place, far removed from the chaos of neighbouring San José. Located five minutes from the airport, it is a popular pit-stop for those on early flights and late arrivals, and a good base for exploring the surrounding countryside, including down-to-earth villages, verdant hills, vertiginous waterfalls and nature reserves full of brightly feathered avian life.

### Sights

The social and spiritual heart of Alajuela is the shady Parque Central, home to the 19th-century neoclassical cathedral with its red metal dome. Five blocks east, the unusual church of La Agonía exhibits an interesting mix of architectural styles. One block south of the Parque Central, a monument commemorates Juan Santamaría, the drummer boy and national hero who set ablaze the building in Rivas (Nicaragua) where William Walker's filibusters were entrenched in 1856. The **Museo Histórico Juan Santamaría** ⓘ *on the north side of the Parque Central, T2441-4775, www.museojuansantamaria.go.cr, Tue-Sun 1000-1800,* tells, somewhat confusingly, the story of this war.

**Best** for
Birdwatching ▪ Flowers ▪ Hiking ▪ Volcanoes

## ON THE ROAD
## Nature tourism

Most tour operators listed in this guide will offer nature-oriented tours. There are many well-kept and well-guarded national parks and nature reserves that protect some samples of the extraordinarily varied Costa Rican ecosystems. In the north the variety is daunting and includes some of the last patches of dry tropical forest in the Parque Nacional Santa Rosa, the cloudforest of Monteverde and the Talamanca Mountains, and nine active volcanoes including Rincón de la Vieja, Poás, Irazú and of course Arenal. For volunteering opportunities, see ASVO and FPN below and Volunteering, Costa Rica, in the Practicalities chapter.

Birdwatchers and butterfly lovers have long flocked to Costa Rica to see some of the 850 or so species of bird and untold varieties of butterfly. All of these can best be seen in the parks, together with monkeys, deer, coyotes, armadillos, anteaters, turtles, coatis, raccoons, snakes, and, more rarely, wild pigs, wild cats and tapirs.

Although the national parks and other privately owned reserves are a main tourist attraction, many are in remote areas and not easy to get to on public transport; buses or coaches that do go tend to stay for a short time. There is a tendency for tour companies to dominate the National Park 'market' to the exclusion of other public transport. For tight budgets, try making up a party with others and sharing taxis or hiring a car.

**Asociación de Voluntarios (ASVO)**, T2258-4430, www.asvocr.org. Contact if you want to work as a volunteer in the parks, with a small daily fee for lodging and food.
**Fundación de Parques Nacionales (FPN)**, T2257-2239, www.fpn-cr.org. Contact for information and permits to visit and/or camp, conduct research or volunteer in the parks. Check in advance if your trip depends on gaining entrance.
**Sistema Nacional de Areas de Conservación (SINAC)**, T2283-8004, www.costarica-nationalparks.com, administers the national park system. Contact them for information, maps and permits.

On the southeastern outskirts of Alajuela, the **Ara Project** ⓘ *Desamparados, T8389-5811, www.thearaproject.org*, is a breeding and release centre for endangered great green and scarlet macaws. To tour the facilities and meet some of the cheeky parrots in person, contact the administrators through their website.

### Parque Nacional Volcán Poás
*Tue-Sun, 0700-1600, US$15, good café next door, and toilets further along the road to the crater. If you wish to get in earlier you can leave your car/taxi at the gates, walk the 3 km up the hill and pay on your way out. The volcano is very crowded on Sun so go in the week if possible. Arrive early as clouds often hang low over the crater after 1000, obstructing the view. Wear good shoes, a hat and suncream.*

Volcán Poás (2708 m) sits in the centre of the Parque Nacional Volcán Poás (6506 ha), where the still-smoking volcano and bubbling turquoise sulphur pool are set within a beautiful forest. The crater is almost 1.5 km across – the second largest in the world. The park is rich with abundant birdlife, given the altitude and barren nature of the terrain, and home to the only true dwarf cloudforest in Costa Rica. Trails are well marked to help guide you from the visitor centre to the geysers, lake and other places of interest. The main crater is 1 km along a road from the car park. There is a visitor centre by the car park with explanations of the recent changes in the volcano. There is also a good café run by **Café Britt**; alternatively, bring your own food and water.

## La Paz Waterfall Gardens

*6 km north of Vara Blanca, T2482-2720, www.waterfallgardens.com. Daily 0800-1700, US$38 (buffet lunch US$13), children US$22 (buffet lunch US$7).*

La Paz Waterfall Gardens, 32 km north of Alajuela on Highway 126, has forest trails, five huge waterfalls, one of the world's largest butterfly and hummingbird gardens, a restaurant with buffet lunch and the **Peace Lodge Hotel** (**$$$$**). The road is twisty, winding through lush forest down to the lowlands at **San Miguel**. Here the road leads either northeast heading to La Virgen and eventually Puerto Viejo de Sarapiquí (see page 833), or northwest to Venecia (see below).

## La Virgen

Some 10 km northeast of San Miguel is La Virgen, near the Río Sarapiquí, a good spot for Grade I, II and III rafting, which is organized by the hotel **Rancho Leona**. From San José, take the Río Frío bus which passes through San Miguel, or a bus from Ciudad Quesada (San Carlos), and ask to get off at **Rancho Leona**. Juan Carlos in La Virgen has been recommended as a guide for rafting, T2761-1148, from US$30 per person.

## Venecia and around

Heading west from San Miguel, Venecia (two buses daily from San José, 4½ hours, US$3) has an interesting church. Near Venecia are the pre-Columbian tumuli of **Ciudad Cutris**. A good road goes to within 2 km of Cutris, from where you can walk or take a 4WD vehicle; get a permit to visit from the local finca owner.

West of Venecia is Aguas Zarcas, where the road splits. Heading directly north, the roads descends into the jungle lowlands, following the Río San Carlos towards the Nicaraguan border, passing through several small towns. After about 40 km, in Boca Tapada, is **La Laguna del Lagarto Lodge** (**$$**, www.lagarto-lodge-costa-rica.com).

## Grecia

The road from Alajuela northwest to Ciudad Quesada (San Carlos) (see page 757) passes through Grecia and several towns, the surrounding hills covered with green coffee bushes. Grecia is also a major pineapple producer, and has an interesting church made entirely of metal. A short distance along the road to Alajuela is **El Mundo de las Serpientes** ① *T2494-3700, www.theworldofsnakes.com, 0800-1600, US$11, children US$6, reductions for biology students*, a snake farm with more than 50 species. On the old road about 10 km towards Tacares is **Los Chorros Recreational Park** ① *US$4*, with two massive waterfalls and picnic spots.

## Sarchí and around

Heading west from Grecia is the town of Sarchí, the country's artisan centre, where you can visit the *fábricas* that produce the intricately geometric and floral designs painted on ox-carts, which are almost a national emblem. The town is divided in two, Sarchí Norte and Sarchí Sur, separated by some 4 km. The green church (until they paint it again) in Sarchí is especially attractive at sunset. Travel agents in San José charge around US$75 for a day trip to Sarchí usually combined with a trip to Volcán Poás and a coffee finca.

The road continues north to **Naranjo**, a quiet agricultural town with an exquisite bright white church and a shocking post-modern pyramidal structure in the main square.

## Zarcero

Frequent bus services from San José/Alajuela pass through Zarcero, on the lip of the continental divide, en route to Ciudad Quesada (San Carlos). The town is famous for vegetable farming, dairy products and notable for the topiary creations of Evangelista Blanco Breves that fill the main plaza. Bushes are clipped, trimmed and shaped into arches leading up to the white church with twin towers, with shapes of animals, dancing couples, a helicopter, many designs of Henry Moore-like sculptures and a small grotto. The interior of the quaint church, overshadowed somewhat by the plaza, is made entirely of wood.

## Bajos del Toro and around

Encompassing a reasonably remote and loosely defined area on Highway 708, Bajos del Toro is enviably positioned between Poás volcano, Parque Nacional Castro Blanco and the Bosque de Paz biological reserve. With such stunning natural scenery in every direction, it's no surprise that a slew of upscale ecolodges have opened their doors here, but ideally you'll need your own vehicle to explore the area.

## San Ramón and around

West of Naranjo along the Pan-American Highway is the town of San Ramón, known locally as the City of Poets, with an attractive Parque Central and a street market on Saturday mornings. The **Museo de San Ramón** ① *opposite the park, Tue-Sat 1000-1800, T2447-7137, www.so.ucr.ac.cr, voluntary donation,* records the history and culture of the local community. There's good walking in the surrounding area. You can visit the coffee-processing plant (in season) at the **Cooperativa de Café** ① *US$15-39,* in San Ramón. The local fiesta is around the day of San Ramón, 30 August, when local saints are carried on litters to the town's church.

**Palmares**, 7 km southeast of San Ramón, has a pretty central park with lovely tall trees, where sloths are occasionally spotted. The quiet town comes alive in January for the annual Fiestas de Palmares, with food, carnival rides, concerts and parades.

## Atenas

After Palmares you can return to the Pan-American Highway and head to the coast, or go back to San José via Atenas. The church and main plaza in Atenas lie on an earthquake fault. The local speciality, *toronja rellena*, is a sweet-filled grapefruit. Atenas is reputed to have the best climate in the world, with stable temperatures of between 17 and 32°C year round.

## Los Angeles Cloud Forest Reserve

Heading north from San Ramón the road forks, left to Zarcero. The right fork heads north to La Tigra and La Fortuna, passing the Los Angeles Cloud Forest Reserve (20 km from San Ramón). The private 800-ha reserve (see **Hotel Villablanca**, Where to stay, below) offers hiking, guided tours, horse riding and canopy ascents.

## Where to stay

### Alajuela

Hotel prices in Alajuela are generally higher than those of San José, and an 'economical' room for 2 will set you back US$40-50. Business-class lodgings within walking distance of the airport include **Hampton Inn & Suites** and the **Holiday Inn Express**.

### $$$$ Xandari

*T2443-2020, www.xandari.com.*
Once an old coffee finca overlooking the Central Valley, this architectural treasure has 24 individually designed private villas nestled in its rambling estate. One of the best hotels in Costa Rica, complete with organic gardens, trails and waterfalls, and spa treatments. Sumptuous and sublime.

### $$$ Hotel 1915

*Calle 2, Av 5-7, 300 m north of Parque Central, T2440-7163, www.1915hotel.com.*
An old family home, smartly refurbished with stylish decor and tasteful rooms. There's also a pleasant terrace and garden patio for chilling out. One of the best in town.

### $$ Hotel Casa Tago

*Del Seguro Social Antiguo, 75 m al este, Av de Las Provincias, T2431-3121, www.hotelcasatago.com.*
A welcoming little hotel with simple but spacious rooms, some with windows, others without. Breakfast is included. No frills, friendly and family run. Recommended.

### $$ Hotel Pacandé

*T2443-8481, del Parque Central, 200 m al norte, 50 m oeste, www.hotelpacande.com.*
An excellent downtown option with a mix of economical quarters with shared bath and 'superior' suites for those seeking extra comfort. A fresh fruit breakfast is served every morning in a lovely patio-garden. Very helpful staff and friendly management. Recommended.

### $$-$ Cortez Azul

*Av 5, Calle 2-4, T2443-6145, www.hotelcortezazul.com.*
Funky backpacker joint with a range of dorms ($) and private rooms, with ($$) or without ($) private bath. The quality varies, so check before accepting. Sociable, bohemian vibe.

### $$-$ Maleku Hostel

*Del Hospital Nuevo, 50 m al oeste, T2430-4304, www.malekuhostel.com.*
Friendly, low-key, down-to-earth hostel with a mix of private rooms ($$) and dorms ($), all with shared bath. Clean and efficient, with good service and helpful staff. Near the bus station.

### Parque Nacional Volcán Poás

Camping in the park is not permitted but there are several places advertising cabins on the road up to Poás and nearby.

### $$$$-$$$ Poás Volcano Lodge

*West of Poasito, 500 m from Vara Blanca junction on road to Poasito, at El Cortijo farm, sign on gate, 1 km to house, T2482-2194, www.poasvolcanolodge.com.*
A superb luxury mountain lodge steeped in rolling pastures and expansive views of Poás, the mountains and the northern Caribbean plains. The estate is criss-crossed by hiking trails with some rooms opening onto the edge of the cloudforest. Recommended.

### $$$ Altura Hotel

*Access road on the left after the 3rd bridge past the gas station in Poasito, T2482-1124, www.alturahotelcr.com.*
An excellent small hotel located 5 mins from Poás volcano. Modern rooms are fully equipped with electric stoves, coffee-makers, fridges and cable TVs. Extras include great views of the Meseta, walking trails, and a roaring fireplace that's brought to life every evening. Breakfast included.

## Grecia

### $$ B&B Grecia
*150 m south of Parque Central, T2444-5326,*
*www.bandbgrecia.com.*
This centrally located, low-key B&B has
just 4 rooms, all light and breezy, simple,
comfortable and clean. There's a small back
garden with soft seats and hammocks for
chilling out. Helpful and knowledgeable.

## Sarchí and around

### $$ Cabinas Daniel Zamora
*Sarchí, T2454-4596.*
Basic rooms with bath, fan, hot water, very
clean and extra blankets if cold at night. Also
owns **Hotel Villa Sarchí**, 800 m west of town.

### $$ Hotel Paraíso Río Verde
*San Pedro de Sarchí, de la Iglesia Católica,*
*200 m al sur, T2454-3003,*
*www.hotelparaisorioverde.com.*
Pleasant little bungalows and a couple
of private rooms overlooking the rolling
countryside. Services include Wi-Fi, breakfast
and parking. You'll need your own vehicle
to get here.

## Zarcero

### $$-$ Don Beto
*By the church, T2463-3137,*
*www.hoteldonbeto.com.*
A friendly little guesthouse with a
whitewashed exterior. They have a handful
of simple, homely, peaceful rooms with
($$) or without ($) private bath. Amenities
include Wi-Fi, hot water, cable TV.

## Bajos del Toro

### $$$$ El Silencio
*T2231-6122, www.elsilenciolodge.com.*
A top-tier ecolodge nestled in the forested
hills. Lodging is in luxury suites and villas,
some equipped with outdoor whirlpools and
viewing decks. Amenities include an excellent
restaurant with a mirador, spa facilities and
yoga deck. Romantic and secluded.

### $$$$-$$$ Bosque de Paz
*T2234-6676, www.bosquedepaz.com.*
Highly recommended for birdwatchers and
nature photographers, Bosque de Paz is an
intimate and ethically managed ecolodge set
inside a 1000-ha private nature reserve. The
grounds extend into lush cloudforests and
boast their own hummingbird and butterfly
gardens. Rates are per person.

### $$ Catarata del Toro
*6 km north of the church, T2476-0800,*
*www.catarata-del-toro.com.*
A 100-ha private nature reserve and
biological corridor bordering both Juan
Castro Blanco and Poás national parks.
Activities include wildlife observation,
extreme hiking, rappelling and a
hummingbird photo shoot.

## San Ramón and around

### $$$ Casa Amanecer
*North of San Ramón, turn off before*
*Concepción, T2445-2100, www.casa-*
*amanecer-cr.com.*
Nestled amid rambling coffee plantations,
this tasteful teak and stone-built lodging
featured in *Su Casa* architecture magazine.
Along with 5 well-appointed rooms, it boasts
verdant gardens and fine views. Costa Rican-
style breakfast included.

### $$ La Posada
*400 m north of the cathedral, T2445-7359,*
*www.posadahotel.net.*
Locally owned and well-established, a
reliable mid-range option with 34 rooms in
typical Tico style. Amenities include Wi-Fi,
kitchen, garden, mini-gym, laundry, parking.

### $$-$ Hostel Sabana
*Del Hospital, 700 m al oeste, opposite*
*the transit police, T2445-8105, www.*
*hostelsabana.com.*
A friendly, family-run hostel with an ultra-
clean dorm ($) and guestrooms ($$). Very
friendly and helpful, the best budget option
in town. Recommended.

## Atenas

### $$$ Orchid Tree
*Calle Oratorio, T2446-0852,*
*www.orchidtreecostarica.com.*
An excellent, intimate B&B, conveniently
located in the village. The property boasts
a lush garden, popular with local birdlife, a
small pool, hammocks and restful enclaves. A
romantic option for couples. Recommended.

### $$$-$$ El Cafetal Inn
*Out of Atenas, in St Eulalia, 4.7 km towards*
*Grecia, T2446-5785, www.cafetal.com.*
A rural B&B with an appealing setting on
a rambling coffee plantation. They have
14 tranquil rooms and suites, bungalows,
a lush garden, fine views, and a large pool.
Airport transfer available. Recommended.

## Los Angeles Cloud Forest Reserve

### $$$$ Hotel Villablanca
*North of town set in the 800-ha Los*
*Angeles Cloud Forest Reserve, T2461-0300,*
*www.villablanca-costarica.com.*
Boutique mountain hotel and spa with
luxury *casitas* and suites, a sublime setting,
one of the best in Central America, very
romantic and popular with honeymooners.
Lots of outdoor activities and tours available.

## Restaurants

### Alajuela
Finding a casual meal in Alajuela is not
difficult, most restaurants, cafés and *sodas*
are within 1 or 2 blocks of the Parque Central
and down Calle Central.

### $$$-$$ El Chante Vegano
*25 m oeste de la Oficina de Correos, www.*
*elchantevegano.com. Tue-Sun 1100-2000.*
This fantastic vegan restaurant offers a
delicious array of healthy options that includes
portobello mushroom burgers, vegetable
pizza, quesadillas, vegan sushi, and fantastic
fresh fruit smoothies (try the watermelon and
mint). Casual outdoor seating, lovely owners
and attentive service. Recommended.

### $$$-$$ Jalapeños Central
*Calle 1, Av 3-5, T2430-4027, 50 m south of the*
*Post Office.*
A very popular family restaurant that's often
buzzing with locals and tourists alike. They
serve reliable Tex Mex, including hearty
burritos, enchiladas, quesadillas and nachos.
Fun and friendly.

### $$ La Sandwichería
*100 m north of the Iglesia Agonía.*
Interesting and creative sandwiches served
on tasty ciabatta bread with a side of home-
made vegetable crisps. There are also stuffed
pittas, wraps, and mainly Italian *platos fuertes*.
Take-away available.

### $$-$ Cevichitos
*Calle Central and Av 3, 100 m north of*
*Heladería Pops, Parque Central.*
A very casual little seafood eatery on the
corner with fast service and good-value
grub. The *ceviche de corvina*, breaded fish
fillet, and *licuado de guanábana* (milkshake);
are all delicious. Recommended.

## Cafés

### Coffee Dreams
*Calle 1 and Av 3.*
The coffee and desserts are very good, but
the food is average. Good for a quick stop or
a morning buzz.

### Zarcero
The town is known for cheese and fruit
preserves.

### $ Soda/Restaurant El Jardín
*1st floor, overlooking the plaza.*
Local lunches and breakfasts.
Good view of topiary.

### San Ramón

### $$$ Musashi
*Opposite the Banco de Costa Rica.*
Something different: good, fresh, authentic
sushi in San Ramón. Sake and Japanese beers
too. Pleasant interior, good for a romantic meal.

### $$-$ Mi Choza
*Opposite the cemetery.*
Also known as **Los Negritos**, they serve hearty *bocas* on cooking boards, including tacos, whole fish and omelettes. A fun place for groups. Simple and unpretentious.

## Festivals

### Alajuela
**11 Apr** **Juan Santamaría Day**, a week of bands, concerts and dancing in celebration of the life of the town's most famous son. **Mid-Jul** The fruitful heritage comes to the fore with a **Mango Festival** of parades, concerts and an arts and crafts fair.

## Shopping

### Alajuela
**Goodlight Books**, *Calle 1-3, T2430-4083.* Quality used books, mostly English, as well as espresso and pastries. Internet available.

### Sarchí and around
One of the largest *artesanías* is **Fábrica de Chaverri** in Sarchí Sur. **Taller Lalo Alfaro**, the oldest workshop, is in Sarchí Norte and worth a visit to see more traditional production methods. Both sell handmade furniture, cowhide rocking chairs and wooden products as well as ox-carts, which come in all sizes.

## Transport

### Alajuela
**Bus** Service to **San José**. Depart Alajuela from main bus terminal Calle 8, Av Central-1, or Av 4, Calle 2-4 every 10 mins, 30 mins, US$0.90, with both services arriving on Av 2 in the capital. To **Heredia** from 0400 until 2200, 30 mins, US$0.70. 1 block south of the terminal buses depart for several small villages in the area including **Laguna de Fraijanes** and **Volcán Poás**.

### Parque Nacional Volcán Poás
The volcano can be reached by car from **San José**. A taxi for 6 hrs with a side trip will cost about US$50-60. There is a daily excursion bus from the main square of Alajuela right up to the crater, leaving at 0915 (or before if full), connecting with 0830 bus from San José (from Av 2, Calle 12-14); be there early for a seat, although extra buses run if necessary; the area gets very crowded, US$4 return. The bus waits at the top with time to see everything (clouds permitting), returning 1430. For **Poasito** organize a taxi, hitch or take the 0600 or 1600 bus from Alajuela to **San Pedro de Poás**, hitch/ taxi to Poasito and stay overnight, hiking or hitching up the mountain next morning.

### Sarchí and around
Express bus from **San José** to Sarchí, Calle 16, Av 1-3, 1215, 1730 and 1755, Mon-Fri, returning 0530, 0615, 1345, Sat 1200, 1½ hrs, US$1.80. **Tuan**, T2441-3781, buses every 30 mins, 0500-2200 from Alajuela bus station, 1½ hrs, US$1.30.
 **Transportes Naranjo**, T2451-3655, run buses to/from **San José**'s Coca Cola terminal every 40 mins, US$1.25. Buses connect other towns and villages in the area.

### San Ramón and Los Angeles Cloud Forest Reserve
San Ramón is a transport hub. A regular service from **San José Empresarios Unidos**, T2222-0064, at Calle 16, Av 10-12, go to **Puntarenas**, 10 a day, every 45 mins or so, US$2.30. There is also a regular service to **La Fortuna** and **Alajuela**. Buses run to surrounding villages and towns.

### Atenas
The library on the plaza in Atenas also serves as the bus office, **Cooptransatenas**, T2446-5767. Many daily buses to **San José**, either direct or via **Alajuela**, US$1.40.

Some 10 km north of San José, Heredia is capital of the province of the same name and an important coffee centre. It is away from the pollution of San José but close to the capital and the airport, and with good public transport. The central area is laid out in a grid, relatively compact and easily explored on foot.

## Sights

The town is mostly new with only the main square maintaining a colonial atmosphere in its architecture. The short squat **Basílica de la Inmaculada Concepción**, built in 1797, has survived countless earthquakes. To the north of the central plaza, with a statue to the poet Aquileo Echeverría (1866-1909), is the solitary defensive structure of **El Fortín**. Across the street the **Casa de la Cultura** is a fine colonial home that now hosts concerts and exhibitions. The School of Marine Biology at the Universidad Nacional campus has a **Museo Zoológico Marino**.

## Britt's Coffee Farm

*US$22, tours 1100, 1½ hrs, includes lunch and show, T2277-1500, www.coffeetour.com.*

One of the region's largest coffee *beneficios* is Café Britt's coffee farm, near Barva de Heredia, where you can see the processing factory, tasting room and a multimedia presentation of the story of coffee. You can be picked up from Heredia or at various points in San José. The **Teatro Dionisio Chaverría** at Café Britt hosts weekend theatre and a children's show on Sunday afternoons.

## Barva and around

North of Heredia is the historic town of Barva, on the slopes of Volcán Barva; there are frequent buses to/from Heredia. At Barva, the **Huetar Gallery** is recommended for arts, crafts and delicious food. There is also a **Museo de Cultura Popular** ① *Mon-Fri 0900-1600, US$3*, 500 m east of the Salón Comunal de Santa Lucía de Barva. North of Heredia through San Rafael, above Los Angeles, is **Galería Octágono** ① *T2267-6325 www.galeriaoctagono. com*, an arts gallery with textiles handmade by a women's community cooperative, and also a B&B (see Where to stay, below). Beyond Barva, to the west, is **Santa Bárbara**, where you can find good seafood at the **Banco de los Mariscos** (T2269-9090), 500 m west from the central plaza. Five kilometres west of Heredia is **San Joaquín de Flores**, a small rural town with views of Barva and Poás volcanoes.

## INBio Parque

*South of Heredia on the road to Santo Domingo, T2507-8107, www.inbio.ac.cr, Fri 0800-1700, Sat-Sun 0900-1730, US$44.*

INBio Parque is an educational and recreational centre that explains and gives insight into Costa Rica's biological diversity. In a small area you can visit the ecosystems of central highland forest, dry forest and humid forest, with trails set out for bromelias and *guarumo*.

## Volcán Barva

**Parque Nacional Braulio Carrillo** ① *park entry US$15, no permit needed (see page 832)*, to the north of Heredia, includes Volcán Barva, at 2906 m. This section of the park is ideal for hiking with a good trail leading up to the summit with three lagoons nearby, and excellent views and wildlife encounters for the few that make the effort. The really enthusiastic can hike all the way down to the lowlands arriving close to La Selva Biological Station near Puerto Viejo de Sarapaqui, but careful planning is required. There is a ranger station and campsite near the entrance, 4 km north of Sacramento, from where it's a 3-km easy climb to the top – still a treasure and, amazingly, a well-kept secret from the hordes.

## Aserrí to San Pable de Turrubares

Some 10 km south of San José is Aserrí, a village with a beautiful white church. On Friday and Saturday evenings, street bands begin the fiesta with music from 2000, followed by marimbas. Extremely popular among locals, the dancing is fabulous, with *chicharrones*, tortillas and plenty of other things to eat and drink. Further along the same road is **Mirador Ram Luna**, a restaurant with a fine panoramic view. At the end of the road is **San Ignacio de Acosta**, again with a good church containing life-size Nativity figures. Buses go there from San José (Calle 8, Avenida 12-14 in front of the Baptist church) via Aserrí hourly from 0500 to 2230, return 0430 to 2100, one hour. The unpaved road continues to **Santiago de Puriscal**, which was the epicentre for many earthquakes in 1990. Although the church is now closed as a result, there are excellent views from the town and the road. From here it is possible to take a dirt road to the Pacific coast, joining the coastal road near Parrita (see page 806). Alternatively, take the road to **San Pablo de Turrubares**, from where you can either head west for Orotina, via an unpaved road through San Pedro and San Juan de Mata, or for Atenas (see page 742) via Quebradas, then east to Escobal, next stop on railway, then 4WD necessary to Atenas.

## Listings Heredia and around

### Where to stay

#### Heredia

**$$$ Valladolid**
*Calle 7, Av 7, T2260-2905,*
*www.hotelvalladolid.net.*
A smart and long-standing business hotel with 11 spacious rooms and suites, all with a/c, private bath, telephone and cable TV. 5th floor has sauna, jacuzzi and **Bonavista Bar** with fine views overlooking the Central Valley.

**$$$-$$ Hotel and Boutique Hojarascas**
*Av 8, Calle 4-6, opposite Mas x Menos car park, T2261-3649, www.hotelhojarascas.com.*
A very professional, comfortable, family-run hotel with good service and attention to detail. Rooms are tasteful, restful and immaculately clean, with solid wooden furniture, fast Wi-Fi, hot water, cable TV. Breakfast included, but cheaper without. Recommended.

**$$ Apartotel Vargas**
*800 m north of Colegio Santa Cecilia and San Francisco Church, T2237-8526, www.apartotelvargas.com.*
9 large, well-furnished apartments with cooking facilities, hot water, laundry facilities, TV, internet. Sr Vargas will collect you from the airport. Excellent choice if taking language classes and in a group. Best option in town.

**$ Las Flores**
*Av 12, Calle 12-14, T2261-8147.*
Quiet, low-key, family-run guesthouse with cheap, clean rooms with private bath. Friendly and helpful. Recommended.

#### Barva and around

**$$$$ Finca Rosa Blanca**
*1.6 km from Santa Bárbara de Heredia, T2269-9392, www.fincarosablanca.com.*
Deluxe suites in an architectural explosion of style and eloquence. Romance and exclusivity at the extremes of imagination.

Spa facilities for comfort. Quality restaurant and bar.

## $$$$-$$$ Bougainvillea de Santo Domingo
*just west of Santo Domingo, T2244-1414, www.hb.co.cr.*
An award-winning mountain lodge with a commitment to sustainability and acres of dazzling landscaped tropical gardens. Excellent service, pool, sauna, spectacular setting, free shuttle bus to San José. Highly recommended.

## $$$ Galería Octágono
*T2267-6325, www.galeriaoctagono.com.*
An arts gallery and B&B; other meals and transport available at additional cost, wonderful cypress cabin, hikes, and friendly and informative owners.

## $$$ Hotel Chalet Tirol
*3 km north of Castillo Country Club, T2267-6222, www.hotelchaleteltirol.com.*
Colourful Alpine-style chalets and well-appointed suites set in flowery gardens and pine trees. This intriguing lodge is also home to a very reputable restaurant serving French fusion and international gourmet.

## Restaurants

### Heredia
There are lots of cheap *sodas* and food stalls inside the market, Calle 4 and Av 8, where you can pick up a carb-rich breakfast or set lunch ($$-$). On the eastern outskirts of town, Calle 9 is a small 'Zona Rosa' with several fun restaurants and a few bars.

## $$$ Baalbek Bar & Grill
*San Rafael de Heredia on the road to Monte de la Cruz, T2267-6482, www.baalbekbaryrestaurante.com.*
A well-established Lebanese restaurant recommended chiefly for its romantic views of the Central Valley. A good place for a date. Belly dancing on Fri, live music on Sat.

## $$$-$$ L'Antica Roma
*Calle 7 and Av 7.*
The best Italian restaurant in town, serving good wood-fired pizzas, various pastas, and cold beer. Seating indoors or out. Recommended.

## $$-$ Las Espigas
*Corner of Parque Central.*
A convenient central location. Drop in for a cheap set lunch, coffee or pastries. There's also a fruit smoothie stand by the main door offering takeaway.

## What to do

### Language schools
**Centro Panamericano de Idiomas**, *San Joaquín de Flores, T2265-6306, www.cpi-edu. com.* Accommodation with local families.
**Intercultura Language and Cultural Center**, *T2260-8480, www. interculturacostarica.com.* Intensive Spanish courses with excursions to beaches, volcanoes, rainforest and a volunteer programme. Also with a campus at Playa Samara.

## Transport

### Heredia
Buses from **San José**, from Av 2, Calle 12-14, every 10 mins daily, 0500-0015, then every 30 mins to 0400, 25-min journey, US$0.70. Return buses from Av 6, Calle 2-1.
  Local buses leave from Av 8, Calle 2-4, by the market.

### Volcán Barva
Accessible from **Heredia**, there is no route from the San José–Limón Highway. Buses leave from the market at 0630, 1230 and 1600, returning at 0730, 1300, 1700. Arriving at **Porrosati** (a town en route to Volcán Barva). Some continue as far as Sacramento, otherwise walk 6 km to park entrance, then 4 km to lagoon. Be careful if leaving a car; there are regular reports of theft from rental cars.

**earthquake-damaged town with a famous basilica**

Encircled by mountains, Cartago (altitude 1439 m) is at the foot of the Irazú Volcano and 22.5 km from San José on a toll road (US$0.75). Founded in 1563, it was the capital of Costa Rica for almost 300 years until San José assumed the role in 1823. Since then the town has failed to grow significantly and remains small, though densely populated. Earthquakes in 1841 and 1910 destroyed many of the buildings and ash from Irazú engulfed the town in 1963. While colonial-style remnants exist in one or two buildings, the town feels as if it is still reeling from the impact of so much natural devastation and is keeping quiet, waiting for the next event.

## Sights

The most important attraction in town, and the focal point for pilgrims from all over Central America, is the **Basílica de Nuestra Señora de Los Angeles**, the patroness of Costa Rica, on the eastern side of town. Rebuilt in 1926 in Byzantine style, it houses the diminutive **La Negrita**, an indigenous image of the Virgin under 15 cm high, worshipped for her miraculous healing powers. The basilica also houses a collection of finely made *milagros* (miracles) – silver and gold charms, no larger than 3 cm high, of various parts of the human anatomy, offered in the hope of being healed. The most important date in the pilgrims' calendar is 2 August, when the image of La Negrita is carried in procession to churches in Cártago with celebrations throughout Costa Rica.

Also worth seeing is **La Parroquia** (the old parish church), roughly 1 km west of the basilica, ruined by the 1910 earthquake and now converted into a delightful garden retreat with flowers, fish and hummingbirds.

## Around Cartago

**Aguas Calientes**, 4 km southeast of Cartago and 90 m lower, has a warm-water *balneario* ideal for picnics. On the road to Paraíso, 8 km from Cartago, is an orchid garden, the **Jardín Botánico Lankester** ⓘ *10 mins' walk from the main road, T2552-3247, daily 0830-1630, US$7.50*, run by the University of Costa Rica. The best displays are between February and April. The Cartago–Paraíso bus departs every 30 minutes from the south side of central park in Cartago (15 minutes); ask the driver to drop you off at Campo Ayala. Taxi from Cartago, US$5.

## Volcán Irazú

*US$15, 0800-1530 most of the year.*

The crater at the top of Irazú (altitude 3432 m) is an impressive half-mile cube dug out of the earth, surrounded by desolate grey sand, which looks like the surface of the moon. President Kennedy's visit in 1963 coincided with a major eruption and, in 1994 the north wall of the volcano was destroyed by another eruption that sent detritus down as far as the Río Sucio. The views of the valley are stupendous on a clear day, but the clouds normally move in, enveloping the lower peaks and slopes by 1300 (sometimes even by 0900 or 1000 between July and November); so get there as early. There's little wildlife other than the ubiquitous Volcano Junco bird and the few plants which survive in the barren landscape.

## Orosí Valley

Further east from Cartago a trip round the Orosí Valley makes a beautiful circular trip, or a fine place to hang out for a while in a valley that is often overlooked as the crowds rush to the more popular spots on the coast. The centrepiece of the valley is the artificial Lake Cachí used for hydroelectric generation. Heading round the lake anti-clockwise, the road passes through Orosí, clips the edge of Parque Nacional Tapantí, continuing to the Cachí Dam and completes the circuit passing through Ujarrás. Along the way there are several miradors which offer excellent views of the Reventazón Valley. For transport, see each destination. Day trips can be easily arranged from San José.

In **Orosí** there is an 18th-century **mission**① *Tue-Sun, closed Mon*, with colonial treasures, and just outside the town are two **balnearios** ① *US$2.50*, with restaurants serving tasty meals at fair prices. It's a good place to hang out, take some low-key language classes, mixed with mountain biking and trips to the national park and other sites of interest.

## Parque Nacional Tapantí-Macizo de la Muerte
*Daily 0700-1700, US$10.*

Some 12 km beyond Orosí is the Parque Nacional Tapantí-Macizo de la Muerte, one of the wettest parts of the country (some parts reportedly receiving as much as 8 m of rain a year). From June to November/December it rains every afternoon. Approached from Orosí, and just 30 km from Cartago, the national park is surprisingly easy to reach and packs in the interest.

Covering 58,000 ha, Tapantí-Macizo includes the former Tapantí National Park and much of the Río Macho Forest Reserve. The park protects the Río Orosí basin which feeds the Cachí Dam hydro power plant. Strategically, the southern boundary of the park joins with Chirripó National Park, extending the continuous protected area that makes up La Amistad Biosphere Reserve. The park incorporates a wide range of life zones with altitudes rising from 1220 m to over 3000 m at the border with Chirripó. The diverse altitudes and relative seclusion of the park has given rise to an impressive variety of species including 260 bird species and 45 mammals. There are picnic areas, a nature centre with slide shows (ask to see them) and good swimming in the dry season (November-June), and trout fishing season (1 April-31 October).

## Cachí

Continue around the lake to Cachí and the nearby **Casa del Soñador** (Dreamer's House), which sells wood carvings from the sculpture school of the late Macedonio Quesada. The road crosses the dam wall and follows the north shore to Ujarrás, then back to Cartago. The **Charrarra tourist complex**, 30 minutes' walk from Ujarrás, has a good campsite, restaurant, pool, boat rides on the lake and walks. It can be reached by direct bus on Sunday. Buses leave from Cartago, one block north of the Cartago ruins.

## Ujarrás

Ujarrás (ruins of a colonial church and village) is 6.5 km east of Paraíso, on the shores of the artificial Lago Cachí. There is a bus every 1½ hours from Paraíso that continues to Cachí. Legend has it that in 1666 English pirates, including the youthful Henry Morgan, were seen off by the citizens of Ujarrás aided by the Virgin. The event is now celebrated annually in mid-March when the saint is carried in procession from Paraíso to the ruined church.

## Tourist information

### Cartago

**Mercatur**, *next to Fuji at Av 2, Calle 4-6.*
Provides local tourist information.

## Where to stay

### Cartago

**$ Dinastia**
*Calle 3, Av 6-8, close to the old railway station, at the Las Ruinas end of town, T2551-7057.*
Slightly more expensive with private bath.
The rooms are small although better with a window.

**$ Los Angeles Lodge B&B**
*Near the Basílica at Av 4, Calle 14-16, T2591-4169.*
Clean, nice rooms, restaurant.

### Around Cartago

**$$$ Sanchirí Mirador and Lodge**
*2 km south of Parque Paraíso, Orosi road, T2574-5454, www.sanchiri.com.*
Commanding views at this highland lodge where guests can rest up in pleasant wooden *cabañas* or modern rooms with balconies. A certified sustainable business with organically farmed produce and environmentally friendly technology.

### Volcán Irazú

**$$$ Grandpa's Hotel**
*7 km north of Cartago on the Irazú road, 500 m west of 'El Cristo' in the village of Cot, T2536-6666, www.grandpashotel.com.*
A cosy Victorian house with fine views and a well-tended flower-filled garden. Lodging includes a range of pleasant rooms, suites, rustic log cabins and an apartment.

### Orosí Valley

**$$$ Chalet Orosí**
*1.5 km south of Orosí, turn west off the highway at Planta Santa María, T2533-3268, www.chaletorosi.com.*
A French-run guesthouse near Tapantí National Park, close to a river and nestled amid coffee plantations and forests. Accommodation is in a range of well-appointed wooden chalets with amenities including solar-heated spa, barbecue and Wi-Fi.

**$$ Orosí Lodge**
*T2533-3578, www.orosilodge.com.*
6 rooms and a house with balcony overlooking the valley towards Volcán Irazú. Just about everything you could want: divine home-baked cookies, mountain bikes, kayaks and horses for rent, and internet service. Credit cards accepted. Excellent value.

**$ Montaña Linda**
*T2533-3640, www.montanalinda.com.*
A classic and well-run backpackers' place, with a range of options. Dormitory rooms, camping, and B&B service if you just can't get out of bed. There is also a language school, with package deals for lodgers. Great spot with a very friendly, knowledgeable team.

### Parque Nacional Tapantí-Macizo de la Muerte

**$$ Kiri Lodge**
*1.5 km from the park entrance, T2533-2272, www.kirilodge.net.*
Excellent lodging and food, breakfast included. Peaceful, trout fishing, very friendly, good trails on 50-ha property.

## Restaurants

### Volcán Irazú

**$$-$ Restaurante Linda Vista**
Spectacular views, as you'd expect from
Costa Rica's highest restaurant, serving good
food and drinks. But most people stop to
post, stick, pin or glue a business card, or
some other personal item, to the wall.

## What to do

### Orosí Valley
**Language schools**
**Montaña Linda Language School**, *T2533-
3640, see Where to stay, above*. Uses local
teachers with a homestay option if you
want total submersion. Recommended.

## Transport

### Cartago
**Bus** To **San José** every 10 mins from Av 4,
Calle 2-4. Arrives and departs San José from
Calle 5, Av 18-20 for the 45-min journey,
US$0.90. After 2030 buses leave from Gran
Hotel Costa Rica, Av 2, Calle 3-5. **Orosí/Río
Macho**, for **Parque Nacional Tapantí** every
30 mins from Calle 6, Av 1-3, 35-55 mins,
US$0.95. **Turrialba**, every hour from Av 3,
Calle 8-10, 1 hr direct, US$1.40, 1 hr 20 mins
colectivo. **Cachí**, via **Ujarrá** and **Paraíso** from
Calle 6, Av 1-3, every 1½ hrs, 1 hr 20 mins.
**Paraíso**, every 5 mins from Av 5, Calle 4-6.
**Aguacalientes**, every 15 mins from Calle
1, Av 3-5. **Tierra Blancas** for **Irazú**, every
30 mins from Calle 4, Av 6-8, US$2.

Closest bus for **Irazú** rides to San Juan de
Chichua, still some 12 km from the summit.
The bus leaves Cartago from north of the
central market, Av 6, Calle 1-3, at 1730,
returning at 0500 the next day, so you have
to spend at least 2 nights on the volcano
or in a hotel if you can't get a ride. To visit
**Volcán Turrialba** take a bus from Calle 4 y
Av 6 to the village of San Gerardo.

### Volcán Irazú
**Bus** It is possible to get a bus from Cartago
to Tierra Blanca (US$0.33) or San Juan de
Chicúa (which has 1 hotel) and hitch a ride in
a pickup truck. Or you can take a Cartago–
Sanatorio bus. Ask the driver to drop you at
the crossroads outside Tierra Blanca. From
there you walk 16 km to the summit. If you're
looking for a day trip from San José, a yellow
'school' express bus (**Buses Metropoli SA**,
T2530-1064), runs from Gran Hotel Costa
Rica, **San José**, daily 0800. It stops at Cartago
ruins 0830 to pick up more passengers,
returns 1230 with lunch stop at **Restaurant
Linda Vista**, US$3.90.

**Taxi** From **Cartago** is US$32 return. A taxi
tour from **Orosí** costs US$10 per person,
minimum 3 people, and stops at various
places on the return journey, eg Cachí dam
and Ujarrás ruins. Since it can be difficult
to find a decent hotel in Cartago, it may be
easier to take a guided tour leaving from **San
José**, about US$44, 5½ hrs includes lunch,
transport from San José. If driving from San
José, take the turn-off at the Ferretería San
Nicolás in Taras, which goes directly to Irazú,
avoiding Cartago.

### Orosí Valley
**Bus** From **Cartago** to Orosí/Río Macho from
Calle 6, Av 1-3, every 30 mins, journey time of
35-55 mins, US$0.90.

### Parque Nacional Tapantí-Macizo de la Muerte
**Bus** The 0600 bus from Cartago to Orosí gets
to Puricil by 0700, then walk (5 km), or take
any other Cartago–Orosí bus to Río Macho
and walk 9 km to the refuge. Alternatively
take a taxi from **Orosí** (US$7 round trip, up
to 6 passengers), or **San José**, US$50.

ecologically diverse zone with many fine coffee farms and whitewater rafting

Turrialba (altitude 646 m, 62 km from San José) connects the Central Valley highlands and Caribbean lowlands, and was once a stopping point on the old Atlantic railway between Cartago and Puerto Limón. The railway ran down to Limón on a narrow ledge poised between mountains on the left, and the river to the right, but no longer operates.

## Sights

The **Centro Agronómico Tropical de Investigación y Enseñanza (CATIE)** ① *about 4 km southeast of Turrialba, T2558-2000 ext 2275, www.catie.ac.cr, botanical garden open daily 0700-1600, T2556-2700, US$6,* covers more than 800 ha. It has one of the largest tropical fruit collections in the world and houses an important library on tropical agriculture; visitors and students are welcome for research or birdwatching. Past CATIE on the south side of the river, a large sugar mill makes for a conspicuous landmark in Atirro, the centre for macadamia nuts. Nearby, the 256-ha **Lake Angostura** has now flooded some of the whitewaters of the Río Reventazón.

## Around Turrialba

Many whitewater rafting companies operate out of Turrialba, with trips to the **Río Reventazón and Río Pacuare**. The rafting is excellent; the Pascua section of the Reventazón can be Grade V at rainy times. The Pacuare is absolutely perfect with divine scenery. By contacting the guides in Turrialba you can save about 30% on a trip booked in San José, provided they are not already contracted.

**Volcán Turrialba** (3329 m) may be visited from Cartago by a bus from Calle 4 y Avenida 6 to the village of San Gerardo. From Turrialba take a bus to Santa Cruz. From both, an unpaved road meets at **Finca La Central**, on the saddle between Irazú and Turrialba.

## Monumento Nacional Guayabo
*T2559-1220, Tue-Sun 0800-1530, US$10, local guides available, water, toilets, no food.*

About 19 km north of Turrialba, near Guayabo, is a 3000-year-old ceremonial centre excavated with paved streets and stone-lined water channels. The archaeological site, 232 ha and 4 km from the town of Guayabo, dates from the period 1000 BC-AD 1400. There are excellent walks in the park, where plenty of birds and wildlife can be seen. Worth a trip to see Costa Rica's most developed ancient archaeological site but small in comparison to the great sites of the Maya.

## Listings Turrialba and around

### Where to stay

#### Turrialba

**$$$ Wagelia**
*Av 4, entrance to Turrialba, T2556-1566, www.hotelwageliaturrialba.com.*
Comfortable lodging with 18 rooms, bath, some a/c, restaurant. Overpriced, but not much else to choose from at this level.

**$$-$ Hostel Casa de Lis**
*Av Central, south of Bancrédito, next to ICE, T2556-4933, www.hostelcasadelis.com.*
An excellent 'boutique' hostel offering comfort, style and service a cut above the rest. Accommodation options include economical dorms ($) and private rooms ($$), all kitted with orthopaedic mattresses and hot water. Recommended.

### $$-$ Interamericano
*Facing the old railway station on Av 1, T2556-0142, www.hotelinteramericano.com.*
A basic but friendly place, family-run, home to a few dogs, popular with kayakers. Clean, private ($$) or shared bath ($). Safe for motorbikes. Communal area with TV and books.

## Around Turrialba

### $$$$ Casa Turire
*14 km southeast of Turrialba, follow the signposts, T2531-1111, www.hotelcasaturire.com.*
Overlooking Lake Angostura, 12 luxury rooms with bath, 4 suites, cable TV, phone, restaurant, pool, library, games room, in the middle of a 1620-ha sugar, coffee and macadamia nut plantation. Virgin rainforest nearby, trails, horses, bike rental, excursions.

### $$$$ Pacuare Lodge
*On the banks of the Pacuare river, T7016-3147, www.pacuareriverlodge.com.*
An intriguing jungle lodge with a very solid reputation, popular with adventurers and honeymooners alike. Accommodation is in range of wooden cabins and luxury suites, all perched on a hillside overlooking the river. No drop-ins or independent visits, package stays only. Rafters can access the lodge as part of a whitewater trip.

### $$$$ Rancho Naturalista
*1.5 km south of Tuis, turn-off signed, T2100-1855, www.ranchonaturalista.net.*
A premier birdwatching lodge surrounded by forests, family-run with 14 good rooms and a range of *casitas*. The main building has an observation balcony where 250 species have been recorded. Rates per person, guides cost extra.

### $$$-$$ Turrialtico
*On road to Siquirres, T2538-1111, www.turrialtico.com.*
On top of hill with extensive views. Rooms are clean with private bath, comfortable, friendly. Going northeast from Turrialba, the main road follows the Río Reventazón down to Siquirres (see page 834).

## Monumento Nacional Guayabo

### $$$ Hotel Guayabo Lodge
*300 m south of Santa Cruz cemetery, T2538-8492, www.guayabolodge.co.cr.*
An airy mountain lodge with expansive views of the surrounding valleys and volcanic cones. They offer 22 standard rooms and 4 suites. Cooking classes, various tours and packages available.

## What to do

### Around Turrialba
See also the companies in San José (eg **Ríos Tropicales**, page 735).
**Serendipity Adventures**, *T2558-1000, www.serendipityadventures.com.* Canyoning, rappelling and hot-air ballooning. Recommended.
**Tico's River Adventures**, *T2556-1231, www.ticoriver.com.* With recommended local guides.

## Transport

### Turrialba
**Bus** From **San José** every hour 0530-2200 from Terminal Turrialba, Calle 13, Av 6-8, 1½ hrs, US$2.40 from **Cartago**, 1 hr, US$1.40, runs until about 2200. Service to **Siquirres**, for connections to Caribbean lowlands, hourly, 40 mins, US$2.

### Monumento Nacional Guayabo
**Bus** From **Turrialba**, there are buses at 1100 (returning 1250) and 1710 (returning 1750), and on Sun at 0900, return 1700 (check times, if you miss it is quite difficult to hitch as there is little traffic), US$0.95 to Guayabo. Several daily buses pass the turn-off to Guayabo; the town is a 2-hr walk uphill (taxi US$10, easy to hitch back). **San José** tour operators offer day trips to Guayabo for about US$65 per person (minimum 4 people), cheaper from Turrialba.

# Northern
## Costa Rica

North of the Meseta Central, the land descends to languid tropical plains as far as the Nicaraguan border, a sweltering sprawl of fruit farms and cattle ranches framed by the teeming wetlands of the Caño Negro nature reserve in the north and two rugged mountain chains in the west: the Cordillera Tilarán and the Cordillera Guanacaste. At the heart of the region lies the iconic peak of Arenal volcano, rising above the waters of Costa Rica's largest lake. It continues to draw adventurers and eco-tourists despite falling dormant in 2011, its environs peppered with scores of protected areas, hiking trails, zip-lines, butterfly reserves and eternally soothing hot springs.

West of Arenal, the land climbs skyward to craggy peaks and gorges, a rolling patchwork of innumerable shades of green. Tempered by shifting veils of mist and sunshine, the region's remote rural villages are steeped in flowery meadows and cloaks of pine. Here, the primeval cloudforests of Monteverde are the principal draw, clothed in thick green mosses, lichens and fiery bromeliads.

In the far northwest, the land descends to Guanacaste, Costa Rica's macho Sabanero heartland. Dominated by rambling haciendas and wide open pastures, it could easily be the backdrop to a Hollywood Western.

**Best** for
Adventure tours ▪ Ecotourism ▪ Volcanoes ▪ Wildlife

**unpretentious town, an important transport and service regional hub**

Also known as San Carlos, Ciudad Quesada is the regional capital of Costa Rica's slow-paced northern lowlands, an area historically grounded in farming and ranching. True to form, it has a frontier feel with an air of bravado and a pinch of indifference. The huge church overlooking the main plaza stands out as the sole point of interest in Quesada, but its bus terminal, 1 km north of town, is seen by many travellers on their way to La Fortuna or Los Chiles.

### Los Chiles

Heading north from Quesada, Highway 35 steers through rich red laterite soils in an almost straight line for 74 km, passing fragrant orange and citrus groves until finally arriving at the languid river port of Los Chiles. The days are hot and sluggish in this remote fishing outpost sprawled indolent on the banks of the Río Frío. There are two main reasons for visiting: one is to take a public boat onwards to the Río San Juan and the Nicaraguan border (see Nicaragua–Costa Rica border box in the Practicalities chapter); the other is to commission a private vessel to explore the humid wetlands of the Refugio Natural de Vida Silvestre Caño Negro.

### Refugio Natural de Vida Silvestre Caño Negro

*Caño Negro park administration, T2471-1309, for information and reservations for food and lodging; US$15 entrance to the park. The entrance to the park is via the village of Caño Negro on the road between Upala and Los Chiles.*

Shrouded in dense tropical vegetation, the 10,171-ha Refugio Natural de Vida Silvestre Caño Negro encompasses a variety of watery habitats, including the 800-ha Caño Lake, which swells to life in the wet season. However, the drier months of January to March signal annual bird migrations and are the best time for observing the park's 365 avian species. You can join an organized expedition from La Fortuna (see page 759), but it is cheaper to commission a guide from the dock in Los Chiles. A three- to four-hour tour costs US$60-100 per group, depending on the size of the vessel, its engine, and the quantity of gasoline burned; Esteban, Oscar Rojas (T2471-1090) and Enrique have all been recommended. Fishing in the park is better than good with easily snagged giant snook and 2-m tarpon. Fully equipped sports fishing expeditions can be organized with professional tour operators in La Fortuna, starting at around US$100 per person for half a day.

## Listings Ciudad Quesada (San Carlos) and around

### Where to stay

#### Ciudad Quesada (San Carlos)

**$$$ Hotel La Garza**
*Platanar de San Carlos, 8 km from Florencia, north of Ciudad Quesada, T2475-5222, www.hotellagarza.com.*
12 charming bungalows with bath and fan, overlooking river. Idyllic spot with good views of Arenal, a 20-min drive from La Fortuna. Guided tours, boat trips, fishing, 230 ha of forest and cattle ranch.

**$$$ Tilajari Resort Hotel**
*Muelle San Carlos, 13 km north of Platanar de San Carlos, T2462-1212, www.tilajari.com.*
Resort-style lodge on the edge of the river. Luxury rooms and suites, a/c, private bath,

tennis courts, 2 pools, sauna, bar, restaurant, horses and excursions available. Popular with groups.

## $$ La Central
*On west side of park, Ciudad Quesada, T2460-0301, www.hotellacentral.net.*
As the name suggests, a central option. Private bath, hot water, fan, TV and phone in room.

## Los Chiles

### $$ Hotel Wilson Tulipán
*1 block west of the Parque Central opposite the immigration offices, T2471-1414, www.hoteleswilson.com.*
10 clean well-appointed rooms with a/c, TV, bath and hot water, breakfast and taxes included. Can arrange a wide variety of tours in the area including river safaris and fishing trips. Restaurant-bar.

### $ Hotel Carolina
*Close to main highway, T2471-1151.*
Clean and well maintained – the best of the budgets. Accommodation ranges from small, fairly dark rooms with shared bath to a/c cabins with TV.

## Restaurants

### Ciudad Quesada (San Carlos)
Variety of *sodas* in the central market offer *casados*, check out the great sword collection displayed at **La Ponderosa**.

### $$$ Coca Loca Steak House
*Next to Hotel La Central, T2460-3208.*
Complete with Wild West swing door.

### $$ Los Geranios
*Av 4 and Calle.*
Popular bar and restaurant serving up good *bocas* and other dishes.

### $$ Restaurant Crystal
*On the western side of the plaza.*
Sells fast food, snacks, ice cream and good fruit dishes.

## Transport

### Ciudad Quesada (San Carlos)
**Bus** To **La Fortuna**, 12 daily, 1½ hrs, US$1.50; to **Los Chiles**, hourly, 3 hrs, US$4.30; to **San José**, hourly, 0500-1930, 2½ hrs, US$3.60; to **Tilarán** via La Fortuna and Arenal, 0630, 1400, US$4. Regular buses also travel northeast to towns on the Río San Carlos and Río Sarapiquí, including **Puerto Viejo de Sarapiquí**, 5 daily, 3 hrs and east to the **Río Frío** district.

### Los Chiles
**Bus** To **San José**, 2 daily, 0500, 1500, 5 hrs, US$4.20. Alternatively, travel to **Ciudad Quesada** and take one of the more frequent services. To get to Los Chiles from **La Fortuna**, take the bus towards Ciudad Quesada, get off at Muelle and wait for a connection. For more information on crossing from Los Chiles to Nicaragua, see Nicaragua–Costa Rica box in the Practicalities chapter.

★ With its perfectly proportioned conical peak rising 1633 m above the plains, Volcán Arenal forms an eternally aesthetic backdrop to the windswept waters of Arenal Lake, when it isn't completely obscured by clouds of course. Due to inclement weather, May to December are poor months to admire the volcano but the best times to avoid the hordes of package tourists, a ubiquitous presence in the dry season.

Historically, Arenal was not always so popular. Long thought to be little more than an innocuous hill, it was completely ignored by the Costa Rican institute of tourism – and almost everyone else – until one fateful day in July 1968 when it suddenly exploded to life and destroyed three villages. For more than four decades thereafter, constant volcanic drama ensued with perpetual roars and rumblings, ominous emissions of gas, steam and smoke, and earth-shuddering detonations accompanied by violent ribbons of blood-red lava weaving down its face. The 7500-year-old volcano was quickly dubbed one of the world's most active, and touristic infrastructure mushroomed at its base. Cavalcades of international travellers made their way to behold Arenal's eruptions, until suddenly, in 2011, for no explicable reason, the eruptions stopped.

Activity may or may not resume anytime soon, with or without the explosive violence of the 1968 eruption; but until then, Arenal remains set up for ecotourism and outdoor adventures. Importantly, numerous mineral-rich therapeutic hot springs continue to bubble to the surface throughout the region – places where you can soak your weary bones and, if the weather is right, admire gently slumbering Arenal, the epitome of classic volcanic beauty.

## La Fortuna  *See map, page 760.*
The small town of La Fortuna (altitude 254 m) is a service, transport and tourism hub, and the conventional base for exploring the Arenal region. Once a humdrum village that shuddered in the shadow of the volcano's power, it has grown rapidly to accommodate visitors. The town's slew of modest hotels and *cabinas* best serve budget travellers, as well as those without independent transport. Those with the means may prefer to stay in one of the resort-style lodgings out of town. As a destination, La Fortuna lacks personality, but it is a convenient place to stage forays into the surrounding countryside: hiking, biking, windsurfing, canyoning, birdwatching, caving, canopy tours, kayaking, whitewater rafting and more can all be organized with the town's multitude of tour operators (for more information, see What to do, below).

## Parque Nacional Volcán Arenal
*Open 0800-1600, entrance US$15. Access is northwest of La Fortuna, follow the signs 14 km on the paved road towards Lago Arenal, then turn south 2 km on a gravel track; taxi US$25. Reception has maps and toilets.*

Established in 1991, the Parque Nacional Volcán Arenal encompasses 12,124 ha of forested terrain, including the volcanic peaks of Arenal and Cerro Chato. Home to more than 450 avian species, it is one of Costa Rica's 21 Important Bird Areas – the three-wattled bell bird, the great curassow, the bare-necked umbrella bird, the keel-billed mot mot and the resplendent quetzal are all resident. From the reception area, hikers have a few options, all of them undemanding. The **Sendero Heliconias** is a flat, linear jaunt through early secondary forest, 1-km long. More interesting is the **Sendero Las Coladas**, flat for 1.5 km until it enters lava fields forged by Arenal's eruptions, whereupon it becomes steep and irregular for 500 m. The **Sendero El Ceibo**, 1.8 km, loops off Las Coladas throughout mature secondary forest and is 95% flat. A trail with vehicular access leads from the reception 1.3 km to a mirador with a parking area, benches and striking views. It is not permitted to climb to the summit of Arenal, but **Cerro Chato**, near Río Fortuna waterfall, can be scaled for expansive views of the surrounding area (see below).

## Catarata Río Fortuna and Cerro Chato
*Administered by ADIFORT, T2479-8338, www.arenaladifort.com, open 0800-1700, entrance US$10.*

About 6 km southwest of La Fortuna is the numinous spectacle of Catarata Río Fortuna (**Río Fortuna Waterfall**) plunging 70 m into a cloud of swirling mist and spray. To get there, head south out of town for 2 km before turning west uphill through yucca and papaya plantations for another 4 km. From the entrance, a steep and slippery path leads 600 m down to the falls, so take shoes with a good tread. Bathing is possible, but it's safer 50 m downstream. If you don't want to walk, you can drive, but 4WD is necessary. Bicycle hire (US$3 per hour, US$15 per day) is another option and hard work, or you can hire a horse for the day at around US$55. Two- to three-hours' climb above the falls is the crater lake of Cerro Chato. The top (1100 m) is reached through mixed tropical/cloudforest, a demanding hike with a good view (if you're lucky); bring some cash to pay fees for crossing private land. Organized trips from La Fortuna US$75.

## Hot springs
From rustic pools to luxury spas, there are scores of hot springs around Arenal. Almost 5 km north of La Fortuna is the **Baldi Thermae complex** ① *T2479-9651, daily 1000-2200, US$41*, with several thermal pools ranging from 37° up to 63°C – the limits of endurance

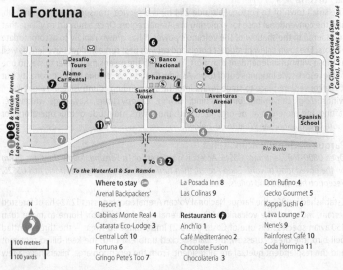

**La Fortuna**

| Where to stay 🛌 | La Posada Inn **8** | Don Rufino **4** |
| --- | --- | --- |
| Arenal Backpackers' Resort **1** | Las Colinas **9** | Gecko Gourmet **5** |
| Cabinas Monte Real **4** | | Kappa Sushi **6** |
| Catarata Eco-Lodge **3** | Restaurants 🍴 | Lava Lounge **7** |
| Central Loft **10** | Anch'io **1** | Nene's **9** |
| Fortuna **6** | Café Mediterráneo **2** | Rainforest Café **10** |
| Gringo Pete's Too **7** | Chocolate Fusion Chocolatería **3** | Soda Hormiga **11** |

without being poached. It's a fun, popular place and there are slides and poolside drinks available. A taxi from town costs US$4, a bus is US$1. Around 5 km west of La Fortuna is **Eco Termales** ① *T2479-8787, www.ecotermalesfortuna.cr*, a much more intimate locale with six tastefully presented thermal pools. A limited number of guests are permitted entry, reserve in advance, around US$50 with a meal. Some 13 km northwest of La Fortuna, **The Springs Resort** ① *T2401-3313, www.thespringscostarica.com*, has five-star treatment in its immaculately landscaped grounds. It has numerous hot- and cold-water pools connected by a system of trails, all of them surrounded by fiery heliconias and other lush rainforest plants; a two-day pass costs US$50. Off the road to Lago Arenal, approximately 10 km northwest of La Fortuna, is **Balneario Tabacón** ① *T2519-1999, daily 1000-2200, day guests welcome but limited, reserve in advance, entry from US$75*, a kitsch complex of thermal pools, waterfalls and (for residents) beauty treatments, with three bars and a restaurant. The water is hot and stimulating; there are pools at descending heights and temperatures as well as water slides and a waterfall to sit under. A taxi from La Fortuna to Tabacón is US$6. Cheaper are the hot waters about 4 km further along the road at **Quebrada Cedeña**, which are clean and safe. There is no sign but look for local parked cars.

## North to Upala

A quiet route north leads from La Fortuna to **San Rafael de Guatuso**. There is a 'voluntary' toll of US$1 between Jicarito and San Rafael. You can come back to the lake by turning off at **Venado**, where there are spooky caves filled with limestone stalactites and stalagmites, squeaky bats, spiders and other creepy crawlies; a day tour from La Fortuna including guide and transport costs US$75. Alternatively, you can return to La Fortuna via San Rafael, where there are a couple of basic hotels. If you continue along the road from San Rafael northwest towards the Nicaraguan border you come to unpretentious **Upala** and a poor road east to **Caño Negro** (see page 757). There is a direct bus from San José to Upala, T2221-3318 (from Avenida 3-5, Calle 10 at 1000 and 1700, four hours).

## Around Lago Arenal

Lago Arenal, Costa Rica's largest lake, was artificially expanded by three times its original size with the construction of the Arenal dam on its eastern side in 1979. Today, stretching west from the foot of Volcán Arenal, it covers an area of approximately 85 sq km. It is a very blustery lake and both windsurfers and turbine builders exploit its gales and gusts. On its southeastern shore, 12 km by road from La Fortuna, the tiny community of El Castillo makes a viable low-key base for exploring the Arenal region, but only if you have your own transport. Here you'll find the **El Castillo Butterfly Conservatory** ① *T2479-1149, www.butterflyconservatory.org, daily 0800-1600*, offering popular educational tours of their laboratories, reproduction greenhouses, exotic frog habitats, host plant gardens and orchid collections. More ecological wonders can be discovered nearby at **Arenal Eco Zoo** ① *T2479-1058, www.arenalecozoo.com, 0800-1900*, home to some 70 reptile species, including a 5.5-m Burmese python called Eliza. On the northern side of Volcán Arenal, a paved road twists and winds from La Fortuna, passing scores of hotels and resorts until arriving at the lake and the dam, where boats making the 'jeep-bus-jeep' journey between Arenal and Santa Elena/Monteverde land. Further west, the road skirts the shore, soon arriving at **Nuevo Arenal**, a small town that was created to replace the one destroyed by the flooding of the lake. There is plenty of good accommodation in the area, much of it in the higher price brackets.

Continuing west towards Tilarán, the western side of the lake is popular with windsurfers throughout the year, and between December and April the conditions are world class. A batch of hotels cater for windsurfers of all levels; there are many other options in the area so take your pick if you want to stop. Whether travelling by bus or car, you can get from La Fortuna to Monteverde via Tilarán in a day, but set out early to make your connection with the 1230 bus in Tilarán or to avoid driving after dark.

**Tilarán** would not appear on the list of destinations for travellers were it not for its role as a small regional transport hub for people journeying between La Fortuna, Santa Elena/Monteverde and Cañas on the Pan-American Highway. In town there is pretty much nothing to do and, with luck, the connecting buses will be timed perfectly to avoid you having to wait too long. But if you do, there are several places to catch a bite to eat, and several good places to stay if you need a bed for the night.

## Listings Volcán Arenal and around *map p760*

### Where to stay

**Volcán Arenal and around**

La Fortuna (see below) is the easiest place to stay if you don't have your own transport, but the whole area west of the town is littered with decent hotels, far too many to mention here.

**$$$$ The Springs Resort and Spa**
*12.9 km northwest of La Fortuna, T2401-3313, www.thespringscostarica.com.*
A world class luxury resort with 18 artisan hot springs, 5 bars, 4 restaurants, and a range of sumptuous wood-built rooms, suites and bungalows. Very expensive, excellent service and highly romantic.

**$$$$-$$$ Arenal Observatory Lodge**
*northwestern side of the volcano, 4 km after El Tabacón, a turn towards the lake down a (signposted) gravel road, T2290-7011, www.arenalobservatorylodge.com.*
4WD recommended along this 9-km stretch. Set up in 1973, the observatory was purely a research station but it now has private rooms, suites and a villa. There are stunning views of the volcano, Lake Arenal and across the valley of Río Agua Caliente. Recommended.

**$$$$-$$$ Los Lagos**
*T2479-1000, www.hotelloslagos.com.*
98 comfortable cabin rooms sleeping up to 4, day visits US$20, excellent food and spectacular views of the volcano over the

lake, good facilities and small café, spa, numerous spring-fed pools, canopy tour, trails and a frog farm.

**$$$ Cabañas Brisas Arenal**
*1.6 km southwest of La Fortuna, T2479-9225, www.brisasarenal.com.*
Family-run lodging committed to sustainability. Tasteful wood-built cabins set in a leafy garden, home to lots of colourful birdlife. Rustic chic, but very comfortable.

**$$$-$$ Hotel Arenal Green**
*1 km south and 1 km west from La Fortuna, towards Río Fortuna waterfall, T2479-8585, www.arenalgreen.com.*
6 modern cabins and 1 villa built with native wood, all equipped with a/c, hot water, cable TV, coffee-maker, mini-fridge and chill-out porch with volcano or garden views. Tranquil, leafy grounds.

**$$ Vista del Cerro**
*3.5 km west of La Fortuna, T2479-7029, www.hotelvistadelcerro.com.*
Simple, comfortable, affordable and unpretentious rooms with volcano views, as the name suggests. Amenities include restaurant, garden and pool. Very helpful, friendly and down-to-earth.

### La Fortuna

As one of the most popular destinations in the country, accommodation tends to be quite pricey in high season. Conversely, generous discounts in the green/low season are common.

### $$$ Catarata Eco-Lodge
*2 km from town, T2479-9522,*
*www.cataratalodge.com.*
Reservations essential for the 21 rooms and cabins in this cooperative with organic garden. Home-made soaps and shampoos, good fresh food, butterfly farm, hot water, laundry and all meals. Run by community association and supported by WWF Canada and CIDA Canada.

### $$$ Hotel Central Loft
*100 m west of the Parque Central,*
*T2479-9004, www.hotelcentralloft.com.*
One of the best hotels in town, centrally located near the main plaza. Rooms are spacious and well-appointed with solid wood furniture – ask for one with views of the volcano. There's also a small pool for cooling off.

### $$$ Hotel Fortuna
*1 block east and 1 block south of the Parque Central, T2479-9197, www.lafortunahotel.com.*
A popular downtown hotel with 44 comfortable rooms (12 wheelchair accessible), some have impressive views of the volcano. All comforts and amenities; price includes breakfast.

### $$$-$$ Cabinas Monte Real
*100 m south and 300 m east of the Parque Central, T2479-9357, www.monterealhotel.com.*
Bordering the Burio river close to a small forest, Cabinas Monte Real is a quiet and friendly place, visited by sloths, iguanas and colourful birds fluttering about the garden. Rooms are large (premium rooms have volcano views). Pool and Wi-Fi. Helpful staff, parking available. Recommended.

### $$$-$$ Las Colinas
*Half a block south of the Parque Central, T2479-9305, www.lascolinasarenal.com.*
A Rainforest Alliance-certified 'eco-friendly' option with 20 tidy rooms, some with incredible views. Family-run, friendly management, good discounts in the low season. Breakfast included and served on an open-air terrace looking out to the volcano. Recommended.

### $$-$ Arenal Backpacker's Resort
*A short distance north of town on the main road, T2479-7000, www. arenalbackpackersresort.com.*
Popular with 20-somethings, a resort-style hostel with a relaxing garden and pool, views of Arenal, hammocks, wet bar, comedy tight-rope, evening activities like ping-pong and twister. Lodging is in mixed or single-sex dorms ($), 'safari tents' ($$) or private rooms ($$).

### $ Gringo Pete's Too
*1½ blocks west of the bus station, T2479-8521, www.gringopetes.com.*
Undoubtedly the cheapest option, very popular with thrifty backpackers, but also quite rule-orientated. Lodgings include basic dorms and private rooms with kitchen facilities and communal areas for relaxing.

### $ La Posada Inn
*250 m east of the Parque Central, opposite the Colegio, T2479-9793, www.posadainncr.com.*
Simple, spartan and spotless rooms, with or without private bath, fans included but mosquitoes reported. Small communal area out front. Low-key, family-run and relaxed.

## North to Upala

### $$$$ Río Celeste Hideaway
*2 km from the entrance of Tenorio National Park, beyond San Rafael, T2206-5114, www.riocelestehideaway.com.*
Luxury rainforest *casitas* with wooden floors and bamboo ceilings. All comforts and amenities, and the chattering sounds of the jungle to lull you to sleep.

## Around Lago Arenal
Hotels in El Castillo on the southern side of the lake are slightly cut off but have fantastic views.

#### $$$$ La Mansión Inn
*Highway 142, T8763-2088,*
*www.lamansionarenal.com.*
Luxury boutique villas set in 10 ha of tropical gardens. Overlooks the lake with a beautiful spring-fed infinity pool, jacuzzis, mirador. Well-appointed rooms with lovely hand-painted murals. Very relaxing.

#### $$$$ Toad Hall
*Highway 142, T8534-3605,*
*www.toadhallarenal.com.*
Nestled in the jungle and overlooking the lake, 4 superb stylish themed villas that will suit couples or families, all very tasteful and artistic. Great restaurant. Recommended.

#### $$$ Hotel Linda Vista
*El Castillo, T2479-1551,*
*www.hotellindavista.com.*
A well-established Castillo favourite owned by the Badilla Picado family. Nice views, several good, unspoilt trails in the area, horse-riding tours, restaurant, pool, attentive service. Recommended.

#### $$$-$$ Hotel Los Héroes (Pequeña Helvecia)
*10 km from Arenal towards Tilarán, T2692-8012, www.hotellosheroes.com.*
Delightful Swiss owners with inspiring energy. A superb hotel, complete with Swiss train service.

#### $$$-$$ La Ceiba
*6 km from Arenal, T2692-8050,*
*www.ceibatree-lodge.com.*
Overlooking Lake Arenal, La Ceiba is set in a 15-ha private nature reserve with 5 bright, comfortable rooms. Tico-owned and run, good, helpful, great panoramic views, good breakfast. Recommended.

### Tilarán

#### $ Cabiñas El Sueño
*1 block north of bus terminal/Parque Central, T2695-5347.*
Clean rooms around central patio, hot water, fan, TV and free coffee. Good deal and friendly.

### La Fortuna

#### $$$ Anch'io Restaurant
*350 m west of the Catholic church.*
Several restaurants in town serve pizza and this is possibly the best. Stone-baked, authentic and complemented by a menu of tasty pasta dishes. Open-air seating on a covered patio. Pleasant and romantic.

#### $$$ Don Rufino
*1 block east of the Parque Central, T2479-9997, www.donrufino.com.*
A very presentable establishment with solid wood tables and a diverse international menu. Salads, steaks, chicken Kiev, risotto, seafood platter, lasagne and sandwiches are among the offerings. One of the better places in town, popular with the tourist crowd.

#### $$$ Kappa Sushi
*Diagonally across from the Parque Central, 25 m north of the Banco Nacional.*
This low-key and intimate little restaurant serves winning sushi – try the rolls. Modern decor, pleasant atmosphere and owners. Recommended.

#### $$$ Nene's
*Calle 5, an alleyway east of Parque Central, T2479-9192.*
The best *comida típica* in town, including grilled meats, brocheta, chicken, pork ribs and prawns. Informal, but not downscale. Popular with local families and tourists. Try the ceviche.

#### $$$-$$ Café Mediterráneo
*400 m south of the roundabout, T2479-7497.*
Another strong contender for the best pizza joint in town, Café Mediterráneo serves as a coffee house in the daytime. In addition to delicious thin-crust Italian-style pizza, they serve tasty wraps, salads, panini, hot and cold coffee and cake.

#### $$$-$$ Lava Lounge
*25 m west of the Catholic church,*
*www.lavaloungecostarica.com.*

Funky bar and grill serving hearty international fare, including salads, wraps, pizza and pasta. House specialities include coconut chicken and grilled pork with 'tropical chutney'. Popular hangout with backpackers and other wandering souls.

### $$ Gecko Gourmet
*Across the street from Lava Lounge, www.geckogourmet.com.*
La Fortuna's only deli-style eatery serves a variety of salads, wraps and sandwiches. Tempting fillings include Caprese chicken, meatloaf and barbecue pork. Also bagels, breakfasts, smoothies, ice coffee and sweet snacks.

### $ Soda Hormiga
*Next to the bus station.*
Bustling and casual *soda* serving the best-value *casados* in town. Come with an appetite, the servings are on the large side.

## Cafés

### Chocolate Fusion Chocolatería
*West of the Parque Central on the main road, next to Anch'io Restaurant.*
The aroma of roasted cacao here is irresistible. As well as good coffee, they sell delicious artisan chocolates and ice cream. Tasty and extravagant.

### Rainforest Café
*125 m south of the Parque Central.*
Travellers come here for the breakfasts, *casados*, coffees, smoothies, cakes and Wi-Fi. Casual Tico place.

### Around Lago Arenal

### $$$ Caballo Negro
*A couple of kilometres west of (Nuevo) Arenal, T2694-4515, www.luckybugcr.net.*
Overlooking a lush tropical garden, the best restaurant for miles, serving vegetarian, Swiss and German favourites, include *jaeger schnitzel*, *brawurst* and home-made *spaetzle*. Warm family atmosphere.

### $$$ Gingerbread Restaurant
*Nuevo Arenal, T2694-0039, www. gingerbreadarenal.com. Tue-Sun, 1700-2100, reservations essential.*
Attached to the boutique **Gingerbread Hotel**, the most popular restaurant in the area, recommended by many. They serve eclectic international fusion cuisine by chef Eyal Ben-Menachem, including a changing daily menu and lots of fresh seafood. Recommended.

### $$$-$$ Moya's place
*Nuevo Arenal.*
A funky and laid-back pizzeria with colourful murals. They also serve good wraps and salads. Good ambiance. Recommended.

### $$$-$$ Tinajas Arenal
*Rancho Las Tinajas, Highway 142.*
Tasty and reasonably priced international fare, including vegan, fish and meat dishes. A verdant setting on an organic farm with fine views of the lake. Tricky to reach without your own transport; follow the signs on the highway. Great place. Recommended.

### Tilarán

### $$ Restaurant La Carreta
*At the back of the church, T2695-6593.*
The place to go and relax if you have time to kill. Excellent breakfast and lunch only, North American food, pancakes, coffee and good local information.

### $ Stefanie's
*Out of the bus station to the left on the corner of the main plaza.*
Good and quick if you need a meal between buses.

## What to do

### La Fortuna
**Boat tours**
Available from several tour operators, safari river floats down the Río Peñas Blancas cost US$55 and offer the chance of glimpsing crocodiles, monkeys, sloths and birds

(kayaking is also an option). Day trips to Caño Negro reserve along the Río Frío involve travelling to Los Chiles and taking the boat from there, US$65. Prices include transport, guide and snacks as a minimum.

## Canoeing, kayaking and whitewater rafting

The lake, Río Aguacate and Río Peñas Blancas are popular destinations for canoeing and kayaking. Whitewater rafting, best in the wet season, is available on several rivers, including:

**Arenal Kayaks**, *Nuevo Arenal, T2694-4336, www.arenalkayaks.com.* A range of 2- to 4-hr kayak tours, including a trip to a small island in the lake where you can see ancient artefacts. They can also manufacture kayaks by hand, if you're in the market.

**Canoa Aventura**, *Highway 142, 500 m west of downtown, T2479-8200, www.canoa-aventura.com.* Safari floats on kayak and canoe, whitewater rafting and hikes. Owned by a Costa Rican family with 25 years' experience in the industry.

**Wave Expeditions**, *behind the Catholic church, T2479-7262, www.waveexpeditions.com.* Wide range of whitewater trips, Class II-V, as well as local tours and longer tailored trips around the Meseta Central, Northern zone, Guanacaste and the Pacific.

## Canopy tours

From high-speed zip-lines to high-altitude suspension bridges, there are many options for exploring the jungle canopy – more than can be listed here.

**Arenal Hanging bridges**, *access road off Highway 142, near Arenal dam, T2290-0469, www.hangingbridges.com.* No zip-line, but a complex network of trails and bridges snaking through 250 ha of tropical forest. Entrance US$24, children free; natural history/ birdwatching packages, plus transport at extra cost.

**Arenal Mundo Aventura**, *2 km south of the Catholic church over the Río Fortuna, T2479-9762, www.arenalmundoaventura.com.*

The only zip-line to pass in front of the Río Fortuna waterfall. 10 cables, 200-800 m. Horse riding option. US$70, children US$50, transport included.

**Ecoglide**, *turn-off on Highway 142, 6 km west of La Fortuna, T2479-7120, www.arenalecoglide.com.* Ecoglide's unique selling point is its Tarzan swing. 13 cables, 15 platforms, 10-430 m. US$55, transport included.

**Sky Adventures Arenal**, *access road off southeastern side of the lake, 2 km east of El Castillo, T2479-4100, www.skyadventures.travel.* Sky Adventures features a sky tram aerial tram ride and a suspension bridge tour (extra cost), as well as a complimentary butterfly and orchid garden. Their zip-line runs 10 cables, 200-750 m. US$77. Transport available at extra cost.

## Horse riding

Horse riding to Río Fortuna waterfall is popular, US$55 per person. Riding through the forest to Monteverde costs around US$85 per person for the day trip; luggage is taken on pack animals or by vehicles. Some operators seem to change the route once underway due to some 'unforeseen problem', so agree the route and try to arrange compensation if there are major changes. Due to competition for business, many horses are overworked. Try not to bargain down the price and do ask to see the horses before beginning the journey.

## Tour operators

Scores of tour operators are based in La Fortuna and they offer a broad range of local trips, including: hiking Arenal volcano, US$50; hiking and hot springs, from US$85; birdwatching, US$65; night tours, US$65; canyoning, US$95. Trips are flexible and can be combined with canopy tours.

**Aventuras Arenal**, *main street, T2479-9133, www.aventurasarenal.com.* Provides all tours in the area and has been around for many years. Can help with enquiries about other parts of Costa Rica.

**Desafío**, *behind the Catholic church, T2479-9464, www.desafiocostarica.com*. Reputable travel agency with an office also in Monteverde offering a full range of tours.

## Tilarán

### Kitesurfing and windsurfing
**Tico Wind**, *Highway 142, west side of Lake Arenal, T2692-2002, www.ticowind.com*. The country's foremost kitesurfing and windsurfing operation. Classes and equipment rental.

## Transport

### Volcán Arenal and around
Volcán Arenal is most easily reached on a paved road running west from Ciudad Quesada (San Carlos). Getting there from Santa Elena/Monteverde by bus demands an 8-hr haul on rough roads via Tilarán, where you must change. The so-called 'jeep-boat-jeep' service takes a short cut across Arenal Lake and cuts the journey time in half. Public transport arrives in La Fortuna, the region's main service town (see below).

### La Fortuna
**Bus** To **Ciudad Quesada**, 14 daily, 1½ hrs, US$1.50. To **San José**, 2 daily, 1245, 1445, 4 hrs, US$4.50 (or go to Ciudad Quesada and change). To **Tilarán** there are 2 buses daily at 0800 (connecting to 1230 bus Tilarán–Santa Elena/Monteverde and 1300 bus Tilarán–Puntarenas) and 1630, US$2.90, 4 hrs.

**Jeep-boat-jeep** The service to **Santa Elena/Monteverde** can be booked with any tour operator (reserve 48 hrs in advance), 4 hrs, US$25-30; they should pick you up and drop you off at your chosen lodgings.

### Tilarán
**Bus** To **Cañas**, 10 daily, 40 mins, US$1.50, from where buses head north and south of the Pan-American highway; to **La Fortuna**, 2 daily, 0700, 1230, 3 hrs, US$2.90; to **Puntarenas**, 2 daily, 0600, 1300, 3 hrs, US$3, or go to Cañas and change; to **Santa Elena/Monteverde**, 2 daily, 0700, 1600, 2½ hrs, US$2. For more information on getting to Monteverde, see page 775.

## Monteverde and Santa Elena  *Colour map 4, B3.*
> plants, insects, birds and mammals in grand profusion

Monteverde Cloud Forest Reserve is one of the most precious natural jewels in Costa Rica's crown. Protected by law, this private preserve is also protected by appalling access roads on all sides (the nearest decent road is at least two hours from the town). Santa Elena and Monteverde, although separate, are often referred to as the same place; most sites of interest are between the town of Santa Elena at the bottom of the hillside and Monteverde Cloud Forest Reserve at the top.

Travelling between La Fortuna and Santa Elena, you can travel overland by horse, jeep, boat or combinations of the three. It's adventurous, challenging and enjoyable depending on the weather conditions at the time. Travel agents in either location can advise and organize. See also Transport, below.

### Santa Elena and around
Santa Elena is a rugged and busy place, often packed with visitors exploring options or just passing time. It is cheaper to stay in town rather than along the single, unpaved road that twists and turns for 5 km through the village of Monteverde, with hotels and places of interest situated along the road almost to the reserve itself. **Santa Elena Reserve**, **Sky Trek** and **Sky Walk** are to the north of Santa Elena, all other places of interest are east, heading up the hill.

Very close to Santa Elena, at the start of the climb to Monteverde, is the **Herpetarium Adventures** ① T2645-6002, daily 0900-2000, US$13, children US$8, with specimens of snakes and amphibians found in the nearby cloudforest. Other natural history places of interest include the **Frog Pond** ① T2645-6320, daily 0900-2030, US$12, with 25 species of

# Monteverde & Santa Elena

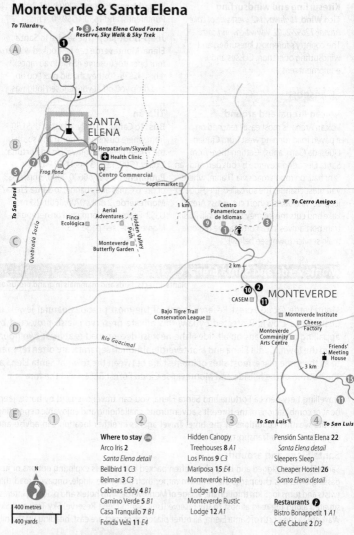

**Where to stay** 🛏
Arco Iris **2**
 *Santa Elena detail*
Bellbird **1** *C3*
Belmar **3** *C3*
Cabinas Eddy **4** *B1*
Camino Verde **5** *B1*
Casa Tranquilo **7** *B1*
Fonda Vela **11** *E4*

Hidden Canopy
 Treehouses **8** *A1*
Los Pinos **9** *C3*
Mariposa **15** *E4*
Monteverde Hostel
 Lodge **10** *B1*
Monteverde Rustic
 Lodge **12** *A1*

Pensión Santa Elena **22**
 *Santa Elena detail*
Sleepers Sleep
 Cheaper Hostel **26**
 *Santa Elena detail*

**Restaurants** 🍴
Bistro Bonappetit **1** *A1*
Café Caburé **2** *D3*

frog, and the **Bat Jungle** ⓘ *daily 0900-2000, T2645-5052, www.batjungle.com, US$11*, where you can learn about the nocturnal habits of over 40 bats.

A dirt road opposite the **Hotel Heliconia** leads to the **Monteverde Butterfly Garden** ⓘ *T2645-5512, www.monteverdebutterflygarden.com, daily 0930-1600 (best time for a visit 1100-1300), US$15, US$10 students, including guided tour*, a beautifully presented large garden planted for breeding and researching butterflies. Near the Butterfly Garden is **Finca Ecológica** ⓘ *T2645-5869, www.santuarioecologico.com, daily 0700-1730, US$10, night tours US$15, free map, guides available*, with three trails totalling around 5 km with bird lists for birdwatching and varied wildlife in this transitional zone between cloud and tropical dry forest. Recommended for night tours as one of the few companies that does not lure the wildlife with food.

**Santa Elena detail**

## Santa Elena Cloud Forest Reserve

*Offices are 200 m north of the Banco Nacional, T2645-5390, www.reservasantaelena.org, 0700-1600, entrance US$14, students US$7. It is a long, steep hike from the village; alternatively hire a taxi, US$6.50.*

One kilometre along the road north from Santa Elena to Tilarán, a 5-km track is signposted to the reserve, managed by the **Centro Ecológico Bosque Nuboso de Monteverde**. It is 83% primary cloudforest and the rest is secondary forest at 1700 m, bordered by the Monteverde Cloud Forest Reserve and the Arenal Forest Reserve. There is a 12-km path network and several lookouts where, on a clear day, you can see Volcán Arenal. There are generally fewer visitors here than at Monteverde. The **Centro Ecológico Bosque Nuboso** is administered by the local community and profits go to five local schools. It was set up by the Costa Rican government in 1989 with collaboration from Canada. The rangers are very friendly and enthusiastic. There is a small information centre where rubber boots can be hired and a small café open at weekends. Hand-painted T-shirts are for sale.

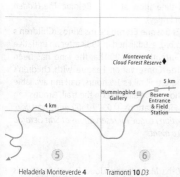

*Monteverde Cloud Forest Reserve* ◆

5 km

*Hummingbird Gallery*

*Reserve Entrance & Field Station*

4 km

⑤    ⑥

Heladería Monteverde **4**
*Santa Elena detail*
Orchid Coffeeshop **5**
 *Santa Elena detail*
Stella's Bakery **11** *D3*
Taco Taco **7**
 *Santa Elena detail*
Tico y Rico **9**
 *Santa Elena detail*

Tramonti **10** *D3*
Treehouse **12**
 *Santa Elena detail*
Trio by Aborigen **13**
 *Santa Elena detail*

## Monteverde and around

Strung out along the road to the cloudforest, the settlement at Monteverde – between Santa Elena and the reserve – was founded by American Quakers in the 1950s. Without a centre as such, it started life as a group of dairy farms providing milk for a cooperative cheese factory. The **cheese factory** (shop closes at 1600), now privately owned, still operates selling excellent cheeses of various types, fresh milk, ice cream, milkshakes to die for and *cajeta* (a butterscotch spread).

Today, Monteverde maintains an air of pastoral charm, but tourism provides more revenue for the town than dairy produce ever could. It was the vision of the dairy farmers that led to the creation of the reserve to protect the community watershed. When George Powell and his wife spent time in the region studying birds they realized the importance of protecting the area. Working with local residents they created the reserve in 1972 – foresight that has spawned the creation of many other natural attractions locally and throughout the country.

The best way of getting the full low-down on the place is at the **Museum of Monteverde History** ① *daily 0930-1930, US$5*. This spacious museum records the history of Monteverde, from the creation of the Central American isthmus three million years ago to its settlement by indigenous people and then the arrival of the Ticos, followed by the Quaker settlers, and then biologists, conservationists and ecotourism.

**Reserva Sendero Tranquilo** ① *daily, T2645-5010, entry restricted to 12 people at any one time,* is a private 200-ha reserve near the Monteverde cheese factory. Reservations and guides should be arranged through **El Sapo Dorado** hotel, which also offers night tours for US$25 per person.

Just before the entrance to Monteverde Cloud Forest is the **Hummingbird Gallery** ① *T2645-5030, daily 0700-1700*, where masses of different hummingbirds can be seen darting around a glade, visiting feeding dispensers filled with sugared water. Outside the entrance is a small shop/photo gallery that sells pictures and gifts, as well as **Bromeliads Nature Bookstore and Café**. There is also a slide show at Hotel Belmar, *The Hidden Rainforest*, by Bobby Maxson (1930 daily except Friday).

Adjoining the Monteverde Cloud Forest is **El Bosque Eterno de los Niños (Children's Eternal Rainforest)** ① *T2645-5003, www.acmcr.org*, established in 1988 after an initiative by Swedish schoolchildren to save forests. Currently at 22,000 ha, the land has been bought and is maintained by the **Monteverde Conservation League** with children's donations from around the world. The **Bajo Tigre** trail takes 1½ hours, parking available with notice, a guide can be arranged, but no horses are allowed on the trail. Groups can arrange trips to the **San Gerardo** and **Poco Sol Field stations** ① *0800-1600, entrance US$6, students US$2, contact the Monteverde Conservation League for reservations at San Gerardo or Poco Sol, T2645-5003, www.acmcr.org, US$50 a night*.

## ★ Monteverde Cloud Forest Reserve

Straddling the continental divide, the 10,500-ha Monteverde Cloud Forest Reserve is privately owned and administered by the **Tropical Science Centre** – a non-profit research and educational association. The reserve is mainly primary cloudforest and spends much of the year shrouded in mist, creating stunted trees and abundant epiphytic growth. The best months to visit are January to May, especially February, March and April. The reserve contains more than 400 species of bird, including the resplendent quetzal, best seen in the dry months between January and May, especially near the start of the Nuboso trail; the three-wattled bellbird with its distinctive 'bonk' call; and the bare-necked

# Essential Monteverde Cloud Forest Reserve

## Park information

www.reservamonteverde.com. Office open daily 0700-1630; the park opens at 0700 and closes at 1700. Entrance fee US$18 (students with ID US$9) valid for multiple entry during the day, cannot be purchased in advance. The reserve entrance is at the field station at the top of the road. Bus from Santa Elena heads up the hill leaving at 0600 and 1100 returning at 1400 and 1700. The total number of visitors to the reserve at any one time is 150, so be there before 0700 to make sure of getting in during high season (hotels will book you a place for the following day). Tour buses come in from San José daily. A small shop at the office sells various checklists, postcards and APS film, gifts and excellent T-shirts, the proceeds of which help towards the conservation project.

## Guides

Natural history walks with biologist guides leave every morning and afternoon, three to four hours, US$32; birdwatching tours, US$64; advance reservations at the office or through your hotel are strongly recommended. If you use a private (non-reserve) guide you must pay his entrance fee too. An experienced and recommended guide who also does night tours is **Gary Diller** (T2645-9916). There are 25 others operating, of varying specialization and experience. Excellent night tours in the reserve are available normally with **Ricardo Guindon** or call **Monteverde Reserve** (T2645-5112, US$17), at 1900 sharp. Day or night, a guide is recommended if you want to see wildlife, since the untrained eye misses a lot.

## Donations and volunteer work

Donations are welcomed for purchasing additional land and maintaining and improving existing reserve areas. If you are interested in volunteer work, from non-skilled trail maintenance to skilled scientific assistance work, surveying, teaching or studying on a tropical biology programme, contact the reserve (US$14 per person, board and lodging, two weeks minimum). The Conservation League works with schools in the area on education regarding conservation. Donations can be made at the **Monteverde Cloud Forest Reserve office** (see above), **Tropical Science Centre** (San José, T2253-3267, www.cct.or.cr), or **Monteverde Conservation League** (Apdo Postal 124-5655, San José, Costa Rica, T2645-5003, www.acmcr.org).

umbrella bird. There are more than 100 species of mammal, including monkeys, Baird's tapir, six endangered cats (jaguar, jaguarundi, margay, ocelot, tigrillo and puma), reptiles and amphibians. But be warned, travellers frequently report there is little chance of seeing much wildlife. The reserve also includes an estimated 2500 species of plant and more than 6000 species of insect. The entrance is at 1500 m, but the maximum altitude in the reserve is over 1800 m. Mean temperature is between 16° and 18°C and average annual rainfall is 3000 mm. The weather changes quickly and wind and humidity often make the air feel cooler.

The commonly used trails are in good condition and there are easy, short and interesting walks for those who do not want to hike all day. Trail walks take from two hours but you could easily spend all day just wandering around. Trails may be restricted from time to time if they need protection. There is a trail northwards to the Arenal volcano that is increasingly used, but it is not easy. There are three refuges for people wishing to spend the night within the reserve boundaries, see Where to stay, below. Free maps of the reserve are available at the entrance. Follow the rules, stay on the paths, leave nothing behind, take no fauna or flora out; no radios/CD players/iPods, etc are allowed.

## Where to stay

### Santa Elena

**$$$ Arco Iris**
*Southeast of Banco Nacional, T2645-5067, www.arcoirislodge.com.*
Stone- and wood-built cabins set among preserved forest fragments and landscaped gardens filled with ornamental and fruit trees. Verdant and tranquil. One of the best in Santa Elena.

**$$$ Monteverde Rustic Lodge**
*1 km north of the church, T2645 6256, www.monteverderusticlodge.com.*
A low-key Monteverde mountain lodge with a leafy garden, rustic wood finishes and spacious rooms equipped with Wi-Fi. Managed by the Badilla brothers. Breakfast included.

**$$ Camino Verde**
*300 m southwest of SuperCompro supermarket, T2645-5641, www.hotelcaminoverde.com.*
A friendly family-style B&B with a *'mi casa es tu casa'* philosophy. Amenities include free tea and coffee all day, shared kitchen, maps, parking. Most rooms have TV and Wi-Fi. Helpful and hospitable.

**$$-$ Cabinas Eddy**
*150 m south of SuperCompro supermarket, T2645-6635, www.cabinas-eddy.com.*
This place has a great balcony for sipping morning coffee and enjoying the birdsong and sunshine. The owner, Eddy, is very helpful and friendly. He offers 14 rooms, some with kitchenette, cheaper without private bath. Breakfast included.

**$$-$ Monteverde Hostel Lodge**
*100 m west of the Centro Comercial, T2645-5989, www.monteverdehostel lodge.com.*
The only hostel in town that's perched right on the edge of the cloudforest. They have dorms ($), private rooms ($$), bungalows ($$), parking, internet, kitchen. Architecture is classic wood walls and floors.

**$$-$ Pensión Santa Elena**
*250 m southeast of Banco Nacional, T2645-5051, www.pensionsantaelena.com.*
Good range of rooms of varying standards and quality – all good value for the money. Very popular with backpackers, clean, good food, kitchen available.

**$ Casa Tranquilo**
*200 m south of SuperCompro supermarket, next to Cabinas Eddy, T2645-6782, www.casatranquilohostel.wix.com/tranquilobackpackers.*
A funky, rustic little hostel, Tico-owned, just out of town and away from the hoi poloi. They have private rooms with or without private bath and an 8-bed mixed dorm. Relaxed, sociable and friendly, with breakfast included. Good reports.

**$ Sleepers Sleep Cheaper Hostel**
*Main St, 150 m from the public bus stop, T2645-6204, www.sleeperssleepcheaperhostels.com.*
Cheap budget accommodation with both private and dorm rooms. Top floor is best for the balcony and views. Kitchen and internet access too. Breakfast included, helpful, good value.

### Monteverde

**$$$$ Fonda Vela**
*T2645-5125, www.fondavela.com.*
40 beautiful rooms and suites spread around 5 buildings. A 25-min walk, 5-min drive to the reserve, on a 14-ha farm with forest and trail system, good birding, 2 excellent restaurants (open to public), bar, TV room, art gallery and conference room.

#### $$$$ Hidden Canopy Treehouses Boutique Hotel
*300 m east of Camino Sky Trek crossroads, T2645-5447, www.hiddencanopy.com.*
You'll enjoy impeccable views of the cloudforest canopy from these sumptuous treehouse chalets constructed with fine hardwoods and other natural materials. Blissful and romantic. Recommended.

#### $$$ Belmar
*300 m behind service station, T2645-5201, www.hotelbelmar.net.*
Established in Monteverde more than 30 years ago, Hotel Belmar has a proven commitment to the environment and sustainability. Lodging is in a fantastic Swiss-style chalet with astounding views of the canopy reaching out as far as Nicoya.

#### $$$-$$ Los Pinos
*200 m east of Cerro Plano school, T2645-5252, www.lospinos.net.*
Comfortable wood cabins (accommodates 2-6) with fully equipped own kitchen, Wi-Fi, hot water, cable TV; ask for one with a fireplace. Set on a private reserve with a mirador, hiking trails and hydroponic vegetable garden. Sustainable ethos. Recommended.

#### $$ Mariposa bed and breakfast
*1 km past Monteverde cheese factory, T2645-5013, www.mariposabb.com.*
Has 3 rooms in a single block sleeping up to 3 people, with private bath. A family atmosphere with breakfast included in the price. Cosy and down to earth.

#### $ Hotel Bellbird
*Just before the gas station, T2645-5518, www.hotelbellbird.com.*
Low-key and economical, Hotel Bellbird offers private rooms with wood-panelled walls, hot water and Wi-Fi. Built by Monteverde pioneers in 1958. Breakfast included.

### Monteverde Cloud Forest Reserve
Shelter facilities throughout the reserve cost US$3.50-5 a night, reserve entry fee for each night spent in the park, plus key deposit of US$5. Bring sleeping bag and torch. You can make your own meals. Dormitory-style accommodation for up to 30 people at entrance, **Albergue Reserva Biológica de Monteverde** (T2645-5122, US$40 full board only, includes park entrance fee). Reservations only for all reserve accommodation (usually booked up by groups).

## Restaurants

### Santa Elena

#### $$$ Trio by Aborigen
*25 m south of the SuperCompro supermarket, T2645-7254, www.aborigencr.com.*
Creative offerings from a Costa Rican chef trained in the Basque Culinary Center in Spain. Try the pork spare ribs with guava, grits and barbecue sauce, and for dessert, the chocolate brownie with mint glaze.

#### $$$-$$ Bistro Bonapetit
*Carretera a Tilarán, 10 mins' walk out of town, take a taxi at night.*
A Tico-Italian restaurant serving good wood-fired pizzas and wholesome *casados*. Pleasant setting in an octagonal building; friendly and efficient service.

#### $$$-$$ El Marquez
*On the northern edge of town, near the exit for the Carretera a Tilarán.*
This modest eatery sells superb ceviche, shrimp, fish fillets and more – don't leave without trying the *mojitos*. Local, affordable and unpretentious.

#### $$$-$$ The Treehouse
*Opposite the Catholic church, www.treehouse.cr.*
The unique selling point of The Treehouse is the large ficus tree growing right through the dining area and the overall effect of sitting among the branches is somehow relaxing. They serve good international cuisine.

#### $$ Tico y Rico
*50 m north of the Catholic church, opposite side of the road.*

Reliable *comida típica*, including lunch time *casados*. Friendly service and unpretentious ambiance.

### $$-$ Taco Taco
*50 m southeast of the Banco Nacional, next to Pensión Santa Elena.*
Popular hole in the wall selling a wide variety of tasty burritos and tacos, including slow-roasted beef, vegetarian and pork *al pastor*.

### Coffee shops and ice cream parlours

Heladería Monteverde
*Next to the Catholic church.*
Owned by the cheese factory on the way to Monteverde, great locally produced ice cream.

Orchid coffeeshop
*200 m west of the Centro Comercial.*
Lovely little café selling excellent coffee, tasty sandwiches and pretty good *huevos rancheros* for breakfast. The best smoothies in town. Recommended.

### Monteverde

### $$$ Tramonti
*3 km from Monteverde reserve before CASEM, T2645-6120, www.tramonticr.com.*
Traditional Italian and completely authentic, including penne, fettuccini, spaghetti and other pastas, good wines and quite probably the best pizzas in the region. Beautiful setting on the edge of the forest.

### $$$-$$ Café Caburé
*Altos de Paseo, 150 m west of CASEM, T2645-5020, www.cabure.net.*
An Argentine restaurant, coffee shop and chocolatier with a breezy veranda on top of a hill. They serve eclectic cuisine from Chinese soups to Mexican *moles*. Don't leave without trying the artisan chocolates.

### $ Stella's Bakery
*Opposite CASEM, T2645-5560.*
Excellent wholemeal bread, cakes and good granola – there's a café if you want to eat in.

## Festivals

**Dec-Mar Monteverde Music Festival**, T2645-5053. Classical and jazz concerts at sunset, local, national and international musicians. Programme available from local hotels.

## Shopping

**CASEM**, *located just outside Monteverde on the road to the reserve next to El Bosque restaurant, T2645-5190.* A cooperative gift shop selling embroidered shirts, T-shirts, wooden and woven articles and baskets. Next door, there's a shop selling Costa Rican coffee.

## What to do

### Canopy tours
Monteverde is the canopy tour capital of Costa Rica. Thanks to the stiff competition for tourist dollars, every operator has at least 1 unique selling point. All cost US$45, except **Zip-line Monteverde**, US$35; 3-4 tours daily. Most companies have offices in Santa Elena (see map), advance booking essential.
**100% Aventura**, *3 km north of Santa Elena, T2645-6388, www.aventuracanopytour.com.* Home to the longest single zip-line in Latin America, 1590 m. Other attractions include a rope bridge, 2 'Superman'-style cables, a Tarzan swing (45 m), ATV tour, horse riding.
**Extremo**, *office in Calle Central, T2645-6058, www.monteverdeextremo.com.* Extremo is the longest canopy tour in Monteverde, covering a total of 4 km. It is a high-speed, high-altitude tour crossing farmland but no forest, 14 cables, 500-1000 m long. Options include the soaring 'Superman' harness, the biggest Tarzan swing in Costa Rica (60 m), a bungee jump of 143 m and horse riding. Recommended for all your adrenalin needs.

**Selvatura**, *office in Calle Central, T2645-5929, www.selvatura.com.* The only canopy tour in primary cloudforest, with 15 cables, 1 'Superman' cable and a Tarzan swing. A great option to see nature up close with 8 suspension bridges, the 3rd largest private insect collection in the world (fascinating, recommended), a dome butterfly garden with 50 live species, the biggest hummingbird garden in Monteverde and a reptile and amphibian exhibition, with 25 species from around Costa Rica. Transport included. Recommended.

**Sky Adventure**, *office in Calle Central, T2479-4100, www.skyadventures.travel.* The sister theme park to **Sky Adventure Arenal**, Sky Adventure Monteverde has 3 components. **Sky Trek** is the zip-line, with all cables and platforms interconnected, so there's no walking; the longest cable is 850 m. **Sky Tram** is a cable car ride over the cloudforest canopy and a part of the zip-line package. **Sky Walk** consists of suspension bridges and can be done independently of the zip-line or tram. They also manage the herpetarium downtown near the bus station.

**The Original Canopy Tour**, *office next to the Catholic church, T2645-5243, www.theoriginalcanopy.com.* As the name suggests, the first ones to set up in Monteverde, offering an exhilarating 40-m rappel down a strangulated fig tree and into the cloudforest. They have 15 cables, 60-800 m long, Tarzan swing, horseback and hot springs tours. Small groups, uncrowded and exclusive.

**Zip-line Monteverde**, *5 mins south of Santa Elena, T2645-6320, www.monteverdetheme park.com.* The cheapest option in town with 15 platforms, 9 cables, 2 rappels and a Tarzan swing. Short lines, undemanding and suitable for children and families.

## Transport

**Bus** To get from Santa Elena to the Monteverde reserve, **Transmonteverde** operates 4 buses daily, 0615, 0730, 1320, 1500, US$1.50; returning 0645, 1130, 1400, 1600. Long-distance to **Puntarenas** via the Km 149 route, 3 daily, 0420, 0600, 1500, 3 hrs, US$2.50; to **San José**, 2 daily, 0630, 1430, 5 hrs, US$5.10, or take the Puntarenas bus and change on the Pan-American Highway; to **Tilarán**, 2 daily, 0400, 1230, 2½ hrs, you must catch the early bus to connect with the bus to La Fortuna. **Note**: if taking the regular bus to **San José**, keep your bag with you at all times; several cases of theft have been reported.

**Car** From the Pan-American Highway northwest to Km 149, turn right (just before the Río Lagarto). Continue for about 40 km on mostly gravel road (allow 2½ hrs) to Santa Elena. Parts of the road are quite good, but in wet weather 4WD is recommended for the rough parts. If driving, check that your car rental agreement allows you to visit Monteverde. A 33-km shorter route is to take the Pipasa/Sardinal turn-off from the Pan-American Highway shortly after the Río Aranjuez. At the park in Sardinal, turn left, then go via Guacimal to the Monteverde road.

There is a service station, Mon-Sat 0700-1800, Sun 0700-1200.

**Horse** Several places rent horses; look for signs between Santa Elena and Monteverde or ask at your hotel. Try not to hire horses that look overworked.

**Jeep-boat-jeep** The service to **La Fortuna** is faster, more convenient and comfortable than the bus, worth the extra dollars, 4 hrs, US$25; book with local tour operators (48 hrs' advance reservation).

**Taxi** Santa Elena to Monteverde, US$6, and Monteverde to the reserve, US$5.75 (hunt around for good prices). Not so easy to find a taxi for return trip, best to arrange in advance.

North of Barranca, the Pan-American Highway heads towards the province of Guanacaste, the cultural heartland of Costa Rica. The province also includes the Peninsula of Nicoya and the lowlands at the head of the gulf. Rainfall is moderate; 1000-2000 mm per year. The long dry season makes irrigation important, but the lowlands are deep in mud during the rainy season.

Guanacaste, with its capital Liberia, has a distinctive people, way of life, flora and fauna. The smallholdings of the highlands give way here to large haciendas and great cattle estates. The rivers teem with fish and there are all kinds of wildlife in the uplands.

The people are open, hospitable and fun-loving, and are famed for their music and dancing; in fact, the *punto guanacasteco* has been officially declared the national dance. There are many fiestas in January and February in the local towns and villages, which are well worth seeing.

Heading northwest on the Pan-American Highway, turn right just after the Río Aranjuez at Rancho Grande (or just south of the Río Lagarto at Km 149) to access a dramatic and at times scenic route to Santa Elena-Monteverde.

## Guanacaste Conservation Area

*Pacific Ocean*

To Peñas Blancas
La Cruz
La Garita
Refugio Nacional de Fauna Silvestre Isla Bolaños
Bahía Salinas
Puerto Soley
Bahía Jobo
Volcán Orosí (1487m) ▲
Refugio de Vida Silvestre Bahía Junquillal
Maritza Station
Bahía Junquillal
Bahía Playa Blanca
Cuaijiniqguil
Parque Nacional Guanacaste
Murciélago Sector
Parque Nacional Santa Rosa ◆
Casona del Santa Rosa
Quebrada Grande
Islas Murciélago
Bahía Potrero Grande
Potrerillos
Playa Nancite
Peña Bruja
Playa Naranjo
Horizontal Experimental Forestry Station ◆
Cañas Dulces
Marine Area

**N**

20 km
20 miles

**Where to stay**
Buena Vista
  Mountain Lodge **2**
Hacienda Lodge
  Guachipelín **1**
Miravieja Lodge **3**

Some 43 km north of Barranca is the turn-off for **Las Juntas**, an alternative route to Monteverde for those using the Tempisque ferry or arriving from Guanacaste; a third of it is paved. After Las Juntas, there is a **mining ecomuseum** ⓘ *daily 0600-1800, US$1.80*, at **La Sierra de Abangares** with mining artefacts from a turn-of-the-20th-century gold mine.

Four kilometres north is a bridge crossing the Tempisque River. After about 6 km, a road to the right at San Joaquín leads to the **Hacienda Solimar Lodge** (see Where to stay, below), a 1300-ha cattle farm with dry tropical virgin forest bordering Parque Nacional Palo Verde (see below) near Porozal in the lower Tempisque River basin. The freshwater Madrigal estuary on the property is one of the most important areas for water birds in Costa Rica (only guests staying at the Hacienda can visit). Also surrounded by gallery forest, it is recommended for serious birdwatchers. Reservations are essential, contact **Birdwatch** ⓘ *T2228-4768, www.birdwatchcostarica.com.*

Some 67 km north of Barranca, Cañas has little to keep the visitor for long. There are a number of interesting sights nearby and, for the those arriving from the north, this is the cut-through to Tilarán and connecting buses to Arenal or La Fortuna. **Las Pumas** ⓘ *behind Safaris Corobicí, Cañas, free but donations welcome and encouraged*, is a small, private, Swiss-run animal rescue centre which specializes in looking after big cats, including jaguar. It's an unmissable if rather sad experience.

### Parque Nacional Palo Verde
*Colour map 4, B2.*
*Administration offices, in Bagaces next to the service station, T2661-4717; park entrance US$15. There are 2 ranger stations, Palo Verde and Catalina. Check roads in wet season.*

At the south of the neck of the Nicoya Peninsula is Parque Nacional Palo Verde, currently over 18,650 ha of marshes with many waterbirds. Indeed, more than 50,000 birds are considered resident in the *laguna*. The views from the limestone cliffs are fantastic. **Palo Verde Biological Station** ⓘ *T2661-4717, reservations on T2524-0607, www.ots.ac.cr,* is a research station run by the **Organization for Tropical Studies**. It organizes natural history walks and basic accommodation; US$89 with three meals and one guided walk per stay, cheaper for researchers; make advance reservations. Turn off the Pan-American Highway at **Bagaces**, halfway between Cañas and Liberia. There is no public transport.

NICARAGUA

Santa Cecilia

Brasilla

Birmania

Pitilla
Station

Volcán Cacao
(1659m)
Cacao
Station

Rincón
Cacao
Biological
Corridor

Rincón
Rainforest
Reserve

Von Seebock (895m)

Volcán Rincón
de la Vieja (1806m)

Parque Nacional
Rincón de la Vieja

Volcán Santa María (1916m)

Santa
María

Colonia
Blanca

Las Pailas

Buenavista

Curubande

San Jorge

Liberia

↖ To San José

## Where to stay

**\$\$ Hacienda Solimar Lodge**
*solimar@racsa.co.cr.*
8 rooms with private or shared bathroom,
includes meals, minimum 2 nights, transport
on request, local guide, horse riding.
Recommended for serious birdwatchers,
contact **Birdwatch** (T2228-4768, www.
birdwatchcostarica.com), see above.
Reservations essential.

## Restaurants

**\$\$\$ Rincón Corobicí**
*Next to La Pacífica, Cañas, T2669-6191.*
Clean and pleasant, with a small zoo and
offers rafting down Río Corobicí.

## Transport

**Bus** The Cañas bus station is 500 m north
of the centre, where all buses depart from
except for those to San José, which leave
from the terminal 300 m west of Parque
Central on the Pan-American Highway.
To **San José**, 5 daily from 0400, 3½ hrs,
US\$5.40. To **Liberia**, hourly, 2 hrs, US\$2.50.
To **Puntarenas**, 8 daily from 0600. To **Upala**,
for Bijagua and Volcán Tenorio, 7 daily from
0500, 1¾ hrs, US\$1.50. To **Tilarán**, 7 daily
from 0600. Buses to Tilarán for **Nuevo
Arenal**, past the volcano and on to **La
Fortuna**, or for connections to **Santa Elena**
and **Monteverde**. If going by road, the turn-
off for Tilarán is at the filling station, no signs.

# Liberia and around *Colour map 4, B2.*

neat, clean cattle town

Known as the 'White City', Liberia (population 40,000) has a triangular, rather
unattractive modern church, and single-storey colonial houses meticulously laid
out in the streets surrounding the central plaza. The town is at the junction of
the Pan-American Highway and a well-paved branch road leads southwest to the
Nicoya Peninsula.

### Parque Nacional Rincón de la Vieja
*Park entry US\$15. Day trips are possible to all areas, US\$15 for Rincón de la Vieja, US\$40 for
Santa Rosa and US\$50 for Palo Verde. Minimum of 4 required, prices per person. Park is closed
Mon for maintenance.*

Most easily visited from Liberia, Parque Nacional Rincón de la Vieja (14,161 ha) was created
to preserve the area around the Volcán Rincón de la Vieja, to the northeast of the town.
There are two ways into the park: the southern route, which has less traffic, goes from
Puente La Victoria on the western side of Liberia and leads, in about 25 km, to the Santa
María sector, closest to the hot springs. In this part, you can hike 8 km to the boiling mud
pots (**Las Pailas**) and come back in the same day; the sulphur springs are on a different trail
and only one hour away. The northern route turns right off the Pan-American Highway
5 km northwest of Liberia, through **Curubandé** (no public transport on this route).
Beyond Curubandé, you cross the private property of **Hacienda Lodge Guachipelin** (US\$2
to cross), beyond which is **Rincón de la Vieja Lodge**.

The park includes dry tropical forest, mud pots, hot sulphur springs and several other
geothermal curiosities. The volcanic massif reaches to 1916 m and can be seen from a

wide area around Liberia when not shrouded in clouds. The area is cool at night and subject to strong, gusty winds and violent rains; in the day it can be very hot, although always windy. These fluctuations mark all of the continental divide, of which the ridge is a part. From time to time the volcano erupts, the last eruption being in November 1995, when it tossed rocks and lava down its slopes.

The park is home to over 350 recorded species of bird, including toucans, parrots, three-wattled bellbirds and great curassows, along with howler monkeys, armadillos and coatis, ticks and other biting insects. It also has the largest density of Costa Rica's national flower the *guaria morada* or purple orchid. Horses can be rented in the park from some of the lodges. If you want to climb the volcano you will need to camp near the top, or at the warden's station, in order to ascend early in the morning before the clouds come in. Trails through the park lead to most sights of interest, including beautiful waterfalls and swimming holes. There are several accommodation options in or near the park, and shorter trips can easily be arranged from Liberia.

### Parque Nacional Santa Rosa

About halfway to the Nicaraguan border from Liberia is Parque Nacional Santa Rosa (38,673 ha). Together with the **Murciélago Annex**, the peninsula to the north of the developed park, it preserves some of the last dry tropical forests in Costa Rica, and shelters abundant and relatively easy-to-see wildlife. During the dry season, the animals depend on the water holes and are thus easy to find until the holes dry up completely.

# Liberia

To Enrique Baltodano Hospital

To Nicaragua

Regional Buses

Buses to San José

Toyota Car Rental

Sol Car Rental

To ③, Nicoya Peninsula & Airport

Pan-American Highway

25 de Julio

Ciberm@nia

Plaza

Supermarket

La Inmaculada

Mayorga Rivas

Rafael Iglesias

Río Liberia

To Parque Nacional Rincón de la Vieja

Av 11 · Av 9 · Av 7 · Av 5 · Av 3 · Av 1 · Av Central · Av 2 · Av 4 · Av 6 · Av 8 · Av 10

C Central

To San José

**N**

200 metres
200 yards

| **Where to stay** |
|---|
| Del Aserradero **2** |
| Garden Inn **3** |
| Hospedaje Dodero **4** |
| La Posada del Tope **9** |
| Liberia **12** |

Wilson **5**

**Restaurants**
Café Liberia **1**
Copa de Oro **4**
El Mesón Liberiano **2**

Los Comales **3**
Pizza Pronto **6**
Tierra Mar **5**
Toro Negro **7**

Conservation work in the area is also trying to reforest some cattle ranches in the area – helped by the fact that cattle have not been profitable in recent years.

Close to the park headquarters and research buildings, the historically important **La Casona** was where, in 1856, the patriots repelled the invasion of the filibuster William Walker, who had entrenched himself in the main building. The old hacienda building, once the Museo Histórico de Santa Rosa, was rebuilt in 2002 having been almost completely destroyed by fire the previous year. There are several good trails and lookouts in the park, the easiest of which is close to La Casona. Lasting a couple of hours, it leads through dry tropical forest with many Indio Desnudo (naked Indian) trees, which periodically shed their red flaky bark.

Deeper in the park, **Playa Naranjo** (12 km, three hours' walk or more, or use 4WD, park authorities permitting) and **Playa Nancite** (about the same distance from the entrance) are major nesting sites of **leatherback** and **olive ridley sea turtles**. The main nesting season is between August and October (although stragglers are regularly seen up to January) when flotillas of up to 10,000 ridley turtles arrive at night on the 7-km-long Playa Nancite. Females clumsily lurch up the beach, scoop out a deep hole, deposit and bury an average of 100 ping-pong-ball-sized eggs before returning exhausted to the sea. Playa Nancite is a restricted-access beach; you need a written permit to stay plus US$2 per day to camp, or US$15 in dormitories. Permits from **SPN** in San José, and the **Park Administration building** ⓘ *Santa Rosa, T2666-5051, make sure you have permission before going*. Research has been done in the Playa Nancite area on howler monkeys, coatis and the complex interrelation between the fauna and the forest. Playa Naranjo is one of the most attractive beaches in the country. It is unspoilt, quiet and very good for surfing. There is good camping, drinking water (although occasionally salty) and barbecue facilities.

### La Cruz and Isla Bolaños *Colour map 4, B2.*

The last town before Peñas Blancas and the border, La Cruz has a bank (for cash, traveller's cheques or credit card transactions), a handful of hotels and absolutely incredible sunsets from the hilltop overlooking the Bahía de Salinas. Down in the bay is the Islas Bolaños Wildlife Refuge and some of the best conditions for windsurfing in Costa Rica.

Isla Bolaños is a 25-ha National Wildlife Refuge protecting the nesting sites of the brown pelican, frigate bird and American oystercatcher. The island is covered with dry forest and you can only walk round it at low tide. The incoming tidal surge is very dangerous; make sure you're off the island before the tide comes in. No camping is allowed.

## Listings Liberia and around *map p779*

### Where to stay

### Liberia

**$$$ Hotel Garden Inn**
*Ruta 21, opposite the airport, T2690-8888, www.hiltongardeninn3.hilton.com.*
The Hilton's contribution to Liberia is a charmless monstrosity on the outside but predictably comfortable on the inside. Located close to the airport.

**$$ Hotel del Aserradero**
*Pan-American Highway and Av 3, T2666-1939, www.hoteldelaserradero.com.*
A highway option, this one set back a short distance so you don't endure the noise of traffic. They have 16 large rooms with cable TV, Wi-Fi and hot water. The garden at the back is good for relaxing. Simple, spartan and quiet.

## $$ Hotel Wilson
*Calle 5, Av Central-2, T2666-4222,*
*www.hoteleswilson.com.*
The colourfully illuminated plastic palms
out front add a touch of pazzaz to this
otherwise generic downtown option. Rooms
are small and well kept. Secure parking and
restaurant downstairs. Lacks personality, but
otherwise good.

## $$-$ La Posada del Tope
*Calle Real, 1½ blocks south from church,*
*T2666-3876, www.laposadadeltope.com.*
A haphazard guesthouse adorned with
antique contraptions. They have basic rooms,
with or without private bath. The owner
Dennis also has a telescope for star gazing.
OK, would suit backpackers.

## $$-$ Liberia
*½ block south of main square, T2666-0161,*
*www.hotelliberiacr.com.*
A lovely old house and long-standing
cheapie, almost a century old. Rooms are
simple, comfortable and quiet. Dorms are
also available ($) and there's an internal
garden and courtyard serving as a restaurant.
Recommended.

## $ Hospedaje Dodero
*Av 11, Calle 12-14, T2665-4326,*
*www.hospedajedodero.yolasite.com.*
Close to the bus terminal, this intimate
and well-kept little guesthouse has simple
private rooms, a little garden at the back
and a basic shared kitchen. Very cheap,
relaxed and friendly. Similar options can
be found on the same street.

### Parque Nacional Rincón de la Vieja

## $$$$-$$$ Hacienda Lodge Guachipelin
*Accessed through the northern route,*
*T2690-2900, www.guachipelin.com.*
50 rooms, internet, meals available. Canopy
tour, naturalist guides, riding, hot springs,
sulphur springs, mud pools, waterfalls
(transport from Liberia arranged, US$50 per
person round trip).

## $$$ Buena Vista Mountain Lodge
*accessed through the Santa María sector,*
*T2690-1414, www.buenavistalodgecr.com.*
Rooms, waterslide, canopy tour, spa, internet,
restaurant/bar.

## $ Miravieja Lodge
*Accessed through the Santa María sector,*
*T8383-6645, www.miravieja.co.cr.*
Rustic lodge in citrus groves, meals, transport
and tours.

### La Cruz and Isla Bolaños

## $$$ Ecoplaya Beach Resort
*Bahía Salinas, T2676-1010, www.ecoplaya.com.*
All-inclusive resort, well maintained with
nice restaurant.

## $$$ Hotel La Mirada
*On road out to the Pan-American Highway,*
*T2679-9702, www.hotellamirada.com.*
Clean, tidy rooms, ample parking.

## $$ Amalia's Inn
*100 m south of Parque Central.*
Stunning views, small pool, very friendly
and excellent local knowledge. Extra person
US$5 and 1 room sleeps 6. Excellent value for
groups and recommended.

## $ Cabinas Santa Rita
*150 m south of Parque Central, T2679-9062.*
Nice, clean, secure with good parking.
Cheaper with fan. Would be great in any
other town not competing with **Amalia's**.

### Restaurants

### Liberia

## $$$ Toro Negro
*Corner of Av Central and Calle 1, T2666-2456.*
The best steakhouse in town, offering a
selection of succulent beef cuts grilled to
order, as well as some lighter fare, including
wood-fired pizzas and chicken cordon
bleu. A convivial family atmosphere.
Recommended for groups and carnivores.

### $$$-$$ Café Liberia
*Calle Real, 150 m sur de la Antigua Gobernación
Casa Zúñiga-Clachar, T2665-1660,
www.cafeliberia.com. Mon-Sat 1000-1800.*
An intimate café-restaurant with a diverse
menu of coffee, snacks and full meals,
including sandwiches, *fajitas*, ceviche and
not-to-be-missed lava cake. The setting
is a handsome colonial building with an
interesting ceiling fresco and a relaxed patio
at the back. Lovely owner and staff, attentive
service. Highly recommended.

### $$$-$$ El Mesón Liberiano
*Calle 3, Av 1-3, T2666-1819, www.elmeson
liberiano.com. Mon-Sat 1100-2300.*
Popular with local families, El Mesón
Liberiano serves hearty ceviches, soup,
steaks, chicken and seafood. Solid wooden
tables and a pleasant open-air patio, very
typical of traditional Guanacaste architecture.

### $$$-$$ Pizza Pronto
*Calle 1, Av 4.*
Classier than the name might suggest,
authentic stone-baked pizzas served in
an atmospheric colonial house. Tasty, but
servings are small for the price.

### $$$-$$ Tierra Mar
*Next to Parque El Pulmón.*
An understated seafood restaurant with a
tempting menu of finely prepared fish and
shellfish, including snapper, clams, shrimp
and ceviche. Open-air seating, good service
and tasty cooking. Recommended.

### $$ Copa de Oro
*Calle Real, 100 m south of Parque Central,
next to Hotel Liberia.*
Good-value *comida típica*, including a
range of wholesome meat, chicken and
seafood *casados*. Think comfort food, not
gourmet. Large portions, good service,
friendly atmosphere and a pleasant setting
in a colonial edifice.

### $ Los Comales
*Calle Central, Av 5-7. Open 0630-2100.*
Traditional Guanacaste dishes prepared
with maize, run by a women's cooperative.
Bustling, low-key, economical.

## La Cruz and Isla Bolaños

### $ La Orquídea
*La Cruz, T2679-9316. Daily 0630-2200.*
Seafood, cheap.

### $ Restaurant Telma
*La Cruz, T2679-9150.*
Tico food, cheap.

### $ Soda Marta
*La Cruz, T2679-9347.*
Cheap Tico fare.

## Festivals

### Liberia
**25 Jul Guanacaste Day** sees dancing,
parades and cattle-related festivities.

## Shopping

### Liberia
**Mini Galería Fulvia**, *on the main plaza*. Sells
English papers and books. English spoken
and helpful.
**Tiffany's**, *Av C-2, Calle 2*. General gifts, cigars.

## What to do

### Liberia
**Hotel Liberia** and **La Posada del Tope** (see
Where to stay, above) can organize tours,
rent out bikes and assist with enquiries.

## Transport

### Liberia
**Air** The **Aeropuerto Daniel Oduber
Quirós**, about 13 km from Liberia (LIR)
on the road to the Nicoya Peninsula, was
named after the former president who
came from Guanacaste. The runway can

handle large jets and charter flights and has become a popular alternative entry point to the country.

**Bus** San José buses leave from Av 5, Calle 10-12, with 14 a day, US$4.25, 4 hrs. Other buses leave from the local terminal at Calle 12, Av 7-9. Liberia to **Playa del Coco**, hourly, 0500-1800, **Playa Hermosa** and **Panama**, 5 daily 0730-1730, 1½ hrs, **Puntarenas**, 7 a day, 0500-1530, **Bagaces/Cañas**, 4 a day, 0545-1710, **Cañas Dulces**, 3 a day, 0600-1730, **La Cruz/Peñas Blanca**, 8 a day 0530-1800. **Filadelfia–Santa Cruz–Nicoya**, 0500-2020, 20 a day.

**Car** Sol and **Toyota** car rental agencies (see map) offer the same prices and allow you to leave the vehicle at San José airport for US$50.

## Parque Nacional Rincón de la Vieja
A taxi costs US$30 1-way from Liberia. Most hotels will arrange transport for US$15 per person, minimum 6 passengers. Departure at 0700, 1 hr to entrance, return at 1700; take food and drink. You can also hitch; most tourist vehicles will pick you up. If you take your own transport a 4WD is best, although during the dry season a vehicle with high clearance is adequate.

## Parque Nacional Santa Rosa
Parque Nacional Santa Rosa is easy to reach as it lies west of the Pan-American Highway, about 1 hr north of Liberia. Any bus going from Liberia to Peñas Blancas on the Nicaraguan border will drop you right at the entrance (US$0.70, 40 mins), from where it's a 7-km walk, but you may be able to hitch a ride. Last bus returns to Liberia about 1800. Coming from the border, any bus heading south will drop you off at the entrance.

## La Cruz and Isla Bolaños
**Bus** Regular buses to **San José** from 0545 until 1630, 5½ hrs. To **Liberia**, 5 daily 0700-1730, 1½ hrs. To **Peñas Blancas on the Nicaraguan border**, 5 daily 0730-1730, 1 hr; for more on the crossing to Nicaragua, see Nicaragua–Costa Rica box in the Practicalities chapter. To **Playa Jobo** in Bahía Solanos, at 0530, 1030 and 1500, from main plaza.

# Península
## de Nicoya

Fringed by idyllic white-sand beaches along most of the coastline, the Nicoya Peninsula is hilly and hot. There are few towns of any size and most of the roads not connecting the main communities are in poor condition. While several large hotel resorts are increasingly taking over what were once isolated coves, they are generally grouped together and there are still many remote beaches to explore. A few small areas of the peninsula are protected to preserve wildlife, marine ecosystems and the geological formations of Barra Honda.

Even in high season, you will be able to find a beautiful beach that is uncrowded. There are so many of them, you can just walk until you find what you want. You will see plenty of wildlife along the way, monkeys, iguanas and squirrels as well as many birds. There can be dangerous undertows on exposed beaches; the safest bathing is from those beaches where there is a protective headland, such as at Playa Panamá in the north.

**Best** for
Beaches ▪ Folklore ▪ Surfing ▪ Sunsets

## Santa Cruz and around
### famous for fiestas, dancing and regional food

Heading south from Liberia by road, the first town you reach is Santa Cruz, known as Costa Rica's National Folklore City. January is the month for the fiesta dedicated to Santo Cristo de Esquipulas, when it can be difficult to find accommodation. There is also a rodeo fiesta in January. But for the rest of the year, it's a quiet little town, with a charming modern church, providing supplies for the beach tourism industry. If you need to buy food, Santa Cruz is a good place to stock up.

In **Guaitil**, 9 km east of Santa Cruz and 19 km north of Nicoya, local artisans specialize in reproductions of indigenous Chorotegan pottery. They work with the same methods used by the indigenous long ago, with minimal or no use of a wheel and no artificial paints. Ceramics are displayed at the local *pulpería*, or outside houses. At **San Vicente**, 2 km southeast of Guaitil, local craftsmen work and sell their pottery.

### Listings Santa Cruz and around

### Where to stay

**Santa Cruz**
If stuck, there are few cheap *pensiones* about town in addition to options below:

**$$$ La Calle de la Alcalá**
*Av 7, Calle 1-3, 25 m east of the Plaza de Los Mangos, T2680-0000, www.hotellacalledealcala.com.*
A reliable downtown option with clean, comfortable, spacious and generally decent rooms and suites, all with a/c, hot water, cable TV, Wi-Fi and wicker furniture. There's also a pool and restaurant.

## Essential Península de Nicoya

### Finding your feet

There are several ways of getting to the Nicoya Peninsula and most travellers use ferries from Puntarenas (see page 803). For the northern region, the car ferry crosses the Gulf of Nicoya to Playa Naranjo, where buses wait to take foot passengers to Nicoya (US$1.25, 2¼ hours), Sámara (US$1.30), Coyote, Bejuco and Jicaral. For the southern region, a ferry departs from Puntarenas to Paquera from the dock at Calle 35. On arrival, get on the bus as quickly as possible (to Cóbano, two to three hours, US$1.25, bad road, to Montezuma US$2.60, 1½ hours at least).

Drivers coming from Nicaragua have the option of entering the Peninsula overland. From Liberia, head west along the Highway 21 towards Santa Elena. The Taiwan Friendship Bridge over the Río Tempisque, leaving the Pan-American Highway roughly halfway between Puntarenas and Liberia, provides a short cut, saving time and gas money getting to the peninsula and eliminating the ferry. Just across the river is **Hotel Rancho Humo**, T2255-2463, www.ranchohumo.com, with boat trips on the Tempisque and Bebedero rivers, visits to Palo Verde and Barra Honda national parks. See also Transport, below.

### Getting around

All the beaches on the Nicoya Peninsula are accessible by road in the dry season. Most places can be reached by bus from Nicoya. However, the stretch from Paquera to Montezuma and the Cabo Blanco Reserve is connected to Playa Naranjo and the north only by very poor roads. There is no bus connection between Playa Naranjo and Paquera and the road is appalling even in the dry season.

**$$ Hotel Diriá**
*On the highway, 3 km north of the Banco
Nacional, www.hoteldiria.co.cr.*
Bath, restaurant, pools.

## Restaurants

**Santa Cruz**

**$ Coopetortilla**
*3 blocks east of the church.*
A local institution– a women's cooperative
cooking local dishes. Cheap and enjoyable.

## Transport

**Santa Cruz**

**Bus**  Buses leave and arrive from terminals on
Plaza de los Mangos. From **San José**, 9 daily,
0700-1800, 4½ hrs, US$8, Calle 18-20, Av 3,
½ block west of Terminal Coca Cola, return
0300-1700. To **Tamarindo**, 2030, return 0645,
US$0.80, also to **Playa Flamingo** and nearby
beaches, 0630, 1500, return 0900, 1700, 64
km. To **Liberia** every hour, US$1.60, 0530-
1930. To **Nicoya** hourly 0630-2130, US$0.70.

**Taxi**  To **Nicoya**, US$10.50 for 2 people.

## West coast beaches  *Colour map 4, B2.*

**a series of beaches with nesting turtles, surfing and spectacular sunsets**

★ A number of beaches are reached by unpaved roads from the Santa Cruz–
Liberia road. Many can be accessed by bus from the Liberia bus station, others
may require you to change buses at Santa Cruz. Each of the beaches has its appeal:
Tamarindo and Playa del Coco for partying, Flamingo to the north and Junquillal
for their greater seclusion and Grande for turtles and surfing.

### Playa del Coco and around

After the town of **Comunidad**, a road leads east to Playa del Coco and Playa Hermosa and
the ever-pending resort development of Playa Panamá, see below.

Playa del Coco is a popular resort some 8 km from the highway, set in an attractive
islet-scattered bay hemmed in by rocky headlands. It's a good place to chill out, with a
mix of good services without being too developed. The best beaches are to the south.
All activities concentrate on the beach and fishing. Coco is the starting point for surf
trips to Santa Rosa spots by boat, such as **Witch's Rock**. Snorkelling and diving are
nothing special, but for a diving expedition to the **Islas Murciélago**, see What to do,
below. Sightings of manta rays and bull sharks are common around Islas Catalinas and
Islas Murciélago.

There are bars, restaurants and a few motels along the sandy beach. It is too small to
get lost. To reach it, leave the road at Comunidad (road paved). Be wary of excursions
to secluded Playa Verde, accessible by boat only, as some boatmen collaborate with
thieves and reap the rewards later. A 2.5-km road heads southwest from Playa del Coco
to **Playa Ocotal**.

### Playa Hermosa and Playa Panamá

A spur road breaks from the main road to Playa del Coco heading north to Playa Hermosa.
This is one of the best resorts and is served by a paved road. Accommodation is mixed, but
it's a good quiet alternative to other beaches in the region. Walking either to the left or
the right you can find isolated beaches with crystal-clear water. The big **Papagayo** tourist
complex near Playa Panamá, which once planned to provide as many as 60,000 hotel
rooms, started years ago.

## Playa Tamarindo and around

South of Filadelfia, close to Belén, a mostly paved but poor road heads east to the beach and popular surf spot of Playa Tamarindo (www.tamarindobeach.net) and other beaches. The sunsets are incredible and while most people make their way to the beach for that magic moment, there's a strong beach culture and this is a popular place just to hang out.

Either side of the sunset, Tamarindo is a flurry of activity, easily the liveliest beach resort on the Nicoya Peninsula and development is quickly changing the place. The beach is attractive with strong tides in places so take care if swimming. Three good breaks provide a variety of options for the surf crowd. Beyond surf and sun, the most popular excursion is an evening trip to Playa Grande and the leatherback turtle nesting sights from October to March. There's a good blend of hotels and bars to make it a good beach stop – not too busy, but not dead.

Close to Tamarindo, to the south, **Playa Avellana** is a quiet beach with good surfing for those who want to get away from the service culture of Tamarindo. Shuttle buses run from Tamarindo and there are a handful of accommodation options.

## Playa Grande

North of Playa Tamarindo is Playa Grande and the **Parque Nacional Marino Las Baulas de Guanacaste** (485 ha terrestrial, 22,000 ha marine), well known as a nesting site for **leatherback turtles** (October-February). Organized trips are only available from Tamarindo or from hotels in Playa Grande. Also in town is **El Mundo de La Tortuga** ① *T2653-0471*, an unusual turtle museum. The road from the main highway at Belén leads directly to Playa Grande, a sleepy town with almost no transport and no way of getting around.

## Playa Flamingo and beaches to the north

North of Tamarindo and Playa Grande are the beaches of Conchal, Brasilito, Flamingo and Potrero. It's a collection of beaches with subtle changes of atmosphere. **Conchal** is a beautiful 3-km beach full of shells, but with only luxury accommodation; most budget travellers stay at **Brasilito** and walk along the beach. Further north, the bay around **Playa Flamingo** has white sand, although the actual beach has some fairly intrusive developments with a grab-all approach to beachfront properties; in fact, the beach is now polluted and not as beautiful as it was. Several smaller beaches retain a relaxed atmosphere where life is governed by little more than the sunrise and beautiful sunsets. Further north is the isolated beach of **Potrero** with pockets of visitors.

## Playa Junquillal

South of Tamarindo, Playa Junquillal is one of the cleanest beaches in Costa Rica and is still very empty. Completely off the beaten track with almost no tourist facilities, it does have a selection of stylish hotels, most of which are quite pricey, but there is also camping if you have a tent.

## Where to stay

### Playa del Coco and around
Good discounts (up to 40%) in green season. Playa Ocotal has only top-end accommodation, but good diving services.

#### $$$ Villa Casa Blanca
*Playa Ocotal, T2670-0518, www.hotelvillacasablanca.com.*
15 idyllic rooms, with breakfast, friendly, informative, family atmosphere, small pool. Pricey but very good.

#### $$$-$$ Coco Palms
*Next to the soccer field, Playa del Coco, T2670-0367, www.sites.google.com/site/hotelcocopalms.*
Coco Palms has good location near the beach and downtown area. They offer a wide range of rooms, from simple economies to fully kitted apartments, all with a/c and cable TV. Amenities include large pool, computers, Wi-Fi, Sushi restaurant and bar, garden and supermarket.

#### $$$-$$ La Puerta del Sol
*North of Playa del Coco, T2670-0195.*
Great little family-run hotel. Good food in Italian restaurant, small pool and gym, friendly atmosphere and free scuba lesson in hotel pool.

#### $$ Cabinas Coco Azul
*Playa del Coco, from the church, 100 m northeast, 25 m south, T2670-0431, www.cabinascocoazul.co.*
Great hosts at this lovely little guesthouse, very homely, helpful and hospitable. Rooms are simple but immaculately clean and comfortable and there's a hot tub too. 2 mins from the beach. Recommended.

#### $$ Pato Loco Inn
*Playa del Coco, T2670-0145.*
Airy rooms, Italian restaurant, internet for guests.

#### $$ Villa del Sol
*At northern end of Playa del Coco, T2670-0085, www.villadelsol.com.*
Canadian-owned (from Quebec), with pool, clean, friendly, safe, big garden with parrots. Recommended.

#### $$-$ Cabinas Chale
*North of Playa del Coco, T2670-0036.*
Double rooms and villas, with private bath. Pretty quiet, small resort-style spot, small pool, 50 m from beach. Good deal, especially villas, which sleep up to 6.

### Playa Hermosa and Playa Panamá
Playa Panamá area has several all-inclusive resort-style hotels ($$$$).

#### $$$$-$$$ La Finisterra
*Playa Hermosa, end of 1st beach road, T2672-0227, www.lafinisterra.com.*
Perched on a beachfront hill 100 m from the ocean, Hotel La Finisterra basks in expansive views and refreshing sea breezes, a comfortable option, in their own words, 'sophisticated but unpretentious'.

#### $$$ La Gaviota Tropical
*Playa Hermosa, 2nd beach road to end, then right 75 m to Roberto's, T2672-0011, www.lagaviotatropical.com.*
This boutique B&B offers 5 comfortable rooms, each tastefully decorated in its own tropical theme, including beach, bird and rainforest rooms. Great hosts, attentive service. Highly recommended.

#### $$-$ Congo's Hostel
*Main street, 50 m before the beach, T2672-1168, www.congoshostel.com.*
Easy-going, friendly hostel with helpful owners and chilled-out vibe. Amenities include kitchen and leafy garden complete with a wooden deck. Simple rooms, family atmosphere. Camping is an option.

## Playa Tamarindo and around

Plenty of accommodation – best in each price range listed. Book in advance at Christmas and New Year.

### $$$$ Capitán Suizo
*A long way south of the centre towards Playa Langosta, T2653-0075, www.hotelcapitansuizo.com.*
8 bungalows, 22 rooms with patio or balcony, a/c, pool, restaurant, kayaking, scuba-diving, surfing and sport fishing available, riding on hotel's own horses, Swiss management. One of Costa Rica's distinctive hotels.

### $$$$-$$$ Tamarindo Bay Boutique Hotel
*100 m south of the Banco Nacional de Costa Rica, west of Hotel Arco Iris, T2653-2692, www.tamarindobayhotel.com.*
Crisp minimalist design, with deluxe rooms being especially 'Zen' and boasting outdoor showers and mini espresso-makers. Swish, intimate and professional.

### $$$ 15 Love
*1 block behind the main road, 200 m before Hotel Jardín del Edén, T2653-0898, www.15lovebedandbreakfast.com.*
15 Love is the hippest hotel in town, boasting spacious standard rooms and sumptuous suites with all modern conveniences and an ocean-view patio shaded by a native tree. Superb design, charming and stylish.

### $$$ Witch's rock surf camp
*Opposite Economy Rental Car, T2653-1238, www.witchsrocksurfcamp.com.*
One of the most popular surf camps in Costa Rica, widely celebrated and built up over the years with a lot of hard work. Various packages and tours available and there's a beginners' break right on the doorstep.

### $$ Hotel Mahayana
*150 m northeast of Hotel Pasatiempo, T2653-1154, www.hotelmahayana.com.*
Simple, tranquil and homely, rooms at Hotel Mahayana feature terracotta floor tiles, private terraces and solid wood beams. Amenities include jacuzzi, kitchen, garden with hammocks, Wi-Fi, tours.

### $$ Villas Macondo
*1 block back from the beach, T2653-0812, www.villasmacondo.com.*
Rooms with shared kitchen and apartments. Pool, washing machine, safety boxes, fridge and friendly people too.

### $$-$ Chocolate Hotel and Hostel
*50 m east from **Stella** restaurant, T2653-1311, www.thechocolatehostel.com.*
The appetizingly named Chocolate Hotel and Hostel boasts 9 large apartment-style suites with private balconies and patios. For the thrifty, there's 'upscale' hostel-style lodging in shared dorms. Pool.

### $ Blue Trailz
*Main street, next to Alamo rent a car, T2653-1705, www.bluetrailz.com.*
Good location near the beach and breaks, this highly popular surf school and hostel has cheap 6-bed dorm rooms ($) with a/c, shared kitchen, hot water, microwave and fridge. Surf-camp packages, board rental, lessons and tours available. For extra comfort, there are also studio apartments ($$$).

### $ Botella de Leche
*300 m from the beach, 2653-0189, www.labotelladeleche.com.*
This self-described '5-star hostel' boasts funky cow decor and a bean bag common room, a 'paradise for the free spirit'. There are dorms and affordable private rooms, all the usual amenities including kitchen and pool. Cosy and sociable.

## Playa Grande

### $$$ La Marajeda
*200 m sur de Minae, T2653-0594, www.hotelswell.com.*
This cosy boutique hotel is a short 3-min walk from the beach. It has 8 crisp, clean, quiet and comfortable rooms with balconies

and terraces overlooking a leafy garden and pool. A simple, tranquil spot.

### $$$-$$ Hotel Las Tortugas
*Right on the beach in the centre of town, T2653-0423, www.lastortugashotel.com.*
11 rooms with bathroom, pool, restaurant, meals included, tours arranged.

### $$$-$ Hotel El Manglar
*Palm Beach Estates, T2653-0952, www.hotel-manglar.com.*
Beachside hostel-hotel, professionally managed by 3 Costa Rican brothers and a sister. Accommodations include dorms ($), good-value split-level standards ($$) and, for those seeking extra comfort, private villas fully kitted with kitchen, living room, hammocks and more ($$$). Recommended.

### $$ Playa Grande Inn
*T2653-0719, www.playagrandeinn.com.*
Formerly **Rancho Diablo**. 10 rooms with fan, good set up for surfers.

## Playa Flamingo and beaches to the north

### $$$$ Casa del Sol
*Playa Portrero, T2296-0375, www.resortcasadelsol.istemp.com.*
Lavish condo units with 2 bedrooms, 2 bathrooms, fully equipped kitchen, washer-dryer, private terrace and patio furniture. Contemporary decor, very swish.

### $$$ Conchal Hotel
*Playa Brasilito, 200 m south of the school, T2654-9125, www.conchalcr.com.*
A 9-room boutique hotel a short walk from Brasilito and Conchal beaches. Tastefully decorated rooms with secluded patio areas, views of the garden and pool.

### $$$ Mariner Inn
*Playa Flamingo, T2654-4081.*
Has 12 rooms with bath, a/c, free camping on the beach.

### $$-$ Hotel Brasilito
*Playa Brasilito, close to beach on plaza, T2654-4237, www.brasilito.com. Closed Mon.*
Good rooms. Horses, kayaks and bikes to rent. **Los Arcades Restaurant**, run by Charlie and Claire, mixes Thai and local dishes.

## Playa Junquillal

### $$$ Casas Pelicano
*300 m north of the school, T2658-9010, www.casaspelicano.cr.*
Overlooking the Pacific Ocean, 2 villas with private access to the beach. Well equipped with hammocks, fans, kitchen, safe. Cooking classes available from Sibyl, the owner, a classically trained chef.

### $$$ Mundo Milo Eco-lodge
*Calle Mundo Milo, T2658-7010, www.mundomilo.com.*
Dutch-owned lodge with interesting African, Mexican and Persian-style *cabinas* built amidst the trees. Very comfortable and creative with a solid sustainable ethos. Breakfast included.

### $$-$ El Castillo Divertido
*T2658-8428, www.costarica-adventureholidays.com.*
Castle rooms, restaurant, gardens, rooftop star-gazing deck, music.

### $$-$ Guacamaya Lodge
*T2658-8431, www.guacamayalodge.com.*
Immaculate bungalows and 1 fully equipped house with pool, ocean views, Swiss cuisine.

### $ Hibiscus
*Cose to the beach, T2658-8437.*
Big rooms with big windows, seafood restaurant with German specialities, garden, 50 m to beach, German-run.

## Playa del Coco and around

**$$$ Mariscos la Guajira**
*On southern beach.*
Popular and beautiful beachfront location.

**$$$ Papagayo**
*Near the beach, T2670-0298.*
Good seafood. Recommended.

**$$ Bananas**
*On the road out of town.*
The place to go drinking and dancing until the early hours.

**$$ Cocos**
*On the plaza, T2670-0235.*
Bit flashy and pricey for the area, but good seafood.

**$$ El Roble**
*Beside the main plaza.*
A popular bar/disco.

**$$ Playa del Coco**
*On the beach.*
Popular, open from 0600.

**$ Jungle Bar**
*On the road into town.*
Another lively, slightly rougher option.

## Playa Tamarindo and around

**$$$ Fiesta del Mar**
*On the loop at the end of town.*
Large thatched open barn, good food, good value.

**$$$ Ginger**
*At the northern end of town, T2672-0041. Tue-Sun.*
Good Thai restaurant.

**$$ Iguana Surf Restaurant**
*On road to Playa Langosta.*
Good atmosphere and food.

**$$ Coconut Café**
*On beach near Tamarindo Vista.*
Pizzas, pastries and good fish. Check for good breakfasts and cheap evening meals.

**$$ El Arrecife**
*On roundabout.*
Popular spot to hang out, with Tico fare, good chicken and pizzas.

**$$ The Lazy Wave**
*On road leading away from the beach, T2653-0737.*
Menu changes daily, interesting mix of cuisine, seafood.

**$$ Portofino**
*At end of road by roundabout.*
Italian specialities and good ice cream.

**$$ Stellas**
*On road leading away from the beach.*
Very good seafood, try *dorado* with mango cream. Recommended.

**$ Arco Iris**
*On road heading inland.*
Cheap vegetarian, great atmosphere.

**$ Frutas Tropicales**
*Near Tamarindo Vista.*
Snacks and breakfast.

## Playa Flamingo and beaches to the north

**$$ La Casita del Pescado**
*Playa Brasilito.*
Some reasonably priced fish dishes which you have to eat quickly because the stools are made of concrete.

**$$ Marie's Restaurant**
*Playa Flamingo, T2654-4136.*
Breakfast, seafood, *casados* and international dishes.

**$$ Pizzeria Il Forno**
*Playa Brasilito.*
Serves a mean pizza.

**$$ Restaurant La Boca de la Iguana**
*Playa Brasilito.*
Good value.

**$$-$ Las Brisas**
*At the northern end of Playa Potrero.*
A great spot for a beer and a snack,
surprisingly popular for its cut-off location.

**$ Costa Azul**
*Playa Potrero, by the football pitch.*
One of several restaurants in the area,
popular with locals.

**$ Cyber Shack**
*Playa Brasilito.*
Internet, coffee, breakfast and UPS service.

### Playa Junquillal

**$$$ La Puesta del Sol**
*T2658-8442.*
The only restaurant along the strip, but then
nothing could compete with the dishes from
this little piece of Italy. Spectacular setting.
Very popular so reservations required.

## Entertainment

### Playa Tamarindo and around
With a long beachside strip, it's a question of
exploring town until you find something that
works. Call it bar surfing if you like.

## Shopping

### Playa Tamarindo and around
The town is increasingly a retail outlet selling
everything you need for the beach. There are
also a couple of general stores in the centre.

## What to do

### Playa del Coco and around
**Agua Rica Charters**, *T2670-0473, or contact
them through the internet café.* Can arrange
transport to Witch's Rock for surfers,
approximately US$400 for up to 10.

**Deep Blue Diving**, *beside Hotel Coco Verde,
T2670-1004, www.deepblue-diving.com.*
Has diving trips to Islas Catalinas and Islas
Murciélago, where sightings of manta rays
and bull sharks are common. 2-tank dive
from US$79. Will also rent gear.
**Rich Coast Diving**, *T2670-0176,
www.richcoastdiving.com.*

### Playa Hermosa and Playa Panamá
**Diving Safari**, *based at the Sol Playa Hermosa
Resort on Playa Hermosa, T2453-5044,
www.billbeardcostarica.com.* One of the
longest-running diving operations in the
country, offering a wide range of options
in the region.

### Playa Tamarindo and around
**Diving**
Try the **Pacific Coast Dive Center** (T2653-
0267), or **Agua Rica Dive Center** (T2653-0094).

**Surfing and yoga**
**Iguana Surf Tours**, *T2653-0148.* Rent
surfboards, they have one outlet near the
beach, opposite the supermarket, the other
in the restaurant of the same name.
**VOEC**, *on the beach, T2653-0852, www.
voecretreats.com.* A women's retreat that
offers 6-night packages, which include surf
and yoga lessons.

**Tour operators**
There are many tours on offer to see the
turtles nesting at night in Playa Grande.
**Hightide Adventures and Surfcamp**,
*T2653-0108, www.tamarindoadventures.net.*
Offers a full range of tours.

## Transport

### Playa del Coco and around
**Bus** From **San José** from Calle 14,
Av 1-3, 0800, 1400, 5 hrs, return 0800,
1400 US$7. 6 buses daily from **Liberia**,
0530-1815, return 0530-1800.

**Playa Hermosa and Playa Panamá**

**Bus** From **Liberia**, Empresa Esquivel, 0730, 1130, 1530, 1730, 1900, return 0500, 0600, 1000, 1600, 1700, US$1.20.

**Playa Tamarindo and around**

**Air** Several daily flights from **San José** with Sansa (US$71, 1 way) and NatureAir (from US$83 to US$111) from **San José**. Daily flight from **La Fortuna** with Sansa.

**Bus** From **Santa Cruz**, 0410, 1330, 1500 daily. To Santa Cruz 1st bus at 0600, US$0.70. Express bus from **San José** daily from Terminal Alfaro, 1530, return 0600 Mon-Sat, 0600, Sun 1230, 5½ hrs. Bus back to San José, can be booked through Hotel Tamarindo Diria, T2653 0032, US$9.60.

**Playa Flamingo and beaches to the north**

**Bus** From **San José** to Flamingo, Brasilito and Potrero, daily from Av 3, Calle 18-20, 0800, 1000, 6 hrs, from US$9.50, return 0900, 1400. From **Santa Cruz** daily 0630, 1500, return 0900, 1700, 64 km to Potrero.

**Playa Junquillal**

**Bus** Daily from **Santa Cruz** departs 1030, around US$9.80, returns to Santa Cruz at 1530.

## Nicoya and around   *Colour map 4, B2.*

*pleasant little town at the heart of the peninsula*

Nicoya is distinguished by possessing the country's second oldest church, the 17th-century church of San Blas. Damaged by an earthquake in 1822 it was restored in 1831 and is currently undergoing renovations. The Parque Central, on Avenida Central, is leafy and used for occasional concerts. Buses arrive at Avenida 1, Calle 3-5. Most hotels and banks are within a couple of blocks of the central park. The area Conservation Offices (ACT) are on the northern side of Parque Central. There is no general information for visitors, but they can assist with specific enquiries.

### Parque Nacional Barra Honda
*Entry US$10, no permit required.*

A small park in the north of the Nicoya Peninsula, Barra Honda National Park (2295 ha) was created to protect a *mesa* with a few caves and the last remains of dry tropical forest in the region. The park office is near Barra Honda at **Santa Ana**, at the foot of the *mesa*, and there are two different trails to the top; two hours' hiking.

### Sámara and Playa Carrillo
Sámara (www.samarabeach.com) is a smallish Tico village that has maintained some of its regular way of life alongside tourist development. The beautiful beach, 37 km from Nicoya on a paved road, is probably the safest and one of the best bathing beaches in Costa Rica. Playa Carrillo is 5 km away at the south end of the beach. The litter problem is being tackled with rubbish bins, warning signs, refuse collections and bottle banks. Both places have airstrips served by scheduled services from San José.

### Nosara
Nosara (www.nosara.com) is a small village about 26 km north of Sámara without much to see or do in it – which makes it ideal if you like lying around on beaches. Indeed most come for the three unspoiled beaches which are not particularly close to the village.

**Playa Nosara** is north of the village across the Río Nosara where you may see turtles (see below); **Peladas** is the prettiest and smallest, south of the river, and **Guiones** is safe for swimming and good for surfing. Expatriates have formed the **Nosara Civic Association** to protect the area's wildlife and forests and prevent exploitation.

## Playa Ostional

North of Nosara is Playa Ostional where olive ridley turtles lay eggs July-November along the coastal strip of the **Refugio Nacional de Vida Silvestre Ostional**. The turtles arrive for nesting at high tide. The villagers are allowed to harvest the eggs in a designated area of the beach, the rest are protected and monitored. Outside the egg-laying period it is very quiet. Contact the MINAE (Ministry of Environment and Energy) ① *T682-0470*, ranger station for details.

## Listings Nicoya and around

### Where to stay

#### Sámara

**$$$$-$$$ El Pequeño Gecko Verde**
*600 m west and 100 m south of*
*Hotel Samara Pacific Lodge, T2656-1176,*
*www.gecko-verde.com.*
Set in a lush tropical garden, 7 luxurious bungalows and 2 spacious rooms, all constructed using locally sourced wood. 5 mins by car from the village. Restful, recommended.

**$$$ Lodge Las Ranas**
*800 m al oeste del Cruce de Cangrejal,*
*T2656-0609, www.lodgelasranas.com.*
A 10-room hotel set up on a hill to enjoy fine views of the mountains, ocean and jungle canopy below. Internet, kitchenette, breakfast, pool, private balconies.

**$$$ Samara Tree House**
*Playa Sámara, T2656-0733,*
*www.samaratreehouse.com.*
6 luxury wood-built *casitas* on stilts, arranged in a neat row at the edge of the sand. Lush tropical gardens and an adults-only pool.

**$$$-$$ Belvedere**
*Sloping up the hill, T2656-0213.*
Very friendly German owners. A cosy hotel with 10 small rooms, very clean. Recommended.

**$$$-$$ Hotel Giada**
*Main street, T2656-3232, www.hotelgiada.net.*
24 rooms with a/c, cable TV, private bath and balcony. Amenities include pizza restaurant, Wi-Fi, jacuzzi, a smart green lawn and pools.

**$$ Hotel Entre Dos Aguas**
*1st property in Sámara, T2656-0998,*
*www.hoteldosaguas.com.*
A tranquil 8-room hotel a short walk from the beach. Good-value rooms are spacious and include furniture crafted from local wood, stone and mosaic hot water showers. Lovely garden with a pool and hammocks.

**$$-$ Hostel El Cactus**
*10 m south of Casa Coba, T2656-3224,*
*www.samarabackpacker.com.*
Located in the village, with good access to all the local services. A modern hostel with a large living room, TV, communal kitchen, garden and pool. Dorms, private rooms and bungalows available.

#### Nosara

**$$$$ The Harmony Hotel**
*Playa Guiones, T2682-4114,*
*www.harmonynosara.com.*
Secluded and upscale surf lodge situated on a pristine break from any paved roads. Beautiful stylish rooms, suites and bungalows. Very tranquil. Recommended.

### $$$ Lagarta Lodge
*Reserva Biológica Nosara, Playa Pelada,*
*T2682-0035, www.lagarta.com.*
Situated on a commanding elevated bluff
overlooking the ocean. Lodgings include
6 cosy standards and 6 superiors with views.
Lots of wildlife in the area thanks to the
adjacent nature reserve, including 270 bird
species. Pool and restaurant.

### $$$ Living Hotel
*G-Section, Playa Guiones, T2682-5201,*
*www.livinghotelnosara.com.*
The epitome of rustic chic with boutique-
styled wooden ranchos, spa treatments,
yoga and surf retreats. Concierge service,
saltwater pool, organic restaurant and Wi-Fi.

### $$$-$$ Gilded Iguana Hotel
*Playa Guiones, T2682-0259,*
*www.thegildediguana.com.*
Established in 1986, one of the oldest hotels
in the area. Located 200 m from the beach
with pool, Wi-Fi, free coffee, rooms with or
without a/c. Family friendly.

### $$-$ Almost Paradise
*Playa Pelada, T2682-0172,*
*www.almostparadise2012.com.*
Fun, funky hostel with affordable
dorms and private rooms, bar, restaurant,
occasional spit-roasted pig.

### $$-$ Jungle's Edge
*200 m south of Nosara Yoga Institute then 200 m*
*west, T2682-5314, www.jungles-edge.com.*
A wide range of lodging from luxury suites to
tents. Amenities include communal rancho
with kitchen, juice bar, Wi-Fi and an open-air
workout area for yoga, dance and martial arts.

### $ Nosara Beach Hostel
*200 m south of Harbor Reef Hotel, Punta*
*Guiones, T2682-0238, www.nosarahostel.com.*
Clean, sociable hostel with affordable bunk
beds and 2 private rooms. Wi-Fi, board
games and play station.

### Playa Ostional
You can camp on the beach.

### $ Cabinas Guacamaya
*T2682-0430.*
With bath, clean, good food on request.
Price per person.

### $ Cabinas Ostional
*Next to the village shop.*
Very cheap and basic accommodation in
cabins with bath, clean, friendly.

## Restaurants

### Nicoya

### $$ Café de Blita
*2 km outside Nicoya towards Sámara.*
Good.

### $$ Soda El Triángulo
*Opposite Chorotega.*
Good juices and snacks, friendly owners.

### $$ Teyet
*Near Hotel Jenny.*
Good, with quick service.

### $ Daniela
*1 block east of plaza.*
Breakfast, lunches, coffee, *refrescos*, good.

### Sámara
There are several cheap *sodas* around the
football pitch in the centre of town.

### $$$ Restaurant Delfín
*On the beach.*
Very good value and French-owned.
They also rent out *cabinas*.

### $$ El Ancla Restaurant
*On the beach, T2656-0716.*
Seafood.

### $$ Las Brasas
*By the football pitch, T2656-0546.*
Spanish restaurant and bar.

### $$ Restaurant Acuario
*On the beach.*
Serves Tico and other food.

**$ Soda Sol y Mar**
*On the road to Nosara.*
Costa Rican and international food.

## Nosara

**$$$ Gilded Iguana**
*Playas Guiones.*
Gringo food and good company.

**$$$ La Dolce Vita**
*South along the road out of town.*
Good but pricey Italian food.

**$$ Casa Romántica**
*Playas Guiones.*
The European restaurant.

**$$ Corky Carroll's Surf School**
*T2682-0385.*
Surf lessons and a good Mexican/Thai
restaurant (closed Sun).

**$$ Giardino Tropicale**
*In the middle section.*
Pizza.

**$$ Hotel Almost Paradise**
*Playas Guiones, T2682-0173.*
Good food with a great view.

**$$ La Luna**
*Slightly up the hill.*
Good food and ambience.

**$$ Olga's**
*Playa Peladas.*
Seafood on the beach.

**$ Soda Vanessa**
*Playas Guiones.*
One of several *sodas* in the village.
Good, very cheap.

## Playa Ostional

**$$-$ Mirador de los Tortugueros**
*1 km south of Cabinas Guacamaya.*
Good restaurant with coffee and pancakes.
Great atmosphere. Recommended.

### Sámara
**Bar La Góndola** is popular and has a dart
board. Opposite is **Bar Colocho**. **Dos
Lagartos** disco is on the beach near Al
Manglar; and the disco at **Isla Chora** is the
place to be during the season if you like
resort discos.

### Nosara
Some of the nightlife is in the village as well;
**Bambú**, **Disco Tropicana** and various others
line the football pitch.

### Sámara
Most hotels will arrange tours for you.
You can rent bikes from near the *ferretería*
on the road to Cangrejal. Recommended,
though are:
**Tip Top Tours**, *T2656-0650*. Run by a very
nice French couple, offering dolphin tours
(from US$45 per person), mangrove tours
(US$43 per person) and waterfall tours
(US$20 per person). Naturalist guided tours
to Barra Honda and Isla Chora (US$70 per
person), as well as slightly more unusual trips
like *Journée Cowboy* where you spend a day
on the ranch roping cattle and eat with a
Tico family.
**Wing Nuts Canopy Tour**, *T2656-0153.*
*US$40, kids US$25.* Family-run, friendly
service, spectacular ocean views from
the treetops, with 12 platforms, lots of
wildlife close up, great photo opportunity,
1st-class equipment.

### Nosara
**Casa Río Nosara** for horse or river tours and
**Gilded Iguana** for kayaking and fishing. For
turtle tours, try **Rancho Suizo** (T2682-0057),
or **Lagarta Lodge** (T2682-0035), who are
both sensitive to the turtles and don't exploit
or bother them.

## Transport

### Nicoya
**Bus** From **San José**, 8 daily from Terminal Alfaro, 6 hrs, US$6.70-9; from **Liberia** every 30 mins from 0430-2200; from **Santa Cruz** hourly 0630-2130. To **Playa Naranjo** at 0500 and 1300, 2¼ hrs, US$3. 12 buses per day to **Sámara**, 37 km by paved road, 1 to **Nosara**.

### Sámara
**Air** Daily flights from **San José**, Sansa US$71, **Nature Air**, US$83-111.

**Bus** From **Nicoya**, 45 km, 1½ hrs, US$2.20, 0800, 1500, 1600, return 0530, 0630, 1130, 1330, 1630. Express bus from Terminal Alfaro, **San José** daily at 1230, return Mon-Sat 0430, Sun 1300, 5-6 hrs. School bus to **Nosara** around 1600; ask locally for details. It is not possible to go from Sámara along the coast to Montezuma, except in 4WD vehicle; not enough traffic for hitching.

**Taxi** Official and others stop outside bus station (US$20 to **Nosara**, US$10 to **Nicoya**).

### Nosara
**Air** Sansa has daily flights to **San José**, US$71, **Nature Air**, US$83-111.

**Bus** Daily from **Nicoya** to Nosara, **Garza**, **Guiones** daily from main station, 1300, return 0600, US$3, 2 hrs; from **San José** daily from Terminal Alfaro at 0600, 6 hrs, return 1245.

### Playa Ostional
**Bus** 1 daily at 0500 to **Santa Cruz** and **Liberia**, returns 1230 from Santa Cruz, 3 hrs, US$1.75.

---

## Southern Península de Nicoya  *Colour map 4, B2.*

**low-key coastal villages, waterfalls and wildlife reserves**

The southern Nicoya Peninsula is almost completely cut off from the north. Roads are appalling and those that exist are frequently flooded in part. For this reason most access the region by ferry from Puntarenas. Beaches and stopping points are dotted along the southern shore of the peninsula, passing through Tambor, Montezuma, Cabuya, Mal País and Playa Santa Teresa.

### Playa Naranjo and Paquera
Arriving at **Playa Naranjo** there are several expensive eating places by the dock and a gas station. **Paquera** is a small village 22 km along the coast from Playa Naranjo. There are a few shops and some simple lodgings; for example, **Cabinas Rosita** on the inland side of the village. It is separated from the quay by 1 km or so; apart from a good *soda*, a restaurant, a public telephone and a branch of **Banco de Costa Rica**, there are no facilities.

### Tambor, Curú National Wildlife Refuge and Cóbano
The small village of **Tambor**, 19 km from Paquera, has a dark-sand beach, some shops and restaurants. The beach is beautiful, 6 km long with rolling surf, but 1½ hours on a bone-shaking road from the ferry. However, cruise ships from Puntarenas come here and part of the beach has been absorbed by the large and controversial **Hotel Playa Tambor**. Built around a cattle farm by the Barceló group of Spain, the resort is alleged to have encroached on the public beach and drained a swamp that was a wildfowl habitat. A second stage is planned at **Punta Piedra Amarilla**, with a 500-boat marina, villas and a total of 1100 rooms. Buses travelling from Paquera to Montezuma, pass through Tambor, connecting with the car ferry arriving from Puntarenas, US$2.60, two hours.

North of Playa Tambor is the **Curú National Wildlife Refuge** ⓘ *T2661-2392, in advance and ask for Doña Julieta*, which is only 84 ha, but has five different habitats and 110 species of bird. Access is through private land.

**Cóbano**, near Montezuma, can be reached by bus from Paquera ferry terminal and buses for Tambor, Cóbano and Montezuma meet the launches from Puntarenas (there is an airstrip with flights from San José). Roads north, west and south out of Cóbano, require 4WD. Cóbano has a petrol/gas station.

## ★ Montezuma

No longer a sleepy hamlet, Montezuma is a very popular small village on the sea. It is a well-liked backpacking destination and at busy periods hotels fill up every day, so check in early. Although it gets crowded, there are some wonderful beaches; many are rocky, with strong waves making it difficult to swim, but it's very scenic. There are beautiful walks along the beach – sometimes sandy, sometimes rocky, always lined with trees – that visit impressive waterfalls. The village can be reached in four hours from Puntarenas if you get the early launch. There is a tourist office at **Aventuras Montezuma**, which is very helpful and often knows which hotel has space; ask here first before looking around. The once-popular **Cabinas Karen** are now closed. Prior to her death in 1994, Doña Karen donated her land to the National Parks in memory of her late husband, creating what was to become Reserva Natural Absoluta Cabo Blanco (see below). **Cabinas Karen** now houses park guards.

### Around Montezuma

Close to the village, 20 minutes up the Río Montezuma, is a beautiful, huge **waterfall** with a big, natural swimming hole, beyond which is a smaller waterfall. Intrepid walkers can carry on up to further waterfalls but it can be dangerous and accidents have been reported. There's another waterfall, 6 km north of Montezuma, with a pool right by the beach – follow the road out to the beach at the north end of town and keep going past three coves for about half an hour until you reach the trail off to the left (you can't miss it). See Tour operators, below.

You can use Montezuma as a base for exploring the **Reserva Natural Absoluta Cabo Blanco** ⓘ *Wed-Sun 0800-1600, US$6, jeep/taxi from Montezuma US$7, first at 0700, returns 1600*. The 1172-ha reserve is 11 km from Montezuma. The marine birds include frigate birds, pelicans and brown boobies; there are also monkeys, anteaters, kinkajou and collared peccary. You can bathe in the sea or under a waterfall. At the beautiful **Playa Balsitas**, 6 km from the entrance, there are pelicans and howler monkeys.

At **Cabuya**, 2 km from Cabo Blanco Reserve, the sea can be cloudy after rough weather. Cabuya Island can be visited on foot at low tide. On the road west out of Cabuya, **Cafetería El Coyote** specializes in local and Caribbean dishes. On the west coast of the peninsula is the fast-growing village of **Mal País**. The coast here is virtually unspoilt with long white beaches, creeks and natural pools, and the facilities stretch north up the beach to blend with **Santa Teresa**. The surfing appeal of the area is growing with Mal País best suited for beginners, with the more experienced crowd going up to Santa Teresa. It's a fast-changing area.

You can also arrange tours to **Isla Tortuga**. Many businesses rent horses; check that the horses are fit and properly cared for. Recommended for horses are **Cocozuma Traveller** and **Aventuras Montezuma**.

## Where to stay

### Playa Naranjo

**$$ Oasis del Pacífico**
*On beach, T2661-0209.*
A/c, old building, clean, quiet, with pool, good restaurant and free transport from ferry. Recommended.

**$ Cabinas Maquinay**
*1.3 km towards Jicaral, T2661-1763.*
Simple rooms with a pool and the attached **Disco Maquinay**.

**$ El Paso**
*North of ferry, T2641-8133.*
With bath, cheaper without, cold water, clean, restaurant and pool.

### Tambor, Curú National Wildlife Refuge and Cóbano

**$$$$ Tango Mar**
*3 km from Tambor, T2683-0001, www.tangomar.com.*
All services including golf course and its own waterfall.

**$ Cabinas Cristina**
*On the beach, Tambor, T2683-0028.*
With bath, cheaper without, good food.

**$ Dos Lagartos**
*Tambor, T2683-0236.*
Cheap, clean, good value.

### Montezuma

Montezuma is a very small place; hotels furthest from the centre are a 10-min walk.

**$$$ El Tajalín**
*T2642-0061, www.tajalin.com.*
Very smart hotel, spotlessly clean, rooms come with private hot water shower and a/c, located in a quiet out of the way spot and yet moments from the high street. Hammock terrace for relaxing.

**$$$-$$ Amor de Mar**
*T2642-0262, www.amordemar.com.*
This well-loved hotel has the feeling of a special place. Rooms are pristine with private bath and hot water. Breakfast and brunch is served on a very pretty terrace that joins well-manicured gardens, where visitors can recline in hammocks and gaze out to sea.

**$$$-$$ El Jardín**
*T642 0074, www.hoteleljardin.com.*
15 rooms and 2 fully equipped villas located on the hill overlooking the town and ocean beyond. Shower, hot water, a/c, private terraces and hammocks. In the grounds is a pool with a little waterfall, very restful and great views, superb spot.

**$$$-$$ Los Mangos**
*A short walk south of the village, T2642-0076, www.hotellosmangos.com.*
Large site comprising 9 bungalows, each accommodating 3 people. Also 10 rooms, some with shared bath, some for 4 people. Yoga classes run from an open-sided pagoda on the grounds. Different and fun and lots of free mangos (when in season).

**$$ Cabinas Mar y Cielo**
*On the beach, T2642-0261.*
Has 6 rooms, sleeping 2-5 people, all with bath, fan and sea view. Recommended.

**$$ Horizontes**
*On road to Cóbano, T2642-0534, www.horizontes-montezuma.com.*
Language school, restaurant, pool, hot water. Highly recommended.

**$$ Montezuma Paradise**
*10 mins' walk out of town, on the road to Cabuya, past the waterfall entrance, T2642-0271.*
Very friendly owners have rooms with shared bath and 1 with private bath, overlooking the ocean and minutes from a secluded beach cove.

### $$-$ La Cascada
*5 mins' walk out of town, on the road to Cabo Blanco, close to the entrance to the waterfalls, T2642-0057.*
Lovely hotel with pretty, well-kept rooms and a wide hammock terrace overlooking the ocean for relaxing. Restaurant serves local food for breakfast, lunch and dinner.

### $ El Tucán
*At the top of the road down to the beach, T2642-0284.*
Wooden hotel on stilts, clean, small wood-panelled rooms, shared shower and toilet, fan, mosquito net on window. Recommended.

### $ Hotel El Capitán
*On the main street, T2642-0069.*
Old wooden house with an endless variety of rooms, most with shared cold-water bath, but some with private bath. Very friendly owners and good location, can get a little noisy, good for backpackers.

### $ Lucy
*Follow road south past Los Mangos, T2642-0273.*
One of the oldest hotels in town and one of the most popular budget options, due to its location on the sea. 10 rooms with fans, some with sea view. Shared bath, pleasant balcony. Ultra-friendly Tica owner. Restaurant next door opens during high season. Recommended.

### $ Pensión Arenas
*On the beach, T2642-0308.*
Run by Doña Meca, rustic small rooms, with fan, shared bath, no frills but pleasant balcony and sea view. Free camping. Laundry service. Cheap.

---

### Around Montezuma

### $$$$ Milarepa
*Playa Santa Teresa, on beach, T2640-0023, www.milarepahotel.com.*
Nice bamboo bungalows, open-air bathroom.

### $$$ Celaje
*Cabuya, on beach, T2642-0374, www.celaje.com.*
Very good Italian restaurant. Pool, rooms with bath, hot water, good.

### $$$-$$ Los Caballos
*3 km north on road to Cóbano from Montezuma, T2642-0124.*
Has 8 rooms with bath, pool, outdoor restaurant, ocean views, gardens. 5 mins from beach. Great horse-riding trips.

### $$$-$ Funky Monkey Lodge
*Santa Teresa, T2640-0317, www.funky-monkey-lodge.com.*
The very friendly and hospitable owners have extended their relaxed and very attractive resort. They now have 1 bungalow sleeping 8 people, 3 private bungalows and 2 apartments, sleeping 2-4 and a suite with a large balcony overlooking the ocean. They also have a rather upmarket dormitory with beds rather than bunks. Recommended.

### $$$-$ Mal País Surf Camp
*Mal País, T2640-0031, www.malpaissurfcamp.com.*
Restaurant, pool, also has camping.

### $$-$ Cabañas Bosque Mar
*Mal País, T2640-0074.*
Clean, large rooms, hot-water shower, attractive grounds, good restaurant on beach nearby, 3 km to Cabo Blanco Reserve.

### $$-$ Cabinas Las Rocas
*20 mins south of Montezuma, T2642-0393, www.caboblancopark.com.*
Good but quite expensive meals, small, seashore setting, isolated.

### $$-$ Frank's Place
*Mal País, the road junction, T2640-0096.*
Set in tropical gardens. Wide variety of rooms with private or shared bath and self-catering options available. Good range of services and local advice.

### $ Cabañas Playa El Carmen
*Playa Santa Teresa, T2683-0281.*

Basic, very cheap cabins and camping, shared bath and kitchen. **Jungle Juice**, vegetarian restaurant, serves smoothies and meals from US$4.

**$ Cabinas y Restaurante El Ancla de Oro**
*Cabuya, T2642-0369.*
Some cabins with bath, others shared bathroom, seafood restaurant, lobster dinners US$10, filling breakfasts, owned by Alex Villalobos, horses US$20 per day with local guide, mountain bike rental, transport from Paquera launch available.

**$ Casa Zen**
*Santa Teresa.*
Smart, budget accommodation with shared bath and 1 fully furnished apartment. Camping area also available. Close to the beach, restaurant on site.

**$ Mochila Inn**
*300 m outside Montezuma, T2642-0030.*
*Cabinas* from US$30, also houses and apartments for around US$350 per month.

## Restaurants

### Montezuma

**$$$ Playa de Los Artistas/Cocina Mediterránea**
*About 5 mins south of town on the road to Cabuya.*
Best restaurant in town.

**$$ Bakery Café**
*North end of town.*
Great for breakfast, with bread, cakes and excellent vegetarian food.

**$$ Brisas del Mar**
*Just south of the soccer ground in Santa Teresa.*
Offers great local seafood – tuna or *mahi mahi* straight from the boats at Mal País. Great service and atmosphere. Highly recommended.

**$$ Chico's Playa Bar**
*On the beach.*
Popular hangout, great sushi. They stop serving food in the low season.

**$$ Cocolores**
*On the beach behind El Pargo Feliz, T2642-0096. Closed Mon.*
Good for seafood and veggie options.

**$ El Pulpo Pizzeria**
*Santa Teresa*
Good-value pizzeria that also delivers.

**$$ El Sano Banano**
*On the road to the beach.*
Healthfood restaurant, good vegetarian food, large helpings, daily change of menu, milkshakes, fresh fruit and yoghurt, owned by Dutch/Americans, free movies with dinner.

**$$ Pizza Romana**
*Opposite El Capitán.*
Good Italian food cooked by Italians, pizzas, pesto, fresh pastas, etc.

**$$-$ Tayrona**
*Behind Taganga.*
Great pizza, Italian-owned, attractive restaurant off the main street.

**$ Soda El Caracol**
*Located by the football field.*
One of several *sodas* around town serving good Tico food, very cheap.

**$ Soda Monte Sol**
*On the road to Cabo Blanco.*
Recommended for good Mexican burritos, good value, big helpings.

**$ Taganga**
*Located at the top of the high street, opposite El Tucán hostel.*
Argentine grills, chicken and meat.

## Entertainment

### Montezuma

**Bar Moctezuma**, usually open the latest, but not as loud as the others.
**Chico's Bar** and **Chico's Playa Bar**, cocktail by the beach, or late-night salsa dancing and very loud reggaeton parties.
**Congo Azul Bar**, reggae nights Thu and Sat.

## Around Montezuma

New bars are opening up every year along the beachfront at Mal País. For a treat, try a *mojito* on the terrace at the exclusive resort of **Flor Blanca** at the northern edge of Santa Teresa.

**Bar Tabu**, *Santa Teresa*. Probably the most popular bar in the area, great location on the beach; good music, always lively, open late.

**La Llora Amarilla**, *Santa Teresa*. Now very popular, large venue that hosts regular disco and party nights.

**Mal País Surf Camp**, *Mal País*. Bar open every night, live jam night on Wed.

## Shopping

### Sámara

**Free Radical** supermarket/*soda* on main road, 1 km east of town centre. Fresh ceviche, delightful pastries, beer, wine, natural juices, local honey and unusual hand-blown glass products.

**Supermarket**, *near Casa del Mar*. Well stocked and you can get fresh bread and croissants from **Chez Joel**.

### Montezuma

There are rather pricey boutique-style souvenir and clothes shops in Montezuma, most selling a very similar range.

**Librería Topsy**, *T2642-0576. Mon-Fri 0800-1400, Sat 0800-1200*. Sells books and maps and will take postcards and small letters to the post office for you.

## What to do

### Montezuma

**Aventuras en Montezuma**, *T2642-0050*. Offers a similar range, snorkelling to Tortuga Island, canopy, sunset and wildlife tours for similar prices, also taxi boat to Jacó, US$35, minimum 5 people. Ivan and his staff are also very helpful as a tourist office and can advise on hotels and other matters locally and nationally. They also book and confirm flights.

**Cocozuma Traveller**, *T2642-0911, www. cocozumacr.com*. Tico-owned company, now one of the best in Montezuma. Runs all the usual tours including horse rides and Isla Tortuga. Their boat taxi now runs to Jacó (US$40), Sámara (US$40) and Tamarindo (US$40). They will also arrange hotels, transfers, car rental and have quadbikes for hire. Very helpful staff are happy to give information about the area.

**Montezuma Eco Tours**, *on the corner opposite Soda Monte Sol, T2642-1000, www. montezumaecotours.com*. Offer a wide range of tours, including shuttle to Cabo Blanco (US$3), kayaking/snorkelling at Isla Cabuya (US$25 per person), day trip to Isla Tortuga (US$40 per person), horse rental (US$25) and bike rental (US$5 per day). Also boat/ road transfers to Jacó/Tamarindo for around US$150 for up to 6 people.

**Montezuma Expeditions**, *top of the high street, T2642-0919, www.montezuma expeditions.com*. Very efficient set up organizing private and group transport around the country. Trips cost US$35-US$48 per person, and include San José, La Fortuna (Arenal), Monteverde and Jacó.

**Zuma Tours**, *Cóbano, T8849-8569, www. zumatours.net*. Lots of information available on their website.

## Transport

### Montezuma

**Bus** To **Paquera** daily at 0530, 0815, 1000, 1215, 1400 and 1600, connecting with the car and passenger ferry to **Puntarenas** central docks. Tickets available in advance from tourist information centre; be at bus stop outside **Hotel Moctezuma** in good time as the bus fills up quickly, US$2.60, 1 hr (paved road). To **Cabuya** US$1, buses run 4 times a day. Change at Cóbano for **Mal País** – 2 buses run daily from Cóbano, 1100 and 1400 (check as times can change).

**Taxi** To **Cóbano** US$5. To **Paquera** US$20.

# Central
## Pacific coast

West of the central highlands lies a narrow lowland strip of African palm with just the occasional cattle ranch. But, for the visitor, it is the miles of beaches stretching from Jacó almost continuously south to Uvita that are the real attraction. Parque Nacional Manuel Antonio is a major destination with developed services. Further south, the beaches are quieter and the Parque Nacional Marino Ballena, which is harder to get to, is barely developed; but it's of interest to divers and whale watchers.

## Puntarenas and around  *Colour map 4, B3.*

### a decaying port and pleasure resort

West of San José and the Meseta Central, the Pan-American Highway descends 800 m to Esparza, an attractive town that was repeatedly sacked by pirates in the 17th century, belying its peaceful nature today. A further 15 km west, Barranca marks the turning for Puntarenas, no more than six avenues wide, which fills a 5-km spit thrusting east–west into the Gulf of Nicoya. Once the country's main Pacific port with rail links to the Central Highlands, it has since been superseded by Caldera a few kilometres to the south.

The northern side of the peninsula, around Calle Central, has a market, banks, a few grimy hotels and the fishing docks. It is run-down and neglected, typical of small tropical ports. In an effort to reinvent itself as a tourist destination, the southern side is made up of the **Paseo de las Turistas**, a seafront esplanade that draws crowds to the hot, sometimes dirty beach, especially at weekends.

Most people come to Puntarenas to party, but the town boasts a handful of modest attractions. In the cultural centre by the main church and tourist office, you'll find the mildly diverting **Museo de la Historia Marina** ① *T2661-5036, Tue-Sun 0945-1200, 1300-1715, US$1.80.* **Puntarenas Marine Park** ① *T2661-5272, www.parquemarino.org, daily 0900-1700, US$10 children US$5,* offers 28 large aquariums showing Costa Rica's marine life. In

**Best** for
Adventure sports ▪ Beaches ▪ Diving ▪ Whale watching ▪ Wildlife

the gulf are several islands including the **Islas Negritas**, a biological reserve reached by passenger launches.

Puntarenas is popular with Tico tourists, but largely overlooked by foreign travellers, who use it as nothing more than a transport hub; from Puntarenas, you can take the ferry to the southern Nicoya Peninsula, or a bus north or south to other parts of the country without returning to San José. If heading for Nicoya, see page 793. If heading to Santa Elena/Monteverde, see page 767.

### Esparza to the Pacific coast

From Esparza on the Pan-American Highway a road runs 21 km southeast to **San Mateo** (from where a road runs northeast to Atenas and the Central Highlands; see page 742). Just before San Mateo, at Higuito de San Mateo, is **Las Candelillas** ① T2428-9157, a 26-ha farm and reforestation project with fruit trees and sugar cane. There is a day use recreational area with showers, pool and riding, trails and bar/restaurant.

From San Mateo a road runs south to **Orotina**, which used to be an important road/rail junction on the San José–Puntarenas route. Today the area is home to **Original Canopy Tour** at **Mahogany Park** ① T2257-5149, www.canopytour.com, which charges US$45 to fly through the trees; transportation is available.

West of Orotina the road forks northwest to the port of **Caldera**, via Cascajal, and southwest to the Pacific coast at Tárcoles.

### Listings Puntarenas and around

### Where to stay

#### Puntarenas

Accommodation is difficult to find from Dec-Apr, especially at weekends.

**$$$$-$$$ Tioga**
*On the beachfront with Calle 17, T2661-0271, www.hoteltioga.com.*
54 rooms; those with balconies are much better, with views. Private bath, a/c, TV and telephone. Restaurant, pool, very good.

**$$ La Punta**
*Av 1, Calle 35, T2661-0696.*
Good spot 1 block from car ferry, with bath, hot water, secure parking, good pool. American-owned, big rooms, friendly, clean.

**$$-$ Gran Hotel Chorotega**
*On the corner of Calle 1, Av 3 near the banks and market, T2661-0998, www.hotelchorotega.com.*
Clean rooms with private bath, cheaper with shared. Efficient and friendly service. Popular with visiting business people. A good deal.

### Restaurants

#### Puntarenas

**$$ Casa de Mariscos**
*Calle 7-9, T2661-1666. Closed Wed.*
On the beachfront, good seafood, reasonable prices.

**$$ La Yunta**
*On the beachfront at Calle 19, T2661-3216.*
A popular steakhouse, open all night.

**$ Soda Macarena**
*Opposite the Muelle de Cruceros (dock).*
Handy while waiting for buses.

### Transport

#### Puntarenas

**Bus** Terminal for San José is at Calle 2, Av 2-4. Buses every 40 mins, 0415-1900 to **San José**, 2 hrs, US$4.30. Daily bus to **Santa Elena** for Monteverde, 0750, 1350, 1415, 5 hrs, US$2.50. Buses south to **Quepos** from main bus station, 6 daily via **Jacó**, US$$2.00, 4 hrs, return 0430, 1030, 1630. To **Liberia** with

Empresa Pulmitan, first at 0600, last 1500, 4 hrs, US$1.50. To Tilarán via Cañas at 1130 and 1630, US$2. Good café at bus terminal.

**Ferry** The ferry dock is about 1 km from Puntarenas bus station, local buses run between the 2, otherwise walk or get a taxi (US$2-3).

Check which dock your ferry leaves from. For the **Nicoya Peninsula** see page 793. To **Playa Naranjo** at 0630, 1000, 1420, 1930, returning at 0800, 1230, 1730, 2100, 1½ hrs. T2661-1069, www.coonatramar.com, for exact times. Pedestrians US$1.70, motorbikes US$6, cars US$24.

Buses meet the ferry for **Nicoya** (through Carmona, 40 km unpaved, 30 km paved road, crowded, noisy, frequently break down, US$1.25, 2¼ hrs), **Sámara** (US$1.30), **Coyote**, **Bejuco** and **Jicaral**.

From the same dock a car ferry goes to **Paquera** at 0500, 0900, 1100, 1400, 1700, 2030, returning at 0530, 0900, 1100, 1400, 1700, 2000, 1½ hrs, US$1.70, T2661-2084, www.navieratambor.com, to check the times. On arrival, get on the bus (which waits for the ferry) as quickly as possible (to **Cóbano**, 2-3 hrs, US$1.25, bad road, to **Montezuma** US$2.60, 1½ hrs at least); pay on the bus, or get a taxi. Note: last bus meets the 1700 ferry only.

## The Costanera to Quepos  *Colour map 4, B3.*

**wildlife reserves and attractive surf beaches**

The Costanera or coastal road passes through Jacó, Manuel Antonio and Quepos and on to Dominical before heading inland to San Isidro de El General, or continuing south to Palmar Norte. If you want a popular beach, pick somewhere before Manuel Antonio. Beyond Manuel Antonio, although not deserted, you'll find things a lot quieter. If driving, leave nothing of value in your vehicle; thefts, robberies and scams are regularly reported. The Costanera is plied by all long-distance buses heading to the southern zone.

### Reserva Biológica Carara
*Daily 0700-1600, US$15.*

Between Orotina and Jacó the Carara Biological Reserve (5242 ha) is rich in wildlife. Three trails lead through the park: one, lasting a couple of hours, leaves from close to Tarcoles bridge; the others, lasting a little over one hour, leave from the ranger station to the south. The reserve protects a transitional zone from the dry north coast of the country to the very humid region of the southeast. Spider monkeys, scarlet macaws and coatis can all be seen in the reserve.

One of the most popular free experiences in Costa Rica is to peer over the side of the Río Tárcoles bridge to see the opaque sediment-filled waters broken by the bony backs of the somnolent crocodiles below. It's easy to find the spot to stop, as cars cram the roadside, especially at dawn and dusk when scarlet macaws can be seen returning to their roosts from Carara Biological Reserve on the southern banks of the river.

You can get a closer look by taking a boat tour with Jungle Crocodile Safari ⓘ *T2241-1853, www.junglecrocodilesafari.com,* or José's Crocodile River Tour ⓘ *T2637-0795, www.crocodile rivertour.com, US$25 per person from the dock in Tárcoles, US$35 round trip from Jacó.*

Next to Carara is La Catarata ⓘ *T2236-4140, 0800-1500, 15 Dec-15 Apr, US$7.50,* a private reserve with an impressive waterfall with natural pools for bathing. Take the gravel road up the hill beside Hotel Villa Lapas: it's 5 km to the entrance and a 2.5-km hike to falls and pools, but it's worth the effort. There are signs on the main road.

## Jacó

A short distance from Carara is Jacó, a large stretch of sandy beach, with a lively and youthful energy. It's popular with surfers and weekenders from San José and comes with a rough'n'ready, earthy commercial appeal. If you want to learn to surf, it's as good a place as any, with several surf shops offering courses and board rental. If you want to party with crowds on holiday, it's a great spot. If you're looking for peace and quiet, go elsewhere.

### Jacó to Quepos

From Jacó the potholed road runs down the coastline with lovely views of the ocean. The beaches are far quieter and, if you have a car, you can take your pick. A few kilometres south is **Playa Hermosa**, which is right on the main road and has a popular surfing beach. If travelling by car, 20 km further and a few kilometres off the road is **Playa Bejuco**, **Esterillos Centro** and **Playa Palma**, near Parrita; definitely worth exploring. Beyond **Parrita** (Banco Nacional, Banco de Costa Rica, a gas station and a few stores) the road travels through a flat landscape of endless African palm plantations. Many of the plantation villages are of passing interest for their two-storey, balconied houses laid out around a central football pitch, a church of some denomination and the obligatory branch of AA. The carriageway narrows to single track on bridges along this road so take care if you're driving, especially at night.

### Quepos

Developed as a banana exporting port by United Brands, Quepos was forced to reinvent itself following the devastation of banana plantations in the region overwhelmed by Panama disease, in the early 1950s. Endless rows of oil-producing African palm have replaced the bananas and Quepos has long since shrugged off the portside image, to the extent that few even bother to explore the dock at the southern end of town.

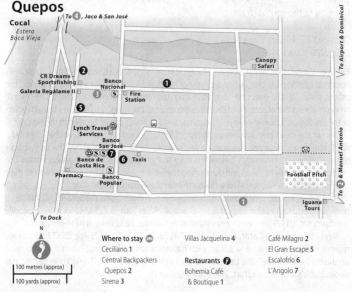

# Quepos

Cocal
Estero
Boca Vieja

To ④, Jaco & San José

To Airport & Dominical

CR Dreams Sportsfishing **②**
Galería Regálame II **③**
**⑤**

Banco Nacional **①**
Fire Station

Canopy Safari

Lynch Travel Services **@**
Banco San José
**@⑤⑤⑦**
Banco de Costa Rica
Pharmacy
Banco Popular
**⑥** Taxis

To ② & Manuel Antonio

Football Pitch

**①**

Iguana Tours

To Dock

N

100 metres (approx)
100 yards (approx)

**Where to stay** 🛏
Ceciliano **1**
Central Backpackers Quepos **2**
Sirena **3**
Villas Jacquelina **4**

**Restaurants** 🍴
Bohemia Café & Boutique **1**

Café Milagro **2**
El Gran Escape **5**
Escalofrío **6**
L'Angolo **7**

Southeast of Quepos, a winding road, lined with hotels, bars, restaurants and stores rises and falls for 7 km before reaching the stunning coastline of Parque Nacional Manuel Antonio (see below) and nearby beautiful beaches. Quepos plays an important role as a service town for local and foreign tourists. It is cheaper than the Manuel Antonio road, there is no shortage of restaurants, bars and shops, and regular buses make the journey to the national park. Tell the bus driver where you are going and you'll be dropped at your chosen hotel.

## Listings The Costanera to Quepos *map p806*

### Where to stay

#### Reserva Biológica Carara

**$$$$ Villa Caletas**
*Punta Leona, to the south of the reserve,*
*T2637-0505, www.hotelvillacaletas.com.*
One of Costa Rica's most distinctive hotels. French-owned, divine rooms and 14 villas atop a mountain with amazing views, spectacular sunsets, lush gardens, pool, restaurant, boat and nature tours.

#### Jacó

Accommodation in Jacó is overpriced; look for discounts May-Nov.

**$$$$ Doce Lunas Hotel**
*Quebrada Seca, 400 m east of the Costanera,*
*T2643-2211, www.docelunas.com.*
Located on the edge of the jungle, 2 km from the beach, Doce Luna is a tranquil and verdant retreat. Rooms are spacious and tastefully attired with hardwood furniture and all modern conveniences including cable TV, minibar, coffee-maker, a/c. Wedding and yoga packages available.

**$$$ Hotel Mar de Luz**
*Av Pastor Díaz, next to the Subway,*
*T2643-3000, www.mardeluz.com.*
A family-orientated hotel with a sustainable ethos, solar panels, pool and comfortable rooms with all the usual amenities, some with kitchenettes. Cool, clean, quiet and secluded from the downtown mayhem.

**$$$ Hotel Paraíso Escondido**
*150 m east of the Catholic church on Calle Los Cholos, T2643-2883, www.hoteljaco.com.*

Romantic villa-style lodging. All rooms with a private bath, patio and a/c, rooms cheaper with fan. Pool and laundry service. The owner often meets arriving buses. Good spot and worth the price.

**$$$ Posada Jacó**
*Calle Bohío, T2643-1951, www.posadajaco.com.*
Hidden on a quiet side street next to a river, Posada Jacó is a low-key option with limited ocean views and a small pool. They have 6 comfortable suites equipped with a/c, cable TV, safe, kitchenette, fridge, microwave, phone and coffee-maker. Intimate and easy-going.

**$$$-$ Room2board hostel and surf school**
*10 m south of Bahía Azul, in front of the beach, T2643-4949, www.room2board.com.*
Upscale 'boutique' hostel with stylish private rooms ($$$), shared rooms ($$) and dorms ($). Lots of amenities including Wi-Fi, TVs, pool, yoga room, lockers, laundry. Surf camp crowd and atmosphere.

**$$-$ Buddha House Boutique Hostel**
*Av Pastor Díaz, T2643-3615,*
*www.hostelbuddhahouse.com.*
A cheery 'boutique' party hostel with a mixture of rooms, with or without private bath ($$), and spacious 5-bed dorms ($). Services include surfboard rental, surf lessons, yoga, massage, tours, pool and hammocks. Laid-back and friendly.

**$$-$ Hotel Kangaroo**
*At the southern end of town, T2643-3351,*
*www.hotelkangaroo.info.*
Mix of dorms and private rooms, but it's the atmosphere that keeps people happy and recommending this place.

### Jacó to Quepos

### $$$ Beso del Viento
*Playa Palo Seco, 5 km, T2779-9674,*
*www.besodelviento.com.*
Surrounded by palm trees a block from the
beach, French-owned Beso del Viento is an
intimate little B&B with 12 stylish rooms, a
restaurant and an oval-shaped pool.

### $$$ Hotel Pelícano
*Esterillos Este, T2778-8105, www.*
*pelicanbeachfronthotel.com.*
50 m from the Pacific Ocean, with
13 boutique rooms, café-restaurant, pool,
private airstrip at the back, beach at the
front. French/Canadian owners, great spot.
Recommended.

### $$$ Hotel Sandpiper Inn
*T2643-7042, www.sandpipercostarica.com.*
A 2-storey hotel with 2 spacious oceanfront
rooms with custom-made furniture and
rustic tile work, all well equipped, a/c,
coolers, Wi-Fi and cable TV. Also pool,
restaurant, sportfishing.

### Quepos
It's difficult to find accommodation on Sat
Dec-Apr and when schools are on holiday.
There are many cheap *cabinas* ($), some
clean, some grungy, most of them clustered
on the east side of town.

### $$$ Hotel Sirena
*Near bus station, T2777-0572,*
*www.lasirenahotel.com.*
The best option in town for its price
bracket. La Sirena has 14 quite good rooms
overlooking a small pool, restaurant/tiki bar
and garden, all with mini-fridge, digital safe,
a/c, cable TV. Breakfast included.

### $$ Villas Jacquelina
*550 m north of Puente Lolo, T8345-1516,*
*www.villasjacquelina.com.*
A villa-style B&B with an eco-friendly ethos,
pool, patios, balconies and mountain views.

Comfortable no-frills rooms feature crisp
sheets and bright artwork, cheaper with
shared bath. Friendly, clean, US/Tico-owned.

### $$-$ Central Backpackers Quepos
*Playa Manuel Antonio road,*
*in front of the INVU, T2777-2321,*
*www.centralbackpackers.hostel.com.*
Friendly, quiet, low-key hostel, simple and
economical. Dorms and private rooms
available. Friendly, basic, family-run.

### $ Ceciliano
*Towards the eastern side of town, on the road*
*leading to Manuel Antonio, T2777-0192.*
Family-run, quiet, small rooms, with bath,
hot. One of many cheapies, not great, but OK
for budget wanderers. Good central location.

## Restaurants

### Jacó
There are lots of *sodas* in Jacó.

### $$$ Sunrise Grill Breakfast Place
*Centre of town. Closed Wed.*
Breakfast from 0700.

### $$$ Wishbone
*On the main street.*
Big plates of Mexican food, from US$6.

### $$ Chatty Cathy's
*On the main drag.*
A popular dining spot.

### $$ La Ostra
*Centre of town.*
Good fish in this pleasant open-air restaurant
open all day.

### $$ Wahoo
*Just within the centre to the north.*
Good Tico food, mainly fish.

### Jacó to Quepos

### $ Doña María's Soda
*Parrita, T8842-3047.*
Small central market, tasty *casados*.

## Quepos

There are many good restaurants along the road towards Manuel Antonio.

### $$$-$$ Bohemia Café & Boutique
*Av 3, Calle Central-2. Tue-Sun.*
Friendly healthfood restaurant with a bohemian ambiance and indie clothing for sale. The coconut Mahi Mahi is a good choice, followed by the chocolate volcano. Flavourful.

### $$$-$$ El Gran Escape
*Central, T2777-0395.*
Lively collection of restaurants and bars offering Tex Mex, pizza and sushi. Good food and service, recommended.

### $$ Escalofrío
*Next to Dos Locos.*
Pizza, pasta and ice cream to die for from US$4.

### Cafés, snacks and bakeries
The municipal market (for fruit and bread) is at the bus station.

### Café Milagro
*On the waterfront, T2777-0794, www.cafemilagro.com.*
Best espresso, cakes, pies, Cuban cigars, souvenirs, freshly roasted coffee for sale; another branch on the road to Manuel Antonio.

### L'Angolo
*Opposite Dos Locos.*
Serves a mix of breads, olives, hams and everything you'd need for self-catering or picnicking in style.

## What to do

### Quepos
**Language schools**
Costa Rica Spanish Institute, *T2234-1001, www.cosi.co.cr.*

Escuela D'Amore, *halfway between Quepos and the national park, T2777-1143, www. escueladamore.com.* Immersion school, living with local families, in a great setting overlooking the ocean.

### Tour operators
**Amigos del Río**, *opposite the football pitch, T2777-0082, www.amigosdelrio.net.* River rafting, kayaking, canopy and horse-riding tours, good guides.
**Iguana Tours**, *close to the church on the football pitch, T2777-2052, www.iguanatours. com.* Excellent local knowledge with many tours available. Friendly and helpful.
**Lynch Travel Services**, *right in the centre of town, T2777-0161, www.lynchtravel.com.*

## Transport

### Jacó
**Bus** From **San José** Coca Cola bus station, Calle 16, Av 1-3, 7 daily, 2½ hrs, US$4.30, arrive at Plaza Jacó-Complex terminal at north end of town, next to **Pizza Hut**. Also several buses to/from Puntarenas and **Quepos**.

### Quepos
**Air** There are several daily flights from **San José**, with **Sansa** (US$63-79) and **Nature Air**, from around US$50 one-way. The **Sansa** office is under Hotel Quepos, T2777-0683.

**Bus** There are 6 buses to Quepos daily from the Terminal Tracopa, Calle 5, Av 18-20, 4 hrs, US$6.30. From Quepos, there are buses northwest along the coast to **Puntarenas**, 7 daily, 3½ hrs, 2 daily buses via **Dominical** to **San Isidro de El General**, T2771-4744, 0500 and 1330, 3½ hrs, US$4, connections can be made there to get to the Panamanian border, return 0700, 1330.

**Taxi** Taxis congregate opposite the bus terminal, just up from **Dos Locos** restaurant. Minibuses meet flights.

From the southeastern corner of Quepos, a road winds up, over and round the peninsula of Punta Quepos, passing the flourishing hotels, restaurants, bars and stores along the length of this rocky outcrop.

Travelling the road for the first time, you can't fail to be impressed by the beauty of the views. And at night, you can't help being blinded by the neon lights that speckle the hillside – evidence of the vibrant tourist trade. At times it is difficult to believe a national park flourishes on the other side of the watershed. The impact on what was once an attractive stretch of jungle-clad coastline is indisputable. For some it is an environmental catastrophe, for others it is a demonstration of the importance of planning to protect.

With 683 ha of mangrove swamps and beaches, home to a rich variety of fauna and flora, Manuel Antonio National Park can rightly claim to be the country's second best wildlife reserve, after Volcán Poás. Just 7 km south of Quepos on a paved road, three beautiful, forest-fringed beaches stretch along the coastline and around the headland of Punta Catedral: **Espadilla Sur**, **Manuel Antonio** and **Puerto Escondido**. Iguanas and white-faced monkeys often come down to the sand.

In addition to enjoying the beaches, hiking is also good in the park. A 45-minute trail, steep in places, runs round the Punta Catedral between Espadilla Sur and Manuel Antonio beaches. If you're early and quiet, it is possible to see a surprising amount of wildlife. A second walk to Puerto Escondido, where there is a blowhole, takes about 50 minutes. The map sold at the entrance shows a walk up to a mirador, with good views of the coastline.

Manuel Antonio has been a victim of its own success, with some of the animals becoming almost tame. But for all the criticism of recent years, it is still beautiful and highly enjoyable. Overdevelopment outside the park and overuse within has led to problems of how to manage the park with inadequate funds. You are not allowed to feed the monkeys but people do, which means that they can be a nuisance, congregating around picnic tables expecting to be fed and rummaging through bags given the chance. Leave no litter and take nothing out of the park, not even seashells.

The range of activities in the area outside the park is slightly bewildering. Sea kayaking is possible, as is mountain biking, hiking, canopy tours, canyoning, deep-sea fishing and even quad biking. Most hotels will assist with booking trips and there are

## Essential Parque Nacional Manuel Antonio

### Opening hours and entry fee

Tuesday-Sunday 0700-1600. US$15.

### Services and facilities

Guides are available, but not essential, at the entrance. You can buy breakfast and other meals from the stalls just before the river, where cars can be parked and minded for US$1 by the stallholders. Basic toilets, picnic tables and drinks are available by the beaches. Cold water showers can be found at Manuel Antonio and Espadilla Sur beaches.

### When to go

It's best to go early or late in the day to see the wildlife.

agencies in Quepos that can also advise. **Note** The beaches in the park are safer than those outside, but rip tides are dangerous all along the coast. Beaches slope steeply and the force of the waves can be too strong for children.

## Listings Parque Nacional Manuel Antonio

### Where to stay

There are hotels all along the road from Quepos to Manuel Antonio, many of them expensive. Many shut in the low season; in high season, it's best to book ahead. The area is full to bursting at weekends with locals camping on the beach.

**$$$$ Makanda by the Sea**
*Down a dirt road leading to Punta Quepos from opposite Café Milagro, T2777-0442, www.makanda.com.*
11 villas and studios with superb open design. An idyllic and romantic paradise spot.

**$$$$ Sí Como No**
*T2777-0777, www.sicomono.com.*
A superb hotel with beautiful touches of design using stunning stained glass, all the comforts you would expect, and service par excellence plus a cinema.

**$$$$-$$$ Costa Verde**
*At the train carriage restaurant and reception, T2777-0584, www.costaverde.com.*
Apartments for 2-4 people, with kitchenette and bath, 2-bedroom villas available, well appointed, pool and a couple of restaurants. Several nature trails out the back. Recommended.

**$$$ Coyaba Tropical**
*Manuel Antonio road, 1 km south of Quepos, T2777-6279, www.coyabatropical.com.*
This excellent, homely B&B is housed in a tastefully restored Spanish colonial building, complete with pool, jacuzzi and lush gardens. Tasteful rooms and friendly hospitable hosts.

**$$ B&B Casa Buena Vista**
*T2777-1002, www.casabuenavista.net.*
A private house offering a breathtaking view and wonderful breakfast terrace, friendly owner. Shared kitchen, breakfast included.

**$$ Hotel Manuel Antonio**
*T2777-1237, www.hotelmanuelantonio.com.*
Good breakfast, camping possible nearby, ask in the restaurant. Handy, just minutes from the national park and the beach.

### Transport

**Bus** There are several buses to the park daily from the Terminal Tracopa in **San José**. At weekends buy your ticket the day before; buses fill to standing room only very quickly. Roads back to San José on Sun evening are packed. A regular bus service runs roughly ½-hourly from beside **Quepos** market, starting at 0545, to Manuel Antonio, last bus back at 1700, US$0.35.

**Car** If driving, there is ample guarded parking in the area, US$6.

**Taxi** From **Quepos**, approximately US$10. Minibuses meet flights from San José to the airport at Quepos (see above), US$2.25.

### ★Playa Matapalo

Some 30 km southeast from the congestion of Quepos towards Dominical the unpaved coastal road drifts almost unnoticed through Playa Matapalo, where you'll find an expansive, beautiful sandy beach recommended for surfing, relaxing and playing with your ideas of paradise. Other activities, in an overwhelmingly Swiss community, include fishing, horse riding and hiking to mountain waterfalls.

### Dominical

Some 12 km further on, at the mouth of the Río Barú, is Dominical, a small town with a population of a few hundred. No more than 500 m from one end to the other it's popular with surfers and often busy. Hotel prices soar in high season and most hotels are close to noisy bars. Treks and horse-riding trips to waterfalls are possible if the beach is too much to bear. Just north of the town **Hacienda Barú** has a **national wildlife preserve**, with activities like abseiling, canopy tours and nature walks (see below). If you want to brush up your Spanish try the **Adventure Education Center** ① *T2787-0023, www.adventurespanishschool.com*, with an immersion Spanish school. They have schools in Arenal and Turrialba as well. But most people come here for the surfing; if you want to learn, visit the **Green Iguana Surf Camp** ① *T8825-1381, www.greeniguanasurfcamp.com*, who provide board hire, group lessons, individual lessons and package deals.

**Punta Dominical** is 4 km south of town (no transport). A poor dirt road follows a steep path inland up the Escaleras (stairs) to some secluded accommodation blending beach and rainforest.

### Uvita

If you get the impression the southern Pacific coast is about beaches, you'd be right. The village of Uvita, 18 km south of Dominical, has beautiful beaches all along the coastline. You can walk in the nearby forests, swim in nearby waterfalls or at the beach, take a boat trip and watch birds. Ballena Marine National Park (see below) protects over 5000 ha of Pacific coral reef and humpback whales can be sighted at nearby Isla Ballena between December and April.

The road south from Uvita is paved all the way to Palmar Norte and access to the beaches of Playa Ballena and Playa Bahía has become easier in recent years with development of the area.

### Parque Nacional Marino Ballena

*There is a nominal entrance fee of US$6 which is rarely collected.*

The vast majority of Ballena (Whale) Marine National Park is coastal waters – 5161 ha against 116 ha of protected land – which may go some way to explaining why there isn't a lot to see at this least-developed national park. The underwater world is home to coral reefs and abundant marine life that includes common and bottle-nosed dolphins as well as occasional visits from humpback whales at times seen with their calves.

Although there is a rarely staffed **rangers station** ① *T2786-7161*, in Bahía, and signposts line the Costanera, the infrastructure in the park is non-existent. Along the beach at Bahía is a turtle-nesting project administered by the local community. As with the park itself, the organization is very ad hoc – visitors and volunteers are welcome. Beachcombing is good, as is snorkelling when the tides are favourable. Boat trips to the island can be arranged from Bahía and diving is starting up with the most recommended local being Máximo Vásquez, or Chumi as he is known. The coastal road continues south beside **Playa Tortuga**, passing small communities of foreigners hiding and enjoying one of the quietest spots near a beach in Costa Rica, to join the Pan-American Highway at Palmar Norte (see page 818).

## Listings Quepos to Palmar Norte

### Where to stay

#### Dominical

**$$$$ Cascadas Farallas**
*About 5 km from Dominical, T2787-4137, www.waterfallvillas.com.*
Wonderfully romantic Balinese-style villas overlooking the falls. Set up for spiritual work, including yoga retreats, spa treatments, weddings and honeymoons.

**$$$ Bella Vista Lodge**
*Punta Dominical, T305-975 0003, www.bellavistalodge.com.*
Great view, good large meals, owned by local American, organizes trips in the area. There are also houses to rent.

**$$$ Hacienda Barú**
*About 2 km north of Dominical, T2787-0003, www.haciendabaru.com.*
A 332-ha reserve that began life as a private reserve in 1972. Cabins sleeping 3 or more with private bath, hiking and riding. So much to see and do in such a small area. There is a canopy observation platform, tree climbing, night walks in the jungle, several self-guided trails and a butterfly garden.

**$$$ Pacific Edge**
*Costanera Km 48, Punta Dominical, T2200-5428, www.pacificedge.info.*
4 large cabins with great views of ocean and rainforest.

**$$$ Villas Río Mar Jungle and Beach Resort**
*Out of town, 500 m from beach, T2787-0052, www.villasriomar.com.*

40 bungalows with bath, fridge and fan, pool, jacuzzi, tennis court, trails, riding, all-inclusive.

**$$-$ Tortilla Flats**
*Formerly Cabinas Nayarit, right on the seafront, T2787-0033.*
Rooms sleeping up to 3 people, with private bath and hot water. A bit overpriced if just for 2.

**$ Cool Vibes Beach Front Hostel**
*Main street, 100 m south of Restaurante El Coco, T8353-6428, www.hosteldominical.com.*
Funky backpackers' place with a rustic open dorm, ocean views and friendly crowds. No private rooms. Kitchen, Wi-Fi, coffee, lockers, surfboard rental and lessons. Cheap and cheerful.

#### Uvita

**$$$$ La Cusinga Eco-Lodge**
*Km 166 Costanera Sur, T2770-2549, www.lacusingalodge.com.*
Situated on a 240-ha private nature reserve, La Cusinga Eco-Lodge has several luxury rooms surrounded by forest, some with expansive views of the Pacific ocean. 3 meals included.

**$$$-$$ Canto de Ballenas**
*6 km south of Uvita, close to Parque Nacional Marino Ballena, T2248-2538, www.hotelcantoballenas.com.*
Rustic but fine wooden cabins in a simple landscaped garden. Great spot in a quiet location.

**\$\$\$-\$ Flutterby House**
*In Bahía near Uvita, T2743-8221,*
*www.flutterbyhouse.com.*
A funky, quirky hostel with a chilled-out
scene. A range of accommodation is
available from simple wooden shacks and
dorms to tree houses or private rooms.
Home-grown veg and an emphasis on
sustainability. Rustic and low-key.

**\$\$ La Ballena Roja Beach Bungalows**
*200 m from Marino Ballena National Park,*
*Playa Chaman–Playa La Colonia, T8361-*
*4829, www.laballenarojauvita.com.*
Charming and simple rooms, rustic chic, with
modern amenities and access to a shared
balcony where you can catch sea breezes.

**\$\$-\$ Cabinas Los Laureles**
*Uvita village, 400 m northeast of*
*Banco de Costa Rica, T2743-8008.*
Nice location, *cabinas* and rooms with
private bathroom, simple and quite good.

**\$\$-\$ Cascada Verde**
*Uvita village, up the hill,*
*www.cascadaverde.org.*
*Hostal*, educational retreat and organic farm,
German-run, vegetarian food, yoga and
meditation workshops available. Pay for a
bed, hammock or camp, or work for your
lodgings. Long-term lodgings preferred,
great spot if you take to the place.

**\$\$-\$ The Tucan Hotel**
*Uvita village, just off the main road,*
*T2743-8140, www.tucanhotel.com.*
Low-key and pleasant spot in Uvita. Dorm
and private rooms, kitchen available, Wi-Fi
and advice on local travel.

## Restaurants

### Dominical

**\$\$ Jazzy's River House**
*Down the main street.*
More an open-house-cum-cultural-centre,
occasionally have meals followed by an
open-mic set up on Wed.

**\$\$ Restaurant El Coco**
*In town.*
Serves good food and rents budget rooms.

**\$\$ San Clemente**
*In town.*
A good mix of Tex Mex with big servings.

**\$\$ Thrusters**
*In town.*
A hip spot for the surf crowd, front restaurant
offers sushi.

**\$ Soda Nanyoa**
*In town.*
Offers Costa Rican specialities.

## Transport

### Dominical
**Bus** To **Quepos** 0545, 0815, 1350 (Sat and
Sun) and 1450, US\$3.20. To **San Isidro**, 0645,
0705, 1450, 1530, 1 hr, US\$2.50. To **Uvita** at
0950, 1010, 1130 (weekends) 1710 and 2000,
US\$1.10. To **Ciudad Cortés** and **Ciudad Neily**
0420 and 1000. To **San José**, 0545, 1340 (Sat
and Sun), 7 hrs.

### Uvita
**Bus** From **San José** Terminal Coca Cola,
Mon-Fri 1500, Sat and Sun 0500, 1500, return
Mon-Fri 0530, Sat and Sun 0530, 1300, 7 hrs,
US\$8.90. From **San Isidro** daily 0800, 1600,
return 0600, 1400. From **Dominical**, last bus
1700 or 1800, US\$1,10.

# Southern
## zone

Heading through the Talamanca mountains, the Pan-American Highway reaches its highest point at Cerro de la Muerte (Peak of Death) and passes El Chirripó, Costa Rica's highest peak at 3820 m, as the scenic road drops down through the valley of the Río de El General to the tropical lowlands of the Pacific coast and the border with Panama. Private reserves along the route are ideal for birdwatching – here the resplendent quetzal enjoys a quieter life than its Monteverde relations – and mountain streams are stocked with trout providing both sport and food. Lodges and hotels are usually isolated, dotted along the highway. Towards Costa Rica's most southerly point, the Península de Osa is a nature haven of beautiful pathways, palm-fringed beaches and protected rainforest, well worth the effort if you have the time.

The Pan-American Highway runs for 352 km from San José to the Southern Zone and on to the Panama border. It's a spectacular journey along a generally good road but challenging if you're driving, with potholes, occasional rockslides during the rainy season, roadworks and generally difficult conditions.

From Cartago, the route heads south over the mountains, beginning with the ascent of **Cerro Buena Vista** (3490 m), a climb of almost 2050 m to the continental divide. A little lower than the peak, the highest point of the road is 3335 m at Km 89, which travels through barren *páramo* scenery. Those unaccustomed to high altitude should beware of mountain sickness brought on by a too-rapid ascent. For 16 km the road follows the crest of the Talamanca ridge, with views of the Pacific 50 km away and, on clear days, of the Atlantic, 80 km to the east.

Some 4.5 km east of Km 58 (Cañón church) is **Genesis II**, a privately owned 40-ha cloudforest National Wildlife Refuge, at 2360 m, bordering the **Tapantí-Macizo de la Muerte National Park**. Accommodation is available here and at several other places along the way. At Km 78 is **Casa Refugio de Ojo de Agua**, a historic pioneer home overlooked but for a couple of picnic tables in front of the house. At Km 80 a steep, dramatic road leads down the spectacular valley of the Río Savegre to **San Gerardo de Dota**, a birdwatchers' paradise. The highest point is at Km 89.5, where temperatures are below zero at night.

## San Isidro de El General

The drop in altitude from the highlands to the growing town of San Isidro passes through fertile valleys growing coffee and raising cattle. The huge **cathedral** on the main plaza is a bold architectural statement, with refreshing approaches to religious iconography inside. The **Museo Regional del Sur** ⓘ *Calle 2, Av 1-0, T2771-5273, Mon-Fri 0800-1200, 1330-1630, free,* is in the old marketplace, now the **Complejo Cultural**. The 750-ha **Centro Biológico Las Quebradas** ⓘ *7 km north of San Isidro, T2771-4131, Tue-Fri 0800-1400, Sat and Sun 0800-1500, closed Oct,* has trails and dormitory lodging for researchers. San Isidro de El General is also the place to stock up for a trip into Parque Nacional Chirripó and to climb Cerro Chirripó Grande (3820 m), see below.

## ★ Parque Nacional Chirripó

*US$15 plus US$10 per night, crowded in season, make reservations through the Oficina de los Parques Nacionales (OPN) in San Gerardo, T2742-5083, open 0630-1200, 1300-1630. Get the latest information from www.sangerardocostarica.com. If you want to walk or climb in the park, get food in San Isidro and book accommodation at the OPN. The bus to San Gerardo leave from the bus station in the market south of the cathedral plaza. The blue and white bus marked San Gerardo leaves at 0930, 1400 and 1845, taking 1½ hrs, US$1.60. Return buses at 0515, 1130 and 1600.*

San Isidro de El General is west of Costa Rica's highest mountain **Cerro Chirripó Grande** (3820 m) in the middle of Parque Nacional Chirripó (50,150 ha). Treks starts from San Gerardo de Rivas (see below). The views from the hilltops are splendid and the high plateau near the summit is an interesting alpine environment with lakes of glacial origin and diverse flora and fauna. The park includes a considerable portion of cloudforest and the walk is rewarding.

## ON THE ROAD

### Climbing the Chirripó peaks

The early morning climb to the summit of Cerro Chirripó, Costa Rica's highest mountain (3820 m), is a refreshing slog after the relative comforts often encountered in Costa Rica. The hike takes you through magnificent cloud forest draped in mosses and ephiphytes before entering a scorched area of *páramo* grasslands with incredible views to the Pacific and Atlantic coastlines on clear days. The widlife – birdlife in particularly – is incredible and, even if you don't see it, you will certainly hear it. The trek itself is not difficult but it is tiring, being almost consistently uphill on the way and a knee-crunching, blister-bursting journey down.

From the *refugio* inside the park, you can also explore the nearby Crestones, a volcanic outcrop that has been etched on to the minds of every Costa Rican, and the creatively named Sabana de los Leones and Valle de los Conejos. There are useful orientation maps on www.sangerardocostarica.com.

If you wish to climb Cerro Chirripó you must make advance reservations by calling the **MINAE** park service office in San Gerardo (T2771-5116), the access town to Chirripó, around 12 km northeast of San Isidro de El General. After phoning for reservations you are given a couple of days to pay by bank deposit to guarantee your space. Visitors are not allowed into the park without reservations at the *refugio*. During the dry season it's often full, so it's a good idea to make arrangements as soon as possible. Start in the early morning for the eight- to 10-hour hike to the *refugio*. The cost is US$15 entry for each day spent in the park, plus US$10 shelter fee per night. Guides are available. The *refugio* has simple but adequate accommodation, with space for about 80 people and a large kitchen area.

The cold (it's often frosty in the morning) comes as a bit of a shock after other regions of Costa Rica, but you can rent blankets and sleeping bags from the *refugio*; gas cookers are also available for hire (US$2). There are sufficient water supplies en route although you will need to carry your food supplies. Electrical power at the *refugio* is only for a couple of hours each night, so be sure to bring a torch/flashlight. The top of Chirripó is located a further 5 km beyond the Crestones base camp.

In addition to the high camp there is a shelter about halfway up, Refugio Llano Bonito (2500 m), which is simple and occasionally clean, with a wooden floor, two levels to sleep on, no door but wind protection, drinking water and toilet. It's about four hours' walk from San Gerardo and three hours' walk on to Refugios Base Crestones. Plan for at least two nights on the mountain, although you can do it with only one night if you're tight for time, rising very early to summit on the second day in time to go all the day down in one hit. While nights can be cold, daytime temperatures tend to be warm to hot, so go prepared with sunscreen and hat. In the rainy season, trails up the plateau are slippery and muddy, and fog obscures the views. Time your descent to catch the afternoon bus back to San Isidro.

For a general update on San Gerardo and climbing Chirripó, visit www.sangerardo costarica.com.

Parque Nacional Chirripó neighbours **Parque Internacional La Amistad** (193,929 ha), established in 1982, and together they extend along the Cordillera de Talamanca to the Panamanian border, comprising the largest area of virgin forest in the country with the greatest biological diversity.

## San Gerardo de Rivas

*There's full information about the town, including accommodation, at www.san gerardocostarica.com.*

In a cool, pleasant spot, San Gerardo de Rivas is at the confluence of the Río Blanco and the Río Pacífico Chirripó. Close to Parque Nacional Chirripó entrance, it is the starting point for the climb up **Cerro Chirripó Grande** (3820 m). If you haven't booked accommodation at the *refugio* in San Isidro you can try booking at the MINAE office (see box, page 817).

As interest in this quiet area grows, new tours are appearing, including trips to local waterfalls (US$40) and nature tours.

Handy for weary legs after the climb, there are **hot springs** ① *daily 0700-1800, entrance US$5*, in the area. Before crossing the concrete bridge turn left to 'Herradura' for 10 minutes then look for the sign after Parque Las Rosas; go down to the suspension bridge, cross the river and continue for 10 minutes to the house where you pay.

## Buenos Aires to Paso Real

Continuing southeast, a good road sinks slowly through the Río General valley where the Talamanca Mountains dominate the skyline. At Km 197 (from San José), the change from coffee to fruit is complete; at the junction for **Buenos Aires** is the huge **Del Monte** cannery. The town, a few kilometres off the Pan-American Highway, has some simple accommodation.

Heading 17 km east towards the mountains is the **Reserva Biológica Durika**, a privately owned reserve of roughly 800 ha, aiming to create a self-sustained community in the Talamanca mountains. Accommodation is available in some rustic cabins.

South along the highway, the small towns of Térraba and Boruca are the most prominent remains of the nation's indigenous population. The community of **Boruca**, with a small *hostal* ($), has a small, poorly maintained museum, but every year the **Fiesta de los Diablitos** on the last day of December and first two days of January, and the last day of January and the first two days of February in **Rey Curre**, see the culture come alive in a festival of music, dance and costume. There is a daily bus to Boruca from Buenos Aires at 1130 (1½ hours).

At **Paso Real** the highway heads west to Palmar Norte, with a turning towards San Vito (see below) and the Panamanian border.

## Palmar Norte and Palmar Sur

Taking a sharp turn at Paso Real (straight on for San Vito, see below), the Pan-American Highway heads west to Palmar Norte (Km 257, with gas station) from where the Costanera leads to Ciudad Cortés and the beach towns of the Central Pacific coast (see page 803).

Crossing the Río Grande de Terraba leads to Palmar Sur, which is 90 km from the Panamanian border. There are several very large pre-Columbian stone spheres in the area. Some, measuring 1.5 m in diameter and accurate to within 5 mm, are in a banana plantation close to town. Their purpose is a matter of conjecture although recent theories claim that they represented the planets of the solar system, or that they were border markers.

## South of Palmar Sur

Through a matrix of cooperative banana and African plantations, a road leads south from Palmar Sur to **Sierpe**, on the Río Sierpe, where there are several small hotels and the departure point for boats to Bahía Drake, see page 826.

The Pan-American Highway heads southeast from Palmar Sur first to **Chacarita** (33 km), where a road turns off to the Osa Peninsula; it continues to **Río Claro** (another 26 km) where a road leads to Golfito; and then, another 15 km further on, the highway reaches **Ciudad Neily**, which is 16 km from the border at **Paso Canoas** (see Costa Rica–Panama box in the Practicalities chapter).

## Listings Travelling the Pan-American Highway

### Where to stay

**$$$$ Hotel de Montaña Savegre**
*San Gerardo de Dota, T2740-1028,*
*www.savegre.com.*
Set in a private nature reserve 9 km from Los Quetzales National Park, complete with waterfalls and trout fishing. Prices include meals.

**$$$ Trogón Lodge**
*San Gerardo de Dota, T2740-1051,*
*www.grupomawamba.com.*
23 fine wooden cabins with private bathroom, set in beautiful gardens connected by paths and used by dive-bombing hummingbirds.

**$$ Hotel and Restaurant Georgina**
*Km 95, T2770-8043.*
At almost 3300 m, Costa Rica's highest hotel, basic, clean, friendly, good food (used by southbound **Tracopa** buses), good birdwatching; ask owners for directions for a nice walk to see quetzals.

### San Isidro de El General

**$$$-$$ Talari Mountain Lodge**
*10 mins from San Isidro on the road to San Gerardo, T2771-0341, www.talari.co.cr.*
8-ha farm, with bath, riverside cabins, known for birdwatching, rustic.

**$$ Rancho La Botija**
*Out of town on the road to San Gerardo, T2770-2147, www.rancholabotija.com.*

Restaurant, pool, hiking to nearby petroglyphs, open 0900 at weekends, great restaurant littered with fragments of *botijas*. Recommended.

**$$-$ Hotel Los Crestones**
*In town, T2770-1200,*
*www.hotelloscrestones.com.*
Big rooms have a TV, plus there's a pool. Wheelchair accessible.

**$ Hotel Chirripó**
*South side of Parque Central, T2771-0529.*
Private or shared bath, clean, very good restaurant, free covered parking, recommended.

### San Gerardo de Rivas

Accommodation is on road to the park.

**$$$-$$ Pelícano**
*T2742-5050, www.hotelpelicano.net.*
11 rooms sleeping between 2 and 5 people, with great views, a bar and restaurant. Beautiful setting with countless birds. Also has a pool.

**$$-$ Casa Mariposa Hostel and Guesthouse**
*50 m noth of entrance to Parque Nacional Chirripó, T2742-5037,*
*www.hotelcasamariposa.net.*
A rustic family-run guesthouse with staggering views and affordable dorm beds ($), private rooms ($$), kitchen, internet, free tea and coffee and hot bath tub. Good reports. Recommended.

### $$-$ El Urán
*At the very top, closest to the park entrance,*
*T2742-5003, www.hoteluran.com.*
Simple, clean rooms, lots of blankets and
a restaurant that will feed you early before
setting out.

### Buenos Aires to Paso Real

### $$-$ Cabañas
*Durika Biological Reserve, T2730-0657,*
*www.durika.org.*
Rustic cabins. Includes 3 vegetarian meals a
day, with a wide range of activities including
walks, hikes to the summit of Cerro Durika
and cultural tours (around US$10 per person
on top of the daily rate).

### South of Palmar Sur

### $$ Río Sierpe Lodge
*Sierpe, T2384-5595, www.riosierpelodge.com.*
All-inclusive plan with an emphasis on fishing.

## Restaurants

### San Isidro de El General

### $$ La Cascada
*Av 2 and Calle 2, T2771-6479.*
Balcony bar where the bright young things
hang out.

### $$ Restaurant Crestones
*South of the main plaza, T2771-1218.*
Serves a good mix of snacks, drinks and
lively company.

### $$ Restaurant El Tenedor
*Calle Central, Av Central-1, T2771-0881.*
Good food, big pizzas, friendly.
Recommended.

### $$ Soda Chirripó
*South side of the main plaza.*
Gets the vote from the current gringo
crowd in town.

### $ La Marisquería
*Corner of Av 0 and Calle 4.*
Simple setting but great ceviche.

### $ Soda J&P
*Indoor market south of the main plaza.*
The best of many.

## What to do

### San Isidro de El General
**Ciprotur**, *Calle 4, Av 1-3, T2771-6096, www.*
*ecotourism.co.cr.* Good information on
services throughout the southern region.
**Selvamar**, *Calle 1, Av 2-4, T2771-4582, www.*
*exploringcostarica.com.* General tours and the
main contact for out-of-the-way destinations
in the southern region.

## Transport

### San Isidro de El General
**Bus** Terminal at Av 6, Calle Central-2 at the
back of the market and adjacent streets but
most arrive and depart from bus depots
along the Pan-American Highway. To
**Quepos** via **Dominical** at 0500 and 1330,
3 hrs, US$4. However, **Tracopa** buses coming
from **San José**, going south go from Calle
3/Pan-American Highway, behind church,
to **Palmar Norte**, US$5.20; **Paso Canoas**,
0830-1545, 1930 (direct), 2100; **David**
(Panama) direct, 1000 and 1500; **Golfito**
direct at 1800; **Puerto Jiménez**, 0630, 0900
and 1500. Waiting room but no reservations
or tickets sold. **Musoc** buses leave from the
intersection of Calle 2-4 with the Pan-
American Highway.
   Most local buses leave from bus terminal
to the south of the main plaza. Buses to **San
Gerardo de Rivas** and **Cerro Chirripó** leave
0500 and 1400, return 0700 and 1600.
**Taxi** A 4WD taxi to San Gerardo costs about
US$20 for up to 4 people.

### Palmar Norte and Palmar Sur
**Air** Daily flights with **Sansa** (from US$65)
and **Nature Air**, **San José**–**Palmar Sur** (from
US$101, 1 way).

**Bus** Express bus to **Palmar Norte** from
Terminal Alfaro, with **Tracopa** from **San
José**, 7 daily 0600-1800, 5 hrs, US$9.70, via

**San Isidro de El General**, 5 buses return to the capital 0445-1300. 5 buses daily to **Sierpe** for the boat to **Bahía Drake** (page 826) 45 mins, US$0.30. Also buses north to **Dominical** and south to the **Golfito** and the Panamanian border.

## Sierpe

**Bus and boat** 5 buses daily to **Palmar Norte**, 0530-1530, 45 mins, US$0.30. Boats down Río Sierpe to **Bahía Drake**, 1½ hrs, US$70 per boat. Many hotels in Drake have boats; may be able to get a lift, US$15 per person.

## Paso Real to San Vito *Colour map 4, B4.*

*some of the country's best coastal views*

The road from Paso Real to San Vito is paved, in good condition and offers some great views as the road rapidly falls through the hills. La Amistad International Park has few facilities for visitors at present, but one secluded lodge is found way up in the hills beyond Potrero Grande, just south of the Paso Real junction on the way to San Vito. Near the border is San Vito. Originally built by Italian immigrants among denuded hills, it is a prosperous but undistinguished town.

On the road from San Vito to Ciudad Neily at Las Cruces are the world-renowned **Wilson Botanical Gardens** ① *T2773-4004, www.ots.ac.cr*, owned by the **Organization for Tropical Studies**, 6 km from San Vito. In 360 ha of forest reserve are over 5000 species of tropical plants, orchids, other epiphytes and trees with 331 resident bird species. It is possible to spend the night here if you arrange it first with the **OTS** ① *San José, T2240-6696 ($$$$ per person all-inclusive), US$32 per person for day visits with lunch*. On the same road is **Finca Cántaros** ① *T2773-3760*, specializing in local arts and crafts, owned by Gail Hewson Gómez. It's one of the best craft shops in Costa Rica – worth a look even if you don't buy anything.

### Border with Panama–Sabalito

Heading east from San Vito, a good gravel road, paved in places, runs via Sabalito (Banco Nacional) to the Panama border at Río Sereno (see border crossing box in the Practicalities chapter for Costa Rica–Panama). There are buses from Sabalito to San José.

## Listings Paso Real to San Vito

### Restaurants

#### Paso Real to San Vito

**$$ Lilianas**
*San Vito.*
Still showing homage to the town's Italian heritage with good pasta dishes and pizza.

**$ Restaurant Nelly**
*San Vito, near Cabinas Las Huacas.*
Good wholesome truck-drivers' fare.

### Transport

#### Paso Real to San Vito

**Bus** Direct buses **San José** to San Vito, 4 daily, 0545, 0815, 1130 and 1445, from Terminal Alfaro, Calle 14, Av 5; direct bus San Vito–San José 0500, 0730, 1000, 1500, 6 hrs, *corriente* buses take 8 hrs, US$11. Alternative route, not all paved, via Ciudad Neily (see below); from San Vito to **Las Cruces** at 0530 and 0700; sit on the left coming up, right going down, to admire the wonderful scenery; return buses pass Las Cruces at 1510.

Some 31 km north of the border a road branches south at Río Claro (several *pensiones* and a fuel station) to the former banana port of Golfito, a 6-km-long linear settlement bordering the Golfo Dulce and steep forested hills. While elements of hard sweat and dock labour remain, Golfito's prominence today comes from being a free port, set up in 1990, selling goods tax free at about 60% of normal prices. Check out www.golfito.info for information on lodging and activities in the area.

Golfito also provides boat and ferry access to Puerto Jiménez and the Osa Peninsula, and popular fishing and surfing beaches to the south of the town.

Entering the town from the south heading north there are a few hotels where the road meets the coast. In 2 km is the small town centre of painted buildings with saloon bars, open-fronted restaurants and cheap accommodation – probably the best stop for budget travellers. Nearby is the dilapidated *muellecito* used by the ferries to Puerto Jiménez and water taxis. One kilometre north are the container port facilities and the **Standard Fruit Company**'s local HQ, though many of the banana plantations have been turned over to oil palm and other crops. Beyond the dock is the free port, airstrip and another set of hotels.

The **Refugio Nacional de Fauna Silvestre Golfito**, in the steep forested hills overlooking Golfito, was created to protect Golfito's watershed. Rich in rare and medicinal plants with abundant fauna, there are some excellent hikes in the refuge. Supervised by the University of Costa Rica, they have a field office in Golfito.

Thirty minutes by water taxi from Golfito, you can visit **Casa Orquídeas** ⓘ *T2775-1614, tours last about 2½ hrs, US$5 per person, US$20 minimum, closed Fri,* a family-owned botanical garden with a large collection of herbs, orchids and local flowers and trees, that you can see, smell, touch and taste.

To the north of Golfito is the **Parque Nacional Piedras Blancas** tropical wet forest. The area was being exploited for wood products, but has been steadily purchased since 1991 with help from the Austrian government and private interests, notably the classical Austrian violinist Michael Schnitzler. All logging has now ceased and efforts are devoted to a research centre and ecotourism, concentrated in an area designated **Parque Nacional Esquinas**. Near the village of **La Gamba** a tourist lodge has been built (see Where to stay, below). La Gamba is 6 km along a dirt road from Golfito, or 4 km from Briceño on the Pan-American Highway between Piedras Blancas and Río Claro.

### Beaches around Golfito

**Playa de Cacao** is about 6 km (1½-hour walk) north of Golfito round the bay, or a short trip by water taxi. Further north is the secluded beach of **Playa San Josecito** with a couple of adventure-based lodges.

About 15 km by sea south of Golfito, and reached by water taxi or a long bus journey (US$2 by colectivo ferry from the small dock; 0600 and 1200, return 0500, 1300), **Playa Zancudo** is a long stretch of clean golden sound, dotted with a few rustic hotels ideal for relaxing and lazing away the days. Still further south is **Pavones**, where a world record left-hand wave has elevated the rocky beach to the realm of surfing legend. South of Pavones, towards the end of the peninsula and at the mouth of the Golfo Dulce is **Punta Banco**.

## Ciudad Neily, Paso Canoas and the Panama border

Ciudad Neily is an uninspiring town providing useful transport links between San Vito in the highlands and the coastal plain, and is roughly 16 km from Paso Canoas on the border with Panama (see Costa Rica–Panama box in the Practicalities chapter). Paso Canoas is a little piece of chaos with traders buying and selling to take advantage of the difference in prices between Costa Rica and Panama. With little to hold you, there's not much reason to visit unless you're heading to Panama. If misfortune should find you having to stay the night, there are some reasonable options.

## Listings Golfito and around

### Where to stay

#### Golfito

It can be difficult to get a hotel room at weekends.

**$$$ Esquinas Rainforest Lodge**
*Near La Gamba, 6 km from Golfito,*
*T2741-8001, www.esquinaslodge.com.*
Full board, private baths, verandas overlooking the forest, tours, all profits to the local community.

**$$ Sierra**
*Northernmost part of town, near the airport*
*and free zone, T2775-0666.*
With 72 double rooms, a/c, a couple of pools and a restaurant. Rooms are better than you'd think from the outside.

**$ Del Cerro**
*Close to the docks, T2775-0006.*
Offering 20 simple rooms sleeping 1-6, private bathroom, laundry services, fishing boat rentals.

**$ Golfo Azul**
*T2775-0871.*
Has 20 large, comfortable rooms, with bath and a/c, good restaurant.

**$ La Purruja Lodge**
*4 km south of Golfito, T2775-5054,*
*www.purruja.com.*
5 duplex cabins with bath, plus camping US$2 per tent.

**$ Mar y Luna**
*T2775-0192.*
Has 8 rooms sleeping 2-4, with bath, fan, restaurant on stilts above the sea, quiet spot, good deal.

**$ Melissa**
*Behind Delfina, T2775-0443.*
Has 4 simple rooms, with private bath, clean and quiet, great spot overlooking bay. Parking available. Recommended.

#### Beaches around Golfito

**$$$ Tiskita Jungle Lodge**
*Punta Banco, T2296-8125, www.tiskita.com.*
A 162-ha property including a fruit farm, with excellent birdwatching, 14 cabins overlooking the ocean. Cool breezes, waterfall, jungle pools, trails through virgin forest – great spot.

**$$$-$$ Cabinas La Ponderosa**
*Pavones, T2776-2076,*
*www.cabinaslaponderosa.com.*
Owned by 2 surfers, large cabins, fan or a/c, with bath (hot water), walking, horse riding, fishing, diving and surfing; also house for rent (sleeps 6), restaurant.

**$$ Los Cocos**
*Playa Zancudo, Golfito, T2776-0012,*
*www.loscocos.com.*
Beachfront cabins with private bathroom, hot water, mosquito net, fan, kitchenette, refrigerator, veranda. Also provide boat tours and taxi service. Discounts for longer stays. Heavenly.

### $$-$ Mira Olas
*Pavones, T2776-2006, www.miraolas.com.*
Comfortable cabins with kitchen and fan, low monthly rates, jungle trail, peaceful garden filled with colourful birdlife, 5 mins from the beach. Highly recommended.

### $$-$ Sol y Mar
*Playa Zancudo, T2776-0014, www.zancudo.com.*
4 screened cabins, hot water, fan, 3-storey rental house (US$700 per month), 50 m from ocean, bar/restaurant, meals 0700-2000, home-baked bread, great fruit shakes, volleyball with lights for evening play, badminton, paddleball, boogie boards, library. Highly recommended.

### $ The Yoga Farm
*Punta Banco, www.yogafarmcostarica.org.*
A laid-back retreat, set on a mountainside surrounded by primary rainforest and near the beach. A great place to get back to nature. Price (per person) includes accommodation, food and yoga.

## Restaurants

### Golfito
Many seafood places along the seafront.

### $$ Cubana
*Near post office.*
Good, try *batidos*.

### $$ El Uno
*Near Cubana.*
Good, reasonably priced seafood.

### $$ La Dama del Delfín Restaurant
*Downtown. Closed for dinner and Sun.*
Breakfast from 0700. Snacks, home-baked goods.

### $ La Eurekita
*Centre.*
Serves a mean breakfast of *huevos rancheros*.

### Beaches around Golfito

### $$ Bar y Restaurant Tranquilo
*Playa Zancudo.*
A lively spot between **Zancudo Beach Club** and **Coloso del Mar**.

### $$ Macondo
*Playa Zancudo.*
Italian restaurant which also has a couple of rooms.

### $ Soda Katherine
*Playa Zancudo, T2776-0124.*
From US$4, great Tico fare; also simple cabins.

## What to do

### Beaches around Golfito
**The Yoga Farm**, *Punta Banco, www.yogafarmcostarica.org.* Yoga, horse riding and hikes through the rainforest. Also organize homestay with an indigenous family.

## Transport

### Golfito
**Air**  Several daily flights to **San José**, with Sansa (US$71 one-way). Runway is all-weather, tight landing between trees; 2 km from town, taxi US$0.50.

**Boat**  There is a boat service between Golfito and **Puerto Jiménez**, leaving the dock in Golfito at 1130, US$2.50, 1½ hrs, returning at 0600, or chartering a water taxi for US$60, up to 8 passengers, is possible.
　　Water taxis in and around Golfito, **Froylan Lopez**, T8824-6571, to **Cacao Beach**, **Punta Zancudo**, **Punta Encanto** or to order, US$20 per hr up to 5 persons.
　　**Docks**  Banana Bay Marina (T2775-0838, www.bananabaymarina.com) accommodate boats up to 150 ft and might be an option if heading south on a boat, but you'll need to ask nicely and be a bit lucky.

**Bus** From **San José** 0700 (8½ hrs) and 1500 (6 hrs express) daily from Terminal Alfaro, return 0500 (express), 1300, US$12.40; from **San Isidro de El General**, take 0730 bus to Río Claro and wait for bus coming from Ciudad Neily. To **Paso Canoas**, US$1.30, hourly from outside Soda Pavo, 1½ hrs. To **Pavones** at 1000 and 1500, return at 0430 and 1230, 3 hrs, US$1.80. A spit of land continues south to Punta Burica with no roads and only a couple of villages.

## Ciudad Neily, Paso Canoas and the Panama border

**Bus** The terminal in Ciudad Neily is at the northern end of town, beside the Mercado Central. Daily bus to **San José**, with **Tracopa**, from main square (6 daily, US$12.40, 7 hrs, on Sun buses from the border are full by the

time they reach Ciudad Neily). Buses arrive at Av 5 and Calle 14 in San José. Services to **San Vito** inland and to **Palmar**, **Cortés** and **Dominical** (0600 and 1430, 3 hrs). Also to **Puerto Jiménez** at 0700 and 1400, 4 hrs. Bus for **Golfito** leaves from town centre every 30 mins. The Pan-American Highway goes south (plenty of buses, 20 mins, US$0.65) to Paso Canoas on the Panamanian border; see also Costa Rica–Panama box in the Practicalities chapter. Colectivo US$1.80, very quick.

To **San José**, 0400, 0730, 0900, 1500 (T2223-7685), or go to Ciudad Neily and change. International buses that reach the border after closing time wait there till the following day. Hourly buses to **Ciudad Neily**, ½ hourly to **Golfito**.

**home to a park world famous for its diversity of wildlife**

★ Across the Golfo Dulce is the hook-shaped appendage of the Osa Peninsula. Some distance from most other places of interest in the country, the journey is worthwhile for the peninsula's Parque Nacional Corcovado, with some of the best rainforest trekking and trails in the country.

Getting to the peninsula is becoming easier. There is a daily ferry service from Golfito arriving at the small dock in Puerto Jiménez; bus services run from San José, passing through San Isidro de El General, Palmar North and from the south at Ciudad Neily; and boats ply the coastal route from Sierpe to Bahía Drake. You can also fly from San José.

### Puerto Jiménez *See map, page 827.*

Once a gold-mining centre, Puerto Jiménez still has the feel of a frontier town although most miners were cleared from the Parque Nacional Corcovado area over 20 years ago.

Today, Puerto Jiménez is a popular destination with its laid-back, occasionally lively atmosphere, reasonable beaches nearby and, of course, the beautiful national park on the Pacific side of the peninsula. Look out for *El Sol de Osa* (www.soldeosa.com), an up-to-date community-information service. A particular charm of Puerto Jiménez, barely five blocks square, is its relative freedom from road traffic; scarlet macaws can be seen roosting in the trees around the football pitch. There are good local walks to the jungle, where you will see monkeys and many other birds, and to beaches and mangroves as well. There is a seasonal migration of humpbacks between October and March.

### Around Puerto Jiménez

Geological treasures can be seen at the gold mine at **Dos Brazos**, about 15 km west of town; ask for the road that goes uphill beyond the town, to see the local gold mines. Several colectivo taxis a day go to Dos Brazos, last bus back at 1530 (often late); taxi

## Essential Península de Osa

Avoid the rainy season. Bring umbrellas (not raincoats, which are too hot), because it will rain, unless you are hiking, in which case you may prefer to get wet. There are a few shelters, so only mosquito netting is indispensable. Bring all your food if you haven't arranged otherwise; in the whole peninsula you'll only find food and accommodation in Puerto Jiménez and Agujitas. The cleared areas (mostly outside the park, or along the beach) can be devastatingly hot. Chiggers (*coloradillas*) and horseflies infest the horse pastures and can be a nuisance, similarly sandflies on the beaches; bring spray-on insect repellent. Another suggestion is vitamin B1 pills (called thiamine, or *tiamina*). Mosquitoes are supposed to detest the smell and leave you alone. Get the Instituto Geográfico maps, scale 1:50,000. Remember finally that, as in any tropical forest, you may find some unfriendly wildlife, like snakes (fer-de-lance and bushmaster snakes may attack without provocation), and herds of peccaries. You should find the most suitable method for keeping your feet dry and protecting your ankles; for some, rubber boots are the thing, for others light footwear that dries quickly.

US$7.25. You can also take a long walk to **Carate** (see below), which has a gold mine. Branch to the right and in 4 km there are good views of the peninsula. A topographical map is a big help, obtainable from Instituto Geográfico in San José. At **Cabo Matapalo** on the tip of the peninsula, 18 km south of Puerto Jiménez, are several expensive sleeping options.

To reach Puerto Jiménez from the Pan-American Highway (70 km), turn right about 30 km south of Palmar Sur; the road is paved to Rincón, thereafter it is driveable with many bridge crossings. There is a police checkpoint 47 km from the Pan-American Highway.

### Bahía Drake

Arriving by boat from Sierpe, Bahía Drake provides a northern entrance point to the Osa Peninsula and Parque Nacional Corcovado. In March 1579, Sir Francis Drake careened his ship on Playa Colorada in Bahía Drake. There is a plaque commemorating the 400th anniversary of the famous pirate's nautical aberration in **Agujitas**. Life in the bay is not cheap and, combined with transport, costs can quickly mount up. Bahía Drake, which continues south merging seamlessly with Agujitas, is a popular destination for divers with Isla del Caño nearby. Open Water PADI courses (US$340) are available at **Cabinas Jinetes de Osa** or through **Caño Divers** at Pirate Cove.

## Listings Península de Osa *map p827*

### Where to stay

**Puerto Jiménez**
For more Jiménez hotels, see www.jimenezhotels.com.

**$$$$ Iguana Lodge**
*5 km southeast of Puerto Jiménez behind the airstrip, T8829-5865, www.iguanalodge.com.*
4 cabins, good swimming and surfing.

**$$$-$$ Cabinas Puerto Jiménez**
*On the gulf shore with good views, T2735-5090, www.cabinasjimenez.com.*
Remodelled big rooms, many with private decks looking out to the gulf, spotless. Wi-Fi.

**$$-$ Cabinas Marcelina**
*Main street, T2735-5007.*
With bath, big, clean, friendly and totally renovated, nice front yard, small discount for youth hostelling members.

## $ Hotel Oro Verde
*Main street, T2735-5241.*
Run by Silvia Duirós Rodríguez, 10 clean,
comfortable rooms, with bath and fan,
some overlooking the street.

## $ Pensión Quintero
*Just off main street, T2735-5087.*
Very simple wooden building, but clean,
cheap and good value (price per person);
will store luggage. Ask for Fernando
Quintero, who rents horses and has a boat
for up to 6 passengers, good value; he is also
a guide, recommended.

## Around Puerto Jiménez
## Cabo Matapalo

### $$$$ El Remanso Rainforest Beach Lodge
*T2735-5569, www.elremanso.com.*
Houses and cabins for rent, all fully equipped
and with ocean views, an oasis of peace.

### $$$$ Lapa Ríos Wilderness Resort
*T2735-5130, www.laparios.com.*
The cream of the crop. Includes meals.
14 luxury palm-thatched bungalows on
private 2400-ha reserve (80% virgin forest,
US owners Karen and John Lewis), camping
trips, boats can be arranged from Golfito.
Idyllic, fantastic views. Recommended.

**Puerto Jiménez**

N
100 metres
100 yards

**Where to stay** 🛏
Cabinas Marcelina **3**
Cabinas Puerto
  Jiménez **4**
Iguana Lodge **1**
Oro Verde **9**

Pensión Quintero **11**

**Restaurants** 🍴
Agua Luna **1**
Carolina &
  Escondido Trex **2**

Il Giardino **3**
Juanita's Mexican
  Bar & Grille **4**
Marisquería Corcovado **5**
Pizzamail.it **6**

## Bahía Drake

### $$$$ Aguila de Osa Inn
*The normal landing point, T2296-2190,*
*www.aguiladeosa.com.*
Includes meals; fishing, hiking, canoeing
and horse riding available, comfortable
cabins made with exotic hardwoods.
Recommended.

### $$$$ La Paloma Jungle Lodge
*T2239-0954, www.lapalomalodge.com.*
Price per person includes meals. 9 cabins
with bath, guided tours with resident
biologist. Packages.

### $$$ Cabinas Jinete de Osa
*T2236-5637, www.costaricadiving.com.*
Good hotel, run by 2 brothers from Colorado.
Diving a speciality, PADI courses offered.
Spacious and airy rooms, all with bath, hot
water, fan. Recommended.

### $$$ Rancho Corcovado Lodge
*In the middle of the beach, T2786-7059.*
www.ranchocorcovado.com. Price per
person. Simple, rustic rooms, many with
view, all with bath. Friendly Tico owners, nice
open-air restaurant on beach serves *comida*
*típica*. Camping permitted.

### $$$-$$ Pirate Cove
*Northern end of the beach, T2786-7845,*
*www.piratecove.com.*
Very nice tent-like cabins emulate an
outdoor experience minus the mud. US$55
per person shared bath, US$70 with bath,
3 meals included.

### $ Bella Vista Lodge
*On the beach at the southern end of town,*
*T2770-8051.*
The only budget option in town and
disappointing. Basic rooms, 2 with bath,
3 shared (even more basic), meals (US$3-5)
not included.

## Restaurants

### Puerto Jiménez

### $$$ Agua Luna
*On the seashore near the dock, T2735-5033.*
Stylish setting, beautifully presented
but pricey.

### $$$ Il Giardino
*Just off the main street.*
Quiet little Italian, intimate setting and
good food.

### $$$-$$ Carolina
*Main street, T2735-5185.*
Highly recommended for fish (everything
actually), good prices. **Escondido Trex** office
at back of restaurant.

### $$$-$$ Pizzamail.it
*Parque Central.*
Authentic, Italian-style stone-baked pizzas,
thin crusts and tasty.

### $$ Juanita's Mexican Bar and Grille
*Central, T2735-5056.*
Happy hour, crab races, good Mexican fare,
seafood from US$4.

### $$-$ Marisquería Corcovado
*Seafront, east of the dock.*
An unpretentious local eatery where you
can pick up some of the best seafood in
town, including great ceviche and fish fillets.
Good value.

## What to do

### Puerto Jiménez
**Aventuras Tropicales**, *opposite the football*
*pitch, T2735-5195, www.aventurastropicales.*
*com.* Can book accommodation and has a
couple of computers with internet.
**MINAE office**, *facing the airstrip, T2735-5036,*
*for booking dormitory lodging and camping*
*facilities in Corcovado National Park.*
**Surcos Tours**, *T8603-2387, www.surcostours.*
*com.* Single and multi-day hiking tours of
Corcovado National Park, birdwatching

tours and trips to Matapalo rainforest. Recommended.

**Tonsa Tours**, see map. Run by the quiet Jaime, provides many of the normal tours and also jungle treks across to Carate. Not for the faint-hearted, but certain to be fascinating.

## Transport

### Puerto Jiménez

**Air** There are daily flights to Puerto Jiménez and **Golfito** with Sansa (US$71) and **Nature Air** (from US$114 one-way) from **San José**.

**Bus** 1 block west of the main street. A café by the bus terminal is open Sat 0430 for a cheap and reasonable breakfast. From **San José**, just outside Terminal Atlántico Norte (C 12, Av 9-11), there are 2 buses daily to Puerto Jiménez at 0600 and 1200 via San Isidro, US$12.60, 8 hrs, return 0500, T2735-5189. There are also buses from **San Isidro**, leaving from the Pan-American Highway at 0930 and 1500, US$8, returns at 0400 and 1300, 5 hrs. To **Ciudad Neily** at 0500 and 1400, 3 hrs, US$3.80. A few colectivos to **Carate** depart from outside **Restaurant Carolina** daily 0530 and 0600, cost US$7. Service may be restricted in the wet season. Local bus is US$1.80.

**Sea** There is a boat service between **Golfito** and Puerto Jiménez, leaving the dock in Golfito at 1130, US$2.50, 1½ hrs, returning at 0600, or chartering a water taxi for US$60, up to 8 passengers, is possible.

## Parque Nacional Corcovado  Colour map 4, C4.

### an ideal spot for just walking along endless beaches

★ Corcovado National Park, including Reserva Biológica Isla del Caño (84 ha), comprises over 42,469 ha – just under half the Osa Peninsula. Consisting largely of tropical rainforest, swamps, miles of empty beaches and some cleared areas now growing back, it is located on the Pacific Ocean at the western end of the peninsula. The park is also filled with birds, mammals and six species of cat.

At **Carate** there is a dirt airstrip and a store, run by Gilberto Morales and his wife Roxana (they rent rooms, but they are often full of gold miners; they also have a tent for hire, but take a sleeping bag). There are several luxury options here and a couple more lodges 30 minutes' walk west along the beach.

Five minutes' walk further down the beach is **La Leona** park wardens' station and entrance to the park. To go beyond here costs US$7 per day, whether you are walking along the beach to La Sirena (18 km, six hours, take sun protection), or just visiting for the day. Beyond here to the end of **Playa Madrigal** is another 2½ hours' walk, partly sandy, partly rocky, with some rock pools and rusty shipwrecks looking like modern sculptures. The shore rises steeply into the jungle, which grows thickly with mangroves, almonds and coconut palms. Check with wardens about high tide so you don't get stuck. There are a couple of rivers along the beach, the first, Río Madrigal, is only about 15 minutes beyond La Leona (lovely and clear, deep enough for swimming about 200 m upstream, a good place for spotting wildlife). The best place for seeing wildlife, though, is La Sirena, where there are paths inland and the terrain is flatter and more isolated.

You can head inland from Sirena on a trail past three conveniently spaced shelters to **Los Patos**, after passing several rivers full of reptiles (20 km, six to nine hours depending on conditions). The wooden house is the ranger station with electricity, TV and four beds available at US$1.75 per night; meals are possible if you don't bring your own

# Essential Parque Nacional Corcovado

### Park information

If short of time and/or money, the simplest way to the park is to take the pickup truck from outside **Tonsa Tours** in Puerto Jiménez to Playa Carate (most days at 0600 and 1400, 2½ hours, US$7 one way, returning at 0800 and 1600, ask in advance about departure). Or call Cirilo Espinosa (T2735-5075), or **Ricardo González** (T2735-5068) for a 4WD jeep taxi. It is possible to book a flight from Puerto Jiménez to Carate or La Sirena in the park for US$99 per person, minimum five people. Ask at the airstrip or call T2735-5178.

The **MINAE office** (Puerto Jiménez, near the airport, T2735-5036, daily 0830-1200, 1300-1700), will give permits for entering the park (US$7) and will book accommodation at La Sirena, see Where to stay, below. Hiking boots and sandals are useful if you are walking in the park.

food. Its balcony is a great observation point for birds, especially the redheaded woodpecker. From Los Patos you can carry on to the park border then, crisscrossing the Río Rincón to **La Palma** (small *hostal*), a settlement on the opposite side of the peninsula (13 km, six more hours), from where there are several 'taxis' making the one-hour trip to Puerto Jiménez (see above). An offshoot of this trail will lead you to a raffia swamp that rings the **Corcovado Lagoon**. The lagoon is only accessible by boat, but there are no regular trips. Cayman and alligator survive here, sheltered from the hunters.

From Sirena you can walk north along the coast to the shelter at **Llorona** (plenty of waterfalls), from which there is a trail to the interior with a shelter at the end. From Llorona you can proceed north through a forest trail and along the beach to the station at **San Pedrillo** on the edge of the park. You can stay here, camping or under roof, and eat with the rangers, who love company. From San Pedrillo you can take the park boat (not cheap) to **Isla del Caño**, a lovely (staffed) park outpost.

## Listings Parque Nacional Corcovado

### Where to stay

See also details of the MINAE office, under Park information above.

**$$$$ Casa Corcovado Jungle Lodge**
*Along the coast from San Pedrillo, T2256-3181, www.casacorcovado.com.*
Outside the park in the forest, but with 500 m of beach more or less opposite Isla del Caño, 14 bungalows, many facilities, packages from 2 nights full board with boat transport (2 hrs) from Sierpe.

**$$$ Corcovado Lodge**
*30 mins' walk west of Carate along the beach, T2257-0766, www.costaricaexpeditions.com.*
20 walk-in tents with 2 campbeds in each, in a beautiful coconut grove with hammocks

overlooking the beach; to be sure of space book through **Costa Rica Expeditions** in San José, see page 735.

**$$$ La Leona Eco-Lodge**
*30 mins' walk west of Carate along the beach, T2735-5705, www.laleonaecolodge.com.*
Rustic tent cabins, crocodile spotting, rappelling, yoga and night hikes. Price per person.

**$ La Sirena**
*Book through MINAE, Puerto Jiménez, near the airport, T2735-5036.*
In dorms, maximum 20 people (reservation essential), take sheets/sleeping bag. Also camping, no reservation needed, 3 meals available. Bring mosquito netting.

**one of the world's most distant island destinations**

This steep-sided and thickly wooded island and national park of 24 sq km lies 320 km off the Osa Peninsula, on the Cocos Ridge, which extends some 1400 km southwest to the Galápagos Islands. There is virtually nothing on the island, apart from a few endemic species, but you can visit for some of the world's best diving.

The BBC Discovery Channel shot some dramatic silhouetted images of tiger sharks here for their *Blue Planet* series. Historically, though, it was a refuge for pirates who are supposed to have buried great treasure here, though none has been found by the 500 or so expeditions looking for the 'x' that marked the spot. Travel by chartered boat can be made in Puntarenas, after a government permit has been obtained, or you can take a scuba-diving cruise on the **Okeanos Agressor** ⓘ *T2232-0572 ext 60 (in US: PO Drawer K, Morgan City, LA 70381, T504-385-2416)*. The twice-monthly 10-day trips are understandably expensive (about US$4235 for 10 days).

# Caribbean
## coast

Heading east from San José, the central highlands quickly fall away to the sparsely populated flat Caribbean lowlands. The tropical rainforest national parks of Tortuguero and Barra del Colorado, leading through coastal canals and waterways, are a nature lover's paradise with easily arranged trips, normally from San José, into the rainforest. South of the distinctly Caribbean city of Puerto Limón, coastal communities have developed to provide comfortable hangouts and laid-back beachlife for all budgets.

## San José to the coast  *Colour map 4, B3.*

*the third largest of Costa Rica's national parks, with abundant wildlife*

### Parque Nacional Braulio Carrillo

The Parque Nacional Braulio Carrillo was created to protect the high rainforest north of San José from the impact of the San José–Guápiles–Puerto Limón highway. It extends for 47,583 ha and encompasses five different types of forest with hundreds of species of bird, jaguar, ocelot and Baird's tapir. Various travel agencies offer naturalist tours, approximately US$75 from San José. San José to Guápiles and Puerto Limón buses go through the park.

The entrance to the **Quebrada González centre** ⓘ *daily 0800-1530, US$15*, is on the highway, 23 km beyond the Zurquí tunnel, just over the Río Sucio at the Guápiles end and has an administration building. To get there, take any bus to the Atlantic and ask to be dropped off. There are three trails: **Las Palmas**, 1.6 km (you need rubber boots); across the road are **El Ceibo**, 1 km, circular; and **Botarrama**, entry 2 km from Quebrada González. The trail has good birdwatching and the views down the Río Patria canyon are impressive. The Zurquí centre near the tunnel has been closed but may open again soon, so ask at headquarters. It has services and the 250-m **Los Jilqueros** trail to the river.

Beyond Quebrada González (1.5 km) is **Los Heliconios** ⓘ *entry US$7*, a butterfly garden with an insect museum and amphibians. Adjoining it, **Reserva Turística El Tapir** ⓘ *entry US$7*, has a 20-minute trail and others of one to two hours.

**Best** for
Beachlife ▪ Rainforest ▪ Turtles ▪ Volunteering

An ingenious **Rainforest Aerial Tram** ⓘ *Tue-Sun 0630-1600, Mon 0900-1530, 90 mins' ride costs US$60, students with ID and children half price, children under 5 are not allowed; office in San José, Av 7, Calle 7, behind Aurola Holiday Inn, T2257-5961, www.rainforestadventure. com*, lifts visitors high into the rainforest, providing a fascinating up-close and personal view of the canopy life. The price includes a guided nature walk. It's best to go as early as possible for birds. Tourist buses arrive from 0800. There's also a zip-wire, trekking tour, birding tour and serpentarium. US$114 covers everything. There's a guarded car park for private vehicles and restaurant for meals in the park. It can be difficult to get reservations during the high season. The San José office organizes an all-inclusive package leaving around 0800 daily, with pickups at most major hotels.

Further on, at the Soda Gallo Pinto is the **Bosque Lluvioso** ⓘ *T2224-0819, daily 0700-1700, entry US$15*, a 170-ha private reserve. It is at Km 56 on the Guápiles highway (**Rancho Redondo**), with a restaurant and trails in primary and secondary forest.

The turn-off at Santa Clara to Puerto Viejo de Sarapiquí is 13 km before Guápiles. At the junction is **Rancho Robertos** (T2711-0050), a good, popular and reasonable roadside restaurant. For Guápiles, see below. Nearby is a **Tropical Frog Garden**, an interesting short stop if you have the time.

There is a private reserve bordering the Parque Nacional Braulio Carrillo called **Río Danta**, with 60 ha of primary rainforest and short limited treks (US$4) arranged with meals (US$6-9). For information contact **Mawamba Group** ⓘ *T2223-2421, must be pre-arranged, no drop-ins.*

## Puerto Viejo de Sarapiquí

Puerto Viejo de Sarapiquí is 40 km north of the San José–Limón highway and 20 km from La Virgen to the southwest. Once an important port on the Río Sarapiquí, only occasionally do launches ply the Río Colorado to the Canales de Tortuguero. There is reported to be a cargo boat once a week to Barra del Colorado (no facilities, bring your own food, hammock, sleeping bag) and on to Moín, about 10 km by road from Puerto Limón. There is little traffic, so you will need luck and a fair amount of cash. There is good fishing on the Río Sarapiquí.

**La Selva Biological Station** ⓘ *T2766-6565, www.ots.ac.cr, 3½-hr guided natural history walk with bilingual naturalists daily at 0800 and 1330-1600, US$30 per person*, on the Río Puerto Viejo, is run by the **Organization for Tropical Studies**. The floral and faunal diversity is unbelievable. Several guided and self-led walks, including a **Sarapiquí River Boat Tour**, are available, but to visit it is essential to book in advance. Accommodation is also available.

The Río Sarapiquí flows into the San Juan, forming the northern border of Costa Rica. The Río San Juan is wholly in Nicaragua, so you technically have to cross the border and then return to Costa Rica. This will cost US$5 and you will need a passport and visa. Trips on the **Río Sarapiquí** and on the **Río Sucio** are beautiful (US$15 for two hours); contact William Rojas in Puerto Viejo (T2766-6108) for trips on the Río Sarapiquí or to Barra del Colorado and Tortuguero. There is a regular boat service to Tortuguero on Monday and Thursday, returning on Tuesday and Friday, costing US$55 per person.

## Las Horquetas de Sarapiquí

Some 17 km south of Puerto Viejo, near Las Horquetas de Sarapiquí, is **Rara Avis** ⓘ *T2764-1111, www.rara-avis.com*, rustic lodges in a 600-ha forest reserve owned by ecologist Amos Bien. This admirable experiment in educating visitors about rainforest conservation takes small groups on guided tours (rubber boots provided), led by biologists. You must be prepared for rough and muddy trails, lots of insects but great birdwatching and a memorable experience.

## Guápiles, Guácimo and Siquirres

One hour from San José, Guápiles is the centre of the Río Frío banana region. It is another 25 km from Guácimo to Siquirres, a clean, friendly town and junction for roads from Turrialba with the main highway and former railways.

## Matina

Some 28 km beyond Siquirres, heading north at the 'techo rojo' junction is Matina, a small, once-busy town on the railway but off the highway. Today, it is an access point to Tortuguero and the less well-known private **Reserva Natural Pacuare**, 30 km north of Puerto Limón, which is accessible by canal from Matina. Run by Englishman John Denham, the reserve has a 6-km stretch of **leatherback turtle-nesting beach** protected and guarded by the reserve. Volunteers patrol the beach in May and June, measuring and tagging these magnificent marine turtles. For volunteer work, contact Carlos Fernández, **Corporación de Abogados** ① *Av 8-10, Calle 19, No 837, San José, T2234-5890, c.fernandez@turtleprotection. org, organization information at www.turtleprotection.org.*

### Where to stay

#### Puerto Viejo de Sarapiquí

**$$$$-$$$ Selva Verde Lodge**
*Out of town, heading west a few kilometres towards La Virgen, T2761-1800, www.selvaverde.com.*
On over 200 ha of virgin rainforest reserve, 40 double rooms, 5 bungalows for 4, includes meals, caters mainly for tour groups. Sensitively set in the rainforest with extensive trail system, rafting, canoeing and riding through property; tours with biologists organized.

**$$$ El Bambú**
*In centre north of park, T2766-6359, www.elbambu.com.*
Mini-resort-style lodgings with 40 comfortable rooms, fan, cable TV, pool, gym, including breakfast, very pleasant.

**$$$ El Gavilán Lodge**
*On the southern bank of the Río Sarapiquí, reached by taxi, T2234-9507, www.gavilanlodge.com.*
Includes breakfast, set in 100-ha private reserve by the river pier, good restaurant, good jungle paths, riding and river tours, 12 rooms private bath, garden jacuzzi, special group and student/researcher rates, day trips and overnight trips from San José.

**$$ Posada Andrea Cristina**
*Just out of town near the main road junction, T2766-6265, www.andreacristina.com.*
Comfortable small cabins, set amongst tropical gardens, and a fantastic treehouse for those who want to get close to the canopy. Good local knowledge.

**$ Mi Lindo Sarapiquí**
*Overlooking park, T2766-6074.*
Has 6 spotless rooms with bath, fan, hot water and restaurant downstairs. Recommended.

#### Las Horquetas de Sarapiquí

**$$$ River-Edge Cabin and Waterfall Lodge**
*T2764-1111, www.rara-avis.com.*
Accommodation at **Rara Avis**, the lodge is a beautiful 8-room jungle lodge in an idyllic setting, the cabin is deeper in the rainforest

for even more seclusion. There is also treetop accommodation and rates for backpackers at **Las Casitas**.

### Guápiles, Guácimo and Siquirres

**$$$ Casa Río Blanco**
*About 6 km west of Guápiles look out for the big yellow road sign, take 1st right before the Río Blanco bridge and follow signpost for 1 km, T2710-4124, www.casarioblanco.com.*
Accommodates 12 guests in comfortable cabins, with breakfast, run by Herbie and Annette from Amsterdam. Beautiful gardens and a great spot for people interested in the environment. Recommended.

**$$ Centro Turístico Pacuare**
*Siquirres, T2768-8111, www.centroturistico pacuare.com.*
Motel-style lodging with 60 reasonable, functional rooms, with or without a/c. Amenities include restaurant, bar, pool table, café, soccer field and large pool.

## Transport

### Puerto Viejo de Sarapiquí
**Bus** Buses stop on north side of park. From **San José** 7 daily from Gran Terminal del Caribe, 1½ hrs, US$3.45, through PN Braulio Carrillo, or through Heredia, 4 daily, 3½ hrs, US$4.20. From **Ciudad Quesada**, 5 daily, 2½ hrs.

**Car** To get there by car from **San José**, after passing through the Parque Nacional Braulio Carrillo take Route 4, a paved road which turns off near Santa Clara to Puerto Viejo; it bypasses Río Frío and goes via Las Horquetas. A more scenic but longer route leaves from **Heredia** via San Miguel and La Virgen, and on to Puerto Viejo.

### Guápiles, Guácimo and Siquirres
**Bus** In Guápiles, buses leave from a central terminal a block to the north of the church. Regular buses to **San José** and **Puerto Limón**. Buses to **Puerto Viejo de Sarapiquí** every 2½ hrs, and to **Río Frío** every 1½ hrs.
For Siquirres, at least 1 bus per hr leaves Gran Terminal del Caribe in **San José**, 2½-hr journey, US$2.90.

## Puerto Limón and the Caribbean coast   Colour map 4, B4.

### the country's most important port and biggest carnival

Puerto Limón is on a rocky outcrop on an almost featureless coastline. Between Puerto Limón and the Río San Juan on the Nicaraguan border, the long stretch of Atlantic coastline and its handful of small settlements is linked by a canal system that follows the coastline.

The region encompasses Parque Nacional Tortuguero (page 837), famed for its wildlife and turtle-nesting beaches, and Refugio Nacional de Fauna Silvestre Barra del Colorado (page 841). The Río San Juan forms the border between Costa Rica and Nicaragua; however, the border is not mid-river, but on the Costa Rican bank. English is widely spoken along the coast.

### Puerto Limón See map, page 836.
Built on the site of the ancient indigenous village of Cariari, Columbus dropped anchor at Punta Uvita, the island off the coastline, on his fourth and final voyage. The climate is very humid and it rains almost every day. With a mainly black population and a large Chinese contingent, the town has a distinctly Caribbean feel, expressed particularly during carnival but in most bars every weekend. Puerto Limón is not a popular stopover,

but experienced travellers may have an interest in exploring Limón. Beware of theft at night and remember it is a port; there are a lot of drunks roaming the streets.

**Parque Vargas** and the seafront promenade at the rocky headland are popular places for social gatherings and killing time, making for ideal people-watching territory, especially in the evening. Parque Vargas, sadly rather run-down, has an impressive botanical display with a colourful mural depicting the history of Limón and a bandstand.

On the upside, the nightlife is good, particularly for Caribbean music and dancing, culminating in carnival every October, Costa Rica's largest festival (see Festivals, below). There is a small **Museo Etnohistórico de Limón** ① *Calle 2, Av 2, Mon-Fri 0900-1200, 1300-1600*, featuring material relating to Columbus' arrival in Limón. The cargo docks are still active with international crews making regular journeys, as well as being the landing point for pristine floating palaces cruising the Caribbean.

### Around Puerto Limón

**Playa Bonita** and **Portete** have pleasant beaches about 5 km along the coastal road from Puerto Limón. **Moín**, a further 1.5 km east along the road, is the sight of the international docks, which exports some 2.8 million bunches of bananas annually. The docks are also the departure point for barges to Tortuguero and Barra del Colorado (eight hours). Boats also run from Moín to Tortuguero (see below) and may be hired at the dockside. Buses run to Moín every 40 minutes from 0600-1740, 30 minutes, US$0.10. If shipping a vehicle, check which dock. Some simple accommodation options are available if you end up waiting here.

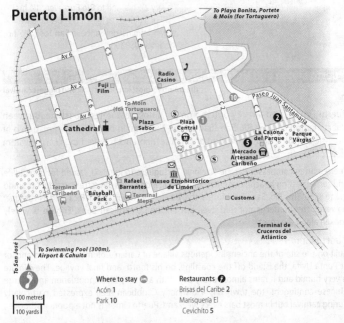

**Puerto Limón**

*To Playa Bonita, Portete & Moín (for Tortuguero)*

Av 6
Av 5
Av 4
Av 3
Av 2
Av 1

Radio Casino
Fuji Film
To Moín (for Tortuguero)
Cathedral
Plaza Sabor
Plaza Central
Paseo Juan Santamaría
La Casona del Parque
Parque Vargas
Mercado Artesanal Caribeño
Rafael Barrantes
Museo Etnohistórico de Limón
Terminal Caribeño
Baseball Park
Terminal Mepe
Customs
Terminal de Cruceros del Atlántico

To San José

N

To Swimming Pool (300m), Airport & Cahuita

100 metres
100 yards

**Where to stay** 🛏
Acón **1**
Park **10**

**Restaurants** 🍴
Brisas del Caribe **2**
Marisquería El Cevichito **5**

## Where to stay

### Puerto Limón

**$$ Park**
*Av 3, Calle 1-2, T2798-0555.*
Neat little hotel with 34 rooms, sea-facing, quiet and cool, restaurant good.

**$$-$ Acón**
*On corner of main square, Calle 3, Av 3, T2758-1010.*
Big rooms with private bath, a/c, clean, safe, good restaurant, a bit run-down, popular daily disco **Aquarius** except Mon.

## Restaurants

### Puerto Limón

**$$ Brisas del Caribe**
*Facing Parque Vargas, Av 2, Calle 1, T2758-0138.*
Cheap noodles, meat and seafood, and good service.

**$$ Marisquería El Cevichito**
*Av 2, Calle 1-2, T2758-1380.*
Good fish, steaks and ceviche and good spot for people-watching.

## Festivals

### Puerto Limón

**Just before 12 Oct Carnival** is Costa Rica's biggest; it's crowded and prices rise, but it's definitely worth seeing.

## Transport

### Puerto Limón

**Bus** Town bus service is irregular and crowded. Service from **San José** with **CoopeLimón**, T2233-3646 and **Caribeño**, T2222-0610, at least every hour, 0500-2000, daily. Arrive and depart from Calle 2, Av 1-2, 2½ hrs, US$5.30. Also services to **Guápiles** and **Siquirres**, US$1.30. From same stop buses to Siquirres/Guápiles, 13 daily, 8 direct. Near Radio Casino on Av 4, Calle 3-4, buses leave for **Sixaola** on the Panamanian border, 1st 0500, last 1800, US$5.30, stopping at **Cahuita. Puerto Viejo** and **Bribri** en route; for more on crossing the border at Sixaola to Panama, see border crossing box in the Practicalities chapter for Costa Rica–Panama). To **Manzanillo**, at 0600, 1430, returning 1130, 1900, 1½ hrs, US$4.20. To **Moín** from Calle 5, Av 3-4, every 30 mins from 0600-2200, US$0.40.

## Parque Nacional Tortuguero  *Colour map 4, B4.*

### extensive park protecting turtle-nesting sites and rainforest

★ Tortuguero (Tortuguero Information Centre, T8833-0827, safari@racsa.co.cr) is a 29,068-ha national park, with a marine extension of over 50,000 ha, conserving the Atlantic nesting sites of the green and leatherback turtle and the Caribbean lowland rainforest inland. As with much of Costa Rica, getting the timing right to see this natural phenomenon is essential. The green turtles lay their eggs at night on the scrappy, rather untidy beach from June to October, with the hatchlings emerging from the depths of their sandy nests until November at the latest. Leatherbacks can be seen from March to June. Hawksbill and loggerheads also nest at Tortuguero but numbers are minimal. Trips to look for nesting turtles are carefully monitored and you must be accompanied by a licensed guide at all times. For details, see Tour operators and Transport, in Listings section, below.

While your visit may not coincide with those of the turtles, the canals of jungle-fringed waterways behind the beach, full of abundant bird and insect life, are always a pleasure.

A **visitor centre**, close to the village of Tortuguero, has information on the park and the turtles. Round the back of the headquarters there is a well-marked and recommended 1.4-km nature trail. In the centre is a small gift shop. To the northern end of the village is the **Caribbean Conservation Corporation**, which has played a fundamental role in the creation and continued research of the turtle nesting grounds. There's an interesting and very informative **Natural History Museum** ⓘ *T2224-9215 (San José), www.conserveturtles. org, daily 1000-1200, 1400-1730, donation US$1.* Information about all this and more can be found on the village website, www.tortuguerovillage.com.

A guide is required for trips along the beach at night and is recommended for trips through the waterways. If travelling with a lodge, tours will be arranged for you. If organizing independently, contact the information kiosk in the village for instructions and to link up with a registered guide. To visit the turtles at night you must pay US$15 park entrance fee and US$5 each for a guide. A guide and tour in no way guarantees you will see a turtle or hatchlings. **Note** Do not swim at Tortuguero as there are sharks.

Tours through the water channels are the best way to see the rainforest, ideally in a boat without a motor. The canal, bordered with primary rainforest, gives way to smaller channels and, drifting slowly through forest-darkened streams, the rainforest slowly comes alive with wildlife including birds – over half of those found in Costa Rica – monkeys, sloths and, for the lucky, alligators, tapirs, jaguars, ocelots, peccaries, anteaters and even manatees. You can hire a canoe and guide for about US$8 per hour per person in a boat without motor, or US$15 with a motor, minimum of four people. Night tours cost US$20 per person per hour. Fishing tours, with all equipment included, cost US$35 per person, with a minimum of two people. Take insect repellent. See Tour operators, below.

## Listings Parque Nacional Tortuguero

### Where to stay

Top-end hotels normally target package deals; walk-in rates given where available. There are many cheap *cabañas* in town; the boatmen or villagers will help you find them. Staying in town is better for the local economy.

#### Tortuguero village

**$$ Casa Marbella**
*In front of the Catholic church, T2709-8011, http://casamarbella.tripod.com.*
B&B with 4 small rooms, with private bath. Run by local guide Daryl Loth. Good source of information and in the centre of the village.

**$$ Miss Junie's**
*T2709-8102.*
Has 12 good cabins at the north end of town.

**$ Cabinas Tortuguero**
*T2709-8114, tinamon@racsa.co.cr.*
5 little cabins, each sleeping 3 with private bath, pleasant garden with hammocks. Nice spot.

#### Beyond Tortuguero village

Places out of the village, best visited as part of a package, include:

**$$$$ Mawamba Lodge**
*T2293-8181, www.grupomawamba.com.*
Comfortable cabins with fans, pool, walking distance to town. Turtle beaches are behind the property.

**$$$$-$$$ Pachira Lodge**
*Across the canal from town, T2257-2242, www.pachiralodge.com.*

3-day/2-night package includes transport, food, tours with bilingual guide, US$309 per person.

### $$$ Laguna Lodge
*T2272-4943, www.lagunatortuguero.com.*
50-odd cabins, with bath and fan, restaurant, bar, beautiful gardens, pool and conference room.

### $$$ Tortuga Lodge
*T2521-6099 (San José), www. costaricaexpeditions.com.*
Price per person includes meals. Very comfortable accommodation, in big rooms, each with veranda or balcony.

### $$$ Turtle Beach Lodge
*T2248-0707, www.turtlebeachlodge.com.*
2- to 7-day packages from US$210 in 48 ha of beautifully landscaped tropical grounds.

### $$ Caribbean Paradise
*1 channel back from Tortuguero, T2232-2174, www.caribbeanparadisetortuguero.com (difficult to reach, try going direct when you arrive).*
Run by Tico Carlos and his wife Ana, includes 3 meals. 20 simple rooms, no set itinerary, personal service, activities as you want them. A refreshing change from the general offering and very enjoyable.

### $ Caño Palma Biological Station
*6 km north of Tortuguero, administered by the Canadian Organization for Tropical Education and Rainforest Conservation (in Canada T905-683-2116).*
Basic rooms for volunteer staff. Price per person, includes meals. A good place for serious naturalists or just for unwinding, accommodation for up to 16 in wooden cabin, freshwater well for drinking and washing. Minimum stay 2 weeks.

### Tortuguero village

### $$ Café Caoba
Cheap and has excellent pizza, sandwiches and shrimp.

### $$ Miss Junie's
*North end of the village.*
Very popular, has good local dishes, reservation necessary.

### $$ The Vine
Pizzas and sandwiches.

### $ El Dolar
Simple restaurant, small menu, good *casado*.

### $ Restaurant El Muellecito
*T2710-6716.*
Also has 3 simple cabins.

### What to do

**Tour operators**
**From San José** Most people visit Tortuguero as part of a tour from San José flying into the airport, or catching an agency bus and boat from Matina. It is possible to travel to Tortuguero independently (see Transport, below). Tours from San José include transport, meals, 2 nights' lodging, guide and boat trips for US$215-330 per person (double occupancy).

**Caño Blanco Marina**, *2 Av, 1-3 C, San José, T2256-9444 (San José), T2710-0523 (Tortuguero).* Runs a daily bus-boat service San José–Tortuguero at 0700, US$50 return. Book in advance – if you miss the boat, there is nothing else in Caño Blanco Marina.

**Mawamba**, *T2223-2421, www.grupo mawamba.com.* Minimum 2 people, 3 days/2 nights, daily, private launch so you can stop en route, with launch tour of national park included. Accommodation at the very comfortable **Mawamba Lodge**, 3-day/2-night package, Tue, Fri, Sun US$330. Other accommodations have very similar packages, with the difference being the level of comfort in the hotel. **Ilan Ilan Lodge**

(T2255-3031, www.ilan-ilanlodge.com), is one of the more affordable at US$215 for 2 nights, US$160 for 1 night (but not really long enough to make it worth it).

Tours from Puerto Viejo de Sarapiquí, including boat trip to Tortuguero, meals, 2 nights' lodging, guide and transport to San José cost US$275-400 per person (double occupancy). *Riverboat Francesca* (T2226-0986, www.tortuguerocanals.com), costs US$200-220 per person 2-day, 1-night trips exploring the canals for exquisite wildlife, sportfishing. Longer packages are also available.

**From Puerto Limón** Organizing a package trip from **Puerto Limón** is more difficult. **Viajes Tropicales Laura** (T2795-2410, www.viajestropicales laura.net), have been highly recommended, daily service, open return US$60 if phoned direct, more through travel agencies, pickup from hotel, will store luggage, lunch provided, excellent for pointing out wildlife on the way. An inclusive 2-day, 1-night package a from Puerto Limón with basic accommodation, turtle-watching trip and transport (no food) costs from US$99 per person.

**Guides** Several local guides have been recommended, including **Johnny Velázquez**; **Alberto**, who lives next to Hotel Mary Scar; **Rubén Bananero**, who lives in the last house before you get to the National Park office, sign on pathway, recommended for 4-hr tour at dusk and in the dark; **Chico**, who lives behind Sabina's Cabinas, US$2 per hr, and will take you anywhere in his motor boat; **Ernesto**, who was born in Tortuguero, and has 15 years' experience as a guide, contact him at Tropical Lodge or through his mother, who owns Sabina's Cabinas; **Rafael**, a biologist who speaks Spanish and English (his wife speaks French), and lives 500 m behind Park Rangers' office (ask rangers for directions); he also rents canoes. **Ross Ballard**, a Canadian biologist who can be contacted through Casa Marbella.

Daryl Loth lives locally and runs **Tortuguero Safaris** (T8833-0827,

safari@racsa.co.cr). **Barbara Hartung** of **Tinamon Tours** (T2709-8004, www.tinamontours.de), a biologist who speaks English, German, French and Spanish, is recommended for boat, hiking and turtle tours in Tortuguero (US$5 per person per hr; all-inclusive trips from Limón 3 days, 2 nights, US$140 per person). Both Daryl and Barbara are strong supporters of using paddle power, or at most electric motors. There are several boats for rent from Tortuguero, ask at the *pulpería*. The use of polluting 2-stroke motors is outlawed in Tortuguero, and the use of 4-stroke engines is limited to 3 of the 4 main water channels.

## Transport

**Air** Daily flights from **San José** with **Nature Air** (US$91).

**Boat** It is quite possible to travel to Tortuguero independently, but more challenging than the all-inclusive packages. There are a couple of options. From **Limón**, regular vessels leaves from the Tortuguero dock in **Moín**, north of Limón, US$50 return. It is a loosely run cooperative, with boats leaving at 1000. There is also a 1500 service that runs less frequently. If possible, book in advance through the Tortuguero Information Centre (check the times; they change frequently). If you are in a group you may be able to charter a boat for approximately US$200.

An alternative route is between **Puerto Veijo de Sarapiquí** and Tortuguero. Boats leave Puerto Viejo on Mon and Thu, returning on Tue and Fri. US$55 per person.

**Bus and boat** From **San José**, the bus/boat combination is the cheapest option and a mini-adventure in itself. Take the 0900 bus to Cariari from the Terminal Gran Caribe, arriving around 1045. Walk 500 m north to the ticket booth behind the police station where you can buy you bus/boat ticket to Tortuguero. Take the 1200 bus to **La Pavona**, arriving around 1330. Take 1 of the boats to Tortuguero, which will arrive about 1500. The journey is about US$10 1-way. Don't be talked intoa package if you're not interested – there are plenty of services to choose from in Tortuguero. The return service leaves at 0830 and 1330 giving you 1 or 2 nights in Tortuguero.

Alternative routes include the 1030 bus from San José to Cariari, changing to get the 1400 bus to La Geest and the 1530 boat to Tortuguero. Or 1300 bus San José–Cariari, 1500 bus Cariari to La Pavona, 1630 boat La Pavone to Tortuguero.

It is also possible to take a bus from Siquirres to **Freeman** (unpaved road,

US$1.70), a Del Monte banana plantation, from where unscheduled boats go to Tortuguero; ask around at the bank of the Río Pacuare, or call the public phone office in Tortuguero (T2710-6716, open 0730-2000) and ask for **Johnny Velázquez** to come and pick you up, US$57, maximum 4 passengers, 4 hrs. Sometimes heavy rains block the canals, preventing passage there or back. Contact **Willis Rankin** (T2798-1556) an excellent captain who will negotiate rampaging rivers. All riverboats for the major lodges leave from Hamburgo or Freeman. If the excursion boats have a spare seat you may be allowed on.

## Barra del Colorado  Colour map 4, B3.

#### secluded national wildlife refuge

The canals here are part artificial, part natural; originally they were narrow lagoons running parallel to the sea separated by a small strip of land. Now the lagoons are linked and it is possible to sail as far as Barra del Colorado, in the extreme northeast of Costa Rica, 25 km beyond Tortuguero. They pass many settlements. The town is divided by the river, the main part being on the northern bank.

The **Refugio Nacional de Fauna Silvestre Barra del Colorado** (81,213 ha) is difficult to access. The reserve and the Parque Nacional Tortuguero share some boundaries, making for a far more effective protected zone. The fame of the region's fauna extends to the waters, which are world renowned for fishing.

Once across the Río Colorado (which in fact is the south arm of the Río San Juan delta), you can walk to Nicaragua along the coast, but it is a long 30-km beach walk; take food and lots of water. Most hikers overnight en route. Seek advice before setting out.

## Listings Barra del Colorado

### Where to stay

**$$$$-$$$ Silver King Lodge**
*T2711-0708, www.silver kinglodge.com.*
Price per person. Deluxe sport-fishing hotel, 5-night packages includes flights, meals, rooms with bath and a/c. Pool.

**$ Tarponland Lodge**
*T2710-2141.*
Cabins, run by Guillermo Cunningham, very helpful and knowledgeable. If you have a tent you may be able to camp at **Soda La Fiesta**, lots of mosquitoes.

### Penshurst

South of Limón, a paved road shadows the coastline normally separated by little more than a thin line of palms. Beyond Penshurst is the **Hitoy Cerere Biological Reserve**. If you have time, camping is easy in the hills and there are plenty of rivers for swimming. Further south the road leads to Cahuita, Puerto Viejo and on towards Manzanillo – low-key beach resorts, with lively centres, comfortable hideaways and coastal and nature opportunities to explore. If heading for the Panamanian border, going inland just north of Puerto Viejo takes you through Bribri and on to Sixaola; see also the border crossing box in the Practicalities chapter for Costa Rica–Panama). From Penshurst it is 11.5 km to Cahuita.

### Cahuita and Parque Nacional Cahuita

*Entry to the park US$15. The official entrance to the park is at Puerto Vargas, about 5 km south of Cahuita, where the park headquarters, a nature trail, camping facilities and toilets are situated. Take the bus to Km 5, then turn left at the sign. You can enter the park for free from the southern side of Cahuita, which is ideal for relaxing on the beach, but leave a donation. If you have the option,*

Cahuita

**Where to stay**
Bungalows Aché **4** *C6*
Cabinas Iguana **3** *B1*
Cabinas Nirvana **25** *B1*
El Encanto B&B Inn **7** *B3*
Jenny's Cabinas **12** *B6*
Kelly Creek **13** *C6*
La Casa de las Flores **1** *B5*
La Diosa **2** *A1*
Magellan Inn **15** *A1*
Restaurant & Bungalows
  Bluspirit **8** *B4*
Sol y Mar **22** *C6*

**Restaurants** 🍴
Chao's Paradise **3** *A1*
Coral Reef **1** *B5*
La Casa Creole **5** *A1*
La Fe **8** *B5*
Mango Tango Pizzeria **17** *B5*
Miss Edith's **6** *A5*

*visit during the week when it is quieter. There is a tourist complex in the area and the marisquería (seafood restaurant), at Puerto Vargas park entrance has a jovial host who also has rooms.*

The small town of **Cahuita** hides 1 km back from the main road and has a sleepy feel. A laid-back community, it's a good place to hide away in one of the secluded spots or to party in the centre of town. There are no banks; money exchange is difficult except occasionally for cash dollars (**Cahuita Tours** changes dollars and traveller's cheques). Take plenty of colones from Limón. The nearest banks are in **Puerto Viejo** and **Bribri** (20 km away) but several places accept credit cards.

North of the town is **Playa Negra**, a beautiful black-sand beach ideal for swimming or just lazing about in a hammock, while to the south is the national park. Most people stay in Cahuita to explore the park.

**Cahuita National Park** (1068 ha) is a narrow strip of beach protecting a coral reef offshore and a marine area of 22,400 ha. The length of the beach can be walked in about three hours; you'll pass endless coconut palms and interesting tropical forest, through which there is also a path. It is hot and humid, so take drinking water, but a wide range of fauna can be seen, as well as howler monkeys, white-faced monkeys, coatis, snakes, butterflies and hermit crabs. Over 500 species of fish inhabit the surrounding waters and reef tours are available. An old Spanish shipwreck can be seen and reached without a boat. Snorkellers should take care to stay away from the coral, which is already badly damaged by agricultural chemicals and other pollutants. The park extends from the southern limit of Cahuita town southeast to Puerto Vargas.

**Note** Cahuita and Puerto Viejo have suffered from what locals believe is a lack of support and investment from central government. An undercurrent of problems, partially based on the perception that everyone on the Caribbean coast takes drugs, does mean that you may be offered drugs. If you are not interested, just say no.

★ **Puerto Viejo de Talamanca**
Puerto Viejo is a good base and a quietly happening party town, with a number of good beaches stretching out to the south. Activities in the area are numerous and you could spend many days exploring the options. There is reef diving nearby, or you can head south to Mandoca for lagoon diving from canoes. Surfers seek out the glorious **Salsa Brava** wave, which peaks from December to February. Away from the beach, nature trips range from tough treks

School

Laundrette

& Willies
Tours

Roberto's
Tours

To Coastal Path

Parque
Nacional
Cahuita

Palenque Luisa **4** *B5*
Pastry Shop **7** *B3*
Pizzeria Cahuita **2** *A5*
Soda Priscilla **16** *C6*
Sol y Mar **2** *C6*

Bars & clubs 🎵
Cocos **14** *B5*

in Gandoca–Manzanillo Wildlife Refuge (see below) through to gentle strolls around the self-guided botanical gardens to the north of town. There are also several cultural trips to KeKöLdi and Bribri indigenous reserves and options to take dug-outs to the inland town of Yorkin. The Asociación Talamanqueña de Ecoturismo y Conservación ① *ATEC, main street, T2750-0398, www.ateccr.org,* provides tourist information, sells locally made crafts and T-shirts, and also offers guide services, rainforest hikes, snorkelling and fishing trips. The **South Caribbean Music Festival** takes place in the lead up to Easter.

## Around Puerto Viejo

There are a number of popular beaches southeast along the road from Puerto Viejo. Traffic is limited, buses occasional, but it is walkable. About 4 km away is **Playa Cocles**, which has some

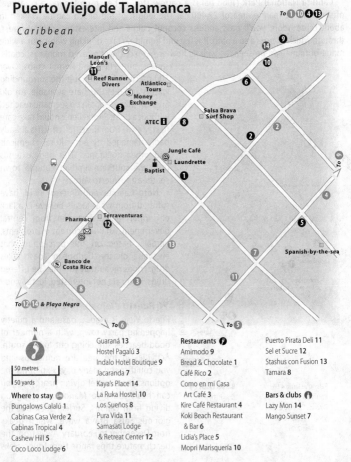

## Puerto Viejo de Talamanca

*Caribbean Sea*

To ① ⑩ ④ ⑬

Manuel León's ⑪
Reef Runner Divers
Atlántico Tours
$ Money Exchange
③
ATEC ⓘ
Salsa Brava Surf Shop
⑧
⑥
②
②
⑭
⑨
⑩

Jungle Café
⑪ Laundrette
Baptist
①

⑦

Pharmacy
Terraventuras
⑫
⑬
⑦
⑤
Spanish-by-the-sea

@
$ Banco de Costa Rica
③
⑪

⑧

To ⑫ ⑭ & Playa Negra

To ⑥    To ⑤

To ⑨
④

**N**

50 metres
50 yards

### Where to stay 🛏
Bungalows Calalú 1
Cabinas Casa Verde 2
Cabinas Tropical 4
Cashew Hill 5
Coco Loco Lodge 6

Guaraná 13
Hostel Pagalú 3
Indalo Hotel Boutique 9
Jacaranda 7
Kaya's Place 14
La Ruka Hostel 10
Los Sueños 8
Pura Vida 11
Samasati Lodge & Retreat Center 12

### Restaurants 🍴
Amimodo 9
Bread & Chocolate 1
Café Rico 2
Como en mi Casa Art Café 3
Kire Café Restaurant 4
Koki Beach Restaurant & Bar 6
Lidia's Place 5
Mopri Marisquería 10

Puerto Pirata Deli 11
Sel et Sucre 12
Stashus con Fusion 13
Tamara 8

### Bars & clubs 🍸
Lazy Mon 14
Mango Sunset 7

of the best surfing on this coast, and 2 km further on is **Playa Chiquita**, with many places to stay. Next is **Punta Uva**, beyond which, after another 5 km, you arrive in **Manzanillo**, followed by white-sand beaches and rocky headlands to **Punta Mona** and the **Gandoca-Manzanillo Wildlife Refuge** ① *ANAI, T2224-6090*, a celebration of Costa Rican diversity largely left alone by prospectors and tourists alike. Among other projects, marine scientists are interested in the protection of the giant leatherback turtle. Volunteer work is possible.

## Bribri

At **Hotel Creek**, north of Puerto Viejo, the paved road heads through the hills to the village of Bribri, at the foot of the Talamanca Range Indigenous Reserve. Halfway between is **Violeta's Pulpería**. From Limón, **Aerovías Talamaqueñas Indígenas** fly cheaply to **Amubri** in the reserve (there is a *casa de huéspedes* run by nuns in Amubri). Villages such as Bribri, Chase, Bratsi, Shiroles and San José Cabécar can be reached by bus from Cahuita. There are several buses daily to Bribri from Limón. Continuing south is Sixaola, on the border with Panama; see also border crossing box in the Practicalities chapter for Costa Rica–Panama).

**Listings** South from Puerto Limón *maps p842 and p844*

### Where to stay

#### Penshurst

**$$$ Los Aviarios del Caribe**
*30 km south of Limón just north of Penshurst, T2750-0775, www.slothsanctuary.com.*
A sloth rescue sanctuary with a small nature reserve. The friendly owners offer canoe trips in the Estrella river delta and there's a volunteer programme if you have time to spare. Recommended.

**$$$ Selva Bananita Lodge**
*20 km from Puerto Limón at Cerro Mochila heading inland at Bananito, T2253-8118, www.selvabananito.com.*
7 cabins on secluded farm, solar heating, primary rainforest tours, tree climbing, horses and bikes to rent.

#### Cahuita and Parque Nacional Cahuita
Beware of theft on the beach and drug pushers who may be undercover police.

**$$$ El Encanto Bed and Breakfast Inn**
*Playa Negra, T2755-0113, www.elencantocahuita.com.*
Attractive place built by very stylish French owners, among shady gardens with pool. 3 bungalows with private bath, hot water,

fan, mosquito net, terrace and hammocks and 1 3-bedroom apartment. Yoga and massage are available.

**$$$ La Casa de las Flores**
*Cahuita, T2755-0326, www. lacasadelasfloreshotel.com.*
Centrally located, 200 m north of park entrance, this Italian-run hotel is modern and very clean. The black and white minimalism is quite harsh in the bedrooms.

**$$$-$$ La Diosa**
*Playa Grande, past Playa Negra, T2755-0055, www.hotelladiosa.net.*
Colourful bungalows with luxury jacuzzi, a/c, private hot-water bath, hammocks, pool, gym, massage, games room, internet, surf/ kayak equipment – all this and on the beach. Cheaper out of season.

**$$$-$$ Magellan Inn**
*2 km north of Cahuita, T2755-0035, www.magellaninn.com.*
Includes breakfast, 6 beautifully decorated rooms with bath and fan, and 10,000-year-old pool (honestly) set in peaceful gardens and with renowned French Creole restaurant.

**$$ Bungalows Aché**
*By the entrance to the national park, T2755-0119, www.bungalowsache.com.*

A little off the beaten track in a very tranquil and attractive location. Well-kept bungalows with private hot-water bath, mosquito nets, coffee-maker, fridge and hammocks, friendly owners.

## $$ Kelly Creek
*Within a couple of blocks of the centre of town, by entrance to national park, T2755-0007, www.hotelkellycreek.com.*
Large rooms with veranda, ceiling fan to assist fresh sea breezes, good service and great spot.

## $$ Restaurant and Bungalows Bluspirit
*Just out of town on the road to Playa Negra, T2755-0122, www.bungalowsbluspirit.com.*
Gorgeous split-level bungalows with private bath, hot water and hammocks, by the beach. Run by a very friendly couple who also serve fresh fish and Italian home-cooked meals in their bar and restaurant.

## $$-$ Cabinas Iguana
*800 m north of Cahuita, T2755-0005, www.cabinas-iguana.com.*
Swiss-owned, very friendly, cabins or houses to rent, kitchen, fan, mosquito netting, balcony, clean, waterfall-fed pool, nice location. Big 2-for-1 book swap. Very good value.

## $$-$ Cabinas Nirvana
*Towards Playa Negra, T2755-0110, www.cabinasnirvana.com.*
Wooden rooms in a very tranquil spot, hot water private bath, pool in gardens.

## $$-$ Jenny's Cabinas
*Heading to the beach, T2755-0256, www.cabinasjenny.com.*
Balconies with view, Canadian-owned, bath, fan, breakfast available, running water, close to the sea but surrounding area a bit scruffy.

## $ Sol y Mar
*On the road to national park, T2755-0237.*
Friendly owners have rooms that sleep 2-6 people, with private hot-water bath. Rooms are a little tatty, but fine and some very spacious. Their local restaurant is good for breakfast.

## Puerto Viejo de Talamanca
Discounts are often available May-Nov.

## $$$$ Samasati Lodge & Retreat Center
*Near Hone Creek on junction between Cahuita and Puerto Viejo, T2224-1870, www.samasati.com.*
Beautiful mountain location with 100-ha reserve, vegetarian restaurant, meditation courses, reservation recommended. Rates per person.

## $$$ Cabinas Casa Verde
*Central, T2750-0015, www.cabinascasaverde.com.*
Comfortable rooms with hammocks, private bath, cracked tile showers in beautiful gardens. A pool and open-air jacuzzi add to the relaxation. The owner collects Central American poison dart frogs and keeps them in tanks dotted around the grounds; ask to take a look, even if you are not a guest. Very nice owners and staff. Recommended.

## $$$ Cashew Hill
*South of town, T2750-0256, www.cashewhilllodge.co.cr.*
Redeveloped in the last few years, although retaining rustic charm. 6 family-orientated rooms, with both private and shared bath, fans and mosquito nets. Set in 1 ha of beautiful gardens on the rolling hills above the town; a mirador looks out over the jungle tops to the sea. Yoga massage retreats and classes available. Quiet, very chilled atmosphere.

## $$$ Coco Loco Lodge
*South of town, T2750-0281, www.cocolocolodge.com.*
Quiet spot in expansive garden south of town, nice thatched wooden and stone cabins, some fully equipped with kitchen and cable TV. Popular. English, German and Spanish spoken.

## $$$-$$ Bungalows Calalú
*On the road to Cocles, T2750-0042, www.bungalowscalalu.com.*
A range of bungalows with and without kitchen, also pool and beautiful butterfly garden in the grounds.

### $$$-$$ Kaya's Place
*Playa Negra, T2750-0690,*
*www.kayasplace.com.*
Beautifully hand built with reclaimed wood, each room is a little different and accommodation ranges from simple to more luxurious *cabinas*. Opposite the beach, a nice chilled spot.

### $$ Cabinas Tropical
*Close to the coast, T2750-2064,*
*www.cabinastropical.com.*
8 spotless rooms, some with fridges, with good mattresses, private bath and hot water. Pleasant gardens with shaded garden house for relaxing. The German owner, Rolf Blancke, a tropical biologist, runs tours.

### $$ Guaraná
*Opposite Lulu Berlu Gallery, T2750-0244,*
*www.hotelguarana.com.*
Very attractive hotel if a little pricey, well kept. All rooms with private, hot water bath, fans, mosquito nets, private balconies and hammocks. They also have a communal kitchen and parking space.

### $$ Indalo Hotel Boutique
*Corner of Calle 219A and Av 67, T2750-0826,*
*www.hotelboutiqueindalo.com.*
Simple but tasteful rooms with youthful, minimalist contemporary decor, outdoor decking and gravel veranda. Spanish-owned, quiet, friendly, hospitable and good value.

### $$ Jacaranda
*A few blocks back (see map), T2750-0069,*
*www.cabinasjacaranda.net.*
A very relaxed spot away from the beach set in beautiful gardens, with mosaic pathways and private areas to relax. Rooms are fixed with colourful throws and side lights, showers are spacious. Very attractive place, hot water throughout, fans, mosquito nets. Communal kitchen. Massages can be booked to take place in a pagoda in their flower garden.

### $$-$ Pura Vida
*A few blocks back from the main street (see map), T2750-0002, www.hotel-puravida.com.*

German/Chilean-run, friendly, very clean, hammocks. Sadly lacking in character but recommended.

### $ Hostel Pagalú
*2 blocks from the bus stop towards the MegaSuper, T2750-1930, www.pagalu.com.*
Clean, decent, professional, chilled-out hostel. Accommodation is in tidy 4- to 6-bed dorms with clean sheets and hot-water showers, or simple but comfortable private rooms, with ($$) or without private bath. Also common areas, free coffee and tea, parking, lockers, Wi-Fi.

### $ La Ruka Hostel
*500 m south of Salsa Brava, just out of town, T2750-0617, www.larukahostel.com.*
Laid-back and friendly backpacker place, fun and sociable, but not crazy wild. Lodging includes 3 dorms sleeping 6-8 persons and 2 private double rooms, all with private bath. There are also hammocks, snorkel and fin rentals, surf board rentals, dogs, cats.

### $ Los Sueños
*Main street (on map), T2750-0369,*
*www.hotellossuenos.com.*
Laid-back and very relaxing, just 4 colourful and bright rooms.

## Around Puerto Viejo

### $$$$ Tree House Lodge
*Punta Uva, T2750-0706,*
*www.costaricatreehouse.com.*
Dutch owner Edsart has 4 apartments – 2 of which are the most unusual in Costa Rica: the treehouse and the beach suite (there is also a beach house). All are fully equipped with kitchen facilities and hot water, and all are equally luxurious.

### $$$$-$$$ Aguas Claras
*4.5 km from Puerto Viejo on road to Manzanillo, T2750-0131, www.aguasclaras-cr.com.*
5 beautiful cottages each painted a different colour with pretty white wooden gables and balconies. All fully equipped and very close to the beach. **Restaurant Miss**

**Holly** serves gourmet breakfast and lunch. Recommended.

### $$$ La Finca Chica
*Playa Cocles, T2750-1919, www.fincachica.com.*
A good choice for couples or families, very attractive wooden *casitas* and bungalows dotted around a verdant 1-ha jungle property. Rustic but comfortable, with all modern amenities. Recommended.

### $$$ La Kukula
*Playa Chiquita, T2750-0653,*
*www.lakukulalodge.com.*
Located 300 m from the beach, a 'tropical-contemporary' jungle-shrouded lodge with a range of rooms, suites and bungalows, all with hot water, mosquito nets and private terraces. Amenities include a rancho-bar and pool.

### $$$ Pachamama Jungle River Lodge
*Punta Uva, T8486-7086,*
*www.pachamamacaribe.com.*
Managed by a happy couple from southern France, Pachamama is located 200 m from the beach at the mouth of a jungle river. Great *casas* and *casitas* equipped with modern appliances and, most importantly, hammocks.

### $$$ Physis Caribbean
*Playa Cocles, T2750-0941,*
*www.physiscaribbean.net.*
A hospitable B&B with a tropical garden and a range of comfortable wood-panelled rooms equipped with a/c, TV, Wi-Fi, dehumidifier and stereo system. Cosy place, helpful owners.

### $$$ Shawandha
*Playa Chiquita, T2750-0018,*
*www.shawandhalodge.com.*
Beautiful bungalows in the jungle with a calm and private feel and fantastic mosaic showers. Massages available. Very stylish restaurant serving French-Caribbean fusion, pricey.

### $$$-$$ La Costa de Papito
*Playa Cocles, T2750-0080,*
*www.lacostadepapito.com.*
11 beautifully designed bungalows with all the style you'd expect from Eddie Ryan

(**Carlton Arms Hotel**, New York). Rooms with fan and bath. Great owners who love to make their guests happy. Recommended. They now host **Pure Jungle Spa** (T2750-0536, www.purejunglespa.com, Tue-Sat), or by appointment. Treatments are organic, handmade and sound good enough to eat, from chocolate facials to banana body wraps.

### $$ Selvin Cabins and restaurant
*Playa Uva, T2750-0664.*
With room and dormitory accommodation. Cheap.

### $$-$ Walaba Hostel
*Punta Uva, T2750-0147,*
*www.walabahostel.com.*
Close to nature, this bohemian hostel has 2 dorms with bunks, a large living room with TV and DVD, shared kitchen and 1 private attic with views of the garden.

## Restaurants

**Cahuita and Parque Nacional Cahuita**
If the catch is good restaurants have lobster.

### $$$ La Casa Creole
*Playa Negra, by the* **Magellan Inn**, *2 km north of Cahuita, T2755-0104 (for reservations). Mon-Sat 0600-0900.*
A culinary feast of French and Creole creations, from US$8. Recommended.

### $$$-$$ Pizzeria Cahuita
*Beach road, next to the police station.*
Thin-crust Italian-style pizzas and pastas. Great desserts too, try the tiramisu.

### $$ Chao's Paradise
*T2755-0421, Playa Negra.*
Typical Caribbean food and seafood specials, good little reggae bar, with oropendula nests overlooking the beach.

### $$ Coral Reef
*Next to Coco's Bar, Cahuita.*
Very accommodating local management can cook to your tastes, great local food with seafood specialities.

## $$ Mango Tango Pizzeria
*Cahuita.*
Great home-made pasta with a wide variety
if Italian sauces, quite a rarity in these parts,
good pizza, good restaurant.

## $$ Miss Edith's
*Cahuita, T2755-0248. Daily until 2130.*
Almost legendary. Delicious Caribbean and
vegetarian food, nice people, good value,
no alcohol licence, take your own, many
recommendations for breakfast and dinner,
but don't expect quick service.

## $$ Restaurant Palenque Luisa
*Cahuita.*
Has the distinctly tropical feel with split-
bamboo walls, sand floors and a good
*menú típico.*

## $$ Sol y Mar
*Cahuita. Open 0730-1200, 1630-2000, need to
arrive early and wait at least 45 mins for food.*
Red snapper and volcano potato are especially
wicked, US$5; also good breakfasts, try cheese,
egg and tomato sandwich, US$2. Good value.

## $$-$ La Fe
*Opposite Coco's Bar, Cahuita.*
Large variety of dishes all centred round rice
and beans, good typical food.

## $ Soda Priscilla
*Opposite Sol y Mar, Cahuita.*
Good budget breakfast *pinto*, eggs and
fresh juices.

---

## Puerto Viejo de Talamanca

## $$$ Amimodo
*North end of town, overlooking the beach,
beyond Standord's.*
Fine Italian restaurant with prices to match.
Reputedly fantastic. Weekend Latin nights.
Doesn't always come with a smile.

## $$$ Koki Beach Restaurant and Bar
*Downtown waterfront, www.kokibeach.
blogspot.com.*
If you want to splash out, a very popular
bar-restaurant, style and interior a cut above

most places in Puerto Viejo. They serve
mainly seafood and meat dishes, including
mussels, filet mignon, sea bass in jalapeño
sauce and sautéed octopus.

## $$$-$$ Mopri Marisquería
*Waterfront, opposite Lazy Mon.*
This unpretentious open-air restaurant
serves really excellent, fresh seafood – try
the fish fillet in coconut sauce. If you were
wondering, Mopri is Caribbean slang for
cousin, the Spanish word *primo* reassembled.
Highly recommended.

## $$$-$$ Stashus con Fusion
*200 m south of town towards the beaches,
T2750-0530.*
Flavourful international offerings include
tandoori coconut fish, Mexican smoked
chipotle chicken and guava green vegetable
curry. Convivial outdoor seating with
candles and occasional live music. Romantic
and intimate.

## $$ Café Rico
*Corner of Calle 217 and Av 69, opposite
Cabinas Casa Verde.*
Great coffee and breakfasts at this funky café
owned by a friendly Englishman. Also book
exchange, laundry and tourist information.
Recommended.

## $$ Como en mi Casa Art Café
*Behind Cabinas Los Almendros, near the
Sat organic market, www.comoenmi
casacostarica.wordpress.com.*
Small, friendly, bohemian café serving fresh
food prepared with love. Offerings include
salads, smoothies, hummus dips, breakfasts,
coffee and home-made chocolate. An
emphasis on local organic ingredients.

## $$ Kire Café Restaurant
*Av 71.*
Affordable and friendly open-air eatery. They
serve smoothies, salads, pizzas, burgers,
*casados* and *comida típica*, all prepared and
served Argentine-style.

## $$ Puerto Pirata Deli
*On the beach, 50 m east from the bus station.*

Funky, friendly place on the beach. They serve raw food and Ayurvedic-inspired Mediterranean dishes, organic, vegetarian, wheat-free. Chilled-out, great place. Try the smoothies.

### $$ Sel et Sucre
*100 m south of the bus stop, www.seletsucrecr.com.*
Delicious sweet and savory crêpes, salads, waffles, chocolate fruit fondues, coffee, cocktails and smoothies. Authentically French, recommended.

### $$ Tamara
*Main street, T2750-0148. Open 0600-2100.*
Local good fish dishes, popular throughout the day and packed at weekends.

### $$-$ Bread and Chocolate
*Centre of town (see map).*
A breakfast café well-known for its home baking and the morning menu is filled with good, home-made choices, ranging from eggs, bacon and fresh bread to oatmeal with apple and cinnamon. Cakes, mint and nut brownies and divine chocolate truffles are also home-made and the café is well recommended.

### $ Lidia's Place
*South of centre.*
Good typical food and to-die-for chocolate cake that does not hang round.

## Cafés and bakeries

### Pan Pay
*Beachfront.*
Good bakery. Also serve great breakfasts: eggs with avocado, fresh bread and tomato salsa, omelettes, pastries, etc. A good place to read the paper and nod at the locals – a very popular spot in the morning.

### Around Puerto Viejo

### $$ El Living
*Playa Cocles.*
Pizza, drinks and music, very laid-back and good prices.

### $$ La Isla Inn
*Playa Cocles.*
Serves Japanese Caribbean fusion, including sushi, soups, salads and stir-fry.

### $$ Magic Ginger
*Hotel Kasha, Playa Chiquita.*
Restaurant and bar serving gourmet French cooking, seafood specials and exotic salads.

### $$ Rest Maxi
*Manzanillo.*
Reggae-style restaurant serving typical Caribbean food and seafood specials.

### $ Aguas Dulce
*Playa Cocles.*
Ice creams, pastries and sandwiches.

## Bars and clubs

### Cahuita and Parque Nacional Cahuita
**Rikki's Bar** and **Cocos Bar** in the centre of Cahuita; the latter is the livelier of the two and hosts reggae nights on Fri and live music.

### Coffee Bar
*On the shore near Cabinas Jenny.*
A good reggae spot.

### Puerto Viejo de Talamanca
Puerto probably has the most lively nightlife on Costa Rica's entire Caribbean coast and has always run on an unspoken rota – each bar having a particular night, and this is still (loosely) the case. 2 solid fail-safes are **Lazy Mon,** on the downtown beach front, and **Mango Sunset,** 20 m from the bus stop.

## What to do

### Cahuita and Parque Nacional Cahuita
**Snorkelling** equipment and **surfboards** available for rent. **Horses** can be hired, but try to ensure they are in good shape. **Bicycles** can be hired for about US$7 per day and you can cycle to Puerto Viejo and the Panamanian border through some beautiful scenery.

## Tour operators

Wide range of activities available including water sports and nature tours.

**Cahuita Tours**, *T2755-0232, exotica@racsa. co.cr.* Excursions by jeep and glass-bottomed boat tours over the reefs, bike, diving and snorkelling equipment rental, international telephone service (ICE) and Western Union money transfer. **GrayLine** bus travel can be arranged here.

**Roberto's Tours**, *office located at his restaurant (Roberto's) on the main street.* Very nice people run all the usual tours of the area including snorkelling and diving.

**Willies Tours**, *T2755-0267, www.willies-costarica-tours.com.* Willie is most helpful and knows everything about Cahuita and surrounding areas. He runs tours to Tortuguero, Panama, Bribri indigenous reserve and whitewater rafting in the Pacuare river. The office is located opposite Restaurant Palenque on the main street, where he also runs an internet café.

## Puerto Viejo de Talamanca

Tours in Puerto Viejo include canopy, snorkelling, boat trips and diving in Cahuita and Manzanillo, trips to an indigenous reserve, rafting in Pacuare, kayaking, birdwatching, etc.

**ATEC** is the easiest source of information (www.ateccr.org) and the original provider of information and tours combining eco-tourism and conservation but you can also try **Terraventuras** (T2750-0750, www. terraventuras.com); **Exploradores Outdoors** (T2750-6262, www.exploradoresoutdoors. com); **Atlántico Tours** (T2750-0004); **Reef Runner Divers** (T2750-0480, www. reefrunner divers.com); **Yuppi and Tino** (T2750-0621) in Puerto Viejo; and **Aguamar Adventures**, in Manzanillo, who have been operating since 1993, and offer diving courses and local trips. Snorkel tours from US$35, tank dives from US$50.

### Penshurst

**Bus** Small buses leave **Limón** (Calle 4, Av 6) for **Valle de Estrella/Pandora**, 7 a day from 0500, at 2-hourly intervals, last at 1800, 1½ hrs (returning from Pandora at similar times).

### Cahuita and Parque Nacional Cahuita

**Bus** Service direct from **San José**'s Terminal del Caribe, to **Cahuita** at 0600, 1000, 1200, 1400 and 1600, return 0700, 0800, 0930, 1130 and 1630, 3½ hrs, US$7.90, T2257-8129, **Trans Mepá**, 4 hrs, US$4.50, and from **Puerto Limón**, in front of Radio Casino, 0500-1800, return 0630-2000, 1 hr, US$2, T2758-1572, both continuing to Bribri, and Sixaola (dirt road) on the Panamanian border (US$1, 2 hrs); see also border crossing box in the Practicalities chapter for Costa Rica–Panama). The bus drops you at the crossing of the 2 main roads in Cahuita.

### Puerto Viejo de Talamanca

**Bus** Daily services from **San José** from Gran Terminal del Caribe at 0600, 1000, 1200, 1400 and 1600, return at 0730, 0900, 1100 and 1600, 4 hrs, US$9; from **Limón** daily from Radio Casino, 0500-1800, return 0600-2000, 1½ hrs; 30 mins from **Cahuita**, US$0.80. To **Manzanillo** at 0700, 1530, 1900, returning 0500, 0830, 1700, ½ hr, US$0.80. To **Sixaola (on the Panamanian border)** 5 daily, 0545 until 1845, 2 hrs, US$2; see also border crossing box in the Practicalities chapter for Costa Rica–Panama).

### Around Puerto Viejo

**Bus** Express bus to **Manzanillo** from Terminal Sixaola, **San José**, daily, 1600, return 0630. From **Limón** daily 0600, 1430, return 1130, 1900, 1½ hrs.

# This is
## Panama

On the edge of the world stage and at the heart of global capitalism, the isthmus of Panama is a paradoxical place. It has long been a conduit for powerful international forces, but it is also a peripheral Central American state, often overlooked, and home to some of the most remote wilderness on the planet.

As a nation, it is both globally and locally orientated, gazing outward to the world and inward to its own soul. It is bound by patriotism, but sustained by foreign influence; united under the flag, but fragmented into a multitude of enclaves. Throughout history, the isthmus played a key role in facilitating shifts in geopolitical power. When Spanish conquistadors washed up in the Americas in the 16th century, Panama became a base for their expansive colonial enterprise; the birthplace of the world's first truly global empire. Centuries later, the country's fate as a transnational crossroads was sealed when the US carved out the Panama Canal and joined the oceans as one.

Today, the isthmus is a fiercely multi-ethnic place, blending vibrant traditions from Europe, Asia, Africa and indigenous America. As a bridge between the continents, it is a bastion of ecological diversity too. A third of the national territory is an officially protected area with tropical rainforests, wetlands, rivers, mountains, cloudforests, offshore islands and coral reefs playing host to some of the most biologically varied and brilliantly coloured wildlife anywhere. But sadly, as Panama's economy powers forth into the 21st century, its outstanding natural spaces are under threat from uncontrolled development. The coming years will be critically important. Will Panama embrace sustainability? Or will it sell out to big business and heavy polluters? There has never been so much to gain – or so much to lose. Panama, the great crossroads of the world, has arrived at its own urgent and ethical crossroads.

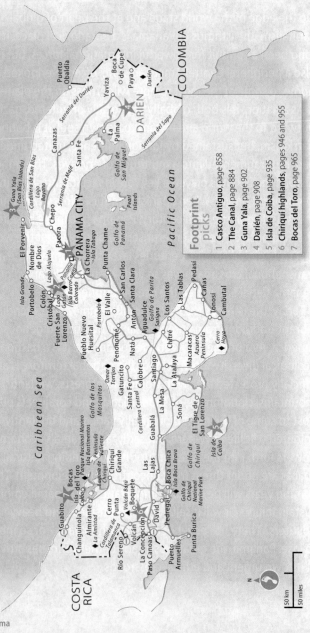

## Footprint picks

1. **Casco Antiguo**, page 858
2. **The Canal**, page 884
3. **Guna Yala**, page 902
4. **Darién**, page 908
5. **Isla de Coiba**, page 935
6. **Chiriquí highlands**, pages 946 and 955
7. **Bocas del Toro**, page 965

# Footprint picks

★ **Casco Antiguo**, page 858

There are fine restaurants and colonial plazas to enjoy in Panama City's gentrified old quarter.

★ **The Canal**, page 884

The engineering marvel of the Panama Canal at Miraflores Locks.

★ **Guna Yala**, page 902

This idyllic Caribbean archipelago is the fabled homeland of Latin America's most vibrant and successful indigenous group.

★ **Darién**, page 908

For the true adventurer, the wilderness of the Darién frontier still offers one of the great challenges this side of space travel.

★ **Isla de Coiba**, page 935

Whales, dolphins and dazzling coral reefs.

★ **Chiriquí highlands**, pages 946 and 955

Cool misty cloudforests, with hiking trails and coffee plantations.

★ **Bocas del Toro**, page 965

An invitation to soak up the Caribbean vibe and kick back on the white-sand beaches.

# Essential Panama City

## Finding your feet

The best part of Panama City is framed by two wave-swept points. In the west, the historic district of San Felipe, also known as Casco Viejo, is the opulent symbol of Old Panamá, with a mix of newly restored colonial mansions and elegant public squares, chic new guesthouses and upmarket eateries. In the east, the burgeoning Area Bancaria is the dynamic reality of New Panamá, home to luxury condos and high-rise office blocks, frenetic urban boulevards and rapidly evolving horizons. Beyond and between these two points lies an intriguing patchwork of disparate and self-contained neighbourhoods. The working-class districts of Santa Ana and Calidonia are places to glimpse the barter and hustle of authentic Panamanian street life. The planned community of Balboa is home to a slew of functional canal-zone architecture.

## Getting around

The city's mass transit system has received an impressive overhaul in recent years with a brand new underground Metro system and a fleet of air-conditioned Metrobuses. Fares are pre-paid using rechargeable Metrocards, available from kiosks, shops, or subway stops. Taxis are not metered but fares are based on a zone system. Overcharging is very common. For short trips in the centre, hand the driver US$2 and look like you expect change. Fares for longer trips should be agreed in advance. Tourist taxis waiting outside hotels are exorbitant; avoid them.

Driving in the capital is not recommended. If you must drive, avoid travelling during rush hours 0700-0930 and 1600-1830. A few parts of the city are conducive to strolling, including the historic quarter of Casco Antiguo, but generally the capital is not very pedestrian friendly.

## Safety

You should strictly avoid the neighbourhoods of Curundú, El Chorrillo and Hollywood, where the risk of robbery is high. The security situation in Casco Antiguo (San Felipe) has greatly improved in recent years, but stay alert. You should avoid the backstreets of Santa Ana, including Chinatown. In both districts, take special care at night. Many cheap hotels are concentrated in Calidonia, but the area is insalubrious after dark. The streets of Bella Vista and the Area Bancaria are generally OK to wander, but they are also poorly policed. Use registered taxis wherever possible. Tourist police on mountain bikes are present in San Felipe during the day, but most of them don't speak English.

## Weather Panama City

| January | February | March | April | May | June |
|---|---|---|---|---|---|
| 31°C 24°C 48mm | 32°C 24°C 25mm | 32°C 25°C 10mm | 31°C 25°C 63mm | 30°C 25°C 239mm | 30°C 25°C 180mm |

| July | August | September | October | November | December |
|---|---|---|---|---|---|
| 30°C 25°C 199mm | 30°C 25°C 216mm | 30°C 24°C 200mm | 29°C 24°C 305mm | 30°C 24°C 268mm | 30°C 24°C 151mm |

# Panama City
## & around

Founded five centuries ago as the Pacific terminus of Spain's pioneering transcontinental trade routes, Panama City has always thrived on the flow of commerce and imperial power. Today, perched at the entrance to the Panama Canal, its multinational banks and corporate headquarters are driving rapid development across the isthmus. Extravagant high-rise condos, boutique shopping malls, luxury car dealerships, showy international bars, restaurants and clubs all cater to the city's booming nouveau riche. With the gentrification of the city's most historic neighbourhoods, lavish colonial mansions are receiving multimillion dollar renovations. Elsewhere, brand new mass transit systems, bold contemporary architecture, and a slew of modern festivals all signal Panama City's emergence as a dynamic regional player.

But significant challenges remain if the city is to transform into a world-class destination. Haphazard urban planning has left many avenues clogged with traffic, while mass consumerism has stifled more authentic cultural expression.

And as the financial towers compete for a piece of the ever-diminishing skyline, many working-class Panamanians are left wondering what the view must be like from way up there.

**Best** for
Colonial architecture ▪ Nearby islands ▪ Nightlife ▪ Restaurants

★ A UNESCO World Heritage Site since 1997, the historic district of San Felipe – popularly known as Casco Antiguo (Old Compound) – was built in 1673. The so-called 'city from within' was a heavily fortified and impenetrable compound until the mid-19th century, when its defensive walls and sentry towers were finally dismantled. Today, diverse architectural influences find expression in San Felipe's increasingly exclusive grid of narrow streets and plazas, including baroque, art deco, neoclassical, Spanish and French colonial styles.

## Around Plaza Independencia

Plaza Independencia, also known as Plaza Catedral, is the geographic and spiritual heart of Casco Antiguo, where Independence from Spain was declared in 1821, and separation from Colombia in 1903. Filled with shady trees, benches, pathways and bronze busts of the

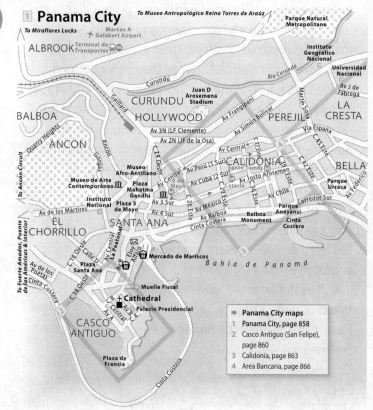

Panama City maps
1  Panama City, page 858
2  Casco Antiguo (San Felipe), page 860
3  Calidonia, page 863
4  Area Bancaria, page 866

republic's founders, the plaza is the site of occasional civic ceremonies and public fiestas. On its west side, the cathedral, built 1688-1794, features a classical façade with attractive multi-toned stone work. Its towers, partially encrusted with mother-of-pearl from the Islas Perlas, house three bells from the city's original (now ruined) cathedral in Panamá La Vieja. On the plaza's south side stands the comprehensive and highly recommended **Museo del Canal Interoceánico** ⓘ *Plaza Independencia, T211-1649, www.museodelcanal.com. Tue-Sun 0900-1700, US$2,* nearly all exhibits are in Spanish, but English audio-guides are available, US$5. The building, originally the opulent Grand Hotel, dates from 1874 and served as the headquarters of both French and North American canal companies. Organized chronologically, exhibitions explore Panama's historic development as a bridge between the oceans, and a link between the worlds. Also on the south side of the plaza is the **Museo de Historia de Panamá** ⓘ *Plaza Independencia, T228-6231, Mon-Fri 0800-1600, US$1,* inside the neoclassical **Palacio Municipal**, where the historic Separation Act of Panama from Colombia was signed on 3 November 1903. The museum's exhibits comprise a small, subtle and precious collection of artefacts from significant moments in Panama's history, including one of the original Panamanian flags stitched by María Ossa de Amador.

## Plaza Bolívar

Filled with restaurants and terraced cafés, the popular and often buzzing haunt of Plaza Bolívar, one block north and one block east of Plaza Independencia, is marked by a statue of the Venezuelan liberator in civilian clothing. On the plaza's east side stands the church of San Francisco, originally built in 1678 and restored after fire damage in 1737 and 1756. Next door, the Convent of San Francisco houses the ministry for foreign affairs and the Salón Bolívar, where Símon Bolívar chaired the historic Congress of Panama in 1826. The event drew leaders from all the newly independent nations of Latin America with the hope of forging a single federal government like the United States. You can tour the building with a guide from the Bolívar Institute. Located just off the southwest corner of Plaza Bolívar, the Iglesia de San Felipe Neri is one of the city's oldest structures with a beautiful tower laden with mother-of-pearl.

Off the southeast corner Plaza Bolívar is Panama's **National Theatre** ⓘ *T262-2535, open 0800-1700, US$1,* commissioned by the republic's first president, Dr Manuel Amador Guerrero, who rightly declared that no independent nation should be without proper national arts facilities. Built by Genaro Ruggieri on the site of an old 18th-century convent, the theatre opened in 1908 with a performance of Verdi's Aida. The interior is sumptuous and operatic with the main ceiling adorned with a striking and spiritually charged fresco by Roberto Lewis. A major restoration of the building was required in 1974 and Dame Margot Fonteyn, who had married into the prominent Panamanian Arias family, danced for the public during the subsequent re-inauguration.

### Avenida Alfaro

On the seafront Avenida Alfaro, two blocks north and two blocks west of the theatre, stands the neoclassical Presidential Palace, built in 1673 as a residence for colonial governors and auditors. Originally built of wood, the building was heavily renovated in 1922 under President Belisario Porras, who received a gift of nine herons upon the project's completion, said to symbolize the nine provinces of Panama. He allowed them

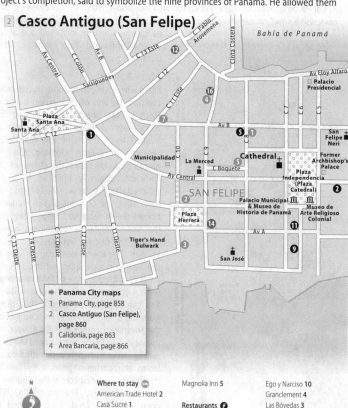

## ② Casco Antiguo (San Felipe)

**Panama City maps**
1 Panama City, page 858
2 Casco Antiguo (San Felipe), page 860
3 Calidonia, page 863
4 Area Bancaria, page 866

| Where to stay | Restaurants | |
|---|---|---|
| American Trade Hotel 2 | Café Coca Cola 1 | Ego y Narciso 10 |
| Casa Sucre 1 | Cedros Grill & Tavern 2 | Granclement 4 |
| Hostel Panamericana 3 | Diablo Rosso 9 | Las Bóvedas 3 |
| Las Clementinas 7 | | Super Gourmet 11 |
| Luna's Castle 4 | | Tantalo Kitchen 5 |
| Magnolia Inn 5 | | |

100 metres
100 yards

to wander freely around the palace and it was subsequently nicknamed **El Palacio de las Garzas** (Herons' Palace). If you wish to view the exterior of the building, the street is heavily policed and you will need to present your passport. The public are not normally permitted to enter inside, but the Alcaldía can grant permission on an individual basis; ask a tour guide to arrange this in advance. The president no longer lives in the palace, but it is still used for government purposes.

## Plaza de Francia

Perched at the southern tip of San Felipe with a bloom of fiery Poinciana trees, the well-restored Plaza de Francia is surrounded by remnants of the city's old sea walls. For many years it was the site of a notorious dungeon, and grizzly stories recall the fate of prisoners who were left to drown when the high tide flooded their cells. Today, *las bóvedas* (the vaults) serve much less sinister purposes: one has been converted into a French restaurant; another is used as a small contemporary art gallery. In memory of the failed French attempt to build the canal, the plaza features a large obelisk crowned by cockerel, symbol of the Gallic nation. The **Instituto Nacional de Cultura**, used as a set in the James Bond film, Quantum of Solace, stands on the north side of the plaza; in the reception area, you can admire dramatic murals by Esteban Palomino. From Plaza de Francia, the Paseo de las Bóvedas follows an old sea wall around the southeast corner of San Felipe to connect with Avenida Central. Sadly, its once expansive views are now obstructed by the Cinta Costera III highway, but it's still a good place to admire the bougainvillea and shop for souvenirs at the market stalls.

## Church and Convent of Santo Domingo

*Av A and Calle 3a, Tue-Sat 0800-1600, US$1.*

These were built in 1673 and razed by fires in 1737 and 1756. A single original feature survived the infernos; the legendary **Arco Chato** (Flat Arch). In the early 20th century, when America was debating where to build a transoceanic canal, propagandists famously used an image of the arch to illustrate the geological stability of Panama. The arch was so well constructed and resilient it remained upright for over 300 years, until 2003, when it tragically collapsed. It has since been rebuilt, but for obvious reasons, it's not as significant as it was.

## Iglesia de San José

*Av A, between Calle 8a and Calle 9a, Mon-Sat 0500-1200 and 1200-2000, Sun 0500-1200 and 1700-2000.*

Five blocks west of the flat arch (see above) stands this church, home to the famous **Altar de Oro**, a massive baroque altar carved from mahogany and veneered with gold. It is one of the few treasures of Panamá La Vieja to have survived Henry Morgan's attack. Different legends recall how it was concealed from the pirates. Some say it was whitewashed by the priest, others that it was hidden by nuns, but whatever the truth, a remark attributed to Morgan hints he was not deceived: "I think you are more of a pirate than I", he reportedly said to the Father.

## Santa Ana

**gritty and lightly crumbling working-class district**

Santa Ana grew up as a colonial suburb of Casco Antiguo, but it lacks the aesthetic charm of its neighbour and has not yet been gentrified. Life gravitates to the Parque Santa Ana, a bustling plaza with itinerant salesmen and shoe-shiners located at the western fringe of Casco Antiguo. North of the plaza, a large gateway marks the entrance to La Peatonal, a thronging and unpretentious pedestrianized shopping street that lurches for nearly a kilometre with thrifty store fronts, fast-food joints, cut-price clothing stalls and booming loud speakers; a great place to observe the authentic day-to-day bustle of the city.

One block north on La Peatonal, a narrow street called **Bajada Salsipuedes** (Get-out-if-you-can) heads east with a mildly diverting array of cramped market stalls which informally flog everything from herbal medicines to school text books. A block from the seafront, a side road turns into the city's Barrio Chino, or Chinatown, but aside from a large red gate at the barrio's eastern entrance, you'll have to make do with the authentic aroma of Chinese spices as evidence you're in an ethnic enclave. **Note** The barrio is very sketchy and not recommended for inexperienced urban explorers.

La Peatonal concludes at Plaza 5 de Mayo, a busy junction roaring with traffic and frenetic activity. At the centre of the plaza, a large obelisk honours firemen who died in a gunpowder explosion at El Polvorín munitions house in May 1914. To the east stands the former terminus of the Panama railway, inaugurated in 1912 and now occupied by a theatre school. To the west, an important monument commemorates slain President José Antonio Remón Cantera, who met his demise under a hail of machine gun fire at the Panama City racetrack in 1955. The assassins were never caught and the monument, designed by Juan Pardo de Zela and Joaquín Roca Rey and entitled *The Allegoric Frieze of Justice*, includes 17 small bronze figures backed by fountains and a large monolith. Behind the monument lies the **Palacio Legislativo Justo Arosemena**, headquarters of the legislative assembly.

## Calidonia

#### hodgepodge district that is neither deeply historic nor especially modern

Beyond Santa Ana (see above), Calidonia's broad avenues march northeast along the Bay of Panama, bridging the old and new. Bordering Plaza 5 de Mayo, the lightly decaying barrio of Marañón, now the site of a Metro station, was once home to thriving communities of Afro-Antillean migrants, who were charged with the most physical, dangerous, and punishing tasks of the Panama Canal's construction.

Their story is told in the small but intriguing **Museo Afro-Antillano** ① *Calle 24 Este y Av Justo Arosemena, T262-5348, www.samaap.org, Tue-Sat 0830-1630, US$1,* housed by an Old Christian Mission Chapel built by Barbadians in 1910. The museum exhibits antique furniture, household tools, musical instruments and other period pieces to explore different dimensions of West Indian culture.

Enclosed in a dense shroud of awnings a few blocks northwest of Marañón, the thoroughfare of **Avenida Central** proceeds from Plaza 5 de Mayo in a helter-skelter fashion into the heart of Calidonia. Thronging with a commotion of pedestrians, traffic and vociferous street vendors, its rough-and-ready entrepreneurial zeal promises some fascinating close-up encounters with local street life, but it's also a mean place, so watch your pockets and take care.

Northeast of the Avenida, the cleaner and more stately neighbourhood of **La Exposición** is built on the site of the famous 1915 Exposition, an acclaimed international

### 3 Calidonia

➡ **Panama City maps**
1 Panama City, page 858
2 Casco Antiguo (San Felipe), page 860
3 Calidonia, page 863
4 Area Bancaria, page 866

**Where to stay** 🛏
Arenteiro **1**
Centro Americano **6**
Hostel Mamallena **2**

**Restaurants** 🍴
Mercado de Mariscos **1**
Romanaccio Pizza **5**

## BACKGROUND
## Panama City

In 1517, under orders from Pedro Arias Dávila (aka Pedrarias the Cruel), Gaspar de Espinosa established a garrison in the indigenous fishing village of Panamá. Two years later, on 15 August 1519, the Spanish town of Nuestra Señora de la Asunción de Panamá was officially founded in its place. It was the first European colony on the American Pacific coast and it soon grew in stature as an embarkation point for expeditions to Peru, Chile and Mexico. As the conquest of the New World advanced, plundered mineral wealth began arriving in volume. Second only to Mexico City and Lima, the city of Panamá expanded exponentially. Disaster struck on 28 January 1671, when the Welsh privateer Henry Morgan launched an unprecedented attack from which the city never recovered. Consumed by fires of uncertain cause, Panamá fell into ruin and was eventually rebuilt at a new location several kilometres away.

Established on 21 January 1673, the new Panama City – today's Casco Antiguo (San Felipe) – occupied a defensive position on an ocean-swept promontory. By the 18th century, the Spanish had ceased transporting gold across the isthmus, instead rounding Cape Horn. The city's importance began to wane and by the time Panama gained Independence from Spain in 1821, there were just 5000 inhabitants left. The city's fortunes were reversed in 1848, when the California gold rush signalled boom times. A massive influx of Yankee 49ers brought new wealth and investment, including the Panama railroad. In 1882, the French arrived on the scene to much fanfare and jubilation. Their grand plan to build a trans-isthmian canal was destined to end ingloriously, but they did leave behind numerous elegant French mansions. In 1903, the US took up the gauntlet and the city grew exponentially. The Americans are credited with improving the capital's sanitation and constructing several new neighbourhoods, including Ancón, Balboa and Amador, which all fell under the jurisdiction of the US-controlled Canal Zone. Waves of immigrant workers arrived, particularly from Barbados, and social tensions rose once again. In 1964, Panamanian anger at six decades of American occupation sparked riots in the capital.

In the 1970s and 1980s, Panama City's skyline mushroomed as it gained prominence as a centre of offshore banking and international cocaine trafficking. General Manuel Noriega and his Colombian business associates enjoyed several years of prosperity until US President George Bush initiated a full-blown invasion on 20 December 1989. The historic quarter of El Chorrillo was virtually destroyed and riots broke out in the aftermath. In recent years, the accelerated pace of change has put significant strain on the city's infrastructure, demanding an overhaul of the public transit system. Developers continue to construct new tower blocks and gated communities at a breathless pace.

science and technology fair commissioned by the pioneering liberal and thrice-elected president Dr Belisario Porras. Since its foundation in the early 20th century, it has functioned as a hub of government offices, embassies, hospitals and other civic services. Life revolves around the shady Plaza Belisario Porras, flanked by sumptuous mansions.

Panama City's Area Bancaria (banking area) has the highest property prices in the city. The construction boom of the last two decades has radically transformed its energy and appearance and today dense traffic, air pollution and the almighty dollar reign.

Rolling almost imperceptibly into the district of Calidonia, the residential neighbourhood of Bella Vista – not to be confused with the wider corregimeinto (district) of Bella Vista, which broadly corresponds to the entire banking area – is a lightly faded middle-class enclave with a scattering of 1930s art deco mansions. From here, Avenida Central changes its name to Vía España. Continuing northeast, the Via passes the **Iglesia del Carmen** (1955) with its neo-Gothic spires and Byzantine-style altar, and soon grows lively with billboards, department stores and other commercial outlets as it enters the neighbourhood of El Cangrejo. The residential areas north and west are filled with a web of back roads, including **Vía Argentina**, which boasts a high concentration of international restaurants and bars, and the gaudily illuminated **Vía Veneto**, home to a big casino, many souvenir shops and a seedy red-light district.

South and east of Vía España, the neighbourhood of **Obarrio** is punctuated by an ordered grid of roads, including Calle 50, a busy boulevard flanked by offices, banks, imposing skyscrapers and corporate headquarters. Southeast of Obarrio, three prestigious neighbourhoods sit side-by-side on the Pacific waterfront: Marbella, Punta Paitilla and Punta Pacífica, all of them characterized by upscale residences, exclusive shops, shimmering skyscrapers and gleaming business hotels. Marbella, buffered by Bella Vista to the west, is the most down-to-earth of the three and notable as the epicentre of Panama City's exuberant party scene. The action is focused on and around **Calle Uruguay**, also a great area for eating out.

The fastest route between Casco Antiguo and the oceanfront neighbourhoods is via the Cinta Costera (Coastal Belt). Completed in 2009 at a cost of US\$189 million, the highway not only accommodates 10 lanes of high-speed traffic, but provides pedestrians, joggers and roller bladers a pleasant seafront promenade to enjoy, complete with plentiful palm trees, cycle lanes, basketball courts, cafés and park spaces. Sunday evening is a good time to soak up the family atmosphere, or simply observe the scramble of skyscrapers illuminated against the evening sky.

## Panamá La Vieja

**weathered and highly photogenic ruins**

Panamá La Vieja, often referred to as Panamá Viejo, are a UNESCO World Heritage Site and all that remains of the original Panama City founded in 1519. Sadly, the site's burnt-out edifices have suffered centuries of damage and vandalism and today it's hard to believe that its crumbling walls and broken foundation stones once belonged to one of the finest cities in the Spanish Empire.

The site is relatively compact and its highlights can be explored in an hour or two. Vía Cincentenario divides the archaeological zone in two with the lion's share of interesting structures on the east side, which carries an entrance fee. The west side is free to explore and here it's worth checking out the **Convento de las Monjas de la Concepción**, founded by nuns in 1597 and one of the city's best restored structures. Under the direction of Beatriz de Silva, a noble Spanish woman who would later be canonized, the nuns were the first Catholic mission to establish themselves in the Americas. Nearby, the **Iglesia**

## 4 Area Bancaria & around

Where to stay
Baru Lodge **1** A3
Bristol **6** C2
California **2** D1
De Ville **7** C3
Euro **4** D1
Milán **13** B2
Panama House Bed
& Breakfast **5** A3
Torres de Alba **16** B2
Toscana Inn **17** B2

Restaurants
Beirut **1** C3
El Burger Bar **5** B2
El Trapiche **4** A2
La Posta **9** C2
Loving Hut **18** B1
Market **10** D3
New York Bagel
Café **11** A2
Plaza Concordia
Food Court **16** B2
Sake **23** D3
Sukhi **19** C3

Bars & clubs
La Rana Dorada **26** A2
Privé & S6IS **23** C2

y Convento de la Compañía de Jesús was dedicated to evangelizing the natives and the ruins visible today were part of the main church and cloister. On the east side of Vía Cincuentenario, the large open space between the ruins is the site of the former **Plaza Mayor** (Main Plaza), which measured 69 m by 57 m and served as the social and geographic centre of the city. On its north side, the 27 m high iconic stone cathedral tower is the city's most prominent and archaeologically significant structure. Constructed between 1619 and 1626 under Bishop Francisco de Cámara, it represents the third version of the city's main church, built in the classic shape of a crucifix. An internal staircase permits visitors to climb to the top for good views over the site. North of the cathedral, the **Casa Alarcón** is a large and relatively well-preserved colonial house, formerly the property of Pedro de Alarcón, a wealthy and powerful nobleman who helped fund the building of the cathedral. To the east, the crumbling **Casa de los Genoveses** served as the city's slave market, housing some 3000 slaves in 1610, each one valued at 300 pesos. Further north stands the **Iglesia y Convento de Santo Domingo**, founded in 1571 and originally built of wood. At the exit of the site, the **Puente del Rey** (1620) marks the beginning of three trails running to the Caribbean coast, including the Camino Real.

## Essential Panamá La Vieja

### Site information

Vía Cincuentenario, T226-8915, www. panamaviejo.org. Most of the area is free to stroll, but access to the museum and cathedral is restricted to Tuesday-Sunday 0830-1800, US$6, children US$2. A taxi to the ruins should cost US$3-4. Buses depart from Vía Israel outside the multi-plaza, 30 minutes, US$0.25. For safety reasons, avoid visiting at night. For a useful pre-trip grounding in the city's history and development, it's worth visiting the **Centro de Visitantes de Panamá Viejo** (Avenida Cincuentenario), Spanish exhibits only.

## Parque Natural Metropolitano and around
### one of Central America's last remaining Pacific tropical dry forests

The 232-ha Parque Natural Metropolitano is home to some 208 bird species, including crimson-crested woodpeckers, keel-billed toucans, and squirrel cuckoos, all very easy to spot. During the migratory months, May to September, an additional 53 species can be seen, including yellow and blackburnian warblers, barn swallows and Baltimore orioles.

There are four easy trails in the park and an old road which can be casually explored in a few hours. For an undemanding stroll, try the circular 0.7 km **Sendero Momotides**, named after the blue-crowned motmot bird, or the 1.1-km Sendero Caobos; both start near the visitor cenrte. The **Sendero Roble** connects with some of the more interesting areas of the park, running north past a turtle-filled pond and bonsai nursery before arriving at a junction marked by a security station. The 1.1-km **Sendero La Cienaguita**, the park's best trail, bears left here and gently climbs through the forest. It concludes at the summit of **Cedar Hill**, where you can glimpse the Calzada Amador, Panama Canal and Bridge of the Americas. From Cedar Hill, the Mono Tití Road gently descends past a viewing platform, **Los Trinos**,

# Essential Parque Natural Metropolitano

## Park information

Between Avenida Juan Pablo II and the Camino de la Amistad, along the Río Curundú, T232-5552, www.parquemetropolitano.org. The visitor centre is open Monday-Friday 1030-1630, the park Monday-Sunday 0600-1700, US$2. A taxi from the city centre costs US$3-4. The park's public services are exemplary and include tours, workshops, internships, volunteering opportunities, and a decent environmental library, the **Biblioteca Ambiental Corotú**. For unrivalled views of the canopy, an ascent in the Smithsonian construction crane is recommended; reserve in advance through the visitor centre or Smithsonian Institute (see page 869).

where you can spot numerous birds. After bearing south, it reconnects with Sendero Roble close to a derelict Second World War US aircraft workshop known as 'El Castillo'.

**Museo Antropológico Reina Torres de Araúz** ① *Av Ascanio Villalaz, Altos de Curundú, Tue-Fri 0900-1600, US$2*. Named after the pioneering Panamanian anthropologist, Reina Torres de Araúz, this good museum – a five-minute walk from the park – is home to an intriguing archaeological collection, including dazzling gold huacas and eerie statues from the country's pre-Columbian sites, although many items were not on display at the time of research.

## Cerro Ancón

### a welcome refuge from the restless swelter below

The verdant slopes of Ancón Hill overlook the capital from the west. During the colonial era, the hill supplied San Felipe with spring water and was a place of weekend recreation, but after the establishment of the Canal Zone it fell under control of the US military, who barred public access for over 60 years.

At the summit, where the Panamanian flag now billows proudly, you can bask in refreshing breezes and commanding views. To the east lies the Bay of Panama, the Amador Causeway, Casco Antiguo and the Area Bancaria. To the west, you can see the Panama railway, canal, locks and port operations. The 2-km road to the summit starts in Quarry Heights, where much of the stone to build the canal's locks was mined. The 30- to 40-minute walk is moderately strenuous, good for wildlife spotting, and best accomplished in the early morning or late afternoon; bring water. Along the way you will pass many attractive US-style Canal Zone-era houses, including the offices of the environmental organization ANCON. A taxi can also take you up, US$3-4 from downtown.

At the base of the hill, there are a few interesting sights too. Housed in a former Masonic lodge, the privately owned **Museo de Arte Contemporáneo** ① *Av de los Mártires, Calle San Blas, T262-8012, www.macpanama.org, Tue-Sun 0900-1600, US$3*, contains a small but diverting collection of contemporary work by national and international artists, including paintings, sculptures, ceramics and photography. Art students can browse their library of contemporary visual art and participate in workshops. On the same road, **Mi Pueblito** ① *Av de los Mártires, T228-9785, Tue-Sun 0900-2100, US$1*, offers a touristy but not unpleasant glimpse of village life in Panama. Essentially an ethnic theme park, it features a series of cheesy but good-natured replica settlements. The **Smithsonian Tropical Research Institute (STRI)** ① *Av Roosevelt, Tupper Building 401, T212-8000, www.stri.si.edu, Mon-Fri 0900-1700, guided tours of the arboretum Wed and Fri 1230, free*, is dedicated to the study of tropical diversity and one of the world's leading centres of scientific research. It has programmes in behaviour, conservation, ecology, evolution, archaeology and anthropology. The STRI headquarters in Ancón have an **arboretum** where you can see examples of native flora including numerous trees, shrubs, orchids and epiphytes. The **Tupper Research and Conference Centre** is located next to the main office. It is home to the excellent **Tupper Tropical Sciences Library**, with over 66,000 volumes, and hosts seminars by resident or visiting scientists every Tuesday (1600-1700, free; see their website for a schedule).

## Balboa  Colour map 5.
### historic Canal neighbourhood with a fascinating utilitarian character

Nestled between Cerro Ancón and the quays of the Panama Canal, the township of Balboa enjoys an illustrious history as the one-time capital of the Canal Zone. Ordered, sterile, and efficient, it was a typical American answer to the wilfulness and riot of the tropics. Once with its own exclusive schools, banks, police stations, churches, cinema and baseball stadium, Balboa was incorporated into the rest of the city in 1999. Most of the town's apartment blocks have now been converted to office space.

Designed by Austin Lord of New York, the **Canal Administration Building** ① *www.pancanal.com, Mon-Fri 1000-1500, free*, was inaugurated in 1914 and continues to function as the hub of canal operations. It boasts several marbled halls, a large domed ceiling, and a series of striking murals by William Van Ingen, who designed artwork for the Library of Congress in Washington DC. Replete with drama and heroism, the murals depict the great engineering trials of the canal's construction. Behind the building, a flight of stairs leads to a monolithic marble monument commemorating George Goethals, the canal's chief engineer and administrator from 1907 to 1916. It features a frieze dedicated to David du Bose Gaillard, who was charged with the immense challenge of cutting a channel through the continental divide.

Lined with lightly weathered Canal Zone apartments, a street called The Prado proceeds in an orderly fashion south of the monument. On the west stands the former **High School**, the site of an eternal flame honouring 21 fallen 'martyrs' who died during the flag riots of 1964. The Prado concludes at a dull monument dedicated to John Stevens, the canal's chief engineer from 1905 to 1907, and opposite stands the **Balboa Theatre**, formerly an art deco cinema and now home to the National Symphony Orchestra. South on Calle Balboa is an interesting sculpture dedicated to the ill-fated nationalist President Arnulfo Arias Madrid, who was thrice elected and thrice overthrown in military coups.

## Calzada Amador

**breezy palm-fringed boulevard with brassy clubs, restaurants and boutique malls**

Only faintly reminiscent of Miami and perhaps not as glamorous as it would like to be, the Calzada Amador (Amador Causeway) extends 2 km across the Bay of Panama with an international marina and a cruise ship terminal. Built in 1911 using rubble from the excavation of Culebra Cut, the causeway joins the mainland with three tiny offshore islets – Naos, Perico and Flamenco – acting as a buffer to prevent the build-up of sediment at the canal's entrance. Formerly a military asset, it has been rigorously developed for tourism, business and conventions since 1994.

Near the start of the causeway stands the long-awaited **Bridge of Life Biodiversity Museum** ⓘ *www.biomuseopanama.org, tours on request*. Designed by acclaimed architect Frank Gehry – whose previous works include the Guggenheim Museum in Bilbao, Spain, and the MIT Stata Center in Cambridge, Massachusetts – the museum explores the natural history of Panama and its important role as a major ecological crossroads using a range of interactive and technological exhibits. Labelled a learning centre and 'hub of interchange of nature, culture, the economy and life', the Bridge of Life Biodiversity Museum has long been trumpeted as the city's most iconic and cutting-edge new development, but it was still closed to the public at the time research.

On Isla Naos, The **Punta Culebra Nature Center** ⓘ *www.stri.si.edu, Tue-Fri 1300-1700, Sat-Sun 1000-1800, US$5, children and retirees US$1, signs in Spanish and English, guides available*, is owned and managed by the excellent Smithsonian Tropical Research Institute. It maintains a diverse range of exhibits intended to educate, raise awareness and promote conservation of Central and South American marine environments, including aquariums with colourful specimens from the Caribbean and the Pacific. Children will enjoy the 'touching pools' where they can handle starfish and other aquatic fauna and there is an observation area outside with telescopes for watching the ships enter the canal.

## Isla Taboga  *Colour map 5.*

**appealing island with a faintly Mediterranean feel**

Isla Taboga, 19 km from Panama City, is draped in swathes of colourful bougainvillea, scented jasmine, and other vibrant flora. The artist Paul Gauguin was so taken with the place when he visited in 1887 that he tried to buy land there. Today, Taboga is well known for its super-sweet pineapples, mangoes, lazy beaches, pelicans and an ancient church.

Originally built of wood in the 16th century, the tiny whitewashed **Iglesia de San Pedro**, situated on the village's main plaza, is believed to be the second oldest church in the western hemisphere. Nearby, there's a plaque commemorating Gauguin and a small garden with a shrine to the island's patron saint, **Nuestra Señora del Carmen**, who is honoured with a procession and ceremonial boat ride around the island on 16 July every year.

There are a few pleasant beaches on Isla Taboga, but nothing spectacular. Most people head to Playa Restinga, around 150 m north of the main pier, where you will be quickly approached with offers of sun loungers and umbrellas, US$5-10 per day.

Nearby, a small spit of sand emerges at low tide to join Playa Restinga to the tiny islet of **El Morro**. A bit of casual snorkelling is possible around the islet, but more interesting underwater experiences can be had in the caves on the west side of the island; hire a fisherman to take you over, around US$20-30. A good hike leads to Cerro de la Cruz with its commanding ocean views and fresh sea breezes. There are two routes to the top. The shorter, harsher path begins on the south side of the island on the edge of the village. The longer, more scenic route begins just south of the pier; ask a local how to get to there.

Roughly 30% of the island is a wildlife refuge for brown pelicans, which can be seen on the hill in their thousands from January to June. Note the heat can be fierce, so don't set out without adequate supplies of water and sunscreen. Ferries to Isla Taboga, 45 minutes, depart two or three times a day from La Playita de Amador, behind the Smithsonian Marine Center on the Amador Causeway (see Transport, page 881).

## Islas Perlas *Colour map 5.*
### scattered archipelago of over 100 mostly uninhabited islands and islets

Known for their prolific pearl fishing in colonial times, the Islas Perlas are 75 km southeast of Panama City. Pearls, the mainstay of the islands' economy during the colonial era, are less common than they used to be, but the surrounding waters remain rich in Pacific mackerel, red snapper, corvina, sailfish, marlin, shark, and many species of game.

Touristic development on the Pearl Islands began in the 1960s and 1970s. They earned some international notoriety in 1979, when the former Shah of Iran took exile on Isla Contadora, the historic headquarters of Panama's now-declining pearl industry. Its name means 'counter' (or 'accountant') and refers to the island's former role as a counting station for harvested pearls. Today it is a wealthy island resort, popular with rich Panameños and crowds of Canadian, Spanish, US and Italian holidaymakers, the most developed and visited place in the archipelago. Island infrastructure includes a runway, a marina, a dive shop, numerous upscale hotels and scores of wealthy villas, and no less than 13 powdery white beaches, several of them flanked by colourful coral gardens.

Other islands include Isla Saboga, home to approximately 700 inhabitants. Trails to various secluded beaches fan out from the island's main settlement, **Pueblo Nuevo**, which is also home to a very old church. Isla San José is a private island with waters rich in marine life, especially black marlin. It attracts wealthy sports fishers keen to snag a world record; no less than 16 have been bagged here already. Unfortunately, the island is as exclusive as it is beautiful; the only lodging is an upmarket resort, Hacienda del Mar, www.haciendadelmar.net, and the only way in is by chartered plane. **Isla Viveros** is a particularly idyllic spot filled with turquoise lagoons and white-sand beaches. **Isla San Telmo** is one of the more pristine islands, home to lush primary forests, prolific bird species and nesting turtles. **Isla del Rey** is the second largest island in Panama after Isla de Coiba. It is home to several towns and fishing villages, as well as numerous rivers and waterfalls. Unfortunately, like many other of the Islas Perlas, it is slated for development. If you're looking to buy pearls, head for **Isla Casaya** and **Isla Casayeta**, 12 km south of Contadora; your hotel should be able to arrange transit. Closer to the mainland, **Isla Taborcillo** is home to John Wayne's hotel, www.isla-taborcillo.com.

## Tourist information

### Autoridad de Turismo Panamá (ATP)
*Av Balboa y Aquilino De La Guardia, Edificio BICSA Financial Center, Piso 29, T526-7000, www.atp.gob.pa or www.visitpanama.com.*
The central office of Panama's tourist board. Additional ATP booths can be found in Tocumen and Albrook airports.

### Autoridad Nacional del Ambiente (ANAM)
*Calle Broberg, Albrook, T500-0855, www.anam.gob.pa.*
This environment agency is a crucial stop for anyone wishing to visit remote national parks or protected areas.

## Where to stay

### Casco Antiguo (San Felipe)

#### $$$$ American Trade Hotel
*Plaza Herrera, Calle 10a, T211-2000, www.acehotel.com.*
A well-presented and professional new addition to Casco's burgeoning luxury hotel scene, set in an exceptional and immaculately renovated mansion property. Rooms are tasteful, spacious, light, airy, some with balconies overlooking the plaza.

#### $$$$ Casa Sucre Hotel
*Calle 8 and Av B, T6679-7077, www.casasucreboutique hotel.com.*
This restored 1873 guesthouse is one of the district's finer boutique options. It has 4 bedrooms and 3 apartments, all well equipped with Wi-Fi, cable TV, fridge, microwave, balcony, fully fitted kitchens and great stonework.

#### $$$$ Las Clementinas
*Calle 11 and Av B, T228-7613, www.lasclementinas.com.*
This tastefully furnished 4-floor townhouse has 6 comfortable, modern suite-apartments

with fully fitted kitchens, high-speed internet, cable TV and safe. A European atmosphere with good views from the rooftop patio.

#### $$$-$ Magnolia Inn
*Calle 8a y Calle Boquete, T202-0872, www.magnolia panama.com.*
A handsomely restored French colonial mansion with a handful of well-attired deluxe rooms ($$$), and for the thrifty traveler, 'luxury' hostel dorms ($). Amenities include a fully equipped kitchen, Wi-Fi, ballroom, a/c, orthopedic mattresses. Good reports.

#### $$-$ Hostel Panamericana
*Plaza Herrera, Calle 10a y Av A, T202-0851, www.panamericanahostel.com.*
A friendly hostel with simple and moderately stylish rooms and dorms, complete with chequered floors, murals, semi-orthopaedic mattresses, lockers and fans. Excellent rooftop terrace with views of Casco below, spacious common areas, kitchen.

#### $$-$ Luna's Castle
*9a Este, between Av B and Av Alfaro, T262-1540, www.lunascastlehostel.com.*
A very popular, busy backpacker hostel in a beautiful old colonial mansion. There are comfortable communal spaces, Wi-Fi, table tennis, guitars, book exchange, movie room and a kitchen. Dorms ($) and private rooms ($$) available, rates include pancake breakfast. Often packed, book ahead, party ambience with bar downstairs.

### Calidonia
If your standards are modest, there are dozens of 'cheap' hotels in this area (ie under US$50). Note many of them charge by the hour as well as the night. Always inspect the room before accepting.

#### $$ Centro Americano
*Av Justo Arosemena y Av Ecuador, T227-4555, www.hotelcentroamericano.com.*

The 61 rooms here are very clean, smart and well appointed, with Wi-Fi, hot water, plasma screen cable TV. Some have balconies and views of the bay. Restaurant, business centre and parking available.

### $ Hostel Mamallena
*Casa 7-62, Calle Primera, T6676-6163,*
*www.mamallena.com.*
A backpacker hostel with private rooms and dorms, kitchen and plenty of places to hang out. Often full. They've done their research, and have details about sail boats to Colombia on the website.

---

### Area Bancaria and around
Most hotels are glitzy, well-appointed and marketed to high-end travellers.

### $$$$ Hotel Bristol
*Av Aquilino de la Guardia, T264-0000,*
*www.thebristol.com.*
The interior of the Bristol Panama is a paragon of style and luxury. Guests are assigned a personal 24-hr butler to meet their every need, while elegantly attired guestrooms include fine Frette linens, Molton Brown toiletries and Hungarian goose down pillows.

### $$$ Baru Lodge
*Calle 2a Norte, El Carmen, T393-2340,*
*www.barulodge.com.*
An oasis of calm and balance. Rooms are classy, comfortable and minimalist, and include a kitchen area with a fridge and microwave. The real draw is the garden, complete with bubbling fountain, koi pond and lush vegetation. A great place to unwind after the frenetic challenges of the city. Recommended.

### $$$ Hotel De Ville
*Calle 50 y Beatriz M De Cabal, T206-3100,*
*www.devillehotel.com.pa.*
Recalling the elegance and opulence of a bygone era, Hotel De Ville is adorned with fine antique furniture imported from former French colonies. Tasteful rooms and suites

have a simple, romantic air but also enjoy modern amenities like Wi-Fi and DVD.

### $$$ Torres de Alba
*Calle Eusebio Morales 55, T269-7770,*
*www.torres dealba.com.pa.*
Slick, stylish, self-contained apartments with a minimalist touch. Some have great views over the city and all are equipped with a fully fitted kitchen, lounge, sofas, plasma TVs, internet and a/c. There's also a pool, gym and a so-so buffet breakfast, if you desire. Ask for a suite in the new tower, worth the extra dollars. Generally good value, comfortable and recommended.

### $$$ Toscana Inn
*Vía España y Calle D, T265-0018,*
*www.toscanainnhotel.com.*
A comfortable and reliable option with lots of good reports from former guests. Rooms are clean, modern and well equipped with a/c, cable TV, minibar and Wi-Fi. Other amenities include computer and business centre, conference room and café. Professional service, friendly, tasteful and highly recommended.

### $$$-$$ California
*Vía España y Calle 43, T263-7736,*
*www.hotelcaliforniapanama.net.*
A good, clean, professional hotel with friendly, English-speaking staff. Rooms are modern, with a/c, cable TV, Wi-Fi and hot water. There's a restaurant attached and gym upstairs. Good value and recommended, but rack rates are steep.

### $$ Euro Hotel
*Vía España 33, T263-0802,*
*www.eurohotelpanama.com.*
Located on a busy street on the edge of Calidonia district, this hotel has over 100 large, comfortable rooms with a/c, hot water and cable TV. There's also a pool, restaurant and bar. Generic and reliable.

### $$ Hotel Milán
*Calle Eusebio A Morales 31, T263-6130,*
*www.hotelmilan.com.pa.*

A reliable and economical option conveniently located. Rooms are clean, functional, comfortable and quiet, and include a/c, cable TV and Wi-Fi. They are currently expanding their premises. Unexciting but safe and good value. Lots of satisfied reports.

### $$ Panama House Bed and Breakfast
*Calle 1a, El Carmen, Casa 32, T263-4366, www.lacasadecarmen.net.*
3 friendly Panamanian ladies run this good-value option close to the action. Rooms have a/c and come with or without private bath. Dorms are also available ($). The garden provides blissful refuge from the city.

## Isla Taboga

### $$$ Cerrito Tropical
*T6489-0074, www.cerritotropicalpanama.com.*
Managed by Cynthia and Hiddo Mulder from Canada and the Dutch Caribbean, Cerrito Tropical is a short walk from the village and boasts nice views from its balcony. Accommodation includes clean, simple, comfortable rooms and apartments. Lots of good information.

## Islas Perlas

### $$$ Casa del Sol
*Isla Contadora, T250-4212, www.panama-isla-contadora.com.*
Casa del Sol offers a range of comfortable B&B accommodation, as well as apartment, villa and house rental ($$$$). Amenities include Wi-Fi, a/c, fridge, fan, hot water. Knowledgeable owners can hook you up with reputable guides and other services.

### $$$ Contadora Island Inn
*T250-4161, www.contadoraislandinn.com.*
This attractive B&B in a spacious remodelled home offers several clean, tidy, tastefully decorated rooms and suites with private bath, hot water, a/c and orthopaedic mattresses. Good reports.

## Restaurants

Panama's restaurant scene is booming and there are few more decent establishments than can be listed here. For additional Spanish-language reviews, try Degusta, www.degustapanama.com.

## Casco Antiguo (San Felipe)
Restaurants in Casco take themselves a bit seriously and are mostly aimed at upmarket clientele. Reservations may be necessary for dinner, especially at weekends.

### $$$ Ego y Narciso
*Calle 3a y Plaza Bolívar, T262-2045.*
Dinner daily, lunch Mon-Fri only. Ego y Narciso has stood the test of time and is now celebrated as one of San Felipe's finest and most popular restaurants. Their menu is eclectic and includes lots of Spanish tapas, Italian pasta and Peruvian-style seafood. The interior is modern and comfortable, but nothing beats the romance and atmosphere of dining outdoors on the plaza, especially after dark.

### $$$ Las Bóvedas
*Plaza de Francia, T228-8058.*
*Mon-Fri 1800-2300, Sat 1200-2300.*
Located in the converted dungeons at the seaward end of Casco Viejo, this long-standing and very atmospheric restaurant serves up French cuisine beneath intimate, arched stone ceilings. An interesting spot, with an adjoining art gallery and live jazz Fri-Sat.

### $$$ Tantalo Kitchen
*Av B y Calle 8a, T262-4030, www.tantalohotel.com.*
Superb Tapas-style dishes and diverse international mains from Chef Pierre DeJanon, all served at long communal tables in a tasteful contemporary dining hall. Buzzing in the evening, check out the rooftop bar too. Recommended.

### $$ Cedros Grill and Tavern
*Av Central, between Calle 4a and 5a, T228-6797.*

This American-style grill house is a casual and easygoing addition to the scene. They serve decent burgers, excellent pizzas and other wholesome pub grub. Friendly and fun, with outdoor seating and sports TV.

## $$ Diablo Rosso
*Av A y Calle 7a, T228-4833, www.diablorosso.com. Tue-Sat.*
Injecting some much-needed creativity into the local scene, kitsch and bohemian Diablo Rosso is a breath of fresh air. Its premises are a multifunctional artistic space, serving as a gallery, concept store and colourful café.

## $ Café Coca Cola
*Av Central and Plaza Santa Ana.*
A bustling, friendly little locals' haunt with good coffee, breakfasts and reasonably priced set lunches. Opened in 1875, Café Coca Cola is the oldest café in the city and something of an institution, boasting numerous Panamanian politicians and Che Guevara among its former diners. Great neighbourhood colour. Recommended.

### Bakeries, delis and ice cream parlours

### Granclement
*Av Central y Calle 3a, T228-0737, www.granclement.com.*
Fantastic gourmet ice cream to soothe your soul and take your taste buds to another level. Not cheap, but delicious. Recommended.

### Super Gourmet
*Av A y Calle 6a, T212-3487, www.supergourmetcascoviejo.com.*
A haven for foodies with a delectable range of imported cheeses, fruits, fine wines and other delicious fare. There are also gourmet sandwiches, salads and tasty breakfasts, such as eggs Benedict. Wi-Fi available.

### Santa Ana
Most hotels have a mediocre restaurant attached.

## $$-$ Mercado de Mariscos
*Av Balboa y Av Eloy Alfaro.*
The Japanese-built fish market is the place to sample Panama's rich and varied seafood offerings. Stalls downstairs sell a staggering array of ceviche for a little over US$1 a tub. Upstairs, a bustling and unpretentious restaurant offers delicious sit-down meals, including crab, lobster, fish fillet and more. It doesn't get any fresher than this. Highly recommended.

## $$-$ Romanaccio Pizza
*Calle 29, between Av Cuba and Av Perú. Mon-Sat.*
Good, tasty Italian-style pizzas with authentic crusts, but forget the burgers. Dining is casual and down-to-earth. Takeaways available.

### Area Bancaria and around

## $$$ Sake
*Torre de las Américas, also in the Metro Mall.*
The best sushi in the city, including some particularly tasty white tuna sashimi. The surroundings are clean, calm and contemporary. Excellent, but quite pricey.

## $$$-$$ La Posta
*Calle 49 y Calle Uruguay, T269-1076, www.lapostapanama.com.*
La Posta is one of Panama City's great culinary pioneers. It boasts a creative menu of mostly meat, seafood and pasta, including temptations like jumbo prawns and passion fruit served with smoked bacon and hearts of palm, or organic wood oven roasted chicken with lemon, herbs and polenta. The interior is smart and tasteful, but not fussy.

## $$$-$$ Market
*Calle 48 near the intersection with Calle Uruguay, T264-9401, www.marketpanama.com.*
Market has a smart interior reminiscent of a New York steakhouse. They serve superb prime Angus beef burgers and enormous mouth-watering steaks, as well as really delicious desserts, such as coconut pavlova

and key lime pie. Buzzing ambience and attentive service. Affordable and recommended.

## $$ Beirut
*Calle 52, T214-3815. Daily 1200-2300.*
Beirut stands out as the city's best Lebanese restaurant with really good hummus, falafels, kebabs and other wholesome Middle Eastern fare. The decor is overdone, but service is prompt, friendly and professional. There's also some seating on a balcony overlooking the street where you can enjoy a mint tea, smoke a hookah and watch the world go by.

## $$ El Trapiche
*Vía Argentina 10, T221-5241.*
This popular restaurant specializes in classic Panamanian fare, including some of the best *caramiñolas* in the country. They often host traditional music and dance programmes; call for information.

## $$ Sukhi
*Calle Beatriz M Cabal, next to the Marriott, T395-6081, www.sukhionline.com. Mon-Sat 1200-2230.*
Sukhi offers excellent, authentic and affordable southeast Asian cuisine, including tasty Vietnamese summer rolls, spicy Penang curry and Teriyaki noodles. So delicious it's almost addictive.

## $ Loving Hut
*Calle Manuel Espinosa Batista, www.lovinghut.com/pa. Open 1200-2000.*
Very fresh, tasty and affordable vegan and vegetarian buffet food with an Oriental twist. A clean, simple interior and friendly service. Excellent fruit juices (try the *maracuyá*) and free fresh jasmine tea. Highly recommended for budget travellers.

## $ Plaza Concordia Food Court
*Vía España. Mon-Fri.*
Head to the back of the arcade to find this large, unpretentious food court with several cheap restaurants serving wholesome buffet fare. One of the few places in the Area

Bancaria where you can eat for under US$5 and packed with office workers 1230-1330.

## Cafés and bakeries

### New York Bagel Café
*Plaza Einstein, off Vía Argentina, T390-6051, www.newyorkbagelcafe.com.*
A popular spot for coffee and bagels, as the name suggests. There's also Wi-Fi, soft sofas and a great bakery selling fresh bread and brownies. Service can be poor during busy times.

## Bars and clubs

Panameños love a good party. Pounding dance clubs, slick lounge-bars, swinging salsa halls, boozy pubs and bohemian jazz haunts are among Panama City's varied venues. When visiting clubs, you should dress to impress and keep a healthy stock of dollars to hand; most places charge a cover of US$10-25.

### Casco Antiguo (San Felipe)

#### Habana Panamá
*Calle Eloy Alfaro y Calle 12 Este, www.habanapanama.com.*
You'll enjoy astounding glimpses of old Cuba at this swinging bastion of style and 1950s elegance. Live salsa music is performed at weekends by smartly attired bands. Pass through the red velvet curtains to the dance floor or head upstairs to sit in one of the red booths. Very cool and highly recommended. Smart attire only, including shoes.

#### Mojitos sin Mojitos
*Av A y Calle 9a, Plaza Herrera, www.mojitossinmojitos.com.*
An atmospheric outdoor patio surrounded by crumbling old city walls and tropical plant life. Laid back and hospitable, great for a cold beer and meeting new friends. They do barbecue burgers too. Occasional live music. Recommended.

## Platea Jazz Bar

*Calle 1a, opposite the old Club Unión, T228-4011.*

An intimate and well-established San Felipe bar, widely celebrated for its live music sets. Jazz plays on Thu, live salsa, complete with spirited dancing, on Fri, and rock on Sat. Check the website to see what's new.

## Relic Bar

*Calle 9a, www.relicbar.com.*

Relic Bar is a hugely popular place that sees an eclectic mix of foreign travellers. It's located in the distinctive stone-walled cellars of **Luna's Castle**, a backpackers' hostel well known for its party-loving clientele (see Where to stay, above). There's a garden with outdoor seating where you can enjoy the tropical night.

## Area Bancaria and around

Calle Uruguay in Marbella is the heart of Panama City's nightclub scene where establishments come and go with the seasons. Two that have stood the test of time are **Privé** and **S6IS (Seis)**, both swish, young, and beautiful. For casual imbibing, try:

## La Rana Dorada

*Plaza Einstein, just off Vía Argentina.*

This Irish-owned pub boasts a great terrace for watching the world go by. Aside from a refreshing array of artisan beers, good pub food is available, including excellent burgers and fish and chips. Now with a branch in Casco Antiguo.

## Entertainment

### Cinema

There are plenty of cinemas and most of them show trashy Hollywood flicks. All of the major malls have screens (see Shopping, below). For listings, consult www.cinespanama.com.

### Theatre

Panama's theatre scene is surprisingly vibrant, including everything from amateur plays to symphony concerts. *La Prensa* and other newspapers publish daily programming (*cartelera*) of cultural events. The most popular venues (there are several others) are:

**Teatro Balboa**, *Av Arnulfo Arias Madrid, Edif 727-C, near Steven's Circle and post office in Balboa, T228-0327.* A fantastic art deco building which originally served as a Canal Zone cinema. It is the headquarters of the **National Symphony Orchestra**.

**Teatro Nacional**, *Av B y Calle 3a, T262-3525.* Panama's elegant National Theatre stages folklore sessions every other Sun and monthly National Ballet performances when not on tour. Check press for details. For more on the theatre, see page 859.

**Theatre Guild of Ancón**, *next to the judicial police headquarters, Ancón, T212-0060, www. anconguild.com.* The Theatre Guild of Ancón opened its doors in 1950 and continues to host English-language productions that prove very popular with the city's expats.

## Festivals

**Jan** Panama City's annual 6-day **Jazz Festival**, www.panamajazzfestival.com, takes place at various locations around the city, drawing crowds of 25,000. One of Central America's finest live music events – don't miss it!

**Feb/Mar** **Carnaval** is staunchly celebrated in the capital, Sat-Tue before Ash Wed. Stages are set up all over the city, including the Cinta Costera, where you can catch live music and dance. Colourful parades, which culminate in the crowning of a Carnival Queen, occur most days. Keep your passport handy to enter some parts of the festivities.

**Apr** Panama's week-long annual **film festival** showcases national and international talent, a promising new cultural event that gets stronger with every year. For more information, see www.iffpanama.org.

**3 Nov** **Independence Day**, practically the whole city – or so it seems – marches in a colourful and noisy parade lasting over 3 hrs. Another parade takes place the following day.

**Dec** Annual **Christmas parade**, with US influence much in evidence, rather than the Latin American emphasis on the *Nacimiento* and the Three Kings.

## Shopping

### Artesanía
*Artesanía* is widely available in specialized craft markets and street stalls. Casco Antiguo has fine products and prices to match in its boutique art shops.

**Flory Salzman**, *Vía Veneto, El Cangrejo, at the back of Don Lee, T223-6963, www.florymola. com.* The best place outside Guna Yala for *molas*, a huge selection sorted by theme, recommended. Many other souvenir shops on this street, mixed quality.

**Mercado de Artesanías Panamá Viejo**, *Vía Cincuentenario, by the visitor centre, T222-0612.* A small, clean, easy-to-navigate craft market with products sourced from indigenous Guna, Emberá, Wounaan and Ngäbe communities. Convenient if visiting the ruins.

**Mercado de Buhonería**, *behind the old Museo Antropológico on Plaza 5 de Mayo, Calidonia.* A small, friendly market selling indigenous and Azuero crafts, hammocks and artefacts from neighbouring countries. Worth a look.

### Jewellery
Av Samuel Lewis in Obarrio is the place to shop for high-quality jewellery. Particularly recommended is:

**Reprosa**, *Av Samuel Lewis y Calle 54, T269-0457, www.reprosa.com.* A unique collection of pre-Columbian gold artefacts reproduced in sterling silver and gold vermeil. They offer interesting tours of their workshop in Panamá Viejo where you can learn about the production process, daily US$10.

### Malls and shopping centres
The spirit of consumerism is alive and well in Panama City. Scores of gaudy

shopping centres, commercial plazas and US-style malls cater to your wanton material needs, including:

**Albrook Mall**, *next to the Terminal de Transporte in Albrook, www.albrookmall.com.* Squarely marketed to the masses and packed at weekends.

**Flamenco Shopping Plaza**, *Isla Flamenco, Calzada Amador.* Duty-free shopping at the cruise-ship terminal on the causeway. Bring your passport to enter.

**Multicentro Mall**, *Av Balboa, near Punta Paitilla, www.multicentropanama.com.pa.* The largest mall in Central America.

**Multiplaza Mall**, *Punta Pacífica, www. multiplaza.com.* The most upmarket mall in the country with brand names like **Calvin Klein**, **Lacoste** and **Apple**.

## What to do

### Adventure and extreme sport
**Aventuras Panamá**, *T6679-4404, www. aventuraspanama.com.* Specialists in hiking, rock climbing and canyoning. Very knowledgeable about Darién and the old colonial roads. Many trips focus on the nearby Chagres National Park including the 'Jungle Challenge' which involves rappelling off a series of waterfalls. For all your adventuring and extreme sport needs.

### Birdwatching
**Advantage Tours**, *T221-4123, www. advantagepanama.com.* Founded by a group of biologists, Advantage Tours offers a range of reliable birding and wildlife tours, including expeditions to Darién. All guides are experienced and usually have a background in biology or tourism. Sponsors of the **Audubon Society**.

**Panama Audubon Society**, *Casa 2006-B, Llanos de Curundú, T232-5977, www. audubonpanama.org.* Panama's oldest and most prestigious bird conservation society. They run regular field trips as well as lectures and reasonably priced tours of the Parque Metropolitano and Parque

Soberanía. Don't miss their Christmas bird count. Highly recommended.

## Fishing

**Panama Canal Fishing**, *T315-1905, www. panamacanalfishing.com.* A very reputable and experienced operation headed by Rich and Gabby Cahill. They offer fishing trips on world-class Lago Gatún where you can catch abundant peacock bass and snook (see also page 889). They claim to reel in 20-30 per person. All equipment, food and drinks included. Recommended.

## Kayaking

**Expediciones Tropicales**, *T317-1279, www. xtrop.com.* Headed by conservationists and indigenous leaders, Expediciones Tropicales is fiercely committed to the preservation of Panama's natural and cultural heritage. They have exclusive access to several remote areas and offer kayak trips in the Chagres River, Panama Canal, Guna Yala and others. Recommended.

## Language schools

**ILERI Language Institute**, *Altos de Betania, Av 17C Norte, house 20H, El Dorado, T392-4086, www.ileripanama.com.* Is a small, friendly school located 20 mins from downtown. They have a range of programmes and can organize homestays.

**Spanish Panama**, *Vía Argentina, El Congrejo, T213-3121, www.spanishpanama.com.* Offers small group or flexible one-to-one classes

with options for volunteering, homestays and/or cultural activities.

## Tour operators

**Ancon Expeditions**, *Calle Elvira Méndez, Edif Dorado, next to Marriott Hotel, T269-9415, www.anconexpeditions.com.* This is the tour operator of the famous environmental NGO, Ancón. Excellent guides and service, including tailor-made culture, history, and wildlife tours. Highly recommended for its Darién trips and multi-day Camino Real treks. One of the best.

**Blue Sailing**, *Calle San Andrés 30-47, Getsemani Cartagena, T05-668 6485/ US 203660 8654, T507 310 704 0425 (mob), www.bluesailing.net.* Travel agency handling boating and sailing trips between Colombia and Panama.

**EcoCircuitos**, *Albrook Plaza, 2nd floor No 31, Ancón, T315-1305 (T1-800-830-7142 from the US), www.ecocircuitos.com.* Expertly run with conservation and sustainability an utmost priority, EcoCircuitos offers a broad range of creative tours to destinations across the country. Activities include hiking, kayaking, cultural exchange, and educational programmes. A founding member of the Panamanian Association of Sustainable Tourism. Great Darién trips and volunteer vacations. Excellent, highly recommended.

**Emberá Tours Panama**, *T6519-7121, www. emberatourspanama.com.* Managed by Garceth Cunampio, an English-speaking Emberá guide who leads adventurous trips

to his home community. Options include journeys in dugout canoes, trips to see shamans, hiking and cultural presentations. Professional service and lots of good reports. Recommended.

**Margo Tours**, *Plaza Paitilla, ground floor, in front of Banco General, Oficina 36, T264-8888, www.margotours.com*. Specializes in tourism for small groups with an emphasis on using local guides. Professional and well established with over 30 years' experience.

**Xplora Eco-Adventures**, *Calle 50 y Vía Brasil, Plaza 50 Building, ground floor, T6526-0567, www.panamatraveltours.com*. A strong emphasis on ecology and good reports from past clients. They offer day trips and multi-day tours to a wide range of destinations including the Panama Canal, Bayano Caves, Guna Yala and Isla Grande.

## Transport

### Air

**International flights** Tocumen International Airport (PTY), www.tocumenpanama.aero, is located 35 km east of Panama City. A taxi to the centre costs US$25-30 for 2 people, 30-45 mins or 1-2 hrs in rush hour. Cheap Metrobuses ply the highway outside, but at the time of research, Metrocards were not available at the airport. To get to the airport on public transport,

take a 'Albrook–Corredor Sur–Tocumen' Metrobus from the Cinta Costera or Terminal de Transporte, every 15-30 mins, 45 mins, US$1.25. Allow extra time if travelling during rush hour. Tumba Muerto and Transísmica buses to Tocumen can take twice as long.

**Domestic flights** Panama's domestic flight hub is Marcos A Gelabert International Airport, commonly known as Albrook Airport, roughly 2 km outside the city centre (taxi US$4-5). There is no convenient bus service; a taxi costs from the Terminal de Transport costs US$2; beware overcharging. Panama's domestic airline, **Air Panama**, T316-9000, www.airpanama.com, flies to several regional airports.

**Tickets** Buy tickets direct from the airline, travel agents or tour operators at least 48 hrs prior to travel, or 3 weeks prior during peak holiday periods. The schedules below are subject to frequent change. All fares are one way and include taxes and charges.

**Schedules** Air Panama: To **Bocas del Toro**, Mon-Sat 0630, 1530, 1 hr, with a stop in **Changuinola** if there is demand, from US$140. To **David**, Mon-Fri 0700, Mon-Sat 0915, Sun 0830, daily 1620, 1 hr, from US$140. To **Guna Yala**, including **Achutupo**, **Playón Chico**, **El Porvenir**, **Corazón de Jesús**, **Ogobsucum**, **Mulatupo**, **Puerto**

**Obaldía**, 0600, 1-1½ hrs, from US$80. To **Isla Contadora**, Mon-Sat 0830, Fri and Sun 1630, 1 hr, from US$82. To **Pedasí**, Wed, Fri, Sun, 1500, 1 hr, from US$112. To **Darién**, including **Sambú** and **Garachine**, Wed, Sat, 1015, 1 hr, from US$96. To **Jaque** and **Bahía Piñas**, Mon and Fri 1030, 1 hr, from US$104. **Air Panama** always flies internationally to **Medellín** (Colombia) and **San José** (Costa Rica), see website for schedules.

## Boat and ferry

'Calypso' ferries to **Isla Taboga** depart from the Playita de Amador on the Causeway, just behind the **Smithsonian Marine Center**, T314-1730, Mon-Thu 0830, Fri 0830, 1500, Sat-Sun 0800, 1030, 1600, 1-1½ hrs, US$16 return, children US$9. Arrive 30 mins prior to departure to be assured a seat. Taxi to the causeway, US$8-15, bargain hard. Return services depart Mon-Thu 1630, Fri 0930, 1630, Sat-Sun 0900, 1500, 1700. Schedules are subject to seasonal changes, confirm times locally or call ahead T314-1730.

To the **Islas Perlas**, Sea Las Perlas, www. sealasperlas.com, T391-1424, operate services from Balboa Yacht Club. To **San Miguel** and **Viveros**, Mon, Wed, Fri-Sun, 0700, 1½ hrs, US$45 one way, US$90 same day return.

## Bus

**Local** Most city buses depart from 1 of 3 pick-up zones outside the Gran Terminal de Transporte in Albrook, as well as from a busy new station at Plaza 5 de Mayo. Outbound (east) buses travel along Av Perú in Calidonia before fanning out to their various destinations. Inbound (west) buses usually travel along Vía España and Av Central. You can check routes at www.mibus.com.pa. The basic fare is US$0.25; routes on the Corredor Sur (Cinta Costera) and Corredor Norte are US$1.25. Cash is no longer accepted. Metrocards are available widely for US$2; bring passport ID when purchasing for the first time. Cards work with both Metro and Metrobuses, but not with the long-distance turnstiles at Albrook (see below).

**Long distance** All long-distance buses depart from the **Gran Terminal de Transporte** 2 km northwest of the city centre in the suburb of Albrook, T303-3030, www. grantnt.com, a hub for all long-distance and international buses, including **Ticabus**. The terminal is clean and modern with numerous facilities. Line 1 of the city's new Metro system runs to the terminal and local buses go to all parts of the city from the road outside. A taxi to the city centre should cost no more than US$5.

For journeys of under 5 hrs, it's normally fine to just turn up. For longer trips (including David), or if travelling during holiday periods, you should allow 1-2 hrs for queuing and waiting. There is a 10 cent turnstile charge for accessing the platforms, payable with a Rapi-pass top-up card, or with a 3-in-1 card, which also valid on the Metro and Metrobuses. No left luggage.

**Bus schedules**: To **Bocas del Toro** (including Almirante and Changuinola), 2000, 2030, 9 hrs, US$28; to **Chame/San Carlos**, every 15 mins, 0530-2000, US$2.60; to **Chitré**, hourly, 0600-2300, 4 hrs, US$9.05; to **Colón**, every ½ hr, 0330-2130, 2 hrs, US$3.15 (expreso); to **David**, hourly, 0530-2400, 7 hrs, US$15.25 (express 2245, 2400, 6 hrs, US$18.15); to **El Valle**, every 30 mins, 0600-2100, 2½ hrs, US$4.25; to **Las Tablas**, hourly, 0600-1900, 5 hrs, US$9.70; to **Metetí**, 5 daily, 1230-1645, 6 hrs, US$9; to **Penonomé**, every 15 mins, 0445-2245, 2 hrs, US$5.25; to **Santiago**, every 30 mins, 0400-2100, 3½ hrs, US$9.10; to **Yaviza**, hourly, 0300-1130, 7 hrs, US$14. For the former **Canal Zone**, including **Miraflores locks** and **Gamboa**, take a SACA bus, every 1-3 hrs, US$0.50-1.50.

**International** Buses going north through Central America get booked up so reserve a seat at least 4 days in advance in low season (or 1-3 months if travelling during Dec).

**Ticabus**, T314-6385, www.ticabus.com, is the main international carrier. It runs daily buses to **San José** at 1100 (executive class) arriving 0200 the next morning, US$55 one way; economy class departs 2355, US$40 one way. Services continue to **Managua**, US$66-95. Tickets are refundable and pay on the same day, minus 15%. Dates are open and easily changed. **Expreso Panama**, T314-6837, www.expresopanama.com, also runs daily buses to **San José** from the Gran Terminal de Transporte, departing at 2300 and arriving 1600 the next day, US$40 one way.

## Car rental

**Avis**, Calle D, El Cangrejo, T264-0722, www.avis.com.pa; additional offices at Tocumen Airport, Albrook Airport and Transístmica. **Budget**, Vía España, Calle Gabriela Mistral, entrada a la Cresta, T294-2300, www.budgetpanama.com; additional offices in Tocumen Airport, Albrook Airport, Hotel El Panamá, Hotel Sheraton, Metromall and Multiplaza. **Dollar**, Vía Veneto, Torre de Alba Hotel, El Cangrejo, T214-4725, www.dollarpanama.com. Additional offices at Tocumen Airport, Albrook Airport, Tumba Muerto, Vía Israel.

## Metro

Construction of Linea Uno (Line 1) of Panama City's new Metro, www.elmetrodepanama.com, was completed in May 2014, just in time for the general election. The line connects the Terminal de Transporte in Albrook with the suburb of Los Andes in under 25 mins, passing through 5 de Mayo, Calidonia, and various neighbourhoods in the Area Bancaria. The flat fare for all journeys is US$0.35, payable with Metrocards only, US$2, available for purchase and recharge at station vending machines and ticket booths, some supermarkets and pharmacies. Operating hours are Mon-Sat 0500-2200, Sun 0700-2200. More lines are planned for coming years.

## Taxi

Taxis can be scarce during peak hours. Many drivers have little clue where some streets are so it's good to have a rough idea of the address location. Voluntary sharing is common but not recommended after dark. If a taxi already has a passenger, the driver will ask your destination to see if it coincides with the other passenger's. If you do not wish to share, waggle your index finger or say 'No, gracias'. Similarly, if you are in a taxi and the driver stops for additional passengers, you may refuse politely. Official fares are based on a zone system. If you get into a dispute over fares, ask to see the driver's zone map.

## Train

A train runs daily from Corozal Passenger Station in Panama City to **Colón** US$25 one way, US$44 return, 0715, returns 1715, 1 hr. See also www.panarail.com. A taxi to the station costs US$5.

# Panama Canal
## & around

The completion of the Panama Canal in 1914 heralded a bold new era of American ascendancy and international trade. Today, however, the canal is the sole property of Panama and a source of immense national pride; its handover symbolized the true beginnings of autonomy and nationhood.

Standing at its edge, watching the vast ocean-going vessels transit its length, it's hard not to marvel at its extraordinary ambition. Impenetrable rainforests, raging rivers, malaria-infested swamps and an entire mountain range were among the obstacles facing its builders, who perished by their thousands in a mire of torrential rain, mud and disease. Vast regions of the landscape that so troubled the canal's architects have been preserved as a vital natural watershed.

In addition to draining all the water necessary for the canal's operations, the protected forests of central Panama provide a refuge for untold flora and fauna, including hundreds of species of brilliantly coloured neotropical birds. The canal stands as a testament to human fortitude, but it will always be framed by power and beauty of nature.

**Best** for
Birdwatching ▪ Engineering history ▪ Hiking ▪ Photo opportunities

**a crowning endeavour of the age of engineering**

★ The Panama Canal is a key component in the world trade system and runs for 80 km from deep water to deep water, crossing the isthmus to connect the Port of Balboa in Panama City with the Port of Cristóbal in Colón.

Unlike the canal in Suez, the Panama Canal is not a sea-level canal; it employs a series of enormous mechanized locks to raise and lower ships between the oceans and its channels. Prodigious quantities of water are required for their operation. Each time a ship transits, approximately 197 million litres are flushed out to sea. At present, some 13,000 ships transit the canal annually, requiring an astonishing 2.5 trillion litres of $H_2O$ – an impossible demand were it not for Panama's tremendous levels of rainfall. All the water required for the canal's day-to-day operations is stored in the vast man-made lakes of Gatún and Alajuela, whose levels are controlled by dams. In recent years, the growing populations of Panama City and Colón – which are serviced with drinking water from the lakes – have created concerns about the canal's long-term water supplies. The Panama Canal – currently undergoing an ambitious expansion to meet 21st-century shipping needs – represents the final manifestation of a transcontinental trade route that began over 400 years ago with a simple overland mule trail.

Few achievements can match the bravado of cutting a passage between the oceans and words like 'fortitude', 'ingenuity', 'perseverance' and 'bravery' became inscribed in the US national narrative. But the canal was instrumental in forging Panamanian identity too. Formerly a rebellious province of Colombia, the isthmus of Panama was wrestled free in a US-backed bloodless revolution in 1903. The price of American intervention included the creation of a sovereign 'Canal Zone' – a state within a state – owned and operated by the US in perpetuity. Thus the Republic of Panama began life divided and colonized, until treaty revisions saw the Canal Zone's complete dissolution in 1999. For more information on the history of the canal and its construction, see the Panama section in Background chapter.

## Transiting the canal

Around 30-40 ships pass through the canal each day. A complete transit requires only eight hours, but most vessels spend 16 hours or more queueing in canal waters. From the Pacific, ships enter near the **Amador Causeway** and sail directly under the iconic **Bridge of the Americas**. After the port of Balboa in Panama City, they arrive at **Miraflores Locks** where they are raised 16.5 m to man-made **Miraflores Lake**. Shortly after, they arrive at **Pedro Miguel Locks** and are lifted a further 9.5 m before entering **Culebra Cut**, formerly known as Gaillard Cut, a narrow rock gorge that crosses the continental divide to **Lake Gatún**. On the other side of Lake Gatún, ships are lowered 26.5 m to sea level and exit the canal at the city of Colón. The transit occurs with the aid of tug boats. A range of companies offer canal tours (see What to do, below) and most people find a partial transit, four or five hours, is sufficient.

## The Panama Railway

*Corozal One West, Panama City, T317-6070, www.panarail.com.*

The Panama Railway is a highly recommended and affordable alternative to a ship transit. Rushing past jungle foliage and the misty morning waters of Lake Gatún, you´ll cross the isthmus in just one hour. Return services from Colón don't depart until the late afternoon, giving you several hours to explore the Caribbean coast. Trains depart from

Panama City Monday to Friday at 0715 and return at 1715, one hour, US$25 one way. The station is located near the Terminal de Transportes in Albrook, from where you can catch a cab, US$2-3. Before venturing into the city of Colón, please consult the safety section, page 892.

## Miraflores Locks

*T276-8325, www.visitcanaldepanama.com, daily 0900-1630, restaurant 1200-2300, US$15, students and children US$10. See also Transport, below.*

Completed in 1913, the two-step Miraflores Locks have a lift of 16.5 m and are supported by two dams with a concrete spillway. Receiving more than 300,000 visitors each year, Miraflores boasts an excellent **observation deck**. Its museum is spread over four floors, starting with the 'History Hall', which includes exhibits on the French and American eras. The next hall, 'Water: Source of Life', deals with the hydrology of the canal's watershed and showcases specimens of creepy-crawlies that live in the forests around the canal. The 'Canal in Action' hall chronicles the canal's day-to-day operations, whilst the final hall, 'The Canal and The World', explores international trade. The restaurant upstairs is quite smart and has a daily lunch buffet ($$$) with commanding views of the ships. Around 4 km north of Miraflores, the one-step Pedro Miguel Locks offer a poor man's experience of the canal, where you can watch the ships for free through a wire fence.

## Gatún Locks

*T276-8325, www.visitcanaldepanama.com, 10 km south of Colón, daily 0800-1600, US$5. See also Transport, below.*

Gatún Locks on the Caribbean side are the largest of the canal's three sets. Spanning a length of 1.5 km, a staggering 1.82 million cubic metres of concrete were used in their construction. Although less visited than Miraflores, Gatún offers the best views, with an observation deck that's right up close to the action. The locks integrate three steps and lift ships 29.5 m; duplicate flights allow ships to pass in opposite directions simultaneously. The passage takes around one hour. At Fort Davis just outside Gatún, a road branches south for 4 km to the **Centro de Observación de la Ampliación del Canal** ① *www.visitcanaldepanama.com, 0800-1600, US$15, children US$10*, where a 60-m-high platform supplies views of the construction of the canal's fourth set of locks. Originally scheduled for completion in 2014 and now considerably delayed, the locks will expand the canal's capacity and accommodate the modern ocean-going giants known as 'post-Panamax' ships.

## Listings The Canal

### What to do

#### Transiting the canal
#### Tour operators

Services aren't luxurious, but they do include food, drinks and bilingual guide. Additionally, bring sun block, hat, umbrella, binoculars and, for full transits, warm clothing. Both companies below accept online bookings: full transit, 8-9 hrs, around US$180, children

US$95; partial transit US$135, children US$85. All schedules are subject to change.
**Canal and Bay Tours**, *Playita de Amador, Calzada Amador, T209-2009, www.canaland baytours.com*. Full transit of the canal on the 1st Sat of the month; partial transit every Sat.
**Panama Marine Adventures**, *Vía Porras y Calle Belén 106, T226-8917, www.pmatours.net*. Full transit of the canal is usually offered once a month on the *Pacific Queen*. Partial transit

Jan-Mar, Thu-Sat; Apr-Dec, Fri-Sat. Transport departs from Isla Flamenco, Calzada Amador. Good reports, recommended.

## Transport

**Miraflores and Pedro Miguel locks**
**Bus** Beaten up old **SACA** buses travel from **Panama City** to the former Canal Zone, passing Miraflores and Pedro Miguel locks en route. They depart from Terminal de Transportes, Albrook, every 1-3 hrs, 0500-2230, US$0.35-1.50. For Miraflores, ask the driver to drop you at 'Las Esclusas de Miraflores', from where it's a 5-min walk.

**Taxi** A taxi to Miraflores locks should cost around US$10 from downtown **Panama City**, but overcharging is common, especially on the return trip. Bargain hard and try to avoid unscrupulous *taxistas* by hailing a cab from the highway, not the Miraflores car park. Fares to/from Pedro Miguel, a few mins further on, are comparable.

**Gatún Locks**
Gatún Locks are best accessed from the city of Colón on the Caribbean coast. A taxi from **Colón** should cost around US$20 return, but many *taxistas* will try to sell you a 'tour' for US$50. 'Costa Abajo' buses pass the locks, every 1-2 hrs, 30 mins, US$0.50. For more information on Colón, see page 892.

# Panama Canal watershed  Colour map 5.
**pristine tropical forests with superb hiking, birdwatching and fishing**

The luxuriant Panama Canal watershed drains the vast quantities of rain and groundwater necessary for the canal's daily functioning. Concealed in the swathes of forests blanketing the watershed from north to south are some of Central America's finest hiking and birdwatching trails. Remnants of old colonial gold routes can even be traced in the thickets and undergrowth. Fishing, boating, kayaking and diving are all possible in the canal watershed.

Between the teeming pockets of natural exuberance, the watershed is populated by numerous Emberá communities whose multi-hued traditions and communal way of life offer a vivid contrast to the urban living of the capital.

The area is strictly managed by the Panama Canal Authority, which is closely assisted by the environment agency ANAM, who have established no less than four national parks in the region.

## Parque Nacional Camino de Cruces
*Visitor centre is on Vía Centenario to the east of the Centanario Bridge, T500-0855, 0800-1600, US$5. Parking, toilets, guides and maps available. Take a SACA bus from Panama City, every 1-3 hrs, 40 mins, US$0.50. A taxi should cost US$15 one way.*

Replete with grand ceiba, nance and fig trees, the Parque Nacional Camino de Cruces encompasses 4590 ha of protected rainforest between the Parque Metropolitano and the Parque Nacional Soberanía, the central zone in the biological corridor linking Panama's Caribbean and Pacific coasts. It derives its name from a trans-isthmian trade route established by the Spanish in 1533, which ran from Panama City to the village of Las Cruces on the Río Chagres (see the Panama section in Background chapter). Although much of the original trail now lies under the waters of manmade Lake Gatún, sections within the park have been partially reconstructed and lead into neighbouring Parque Nacional Soberanía as far as the lake shore (see below).

## Parque Nacional Soberanía

Enclosing the eastern bank of the canal from Bahía Limón on Lago Gatún to the town of Paraíso on the Gaillard Highway, the Parque Nacional Soberanía encompasses 19,545 ha of vivid lowland rainforest. It is one of the easiest parks to get to in Costa Rica. The 525 bird species here are too many to list, but on a single visit you will easily see parrots, woodpeckers, wrens, manakins, toucans and aracaris. If you're lucky, you may glimpse rarer species like the yellow-eared toucanet or the harpy eagle. Arrive at dawn for an unforgettable display of birdsong.

Administrative offices at the intersection of the Carretera Gaillard (Avenida Omar Torrijos) and the Carretera Madden, T232-4192, US$5. To get there from Panama City, take a SACA bus or a taxi.

Soberanía has six different trails. They are generally well maintained, but sometimes subject to flood damage. It's worth checking their status with ANAM before setting out. Note that some of the trailheads are far from the administrative offices; if travelling by taxi, ask it to wait while you pay entrance fees. If you arrive before office hours, you should be able to pay upon exit.

**The Pipeline Road** 17 km, eight hours round-trip, access from Gamboa (see page 889). The Pipeline Road (Camino Oleoducto) is an exceptional birding trail and the **Panama Audubon Society's Christmas count here consistently breaks** world records. The trail is flat and paved and the first 6 km are secondary forest. A guide is recommended to make the most out of your bird sightings; try the **Rainforest Discovery Center**, 1.5 km from the trailhead (see page 889).

**The Plantation Trail** 13 km, four to six hours round trip, access from the Gaillard Highway, near the entrance to the Canopy Tower. The moderately strenuous Plantation Trail began life as an access road for local coffee and cacao plantations. Wildlife is relatively easy to spot and you can also connect with the Camino de Cruces.

**Camino de Cruces** 10 km, 12 hours round trip, access from the Plantation Trail or Madden Highway; look for the parking area with picnic tables. A tough hike that leads into the adjoining Parque Nacional Camino de Cruces and concludes near the ruins of Venta de Cruces.

**Spirit of the Forest** 1.7 km, one-hour round-trip, access from opposite the administrative offices. The park's newest trail is an easy stroll that includes plenty of interpretive signage.

**El Charco** 0.8 km, 20 minutes, access from Gaillard Highway. A very tame and easy trail that leads to waterfalls and swimming holes. There is a family picnic area.

**Cicloruta** 17.5 km. This road commences 2 km from the administrative office on the Madden Highway. It is designed for mountain bikes.

## Summit Botanical Gardens and Zoo

*Carretera Gaillard (Av Omar Torrijos), T232-4854, 0900-1700, US$1. There are food stalls, but the zoo is a great place for a picnic.*

## ON THE ROAD

### Nature tourism

Some 43% of Panama remains forested and a quarter of the land has protected status, which includes 14 national parks, wildlife refuges and forest reserves that are home to over 900 recorded bird species – including the endangered great green macaw and the harpy eagle, the national bird. Most national parks can be visited without hindrance if you can get there – there is supposed to be a small entry fee but it is rarely charged.

Transport can be very difficult and facilities non-existent; the largest, Darién National Park, is a good example. Slowly the value of the national park system to tourism is being realized and some parks now have cheap accommodation in huts.

A useful organization is Asociación Nacional de Conservación de la Naturaleza (ANCON), T314-0050, www.ancon.org. They run conservation projects and offer voluntary work. For more wildlife volunteering opportunities, see Volunteering, Panama, in the Practicalities chapter.

The Summit Botanical Gardens were created by the Canal company in 1923 for the study of plants. Today, the site houses some 40 species of animal, including tapirs, jaguars, deer, monkeys and crocodiles. The star attraction is the harpy eagle enclosure, where the zoo worked with the Peregrine Fund (www.peregrinefund.org) for many years, breeding and releasing new eagles into the forests of Soberanía. The zoo has some great bamboo specimens and one of the world's largest palm collections.

### Canopy Tower
*Semaphore Hill, signed off Carretera Gaillard (Av Omar Torrijos), T264-5720, www.canopytower.com.*

Perched atop Semaphore Hill with commanding views of the rainforest, the Canopy Tower began life in 1965 as a US Air Force radar tower. The tower retired in 1995 and was transferred to Panamanian control in 1996. When businessman Raúl Arias de Para acquired the site in 1997, he set about converting the former military structure into one of Central America's finest ecolodges. Day visitors are welcome (contact in advance), but to really appreciate the forested surroundings, an overnight stay ($$$$) and early rise is recommended. Amenities include a great library with field guides, a restaurant and observation deck equipped with Leica 77-mm scopes. All guides are bilingual and some of them are able to call the birds directly.

### Panama Rainforest Discovery Center
*Pipeline Rd, 1.6 km from entrance, access from Gamboa, T314-1141, www.pipelineroad. org, Fri-Sun 0600-1600, US$30 peak hours (0600-1000), US$20 off peak; numbers limited, reservations recommended. Visits Mon-Thu must be booked 48 hrs in advance.*

Managed by the Fundación Avifauna Eugene Eisemann (www.avifauna.org.pa), this interpretive centre specializes in environmental education. The central attraction is a 32-m-high observation tower with intimate views of the forest canopy, which is often teeming with birds, monkeys and sloth. There's also a well-maintained 1.2-km circuit of forest trails, gift shop and a viewing deck on the banks of Calamito Lake, where you might spot caimans and aquatic birds. The centre conducts an annual 'raptor count', 1 October-15 November, when vultures, hawks and other birds of prey fill the skies. Their most exciting research project is a study exploring the feasibility of reintroducing green macaws to the area.

## Gamboa and around

Located roughly halfway across the isthmus, the sleepy township of Gamboa is home to the canal authority's Dredging Division. Its proximity to the pipeline road makes it a good base for early morning forays into the Parque Nacional Soberania and a handful of decent guesthouses have sprung up to service birdwatchers. The Smithsonian Tropical Research Institute also maintains laboratories and residential accommodation in town, along with a small pier for the transportation of scientists, visitors and supplies to its research station on Isla Barro Colorado (see below).

The long-running **Gamboa Rainforest Resort** ⓘ *Goethals Blvd, 1st right after crossing the bridge into Gamboa, T314-5000, www.gamboaresort.com*, is a hit with families and those seeking tame adventures within the safe confines of a resort development ($$$$). An orchid nursery, serpentarium, butterfly house, freshwater aquarium and staged Emberá village are among its draws, but the star attraction is a cable-car ride over the forest canopy.

## Lago Gatún

Serene Lake Gatún was formed by the damming of the Río Chagres at the village of Gatún. Some 422 sq km were permanently flooded, washing away abandoned villages and transforming hilltops into islands. At the time of its creation, it was the world's largest man-made lake. As well as supplying Colón and Panama City with drinking water, it is home to a very large population of peacock bass known as *sargentos* (sergeants) due to the stripes on their sides. They are prized game fish, aggressive and, owing to their numbers, easy to snag. **Rich Cahill** ⓘ *T6678-2653, www.panamacanalfishing.com*, offers reputable expeditions and dawn is the best time to go, as after mid-morning the fish don't bite. Kayaking on the lake is offered by a few tour operators in Panama City, including **Eco Circuitos** (see page 879). **Diving** is also interesting, with an old Belgian locomotive and ruined towns resting in the murky depths. There are numerous islands on Lake Gatún, some of them home to rescue monkeys; please approach with a qualified naturalist only.

## Monumento Isla Barro Colorado

*T212-8951, www.stri.org, office hours 0800-1500, tour US$70, students US$40. Boats to the island depart Tue, Wed, Fri 0715; Sat-Sun 0800; be on time, the boat won't wait. The dock in Gamboa is on a gravel track just past the dredging dock. Taxi from Panama City, US$30 one way.*

Isla Barro Colorado is the largest island in Lake Gatún and one of the most studied habitats on earth, a world-class field station that sees over 200 visiting scientists per year. Facilities include labs, growing houses, insectaries and dark rooms. Long-term and short-term research is conducted at various sites, including a 50-ha forest plot that's part of the **Center of Tropical Science's** 'Earth Observatory' ⓘ *www.sigeo.si.edu*; an ambitious project that explores the dynamics of tropical forests on three different continents. Visitors to the island will experience a tour of the facilities, a guided walk on a two- to three-hour interpretative trail and lunch. Places are limited so you are advised to organize your trip well in advance, two to three weeks if possible, directly through the Smithsonian Institute or a Panama City tour operator.

## Where to stay

### Gamboa

**$$$$ Panama Lodge**
*Lake Gatún, accessed by 2 daily boats from Gamboa, T213-1172, www.junglelandpanama.com.*
This floating jungle lodge is nestled in a secluded cove on the lake, complete with simple but comfortable wood-built rooms and tranquil balconies overlooking the water. Fishing, swimming, kayaking, hiking, and night tours are available. Prices are all inclusive, including tours and meals.

**$$$ Canopy B&B**
*Harding Av and Jadwin Av, T264-5720, www.canopytower.com.*
Part of the prestigious Canopy Tower group, Canopy B&B is a very attractive 1930s Canal Zone-era building that has been artfully restored to its former glory. It has just 5 rooms, all very comfortable, quiet and cosy, some with great views over the surrounding vegetation. Staff are very helpful and hospitable. Numerous tours available.

**$$ Mateo's B&B**
*Calle Humberto Zarate, Casa 131A, T6690-9664, www.gamboabedandbreakfast.com. Friendly, welcoming, down-to-earth B&B accommodation with a host of visiting wildlife in the garden, including agoutis, hummingbirds and monkeys.*
Simple rooms and cabins are available, along with a 2-room apartment for longer-term visitors. Meals can be arranged for US$6. Very tranquil and easy-going. Staying with Mateo and Beatrice is like staying with your grandparents. Recommended.

## Transport

**Bus** Exploring the area by bus is possible, but it can involve long waits on empty highways. Hitching is an option for groups and couples, but not for lone women.
**SACA** buses depart from the Terminal de Transportes in Albrook, every 1-3 hrs, 0500-2230, US$0.35-1, and travel through the former Canal Zone, passing Ciudad de Saber, Miraflores, Pedro Miguel and Paraíso, before branching west onto Av Omar Torrijos to the Parque Soberanía, Summit gardens, Canopy Tower and finally Gamboa. Bus services are reduced on Sun, always check the destination on the windscreen as not all of them terminate in Gamboa.

# Central
# Caribbean coast

The Caribbean coast of Panama has always been valued
as a strategic link between the Old World and the New.

Today, at the point where the Panama Canal empties into
the Bay of Limón, the historic city of Colón is home to a
sprawling and heavily fortified Free Trade Zone: the largest
in the Americas. But, despite this, life on Panama's 'other
side' is often marked by economic hardship. Fortunately,
the region's lack of development does not detract from
its easy-going ambience or lavish natural beauty.

Punctuated by deserted beaches and lost-in-time
fishing villages, the Caribbean coast is a world of few
roads and fewer worries. Part of its special appeal lies
in its swaggering sense of history. A string of well-
preserved Spanish fortresses recall the fact that for over
250 years, the region was beset by pirates keen to plunder
Spain's wealthy fleet. The coast's swashbuckling history
is well complemented by a fusion of cultures that hail
predominantly from Africa. Raucous festivals recall the
era of colonial slave trading with feisty Congo dances
and fervent drum beats. English-speaking Afro-Antilleans
add lilting calypso music and delicious cooking. Rambling
along the shores, ramshackle and content, few places are
as distinct or romantic as Panama's Caribbean coast.

**Best** for
Beaches ▪ Diving ▪ Swashbuckling stories

Sadly, there is no shortage of horror stories about Colón. The city began life in the 19th century as a lawless and dismal frontier town, impressively branded 'the wickedest city in the Americas'. In some respects, little has changed. Despite historic moments of affluence – first as a terminal for the Panama railway, more recently as a hub for the nation's maritime industries – Colón has failed to shake off its negative image.

Decades of neglect have left swathes of the city in disrepair, riddled with violence and crime, its population terminally deprived and marginalized. The scenes of destitution and urban decay are the legacy of Panama City elitism, for the vast wealth generated by Colón's Free Trade Zone is funnelled straight to the capital, never reaching the streets outside.

However, despite its problems, there is much to celebrate about Colón. Beyond the ghettoes, it boasts lively pockets of colour and, in some places, there are optimistic signs of gentrification. It is hoped that, in the not-too-distant future, Colón will once again rise to glory. For now, it is assuredly off the tourist trail, but a fascinating destination nonetheless.

Located on Isla Manzanillo, the city is connected to the mainland by two main arteries: Avenida Amador Guerrero and Avenida Bolívar. Walking around the city is not recommended, but it is useful to remember that streets are laid out in a compact grid with numbered *calles* running east–west and named *avenidas* running north–south. Most taxis charge US$1-2 for destinations within the city. See Transport, below.

### Safety

Attached to Colón's Home Port and second cruise-ship terminal, Colón 2000 is a well-guarded shopping and entertainment complex. Although lacking in personality, this tourist enclave is one of the safest and most-visited places in the whole city. Beyond it, Colón is a dangerous place and the risk of robbery is high. You are strongly advised to use a taxi to get around. If you must walk, stick to the main thoroughfares, leave all valuables in your hotel and strictly avoid deserted areas and backstreets. Under no circumstances go walking at night. Colón is not for the faint hearted and less experienced travellers may want to skip it altogether.

### Sights

**Avenida Bolívar** is one of Colón's main commercial streets and a great place to witness the bustle of day-to-day life. The crowded *avenida* is home to lots of weathered old shops and enters the city from the southwest, heading north until it concludes at the oceanfront **Paseo de Washington**, which fronts the Atlantic Ocean and has views of the ships waiting to enter the canal. The surrounding neighbourhood, known as **Nuevo Cristóbal**, is currently becoming gentrified and is home to numerous structures dating from the early 20th century. Among them is the historic **Washington Hotel**, constructed in 1913 on the site of an old railway building. Just west of the hotel lies **Fuerte de Lesseps**, a former American artillery post. The old **Episcopal Church**, known locally as the Church-by-the-Sea, is located directly opposite, built in 1865 for railway workers.

Encompassing a staggering 400 ha, the sprawling **Colón Free Trade Zone** ⓘ *www.colonfreetradezone.com*, is a major distribution hub for shipments throughout the Americas. Established in 1948 in the southeast of the city, it receives 250,000 visitors annually and has imports and exports valued at over US$5 billion. A city within a city, the zone is home to some 1750 commercial outlets, including purveyors of fine perfume and liquor, designer clothing, jewellery, electronics and more. Virtually all trade, however, is wholesale. You will need your passport to enter and any purchases you make will be forwarded to Tocumen International Airport for collection when you leave Panama.

## Gatún and around

From Colón, Avenida Bolívar heads south and passes through the colourful old Canal Zone township of **Margarita**, Fort Davis (now the Colón campus of the Technological University of Panama), and Gatún with its impressive locks (see page 885). West of Fort Davis, the highway continues to Gatún locks and a swing bridge over the Panama Canal, but it is often closed for long periods when canal traffic is high. On the opposite bank, the road divides. One route heads south and skirts the shores of Lake Gatún, offering access to the protected forests of San Lorenzo, and eventually, the remote coast-road of the **Costa Abajo**. A northbound branch heads to **Fort Sherman** (now an international marina) and the ruined Spanish fortress of **San Lorenzo** (see below).

### Fuerte San Lorenzo

*0800-1600, free. The fort is situated about 1 hr from Colón on a winding road. To get there, go to Gatún, cross over the bridge and turn north. There is no public transport to the fort. A taxi from Colón should cost US$40-60 return; bargain hard.*

Perched on a cliff-top promontory overlooking the coast, Fuerte San Lorenzo is one of the oldest and best-preserved Spanish fortifications in the Americas, although it has been destroyed and rebuilt several times since its foundation in 1595. Situated close to the outlet of the Río Chagres, the fort was designed to protect the **Camino Las Cruces** (see the Panama section in Background chapter). In 1596, the Englishman Sir Francis Drake launched a 23-ship attack on San Lorenzo and destroyed it. He proceeded up the Chagres but failed to reach Panama City. In 1671, Henry Morgan fought a bloody 11-day battle to take the fort as a prelude to his decisive swoop on Panamá La Vieja. Today, the site has undergone an extensive UNESCO renovation programme and is well worth a visit. It has moats, cannons, arched rooms, and commanding views of the Chagres and Caribbean Sea. Like Portobelo, most of the fortress is constructed from cut coral.

## Costa Abajo

The rural hamlet of **Achiote** is set in a flower-filled valley, a great place for hiking and birdwatching and hiking. Trips are best organized through **El Tucán Visitor Centre** ⓘ *www.ceaspa.org.pa*, an excellent NGO dedicated to sustainable development and environmental education. Beyond Achiote, the languorous village of **Piña** marks the start of the Costa Abajo, a remote and sparsely populated stretch of Caribbean shoreline with an end-of-the-world ambience and friendly Afro-Antillean inhabitants. The coast road connects a string of palm-fringed fishing villages, including **Nuevo Chagres** and **Palmas Bellas**, before finally petering out around **Miguel de la Borda**. You'll need a sturdy 4WD to continue to the communities beyond. On public transport, you can reach the area with a Costa Abajo bus, which passes through Achiote. If driving (recommended), come prepared with your own supplies of food and water.

## Tourist information

In addition to the 2 offices listed below, any decent hotel will also be able to offer advice and information on visiting the Colón Free Trade Zone.

**ATP office**
*Colón 2000, T475-2300. Open 0800-1600.*

**CEFATI office**
*Paseo Washington, T448-2200.
Open 0800-1600.*

## Where to stay

### Colón

There are lots of dirt-cheap *pensiones* in Colón, but security is an issue and none have been recommended here.

**$$$ Radisson Colón 2000**
*Paseo Gorgas, Calle 13, T446-2000,
www.radisson.com/colonpan.*
A decent hotel, popular with cruise ship passengers and people conducting business in the Free Trade Zone. Amenities include restaurant, bar, pool, sauna and casino. Conveniently located in the Colón 2000 cruise ship terminal with access to shops and restaurants.

**$$$ Sierra Llorana Ecolodge**
*Signposted from the Santa Arriba turn-off, south of Sabanitas, T6574-0083,
www.sierrallorana.com.*
Nestled in the heart of a 400-ha private nature reserve, the Sierra Llorana is ideal for birdwatchers and other wildlife enthusiasts. Accommodation consists of clean, simple, tastefully adorned suites with balcony. They also have 1 slightly cheaper room ($$). Tours to San Lorenzo and birding sites are available. Recommended.

**$$ Andros**
*Av Herrera, between Calle 9a y 10a,
T441-0477, www.hotelandros.com.*

Located in downtown Colón, Hotel Andros has 60 clean, comfortable, modern rooms equipped with TV, a/c, hot water and Wi-Fi. Good service and reasonable value. Recommended.

### Fuerte San Lorenzo

**$$$ Marina Hotel**
*30 Butner St, Fort Sherman, T433-0471,
www.shelterbaymarinahotel.com.*
Affiliated with the modern yachting marina at Fort Sherman, the Marina Hotel is located a short drive from the ruins of San Lorenzo. It has 11 rooms complete with satellite TV, efficient a/c and hot water. A quiet spot in attractive surroundings.

### Achiote

**$ Centro El Tucán**
*Achiote, www.sanlorenzo.org.pa, arrange your visit through CEASPA, T226-4529.*
The Toucan Centre is a community project with 2 dormitories and a total capacity for 20 people. There are toilets, showers, drinking water, an outdoor terrace, dining room and kitchen. The grounds are green and peaceful and filled with coffee and banana plants. Unrivalled access to the Achiote Rd birdwatching trail.

## Restaurants

### Colón

There are plenty of cheap eateries offering locally flavoured *comida criolla*; ask a taxi driver for recommendations. Otherwise head to the Colón 2000 terminal:

**$$ Grand Café**
*Colón 2000, Calle 11 and Av Roosevelt.*
Excellent, authentic Lebanese cuisine including tasty falafels, hummus, Turkish coffee and kofta kebabs. A very safe location with a pleasant outdoor terrace. Highly recommended.

## What to do

### Colón

**Canopy tours**

**Panama Outdoor Adventures**, *Río Piedra, T6605-8171, www.panamaoutdooradventures, look for the turning by the orange bus stop 5 mins past María Chiquita.* One of Panama's best canopy tours. Their circuit features 11 platforms and 9 cables, the longest running 225 m. They also offer a range of outdoor activities, including hiking, horse riding, camping trips and river tubing. Recommended.

## Transport

### Colón

**Bus** Bus station is on Av Bolívar and Calle Terminal on the south side of town; use a taxi to get there. To **Panama City**, every 20 mins, express (recommended) US$3.15, 1½ hrs; to **La Guaira** (including Puerto Lindo), 5 daily, 2 hrs, US$3.20; to **Portobelo**, every 30 mins, US$2.80, 1½ hrs; to the Costa Arriba (including Portobelo and Nombre de Dios, but check final destination with driver), hourly, 1-4 hrs, US$1-5; to the **Costa Abajo** (including Gatún Locks and Achiote), every 1-2 hrs, 1-3 hrs, US$1-3. Note if travelling from Panama City to Portobelo, you can skip Colón entirely by changing buses in Sabanitas.

**Car** If driving from Panama City, the **Corredor Norte** connects with a rapid 4-lane toll highway, Ruta 3.

**Car rental** Europcar, Millennium Plaza, inside Four Points Sheraton, T447-1408, www.europcar.com. **Hertz**, T441-3272, Plaza Colón 2000, www.hertzpanama.com.pa.

**Taxi** Because of safety concerns, a taxi is highly recommended for getting around the city. Tariffs vary; US$1 in Colón, US$1.25 to outskirts, US$10 per hr.

**Train** US$22 one way to **Panama City**, leaves 1715, station on west side of town just south of the centre. See page 882.

---

## Portobelo and the Costa Arriba  *Colour map 5.*
### wrapped in tropical torpor, a poor settlement on the Caribbean coast

Once upon a time, Portobelo was an affluent and important colonial stronghold, the Caribbean coast terminus of Spain's transcontinental trade routes and a bustling imperial port where bars of plundered indigenous gold were piled up like firewood in the Royal Customs House. Today, it has a sleepy atmosphere and just a few thousand inhabitants.

Designated a UNESCO World Heritage Site in 1980, its ruined fortifications were built in the 16th century as a defence against marauding buccaneers, a weathered symbol of colonial authority that has withstood numerous onslaughts by pirates. A fierce guardian of its African-colonial heritage, Portobelo is the region's most important cultural centre too.

The village is very small and easily explored on foot. The ATP, just west of the square behind the Alcaldía, can supply guides, schedules of Congo dances and other performances, as well as comprehensive information about many local points of interest.

Unravelling with a succession of sheltered bays and secluded villages, the entire Costa Arriba is the heartland of Panama's Cimarrón people, who are directly descended from escaped African slaves; their traditional music, dances and stories add spice to a region already packed with swashbuckling intrigue. East of Portobelo, the landscape becomes increasingly remote as it enters the Parque Nacional Portobelo, replete with challenging hiking trails, brilliantly coloured birds, rugged peaks, copious waterfalls and

## BACKGROUND

## Portobelo

Following the destruction of Nombre de Dios, a colonization drive pushed settlers to Puerto Bello, which was officially founded San Felipe de Puertobelo in 1597. Puertobelo – later contracted to Portobelo – was built in a crescent shape around the bay. By the beginning of the 17th century, several fortresses had been constructed from cut coral stone. El Castillo de San Felipe de Todo Fierro – nicknamed 'the iron castle' – was built at the base of a large hill. There were other fortresses and small garrisons controlling the approach to the city.

Assigned the role of Spanish treasure house, Portobelo flourished. Gold, silver and other treasures from the New World piled up in its warehouses. An annual trade fair – for which 300 soldiers were garrisoned – brought crowds of international travellers. Inevitably, its wealth made it a target for pirates. In 1602, William Parker slipped into the bay, torched the district of Triana and marched on the city, looting 10,000 ducats from the royal treasure house. In June 1668, Henry Morgan, the ever-ambitious Welsh privateer, sacked the settlement entirely. In 1739, Admiral Edward Vernon attacked Portobelo with a formidable force of six ships, 370 cannons and 2735 men. He bombarded the forts non-stop until the inhabitants were forced to surrender. The fortifications were rebuilt, but were never again seriously challenged. The re-routing of trade routes around Cape Horn spelled the end of Portobelo's eventful career.

rivers. Offshore, the clear Caribbean waters conceal an intriguing underwater world of old shipwrecks and coral reefs.

### Sights

The ruined forts of Portobelo overlook the bay with crumbling walls and wistful old cannons; with enough imagination, you can make out the treasure ships in the distance.

On the coast road on the western outskirts of town, **Fuerte Santiago** was constructed after Admiral Vernon's devastating attack in 1739. It boasts security-conscious 3-m-thick walls, officers' quarters, a sentry box, barracks, watchtowers and artillery sheds. Nestled on the bay at the centre of town, Portobelo's largest and most impressive fortress is **Fuerte San Jerónimo**. It features an impressive gateway, officers' quarters, barracks and guardroom, as well as 18 cannon embrasures where some cannons have not been moved since the Spanish left in 1821. Across the bay, **Fuerte San Fernando** was built to replace Fuerte San Felipe and San Diego, also destroyed by Vernon. Much of the structure was dismantled to build the breakwater at the northern end of the canal.

Built in 1814, the Iglesia de San Felipe is a historic national landmark and the most important church in Portobelo. It is home to the highly revered Black Christ – also known as **El Nazareno** – a 17th-century cocobolo-wood statue that draws over 50,000 pilgrims each year on 21 October. Behind the church, inside the Iglesia de San Juan de Dios, the **Museo del Cristo Negro** ① *T448-2024, daily 0900-1700, US$1*, is home to a collection of over 60 of the Black Christ's ceremonial robes. Some of them are over a century old and boast lavish materials and ornate needlework.

On the village's main street stands the **Real Aduana de Portobelo (Royal Customs House)** ① *T448-2024, Tue-Sun 0800-1600, US$1*. Built 1630-1634, this handsome colonial structure was painstakingly restored to glory in 1998. It originally served as the king's counting house, where careful inventories for Portobelo fairs were made. Today, it is home to a good local museum with expositions on Portobelo's turbulent past. There is a collection of antique weaponry and, on the second floor, interesting illustrations of the village in its heyday. The bronze cannon at the entrance of the museum was found on a sunken galleon in the bay.

## Around Portobelo

**Playa Blanca** is a great swimming beach. It's located on a peninsula just northeast of Portobelo Bay and the only way to get there is by boat, 20 minutes from Portobelo, around US$5 per person. The beach is surrounded by forests and there are some good coral reefs just offshore. **Playa La Huerta** is a small, sheltered cove flanked by thick vegetation. It's a very calm spot and dive shops sometimes use the area to train students. To get there, hire a boatman from the dock in Portobelo, around US$5 per person. **Puerto Francés** has also been recommended for swimming. In all cases, pay the boatman on return and take adequate supplies of food and water with you.

Beyond Portobelo, the coastal highway strikes inland for several kilometres before branching north into the heart of the Parque Nacional Portobelo. Around 6 km before **La Guaira** – the jumping off point for Isla Grande (see below) – the road forks near **Puerto Lindo**, a tiny fishing village hidden inside a bay. Puerto Lindo is becoming popular as a stopover for vessels travelling to the fabled islands of Guna Yala and beyond, to Colombia.

## Isla Grande

It would be a stretch of imagination to call Isla Grande 'paradise', but it is a popular and agreeable destination with a tropical island ambience. Despite its name, it is not a big place – just 5 km long and 1.5 km wide. Most of the action is concentrated on the south side of the island, where a ramshackle village clings to the shore with a string of hotels, restaurants and holiday homes. If you like to party, head over at the weekend, when the place is thronging with revellers from the capital. If you like it quiet, come in the week, when it's virtually deserted. The best and only really feasible beach is **La Punta**. Head left after landing on the pier and you'll discover it beyond a spit of sand at the island's southwest tip. The beach enjoys the shade of palms, but unfortunately, a large hotel also overlooks it. If you fancy a short stroll, 10-20 minutes, a steep path commences on the northeast side of the island and leads to a mirador and French-built **lighthouse**. Isla Grande lies just a few hundred metres off the mainland, with *lanchas* departing from the tiny village of La Guaira, 10 minutes, US$3. Buses to La Guaira depart five times daily from Colón, US$3.20, passing through Sabanitas and Portobelo. A taxi from Portobelo to La Guaira costs US$10.

## Nombre de Dios and beyond

Nombre de Dios was established in 1509 by the Spanish nobleman Diego de Nicuesa, who found himself lost off the coast of Panama with 520 of his 800-strong crew dead to starvation and disease. Upon arriving in a sheltered harbour, the bedraggled Nicuesa is reported to have cried out, 'Paremos aquí, en el nombre de Dios!' (We stop here, in the name of God!)

The colony soon fell into ruin, however, until 1519, when Diego de Albites revived it. As the northern terminus for the Camino Real, Nombre de Dios grew and prospered, serving as Spain's foremost Caribbean trading hub for over 60 years. But despite its good fortunes, it earned a reputation for thievery and disease, and was dubbed the 'Graveyard of Spaniards'. On 29 July 1572, Sir Francis Drake attacked and captured the settlement, but

Spanish reinforcements forced him into an early and empty-handed retreat. A year later, he attacked again, capturing a mule train and making off with much treasure. In August 1595, he embarked on an ambitious scheme to take Panama City, but found himself ambushed on the Camino Real. He retreated, burning Nombre de Dios to the ground as he fled, and dying of dysentery soon after. The colony itself was abandoned for Portobelo.

There isn't much to see or do in Nombre de Dios itself, today a tiny end-of-the-world village. There's a good beach, **Playa Damas**, around 1.5 km from town, but it's best to take a boat, as the trail demands you cross a deep river. If you can locate a guide, it's also possible to hike in the surrounding hills and forests, where excavations have revealed parts of the **Camino Real**, a broken cannon and other historical objects.

## Beyond Nombre de Dios

The settlements beyond Nombre de Dios become increasingly isolated the further east you travel. The first village you'll pass is **Viento Frío**, a small fishing community with a large beach. Beyond it, **Palenque** is a very remote and unspoilt community with calm waters and mangroves. **Miramar** is the cleanest of the *pueblitos* on this stretch of coastline and the occasional smuggling boat puts in here. At the end of the road lies **Cuango**, a bit run-down and dusty between the rains. If you want to go any further, you will need to hire a boat. For the very determined, it's possible to reach Guna Yala.

## Listings Portobelo and around

### Where to stay

#### Portobelo

Nearly all accommodation is situated west of Portobelo on the highway to Sabanitas.

#### $$ Coco Plum Cabañas
*Buena Ventura, 5 km west of Portobelo, T448-2102, www.cocoplum-panama.com.*
Colourful, nautically themed rooms adorned with fishing nets and shells. There's a small dive shop attached and they offer snorkelling tours and transit to the beaches. A pretty, relaxing spot, but reports on service are mixed.

#### $$ Octopus Garden
*Can Can, 8 km west of Portobelo, T448-2293, www.octopusgardenhotel.panamadivers.com.*
A laid-back and sociable diving resort with a range of simple, comfortable rooms with a/c and hot water. Their restaurant serves ultra-fresh seafood and boasts a deck overlooking the water – the perfect place to knock back a beer and enjoy the sunset.

#### $ Hospedaje Sangui
*T448-2204, on the highway in Portobelo, close to the church.*
Economical and basic quarters with shared bath and cold water.

#### Puerto Lindo

#### $$ Bambu Guest House
*Puerto Lindo, T448-2247, www.panamaguesthouse.com.*
A comfortable guesthouse built on the side of a mountain overlooking the sea. They have a handful of large rooms, all with own bathroom. Can help arrange excursions.

#### $ Hostel Wunderbar
*Puerto Lindo, T448-2433, www.hostelwunderbar.com.*
This laid-back hostel features a traditional Guna-style 'house of congress' made of cane and thatch. Activities include canoes, cycles and horse riding. This is also the place to enquire about sailing trips to the Guna Yala archipelago and Cartagena, Colombia. All accommodation is in simple dorms.

## Isla Grande

During holidays and dry season weekends, make reservations in advance; prices often double during high season. All hotels have bars and simple restaurants.

### $$$ Sister Moon
*5-10 mins east of Super Jackson, T6948-1990 (reservations), www.hotelsistermoon.com.*
Sister Moon occupies a privileged position on a hill overlooking the ocean. It has comfortable, simple cabins with private bath and fan. There's a pool, common rooms, terrace, restaurant and billiards room.

### $$ Cabañas Jackson
*Immediately behind main pier, T441-5656.*
Clean, basic and economical lodgings. Rooms have fan, cold water and spongy beds. Grocery shop attached.

### $$ Villa Ensueño
*East of the main pier, T448-2964, www.hotelvillaensueno.com.*
Big lawns (big enough to play football), colourful cabins and picnic tables overlooking the water. There are also hammocks, table tennis and *artesanía*.

## Restaurants

### Portobelo
A number of small *fondas* serve coconut rice with fresh shrimps, spicy Caribbean food with octopus or fish, or *fufú* (fish soup cooked with coconut milk and vegetables).

### $$ Las Anclas
*Buena Ventura, 5 km west on the road to Colón.*
**Coco Plum**'s restaurant is pleasant, brightly decorated and overlooks the waves. They serve breakfasts, lunches and seafood dinners but aren't always open in low season.

### $$ Los Cañones
*in Buena Ventura, 5 km west on the road to Colón.*
Good food in a lovely setting by the water, but not cheap. Good reports.

### $ La Torre
*T448-2039, in La Escucha, 3 km west on the road to Colón.*
Large wooden structure serving good seafood and burgers. Large portions and highly praised by some.

### Isla Grande
You'll find lots of good fresh fish at a host of places on the waterfront.

### $$ Kiosco Milly Mar
*Just west of landing pier.*
A cute little place serving excellent fish dishes at moderate prices.

### $$-$ Bar-Restaurant Congo
*West of the pier.*
This restaurant juts out over the water on its own small pier. They serve up the usual Caribbean treats, rum, beer and fresh fish.

## Festivals

### Portobelo
**Jan-Apr** Several important fiestas in the first part of the year provide opportunities to experience the unfolding Congo dramas that run from the **Día de los Reyes** (6 Jan) until **Easter**. Unlike the dance of the same name, Congo here refers to the main male participants who are conversant in festival dances, customs and a secret Congo dialect. The various elements of Congo symbolism relate the people's original African religions, their capture into slavery, their conversion to Catholicism and the mockery of the colonial Spaniards, who are often depicted as gruesome devils. Members of the audience are sometimes 'imprisoned' in a makeshift palisade and have to pay a 'ransom' to be freed (some spare change will do!). The major celebrations of Carnaval and the Patron Saint Day (20 Mar) are good times to witness the exuberant Congo festivities, but none are as lively or well attended as the Festival de los Diablos y Congos, celebrated every 2 years 2 weeks after Carnaval.

**21 Oct** The miraculous reputation of the **Black Christ** is celebrated annually when tens of thousands of purple-clad pilgrims arrive from all over the country. Some of them will walk great distances and cover the last stretch on their hands and knees. Mass is celebrated at 1800, but you should be inside the church by 1600 if you want to witness it. From 2000, the statue of El Nazareno is paraded through town on pathways strewn with flowers and flickering candles. The procession is led by 80 men who take 3 steps forward and 2 steps back to musical accompaniment. There's feasting and dancing till dawn.

## What to do

### Portobelo
### Diving
**Panama Divers**, *Can Can, 8 km west of Portobelo, T448-2293, www.panamadivers. com.* Experienced staff and instructors with PADI-certification up to Dive Master. Various speciality dives available, including deep, drift and wreck dives. Snorkel trips available too. Same owners as **Octopus Garden** (see Where to stay, above).
**Scuba Panama**, *Buena Ventura, 5 km west of Portobelo, T261-3841, www.scubapanama. com.* PADI-certification up to Dive Master. Snorkelling, fishing, boat tours and trips to Guna Yala archipelago are also available. Same owners as **Sunset Cabins**.

### Portobelo
**Bus** To **Colón**, hourly, 1½ hrs, US$2.80. If you're coming from Panama City, you can skip Colón altogether by exiting at the town of Sabinatas, 13 km south of Colón on the main highway. Buses to Portobelo pass outside the Rey Supermarket every 30 mins.

To **La Guaira** (including Puerto Lindo), 5 daily, US$1.50, 45 mins (taxi is also a possibility, US$10). To villages further east, take buses marked 'Costa Arriba' from stop at back of square: **Nombre de Dios**, 45 mins, US$1.20; **Palenque**, 70 mins, US$1.75; **Miramar**, 80 mins US$2, **Cuango**, 1½ hrs, US$3.50. The road is paved until just beyond Nombre de Dios.

### Puerto Lindo
**Boat** Puerto Lindo is an increasingly popular departure point for trips to Guna Yala and Colombia. Enquire at hotels or hostels to see if any captains are moored in the vicinity.

### Isla Grande
**Bus** Buses drop you at La Guaira on the mainland from where *lanchas* (motor boats) nip across to the island, US$3. Tell the boatman if you need a particular locale, Bananas Resort, for example. From La Guaira 5 buses per day go to **Colón**, hourly 0530-0830, the last at 1300, US$3.20. There may be later buses on Sun and you should expect crowding at such times. Hitching with weekend Panamanians is also possible, all the way to **Panama City** if you're lucky!

# Eastern
## Panama

The impenetrable rainforests and serene desert isles have long divided Eastern Panama from the world outside. Few destinations are so pristine and isolated but, historically, eastern Panama was the first place on the continent to be colonized by Europeans in the 16th century. At every turn, the incipient empire threatened collapse under tribal skirmishes, feverish epidemics, and the sheer ferocity of tropical nature. The region was ultimately abandoned for a more strategic foothold further west, and the forests were left to bloom unhindered for centuries.

Today, eastern Panama is home to lost-world landscapes filled with giant trees and snaking rivers, mist-swathed mountains and crashing shorelines. It is one of the most biologically diverse places on earth and celebrated as the fabled heartland of the Guna, Emberá and Wounaan people, whose cultures have not been broken by the passage of time. Sadly, modernity has brought new and deadly forces to the region in the form of loggers, ranchers, and colonists. What the conquistadors could never accomplish with greed alone, 21st-century humans are now realizing with bulldozers and chainsaws.

**Best** for
Adventure ▪ Fishing ▪ Isolation ▪ Wildlife

★ The Guna are one of Latin America's strongest and most successful indigenous groups. Their homeland, Guna Yala, is a semi-autonomous *comarca* that encompasses an archipelago (also known as the San Blas islands) and Caribbean shore. Conforming to the easy rhythms of tide and harvest, daily life is refreshingly pure and simple: men cast their fishing lines from dugout canoes, children scale coconut trees, and women chatter outside cane-and-thatch houses whilst sewing brilliantly coloured *molas*. Despite the recent intrusion of a modern cash economy, Guna society continues to be driven by the age-old values of family, community and ancestral tradition.

Administration of the *comarca* and its islands – of which only 40 are permanently inhabited – is strictly controlled. No large-scale developments blight the landscape, neither resorts nor gated communities.

**What to expect**  You will not be free to roam unguided and the number of islands open to foreign visitors is limited. Tax is payable when you land on any island for any length of time, usually US$3-15. Bring your passport for registration with the Sahlia (local chief). Most rates for lodging include meals and one daily excursion. Even the most expensive accommodation is rustic. Electricity may be limited or nonexistent. There are no ATMs in the region so bring all the cash you need, preferably in small notes. Camping is possible but needs to be cleared with the Sahlia. Due to the presence of drug traffickers in the region, camping on uninhabited islands is not recommended. There are payphones in the larger communities.

**Customs and etiquette**  The Guna are very conservative and you will be expected to behave politely. Please dress appropriately when visiting communities and avoid exposing too much flesh, except on the beach. You must ask permission before photographing anyone and will typically be charged US$1 per subject, but US$1 per photo is not uncommon. Fees for using video cameras are quite high, sometimes up to US$50.

### El Porvenir and around

El Porvenir is the western gateway to the archipelago. It has a small landing strip, a simple grocery store, a basic hotel and a tiny beach. The **Museo de la Nación Kuna** ① *open on demand, US$2*, has some intriguing displays on Guna culture, including exhibitions relating to their ceremonial life and some traditional *artesanía*. Apart from that, there's not much to detain you and most travellers head to one of the other nearby islands, including bustling **Isla Wichub-Wala** and **Isla Nalunega** (Red Snapper Island). Both have their own Casa de Congreso, a range of simple accommodation, sparsely stocked general stores and basketball courts.

Between Wichub-Wala and Nalunega lies the artificial island of **Ukuptupu**, formerly a Smithsonian Institute research station and now the site of a popular hotel. It's a great place to watch the comings and goings of yachts, motorboats, and dugout canoes. Around 15 to 30 minutes away lie several small islands, often visited as day excursions. They include **Isla Pelícano**, with its gorgeous beach and colourful coral reef, and **Isla Perros**, with its sunken ship teeming with marine life.

# BACKGROUND
## Guna Yala

The Guna trace their roots to the region of Urabá in Colombia, where they were heavily concentrated at the time of European contact. They are believed to have migrated to the Darién region following inter-tribal wars in the 16th century, and after settling into rainforest communities, established trade relationships with European pirates and adventurers. By the mid-1800s, the Guna began moving offshore to the islands, where they could escape the insect-borne diseases sweeping across the isthmus.

In 1870, Colombia granted the Guna their own semi-autonomous region, including a large swathe of coast from eastern Colón as far the Gulf of Urabá, but in 1903, the nation of Panama was formed and their territorial area was dissolved. The region saw an influx of prospectors, fishermen, fruit companies and US Baptist missionaries, who began intermarrying with the Guna. In the 1920s, the Panamanian government launched a programme of forced assimilation, including the suppression of age-old Guna traditions. On 25 February 1925, two chiefs – Olgintipipilele and Nele Kantule – led a rebellion, killing several Panamanian policemen and ethnically cleansing non-Guna or mixed-blood children. A few days later, the flag of the Independent Republic of Dule was raised, with its orange stripes and black swastika symbolizing the four winds. In 1938, the Kuna District of San Blas was officially recognized as Panama's first self-governing Comarca.

## Los Cayos

Around 7 km east of El Porvenir lie the idyllic islands of the **Cayos Chichime**, also known as Wichudup or Wichitupo. The deep-water channel entering the harbour is only 30 m wide with reefs on both sides, requiring extremely careful navigation. The islands are beautiful and inhabited by only a handful of Guna families. To the northeast lies another long chain of sparsely inhabited islands known as **Cayos Holandeses** or Dutch Keys. Washed by strong Caribbean swells, they are quite far from the mainland and have a remote, rugged feel. They harbour abundant marine life inside a large barrier reef. Towards the eastern side, there is protected anchorage known to yachters as the 'swimming pool'. As with Chichime, caution and good navigational charts are required when entering this area.

## Cartí

The communities of Cartí, south of El Porvenir, consist of several densely inhabited island villages and a mainland settlement with a landing strip and road access to El Llano on the Pacific. **Cartí Suitupo** is the usual port of call, with its interesting folkloric museum and crowds of *mola* vendors. If you're looking for an encounter with traditional Guna culture, this isn't the best place. Many people here have exchanged their traditional clothing for Western-style attire and cruise ships frequently descend on the area, bringing crowds of gawping tourists, which, perversely, is the best time to see the locals dressed like Gunas. If you're looking for a more natural locale, the rather lovely **Isla Aguja** lies nearby, with its beaches, palm trees and handful of inhabitants.

## Río Sidra and around

The island of Río Sidra lies around 16 km east of Cartí and is composed of two densely populated communities: **Marmatupo** and **Urgandí**. The island has some basic amenities, including a telephone and general store, and is mainly used as a departure point for

## ON THE ROAD

## The mola: a synthesis of modernity and tradition

*Molas* are a type of reverse appliqué decorative textile made by Guna women. They are traditionally worn as panels on the front and back of a blouse (the word *mola* actually means 'blouse' in the Dulegaya language), but they also make great wall-hangings and cushion covers. The art of *mola*-making is thought to have begun with the arrival of Christian missionaries. Scandalized by the ancient Guna practice of body painting, the moral-minded preachers persuaded them to cover up their skin and instead switch to the medium of cloth. Early *mola* designs replicated the geometric shapes and abstract patterns of their body art, while later productions incorporated psychedelic birds, animals, fish, spirits and other totemic figures. Some of the most modern *molas* feature aeroplanes, flags, political ideas or scenes, which can be quite intriguing. Another recent development is machine-made *molas* with simplistic motifs and gaudy colours. Usually measuring 40 by 33 cm, *molas* are made out of up to seven (but on average three to four) superimposed, differently coloured cloths. Each layer is cut to make up a design element constituted by the unveiled layer beneath it. The ragged hem is folded over and sewn down with concealed stitching and step-by-step, layer-by-layer, the process slowly reveals the design.

*Molas* are quintessential souvenirs and have the advantage of being light and small, so they don't take up precious luggage space. It's worth seeking out a good quality one, but be aware that the very best *molas* take months of work and may set you back hundreds of dollars. Generally, most people settle for something in the region of US$20-50; anything less and the quality starts to suffer. As a rule, the more layers a *mola* has, the higher its cost. Stitching should be fine, even and hidden, and never substituted with tape. Where there is decorative surface stitching, it shouldn't compete with the more graphic cut-away. Some *molas* have appliqué sewn on, as opposed to cut away, and they can create additional depth and enliven the surface. However, try to avoid those with dots, triangles and small circles roughly applied to fill up space. Don't worry about exact symmetry, but do look for fine and even outlines, the narrower the better. Check the quality of the material in the lower layers and run your hand across the surface of the *mola* to make sure the layers don't scrunch up. Finally, beware *molas* that have been left out in the sun for weeks on end as their colours will be bleached.

A bit of playful barter is appropriate when making multiple purchases, but generally Guna are astute business people and won't budge too much on prices.

some rather splendid and secluded destinations, such as **Isla Kuanidup** which has rustic lodgings, blissful hammocks and beaches. **Isla Nusatupo** is a less visited spot offering access to the **Cayos Los Grullos**, with fine snorkelling around the islands and coral reefs. **Isla Máquina** is a quiet, traditional island that's worth visiting as a day trip, but no tourist facilities exist for longer stays. The **Islas Robinson** are becoming very popular with backpackers, especially **Isla Naranjo Chico**. Jeep transport from the hostels in Panama City usually unloads in Cartí for dispatch directly to the Islas Robinson.

## Corazón de Jesús and around

Around 30 km east of Río Sidra, Corazón de Jesús is the archipelago's main trading centre, home to a large grocery store, airstrip and lots of built-up areas. Connected to Corazón de Jesús by a long footbridge, **Narganá** is the Comarca's administrative centre, with the only courthouse, jail and bank for miles. Both communities are Westernized, with concrete the preferred construction material. Although you won't encounter traditional 'cane-and-thatch' villages here, a visit to these communities is still an intriguing experience.

## Playón Chico and around

Playón Chico lies around 40 km east of Corazón de Jesús. It is a large inhabited island, relatively modern and the jumping-off point for more idyllic destinations, including **Isla Iskardarp**, which is home to the **Sapibenega Kuna Lodge**, regarded as one of the archipelago's premier lodgings. **Isla Yandup**, about five minutes from Playón Chico, is also very comfortable.

## Listings Comarca Guna Yala

### Tourist information

There are no official tourist information offices in Guna Yala, but the **Guna Congreso General** (Calle Crotón, Edif 820-XB, Balboa, Panama City, T314-1293, www.congresogeneralkuna.com), maintains some modest material on their website, www.turismokunayala.com.

### Where to stay

In Guna Yala, you are strongly advised to book ahead, especially during major holidays when most accommodation is likely to be full. Lodgings below are grouped by point of entry, but many require onward transport (assuming you've booked ahead, this should be waiting for you). All rates are per person and all but the very cheapest include meals, transport and excursions.

### El Porvenir and around

**$$$ Cabañas Coco Blanco**
*Isla Ogobsibu, 15 mins from El Porvenir, T275-2853 or T6700-9427, cocoblanco.wordpress.com.*
Secluded private island with a handful of traditional cane-and-thatch *cabañas* right on the beach. Interestingly, they prepare a lot of Italian food.

**$$$ Cabañas Wailidup**
*Isla Wailidup, 25 mins from El Porvenir, T259-9136 (Panama City) or T6709-4484.*
Exclusive *cabañas* on a private island, all powered by solar energy. Guests enjoy their own personal beach, bar-restaurant and pier. Sandflies may be an issue during certain months. The owner, Sr Juan Antonio Martínez, also owns **Kuna Niskua** on Wichub-Wala.

**$$ Cabañas Ukuptupu**
*Isla Ukuptupu, 5 mins from El Porvenir, T6746-5088, www.ukuptupu.com.*
Housed in the former Smithsonian Institute research station, these wooden cabins are built on platforms over the water. Some walkways have hammocks and interesting views of the boats arriving at Wichub-Wala. The owner, Don Juan García, speaks some English and is very hospitable. The bathroom is shared with barrel and bucket showers. Recommended.

**$$ Hotel Corbiski**
*Isla Corbiski, T6708-5254, www.hospedaje corbiskikunayala.blogspot.com.*
Located on a community island near El Porvenir, simple cane-and-thatch cabins with shared bath. English-speaking owner Elias Martínez is a school teacher and very knowledgeable about the community.

## $$ Hotel El Porvenir
*El Porvenir, T221-1397 (Panama City) or T6692-3542, hotelelporvenir@hotmail.com.*
Managed by the friendly Miss Oti. Simple, solid rooms close to the airstrip, with a handy grocery store attached. Rates include 3 meals, but lobster is extra. All rooms have a private bathroom. For large groups, call the Panama City number.

## $$ Hotel San Blas
*Isla Nalunega, 5 mins from El Porvenir, T344-1274 (Panama City) or T6063-6708.*
Located inside a Guna community. The traditional cane-and-thatch *cabañas* here are more interesting than the solid brick wall rooms upstairs, which are simple and smallish. The hotel's guide, Lucino, is very friendly and scouts for guests at El Porvenir airport; he speaks English and French. There's a small beach out front.

## Cartí

## $$ Cartí Homestay
*T6734-3454, www.cartihomestay.info.*
A new, family-run hostel with a laid-back ambience and backpacker clientele. Lodging is rustic and consists of hammocks, bunks and double beds. The owners also offer transportation to Colombia and lodging on other islands.

## Río Sidra and around

## $$$ Cabañas Kuanidup
*Isla Kuanidup, 25 mins from Río Sidra, T6635-6737, www.kuanidup.8k.com.*
An idyllic, isolated spot with rustic *cabañas*, swaying hammocks, lovely coral reef and achingly picturesque white-sand beaches. The perfect castaway desert island.

## $$ Cabañas Narascandub Pipi
*Isla Naranjo Chico, T6501-6033, www.sanblaskunayala.com.*
Rustic cabins and dorm beds by the beach.

## $ Robinson Cabins
*Isla Naranjo Chico, T6721-9885, www.robinsoncabins.blogspot.com.*
A popular backpacker option with lots of chill-out spots. Private cabins and dorms are available.

## Playón Chico and around

## $$$$ Sapibenega Kuna Lodge
*Isla Iskardup, 5 mins from Playón Chico, T215-1406, www.sapibenega.com.*
One of the most expensive and exclusive lodgings in the entire *comarca* with solar-powered cane-and-thatch *cabañas* on stilts, all with private baths, balconies and hammocks.

## $$$ Yandup Lodge
*Isla Yandup, T202-0854, www.yandupisland.com.*
Situated on a private island and one of the best lodgings in Guna Yala. Isla Yandup boasts its own white-sand beach and offshore coral reefs. Cabins are rustic but comfortable and fully kitted with lights, fans and mosquito nets. Recommended.

## Festivals

### Guna Yala
All the following fiestas involve dances, games, meals and speeches, and are traditional. Those on Narganá have a stronger Western element (but also typical dancing and food).
**25 Feb Anniversary of the Dule Revolution**, at Playón Chico, Tupile, Ailigandi and Ustupu.
**19 Mar Fiesta patronal** on Narganá.
**8 Jul Anniversary of Inakiña** on Mulatupo.
**29-31 Jul Fiesta patronal** on Fulipe.
**20 Aug Charles Robinson anniversary** on Narganá.
**3 Sep Anniversary of Nele-Kantule** on Ustupo.
**11 Sep Anniversary of Yabilikiña** on Tuwala.

## Transport

### Guna Yala

**Air** Air Panama, www.airpanama.com, flies from Panama City to **El Porvenir**, **Achutupo**, **Mulatupo**, **Playón Chico**, **Corazón de Jesús**, **Ustupo Ogobsucum** and **Puerto Obaldía**, daily 0600, from US$82 one way including taxes; return flights leave 0600-0700. Costs and schedules subject to change, buy a return or you may get stranded.

**Boat** Long-distance boats to Colombia usually involve a stop in the islands. Unless you have your own yacht, you will be obliged to use local boatmen to get around. Public *lanchas* depart regularly from major settlements, including Cartí, but there's no official schedule. Trips to the backpacker islands around Río Sidra should cost US$20-30 per person one way. If you have a specific journey in mind, discuss your plans with your hotel.

**Car** Overland transport to Cartí is provided by several hostels in Panama City including **Luna's Castle**, www.lunascastlehostel.com, and **Hostel Mamallena**, www.mamallena.com, and by **Robinson Cabins**, www.robinsoncabins.blogspot.com. The 3-hr journey costs US$20-35 one way and you must pass several Guna-controlled tolls, US$2-10 each. After additional taxes and boat charges, a return flight may work out only slightly more expensive. For overland travellers, there is a highway from **El Llano** to **Cartí**; only 4WD vehicles are permitted and there are tolls.

## Isla Achutupo and beyond

*very traditional island with lots of unspoilt culture*

Isla Achutupo, around 30 km east of Playón Chico, has its own airstrip. Nearby, about a minute away, Isla Uaguitupo (Dolphin Island) is home to an upmarket ecolodge. Isla Ustupo, 15 km away, is the largest island in the *comarca* with a population of 5000, lots of social amenities and a grocery store. Isla Ailigandi lies around 35 minutes from Achutupo and has an array of murals and political statues devoted to the Guna nation. Much further east, Mulatupo has its own airstrip but is rarely visited by tourists and is virtually off the radar. Puerto Obaldía, close to the Colombian border, is a very interesting frontier town with lots of sketchy traffic passing through; seek advice before setting out.

## Listings Isla Achutupo and beyond

### Where to stay

**$$$$ Akwadup Lodge**
*Isla Akwadup, T396-4805,*
*www.sanblaslodge.com.*
More private island 'luxury' among the top-end of Guna Yala's accommodation. Lodgings consist of *cabañas* over the water, relatively modern and fully equipped with running water and Wi-Fi. Very comfortable and idyllic, but not cheap.

**$$$ Uaguinega Ecoresort**
*Isla Uaguitupu, T838-9885,*
*www.dolphinlodgesanblas.com.*
Also known as Dolphin Island Lodge. A range of upmarket wooden cabins and cane-and-thatch *cabañas*. Amenities include bar-restaurant, hammocks and volleyball. This is the only hotel in the *comarca* with satellite internet.

**a land of vast rainforests and vibrant cultures**

★ The province of Darién is the place to witness neotropical nature in all its glory and to reflect on humanity's reckless relationship with the environment. Having traversed the entire North American continent from Alaska, the Panamerican Highway promptly ends in Darién. Beyond it, a consuming wilderness sprawls east into Colombia, known notoriously as the Darién Gap, a graveyard of failed explorers, missionaries and colonists. Within its rainforests, nature's unbridled energy manifests in a dazzling profusion of weird flora and fauna. The art and culture of the Emberá and Wounaan are tied to the land in all its diversity too.

But the risks of travelling in the region should not be underestimated and the overland route to Colombia is presently too dangerous to travel. Safely navigating the region independently requires careful planning, plenty of funds and, ideally, a strong constitution and sense of adventure.

## Panama City to Yaviza

The Interamericana highway is paved as far as Yaviza and passes through a string of sleepy communities en route to its conclusion at the edge of the jungle. About 18 km east of Chepo, you'll pass the turning for the 30-km-long El Llano–Cartí highway, which connects with Guna Yala and also offers access to the reputable and luxury **Burbayar Lodge**, see Where to stay, below, where there is world-class birdwatching.

Another 22 km east on the Interamericana lies Lago Bayano, created in 1976 with the damming of the Bayano River. Beyond it, the highway rolls east to the provincial border with Darién, flanked by the folded ridges of the **Serranía de Majé** to the south. The settlement of Ipetí is composed of three ethnically distinct Guna, Emberá and Latino townships and the Emberá contingent have established a good community tourism project, worth a stop if you have time. Continuing east, you'll pass the towns of **Tortí, Cañazas**, and **Agua Fría No 1**. At Santa Fe, **Ecotur Darién** ① *T6736-1607*, has been recommended as a reliable local tour operator; they can help organize lodgings and excursions further afield. About 10 km further east lies **Quebrada Honda**. If you have a 4WD, you can turn south here and head 11 km on a bumpy track to the excellent community tourism project of **Puerto Lara** ① *www.puertolara.com*. This friendly Wounaan village offers a host of fun activities including body painting, traditional dancing, hiking and fishing. Taxi pickup available, book in advance.

It's another 26 km on the Interamericana until you arrive at Metetí, a major town and stopover just 50 km from the end of the highway. It is home to convenience stores, restaurants, hotels and colonists. Many travellers pass through **Metetí** on their way to La Palma, the capital of Darién (see below); public boats depart from **Puerto Quimba**, 20 km away on the Río Iglesias (0730-1830, 30 minutes, US$3). To get to the port, catch a local bus (US$1.50) or a taxi (US$10).

Should you need to stay overnight in Metetí, there are a few cheap, basic hotels and one outstanding option ($$$$), the **Filo de Tallo** ecolodge ① *T314-3013, www.panamaexoticadventures.com*. In nearly every way, Metetí is a preferable place to Yaviza, the rough-and-ready frontier town at the end of the highway. Here, you'll find numerous cheap hotels, stores, restaurants and seedy bars, along with a police station where you must check in upon arrival. If you intend to visit the Parque Nacional Darién, you must also register with **ANAM** and pay park entrance fees. From Yaviza, it's possible to hire a boat to **El Real** (one hour, US$60-80).

## Parque Nacional Darién

*US$5. The park is not always open due to security issues. If you are allowed to proceed, you will require a guide and the official permission of the environment agency. Do not leave Panama City without first consulting ANAM and organizing any necessary paperwork.*

Punctuated by vast lowland rainforests, cloudforests, mountain ranges, rambling coastline, rugged ravines and gorges, the Parque Nacional Darién encompasses 579,000 ha of pristine wilderness along the Panama–Colombia border. It is the largest protected area in Central America and a UNESCO Biosphere Reserve since 1983. Dispersed Guna, Emberá, Wounaan and African-descendent settlements lie within the park, mostly along the banks of river systems such as the Tuira, Balsas, Sambú and Jaqué rivers. Some 450 bird species are known to inhabit the park, including harpy eagles, macaws, parakeets, quetzals and the virtually ubiquitous toucans. Resident mammals include rare jaguars, peccaries, bush dogs, tapirs, capybaras, anteaters, agoutis, coatis, deer and scores of different monkeys. Botanists, too, will find plenty to inspire them in the primeval forests, which are home to towering virgin trees and untold species of orchid.

Inside the park, the Pirre Field Station is managed by **ANAM** ① *T299-6965*, in El Real, and offers rustic accommodation ($), a simple dining area and cooking facilities. Camping and hammocks are an option if you bring your own gear. Note you will not be able to buy food at the station, so bring enough for yourself and your guide, and a bag of good coffee for the guards too. The field station is located at Rancho Frío, 13 km south of the town of **El Real,** a fairly large frontier settlement that's best accessed from Yaviza (see above). El Real is your last

## Essential Darién

### Safety and precautions

Panama's tourism board (ATP) advises against independent travel in the region. If you do decide to go it alone, you will be required to present identification regularly at security checkpoints, and in some cases, an official permit to travel. It is essential to plan ahead and consult ANAM in Panama City for up-to-date information. If you intend to stay the night anywhere, notify the police upon arrival. A guide is obligatory if trekking; find one through the local ANAM office and do not travel with persons you do not know. Due to banditry, never discuss your journey with strangers. Broadly speaking, the forests east of **Yaviza**, with a few exceptions, are considered unsafe for tourists. It has been dangerous to cross the Darién Gap into Colombia for many years and you will risk kidnapping or murder if you try.

Conditions in Darién are challenging. Malaria is endemic, as is rabies, carried by vampire bats. Tap water is not potable, bring purification tablets. Blackouts are common so torches, matches, candles and batteries are essential. There are no banks or ATMs beyond Yaviza and La Palma. Using an established tour operator is the safest and easiest option; **Ancon Expeditions** and **Eco Circuitos** are particularly recommended (see Panama City tour operators, page 879).

Hiking between destinations is very common but subject to important safety concerns described above. Always use a guide and be aware the going is rough and muddy in the wet season.

## BACKGROUND

### Darién

Darién's riverine interior is home to communities of Emberá and Wounaan, who maintain their own self-governing Comarca. It is divided into two districts: Cémaco in the north and Sambú in the south. The two indigenous groups are linguistically distinct but culturally homogenous and are believed to have migrated to Panama from the Amazon rainforest. The Emberá and Wounaan tend to live in small villages of several households clustered on riverbanks. Prior to the 20th century, their society lacked any formal political structure, instead operating on broadly egalitarian lines with shamans and elders maintaining the highest authority. In 1963, an adventurer called Harold Baker Fernández spent a considerable time with the Emberá and informed them that by settling into villages they could petition the government for schools, clinics and other social amenities. They subsequently constructed their political life around the Guna model, which includes a hierarchy of local and regional caciques, as well as communal decision-making through a Casa de Congreso (House of Congress).

The Emberá and Wounaan are not squeamish about nudity – women are usually bare-chested and most children go naked until puberty. Both sexes like to paint themselves with semi-permanent tattoos using juice from inedible jagua fruits. Etched on the skin with a bamboo stick, designs often include intricate geometric lines or dark blocks, bands and zig-zags. Unfortunately, the traditional art of Emberá and Wounaan ceramics has now been lost, but both groups continue to create excellent baskets and carved ornaments from cocobolo wood and tagua nuts. Traditional music includes the use of drums, flutes and conches, frequently accompanied by dances that mimic the movements of wild animals. Traditional religion is broadly animistic and based on a belief in natural spirits.

chance to pick up supplies, including anti-malarial medicine. From there, you need to hire a guide for the two- to three-hour trek to Rancho Frío; ANAM charges US$20-30. In the wet season the trip can take four hours and you will certainly need rubber boots or wellingtons.

### La Palma and around

La Palma, the diminutive capital of Darién, is perched inside the gulf of San Miguel at the place where the first European, Vasco Núñez de Balboa, emerged to 'discover' the Pacific coast of the Americas. It is a hot, grubby, indolent place that's not exactly friendly or inviting, but is interesting nonetheless. It has the best facilities for miles, including a bank, airstrip, simple hotels, bars, eateries and general stores.

South of La Palma, the **Reserva Natural Punta Patiño** encompasses 263 sq km of primary and secondary forests, black-sand beaches and extensive Ramsar-listed wetlands, including red and black mangroves around the mouth of the **Río Mogué**. It is the largest private nature reserve in Panama, managed by ANCON, who also maintain a very pleasant lodge ($$$$) inside the park, **Punta Patiño Lodge** ① *Reserva Natural Punta Patiño, T269-9415 (Panama City booking office), www.anconexpeditions.com.* Perched between jungle and riverbank, the colourful Emberá village of Mogué is a popular excursion for ANCON's guests and other tour groups; traditional dances, crafts and tattoos are among the offerings, along with trips to find harpy eagles. Mogué is about 1½ hours from La Palma, or 30 minutes from Punta Patiño.

A journey up the jungle-shrouded Río Sambú – home to several authentic Emberá and Wounaan communities – is one of the most interesting river journeys in Panama. The largest and most important village in the region, **Sambú**, has an airstrip, medical centre, hotels and payphone. It makes a good base for exploring destinations further upstream, including

**Puerto Indio** and **Pavarandó**. The best place to stay in town is **Sambú Hause** ⓘ *T6687-4177, www.sambuhausedarienpanama.com*, operated by a friendly American expat who knows the best guides and destinations. Sambú can be reached by thrice-weekly *panga* from La Palma (US$20, schedules vary). Expect to pay around US$100 round-trip to travel from Sambú to the furthest communities upstream.

## Bahía Piña

Bahía Piña on the Pacific coast is known for its superb fishing; more **International Game Fish Association** records have broken here than anywhere else in the world. The bay owes its large fish population to the **Zane Grey Reef**: a seamount that gathers plankton and attracts large predators. Flush fishermen like to stay at the world-class **Tropic Star Lodge** ⓘ *T800-682-3424 (US booking), www.tropicstar.com* ($$$$). Around 8 km from the Tropic Star lies the very small community of **Jaqué**, home to indigenous refugees who fled the fighting in Colombia. It's possible to catch a boat from Jaqué to Buenaventura in Colombia, US$100, but it's a rough trip and you may have to wait five days for an available passage. As ever, check on current safety before setting out.

## Listings Eastern Panama

### Where to stay

**Panama City to Yaviza**

**$$$$ Burbayar Lodge**
*Llano Cartí, T236-6061, www.burbayar.com.*
An upmarket but pleasantly rustic ecolodge with good forest trails and some of the world's best birding.

### Transport

**Air** By plane, **Air Panama** flies from Albrook Airport to Garachiné, Jaqué, Bahía Piñas and Sambú (see Panama City transport, page 880).

**Boat** Most river travel is on motorized long-boats called *piraguas*. These can be hired privately for approximately US$80-150 per day, depending on gasoline burned. If travelling long distances, pack a barrel or tank for the return leg.

**Bus** There are several daily buses from Panama City to Yaviza, where the road ends.

# **Central** provinces

Panama's central provinces – Coclé, Herrera, Los Santos and Veraguas – were the first areas of the isthmus to be settled after the foundation of Panama City in the 16th century. Home to ancient colonial churches and lost-in-time villages, they remain a bastion of traditions, folklore, and old-world Spanish charm. This is Panama's bucolic heartland, feisty, gregarious, conservative and proud – the geographic and spiritual centre of the nation.

Around the Interamericana highway, the landscape is punctuated by rolling cattle pastures and sweltering fields of sugar cane, sleepy cowboy towns and bustling farming communities. Climbing towards the lonely peaks of the continental divide, the roads and settlements grow increasingly remote, before finally surrendering to a wilderness of tropical forests.

Panama's central provinces maintain a seamless cultural character grounded in the style and history of the region. Panamanians call it *típico* – a rustic brand of national expression that permeates the *campesino* way of life from lowlands to highlands. The best way to experience it is during a fiesta, when sleepy village plazas spark to life with explosions of music, dance, fireworks and pageantry. Travelling in Panama's hospitable central provinces, one cannot help feeling far removed from the modern world, and at the same time, at the heart and soul of everything.

**Best** for
Birding ▪ Diving ▪ Orchids ▪ Traditional fiestas ▪ Whale watching

The clean, laid-back towns of Coclé province are often a welcome relief after the madness and hustle of the capital, a mere two hours away. Its Pacific coastline, among the most visited in the country, rambles westward from Punta Chame to Farallón with a procession of ocean-front communities and upmarket beach resorts. In the mountains, the flower-festooned spa town of El Valle overlooks a rolling landscape of verdant highland forests and thundering waterfalls.

Further west, the bustling market town of Penonomé is the down-to-earth provincial capital of Coclé. It is the gateway to a host of destinations including magnificent nature reserves, intriguing pre-Columbian ruins, ancient churches and a cigar factory.

## West on the Interamericana: the central Pacific coast

The well-plied Interamericana highway heads west out of Panama City and into the heart of Panama's rural interior. The first place of any size you'll encounter is the virtual suburb of **Arraiján**, closely followed by the bustling and unpretentious township of **La Chorrera**, around 34 km from the capital, before the Interamericana aligns with the Pacific coast and a string of beach communities. The region is a consistent hit with surfers, foreign tourists, Panama City weekenders, Floridian retirees and, unfortunately, large-scale property and resort developers. If you're looking for quick and easy beach time, the salt-and-pepper sands are generally well serviced, but they are not the country's finest.

The narrow windswept peninsula of **Punta Chame** has desolate white-sand beaches and far-off views of Taboga Island. From December to May, it receives consistent 15- to 25-knot winds and is a popular spot with kitesurfers; contact Shokogi ① *T6921-1532, www. shokogi.com*, if you would like to try it yourself. The turn-off to Punta Chame is just before the town **Bejuco** on the Interamericana; buses to the beach run from the junction, hourly, 20 minutes, US$2. (**Note** Punta Chame should not be confused with the settlement of Chame). Several kilometres after Bejuco, **Playa Coronado**, is one of the largest and most developed destinations on the Pacific. High-rise condos, gated communities, a resort, golf course and wealthy vacation villas make it a popular haunt of moneyed Panameños and US retirees. Look out for the mall and shopping complex on the Interamericana. Starting with the village of San Carlos, around 10 km from Coronado, a string of quiet communities front the ocean, but most are slated for big, bold developments. They include **El Palmar** and **Rio Mar**, both recommended for surfing, and **Santa Clara**, a down-to-earth fishing village that is rapidly transforming into a resort town, but is still quiet and empty during the week. The turning for Santa Clara is just 11 km west of the turning for El Valle (see below) from where it is a 2-km walk to the beach; taxi, US$2. Beyond Santa Clara, the tiny hamlet of **Farallón** is home to the famous **Royal Decameron**, a favourite haunt of retired Canadians and package tourists. The nearby powder-white sands of Playa Blanca are marketed at an altogether moneyed clientele.

On the highway, the town of **Río Hato** signifies the gateway to the agricultural heartlands of Coclé province. It has some useful amenities including supermarkets and internet. Several kilometres beyond it, you'll pass the cowboy town of **Antón**, a quiet place of rice fields and cattle ranches.

## El Valle

Surrounded by brooding peaks, rumbling rivers, expansive lookouts, and mysterious stone petroglyphs, El Valle is a refreshing mountain retreat nestled in the crater of an extinct volcano. Hikers, birders, climbers and other outdoor types are well serviced by its network of hiking trails, along with a well-developed tourist infrastructure that offers everything from rappelling to horse riding to zip-lining. The town itself is quiet, slow-paced and great for strolling. For information, there is an ATP kiosk on the main street, which may or may not be open.

On Avenida Central, El Valle's *artesanía* market draws talent from the nation's artisan and indigenous communities, including the Ngäbe, Emberá, Wounaan and Guna. Soapstone animal carvings, ghoulish masks, painted gourds (totumas), carved wooden tableware, pottery, molas, palm baskets, ceramic flowerpots and traditional Panama

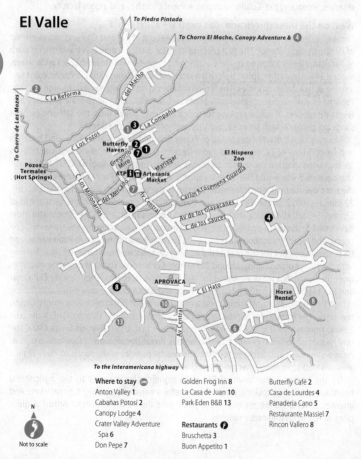

**El Valle**

To Piedra Pintada

To Chorro El Macho, Canopy Adventure & ④

To Chorro de Las Mozas

C La Reforma

C del Macho

C La Compañia

To Chorro de Las Mozas

C Los Pozos

Butterfly Haven ② ①
⑦
Gregorio Miró
ATP ⓘ ⓗ
C Marirgar
Artesanía Market

El Níspero Zoo

Pozos Termales (Hot Springs)

C del Mercado

⑦
Av Central
⑤

Carlos A Rosemena Guardia

Av de los Guayacanes
C de los Sauces

④

C Los Millonario

③ C La Compañia
①

⑧

APROVACA
C El Hato

⑩
⑬

Av Central

⑥

Horse Rental
⑧

To the Interamericana highway

N
Not to scale

**Where to stay** 🛏
Anton Valley **1**
Cabañas Potosí **2**
Canopy Lodge **4**
Crater Valley Adventure Spa **6**
Don Pepe **7**

Golden Frog Inn **8**
La Casa de Juan **10**
Park Eden B&B **13**

**Restaurants** 🍴
Bruschetta **3**
Buon Appetito **1**

Butterfly Café **2**
Casa de Lourdes **4**
Panadería Cano **5**
Restaurante Massiel **7**
Rincon Vallero **8**

## ON THE ROAD

### Know your Panama hat

Favoured by socialites at summer garden parties, Al Capone and English cricket spectators, the cream-coloured Panama hats of public imagination actually hail from Ecuador. Woven from the leaves of the *toquilla* plant, the hats first arrived on the isthmus in the 19th and 20th centuries. They were an instant hit among transient 49ers, who took them home to the US and erroneously called them 'Panamas'. During the construction of the canal, the hats proved an ideal working accessory – lightweight, breathable and perfect for keeping off the sun and rain. In 1906, they became all the rage in Europe and the US when President Roosevelt famously donned one during his historic visit to the canal construction site.

Traditional Panama hats – as worn by the rural populations of Panama's central provinces – are an altogether different garment and commonly known as *sombreros pintados*. Woven from the braided fibres of *junco*, *bellota* and *pita* plants, the hats are a vital element in traditional dress codes and essential for festivals and public gatherings. They are also worn by many on a casual daily basis, as a visit to Panama's interior quickly reveals. Style of *sombrero pintado* varies between villages and artisans, but very simple, coarse versions can be bought for around US$5 and serve as robust working hats; the preferred attire of agricultural labourers. The very best hats require a month or more of careful construction and can fetch several hundred dollars on the local market. If you're interested in acquiring a *sombrero pintado* – fine or coarse – try the stalls on the highway near Penonomé, or travel to a specialized village (for example, La Pintada in Coclé or Ocú in the Azuero Peninsula) to buy directly from an artisan. Prices are based on the number of *vueltas* or lines of braiding along the rim and you should generally look for a fine and even weave.

Wearing your *sombrero pintado* is an art in itself. Perhaps the best way (and the way least likely to cause offence) is with the front and back turned up just so, denoting a successful, happy and handsome wearer. Turning up only the back is said to indicate specialized intellectual knowledge, while turning up just the front is said to be the preferred style of a ladies' man. Turning down the front, meanwhile, can be a sign of mourning or unhappiness. Panama has been staging a festival dedicated to the *sombrero pintado* since 2011. It is a joyous occasion filled with ox-cart processions, traditional dancing, music and, of course, plentiful hats.

---

hats are some of the items on sale. Although open daily, it is most vibrant and well attended on Sunday mornings. Established in 2001, the **Asociación de Productores de Orquídeas El Valle y Cabuya (APROVACA)** ⓘ *signposted off Av Central, next to ANAM, T983-6472, www.aprovaca.webs.com, entrance US$2, students US$1, children US$0.75*, works to protect endangered endemic orchids, which sadly are being threatened by poachers. It manages one of the best nurseries in the country with specimens of some 147 species, including the Holy Ghost orchids (Panama's national flower). El Valle's zoo, **El Níspero** ⓘ *1 km east of Av Central, look for the signs, daily 0700-1700, US$3, children US$2*, is home to some 55 species of captive birds and numerous exotic fauna. Its highlight is the excellent **El Valle Amphibian Conservation Center**, which is working with Houston, San Antonio and San Diego zoos to propagate El Valle's golden frogs, now extinct in the wild. The **Butterfly Haven** ① *turn north at Melo on Av Principal and follow the signs, www. butterflyhavenpanama.com, Wed-Mon 0900-1600, US$5*, is a charming butterfly house that's home to some 350 brightly coloured species.

Located on the northeast side of town, 40 minutes' walk from the centre, **El Chorro Macho** ① *US$3.50*, is a powerful waterfall surrounded by verdant forests and some easy walking trails where you can spot birdlife in the trees. Adventurous types may prefer to experience the falls from a high-speed zipline. Incorporating four elevated platforms and a line that passes directly over the 80-m-high crashing waters, the **Canopy Adventure** ① *T983-6457, www.adventure.panamabirding.com, US$50*, is a popular 1½-hour canopy tour. Nearby on the north side of town is the **Piedra Pintada (painted stone)** ① *US$1.50*, an ancient cliff face etched with obscure lines and interconnected symbols. Their meaning is hotly debated, but most agree that they are likely to be a map of some kind. After you've scrutinized the weird symbols, it's worth continuing on the trail for a while to enjoy a series of lively waterfalls. If all that walking has left you tired, there's no better way to relax than soaking in El Valle's mineral-rich, thermally heated **Pozos de Aguas Termales (hot springs)** ① *daily 0800-1700, US$2, children US$1*. Bring small notes or the exact money. During busy times, bathing sessions may be restricted to 20 minutes. The water at these public baths has been channelled into two large concrete pools surrounded by tropical vegetation. Various types of local mud are freely supplied if you wish to indulge in a face mask. The facilities include a picnic area, cold showers and changing rooms.

## Around El Valle

A variety of trails criss-cross the hills and pastures around El Valle – some, not all, can be accomplished without a guide. A very popular hike leads to the **India Dormida** (Sleeping Indian), a jagged mountain ridge overlooking the town to the north. The ridge derives its name from a local myth of an indigenous girl who fell in love with a Spanish conquistador. When her father refused to let her marry him, she climbed into the hills and committed suicide. As a mark of respect for her eternal love, the gods transformed her body into the eternal form of a mountain. Another popular hike leads to **Cerro Gaital Natural Monument** with its stunning views of the Pacific Ocean. A tough trail leads to the summit from behind **Hotel Campestre**, but you will need climbing experience, equipment and a guide. Numerous other peaks can be scaled including **Cerro Pajita**, **Cerro Guacamayo**, **Cerro Iguana**, **Cerro Tagua** and **Cerro Cara Coral**; seek advice before setting out.

## Penonomé and around

Penonomé is an agricultural trading hub, the conservative capital of Coclé province and an architecturally inconsistent place that blends functional commercial edifices, modern residences and a handful of much older structures dating from the early republic and colonial era. After the sacking of Panama City by Henry Morgan, it became Panama's temporary administrative centre while Nueva Panamá was constructed. It is also the birthplace of the outspoken and ill-fated nationalist Arnulfo Arias, who served as president on three occasions and was deposed each time by a military junta. The surrounding communities are famed for their *sombreros pintados*, or 'painted hats', which are still popular with Coclé's rural population and available for sale on the Interamericana highway (see box, page 915).

Located 1 km out of town, the Balneario Las Mendozas is a recreational complex built on the edge of a lake. The water is deep, good for swimming and very refreshing on a hot day. Nearby, the **Río Zaratí**, also known as the Santa María, is the site of an annual water carnival. Approximately 45 minutes north of Penonomé, the Reserva Natural

Privada Tavida is an enchanting highland nature reserve privately owned and maintained by **Posada Cerro La Vieja** (see Where to stay, below). A variety of hiking trails lead to petroglyphs, the summit of **Cerro La Vieja**, and to **Cascada Tavida**, a refreshing waterfall with some very romantic cabins close by. To get to **Posada Cerro La Vieja**, take one of the old-fashioned *chivas* marked Chiguiri Arriba; they depart roughly every two hours from behind Penonomé market. If you're visiting on a day trip, it's best to book guides at least 24 hours in advance.

Nestled in the foothills 10 km outside of Penonomé, the sleepy village of La Pintada is a good staging post for hiking or horse-riding trips in the countryside. The **Mercado de Artesanías**, next to the football pitch, is a good place to enquire about local guides. Near the southern entrance to town, a signed slip road leads to **Cigars Joyas de Panamá** ⓘ *La Pintada, www.joyasdepanamacigars.com, free tours*. Established in 1982 by Miriam Padilla, who learned her craft from Cuban exiles, Cigars Joyas de Panamá is one of the country's few surviving cigar manufacturers. Even non-smokers may find the factory's rich aroma quite delicious. The plants are cultivated organically in Chiriquí from Cuban seed tobacco, harvested, dried, then rolled at wooden tables. Many are exported to the USA where they can sell for over US$200 a box. Visitors to the factory can purchase them individually or in bulk at excellent prices.

### Parque Nacional Omar Torrijos (El Copé) *Colour map 4, B6.*
*Open 0600-2000, entrance US$5. To get to the park, first take a bus from Penonomé to El Copé, every 30-60 mins, 1 hr, US$2.40. From there, catch a connection to Barrigón, 15 mins, US$0.40, then walk 4 km uphill to the gate. If you wish to stay overnight, there is a rangers' station with four beds and cooking facilities, US$5 per person, bring own food and a warm sleeping bag. Alternatively, basic homestays may be available in Barrigón and La Rica; enquire locally. Three interesting trails snake out from the rangers' station inside the park.*

Named after General Omar Torrijos – who died in a plane crash in the Coclé mountains in 1981 – the Parque Nacional Omar Torrijos (also known as El Copé) encompasses 25,275 ha of challenging highland terrain. It is punctuated by several formidable peaks, including **Cerro Peña Blanca**, the park's highest at 1314 m. The park's many life zones include lower montane and pre-montane rainforests on the Pacific side and tropical wet forests on the Caribbean – delicate orchids, bromeliads and towering ceiba trees abound. Among its numerous rare (but infrequently sighted) animal species are jaguars, pumas, ocelots and tapirs. Birdlife is prolific and comes in its usual multicoloured glory. Due to its remoteness, El Copé is rarely visited. Nonetheless, it has good trails and fantastic potential for hiking, climbing, birding and other outdoor adventures.

### Natá and around *Colour map 4, C6.*
Established on 20 May 1522 by Pedro Arias de Avila, the town of Natá – or Natá de Caballeros – is the oldest surviving colonial settlement in Panama and one of the oldest in all the Americas. Named after a local indigenous chief who once ruled the region, Natá served as a strategic military base for one hundred of Spain's fiercest conquistadors, known as the 'Caballeros' (gentlemen) of the town's namesake. Today, Natá is a quiet place of 6000 inhabitants. It is situated 31 km west of Penonomé on the Interamericana.

Work on the town church, the Iglesia de Natá (properly known as the Iglesia de Santiago Apóstol), began in 1522 using indigenous slaves. It is a very old, mysterious structure imbued with an intriguing mix of Catholic and pre-Columbian motifs. During restoration work in 1995, three human skeletons were uncovered beneath the floor and their identity remains a mystery. For examples of religious syncretism, look for the feathered serpents carved into the altars along with the distressed indigenous Cherubim and Seraphim. If the church is locked, ask for the key from the houses opposite.

Located about 8 km north of Natá is one of Panama's only two pre-Columbian archaeological sites, the **Parque Arqueológico del Caño** ① *Tue-Sat 0900-1600, Sun 0900-1300, US$1*. Although it provides evidence of a well-developed pre-Columbian culture dating to 500 AD, it has suffered from looting and vandalism. The museum has a modest collection of pottery, arrowheads and other local finds. Since 2005, Dr Julia Mayo, a research associate at the Smithsonian Tropical Research Institute, has been uncovering stunning gold jewellery in El Caño's ancient burial pits, most of it dating to around 900 AD. The *National Geographic* featured photographs of her discoveries in its January 2012 edition. There are no buses to the site; a taxi from Natá costs US$7.

## Listings Coclé *map p914*

### Where to stay

**West on the Interamericana: the central Pacific coast**

#### $$$$ Togo B&B
*Calle La Venta, Playa Blanca, T264-7845, www.togopanama.com.*
A very comfortable and stylish boutique B&B with clean, modern, tasteful rooms, all kitted out with contemporary artwork, kitchenette, private balcony and sofa bed. Tranquil and inviting with great hosts and consistently good reports. Recommended.

#### $$$ Cabañas Las Sirenas
*Santa Clara, T993-3235, www.lasirenas.com.*
A range of clean, comfortable, well-kept cottages set high up in breezy leafy grounds or, if you prefer, close to the beach. Each is equipped with kitchen, cable TV, Wi-Fi, porch and hammock. Pleasant, with good reports, but not great value.

#### $$$ El Litoral
*Av Punta Prieta, Playa Coronado, T6658-1143, www.litoralpanama.com.*
A modern and homely B&B with a terrace and small pool, 10 mins from the beach. Rooms are clean, comfortable and agreeably attired. El Litoral offers yoga programmes, massage and very tasty, healthy breakfasts. Great hosts and good reports. Maximum

2 persons per room and a 2-night minimum stay. Recommended.

#### $$$-$$ Río Mar Surf Camp
*Río Mar, T345-4010, www.riomarsurf.com.*
A great beachside location with access to the breaks. Pool and a mini-ramp for skateboarding. They have 8 rooms with cable TV, Wi-Fi and fan (a/c extra). Board rental, tours and surf lessons available. Good café/ restaurant attached.

#### $$ Hostal Casa
*Amarilla, Punta Chame, T6032-7743, www.hostalcasaamarilla.com.*
Located about 300 m from the sea in the main village, this is a comfortable B&B with 2 tastefully decorated rooms in the main house ($$$), 4 rooms in an annexe and 3 rooms in cabins. Amenities include pool, bar and restaurant serving French, Mediterranean and Creole food. Hospitable and attentive. Good reports.

#### $$ Palmar Surf Camp
*Playa El Palmar, T6615-5654, www.palmarsurfcamp.com.*
Comfortable rooms and comfortable ocean-front *cabañas* for 2-4 persons, all equipped with cable TV, DVD, private bath and kitchen. Surf board rental, classes and lots of outdoor activities including kayaking, snorkelling, camping and fishing. Relaxing palapas with hammocks. Recommended.

## El Valle

Accommodation is more expensive and harder to find at weekends; you should definitely book ahead Fri-Sat, especially in high season.

### $$$$ Canopy Lodge
*On the road to Chorro El Macho, T264-5720, www.canopylodge.com.*
Part of the excellent 'Canopy family' and a very popular place with birders, including Sir David Attenborough. Rooms are large, comfortable and well equipped, overlooking beautiful tranquil grounds that are invariably fluttering with dazzling local birdlife. Birdwatching packages are available and reservations required. Great reputation, good guides and highly recommended.

### $$$$ Crater Valley Adventure Spa
*Vía Ranita Dorada, T983-6167, www.crater-valley.com.*
This small but comfortable hotel offers a range of adventure activities including horse riding, trekking, climbing, biking and rappelling. More sedate types might want to take advantage of the spa options, which include skin treatments, salon services, massage and a great outdoor hot tub. Prices rise at the weekends.

### $$$ Anton Valley Hotel
*Av Central, T983-6097, www.antonvalleyhotel.com.*
Comfortable, well-attired lodgings with clean, restful, presentable rooms, all equipped with cable TV, hot water and orthopaedic mattresses. Deluxe rooms and the suite are much more attractive than standards. Good internet rates in low season. Helpful and professional. Recommended.

### $$$ Park Eden B&B
*Calle Espave 7, T983-6167, www.parkeden.com.*
This very romantic country house is set in 1 ha of lush gardens. Look out for lots of colourful birds fluttering around. Hosts Lionel and Monica are very gracious and friendly;

rooms are very clean, comfortable and well equipped. Good reports, recommended.

### $$$-$$ Golden Frog Inn
*Off Calle El Ciclo, T983-6117, www.goldenfroginn.com.*
You'll find tranquil, beautifully landscaped grounds at the Golden Frog Inn. Accommodation includes tasteful Mediterranean-style suites with lush verandas, own kitchens, bedrooms and hammocks. Guestrooms are cheaper ($$), but comfortable, with use of shared kitchen and pool. Great hosts and reports. Recommended, but reserve in advance.

### $$ Cabañas Potosí
*Calle La Reforma, T983-6181, cabanas.potosi@elvalle.com.pa.*
Comfortable, clean, secluded cabins with mini-fridges, porches, hot water and hammocks. Very restful and lots of colourful birds in the well-tended garden. Friendly, helpful hosts Dennis and Mireya can arrange good birdwatching trips or anything else you need. A short way out of town. Lots of good reports. Recommended.

### $$ Hotel Don Pepe
*Av Principal, T983-6425, www.hoteldonpepe.com.*
Owned and operated by the gregarious Don Pepe, who can often be found in the well-stocked *artesanía* store below. Rooms are clean and reasonable with hot water and TV. Additional services include internet, laundry and guide. Friendly.

### $ La Casa de Juan
*Calle Cocorron 4, T6453-9775, www.lacasade juanpanama.blogspot.com. Friendly budget lodgings with very simple rooms, all equipped with own bath and hot water.*
Shared facilities include internet, table tennis, kitchen, treehouse, TV, DVDs and billiards. Ultra-cheap for El Valle and a good choice for backpackers.

## Penonomé

### $$$ Posada Cerro La Vieja
*T6627-4921, www.posadalavieja.com.*
A beautifully secluded ecolodge set in the
rambling grounds of the Reserva Natural
Privada Tavida, with stunning mountain
views and lots of colourful birdlife. Lodgings
consist of comfortable rooms and suites
with a/c, cable TV and hot water. There's also
one superb private cabin overlooking Tavida
waterfall ($$$$). Additional facilities include
a great spa with a hot tub, sauna and steam
room. Very tranquil, recommended, but
book ahead.

### $ Dos Continentes
*Carretera Interamericana, near the entrance
to town, T997-9325.*
Large, comfortable rooms with hot showers,
cable TV and a/c. There's a good little
restaurant downstairs, popular with the
locals at most times. Clean and functional.
Good value, but avoid noisy rooms facing the
main road.

## Restaurants

### El Valle

### $$$ La Casa de Lourdes
*Calle El Ciclo, next to Los Mandarinos,
T983-6450, www.lacasadelourdes.com.*
The finest restaurant in town, very
elegant and romantic. A changing menu
includes delicious offerings like shrimps
in Grand Marnier and plantain croquettes
in goat's cheese sauce. The desserts are
to die for. Reservations are required,
please dress smartly.

### $$ Bruschetta
*Av Central, inside the Antón Valley Hotel,
T983-6097, www.antonvalleyhotel.com.
Open for breakfast, lunch and dinner.*
Very buzzing and busy on Fri and Sat
evenings, when you should book in
advance. They serve an eclectic mix of

Italian and international food, including
good seafood, salads and, if in season,
sublime passion-fruit mousse. Service is
helpful but sometimes overstretched.

### $$ Buon Appetito
*150 m behind Panaderia Cano.*
An authentic Italian restaurant serving
tasty stone-baked pizzas and pastas, great
desserts too, including Tiramisu. A warm
and friendly restaurant with seating indoors
and out. Recommended.

### $$ Rincón Vallero
*Calle Espavé, T983-6175,
www.hotelrinconvallero.com.*
Outdoor dining in a fabulous garden
complete with a well-stocked carp pool,
romantic lighting and singing frogs.
They serve a range of Panamanian and
international fare, including good seafood;
try the *corvina*. A fair wine selection too.

### $ Restaurante Massiel
*Av Central.*
A relaxed and friendly cafeteria serving
reliable set meals and Panamanian staples
like *ropa vieja* and *sancocho*. Wholesome
and economical.

## Cafés and bakeries

### Butterfly Café
*14 Calle La Planta, attached to the
Butterfly Haven. Opens 1000.*
A pleasant little café where you can
enjoy a good cooked breakfast or brunch
overlooking the butterfly garden. Other
offerings include smoothies, fruit and
granola, wraps, sandwiches and various
vegetarian options. Recommended.

### Panaderia Cano
*Av Central.*
Good hot bread, buns, pastries, strudels,
cinnamon bread, and coffee. A cheap
and reliable pit-stop, with an internet
café attached.

## Festivals

### West on the Interamericana: the central Pacific coast

**13-16 Jan** **Patron Saint Feast in Antón** with much traditional dancing and revelry.

**13-15 Oct** **Antón's Toro Guapo** festivities.

### El Valle

**19 Jan** **El Valle's Patron Saint Feast**, dedicated to San José.

**Sep** The **Semana de Campesino** is a very typical fiesta, complete with processions, ox-carts and dances.

### Penonomé

**Feb/Mar** **Carnaval** is big in Penonomé with a flotilla on the Río Zaratí.

**Dec** Penonomé's **Patron Saint Feast** involves a traditional church service, religious procession and street party; dates change, usually 1st or 2nd weekend of Dec.

## What to do

### El Valle
#### Hiking and birding

Plenty of casual hiking and birdwatching can be done in the hills around El Valle, but more ambitious treks may require a guide. The ATP office on Av Central, or your hotel, can usually point you in the right direction. For specialized birding guides, speak to **Ken Allaire**, T6873-1772, **Mario Bernal**, T6693-8213 or **Mario Urriola**, T6569-2676; all speak English and Spanish.

## Transport

### El Valle

**Bicycle** Bikes are a great way to get around town and explore the surrounding countryside. Many hotels rent them out on an hourly/daily basis, try **Don Pepe**, Av Central.

**Bus** Buses to **Panama City** depart every 30-45 mins, 0630-1830, 2½ hrs, US$4.25. For other destinations, take any bus heading to the Interamericana and change at the El Valle turn-off.

**Taxi** Roaming cabs can be found on Av Central, but in the evening it may be best to book in advance. Ask your hotel to make arrangements, or try **Alfredo** T6639-1090 or **Efraín** T6609-0371.

### Penonomé

**Bus** Buses to **Panama City** depart from their own bus shelter on the Interamericana, opposite Hotel Dos Continentes, every 20 mins, 2½ hrs, US$5.25. For the **Azuero Peninsula**, take a passing Santiago bus on the Interamericana highway and change at Divisa. For **David**, catch a passing bus or go to Santiago and change. To **La Pintada**, catch a bus at the turn-off on the southwest corner of the Plaza Central, every 15 mins, 20 mins, US$1.35. For short-haul destinations west of Penonomé – including **Aguadulce**, every 15 mins, 30 mins, US$1.80 and **El Copé** (Parque Nacional Omar Torrijos), every 30-60 mins, 1 hr, US$2.40 – wait on the Interamericana or enquire at the chaotic local bus station, south of the plaza near the market. To **Chiguiri Arriba** (including Churquita Grande/Reserva Tavida), every 1-2 hrs, 1-2 hrs, US$1.65, rough rural buses depart from behind the market.

The twin provinces of Herrera and Los Santos comprise the fabled, folkloric heartland of Panama's Azuero Peninsula. The whole region with its sprawling rural communities is revered for its fine artistic output, with entire families specializing in the production of intricate embroidered dresses, devilish masks, fine pottery or musical instruments.

Equally, Herrera and Los Santos maintain a staunch devotion to traditional modes of worship. Religious feast days draw crowds of pilgrims and miracle-seekers with dazzling public performances that recall the passion of Christ, the conquest of the Americas, or the trials of the human soul and its descent into purgatory. The scenes of ritual Catholic penitence are matched only by scenes of ritual inebriation, including the wildest Carnival celebrations this side of Río.

Thanks to its hazy fruit-filled pastures, the Azuero is often compared to the bucolic backwaters of Italy. Some complain that 500 years of intensive agriculture have left little space for the natural world, but this is not true. The peninsula has long been a refuge for migratory birds and endangered sea turtles, with teeming wetlands, marshes, mudflats, offshore islands and coral reefs among its diverse natural landscapes. Likewise, the Azuero's Pacific shoreline is singularly beautiful and has not gone unrecognized by the international surf crowd.

### Chitré and around

The laid-back city of Chitré is the capital of Herrera province and the largest urban settlement in the Azuero. It has a handsome central plaza with a stately cathedral, an affable population, and a scattering of historic buildings dating from the 19th and early 20th centuries. Day-to-day life proceeds in a rambling, easy-going fashion and although Chitré is not a beautiful city, it is quite likeable and also makes an inexpensive base for exploring the surrounding countryside. For maps and information, there is a **CEFATI office** ⓘ *2 km out of town in La Arena, Vía Circunvalación, T974-4532, www.chitrenet.net/chitre. html, Mon-Fri 0900-1600.*

The spiritual heart of the city is the Parque Unión, beautified with trim green lawns and colourful flowers. On its east side stands the **Catedral de San Juan Bautista**, one of the city's finest historic structures. Inaugurated in 1910, the cathedral was carefully restored to its current condition in the 1980s. Housed in the city's elegant old post office, Chitré's only museum, the **Museo Herrera** ⓘ *Paseo Enrique Geenzier, Mon-Sat 0800-1600, US$1,* is dedicated to local history and anthropology. Exhibits are on the dusty side with signs in Spanish only, but offer a mildly diverting account of the region's development. Artefacts include an enormous thigh bone from a giant prehistoric sloth and pre-Columbian remains from the **Sarigua** and **Monagrillo** cultures. The reproduction gold *huacas* are the most beautiful items on display.

The tiny hamlet of **La Arena**, 2 km west of Chitré, is a renowned pottery centre and a virtual suburb of the city. Rows of workshops flank the Carretera Nacional, where you'll find exuberant displays of local craftwork: giant earthen flowerpots, colourful wind chimes, vases, mushrooms, bells and a menagerie of brilliantly coloured clay geese, macaws, toucans, butterflies and frogs all vie for attention. For ceramic purists, fine monochrome pre-Columbian reproductions are widely available. To get to La Arena, walk along the

Carretera Nacional for 40 minutes; catch a local bus, five minutes, US$0.25; or take a taxi, US$1.50. The vast tidal mudflats of Playa El Aguillito, 7 km from Chitré, are the site of mass bird migrations. Thousands of terns, egrets, sandpipers and other shore birds – most of them from the western USA and Canada – converge on the beach each year to feed on the tiny shrimps exposed by the low tide. You can get to the **Playa Aguillito** by frequent bus, 0600-1800, US$0.50, or taxi, US$3.

Some 10 km out of town, the **Parque Nacional Sarigua** ① *US$5, to get here, take a taxi, US$5-10*, is a man-made wasteland that's optimistically peddled as Panama's only desert. Once upon a time, dense tropical forests consumed the park's 4729-ha area, but decades of intensive farming effectively destroyed it. Today, visitors will encounter desolate landscapes of cracked earth and dune-like formations, as striking as they are eerie. Interestingly, sparse life is now beginning to colonize the park, including several species of cacti and other thorny plants. Its greatest value, however, is as an archaeological site. Fishing and farming settlements thought to be between 5000 and 11,000 years old were recently discovered in Sarigua and ancient arrow heads can sometimes be seen in its exposed subsoil. Ironically, the area's status as a national park prohibits large-scale excavation.

## Parita

The well-preserved colonial village of Parita derives its name from 'Paris', a Spanish nickname for a local indigenous chief properly known as Antataura. The town is home to around 3000 inhabitants and, despite its disarming aesthetic charms, rarely visited by tourists. Semana Santa, Corpus Christi and Carnaval are all attended with great gusto in Parita with activities focused on the expansive main plaza, a traditional gathering place for bullfights, dances and fireworks displays. Parita's patron saint is **Santo Domingo de Guzmán**, honoured each year in an extensive festival, 26 July to 4 August.

Parita is best known for its diminutive Iglesia de Santo Domingo de Guzmán. Built in 1656, it is one of the finest colonial structures on the peninsula and a national landmark. Its interior conceals numerous hand-crafted wooden altars carved in typically exuberant Churrigueresque style, while the south-facing façade features an interesting bell tower laden with mother-of-pearl. Next to the church, the Rodríguez-López workshop specializes in the painstaking restoration of religious art and antiques. There are only a few artisans in Panama with the highly specialized skills for this type of work and ancient altars arrive at the workshop from all kinds of far-flung places. On the Carretera Nacional on the northern edge of town is the home of **Darío López** ① *T974-2933*, the Azuero's chief mask-maker. He has been crafting brilliantly ghoulish *diablico* masks for almost 50 years now, most of them for Herrera's resplendent Corpus Christi festivities. The masks are made from papier mâché overlaid onto a clay mould. Darío ships his creations to the international market and is happy to receive visitors; prices vary from a few dollars for a tiny souvenir up to US$30-50 for a large mask. To find him, look for the house with masks outside.

Around 25 km north of Parita, the 2000-ha **Ciénaga de las Macanas** wildlife reserve is the largest wetland in the Azuero Peninsula. Encompassing the floodplains of the Santa María River, it is an officially designated Important Bird Area. Visitor services include a wood-built observation deck, several hiking trails, and the option of boat tours on the lake, where you might spot green iguanas and boa constrictors on the islands. The small fishing and farming community of El Rincón manages the reserve's visitor centre. To get there, look for the turning 3 km south of Santa Maria on the Divisa–Chitré highway, taxi US$10-20 from Parita.

## Pesé

Steeped in dense sugar cane plantations, the friendly farming town of Pesé is the proud birthplace of Panama's national tipple, Seco Herrerano. Its creation is credited to a Spanish immigrant, Don José Varela Blanco, who founded Panama's first sugar mill in in 1908. Some 28 years later, his three eldest sons encouraged him to distil the sugar-cane juice into a potent liquor, and so began a long and lucrative family business. Devout drinkers can visit the distillery, **Varela Hermanos Seco Factory** ⓘ *T974-9491, www.varelahermanos.com, Jan-Mar Mon-Sat 0900-1700, free*, but contact well in advance. Religious types may find more interest in Pesé's pious enactment of Christ's Passion, performed on the main plaza every Semana Santa. The play spans four days, several stages and involves over 100 members of the community. It concludes with a mock crucifixion and a roaring good fiesta in true Latin spirit.

## Ocú

The town of Ocú, 22 km west of Pesé, is a friendly agricultural community enclosed by hot, sprawling fields of yam, yucca, watermelon and sugar cane. It is chiefly celebrated for its time-honoured customs and cultural life, including its own forms of music, dance, mask-making and, in particular, the manufacture of traditional hats. Although Ocú's fame has recently been eclipsed by its commercial rival Penonomé, many artisans in and around town continue to weave for pleasure and profit. Most trading of Ocú hats – along with distinctive Ocú *polleras* and *montunos* – is done on the **Carretera Interamericana**, reached along the direct northbound road out of town. Alternatively, you are welcome to visit artisans in their workshops. If you're in the region during August, the three-day **Festival de Manito** is a particularly evocative and interesting time (see Festivals, below).

## Villa de Los Santos

The Río Villa, 4 km south of Chitré, forms the official boundary between Herrera and neighbouring Los Santos province. Perched on its southern bank, Villa de Los Santos is an historic Santeño settlement with pastel-shaded colonial architecture and a terminally soporific ambience. Founded on 1 November 1569 by 18 rebellious families who broke away from the royalist stronghold of Natá, Los Santos has always been a bastion of liberalism and non-conformity. True to its anti-royal roots, it was the first town in Panama to issue a call for Independence from Spain. The famous *grito* is said to have originated with a peasant woman, Rufina Alfaro, on 10 November 1821, and the event is commemorated each year with a presidential visit and a civil parade. The town is also famed for its Corpus Christi celebrations, 40 days after Easter, which are some of the most vivid and fascinating in all Latin America.

Panama's Declaration of Independence was signed in a building now housing the **Museo de la Nacionalidad** ⓘ *Calle José Vallarino, Tue-Sat 0930-1630, Sun 0930-1300, US$1*, all signs in Spanish. Formerly occupied by Franciscan monks, prisoners of war and, later, the Vásquez family, it has served as a museum of local history since 1974. Exhibits are sparse and it's not worth making a special trip to see them, but it's worth a browse if you're already in town. Located on the main plaza, the Iglesia San Atanasio is a widely regarded as one of Panama's most beautiful churches. It bears the date 1782, although other records suggest it was founded in 1569. Its interior features a beautiful vaulted ceiling with painted wooden ribs and rows of geometric patterns. The baroque-style altar and attendant images are carved from precious woods and gilt with gold leaf.

## Guararé

Named after an old indigenous chief, Guarari, the quintessential Azuero town of Guararé stages one of the country's finest annual folkloric festivals, the **Feria de la Mejorana**, founded in 1949 by Profesor Manuel F Zárate, who dedicated his life to preserving and revitalising Azuero culutre. The event supplies a wonderfully spirited overview of the region's traditions, with dances, singing, storytelling, plays, beauty contests, bull fighting and ox-cart parades. A good place to learn more is the **Museo Profesor Manuel F Zárate** ① *Calle 21 de Enero, T994-5644, Tue-Sat 0900-1600, US$0.75.* Exhibits include fine examples of traditional *campesino* clothing, intricate and delicate *polleras*, photos of *mejorana* queens, dirty devil masks and traditional musical instruments.

## Las Tablas

Las Tablas, 31 km south of Chitré, is the fabled capital of Los Santos province and the second largest urban settlement on the peninsula. That's not saying much in the Azuero and it actually feels more like a provincial town than a city. Although it has a thriving plaza and a smattering of handsome architecture, there isnLt much to see or do – until festival time that is. Las Tablas has a fearsome reputation for the wildest and most debauched Carnaval party in the country, where thousands of revellers descend for several days of non-stop dancing, parades and intoxicated grandeur. At other times, the city is feted as the home of one of Panama's most important Catholic icons, Santa Librada, who is depicted in crucifixion wearing trademark red and blue robes. For most of the year she is kept inside the baroque Iglesia Santa Librada, which was added to the main plaza in 1789, damaged by a fire in 1958 and subsequently rebuilt. Her spirited official saint's day is 20 July and Las Tablas receives around 25,000 pilgrims for the event. Las Tablas is also famed as the birth place of the liberal president Belisario Porras, who elected to office on no less than three separate occasions. He is remembered chiefly for his bold contribution to the nation's infrastructure, including the national archives, the Chiriquí railway system, and Santo Tomás Hospital in Panama City. The house where he was born has been converted to a museum in his honour, **Museo Belisario Porras** ① *Av Belisario Porras, on the main plaza, T994-6326, Tue-Sat 0900-1700, US$1; Spanish-only,* includes an explanation of all the exhibits.

## Pedasí and around

Pedasí has spent most of its sleepy existence ignored by the outside world, but times are fast changing for this remote agricultural community. Word got out about its pristine beaches and now the property developers have moved in, the gated communities have plotted down, and several Hollywood celebrities have even pitched in and bought up tracts of land. Fortunately, amid the flurry of speculation, Pedasí has managed to retain its small-town friendliness. For now, backpackers can still find cheap accommodation and surfers can still stake claim to miles of deserted coastline.

The town is a very small place and although it is pleasant rambling up and down its soporific streets, the best attractions are a way out. For tourist information, there is a very good **ATP office** ① *just off the main road near the north entrance to town, T995-2339, open 0900-1700.* **Playa Lagarto** (also known as Playa Pedasí) is a popular surf spot with good left and right beach breaks; it is located 10-minute drive from the cente, taxi US$3-5. Also good for surfing, **Playa El Toro** has left and right rock bottom point breaks (snorkelling and swimming are not so good); to get there, take a taxi, five minutes, US$3, or walk 30 minutes east from the plaza. **Playa La Garita**, next to El Toro, has rocks and strong currents, little surf or swimming appeal, but it is pleasantly secluded; to get there, follow the same road towards El Toro, follow the signs and hike the last 100 m through scrub. **Playa El Arenal** (also called El Bajadero) – from where lanchas leave to **Isla Iguana** (see below) – is a vast sweeping beach with gold sand and moderately powerful waves. It's the best beach for swimming and usually quite empty except for a few kitesurfers January to April. You can walk there in 30-40 minutes via the access road near the north entrance to town or take a taxi, US$3-4.

The white-sand beaches of the **Refugio de Vida Silvestre Isla Iguana (Isla Iguana Wildlife reserve)** ⓘ *ANAM entrance fee US$10, boats to the island depart from Playa El Arenal (see above), 30 mins, US$60 return, you have to wade into the water to board, camping is possible, bring own supplies and inform ANAM upon arrival*, are surrounded by clean, clear tropical waters and 16 ha of dazzling multicoloured reefs. Diving or snorkelling offshore is fantastic, thanks partly to the island's location near the edge of a continental shelf. The 55-ha nature reserve is also home to the largest great frigate colony in Panama.

A 10-minute drive from Pedasí, the golden sands of **Playa Los Destiladeros** are backed by low hills and a scattering of high-end hotels and vacation villas. It is a popular surf spot, with a strong left break known as 'The French', but is not so good for swimming. **Playa Venado** is the Azuero Peninsula's premier surf destination, a regular stop on the international tournament circuit and one of the country's finest beaches. Sadly, it has also been sold out to grandiose developers; see it while you can. The beach is 4 km long and set in a perfect horseshoe cove with vast tubes that break left and right with perfect consistency. Around 4 km east of Playa Venado is **Playa Ciruelo**, rarely visited but also recommended for its rock bottom left break. A few kilometres further, **La Playita** has calm waters good for snorkelling or swimming.

The remote and tranquil shores of **Isla Caña** are frequented by five species of endangered marine turtles and the 14-km-long beach sees up to 5000 arrivals of olive ridleys between July and November. Swept with thorny vegetation and tropical savannah, Isla Caña has an area of 832.5 ha. Its 900 inhabitants are closely involved with conservation and maintain a modest tourism programme for those who would like to witness the nocturnal spectacle of turtles arriving to lay their eggs. Contact the ANAM-trained **Grupo de Ecoturismo** ⓘ *T6718-0032*, who offer *cabañas*, homestays and tours. To get to the island from Pedasí, take a bus to Cañas, then to Tonosí, asking to be let out at the turning for Isla Cana. It's an 8-km hike from the bus drop-off, admission US$10.

The tiny and remote cowboy town of **Tonosí**, 48 km west of Pedasí, is a picture of Azuero indolence. There isn't much to do in town itself, but surfers may want to head out to one of the region's fantastic beaches, including **Playa Guánico** and **Playa Cambutal**. From Tonosí, a highway bears north and eventually connects with the village of **Macaracas**, the site of a well-attended folklore festival in January. From there, a web of roads connects with Las Tablas and Chitré.

## Parque Nacional Cerro Hoya

*The road ends at Restigue, a village just south of Arenas, from where you must walk. You will need a 4WD to get there. Alternatively, you can enter the park via the coastal village of Cambutal, boat hire US$70. For a reputable guide, speak to Tanager Tourism (see What to do, below).*

From Santiago, the capital of Veraguas province (see page 933), a highway branches south along peninsula's isolated western coast, buffered by a chain of mountains. Infrequently travelled by outsiders, the road winds through rolling cattle pastures and a string of rural villages, including Malena, home to an excellent ecotourism and turtle conservation project. Nearby, Palmilla plays host to waterfalls and the excellent ecotourism operator **Tanager Tourism** (see What to do, below), who specialize in trips to Parque Nacional Cerro Hoya. A bastion of rugged natural beauty, the park protects 326 sq km of diverse and challenging terrain, including mangrove swamps, coastal cliffs, offshore reefs, islands, uplands, and the highest peak in the Azuero, **Cerro Hoya** (1559 m), which is home to lower montane wet forests, pre-montane forests, and tropical rainforests. Some 30 endemic plant species have been recorded inside the park, along with 95 bird species – ospreys, hawks and scarlet macaws among them. The park is quite remote and there is poor infrastructure in the area. Hiking is tough and a guide is absolutely necessary.

## Listings Herrera and Los Santos: Azuero Peninsula

### Where to stay

#### Chitré
Prices can rise by 50-100% during festivals.

#### $$$ Gran Hotel Azuero
*Paseo Enrique Geenzier, T970-1000,*
*www.hotelazuero.com.*
A large, new hotel on the outskirts of town, with a range of amenities including gym, pool, restaurant and bar. Rooms are modern, immaculately clean and kitted with a/c, cable TV, hot water, phone and safe. Professional service and the best hotel in Chitré. A 5- to 10-min walk from the centre.

#### $$ Hotel Bali Panama
*Av Herrera and Calle Correa, T996-4620,*
*www.hotelbalipanama.com.*
This friendly, helpful hotel has 28 clean, functional, windowless rooms with a/c, cable TV, safe and hot water. There's Wi Fi in the lobby and a restaurant attached. Good coffee and parking available.

#### $$ Versalles
*Paseo Enrique Geensier, near entry to Chitré,*
*T996-4422, www.hotelversalles.com.*
An uninspired modern exterior gives way to a pleasant interior complete with cool, lush gardens and pool. Rooms are bland, but ultimately decent and comfortable. It's a 5- to 10-min walk from the centre.

#### $ Miami Mike's Backpackers' Hostel
*Av Herrera and Calle Manuel Correa,*
*T910-0628, www.miamimikeshostel.com.*
A friendly and laid-back budget hostel with mixed and single-sex dorms, all strikingly adorned with murals of history's greats, Marilyn Monroe, Che Guevara and Bob Marley among them. Fully equipped kitchen, lounge, Wi-Fi and lots of information. Located right on the Carnaval parade route with unsurpassed views from the breezy rooftop bar and terrace. You're welcome to sling a hammock. Highly recommended for budget travellers.

#### Las Tablas

#### $$ Hotel Don Jesús
*Vía al Montero, Entrada Bda La Ermita,*
*T994-5693, www.hoteldonjesus.com.*
A pleasant and well-kept lodging with 21 homely rooms, all equipped with a/c, fan, hot water, cable TV, phone and Wi-Fi. There's also a shared terrace, restaurant, pool and private parking.

#### $$-$ Hotel Piamonte
*Av Belisario Porras, T923-1903,*
*hotelpiamonte@hotmail.com.*
A clean, friendly, helpful hotel with 2 buildings and 34 rooms; those with hot water cost slightly more. Amenities include a/c, cable TV, Wi-Fi, restaurant-bar, parking and safe deposit. They run a wide range of tours, including folkloric, agro-touristic, beach and islands.

## Pedasí

### $$$ Casa de Campo
*Calle Principal, T6780-5280,*
*www.casacampopedasi.com.*
Impeccable interior design with rich wooden finishes, solid furniture, earth tones and hints of colonial Spain. This villa-style boutique hotel features 5 extremely comfortable and well-presented rooms along with an attractive garden, pool, palapa and stylish dining hall.

### $$$ Casita Margarita
*Calle Principal, T995-2898, pedasihotel.com.*
A very handsome boutique hotel in an artfully remodelled colonial building. They have 6 comfortable, well-attired rooms and a host of amenities including Wi-Fi, restaurant and tour. Lots of attention to detail with very tasteful furnishings. Breakfast included. The best in town, recommended.

### $$$ Hostal Lajagua
*Vía El Arenal, after Buzo Azuero scuba centre,*
*T995-2912, www.casalajagua.com.*
A stylish property with long, shady verandas, colonial-style walkways, rustic wooden furniture, a lush green garden and refreshing circular pool. Rooms are simply furnished but large and restful. Lajagua can organize a range of activities from ATV rental to fishing. Great hosts, good reports.

### $$ Dim's Hostel
*Calle Principal, T995-2303.*
A lovely hostel with a peaceful leafy garden, hammocks, restaurant, internet and good clean rooms. Transportation to Playa Venado and Isla Iguana available. Very friendly and hospitable. Highly recommended.

### $$ Hostal Doña María
*Calle Principal, T995-2916,*
*www.hostaldonamaria.com.*
A friendly guesthouse with 6 rooms and lots of lounge space, including a pleasant balcony and tranquil garden with hammocks and barbecue pit. Rooms have TV, internet, fan and hot water. Friendly and hospitable. Good reports.

### $$ La Rosa de los Vientos
*Camino a Playa de Toro, 2 km out of town,*
*T6778-0627, www.bedandbreakfastpedasi.com.*
You'll find tranquil tropical grounds and stunning ocean views at this intimate and well-presented B&B. Rooms are comfortable and tasteful and feature sliding doors with shady verandas. Very romantic and reasonably priced. Recommended.

## Around Pedasí

### $$$$-$$$ Hotel Villa Romana
*Puerto Escondido, T995-2922,*
*www.villapedasi.com.*
A very romantic boutique hotel with rustic Italian architecture and stunning ocean views. They offer a range of very comfortable and well-attired suites, all with therapeutic queen-size beds, a/c, Wi-Fi and minibar. Amenities include pool and restaurant.

### $$$ Hostal Boom Shiva
*Playa Cambutal, no phone,*
*www.boomshivapanama.com.*
An Eastern-flavoured surf lodge with 2-storey wooden bungalows on the beach, an authentic Italian restaurant and a spa offering massage therapy. Contributes to local turtle conservation.

### $$$ Hotel El Sitio
*Playa Venado, T832-1010,*
*www.elsitiohotel.com.*
The 14 modern rooms have solid contemporary furnishings and attractive wooden balconies overlooking the ocean. Activities include yoga, horse riding and fishing. Good restaurant serves dishes such as shrimps in tartar sauce and basil pesto pasta.

### $$$ Hotel Playa Cambutal
*Playa Cambutal, T832-0948,*
*www.hotelplayacambutal.net.*
Clean, modern luxury lodging in the remote environs of Playa Cambutal. Rooms are comfortable and well attired with a/c, hot water and Wi-Fi. Activities include surfing, horse riding and sports fishing.

### $$$ Sereia do Mar
*Playa Ciruelo, sereiadomar.net.*
An attractive fishing and surfing lodge
with 4 comfortable, well-equipped rooms
with orthopaedic mattresses, a/c, TV, DVD
and fridge. Garden hammocks and a fine
veranda with striking ocean views, a great
place to bask in the sunset. Good staff,
friendly and hospitable.

### $$$-$ Hostal Eco Venao
*Playa Venado, T832-0530, www.ecovenao.com.*
Set in 140 ha of lush, reforested grounds,
this self-styled surf lodge caters to a range
of budgets. It features attractive and well-
furnished guesthouses ($$$), romantic
wooden *cabañas* on stilts ($$), a rustic hostel
complete with dorm beds ($) and, for the
truly adventurous, camping ($). Ecologically
minded and recommended.

## Parque Nacional Cerro Hoya

### $$$ Hotel Heliconia B&B
*Palmilla, T6676-0220,*
*www.hotelheliconiapanama.com.*
Offering easy access to stunning attractions
such as the Cerro Hoya National Park, Isla
de Coiba and Isla Cebaco, this excellent
B&B has clean, comfortable guestrooms,
all with hot water and fan, 1 with a/c.
Owned and operated by 2 Dutch biologists,
Kees Groenedijk and Loes Roos, who also
offer a range of nature and community
tours. Beautiful lush grounds filled with
wildlife and great food in the restaurant.
Highly recommended.

## Restaurants

### Chitré

### $$$-$$ Memories
*Paseo Enrique Geenzier, western outskirts
of town.*
American-style sports-themed restaurant-
bar with big-screen TVs and artery-
hardening comfort food, including burgers,
fried chicken, enchiladas and kebabs.

### $$ Ebeneezer
*Julio Botello, near the stadium.*
A friendly and unpretentious family restaurant
serving burgers, pizzas, pasta and other
international fare. Good specials and a small
café-bar for caffeinated drinks on the go.
Some outdoor seating too. Recommended.

### $$ El Anzuelo
*Paseo Enrique Geenzier, western outskirts
of town.*
Rancho-style outdoor restaurant with a
convivial evening atmosphere. They serve
very good fresh seafood and some tasty
burgers. Friendly and popular, but service
may be slow at busy times. Recommended.

### $ El Aire Libre
*On the plaza.*
Popular little locals' place that's always
busy. They serve good cheap breakfasts
and reliable *comida del día* for a few dollars.
Friendly service and consistent quality.
Recommended.

## Bakeries and cafés

### Pan and Cake
*Nueva Provincia.*
Cheap sweet treats and snacks, including
good-value pizzas. The *maracuyá* (passion-
fruit) ice cream is sensational.

## Las Tablas
Dining options aren't extensive. You'll find
cheap and cheerful bakeries scattered
around town, along with some economical
locals' eateries concentrated near the market
on Av Belisario Porras.

### $$-$ El Caserón
*A good clean place, the best in town.*
They serve chicken, meat, pork and seafood,
including lobster. Indoor and outdoor
seating and attentive service.

### $ Los Portales
*Av Belisario Porras.*
A great old colonial building with
indoor and outdoor seating. They serve

economical home-cooked fare and *comida típica*. Rustic ambience.

## Pedasí

### $$ Pasta e Vino
*4 blocks east of the Plaza Central, T6695-2689. Tue-Sun, dinner only.*
Simple, authentic Italian food served in the home of the owners, Danilo and Elena. A changing menu includes a selection of pasta, salads and wines. Good service and desserts. Paella is available, but give advance notice earlier in the day. Only a few tables so make advance reservations. Good reports.

### $$ Restaurante Isla Iguana
*Calle Principal, southern exit of town.*
A large restaurant with some seating outside by the road. They serve good fresh seafood Panamanian-style, including tasty fish fillets.

### $$-$ Smiley's
*Calle Principal, northern entrance to town.*
American comfort food including burgers, chicken wings and fries. A popular expat hang-out and good for a beer with live music and buzzing atmosphere on Tue and Fri. Friendly and hospitable.

### $ Bienvenidush
*Calle Agustín Moscoso.*
A lovely Mediterranean and Milddle Eastern restaurant serving delicious tapas, hummus, falafel, cheese platters and boutique wine. Stylish, bohemian interior, romantic ambience after dark.

### $ Restaurante Ejecutivo
*Plaza Central.*
Extremely unpretentious locals' haunt serving very cheap high-carb buffet food and *comida típica*. A bit charmless, but suitable for thrifty travellers.

## Cafés and bakeries

### The Bakery
*Calle Principal.*
A good stop for fresh baked bread and sweet treats. They also do popular (if pricey) breakfasts and snack food at lunch-time. Some outdoor seating.

### Dulcería Yely
*Calle Ofelia Reluz, just off Calle Principal.*
A Pedasí institution that's been visited by politicians and dignitaries from afar. A good place for sweet cakes and coffee. Breakfast served.

### Maudy's
*Calle Principal.*
A very cute little café with some outdoor seats and a good notice board. They serve the best smoothies on the Azuero. Wi-Fi enabled. Recommended.

## Festivals

### Chitré
**Feb/Mar** Chitré's raucous **carnival** celebrations are second only to Las Tablas. Expect non-stop party action and bring a spare liver.
**24 Jun** Chitré's patron saint is honoured in the **Fiesta de San Juan Bautista**. Also in the preceding week.
**19 Oct** The **foundation of Chitré** (1848) is celebrated with colourful performances and historically themed parades.

### Parita
**3-7 Aug** Parita's patron saint, **Santo Domingo**, has a lengthy and well-attended festival with lots of bullfighting, dancing and merry-making.
**18 Aug** Colourful processions commemorate **Parita's founding** in 1558.

### Pesé
**Mar/Apr** Pesé sees a dramatic re-enactment of Christ's Passion and Crucifixion during annual **Semana Santa** celebrations.

### Ocú
**18-23 Jan** **San Sebastián**, the district's patron saint, is celebrated in Ocú with costumed folklore groups and the ritual burning of his effigy.

**Aug  Festival del Manito** is a 3-day festival straight from medieval Spain and well worth attending. Dramatic performances include the Duelo del Tamarindo and the Penitente de la Otra Vida.

## Villa de los Santos

**End Apr**  The **Feria de Azuero** takes place in its own grounds just outside Villa de los Santos. It is an important and well-attended event that showcases the region's agriculture, culture, crafts and gastronomy.
**May/Jun  Corpus Christi** (40 days after Easter) is a 4-day Catholic feast celebrated with astonishing vigour in Los Santos. Lots of firecrackers, processions, theatrical performances and dance contests, especially from the grotesque *diablos sucios* (dirty devils). Very popular and a glorious distillation of the peninsula's Spanish roots.
**10 Nov**  Hearty celebrations commemorate Los Santos's **Grito de Independencia**.

## Guararé

**23-28 Sep**  The **Feria de la Mejorana** is an important folk music festival that attracts great crowds to Guararé. A *mejorana* is a stringed instrument, much like a guitar.

## Las Tablas

**Feb/Mar**  Commencing the Sat before Ash Wed, **Carnaval** is celebrated all over the Azuero Peninsula with great gusto, but Las Tablas takes the crown. Expect 5 days of spirited celebrations, with lots of dancing, drinking and water fights. Calle Arriba and Calle Abajo famously compete for the best floats and beauty queens.
**19-23 Jul**  The **Fiesta de Santa Librada** is a very important patron saint feast that draws thousands of pilgrims from all over the country. It combines religious services and street parties and is now incorporated into the **Fiesta de la Pollera**, a competitive celebration of Panama's intricately embroidered national dress.

## Pedasí

**29 Jun**  Celebrations with folkloric dancing honour the **patron saint of Pedasí**.
**16 Jul**  Playa El Arenal, near Pedasí, is the site of an annual **fishing tournament**.
**25 Nov**  More music and dancing in honour of the patron saint.

## What to do

### Chitré

**Cubitá Tours**, *PH Cubitá La Plaza, Office 3, Vía Roberto Ramírez de Diego, T910-0188, www.cubitatours.com*. Tour operator specializing in the Azuero Peninsula, offering authentic cultural and historical experiences, adventure and eco tours as well as guided visits to local festivals.

### Pedasí
#### Diving, snorkelling and fishing

**Buzos de Azuero**, *Vía El Arenal, inside Pedasí Sports Club, T995-2894, www.pedasisportsclub. biz*. Dive and snorkel trips to Isla Iguana and Isla Frailes, as well as PADI certification up to Dive Master. They also offer sports fishing, spear-fishing, kayaking, turtle observation and whale watching. Very experienced.

#### Kitesurfing

**Shokogi**, *T6701-5476, www.shokogi.com*. Playa El Arenal is a popular kitesurfing spot Dec-Apr. If you've never tried it before, Shokogi offer a 4-day training course to get you started, including safety and kite control, as well as equipment rental and second-hand sales for experienced kitesurfers. Contact Gigi.

#### Language schools

**Buena Vida**, *T6886-1022, www.pedasispanish school.com*. Individual instruction from US$12-15 per class; or group lessons, US$230 per week. All teachers have university degrees in education.

### Parque Nacional Cerro Hoya

**Tanager Tourism**, *Palmilla, T6676-0220, www.tanagertourism.com*. This socially and environmentally aware ecotourism project is operated by 2 knowledgeable Dutch biologists. They offer a diverse range of interesting tours including snorkelling trips to Isla Cebaco and Isla de Coiba, hiking in Cerro Hoya National Park, turtle watching on the beach, community tourism, birdwatching and swimming in local waterfalls. Very professional and experienced. Highly recommended.

## Transport

### Chitré

**Bus** Chitré is the transport hub of the peninsula. The bus terminal is on Vía Circunvalación on the south side of town; taxi to/from the centre US$2. Most buses run from sunrise to sunset. For **Las Arenas** and **Playa Aguallito**, use city buses.

To **Las Tablas**, every 15 mins, 1 hr, US$1.50; to **Parita**, every 30 mins, 15 mins, US$1; to **Pesé**, every 20 mins, 20 mins, US$1.20; to **Pedasí**, go to Las Tablas and change; to **Ocú**, 0430-1900, every 30 mins, US$3; to **Panama City** (250 km), every 1-2 hrs or when full, 0600-2300, 4 hrs, US$9.05; to **Santiago**, every 30 mins, 1½ hrs, US$3; to **Villa de Los Santos**, every 15 mins, take a Las Tablas bus, 10 mins, US$0.35.

**Car hire** The Azuero is perfect for driving, but you may need a 4WD to reach its most remote stretches. There are few rental agencies in town, try: **Hertz**, T996-2256, www.rentacarpanama.com; **Thrifty Car Rental**, T996-9565, www.thrifty.com.

### Ocú

**Car** Ocú can be reached directly from the Interamericana (19 km) by a paved turn-off south just past the Río Conaca bridge (11 km west of Divisa); colectivos run from here for US$1.20. Alternatively, a mostly gravel road runs west from Parita along the Río Parita valley, giving good views of the fertile landscapes of the northern peninsula.

### Las Tablas

**Bus** Buses to **Panama City** depart from their own bus station on Av 8 de Noviembre and Calle Emilio Castro, hourly, 0600-1630, 5 hrs, US$9.70. To **Chitré** (including **Guararé** and other destinations north on the highway) wait for passing services on Av 8 de Noviembre, 0600-1900, every 10-20 mins, 45 mins, US$1.50. Buses to **Pedasí** depart from the market on Av Belisario Porras, 0600-1900, every 45 mins, 1 hr, US$2.40.

### Pedasí

**Boat** Boats to **Isla Iguana** depart from Playa El Arena, around US$60-70 return; prices negotiable. Always pay upon return.

**Bus** Buses to **Las Tablas** depart from Calle Principal outside The Bakery, 0600-1615, every 45 mins, 1 hr, US$2.40. For **Playa Los Destiladeros**, **Achitones Laboratory** and **Playa Venado** and around, take a bus bound for Las Cañas, 0700, 1200, 1500 (Las Tablas service), 45 mins, US$2.40, and inform the driver of your intended destination. Buses return from **Las Cañas to Pedasí** at 0700 (Las Tablas service), 0900, 1500. If travelling in a group, it may be better to share the cost of a taxi (see below).

For **Reserva de Vida Silvestre Isla Caña** and **Tonosí**, you must take the 0700 bus to Las Cañas and catch a connecting service towards Tonosí, hourly, 1 hr, US$2 – the last one leaves Las Cañas at 1200 (the last returns to Las Cañas at 1400).

**Taxi** Due to irregular bus timetables, taxis are often the easiest way to get to and from the beaches. To **Playa Los Destiladeros**, US$10; to **Playa Venado**, US$20; to **Reserva de Vida Silvestre Isla Caña**, US$30; to **Tonosí/Playa Cambutal**, US$40.

### a staggering and blissfully remote coastline

Veraguas is one of the least populated, least developed and least visited provinces in Panama, and the only one to touch both Caribbean and Pacific shores. It's the preserve of intrepid wave-seekers who congregate at the fabled surf haunt of Santa Catalina. Offshore, adventurous divers head to the pristine waters of Isla de Coiba, where a scintillating underwater world is inhabited by large marine species like hammerhead sharks, sailfish, bottlenose dolphins and humpback whales. Inland, hikers head to the lofty peaks of Santa Fe, rich in cloudforests, colourful birdlife, remote communities and delicate orchids.

## Santiago and around

Santiago, the provincial capital of Veraguas, was founded in 1632 by migrant families from Santa Fe and Montijo. Located halfway between Panama City and David, it is an importanTransport hub and pit-stop for motorists and long-distance buses, which often pause for fuel, food and refreshments on the Interamericana highway. Santiago is home to approximately 75,000 inhabitants and has a thriving economy grounded in agriculture, livestock and banking. Although rapidly modernizing, it is a hot, grubby, terminally humdrum place with little to offer the casual explorer. With time to burn, you could check out the city's baroque-style **Escuela Normal Superior Juan Demóstrenes Arosemena** on Calle 6 and 7. Opened in 1938 as a model education institution and teaching college, it is a national landmark and one of the most aesthetic buildings in all Panama.

Roughly 16 km north of Santiago, the small agricultural community of **San Francisco**, founded in 1621 by Fray Pedro Rodríguez and Valderas of the Santo Domingo order, is well known for its ancient baroque church, the Iglesia San Francisco de Asís de la Montaña, which draws pilgrims from afar. Completed in 1727, it features striking frescoes and several altars blending indigenous and Catholic motifs. To get to San Francisco, take a bus from Santiago's regional bus station, every 15 minutes, 20 minutes, US$0.65. A few kilometres east of Santiago lies the diminutive village of Atalaya, best known for its church of **Jesús Nazareno de la Atalaya**, the focus of fervent and well-attended Lent celebrations.

## Santa Fe and around   Colour map 4, B6/C6.

Nestled in the shadow of the continental divide, the highland town of Santa Fe, 52 km north of Santiago, is steeped in rugged peaks, rolling valleys, pine trees, cloudforests and innumerable waterfalls; superb country for walking and birdwatching. Hard-core adventurers can even attempt to hike over the continental divide to **Calovébora** on the Caribbean coast (guide required). It is possible to drive too, but the road is extremely rough and you will need a 4WD with high clearance and a winch, a spare tyre or two and excellent off-road skills.

Founded by Francisco Vásquez in 1557, Santa Fe first flourished as a gold-mining camp. Today it is better known for agriculture, especially coffee. The processing plant of Café El Tute is managed by the **Co-operativa La Esperanza de los Campesinos**, a famous collective established in 1969 by the good Father Héctor Gallego. Tours of the roasting facilities are in Spanish, just turn up, US$5 per person. If you would like to combine your visit with a tour of a finca, contact the **Fundación Héctor Gallego** ⓘ *near Hostal La Qhia, T954-0737.* Santa Fe is also known for its well-attended annual orchid festival. **Berta de Castrellón** ⓘ *T954-0910,* is Santa Fe's most experienced and creative horticulturalist. She keeps a collection of over 250 orchids in her garden, all quite stunning and unique to the surrounding highlands. October to November are the best months for seeing them in bloom. A few doors down, **Anayansi Vernaza** ① *T6129-2991*, maintains a smaller but equally lively orchid collection.

On a hot day, there's no better way to cool off than visiting the swimming hole of Quebrada Bulavá. If you're feeling lazy, you can hire an inner tube and drift through the creek. A local entrepreneur, **William Abrego**, rents them for US$5 including a life jacket and can arrange a taxi to pick you up downstream. The *quebrada* is located about 20 minutes out of town. To get there, cross over the bridge on the east side of the village, then take the second dirt road on the right.

**El Bermejo** is the highest and most spectacular of the region's many waterfalls. To get there, cross over the Río Bulavá and continue past William's Inner Tubes. When the road divides, turn left and begin climbing uphill, following the signs for 'Cascada de Bermejo'. When you arrive at the trailhead, look out for the yellow arrows and be prepared to cross several streams. Stick to the left whenever the trail divides. Note that accidents have occurred at the falls so it is recommended you visit with at least one other person. Beware slippery rocks and strong currents and seek local advice before setting out in the wet season.

Several kilometres south of Santa Fe, **El Salto** consists of three enchanting side-by-side waterfalls. There are lots of petroglyphs in the area and the local *campesino* community has interesting organic gardens. To get there, take a bus towards Santiago and exit at the bridge over the Río Santa María. Take the road towards El Carmen/El Alto for around 1 km until you see El Salto signed on the right. After another kilometre, the road forks; take the right path. The road will continue climbing for around 5 km and you'll cross several streams. Look out for the waterfalls on your left, or descend to the village, where **Egberto Soto** will be happy to take you on a tour of his community. This hike should not be attempted unguided in the wet season when streams are deeper and more powerful, and prone to flash floods.

There are many other interesting hikes to be had in the region, especially inside the cloudforests of the 72,636 ha **Parque Nacional Santa Fe**, an extensive and somewhat remote protected area adjoining the Parque Nacional Omar Torrijos; consult Hostel Qhia for recommended guides.

## Santa Catalina

It was only a matter of time before word got out: Santa Catalina is epic. 'Discovered' in the 1970s by intrepid vagabond surfers, this obscure fishing village with Hawaiian-style waves was a closely guarded secret for more than three decades. Today, soaring land values, upscale surf lodges, and an established international tournament all point to its growing prestige.

If you are still learning, head to **Playa El Estero** at the end of a dirt road on the edge of town; the waves are easy and break left and right over the sand. Otherwise try the popular **Playa Santa Catalina**, where you'll find strong, consistent left and right hollows breaking over volcanic rocks. If you're prepared to travel, there are plenty of other less crowded and equally awesome local breaks. **Punta Brava**, about half an hour southwest of Santa Catalina, has two left breaks and one right – the main break is a left over a rocky bottom. About 45 minutes northeast, or 10 minutes by boat, **Punta Roca** offers a similar hollow left break over rocks. There are numerous other sites, some of them secret, that local hotels and operators (see Where to stay, below) can guide you to. The waves in Santa Catalina are highest between February and August, when they can reach a staggering 9 m.

★ **Parque Nacional Isla Coiba** *Colour map 4, C5.*

*Isla de Coiba lies 20 km off shore and is most frequently accessed from Santa Catalina with professional tour operators (recommended). You can travel to the island independently, but you must get permission and pay park fees with ANAM in Santiago, T998-4387; they will also be able to advise on lodging and boat captains. Camping is possible with advance permission.*

Isla de Coiba is the largest and most resplendent of Panama's islands, almost entirely covered in virgin rainforests, and so biologically diverse it has been compared to the Galápagos of Ecuador. It shelters dozens of endemic bird species and mammal species, but it is offshore, where warm ocean currents and stunning geological formations converge, that Coiba is so truly extraordinary. Frequenting its waters are 23 species of whale and dolphin, four types of turtle, prolific sharks, untold manta rays, plentiful schools of snapper, jacks and barracuda, and the second largest coral reef in the Eastern Pacific Ocean, **Bahía Damas**, which covers an area of 135 ha off Coiba's eastern shore. Great ocean canyons, which are plied by large sea mammals and pelagic species, lie off the untouched southern coast, where you'll also find fine sandy beaches and giant waves to please any surfer. Sports fishers will not be disappointed by Coiba either: the underwater cliffs of **Hannibal Bank**, which mark the edge between ocean environments, are reportedly home to giant marlin. Don't forget to acquire a catch-and-release permit from ANAM, US$50, valid for one week. The island owes much of its pristine state to its former role as a penal colony, which kept settlers out as much as prisoners in. During the years of Guardia dictatorship, numerous dissidents were interred on Coiba and some of them ended up as shark fodder. The prison closed completely in 2004 and the old cells on the northeast shores are now home to an ANAM station. From here, several hiking trails wind through the forests with opportunities for viewing wildlife, including crested eagles and numerous red macaws. An alternative way to spot wildlife is to kayak among the mangroves and jungle-shrouded rivers, where dazzling poison dart frogs, giant boa constrictors, and crocodiles are reported to lurk.

## Listings Veraguas

### Where to stay

#### Santiago

**$$ Gran David**
*Carretera Interamericana, T998-4510.*
A reliable highway lodging close to the centre of town, but not as economical as it once was. Rooms are clean and comfortable with private bath, a/c and hot water. There's a reasonable restaurant with good set-price lunches. Wi-Fi in some areas. Recommended.

#### Santa Fe

**$$-$ Hostal La Qhía**
*T954-0903, www.panama mountainhouse.com.*
A popular international hostel in the style of a handsome highland lodge. They offer dorms ($) and private rooms ($$) with shared bath, cane walls and little privacy. Rooms with stone walls cost extra and include own bath with attractive tilework. There is a tidy outdoor kitchen with fridge; breakfast available at extra cost. Good local information, book exchange and videos. Green grounds and a great palapa with hammocks, perfect for chilling out.

**$$-$ Hotel Santa Fe**
*500 m south of the entrance to town, T954-0941, www.hotelsantafepanama.com.*
This hospitable motel-style lodging on the outskirts of town boasts superb mountain views and a very good restaurant. Rooms

are clean, comfortable and generally good value; one has a/c and hot water. Friendly and helpful management with lots of excellent local information. Relaxed, professional and recommended.

### $ Tierra Libre
*Behind the Iglesia de Santa Fe, T6911-4848, www.santafepanama.info.*
Friendly, low-key hostel with a clean 6-bed dorm and some very spacious private rooms with own bathroom and hot water. Great food at the restaurant, including breakfast for US$5. Laundry, restaurant, bar and reference books on the region. Clean and quiet.

## Santa Catalina

### $$$ Hotel Santa Catalina
*Road to Playa El Estero, T6781-4847, www.hotelsantacatalinapanama.com.*
A friendly, long-running surf hotel originally established by Kenny Myers, one of Catalina's early pilgrims and a local legend. It boasts a low-impact design and a handful of clean, comfortable rooms, all equipped with hot water, a/c, fan, mini-fridge, terrace and hammock. Good location by the beach. Recommended.

### $$$ Sol y Mar
*Calle Principal, near the entrance to town, T6920-2631, www.solymarpanama.com.*
Perched on a hill with superb sea views, laid-back Sol y Mar has clean, comfortable cabins, all equipped with a/c, satellite TV, hot water and mini-fridge. Facilities include pool, table tennis and a good restaurant serving tasty seafood. The owner, Luis, is very helpful and a great host. Lots of good reports, recommended.

### $$ Hibiscus Garden
*Playa Lagartero, 10 km before Santa Catalina, T6615-6097, www.hibiscusgarden.com.*
Simple, friendly guesthouse with clean, comfortable rooms, all equipped with a/c, fan, private bath, hot water and private terrace. Located out of town close to a

good swimming beach. Tranquil, helpful and very hospitable, good reports.

### $$ Rancho Estero
*Playa Estero, T6415-6595, www.ranchoestero.com.*
Situated on a bluff overlooking the beach, Rancho Estero offers simple cane-and-thatch 'Tiki' cabins. Most facilities are shared, including hot-water showers and sun terrace. Great views, with lots of hammocks and chill-out spaces.

### $$ Santa Catalina Inn
*Centre of town, 5 mins from the beach, T6571-3125, www.santacatalinainn.com.*
A new hotel, home to **Scuba Coiba Dive** shop and the very good **Chili Rojo** restaurant. They offer comfortable, simple, straightforward rooms with good balconies, a/c, fan and hot water. Good central location and friendly owner. Not bad.

## Restaurants

### Santa Fe

### $ El Terminal
*At the bus terminal.*
Simple grub, locals' fare and carb-rich offerings, including ultra-economical breakfasts and lunch, best washed down with a sugary cup of instant coffee.

### $ Hotel Santa Fe
*500 m south of the entrance to town. Open for breakfast, lunch and dinner.*
Tasty and reasonably priced local and international fare made with fresh, locally sourced ingredients. Dishes include chicken, pork, beef and fish specials, and a refreshing wild lemongrass tea. Recommended.

### $ Tierra Libre
*Behind the church. Tue-Sun lunchtime only.*
Really excellent chicken sandwiches, falafels, lunchtime snacks, fresh fruit smoothies and other tasty delights, all prepared with love and highly recommended.

## Santa Catalina

### $$-$ Los Pibes
*Towards Playa Estero, 2nd dirt road on the right.*
Friendly, funky open-air restaurant serving
wholesome Argentine fare including tasty
grilled steaks, burgers and delicious fresh
fish. Recommended.

### $ Donde Viancka's
*On the road to Playa Estero.*
Friendly open-air restaurant serving ultra-
fresh seafood and catch of the day, including
lobster (if in season), shrimps and tasty
corvina. Panamanian and locally flavoured.

### $ Jammin' Pizza
*Towards Playa Estero, 1st dirt road on the right.*
Buzzing little eatery serving tasty
stone-baked pizza and ice cold beer.
Well established and very popular in
the evenings, recommended.

### $ Restaurante Vásquez
*Towards Playa Estero, next to the*
*general store.*
Cheap *comida típica* and other local grub.
Simple, unpretentious and good for a
scrambled egg breakfast in the morning.

## Festivals

### Santiago and around
**Feb** Celebrations dedicated to **Jesus
of Nazareth**, Atalaya. A major religious
festival with around 50,000 pilgrims
arriving in the village.
**25 Jul** Santiago's **patron saint festival**,
including folk parades, dancing and religious
service. Well attended and very festive.
**4 Oct** **Patron saint feast** in the village of
San Francisco.

### Santa Fe
**Aug** Santa Fe's **Feria de Orquídeas** sees
beautiful presentations of highland orchids
and thousands of horticulturists from all the
over country.

## What to do

### Santa Fe
#### Agro-tourism
**Chon and María**, *T6525-4832*. Friendly Chon
and María offer intriguing and personable
tours of their organic gardens and farm.
Most visitors leave with a smile on their face.

#### Hiking and birding
**Aventuras Cesama**, *T6792-0571, www.
aventurascesamo.blogspot.com*. Managed
by experienced guide César Miranda,
who knows the mountains intimately. He
offers a wide range of walking and riding
tours to local waterfalls, forests and rural
communities, including **Alto de Piedra**,
where he maintains a pleasant finca.

### Santa Catalina
#### Diving
A 2-tank dive in Coiba National Park costs
around US$115; 3-tanks US$140. A snorkel
tour costs US$55-65 per person, 4-5 person
minimum. Multi-day trips cost upwards of
US$500; consult individual operators for
schedules. Open-water PADI certification
is comparable to other places in Panama;
around US$325 including all materials. All
prices are exclusive of park entrance fees,
US$20-35 depending on length of visit.
**Coiba Dive Center**, *Calle Principal, T6780-
1141, www.coibadivecenter.com*. Well
established and reputable, **Coiba Dive
Center** offers 2-tank and 3-tank dives, multi-
day expeditions (consult website), snorkelling
and certification up to Dive Master. Owned
by Canadian Glenn Massingham.
**Scuba Coiba**, *Calle Principal, T6980-7122,
www.scubacoiba.com*. Managed by Austrian
Herbie Sunk, Scuba Coiba is Santa Catalina's
1st dive shop. They offer 2-tank dives to
Coiba, snorkelling trips and multi-day
expeditions, including an overnight stay
on the island. Certification is available from
Open Water to Dive Master.

## Sea kayaking

**Fluid Adventures**, *Calle Principal, T6560-6558, www.fluidadventurespanama.com.* Day trips and multi-day trips to Isla de Coiba and beyond. Very well equipped and professional with rental of high-quality single and tandem kayaks and other equipment, including surfboards. Lessons are available.

## Transport

### Santiago

**Bus** Santiago's bus station is located on Calle 10, 15-30 mins walking from the Interamericana; taxi US$1.50. To **Panama City**, www.playamalena.org, 0600-2300, 3½ hrs, US$9.10; for **David**, buses stop outside the **Hotel Piramidal**, hourly, 3½ hrs, US$9; to **Chitré**, every 30 mins, 0600-1700, 1½ hrs, US$3; to **San Francisco**, every 30 mins, 0700-1600, 1 hr, US$0.90; to **Santa Fe**, every hour, 0700-1600, 30 mins, US$2.90; to **Palmilla**, 10 daily, 0600-1730, 2 hrs, US$4.25; for **Santa Catalina** first go to Soná, every 30 mins, 1 hr, US$1.10, then take a connecting bus, 0700, 1200, 1600, 2 hrs, US$4.25.

### Santa Catalina

**Bus** Return service to **Soná** departs at 0700, 0800, 1400, 2 hrs, US$4.25; subject to change, check times locally.

# Chiriquí

Historic dealings with the United Fruit Company, foreign coffee barons, cattle ranchers and the oil industry have all delivered economic stability to the Chiriquí region, which is today rediscovering itself as a world-class tourist destination.

On the Pacific coast, the rambling Gulf of Chiriquí embraces a procession of surf-swept beaches and deserted offshore islets. Rolling inland, the steamy lowlands relent to a rugged canopy of rambling hills, mist-swathed valleys, forests, whitewater rivers and formidable peaks.

But sadly, the region's unique promise is today being overshadowed by aggressive hydroelectric concessions, which threaten to devastate its watershed.

To the east of Chiriquí, encompassing 7000 sq km of remote mountainous terrain, the Comarca Ngäbe-Buglé is the largest indigenous landholding in Panama, home to immense mineral deposits and one of the most solitary places in Central America. Devoid of roads or electricity, its Ngäbe and Buglé inhabitants maintain an intimate relationship with the natural world. Diverse plants are used in their traditional forms of medicine and crafts, while daily survival depends upon cultivation of staples such as yucca. Thus the land symbolizes life itself, and in the spiritually charged Comarca Ngäbe-Buglé, land, people and life are one single indivisible entity.

**Best** for
Coffee tours ■ Flora & fauna ■ Hiking ■ Kayaking

Steamy David is Panama's second city and the capital of Chiriquí province. International trade with Costa Rica, a mere hour away, has long brought a special prosperity to this growing hub of ranching and commerce. Its affluence has only intensified in recent years thanks to international property speculation in the surrounding countryside.

David's journey from cow town to boom town has been remarkable, but at its heart it remains a down-to-earth city with bustling street life and hodgepodge urban planning. Its abundance of banks, shops, hotels, restaurants and other useful amenities – along with its transportation links and a convenient location halfway between Panama City and San José in Costa Rica – make it a practical and comfortable place to pause. More compelling are the languid lowlands east and west of the city, where you'll encounter

# David

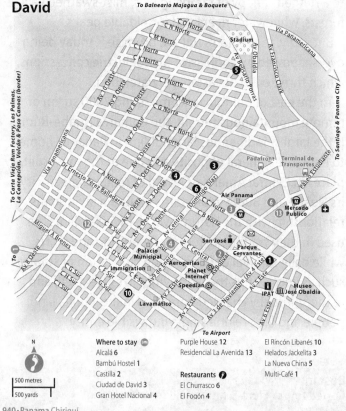

**Where to stay**
Alcalá **6**
Bambú Hostel **1**
Castilla **2**
Ciudad de David **3**
Gran Hotel Nacional **4**
Purple House **12**
Residencial La Avenida **13**

**Restaurants**
El Churrasco **6**
El Fogón **4**

El Rincón Libanés **10**
Helados Jackelita **3**
La Nueva China **5**
Multi-Café **1**

an arresting labyrinth of scattered tiny islands, beaches, tangled mangroves, yawning estuaries, marshlands, rainforests and swamps.

Although David's downtown area is easily explored on foot, it can nonetheless pose navigational challenges. The central plaza is not central, there are few street signs, some streets have two names or no pavements and some locals prefer to use nostalgic points of reference when giving directions (eg two blocks from where the tamarind tree used to be). **Taxis** are useful; most fares rarely exceed US$3.

## Sights

Although geographically off centre, Parque Miguel de Cervantes Saavedra (known simply as El Parque or Parque Cervantes) is the heart of the city, an ideal place to unwind and quietly observe the comings and goings of daily Davidian life. At its heart stands a blue-grey diamond-shaped fountain, designed by Osmeida Ferguson in 2007. A few blocks southeast of the plaza lies the city's tiny historic quarter, Barrio Bolívar, formerly known as Barrio El Peligro. There's not much to see beyond a handful of historic buildings, but strolling around is pleasant and with enough imagination you can get a sense of old David. The barrio's centre is the sedate **Plaza Bolívar**.

---

**Listings** David and the Chiriquí lowlands *map p940*

### Tourist information

#### ATP office
*Calle Central, between Av 5a Este and Av 6a Este, T775-4120, www.visitpanama.com. Mon-Fri 0900-1600.*
Friendly and helpful.

### Where to stay

#### $$$$ Ciudad de David
*Calle D Norte and Av 2a Este, T774-3333, www.hotelciudaddedavid.com.*
This slick new business hotel has 103 impeccably attired rooms, pool, gym, spa, restaurant and business centre. Rack rates are high, but they often offer discounts of nearly 50%. The breakfast buffet, US$10 for non-guests, is worth sampling. The best in town. Recommended.

#### $$$ Gran Hotel Nacional
*Av Central and Calle Central, T775-2221, www.hotelnacionalpanama.com.*
A landmark David hotel. Rooms are comfortable, generic and overpriced. New rooms and poolside rooms cost extra. The facilities are generally excellent, including

garden, pool, casino and 3 restaurants. The lunch buffet is good, US$7.25.

#### $$ Alacalá
*Av 3a Este and Calle D Norte, T774-9018, www.hotelalcalapanama.com.*
Rooms are clean, pleasant and functional, if unexciting. All are equipped with a/c, telephone, Wi-Fi, hot water and cable TV. Restaurant, bar, parking and room service. Discounts available.

#### $$ Castilla
*Calle A Norte, between Av 2a Este and Av 3a Este, T774-5260, www. hotelcastillapanama.com.*
A clean, quiet hotel with an attractive lobby and 68 well-appointed rooms. Services include Wi-Fi, parking, a/c, cable TV and hot water. The restaurant serves Spanish and Panamanian food. Friendly, helpful staff and discounts off-season. Recommended.

#### $$-$ The Purple House
*Calle C Sur and Av 6a Oeste, T774-4059, www.purplehousehostel.com.*
Hostel close to the town centre with private rooms and dorms, all equipped with orthopaedic mattresses. A wealth of

amenities include book exchange, *artesanías*, DVD, kitchen, Wi-Fi and stacks of travel information. Very helpful and attentive. Located away from the centre; take a taxi.

### $ Bambú Hostel
*Calle de la Virgencita, San Mateo Abajo, T730-2961, www.bambuhostel.com.*
A friendly, sociable hostel with a pleasant landscaped garden, pool and 'Mayan-style' rancho bar. Small dorms and a few well-equipped double rooms are available. Lots of amenities, including TV, DVD, Wi-Fi, gym, barbecue, table tennis, lockers and hot shower, to name a few. Located in the suburbs; take a taxi to get there.

### $ Residencial La Avenida
*Av 3a Este and Calle D Norte, T774-0451, residencialavenida@hotmail.com.*
One of David's best budget hotels. It has clean, pleasant rooms with lots of space and natural light. They come equipped with a/c, cable TV, phone and Wi-Fi. Cheaper quarters have fan. Quiet, relaxed and good value.

## Restaurants

### $$ El Churrasco
*Av Central, between Calle C Norte and Calle D Norte.*
This popular restaurant serves a very decent lunch buffet with a broad selection of wholesome, economical Panamanian fare. In the evening there are stone-baked pizzas, as well as the restaurant's namesake, beef *churrasco*. Highly recommended.

### $$ El Fogón
*Calle D Norte and Av 2a Oeste.*
A popular, brightly decorated David institution. They serve Panamanian and international food, such as ceviche, burgers, whole chicken and pasta. The seafood menu is extensive with a range of lobster, prawn, fish fillet and octopus dishes.

### $$ El Rincón Libanés
*Calle F Sur, between Av Central and Av 1a Este.*
Arabic and Lebanese cuisine, including kebabs and other grilled meat, tasty hummus and tzatziki. They have shisha pipes and molasses tobacco, if you fancy an after-dinner smoke. Recommended.

### $$ La Nueva China
*Av Olbadía.*
The best Chinese restaurant in David. Try the *pescado con hojas* (fish in black bean sauce served on a bed of pak choy). The sweet and sour chicken isn't bad either.

### $ Multi-Café
*Plaza Cervantes, Av 4a.*
Economical breakfasts, lunches and dinners served from a buffet. Cheap and filling, but pick something that looks fresh and hot. OK for a quick meal, but nothing special. Popular with locals.

## Cafés, bakeries and juice bars

Helados Jackelita
*Calle E Norte, between Av Central and Av 1a Oeste.*
Very good fresh fruit ice creams and smoothies. Recommended.

## Entertainment

### Cinemas
**Cine Moderno**, *Chiriquí Mall, Vía Interamericana, T774-9895.*
**Multi-Cines Nacional**, *Hotel Gran Nacional, Av Central and Calle Central, T774-7887.*

## Festivals

Mid-Mar   Fería Internacional de David. A major 10-day festival that sees over 300,000 visitors and over 500 exhibitors in the fields of industry, commerce and agriculture. Everything from heavy machinery to *artesanías* to flowers and livestock is sold. The entrance to the festival is marked by a large traditional gate specifically built for the occasion. Dates change each year, but always include the city's patron saint's day on 19 Mar. For more information, see www.feriadedavid.com.

## La Concepción

**Late Jan-early Feb Fiesta de Candelaria.**
A very large and popular 10-day Catholic
Candelmas festival in honour of the city's
Virgen de la Candelaria. Lots of dancing,
drinking, feasting, horse riding, fireworks
and bullfights..

Transport

**Air** Aeropuerto Internacional Enrique
**Malek (DAV)**, Vía Aeropuerto, 5 km from
centre, *T721-1072*, is being expanded and
will soon handle long-haul international
flights. To **Panama City**, Air Panama,
0800, 1400, 1800, from US$140 one-way,
including tax. There are also flights to Costa
Rica. You can acquire tickets at the airport,
or downtown: **Air Panama**, Av 2a Este and
Calle D Norte, T775-0812, www.airpanama.
com. To get to the airport, take a taxi,
US$3-4; or a Pedregal bus from the corner
of Parque Cervantes, US$0.30.

**Bus Long distance** David is framed
by the Interamericana highway, where
international buses bound for Panama City
make a stop. The downtown long-distance
**bus station**, Paseo Estudiante, 1 block
north of Av Obaldía, is a 5-min walk from
Plaza Cervantes; taxi to city centre, US$1.
The **Padafront** terminal is at Av 2a Este and
Av Obaldía. To **Almirante**, every 30 mins,
0300-1900, 4-5 hrs, US$8.45; to **Boquete**,
every 20 mins, 0525-2125, 1 hr, US$1.75;
to **Caldera**, every 1-2 hrs, 0610-1915, 1 hr,
US$2.45; to **Changuinola**, every 30 mins,

0300-1900, 5-6 hrs, US$9.70; to **Cerro Punta**,
every 15 mins, 0445-2030, 2 hrs, US$3.50; to
**Dolega**, every 10 mins, 0520-2330, 30 mins,
US$1.35; to **Panama City**, Terminales
David–Panama, 16 daily, 0300-0000, 7-8 hrs,
US$15.25; Express 2245 and 0000, 5-6 hrs,
US$18.50; Padafront, 5 daily, 0500-2000,
US$15; to **Paso Canoas**, every 15 mins, 0600-
2130, 1 hr, US$2.15; to **Puerto Armuelles**,
every 20 mins, 0600-2130, 1½ hrs, US$3.75;
to **Río Sereno**, every 40 mins, 0430-1800,
2½ hrs, US$5.25; to **San Félix**, hourly,
0700-1820, 1½ hrs, US$2.70; to **Soloy**, hourly,
0800-1200 and 1400-1700, 1½ hrs, US$3;
to **Tolé**, every 40 mins, 0700-1945, 1½ hrs,
US$3.35; to **Volcán**, every 15 mins, 0445-
2030, 1½ hrs, US$3.

**International** Expreso Panama
(formerly Panalines) and **Ticabus** services
travelling from **San José** (Costa Rica) to
**Panama City** drop off passengers on the
Interamericana in David, but there is no way
to board a bus. The quickest and cheapest
way of reaching Costa Rica is to take a
bus to **Paso Canoas**, cross the border on
foot and pick up a bus on the other side
(recommended). If you don't want to change
buses, **Tracopa** offer services David–San
José, 0830, US$14, 8 hrs. **Tracopa** have their
own terminal next to the main bus station.
See also Costa Rica–Panama box in the
Practicalities chapter.

**Car hire** Hertz, Aeropuerto Enrique Malek,
T721-8471, www.rentacarpanama.com.
**Nacional**, Aeropuerto Enrique Malek,
T721-0000, www.nationalpanama.com.

## Chiriquí lowlands *Colour map 4, C5.*

green islets and mangroves, vast sandy beaches and tropical forests

### Playa Barqueta

Playa Barqueta is the closest beach to David, but infrequently visited off-season when
there may not be another soul for miles on its grey-black sands. Backed by a string of
wealthy vacation homes, the beach is baking hot and pounded by strong waves, but
has few public facilities. Around 300 m west of Las Olas resort you'll find a mediocre
beachfront restaurant with showers and toilets, US$0.25. Getting to Playa Barqueta by
public transport is tricky; take a taxi, US$10-15 one way. Part of the beach is protected

as the 5935-ha Refugio de Vida Silvestre Playa de la Barqueta Agrícola, home to nesting sea turtles and aquatic birds like the black-bellied whistling duck. Access to the reserve is officially via a long dirt road that follows the coast until it ends close to an ANAM ranger station; you will need a sturdy 4WD to traverse it. Alternatively, you can just keep walking east on the beach, but pack food and water, start early, and dress for the heat.

## Pedregal

The diminutive port of Pedregal, 8 km south of David's city centre, is perched on the serpentine **Río Platanal**, close to the estuary of the mighty Río Chiriquí. The port acquired brief commercial importance after the construction of the Chiriquí railway in 1916. Today, it hosts a modest marina with mooring and basic facilities, and a scattering of restaurants. To get there, take a bus from the corner of Parque Cervantes, US$0.50, 20 minutes; or a taxi, US$4-5. The small town of Dolega, whose name means 'place of winter', lies 13 km north of David on the highway to Boquete. The town is known principally for its hydroelectric plant, church, orchids and the **Bookmark Secondhand Bookshop** ⓘ *David–Boquete highway, T776-1688, Tue-Sun 0900-1700*, which contains the country's best collection of second-hand English-language books. Roughly 4 km south of town on the highway you'll find the entrance to the refreshing **El Majagua** waterfall, part of a popular resort complex that opens only during high season (off season it's best avoided).

## David to Costa Rica

La Concepción lies 25 km west of David on the Interamericana highway, roughly halfway to the Costa Rican border. Sometimes referred to as **Bugaba**, after the surrounding district, it is an important agricultural shipping point and the gateway to the western Chiriquí highlands. The frontier itself, 52 km from David, is marked by the frenetic and insalubrious border town of Paso Canoas, where travellers must submit to formalities before proceeding. International buses take two or three hours to process and immigration officials on the Panamanian side are now quite overzealous (see Costa Rica– Panama box in the Practicalities chapter). At **Gariche**, a few kilometres east of Paso Canoas, there is a checkpoint where cars and buses are inspected. Have passport, vehicle permit and driver's licence handy in case they are asked for (usually hassle-free).

## Boca Chica and around

*To get to Boca Chica from David, take a bus 39 km east to Horconcitos; if there are no direct buses, you can catch any eastbound service and ask to be let out at the Horconcitos turning on the Interamericana, where you can take a taxi to the village, US$3. Infrequent buses travel the extra 13 km from Horconcitos to Boca Chica, US$3. If there's no bus, the restaurant opposite the Boca Chica turning can call you a taxi, US$8. You can also take a boat to Boca Chica from Pedregal, 30-60 mins.*

The obscure fishing village of Boca Chica lies on the Bahía de Muertos, just east of the Río Chiriquí's yawning estuarine outlet, a gateway to the soporific Isla Boca Brava and the pristine **Parque Nacional Marino Gulfo de Chiriquí**, whose waters are home to diverse marine species including white-tipped sharks, angel kingfish, leatherback and hawksbill turtles, moray eels, lobsters, dolphins, prized game like marlin, sailfish and dorado and, between September and November, migrating humpback whales.

Just across the water from Boca Chica, **Isla Boca Brava** is a tranquil offshore retreat cloaked in tropical foliage. There are dirt roads, good for hiking, and several kilometres of walking trails, some of which are overgrown and hard to follow. Two decent crescent-shaped beaches can be found on the southern side of the island; those on the northern side are rocky and less pleasant. Around 280 bird species make their home on Isla Boca Brava, including the lance-tailed manakin, renowned for its courtship dances that are uniquely performed by pairs of cooperative males. To get to Isla Boca Brava, water taxis cross the narrow channel from Boca Chica, five to 10 minutes, US$2-3.

Your hotel should be able to help organize fishing, surfing, snorkeling, or whale-watching trips further afield in the Parque Nacional Marino Golfo de Chiriquí (see What to do, below). Created in 1994, this ladle-shaped protected area encompasses 14,740 ha of ocean space, including a dozen coral reefs and the 22 densely vegetated islands of the Parida archipelago. The largest, **Isla Parida**, has a source of fresh water and some lodgings. Most of the others are uninhabited, but easily visited. Several of them, such as **Isla Bolaños**, boast scintillating white-sand beaches and verdant forests replete with oak, cedar, wild cashew and guanacaste trees. On the larger islands you might spot howler monkeys, agoutis, green and black frogs and iguanas. For more on activities in the area, see What to do, below.

## Playa Las Lajas
*To get there from David, catch a Las Lajas bus, or any eastbound service that passes Las Lajas. Exit at the beach turn-off and take a taxi south, US$6.*

Located 62 km east of David and 13 km south of the Interamericana highway, the broad expanse of Playa Las Lajas stretches for 14 km with grey sands, palm trees and burgeoning beachfront developments. It has large waves which might suit beginner body-boarders, but little for the surfing pro. During high season, especially on Sundays, Panamanian day-trippers descend on the area to eat, drink and make merry. During low season, particularly on weekdays, it's blissfully deserted. Be warned, high tide consumes most of the sand.

## Listings Chiriquí lowlands

### Where to stay

**$$$$ Boutique Hotel Cala Mia**
*Isla Boca Brava, T851-0059,*
*www.boutiquehotelcalamia.com.*
A beautifully presented and exclusive boutique lodging with 11 elegant bungalows with handmade furniture, ocean views and outdoor rancho terraces. Some have direct access to the beach. Spa treatments, infinity pool and a fine restaurant serving organic food sourced from their own farm. Completely powered by solar. Good reports.

**$$$ Gone Fishing**
*Boca Chica, T851-0104,*
*www.gonefishingpanama.com.*
This comfortable and relaxing lodging on a cliff top boasts awesome views of the ocean. They can organize a range of outdoor activities, including fishing (as the name

suggests). There's an infinity pool, garden and a restaurant serving the catch of the day.

**$$ Hotel Boca Brava**
*Isla Boca Brava, T851-0017,*
*www.hotelbocabrava.com.*
The hotel boasts a range of quirky rooms and bungalows, some much better than others. The grounds are rambling and leafy and offer access to the island's main trails. The restaurant has superb views and breezes. Various tours available, including surfing, whale watching and fishing. Hospitable and helpful owners. Recommended.

### What to do

#### Diving
**Boca Brava Divers**, *T775-3185*. Managed by reputable dive expert Carlos Spragge, who has many years of experience in the waters of Chiriquí. His dive packages start at US$150

per day, 4-person minimum, including boat, tanks, weight and lunch. Tours to Isla de Coiba are also available.

### Fishing

Casual fishing is as easy as finding a boatman to take you out for the day. Prices vary with the amount of fuel used, but you should expect to pay around US$100-150 for around 6 hrs. If you don't have your own equipment, or if you want to conduct a serious deep-sea expedition, contact one of the fishing lodges mentioned in Where to stay, above.

### Whale watching

Whale watching is possible Sep-Nov. Any hotel should be able to hook you up with a boatman; most charge around US$50-60 per person, 4-person minimum. Trips include a 1- to 2-hr stopover on a secluded beach and can usually be combined with snorkelling/fishing.

### Transport

**Boat** Private water taxis run to **Isla Boca Brava** for around US$5 one way. If no one is waiting at the main pier, enquire at a local bar or store and they should call in a boatman.

**Bus** Buses run infrequently to **Horconcitos**, US$3. Alternatively, take a taxi, US$8.

## Boquete and the eastern highlands   Colour map 4, C5.

highland town feted as Panama's premier outdoor destination

★ Nestled in the verdant valley of Caldera, the mountains surrounding Boquete are green and rugged, thickly forested in parts, home to thunderous rivers, piping hot springs and abundant birdlife. At 1060 m, the cool climate allows for the production of orchids, strawberries, root vegetables and, most importantly, coffee – the basis of the local economy since the late 19th century.

In more recent years, the town has been the focus of a prodigious property boom with a cavalcade of foreign baby-boomers arriving to live out their retirement. Increasingly, Boquete looks and feels like a well-heeled North American suburb. The region's changing demographics, along with rock-bottom coffee prices, mean many locals are turning to tourism as an alternative source of income. The town's lodgings run the gamut from backpacker hostels to luxury spas, and it is a great base for organizing whitewater rafting, hiking, horse riding, birding and other adventures.

Boquete is small and easily navigated on foot. The town's principal artery is **Avenida Central**, where you'll find most shops, hotels, restaurants and the plaza. Taxis are feasible for reaching some remote locations, but in some cases you will need a 4WD, or the services of a tour operator

### Sights

Boquete is a tranquil, predominantly wood-built town with several landscaped gardens and meandering streams. At its heart lies the **Parque de las Madres**, also known as the Parque Central, a shady plaza where the old railway station stood, complete with trees, bandstand and old-fashioned lamp posts. It is not unusual to see lots of Ngäbe people about town, many of them employed as seasonal labourers in Boquete's coffee fincas. On the outskirts of town bridge crosses over the Río Caldera to the fairgrounds of the annual **Feria de las Flores y del Café**, usually held mid-January (see Festivals, below).

On Avenida Central, roughly 500 m north of Parque Central, the acclaimed **Mi Jardín es su Jardín** is Boquete's most famous and striking botanical garden, home to over

200 species of flower. Owned by the González family, the gardens are free to wander. The imaginatively landscaped grounds contain a variety of colourful flower beds, bubbling creeks, teeming carp ponds and a procession of wacky ornaments, including gaudy painted flamingos and giant psychedelic cows. Another interesting garden, but not for all tastes, is the quirky **El Explorador** ① *Jaramillo, 3 km northeast of town, T720-1989, daily 0900-1800, US$3, to get there take a taxi, 5-10 mins, US$3, or walk, 45 mins*, where fine horticultural displays of roses and fruit trees are punctuated with an array of eccentric ornaments and wooden signs proclaiming philosophical truths. There is a café and bakery on site, should all that other-worldly contemplation leave you peckish.

## Hikes around Boquete

There's a wide of variety of potential hikes in Boquete's bucolic surroundings, far more than can be mentioned here. Locals will know secret routes and should be able to point you in the right direction. Many short trips can be undertaken without a guide, but guides can also be very useful for spotting wildlife. Whatever your plans, it's a good idea to start early to avoid getting caught in afternoon showers. Bring water, sunscreen, waterproofs and food, and inform your lodging of your chosen route. The most popular walking is in the **Parque Nacional Volcán Barú**, with one awesome trail leading to the summit and another to **Cerro Punta** (see page 957). Planning is required for both trips and, if you're inexperienced, a guide. Less demanding are the various paved loop roads snaking around the hillsides. They're usually quite empty of traffic and great for biking too, especially on the downhill stretches. Allow three to four leisurely hours to walk the scenic **Volancito loop** up and around the western flank of the Caldera Valley. It begins at the CEFATI visitor centre on the south side of town: just follow the sign to Volcancito and enjoy the views. Likewise, the **Jaramillo loop** offers expansive views from the eastern side of the valley.

# Boquete

San Juan Bautista
Site of Feria de las Flores y del Café
C Central
Av B Este
Av A Oeste
C 1 Sur
Parque de las Madres
C 2 Sur
Palacio Municipal
Parque D Médica
Buses to David
C 4 Sur
Chiriquí River Rafting
Plaza Los Establos
C 5 Sur
Río Caldera
C 6 Sur
C 7 Sur
Av A Este
Hiking Tours
C 8 Sur
Av Central
Av Belisario Porras
Biblioteca Pública
To Tourist Information Centre & David

N

100 metres
100 yards

**Where to stay**
Hostal Gaia **5**
Hostal Mamallena **9**
Hostal Nomba **13**
Hostal Refugio del Río **7**
Panamonte **4**

Pensión Marilos **12**

**Restaurants** ❼
Art Café La Crêpe **10**
Bistro Boquete **14**
Central Park **12**
El Oasis **1**
Machu Picchu **11**
Nelvis **2**
Punta de Encuentro **3**
Sugar & Spice **6**

Cross over the bridge towards the festival grounds and bear right up the hill, sticking to the left when passing any major forks or junctions; three to four hours. The **Alto Lino loop** begins a few kilometres north of the town on an eastbound road heading uphill. Roughly halfway along the road you'll arrive at the **Sendero El Pianista** (Pianist trail), a good but strenuous birdwatching trail which leads uphill from the cattle pastures into mist-swathed cloudforest and the provincial border with Bocas del Toro; a guide may be necessary if you are not confident. The trail is a four- to five-hour walk to the top and back down, so you might want to get a taxi (US$3) to shuttle you to and from the trailhead. True adventurers should consider the four-day odyssey to **Bocas del Toro**, which is not for the faint of heart; a guide is absolutely necessary.

## Parque Nacional Volcán Barú

At 3474 m, **Volcán Barú** is Panama's highest peak and the views from its summit are astounding: on an exceptional day, you can glimpse both Pacific and Atlantic oceans and breathe in one of the most expansive vistas anywhere. The surrounding Parque Nacional Volcán Barú shelters seven craters and no less than 10 different rivers, among them the Río Caldera and Río Chiriquí. Local fauna includes some 40 endemic species, five species of big cat, numerous endangered mammals, amphibians, reptiles and over 400 species of bird, including black and white hawk eagles, volcano juncos and, between January and

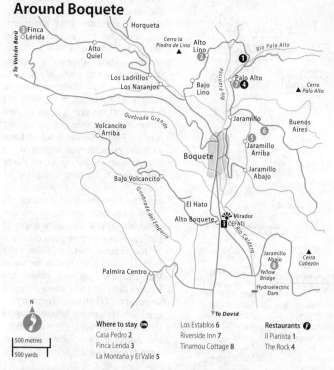

# Around Boquete

**Where to stay** 🛏
Casa Pedro **2**
Finca Lerida **3**
La Montaña y El Valle **5**

Los Establos **6**
Riverside Inn **7**
Tinamou Cottage **8**

**Restaurants** 🍴
Il Pianista **1**
The Rock **4**

## ON THE ROAD

## Coffee fincas around Boquete

The mountains and hills around Boquete are the misty heartland of Panama's coffee industry. Fans of the black stuff should not miss the opportunity to visit one of the many local *fincas* and learn about the processes of production, from bean to cup. Each producer has a slightly different approach and there are too many to list entirely.

The most famous is **Café Ruiz**, 500 m north of the plaza in Boquete, T720-1000, www.caferuiz-boquete.com, daily tours such as quick 'coffee appreciation' taster session, 45 minutes, US$9, or full three-hour tour, US$30, advance reservation necessary. Established in 1979 as a family business, the company has won numerous international awards. Today, **Café Ruiz** is the largest exporter of speciality coffee in Panama with some 90% of its beans shipped to Europe and the US for roasting.

If you'd like to combine your coffee tasting with some world-class birdwatching, head to **Finca Lérida**, northwest of town, T720-2285, www.fincalerida.com, tours two hours, US$31, reserve in advance. The sprawling estate, established by Tollef Monniche in 1922 and bought by Alfred Collins in 1957, features moss-draped cloud forests which are home to hundreds of bird species, including the rare resplendent quetzal. Luxury lodgings are available if you want to make a dawn start on the trails. The *finca* itself is one of the oldest coffee operations in Boquete and its beans are still processed in the pioneering plant designed by Mr Monniche.

Those familiar with the streets of Boquete or David may have already noticed the Western-style coffee houses of **Kotowa Coffee**, www.kotowacoffee.com. The Kotowa estate was founded in 1918 by Canadian entrepeneur Alexander MacIntyre, who notably channelled the Río Cristal to drive his hydraulic mill. Kotowa coffee, grown without pesticides, has a good body, chocolatey taste and sweet acidity. Tours of the estate are offered by **Coffee Adventures**, T730-3852, www.coffeeadventures.net, Monday-Saturday 1400, US$29.50, advance reservation necessary. They include a visit to the historic processing mill and end with a tasting session.

May, numerous resplendent quetzals. Average temperatures range from a subtropical 20°C on the lower slopes to a distinctly chilly 10°C higher up. During the dry season, frost or even an occasional flurry of snow is not unusual on the summit.

The park can be accessed from Boquete on Barú's east slope, or from Volcán or Cerro Punta in the west. It is easiest to reach the summit from the east side as the trail on the west face is dicey and unclear; if you do choose to begin your trek in Volcán, you are strongly advised to use a guide. On the lower slopes, the famous **Sendero Los Quetzales** is much easier to follow from west to east, starting in **Cerro Punta** (see page 957).

Only experienced hikers should attempt to climb Volcán Barú unguided. Departing from Boquete, it takes six to eight hours to complete the strenuous 21-km trail to the summit, and another five to six hours to return. Begin your ascent at 0500 if you want to make it back before dark. Alternatively, camp halfway and climb to the summit early the next morning – you will have a better chance of seeing both oceans at dawn. Pack dried food, 4-5 litres of water per person, compass, waterproofs and plenty of warm clothing. **Explora Ya** in Boquete can provide tents and sleeping bags, or take a shopping trip to the **Do-it Center** on Plaza Terronal in David. Inform your hotel of your intentions before you set out. The first 7 km of the ascent is paved, passing through rich coffee groves and forests of aromatic pines. It concludes at the ANAM office where you must pay admission. Note you can take a taxi this far, US$3-5. From the park entrance, the trail climbs through cloudforest draped with creepers, lichen and bromeliads. At the summit you'll find a forest of TV and radio aerials in a fenced enclosure. A small path leads to a cross and trigonometric point where you'll enjoy the best views of the craters, and sometimes, rainbows formed by the *bajareque* drizzle.

## Los Pozos de Caldera

*Daily 0800-1900, US$2. Follow the signs from Caldera village, a 60-min hike on dirt roads; driving is possible with 4WD. A taxi from Boquete should cost US$40 return, including a wait.*

The hot springs of Caldera are the perfect restorative for weary limbs and bones. Four thermally heated pools of differing temperatures, most of them enclosed by foliage and rustic walls of rocks, are said to alleviate rheumatism, arthritis and skin problems. The springs are located on the banks of the Río Chiriquí, where it's possible to dig your own soaking pool in the dry season only. Beware the owner's kleptomaniacal spider monkey – he knows how to get into bags. The springs are located in the village of Caldera, 18 km from Boquete, one of the oldest inhabited settlements in Chiriquí. You can access the village from either Boquete or David, but direct buses are infrequent. The David–Boquete bus passes the Caldera turning (marked Chiriquitos), 11 km south of downtown Boquete; from there it's a 7-km hike, or flag a taxi. The land around Caldera is flat, grassy, wide open and ideal for horse riding, also offered at the springs.

## Comarca Ngäbe-Buglé

Life in the Comarca Ngäbe-Buglé – homeland of the indigenous Ngäbe and Buglé people – obeys its own laws and innate natural rhythms. It is an extraordinarily peaceful place, filled with earthy tones and scenes of rural easiness. Settlements in this sparsely populated semi-autonomous region, which encompasses the rugged Cordillera Central east of Chiriquí, consist of dispersed hamlets and villages connected by rambling mule trails. Women wear colourful traditional dresses called *naguas*, their striking zig-zag patterns said to symbolize the Comarca's mountains and rivers or, according to some accounts, an ancient mythical snake. Most men dress like typical *campesinos*. Slash-and-burn agriculture, livestock and fishing are supplemented by seasonal work in commercial coffee, fruit and vegetable plantations, but wages and conditions tend to be poor.

Tourism in the Comarca is in its very earliest stages, and infrastructure, where it exists, is extremely basic. There is no electricity: a torch is essential. Be prepared for the possibility of bats and bugs in your room, bring a sheet sleeper (or sleeping bag for higher altitudes) and a mosquito net. Do not drink the water without first boiling or sterilizing it. Larger communities have simple shops selling bottled water, sodas, snacks and sundries. Rubber boots are essential for hiking in the wet season. The Ngäbe and Buglé are friendly people, but also quite conservative and reserved. As ever, no photographs should be taken without permission. If you would like to contribute something extra to your host or the community – for example, school books and stationery – it is always welcome. It is better if you don't bring alcohol into the Comarca.

Surrounded by thundering waterfalls and whitewater rivers, the rustic village of Soloy is home to around 6000 Ngäbe inhabitants, a very practical and friendly introduction to the Comarca. Located in the western district of **Besiko**, it is a fairly commercial settlement with paved road access from near the Horconcitos turning on the Interamericana highway; the journey time from David is less than two hours by bus. Amenities include mobile phone reception, running water (not potable), a handful of simple lodgings, restaurants and basic stores. There is talk of electricity arriving in town, but for now, it is assuredly off the grid. Before setting out, you are strongly advised to make contact with the village through the excellent NGO Medo ⓘ www.medo.awardspace.com, run by Adán Bejerano, T6468-5249 (English-speaking). Also see the community's website, www. comarcangobebugle.com.

There are plenty of hikes in the countryside around Soloy. The **Sendero La Esperanza** is a light walk, 1½ hours' round trip, offering fine views of the mountains before concluding at a double waterfall. The **Sendero Salto Mono**, three hours' round trip, leads to a sheer cliff with a powerful waterfall and, if in bloom, swathes of *chichica* (heliconia) flowers. For views of the Pacific Ocean, **Sendero Cerro Miel** is a moderately strenuous uphill hike, three to four hours' round trip. The most impressive of Soloy's many waterfalls is the **Cascada Kiki**, which some say is the highest in the country. The hike is only moderately strenuous, but the final descent into the canyon on a rope is not for the faint of heart; three to four hours' round trip, US$2 entrance fee. The hike to the Caribbean coast is a fascinating odyssey that leads deep into the Comarca. If the trail is open, it requires several challenging days of walking and lots of planning. Guides are necessary for all hikes, US$15 per day. Horses, particularly good for the trail to Kiki, are US$15 per person per day; arrange through Medo.

Adventurous souls can also enjoy a whitewater rafting trip on the **Río Fonseca**, which courses past the community with Grade III-IV whitewater rapids; contact **Eusebio Bejerano** ⓘ T6868-3433, US$30-75 including all safety equipment. Cultural presentations are another possibility, also arranged through Medo (see above), including *artesenía* presentations, a traditional jeki dance and balsería log-throwing, US$25. **Horacio Bejerano** ⓘ T6598-3325, tours US$5, maintains an excellent botanical garden with all kinds of rare orchids and interesting medicinal plants.

There are several co-op stores around town where you can pick up local *artesanía* and produce.

## Listings Boquete and around *maps p947 and p948*

### Tourist information

#### CEFATI visitor centre
*1 km south of Boquete on the highway, T720-4060. Mon-Fri 0900-1700.*
This stunningly positioned Alpine-style office provides local information and has a coffee shop attached.

### Boquete and around

#### $$$$ Finca Lérida
*T720-2285, www.fincalerida.com.*
One of Boquete's most famous and elegant 'ecolodges' and a destination in itself. Finca Lérida has a wide range of rooms and suites,
many in classic Scandinavian style, after the lodge's original owners. The grounds are vast and rambling and a birders' delight.

#### $$$$ La Montaña y el Valle – The Coffee Estate Inn
*Jaramillo Arriba, 2.5 km from central Boquete, T720-2211, www.coffeeestateinn.com.*
Deluxe cottages nestled in 2.5 ha of gorgeous, verdant grounds. Units are fully equipped with kitchen and living area, and have great views of the countryside. Delicious gourmet food is available, including freshly roasted coffee from their farm. Breakfast and tour included. Recommended.

#### $$$$ The Riverside Inn
*Palo Alto, T720-1076, www.*
*riversideinnboquete.com.*
One of Boquete's most exclusive lodgings,
complete with beautifully decorated rooms
and a handsome master suite with a 4-poster
bed and jacuzzi. 'Standard' rooms have
superb mattresses, Egyptian cotton linen
and a wealth of kit such as TV, DVD, coffee-
makers and Wi-Fi.

#### $$$ Boquete Garden Inn
*Palo Alto, T720-2376, www.*
*boquetegardeninn.com.*
Perched on the banks of the Río Palo Alto,
the hospitable Boquete Garden Inn has
received glowing reports from previous
guests. It has 5 spacious *cabañas*, all
tastefully decorated and well equipped with
cable TV, Wi-Fi and kitchenette. Beautiful,
tranquil, flowery grounds, plentiful birdlife
and super-friendly owners. Excellent, one of
the best and highly recommended.

#### $$$ Cabañas Isla Verde
*On main street, follow signs posted just before*
*the Casona Mexi restaurant, Bajo Boquete,*
*T720-2533, www.islaverdepanama.com.*
An interesting option with 6 imaginatively
designed 2-storey 'roundhouse' *cabañas*
and 4 suites overlooking a small stream.
German owner Eva Kipp is friendly and
knowledgeable. Discounts available in the
low season.

#### $$$ Los Establos
*T720-2685, Jaramillo Arriba,*
*www.losestablos.net.*
Very elegant and secluded lodgings in the
style of a traditional coffee hacienda. They
offer a range of deluxe rooms, suites and
cottages, all well attired with local art and
solid wood furnishings. Breakfast, coffee
and wine are included in the rates.

#### $$$ Panamonte
*Av 11 de Abril, Bajo Boquete, T720-1324,*
*www.panamonte.com.*
Built in 1919, this highly attractive hotel
is today managed by the Collins family

(Swedish-American). The rooms are
elegant and comfortable and the garden
is home to over 200 varieties of orchid.
New developments include a day spa
and various tours are available. Charming
and recommended.

#### $$$ Tinamou Cottage
*Jaramillo Abajo, 10 mins from town,*
*T720-3852, www.coffeeadventures.net/*
*tinamou.html.*
A tastefully presented B&B with
3 comfortable, well-equipped and secluded
cottages on a private coffee finca. Perfect
for nature lovers, with expert hosts and
good walking trails. Rates include breakfast
and owners can arrange pickup in town.
Discounts with internet bookings.

#### $$ Casa Pedro
*Alto Lino, Diagonal a Clínica Dental*
*del Dr Rivera, T720-2402,*
*www.casapedroboquete.com.*
A pleasant mid-range option managed by a
friendly American-Panamanian family. Clean,
comfortable, homely double rooms have
shared hot-water bath. There's also a suite
with a great wooden viewing deck and some
fully equipped cottages ($$$).

#### $$-$ Hostal Gaia
*Av Central, behind Sugar and Spice bakery, Bajo*
*Boquete, T720-1952, www.hostalgaia.com.*
Friendly, intimate little *hostal* with small
dorms for 4-6, fully equipped kitchen,
games, books, laundry, lockers and free
coffee. 2 private rooms are also available ($$).
New, clean, pleasant and recommended.

#### $$-$ Hostal Refugio del Río
*from Plaza Los Establos 1 block west,*
*½ block north, Bajo Boquete, T720-2088,*
*www.refugiodelrio.com.*
The friendly Refugio del Río has comfortable
annexed private rooms ($$) with pleasant
riverside porches. For budget travellers,
there are 2 dorms ($) inside the main house,
complete with communal kitchen, internet,
laundry facilities, dining room and TV.

Motorbike, cycle and ATV rental available. Recommended.

### $ Hostal Mamallena
*Parque Central, Bajo Boquete, T720-1260, www.mamallenaboquete.com.*
A popular backpackers' joint with a convenient central location on the plaza. Opened by the same team who own Mamallena in Panama City, the hostel has 17 private rooms and 5 dorms of different sizes. Plenty of amenities including kitchen, luggage storage, Wi-Fi, bar and restaurant. Free tea and coffee and all-day pancake breakfast included. Friendly, helpful and English-speaking.

### $ Hostal Nomba
*100 m west of Parque Central, behind Bistro Boquete, Bajo Boquete, T720-2864, www.nombapanama.com.*
Sociable self-styled 'adventure hostel' that's very popular with backpackers. They offer simple but comfortable dorms and private rooms, communal kitchen, library, in-room security lockers and bike rental. Their onsite tour agency can organize a range of excursions.

### $ Pensión Marilós
*Calle 7 Sur and Av B Este, opposite Rebequet, Bajo Boquete, T720-1380.*
A friendly, economical place with an agreeable home ambience. Rooms are very clean and comfortable with bath and hot water. Guests have use of the kitchen and living areas. The English-speaking management can also organize tours or store luggage. Often full but sharing is permitted. Good value and recommended.

## Restaurants

### Boquete and around

### $$$-$$ Art Café La Crepe
*Av Central, near San Juan Bautista.*
Tasty French crêpes are served at this jazzy, continental eatery, including some very creative ones. Classic French cooking is the house speciality, and dishes include fresh rainbow trout and crayfish in brandy and liqueur. Recommended.

### $$$-$$ El Oasis
*Av Buenos Aires, just over the bridge, Bajo Boquete, T720-1586, www.oasisboquete.com.*
Gourmet dining in a vibrant and sophisticated setting. Tasty offerings include ceviche, king prawn cocktail, Waldorf salad, and tricolour mousse. They have an extensive pasta, sandwich and vegetarian menu, and plenty of meat dishes too. Good service, but mixed reports on the lamb.

### $$$-$$ Restaurante Hotel Panamonte
*Av Central, north end of Boquete.*
*Open for breakfast, lunch and dinner.*
This restaurant is quaint and charming and the meals are fantastic – pricey, but worth the treat. Serves succulent trout, fresh juices and delicious desserts, among others.

### $$$-$$ The Rock
*Av 11 de Abril, Palo Alto, inside the Riverside Inn, www.therockboquete.com.*
The Rock enjoys a reputation as one of Boquete's best eateries. Their gourmet offerings include delicious onion soup, trout fillet, pork ribs, Thai chicken and steak, all beautifully prepared and presented. Beverages include artisan beers and a selection of fine wines. Great service, pleasant setting and highly recommended.

### $$ Bistro Boquete
*Av Central, Boquete.*
US owner Loretta once cooked for a US president in her previous establishment in Colorado. Her bistro here is renowned for excellent filet mignon, good breakfasts, tasty lunches and dinners.

### $$ Il Pianista
*Palo Alto, near Boquete Paradise.*
Located on a hill close to the entrance of the **Pianista hiking trail**, this oft-praised restaurant serves large, tasty Italian dishes including pizza and calzone. Good for a lunch stop after completing the hike.

Romantic and cosy setting, friendly service and reasonable prices. Recommended.

### $$ Machu Picchu
*Av Belisario, Porras.*
Fantastic Peruvian food cooked by a very friendly Peruvian. Pleasant interior, impressive menu, mostly meat, fish and seafood. Heartily recommended by locals as one of the best in town.

### $ Central Park
*Parque Central, Bajo Boquete.*
Intimate but casual little restaurant and coffee shop on the plaza. They offer economical fare, including hearty breakfasts and set lunches, as well as *comida típica*, such as stewed meat, grilled pork and pan-fried fish.

### $ Nelvis
*Av A Oeste, behind Plaza Los Establos, Bajo Boquete.*
Very popular with locals at lunchtime, cheap and cheerful **Nelvis** has crowds queue up for the economical Panamanian buffet. The fried chicken is reportedly the best in town.

### $ Punto de Encuentro
*Av A Este, near Pensión Marilós.*
Breakfast only. Also known as Olga's, a cosy little café with a garden and noticeboard, serving pancakes, fruit salad and juices.

### Bakeries and cafés

#### Sugar and Spice
*Av Central, Bajo Boquete.*
The best café and bakery in town, serving truly delicious fresh bread, pies, cakes, sandwiches, soups and other tasty fare. Highly recommended, don't miss it.

## Entertainment

### Boquete and around
#### Theatre
**Boquete Community Players Theatre**, *across the river near the feria grounds, www. bcpboquete.com.* Popular plays and theatrical events from Boquete's expat crowd. Check their website for the latest.

## Festivals

### Boquete and around
**Jan**  Thousands of visitors descend on Boquete for its annual **Feria de las Flores y del Café** (Flower and Coffee Fair), www. feriadeboquete.com, a 10-day festival showcasing the region's abundance of exotic and colourful flowers. Coffee harvesting is also in full swing and the occasion draws tradesmen from all over Central America. Usually commences 2nd week of Jan and lodgings fill up quickly; book in advance.
**Mar**  Founded in 2007, the Boquete **Jazz and Blues Festival**, www.boquetejazzandblues festival.com, sees a convergence of musical talent. The 2nd most important musical festival in the country after the **Panama City Jazz Festival** (see page 877).
**Apr**  The **Feria de las Orquídeas** (Orchid Fair) is the time and place to shop for orchids, which grow in abundance throughout the Chiriquí highlands. A hit with horticulturalists and a good place to share tips and expertise.

## What to do

### Boquete and around
#### Canopy tours
**Boquete Tree Trek**, *Plaza los Establos, Av Central, T720-1635, www.boquetetreetrek.com.* Known for their high-speed zipline tours of the forest canopy, Boquete Tree Trek also offers hiking, birdwatching, biking and other outdoor adventures, as well as overnight stays on their rural property.

#### Kayaking and whitewater rafting
**Boquete Outdoor Adventures**, *Plaza los Establos, Av Central, T720-2284, www. boqueteoutdooradventures.com.* Various 1-day and multi-day adventure packages in Chiriquí and beyond. Specializes in whitewater kayaking but also offers rafting and sea kayaking.
**Chiriqui River Rafting**, *Av Central, next to Lourdes, T6897-4382, www.panama-rafting. com. Open 0830-1730.* Bilingual father-and-son team Héctor and Ian Sánchez, offer 2- to

4-hr Grade II, III and IV trips with modern equipment. Recommended.

## Language schools

**Habla Ya**, *Plaza Los Establos, Av Central, T720-1294, www.hablayapanama.com.* Very good, professional school that receives good reviews from former students. Class sizes are small and teachers are well trained. Recommended.

**Spanish by the River**, *Alto Boquete, T720-3456, www.spanishatlocations.com.* A little out of town but has also received very good reviews.

## Tour operators

**Boquete Mountain Safari Tours**, *Plaza Los Establos, Av Central, T6627-8829, www.boquete mountainsafaritours.com.* From short hikes to full-on adventures, Boquete Mountain Safari Tours offers a good selection of half- and full-day tours, including horse riding, hot springs, coffee farms, hiking and birdwatching. Uses distinctive vintage Land Rovers. Helpful and friendly with lots of good reports.

**Coffee Adventures**, *T720-3852, www.coffee adventures.net.* A diverse range of hiking, birdwatching and community tours of the areas surrounding Boquete, as well as visits to the Kotowa coffee estate. Expertly run

by Terry Van Niekerk, who speaks English, Spanish and Dutch. Good reports and highly recommended, especially if hiking the Sendero Los Quetzales.

**Explora Ya**, *Plaza Los Establos, Av Central, T730-8344, www.exploraya.com.* Excellent and well-presented new operator that offers a creative range of local adventures, including hiking, rafting, hot springs, horse riding, rocking climbing and ascents of Volcán Barú. Affiliated with the popular **Habla Ya** Spanish school. Very popular, professional and highly recommended.

## Transport

### Boquete and around

Boquete lies 38 km north of David on a paved and newly expanded 4-lane highway.

**Bus** Buses to **David** depart from the southeast corner of the plaza, every 20 mins, 1 hr, US$1.75, and travel south along Av Belisario Porras. (**Note** Buses cease at dusk.) Local buses ply the hills around town and collect passengers along Av Central, irregular schedules, US$0.50-2. The easiest way to reach hotels in the surrounding suburbs – including Palo Alto, Jaramillo Arriba, Jaramillo Abajo – is by taxi; most one-way fares are US$2-5.

## Volcán and the western highlands   Colour map 4, B5/C5.

*less touristy than Boquete, overlooked by the Barú volcano*

★ Nestled in a high plateau formed by an ancient volcanic eruption, the highland town of Volcán basks in the shifting moods of Volcán Barú, its dark peak alternately draped in sunshine, rainbows, and sulking storm clouds. It is the largest settlement in Chiriquí's refreshing western *tierras altas*, 32 km north of La Concepción (Bugaba) on the leeward flank of the volcano.

Bound by the untamed Cordillera Talamanca to the north and the Costa Rican border to the west, the region is steeped in a disparate network of bucolic villages, rolling dairy pastures, desolate lava fields, misty cloudforests and jagged mountain vistas.

Volcán itself is stretched out over a sparse strip of highway where you'll find a handful of shops, restaurants, banks, petrol stations and other amenities. Despite the town's vast outdoors potential – including access to two world-class national parks – it is far less visited than Boquete. Consequently, the area offers an authentic taste of highland life, for the moment unsullied by intensive tourism or grasping property developers.

## Around Volcán

Backed by verdant hills and forests, the tranquil waters of Lagunas de Volcán will please birders and landscape photographers alike. Opened to the public in 1994, the 13-ha area features two large lakes rich in waders and waterfowl, including many ducks, herons, geese and jacanas. At 1240 m, they are the highest lake system in Panama and they fall under the private property of the Janson family, who operate one of the finest coffee fincas in Central America. Their high-altitude plantations enjoy a long growing season that gives their beans a special depth of flavor and a unique butterscotch tang. The family's tour company is **Lagunas Adventures** ① *T6569-7494, www.lagunasadventures. com*, offering guided visits to their finca, kayaking on the lakes, horse riding, hiking and other outdoor excursions. The lagunas are located 4 km from central Volcán. To get there, take a taxi to the old airport, US$2.50, then follow the dirt road for 2 km. Once in the forest, a left branch leads to the lakeshore.

Approximately 6 km from Volcán on the road to Caizán lies the **Sitio Arqueológico Barriles** ① *daily 0900-1700, US$1, several buses daily, US$0.50; or take a taxi, US$4*. The site is very modest compared to the grand Mayan metropolises further north in Central America, but it is intriguing nonetheless, especially if the curator, Edna Houx, is on hand to bring the exhibitions to life. Thought to have been a socio-ceremonial centre with a population of up to 1000 inhabitants, Barriles was part of the Gran Chiriquí culture, which included Western Panama and large parts of southern Costa Rica. It peaked around AD 300-900 and then mysteriously declined. The site's name, which means 'barrels', is derived from several large cylindrical stones believed to have been used to transport boulders from the foot of the Volcán Barú, some 20 km away. Among the most interesting finds at the site are 14 humanoid statues and a giant ceremonial *metate* (grinding stone) with 48 carved human heads – a motif almost certainly connecting the site to human sacrifice. Sadly, many of the best finds at Barriles are now under the care of the **Reina Torres de Araúz Anthropological Museum** in Panama City (see page 868).

## Volcán to Costa Rica

From the police station in Volcán a paved highway winds west towards the Costa Rican border, climbing over Cerro Pando and passing scenic plantations and cattle country. Near Santa Clara, approximately 27 km from Volcán (look for a sign a few hundred metres after the gas station), is the turning for **Finca Hartmann** ① *T6450-1853, www.fincahartmann. com*, specializing in the production of shade-grown boutique coffee. Its organic plantations lie in the buffer zone of the Parque Internacional La Amistad and numerous hiking trails criss-cross the property, highly renowned as a birdwatching and wildlife mecca. Based on observations made by the **Smithsonian Tropical Research Institute**, 282 bird species and 62 mammal species can be spotted on the densely wooded finca. Coffee tours cost US$10, all other tours, including hiking and birding, are individually priced; enquire in advance. The international crossing at Río Sereno, 45 km from Volcán, is extremely quiet, friendly and usually easy, but not recommended if you are entering Costa Rica with your own vehicle (see Costa Rica–Panama box in the Practicalities chapter). Approaching the village from Volcán, abandoned military installations are visible on the right. The bus will drop you a short walk from the frontier. A small handful of Panamanian businesses, including the **Banco Nacional**, are centred around the plaza.

## Volcán to Cerro Punta

On the highway to Cerro Punta, the settlement of Paso Ancho is flanked by wide open spaces and sparsely vegetated lava fields. If you have your own vehicle, you can experience the strange optical illusion for which the area is known: stop the engine, put the car in neutral, then watch it mysteriously roll uphill. Paso Ancho is the starting point of a nine-hour hike to the summit of Volcán Barú. The trail is beautiful, climbing through lush cloudforests and then ascending steeply over loose volcanic rock and scree, but it is poorly marked near the top and a guide is strongly recommended. Roughly halfway between Volcán and Cerro Punta, the diminutive settlement of Bambito is backed by volcanic cliffs and pine forests. Several comfortable hotels dot the area including the reputable **Hotel Bambito**, which manages a famous trout farm beside the highway, **Venta de Truchas** ⓘ *0700-1600, fresh fish straight from the pools at US$5 a kilo*. You can rent a rod to catch them, US$5, or use your own, US$2.60, or just ask the guards to snare one. Trout are not native to Panama; they were introduced in 1925 and make a delicious addition to local rivers and dinner menus.

## Cerro Punta

Surrounded by a patchwork of diminutive farming plots, the sleepy town of Cerro Punta, 25 km north of Volcán, lies at the heart of a vegetable and flower-growing zone. Many of its Alpine-style houses faithfully reflect the influence of former Swiss and Yugoslav settlers; there is even a small settlement nearby called Nueva Suiza. At an altitude of 2130 m, Cerro Punta is one of the few places cool enough in Panama to support the cultivation of cold produce, including prolific cabbages, lettuces, potatoes, carrots and, best of all, strawberries, which are available from local stalls and restaurants. There is no tourist office in Cerro Punta, but **Los Quetzales Lodge & Spa** in Guadalupe, 3 km north of Cerro Punta at the end of the road, sells maps and can hook you up with their guides for hiking trips.

## Sendero Los Quetzales

*US$5. To get to the trail, head north out of Cerro Punta, cross over the bridge and follow the signs to the ANAM station at Alto Respingo, 4 km away; alternatively, take a 4WD taxi, US$10. Total journey time, 5-8 hrs one way.*

Meandering through pristine cloudforests at the foot of **Volcán Barú**, the Sendero Los Quetzales is widely regarded as one of Central America's most stunning hiking trails. Connecting **Cerro Punta** and **Boquete**, the 10-km *sendero* can be followed in either direction, but it is quicker and less strenuous when followed west to east. Note you will have to cover some extra ground between the towns and the rangers' stations, bringing the total distance to 22 km (this can be reduced with 4WD taxis). Commencing at the rangers' station in **Alto Respingo**, 4 km from Cerro Punta, the trail climbs briefly before continuing through the forest in a general downhill fashion. After a few hours, you will arrive at **Mirador La Roca**, a rest point with picnic tables, campsite and expansive views. The final stretch follows the Río Caldera and some roughly hewn dirt tracks as far as the second rangers' station at **Alto Chiquero**. From there, it is another 8 km to Boquete. The trail is much easier in the dry season, but can be enjoyed throughout the year, if properly kitted with rubber boots and raincoat. During the wet season, it can make sense to begin in Boquete, where you have a better chance of a dry morning.

## Finca Drácula

*Guadalupe, 3 km north of Cerro Punta, T771-2070, www.fincadracula.com. Mon-Fri 0800-1130, 1300-1700; entrance US$7, entrance plus guided tours US$10 (reserve in advance). To get there, follow the signs past Los Quetzales Lodge & Spa, 10-15 mins uphill.*

There's no sign of Transylvanian vampires at Finca Drácula, a superb orchid sanctuary named after the *Telipogon vampirus* flower. Said to be the largest collection of orchids in Latin America, the finca is home to 2200 species, some of them very rare and endangered. The sanctuary is particularly renowned for its efforts to protect and propagate native species threatened by temperature change, deforestation or the disappearance of pollinating insects. Their scientific work includes the discovery of 150 previously unknown species. Finca Drácula was established by Andrew Maduro in 1969. Formerly home to extensive cattle pastures, the 10-ha grounds are immaculately landscaped with winding trails, trees, lakes, ponds and streams. The finca offers month-long internships for students from diverse academic backgrounds.

## Parque Internacional La Amistad (PILA)

*The main entrance is at Las Nubes, around 7 km northwest of Cerro Punta, 0800-1600, US$5. If you wish to stay overnight, there is a basic rangers' station with beds, US$12; bring your own sleeping bag and book in advance through ANAM. Another entrance can be found in Guadalupe, 3 km northeast of Cerro Punta, but it is normally only used by guests of Los Quetzales Lodge & Spa (see Where to stay, below). On the lesser visited Caribbean side, access is via the Naso-run Wekso project (see page 964).*

Encompassing 401,000 ha of diverse life zones, the Parque Internacional La Amistad is jointly administered by Costa Rica and Panama. It is home to some of the last remaining highland virgin forests in Central America, including areas that have been untouched for 25,000 years. The park is a designated UNESCO World Heritage Site and enjoys particularly high rates of endemism. Some 180 endemic plant species and 40 endemic bird species have been recorded in the region. The Panamanian section of the park covers approximately 207,000 ha of complex volcanic terrain including the numerous peaks, valleys and cliffs of the **Talamanca** mountain range. Temperatures and altitudes vary greatly, encouraging high biodiversity. Some 400 bird species inhabit La Amistad, including harpy eagles, quetzals, crested eagles and bare-necked umbrella birds. Mammal species number about 100 and include tapirs, ocelots and jaguars.

Several trails commence at the entrance of Las Nubes. For a casual 500-m stroll through the forest, head to **Sendero Puma Verde**. Nearby, **Sendero El Retoño** is a 2.1-km loop trail, also flat and very easy, which crosses streams and rivers and offers good birdwatching opportunities. For a moderately strenuous two- to three-hour hike, the **Sendero La Cascada** leads uphill to a series of miradors with expansive views over the valleys. It concludes at an impressive 50-m-high waterfall. **Vereda la Montaña** is a fairly strenuous 4-km hike up **Cerro Picacho**. It take around six hours to complete the round trip (guide necessary) and you will be rewarded with fine views of the Caribbean. There is a rangers' station at the summit, if you want to stay overnight.

## Tourist information

There is no ATP office in Volcán but tour operators may be able to supply advice, along with the **ANAM** office on the highway to Cerro Punta.

## Where to stay

### Volcán

**$$$ Dos Ríos**
*Río Sereno Highway, on the edge of town, T771-4271, www.dosrios.com.pa.*
A long-standing motel-style place with beautiful lush grounds and slightly tired rooms. Noise is reportedly an issue; get a room upstairs so you don't have to hear the creaky floorboards. OK, good staff, but not great value.

**$$ Cabañas Reis**
*At the entrance to Volcán, T771-5153, www.cabanasreis.com.*
Formerly **Cabañas Señorials**, this pleasant road-side lodging has a row of 10 clean, tidy, concrete cabins, fully kitted with cable TV, Wi-Fi, hot water and comfortable furnishings. Friendly, English-speaking management.

**$$ Volcán Lodge**
*Calle 1, near the entrance to Volcán, southeast side of town, T771-4709, www.volcanlodge.webs.com.*
A very cosy, historic and well-restored wooden guesthouse with a handful of clean, simple, comfortable rooms. The restaurant is one of the best places in town. Warm, friendly and recommended.

**$ Hospedaje Brisas de California**
*Calle 11, Nueva California, T771-4323.*
Budget guesthouse managed by a very friendly and helpful couple, Efraín and Mariela, who do everything they can to make you feel at home. Rooms are simple but pleasant, equipped with TV, hot water,

Wi-Fi and a simple outdoor cooking area. Recommended.

### Volcán to Cerro Punta

**$$$ Cabañas Kucikas**
*Bambito, www.kucikas.com, T771-4245.*
Perched on the banks of Chiriquí Viejo, Cabañas Kucikas offers a range of comfortable cottages complete with fully equipped kitchens, lounges, dining areas and bedrooms. Some of them have capacity for up to 10 people. A pleasant setting.

**$$$ Hotel Bambito**
*Vía Cerro Punta, T215-9448, www.hotelbambito.com.*
Alpine-style resort with 47 rooms and natural landscapes. Luxury amenities include an indoor pool, jacuzzi, sauna, spa facilities, tennis court, health club, restaurant and lounge. Rooms are comfortable, well equipped and decorated in relaxing earthy hues. Breakfast included, packages available.

### Cerro Punta

**$$$$-$$$ Hostal Cielito Sur**
*Nueva Suiza, 2 km before Cerro Punta, T771-2038, www.cielitosur.com.*
A comfortable and hospitable B&B operated by Janet and Glenn Lee. Rooms are comfortable and creatively decorated; some are equipped with refrigerator and microwave. Restaurant, porch and communal area with soft sofas and fireplace, great for unwinding after a day on the trails.

**$$$$-$$ Los Quetzales Lodge & Spa**
*T771-2182, www.losquetzales.com.*
A true forest hideaway with self-contained cabins inside Parque Amistad. A multitude of animals and birds, including quetzals, can be seen from the porches. Back in town, there are dormitories, chalets and some economical rooms, all comfortable and pleasant. Spa facilities and restaurant

are excellent. Very special and highly recommended.

**$ Hotel Cerro Punta**
*Calle Principal, T771-2020, www.cerropunta.zxq.net.*
Needs a lick of paint. 10 tired, slightly cramped rooms with hot water and no TV. There's a dated wood-panelled restaurant offering hot meals. Past its heyday but quite friendly, helpful and OK for budget travellers.

## Restaurants

### Volcán

**$$$ Cerro Brujo Gourmet**
*Av 6 y Calle 7a, Brisas del Norte, T6669-9196.*
Very tasty and creative cooking from chef Patricia Miranda. The menu is constantly changing and features home-grown organic produce from her garden. Lots of praise and good reports.

**$$ Maná**
*Calle 1, inside Volcán Lodge, near the entrance to town, T771-4709, www.volcanlodge.webs.com.*
Delicious home-cooked comfort food including soups, salads, sandwiches and hearty specialities such as filet mignon, beer-battered shrimps and fish of the day. An attractive setting in a historic wooden guesthouse. Affordable prices and highly recommended.

**$ Restaurante Mary**
*Av Central.*
A popular lunchtime haunt where you can pick up a good, economical, wholesome set meals, such as *pollo frito* and *pollo guisado*. A la carte dishes (**$$**) are OK, but not as good value.

### Cafés and bakeries

**Panadería Ortega**
*Av Central.*
Serves a good selection of cakes and cookies. A nice place to warm up with hot chocolate or coffee when the chill twilight sets in.

## Festivals

### Volcán

**Dec** The **Feria de las Tierras Altas** is held during the 2nd week of Dec. Festivities include dancing, a craft fair and general merriment.

## What to do

### Volcán

Despite Volcán's incredible tourist potential, there are few tour operators in town; Boquete remains the main hub of action. Your hotel should be able to recommend a reputable guide (essential for climbing Barú), otherwise try:
**Green Mountain Adventures**, *Av Central, at the northwest exit to town, near Hotel Dos Ríos, T6457-6080, www.gmavolcan.tripod.com.* A good range of outdoor activities, including hiking, biking, rock climbing, agro-tourism and horse riding.

## Transport

### Volcán

You can get around town on foot, but its sprawling layout means buses, every 5 to 15 mins, are a more convenient option if you need to get from one side to the other
Buses to **David** run southeast along Av Central every 15-20 mins, US$3. For **Cerro Punta** and destinations north, buses turn north outside the police station, every 20-30 mins, US$1. To **Río Sereno**, wait for a passing bus on Av Central, every 30 mins, US$2.25. To **Los Barriles**, take a Caizán bus from the station next to Panadería Ortega, about 1 km northwest of the police station on Av Central; every 30 mins, 15 mins, US$0.70.

### Cerro Punta

Buses to **David** depart every 30 mins, US$3.50, passing through Volcán and Concepción (Bugaba) en route. A taxi is recommended to reach **Parque Nacional La Amistad**, US$5.

# **Bocas** del Toro

An obscure Caribbean province of scattered islands and secret enclaves, the remote and sparsely settled backwater of Bocas del Toro plays host to a profusion of ecological niches. Steamy lowland rainforests, highland cloudforests, teeming coastal lagoons, kaleidoscopic coral reefs and rambling jungle rivers punctuate the region, home to rare and exuberant flora and fauna.

Bocas del Toro owes its pristine natural beauty to millennia of isolation. While neighbouring territories succumbed to imperial Spain, Bocas was barely colonized or evangelized. Foreign intrusion was fleeting until the late 19th century, when the United Fruit Company struck 'green gold' and set about radically transforming the region, installing banana plantations, sea ports, railways and settlements. Today, the province's fruit operations are scaled back, but its inhabitants trace their ancestry to such disparate homelands as Jamaica, China, Europe and North America. The local dialect – Guari-Guari – is assuredly multicultural too, fusing elements of the English, Spanish and Ngäbere languages.

But despite its international pretensions, Bocas del Toro, hemmed in between mountains, sea and jungle remains a colourful patchwork of isolated, culturally distinct communities, as varied as the natural world they echo.

**Best** for
Diving ▪ Relaxing ▪ Surfing ▪ Wildlife

★ Mainland Bocas del Toro is a land of few roads and fewer travellers; you'll need sturdy boots and a strong machete to explore it. Stamped with the blue marks of Chiquita Brands, bananas continue to play a major role in the local economy. The grungy city of Changuinola is the region's largest urban settlement, enveloped in steamy plantations and an important centre of cultivation and export.

Beyond bananas, mainland Bocas del Toro is interspersed with intriguing indigenous communities, including Ngäbe and Buglé in the lowlands. Inland, where the Parque Internacional La Amistad rolls upwards to meet the cloud-drenched peaks of the Talamanca mountain range, you'll find determined settlements of Naso and Bri Bri. An expedition to their heartland is one of the most rewarding adventures Panama has to offer.

## Chiriquí to Bocas del Toro

The highway to Bocas del Toro branches north off the Carretera Interamericana around 14 km east of David. As you climb, you will be rewarded with views of the Pacific Ocean and Chiriquí lowlands. Before reaching the continental divide, you'll enter the forested zones of the 19,500-ha Reserva Forestal Fortuna, created in 1976 to protect the river basin of the **Lago Fortuna**. There are multiple trails through the cloudforests and the best way to experience them is by spending a night or two at one of the area's interesting lodges (see Where to stay, below). After the continental divide, the road winds down to sea level, passing the **Fortuna Hydroelectric Plant** and its vast artificial lake. There is a significant shift in humidity, vegetation and architecture as you enter the steamy Bocas lowlands. If travelling by bus to Almirante/Changuinola, you will pause for a break at Chiriquí Grande junction, where there is a busy roadside restaurant.

## The Banana Coast

It's hard to believe that the jungle-cloaked coast of Bocas del Toro was once the thriving economic engine of a banana republic. At the height of its glory, great steamships would ply the waters offshore, laden with fruit and migrant workers. Today, most of the plantations have been abandoned to secondary growth, the 'great white fleet' has been sold, and many of the old banana towns are dwindling as younger generations flee in search of a better life.

The first place of any size is the salty town of Chiriquí Grande, which has weathered boom and bust cycles like a stubborn old sailor. Flourishing and withering as a major port, a banana town and, in the early 1980s, the Caribbean terminus for a transoceanic oil pipeline, it has again fallen on hard times and is today quite depressed. Heading west on the highway to Almirante, at Km 25, the welcoming Ngäbe community of **Silico Creek** is home to 500 inhabitants and the **Urari Community Tourism Project** ① *T6233-8706, www. urari.org*. In addition to hikes, horse riding and accommodation, it offers an excellent cacao tour, US$10, where you'll be led through the process of chocolate production from finca to factory.

The sluggish and sketchy port town of **Almirante**, dredged from malaria-infested swamps in the early 20th century, served as the UFC headquarters between 1912 and 1929. Today it is used for exports by Chiquita Brands, whose blue and white containers can be seen stacked high on the docks, and the town is as rough and seedy as any other desperate backwater. It does, however, see a steady stream of foreign visitors on their way to the Bocas del Toro archipelago; water taxis to **Isla Colón** depart half hourly from the docks, 0600-1830, 25 minutes, US$4.

Close to the Costa Rican border, the only place of any real size in the province is the scruffy, sultry city of **Changuinola**, home to the Bocas Fruit Company, a subsidiary of Chiquita Brands. Most of its 50,000 inhabitants find employment in the surrounding sprawl of banana fincas. As a regional hub of commerce and transportation, some travellers stop in Changuinola on their way to and from Guabito on the Costa Rican border (see Costa Rica–Panama box in the Practicalities chapter).

On the highway to Guabito, 5 km north of Changuinola, are the protected wetlands of **Humedal San San Pond Sak** ① *managed by ANAM but best visited through the Asociación de Amigos y Vecinos de la Costa y la Naturaleza (AAMVECONA), offices at the reserve's entrance, T6666-0892, www.aamvecona.com.* Encompassing an area of 16,125-ha, the reserve is home to a large population of critically endangered manatees, who dwell all year round among the brackish waters of the mangrove swamps. Endangered sea turtles, including green and hawksbill, are also nest on the reserve's beach from March to July. AAMVECONA offer a half-day manatee tour, US$70 per group, including transportation by boat and Spanish-speaking guide. For an extra US$10 per person, you can also take a two-hour aquatic tour by kayak, or visit the turtle beach, if in season. There is a simple wooden ecolodge within the reserve with bunk beds and a shared kitchen, US$10 per person per night plus US$5 for each cooked meal; volunteer opportunities available. To get to the wetlands, catch a bus bound for Las Tablas, US$0.70, 10 minutes, and ask to be dropped off at the entrance; or take a taxi, US$4.

## The Naso Kingdom

*To get to the Río Teribe, first catch a bus to El Silencio, departing from Changuinola's bus terminal every 20 mins, US$0.65, 30 mins. A new bridge, constructed by the Empresas Públicas de Medellín hydroelectric company, now crosses the Río Teribe to connect with a new road to Bonyic, where trucks run to the Naso Kingdom, every 30-60 mins, US$1, 20 mins.*

The Río Teribe – known as Tjer Di ('Grandmother Water') in the Naso language – is the central axis and spiritual heart of the Naso Kingdom, one of indigenous America's last remaining monarchies, headed by a king or queen and supported by a *consejo* (council) of 30 elders. Naso ancestral lands encompass 11 communities on or around the riverbanks as well as the remote **Parque Internacional La Amistad** and the **Bosque Protector Palo Seco**, home to over 400 brilliant bird species, scores of rare mammals, reptiles, amphibians, and more plant and tree species than can be found in the entire European continent. Unsurprisingly, the Naso are masters of bushcraft and jungle medicine, not to mention hunting and fishing.

Although most Naso live like their forebears, surviving on subsistence agriculture, missionary and Western influences have intensified in recent years and the role of the shaman has been marginalized by pastors, ministers, priests and doctors. Traditional clothing has also been exchanged for Western attire and the Naso language, belonging to the Chibchan family, is now declining. Since 2004, the controversial Bonyic hydroelectric project has caused a schism in Naso society, although many Naso continue to campaign for the formation of 130,000 ha of semi-autonomous *comarca*.

The jungle gateway of El Silencio, slung along a muddy river bank at the confluence of the Río Chaguinola and the Río Teribe, offers little in the way of activities, but there are a handful of simple restaurants and a reasonably well-stocked 'super' where you can pick up food, water and sundry items, such as candles, torches, batteries, matches, insect repellent and rubber boots.

The **Wekso Ecolodge** ⓘ *T6569-2844, www.odesen.bocasdeltoro.org*, was established in 1995 by the Naso community tourism initiative, ODESEN. Located on the northern bank of the Río Teribe, opposite the community of Bonyic, it is an essential stop for anyone wishing to penetrate the mysteries of the kingdom. The lodge is conveniently located at the entrance to the Parque Internacional La Amistad, and Adolfo Villagra, ODESEN's highly regarded founder, can expertly organize, assist or advise on a wide range of activities. Popular options include guided hikes in the rainforest, river trips to the Naso heartland, traditional fishing with bows and arrows, community tours of Sieyic and Sieykin, stays with local families and, for the truly adventurous, week-long expeditions to sacred mountains and beyond. Wekso's guides cost US$20 per day (plus tip and, if applicable, transportation costs) and are excellent and informative. The lodge offers rustic accommodation for up to 30 guests in traditional thatch and wood or concrete houses ($). Built on the site of a former 'Pana-Jungla' Panamanian Defence Force training camp, the grounds are littered with intriguing sights. Check out the overgrown helipad where General Noriega touched down, the weathered 'animal warrior' statuary and the crumbling mural where painted verses extol the hardened glories of the Pana-Jungla life. Alternatively, on the opposite side of the river, Bonyic is the base of operations for OCEN ⓘ *T6569-3869, www.ocen.bocas.com*, who offer accommodation ($), guides, tours and transportation; ask around for Raúl Quintero, the project manager.

## Listings Mainland Bocas del Toro

### Where to stay

#### Chiriquí to Bocas del Toro

**$$ Finca La Suiza**
*Hornito, 4 km north of Los Planes, T6794-4462, www.fincalasuizapanama.com.*
A very comfortable and hospitable highland lodge managed by Herbert Brullman and Monika Kohler. Several excellent hiking trails begin in their property where you'll see plentiful birdlife, entrance US$8. Excellent organic food and all-round good reports. Recommended.

**$ Lost and Found**
*T6432-8182, near Valle de la Mina, www.lostandfoundlodge.com.*
A very popular and successful youth hostel located high up on the edge of the continental divide. Verdant grounds encompass 12 ha of rainforest with a variety of tours and volunteer opportunities. Accommodation includes dorms and simple private rooms. Recommended.

#### Changuinola

**$$-$ Semiramis**
*Calle 17 de Abril, diagonally opposite the Alhambra, T758-6006.*
Offers 29 dark rooms with outstandingly kitsch pictures, a/c, hot water, TV and Wi-Fi in the lobby. The restaurant serves seafood. Parking available. Friendly.

### Restaurants

#### Changuinola

**$$ Casa Roma**
*Calle 17 de Abril, next to Residencial Carol.*
Casa Roma serves reasonably priced Turkish and Italian fare, including pizzas, kebabs and hummus. Clean and friendly. Not bad.

**$$ Restaurante Ebony**
*Calle 17 de Abril.*
Authentic Afro-Antillean fare served in an equally authentic, laid-back setting. Lots of tributes to Bob Marley.

## Transport

### Almirante

**Boat** Water taxi to **Bocas** 0600-1830, 25 mins, US$4. Several companies at the *muelle* compete for your custom, including **Bocas Marine Tours and Taxi 25**. A colectivo taxi from the bus station to the *muelle* is US$1, or it can be walked in 5-10 mins. Unofficial guides may request 'tips'.

**Bus** To **David**, every 40 mins, 4-5 hrs, US$8.45; **Changuinola**, every 30 mins, 30 mins, US$1.50.

### Changuinola

**Bus** The SINCOTAVECOP bus station is 1 block behind 17 de Abril, turn up from the Shell station. To **Almirante**, every 30 mins till 2000, 30 mins, US$1.75; to **El Silencio**, every 20 mins, 20 mins, US$0.65; to **Costa Rica**, catch a Las Tablas bus to Guabito, every 20 mins till 2000, 30 mins, US$0.80, cross the border on foot and catch a service from Sixaloa on to Limón. There is also a non-stop service to **San José** 1 daily, 1000 (no office, pay on bus) US$10, 6-7 hrs, but many police checks (note this bus may not always run). See also Costa Rica–Panama box in the Practicalities chapter. For long-distance buses south and east, head to the Terminal Urracá at the north end of town; to **Panama City**, 0700, 10-12 hrs, US$28; to **David**, 4-5 hrs, US$8.45.

## Bocas del Toro archipelago  Colour map 4, B5.

*far-flung islands, tangled rainforests, kaleidoscopic coral reefs and white-sand beaches*

★ The Bocas del Toro archipelago has long drawn adventurers to their languid shores, Christopher Columbus first and foremost among them. When he became the first European to explore the region in 1502, he failed to find gold or a passage to Asia, but he did lay eyes on a pristine natural bounty.

Today, despite the intrusion of modernity, the Bocas archipelago continues to be a bastion of biodiversity, teeming with exuberant and uniquely evolved flora and fauna, including dazzling neon-coloured frogs, sloths, orchids, butterflies and sea turtles. Add the lure of spectacular beaches, world-class waves, authentic Caribbean communities and a robust party scene, and you'll soon understand why so many foreigners are coming here to retire, open businesses or otherwise bask in the laid-back local lifestyle. Sadly, the flurry of international interest has also attracted less benign forces, including aggressive property developers with grandiose plans. Please tread carefully, life is fragile.

**Safety** Most crimes in Bocas are opportunistic. Never leave valuables unattended on the beach and do not wander empty or unlit roads after dark. Take particular care at the bars if you drink too much. The single greatest danger to travellers comes from the ocean itself in the form of rip tides; make sure you familiarize yourself with their hazards. Tap water is not potable.

### Isla Colón

Isla Colón is the most heavily populated of the archipelago's islands and home to the province's jaunty capital, Bocas Town. As a hub of transport, commerce and unfettered hedonism, most visitors wash up on its streets at some stage. Like all good port towns, it manages to exude charm and sleaze in equal measure. Beneath a gentle exterior of brightly painted wooden houses, the town nurtures a dark and feisty predilection for pleasure. Life ambles up and down **Main Street**, also known as **Calle Tercera**, where scores of waterfront restaurants, hotels, bars, cafés and water taxis vigorously compete for your tourist dollars. The geographic and social heart of town is the shady **Plaza Simón Bolívar**, a great spot for people-watching and local interaction. Spark up a conversation and you're likely to meet any number of friendly, talkative, off-the-wall or on-the-edge characters.

On the outskirts of town, Playa Istmito – also known as **La Cabaña** – overlooks the sea with yellow-grey sands and a string of colourful cabins that are empty until the annual **Feria del Mar** celebrations (see Festivals, below). Although cleaner than it's been in many years, the beach is far from pristine and swimming is not recommended. It is quite popular with locals, however, who often gather to play volleyball or sip *cervezas* under the thatched *palapas*. As the name suggests, the beach is situated on a slender isthmus. On the opposite flank is the poor, polluted but authentic neighbourhood of **Saigon**.

Around 1 km north of the Istmito on the main road is the excellent **Smithsonian Tropical Research Institute** ① *T757-9794, www.stri.si.edu, Thu-Fri 1400-1700, free,* dedicated to the study of the archipelago's diverse marine and terrestrial ecosystems; sea-grass meadows, coral reefs, mangroves and sand beaches among them. Members of the public visiting the station can enjoy tours of the laboratories, a nature trail, aquariums, a bookshop and various interpretive displays on local ecology.

Less than 1 km north of the research station is **Finca Los Monos** ① *T757-9461, www.bocasdeltorobotanicalgarden.com, tours depart Mon 1300 and Fri 0830, or by appointment, 2 hrs, US$10, sturdy footwear recommended.* A lot of love and hard work has gone into this 9.3-ha tropical botanical garden created by plant enthusiasts David and Lin Gillingham. Hundreds of brilliantly coloured species are represented in the grounds, rainforest heliconias, ornamentals, gingers, palms, fruit and spice trees among them.

# Bocas del Toro Archipelago

Around 2 km north of Bocas Town, the road forks. The right-hand branch leads to the expat enclave of Big Creek before heading to several beaches, most of them fraught with monster waves that make them bad for swimming but good for surfing. The road peters out at **Playa Paunch**; if you're cycling you'll push along the sand, but you can take a rest at Paki Point restaurant.

Further north, the road picks up again and leads to **Playa Bluff**, 7 km from downtown. The beach is several kilometres long and has hard, fast waves. It is one of the most popular surf spots on the island, but unsuitable for the inexperienced. Note turtles lay eggs on Playa Bluff between May and September; if you would like to observe them, contact the conservation group **Anaboca** ① *Bocas Town Market, 2nd St and Av G, 2nd floor, T6843-7244, www.anaboca.org*. Taxis to the beaches are expensive, US$10-20, 25-30 minutes, depending on which end of the beach you want.

Back on the main road, at the fork, the left-hand branch leads to the interior of the island and the tiny hamlet of **Colonia Santeña**. The community is home to a small, dark cave known as 'La Gruta', US$1, which is revered as a shrine and home to many thousands of bats. If you still wish to see the colony, cover your mouth, follow the stream a short way, and shine a torch on the ceiling.

At the end of the road lies the community of Boca del Drago, 25 km from Bocas Town, overlooking the strait which Columbus navigated five centuries ago. Nearby, **Playa Estrella** (Starfish Beach) is good for swimming, but its ambience has been ruined by several scruffy bars and restaurants. If you manage to find any surviving starfish on the beach, please do not handle them. You can also reach Boca del Drago by water taxi, US$5, or by bus, US$2.50, 30 minutes.

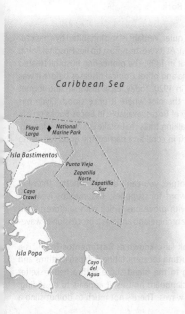

Located a short distance northeast of Boca del Drago, the jagged outcrop and wildlife reserve of Swan's Cay (**Isla del Cisne** or **Isla Pájaros**) is an important ground-nesting site for many indigenous and migratory seabirds including frigates, pelicans, boobies, gulls and the famous red-billed tropic birds. As there's a risk of disturbing the nests and other important elements of the habitat, you'll need ANAM permission to go ashore and you should definitely be accompanied by a qualified naturalist if you choose to do so.

### Isla Caranero

Isla Caranero, or **Careening Cay**, is the site where Christopher Columbus is reported to have careened his vessels (ie tilted them on their side for the purposes of cleaning or repair). The island is visible from the waterfront in Bocas Town and just two minutes away by water taxi, US$1-1.50. It is considerably smaller and calmer than its feisty neighbour. The beaches aren't dazzling, but good enough for lolling

# BACKGROUND
## Bocas del Toro archipelago

In 1899, the United Fruit Company established its headquarters in Bocas Town inside a large wooden mansion that is today the Hotel Bahía. As Bocas boomed, it expanded with wooden walkways over the mangrove swamps, gradually incorporating modern infrastructure. The population was broadly multicultural, consisting of Afro-Antillean migrant workers, European farmers, North American businessmen and others. By 1929, however, Panama disease had ruined fruit agriculture in the region and the UFC shut up shop.

For decades, Bocas dwindled as a far-flung provincial capital with no industry and little purpose. In 1989, at the close of the Noriega years, there were just three hotels in town, a situation that would soon be transformed by the *Tico Times* and other gringo media, who instigated a frenzied land grab of the archipelago's 'paradise islands'. During the intense construction boom that followed, many pristine areas were cleared or otherwise plundered for their precious hardwoods. Unique ecosystems were damaged or destroyed and in some cases bitter disputes over land ownership fuelled local resentments, division and corruption.

quietly in a hammock; bring insect repellent to combat sandflies. More popular with surfers than beachcombers are the island's reef point breaks – most notably **Caranero Point** – suitable for intermediate and advanced surfers. There are also some less challenging 'beginner' waves, including **Black Rock**.

## Isla Solarte

Isla Solarte, also known as **Nancy Cay**, is a small, quiet, verdant island inhabited by a handful of expats and a community of Ngäbe fishermen. At its westernmost tip lies Hospital Point, named after the old UFC medical facilities built in 1899. The pioneering hospital treated many thousands of banana workers for malaria and other tropical diseases before it was decommissioned and removed to Almirante in 1920. Today, local historian and former United Fruit scientist, Clyde Stephens, owns the plot where it once stood. Clyde has written some interesting books on the history of Bocas, available in **Bocas Books** on Isla Colón (see page 975). There are a couple of walking trails that snake Isla Solarte's length, and the surrounding waters are sheltered, rich in coral and particularly good for diving and snorkelling.

## Isla Bastimentos

For verdant nature and swashbuckling adventure, you can't do much better than Isla Bastimentos. Named after an old Spanish word for 'supplies', Bastimentos is where Christopher Columbus re-stocked his ships with provisions. Thick with rainforests and mangroves, it is the second largest island in the archipelago and has a procession of wave-lashed beaches.

The island's principal community, **Old Bank** (also known as **Bastimentos Town**), is a ramshackle Afro-Caribbean settlement of strutting roosters, lilting Calypso rhythms and talkative, terminally idle characters. Clinging to the island shore with a helter-skelter profusion of rickety old piers and teetering clapboard houses, it appears to be sliding, slowly, nonchalantly and inexorably into the waves. There's not much to do but sling a hammock and soak up the carefree vibe. If you need to stretch your legs, a 15-minute uphill walk from the police station leads to an interesting organic farm, **Up In the Hill** ⓘ *T6607-8962, www.upinthehill.com*, where they produce a range of cacao-based products, and coconut oil infused with herbs and wild flowers; highly recommended.

The searing northern coastline of Bastimentos boasts a shifting succession of broad sandy beaches, forested headlands, rugged coves, sheltered bays, teeming coral reefs, and epic surf breaks. The legendary site of Silverbacks, close to the northwest tip of the island, sees 7-m-high Hawaiian-style waves, suitable for advanced surfers only (peaks December to February); take a water taxi to get there, US$5. Further east, **Playa Wizard**, also known as Playa Primera, is the first in a series. To get there from Old Bank follow a path over the hill that starts at the east side of the village, 20 minutes; wear proper shoes as the trail can be muddy. The waves at Playa Wizard are powerful, good for intermediate surfers, but also filled with rip-tides and unsuitable for swimming. Do not leave valuables unattended.

From Playa Wizard, an interesting **hiking trail** heads east, skirting the shore and occasionally ducking into the rainforest where you can spot strawberry-coloured poison dart frogs; check on the trail's safety status before setting out. After approximately 20 minutes, you'll pass **Playa Segunda** or Second Beach, followed shortly after by **Red Frog Beach**, the site of a resort and residential complex that boasts a paved road, and to speed your escape, a marina. Overland, the trail continues east, soon arriving at **Magic Bay** and then the sheltered waters of **Playa Polo**, where several coral reefs can be explored and the waters are generally calm. **Playa Larga** lies another 30 minutes away and is an important nesting site for leatherback and hawksbill turtles, which arrive en masse from March to September. Sea access to this final stretch of coast is generally restricted to the calm months of March to April and September to October.

Created in 1988, the Parque Nacional Marino Isla Bastimentos encompasses an area of 13,226 ha, with over 85% of it marine. Arcing over the island in a rough R shape, the park protects the scintillating **Cayos Zapatillas**, a pair of pristine 'desert isles' fringed by white-sand beaches. They are managed by ANAM, who maintain a rangers' station; admission is US$10, sometimes included in tour costs. The snorkelling and diving in the surrounding waters is worthwhile, with vast shelves of teeming coral, dolphins, sharks, rays and many diverse fish species. The islands' shores are also nesting sites for hawksbill and leatherback turtles and the easternmost island has an easy walking trail.

Isla Bastimentos is home to a few interesting community tourism projects. The friendly Ngäbe village of **Quebrada Sal** (Salt Creek) is perched on its eastern shore. Visitors can enjoy traditional food, dances and *artesanía* presentations, as well as guided hikes on four different trails, each lasting up to an hour. The project is managed by the **Alianza de Turismo de Salt Creek** ⓘ *T6155-0614, www.aliatur.bocas.com; call ahead to arrange your visit*. The Ngäbe village at **Bahía Honda** is home to a small community meeting hall, a chapel, primary school and restaurant. Plentiful *artesanías* are available and you are welcome to stay for lunch, but most people come to experience the **Trail of the Sloth**. Managed by the **Timorogo community tourism project** ⓘ *T6726-0968, www.timorogo. bocasdeltoro.org*, the trail takes visitors along a mangrove creek by traditional dugout *cayuco* (kayak).

Located off the southeast tip of the island, **Cayo Crawl**, also known as **Coral Cay**, is actually a narrow channel between Isla Bastimentos and Isla Popa. It offers excellent snorkelling in the calm waters of a coral garden. Popular with Bocas tour operators, many groups pause for a lunch at Cayo Crawl, mooring at one of the rickety and locally famous restaurants.

## Isla San Cristóbal

Isla San Cristóbal covers an area of 37 sq km and is home to one of the largest Ngäbe villages in the region, **San Cristóbal**, where fishing and subsistence farming are the mainstay of local life. On the southeast shores of the island lies **Laguna Bocatorito**, or **Dolphin Bay**, a bottlenose dolphin breeding ground. In high season, boatloads of tourists often arrive together in the morning and chase the pods around in what must be a very familiar (and probably tedious) ritual for the animals.

## Isla Popa

Isla Popa is one of the largest islands in the archipelago and home to rustic Ngäbe communities who are rarely visited but keen to attract interest. Perched on the island's northwest flank, the village of **Popa 1** is the oldest and most populous of its communities and a good place to start your explorations. Further south, the slightly smaller and younger community of **Popa 2** is composed of Ngäbe migrants from all over the province. Intriguing mangrove and rainforest trails commence in the village, home to the **Meri Ngobe Community Tourism Project** ① www.meringobe.bocasdeltoro.org, which offers simple (but comfortable) accommodation, guides and *artesanías*.

## Listings Bocas del Toro archipelago *map p966*

### Tourist information

The monthly magazine, *Bocas Breeze*, www.thebocasbreeze.com, is an expat-led effort and a good source of local news. You can find it in hotels and restaurants throughout Bocas town.

### Where to stay

#### Isla Colón

#### $$$$ Punta Caracol
*Western side of the island, T757-9410, www.puntacaracol.com.*
Located in a secluded enclave on the western side of the island, Punta Caracol is an exclusive and famous eco-resort consisting of a string of thatched luxury bungalows arcing over the water on their own private pier. The most expensive lodgings in the area, first class and very attentive.

#### $$$$-$$$ Bocas del Toro
*Calle 2a, T757-9771, www.hotelbocasdeltoro.com.*
This attractive boutique hotel on the seafront has been constructed with 11 types of hardwood. It has large clean, comfortable rooms, some with excellent sea views.

There's a restaurant, kayak rental, tours by arrangement and Wi-Fi. Rooms are well equipped with TVs, a/c, orthopaedic mattresses, electronic safes, telephones, coffee-makers and a complimentary bag of organic coffee. Recommended.

#### $$$$-$$$ Tropical Suites
*Calle 1a, T757-9880.*
Boutique hotel in the heart of downtown Bocas. A range of suites have fully equipped kitchens, attractive wood furnishings, Wi-Fi, a/c, TVs and, in some cases, jacuzzis. Rates vary with views and season. Sometimes good internet rates are available. Breakfast included.

#### $$$ Bahía
*South end of Main St, T757-9626, www.ghbahia.com.*
Built in 1905, this interesting historic building was the former HQ of the **United Fruit Company**; check out the intriguing old photos on the walls. All rooms have hot water, TV and a/c; the remodelled rooms are more expensive. There's a Peruvian restaurant in front and Wi-Fi is available. Ask to see a room before accepting.

### $$$ Bocas Inn Lodge
*North end of Main St, T757-9600,*
*www.anconexpeditions.com.*
Run by tour operator **Ancon Expeditions**
(see page 879). Comfortable and simple
with pleasant, spacious bar and terrace,
communal veranda upstairs and platform
for swimming. The water is heated with
solar panels. Crab and lobster off the menu
due to overfishing concerns. Prices include
breakfast. Good reviews.

### $$$ Palma Royale
*Main St, www.palmaroyale.com.*
A new condo-style establishment that's
received good reviews from guests. They
offer a range of designer suites (**$$$**),
studios (**$$$$**) and a penthouse (**$$$$**) with
handsome hand-crafted wood furniture,
TVs, Wi-Fi and all the usual amenities.

### $$ Casa Amarilla
*Calle 5a and Av G, T757-9938,*
*www.casaamarilla.org.*
4 large airy rooms with good beds, a/c,
fridge, digital safe, laptops, Wi-Fi and large
cable TVs. Owner Dennis Fischer lives
upstairs and is helpful and interesting to chat
to. Free coffee and tea all day. A good place
and recommended. Space is limited, so book
in advance.

### $$ Cocomo-on-the-Sea
*Av Norte y Calle 6a, T757-9259,*
*www.cocomoonthesea.com.*
A lovely B&B on the seafront with a lush
tropical garden, sundeck and 4 clean,
simple rooms with a/c and private bath.
A huge all-you-can-eat breakfast is included,
book swap, Wi-Fi, laundry service, free use
of kayaks, refrigerator and beach towels.
US owner Douglas is a superb fellow and
very helpful; he can hook you up with some
of the best guides on the island. Nice place
and recommended.

### $$ Hotelito del Mar
*Calle 1a, T757-9861, www.hotelitodelmar.com.*
Rooms are quiet, sparklingly clean and
adorned with vibrant artwork. They all have
private bath, hot water, cable TV, Wi-Fi
and a/c. Tourist information is available
and tours by arrangement. The owner is
friendly. Good central location. Continental
breakfast included.

### $$ Lula's B&B
*Av Norte, across street from Cocomo-on-the-*
*Sea, T757-9057, www.lulabb.com.*
Old-style, family-run place with a kitchenette
and deck upstairs and a living area
downstairs. This is the base of operations for
**Bocas Surf School**. All rooms come with a/c,
private bath, safe and hot water; Wi-Fi and
full breakfast are included. Owners Bryan
and Jana Hudson are friendly and helpful.
Homely, clean, quiet, safe and very secure.

### $ Casa Verde
*Av Sur, T6633-8050, www.casaverdebocas.com.*
This small, friendly hostel has a range of
simple private rooms, all kitted with a/c,
fridge, electronic safe and shared bath with
hot water. Various cheap dorm beds are also
available. Communal kitchen, Wi-Fi, internet
terminal, a sea deck for swimming, inner
tubes, and a buzzing little bar-restaurant
where you can pick up quesadillas and
other snacks. Affordable tours depart daily.
Recommended.

### $ Heike
*Calle 3a, on the plaza, T757-9708,*
*www.hostelheike.com.*
A friendly, inexpensive backpackers' hostel
with 2 private rooms, 6 dorms, shared
bathrooms, kitchen, communal veranda,
coffee all day and a cosy sun terrace complete
with hammocks, internet terminals, good
breezes and sofas. Surfboards are available
for rent, free use of the guitars, filtered water
and pancake breakfast included.

### $ Sagitarius
*Calle 4a, T757-9578,*
*hsagitario@cwpanama.net.*
Simple, reasonably priced wooden rooms
with hot water, bath, TV and a/c (cheaper
with fan). Locally owned, clean and good
for budget wanderers.

## Isla Caranero

### $$$ Buccaneer Resort
*East side, T757-9042,*
*www.bocasbuccaneer.com.*
Situated close to good surf breaks,
swimming areas and coral reef, Buccaneer
offers a range of simple, wooden lodgings to
suit families, groups and couples. Their suites
sleep 4 and include great sea views, a/c,
fridge, hammocks, balcony and private bath
with hot water. Smaller, cheaper bungalows
sleep 3 and include similar amenities. For
more adventurous types there are rustic
*cabañas*. Wi-Fi available and breakfast
included. Friendly, helpful management.

### $$ Hotel Tierra Verde
*T757-9903, www.hoteltierraverde.com.*
A well-maintained hotel situated among
coconut palms, a stone's throw from the
shore. Rooms have private showers, hot
water and Wi-Fi. Those with ocean view cost
US$10 more. The hotel can arrange tours and
sometimes walk-in rates apply. Continental
breakfast included. Comfortable and friendly.

### $ Aqua Lounge Hostel and Bar
*T6456-4659, www.bocasaqualounge.info.*
A very cool and popular hostel that flies in
DJs for their famous twice-weekly parties. At
most other times the hostel is quiet. Plenty of
useful amenities including a chill-out terrace
on the water, swimming area, hammocks,
movie theatre, ping-pong, water trampoline,
Wi-Fi, restaurant, kitchen, laundry and bar.
Lodgings consist of large dorms and 6 simple
private rooms with shared bath. Happy hour
runs all day and the hostel regularly hosts
special events like barbecues and 'Beer
Olympics'. Prices include buffet breakfast.

## Isla Bastimentos

### $$$$ Al Natural
*Old Point, T757-9004,*
*www.alnaturalresort.com.*
Belgian-owned solar-powered ecolodge
bungalows built using traditional
techniques and native fallen trees.

Bungalows consist of 3 walls, leaving 1 side
open and exposed to a spectacular view
of the ocean and Zapatillas in the distance;
a truly natural experience. Price includes
transport from Isla Colón, 3 lovingly
prepared meals with wine, use of kayaks
and snorkelling gear. Email reservations in
advance. Highly recommended.

### $$$$ Eclypse de Mar
*Offshore, near Old Bank, T6611-4581,*
*www.eclypsedemar.com.*
Attractive 'Acqua-Lodge' in the same vein
as the famous **Punta Caracol**. Secluded
bungalows built over the water, all fully
equipped and with stunning sunset views.

### $$$ Coral Cay
*East of Isla Bastimentos, T6626-1919,*
*www.bocas.com/coralcay.htm.*
Peaceful, rustic cabins built over the
water. Beautiful surroundings and
outstanding seafood. Price includes
2 meals per day, snorkelling equipment
and the use of a traditional dugout canoe.
Watch out for sandflies.

### $$ Caribbean View Hotel
*Old Bank, T757-9442, hotelcaribbeanview@*
*yahoo.com.*
Wooden, traditional-style hotel with lovely
local owners and quite upmarket for rustic
Bastimentos Town. Rooms have a/c or fan,
private shower, hot water and TV. Wi-Fi,
kayaks, boat and cave tours also available.
There is a communal deck over the water.

### $ Hostal Bastimentos
*Old Bank, T757-9053,*
*www.hostalbastimento.com.*
This long-established budget hostel has
lots of interesting statues in the garden and
an elevated position overlooking the town.
Lodgings include ultra-cheap dorm beds
and a wide range of double rooms, cheaper
without private bath and more expensive
with hot water and fridge ($$). Amenities
include 2 shared kitchens, Wi-Fi, internet
terminal and free kayaks.

### $ Tío Tom's Guesthouse
*Old Bank, T757-9831,*
*www.tiotomsguesthouse.com.*
Dutch adventurer Tío Tom is a Bastimentos institution. He offers rustic wooden rooms on the water, all with private bath, and a pleasant bungalow with its own terrace (**$$**). Interesting extras include a small orchid garden, hydroponic crops, own produce, dive school, kayak rental, book exchange and an evening 'family meal' that uses local ingredients as much as possible. Very knowledgeable about Panama and the islands. Recommended.

## Isla Popa

### $$$$ Popa Paradise Beach Resort
*Isla Popa, T832-1498, www.popaparadise beachresort.com.*
High-end cabins and *casitas* with TV, a/c and balconies. 2 'penthouse' suites are also available, with kitchen, balcony, living room and dining area. Personal, professional attention and 'barefoot luxury'.

## Restaurants

### Isla Colón

### $$$ El Pecado
*Calle 3a, under Hotel Laguna.*
Panamanian and international food, including Lebanese. One of the best restaurants in town, and not too expensive. Great drinks and good wines worth splashing out on, also try their early evening hummus with warm Johnny cakes (coconut bread). Recommended.

### $$$ La Casbah
*Av G.*
Popular and intimate evening restaurant with seating inside and out. Dishes are fresh, creative and tasty with both local and Mediterranean inspiration. Catch of the day is good.

### $$ Buena Vista Bar and Grill
*Calle 2a.*
Long-standing restaurant/bar run by a very friendly Panamanian and his American girlfriend. Good menu for both bar snacks and main meals, grills, tacos, fish and veggie options. Good spot over the water to relax with a beer or cocktail.

### $$ El Ultimo Refugio
*Av Sur and Calle 5a.*
A ramshackle and romantic setting on the water with lots of candlelight and a plant-covered wooden deck. Creative dishes include Peruvian ceviche, marlin fillet, pork tenderloin, pineapple and ginger shrimp. Popular and recommended.

### $$ Gringos
*Calle 4a, behind Golden Grill.*
Authentic Tex-Mex menu with some classic recipes imported from Baja California. The nachos and salsa are excellent, the burritos rich and filling. Wholesome comfort food, popular with expats and recommended.

### $$ Lemongrass
*Calle 2a, next to Buena Vista, upstairs.*
One of the best in Bocas. The hospitable English owner has experience of cooking in Asia so expect good, authentic Thai curries and lots of fresh seafood. Good views over the bay and excellent bar for cocktails. Friendly, buzzing and recommended.

### $$-$ La Buguita
*Calle 3a, attached to La Buga dive shop.*
Popular with backpackers and divers, this little café on the water serves fish tacos, deli sandwiches, breakfast burritos, smoothies and mini-pizzas.

### $$-$ Lili's Café
*Calle 1a, next to Tropical Suites Hotel.*
*Open for breakfast and lunch only.*
Chilled-out and friendly café on the water serving Caribbean cuisine with a health food twist. Good range of breakfasts and mains, including pastas, soups, salads and sandwiches.

### $$-$ Om Café
*Av E. Closed Wed and Thu.*

Excellent, home-made Indian food served in very relaxing and ambient surroundings. Tables are available on the balcony or private rooms for larger parties. Om also serves good breakfasts with home-made granola and yoghurt, lassis, fruit salads and bagels. Recommended.

### $ Golden Grill
*Calle 3a, opposite the park.*

The fast-food emporium of Bocas: cheap burgers, chips and hot dogs, best consumed drunk. Takeaway available 24 hrs. Free Wi-Fi for customers.

### $ Restaurant Chitré
*Calle 3a.*

Long-running *fonda* serving cheap and cheerful buffet fare. Friendly owners, and a good spot for watching street traffic.

## Cafés, bakeries, delis and juice bars

### Bocas Blended
*Calle Norte, on the corner opposite Casa Max.*

Quirky old bus converted into a juice bar. There's conspicuous seating on the roof where you can watch the world go by. Juices are good and rich in vitamins, but not cheap. They also do wraps and other snacks.

### Panadería Dulcería Alemana
*Calle 2a.*

This small German bakery does tasty cakes, delicious fresh bread, good coffee and light snacks. Very good.

### Super Gourmet
*Calle 1a, near the ferry for Almirante.*

Deli and gourmet supermarket that does very good, if pricey, sandwiches, pastas and salads. You'll also find tasty local produce and plenty of foreign imports here.

## Isla Caranero

### $$ Bibi's on the Beach
*part of the* **Buccaneer Resort**, *east side of the island near Black Rock, T6785-7984, www. bibisonthebeach.com. Open for breakfast, lunch and dinner every day except Tue.*

Managed by friendly Argentine Luis Bertone, Bibi's has a great location overlooking Bastimentos and Solarte islands. They specialize in fresh, tasty, Creole-style seafood, including ceviche, prawns, lobster, whole fish, fillets, octopus and seafood platters. Salads, pastas, burgers and chicken dishes are also available. Good ambience. Recommended.

### $$ The Pickled Parrot
*facing Isla Bastimentos.*

Draught beers, Thai soups and American barbecues, with a daily happy hour 1500-1700. Owner George is a world-class raconteur and host. Lovely at sunset and great for drinking after dark.

## Isla Bastimentos

### $ Kechas
*Old Bank, north of the police station.*

Reliable Caribbean eatery on the water also known as Alvin's. They serve large plates of hearty local fare, including seafood, chicken and meat, all invariably accompanied by rice and plantain. Good value.

### $ Roots
*Old Bank.*

Locally famous bar and restaurant with a nice terrace over the water. They serve Caribbean seafood and other local fare. Closed for a while but now under new management, back on its feet and doing well.

### $ Sonrisas del Mar
*Old Bank, close to the northern tip.*

Perched on the water, this locals' favourite serves seafood and smoked chicken, as well as occasional 'exotics' and 'bush' meat, which may or may not be ethical depending on the species, source and season. Please order wisely.

## $ Up in the Hill
*15 mins from Old Bank, follow the path next to the police station.*
Intimate and ramshackle café attached to an interesting cacao and coconut farm. They serve hot coffee, fresh herbal teas, juices, brownies and exquisite truffles.

## Bars and clubs

### Isla Colón

#### Barco Hundido
*Calle 1a, next to Cable & Wireless office.*
The **Wreck Deck** (its original name) is built over a wrecked, sunken boat. Once very popular, there have been some negative reports lately.

#### Bocas Books
*Av E, under Om Café.*
One of the best English-language bookshops in Panama, also serving as a popular watering hole. The owner, Dave, is a convivial fellow with lots of interesting insights into island life. Stop by, browse the books, have a chat, drink a beer – or three. Recommended.

#### Bocas Wine Bar
*Av Central.*
The best of the expat hangouts, on the main drag with a breezy balcony overlooking the street below. Fine wines, as the name suggests.

#### La Mama Loca
*Inside Casa Verde (see Where to stay, above).*
Attracting a nice little crowd at the time of research. Beer, cocktails, shooters and shots by the waters' edge, and usually live music from 1800, including reggae. Friendly and recommended.

#### Mondo Taitu
*Av G.*
Busy and often buzzing bar in a backpackers' hostel. Good for beer, cocktails, hookah pipes and meeting other travellers. A young, brazen, party-loving crowd.

#### Rip Tide
*Calle Norte, the waterfront.*
A salty expat bar built into a big old boat on the water. Good for a beer and politically incorrect conversation, but not for innocents.

#### Toro Loco
*Av Central, between Calle 1a and 2a.*
A US-style grill and bar with loud music, sports TV, dartboard and various dark little corners. Popular with expats.

### Isla Caranero

#### Aqua Lounge
*2 mins from Bocas.*
An estimated 300-400 people attend the legendary parties at the Aqua Lounge, hosted every weekend and on an additional night in the week. Happy hour runs all day, giving you plenty of warm-up time. Good security and admission by invitation only (invites are distributed at hostels in Bocas town; otherwise just show up on the night and ask for one). Highly recommended.

### Isla Bastimentos
Every Mon everyone who wants to party heads over to Isla Bastimentos for **Blue Mondays**, a largely local event with live calypso music and the full Caribbean vibe. Hugely popular.

## Festivals

### Isla Colón
**Jul** The **Virgen del Carmen** is honoured in the 3rd week of Jul with pilgrimages to La Gruta.
**28 Sep-2 Oct** The **Feria del Mar** is held on the Playa Istmito with lots of music, dancing and fun.
**16 Nov** Celebrations commemorating the **foundation of Bocas del Toro**.

### Isla Bastimentos
**23 Nov** **Bastimentos Day**, featuring music, parades and good-natured revelry.

## What to do

### Isla Colón
#### Diving and snorkelling

Sep-Oct and Mar-Apr are the best months for diving and snorkelling. Bocas is a good place for beginners and courses are competitively priced during the low season.

**Bocas Watersports**, *Calle 3a, T757-9541, www.bocaswatersports.com*. Dive courses, waterskiing and kayak rental. Local 2-tank dives cost US$50, with longer 2-tank trips to Tiger Rock and the Zapatilla Cayes running at around US$75. Snorkelling gear costs US$5 a day. They offer a day-long snorkelling tour to Dolphin Bay, Crawl Cay, Red Frog and Hospital Point, snacks included, US$20. Training from Open Water Diver to Dive Master.

**La Buga Dive Center**, *Calle 3a, T757-9534, www.labugapanama.com*. An expanding and popular outfit. They offer training from Open Water Diver, US$245, to Dive Master. Specialities include Deep Diver, Night Diver and Underwater Naturalist. They claim to have the biggest, fastest boat in the area, and know special dive sites their competitors don't.

**Starfleet**, *Calle 1a, next to Buena Vista, T757-9630, www.starfleetscuba.com*. A very professional, PADI Gold Palm IDC centre, managed by Brits Tony and Georgina Sanders. They offer training from Open Water Diver, US$175-235, up to Instructor level. A 2-tank dive is US$60, a day-long snorkel tour, US$20. They have over 17 years' experience in Bocas waters and notably sponsored Panama's first and only native PADI course director. Impeccable safety record, with good instructors and equipment. Dive Master internships also available. Highly recommended.

#### Sailing

**Catamaran Sailing Adventures**, *Av Sur y Calle 6a, next to Hotel Dos Palmas, T757-9710 or T6464-4242, www.bocassailing.com*. Owner Marcel offers popular day sailing tours on his 12-m-long catamaran around the Bocas Islands for US$44, including lunch and snorkelling gear. Very knowledgeable when it comes to finding the best reef areas; you can also hire the whole boat from US$400 and do a customized trip. Trips leave daily at 0930, but you will need advance reservation. Environmentally aware and recommended.

#### Surfing

You can rent boards from hostels like Mondo Taitu and Heike. There are 2 surf shops in town, **Tropix**, on Calle 3a (T757-9415) who make custom boards and **Flow**, located under **Om Café**. **Bocas Surf School** operates from Lula's B&B (Av H, T6482-4166, www.bocassurfschool.com).

#### Tour operators

There are numerous tour operators, most have maps and photos to help plan your day. Typical tours visit either Dolphin Bay, Hospital Point, Coral Cay and Red Frog Beach (Bastimentos), or Boca del Drago and Swans Cay (Bird Island). For a little extra you can add Cayos Zapatilla to the 1st tour.

#### Yoga

**Bocas Yoga**, *Calle 4a, the big purple building, www.bocasyoga.com*. Dedicated Yoga studio with daily classes in Hatha, Vinyasa and Anusara-inspired yoga. Drop-in rates US$5 per class, multi-class packages also available. Teachers are certified and experienced. Suitable for all levels, check for the latest schedule.

### Isla Caranero
#### Surfing, kayaking and snorkelling

**Aqua Lounge Surf School**, *T6456-4659, www.bocasaqualounge.info*. Surf coaching from US$40 half day; US$60 full day. A typical session includes surf theory, rules and etiquette, warm-up and actual surfing. They have a specialist surf photographer and your sessions can be combined with yoga lessons.

**Escuela del Mar**, *part of the Buccaneer Resort, east side of the island near Black Rock, T6785-7984, luisbertone@gmail.com.* Passionate surf instructor Luis Bertone has 20 years' experience riding waves. His surf school is perfectly positioned next to Black Rock, an ideal break for learners, and he offers instruction to all ages from US$45 for a half day to US$110 for 3 full days. Lessons can be 'kayak assisted' and rentals include long boards, short boards, body boards, kayaks (very affordable) and snorkel gear. Recommended.

### Isla Bastimentos
#### Diving and snorkelling
**Scuba 6 Dive Center**, *Old Bank, inside Tío Tom's Guesthouse, T6793-2722, www. scuba6diving.com.* An enthusiastic new outfit managed by experienced and adventurous divers. They offer PADI Open Water certification, training up to Assistant Instructor and preparation for IDC. Groups are kept small and course materials are available in German, English, Dutch or Spanish. Recommended.

## Transport

### Isla Colón
**Air** Bocas del Toro can be reached with **Air Panama** twice daily from Albrook Airport, US$140 one-way including taxes. There are also international services with Costa Rica's Nature Air. Call **Bocas International Airport** for details, Av E and Calle 6a, Bocas Town, Isla Colón, T757-9841.

**Bicycles** Bicycles are a good way to get around Isla Colón.

**Boat** To **Almirante**, water taxis run daily 0530-1830, 30 mins, US$3. *Palanga*, the car ferry, runs between **Almirante** and Bocas every day, leaving at 0900 and returning from Bocas at 1200. US$15 per car (more for large vehicles), US$1 for foot passengers. If you're travelling to San José, Costa Rica, set off at dawn.

From Isla Colón to the other islands, including **Caranero**, **Bastimentos** and **Solarte**, water taxis depart from waterfront piers along Calle Primera; ask around The Pirate, Taxi 25, near IPAT or the dock for Bocas Marine Tours. Fares are US$1-5 one way and always rising with the cost of gasoline. On other islands, waving a large flag (provided at piers) should summon a passing taxi, or simply ask the nearest restaurant or hotel to call up a boatman. From Caranero or Bastimentos Town it's easy to flag down a passing boat. If going to remote beaches, always arrange a pick up time. If hiring a boat, try to arrange it the day before, at least US$60-100 per day (4 hrs minimum, can take 9 people or more, depending on boat size).

**Taxi** Taxis cost US$0.50 colectivo, or US$1 at night.

# Background

# Regional
### history

## Arrival of the American people

While controversy continues to surround the precise date humans arrived in the Americas, the current prevailing view suggests the first wave of emigrants travelled between Siberia and Alaska across the Bering Strait ice bridge created in the last Ice Age, approximately 15,000 years ago. Small hunter-gatherer groups quickly moved through the region, and in fertile lands they developed agriculture and settled. By 1500 BC sedentary villages were widespread in many parts of the Americas, including Central America, where stone-built cities and complex civilizations also began to emerge.

## Pre-Columbian civilizations

Despite the wide variety of climates and terrains that fall within Central America's boundaries, the so-called Mesoamerican civilizations were interdependent, sharing the same agriculture based on maize, beans and squash, as well as many sociological traits. These included an enormous pantheon of gods, pyramid-building, a trade in valuable objects, hieroglyphic writing, astronomy, mathematics and a complex calendar system. Historians divide Mesoamerican civilizations into three broad periods, the **pre-Classic**, which lasted until about AD 300, the **Classic**, until AD 900, and the **post-Classic**, from AD 900 until the Spanish conquest.

### Olmecs

Who precisely the Olmecs were, where they came from and why they disappeared is a matter of debate. It is known that they flourished from about 1400-400 BC, lived in the **Mexican Gulf coast** region between Veracruz and Tabasco, and that all later civilizations have their roots in Olmec culture. They are particularly renowned for their carved **colossal heads**, jade figures and altar. They gave great importance to the jaguar and the serpent in their imagery and built large ceremonial centres such as **San Lorenzo** and **La Venta**. The progression from the Olmec to the Maya civilization seems to have taken place at Izapa on the Pacific border of present-day Mexico and Guatemala.

### Maya

The best known of the pre-Conquest civilizations were the Maya, thought to have evolved in a formative period in the **Pacific highlands** of Guatemala and El Salvador between 1500 BC and about AD 100. After 200 years of growth it entered what is known today as its Classic period, when the civilization flourished in Guatemala, El Salvador, Belize, Honduras and southern Mexico. The height of the Classic period lasted until AD 900, after which the Maya resettled in the Yucatán, possibly after a devastating famine, drought or peasant uprising. They then came under the influence of the central Mexican Toltecs, who were highly militaristic, until the Spanish conquest in the 16th century.

Throughout its evolution, Mayan civilization was based on independent city states that were governed by a theocratic elite of priests, nobles and warriors. Recent research has revealed that these cities, far from being the peaceful ceremonial centres once imagined, were **warring adversaries** striving to capture victims for sacrifice. This change in perception of the Maya was largely due to a greater understanding of Mayan **hieroglyphic writing**, which appears both on paper codices and on stone monuments. Aside from a gory preoccupation with sacrifice, Mayan culture was rich in **ceremony, art, science, folklore** and **dance**. Their cities were all meticulously designed according to strict and highly symbolic geometric rules: columns, figures, faces, animals, friezes, stairways and temples often expressed a date, a time or a specific astronomical relationship. Impressively, the Mayan calendar was so advanced that it was a nearer approximation to sidereal time than either the Julian or the Gregorian calendars of Europe; it was only .000069 of a day out of true in a year. The Maya also formulated the concept of 'zero' centuries in advance of the Old World, plotted the movements of the sun, moon, Venus and other planets, and conceived a time cycle of more than 1800 million days.

## Conquest

It was only during his fourth voyage, in 1502, that **Columbus** reached the mainland of Central America. He landed in **Costa Rica** and Panama, which he called **Veragua**, and founded the town of Santa María de Belén. In 1508 Alonso de Ojeda received a grant of land on the Pearl coast east of Panama, and in 1509 he founded the town of San Sebastián, later moved to a new site called Santa María la Antigua del Darién (now in Colombia). In 1513 the governor of the colony at Darién was **Vasco Núñez de Balboa**. Taking 190 men he crossed the isthmus in 18 days and caught the first glimpse of the Pacific; he claimed it and all neighbouring lands in the name of the King of Spain. But from the following year, when **Pedrarias de Avila** replaced him as Governor, Núñez de Balboa fell on evil days, and he was executed by Pedrarias in 1519. That same year Pedrarias crossed the isthmus and founded the town of Panamá on the Pacific side. It was in April 1519, too, that **Cortés** began his conquest of Mexico. Central America was explored from these two nodal points of Panama and Mexico.

### Settlement

The groups of Spanish settlers were few and widely scattered, a fundamental point in explaining the **political fragmentation** of Central America today. Panama was ruled from Bogotá, but the rest of Central America was subordinate to the Viceroyalty at Mexico City, with Antigua, Guatemala, as an Audiencia for the area until 1773, and thereafter Guatemala City. Panama was of paramount importance for colonial Spanish America for its strategic position, and for the trade passing across the isthmus to and from the southern colonies. The other provinces were of comparatively little value.

The small number of Spaniards intermarried freely with the locals, accounting for the predominance of mestizos in present-day Central America. But the picture has regional variations. In Guatemala, where there was the highest native population density, intermarriage affected fewer of the natives, and over half the population today is still purely *indígena* (**indigenous**). On the Meseta Central of Costa Rica, the natives were all but wiped out by disease and, as a consequence of this great disaster, there is a community of over two million whites, with little *indígena* admixture. **Blacks** predominate along the Caribbean coast of Central America. Most were brought in as cheap labour to work as railway builders and banana planters in the 19th century and canal cutters in the 20th. The Garífuna people, living between southern Belize and Nicaragua, arrived in the area as free people after African slaves and indigenous Caribbean people intermingled following a shipwreck off St Vincent.

## Independence and after

On 5 November 1811, **José Matías Delgado**, a priest and jurist born in San Salvador, organized a revolt with another priest, Manuel José Arce. They proclaimed the Independence of El Salvador, but the Audiencia at Guatemala City suppressed the revolt and took Delgado prisoner. Eleven years later, in 1820, the revolution of Spain itself precipitated the Independence of Central America. On 24 February 1821, the Mexican **General Agustín de Iturbide** announced his **Plan de Iguala** for an independent Mexico. Several months later, the Central American *criollos* followed his example and announced their own **Declaration of Independence** in Guatemala City on 15 September 1821. Iturbide invited the provinces of Central America to join with him and, on 5 January 1822, Central America was annexed to Mexico. Delgado, however, refused to accept this decree and Iturbide, who had now assumed the title of **Emperor Agustín I**, sent an army south under Vicente Filísola to enforce it. Filísola had completed his task when he heard of Iturbide's abdication, and at once convened a general congress of the Central American provinces. It met on 24 June 1823, and thereafter established the **Provincias Unidas del Centro de América**. The Mexican Republic acknowledged their Independence on 1 August 1824, and Filísola's soldiers were withdrawn.

### The United Provinces of Central America

In 1824, the first congress, presided over by Delgado, appointed a provisional governing *junta* which promulgated a constitution modelled on that of the United States. The Province of Chiapas was not included in the Federation, as it had already adhered to Mexico in 1821. Guatemala City, by force of tradition, soon became the seat of government.

The first president under the new constitution was **Manuel José Arce**, a liberal. One of his first acts was to **abolish slavery**. El Salvador, protesting that he had exceeded his powers, rose in December 1826. Honduras, Nicaragua and Costa Rica joined the revolt, and in 1828 **General Francisco Morazán**, in charge of the army of Honduras, defeated the federal forces, entered San Salvador and marched against Guatemala City. He captured the city on 13 April 1829, and established that contradiction in terms: a liberal dictatorship. Many conservative leaders were expelled and church and monastic properties confiscated. Morazán himself became President of the Federation in 1830. He was a man of considerable ability; he ruled with a strong hand, encouraged education, fostered trade and industry, opened the country to immigrants, and reorganized the administration. In 1835 the capital was moved to San Salvador.

These reforms antagonized the conservatives and there were several uprisings. The most serious revolt was among the *indígenas* of Guatemala, led by Rafael Carrera, an illiterate mestizo conservative and a born leader. Years of continuous warfare followed, during the course of which the Federation withered away. As a result, the federal congress passed an act which allowed each province to assume the government it chose, but the idea of a federation was not quite dead. Morazán became President of El Salvador. Carrera, who was by then in control of Guatemala, defeated Morazán in battle and forced him to leave the country. But in 1842, Morazán overthrew Braulio Carrillo, then dictator of Costa

Rica, and became president himself. At once he set about rebuilding the Federation, but a popular uprising soon led to his capture. He was shot on 15 September 1842 and with him perished any practical hope of Central American political union.

## The separate states

The history of **Guatemala, El Salvador, Honduras** and **Nicaragua** since the breakdown of federation has been tempestuous in the extreme (**Costa Rica**, with its mainly white population and limited economic value at the time, is a country apart, and **Panama** was Colombian territory until 1903). In each, the ruling class was divided into pro-clerical conservatives and anti-clerical liberals, with constant changes of power. Each was weak, and tried repeatedly to buttress its weakness by alliances with others, which invariably broke up because one of the allies sought a position of mastery. The wars were mainly ideological wars between conservatives and liberals, or wars motivated by inflamed nationalism. Nicaragua was riven internally by the mutual hatreds of the Conservatives of Granada and the Liberals of León, and there were repeated conflicts between the Caribbean and interior parts of Honduras. Despite the permutations and combinations of external and civil war there has been a recurrent desire to re-establish some form of **La Gran Patria Centroamericana**. Throughout the 19th century, and far into the 20th, there were ambitious projects for political federation, usually involving El Salvador, Honduras and Nicaragua; none of them lasted more than a few years.

## Regional integration

Poverty, the fate of the great majority, has brought about closer economic cooperation between the five republics, and in 1960 they established the **Central American Common Market** (CACM). Surprisingly, the Common Market appeared to be a great success until 1968, when integration fostered national antagonisms, and there was a growing conviction in Honduras and Nicaragua, which were doing least well out of integration, that they were being exploited by the others. In 1969 the 'Football War' broke out between El Salvador and Honduras, basically because of a dispute about illicit emigration by Salvadoreans into Honduras, and relations between the two were not normalized until 1980. Hopes for improvement were revived in 1987 when the Central American Peace Plan, drawn up by President Oscar Arias Sánchez of Costa Rica, was signed by the presidents of Guatemala, El Salvador, Honduras, Nicaragua and Costa Rica. The plan proposed formulae to end the civil strife in individual countries, achieving this aim first in Nicaragua (1989), then in El Salvador (1991). In Guatemala, a ceasefire after 36 years of war led to the signing of a peace accord at the end of 1996. With the signing of peace accords, emphasis has shifted to regional, economic and environmental integration.

In October 1993, the presidents of Guatemala, El Salvador, Honduras, Nicaragua and Costa Rica signed a new **Central American Integration Treaty Protocol** to replace that of 1960 and set up new mechanisms for regional integration. The Treaty was the culmination of a series of annual presidential summits held since 1986 which, besides aiming for peace and economic integration, established a Central American Parliament and a Central American Court of Justice. Attempts at further economic and regional integration continue. Plans to create a **Free Trade Area of the Americas** (FTAA) appear to have failed, but the 2003 **Dominican Republic-Central American Free Trade Agreement** (DR-CAFTA) has now been signed by several nations including the Dominican Republic, Guatemala, El Salvador, Honduras, Nicaragua and Costa Rica.

The DR-CAFTA closely compliments the 2001 **Plan Puebla-Panama** (the PPP, also known as the Mesoamerican Integration and Development Project) an economic corridor stretching from Puebla, west of Mexico City, as far as Panama. Supporters of the plan see it as a means for economic development. Critics see it as a way of draining cheap labour and natural resources with little concern for the environment or long-term progress. Today, the PPP simmers on the back burner, but the desire for Central American nations to strengthen ties is regularly voiced. This is most apparent in the creation of Central America 4 (CA-4), a 2006 border control agreement between Guatemala, El Salvador, Honduras and Nicaragua, that opens up travel between the four nations. Regional meetings occur periodically to promote and encourage trust and cooperation, and while the final destination of such cooperation is far from clear, the Central America of today is far more productive and safer than it was in the 1980s and early 1990s.

# Mexico

## History

### Spanish rule

The remarkable conquest of Mexico began when 34-year-old **Hernán Cortés** disembarked near the present Veracruz with about 500 men, some horses and cannon, on 21 April 1519. They marched into the interior and were admitted into the Aztec capital of Tenochtitlán in November. There they remained until 30 June of the following year, when they were expelled after a massacring a group of Aztec nobles. The next year Cortés came back with reinforcements and besieged the city. It fell on 30 August 1521, and was utterly razed. Cortés then turned to the conquest of the rest of the country.

By the end of the 16th century the Spaniards had founded most of the towns that are still important, tapped great wealth in mining, stock raising and sugar-growing, and firmly imposed their way of life and beliefs. Government was by a Spanish-born upper class, based on the subordination of the *indígena* and mestizo populations and there was a strict dependence on Spain for all things. As with the rest of Hispanic America, Spain built up resistance to itself by excluding from government both Spaniards born in Mexico and the small body of educated mestizos.

### Independence

The flag of revolt was raised in 1810 by the curate of Dolores, **Miguel Hidalgo**, who collected 80,000 armed supporters. Had it not been for Hidalgo's loss of nerve, the capital might have been captured in the first month, but 11 years of fighting created bitter differences. A loyalist general, **Agustín de Iturbide**, joined the rebels and proclaimed an independent Mexico in 1821. A federal republic was created on 4 October 1824, with General Guadalupe Victoria as president. In 1836, Texas rebelled against the dictator, Santa Ana, and declared its Independence. It was annexed by the United States in 1845. War broke out and, under the terms of the peace treaty, the US acquired half Mexico's territory.

### Benito Juárez

A period of liberal reform dominated by independent Mexico's great hero, the Zapoteco, Benito Juárez, began in 1857. The church, in alliance with the conservatives, hotly contested his programme and the constant civil strife wrecked the economy. Juárez was forced to suspend payment on the national debt, causing the French to invade and occupy Mexico City in 1863. They imposed the **Archduke Maximilian of Austria** as

Mexican Emperor, but under US pressure, withdrew their troops in 1867. Maximilian was captured by the *Juaristas* at Querétaro, tried, and shot on 19 June. Juárez resumed control of the country and died in July 1872.

## General Porfirio Díaz

Sebastián Lerdo de Tejada, the distinguished scholar who followed Juárez, was soon tricked out of office by **General Porfirio Díaz**, who ruled Mexico from 1876 to 1910. Díaz's paternal, though often ruthless, central authority introduced a period of 35 years of peace. A superficial prosperity followed, but the main mass of peasants had never been so wretched. It was this open contradiction between dazzling prosperity and hideous distress that led to the start of civil war (known as the Mexican Revolution) in November 1910, and to Porfirio Díaz's self-exile in Paris.

## The Mexican Revolution

A new leader, **Francisco Madero**, championed a programme of political and social reform, which included the restoration of stolen lands. Madero was initially supported by revolutionary leaders such as **Emiliano Zapata** in Morelos, **Pascual Orozco** in Chihuahua and **Pancho Villa**, also in the north. During his presidency (1911-1913), Madero neither satisfied his revolutionary supporters, nor pacified his reactionary enemies. After a coup in February 1913, led by General Victoriano Huerta, Madero was brutally murdered, but the great cry, *'Tierra y Libertad'* (Land and Freedom) was not to be quieted until the election of Alvaro Obregón to the Presidency in 1920. Before then, Mexico was in a state of civil war, leading first to the exile of Huerta in 1914, then the dominance of Venustiano Carranza's revolutionary faction over that of Zapata (assassinated in 1919) and Villa.

## The PRI

In 1946, the official ruling party assumed the name **Partido Revolucionario Institucional (PRI)**, and held a virtual monopoly over all political activity. In the late 1980s, disaffected PRI members and others formed the breakaway **Partido de la Revolución Democrática (PRD)**, which rapidly gained support. On New Year's Day of the election year, 1994, at the moment when the North American Free Trade Agreement (NAFTA) came into force, a guerrilla group, The **Ejército Zapatista de Liberación Nacional (EZLN)** briefly took control of several towns in Chiapas. Despite ongoing unrest, PRI candidate **Ernesto Zedillo Ponce de León**, a US-trained economist and former education minister, won a comfortable majority in the August elections.

On 20 December, just after his inauguration, Zedillo devalued the peso, claiming that political unrest was causing capital outflows. On 22 December a precipitate decision to allow the peso to float against the dollar caused an immediate crisis of confidence and investors in Mexico lost billions of dollars as the peso's value plummeted. Mexicans were hard hit by the recession and the ruling position of the PRI was damaged. In Chiapas, Zedillo suspended the controversial PRI governor, but the tension between the EZLN and the army continued as a 72-hour campaign to apprehend the EZLN leader, Subcomandante Marcos, failed. Talks recommenced in April, with the EZLN calling a ceasefire but the first peace accord was not signed until February 1996. Mid-term congressional elections held in July 1997 showed the PRI's grip on power was beginning to fade. The PRD surged to become the second largest party in the lower house.

## The PAN

During the 1999 presidential elections, Zedillo relinquished his traditional role in nominating his successor and the PRI had a US-style primary election to select a candidate. The PAN, meanwhile, chose former Coca-Cola executive **Vicente Fox** to lead their campaign. On 2 July 1999, Mexicans gave power to Fox, former governor of Guanajuato, and the PAN, prising it from the PRI for the first time in 71 years. An admirer of 'third way' politics and of ex-US President Bill Clinton and UK Prime Minister Tony Blair, Fox took office on 1 December 2000 announcing czar-led initiatives that would tackle government corruption, drug-trafficking, crime and poverty, and the economic conditions that drive migration to the US.

Elections in July 2006 saw a new president leading Mexico. Felipe Calderón, the candidate of the ruling conservative National Action Party (PAN) beat Andrés Manuel López Obrador of the centre-left Party of the Democratic Revolution (PRD) by a narrow margin, pushing Roberto Madrazo of the Institutional Revolutionary Party (PRI) into third place. Calderón came to power looking to reduce poverty, violence, tax evasion, corruption and his own salary by 10%. Public infrastructure projects on roads, airports, bridges and dams would also intend to stem outward migration of Mexico's workforce. Ultimately, Calderón's term was dominated by his extremely bloody war on drugs that has marred Mexico's northern states. Calderón's war failed to stem the flow of cocaine over the US border – or the flow of weapons from the opposite direction. The official death toll at the close of his administration in 2012 was 60,000, but some estimates put the figure twice as high, excluding the 27,000 who have gone missing.

### Return of the PRI
Amid civic protests and accusations of electoral fraud, Enrique Peña Nieto, PRI candidate and former governor of Mexico state, was elected with nearly 40% of the vote. Many feared a return to the old-school corruption and repression that characterized former PRI administrations. Despite allegations of corruption and the failure to reduce deaths in the war on drugs, Nieto won another term in Congress in the June 2015 elections.

## Culture

### People
About 9% of Mexico's population are considered white, about 30% *indígena* (indigenous); with about 60% mestizos, a mixture in varying proportions of Spanish and *indígena*. Mexico also has infusions of other Europeans, as well as Arabs and Chinese. There is a national cultural prejudice in favour of the indigenous rather than the Spanish element, though this does not prevent *indígena* from being looked down on by the more Hispanic elements. There is hardly a single statue of Cortés in the whole of Mexico, although he does figure, pejoratively, in the frescoes of Diego Rivera and his contemporaries. On the other hand the two last Aztec emperors, Moctezuma and Cuauhtémoc, are national heroes.

### The Mayans
The Yucatec Maya, occupying the Yucatán Peninsula, number some 2.45 million (with 892,723 Yucatec speakers) and are Mexico's biggest indigenous group after the Nahuas. The Yucatec Maya speak a single language with many distinct (but mutually intelligible) regional dialects. They lead lives with differing degrees of modernity. In eastern Chiapas, the Lacandón are a particularly fascinating, though sparsely numbered, lowland Maya group. Known as Hach Winik in their own language, which means 'real people', they are believed to be descended from refugees who fled Guatemala and Yucatán during the Spanish Conquest. In the highlands of Chiapas, the rugged topography provides niches for a network of 13 distinct ethnic groups, each with their own attire. Tzeltal, Tzotzil,

Tojolabal and Mam are their main languages. Community life is orientated around the family, a cargo system of civic duties, and religion – for which Alteños, as highlanders are called, are especially famous.

## Land and environment

### Geography

The land mass that is Mexico is the result of millions of years of geological moulding, a process that still continues today. The country continues to be regularly ignited by the spectacular eruptions of Popocatépetl, 60 km to the east of the capital, which has been slowly wakening from a 65-year slumber for several years and was most recently active with plumes of ash in January 2015. Likewise to the west of the capital, Colima volcano is closed to climbers, as activity that has been growing steadily in the last few years looks certain to result in an eruption. In April 2015, an impressive 3-km-high plume of ash erupted, with lightning spotted inside.

Mexico is roughly a quarter of the US in size, with which it has a frontier of 2400 km. The southern frontier of 885 km is with Guatemala and Belize. There is 2780 km of coast on the Gulf of Mexico and the Caribbean, and 7360 km on the Pacific. The structure of Mexico's land mass is extremely complicated, but may be simplified as a plateau flanked by ranges of mountains roughly paralleling the coasts. To the south, the Pacific coast of Oaxaca is forbidding and its few ports of little use, though there is tourism. After some 560 km, the highlands fall away into the low-lying Isthmus of Tehuantepec. Very different are the Gulf coast and Yucatán; half this area is classed as flat, and much of it gets enough rain the year round, leading to its having become one of the most important agricultural and cattle raising areas in the country. The Gulf coast also provides most of Mexico's oil and sulphur. Geographically, North America may be said to come to an end in the Isthmus of Tehuantepec. South of the Isthmus the land rises again into the thinly populated highlands of Chiapas, which extend for about 300 km southeast to the border with Guatemala.

East of Chiapas, the Yucatán is a limestone platform, comparatively flat and characterised by natural caverns, wells, sinkholes (*cenotes*) and white, sandy beaches. The northeast corner of Yucatán is the point nearest to Cuba and where the Caribbean Sea meets the Gulf of Mexico. The water passing through this passage initiates the current known as the Gulf Stream.

Perhaps the world's most dramatic geological happening ever recorded took place in Yucatán. It is now generally agreed that the cataclysm that almost ended life on the planet 65 million years ago was a small asteroid, weighing perhaps one billion tonnes, colliding with the earth at 160,000 kph. This left a hole many kilometres deep and over 150 km wide in the Yucatán, now known as the Chicxulub Crater.

# Belize

## History

Throughout the country, especially in the forests of the centre and south, there are many ruins of the Classic Maya period, which flourished here and in neighbouring Guatemala from the fourth to the ninth century and then, mysteriously (most probably because of drought), emigrated to Yucatán. It is estimated that the population was then 10 times what it is now.

The first settlers were English, with their black slaves from Jamaica, who came in about 1640 to cut logwood, then the source of textile dyes. The British Government made no claim to the territory but tried to secure the protection of the wood-cutters by treaties with Spain. Even after 1798, when a strong Spanish force was decisively beaten off at St George's Caye, the British Government still failed to claim the territory, though the settlers maintained that it had now become British by conquest.

When they achieved Independence from Spain in 1821, both Guatemala and Mexico laid claim to sovereignty over Belize, but these claims were rejected by Britain. Long before 1821, in defiance of Spain, the British settlers had established themselves as far south as the River Sarstoon, the present southern boundary. Independent Guatemala claimed that these settlers were trespassing and that Belize was a province of the new republic. By the middle of the 19th century Guatemalan fears of an attack by the United States led to a rapprochement with Britain. In 1859, a convention was signed by which Guatemala recognized the boundaries of Belize while, by Article 7, the United Kingdom undertook to contribute to the cost of a road from Guatemala City to the sea "near the settlement of Belize"; an undertaking that was never carried out.

Heartened by what it considered a final solution of the dispute, in 1862 Great Britain declared Belize, still officially a settlement, a colony, and a Crown Colony nine years later. Mexico, by treaty, renounced any claims it had on Belize in 1893, but Guatemala, which never ratified the 1859 agreement, renewed its claims periodically.

### Independence and after

Belize became independent on 21 September 1981, following a United Nations declaration to that effect. Guatemala refused to recognize the independent state, but in 1986 President Cerezo of Guatemala announced an intention to drop his country's claim to Belize. A British military force was maintained in Belize from Independence until 1993, when the British government announced that the defence of Belize would be handed over to the government on 1 January 1994, and that it would reduce the 1200-strong garrison to about 100 soldiers who would organize jungle warfare training facilities. The last British troops were withdrawn in 1994 and finance was sought for the expansion of the Belize Defence Force. Belize was admitted into the OAS in 1991 following negotiations with Guatemala and Britain. As part of Guatemala's recognition of Belize as an independent nation (ratified by Congress in 1992), Britain will recompense Guatemala by providing financial and technical assistance to construct road, pipeline and port facilities that will guarantee Guatemala access to the Atlantic.

Border friction is an ongoing issue between Belize and Guatemala, and in early 2000 tensions overflowed when Guatemalans took some members of the Belizean Defence

Force hostage for several days, eventually resulting in some Guatemalans being shot. Tensions were stretched to the limit, and periodically continue to rise and fall but now seem to have cooled and Guatemala has agreed to pursue its claim to half of Belizean territory through the international courts. Low-key negotiations continue between the two countries and in 2003 both countries agreed a draft settlement at Organization of American States (OAS) brokered talks. Progress was painfully slow, with Belize and Guatemala only signing up to a negotiation framework at the end of 2005.

## Culture

### People

The 2010 National Census put the population of Belize at 321,115. The urban/rural distribution continues to be roughly 50:50 as it was in 1991.

About 25% of the population are predominantly black and of mixed ancestry, the so-called Creoles, a term widely used in the Caribbean. They predominate in Belize City, along the coast and on the navigable rivers. About half of the population are mestizo; 10% are Maya, who predominate in the north between the Hondo and New rivers and in the extreme south and west. About 5% of the population are Garífuna (black Caribs), descendants of those deported from St Vincent in 1797; they have a distinct language, and can be found in the villages and towns along the southern coast. They are good linguists, many speaking Mayan languages as well as Spanish and 'Creole' English. They also brought their culture and customs from the West Indies, including religious practices and ceremonies, for example Yankanu (John Canoe) dancing at Christmas time. The remainder are of unmixed European ancestry (the majority Mennonites, who speak a German dialect, and are particularly friendly and helpful) and a rapidly growing group of North Americans. The Mennonites fall into two groups, generally speaking: the most rigorous, in the Shipyard area on The New River, and the more 'integrated' in the west, Cayo district, who produce much of Belize's poultry, dairy goods and corn. The newest Mennonite settlements are east of Progresso Lagoon in the northeast. There are also East Indian and Chinese immigrants and their descendants.

### Language

English is the official language, although for some 180,000 the lingua franca is 'Creole' English. Spanish is the lingua franca for about 130,000 people and is widely spoken in the northern and western areas. In addition, it is estimated that 22,000 people speak Mayan languages, 15,000 Garífuna and 3000 German.

## Land and environment

The coastlands are low and swampy with much mangrove, many salt and freshwater lagoons and some sandy beaches. In the north the land is low and flat, while in the southwest there is a heavily forested mountain massif with a general elevation of between 2000 and 3000 ft. In the east are the Maya Mountains, not yet wholly explored, and the Cockscomb Range which rises to a height of 3675 ft at Victoria Peak. Further west are some 250 square miles of the Mountain Pine Ridge, with large open spaces and some of the best scenery in the country.

From 10 to 40 miles off the coast an almost continuous, 184-mile line of reefs and cayes (or cays) provides shelter from the Caribbean, and forms the longest coral reef in the Western Hemisphere (the fifth-longest barrier reef in the world). Most of the cayes are quite tiny, but some have been developed into tourist resorts. Many have beautiful sandy beaches with clear, clean water, where swimming and diving are excellent. However, on the windward side of inhabited islands, domestic sewage is washed back on to the beaches, some of which are also affected by tar.

The most fertile areas of the country are in the foothills of the northern section of the Maya Mountains: citrus fruit is grown in the Stann Creek Valley, while in the valley of the Mopan, or upper Belize River, cattle raising and mixed farming are successful. The northern area of the country has long proved suitable for sugar cane production. In the south bananas and mangoes are cultivated. The lower valley of the Belize River is a rice-growing area as well as being used for mixed farming and citrus cultivation.

# Guatemala

## History

Under Pedro de Alvarado, the Spanish conquered Guatemala bit by bit from 1524 to 1697. The indigenous Maya died in their thousands from Western diseases and the survivors were forced to work and pay tribute under the *encomienda* system. In 1825 Guatemala became the capital of the Central American Federation until its dissolution in 1838. From 1839 to 1842, conservative governments restored Spanish institutions in a hark back to the colonial era. This trend was maintained by fiercely pro-church Rafael Carrera, who became president in 1844. He set about restoring church power and invited the Jesuits back into the country (they had been expelled in 1767). He went into exile in 1848 before returning to power in 1851 where he remained until 1865.

### The 1871 Liberal Revolution
On Carrera's death, Conservative General Vicente Cerna ruled Guatemala until 1871, when General Justo Rufino Barrios successfully overthrew his regime and introduced a wave of Liberal leadership. Miguel García Granados (1871-1873) reigned briefly, expelling leading clerics and overturning Carrera's invitation to the Jesuits. Thereafter, Justo Rufino Barrios (1873-1885) himself was elected president. He too was vehemently anticlerical. He expropriated church property, using the proceeds to found a national bank, secularized education and marriage. New ports and railways were constructed and coffee production was reformed, transforming Guatemala into a major producer. This was largely accomplished through the confiscation of indigenous lands. Barrios also tried to restore the federation and when the idea foundered he resorted to dictatorial methods. He invaded El Salvador when they refused to cooperate and died in a battle at Chalachuapa. Manuel Lisandro Barillas (1885-1892) followed in his footsteps and again tried unsuccessfully to re-establish Central American union. The Liberal trend continued with General José María Reina Barrios (1892-1898), who confiscated his enemies' property and spent much time quashing internal rebellion. During his term the price of coffee crashed on the world market, but public works using public money continued to be built, causing widespread outrage and revolts. He was assassinated.

### Dictatorship and the rise of the United Fruit Company
When Manuel Estrada Cabrera (1898-1920) came to power, his was the longest one-man rule in Central American history. Cabrera encouraged foreign investment, expansion

of the railways and the United Fruit Company's foray into Guatemala, granting it some 800,000 ha for the planting of bananas. The company's privileges included a monopoly on transport and a free rein over their own affairs. American interests in Guatemala grew to the point where 40% of all exports were US controlled. Cabrera was eventually toppled amid widespread discontent. Carlos Herrera followed but the old style military did not like his approach. He was overthrown in a bloodless military coup, bringing José María Orellana to power. Orellana negotiated more concessions for United Fruit and the railway company. However, organized protests over plantation workers' rights grew and periodically met with government crackdowns. Orellana, unlike some of his predecessors, died a natural death in 1926.

## Jorge Ubico

Jorge Ubico was an efficient but brutal dictator who came to power in 1931. He tightened political control, introduced a secret police, clamped down on workers' discontent and Communist movements, persecuted writers and intellectuals, promoted forced labour and fixed low wage rates. He also extended privileges to the United Fruit Company. These, and other issues, and the fact that he sought constant re-election, provoked widespread demonstrations calling for his resignation. In June 1944, following the death of a teacher in a protest demanding university autonomy, Ubico resigned and a triumvirate of generals assumed power.

## October Revolution

On 20 October 1944 there was an armed uprising of La Guardia de Honor, backed by popular support. The military leaders drew up a democratic constitution, abolished forced labour, and upheld the autonomy of the university. Teacher Juan José Arévalo of the Frente Popular Libertador party was then elected president and drew up a plan of social reform. He separated the powers of state, introduced *comedores* for children of poor workers, set up the Department for Social Security, and accepted the existence of the Communist Party. He survived more than 20 military coups and finished his term of five years (1945-1950).

## 1954 US-backed military coup

Jacobo Arbenz Guzmán, a member of the 1944 military triumvirate, became the elected president in 1950. His 1952 Agrarian Reform Law saw the expropriation of large, underutilized estates without adequate compensation awarded to their owners – mainly the United Fruit Company, which for years had been under-declaring the value of its land for tax reasons. According to the company, of its 550,000 acres around the Caribbean, 85% of it was not farmed. It was offered a measly US$2.99 an acre for land (440,000 acres) which it said was worth US$75. The company's connections with high-powered players within the US Government and the CIA, and its constant allegation that Communism was percolating through the Guatemalan corridors of power, eventually persuaded the US to sponsor an overthrow of the Arbenz government. Military strikes were launched on the country in June 1954. At the end of the month Arbenz, under pressure from Guatemalan military and the US ambassador John Peurifoy, resigned.

## Military rule

In June 1954 Colonel Carlos Castillo Armas took over the presidency. He persecuted and outlawed Communists. He was assassinated in 1957, which provoked a wave of violence and instability and for the next three decades the army and its right-wing supporters suppressed left-wing efforts, both constitutional and violent, to restore the gains made under Arévalo and Arbenz. Many thousands of people, mostly leftists but also many Maya without political orientation, were killed during this period.

## The rise of the guerrilla movement

On 13 November 1960, a military group, inspired by revolution in Cuba, carried out an uprising against the government. It was suppressed but spawned the **Movimiento 13 de Noviembre**, which then joined forces with the **Guatemalan Workers' Party**. In 1962, student demonstrations ended in bloodshed, which resulted in the creation of the **Movimiento 12 de Abril**. These movements then merged to form **Fuerzas Armadas Rebeldes** (FAR) in 1962.

During this period, Arévalo made a move to re-enter the political fold. A coup d'état followed. Guerrilla and right-wing violence began to increase in the late 1960s. In the early 1970s the guerrillas re-focused. The FAR divided into FAR and the EGP (Ejército Guerrillero de los Pobres, Guerrilla Army of the Poor), which operated in the north of the country. In 1972 the **Organización Revolucionaria del Pueblo en Armas** (ORPA) was formed. The EGP was led by Rolando Morán, a supporter of the Cuban Revolution. The group's first action took place in the Ixil Triangle in 1975. The ORPA was led by Commandante Gaspar Ilom, also known as Rodrigo Asturias, son of Nobel Prize for Literature winner Miguel Angel Asturias.

## The worst of the conflict

Throughout the 1970s and early 1980s the worst atrocities of the war were committed. **General Kjell Eugenio Laugerud García**'s presidency was characterized by escalating violence, which led the US to withdraw its support for the Guatemalan government in 1974. In 1976, a devastating earthquake struck Guatemala killing 23,000 people. This prompted widespread social movements in the country to improve the lives of the poor. At the same time, guerrilla activity surged. Meanwhile, the US, believing the human rights situation had improved, resumed military sales to Guatemala. But in 1981 the military unleashed a huge offensive against the guerrillas who united to confront it with the formation of the **Unidad Revolucionaria Nacional Guatemalteca** (URNG). The situation worsened when Ríos Montt came to power in 1982 following a coup d'état. He presided over the bloodiest period of violence with the introduction of the scorched-earth policy, massacring whole villages in an attempt to root out bands of guerrillas. Ríos Montt was ousted by his defence minister, General Oscar Mejías Victores, in a coup in August 1983.

## Return of democracy

**Mejía Victores** permitted a Constituent Assembly to be elected in 1984, which drew up a new constitution and worked out a timetable for a return to democracy. He also created numerous 'model villages' to rehouse the displaced and persecuted Maya, who had fled in their thousands to the forests, the capital, Mexico and the US. Presidential elections in December 1985, were won by civilian Vinicio Cerezo Arévalo of the Christian Democrats (DC), who took office in January 1986. He was the first democratically elected President of Guatemala since 1966. In the 1990 elections **Jorge Serrano Elías** of the Solidarity Action Movement made Guatemalan history by being the first civilian to succeed a previous civilian president in a change of government.

## Civil unrest

By 1993, however, the country was in disarray. The social policies pursued by the government had alienated nearly everybody and violence erupted on the streets. Amid growing civil unrest, President Serrano suspended the constitution, dissolved Congress and the Supreme Court, and imposed press censorship. International and domestic condemnation of his actions was immediate. After only a few days, Serrano was ousted by a combination of military, business and opposition leaders and a return to constitutional rule was promised. Congress approved a successor, Ramiro de León Carpio, previously the human rights ombudsman. He soon proved as capable as his predecessors, however, and the public's distaste of corrupt congressional deputies and ineffectual government did not diminish. The reform of election procedures and political parties had been called for by a referendum in 1994, which obliged Congressional elections to be called. The result gave a majority of seats to the **Guatemalan Republican Front** (FRG), led by ex-president Ríos Montt, who was elected to the presidency of Congress for 1994-1996. Ríos Montt's candidate in the 1995 presidential election, Alfonso Portillo, lost by a slim margin to Alvaro Arzú of the National Advancement Party. Arzú proposed to increase social spending, curtail tax evasion, combat crime and bring a speedy conclusion to peace negotiations with the URNG guerrillas.

## Towards peace

One of the earliest moves made by President Serrano was to speed up the process of talks between the government and the URNG, which began in March 1990. The sides met in Mexico City in April 1991 to discuss such topics as democratization and human rights, a reduced role for the military, the rights of indigenous people, the resettlement of refugees and agrarian reform. Progress, however, was slow. In August 1995 an accord was drawn up with the aid of the UN's Guatemala mission (MINUGUA) and the Norwegian government. The timetable proved over-ambitious, but, on taking office in January 1996, President Arzú committed himself to signing a peace accord. In February 1996 he met the URNG leadership, who called a ceasefire in March. On 29 December 1996 a peace treaty was signed ending 36 years of armed conflict. An amnesty was agreed which would limit the scope of the Commission for Historical Clarification and prevent it naming names in its investigations of human rights abuses.

## Peacetime elections and the Portillo Government

The 1999 elections went to a second round with self-confessed killer Alfonso Portillo of the FRG winning. Portillo subsequently promised to reform the armed forces, solve the killing of Bishop Gerardi and disband the elite presidential guard, so implicated in the human rights abuses. Common crime, as well as more sinister crimes such as lynchings, plagued Portillo's term and seemed to increase.

The new millennium generally brought mixed results for justice. The former interior minister Byron Barrientos resigned in 2001 and faced accusations of misappropriating US$6 million in state funds. In June 2002, ex-president Jorge Serrano was ordered to be arrested on charges which included embezzlement of state funds. He remains exiled in Panama. In 2002, a former colonel in the Guatemalan army, Colonel Juan Valencia Osorio, was found guilty of ordering the murder of anthropologist Myrna Mack and sentenced to 30 years' imprisonment. However, the appeal court overturned his conviction in 2003. Also in 2002, the four men imprisoned for their role in the 1998 murder of Guatemalan Bishop Gerardi had their convictions overturned. A retrial was ordered. In 2003 Ríos Montt mounted a legal challenge to a rule which prohibits former coup leaders running for president. The constitutional court ruled he could stand in the autumn parliamentary elections.

## Elections of 2003 and beyond

A new era in Guatemalan politics began with the election of **Oscar Berger** as president in 2003. After coming second to Portillo in the 1999 elections as candidate for PAN, Berger led the newly formed **Gran Alianza Nacional** (GANA) to electoral victory over his centre-left rival Alvaro Colom. Berger promised to improve access to clean water, education and health care. He also persuaded indigenous leader and Nobel Prize winner Rigoberta Menchú to join his government.

Berger's presidency provided slight economic growth and attempts to strengthen the country's institutions, despite low tax revenues, organized crime, discrimination and poverty. Elections in 2007 were also a close affair, with second round run-off providing Alvaro Colom with a narrow victory for the Unidad Nacional de la Esperanza (National Unity of Hope). Colom took office vowing to fight poverty with a government that would have a Mayan face, while promising to reduce organized crime.

In recent years, Los Zetas drug gang, former wing of the Mexican Gulf Cartel, has moved into Guatemala, with smuggling concentrated in northern regions, particularly Petén. Dozens of murders have been linked with the ruthless gang, which is thought to include former members of the Kaibiles – the elite Guatemalan army squad, notorious for its brutalities during Guatemala's civil war.

### Otto Pérez Molina

In January 2012, Otto Pérez Molina was elected to office. A controversial figure, he graduated from the School of the Americas to become Guatemala's director of military intelligence. He was also once a member of Guatemala's notorious Kaibiles, and after becoming president, he was accused of participating in scorched earth policies, torture and genocide during the war, which he denied. Despite his authoritarian background, Pérez Molina took the somewhat liberal stance of proposing the full legalization of drugs during a UN visit. In fact, Guatemala continues to receive considerable military aid for the war on drugs, which critics say is being used to beef up security and crush public dissent against mining, hydroelectric and other foreign-owned projects; indigenous activists and trade unionists continue to be assassinated. In 2013, Efraín Ríos Montt was found guilty of genocide and crimes against humanity. Outrageously, the ruling was subsequently overturned by the constitutional court on a technicality. In January 2015 his re-trail was suspended.

## Culture

### People

The word *ladino* applies to any person with a 'Latin' culture, speaking Spanish and wearing Western clothes, though they may be pure Amerindian by descent. The opposite of *ladino* is *indígena*; the definition is cultural, not racial. Guatemala's population in 2013 was estimated to be 15.47 million. The indigenous people of Guatemala are mainly of Maya descent. The largest of the 22 indigenous Maya groups are K'iche', Q'eqchi' and Mam. When the Spaniards arrived from Mexico in 1524 those who stayed settled in the southern highlands around Antigua and Guatemala City and intermarried with the groups of native subsistence farmers living there. This was the basis of the present mestizo population living in the cities and towns as well as in all parts of the southern highlands and in the flatlands along the Pacific coast; the indigenous population is still at its most dense in the western highlands and Alta Verapaz. They form two distinct cultures: the almost self-supporting indigenous system in the highlands, and the *ladino* commercial economy in the lowlands. About half the total population are classed as Amerindian (Maya) – estimates vary from 40-65%.

## Costume and dress

Indigenous dress is particularly attractive, little changed from the time the Spaniards arrived: the colourful head-dresses, *hiipiles* (tunics) and skirts of the women, the often richly patterned sashes and kerchiefs, the hatbands and tassels of the men vary greatly, often from village to village. Unfortunately a new outfit is costly, the indigenous people are poor, and denims are cheap. While men are adopting Western dress in many villages, women have been slower to change.

## Religion

There is no official religion but about 70% consider themselves Roman Catholic. The other 30% are Protestant, mostly affiliated to evangelical churches, which have been very active in the country over the past 30 years.

## Land and environment

A lowland ribbon, nowhere more than 50 km wide, runs the whole length of the Pacific shore. Cotton, sugar, bananas and maize are the chief crops of this strip. There is some stock raising as well. Summer rain is heavy and the lowland carries scrub forest. From this plain the highlands rise sharply to heights of between 2500 and 4000 m and stretch some 240 km to the north before sinking into the northern lowlands.

A string of volcanoes juts boldly above the southern highlands along the Pacific. There are intermont basins at from 1500 to 2500 m in this volcanic area. Most of the people of Guatemala live in these basins, which are drained by short rivers into the Pacific and by longer ones into the Atlantic. One basin west of the capital, ringed by volcanoes and with no apparent outlet, is Lago de Atitlán.

The southern highlands are covered with lush vegetation over a volcanic subsoil. This clears away in the central highlands, exposing the crystalline rock of the east-west running ranges. This area is lower but more rugged, with sharp-faced ridges and deep ravines modifying into gentle slopes and occasional valley lowlands as it loses height and approaches the Caribbean coastal levels and the flatlands of El Petén. The lower slopes of these highlands, from about 600 to 1500 m, are planted with coffee. Above 1500 m is given over to wheat and the main subsistence crops of maize and beans. Deforestation is becoming a serious problem. Where rainfall is low there are savannahs; water for irrigation is now drawn from wells and these areas are being reclaimed for pasture and fruit growing.

Two large rivers flow down to the Caribbean Gulf of Honduras from the highlands: one is the Río Motagua, 400 km long, rising among the southern volcanoes; the other, further north, is the Río Polochic, 298 km long, which drains into Lago de Izabal and the Bahía de Amatique. There are large areas of lowland in the lower reaches of both rivers, which are navigable for considerable distances; this was the great banana zone.

To the northwest, bordering on Belize and Mexico's Yucatán Peninsula, lies the low, undulating tableland of El Petén almost one-third of the nation's territory. In some parts there is natural grassland, with woods and streams, suitable for cattle, but large areas are covered with dense hardwood forest. Since the 1970s large-scale tree-felling has reduced this tropical rainforest by some 40%, especially in the south and east. However, in the north, which now forms Guatemala's share of the Maya Biosphere Reserve, the forest is protected, but illegal logging still takes place.

# El Salvador

When Spanish expeditions arrived in El Salvador from Guatemala and Nicaragua, they found it quite densely populated by several indigenous groups, of whom the most populous were the **Pipiles**. By 1550, the Spaniards had occupied the country, many living in existing indigenous villages and towns. The settlers cultivated cocoa in the volcanic highlands and balsam along the coast, and introduced cattle to roam the grasslands freely. Towards the end of the 16th century, indigo became the big export crop: production was controlled by the Spaniards, and the indigenous population provided the workforce, many suffering illness as a result. A period of regional turmoil accompanied El Salvador's declaration of Independence from the newly autonomous political body of Central America in 1839: indigenous attempts to regain their traditional land rights were put down by force.

Coffee emerged as an important cash crop in the second half of the 19th century, bringing with it improvements in transport facilities and the final abolition of indigenous communal lands.

The land question was a fundamental cause of the peasant uprising of 1932, which was brutally crushed by the dictator **General Maximiliano Hernández Martínez**. Following his overthrow in 1944, the military did not relinquish power: a series of military coups kept them in control, while they protected the interests of the landowning oligarchy.

## 1980s Civil War

The most recent military coup, in October 1979, led to the formation of a civilian-military junta which promised far-reaching reforms. When these were not carried out, the opposition unified forming a broad coalition, the Frente Democrático Revolucionario, which adopted a military wing, the **Farabundo Martí National Liberation Front (FMLN)** in 1980. Later the same year, the Christian Democrat **Ingeniero José Napoleón Duarte** was named as President of the Junta. At about the same time, political tension reached the proportions of civil war.

Duarte was elected to the post of president in 1984, following a short administration headed by Dr Alvaro Magaña. Duarte's periods of power were characterized by a partly successful attempt at land reform, the nationalization of foreign trade and the banking system, and violence. In addition to deaths in combat, 40,000 civilians were killed between 1979 and 1984, mostly by right-wing death squads. Among the casualties was **Archbishop Oscar Romero**, who was shot while saying mass in March 1980. Nothing came of meetings between Duarte's government and the FMLN, which were aimed at seeking a peace agreement. The war continued in stalemate until 1989, by which time an estimated 70,000 had been killed. The Christian Democrats' inability to end the war, reverse the economic decline or rebuild after the 1986 earthquake, combined with their reputation for corruption, brought about a resurgence of support for the right-wing National Republican Alliance (ARENA). An FMLN offer to participate in presidential elections, dependent on certain conditions, was not accepted and the ARENA candidate, **Alfredo Cristiani**, won the presidency comfortably in March 1989, taking office in June. Peace talks again failed to produce results and in November 1989 the FMLN guerrillas staged their most ambitious offensive ever, which paralysed the capital and caused a violent backlash from government forces. FMLN-government negotiations resumed with UN mediation following the offensive, but the two sides could not reach agreement about the purging of the armed forces, which had become the most wealthy institution in the country following 10 years of US support.

## Peace negotiations

Although El Salvador's most left-wing political party, the Unión Democrática Nacionalista, agreed to participate in municipal elections in 1991, the FMLN remained outside the electoral process, and the civil war continued unresolved. Talks were held in Venezuela and Mexico after initial agreement was reached in April on reforms to the electoral and judicial systems, but further progress was stalled over the restructuring of the armed forces and disarming the guerrillas. There were hopes that human rights would improve after the establishment in 1991 of a UN Security Council human rights observer commission (ONUSAL), which was charged with verifying compliance with the human rights agreement signed by the Government and the FMLN in Geneva in 1990.

Finally, after considerable UN assistance, the FMLN and the Government signed a peace accord in New York in January 1992 and a formal ceasefire began the following month. A detailed schedule throughout 1992 was established to demobilize the FMLN, dismantle five armed forces elite battalions and to initiate land requests by ex-combatants from both sides. The demobilization process was reported as completed in 1992, formally concluding the civil war. The US agreed at this point to 'forgive' a substantial portion of the US$2 billion international debt of El Salvador.

In 1993, the United Nations Truth Commission published its investigation of human rights abuses during the civil war. Five days later, the legislature approved a general amnesty for all those involved in criminal activities in the war. This included those named in the Truth Commission report. The Cristiani government was slow to implement not only the constitutional reforms proposed by the Truth Commission, but also the process of land reform and the establishment of the National Civilian Police (PNC).

By 1995, when Cristiani's successor had taken office, the old national police force was demobilized, but the PNC suffered from a lack of resources for its proper establishment. In fact, the budget for the implementation of the final peace accords was inadequate and El Salvador had to ask the UN for financial assistance.

## 1994 elections and after

Presidential and congressional elections in 1994 failed to give an outright majority to any presidential candidate and **Calderón Sol** of ARENA won the run-off election. Besides his government's difficulties with the final stages of the peace accord, his first months in office were marked by rises in the cost of living, increases in crime, strikes and protests, and occupations of the Legislature by ex-combatants. Frustration at the slow rate of reform came in the form of criticism from the United Nations and in 1997 through the ballot box. Only 41% of the electorate bothered to vote. In the National Assembly, Arena narrowly beat the FMLN. FMLN managed to run neck-and-neck with Arena until within a year of the March 1999 presidential elections. The party's inability to select a presidential candidate, however, caused it to lose ground rapidly. Arena's candidate, **Fransisco Flores**, won the election but still with a poor turn-out of less than 40% of the electorate. In the face of such a huge rejection of the political system Flores could not claim a clear mandate. Most interpreted the abstention as a lack of faith in any party's ability to solve the twin problems of poverty and crime. Elections in 2004 won a five-year term for **Tony**

Saca, the fourth successive victory for the right-wing Arena party. The former radio and TV presenter promised to crack down on criminal gangs and promote ties with the US.

## Into the 21st century

If the devastating earthquakes of early 2001 were not enough for the country to deal with, droughts through the summer months led to a food crisis that required United Nations' intervention. Old rivalries flared briefly as Honduras expelled two Salvadorean diplomats on spying charges, displaying the fragility of the cordial relations with the northern neighbour. El Salvador also hosted the meeting of Mexican and Central America presidents to develop the controversial **Plan Puebla-Panama** regional integration project which would link the Mexican city of Puebla with Panama City along an economic investment corridor.

In 2006 El Salvador continued to lead the way for regional integration as the first country to fully implement the Central American Free Trade Agreement with the US. The regional confidence continued and El Salvador and Honduras inaugurated their newly defined border, bringing to an end the dispute that led to the outbreak of war between the two nations in 1969.

In March 2011, the Inter-American Commission on Human Rights prepared to reopen the court case investigating the massacre of some 1000 civilians in village of El Mozote in December 1981, the bloodiest episode in the country's civil war.

In the same month, US President Barack Obama offered US$200m to help El Salvador fight drug traffickers and gang violence. The money is part of the $1.5bn 'Mérida Initiative' announced in 2007 to combat the drugs cartels. Critics say that the US military aid deployed to Central America is contributing to the reigon's re-militarization, which may have more to do with securing resources for exploitation than with stopping the flow of cocaine.

In 2014, presidential elections were narrowly won by Salvador Sánchez Cerén of the left-wing FMLN, a figure very much moulded by his experiences within revolutionary organizations.

## Culture

### People

The population of 6.7 million people is far more homogeneous than that of Guatemala. The reason for this is that El Salvador lay comparatively isolated from the main stream of conquest, and had no precious metals to act as magnets for the Spaniards. The small number of Spanish settlers intermarried with those indigenous locals who survived the plagues brought from Europe to form a group of mestizos. There were only about half a million people as late as 1879. With the introduction of coffee, the population grew quickly and the new prosperity fertilized the whole economy, but the internal pressure of population has led to the occupation of all the available land. Several hundred thousand Salvadoreans have emigrated to neighbouring republics because of the shortage of land and the concentration of land ownership, and, more recently, because of the civil war.

Of the total population, some 10% are regarded as ethnic indigenous, although the traditional indigenous culture has almost completely vanished. Other estimates put the percentage of the pure indigenous population as low as 5%. The **Lenca** and the **Pipil**, the two surviving indigenous groups, are predominantly peasant farmers. Only 1% are of unmixed white ancestry, the rest are mestizos.

With a population of 322 to the square kilometre, El Salvador is the most densely populated country on the American mainland. Health and sanitation outside the capital and some of the main towns leave much to be desired.

## Music and dance

The Mexican music industry seems to exert an overwhelming cultural influence, while the virtual absence of an indigenous population may also be partly responsible, since it is so often they who maintain traditions and connections with the past. Whatever the reason, the visitor who is seeking specifically Salvadorean native music will find little to satisfy him or her. El Salvador is an extension of 'marimba country', but songs and dances are often accompanied by the guitar and seem to lack a rhythm or style that can be pinpointed as specifically local. An exception is the music played on the *pito de caña* and *tambor* which accompanies the traditional dances called *Danza de los Historiantes*, *La Historia* or *Los Moros y Cristianos*. Over 30 types of dance have been identified, mostly in the west and centre of the country, although there are a few in the east. The main theme is the conflict between christianized and 'heretic' *indígenas* and the dances are performed as a ritual on the local saint's day.

## Land and environment

El Salvador is the smallest, most densely populated and most integrated of the Central American republics. Its intermont basins are a good deal lower than those of Guatemala, rising to little more than 600 m at the capital, San Salvador. Across this upland and surmounting it run two more or less parallel rows of volcanoes, 14% of which are over 900 m high. The highest are Santa Ana (2365 m), San Vicente (2182 m), San Miguel (2130 m), and San Salvador (1893 m). One important result of this volcanic activity is that the highlands are covered with a deep layer of ash and lava which forms a porous soil ideal for coffee planting.

The total area of El Salvador is 21,000 sq km. Guatemala is to the west, Honduras to the north and east, and the Pacific coastline to the south is approximately 321 km long. Lowlands lie to the north and south of the high backbone. In the south, on the Pacific coast, the lowlands of Guatemala are confined to just east of Acajutla; beyond are lava promontories before another 30-km belt of lowlands where the 325-km long Río Lempa flows into the sea. The northern lowlands are in the wide depression along the course of the Río Lempa, buttressed to the south by the highlands of El Salvador and to the north by the basalt cliffs edging the highlands of Honduras. The highest point in El Salvador, Cerro El Pital (2730 m) is part of the mountain range bordering on Honduras. After 160 km the Lempa cuts through the southern uplands to reach the Pacific; the depression is prolonged southeast till it reaches the Gulf of Fonseca.

El Salvador is located on the southwest coast of the Central American Isthmus on the Pacific Ocean. As the only country in the region lacking access to the Caribbean Sea, it does not posses the flora associated with that particular coastal zone. El Salvador nevertheless has a wide variety of colourful, tropical vegetation; for example over 200 species of orchid grow all over the country. As a result of excessive forest cutting, and hence the destruction of their habitats, many of the animals (such as jaguars and crested eagles) once found in the highlands of the country, have diminished at an alarming rate. In response to this problem several nature reserves have been set up in areas where flora and fauna can be found in their most unspoilt state. Among these nature reserves are the Cerro Verde, Deininger Park, El Imposible Woods, El Jocatal Lagoon and the Montecristo Cloud Forest.

# Honduras

Honduras was largely neglected by Spain and its colonists, who concentrated on their trading partners further north or south. The resulting disparity in levels of development between Honduras and its regional neighbours caused problems after Independence in 1821. Harsh partisan battles among provincial leaders resulted in the collapse of the Central American Federation in 1838. The national hero, **General Francisco Morazán** was a leader in unsuccessful attempts to maintain the Federation and the restoration of Central American unity was the main aim of foreign policy until 1922.

## Banana Republic

Honduras has had a succession of military and civilian rulers and there have been 300 internal rebellions, civil wars and changes of government since Independence, most of them in the 20th century. Political instability in the past led to a lack of investment in economic infrastructure and socio-political integration, making Honduras one of the poorest countries in the Western Hemisphere. It earned its nickname of the 'Banana Republic' in the first part of the 20th century following the founding of a company in 1899, by the Vaccaro brothers of New Orleans, which eventually became the Standard Fruit Company and which was to make bananas the major export crop of Honduras. The United Fruit Company of Boston was also founded in 1899 and, 30 years later, was merged with the Cuyamel Fruit Company of Samuel Zemurray, who controlled the largest fruit interests in Honduras. United Fruit (UFCo), known as El Pulpo (the octopus), emerged as a major political influence in the region with strong links with several dictatorships.

## The Great Depression

The 1929 Great Depression caused great hardship in the export-oriented economies of the region, and in Honduras it brought the rise of another authoritarian regime. **Tiburcio Cariás Andino** was elected in 1932 and, through his ties with foreign companies and other neighbouring dictators, he was able to hold on to power until renewed turbulence began in 1948, and he voluntarily withdrew from power a year later. The two political parties, the Liberals and the Nationals, came under the control of provincial military leaders and, after two more authoritarian Nationalist governments and a general strike in 1954 by radical labour unions on the north coast, young military reformists staged a palace coup in 1955. They installed a provisional junta and allowed elections for a constituent assembly in 1957. The assembly was led by the Liberal Party, which appointed **Dr Ramón Villeda Morales** as president, and transformed itself into a national legislature for six years. A newly created military academy graduated its first class in 1960, and the armed forces began to professionalize their leadership in conjunction with the civilian economic establishment. Conservative officers, nervous of a Cuban-style revolution, pre-empted elections in 1963 in a bloody coup which deposed Dr Villeda, exiled Liberal Party members and took control of the national police, which they organized into special security forces.

## Football War

In 1969, Honduras and El Salvador were drawn into a bizarre episode known as the 'Football War', which took its name from its origin in a disputed decision in the third qualifying round of the World Cup. Its root cause, however, was the social tension aroused by migrating workers from overcrowded El Salvador to Honduras. In 13 days, 2000 people were killed before a ceasefire was arranged by the Organization of American States. A peace treaty was not signed until 1980, and the dispute provoked Honduras to withdraw from the Central American Common Market (CACM), which helped to hasten its demise.

Tensions between the two countries can still easily rise. Disputes over the border and fishing rights in the Gulf of Fonseca are a cause of friction, and in August 2001, Honduras expelled two Salvadoreans on spying charges. Honduras also has disputed land claims with Nicaragua to the east. However, regional cooperation is sufficiently well developed for regional conferences to tackle the problems with commitments to non-aggressive solutions.

## Transition to democracy

The armed forces, led chiefly by **General López Arellano** and his protégés in the National Party, dominated government until 1982. López initiated land reform but, despite liberal policies, his regime was brought down in the mid-1970s by corruption scandals involving misuse of hurricane aid funds and bribes from the United Brands Company. His successors increased the size and power of the security forces and created the largest air force in Central America, while slowly preparing for a return to civilian rule. A constituent assembly was elected in 1980 and general elections held in 1981. A constitution was promulgated in 1982 and **President Roberto Suazo Córdoba** of the Liberal Party assumed power. During this period, Honduras cooperated closely with the USA on political and military issues, particularly in covert moves to destabilize Nicaragua's Sandinista government, and became host to some 12,000 right-wing Nicaraguan contra rebels. It was less willing to take a similar stand against the FMLN left-wing guerrillas in El Salvador for fear of renewing border tensions. In 1986 the first peaceful transfer of power between civilian presidents for 30 years took place when **José Azcona del Hoyo** (Liberal) won the elections. Close relations with the USA were maintained in the 1980s, Honduras had the largest Peace Corps Mission in the world, non-governmental and international voluntary agencies proliferated as the government became increasingly dependent upon US aid to finance its budget.

In 1989, the general elections were won by the right-wing **Rafael Leonardo Callejas Romero** of the National Party. Under the terms of the Central American Peace Plan, the contra forces were demobilized and disarmed by June 1990. The Honduran armed forces have come under greater pressure for reform as a result of US and domestic criticism of human rights abuses.

## Liberal government since 1993

In the campaign leading up to the 1993 general elections, the Liberal candidate, **Carlos Roberto Reina Idiáquez**, pledged to provide every citizen *"techo, trabajo, tierra y tortilla"* (roof, work, land and food), arguing for a more socially conscious face to the economic adjustment programme inaugurated by President Callejas. Although many of his economic policies were unpopular, and he was unable to alleviate widespread poverty in the short term, President Reina received approval for his handling of the military and investigations of human rights' abuses.

The 1997 presidential elections were again won by the Liberal candidate, **Carlos Flores Facusse**. He had the support of the business community, who believed he would control public spending and reduce the government deficit in line with IMF targets, but he also campaigned against economic austerity and in favour of bridging the gap between rich and poor. The passage of Hurricane Mitch over Honduras in 1998 forced the Flores administration to refocus all its attention on rebuilding the country at all levels, social, economic and infrastructural.

**Ricardo Maduro** of the National Party was sworn in as president in 2002. Elections in 2005 were won by the Liberal Party's **Manuel Zelaya**. Zelaya had served in the government of Carlos Flores. On taking office he vowed to continue the fight against gang violence along with tackling corruption in government, creation of hundreds of thousands of badly needed jobs and support for CAFTA free trade agreement with the US.

But despite the determination, violence continued to dominate the political agenda, with prison riots and occasional ransoms of high-profile individuals undermining the rule of law.

## The coup

In 2009, President Manuel Zelaya was ousted in a military coup. Troops seized the president early in the morning and sent him – still wearing his pyjamas – into exile in Costa Rica. The move followed the president's proposal to hold a referendum on changing the law to allow him to stand for a second term of office. When the head of the armed forces opposed the plan, Zelaya fired him, which triggered the coup. Zelaya now lives in the Dominican Republic. In the same year, presidential elections were won by **Porfirio 'Pepe' Lobo Sosa** of the right-wing National Party, with the largest number of votes ever recorded in Honduras' history. He took office in January, 2010.

Since then, the country has seen a sharp upturn in violent crime, an escalation of the war on drugs and a general deterioration in infrastructure, along with a marked strengthening of oligarch families, bluntly backed by the police and military. A series of ugly land disputes resulted in a spate of political assassinations, mostly of young peasant activists, and, against the backdrop of a human rights crisis, elections were held in 2013. Juan Orlando Hernández of the ruling National Party was voted to office. However, there has been no significant improvement for the vast majority of everyday Hondurans.

## Culture

### People

2006 estimates put the population at just under seven million. The pure indigenous population is only an estimated 7% of the total population, and the percentage of pure Spanish or other European ancestry is even smaller. The two largest indigenous groups are the Chortis from Santa Rosa de Copán westwards to the border with Guatemala, and the Lencas in the departments of Lempira, Intibucá and, above all, in the highlands of La Paz. There are also about 45,000 Miskito people who live on the Caribbean coast, alongside several communities of Garífunas (black Caribs). The population is 90% mestizo. Some 53% are peasant farmers or agricultural labourers, with a low standard of living.

### Music

Honduras shares with Belize and Guatemala the presence of Garífuna or black Caribs on the Caribbean coast. These descendants of indigenous Caribs and escaped black slaves were deported to the area from St Vincent in the late 18th century and continue to maintain a very separate identity, including their own religious observances, music and dances, profoundly African in spirit and style.

With a territory of 112,100 sq km, Honduras is larger than all the other Central American republics except Nicaragua. Bordered by Nicaragua, Guatemala and El Salvador, it has a narrow Pacific coastal strip, 124 km long on the Gulf of Fonseca, and a northern coast on the Caribbean of 640 km.

Inland, much of the country is mountainous: a rough plateau covered with volcanic ash and lava in the south, rising to peaks such as Cerro de las Minas in the Celaque range (2849 m), but with some intermont basins at between 900 and 1800 m. The volcanic detritus disappears to the north, revealing saw-toothed ranges which approach the coast at an angle; the one in the extreme northwest, along the border with Guatemala, disappears under the sea and shows itself again in the Bay Islands.

At most places in the north there is only a narrow shelf of lowland between the sea and the sharp upthrust of the mountains, but along two rivers (the Aguán in the northeast, and the Ulúa in the northwest) long fingers of marshy lowland stretch inland between the ranges. The Ulúa lowland is particularly important; it is about 40 km wide and stretches southwards for 100 km where the city of San Pedro Sula is located. From its southern limit a deep gash continues across the highland to the Gulf of Fonseca on the Pacific. The distance between the Caribbean and the Pacific along this trough is 280 km; the altitude at the divide between the Río Comayagua, running into the Ulúa and the Caribbean, and the streams flowing into the Pacific, is only 950 m. In this trough lies Comayagua, the old colonial capital. The lowlands along the Gulf of Fonseca are narrower than they are along the Caribbean; there is no major thrust inland as there is along the Ulúa.

The prevailing winds are from the east, consequently the Caribbean coast has a high rainfall and is covered with deep tropical forest. The intermont basins, the valleys and the slopes sheltered from the prevailing winds bear oak and pine down to as low as 600 m. Timber is almost the only fuel available. In the drier areas, north and south of Tegucigalpa, there are extensive treeless savannahs.

Today, land under some form of cultivation is only 18% of the total, while meadows and pastures make up 14% of total land use. Rugged terrain makes large areas unsuitable for any kind of agriculture. Nevertheless, there is undeveloped agricultural potential in the flat and almost unpopulated lands of the coastal plain east of Tela to Trujillo and Puerto Castilla, in the Aguán valley southward and in the region northeast of Juticalpa. The area to the northeast, known as the Mosquitia plain, is largely unexploited and little is known of its potential.

# Nicaragua

Nicaragua was at the crossroads of northern and southern prehispanic cultures. The best understood are the Chorotegas, who came from Mexico around AD 800, and the Nicaraguas, who partially displaced the Chorotegas in the Pacific basin around AD 1200. The Nicaraguas set up a very successful society which traded with people from Mexico to Peru, but the most interesting pre-Columbian remains are the many petroglyphs and large basalt figures left by unnamed pre-Chorotega cultures, in particular on the islands of Zapatera and Ometepe. The Ramas and Mayagna, of South American lowland origin, populated the eastern seaboard regions, but are almost extinct today.

## Conquest and colonization

In 1522, the Spanish explorer Gil González Dávila arrived overland from Panama, and searching for the wealthiest chief of all, arrived on the western shores of Lake Nicaragua to meet the famous Nicaraguas chief, Niqueragua. The chief and Dávila engaged in long philosophical conversations conducted through a translator and eventually the great chief agreed to accept Christianity. The Chorotega chieftain Diriangen, however, was less conducive to religious conversion and subsequently slaughtered Dávila's small force of troops. In 1524 the Spanish sent a stronger army and the local populace was overcome by Francisco Hernández de Córdoba. The colonies of Granada and León were subsequently founded and the local administrative centre was not wealthy Granada, with its profitable crops of sugar, cocoa, and indigo, but impoverished León, then barely able to subsist on its crops of maize, beans and rice. This reversal of the Spanish policy of choosing the most successful settlement as capital was due to the ease with which León could be reached from the Pacific. In 1852 Managua was chosen as a new capital as a compromise, following violent rivalry between Granada and León.

## Walker's expedition

The infamous filibustering expedition of William Walker is an important event in Nicaraguan and Costa Rican history. William Walker (1824-1860) was born in Nashville, Tennessee, graduated and then studied medicine at Edinburgh and Heidelberg, being granted his MD in 1843. He then studied law and was called to the bar. In May 1855, he sailed for Nicaragua, where Liberal Party leaders had invited him to help them in their struggle against the Conservatives. In October he seized a steamer on Lake Nicaragua and was able to surprise and capture Granada. A new government was formed, and in June 1856 Walker was elected president. On 22 September, to gain support from the southern states in America, he suspended the Nicaraguan laws against slavery. Walker then attempted to take control of La Casona in the Guanacaste province of Costa Rica, only to be repelled by a coalition of Central American states. He surrendered to the US Navy to avoid capture in May 1857. In November 1857, he sailed from Mobile, Alabama with another expedition, but after landing near Greytown, Nicaragua, he was arrested and returned to the USA. In 1860 he sailed again from Mobile and landed in Honduras in his last attempt to conquer Central America. There he was taken prisoner by Captain Salmon, of the British Navy, and handed over to the Honduran authorities who tried and executed him on 12 September 1860. Walker's own book, *The War in Nicaragua*, is a fascinating document.

## US involvement

US involvement in Nicaraguan affairs stretches back a long way. In 1909, US Marines assisted Nicaraguan Conservative leaders in an uprising to overthrow the Liberal president, José Santos Zelaya. In 1911 the USA pledged help in securing a loan to be guaranteed through the control of Nicaraguan customs by an American board. In 1912 the United States sent marines into Nicaragua to enforce control. Apart from short intervals, they stayed there until 1933. During the last five years of occupation, nationalists under **General Augusto César Sandino** waged a relentless guerrilla war against the US Marines. American forces were finally withdrawn in 1933, when President Franklin Roosevelt announced the 'Good Neighbour' policy, pledging non-intervention. An American-trained force, the Nicaraguan National Guard, was left behind, commanded by **Anastasio Somoza García**. Somoza's men assassinated General Sandino in February 1934 and Somoza himself took over the presidency in 1936. From 1932, with brief intervals, Nicaraguan affairs were dominated by this tyrant until he was assassinated in 1956. His two sons both served a presidential term and the younger, General **Anastasio Somoza Debayle**, dominated the country from 1963 until his deposition in 1979; he was later assassinated in Paraguay.

## 1978-1979 Revolution

The 1978 to 1979 Revolution against the Somoza Government by the Sandinista guerrilla organization (loosely allied to a broad opposition movement) resulted in extensive damage and many casualties (estimated at over 30,000) in certain parts of the country, especially in Managua, Estelí, León, Masaya, Chinandega and Corinto. After heavy fighting General Somoza resigned on 17 July 1979 and the government was taken over by a Junta representing the Sandinista guerrillas and their civilian allies. Real power was exercised by nine Sandinista *comandantes* whose chief short-term aim was reconstruction. A 47-member Council of State formally came into being in May 1980; supporters of the Frente Sandinista de Liberación Nacional (FSLN) had a majority. Elections were held on 4 November 1984 for an augmented National Constituent Assembly with 96 seats; the Sandinista Liberation Front won 61 seats, and **Daniel Ortega Saavedra**, who had headed the Junta, was elected president. The failure of the Sandinista Government to meet the demands of a right-wing group, the Democratic Coordinating Board (CDN), led to this coalition boycotting the elections and to the US administration failing to recognize the democratically elected government.

## The Sandinistas

Despite substantial official and private US support, anti-Sandinista guerrillas (the Contras) could boast no significant success in their war against the government. In 1988, the Sandinistas and the contras met for the first time to discuss the implementation of the Central American Peace Plan, drawn up by President Oscar Arias Sánchez of Costa Rica and signed in August 1987. By 1989, the contras, lacking funds and with diminished numbers, appeared to be a spent force. The Sandinista Government had brought major improvements in health and education, but the demands of the war and a complete US trade embargo did great damage to the economy as a whole. The electorate's desire for a higher standard of living was reflected in the outcome of the elections, when the US-supported candidate of the free market coalition group National Opposition Union (UNO), Señora **Violeta Chamorro**, won 55.2% of the vote, compared with 40.8% for President Ortega.

The USA was subsequently under considerable pressure to provide aid, but of the US$300 million promised for 1990 by the US Congress, only half had been distributed by 1991. The lack of foreign financial assistance prevented any quick rebuilding of the economy. The Nicaraguan government's scant resources also did not permit it to give the disarmed contra forces the land that had been promised to them. Demilitarized Sandinistas and landless peasants also pressed for land in 1991, with a consequent rise in tension. Factions of the two groups rearmed, to be known as recontras and recompas; there were many bloody conflicts. Divisions within the UNO coalition, particularly between supporters of President Chamorro and those of Vice President Virgilio Godoy, added to the country's difficulties. Austerity measures were introduced in early 1991, including a devaluation of the new córdoba. In 1992, pacts signed between Government, recontras and recompas failed to stop occasional heavy fighting over the next two years. In 1994, however, a series of bilateral meetings, proposed by archbishop Miguel Obando y Bravo, significantly contributed to disarmament.

## Movement towards a real and lasting peace

The achievement of a more peaceful state of affairs, if not reconciliation, did not remove other political tensions. After the UNO coalition realigned itself into new political groupings and returned to the National Assembly following a boycott in 1993, the FSLN began to fall apart in 1994. By early 1995, the Sandinistas had become irrevocably split between the orthodox wing, led by Daniel Ortega, and the Sandinista Renewal Movement (MRS), under Sergio Ramírez. The MRS accused the orthodox wing of betraying Sandinista principles by forming pacts with the technocrats and neo-liberals of the Government. The MRS was itself accused of opportunism. Linked to this was considerable manoeuvring over UNO-inspired constitutional reform.

## The 1996 elections

The front-runner in the 1996 presidential elections was **Arnoldo Alemán**, former mayor of Managua, of the Liberal alliance. His main opponent was Daniel Ortega of the FSLN, who regarded Alemán's policies as a return to Somoza-style government. After reviewing the vote count because of allegations of fraud, the Supreme Electoral Council (CSE) declared Arnoldo Alemán had won 51% compared with 37.7% for Daniel Ortega. The FSLN called for new elections in Managua and Matagalpa as the OAS declared the elections fair but flawed. Ortega announced he would respect the legality but not the legitimacy of the Government of Alemán.

## A new opportunity

In 2001, Daniel Ortega of the FSLN lost to **Enrique Bolaños** of the ruling Liberal Party (PLC). Voters chose Enrique Bolaños in what many believed to be a vote against Ortega rather than approval of the Liberal Party. In Enrique Bolaños' first three months of office in 2002 he shocked many by taking a very aggressive stance against corruption and his administration exposed several cases of embezzlement under the Alemán adminstration. The desire to cleanse the past and clear the way for the future was apparent when in 2003 former president Arnoldo Alemán was sentenced to 25 years in prison, later transferred to house arrest, for corruption including money laundering and embezzlement to a value of nearly US$100m.

President Bolaños' agreement to allow his predecessor to be investigated led to his alienation by some in the Liberal Party. The delicate balance of power in Congress has restricted the president's powers, and further changes were only avoided at the last minute when Bolaños made a pact with Sandinista leader Ortega.

## Ortega returns

Following elections in 2006, Daniel Ortega returned after winning 38% of the vote. Despite ample promises of help from new allies such as Venezuela and Iran, change to Nicaragua's daily reality was initially slow, with the rising cost of living outpacing mandated salary adjustments. Ortega was widely criticized for employing the same neo-liberal policies of the last 17 years. *The Economist* called it "Ortega's Crab Walk": tough revolutionary, anti-imperialist rhetoric combined with a textbook IMF economic policy. Ortega amended the Nicaraguan constitution to allow a president to hold office for two consecutive terms in 2009. Making no secret of his ambitions for perpetual re-election, he ran as the Sandinista candidate in 2011 and won a landslide victory against a poorly organized and divided Liberal opposition. In 2013, congress approved legislation that will allow Ortega to run for a third successive term, stoking opposition criticisms of an incipient 'dictatorship' and cult of personality.

Today, after eight years of Sandinista rule, the party can claim significant reductions in poverty and inequality, sustained growth of GDP and a general strengthening of the national currency. The future looks reasonably bright and many Nicaraguans are hopeful that a US$40 billion Chinese-built transoceanic canal, whose construction started in January 2015 and is due to be completed in 2020, will bring new opportunity and investment. However, there were protests in June 2015 against the canal's potential environmental impact, a concern voiced by scientists in a recent report, and evictions of farmers from their land.

## Culture

### People

With a population of 5.5 million, population density is low: 43 people per square kilometre, compared with El Salvador's 322. Nine out of 10 Nicaraguans live and work in the lowlands between the Pacific and the western shores of Lake Nicaragua, the southwestern shore of Lake Managua, and the southwestern sides of the row of volcanoes. In latter years settlers have taken to coffee-growing and cattle-rearing in the highlands at Matagalpa and Jinotega. Elsewhere, the highlands, save for an occasional mining camp, are very thinly settled.

The densely forested eastern lowlands fronting the Caribbean were neglected, because of the heavy rainfall and their consequent unhealthiness, until the British settled several colonies of Jamaicans in the 18th century at Bluefields and San Juan del Norte. But early this century the United Fruit Company of America (now United Brands) opened banana plantations inland from Puerto Cabezas, worked by blacks from Jamaica. Other companies followed suit along the coast, but the bananas were later attacked by Panama disease and exports today are small. Along the Mosquito coast there are still English-speaking communities of African, or mixed African and indigenous, descent. Besides the mestizo intermixtures of Spanish and indigenous (69%), there are pure blacks (9%), pure indigenous (5%) and mixtures of the two (mostly along the Atlantic coast). A small proportion is of unmixed Spanish and other European descent. For a brief survey of the people of eastern Nicaragua, see box, page 652.

## Music and dance

Nicaragua is 'marimba country' and the basic musical genre is the *son*, this time called the *Son Nica*. There are a number of popular dances for couples with the names of animals, like *La Vaca* (cow), *La Yeguita* (mare) and *El Toro* (bull). The folklore capital of Nicaragua is the city of Masaya and the musical heart of Masaya is the indigenous quarter of Monimbó. Here the marimba is king, but on increasingly rare occasions may be supported by the *chirimía* (oboe), *quijada de asno* (donkey's jaw) and *quijongo*, a single-string bow with gourd resonator. Some of the most traditional *sones* are *El Zañate*, *Los Novios* and *La Perra Renca*, while the more popular dances still to be found are *Las Inditas*, *Las Negras*, *Los Diablitos* and *El Torovenado*, all involving masked characters. Diriamba is another centre of tradition, notable for the folk play known as *El Güegüense*, accompanied by violin, flute and drum and the dance called *Toro Guaco*.

The Caribbean coast is a totally different cultural region, home to the Miskito people and English-speaking black people of Jamaican origin concentrated around Bluefields. The latter have a maypole dance and their music is typically Afro-Caribbean, with banjos, accordions, guitars and of course drums as the preferred instruments.

## Land and environment

Broadly speaking, there are three well-marked geographic regions in Nicaragua. The first is a large triangular-shaped central mountain land beginning almost on the southern border with Costa Rica and broadening northwards; the prevailing moisture-laden northeast winds drench its eastern slopes, which are deeply forested with oak and pine on the drier, cooler heights.

The second geographic region is a belt of lowland plains which run from the Gulf of Fonseca, on the Pacific, to the Costa Rican border south of Lake Nicaragua. Out of it, to the east, rise the lava cliffs of the mountains to a height of 1500-2100 m.

The third region is a wide belt of eastern lowland through which a number of rivers flow from the mountains into the Atlantic. In the plains are the two largest sheets of water in Central America and 10 crater lakes. The capital, Managua, is on the shores of Lake Managua (Xolotlán), 52 km long, 15-25 km wide, and 39 m above sea-level. Its maximum depth is only 30 m. The Río Tipitapa drains it into Lake Nicaragua, 148 km long, about 55 km at its widest, and 32 m above the sea; Granada is on its shores. The 190-km Río San Juan drains both lakes into the Caribbean and is one of 96 principal rivers in the country. The longest at 680 km is the Río Coco, on the border with Honduras. Lying at the intersection of three continental plates, Nicaragua has a very unstable, changing landscape. Through the Pacific basin runs a row of 28 major volcanoes, six of which were active during the 20th century.

# Costa Rica

## Spanish settlement

During his last voyage in September 1502, Columbus landed on the shores of what is now Costa Rica. Rumours of vast gold treasures (which never materialized) led to the name of Costa Rica (Rich Coast). The Spaniards settled in the Meseta Central, where the numbers of several thousand sedentary indigenous farmers were soon greatly diminished by the diseases brought by the settlers. Cártago was founded in 1563 by **Juan Vásquez de Coronado**, but there was almost no expansion for 145 years, when a small number left Cártago for the valleys of Aserrí and Escazú. They founded Heredia in 1717, and San José in 1737. Alajuela, not far from San José, was founded in 1782. The settlers were growing in numbers but were still poor and raising only subsistence crops.

## Independence and coffee

Independence from Spain was declared in 1821 whereupon Costa Rica, with the rest of Central America, immediately became part of Mexico. This led to a civil war during which, two years later, the capital was moved from Cártago to San José. After Independence, the government sought anxiously for some product which could be exported and taxed for revenue.

Coffee was successfully introduced from Cuba in 1808, making Costa Rica the first of the Central American countries to grow what was to become known as the golden bean. The Government offered free land to coffee growers, thus building up a peasant landowning class. In 1825 there was a trickle of exports, carried by mule to the ports. By 1846 there were ox-cart roads to Puntarenas. By 1850 there was a large flow of coffee to overseas markets which was greatly increased by the opening of a railway in 1890 from San José and Cártago to Puerto Limón along the valley of the River Reventazón. From 1850, coffee prosperity began to affect the country profoundly: the birth rate grew, land for coffee was free, and the peasant settlements started spreading, first down the Reventazón as far as Turrialba, then up the slopes of the volcanoes, then down the new railway from San José to the old Pacific port of Puntarenas.

## Banana industry

Bananas were first introduced in 1878 making Costa Rica the first Central American republic to grow them. It is now the second largest exporter in the world. Labour was brought in from Jamaica to clear the forest and work the plantations. The industry grew and in 1913, the peak year, the Caribbean coastlands provided 11 million bunches for export. Since then the spread of disease has lowered exports and encouraged crop diversification. The United Fruit Company turned its attentions to the Pacific littoral, especially in the south around the port of Golfito. Although some of the Caribbean plantations were turned over to cacao, *abacá* (Manila hemp) and African palm, the region has regained its ascendancy over the Pacific littoral as a banana producer. By the end of the century over 50,000 ha were planted to bananas, mostly in the Atlantic lowlands.

In the 1990s Chiquita, Dole and Del Monte, the multinational fruit producers, came under international pressure over labour rights on their plantations. Two European campaign groups targeted working conditions in Costa Rica where, despite constitutional guarantees of union freedom, there was a poor record of labour rights abuse. Only 10% of Costa Rica's 50,000 banana workers were represented by unions. The rest preferred to join the less political *solidarista* associations, which provide cheap loans and promote savings, and thus avoid being blacklisted or harassed. Del Monte agreed in 1998 to talk to the unions after a decade of silence, while Chiquita declared its workers were free to choose trade union representation.

## Democratic government

Costa Rica's long tradition of democracy began in 1889 and has continued to the present day, with only a few lapses. In 1917 the elected president **Alfredo González** was ousted by **Federico Tinoco**, who held power until 1919, when a counter-revolution and subsequent elections brought Julio Acosta to the presidency. Democratic and orderly government followed until the campaign of 1948 when violent protests and a general strike surrounded disputed results. A month of fighting broke out after the Legislative Assembly annulled the elections, leading to the abolition of the constitution and a junta being installed, led by **José Figueres Ferrer**. In 1949 a constituent assembly drew up a new constitution and abolished the army. The junta stepped down and **Otilio Ulate Blanco**, one of the candidates of the previous year, was inaugurated. In 1952, Figueres, a socialist, founded the Partido de Liberación Nacional, and was elected president in 1953. He dominated politics for the next two decades, serving as president in 1953-1958 and 1970-1974. The PLN introduced social welfare programmes and nationalization policies, while intervening conservative governments encouraged private enterprise. The PLN was again in power 1974-1978 (**Daniel Oduber Quirós**), 1982-1986 (**Luis Alberto Monge**), 19861-1990 (**Oscar Arias Sánchez**) and 1994-1998 (**José María Figueres**, son of José Figueres Ferrer).

President Arias drew up proposals for a peace pact in Central America and concentrated greatly on foreign policy initiatives. Efforts were made to expel Nicaraguan contras resident in Costa Rica and the country's official proclamation of neutrality, made in 1983, was reinforced. The Central American Peace Plan, signed by the five Central American presidents in Guatemala in 1987, earned Arias the Nobel Peace Prize, although progress in implementing its recommendations was slow. In the 1990 general elections, **Rafael Angel Calderón Fournier**, a conservative lawyer and candidate for the Social Christian Unity Party (PUSC), won a narrow victory, with 51% of the vote, over the candidate of the PLN. Calderón, the son of a former president who had been one of the candidates in the 1948 disputed elections, had previously stood for election in 1982 and 1986. The president's popularity slumped as the effects of his economic policies were felt on people's living standards, while his Government was brought into disrepute by allegations of corruption and links with 'narco' traffickers.

## PLN government, 1994 and 1998

In the February 1994 elections another former president's son was elected by a narrow margin. **José María Figueres** of the PLN won on economic policies. Figueres argued against neo-liberal policies, claiming he would renegotiate agreements with the IMF and the World Bank, but in his first year of office a third Structural Adjustment Programme was approved. A subsequent National Development Plan and a Plan to Fight Poverty contained a wide range of measures designed to promote economic stability and to improve the quality of life for many sectors of society.

## 1998, 2002 elections

In 1998 the elections were won by the PUSC candidate, **Miguel Angel Rodríguez**. Thirty percent of voters abstained. The new president took office in May 1998, promising to make women, the young and the poor a priority for his government. Typically for Costa Rica, the elections of early 2002 ran on a frenzy of neutrality. **President Pacheco** stimulated just enough support to win after the election went to a run-off.

## 2006 and beyond

Having successfully convinced Costa Rica's Congress to change the constitution and allow re-election, Oscar Arias was elected president in 2006, 16 years after serving his first term.

In the 2010 elections, the PLN put forward Vice-President Laura Chinchilla against the libertarian candidate Otto Guevara, becoming Costa Rica's first female president. She proved to be a socially conservative president, opposing gay marriage and supporting the ban on a morning after pill, but she did declare a moratorium on oil exploration. She ended her term with historically low approval ratings, thanks mainly to her fiscal reforms.

The 2014 elections saw a second round run-off between PLN candidate and former San José mayor, Johnny Araya Monge, and centre-left Citizens' Action Party candidate Luis Guillermo Solís Rivera. But Araya dropped out of the race, leaving Solís to claim the presidency with 78% of the vote.

# Culture

## People

In all provinces over 98% of the population is white and mestizo except in Limón where 33.2% is black and 3.1% indigenous, of whom only 5000 survive in the whole country. There are three groups: the Bribri (3500), Boruca (1000) and Guatuso. Although officially protected, the living conditions of the indigenous population are very poor. In 1992 Costa Rica became the first Central American country to ratify the International Labour Organization treaty on indigenous populations and tribes. However, even in Limón, the percentage of blacks is falling: it was 57.1% in 1927. Many of them speak Jamaican English as their native tongue. Much of the Caribbean coastland, especially in the north, remains unoccupied. On the Pacific coastlands a white minority owns the land on the hacienda system which has been rejected in the uplands. About 46% of the people are mestizos. The population has risen sharply in the mountainous Peninsula of Nicoya, which is an important source of maize, rice and beans.

## Music and dance

This is the southernmost in our string of 'marimba culture' countries. The guitar is also a popular instrument for accompanying folk dances, while the *chirimía* and *quijongo*, already encountered further north, have not yet totally died out in the Chorotega region of Guanacaste Province. This province is indeed the heartland of Costa Rican folklore and the Punto Guanacasteco, a heel-and-toe dance for couples, has been officially decreed to be the 'typical national dance', although it is not in fact traditional, but was composed at the turn of the last century by Leandro Cabalceta Brau during a brief sojourn in jail. There are other dances too, such as the *botijuela*, *tamborito* and *cambute*, but they are not traditional, being are performed on stage when outsiders need to be shown some native culture.

Among the country's most popular native performers are the duet **Los Talolingas**, authors of *La Guaria Morada*, regarded as the 'second national anthem' and **Lorenzo 'Lencho' Salazar**, whose humorous songs in the vernacular style are considered quintessentially Tico.

Some of the Republic's rapidly deculturizing indigenous groups have dances of their own, like the *Danza de los Diablitos* of the Borucas, the *Danza del Sol* and *Danza de la Luna* of the Chorotegas and the *Danza de los Huesos* of the Talamancas. A curious ocarina made of beeswax, the *dru mugata* is still played by the Guaymí people and is said to be the only truly pre-Columbian instrument still to be found. The drum and flute are traditional among various groups, but the guitar and accordion are moving in to replace them. As in the case of Nicaragua, the Caribbean coast of Costa Rica, centred on Puerto Limón, is inhabited by black people who came originally from the English-speaking islands and whose music reflects this origin. The sinkit seems to be a strictly local rhythm, but the calypso is popular and the cuadrille, square dance and maypole dance are also found. There is also a kind of popular hymn called the *saki*. Brass, percussion and string instruments are played, as well as the accordion.

## Land and environment

Costa Rica lies between Nicaragua and Panama, with coastlines on the Caribbean (212 km) and the Pacific (1016 km). The distance between sea and sea ranges from 119-282 km. A low, thin line of hills between Lake Nicaragua and the Pacific is prolonged into northern Costa Rica with several volcanoes (including the active Volcán Arenal), broadening and rising into high and rugged mountains and volcanoes in the centre and south. The highest peak, Chirripó Grande, southeast of the capital, reaches 3820 m. Within these highlands are certain structural depressions; one of them, the Meseta Central, is of paramount importance. To the southwest this basin is rimmed by the comb of the Cordillera; at the foot of its slopes, inside the basin, are the present capital San José, and the old capital, Cártago. Northeast of these cities, about 30 km away, four volcano cones rise from a massive common pedestal. From northwest to southeast these are Poás (2704 m), Barva (2906 m), Irazú (3432 m) and Turrialba (3339 m). Irazú and Poás are intermittently active. Between the Cordillera and the volcanoes is the Meseta Central: an area of 5200 sq km at an altitude of between 900 and 1800 m, where two-thirds of the population live. The northeastern part of the basin is drained by the Reventazón through turbulent gorges into the Caribbean; the Río Grande de Tárcoles drains the western part of it into the Pacific.

There are lowlands on both coasts. On the Caribbean coast, the Nicaraguan lowland along the Río San Juan continues into Costa Rica, wide and sparsely inhabited as far as Puerto Limón. A great deal of this land, particularly near the coast, is swampy; southeast of Puerto Limón the swamps continue as far as Panama in a narrow belt of lowland between sea and mountain.

The Gulf of Nicoya, on the Pacific side, thrusts some 65 km inland; its waters separate the mountains of the mainland from the 900-m-high mountains of the narrow Nicoya Peninsula. From a little to the south of the mouth of the Río Grande de Tercels, a lowland savannah stretches northwest past the port of Puntarenas and along the whole northeastern shore of the Gulf towards Nicaragua. Below the Río Grande de Tercels the savannah is pinched out by mountains, but there are other banana-growing lowlands to the south. Small quantities of African palm and cacao are now being grown in these lowlands. In the far south there are swampy lowlands again at the base of the Península de Osa and between the Golfo Dulce and the borders of Panama. Here there are 12,000 ha planted to bananas. The Río General, which flows into the Río Grande de Térraba, runs through a southern structural depression almost as large as the Meseta Central.

# Panama

## Camino Real

Panama City was founded in 1519 after a trail opened up between what is now the Pacific and the Caribbean. The Royal Road, or the *Camino Real*, ran from Panama City to Nombre de Dios until it was re-routed to Portobelo. An alternative route was used later for bulkier, less-valuable merchandise; it ran from Panama City to Las Cruces, on the Chagres River. Intruders were quickly attracted by the wealth passing over the Camino Real. **Sir Francis Drake** attacked Nombre de Dios, and in 1573 his men penetrated inland to Vera Cruz, further up the Chagres River on the Camino Real, plundering the town. Spain countered later attacks by building strongholds and forts to protect the route: among them San Felipe at the entrances to Portobelo and San Lorenzo at the mouth of the Chagres. Spanish galleons, loaded with treasure and escorted against attack, left Portobelo once a year. Perhaps the most famous pirate attack was by **Henry Morgan** in 1671. After capturing the fort of San Lorenzo, he pushed up the Chagres River to Las Cruces. From there he descended to Panama City, which he looted and burnt. The city was subsequently rebuilt on a new site, at the base of Ancón Hill, and fortified. With Britain and Spain at war, attacks reached their climax with Admiral Vernon's capture of Portobelo in 1739 and the fort of San Lorenzo the following year. Spain abandoned the route in 1746 and began trading round Cape Horn. Nonetheless, crossing between the Atlantic and Pacific became part of a Panamanian tradition and ultimately led to the construction of the Canal.

## Panama Railroad

In 1821, Gran Colombia won Independence from Spain. Panama, in an event celebrated annually on 28 November, declared its own Independence and promptly joined Bolívar's Gran Colombia federation. Though known as the 'Sovereign State' of Panama it remained, even after the federation disintegrated, a province of Colombia. Some 30 years later, streams of men were once more moving up the Chagres and down to Panama City: the forty-niners on their way to the newly discovered gold fields of California, taking a quicker and safer route than the challenges of continental North America. Many perished on this 'road to hell', as it was called, and the gold rush brought into being a railway across the isthmus. The Panama Railroad from Colón (then only two streets) to Panama City took four years to build, with great loss of life. The first train ran on 26 November 1853. The railway was an enormous financial success until the re-routing of the Pacific Steam Navigation Company's ships round Cape Horn in 1867 and the opening of the first US transcontinental railroad in 1869 reduced its traffic.

## Building of the Canal

**Ferdinand de Lesseps**, builder of the Suez Canal, arrived in Panama in 1881 to a hero's welcome, having decided to build a sea-level canal along the Chagres River and the Río Grande. Work started in 1882. About 30 km had been dug before the Company crashed in 1893, defeated by extravagance, corruption, tropical diseases (22,000 people died, mostly of yellow fever and malaria) and by engineering difficulties inherent in the construction of a canal without lift-locks. Eventually the Colombian government authorized the Company to sell all its rights and properties to the United States, but the Colombian Senate rejected the treaty, and the inhabitants of Panama, encouraged by the United States, declared their Independence on 3 November 1903. The United States intervened and, in spite of protests by Colombia, recognized the new republic. Colombia did not accept the severance until 1921.

Within two weeks of its Independence, Panama, represented in Washington by the controversial Frenchman **Philippe Bunau-Varilla**, signed a treaty granting to the USA 'in perpetuity' a 16-km-wide corridor across the isthmus over which the USA would exercise authority 'as if it were sovereign'. Bunau-Varilla, an official of the bankrupt French canal company, presented the revolutionary junta with the *fait accompli* of a signed treaty. The history of Panama then became that of two nations, with the Canal Zone governor, also a retired US general, responsible only to the President of the USA. Before beginning the task of building the Canal, the United States performed one of the greatest sanitary operations in history: the clearance from the area of the more malignant tropical diseases. The name of the physician **William Crawford Gorgas** will always be associated with this, as will that of the engineer **George Washington Goethals** with the actual building of the Canal. On 15 August 1914, the first official passage was made, by the ship *Ancón*.

## 1939 Treaty with USA

As a result of bitter resentment, the USA ended Panama's protectorate status in 1939 with a treaty which limited US rights of intervention. However, the disparity in living standards continued to provoke anti-US feeling, culminating in riots that began on 9 January 1964, resulting in the death of 23 Panamanians (the day is commemorated annually as Martyrs' Day), four US marines and the suspension of diplomatic relations for some months. In 1968 **Arnulfo Arias Madrid** was elected president for the third time and after only 10 days in office he was forcibly removed by the National Guard which installed a provisional junta. **Brigadier General Omar Torrijos Herrera** ultimately became Commander of the National Guard and principal power, dominating Panamanian politics for the next 13 years. Gradually, the theoretically civilian National Guard was converted into a full-scale army and renamed the Panama Defence Forces. Constitutional government was restored in 1972 after elections for a 505-member National Assembly of Community Representatives, which revised the 1946 constitution, elected **Demetrio Basilio Lakas Bahas** as president, and vested temporary extraordinary executive powers in General Torrijos for six years. Torrijos' rule was characterized by his pragmatic nationalism; he carried out limited agrarian reform and nationalized major industries, yet satisfied business interests. Importantly, he reached agreement with the USA to restore Panamanian sovereignty over the Canal Zone and to close the US military bases by the year 2000. In 1978 elections for a new National Assembly were held and the new representatives elected **Arístedes Royo Sánchez** president of the country. General Torrijos resigned as Chief of Government but retained the powerful post of Commander of the National Guard until his death in a small plane air-crash in 1981. There followed several years of rapid governmental changes as tension rose between presidents and National Guard leaders.

## General Noriega's Administration

Following an election in May 1984, **Nicolás Ardito Barletta** was inaugurated in October for a six-year term, though the fairness of the elections was widely questioned. He was removed from office by military pressure in September 1985 and replaced by **Eric Arturo Delvalle**, whose attempts to reduce the Guardia's influence, by then concentrated in the hands of **General Manuel Antonio Noriega Moreno**, led to his own removal in February 1988. **Manuel Solís Palma** was named president in his place. With the economy reeling and banks closed as a result of US economic sanctions, the campaign leading up to the election of May 1989 saw the growing influence of a movement called the *Civilista* Crusade, led by upper- and middle-class figures. When their coalition candidate, Guillermo Endara Galimany, triumphed over Noriega's candidate, Carlos Duque Jaén, the election was annulled by the military. General Noriega appointed Francisco Rodríguez as provisional president in September, but by December, General Noriega had formally assumed power as Head of State. These events provoked the US military invasion **Operation 'Just Cause'** on 20 December to overthrow him. He finally surrendered in mid-January, having first taken refuge in the Papal Nunciature on Christmas Eve.

He was taken to the USA for trial on charges of drugs trafficking and other offences, and sentenced to 30 years in prison. **Guillermo Endara** was installed as president. The Panamanian Defence Forces were immediately remodelled into a new Public Force whose largest component is the civilian National Police. Panama has not had a regular army since. Noriega was released in September 2007 and extradited to France, where he was jailed for two years for money laundering, before being extradited back to Panama. He is currently in prison, serving three 20-year sentences for crimes committed during his rule.

## After 'Just Cause'

After the overthrow of General Noriega's administration, the US Senate approved a US$1 billion aid package including US$480 million in direct assistance to provide liquidity and get the economy moving again. The USA also put Panama under considerable pressure to sign a Treaty of Mutual Legal Assistance, which would limit bank secrecy and enable investigation into suspected drug traffickers' bank accounts. While structural, economic and legal changes impacted Panama in the early 1990s, Panama was still not without problems. Charges of corruption at the highest level were made by Panamanians and US officials. President Endara himself was weakened by allegations that his law firm had been involved with companies owned by drugs traffickers. Though the economy grew under Endara, street crime increased, social problems continued, there were isolated bombings and pro-military elements failed in a coup attempt.

The 1994 elections took place with 2000 local and international observers, and polling was largely incident-free and open. Ernesto Pérez Balladares of the Partido Revolucionario Democrático (PRD), won with less than a third of the popular vote. He gave priority to tackling the problems of social inequality, unemployment, deteriorating education standards and rising crime.

## Into the 21st century

In 1999, **Mireya Moscoso** emerged victorious in presidential elections which saw a 78% voter turnout. Moscoso obtained 45% of the popular vote, ahead of her closest rival Martín Torrijos (son of General Omar Torrijos) with 38%. Moscoso took office on September 1, becoming the first female president of Panama, enjoying the honour of receiving control of the Panama Canal from the US on 31 December 1999, but left office with historically low approval ratings amid allegations of corruption.

Elections in May 2004 saw **Martín Torrijos**, son of former dictator Omar Torrijos, win the presidential elections. His main legacy was the initiation of an ambitious expansion of the Canal, including a fourth set of locks. In 2009, supermarket magnate **Ricardo Martinelli** and his conservative Democratic Change party rode to power as part of a right-wing coalition. Although Martinelli successfully overhauled much of the national infrastructure, his term saw no less than four violent uprisings when he sought to make sweeping changes to labour, environment and mineral codes; his party was voted out in 2014.

The new coalition government, headed by former vice-president and Panameñista candidate Juan Carlos Verala, has reached out to the old oligarchy as well as progressive figures in civil society. Although scheduled for completion in 2014, the Panama Canal expansion remained incomplete at the time of research.

## Culture

### People

The population of 3.2 million is mostly of mixed descent but there are indigenous and black communities and a small Asian population. Most of the rural population live in the six provinces on the Pacific side, west of the Canal. There is only one rural population centre of any importance on the Caribbean: in Bocas del Toro, in the extreme northwest.

Of the 60 indigenous tribes who inhabited the isthmus at the time of the Spanish conquest, only three have survived in any number: the Kunas (also spelt Cunas, particularly in Colombia) of the San Blas islands (50,000), the Guaymíes, who prefer to be called Ngöbe-Buglé, of the western provinces (80,000), and the Emberá-Wunan, formerly known as Chocóes of Darién (10,000). These, and a few others, such as the Naso, Bri-Bri and Bokotá, account for 6% of the total population. Indigenous opposition to the opening of copper mines at Cerro Colorado and demonstrations supporting greater autonomy for indigenous people in the area characterized 1996, but were inconclusive. However, an administrative enclave, the Comarca, providing for some Ngöbe-Buglé home rule, has been created.

Numbers of African slaves escaped from their Spanish owners during the 16th century. They set up free communities in the Darién jungles and their Spanish-speaking descendants, known as *cimarrones*, still live there and in the Pearl Islands. The majority of Panama's blacks, often bilingual, are descended from English-speaking West Indians, brought in for the building of the railway in 1850, and later of the Canal.

There are also a number of East Indians and Chinese, a few of whom, especially in the older generations, tend to cling to their own languages and customs.

### Music and dance

Being at the crossroads of the Americas, where Central America meets South America and the Caribbean backs on to the Pacific, and being one of the smallest Latin American republics, Panama possesses an outstandingly rich and attractive musical culture. Albeit related to that of the Caribbean coast of Colombia and Venezuela, it is very different. The classic Panamanian folk dances are the *tambor* or *tamborito, cumbia, punto* and *mejorana*, largely centred on the central provinces of Coclé, and Veraguas and those of Herrera and Los Santos on the Península Azuero. Towns that are particularly noted for their musical traditions are Los Santos, Ocú, Las Tablas, Tonosí and Chorrera. The dances are for couples and groups of couples and the rhythms are lively and graceful, the man often dancing close to his partner without touching her, moving his hat in rhythmic imitation of fanning. The woman's *pollera* costume is arguably the most beautiful in Latin America and her handling of the voluminous skirt is an important element of the dance. The *tamborito* is considered to be Panama's national dance and is accompanied by three tall drums. The *cumbia*, which has a common origin with the better-known Colombian dance of the same name, has a fast variant called the *atravesado*, while the *punto* is slower and more stately. The name *mejorana* is shared by a small native guitar, a dance, a song form and a specific tune. The most common instruments to be found today are the tall drums that provide the basic beat, the violin, the guitar and the accordion. The *tuna* is a highly rhythmic musical procession with women's chorus and massed hand-clapping.

Turning to song, there are two traditional forms, both of Spanish origin: the *copla*, sung by women and accompanying the *tamborito*, and the *mejorana*, which is a male solo preserve, with the lyrics in the form of *décimas*, a verse form used by the great Spanish poets of the Golden Age. It is accompanied by the ukulele-like guitar of the same name. Quite unique to Panama are the *salomas* and *gritos*, the latter between two or more men. The yodelling and falsetto of the *salomas* are in fact carried over into the singing style and it is this element, more than any other, that gives Panamanian folk song its unique and instantly recognizable sound. There are other traditional masked street dances of a carnavalesque nature, such as the very African *congos*, the *diablicos sucios* (dirty little devils) and the *grandiablos* (big devils). In the area of the Canal there is a significant English-speaking black population, similar to those in Nicaragua and Costa Rica, who also sing calypso, while the Guaymí people (Ngöbe-Buglé) in the west and the Kuna and Chocó (Emberá-Wunan) of the San Blas islands and Darién isthmus possess their own song, rituals and very attractive flute music.

## Land and environment

Panama is most easily visualized as a slightly stretched, horizontal 'S', with the 767-km Caribbean coastline on the north and the 1234-km Pacific coast on the south and lying between 7° and 10° north of the Equator. The Canal, which runs southeast-northwest, bisects the country; the mountains running along the isthmus divide the country from north to south. About one-third of the population lives in Panama City on the east side of the Canal at its southern terminus. Most of the rural population live in the quarter of the country south of the mountains and west of the Canal.

At the border with Costa Rica there are several inactive volcanic cones, the boldest of which is the Volcán Barú, 3475 m high and the highest point in the country. The sharp-sided Cordillera de Talamanca continues southeast at a general altitude of about 900 m, but subsides suddenly southwest of Panama City. The next range, the San Blas, rises east of Colón (the city at the north end of the Canal) running parallel to the Caribbean coastline, into Colombia. Its highest peak Tacarcuna, at 1875 m, is in the heart of the Darién. A third range rises from the Pacific littoral in the southeast, running along the Pacific coast of Colombia as the Serranía de Baudó. Nature decreed a gap between the Talamanca and San Blas ranges in which the divide is no more than 87 m high. The ranges are so placed that the gap, through which the Canal runs, follows a line from northwest to southeast. To reach the Pacific from the Atlantic you must travel eastwards so when travelling through the Canal (as in much of the country) the sun rises over the Pacific and sets over the Atlantic.

The rate of deforestation in Panama accelerated rapidly in the 1980s and early 1990s, but has fallen considerably. 70% of the country is classified as primary forest, more than any other Central American republic except Belize.

# Wildlife

Mexico alone has over 430 mammal species, more than 960 different birds, around 720 reptiles and almost 300 amphibians; as for insects, there are definitely more than you want to know about, from beautiful butterflies to biting bugs. Even the smallest country in the area, El Salvador, which has little natural habitat remaining, can boast a total of 680 species of vertebrates (the UK has just 280 or so). This diversity is due to the fact that the area is the meeting place of two of the world's major biological regions – the Nearctic to the north and the Neotropical to the south. It has a remarkable geological and climatic complexity and consequently an enormous range of habitats, from desert in the north of Mexico to rainforests, dry forests, cloudforests, mangroves and stretches of wetlands further south in the tropical areas of the region.

## When to go

In terms of wildlife, the best time to visit depends, obviously, on where you are and what you want to see, whether it's the sight of hundreds of thousands of migrating raptors passing over Central America between August and December, or that of nesting turtles along the coast from Mexico to Panama. The exact dates of the turtle season vary with the species, but June to October are peak times for many. In practise, planning will be required to get the timing right.

## Spotting wildlife

Use local, experienced guides as these people will know what species are around and where to look for them and will often recognize bird calls and use these as an aid to spotting them. You should take binoculars; get a pair with a reasonable magnification and good light-gathering configurations (ie 10x40 or 8x40) for use in the dim light of the rainforests. They will also need to be reasonably waterproof. Another enormous aid to wildlife watching is a strong torch or, better still, a powerful headlamp. The latter not only leaves your hands free but it also helps when trying to spot eye shine of nocturnal mammals, the light reflected back from their eyes direct to yours. Some places, such as Monteverde Cloud Forest Reserve in Costa Rica and the Community Baboon Sanctuary in Belize, offer excellent night walks with guides, but with care you can equally well arrange your own. Another strategy to use is to select a likely looking spot – such as a fruiting fig or a watering hole (in dry country) – and wait for the animals to come to you.

## Mammals

In Central America and Mexico mammals tend to be secretive, indeed the majority are nocturnal; hence the need for night walks if you are serious about finding them, though, even then, good views are comparatively rare. That said, you will certainly see some delightful creatures, with views of primates being more or less guaranteed. The rainforests throughout the region contain spider monkeys, howler monkeys and/or capuchin monkeys. The howlers are probably the most noticeable because, as their name suggests, they are inclined to make a huge row at times, especially early in the mornings and in the late afternoons. The Community Baboon Sanctuary in Belize was set up especially for the conservation of the black howler monkey and you've a good chance of seeing them in Tikal, Guatemala, in Parque Nacional Pico Bonito in Honduras, on the Omotepe Islands in Nicaragua and the rainforests of Costa Rica. The spider monkey is a much more agile, slender primate, swinging around high in the canopy, using its prehensile tail as a fifth limb and again found throughout the region. The smaller, **white-throated capuchins** are also commonly seen, moving around quite noisily in groups, searching for fruit and insects in the trees and even coming down to the ground to find food. Smaller again, and restricted to Panama and Costa Rica, is the **red-backed squirrel monkey**. The most likely places to see them are Corcovado and Manuel Antonio national parks in Costa Rica. Finally, for the daytime species, you may see a tamarin, both Geoffroy's and the cotton-top tamarin are present, but only in **Panama** (try Darién or Natural Metropolitano national parks). The New World, unlike Africa and Asia, has only one group (10 species) of nocturnal primates and this, appropriately enough, is the **night monkey**. Panama is the only country in the region to contain night monkeys.

Another mammal you are very likely to see in the southern countries of the region are sloths. Good places to look are Reserva Monteverde and the forests of Tortuguero and Manuel Antonio in Costa Rica. As they tend to stay in one area for days at a time, local guides are excellent at pointing them out. The most easily seen of the carnivores is not, sadly, the longed-for **jaguar**, but the ubiquitous **white-nosed coati**, a member of the racoon family. The females and their offspring go around in groups and are unmistakable with their long, ringed tails, frequently held in the air, and their long snouts sniffing around for insects and fruit in trees and on the ground. At many tourist sites, they hang around waiting to be fed by the visitors, in particular around Tikal and in the popular lowland national parks of Costa Rica. Members of the cat family are rarely seen; those in the area include the **bobcat** (in Mexico only), **jaguar**, **puma**, **ocelot** and margay. All are more likely to be seen at night, or, possibly, at dawn and dusk. In Belize, Cockscomb Basin Wildlife Sanctuary is also known as the Jaguar Reserve, so this area is as good a place as any to try your luck. Río Bravo and Chan Chich Lodge in Belize, Corcovado and Tortuguero national parks in Costa Rica and Reserva Biológica Indio Maíz in Nicaragua are also possibilities for the jaguar and the other small cats. The largest land mammal in Central America is **Baird's tapir**, weighing up to 300 kg. It is a forest species and very secretive, particularly so in areas where it is hunted. **Corcovado** and **Santa Rosa** national parks in Costa Rica are all places it might be seen, at least there is a reasonable chance of seeing its hoof prints. It might be seen at waterholes or be spotted swimming in rivers. More likely to be seen are **peccaries**, especially the collared peccary, medium sized pig-like animals that are active both day and night. The **collared peccary** can be found in both dry and rainforests throughout the region, while the **white-lipped peccary** is more common in wetter, evergreen forests. Both live in herds, of up to 100 individuals in the case of the white-lipped species. Found throughout the area, in drier, woodland patches, the **white-tailed deer** can easily be spotted, especially at dawn or dusk, or their bright eyeshine can be seen at night if you are out in a car or on foot with a torch. Also found from Mexico down into South America is the smaller **red brocket**; this, though, is a rainforest species and is more elusive. Rodent species you might come across include the **agouti**, which looks rather like a long-legged guinea pig and can be seen moving around on the forest floor. Considerably larger and stockier is the nocturnal **paca** (**gibnut** in Belize), another forest species found throughout the region, often near water where they hide when chased by predators. The world's largest rodent, the **capybara**, is also found near water, but in this region can be seen only in Panama, in Darién, for instance. **Bats** will usually be a quick fly past at night, impossible to identify but for the jagged flight path which is clearly not that of a bird. The nightly exodus of **bats** from caves near to El Zotz, in Petén, Guatemala is a spectacular sight. Others feed on fish, frogs, fruit and insects; probably the most notorious is the blood-sucking vampire bat, though it rarely attacks humans, instead feeding almost exclusively on domestic stock, such as cattle and goats.

Finally, marine mammals in the area include whales, **dolphins** and **manatees**. The last of these can be seen in Belize's Southern Lagoon, Lago Izabal in Guatemala or Cuero Y Salado Wildlife Reserve in Honduras. Whales and dolphins occur along both the Pacific and Atlantic coasts and can be watched at a number of sites as far south as Isla Iguana Wildlife Reserve in Panama.

## Birds

It is true, the early bird gets the worm and the earlier you get up, the more species you'll see. All countries have very high numbers of birds on their lists but Panama is the haven for birdwatchers in this area; though relatively tiny, it boasts almost as many (922) bird species as Mexico. One of the best places to go in Panama is the Pipeline Road (Sendero Oleoducto) in Parque Nacional Soberanía. In this lowland rainforest area, brilliantly coloured species such as the violaceous and slaty-tailed **trogans** or the blue-crowned **motmot** can be seen, along with parrots, tanagers, hummingbirds, **antbirds** and many others during the day. It is also a good place to see the spectacular keel-billed **toucan**. At night, eight species of owl, including the crested, can be found, along with **potoos** and a variety of **nightjars**. Also, for serious birders, not to be missed in Panama is Parque Nacional Darién with mangroves, lowland and montane rainforest where numerous raptors can be seen, including king and black vultures, crested eagles and, if you're really lucky, the huge, monkey-eating **harpy eagle** with its 2-m wing span. Macaws, **parrots** and **parakeets** are common, along with toucans, hummingbirds, aracaris and **tanagers**. The **golden-headed quetzal** can be seen at higher altitudes in Parque Nacional Darién (Cerro Pirre) and nowhere else in Central America.

Many of these birds can be seen outside Panama. **Toucans** and the smaller **toucanets** are widespread throughout the tropical areas of the region with the ruins of Tikal offering good siting opportunities. Another popular sighting is the **scarlet macaw** easily spotted near Puerto Juárez, Costa Rica, and the region of El Perú and the Río San Juan in Guatemala. Hummingbirds too are a common sighting throughout the region, frequently drawn to sugar-feeders. The **harpy eagle** is extremely rare with sightings on the Osa Peninsula, Costa Rica a possibility and in the rainforest region of northern Guatemala, Belize and southern Mexico.

To find the **resplendent quetzal**, a brilliant emerald green bird, with males having a bright scarlet breast and belly and ostentatious long green streamers extending as much as 50 cm beyond the end of its tail, Monteverde Cloud Forest Reserve or the less atmospheric Eddie Serrano Mirador in Costa Rica are a couple of the best places to go. You'll also have a good chance of spotting the quetzal in the Quetzal Biosphere Reserve in the Sierra de las Minas, Guatemala, where the bird is the national symbol and name of the currency.

In addition to the quetzal, Costa Rica, containing around 850 bird species, follows close on the heels of Panama as being a good country to visit for birdwatchers and **Monteverde** is a hotspot. Species there include black guans, emerald toucanets, violet sabrewings, long-tailed manakins, three wattled bellbirds and the threatened **bare-necked umbrellabird**. Mixed flocks of small birds such as **warblers**, **tanagers**, **woodcreepers** and **wood-wrens** can also be seen in the area. La Selva Biological Station, an area of rainforest in Costa Rica, is another area rich in rainforest species such as the **chestnut-billed toucan**, mealy parrot and squirrel cuckoo. A very different habitat, with, consequently, different birds, is found in the large wetland area of Parque Nacional Palo Verde in Costa Rica. Here one can see the **jabiru**, **black-necked stilt**, **spotted rail**, **bare-throated tiger heron**, **purple gallinule** and many other waterbirds. In the dry season, **ducks**, including the **black-bellied whistling duck**, **blue-billed teal**, **ring-necked duck** and **northern pintail**, congregate in this area in their thousands. More rarely seen here is the **white-faced whistling duck**. Many of these waterbirds can also be seen in Crooked Tree Wildlife Sanctuary in Belize.

Of course, all along the coasts are masses of different seabirds, including **pelicans**, **boobies** and the **magnificent frigate bird**. And in Mexico coastal, wetlands near Celestún and in Río Lagarto on the Yucatán Peninsula provide good sightings of **pink flamingoes**.

If you are looking for real rarities, then try spotting the threatened **horned guam**, a highly distinctive and striking bird, that can be found only in high cloudforests of Mexico and Guatemala, for example, in El Triunfo Biosphere Reserve in Mexico.

## Reptiles

This covers **snakes**, **lizards**, **crocodilians** and **turtles**. Mexico has more of these animals than any other country in the world. Throughout the whole region, though, you are not particularly likely to see snakes in the wild; for those wishing to do so, a snake farm or zoo is the best place to go. You might, though, be lucky on one of your walks and see a **boa constrictor**, or, again, a guide might know where one is resting. In contrast, **lizards** are everywhere, from small geckos walking up walls in your hotel room, catching insects attracted to the lights, to the large **iguanas** sunbathing in the tree tops. The **American crocodile** and **spectacled caiman** are both found throughout the area, with the latter being seen quite frequently. **Morlet's crocodile**, on the other hand, is found only in Mexico, Belize and Guatemala. Several species of both freshwater and sea **turtles** are present in the region. Parque Nacional Tortuguero in Costa Rica is a good place to see freshwater turtles and four species of marine turtle, while at Ostional Beach in Santa Rosa National Park you can watch masses of olive ridley turtles coming in to lay their eggs, particularly in September and October. You'll also be able to see nesting turtles along the Pacific coastal beaches of Nicaragua, in La Mosquitia, Honduras, Monterrico, Guatemala and Mexico.

## Amphibians

You'll certainly hear frogs and toads, even if you do not see them. However, the brightly coloured **poison-dart frogs** and some of the tree frogs are well worth searching out. Look for them in damp places, under logs and moist leaf litter, in rock crevices and by ponds and streams, many will be more active at night. Monteverde and La Selva Reserves are both rich in amphibians, and a visit to Bocas del Toro will also reveal colourful amphibians on appropriately named Red Frog Beach.

## Invertebrates

There are uncounted different species of invertebrates in the area. Probably, most desirable for ecotourists are the **butterflies**, though some of the **beetles**, such as the jewel **scarabs**, are also pretty spectacular. If you are fascinated by spiders, you can always go hunting for nocturnal **tarantulas**; Lamanai in **Belize** harbours four different species. There are **butterfly farms** in some of the countries, including Nicaragua (Los Guatusos Wildlife Reserve) and Costa Rica (eg el Jardín de Mariposas in Monteverde) that will give you a close up view of many different species. Watching **leaf-cutter ants** marching in long columns from a bush they are systematically destroying and taking the pieces of leaf to their nest, huge mounds on the forest floor, can be an absorbing sight, while marching columns of army ants, catching and killing all small beasts in their path, are best avoided.

## Marine wildlife

Predicting the movement and location of marine animals is difficult, and often sightings of sharks and rays is chance. However, the **whale shark** makes a seasonal migration through the coastal waters of Belize and Honduras between March and May. Less natural shark encounters can be had off **Caye Caulker** (Belize) and **Isla Mujeres** (Yucatán, Mexico), where hand-feeding brings in **sting rays** and **nurse sharks** for close but safe encounters.

# Books & films

## Books

### Southern Mexico

**Coe, MD**   *The Maya* (Pelican Books, or large format edition, Thames and Hudson). Essential recommended reading for the Maya archaeological area.

**Franz, Carl**   *The People's Guide to Mexico* (John Muir Publications, Santa Fe, NM). Highly recommended, practical, entertaining and now in its 11th edition. There is also a *People's Guide Travel Letter*.

**Greene, Graham**   *The Lawless Roads*. Greene's classic journey through Chiapas and Tabasco during the anticlerical purges of the 1930s. Also see his masterpiece, *The Power and the Glory*.

**Huxley, Aldous**   *Eyeless in Gaza*. The story of an Oxford graduate who takes up arms with Mexican revolutionaries. By the same author, *Beyond the Mexique Bay* is a journey through the Caribbean, Guatemala and Mexico during the 1930s

**Lawrence, DH**   *The Plumed Serpent*. Lawrence's classic is a fictional exploration of Aztec religion and a criticism of Catholicism.

**Lowry, Malcolm**   *Under the Volcano*. Set in Mexico and apparently inspired by the cantinas of Oaxaca City, Lowry's delirious depiction of alcoholic ruin is a masterpiece and vastly underrated.

**Peterson and Chalif**   *A Field Guide to Mexican Birds* (Houghton Mifflin).

**Thomas, Hugh**   *Conquest: Cortes, Montezuma, and the fall of the Old Mexico*.

**Tree, Isabella**   *Sliced Iguana – Travels in Mexico*. Gets the real flavour of Mexico and is a great travel companion.

### Belize

**King, Emory**   *Hey Dad, this is Belize*. A collection of anecdotes by a local celebrity who found himself in Belize after surviving a shipwreck out on the cayes.

**Association for Belize Archaeology**, *Warlords and Maize Men*. A guide to Mayan sites.

### Guatemala

**Asturias, Miguel Angel**   *Hombres de maíz*, *Mulata de tal* and *El señor presidente*. Classics of Guatemalan literature.

**Daniels, Anthony**   *Sweet Waist of America: Journeys around Guatemala* (Hutchinson). Travelogue.

**Menchú, Rigoberta**   *I, Rigoberta Menchú*. From the Mayan nobel-prize winner.

**Payeras, Mario**   *Los días de la selva*. A first-hand account of the guerrilla movement in the 1970s.

**Schele, L and Friedel, D**   *A Forest of Kings*. Linda Schele's work in deciphering the narratives contained in Classic Mayan monuments has been crucial to our understanding of Mayan history. Highly recommended; there are many other intriguing titles by the same author.

### El Salvador

**Argueta, Manlio**   *One day of Life* and *Cuzcatlán*. A look at peasant rebellion during El Salvador's 20th-century history.

**Raudales, Walter**   *Amor de Jade*. To be published in English too, is a novel based on the life of El Salvador's Mata Hari (now ex-comandante Joaquín Villalobos' wife).

## Honduras

**Theroux, Paul**   *The Mosquito Coast* (Penguin). Was also turned into a film starring Harrison Ford.
**Lewis, Norman**   *The Volcanoes Above.*

## Nicaragua

**Cabezas, Omar**   *Fire from the Mountain: The Making of a Sandinista.* Descriptions of León's fight against the Somoza regime.
**Darío, Rubén**   *Cuentos Completos.* The collected stories of this great Nicaraguan poet, the quintessential Latin American author.
**Marriott, Edward**   *Savage Shore: Life and Death with Nicaragua's Last Shark Hunters.* A look at the life of the shark hunters of Lake Nicaragua.
**Rushdie, Salman**   *The Jaguar Smile.* A romantic view of the Revolution, but maybe that's only with the benefit of hindsight.

## Costa Rica

*Costa Rica: A Guide to the People, Politics and Culture* (In Focus series, Latin America Bureau). A distilled analysis of the country.
**Beletsky, Les**   *Costa Rica: The Ecotravellers' Wildlife Guide.* Great nature book.
**Stiles, Gary and Skutch, Alexander** *Guide to the Birds of Costa Rica* (Cornell University Press). The definitive field guide for birdwatchers.

## Panama

**Dinges, John**   *Our Man in Panama.* For the era of military rule.
**DuFord, D**   *Is there a hole in the boat? Tales of travel in Panama without a car.* A collection of lively travel stories from an award-winning writer.
**Dyke, T & Winder, P**   *The Cloud Garden* (Lyons Press). The true story of a horticulturist and a banker who travel to the Darién Gap in search of rare orchids, only to be kidnapped by Colombian paramilitaries.
**Greene, G**   *Getting to know the General* (Random House). Graham Greene's shameless apology for Omar Torrijos is rather fascinating.
**Howe, J**   *A people who would not kneel: Panama, the United States and the San Blas Kuna* (Smithsonian Books). A fascinating account of Guna history, politics and anthropology.
**Le Carré, John**   *Tailor of Panama.* A cynical but entertaining view of Panama City society.
**McCullough's, David**   *The Path Between the Seas.* For the history of the Canal.
**Ridgely, Robert S and John Gwynn** *Guide to the Birds of Panama* (Princeton University Press). The definitive guide for ornithologists it is richly illustrated and describes 929 species.

## Southern Mexico

**Apocalypto** (2006). Mel Gibson's portrayal of the last days of Mayan civilization is one-sided and violent. Nonetheless, it's a visually diverting production and action-packed.

**Sin dejar huella** (*Without a trace*, 2000). Women's road movie following a journey from north to south Mexico ending up in the Yucatán. Great scenery.

**Sin nombre** (2009). A powerful treatment of illegal immigration and Mexican gang culture. Focuses on the story of a Honduran girl travelling north into Mexico.

**Y tu mamá también** (2002). Another road movie, this time to the beautiful beach of Boca del Cielo, on the coast of Chiapas.

## Guatemala

**El Norte** (1983). Follows the plight of a Guatemalan brother and sister who seek a new life after experiencing the trials of their village massacre.

**La Jaula de Oro** (*The Golden Cage*, 2013). A more recent release, this award-winning tells the story of 3 Guatemalan teenagers and their journey to become illegal immigrants in the US.

**When the Mountains Tremble** (1983). A hard-hitting film demonstrating the desperation of national governments and guerrillas.

## Belize

**Three Kings of Belize** (2007). A great documentary that follows Belizean musicians Paul Nabor, Wilfred Peters and Florencio Mess.

## El Salvador

**Voces inocentes** (*Innocent Voices*) (2004). Academy award-nominated film about the civil war seen through the eyes of an 11-year-old child soldier.

**Romero** (1989). Covers the story surrounding the archbishop's assassination. Starring Raúl Julia.

**Salvador** (1986). Oliver's Stone film takes the journalist's view of events in the country's civil war circa 1980.

## Honduras

**Latino** (1985). Follows the twists, turns, loves and contradictions of a Latino US soldier drafted to Honduras to provide military training in the mid-1980s.

## Nicaragua

**Carla's Song**, set during the Revolution and starring Nick Nolte and Gene Hackman, is an insightful, if feverishly pro-Sandinista portrayal of Nicaragua post-Revolution.

**Under Fire** is a film which mixes a lot of fact with some fiction. While the setting may be Nicaragua, it was filmed in Mexico.

**Walker** (USA, 1987). This counter-culture take on filibuster William Walker was shot in Nicaragua during the Contra War.

## Costa Rica

**El Camino** (2007). By Costa Rican director Ishtar Yasin, El Camino follows the journey of two Nicaraguan children as they travel to Costa Rica to find their long-lost mother.

## Panama

**Canal Zone** (1977). Directed by Frederick Wiseman, a trilogy documentary series looking at life in the Canal Zone.

**The Tailor of Panama** (2001). A lightweight tale of intrigue adapted from John Le Carré's novel. Some great lines: "Welcome to Panama – Casablanca without heroes".

# Practicalities

# **Getting** there

All countries in Latin America (in fact across the world) officially require travellers entering their territory to have an onward or return ticket and may at times ask to see that ticket. Although rarely enforced at airports, this regulation can create problems at land border crossings. In lieu of an onward ticket out of the country you are entering, any ticket out of another Latin American country may sometimes suffice, or proof that you have sufficient funds to buy a ticket (a credit card will do). International air tickets are expensive if purchased in Latin America.

## Air

Certain Central American countries impose local tax on flights originating there. Among these are Guatemala, Costa Rica, Panama and Mexico.

Fares from Europe and North America to Latin American destinations vary. Peak periods and higher prices correspond to holiday season in the northern hemisphere. The very busy seasons are as follows: 7 December to 15 January and July to mid-September. If you intend travelling during those times, book as far ahead as possible. Check with an agency for the best deal for when you wish to travel.

There is a wide range of offers to choose from in a highly competitive environment. An indication of cost is difficult to give due to the large number of variables, not least the current fluctuations in currency and the wide variations in oil prices in recent years. The main factors are frequency of flights and popularity of destination at a particular time of year. As a rough guide a three-month London–Mexico return in August is around US$1200. In November the same flight falls to US$1000. Travellers from Australia and New Zealand are getting an increasingly better deal compared with recent years, with special offers occasionally down to AUS$1900 flying direct to Mexico City. The more regular price is close to AUS$3200.

Fares fall into three groups, and are all on scheduled services: **Excursion** (return) fares: these have restricted validity either seven to 90 days, or seven to 180 days, depending on the airline. They are fixed-date tickets where the dates of travel cannot be changed after issue without incurring a penalty. **Yearly fares**: these may be bought on a one-way or return basis, and usually the returns can be issued with the return date left open. You must, however, fix the route. **Student** (or Under-26) fares: one way and returns available, or 'open jaws' for people intending to travel a linear route and return from a different point from that which they entered.

Note all travellers to the US (including those in transit) who are eligible for a visa waiver must submit to the **Electronic System for Travel Authorization (ESTA)**; see page 1066.

### Flights from Europe

It is worth considering **Mexico City** as an entry/exit point. Air fares between February and June can be very reasonable (although the same does not apply to Cancún, when high season signals a steep price climb) and European carriers include **Air France, British Airways, Iberia, KLM** and **Lufthansa**. With the promotion of **Cancún** as a gateway from Europe, there are a large number of scheduled flights from Europe to the Yucatán peninsula. The best deals can be found from November to January and carriers include **Air Berlin, Air Europa, Air France, Blue Panorama Airways, British Airways, Condor, Jet Airfly,**

Lufthansa, Nordwind, Orbest, Virgin Atlantic and XL Airways. Aeroméxico also offers competitive prices from London. There are some very affordable no-frills seasonal charter flights (for example Thomas Cook, Thomson Airways, TUfly Nordic, LOT, EuroAtlantic Airways and Arkefly).

Beyond Mexico, there are fewer direct flights to the region and you will usually have to travel via the US.

Iberia flies directly to **Guatemala** from Madrid and via Miami, with connecting flights from other European cities. Long-haul operators from Europe will share between airlines, taking passengers across the Atlantic normally to Miami, and using **Taca**, for example, to link to Guatemala City.

The only direct flights to **San Salvador** are from Madrid with **Iberia**. All other European flights go via the US (see below).

There are no direct flights to Tegucigalpa in **Honduras** from Europe, all traffic is routed via the US (see below). There are flights to Roatán from Milan-Malpensa with **Air Italy**.

There are no direct flights to **Nicaragua** from Europe, but connecting flights can be made via Miami (see below).

Iberia have daily flights between Madrid and San José, **Costa Rica**. There are direct charter flights in season from several European cities including Frankfurt (**Condor**). **Martinair**, a subsidiary of KLM, flies Costa Rica–Netherlands, for around US$500 return. From most European cities flights connect in the US; see below.

To **Panama** KLM offers direct flights from Amsterdam, **Iberia** from Madrid, **Air France** from Paris, **Condor** from Frankfurt, and **Avior** from Barcelona. **Lufthansa** is scheduled to begin flights to Panama City from Frankfurt in November 2015. All other flights include a stopover in the US, but Tocumen's expansion plans mean that could change soon.

## Flights from the US and Canada

Flying to **Mexico** from the US offers a very wide range of options. The main US carriers are **American Airlines, US Airways, Delta** and **United**. The main departure points are Atlanta, Miami, Dallas/Fort Worth, Los Angeles and San Francisco. For low-cost flights to Mexico, try **Spirit Air** or **Jet Blue** (recommended). From Canada, the options are less varied, but regular flights serve the main cities with direct flights from Montreal and Toronto with **Air Canada**. Keep an eye out for special offers, which can produce extremely cheap flights (often at very short notice).

**Belize** is served by American Airlines, Delta and United (many travellers find it cheaper to fly into Cancún and travel overland to Belize, see Border crossings box, page 1038).

From the US to **Guatemala**, you can fly with American Airlines, Delta, Spirit Air and United. From Canada connections to Guatemala are made through San Salvador, Los Angeles or Miami.

There are flights to **San Salvador** from Dallas/Fort Worth and Miami with **American Airlines**; from Chicago-O'Hare, Dallas/Fort Worth, Houston-Intercontinental, Los Angeles, Miami, San Francisco, Washington-Dulles, New York and Toronto-Pearson with **Avianca**; from Atlanta and Los Angeles with **Delta Airlines**; from Fort Lauderdale and Houston-Intercontinental with **Spirit Airlines**; and from Houston-Intercontinental with **United Airlines**.

There are flights to Tegucigalpa, **Honduras**, from Miami with **American Airlines**; from Atlanta with **Delta Airlines**; and from Houston-Intercontinental with **United**. There are flights to Roatán from Miami and Dallas/Fort Worth with **American Airlines**; from Atlanta with **Delta Airlines**; from Montreal-Trudeau and Toronto-Pearson with **Air Transat** and

Sunwing Airlines (seasonally); and from Houston-Intercontinental with United Airlines. There are flights to San Pedro Sula from Miami and New York-JFK with Avianca; from Atlanta with Delta; from Fort Lauderdale and Houston-Intercontinental with Spirit Airlines; from Houston-Intercontinental and Newark with United Airlines.

Several US carriers now fly directly to Managua, **Nicaragua**, from a handful of US cities including Atlanta with Delta Airlines; Fort Lauderdale with Spirit Airlines; Houston with United Airlines, Copa, and Air Canada; and Miami with American Airlines, Iberia, US Airways, TACA and British Airways. Return flights cost around US$400-800.

Flights to San José, **Costa Rica**, from North American cities include Atlanta with Delta and Air France; Dallas with American Airlines, British Airways and US Airways; Fort Lauderdale with Spirit Airlines and Jet Blue; Houston with United Airlines and Air Canada; Los Angeles with Delta; Miami with American Airlines and US Airways; Newark with United Airlines; and Orlando with Jet Blue. Non-stop flights to Liberia depart from Atlanta with Delta; Dallas with American Airlines; Houston with United Airlines; Miami with American Airlines; New York with Jet Blue; and Toronto with WestJet. Return flights cost around US$300-800 for either San José or Liberia.

There are daily flights to **Panama City** from Boston with Copa and United Airlines; Chicago with Copa and United Airlines; Fort Lauderdale with Spirit Airlines; Houston with Copa and United Airlines; Las Vegas with Copa and United Airlines; Los Angeles with Copa, United Airlines and Asiana; Miami with Copa, United Airlines, US Airways, American Airlines, British Airways and Iberia; Montreal with Copa; New York with Copa, Asiana and United Airlines; Newark with Copa and United Airlines; Orlando with Copa and United Airlines; Tampa with Copa and United Airlines, and Washington DC with Copa and United Airlines. Return flights cost US$300-800.

## Flights from Central America

Connections are available throughout Central America, in most cases travelling through the capital city. There are exceptions with connections to Belize from Flores. The main regional carriers are **Aeroméxico**, **Copa** and **Avianca** (with its many subsidiaries).

## Flights from South America

To Guatemala, **Avianca** flies from Bogotá via San José, **Copa** via Panama. There are good connections from El Salvador to Colombia with a few flights to Barranquilla and Bogotá. Also available are connections with Buenos Aires, Cali, Caracas, Cartagena, Cúcuta, Guayaquil, Quito, Lima, Medellín, Santa Marta and Santiago. To Nicaragua, there are good connections with **Copa** and **Aeroméxico**. Costa Rica has flights to Bogotá, Cali, Caracas, Cartagena, Guayaquil, Lima, Quito and Santiago; **Avianca** is the main carrier for all these destinations. Panama is also a hub for South America, served mainly by **Copa** and **Avianca**.

## Sea

Following the coastal route doesn't have to be done from the land side, as thousands of sailors who follow the good-weather sailing around the coast of Mexico and Central America can confirm. Indeed there seem to be increasing numbers of people travelling this way. Between California, the Panama Canal and Florida dozens of marinas await the sailor looking to explore the region from the sea. A guide to the marinas and sailing ports of the region is *Cruising Ports: the Central American Route*, and *Mexico Boating Guide* by Captain Pat Rains, published by Point Loma Publishing in San Diego. Captain Rain is an experienced navigator of Mexican and Central American waters with over 30 Panama transits under her cap (www.centralamericanboating.com).

Travelling by freighter to the region is possible as a paid passenger, but since fares include room and board for your time at sea, costs are comparable to international flights. Aside from the obvious adventure appeal, it is really only worth considering if you are shipping a vehicle from Europe or the US. Enquiries regarding passages should be made through agencies in your own country. In the UK, **Strand Voyages** have information on occasional one-way services to the Gulf of Mexico from Europe. For boat travel within the region, see Getting around, page 1030.

### In Europe
**The Cruise People**, T020-7723 2450, www.cruise people.co.uk.
**Globoship**, Switzerland, T31-313 0004, www.globoship.ch.
**Strand Voyages**, T020-7802 2199, www.strandtravel.co.uk.

### In the US
**Freighter World Cruises**, T1-800-531 7774, www.freightercruises.com.

**Travltips Cruise and Freighter Travel Association**, T1-800-872 8584, www.travltips.com.

### In Panama
**Blue Sailing**, Calle San Andrés 30-47, Getsemani Cartagena, T0057-5668 6485, US T203-660 8654, www.bluesailing.net. Travel agency handling boating and sailing trips between Colombia and Panama.

# Getting around

Bus travel is the most popular style of transport for independent travellers. An excellent network criss-crosses the region varying in quality from luxurious intercity cruisers with air conditioning, videos and fully reclining seats, to beaten-up US-style school buses or 'chicken buses' with busted suspension and holes in the floor.

Travelling under your own steam is also very popular. Driving your own vehicle – car, camper van, motorbike and bicycle – offers wonderful freedom and may not be as expensive or as bureaucratic as you think. From the emails we receive, the ever-greater cooperation between the nations of Central America is producing dramatic benefits at border crossings for those who decide to go it alone. Indeed, since 2006, when Guatemala, El Salvador, Honduras and Nicaragua signed the **Central America-4**, it's been even easier (see box, page 1031). With the comprehensive road network it's easy to miss out on other sensible choices. Don't shun the opportunity to take a short flight. While you'll need to enquire about precise costs, the view from above provides a different perspective and the difference in cost may not be as great as you think. Getting around in Central America is rarely a problem whether travelling by bus, car, bike, in fact almost any mode of transport.

There is just one caveat that stands good across all situations: be patient when asking directions. Often Latin Americans will give you the wrong answer rather than admit they do not know. Distances are notoriously inaccurate so ask a few people.

## Air

With the exception of El Salvador, all countries have a domestic flight service and some of the national airlines offer connections throughout Central and Latin America. Prices can be steep due to a lack of competition, but it is definitely worth considering an aerial 'hop' if it covers a lot of difficult terrain and you get the bonus of a good view.

From Mexico City and Cancún, the main regional carriers are **Aeroméxico**, **Avianca**, **Copa**, **Interjet** (recommended), **VivaAerobus** and **Volaris**. From Belize City, **Tropic Air** and **Maya Island Air** serve Cancún, Honduras and Guatemala (Flores and Guatemala City). From Guatemala City, the regional carriers are **Aeroméxico**, **Avianca**, **Copa**, **Interjet**, **Transportes Aereos Guatemaltecos** (Flores, Honduras, El Salvador) and **Veca Airlines** (El Salvador).

In Honduras, for the Bay Islands, there are domestic flights to Roatán from Tegucigalpa with **Aerolíneas Sosa**, **Avianca**, **CM Airlines** and **Easy Sky**; from La Ceiba with **AeroCaribe**, **Aerolíneas Sosa**, **Easy Sky** and **Lanhsa**. The small carrier **Island Air** flies between Utila and Roatán. Flights from La Ceiba connect with the Bay Islands, Guanaja and Puerto Lempira.

**La Costeña** operates services to Bluefields, the Corn Islands, Las Minas (Bonanza/Siuna/Rosita), Bilwi (previously known as Puerto Cabezas), San Juan de Nicaragua (also known as San Juan del Norte) and San Carlos. No seat assignments are given and flights are often fully booked.

From San José in Costa Rica you can fly to Arenal (La Fortuna), Dominical/Palmar Sur, Drake Bay, Golfito, Liberia, Norasa, Puerto Jiménez, Punta Islita, Quepos, Tamarindo, Tambor and Tortuguero. The two domestic airlines are **Sansa** and **Nature Air**.

There are local flights to most parts of the country with **Air Panama**, including David, Bocas del Toro, Pedasí, Islas Perlas, landing strips of Guna Yala (including Achutupo, Playón Chico, El Provenir, Corazón de Jesus, Ogobsucum, Mulatupo and Puerto Obaldía) and Darién province (including Sambú, Garachine, Jaque and Bahía Piñas).

Remote destinations throughout the region are invariably served by small aircraft with stringent weight restrictions and extra charges for large items such as surf boards; check with the airlines before setting out.

## Boat

Keeping all options open, water transport has to be a consideration – although not a very realistic one – in terms of reaching a distant destination. Most water transport consists of small boats with outboard motors. They travel relatively short distances in localized areas, usually along tropical rivers or between off-shore islands, where road transport is otherwise lacking. Due to the high cost of fuel, they are frequently crowded and somewhat expensive compared to buses. If hiring a boat privately, it is best to share costs with other travellers. Overcharging is very possible and when calculating costs you need to consider the weight of cargo (including passengers), distance covered, engine horse-power, fee for the driver, port taxes (if any) and, most importantly, the quantity of fuel used.

You'll find just a few regular ferry schedules that avoid circuitous land routes – the main journey is from the Mexican border town of Chetumal to the northern Cayes of Belize, which skips Belize City; see box, page 1038. Crossing the Usumacinta river between Guatemala and Mexico is a well-established (if remote) option that connects Chiapas with the Petén; see box, page 1038. There are also ferry connections between Punta Gorda in Belize and Lívingston in Guatemala. See box, page 1039.

Other main journeys by boat are from the Bay Islands of Honduras to the mainland; across Lake Nicaragua; and in Costa Rica, where there are connections between the mainland and the Osa and Nicoya peninsulas on the Pacific Coast. If heading from Panama to South America, if determined, you can work your way along the Caribbean coastline to Colombia using a number of small sporadically available vessels.

Beyond this functional one journey stands out: travelling the Panama Canal (as opposed to just seeing it!) and crewing a private yacht. Both of these require flexible schedules and good timing, but you might get lucky. Conditions of 'employment' vary greatly – you may get paid, you may get board and lodgings, and you may even have to pay.

## Road

### Bus and colectivo

**Bus** There is an extensive road system with frequent bus services throughout Mexico and Central America. Costs, quality and levels of comfort vary enormously; see country sections below for an overview. As a general rule, in mountainous country (and after long journeys), do not expect buses to get to their destination anywhere near on time. Avoid turning up for a bus at the last minute; if it is full it may depart early. Try to sit near the front; going round bends and over bumps has less impact on your body near the front axle, making the journey more comfortable and reducing the likelihood of motion sickness (on some long journeys it also means you are further from the progressively smelly toilets, if available, at the back of the bus). Tall travellers are advised to take aisle seats on long journeys as this allows more leg room.

When the journey takes more than three or four hours, meal stops at country inns or bars, good and bad, are the rule. Often no announcement is made on the duration of the stop; ask the driver and follow him, if he eats, eat. See what the locals are eating – and buy likewise, or make sure you're stocked up on food and drink at the start. For drinks, stick to bottled water, soft drinks or coffee (black). The food sold by vendors at bus stops may be all right; watch if locals are buying. Do not leave valuable items on the bus during stops. Importantly, make sure you have a sweater or blanket to hand for long bus journeys, especially at night; even if it's warm outside, the air conditioning is often set to blizzard.

**Southern Mexico** Mexican buses are generally very efficient and put US **Greyhound** buses to shame. In some cities there is a central bus terminal, while in others there are a couple: one for first-class services, one for second. A third variation is division by companies. In southern Mexico, **ADO** ⓘ www.ado.com.mx, is the main operator and it has several subsidiaries, including **OCC** and **ADO GL**. Most intercity routes are served by comfortable first-class buses with reclining seats, air conditioning, Spanish-language movies and toilet. For those seeking extra luxury, **ADO Platino** offers a soft drinks, snacks and almost horizontally aligned seats. It is highly advisable to book your tickets several days in advance when travelling at Christmas, Semana Santa or other national holidays. If your journey is longer than six hours, it is sensible to book 24 hours ahead. First-class fares are usually 10% dearer than second-class ones and the superior classes 30-40% more than first class. On a long journey you can save the price of a hotel room by travelling overnight, but in some areas this is dangerous and not recommended. You can book tickets in advance on the ADO website or with **Boletotal** ⓘ www.boletotal.mx.

**Belize** Public transport between most towns is by bus and, with the short distances involved, there are few long journeys to encounter. Trucks carry passengers to many isolated destinations. Most buses are ex-US school buses with small seats and limited leg room. There are a few ex-**Greyhounds**, mostly used for 'express' services and charters. It is recommended to buy tickets for seats in advance at the depot before boarding the bus. To find out about bus schedules go to www.guidetobelize.info (then select travel and then bus). Most buses have no luggage compartments so bags that do not fit on the luggage rack are stacked at the back. Get a seat at the back to keep an eye on your gear, but rough handling is more of a threat than theft.

**Guatemala** There is an extensive network of bus routes throughout the country. Like Belize, the chicken buses (former US school buses) are mostly in a poor state of repair and overloaded. Faster and more reliable Pullman services operate on some routes. Correct fares should be posted. We receive regular complaints that bus drivers charge tourists more than locals, a practice that is becoming more widespread. One way to avoid being overcharged is to watch for what the locals pay or ask a local, then tender the exact fare on the bus. Many long-distance buses leave very early in the morning. Make sure you can get out of your hotel/*pension*. For international bus journeys make sure you have small denomination local currency or US dollar bills for border taxes. At Easter there are few buses on Good Friday or the Saturday and buses are packed with long queues for tickets for the few days before Good Friday. Many names on bus destination boards are abbreviated; for example, Guate – Guatemala City; Chichi – Chichicastenango; Xela/Xelajú – Quetzaltenango, and so on.

**El Salvador** Bus services are good and cover most areas, although the buses are usually crowded. The best time to travel by bus is 0900-1500; avoid Friday and Sunday afternoons. All bus routes have a number, some also have a letter. Strange as it may seem, the system works and the route numbers don't change. Tickets are still unbelievably cheap, both within cities – usually around US$0.25 – and for long-distance journeys, which rarely cost more than US$1.50. Buses are brightly painted, particularly around San Miguel. The cheaper alternatives to the **Pullman** buses, which cross to Guatemala and Tegucigalpa from Puerto Bus Terminal in San Salvador, have luggage compartments beneath them and the luggage is tagged.

**Honduras** There are essentially three types of service: local (*servicio a escala*), direct (*servicio directo*) and luxury (*servicio de lujo*). Using school buses, a *servicio a escala* is very slow, with frequent stops and detours and is uncomfortable for long periods. *Servicio directo* is faster, slightly more expensive and more comfortable. *Servicio de lujo* has air-conditioned European and Brazilian buses with videos. For safety, it is highly recommended you use direct or luxury services where possible, such as Hedman Alas, www.hedmanalas.com, and Viana Transportes, www.vianatransportes.com. If intending to do a lot of bus travel, consider buying a discount card from Hedman Alas' sister company, **Promodias** ⓘ *www.promodias.com*, available at bus terminals – it offers deals on hotels, restaurants and other tourist services.

Buses set out early in the day, with a few night buses running between major urban centres. Try to avoid bus journeys after dark as there are many more accidents and even occasional robberies.

Minibuses are faster than buses, so the journey can be quite hair-raising. Pickups that serve out-of-the-way communities will leave you covered in dust (or soaked) – sit in or near the cab if possible.

**Nicaragua** Local buses are the cheapest in Central America and often the most crowded. This is how most Nicaraguans get around and, outside Managua, the bus drivers are usually friendly and helpful. Route schedules are pretty reliable except on Sundays. You can flag down most buses that are not marked 'Express'. Fares are collected as you board city buses or en route in the case of intercity buses. For express buses, you need to purchase your ticket in advance at the terminal or from the driver; some buses have reserved seating. Baggage loaded on to the roof or in the luggage compartment may be charged for, usually at half the passenger rate or a flat fee of US$0.50.

**Costa Rica** The good road network supports a regular bus service that covers most parts of the country. Buses are reasonably comfortable by Central American standards, most have reclining seats but no air conditioning or onboard toilets (there are highway breaks every two to three hours). San José is the main hub for buses, although you can skip down the Pacific coast by making connections at Puntarenas. Coming from Nicaragua, direct to Arenal, requires cutting in and travelling through Tilarán. Shuttle bus companies offer transport from the capital to dozens of beach and tourist destinations in comfortable air-conditioned minibuses; they're quicker but more expensive.

**Panama** All major towns and cities are served by an affordable and efficient bus network. Most intercity buses are 28-seater air-conditioned 'coasters', often enlivened with high-volume salsa or reggaeton. There is limited luggage space at the back, but strapping bags to the roof is an option. If departing from Panama City, buy your ticket at one of the booths before boarding. Elsewhere, a *pavo* (assistant) will collect fares after departure. Designated bus stops usually consist of a concrete shelter by the roadside. To get off, simply inform the *pavo* of your desired destination or yell 'parada' (stop). Buses making the haul between Panama City and David are comfortable, modern, air-conditioned coaches. Rickety *diablos rojos* (red devils) are converted US school buses, usually pimped with gaudy artwork and disco lights, and they are gradually being phased out.

**Colectivos (shuttles and taxis)** In parts of Central America, especially Mexico and Guatemala, a colectivo can refer to an economical shuttle van (also called a combi, especially in Chiapas), or to a shared taxi, where the fare is divided between four or five passengers, or where the driver picks up and drops off passengers between destinations. The distances covered are comparatively short with most journey times under four hours. The advantage of colectivos is that they often travel backdoor routes and supply a speedy alternative to conventional buses. They are, however, less comfortable than ADO. For safety and security, it is best to avoid using colectivo taxis in any of the capital cities.

On many popular routes throughout the region there are tourist shuttle vans that can be booked through hotels and travel agencies. These are pricier than regular colectivos but they travel longer distances and can take a lot of the hassle out of journeys that involve several changes or border crossings (for example, San Cristóbal de las Casas to Antigua). They will also pick you up from your hotel. **Belize Shuttles** ⓘ *Belize International Airport, Ladyville, T631-1749, in the USA T757-383 8024 and Canada T647-724 2004, www. belizeshuttlesandtransfers.com*, offer transfers to and from Belize City, to many other parts of the country, and to Cancún in Mexico and Flores in Guatemala (for the ruins at Tikal).

**International buses** These link the capital cities, providing an effective way of quickly covering a lot of ground. There are several companies but the main operator is **Ticabus** ⓘ *www.ticabus.com*, with headquarters in Costa Rica. However, bear in mind that Panama–Guatemala with **Ticabus** takes almost three days and costs over US$100, plus accommodation in Managua and San Salvador. You may want to consider flying if you need to get through more than one country quickly.

## Crossing borders

Travellers who are eligible for tourist cards or their equivalent (including most European, Australian and North American visitors) find that crossing borders in Central America a relatively straightforward process. Those travellers who require visas, however, may not always find them available; approach the relevant consulate (offices in the capital or big cities) before setting out for the border. For Customs and duty free, see page 1046; for Visas and immigration, see page 1066.

Some crossings levy exit and entrance taxes, along with occasional *alcaldía* (municipal) fees; the amounts vary. 'Unofficial' taxes are not uncommon and sometimes it can be easier to pay a few extra dollars than enter into drawn-out dispute. Asking for a '*factura*' (receipt) can help. Many immigration officers will ask for evidence of onward travel – either a return flight or a bus ticket – along with funds. Leaving Mexico, there are no exit fees, but you must present a receipt for your FMM tourist card (often included in air fares) to avoid being charged US$22. The overland departure tax for Belize is BZ$37.50 (not US dollars), payable in cash only (Belizean or US). The fees payable when leaving or entering Guatemala, Honduras, El Salvador, Nicaragua and Panama vary with the crossings, but rarely exceed US$5 including *alcaldía* tax. Sometimes you will pay nothing at all.

If you use international buses, expect long queues and tedious custom searches. If you're light on luggage, it is usually quicker to use local buses and cross the border on your own. Some drivers may be subjected to bureaucratic delays. Preparation is the best guarantee of a speedy crossing; check in advance which documents you will require and make several copies before setting out (see car documents below for more on procedures). The busiest borders are often frequented by unpleasant characters. Changing money is OK, but check the rate and carefully count what you're given; rip-offs can occur. Avoid buying documents from hawkers – these should be available for free from immigration officers. For essential information, see Border crossings on pages 1038-1045.

## Car

If driving, an international driving licence is useful, although not always essential. Membership of motoring organizations can also be useful for discounts such as hotel charges, car rentals, maps and towing charges.

The kind of motoring you do will depend on your car. A 4WD is not necessary, although it does give you greater flexibility in mountain and jungle territory. Wherever you travel you should expect from time to time to find roads that are badly maintained, damaged or closed during the wet season, and delays because of floods, landslides and huge potholes.

Be prepared for all manner of mechanical challenges. The electronic ignition and fuel metering systems on modern emission-controlled cars are allergic to humidity, heat and dust, and cannot be repaired by mechanics outside the main centres. Standard European and Japanese cars run on fuel with a higher octane rating than is commonly available in North, Central or South America. Note that in some areas petrol stations are few and far between. Fill up when you see one as the next one may be out of fuel.

**Documents** Land entry procedures for all countries are simple though time-consuming, as the car has to be checked by customs, police and agriculture officials. All you need is the registration document in the name of the driver or, in the case of a car registered in someone else's name, a notarized letter of authorization. In Guatemala, Costa Rica and Honduras, the car's entry is stamped into the passport so you may not leave the country even temporarily without it. Note that Costa Rica does not recognize the International Driving Licence (you can drive with a regular licence for up to three months), which is otherwise useful. A written undertaking that the vehicle will be re-exported after temporary importation is useful and may be requested in Nicaragua, Costa Rica and Panama.

Most countries give a limited period of stay, but allow an extension if requested in advance. Of course, do be very careful to keep **all** the papers you are given when you enter, to produce when you leave. An army of 'helpers' loiters at each border crossing, waiting to guide motorists to each official in the correct order, for a tip. They can be very useful, but don't give them your papers. Bringing a car in by sea or air is much more complicated and expensive; generally you will have to hire an agent to clear it through.

Insurance for the vehicle against accident, damage or theft is best arranged in the country of origin. In Latin American countries it is very expensive to insure against accident and theft, especially as you should take into account the value of the car increased by duties calculated in real (that is non-devaluing) terms. If the car is stolen or written off, you will be required to pay very high duty on its value. A few countries, such as Costa Rica, insist on compulsory third-party insurance, to be bought at the border; in other countries it's technically required, but not checked up on **Sanborn's**, www.sanborninsurance.com, and other insurers will insure vehicles for driving in Mexico and Central America). Get the legally required minimum cover – which is not expensive – as soon as you can, because if you should be involved in an accident and are uninsured, your car could be confiscated.

If anyone is hurt, do not pick them up (you become liable). Seek assistance from the nearest police station or hospital if you are able to do so. You may find yourself facing a hostile crowd, even if you are not to blame.

Expect frequent road checks by police, military (especially Honduras, where there is a check point on entering and leaving every town), agricultural and forestry produce inspectors, and any other curious official who wants to know what a foreigner is doing driving around in their domain. Smiling simple-minded patience is the best tactic to avoid harassment.

For a good, first-hand overview of the challenges of travelling overland in your own vehicle, get hold of a copy of *Panama or Bust*, by Jim Jaillet, www.panamaorbust.com, which covers the challenges of preparing for and completing a year-long trip from the US to Panama and back.

**Security** Spare no ingenuity in making your car secure. Avoid leaving the car unattended except in a locked garage or guarded parking space. Remove all belongings and leave the empty glove compartment open when the car is unattended. Also lock the clutch or accelerator to the steering wheel with a heavy, obvious chain or lock. Street children will generally protect your car in exchange for a tip. Note down key numbers and carry spares of the most important ones, but don't keep all spares inside the vehicle.

**Shipping a vehicle to Central America** Two recommended shipping lines are **Wallenius Wilhelmsen** ⓘ *head office in Norway, T+47-6758-4100, for other offices visit www.2wglobal. com*, and, in the US, **American Cargo Service Inc** ⓘ *T305-592-8065*. Motorcyclists will find good online recommendations at www.horizonsunlimited.com.

**Shipping a vehicle to South America** Shipping from Panama to mainland South America is expensive; shop around to find the cheapest way. The shipping lines and agents, and the prices for the services from Panama and elsewhere change frequently.

## Car hire

While not everyone has the time or inclination to travel with their own car, the freedom that goes with renting for a few days is well worth considering, especially if you can get a group of three or four together to share the cost. The main international car hire companies operate in all countries, but tend to be expensive. Hotels and tourist agencies will tell you where to find cheaper rates, but you will need to check that you have such basics as a spare wheel, toolkit, functioning lights, etc. If you plan to do a lot of driving and will have time at the end to dispose of it, investigate the possibility of buying a second-hand car locally; since hiring is so expensive it may work out cheaper and will probably do you just as well.

**Car hire insurance** Check exactly what the hirer's insurance policy covers. In many cases it will only protect you against minor bumps and scrapes, not major accidents, or 'natural' damage (for example flooding). Ask if extra cover is available. Also find out, if using a credit card, whether the card automatically includes insurance. Beware of being billed for scratches that were on the vehicle before you hired it. When you return the vehicle make sure you check it with someone at the office and get signed evidence that it is returned in good condition and that you will not be charged.

## Cycles and motorbikes

**Cycling** Unless you are planning a journey almost exclusively on paved roads – when a high-quality touring bike would probably suffice – a mountain bike is recommended. The good-quality ones are incredibly tough and rugged. Although touring bike and to a lesser extent mountain bike spares are available in the larger Mexicana and Central American cities, you'll find that locally manufactured goods are often shoddy and rarely last. In some countries, such as Mexico, imported components can be found but they tend to be very expensive. Buy everything you can before you leave home.

The **Expedition Advisory Centre** ① *T+44-(0)20-7591-3030, www.rgs.org*, has published a booklet on planning a long-distance bike trip titled *Bicycle Expeditions*, by Paul Vickers. Published in March 1990, it is available as a PDF from the website or £5 for a photocopy. In the UK the **Cyclists' Touring Club** ① *T0844-736-8450, www.ctc.org.uk*, has information on touring, technical information and discusses the relative merits of different types of bikes.

**Motorbikes** People are generally very friendly to motorcyclists and you can make many friends by returning friendship to those who show an interest in you. Buying a bike in the States and driving down works out cheaper than buying one in Europe. In making your choice, go for a comfortable bike. The motorcycle should be off-road capable, without necessarily being an off-road bike. A passport, international driving licence and bike registration document are required.

**Security** This is not a problem in most countries. Try not to leave a fully laden bike on its own. A D-lock or chain will keep the bike secure. An alarm gives you peace of mind if you leave the bike outside a hotel at night. Look for hotels that have a courtyard or more secure parking and never leave luggage on the bike overnight or whilst unattended. Also take a cover for the bike.

**Border crossings** All borders in Central America seem to work out at about US$20 per vehicle. The exceptions to this are Mexico. All borders are free on exit, or should be on most occasions. Crossing borders on a Sunday or a holiday normally incurs double the standard charges in Central American countries. It is sometimes very difficult to find out exactly what is being paid for. If in doubt, ask to see the boss and/or the rule book. See also pages 1038-1045.

## Hitchhiking

Hitchhiking involves inherent risks and should be approached sensibly and with caution. Having said that, hitchhiking in Mexico and Central America is reasonably safe and straightforward for males and couples, provided you speak some Spanish. It is a most enjoyable mode of transport: a good way to meet the local people, to improve one's languages and to learn about the country. If trying to hitchhike away from main roads and in sparsely populated areas, however, allow plenty of time, and ask first about the volume of traffic on the road. On long journeys, set out at the crack of dawn, which is when trucks usually leave. They tend to go longer distances than cars.

## Train

Aside from its freight routes, Central America's rail network has all but declined. Some commuter services were recently opened in San José, Costa Rica, but they are not for tourists and are largely uninspiring. The only decent railway worth checking out is the Panama Railway, which connects Panama City with the port of Colón on the Caribbean coast. If you don't have the time or budget to sail the length of the Panama Canal, the train is the best alternative.

## Maps

Maps from the **Institutos Geográficos Militares** in capital cities are often the only good maps available in Latin America. It is therefore wise to get as many as possible in your home country before leaving, especially if travelling overland. An excellent series of maps covering the whole region and each country is published by **International Travel Maps (ITM)** ① *T604-273-1400, www.itmb.com*, most with historical notes by the late Kevin Healey.

An excellent source of maps is **Stanfords** ① *12-14 Long Acre, Covent Garden, London, WC2E 9LP, T+44-020-7836 1321, www.stanfords.co.uk*. Also in Bristol.

# BORDER CROSSINGS

## Mexico–Belize

### Chetumal–Corozal

The main border crossing is Santa Elena for Chetumal/Corozal. Santa Elena is 12 km north of Corozal, from where there are onward connections to Belize City (three to four hours). Chetumal is 11 km north of Santa Elena and has connections to the Yucatán Peninsula and Quintana Roo beaches; see also Chetumal transport in Southern Mexico chapter. There's a modern 24-hour immigration terminal here and formalities are usually swift. If entering Belize, it's not strictly necessary to change dollars as they are accepted everywhere at a fixed rate of 1:2. It is easier to change Mexican pesos at the border than inside Belize.

### La Unión–Blue Creek

A less widely used crossing is at La Unión/Blue Creek (not recommended unless you like a challenge). There are immigration facilities here but officials are only used to dealing with Mexicans and Belizeans, so delays are likely. See also Belize chapter.

## Mexico–Guatemala

### Tapachula–El Carmen/Ciudad Tecún

The principal border town is Tapachula, with a crossing via the international Talismán Bridge or at Ciudad Hidalgo (see El Soconusco section in Southern Mexico chapter). For onward connections, see also Tapachula Transport, Southern Mexico.

The Talismán–El Carmen route rarely sees much heavy traffic. It's better to change money in Tapachula than with money-changers at the border. Both Mexican and Guatemalan immigration (200 m apart) are open 24 hours. Talismán is 16 km from Tapachula, from where ADO buses depart to major destinations in Chiapas and Oaxaca. This crossing also offers easy access to the Soconusco region along the Mexican Pacific coast. Once in Guatemala, there are connections to Malacatán and onwards to Quetzaltenango.

The main Pan-American Highway crossing, which also connects with Tapachula, is Ciudad Hidalgo–Tecún Umán. Both immigration offices are open 24 hours. Tapachula is 40 km from Ciudad Hidalgo, 30 minutes, with connections to the Soconuso and beyond. Once in Guatemala, there are connections to Coatepeque, Mazatenango and Retalhuleu. There are also a few express buses daily to Guatemala, five hours.

### Ciudad Cuauhtémoc–La Mesilla

The fastest, easiest and most scenic route between Chiapas and western Guatemala is via Ciudad Cuauhtémoc. Currency exchange rates are not generally favourable at the border. ATMs are in La Mesilla on the Guatemala side. Immigration offices on both sides are open 0600-2100. On the Mexican side, there is a cheap hotel, a restaurant and ADO bus station, from where infrequent ADO buses operate to major destinations. Frequent colectivo shuttles go to Comitán (with onward connections to San Cristóbal de las Casas). The Guatemalan border is a few kilometres from Ciudad Cuauhtémoc, but cannot be walked; take a taxi/colectivo instead. In Guatemala, buses go to Huehuetenango (two hours) and on to Quetzaltenango (four hours). See also Comitán section in the Southern Mexico chapter.

### Tenosique–El Ceibo

An interesting route is southeast from Palenque via Tenosique and El Ceibo, offering access to the Petén in Guatemala. Try to bring the currency you need, although local shops or restaurants may exchange. Both immigration offices are open 0700-1800. *Colectivos* and taxis travel from El Ceibo to the market at Tenosique and there are onward connections to Palenque (two hours). In Guatemala, there are several daily buses to Flores/Santa Elena (four to five hours). See also Palenque Town section in Southern Mexico chapter.

### Frontera Corozal–Bethel/La Técnica

Alternatively, you can cross at Frontera Corozal–Bethel/La Técnica for Santa Elena/ Flores, a relatively easy crossing on the Río Usumacinta. From Corozal the boat journey to Bethel is 40 minutes, US$30-60 per boat. The journey to La Técnica is five minutes, US$3.50 per person, from where you must take a bus to Bethel for formalities. Immigration on both sides is open 0900-1800. Note robberies have been reported on the road to La Técnica; check the security situation before setting out. In Guatemala there are just a handful of daily buses to Flores/Santa Elena, so arrive early. See also East of Palenque: the Carretera Fronteriza section in Southern Mexico chapter. It is four hours by bus to Palenque from Frontera Corozal, so set out early.

## Belize–Guatemala

### Benque Viejo–Menchor de Mencos

The most commonly used crossing is between Benque Viejo del Carmen and Melchor de Mencos (see San Ignacio section in Belize chapter), popular with those travelling between Belize and Tikal. Taxi rip-offs are common; bargain hard. For currency exchange, there are good rates on the street; or try Banrural at the border (0700-2000). Both immigration offices are open 0600-2000. There are several buses a day from Melchor de Mencos to Santa Elena (Flores), two to three hours; colectivo 1½ hours. In Belize, there are regular buses to Belize City. If you leave Santa Elena, Guatemala, at 0500, you can be in Belize City by 1200. Also direct buses operate from Flores to Chetumal (Mexico) with Línea Dorada.

### Punta Gorda–Puerto Barrios/Lívingston

Another crossing is by sea between Punta Gorda and Puerto Barrios. Boat services go from Punta Gorda in Belize to Puerto Barrios and Lívingston in Guatemala; see Punta Gorda transport section in Belize chapter. They include **Requena Water Taxi**, 12 Front Street, T722-2070, departing from the dock opposite immigration. Schedules change and are irregular; arrive as early as possible or better yet, arrange in advance. It's best to buy quetzals in Guatemala. At Belizean immigration, obtain stamps from the customs house near the pier on Front Street and allow up to two hours for processing. If you arrive in Guatemala by boat, check into immigration immediately. Offices are in Puerto Barrios and Lívingston; both open 24 hours. There are highway connections from Puerto Barrios to Guatemala City and Flores and in Belize, there are connections with southern Belize.

## Belize–Honduras

### Placencia–Puerto Cortés

There is a weekly boat service from Placencia, via Mango Creek, to Puerto Cortés (see Placencia transport listings in Belize chapter); in good weather the crossing takes two hours. Obtain all necessary exit stamps and visas before sailing. There is a weekly boat service from Puerto Cortés to Placencia via Mango Creek every Monday.

### Dangriga–Puerto Cortés

A cabin cruiser, *Nesymein Neydy*, travels from Dangriga to Puerto Cortés every Thursday and Saturday at 0900, arriving in Puerto Cortés around 1400, around US$50. The boat leaves the North Riverside dock. Ensure all your paperwork is in order before departure. Subject to good weather, boat services to Dangriga depart from Puerto Cortés every Monday at 1100 and continue to Belize City; see Belize chapter.

## Guatemala–Honduras

Links with Honduras are possible on the Caribbean near Corinto (see Chiquimula transport listings in Guatemala chapter); for the ruins at Copán the best crossing is El Florido (see Flores and Santa Elena transport listings in Guatemala chapter). The crossing at Agua Caliente is another option.

### El Florido

A popular and busy crossing, but straightforward for pedestrians. If entering Honduras just to visit Copán ruins, you can get a temporary 72-hour exit pass, but you must return on time. There are numerous money-changers, but you'll find better rates in Copán. Immigration offices are open 0700-1900. Minibuses run all day until 1700 to Copán ruins and, on the Guatemalan side, there are numerous minibus services to Guatemala City and Antigua.

### Entre Ríos–Corinto

This is a Caribbean coast crossing. A road connects Puerto Barrios (Guatemala) and Puerto Cortés (Honduras) with a bridge over the Motagua river. Get your exit stamp in Puerto Barrios or Livingston if you are leaving by boat to Honduras. If you arrive by boat, go straight to either of these offices. Honduran immigration is at Corinto if crossing from Puerto Barrios in Guatemala. In Honduras, there are connections to the northern coast. Buses leave Corinto for Omoa and Puerto Cortés every hour or so. In Guatemala there is access to Guatemala City and Santa Elena/Flores.

### Agua Caliente

A busy crossing, but quicker, cheaper and more efficient than the one at El Florido. There are banks, a tourist office, *comedor* and *hospedaje* on the Honduran side. If leaving Honduras, keep some lempiras for the ride from Agua Caliente to Esquipulas. Immigration on both sides is open 0700-1800. In Honduras there are several buses daily from Agua Caliente to San Pedro Sula, six to seven hours, and frequent services to Nueva Ocotepeque. In Guatemala minibuses go to Esquipulas with connections to Guatemala City, Chiquimula and the highway to Flores.

## Guatemala–El Salvador

El Salvador and Guatemala are covered under the CA-4 border control agreement (see box, page 1031) but you must still submit to immigration formalities before proceeding.

### Frontera–San Cristóbal

The main Pan-American highway crossing, used by international buses and heavy traffic. Immigration on both sides is open 0600-2200, but it's usually possible to cross outside these hours with extra charges. **Note** Travelling during the hours of darkness is not recommended. In El Salvador, there are regular buses to Santa Ana, No 201, with connections to San Salvador, 1½ hours. In Guatemala, there are buses to Guatemala City, two to three hours.

### Valle Nuevo–Las Chinamas

The fastest road link from San Salvador to Guatemala City, but it's busy. It's a straightforward crossing though with quick service if your papers are ready. Change currency with the women in front of the ex-ITSU office; there's a good quetzal-dollar rate. Immigration offices on both sides are open 0800-1800. In El Salvador there are frequent buses to Ahuachapán, No 265, 25 minutes, with connecting services to San Salvador, No 202. Alternatively, try to negotiate a seat with an international Pullman bus; most pass between 0800 and 1400. Onwards to Guatemala there are connections to Guatemala City, two hours.

### Ciudad Pedro Alvarado–La Hachadura

This border is at the bridge over the Río Paz, with a filling station and a few shops nearby. It's increasingly popular, thanks to improved roads. Private vehicles require a lot of paperwork and can take two hours to process. It gives access to El Salvador's Pacific Coast, and there are services to San Salvador's Terminal Occidente, No 498, three hours, and to Ahuachapán, No 503, one hour. The last bus to Sonsonate is at 1800. In Guatemala, there is access to the Pacific coast and Guatemala City.

### Anguiatú

Normally a quiet border crossing, except when there are special events at Esquipulas in Guatemala. Immigration offices are open 0600-1900. Once in El Salvador there are buses to Santa Ana, No 235A, two hours, and to Metapán, 40 minutes, from where a rough but very scenic road runs to El Poy. In Guatemala, there's good access north to Tikal. Head for the Padre Miguel junction, 19 km from the border, from where you can make connections to Chiquimula and Esquipulas.

## El Salvador–Nicaragua

### La Unión–Potosí

Tour operators have begun ferrying tourists across the Gulf of Fonseca (two to three times a week, US$65, but you should also allow up to two hours for formalities) between La Union and Potosí with onward connections to León and San Salvador. Try Cruce del Golfo, www.crucedelgolfo.com. Note the route is much more expensive than going overland, but not necessarily faster. You may get a cheaper deal by gathering a group and negotiating with local boatmen (US$60-100), but check the vessel is seaworthy and includes life jackets. Salvadorean immigration is located in La Unión next to the post office, Avenida General Cabañas and Calle 7a Pte, T2604-4375, 0600-2200. Onward transport in Nicaragua includes onward buses to Chinandega, three hours, but tour operators can include shuttles with your passage. In El Salvador, there is a bus to San Salvador every 30 minutes. There are also regular buses to the beaches and San Miguel.

## Honduras–El Salvador

### El Poy

This crossing between northern El Salvador and southwestern Honduras is straight-forward, but it's better to arrive early if you have a long journey ahead. If changing currency, bargain hard with the money-changers. Travelling onwards to Honduras, shuttles carry passengers to Nueva Ocotopeque, 15-20 minutes, where you can catch highway connections north to Santa Rosa de Copán. On the El Salvador side, buses to San Salvador depart hourly, three to four hours, passing La Palma en route, 30 minutes.

### El Amatillo

The Río Goascarán forms the border at El Amatillo. If driving, you will be hounded by *tramitadores*, some of them are unethical, but their services aren't really required here anyway. Expect thorough car searches. Both Salvadorean and Honduran immigration are open 0600-1700 with a break for lunch. In Honduras, there are hourly services to Tegucigalpa, four hours; and to Choluteca, every 30 minutes, three hours. In El Salvador, there are regular bus services to San Miguel, bus 330, 1½ hours.

### Sabanetas–Perquín

The international boundary here has been variously disputed throughout history. A treaty resolved the disagreement in 2006 and the border now lies 3 km north of Perquín in El Salvador, though it may be impassable after heavy rains. Travel early morning for the best chance of transport connections. There is a Honduran immigration office 5 km inside the country. Note: this is not a major crossing and motorists with international plates are being turned away. Irregular onward bus services go to Marcala in Honduras and San Miguel in El Salvador.

## Honduras–Nicaragua

### Guasaule

There are good roads at this crossing, the preferred route of international buses. If driving, it might be worth hiring a 'helper' to steer you through the formalities. There is a bank by Nicaraguan immigration and lots of money-changers (beware children trying to distract you while you make the transaction). Both Honduran and Nicaraguan immigration are open 0800-1600. On the Nicaraguan side, there are buses to Chinandega and León every 30 minutes, one to two hours, along with a few direct services to Managua. In Honduras, there are regular buses to Choluteca, 45 minutes.

### Las Manos–Ocotal

This is recommended as the best route if travelling between the capital cities of Managua and Tegucigalpa. If driving, *tramitadores* will help you through the paperwork (for a US$5 tip). Both Honduran and Nicaraguan immigration are open 0800-1600. Exchange rates are better on the Nicaraguan side. Buses to run Ocotal in Nicaragua every 30 minutes, from there you can connect to Estelí or Managua. In Honduras, there are direct connections to Tegucigalpa.

### El Espino–Somoto

Border formalities are reportedly very tedious at this crossing. There are places to eat, but no hotels at the border itself. In Nicaragua, buses run from the border to Somoto every 30 minutes; taxis also run, but beware of overcharging. There are roughly six daily buses to Managua, 3½ hours. In Honduras, taxis and minibuses shuttle passengers from the border to Choluteca.

### Leimus–Waspam

This is a hardcore crossing in the heart of the Mosquitia and not for fainthearted. You are strongly advised to seek up-to-date advice from immigration officials before attempting the crossing as it may be impossible to travel between border posts on the same day, requiring additional paperwork. There are no banks or ATMs in the region so bring all the cash you need. Shop owners in Waspam may change currency. In Honduras, obtain your stamps in Puerto Lempira. There is no known immigration office in Waspam, the nearest may be in Bilwi (Puerto Cabezas), a gruelling six hours away on rough dirt roads, which may be impassable in wet season. In Honduras, Leimus has road connections with Puerto Lempira.

# Nicaragua–Costa Rica

Entry requirements for Costa Rica include proof of funds (US$300) and an onward ticket.

## Los Chiles–San Carlos

An intriguing crossing, usually hassle free, used by adventurers and itinerant labourers travelling to and from Nicaragua's remote Río San Juan province. Two daily river boats connect San Carlos and Los Chiles on the Río Frio, 45 minutes, check schedules locally.

Banks and money changers are in San Carlos on the Nicaraguan side, but you are strongly advised to bring dollars before setting out. Immigration on both sides is open 0800-1600. If leaving Nicaragua, before proceeding get your exit stamp in San Carlos, US$2. Entrance tax to Nicaragua, US$12. Exit tax for Costa Rica is US$7, payable by credit card only.

To travel into Costa Rica, buses run to La Quesada (San Carlos) with many onward services to La Fortuna. Onwards to Nicaragua, from San Carlos you can travel east up the Río San Juan or take a ferry across Lake Nicaragua to Isla Ometepe or Granada. There are also road connections and a few daily buses to Managua.

## Peñas Blancas

This is the only Nicaragua–Costa Rica road crossing. It's hectic on the Nicaragua side with lots of helpers and hustlers who may try to sell you forms and paperwork; no purchase is necessary, however, as these are free at the immigration window. There's a branch of BCR in the customs building and no shortage of money changers, but beware being short changed.

Immigration on both sides is open Monday-Saturday 0600-2200, Sunday 0600-2000. International buses are subject to customs searches. On the Nicaraguan side, there is a municipality tax, US$1, exit tax US$2 and entrance tax, US$12. On the Costa Rican side, the exit tax is US$7, payable at a machine with passport and credit card only. If your passport in not readable, pay at the BCR.

Onwards to Costa Rica, several daily express buses depart from behind the immigration terminal, five to six hours; also to Liberia, every 30-60 minutes, 1½ hours. To Nicaragua there are buses to Rivas every 30 minutes, where you can catch connections to Granada, Managua, or Isla Ometepe. For San Juan del Sur, exit at La Virgen. Direct buses also run from Peñas Blancas to Managua, every 30 minutes, 3½ hours.

## Costa Rica–Panama

Panama is an hour ahead of Costa Rica. Entry requirements include proof of funds (US$300 for Costa Rica; US$500 for Panama) and an onward ticket. International bus tickets are available at the border, but some overzealous officials may demand to see a ticket to your country of origin. On the Costa Rican side, exit tax is US$7, payable at a machine with credit card and passport prior to processing, or at the BCR. On the Panamanian side there is a municipal tax US$1-3, which is not always collected.

### Paso Canoas

A busy, insalubrious, well-plied crossing on the Interamericana highway. International buses can take two to three hours to process, otherwise it's usually quick and hassle free. The town has lots of amenities, including hotels and restaurants. There are ATMs and plentiful money changers.

Immigration on both sides is open 0600-2200. Onwards to Panama, there are frequent bus connections with David, 1½ hours away, stopping at La Concepción (Bugaba) for connections to Volcán and Cerro Punta. Onwards to Costa Rica, there are connections with the central Pacific coast and direct to San José. More frequent services to the capital run from Ciudad Neilly.

### Río Sereno

A minor crossing providing access to Volcán and the western Chiriquí highlands, it's quiet and cool with some reports of lengthy bureaucratic treatment. Vehicles cannot complete formalities. There's a bank with an ATM, but no exchange; bring local currency or ask who might change it.

Costa Rican immigration is open 0800-1600; Sunday till 1400. Panamanian immigration is open 0500-1700. Onward to Panama, there are dawn to dusk services from Río Sereno to Volcán, La Concepción and David. Onwards to Costa Rica, there are frequent buses to San Vito via Sabilito.

### Sixaola–Guabito

A straightforward and interesting crossing divided by the Río Sixaola, which you must cross by bridge. Basic and undesirable accommodation is available. There are no banks; try money-changers or the stores, but rates are poor.

Immigration on both sides is open 0700-1700. Onwards to Panama, colectivo taxis go to Changuinola, 20 minutes away, where you can catch a bus to David, Panama City or Almirante (for the Bocas archipelago). Sometimes tourist buses go to the docks at Almirante. Onwards to Costa Rica, there is a bus station with regular services to Puerto Limón, Puerto Viejo and San José.

# Essentials A-Z

## Children

Travel with children can bring you into closer contact with Latin American families and generally presents no special problems; in fact, the path is often smoother for family groups. Officials tend to be more amenable where children are concerned. Always carry a copy of your child's birth certificate and passport photos. For an overview of travelling with children, visit www. babygoes2.com.

### Public transport

Overland travel in Latin America can involve a lot of time spent waiting for public transport. It is easier to take biscuits, drinks, bread, etc with you on longer trips than to rely on meal stops where the food may not be to taste. All airlines charge a reduced price for children under 12 and less for children under 2. Double check the child's baggage allowance though; some are as low as 7 kg. On long-distance buses children generally pay half or reduced fares. For shorter trips it is cheaper, if less comfortable, to seat small children on your knee. Often there are spare seats that children can occupy after tickets have been collected. In city and local buses, small children do not generally pay a fare, but are not entitled to a seat when paying customers are standing. On sightseeing tours you should always bargain for a family rate; often children can go free. Note that a child travelling free on a long excursion is not always covered by the operator's travel insurance.

### Hotels

Try to negotiate family rates. If charges are per person, always insist that 2 children will occupy 1 bed only, therefore counting as 1 tariff. If rates are per bed, the same applies.

It is quite common for children under 12 to be allowed to stay for no extra charge as long as they are sharing your room.

## Customs and duty free

Duty free allowances and export restrictions for each country are listed on www. worlddutyfree.com, under Customs Allowances. It goes without saying that drugs, firearms and banned products should not be traded or taken across international boundaries.

## Disabled travellers

In most Latin American countries, facilities for disabled travellers are severely lacking. Most airports and hotels and restaurants in major resorts have wheelchair ramps and adapted toilets. While some cities such as San José in Costa Rica are all ramped, in general pavements are often in such a poor state of repair that walking is precarious.

Some travel companies specialize in exciting holidays, tailor-made for individuals depending on their level of disability. Disabled Travelers, www.disabledtravelers. com, provides travel information for disabled adventurers and includes a number of links, reviews and tips. You might also want to read *Nothing Ventured*, edited by Alison Walsh (Harper Collins), which gives personal accounts of worldwide journeys by disabled travellers, plus advice and listings.

## Dress

Casual clothing is adequate for most occasions although men may need a jacket and tie in some restaurants. Dress conservatively in indigenous communities and small churches. Topless bathing is generally unacceptable.

## Drugs

Users of drugs without medical prescription should be particularly careful, as some countries impose heavy penalties – up to 10 years' imprisonment – for even the simple possession of such substances. The planting of drugs on travellers, by traffickers or the police, is not unknown. If offered drugs on the street, make no response at all and keep walking. Note that people who roll their own cigarettes are often suspected of carrying drugs and are subjected to close searches.

If you are taking illegal drugs – even ones that are widely and publically used – be aware that authorities do set traps from time to time. Should you get into trouble, your embassy is unlikely to be very sympathetic.

## Electricity

Throughout Mexico and Central America, a US-style 2-pin plug is used. The electricity supply is far from stable; important equipment should have surge protectors, especially during storms.

## Embassies and consulates

For a list of Mexican and Central American embassies abroad, see http://embassy. goabroad.com.

## Gay and lesbian travellers

Most of Mexico and Central America is not particularly liberal in its attitudes to gays and lesbians. Having said that, times are changing and you'll find there is a gay scene with bars and clubs at least in most of the bigger cities and resorts. Helpful websites include www.gayscape. com, www.gaypedia.com and www.iglta. org (International Gay and Lesbian Travel Association).

## Health

See your GP or travel clinic at least 6 weeks before departure for general advice on travel risks and vaccinations. Try a specialist travel clinic if your own GP is unfamiliar with health conditions in Mexico and Central America. Make sure you have sufficient medical travel insurance, get a dental check, know your own blood group and if you suffer a long-term condition such as diabetes or epilepsy, obtain a Medic Alert bracelet/ necklace (www.medicalert.co.uk). If you wear glasses, take a copy of your prescription.

### Vaccinations

Vaccinations for tetanus, hepatitis A and typhoid are commonly recommended for all countries covered in this book. In addition, yellow fever vaccination is required if entering from an infected area (ie parts of South America). Vaccinations may also be advised against tuberculosis, hepatitis B, rabies and diphtheria and, in the case of Guatemala, cholera. The final decision, however, should be based on a consultation with your GP or travel clinic. In all cases you should confirm your primary courses and boosters are up to date. Note: If you are travelling to Central America from South America, it is highly likely you will be allowed to proceed without a valid yellow fever certificate.

### Health risks

The most common cause of **travellers' diarrhoea** is from eating contaminated food. In Central America, drinking water is rarely the culprit, although it's best to be cautious (see below). Swimming in sea or river water that has been contaminated by sewage can also be a cause; ask locally if it is safe. Diarrhoea may be also caused by viruses, bacteria (such as E-coli), protozoal (such as giardia), salmonella and cholera. It may be accompanied by vomiting or by severe abdominal pain. Any kind of diarrhoea responds well to the replacement of water and salts. Sachets of rehydration salts can be bought in most chemists and can be dissolved in boiled water. If symptoms persist, consult a doctor. Most towns have at least one laboratory where you can test for parasites (eg amoebas) and other nasties, but be aware that depending on the hatching cycle, you may require several days of consecutive testing before pathogens show up. Tap water in the major cities may be safe to drink but it is advisable to err on the side of caution and drink only bottled or boiled water. Avoid ice in drinks unless you trust that it is from a reliable source.

Travelling in high altitudes can bring on **altitude sickness**. On reaching heights above 3000 m, the heart may start pounding and the traveller may experience shortness of breath. Smokers and those with underlying heart or lung disease are often hardest hit. Take it easy for the first few days, rest and drink plenty of water, you will feel better soon. It is essential to get acclimatized before undertaking long treks or arduous activities.

**Malaria** precautions are essential for some parts of Mexico and Central America, particularly some rural areas. Once again, check with your GP or travel clinic well in advance of departure. Avoid being bitten by mosquitoes as much as possible. Sleep off the ground and use a mosquito net and some kind of insecticide. Mosquito coils release insecticide as they burn and are available in many shops, as are tablets of insecticide, which are placed on a heated mat plugged into a wall socket. **Dengue** fever is carried by mosquitos in urban areas, but it is rare for travellers to contract it. The best prevention is to avoid being bitten, as for malaria. **Chikungunya** is a new disease spreading through Central America, also carried by mosquitos, and its symptoms are similar to dengue (fever accompanied by aches). Most people recover within a week, but a few develop long-term joint pain.

### If you get sick

Contact your embassy or consulate for a list of doctors and dentists who speak your language, or at least some English. Your hotel may be able to recommend a local doctor or hospital. Good-quality healthcare is available in the larger centres but it can be expensive, especially hospitalization. Make sure you have adequate insurance (see below).

### Mexico

Social security hospitals are restricted to members, but they will take visitors in emergencies; they are more up to date than the *centros de salud* and *hospitales civiles* found in most town centres, which are very cheap and open to everyone. A consultation in a private doctor's surgery may cost US$20-40.

### Belize

Insect bites should be carefully scrutinized if not healing or if odd symptoms occur, as the possibilities of Chagas, leishmaniasis, or botfly larvae are all present. Medical services have improved in recent years with the Karl Heusner Memorial Hospital in Belize City, though many Belizeans still seek medical care for serious ailments in Mérida, Mexico, or Guatemala City. The **British High Commission** in Belmopan (T822-2146) has a list of doctors and dentists.

### Guatemala

Carelessness about precautions of drinking water, milk, uncooked vegetables and peeled fruits is likely to lead to amoebic dysentery, which is endemic. In Guatemala City 2 good hospitals are **Bella Aurora**, 10 Calle, 2-31, Zona 14, T2368-1951, and **Herrera Llerandi**, 6 Av, 8-71, Zona 10, T2334-5959, but you must have full medical insurance or sufficient funds to pay for treatment. English and other languages are spoken. Most small towns have clinics. At the public hospitals, which are seriously underfunded and where care for major problems is not good, you may have an examination for a nominal fee, but drugs are expensive.

## El Salvador

Gastroenteritic diseases are most common. Visitors should take care over what they eat during the first few weeks, and should drink purified bottled water. The bags of water sold in the street are not always safe and taste somewhat of rubber. El Salvador has one of the best health systems in Central America, so the capital is a good place to sort out problems. You can get a stool sample taken at the **Pro-Familia Hospital**, 25 Av Norte, near Metro Centro, which gives you the result in about 6-12 hrs.

## Honduras

There is cholera, so eating on the street or at market stalls is not recommended. There are hospitals and private clinics in Tegucigalpa, San Pedro Sula and larger towns.

## Nicaragua

Take the usual tropical precautions with food and drink. Tap water is not recommended for drinking outside Managua, León and Granada and avoid uncooked vegetables and ready-peeled fruit; intestinal parasites abound. Malaria is prevalent, especially in the wet season; high-risk areas are east of the great lakes so take regular prophylaxis. Dengue fever is increasingly present, including in Managua; avoid being bitten by mosquitoes.

## Costa Rica

Drinking water is safe in all major towns; elsewhere it should be boiled, but bottled water is widely available.

Intestinal disorders are prevalent in the lowlands although Chagas disease is now rare. Malaria is on the increase; malaria prophylaxis is advised for visitors to the lowlands, especially near the Nicaraguan and Panama border. If visiting jungle

areas try and prevent insect bites by using repellent and appropriate clothing. Dengue fever has been recorded throughout the country, mostly in coastal cities. Uncooked foods should not be eaten. Having said all that, the standards of health and hygiene are among the best in Latin America.

## Panama

Water in Panama City, David, and Colón is safe to drink. Drink bottled water outside the cities. Bocas tap water is not good. Yellow fever vaccination is recommended before visiting Darién. Travellers to Darién Province and San Blas Province in Panama should treat these as malarial areas in which there is resistance to chloroquine. Treatment is expensive; insurance underwritten by a US company would help considerably.

---

## Useful websites

**www.btha.org** British Travel Health Association.
**www.cdc.gov** US government site that gives excellent advice on travel health and details of disease outbreaks.
**www.fco.gov.uk** British Foreign and Commonwealth Office travel site has useful information on each country, people, climate and a list of UK embassies/consulates.
**www.fitfortravel.scot.nhs.uk** A-Z of vaccine/health advice for each country.
**www.numberonehealth.co.uk** Travel screening services, vaccine and travel health advice, email/SMS text vaccine reminders and screens returned travellers for tropical diseases.

### Insurance

Insurance is strongly recommended and policies are very reasonable. If you have financial restraints, the most important aspect of any insurance policy is medical care and repatriation. Ideally you want to make sure you are covered for personal items too. Read the small print before heading off so you are aware of what is covered and what is not, what is required to submit a claim and what to do in the event of an emergency. Always buy insurance before setting out as your options will be more limited and generally quite costly once you've departed from your home country.

## Internet

Public access to the internet is endemic with cybercafés in both large and small towns. Many hotels and cafés also have Wi-Fi. Speeds and connections are often unreliable, particularly with smart phones and data hungry applications that place strain on the bandwidth. When using public Wi-Fi, please be considerate of other users.

## Language

Spanish is spoken throughout most of Mexico and Central America and, while you will be able to get by without knowledge of Spanish, you will probably become frustrated and feel helpless in many situations. A pocket dictionary and phrase book together with some initial study or a beginner's Spanish course before you leave are strongly recommended. If you have the time, book 1-2 weeks of classes at the beginning of your travels. Some areas have developed a reputation for language classes, including San Cristóbal de las Casas in Mexico, Antigua and Quetzaltenango in Guatemala, or Granada in Nicaragua. The better-known centres normally include a wide range of cultural activities and supporting options for homestay. A less well-known centre is likely to have fewer English speakers around. For details, see Language schools in the What to do sections of individual towns and cities.

Not all the locals speak Spanish, of course. In Belize, English is the official language. In Honduras English is often spoken in the north, in the Bay Islands, by West Indian settlers on the Caribbean coast, and in business communities. In Nicaragua on the Caribbean coast English is widely spoken, but in the rest of the country it's Spanish only. In Costa Rica you will find someone who can speak some English in most places. In the Caribbean the Afro-Caribbean population speak a regional creole dialect with elements of English. In Panama English is widely understood but again, knowledge of Spanish is very helpful. The older generation of West Indian immigrants in Bocas speak Guari-Guari, a dialect of English incomprehensible to most other English speakers. In rural areas indigenous people use their own languages and many are bilingual.

You will find that some indigenous people in the more remote areas – the highlands of Guatemala for example – speak only their indigenous languages, although there will usually be some people in a village who can speak Spanish. Regarding pronunciation in Guatemala, 'X' is pronounced 'sh', as in Xela (shay-la).

### Language tuition

Arranging language tuition internationally is increasingly popular.

**AmeriSpan**, 1334 Walnut St (PO Box 58129), 6th floor, Philadelphia, PA 19107, T1-215-751-1100, T1-800-879-6640, www.amerispan.com (also with offices in Antigua, Guatemala). One of the most comprehensive options, offering Spanish immersion programmes, educational tours, volunteer and internship positions throughout Latin America.

**Cactus Language**, 4 Clarence House, T0845-130-4775, www.cactuslanguagetraining.com. Spanish language courses from 1 week in duration in Mexico and Central America, with pre-trip classes in the UK. Also has additional options for volunteer work, diving and staying with host families.

**Institute for Spanish Language Studies**, in the US on T1-866-391-0394, www.isls.com. Has schools in Mexico, offering innovative and flexible programmes.

**Spanish Abroad**, T1-888-722-7623 (USA and Canada), T1-602-778-6791 (worldwide), www.spanishabroad.com. Intensive Spanish immersion programmes throughout Latin America for those wishing to study abroad.

## Media

Latin America has more local and community radio stations than practically anywhere else in the world; a shortwave (world band) radio (or an equivalent phone app) offers a practical means to brush up on the language, sample popular culture and absorb some of the richly varied regional music. International broadcasters also transmit across Central America in both English and Spanish, these include the **BBC World Service**, www.bbc.co.uk/worldservice/index.shtml for schedules and frequencies, the **Voice of America**, www.voa.gov, and Boston (Mass)-based **Monitor Radio International**, operated by Christian Science Monitor, www.csmonitor.com. **Putumayo World Music**, www.putumayo.com, specializes in the exotic sounds of Mexican music.

### Mexico

The influential daily newspapers are: *Excelsior, Novedades, El Día, Uno Más Uno, El Universal, La Jornada* (www.jornada.unam.mx, more to the left, with *Tiempo Libre*, listing cultural activities in Mexico City), *La Prensa* (a popular tabloid, with the largest circulation) and *El Nacional* (mouthpiece of the government). There are influential weekly magazines: *Proceso, Siempre, Epoca* and *Quehacer Político*.

### Belize

There are no daily newspapers in Belize. News is available in the weeklies, which generally come out on Friday morning, with the forthcoming Sunday's date: *The Belize Times* (PUP supported), *The Guardian* (UDP supported), *The Reporter* and *Amandala*. Good coverage of Ambergris Caye is provided by *The San Pedro Sun*; likewise, *Placencia Breeze* covers Placencia. Small district newspapers are published sporadically. Radio station *Love FM* (95.1FM) is the perfect summary of Belize on the airwaves. Try www.belizeweb.com for Belizean internet radio.

### Guatemala

The main newspaper is *Prensa Libre* (www.prensalibre.com). The *Guatemala Post*, www.guatemala post.com, is published in English online. *Siglo Veintiuno*, www.sigloxxi.com, is a good newspaper. One of the most popular papers is *Nuestro Diario*, a tabloid with more gory pics than copy. The *Revue*, www.revuemag.com, produced monthly in Antigua, carries articles, maps, advertisements, lodgings, tours and excursions, covering Antigua, Panajachel, Quetzaltenango, Río Dulce, Monterrico, Cobán, Flores and Guatemala City.

### El Salvador

Newspapers in San Salvador include *Diario de Hoy* (right wing), www.elsalvador.com, and *La Prensa Gráfica* (centre) every morning including Sun, www.laprensagrafica.com; both have the most complete listings of cultural events in San Salvador. *Co Latino* is a left-wing newspaper. *El Mundo* in the afternoons except Sun. US newspapers and magazines are available at leading hotels.

Of the 80 radio stations, one is government owned and several are owned by churches.

There are 4 commercial TV stations, all with national coverage, and 1 government-run station with 2 channels. There are several cable channels, all with CNN news, etc.

### Honduras

The principal newspapers in Tegucigalpa are *El Heraldo* and *La Tribuna*. In San Pedro Sula they are *El Tiempo* and *La Prensa*. Links on the net at www.honduras.com. The

English weekly paper *Honduras This Week*, is now mainly online at www.hondurasthisweek.com. They're frequently looking for student interns.

There are 6 television channels and 167 broadcasting stations. Cable TV is available in large towns and cities.

## Nicaragua

All newspapers are published in Managua, but many are available throughout the country. Dailies include *La Prensa*, centre, the country's best, especially for coverage of events outside Managua; *El Nuevo Diario*, centre-left and sensationalist; *La Noticia*, right, government paper. *El Seminario* is a left-leaning, well-written weekly with in-depth analysis. The monthy *El País*, pro-government, has good features.

## Costa Rica

The best San José morning papers are *La Nación* (www.nacion.co.cr) and the business-orientated *La República* (www.larepublica. net); there is also *Al Día*, *El Heraldo*, *Diario Extra* (the largest circulating daily) and *La Prensa Libre* (www.prensalibre.co.cr). *La Gaceta* is the official government daily paper.

There are 6 local TV stations, many MW/FM radio stations throughout the country. Local **Voz de América** (VOA) station. **Radio Dos** (95.5 FM) and **Rock Radio** (107.5 FM) have English-language DJs and music. Many hotels and private homes receive one of the 4 TV stations offering direct, live, 24-hr satellite TV from the USA. All US cable TV can be received in San José.

## Panama

*La Prensa* is the major local daily newspaper. Others are *La Estrella de Panamá*, *El Universal de Panamá*, *El Panamá América* and 2 tabloids, *Crítica Libre* and *El Siglo*. *Colón News* is a weekly publication in Spanish and English. In English is the biweekly *Panama News*.

## Money

### Currency and exchange

For up-to-the-minute exchange rates visit www.xe.com.

While most – but not all – countries in Mexico and Central America have their own currencies, the most useful foreign currency in the region is the US dollar. Banks and *casas de cambio* are increasingly able to change euros but the dollar is still the most readily accepted and changed.

The 3 main ways of keeping in funds while travelling are still US dollars cash, plastic (credit cards) and US dollar TCs.

### Mexico

*US$1=$16.34 pesos (Aug 2015).*
The monetary unit is the Mexican peso, represented by '$' – the dollar sign – which provides great potential for confusion, especially in popular tourist places where prices are higher and often quoted in US dollars (US$).

### Belize

*US$1=Bz$2 (stabilized).*
The monetary unit is the Belize dollar. Currency notes issued by the Central Bank are in denominations of 100, 50, 20, 10, 5 and 2 dollars, and coins of 2 dollars and 1 dollar; 50, 25, 10, 5 and 1 cent coins are in use. The American expressions quarter (25c), dime (10c) and nickel (5c) are used, although 25c is sometimes referred to as a shilling. US dollars are accepted everywhere. A common cause for complaint or misunderstanding is uncertainty about which currency you are paying in. The price tends to be given in US$ when the hundred Belizean dollar mark is breached; make sure it is clear from the start whether you are being charged in US or Belizean dollars.

### Guatemala

*US$1=7.64 quetzales (Aug 2015).*
The unit is the quetzal, divided into 100 centavos. There are coins of 1 quetzal,

50 centavos, 25 centavos, 10 centavos, 5 centavos and 1 centavo. Paper currency is in denominations of 5, 10, 20, 50, 100 and 200 quetzales. There is often a shortage of small change; ask for small notes when you first change money to pay hotel bills, transport, etc.

### El Salvador
*US$1=8.7 colones (fixed).*
El Salvador adopted the dollar on 1 Jan 2001. All US coinage and notes are widely used, although you may have problems with US$20 bills and above. Some small shops and street merchants still price their products in colones, but they are a minority.

### Honduras
*US$1=$21.9 lempiras (Aug 2015).*
The unit of currency is the lempira (written Lps and referred to as lemps) named after a famous indigenous chief who lost his life while fighting the invasion of the Spanish. It is reasonably stable against the US dollar. Divided into 100 centavos, there are nickel coins of 5, 10, 20 and 50 centavos. Bank notes are for 1, 2, 5, 10, 20, 50, 100 and 500 lempiras. No one has change for larger notes, especially the 500. Any amount of any currency can be taken in or out of the country. It is advisable to have US dollars in cash, in smaller denominations, US$10-50.

### Nicaragua
*US$1=27.41 córdobas (Aug 2015).*
The unit of currency is the córdoba, divided into 100 centavos. Any bank in Nicaragua will change US dollars to córdobas and vice versa. US dollars are accepted as payment almost everywhere but change is given in córdobas. It is best to carry US dollar notes and sufficient local currency away from the bigger towns. Take all the cash you need when visiting the Caribbean coast or Río San Juan. Carry small bills when travelling outside cities or using public buses. When changing money take some ID or a copy. It is not possible to change currencies other than US dollars and euros (**BanCentro** only). Money changers on the street (*coyotes*) during business hours are legitimate and their rates differ little from banks.

### Costa Rica
*US$1=534.51 colones (Aug 2015).*
The unit is the colón which devalues annually at a rate of about 10%. The small, golden-coloured coins are minted for 5, 10, 25, 50, 100 and 500 colones. Notes in use are for 1000, 2000, 5000 and 10,000 colones. US dollars are widely accepted but don't depend on being able to use them. They can be exchanged in most banks. Most tourist and upmarket hotels will change dollars for guests only; the same applies in restaurants and shops if you buy something. Hardly anyone will change damaged US dollar notes. All state-run banks and some private banks will change euros, but it is almost impossible to exchange any other major currency in Costa Rica.

### Panama
*US$1=1 balboa (fixed).*
The unit of currency in Panama is the balboa, but Panama is one of the few countries in the world which issues no paper money; US banknotes are used exclusively, and US notes and coins are legal tender. There is now a 1 balboa coin (nicknamed 'Martinelli') along with silver coins of 50c (called a *peso*), 25c (*cinco reales* or *cuara*, from the US quarter), 10c, nickel of 5c (called a *real*) and copper of 1c. All coins are used interchangeably with US equivalents, which are the same in size and composition. There is great reluctance in Panama to accept US$50 and US$100 dollar notes because of counterfeiting; you will be asked to produce ID and sign a register when spending them. If travelling north remember that US dollar notes, especially smaller denominations, are useful in all Central American countries and may be difficult to obtain in other republics.

Stocking up on a supply of US$5 and US$1 notes greatly facilitates border crossings and traffic problems in Central America where 'fees' and 'instant fines' can become exorbitant if you only have a US$20 note.

## Cash

The chief benefit of taking US dollars is that they are accepted almost everywhere. However, in some places they are only accepted if they are in excellent condition – no small tears, rips, nicks, holes or scribbles. When ordering money at home bear this in mind. Take a selection of bills including several low-value US dollar bills (US$5 or US$10) which can be carried for changing into local currency if arriving in a country when banks or *casas de cambio* are closed, and for use in out of the way places when you may run out of local currency. They are also very useful for shopping: shopkeepers and *casas de cambio* tend to give better exchange rates than hotels or banks (but see below).

If your budget is tight it is essential to avoid situations where you are forced to change money regardless of the rate; watch weekends and public holidays carefully and never run out of local currency. Take plenty of local currency, in small denominations, when making trips away from the major towns and resorts.

Whenever possible change your money at a bank or a *casa de cambio*. Black markets and street changers have largely disappeared; avoid them if you can as you are unlikely to get a significantly better rate and you place yourself a greater risk of being ripped off. If you need to change money on the street, do not do so alone. If you are unsure about rates of exchange when you enter a country, check at the border with more than one changer, or ask locals or any traveller who may be leaving that country. Whenever you leave a country, sell any local currency before leaving; the further you get away from a country, the less the value of a country's money and in some cases you may not be able to change it at all.

**Note** In Belize, the government has restricted the exchange of foreign currency to government-licensed *casas de cambio*, but these only operate in major towns. You can still find some money changers at the borders, but the exchange rate is not as high as it has been, and there is a risk of both you and the money changer being arrested and fined.

## Debit and credit cards

Debit and credit cards are ideal for travelling, providing ready access to funds without carrying large amounts of cash on your person. In an ideal world taking a couple of cards (one Visa and one MasterCard) will make sure you are covered in most options. It is straightforward to obtain a cash advance against a credit card and even easier to withdraw cash from ATMs (*cajeros automáticos*). Remove your credit card from the machine immediately after the transaction to avoid it being retained; getting it back can be difficult. You may have to experiment with different ATM networks, especially in Guatemala, as they do not work consistently. Keep a backup supply of cash until you figure out which ones support your card. The rates of exchange on ATM withdrawals are the best available for currency exchange but your bank or credit card company imposes a handling charge which is a percentage of the transaction, so try to avoid using your card to withdraw small amounts of cash (check with your bank for details before setting out). If your card is lost or stolen, immediately contact the 24-hr helpline of the issuer in your home country (find out the numbers to call before travelling and keep them in a safe place). Do not rely on ATMs when venturing into the countryside or remote islands – there may or may not be service. Most upscale hotels and restaurants, especially in the capitals, accept payment by credit card. Elsewhere, you will have to rely on cash.

## Currency cards

If you don't want to carry lots of cash, prepaid currency cards allow you to preload money from your bank account, fixed at the day's exchange rate. They look like a credit or debit card and are issued by specialist money-changing companies, such as **Travelex** and **Caxton FX**, and the **Post Office**. You can top up and check your balance by phone, online and sometimes by text.

## Traveller's cheques

Traveller's cheques (TCs) are almost obsolete; shops and restaurants won't change them, but they do provide peace of mind against theft. Several banks charge a high fixed commission for changing TCs because they don't really want the bother. *Casas de cambio* are usually a much better choice for this service. The better hotels will normally change TCs for their guests (often at a poor rate). Denominations of US$50 and US$100 are preferable, with a few of US$20 to increase your options.

## Cost of travelling

Prices vary widely across the region. The most expensive countries are Mexico, Belize, Costa Rica, and increasingly, Panama. Thrifty travellers can get by on US$30-40 a day if they travel in the low season and restrict themselves to dorm beds or shared rooms (US$10-15 per person per night), cheap local eateries (US$3-7 per meal) and no excursions or extra activities. A more realistic and comfortable budget is U$40-80. Outside of the Yucatán, prices in southern Mexico are a bit lower, especially in Chiapas, one of the best value destinations in the country. Note: if you intend to do a lot of travelling in Mexico, bus transport can eat up a significant portion of your

budget. Throughout the region, be aware of seasonal price variations at popular beach destinations, where you may pay 50-100% more for accommodation during the busy months. Off-season, good bargains are available in tourist hubs, but you will need to negotiate the price down (ask if they have anything '*mas económico*'). Discounts are usually available if you intend to stay more than three nights. The nations of Guatemala, El Salvador, Honduras, and Nicaragua, are markedly cheaper than the rest, but are no longer the great bargain they once were. Eating at markets and staying in the cheapest accommodation, a very tight daily budget would be US$20 per day. For more comfort and leisure, it is best to budget around US$40-50 per person per day. As ever, couples and groups make good savings.

## Opening hours

### Mexico
**Banks** Mon-Fri 0900-1330 (some stay open later), Sat 0900-1230.
**Businesses** 0900/1000-1300/1400, then 1400/1500-1900 or later. Business hours vary considerably according to the climate and local custom.

### Belize
**Businesses** 0800-1200, 1300-1600 and Fri 1900-2100, with half day on Wed. Small shops open additionally most late afternoons and evenings, and some on Sun 0800-1000. **Government and commercial offices**
Mon-Fri 0800-1200 and 1300-1600.

### Guatemala
**Banks** Mon-Fri 0900-1500, Sat 0900-1300. Some city banks are introducing later hours, up to 2000; in the main tourist towns and shopping malls, some banks are open 7 days a week. **Shops** 0900-1300 and 1500-1900, often mornings only on Sat.

### El Salvador

**Banks** Mon-Fri 0900-1700, Sat 0900-1200, closed between 29-30 Jun and 30-31 Dec.
**Businesses** Mon-Fri 0800-1200, 1400-1730; Sat 0800-1200.
**Government offices** Mon-Fri 0730-1530.

### Honduras

**Banks** In Tegucigalpa Mon-Fri 0900-1500; on the north coast Sat 0800-1100. **Post offices** Mon-Fri 0700-2000; Sat 0800-1200.
**Shops** Mon-Fri 0900-1200, 1400-1800; Sat 0800-1200.

### Nicaragua

**Banks** Mon-Fri 0830-1200, 1400-1600, Sat 0830-1200/1300.
**Businesses** Mon-Fri 0800-1200, 1430-1730.

### Costa Rica

**Banks** Mon-Fri 0900-1500.
**Businesses** Mon-Fri 0900-1200, 1400-1730 (1600 government offices), Sat 0800-1200. **Shops** Mon-Sat 0800-1200, 1300-1800 (most stay open during lunch hour),

### Panama

**Banks** Open at different times, but are usually open all morning, and often on Sat.
**Government offices** Mon-Fri 0800-1200, 1230-1630. **Shops** Mon-Sat 0700/0800-1200, 1400-1800/1900.

## Photography

There is a charge of US$3-5 for the use of video cameras at some historical sites. For professional camera equipment, including a tripod, the fee is much higher. Never take photos of indigenous people without prior permission.

## Police

Probably the best advice with regards the police in Mexico and Central America is to have as little to do with them as possible.

An exception to this rule are the tourist police, who operate in some of the big cities and resorts, and provide assistance. In general, law enforcement in Latin America is achieved by periodic campaigns, not systematically.

You may be asked for identification at any time and should therefore always have ID on you. If you cannot produce it, you may be jailed. If you are jailed, you should contact your embassy or consulate and take advice. In the event of a vehicle accident in which anyone is injured, all drivers involved are automatically detained until blame has been established, and this does not usually take less than 2 weeks. If a visitor is jailed his or her friends should provide food every day. This is especially important for people on a special diet, such as diabetics.

The giving and receiving of bribes is not recommended. However, the following advice may prove useful. Never offer a bribe unless you are fully conversant with the customs of the country. Wait until the official makes the suggestion, or offer money in some form that is apparently not bribery, for example 'In our country we have a system of on-the-spot fines (*multas de inmediato*). Is there a similar system here?' Do not assume that officials who accept a bribe are prepared to do anything else that is illegal. You bribe them to do their job, or not do it, or to do it more quickly, or more slowly. You do not bribe them to do something which is against the law. The mere suggestion would make them very upset. If an official suggests that a bribe must be paid before you can proceed on your way, be patient (assuming you have the time) and they may relent. Bear in mind that by bribing you are participating in a system that may cause you immense frustration.

## Post

Postal services vary in efficiency from country to country and prices are quite high; pilfering is frequent. All mail, especially packages, should be registered. Check before leaving home if your embassy will hold mail and if so for how long, in preference to the Poste Restante/General Delivery (*Lista de Correos*) department of a country's Post Office. Cardholders can use Amex agencies. If you're expecting mail and there seems to be no mail at the *Lista* under the initial letter of your surname, ask them to look under the initial of your forename or your middle name. If your name begins with 'W', look for letters under 'V' as well, or ask. For the smallest risk of misunderstanding, use title, initial and surname only.

## Punctuality

Punctuality is more of a concept than a reality in Latin countries. The *mañana* culture reigns supreme and any arrangement to meet at, say 1900, will normally rendezvous somewhere between 2000 and 2100. However, the one time you are late to catch a bus, boat or plane, it will leave on time – the rule is hurry up and wait.

## Safety

Generally speaking, most places in Latin America are no more dangerous than any major city in Europe or North America and the people, if anything, are friendlier and more open. In provincial towns, main places of interest, on daytime buses and in ordinary restaurants the visitor should be quite safe. Nevertheless, in large cities (particularly in crowded places such as markets and bus stations) crime exists, mostly of the opportunistic kind. If you are aware of the dangers, act confidently and use your common sense, you will lessen many of the risks. The following tips, endorsed by travellers, are meant to forewarn, not alarm.

Keep all documents secure; hide your main cash supply in different places or under your clothes. Extra pockets sewn inside shirts and trousers, pockets closed with a zip or safety pin, money belts, neck or leg pouches, and elasticated support bandages for keeping money and cheques above the elbow or below the knee have been repeatedly recommended. Pouches worn outside the clothes are not safe. Keep cameras in bags (preferably with a chain or wire in the strap, so it can't be slashed) and don't wear fancy wristwatches or jewellery. Carry your small day pack in front of you.

### Mexico

In recent years, Mexico's feuding drug cartels have been the cause of much unpleasant violence but, despite the horrific scenes reported by the international media, the problem is largely confined to the US border in sketchy barrios you are unlikely to see. Millions of people travel safely to Mexico every year and the Yucatán's homicide rate is actually lower than that in much of rural North America. If you are unfortunate enough to be a victim of crime, it is most likely to be an opportunistic theft, against which you must take the usual sensible precautions. Cars are a prime target; never leave possessions visible inside the car and park in hotel car parks after dark. Avoid travelling at night; if at all possible make journeys in daylight. Avoid lonely beaches, especially if you are a single woman. Speaking Spanish is a great asset for avoiding rip-offs targeting gringos, especially short changing and overcharging (both rife).

### Belize

While attacks on foreigners are extremely rare, precautions are still advised, particularly if travelling alone or at night or in deserted areas. Crimes against travellers are harshly punished. Despite the apparent availability of illegal drugs, the authorities are keen to prevent their use. The penalties for possession of marijuana are 6 months in prison or a US$3000 fine, minimum.

## Guatemala

In some parts of the country you may be subject to military or police checks. Local people can be reluctant to discuss politics with strangers. Do not necessarily be alarmed by 'gunfire', which is much more likely to be fireworks and bangers, a national pastime, especially early in the morning.

Robberies and serious assaults on tourists are becoming more common. While you can do nothing to counter the bad luck of being in the wrong place at the wrong time, sensible precautions can minimize risks. Single women should be especially careful. Tour groups are not immune and some excursion companies take precautions. Do not travel at night if at all possible and take care on roads that are more prone to vehicle hijacks: the road between Flores and the Belizean border, the highway between Antigua and Panajachel and the principal highway between the capital and El Salvadorean border. Assaults and robberies on the public (former US) buses have increased. There have been a high number of attacks on private vehicles leaving the airport.

**Asistur**, T1500/2421-2810 is a 24-hr, year-round tourist assistance programme for any problem or question. There is also a national tourist police force, **POLITUR**, T5561-2073, or for emergencies: T120/122/123. Other useful numbers include: **National police** T110; and **tourist police** in Antigua T832-7290.

## El Salvador

Traditionally El Salvador has a reputation for violence and crime. In part this is a legacy of many years of civil war although this has been improved through a more active role of the police in later years. The reality is that most people visiting El Salvador return with reports of friendly, open people; far from being targeted by criminals, you are much more likely to receive a warm welcome and genuine interest in your visit. Locals will talk incessantly about the country's problems and dangers but few actual examples materialize. Be cautious until you find your own level of comfort and always ask local advice. Statistically El Salvador has the unenviable distinction of having the worst levels of violent crime on the continent. This derives from Salvadorean gang culture (*maras*) and most visitors will see nothing of this activity. If renting a car, buy a steering lock. Visitors to San Salvador should seek advice on where is not safe both inside and outside the city. For general safety updates, consult the UK Foreign Office, www.gov.uk/foreign-travel-advice/el-salvador.

## Honduras

There are serious domestic social problems in Tegucigalpa and San Pedro Sula, including muggings and theft, but there is a Tourist Police service in place – in Copán Ruinas, Roatán, La Ceiba, Tela and San Pedro Sula – that has reduced the problem. Take local advice and be cautious when travelling alone or off the beaten track. It is considered unsafe for tourists to use public transport within the cities of Tegucigalpa and San Pedro Sula – use licensed taxis only. Armed robberies on intercity buses are not unheard of, especially on the routes between Tegucigalpa, San Pedro Sula and La Ceiba, where it is best to use one of the direct services; Hedman Alas and Viana Transportes are highly recommended for their strict security measures. Contrary to the bad press, the vast majority of Hondurans are honest, friendly, warm and welcoming, and the general perception is that tourists are not targeted by criminals. You can check the latest security news at the UK Foreign Office, www.gov.uk/foreign-travel-advice/honduras.

## Nicaragua

Visitors must carry their passports with them at all times. A photocopy is acceptable, but make sure you have a copy of your visa or entrance stamp as well. Pickpocketing and bag slashing occur in Managua in crowded places, and on buses throughout the country. There have been several incidents of ugly taxi robberies in the capital; do not share vehicles with strangers you have just met, no matter how friendly or polite they appear. Most beaches are no go at night, and some should be approached cautiously in the day; seek local advice before setting out. Do not wander the streets of Managua after dark. Most other town centres are safe to stroll until 2300, but common sense rules apply.

## Costa Rica

Generally speaking, Costa Rica is very safe but, as ever, there are some problem areas. Look after your belongings in hotels and use the safe. If hiring a car do not leave valuables in the vehicle and leave nothing unattended on beaches or buses. Theft (pickpockets, grab-and-run thieves and muggings) is on the increase in San José, especially in the centre, in the market, at the Coca Cola bus station, in the barrios of Cuba, Cristo Rey, México, 15 de Setiembre and León XIII. Keep away from these areas at night and on Sun, when few people are around. Street gangs, known as *chapulines*, are mostly kids. The police do seem to be trying to tackle the problem but help yourself by avoiding potentially dangerous situations.

You must carry your passport (or a photocopy) with you at all times.

## Panama

Panama is generally safe and the greatest threats to the average traveller are pickpocketing and other thefts. Carry a photocopy of your passport at all times and take the usual sensible precautions. Certain areas of Panama City should be avoided, including Curundú, El Chorillo and Hollywood. Santa Ana and Calidonia can also be sketchy at night. Tourists attract thieves, so watch your belongings on the beaches of Bocas del Toro. Colón is certainly

very dangerous and you should not go wandering around its streets. Darién cannot be visited without appropriate jungle experience and the help of a qualified guide; the region poses risks for kidnapping or worse.

## Safety on public transport

When you have your luggage with you at a bus station, be especially careful: don't get into arguments with any locals if you can help it and clip, tie or lock all the items together with a chain or cable if you are waiting for some time, or simply sit on top of your backpack. Take a taxi between airport/bus station/railway station and hotel, if you can afford it. Keep your bags with you in the taxi and pay only when you and your luggage are safely out of the vehicle (but keep an eye on it your luggage!). Avoid night buses unless essential or until you are comfortable travelling in the area; avoid arriving at night whenever possible; and watch your belongings whether they are stowed inside or outside the cabin (rooftop luggage racks create extra problems, which are sometimes unavoidable – many bus drivers cover rooftop luggage with plastic sheeting, but a waterproof bag or outer sack can be invaluable for protecting your luggage and for stopping someone rummaging through the top of your bag). Major bus lines often issue a luggage ticket when bags are stored in the hold; this is generally a safe system. When getting on a bus, keep your ticket handy as you will probably have to show it at some point. Finally, be wary of accepting food, drink, sweets or cigarettes from unknown fellow travellers on buses or trains; although extremely rare, they may be drugged, and you could wake up hours later without your belongings. In this connection, never accept a bar drink from an opened bottle (unless you can see that the bottle is in general use); always have it uncapped in front of you. Do not take shared taxis with strangers you have met on the bus, no matter how polite or well-dressed.

## Scams

A number of distraction techniques such as mustard smearers and paint or shampoo sprayers and strangers' remarks like 'what's that on your shoulder?' or 'have you seen that dirt on your shoe?' are designed to distract you for a few critical moments in which time your bag may be grabbed. Furthermore, supposedly friendly assistance asking if you have dropped money or other items in the street work on the same premise. If someone follows you when you're in the street, let him catch up with you and give him the 'eye'. While you should take local advice about being out at night, do not assume that daytime is any safer. If walking after dark on quiet streets, walk in the road, not on the pavement.

Be wary of 'plain-clothes policemen'; insist on seeing identification and going to the police station by main roads. Do not hand over your identification (or money – which they should not need to see anyway) until you are at the station. On no account take them directly back to your lodgings. Be even more suspicious if they seek confirmation of their status from a passer-by. If someone implies they are asking for a bribe, insist on a receipt. If attacked, remember your assailants may well be armed, and try not to resist.

It is best, if you can trust your hotel, to leave any valuables you don't need in a safe-deposit box. Always keep an inventory of what you have deposited. If you don't trust the hotel, lock everything in your pack and secure that in your room. If you do lose valuables, you will need to report the incident to the police for insurance purposes.

## Sexual assault

This is extremely rare, but if you are the victim of a sexual assault, you are advised in the first instance to contact a doctor (this can be your home doctor if you prefer). You will need tests to determine whether you have contracted any sexually transmitted diseases; you may also need advice on post-coital contraception. You should also contact your embassy, where consular staff are very willing to help in cases of assault.

## Student and teacher travellers

If you are in full-time education you will be entitled to an **International Student Identity Card** (ISIC), which is distributed by student travel offices and travel agencies in over 100 countries. ISIC gives you special prices on all forms of transport (air, sea, rail, etc), and a variety of other concessions and services. Contact the **International Student Travel Confederation** (ISTC), T+31-20-421 2800, www.isic.org. Student cards must carry a photograph if they are to be of any use for discounts in Latin America. The ISIC website provides a list of card-issuing offices around the world. Teachers may want to take an **International Teacher Identity Card** (ITIC) distributed by ISTC (above), as discounts are often extended to teachers.

## Tax

Airport departure tax is now normally included in the ticket price. There may also be taxes on international and domestic air tickets sold in individual countries. Sales tax varies from country to country, and is between 10 and 16%. Hotel tax is 3-9%, usually payable just in the more upmarket places.

## Telephone

Many of the telecommunications networks have been privatized and prices have fallen considerably. In some areas, services have even improved. Consequently keeping in touch by phone is no longer prohibitively expensive. International telecom charge cards are useful and available from most countries; obtain details before leaving home. For the US AT&T's **USA Direct**, **Sprint** and **MCI** are all available for calls to the US. It is much cheaper than operator-assisted calls. Internet calls (eg via **Skype**, **Whatsapp** and **Viber**) are also possible if you have access to Wi-Fi.

Using a mobile in most of Mexico and Central America is very expensive. In addition to the hassle of having to charge your phone, research whether it is worth your while. Mobile phone calls will be cheaper if you buy a SIM card for the local network; in-country calls are likely to be considerably cheaper than using your home-based account. The initial cost of the SIM is getting more affordable (as little as US$3 in Honduras), but check the cost of calls. Also bear in mind that the number you use at home will not work. Some networks, eg **O2**, provide an app so you can use the time on your contract if you access the app via Wi-Fi.

## Mexico
*Country code T+52. Operator T020; international operator T090. Directory enquiries T040.*

Most destinations have a 7-digit number and 3-digit regional code (Mexico City is an exception). The format of a number, depending on the type of call, should be as follows: **local** 7- or 8-digit phone number; **regional** long-distance access code (01) + regional code (2- or 3-digit code) + 7- or 8-digit number; **international** international direct-dialling code + country code + regional code + 7- or 8-digit number. Most public phones take phone cards only (**Ladatel**) costing 30 or 50 pesos from shops and news kiosks everywhere. Reverse-charge (collect) calls can be made from any blue public phone; say you want to *llamar por cobrar*. Pre-paid phone cards are expensive for international calls. Of other pre-paid cards, the best value are **Ekofon**, www.ekofon.com.

## Belize
*Country code T+501. International operator T115. Information T113.*

If you have many calls to make, a card phone works out much cheaper. There is a direct-dialling system between the major towns and to Mexico and USA. Local calls cost US$0.25 for 3 mins, US$0.12 for each extra min within the city, US$0.15-0.55 depending on zone. **Belize Telemedia Ltd**, 1 Church St, Belize City, Mon-Sat 0800-1800, Sun and holidays 0800-1200, has an international telephone, telex and internet service. The entire country's telephone directory is online at www.belizetelemedia.net.

Most people now have a mobile phone and most parts of the country have coverage. All towns have a telephone office and in most villages visitors can use the community phone. Payphones and card phones are fairly commonplace in Belize City and elsewhere.

## Guatemala
*Country code T+502. Directory enquiries T154.*

All phone numbers in the country are on an 8-figure basis. There are 2 main service providers – **Telgua** and **Telefónica**. Telefónica sells cards with access codes, which can be used from any private or public Telefónica phone. Telgua phone booths are ubiquitous and use cards sold in values of 20 and 50 quetzales. From a **Telgua** phone, dial 147 before making an international call.

Most businesses offering a phone-call service charge a minimum of US$0.13 for a local call, making a phone card a cheaper option.

International calls can be made from phone booths; however, unlike the local calls, it is cheaper to phone from an internet café or shop, which tend to offer better rates.

Mobile phone SIM cards are affordable, with good deals costing around US$10-20 for the card, which includes free calls. **Comcel** and **PCS** offer mobile phone services. Rates are around US$0.03 per min for a national call, US$1.20 for international.

Operator calls are more expensive. For international calls via the operator, dial T147-110. For calling card and credit-card call options, you need a fixed line in a hotel or private house. First you dial 9999 plus the following digits: For **Sprint USA**, dial 136; **AT&T Direct**: 190; **Germany**: 049; **Canada**: 198; **UK (BT)**: 044; **Switzerland**: 041; **Spain**: 034, **Italy**: 039.

Collect calls may be made from public Telgua phones by dialling T147-120.

## El Salvador
*Country code T+501.*
There are no local area codes within El Salvador. There is a network of public phones for telecommunications companies – all use prepaid phone cards that only work in the company's particular machines. Available at most street corners, supermarkets, petrol stations to small stores they can be used for local and international calls, but make sure the card is from the same company as the public phone. The cards come in several denominations (US$1-3, US$5, US$10, US$25, etc). Mobile phones are very cheap. You can get a SIM card for US$3 and if you need a mobile phone you can get one fromas little as US$12.

Some hotels will provide direct dialling – by far the easiest option. Dial T114 for **Information** (English spoken) and details of phone numbers in capital.

## Honduras
*Country code T+504. International operator T197. Local operator T192. Information T193.*
**Hondutel** provides international telephone services from stations throughout the country. The system has improved dramatically in recent years due to competition, with an increasing majority of Hondurans owning a cell phone. You can buy a cell phone for about US$10 from Tigo, Claro and Digicel, with phone cards from US$2 upwards.

## Nicaragua
*Country code T+505.*
Phone numbers in Nicaragua have 8 digits; those starting 2 are landlines. Phone cards are available from petrol stations, supermarkets and shops. International or national calls can be made at any **Entel** office, 0700-2200. All calls paid for in córdobas. To the USA, US$3 for the 1st minute, US$1 for each following minute. Collect calls (*por cobrar*) to the USA and Europe are possible. For SPRINT, dial 171; AT&T 174 and MCI 166. To connect to phone services in Germany dial 169, Belgium 172, Canada 168, Spain 162, Netherlands 177, UK 175.

## Costa Rica
*Country code T+506. Operator T116.*
There are no area codes in Costa Rica. Costa Rican numbers have 8 digits; numbers starting 2 are landlines, those starting 8 are mobiles.

Standard rates to US, Canada, Mexico and South America are US$0.45 a min; Panama is US$0.40 and Europe and the rest of the world (except Central America and Belize) US$0.60 a min if you dial direct; operator-assisted calls cost up to US$3.12 a min. Only variable rates are to Central America: standard rates between 0700 and 1900 (US$0.40 a min), reduced between 1900 and 2200 (US$0.35) and reduced again between 2200 and 0700 and during the weekend (US$0.28). Add 13% sales tax.

Public phones are maddening to use, various kinds are available: some use 10 and 20 colón silver coins, others use 50 colón gold coins, and still others employ at least 2 types of calling cards, but not interchangeably. The 199 cards are recommended, but it's often easiest to call collect inside (T110) and outside (T116) the country. Assistance for hearing impaired (Spanish only) is T137.

Phone cards with 'Personal Identification Numbers' are available for between US$0.80 and US$10. These can be used for national and international direct dialling from a private phone. Calls abroad can be made from phone booths; collect calls abroad may be made from special booths in the RACSA office, or from any booth nationwide if you dial T116 for connection with the international operator (T175 for collect calls to the USA). Phone cards can be used. Dial T124 for international information. Country Direct Dialling Codes to the USA are: **MCI/World Phone** 0800-012-2222, **AT&T** 0800-0114-114, **Sprint/GlobalOne** 0800-013-0123, **Worldcom** 0800-014-4444.

### Panama
*Country code T+507. International operator T106. Local operator T102.*
**Telecarrier** T088+00; **Clarocom** T055+00. Collect calls are permitted, 3 mins minimum, rates are higher than direct, especially to USA. The cost of direct dialled calls, per minute, are between US$1-3.20. Calls are roughly 20-30% cheaper for most, but not all destinations from 1700-2200. Lowest rates apply Sun all day. There are many cheap international call centres in Panama City, check the internet cafés on Vía Veneto for best offers.

Public payphones take 5, 10 and sometimes 25 cent coins. Phone cards are available in denominations of US$3, 5, 10, 20 and 50, for local, national and international calls. There are prepaid *Aló Panamá* cards – dial 165 for connection in US$10, US$20, US$30 and US$50 denominations, but they are 50% more expensive than payphone cards. For **AT&T** dial T109. For *SPRINT* (collect calls only) T115 and for **MCI** T108. BT Chargecard calls to the UK can be made through the local operator.

### Time
Southern Mexico is in Central Standard Time (CST), 6 hrs behind GMT. Daylight Saving Time runs from the 1st Sun in Apr to the last Sun in Oct (when it is 5 hrs behind GMT). Guatemala, Belize, El Salvador, Honduras, Nicaragua and Costa Rica are also -6 hrs GMT. Panama is -5 hrs GMT.

### Tipping
Normally 10-15%; the equivalent of US$0.25 per bag for porters, the equivalent of US$0.20 for bell boys, and nothing for a taxi driver unless for some kind of exceptional service.

### Tourist information
All countries in the region have a tourist board but not all have an international presence. Fortunately the internet makes it possible to get the latest information on developments in a country.
**South American Explorers**, USA, T607-277-0488, www.saexplorers.org, is a very useful resource. Despite the name, the whole of Latin America is covered and members receive help with travel planning as well as informed access on books and maps covering the region.

#### Useful websites
**www.latinnews.com** Up-to-date site with political comment.
**www.planeta.com** A phenomenal resource, which is staggering for its detail on everything from ecotourism and language schools to cybercafés.
**www.revuemag.com** Growing regional guide in print and online, focusing on Guatemala with coverage of Belize.

#### Mexico
Tourist offices are listed throughout the text. In Europe, information is available in several different languages by calling T00-800-1111-

2266. In North America call T1-800-446-3942.

Mexico's web presence is phenomenal, some of the reliable, informative and useful websites that have been round for a while include:

**www.mexconnect.com** General information.

**www.mexperience.com** Well-constructed site updated daily, with current affairs, feature articles and advice on travel in Mexico. Look out for the forum where comments from fellow travellers are exchanged.

**www.sectur.gob.mx** Tourism Secretariat's site, with less glossy links but equally comprehensive information.

**www.visitmexico.com** Mexico Tourist Board site, a comprehensive multilingual site with information on the entire country.

## Belize

Useful websites on Belize include the following:

**www.belizenet.com**, **www.belize.net** and **www.belize.com** Good search engines with general information.

**www.governmentofbelize.gov.bz** The government site on the country, packed with information on the official angle.

**www.belizeaudubon.org** and **www.pfbelize.org** Cover many protected areas and have a strong conservation focus.

**www.ambergriscaye.com**, **www.gocaye caulker.com** and **www.placencia.com** and **www.southernbelize.com** Useful sites.

**www.belizex.com** Covers the Cayo area.

**www.belizereport.com** The online version of the *Belize Report*.

**www.belizenews.com** Local news and links to the local newspapers (*Amandala*, *The Belize Times*, *The Reporter* and *The Guardian*).

## Guatemala

The country's official tourist office is the **Instituto Guatemalteco de Turismo (INGUAT)**, 7 Av, 1-17, Zona 4, Centro Cívico, Guatemala City, T2421-2800, www.visit guatemala.com. Mon-Fri 0800-1600. INGUAT provides bus times, hotel lists and road maps. Staff are helpful. They also have an office at the airport, open daily 0600-2400.

**The Guatemalan Maya Centre**, 94b Wandsworth Bridge Rd, London SW6 2TF, T020-7371 5291, www.maya.org.uk, has information on Guatemala, the Maya, a library, video archive and a textile collection; visits by prior appointment.

Regional websites covering some of the more popular areas include **www.atitlan. com**, **www.mayaparadise.com** (Río Dulce/ Lívingston), **www.cobanav.net** (Cobán) and **www.xelapages.com** (Quetzaltenango). **Posada Belén** in Guatemala City run a very informative site packed with information, www.guatemalaweb.com. Of the several publications with websites, the *Revue*, **www. revuemag.com**, is probably the most useful to the visitor.

## El Salvador

**www.alfatravelguide.com** Has a comprehensive listings of hotels throughout the country.

**www.elsalvador.com** Site of *El Diario de Hoy*– look in 'Otros Sitios' for tourist info.

**www.diariocolatino.com** Site of the leftist *Co Latino* newspaper.

**www.mipatria.net** and **www.theother elsalvador.com** Access to useful information.

**www.turismo.com.sv** Lists of hotels, restaurants and interesting places to visit.

**www.utec.edu.sv** Site of Centre for Investigation of El Salvadorean Public Opinion (CIOPS) with information in Spanish on El Salvadorean political and social issues.

## Honduras

**www.hondurastips.hn/** A reliable favourite with lots of information about Honduras and hotel, restaurant and transport listings (Spanish only). The biannual publication, *HONDURAS Tips*, edited by John Dupuis in La Ceiba, Edificio Gómez, Local No 2, 4 Calle, T2440-3383, is full of interesting and useful tourist information, in English and Spanish, free (available in Tegucigalpa from Instituto Hondureño de Turismo, and widely distributed around the country in major hotels).

**www.hondurasweekly.com** News, cultural features, travel tips, listings and links.
**www.letsgohonduras.com** The official Tourist Office (IHT) guide on the internet, with basic highlights.
**www.netsys.hn** Good business directory and useful links (in English).

Several regional guides are being developed – these are mentioned within the text.

## Nicaragua

**www.nicanet.org** For activist issues.
**www.nicaragua.com** Has an e-community.
www.nicaraguadispatch.com English-language news.
**www.toursnicaragua.com** Has a good selection of photographs and images.
**www.vianica.com** Good on hotels, transport and itineraries.

## Costa Rica

**www.ticotimes.net** Famous for its English-language news.
**www.infocostarica.com** A Yahoo-style search engine with information, links and maps for all things Costa Rican.

## Panama

**www.bananamarepublic.com** Ascerbic news and satire from journalist Okke Ornstein.
**www.thepanamanews.com** English language news and analysis from Eric Jackson.
**www.businesspanama.com** Economic, political and business information.
**www.panamainfo.com** An excellent site in English with good general information on Panama and links to several other national sites including newspapers, government organizations and tourist services.

## Tour operators

### In the UK

**Condor Journeys and Adventures**, T01700-841 318, www.condorjourneys-adventures.com. Also has offices in France.
**Dragoman**, T01728-861 133, www.dragoman.co.uk.
**Exodus Travels**, T020-8675 5550, www.exodus.co.uk.
**Explore Worldwide**, T0870-333 4001, www.explore.co.uk.
**Galapagos Classic Cruises**, T020-8933 0613, www.galapagoscruises.co.uk.
**Journey Latin America**, T020-3432 5923, www.journeylatin america.co.uk. Leading specialist for tailor-made holidays in Latin America. Also offer a wide range of flight options.

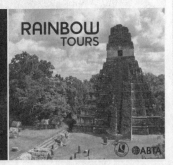

**Last Frontiers**, T01296-653 000, www.lastfrontiers.com. Latin American specialists offering tailor-made itineraries, family holidays and honeymoons.
**LATA**, www.lata.org. Useful country information and listing of UK tour operators, specializing in Latin America.
**Naturally Belize**, T020-8274 8510, www.naturallybelize.co.uk. Small specialist travel business arranging tailor-made holidays in Belize.
**Rainbow Tours**, T020-7666 1260, www.rainbowtours.co.uk/latinamerica. Tailor-made travel throughout Latin America.
**Reef & Rainforest Tours**, T01803-866 965, www.reefandrainforest.co.uk. Specialists in tailor-made and group wildlife tours.
**Select Latin America**, T020-7407 1478, www.selectlatinamerica.co.uk. Tailor-made holidays and small group tours.
**South American Experience**, T0845-277 3366, www.southamericanexperience.co.uk.
**Steppes Travel**, T01285-885 333, www.steppestravel.co.uk. Tailor-made and group itineraries throughout Costa Rica and the rest of Latin America.
**Trips Worldwide**, T0117-311 4404, www.tripsworldwide.co.uk.
**Tucan Travel**, T020-8896 1600, www.tucantravel.com.
**Veloso Tours**, T020-8762 0616, www.veloso.com.

**In North America**
**Exito Travel**, T970-482 3019, www.exito-travel.com.
**GAP Adventures**, T1-800-708 7761, www.gapadventures.com.
**LADATCO tours**, T1-800-327 6162, www.ladatco.com.
**Mila Tours**, T1-800-367 7378, www.milatours.com.
**S and S Tours**, T800-499 5685, www.ss-tours.com.

## Visas and immigration

If you are thinking of travelling from your own country via the USA, or of visiting the USA after Latin America, you are strongly advised to get your visa and find out about any other requirements from a US Consulate in your own country before travelling. If you are eligible for a visa waiver, you are now required to register in advance with the **Electronic System for Travel Authorization** (ESTA), www.esta.cbp.dhs.gov/esta/. You will need to do this before setting out.

For US nationals, the implications of the **Western Hemisphere Travel Initiative**, which came into force on 1 Jan 2008, should be considered if entering Mexico. You will need a passport to re-enter the US once you have left and visited Mexico.

All international travel requires that you have at least 6 months remaining on a valid passport. Beyond a passport, very little is required of international travellers to Mexico and Central America. However, there are a few little tricks that can make your life a lot easier. Latin Americans, especially officials,

are very document-minded. If staying in a country for several weeks, it is worthwhile registering at your embassy or consulate. Then, if your passport is stolen, the process of replacing it is faster and easier. It can also be handy to keep some additional passport-sized photographs together with photocopies of essential documents – including your flight ticket – separately from the originals.

It is your responsibility to ensure that your passport is stamped in and out when you cross borders. The absence of entry and exit stamps can cause serious difficulties; seek out the proper immigration offices if the stamping process is not carried out as you cross. Also, do not lose your entry card; replacing it can cause you a lot of trouble and possibly expense. If planning to study in Mexico or Central America for a long period, make every effort to get a student visa in advance.

In 2006 Guatemala, El Salvador, Honduras and Nicaragua signed a Central America-4 (CA-4) Border Control Agreement; see box, page 1031. Travel between these 4 countries now involves minimal customs control. Nevertheless, always check at these countries' consulates for any changes to the rules.

**Mexico**
Virtually all international travellers require a passport to enter Mexico. Upon entry you will be issued a tourist card known as a **Forma Migratoria Múltiple (FMM)**, valid for up to 180 days. The card comes with a fee,

The **Derecho de No Migrante (DNI)** costs approximately US$22, which you must pay upon exit, or if you prefer, upon entry – be sure to get a stamp and keep all receipts. If arriving in Cancún or Mexico City, the DNI is often included in airfares. Nonetheless, when exiting at land borders, you must present evidence of this to avoid being

charged a 2nd time (this issue has been frequently reported at the Mexico–Belize border). On your plane ticket, the DNI is indicated by the code 'UK' – print the page and highlight it. Note your FMM must be surrendered when leaving the country to avoid problems later. If you are in Mexico for 7 days or less and you return to your country of origin, you are exempt from the DNI.

If your stamp bears less than 180 days, you can extend it up to the limit at any **National Institute of Migration** office; you can find details at www.inm.gob.mx. To renew a tourist card by leaving the country, you must stay outside Mexico for at least 72 hrs.

Take TCs or a credit card as proof of finance. At the border crossings with Belize and Guatemala, you may be refused entry into Mexico if you have less than US$200 (or US$350 for each month of intended stay, up to a maximum of 180 days). Likewise, if you are carrying more than US$10,000 in cash or TCs, you must declare it.

If a person under 18 is travelling alone or with one parent, both parents' consent is required, certified by a notary or authorized by a consulate. A divorced parent must be able to show custody of a child. (These requirements are not always checked by immigration authorities and do not apply to all nationalities.) Further details are available from any Mexican consulate.

## Belize

All nationalities need passports, as well as sufficient funds and, officially, an onward ticket, although this is rarely requested for stays of 30 days or less. Visas are not usually required by nationals from countries within the EU, Australia and New Zealand, most Caribbean states, the USA and Canada. Citizens of India, Israel, Austria and Switzerland do need a visa. There is a **Belizean Consulate** in Chetumal, Mexico, at Armada de México 91, T+52-983-21803, US$25. If you need a visa it is best to obtain

one in Mexico City or your home country before arriving at the border.

## Guatemala

Only a valid passport is required for citizens of all Western European countries; USA, Canada, Mexico, all Central American countries, Australia, Israel, Japan and New Zealand. The majority of visitors get 90 days on arrival.

Visa renewal must be done in Guatemala City after 90 days, or on expiry. Passport stamp renewal on expiry for those citizens only requiring a valid passport to enter Guatemala must also be done at the immigration office at **Dirección General de Migración**, 6 Avenida, 3-11, Zona 4, Guatemala City, T2411-2411, Mon-Fri 0800-1600 (0800-1230 for payments). This office extends visas and passport stamps only once for a further period of time, depending on the original time awarded (maximum 90 days). Since 2006, when Guatemala signed a Central America-4 (CA-4) Border Control Agreement with El Salvador (see box, page 1031), Honduras, and Nicaragua you will have to visit a country outside of these 3 to re-enter and gain 90 days. These rules have been introduced to stop people leaving the country for 72 hrs (which is the legal requirement) every 6 months and returning, effectively making them permanent residents.

## El Salvador

Every visitor must have a valid passport. No visas are required for European, US, Canadian, Australian or New Zealand nationals. The government website www.rree.gob.sv has a full list of country requirements.

Overstaying the limit on a tourist card can result in fines. Immigration officials can authorize up to 90 days stay in the country; extensions may be permitted on application to Migración, Centro de Gobierno (see under San Salvador).

## Honduras

Neither a visa nor tourist card is required for nationals of Western European countries, USA, Canada, Australia, New Zealand, Japan, Argentina, Chile, Guatemala, Costa Rica, Nicaragua, El Salvador, Panama and Uruguay. Citizens of other countries need either a tourist card, which can be bought from Honduran consulates for US$2-3, or a visa, and they should enquire at a Honduran consulate in advance to see which they need. The price of a visa seems to vary depending on nationality and where it is bought. Extensions of 30 days are easy to obtain (up to a maximum of 6 months' stay, cost US$5). There are immigration offices for extensions at Tela, La Ceiba, San Pedro Sula, Santa Rosa de Copán, Siguatepeque, La Paz and Comayagua, and all are more helpful than the Tegucigalpa office.

You will have to visit a country outside of Guatemala, Honduras and Nicargua to re-enter and gain 90 days.

## Nicaragua

Visa rules change frequently, so check before you travel; see www.cancilleria.gob.ni. Visitors need a passport with a minimum validity of 6 months and may have to show an onward ticket and proof of funds in cash or TCs for a stay of more than a week. No visa is required by nationals of EU countries, the USA, Canada, Australia or New Zealand. Most visitors are given 90 days on entrance which can be extended to 180 days. Extensions are obtained at the **Dirección de Migración y Extranjería**, Semáforo Tenderí, 2 1½ c al norte, Managua, T244-3989 (Spanish only), www.migracion.gob.ni. Arrive at the office before 0830. From the small office on the right-hand side you must obtain the *formulario* (3 córdobas). Then queue at the *caja* in the large hall to pay US$23 for each 30-day extension (maximum 90 days). There is also a small *Migración* office in Metrocentro shopping mall where you can also obtain an extension. Another possibility is to leave the country for 72 hrs.

If you need a visa it can be bought before arriving at the border, it costs US$25, is valid for arrival within 30 days and for a stay of up to 30 days; 2 passport photographs are required. A full 30-day visa can be bought at the border, but it is best to get it in advance. Visas take less than 2 hrs to process in Guatemala City and Tegucigalpa, but may take 48 hrs elsewhere.

## Costa Rica

Nationals of most EU nations, the US, Australia, New Zealand, Canada, Israel and Japan do not need visas for visits of up to 90 days. For more information check www.migracion.go.cr. Tourists must show at least US$300 in cash or TCs before being granted entry, along with an onward ticket and/or a ticket to their country of origin. Monetary fines for overstaying your visa or entry permit have been eliminated; tourists who overstay their welcome more than once may be denied entry into the country on subsequent occasions, part of government efforts to crack down on 'perpetual tourists'. For stays longer than the 90-day permitted period, you can ask for a Prórroga de Turismo at Immigration in San José. For this you need 4 passport photos, an airline or bus ticket out of the country and proof of funds (for example TCs); you can apply for an extension of 2 months for US$100. The paperwork takes 3 days. It is may be cheaper and less hassle to leave the country for 72 hrs and re-enter for a new stamp.

## Panama

All visitors to Panama must have a passport valid for a minimum of 6 months, an onward/return ticket and proof of sufficient funds for their stay (US$500 cash or a credit card). Depending on your country of origin, you may or may not require a stamped or authorized visa (see below). Visitors are entitled to a maximum stay of 180 days, no renewals (visas 90 days). However, if your stamp/tourist card expires, you can renew it by leaving the country for 72 hrs and re-entering. Citizens of the United States, Canada, Australia, New Zealand, most European (including the UK), Caribbean, South American, Central American and some Asian countries do not need a visa; simply hand over your passport and receive your entry stamp. Citizens of Egypt, Peru, Dominican Republic, many African, Eastern European and Asian countries require a stamped visa US$85, or an authorized visa, US$100, which must be arranged in advance of travel; check with Panama's **Migración** office, www.migracion.gob.pa, for more information. Visas are typically valid for 30 days but can be extended to 90 days at the Migracion offices on Av Cuba at Calle 29 Este (there are also offices in David, Chitre, Changuinola and Santiago); ask for a Prórroga de Turista.

## Weights and measures

In Mexico and most of Central America, the metric system is official, but in practice a mixture is used of metric, imperial and old Spanish measurements. In Belize, they use imperial and US standard weights and measures.

## Women travellers

Some women experience problems, whether accompanied or not; others encounter no difficulties at all. Unaccompanied Western women will at times be subject to close scrutiny and exceptional curiosity. Don't be unduly scared. Simply be prepared and try not to overreact. When you set out, err on the side of caution until your instincts have adjusted to the new culture. Women travelling alone could consider taking a wedding ring to prevent being hassled. To help minimize unwanted attention, consider your clothing choices. Do not feel bad about showing

offence. When accepting an invitation, make sure that someone else knows the address you are going to and the time you left. Ask if you can bring a friend (even if you do not intend to do so). A good rule is always to act with confidence, as though you know where you are going, even if you do not. Someone who looks lost is more likely to attract unwanted attention. Do not disclose to strangers where you are staying.

## Volunteering

Two main areas provide opportunities for unskilled volunteers: childcare – often at orphanages or schools – and nature projects. Be warned, spontaneous volunteering is becoming more difficult. Organizations that use volunteers have progressed and plan their personnel needs so you may be required to make contact before you visit. Many organizations now charge volunteers for board and lodging and projects are often for a minimum of 4 weeks. Guatemala in particular has fairly well-developed and organized volunteer programmes.

Many developed countries have nationally organized volunteer programmes. The **US Peace Corps**, T1-800-424-8580, www.peacecorps.gov, is the most prominent in the region, working with countries on development projects with 2-year assignments for US citizens in countries throughout Mexico and Central America.

Variations on the volunteering programme are to enrol on increasingly popular gap-year programmes. These normally incorporate a period of volunteer work with a few months of free time at the end of the programme for travel.

**Experiment in International Living**, T+44-1684-562577, www.eiluk.org, is the UK element of a US international homestay programme that arranges stays with families in Mexico and Central America with social projects based on the ethos that if you want to live together, you need to work together.

It's an excellent way to meet people and learn the language.

## Guatemala

**Asociación de Rescate y Conservación de Vida Silvestre (ARCAS)**, T2478-4096, www.arcasguatemala.com. Runs projects involving working with nature and wildlife, returning wild animals to their natural habitat.

**Casa Alianza**, 13 Av, 0-37, Zona 2 de Mixco, Col la Escuadrilla Mixco, Guatemala City, T2250-4964, www.casa-alianza.org. A project that helps street children.

**Casa Guatemala**, 14 Calle, 10-63, Zona 1, Guatemala City, T2331-9408, www.casa-guatemala.org. Runs a project for abandoned and malnourished children at Río Dulce.

**Comité Campesino del Altiplano**, on Lake Atitlán, 10 mins from San Lucas, T5804-9451, www.ccda.galeon.com. This **Campesino Cooperative** now produces Fair Trade organic coffee buying from small farmers in the region; long-term volunteers are welcome but Spanish is required.

**Fundación Mario Dary**, Diagonal 6, 17-19, Zona 10, Guatemala City, T2333-4957, fundary@intelnet.net.gt. Operates conservation, health and education projects on the Punta de Manabique and welcomes volunteers.

**Proyecto Ak' Tenamit**, 11 Av 'A', 9-39, Zona 2, Guatemala City, T2254-1560, www.aktenamit.org, based at Clínica Lámpara, 15 mins upriver from Lívingston. This project was set up to help 7000 civil-war-displaced Q'eqchi' Maya who now live in the region in 30 communities.

**Proyecto Mosaico Guatemala**, 3 Av Norte 3, Antigua. T7832-0955, www.promosaico.org. An information centre and clearing house for volunteers, with access to opportunities all over the country.

**Quetzaltrekkers**, Casa Argentina, 12 Diagonal, 8-43, Zona 1, Quetzaltenango, T7765-5895, www.quetzaltrekkers.com.

Volunteer opportunities for hiking guides and office workers, minimum 3-month commitment.

**UPAVIM**, Calle Principal, Sector D-1, Col La Esperanza, Zona 12, Guatemala City, T2479-9061, www.upavim.org. This project helps poor families, providing social services and education for the workers using fairtrade principles.

There are also opportunities to work in children's homes in Quetzaltenango (Xela). 2 organizations are **Casa Hogar de Niños** and the **Asociación Hogar Nuevos Horizontes**. Also check out Xela-based volunteering information organization **www.entremundos.org**. Several language schools in Xela fund community development projects and seek volunteers. Make enquiries in town or via www.xelapages.com.

The London-based **Guatemala Solidarity Network**, www.guatemalasolidarity.org.uk, can assist with finding projects that look at human rights issues.

## Nicaragua

Volunteer work in Nicaragua is not as common as it was during the Sandinista years. Foreigners now work in environmental brigades supporting the **FSLN (Frente Sandinista de Liberación Nacional)**, construction projects, agricultural cooperatives and environmental organizations. Certain skills are in demand, as elsewhere in the developing world.

To find out about the current situation, try contacting non-governmental organizations in your home country, such as **Nicaraguan Network**, www.nica net.org, and Nicaraguan Solidarity Campaigns, such as **NSC/ENN Brigades**, www.nicaraguasc.org.uk, or **Dutch Nicaragua Komitee**, in Managua.

**Casa Danesa**, T267-8126 (Managua), may be able to help find volunteer work, usually for 3 months, but shorter times are sometimes acceptable. An excellent short-term non-profit volunteer experience can be had with **El Porvenir**, www.elporvenir.org, an outgrowth of **Habitats for Humanity**. Work is on drinking water, latrine and re-forestation projects.

## Costa Rica

Volunteering to help with environmental and conservation work is very popular, well developed and organized. Normally you have to pay for food and sometimes lodgings. (Charges usually vary from US$75-150 a week.) The workload and type varies enormously. Most volunteers organize a placement before arriving. Once working you will normally work a shift pattern with 2- to 4-day breaks for travel.

Volunteering at national parks can be organized through **ASVO**, www.asvocr.org. You can also contact organizations direct: for **Hacienda Barú** near Dominical (see page 813), **Caño Palma Biological Station** in Parque Nacional Tortuguero (see page 839), **Aviarios del Caribe** South from Puerto Limón (see page 845), **ANAI** (see page 845) and the **Talamanca Dolphin Foundation** on the south Caribbean coast close to Puerto Viejo de Talamanca, the **Children's Eternal Rainforest** in Monteverde (see page 770) and **Campanario Biological Reserve** in Bahía Drake and **Rara Avis** near Puerto Viejo de Sarapiquí (see page 833).

## Panama

Panama has plenty of volunteer opportunities in the fields of teaching, conservation and organic farming. Contact NGOs in your own country to find out about the latest schemes. **Summit Garden and Zoo**, www.summitpan ama.org, have an interesting environmental education programme where you'll contribute to the zoo's maintenance and learn about local fauna. **Global Vision International**, www.earthwatch.org, run a programme in the conservation of sea turtles in Bocas del Toro. You'll be required to tag and monitor turtles and pay a fee in addition to your work contribution. **Habitat for Humanity International**, www.habitat.org, are working in the area to provide housing.

# Footnotes

# Basic Spanish for travellers

Learning Spanish is a useful part of the preparation for a trip to Latin America and no volumes of dictionaries, phrase books or word lists will provide the same enjoyment as being able to communicate directly with the people of the country you are visiting. It is a good idea to make an effort to grasp the basics before you go. As you travel you will pick up more of the language and the more you know, the more you will benefit from your stay.

## General pronunciation

Whether you have been taught the 'Castilian' pronunciation (z and c followed by i or e are pronounced as the th in think) or the 'American' pronunciation (they are pronounced as s), you will encounter little difficulty in understanding either. Regional accents and usages vary, but the basic language is essentially the same everywhere.

### Vowels

- *a* as in English *cat*
- *e* as in English *best*
- *i* as the *ee* in English *feet*
- *o* as in English *shop*
- *u* as the *oo* in English *food*
- *ai* as the *i* in English *ride*
- *ei* as *ey* in English *they*
- *oi* as *oy* in English *toy*

### Consonants

Most consonants can be pronounced more or less as they are in English.
The exceptions are:

- *g* before *e* or *i* is the same as *j*
- *h* is always silent (except in *ch* as in *chair*)
- *j* as the *ch* in Scottish *loch*
- *ll* as the *y* in *yellow*
- *ñ* as the *ni* in English *onion*
- *rr* trilled much more than in English
- *x* depending on its location, pronounced *x, s, sh* or *j*

## Spanish words and phrases

### Greetings, courtesies

hello  *hola*
good morning  *buenos días*
good afternoon/evening/night
  *buenas tardes/noches*
goodbye  *adiós/chao*
pleased to meet you  *mucho gusto*
see you later  *hasta luego*
how are you?  *¿cómo está?/¿cómo estás?*
I'm fine, thanks  *estoy muy bien, gracias*
I'm called...  *me llamo...*
what is your name?  *¿cómo se llama?/*
  *¿cómo te llamas?*
yes/no  *sí/no*

please  *por favor*
thank you (very much)  *(muchas) gracias*
I speak Spanish  *hablo español*
I don't speak Spanish  *no hablo español*
do you speak English?  *¿habla inglés?*

I don't understand *no entiendo/
no comprendo*
please speak slowly *hable despacio
por favor*
I am very sorry *lo siento mucho/disculpe*
what do you want? *¿qué quiere?/
¿qué quieres?*

I want *quiero*
I don't want it *no lo quiero*
good/bad *bueno/malo*
leave me alone *déjeme en paz/
no me moleste*

## Questions and requests

Have you got a room for two people?
*¿Tiene una habitación para dos personas?*
How do I get to_? *¿Cómo llego a_?*
How much does it cost?
*¿Cuánto cuesta? ¿cuánto es?*
I'd like to make a long-distance
phone call *Quisiera hacer una llamada
de larga distancia*
Is service included? *¿Está incluido
el servicio?*

Is tax included? *¿Están incluidos
los impuestos?*
When does the bus leave (arrive)?
*¿A qué hora sale (llega) el autobús?*
When? *¿cuándo?*
Where is_? *¿dónde está_?*
Where can I buy tickets?
*¿Dónde puedo comprar boletos?*
Where is the nearest petrol station?
*¿Dónde está la gasolinera más cercana?*
Why? *¿por qué?*

## Basics

bank *el banco*
bathroom/toilet *el baño*
bill *la factura/la cuenta*
cash *el efectivo*
cheap *barato/a*
credit card *la tarjeta de crédito*
exchange house *la casa de cambio*
exchange rate *el tipo de cambio*

expensive *caro/a*
market *el mercado*
note/coin *le billete/la moneda*
police (policeman) *la policía (el policía)*
post office *el correo*
public telephone *el teléfono público*
supermarket *el supermercado*
ticket office *la taquilla*

## Getting around

aeroplane *el avión*
airport *el aeropuerto*
arrival/departure *la llegada/salida*
avenue *la avenida*
block *la cuadra*
border *la frontera*
bus station *la terminal de autobuses/
camiones*
bus *el bus/el autobús/el camión*
collective/fixed-route taxi *el colectivo*
corner *la esquina*
customs *la aduana*
first/second class *primera/segunda clase*
left/right *izquierda/derecha*
ticket *el boleto*
empty/full *vacío/lleno*
highway, main road *la carretera*

immigration *la inmigración*
insurance *el seguro*
insured person *el/la asegurado/a*
to insure yourself against *asegurarse
contra*
luggage *el equipaje*
motorway, freeway *el autopista/
la carretera*
north, south, east, west *norte, sur,
este (oriente), oeste (occidente)*
oil *el aceite*
to park *estacionarse*
passport *el pasaporte*
petrol/gasoline *la gasolina*
puncture *el pinchazo/la ponchadura*
street *la calle*
that way *por allí/por allá*

this way *por aquí/por acá*
tourist card/visa *la tarjeta de turista*
tyre *la llanta*

unleaded *sin plomo*
to walk *caminar/andar*

## Accommodation

air conditioning *el aire acondicionado*
all-inclusive *todo incluido*
bathroom, private *el baño privado*
bed, double/single *la cama matrimonial/ sencilla*
blankets *las cobijas/mantas*
to clean *limpiar*
dining room *el comedor*
guesthouse *la casa de huéspedes*
hotel *el hotel*
noisy *ruidoso*
pillows *las almohadas*

power cut *el apagón/corte*
restaurant *el restaurante*
room/bedroom *el cuarto/la habitación*
sheets *las sábanas*
shower *la ducha/regadera*
soap *el jabón*
toilet *el sanitario/excusado*
toilet paper *el papel higiénico*
towels, clean/dirty *las toallas limpias/ sucias*
water, hot/cold *el agua caliente/fría*

## Health

aspirin *la aspirina*
blood *la sangre*
chemist *la farmacia*
condoms *los preservativos, los condones*
contact lenses *los lentes de contacto*
contraceptives *los anticonceptivos*
contraceptive pill *la píldora anti-conceptiva*
diarrhoea *la diarrea*

doctor *el médico*
fever/sweat *la fiebre/el sudor*
pain *el dolor*
head *la cabeza*
period/sanitary towels *la regla/las toallas femeninas*
stomach *el estómago*
altitude sickness *el soroche*

## Family

family *la familia*
friend *el amigo/la amiga*
brother/sister *el hermano/la hermana*
daughter/son *la hija/el hijo*
father/mother *el padre/la madre*

husband/wife *el esposo (marido)/ la esposa*
boyfriend/girlfriend *el novio/la novia*
married *casado/a*
single/unmarried *soltero/a*

## Months, days and time

January *enero*
February *febrero*
March *marzo*
April *abril*
May *mayo*
June *junio*
July *julio*
August *agosto*
September *septiembre*
October *octubre*
November *noviembre*

December *diciembre*

Monday *lunes*
Tuesday *martes*
Wednesday *miércoles*
Thursday *jueves*
Friday *viernes*
Saturday *sábado*
Sunday *domingo*

## Time

at one o'clock *a la una*
at half past two *a las dos y media*
at a quarter to three *a cuarto para las tres/a las tres menos quince*
it's one o'clock *es la una*
it's seven o'clock *son las siete*

it's six twenty *son las seis y veinte*
it's five to nine *son las nueve menos cinco*
in ten minutes *en diez minutos*
five hours *cinco horas*
does it take long? *¿tarda mucho?*

## Numbers

one *uno/una*
two *dos*
three *tres*
four *cuatro*
five *cinco*
six *seis*
seven *siete*
eight *ocho*
nine *nueve*
ten *diez*
eleven *once*
twelve *doce*
thirteen *trece*
fourteen *catorce*
fifteen *quince*

sixteen *dieciséis*
seventeen *diecisiete*
eighteen *dieciocho*
nineteen *diecinueve*
twenty *veinte*
twenty-one *veintiuno*
thirty *treinta*
forty *cuarenta*
fifty *cincuenta*
sixty *sesenta*
seventy *setenta*
eighty *ochenta*
ninety *noventa*
hundred *cien/ciento*
thousand *mil*

## Food

avocado *la palta*
baked *al horno*
bakery *la panadería*
banana *la banana*
beans *los frijoles/las habichuelas*
beef *la carne de res*
beef steak *el lomo*
boiled rice *el arroz blanco*
bread *el pan*
breakfast *el desayuno*
butter *la manteca*
cake *la torta*
chewing gum *el chicle*
chicken *el pollo*
chilli or green pepper *el ají chile/pimiento*
clear soup, stock *el caldo*
cooked *cocido*
dining room *el comedor*
egg *el huevo*
fish *el pescado*
fork *el tenedor*
fried *frito*

garlic *el ajo*
goat *el chivo*
grapefruit *la toronja/el pomelo*
grill *la parrilla*
grilled/griddled *a la plancha*
guava *la guayaba*
ham *el jamón*
hamburger *la hamburguesa*
hot, spicy *picante*
ice cream *el helado*
jam *la mermelada*
knife *el cuchillo*
lemon *el limón*
lobster *la langosta*
lunch *el almuerzo/la comida*
meal *la comida*
meat *la carne*
minced meat *la carne picada*
onion *la cebolla*
orange *la naranja*
pepper *el pimiento*
pasty, turnover *la empanada/el pastelito*

pork *el cerdo*
potato *la papa*
prawns *los camarones*
raw *crudo*
restaurant *el restaurante*
salad *la ensalada*
salt *la sal*
sandwich *el bocadillo*
sauce *la salsa*
sausage *la longaniza/el chorizo*
scrambled eggs *los huevos revueltos*
seafood *los mariscos*

soup *la sopa*
spoon *la cuchara*
squash *la calabaza*
squid *los calamares*
supper *la cena*
sweet *dulce*
to eat *comer*
toasted *tostado*
turkey *el pavo*
vegetables *los legumbres/vegetales*
without meat *sin carne*
yam *el camote*

### Drink

beer *la cerveza*
boiled *hervido/a*
bottled *en botella*
camomile tea *la manzanilla*
canned *en lata*
coffee *el café*
coffee, white *el café con leche*
cold *frío*
cup *la taza*
drink *la bebida*
drunk *borracho/a*
firewater *el aguardiente*
fruit milkshake *el batido/licuado*
glass *el vaso*
hot *caliente*

ice/without ice *el hielo/sin hielo*
juice *el jugo*
lemonade *la limonada*
milk *la leche*
mint *la menta*
rum *el ron*
soft drink *el refresco*
sugar *el azúcar*
tea *el té*
to drink *beber/tomar*
water *el agua*
water, carbonated *el agua mineral con gas*
water, still mineral *el agua mineral sin gas*
wine, red *el vino tinto*
wine, white *el vino blanco*

### Key verbs

| to go | ir | to be | ser | estar |
|---|---|---|---|---|
| I go | *voy* | I am | soy | estoy |
| you go (familiar) | *vas* | you are | eres | estás |
| he, she, it goes, you (formal) go | *va* | he, she, it is, you (formal) are | es | está |
| we go | *vamos* | we are | somos | estamos |
| they, you (plural) go | *van* | they, you (plural) are | son | están |

(*ser* is used to denote a permanent state, whereas *estar* is used to denote a positional or temporary state.)

| to have (possess) | tener |
|---|---|
| I have | *tengo* |
| you (familiar) have | *tienes* |
| he, she, it, you (formal) have | *tiene* |
| we have | *tenemos* |
| they, you (plural) have | *tienen* |
| there is/are | *hay* |
| there isn't/aren't | *no hay* |

This section has been assembled on the basis of glossaries compiled by André de Mendonça and David Gilmour of South American Experience, London, and the Latin American Travel Advisor, No 9, March 1996.

# Index

*Entries in* **bold** *refer to maps*

# FOOTPRINT

## Features

**Richard Arghiris**

Richard Arghiris is a freelance writer, journalist, blogger and long-term traveller. He has been wandering the highways and unpaved back roads of Central America since 2003, contributing to magazines, newspapers, blogs, websites, documentaries and Footprint guidebooks. The region's diversity of remote landscapes, its vivid tropical ecology, and its patchwork of indigenous, Latin and African-descendant cultures – not to mention its swashbuckling sense of drama – are an ongoing creative inspiration for Richard. His blog, Unseen Americas, www.unseenamericas.com, features news reports, narrative journalism, and street photography from the sketchy US-Mexico border to the teeming rainforests of Panama.

## **Price** codes

**Where to stay**

$$$$ over US$150
$$$ US$66-150
$$ US$30-65
$ under US$30

Price of a double room in high season, including taxes.

**Restaurants**

$$$ over US$12
$$ US$7-12
$ US$6 and under

Prices for a two-course meal for one person, excluding drinks or service charge.

# Credits

**Footprint credits**
**Editor**: Jo Williams
**Production and layout**: Emma Bryers
**Maps**: Kevin Feeney
**Colour section**: Angus Dawson

**Publisher**: Patrick Dawson
**Managing Editor**: Felicity Laughton
**Administration**: Elizabeth Taylor
**Advertising sales and marketing**:
John Sadler, Kirsty Holmes
**Business Development**: Debbie Wylde

**Publishing information**
Footprint Mexico & Central America
20th edition
© Footprint Handbooks Ltd
October 2015

ISBN: 978 1 910120 38 5
CIP DATA: A catalogue record for this book is
available from the British Library

® Footprint Handbooks and the Footprint
mark are a registered trademark of Footprint
Handbooks Ltd

Published by Footprint
6 Riverside Court
Lower Bristol Road
Bath BA2 3DZ, UK
T +44 (0)1225 469141
F +44 (0)1225 469461
footprinttravelguides.com

Distributed in the USA by National Book
Network, Inc.

Every effort has been made to ensure that
the facts in this guidebook are accurate.
However, travellers should still obtain advice
from consulates, airlines, etc about travel
and visa requirements before travelling.
The authors and publishers cannot
accept responsibility for any loss, injury or
inconvenience however caused.

# Footprint Mini Atlas **Central America**

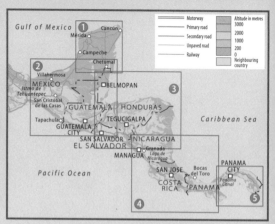

## Map 1

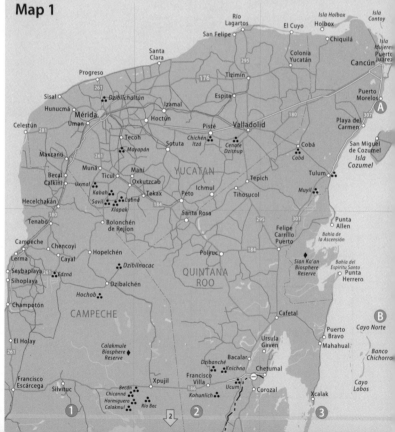

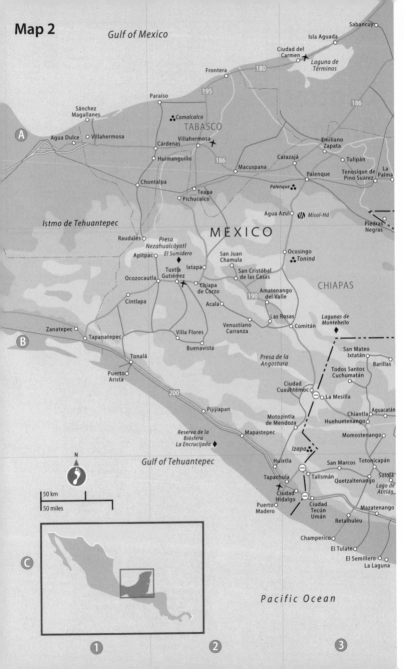

# Map 2

**Gulf of Mexico**

Sabancuy
Isla Aguada
Ciudad del Carmen
*Laguna de Términos*
Frontera
180
195
Paraíso
186
Sánchez Magallanes
*Comalcalco*
**TABASCO**
Agua Dulce
Villahermosa
Villahermosa
Cárdenas
Emiliano Zapata
Tulipán
Huimanguillo
186
Macuspana
Catazajá
Tenosique de Pino Suárez
La Palma
Chontalpa
Palenque
Teapa
Pichucalco
*Palenque*
*Istmo de Tehuantepec*
Agua Azul
*Misol-Há*
Piedras Negras
Raudales
*Presa Nezahualcóyotl*
**MÉXICO**
El Sumidero
Apitpac
San Juan Chamula
Ocosingo
*Toniná*
Ocozocuautla
Ixtapa
Tuxtla Gutiérrez
San Cristóbal de las Casas
**CHIAPAS**
Chiapa de Corzo
Amatenango del Valle
190
Cintlapa
Acala
Las Rosas
*Lagunas de Montebello*
Venustiano Carranza
Zanatepec
Villa Flores
Comitán
San Mateo Ixtatán
Tapanatepec
Buenavista
*Presa de la Angostura*
Barillas
Tonalá
Todos Santos Cuchumatán
Puerto Arista
Ciudad Cuauhtémoc
La Mesilla
Chiantla
Aguacatán
200
Pijijiapan
Motozintla de Mendoza
Huehuetenango
Momostenango
Mapastepec
*Reserva de la Biósfera La Encrucijada*
Izapa
**Gulf of Tehuantepec**
Huixtla
San Marcos
Totonicapán
Tapachula
Talismán
Quetzaltenango
Sololá
*Lago de Atitlán*
Ciudad Hidalgo
Puerto Madero
Ciudad Tecún Umán
Mazatenango
Retalhuleu
Champerico
El Tulate
El Semillero
La Laguna

**N**

50 km
50 miles

**Pacific Ocean**

A
B
C

1
2
3

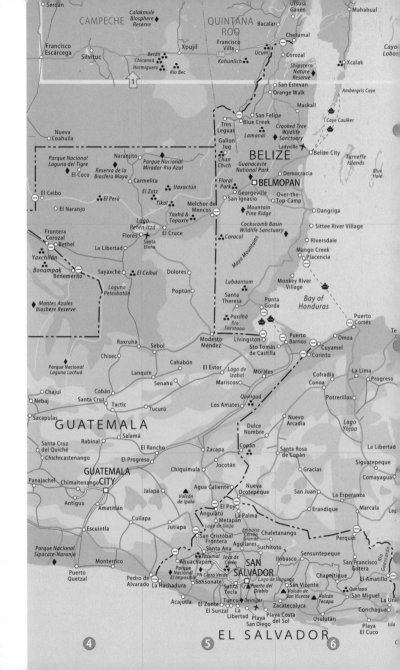

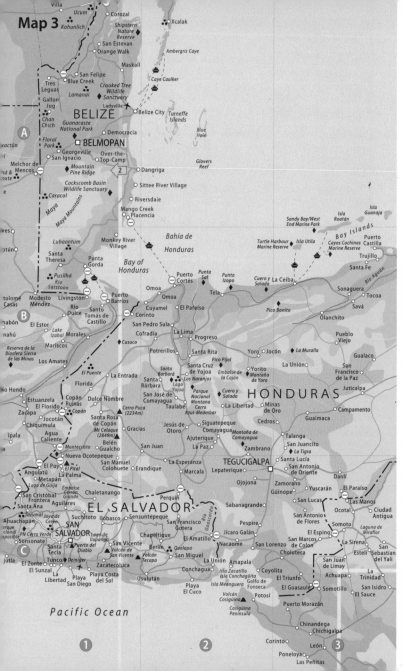

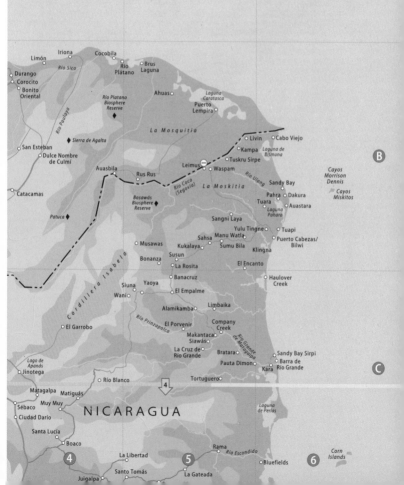

Caribbean Sea

N

50 km
50 miles

A

Limón
Iriona
Cocobila
Río Sico
Río Plátano
Brus Laguna
Durango
Corocito
Bonito Oriental
Ahuas
Río Platano Biosphere Reserve
Laguna Caratasca
Puerto Lempira
La Mosquitia
San Esteban
Dulce Nombre de Culmí
Sierra de Agalta
Livin
Cabo Viejo
Kampa
Laguna de Bismuna
Auasbila
Rus Rus
Leimus
Tuskru Sirpe
Waspam
Río Ulang
Catacamas
Bosawás Biosphere Reserve
Río Coca (Segovia)
La Moskitia
Sandy Bay
Pahra
Dakura
Patuca
Tuara
Laguna Pahara
Auastara
Cordillera Isabela
Sangni Laya
Yulu Tingne
Tuapi
Musawas
Sahsa
Manu Watla
Sumu Bila
Puerto Cabezas/Bilwi
Kukalaya
Klingna
Susun
Bonanza
La Rosita
El Encanto
Banacruz
Haulover Creek
Siuna
Yaoya
El Empalme
Wani
Alamikamba
Limbaika
Río Prinzapolca
El Porvenir
Company Creek
El Garrobo
Makantaca
Siawás
Río Grande de Matagalpa
Sandy Bay Sirpi
La Cruz de Río Grande
Bratarac
Barra de Río Grande
Lago de Apanás
Jinotega
Pauta Dimon
Kara
Matagalpa
Matiguás
Río Blanco
Tortuguero
Sébaco
Muy Muy
Ciudad Darío
Santa Lucía
NICARAGUA
Laguna de Perlas
Boaco
La Libertad
Rama
Río Escondido
Corn Islands
Juigalpa
Santo Tomás
La Gateada
Bluefields

Cayos Morrison Dennis
Cayos Miskitos

B

C

4

4
5
6

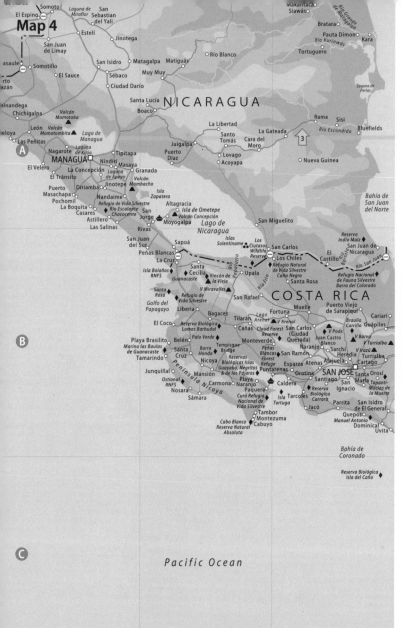

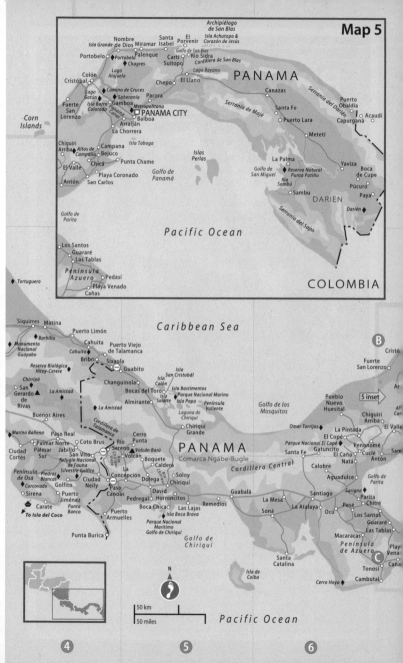